Judicial Review

Judicial Review

Sixth edition

Sir Michael Supperstone
James Goudie QC
Sir Paul Walker

General editor:
Professor Helen Fenwick

Members of the LexisNexis Group worldwide

United Kingdom	LexisNexis, a Division of Reed Elsevier (UK) Ltd, Lexis House, 30 Farringdon Street, London, EC4A 4HH, and 9–10, St. Andrew Square, Edinburgh, EH2 2AF
Australia	LexisNexis Butterworths, Chatswood, New South Wales
Austria	LexisNexis Verlag ARD Orac GmbH & Co KG, Vienna
Benelux	LexisNexis Benelux, Amsterdam
Canada	LexisNexis Butterworths, Markham, Ontario
China	LexisNexis China, Beijing and Shanghai
France	LexisNexis SA, Paris
Germany	LexisNexis Deutschland GmbH, Munster
Hong Kong	LexisNexis Butterworths, Hong Kong
India	LexisNexis India, New Delhi
Italy	Giuffrè Editore, Milan
Japan	LexisNexis Japan, Tokyo
Malaysia	Malayan Law Journal Sdn Bhd, Kuala Lumpur
New Zealand	LexisNexis Butterworths, Wellington
Poland	Wydawnictwo Prawnicze LexisNexis Sp, Warsaw
Singapore	LexisNexis Butterworths, Singapore
South Africa	LexisNexis Butterworths, Durban
USA	LexisNexis, Dayton, Ohio

© RELX (UK) Limited 2017

Published by LexisNexis
This is a Butterworths title

ISBN for this volume: 9781474306966

Printed in Great Britain by CPI Group (UK) Ltd, Croydon, CR0 4YY

Visit LexisNexis at www.lexisnexis.co.uk

Foreword

The jurisdiction of the Queen's Bench judges to supervise the lawfulness of official action is one deeply rooted in history, as evidenced by the names of old prerogative writs. Some of the leading cases were decided long ago. But a glance at almost any page of the text of this new edition provides a powerful reminder of what any lawyer practising in this field instinctively knows, that a very large proportion of the authorities on which applications for judicial review now turn have been decided in the last 30 to 35 years or so. During that period, the field has seen intense activity, which continues apace.

This puts an immense premium on familiarity with the law as it develops. Knowledge of favourite authorities mastered in university or law school years ago is no substitute for knowledge of what has been decided more recently. But the proliferation of decisions and the ready availability of transcripts can all too easily reduce the law to a shapeless jumble of single instances and lead to the citation of decisions, which illustrate the application of a familiar rule and, in truth, decide nothing. So the abundant materials must, to present a coherent picture, be marshalled, dissected and ordered.

This is a task calling for learning, skill and experience, qualities which the contributors to this volume are superbly qualified to provide. The result is a work which will be of great value to all who are called upon to conduct litigation and make decisions in this very important field. It is, after all, important to remember, as Lord Hailsham of St Marylebone pointed out in his 1983 Hamlyn Lectures, that Thomas Fuller's great injunction — "Be you never so high, the law is above you" — applies to judges no less than ministers.

Preface

This new 6th edition of this work, is concerned with the impact of a range of new developments which have now more fully taken effect, rather than with their innovation. I have continued to undertake the editorship which I took over for the 4th edition from The Hon Mr Justice Supperstone, James Goudie QC and The Hon Mr Justice Walker. This edition comes at a point when the Human Rights Act 1998 has been in force for 17 years; it takes account of recent significant developments under that Act affecting judicial review due to thorough revision of CHAPTER 9, on proportionality, which was originally introduced as a new Chapter in the 4th edition. The chapter sets out to provide a rigorous analysis of how proportionality works, examining the way that UK judges have handled it in judicial review cases. CHAPTER 4, explaining the impact of the Act on judicial review, has been considerably revised in this edition to consider a number of recent significant cases on the relationship between the domestic courts and the Strasbourg Court, under the Act. Similarly, CHAPTER 21, dealing with devolution, has been revised to take account of a range of developments in that area over the last eight years, pointing out that the political sensitivities involved and the complexity of the devolution arrangements, have led to quite frequent resort to the courts by way of judicial review.

Developments in the law of judicial review in Scotland, and in European Union law as it affects judicial review, are described in CHAPTERS 22 and 15 respectively, and CHAPTER 15 considers new developments in EU law in respect of fundamental human rights. It covers the (obviously) highly significant matter of 'Brexit': the government's notification in 2017 of the UK's intention to withdraw from the EU and the nature of the 'Great Repeal Bill' to repeal the European Communities Act 1972 and to convert the body of existing directly applicable EU law into domestic law. As regards the substantive and procedural law of judicial review in England and Wales, as described in other chapters of this edition, there have been substantial developments in a number of areas over the last 12 years. In this edition CHAPTER 8 is concerned only with the principle of 'reasonableness', since proportionality receives extended treatment in CHAPTER 9; CHAPTER 8 points out that there is no longer a consistent test as to what makes a decision unreasonable; the intensity of review now depends on the context, which includes the importance of the rights affected by the decision. The chapter focuses in particular on developments in the law relating to 'substantive legitimate expectations'. CHAPTER 11 deals with the rules of natural justice, ending with consideration of the relevance of Article 6 ECHR in this context. In CHAPTER 12, dealing with bias, recent developments relating to the tension between predisposition and predetermination are explored. As CHAPTER 13, considering other grounds of review, explains, the extent to which the courts envisaged review for mistake of fact as independent of review for unreasonableness has recently been clarified. Mistake of fact is now well established as a separate ground of review. CHAPTER 19, dealing with the early stages of procedure, discusses the recent changes to the traditional approach to disclosure which mean that it has become more flexible and less prescriptive.

The objective of this edition has been two-fold. First, it has been to ensure that all recent developments in judicial review have been covered. That I hope has been achieved with the assistance of our distinguished team of contributors to whom I am indebted for their efforts. This edition has welcomed a number of new contributors with whom it has been a pleasure to work. Secondly, it has been to set individual chapters in context with extensive cross-references to relevant discussion elsewhere in the book.

In this regard, I must of course acknowledge the debt this edition owes to the work of The Hon Mr Justice Supperstone, James Goudie QC and The Hon Mr Justice Walker in bringing previous editions of this work to completion. For all the patience, encouragement and support received from the publishers, I am very grateful.

Lord Bingham sadly died as the fourth edition of this work reached completion. We have included his Foreword exactly as it was written in 2005 for the 3rd edition, as a mark of respect for him.

The work endeavours to state the law as at 28 February 2017.

Contributors

Professor Gordon Anthony

Gordon Anthony is a Professor of Law at Queen's University Belfast and a member of the European Public Law Organisation, Athens, Greece. He has published widely in the field of public law. His books include *Textbook on Administrative Law* (Oxford University Press, 6th edn, 2009, with Peter Leyland); *Judicial Review in Northern Ireland* (Hart Publishing, Oxford, 2008); and *UK Public Law and European Law: The Dynamics of Legal Integration* (Hart Publishing, Oxford, 2002).

Aaron Baker

Aaron Baker is Associate Professor (Reader) at Durham Law School at the University of Durham. A discrimination litigator in the US before becoming an academic, he specialises in employment discrimination law and proportionality under the Human Rights Act 1998. He has published extensively on human rights law, in journals such as the *Modern Law Review*, *Public Law*, and the *American Journal of Comparative Law*. Aaron Baker is also the co-author of the latest edition of Smith and Wood's *Employment Law*.

Rachel Barrett

Rachel Barrett is a barrister at Cloisters specialising in human rights, equality, employment and mental health law.

Rupert Beloff MA (Oxon), LLB (Buckingham), PgDip (EC Law) (Kings), Barrister and member of Gray's Inn

Rupert practices from No 5 Chambers in London and Birmingham in the fields of public, commercial, media and sports law.

Tim Buley MA, LLM

Barrister at Landmark Chambers.

Jude Bunting

Jude Bunting is a barrister at Doughty Street Chambers. Jude is a human rights, equality and public law specialist.

Tom Cross

Tom Cross practises as a barrister in the areas of public and human rights law at 11 King's Bench Walk, the Chambers of James Goudie QC and John Cavanagh QC. He has co-authored a number of books (including *The Protections for Religious Rights: Law and Practice* (OUP: 2013)), and has written for a varied range of publications. From 2008-9 he was a Visiting Lecturer at City University, London, teaching the law of torts. He is a member of Lincoln's Inn.

Dilpreet K Dhanoa

Dilpreet K Dhanoa is a tenant (called: 2009) practising from 4–5 Gray's Inn Square. She specialises in General Commercial and Public Law and has a wide range of litigation experience including Financial Services, Tax, Public and Local Government law. Dilpreet regularly appears in the County Courts and High Court and came to the Bar after spending two years at Deloitte LLP. She originally read law as an undergraduate before completing a Masters at the University of Oxford. She is the Assistant Editor and Research Assistant for several other publications, and regularly writes and lectures on a variety of subjects touching upon public and commercial law.

Richard Drabble QC, BA

Barrister at Landmark Chambers.

Professor Gavin Drewry

Professor Gavin Drewry is an Emeritus Professor of Public Administration at Royal Holloway, University of London and is an Honorary Professor in the Faculty of Laws at University College, London. He has published extensively in the inter-disciplinary field of political science and law. Professor Drewry is a former Chair of the Study of Parliament Group and has been a member of the Council of Administration of the International Institute of Administrative Sciences since 2004. He is a former Deputy Editor of the *Statute Law Review* and serves on the editorial committees of several other journals, including *Public Law* and the *International Review of Administrative Sciences*.

Philip Engelman

Philip Engelman is a barrister at Cloisters with extensive experience in public law, human rights and employment law.

Professor Helen Fenwick

Helen Fenwick is a Professor of Law at the University of Durham and previously Co-Director of the University of Durham Human Rights Centre. She is a Human Rights Consultant to Doughty Street Chambers. She is author of: *Civil Rights: New Labour, Freedom and the Human Rights Act* (Longmans/Pearson, 2000); *Media Freedom under the Human Rights Act* (2006: OUP, with G Phillipson); *Text, Cases and Materials on Public Law and Human Rights* (3rd edn, Routledge: 2010, with G Phillipson) and of *Civil Liberties and Human Rights* (4th edn, Routledge: 2007).

Toby Fisher MA, LLM

Barrister at Landmark Chambers.

Alex Gask

Alex Gask is a barrister at Doughty Street Chambers, specialising in public law and human rights. Prior to joining the Bar, he was a public law solicitor at the campaigning organisation Liberty.

James Goudie QC, LLB, FCIArb

Master of the Bench of the Inner Temple, Past President of National Security Panel for Information Rights, Past Chairman of the Administrative Law Bar Association, of the Bar European Group and of the Law Reform Committee of the Bar Council, Joint Head of 11 King's Bench Walk Chambers, Governor of LSE.

Admas Habteslasie

Admas Habteslasie is a barrister at Landmark Chambers, specialising in public law.

Chris Himsworth

Chris Himsworth is Professor Emeritus of Administrative Law at Edinburgh University. His publications have included *Scotland's Constitution: Law and Practice* (2nd edn, 2009) (with CM O'Neill).

Christopher Knight MA, BCL

Christopher Knight is a barrister at 11 King's Bench Walk specialising in public law, information law and employment law. Christopher has written numerous articles on public law and human rights in *Public Law*, the *Cambridge Law Journal* and *Judicial Review*. He is a contributor to the *White Book* and is the co-author of Bradley, Ewing and Knight, *Constitutional and Administrative Law* (2014, 16th edn).

The Hon Mr Justice Lewis, Justice of the High Court, Queen's Bench Division

The Hon Mr Justice Lewis is the editor of the Judicial Review title in *Halsbury's Laws of England* and the author of *Judicial Remedies in Public Law*.

The Rt. Hon. Lord Justice Lloyd Jones

Chairman of the Law Commission of England and Wales

Hugh Mercer QC, MA (Cantab), Licence spéciale en droit européen (Brussels)

Hugh Mercer practises from Essex Court Chambers in London and from Brussels in the fields of EU, public/regulatory law and competition law. He is Chairman of the CCBE Permanent Delegation to the Court of Justice and the General Court of the European Union, the liaison committee between all EU lawyers and the EU courts in Luxembourg.

Katherine O'Byrne, LLM (Cantab)

Katherine O'Byrne is a barrister at Doughty Street Chambers in London with experience in international law, immigration and asylum, judicial review and human rights.

Timothy Pitt-Payne, QC

Timothy Pitt-Payne is a barrister in 11 King's Bench Walk Chambers with extensive experience in public law, information law, local government law and employment law.

Stephen Reeder

Stephen Reeder has specialised in public and administrative law since being called to the Bar in 1991. He is a member of the public law team practising from Doughty Street Chambers in London, Manchester and Bristol.

Vivienne Sedgley, MA (Cantab), Barrister of 4–5 Gray's Inn Square

Vivienne Sedgley MA (Cantab) is a Barrister at 4–5 Gray's Inn Square, specialising in public law. She was called to the Bar in 2011 at Middle Temple with a Certificate of Honour. Before coming to the self-employed Bar, she worked in the Office of Speaker's Counsel at the House of Commons. She is also an Assistant Editor of Parker's Law and Conduct of Elections.

Jonathan Swift QC, BA (Oxon), LLM (Cantab)

Jonathan Swift is a barrister in 11 King's Bench Walk Chambers with extensive experience in a range of public law areas including constitutional law, civil liberties and human rights. He was First Treasury Counsel 2006–2014 leading for the government on major cases concerning public administration. He is a Master of the Bench of the Inner Temple.

Azeem Suterwalla, BA (Oxon), MA Harvard

Azeem Suterwalla is a barrister at Monckton Chambers and specialises in public and human rights' law across a range of subject areas, including community care, children related, data protection and retention of information, education, immigration and asylum support.

Martin Westgate QC, BA (Hons)

Martin Westgate is a barrister in Doughty Street Chambers with extensive experience in public and administrative law.

Former Contributors

Introduction – The Hon Mr Justice Supperstone; The Hon Mr Justice Walker

Nature of judicial review – Sir Louis Blom-Cooper QC, Master of the Bench of the Middle Temple

The Human rights Act and Judicial Review – Anthony Bradley QC (Hon); Sarah Fraser Butlin, Barrister

The Ambit of Judicial Review – The Hon Mr Justice Supperstone; The Hon Mrs Justice Laing; Clive Sheldon QC, LLM

Illegality: the problem of jurisdiction – Lord Justice Laws and Ben Hooper MA (Oxon), Barrister

Discretion and Duty: the Limits of Legality – Peter Wallington MA, LLM, Barrister

Unreasonableness and Proportionality – The Hon Mr Justice Walker; Adam Straw, Barrister

Natural Justice and Fairness: the Audi Alteram Partem Rule – Michael Beloff QC, MA (Oxon)

Procedural Rules and Consultation – The Rt Hon Lord Justice Elias; Andrew Blake BA (Cantab), LLM, Barrister; Stephen Broach MA, MRes Barrister; Lindsay Johnson MA, MPhil, Barrister; Amy Rogers BA (Cantab), Barrister

Procedure: Hearings and Appeals – Joanne Clement, Barrister

Other Grounds of Review – The Hon Mr Justice Walker

Crown Proceedings – Philip Sales MA (Cantab), BCL (Oxon), First Treasury Junior Counsel Common Law

European Union Law – Richard Plender QC, LLD

Remedies: Mandatory, Prohibiting and Quashing Orders – The Hon Mr Justice Walker

Declarations, Injunctions and Money and Restitutionary Remedies – The Hon Mr Justice Walker

Devolution – Rt Hon Lord Justice Richards (Wales); The Hon Mr Justice Maguire;

Contents

Contents

Contents

Chapter 7: Discretion and Duty: the Limits of Legality
Azeem Suterwalla and Katherine O'Byrne

Chapter 8: Unreasonableness
Graeme Hall

Contents

Chapter 9: Proportionality
Aaron Baker

Contents

Contents

Chapter 17: Declarations, Injunctions and Money and Restitutionary Remedies
Martin Westgate QC

Chapter 18: Restrictions on the Availability of Judicial Review
Timothy Pitt-Payne QC

Chapter 19: Procedure: the Early Stages
Tim Buley, Toby Fisher, Admas Habteslasie

Contents

Contents

Table of Statutes

Paragraph references printed in **bold** type indicate where the Act is set out in part or in full.

Table of Statutory Instruments and Codes of Practice

Paragraph references printed in **bold** type indicate where the Act is set out in part or in full.

Table of European and International Legislation

Paragraph or page numbers printed in **bold** type indicate where an Article is set out in part or in full.

SECONDARY LEGISLATION

Directives

Regulations

Table of Foreign Legislation

Table of Cases

C

D

E

F

G

H

I

J

K

M

Table of Cases

c

N

S

T

U

V

W

X

Y

Z

Chapter 1

INTRODUCTION

PRELIMINARY

1.1 The term 'judicial review' can be, and has been, used to describe many types of judicial decision-making. In this book it is used to refer to a specialist jurisdiction of the High Court in England and Wales.[1] Under this jurisdiction a claim in the field of public law can be examined by the court. One possible outcome is the quashing of something done by the defendant – that is, a formal order of the court destroying the validity of the thing in question. Another possible outcome is a declaration as to the lawfulness of action or inaction by a defendant. Yet another possible outcome is the making of an order which obliges the defendant to behave in a particular way. This book broadly aims to describe the legal principles which determine who can make such a claim, against whom, on what grounds, and the remedies available. In order to do this we have asked specialist authors to set judicial review in context, to describe the types of activity that can be the subject of such a claim, to examine the nature of judicial review and the grounds on which the courts will intervene, to explain the role of European Union Law, to describe the remedies that are available and who can seek them, to explain the procedures involved, to examine the impact of devolution, and to give an account of corresponding principles in Scotland.

[1]   The corresponding jurisdiction in Scotland is described in CHAPTER 22.

SETTING JUDICIAL REVIEW IN CONTEXT

1.2 The historical background is described in CHAPTER 2. It is essential to have an understanding of the ancient remedies which gave rise to today's specialist jurisdiction, and of how they developed over time. As well as giving a sketch of the history of relevant remedies, CHAPTER 2 seeks to set this in the context of developments in public administration. It examines the legacy of A V Dicey's opposition to any attempt to introduce a separate system of administrative law. CHAPTER 2 ends with an account of twentieth and twenty-first century developments, including the debate as to how active judges should be in intervening in the business of elected government. What has been described as 'judicial timidity' in the first half of the twentieth century was overtaken by a more activist approach and major procedural reforms.

1.3 Themes from the twentieth century and the first 17 years of the twenty-first are discussed further in Chapter 3. Here there is an overview of trends in judicial activism, and of how the courts began to supervise self-regulatory bodies exercising no statutory powers. This topic is discussed in more detail in Chapters 5 and 6. The overview of judicial activism in Chapter 3 continues by looking at aspects of the courts' approach to the reasonableness of administrative action – another topic discussed in more detail later in the book, in this case in Chapter 8. The chapter concludes its discussion of judicial activism by focusing on the recent tendency of judges in the Human Rights Act era to seek to control even political decisions (it concludes that no one case has illustrated concerns 'about an overactive judiciary more acutely than the recent "Brexit" challenge, *R (Miller) v Secretary of State for Exiting the European Union*',[1] and decisions taken within the context of national security, a theme that is picked up in Chapter 9.

[1]   [2017] 2 WLR 583.

1.4 Chapter 4 describes one of the most significant legislative developments to affect judicial review. This is the Human Rights Act 1998 (HRA), enacted in order to give domestic effect to the European Convention on Human Rights. Chapter 4 was revised in the last two editions to consider a number of the most significant cases on the impact of the HRA, both procedurally and substantively, in the first 14 years of its life; this edition consolidates that revision, in covering developments over the last three years. In Chapter 4 a brief description of the background is followed by an explanation of the structure of the Act. It points out that, while the HRA gives effect to the rights contained in Schedule 1, there is judicial recognition of the possibility that rights protection in the UK could go beyond that apparent from the Strasbourg jurisprudence or could take a stance non-dependent on it. It considers the duty of courts under s 2 and notes the finding of the Supreme Court to the effect that courts would not normally contemplate an outright refusal to follow Strasbourg authority at the Grand Chamber level,[1] but also the signs of a recent 'retreat from *Ullah*'.[2] The implications of the Act for judicial review are then discussed, beginning with its effect on the interpretation of primary and subordinate legislation. The duty of public authorities to act compatibly with Convention rights is examined and consideration is given to a number of recent cases on the interpretation of the term 'public function'. After touching on 'horizontality' – the effects of the Act on the rights of one individual against another – the chapter describes the remedies available under the Act. Judicial review will often be the appropriate means of bringing an alleged breach of Convention rights into court. However, the scope and procedure on the one hand of judicial review, and on the other hand of the remedy under the Act, do not coincide. This leads on to an analysis of the rights conferred by art 6 of the Convention in the context of judicial review, and of the requirement that acts of public authorities are prescribed by law. Chapter 4 ends with a discussion of the 'margin of appreciation', discretionary decisions and the discretionary area of judgment – topics which are further examined in Chapter

9.

¹ Lord Mance, *R (Chester) v Secretary of State for Justice* [2013] UKSC 63, [2014] AC 271 at para 27.

² The phrase was used by Lord Wilson in *Moohan v Lord Advocate* [2014] UKSC 67 at paras 104–105, [2015] AC 901 at paras 104–105. This passage was cited by Lord Kerr in *Keyu v Secretary of State for Foreign and Commonwealth Affairs* [2015] UKSC 69 at para 234; [2016] AC 1355 at para 234.

TYPES OF ACTIVITY THAT CAN BE THE SUBJECT OF JUDICIAL REVIEW

1.5 CHAPTER 5 explains how the courts have focussed not on whether the defendant is, in general terms, amenable to judicial review, but on whether a particular decision is amenable. The exercise of powers conferred by statute will, in many cases, be amenable to judicial review, but this will not always be so. Conversely, the exercise of powers which have no statutory basis may, in an appropriate case, be subject to judicial review. Recent cases have involved consideration of whether a feature or combination of features imposes a public character or stamp upon the act sought to be reviewed. Here there is a strong link with the human rights discussion in CHAPTER 4, for there is considerable overlap between the types of activity to which the Human Rights Act 1998 applies and those which may be the subject of judicial review. In CHAPTER 5 the similarities and differences are discussed. Specific areas of activity examined include commercial transactions, land transactions, the exercise of prerogative powers, and the exercise of powers of visitors to charitable and other institutions. The chapter then turns to the relationship between judicial review and ordinary actions, before concluding with a discussion of whether judicial review can be excluded. Both of these topics are discussed further in CHAPTER 6.

THE NATURE OF JUDICIAL REVIEW

1.6 The principal scope of CHAPTER 6 is the legal and logical nature of judicial review. The chapter begins with the thesis that there are two meanings of 'jurisdiction' in public law. First, there is the High Court's jurisdiction to review the types of activity described in CHAPTER 5. Second, there is the reviewed body's jurisdiction in the sense that there are particular things that the reviewed body is entitled to do. As it is the High Court which determines what the reviewed body can and cannot do, it follows that the jurisdiction of the reviewed body is in part a function of the jurisdiction of the High Court. The chapter then contrasts this thesis with the traditional 'ultra vires' theory, analysing the decision in *Anisminic*.[1] This leads to an extensive discussion of the role of the High Court when statute appears to oust that court's jurisdiction, with emphasis being placed upon the court's role of statutory construction. CHAPTER 6 then considers the thesis in relation to collateral challenges – cases where public law acts or decisions are challenged outside the confines of judicial review. It goes on to discuss the position of the courts and the significance of the debate. The final section of the chapter draws conclusions, in particular that the common law is logically prior to statute,[2] rather than the other way round.

1   *Anisminic Ltd v Foreign Compensation Commission* [1969] 2 AC 147.
2   See *R (Cart) v Upper Tribunal* [2012] 1 AC 663, at paras 32 and 37.

GROUNDS OF REVIEW

1.7 In 1984 Lord Diplock identified a tripartite classification of the grounds of review. He said in *Council of Civil Service Unions v Minister for the Civil Service*[1] that judicial review had developed to a stage when, without reiterating any analysis of the steps by which the development has come about, one could conveniently classify under three heads the grounds upon which administrative action is subject to control by judicial review. The first ground he called 'illegality,' the second 'irrationality' and the third 'procedural impropriety.' He recognised that further development on a case-by-case basis might, in course of time, add further grounds, and had in mind particularly the possible adoption in the future of the principle of 'proportionality', recognised in the administrative law of several Member States of the European Economic Community. That principle has received recognition in this context for some time. Prior to the inception of the Human Rights Act 1998 the primary role of proportionality arose in areas heavily influenced by European Union law, such as indirect discrimination. Now, as CHAPTER 9 explains, the Human Rights Act has made proportionality a more common doctrine in judicial review cases.

1   [1985] AC 374 at 410.

1.8 CHAPTER 7 is largely concerned with Lord Diplock's first head. It deals broadly with the legal framework of the exercise or non-exercise of powers. The distinction between a discretion and a duty is examined. It is a distinction which is superficially, but deceptively, simple. Categories of duty and discretion are described. It is argued that it is possible to analyse almost all discretionary powers as being subject to one or more preconditions, and this leads to a discussion of whether a discretionary power can be regarded as conferring a pure discretion unfettered by legal constraints. The effect on discretionary powers of the Human Rights Act 1998 (discussed more generally in CHAPTER 4) is examined. Discussion of the question whether there are unreviewable discretions leads on to the principal categories within the heading of illegality as a ground of review. The first is unlawful sub-delegation or divestment of the decision-making power. A second category is fettering of discretion in the sense of imposing limits on the decision-taker's future freedom of action – 'temporal fettering'. The third category is challenge by reference to the taking into account of relevant and irrelevant considerations, including the distinction between the identification of those considerations to which regard must be had and the relative weight to be attached to each consideration, and the purposes for which a power may or may not be exercised, including the concept of bad faith.

1.9 The third head of review, which Lord Diplock described as 'irrationality', is discussed in CHAPTER 8 by reference to the principle of 'reasonableness'. The first section of the chapter begins with an overview of the development of the modern principles of review for unreasonableness, pointing out that there is no longer a consistent test as to what makes a decision unreasonable; the intensity of review now depends on the context, which includes the importance of the rights affected by the decision. It notes the recent and increasing enthusiasm to develop the common law so that it reflects Convention rights[1] and finds that in such cases, a proportionality approach equivalent to that applied by the Strasbourg Court will often be applied. The chapter then turns to general questions of terminology, the time at which and evidence with which a decision is to be tested, and the consequences of a finding of unreasonableness. The next section examines the relationship of the principle of reasonableness with the principles governing review based on illegality, procedural impropriety and other grounds. The third section discusses circumstances in which the principle of reasonableness has been said to be inapplicable, or modified in its application. The fourth section surveys aspects of the principle of reasonableness in operation, focusing in particular on recent developments in the law relating to 'substantive legitimate expectations'.

[1]   *Osborn v Parole Board* [2013] UKSC 61, [2013] 3 WLR 1020 at 62.

1.10 The question of review on grounds of proportionality is discussed in CHAPTER 9, originally included in the fourth edition of this book to recognise the growing importance of this concept after the inception of the Human Rights Act 1998. This chapter examines proportionality with a rigour and thoroughness befitting the prominence the principle has achieved under the Human Rights Act over the last 17 years since the Act came into force. Building on the work in the two previous editions, it explains the genesis of the principle in European law, and considers the progress of proportionality as a free-standing ground for review in the UK. The greater part of the chapter, however, is given over to a careful analysis of how proportionality works, how it should work, and how UK judges have handled it in judicial review cases. It sets out the various 'tests' of proportionality, their logic, and the structure of the proportionality analysis in its most refined form. It explores in detail where these tests fit within domestic judicial review, first with regard to the application of EU law and then, through the HRA, the ECHR jurisprudence of the European Court of Human Rights (ECtHR). It concludes by noting that the Supreme Court has recently dropped extensive hints that it could soon take the step of applying proportionality as a general tool of judicial review although the step of declaring proportionality a principle of common law judicial review has not yet been taken. It finds that if 'resistance to accepting proportionality was based on a fear of shifting decision-making authority to the courts, that is not what is happening even in human rights cases'. It proceeds to find that there is therefore 'a very good chance that neither "Brexit" nor the advent of a British Bill of Rights (BBoR) will diminish the role of proportionality in UK courts'. It finds that the British Bill of Rights (referred to in the 2015 and 2016 Queen's Speeches, although no draft Bill has yet appeared) is unlikely to go so far as to withdraw from the ECHR altogether, so proportionality will 'not go away in human rights cases' even if the HRA is repealed and replaced by a BBoR.[1]

[1]   *Pham v Secretary of State for the Home Department* [2015] UKSC 19; [2015] 3 All ER 1015 [94]–[96], [115]–[116]; *Kennedy v The Charity Commission* [2014] UKSC 20; [2015] 1 AC 455 [54]–[55].

1.11 Returning to Lord Diplock's second head of review, procedural impropriety, this is examined in CHAPTERS 10–12. Procedural rules are discussed in CHAPTER 10. Such rules often require consultation with identified bodies, and the courts' approach to this is discussed in detail. CHAPTER 11 deals with the rules of natural justice: minimum standards of procedural fairness imposed by the common law. They may be allied to, and sometimes co-extensive with, the kinds of procedural rules discussed in CHAPTER 10. CHAPTER 11 ends with consideration of the relevance of Article 6 ECHR, scheduled in the Human Rights Act, in this context. Bias is discussed in CHAPTER 12. The well-known rules are that decision-makers should not be judges in their own cause and that there should be no appearance of bias. Decision-makers should be impartial. Not only must they not benefit themselves, they must not favour one party or disfavour another. Where art 6 of the European Convention on Human Rights applies, they must be independent. In all cases they must not have such preconceived views as amount to an unlawful fettering of discretion; recent developments relating to the tension between predisposition and predetermination are explored. The ambit of these principles is discussed, along with countervailing factors which may outweigh them.

1.12 Actual or potential grounds of review which do not easily fall within Lord Diplock's tripartite classification also call for discussion. One possible further ground specifically identified by Lord Diplock was proportionality. As indicated above, it has now become an accepted ground of review in cases concerned with human rights issues. It is therefore considered separately in CHAPTER 9. It is not obvious how other well-recognised grounds of review are to be classified under the three heads identified by Lord Diplock. CHAPTER 13 describes those grounds – bad faith, procedural fraud or mishap, and vagueness – before turning to a recently established ground, mistake of fact, and the ground of breach of fiduciary duty. As the chapter explains, the extent to which the courts envisaged review for mistake of fact independently of review for unreasonableness has recently been clarified.

CROWN PROCEEDINGS

1.13 The position of the Crown is discussed in CHAPTER 14. The first aspect considered is the Crown's immunity from process. This is followed by discussion of the *Carltona* principle, under which ministerial powers and duties may be exercised by departmental officials responsible to the minister. Public interest immunity from disclosure is then examined, including by reference to the provisions of the Justice and Security Act 2013. The chapter describes the role of the Crown where a declaration of incompatibility is sought under the Human Rights Act 1998. The chapter concludes with consideration of the liability of the Crown in damages for legislative or administrative measures.

EUROPEAN UNION LAW

1.14 CHAPTER 15 is concerned with European Union (EU) law. After an initial discussion of treaties and legislation as sources of EU law, the chapter describes general principles of that law. These include equality, proportionality, legal certainty, legitimate expectations and solidarity, as well as certain principles of administrative or procedural fairness. Enforcement of EU law in national courts is examined. There is then an explanation of principles governing preliminary rulings, followed by a discussion of damages in EU law. The position concerning European Court actions against States, and against Institutions, is briefly described. The chapter concludes by explaining how ordinary principles of judicial review may need to be modified so as to protect rights conferred by EU law. This does not mean that the *scope* of judicial review has to be modified, so as to enable judges to substitute their own decisions for those of administrators or scientists, but that additional *grounds* may need to be available where a litigant challenges, as inconsistent with general principles of EU law, a decision having its basis in EU legislation. The chapter considers developments in EU law in respect of fundamental human rights and the position of the Charter of Fundamental Rights in the United Kingdom. It covers the highly significant matter of 'Brexit': the government's notification in 2017 of the UK's intention to withdraw from the EU and the nature of the 'Great Repeal Bill' to repeal the European Communities Act 1972, and to convert the body of existing directly applicable EU law into domestic law.

REMEDIES AND WHO CAN SEEK THEM

1.15 The remedies which the High Court may grant on an application for judicial review are dealt with under three heads. First, CHAPTER 16 describes the remedies which correspond to the ancient prerogative writs: what are now called mandatory, prohibiting or quashing orders, as set out in ss 29, 31(1)(a), and 31(5) of the Supreme Court Act 1981. These remedies can be used to compel administrative action, to prohibit it, and to invalidate it. Second, CHAPTER 17 describes the remaining remedies identified by the 1981 Act as available on judicial review: a declaration or injunction under ss 31(1)(b) and 31(2), an injunction restraining a person not entitled to do so from acting in certain offices of a public nature under ss 30 and 31(1)(c), and other remedies under s 31(4). It covers certain significant changes to the Senior Courts Act 1981 made by the Criminal Justice and Courts Act 2015, covering cases started on or after 13 April 2015 under which the court must refuse relief. Third, CHAPTER 18 explains restrictions on remedies. These restrictions are concerned with the entitlement to seek a remedy and with the circumstances in which a particular remedy may be refused. The chapter covers changes made by the Criminal Justice and Courts Act 2015, including the changes considered in CHAPTER 17.

1.16 Accordingly, CHAPTER 18 begins with a discussion of the question of who can claim judicial review, sometimes described as the question of 'standing'. In this context it discusses when the claimant's own personal interests may be relied on as constituting a sufficient interest to bring a claim, when a claimant may seek judicial review on behalf of some particular section of society or on behalf of the public interest, and when a claimant may have standing to seek judicial review by virtue of the Human Rights Act 1998.

1.17 Next, CHAPTER 18 turns to examine when the court may, as a matter of discretion, refuse relief even though a good ground for judicial review has been shown. Starting with delay by the claimant, the chapter moves on to discuss other conduct of the claimant, the existence of an alternative remedy, the absence of any practical purpose in granting a remedy, and the effect of a remedy on the defendant or on third parties. The chapter considers significant changes made under the Criminal Justice and Courts Act 2015, which placed restrictions on the grant of leave and on the provision of remedies in certain circumstances. It makes provision *inter alia* that the court must refuse to grant leave to make an application for judicial review, and must refuse to grant any relief on such an application, if it appears to the court to be highly likely that the outcome for the applicant would not have been substantially different if the conduct complained of had not occurred. It further provides that leave to apply for judicial review is not to be granted unless the applicant has provided the court with such information about the financing of the application as is specified in rules of court.

PROCEDURE

1.18 The early stages of procedure are dealt with in CHAPTER 19. This chapter describes the procedure involved in a judicial review claim up to the period shortly before the hearing. Procedure from that time onwards is discussed in CHAPTER 20. After a discussion of the pre-action protocol for judicial review, the chapter explains how a claim is begun, taking account of s 85(1) of the Criminal Justice and Courts Act 2015 under which a claimant will be required to provide information about the financing of the claim before an application for judicial review can be made. It then describes the steps to be taken by a defendant, and the procedure under which the court determines both the grant of permission and interim relief. There is also a discussion of costs at the early stages, which takes account of changes made by s 87 of the Criminal Justice and Courts Act 2015, and of the new statutory regime introduced in ss 88–90 of the 2015 Act setting out a comprehensive statutory code governing when a protective costs order (now termed a 'Cost Capping Order') can be made (also discussed in CHAPTER 20). It covers the procedure for urgent applications. The chapter concludes with discussion of disclosure, applications for cross-examination of witnesses, other applications and directions, and listing. The chapter explains that the traditional approach to disclosure has recently changed, becoming more flexible and less prescriptive.

1.19 CHAPTER 20 deals with the hearing and appeals. The focus of the chapter is on specific issues that can arise immediately before or in the course of a final hearing, at the conclusion of the hearing, in relation to orders on costs (both in advance, and at the end, of hearings), and in relation to any appeals (including appeals that arise after permission applications). It covers ss 88–90 of the Criminal Justice and Courts Act 2015 providing new rules governing the circumstances in which Costs Capping Orders can be made, in detail.

THE IMPACT OF DEVOLUTION ON JUDICIAL REVIEW

1.20 Devolution has differing impacts on judicial review which reflect the particular arrangements made for each jurisdiction. In CHAPTER 21 there will be found separate sections examining how the arrangements for devolution in Scotland, Wales and Northern Ireland are having a bearing on judicial review. The chapter begins by considering challenges by way of judicial review in

Northern Ireland concerning devolution issues. As the chapter points out, the political sensitivities involved and the complexity of the devolution arrangements has made it unsurprising that resort to the courts by way of judicial review has been frequent in the short life of the operation of the devolved institutions, and the actions have had a significant political dimension. The chapter moves on to consider judicial review and devolution in Scotland more briefly, since in practice, devolution issues have not arisen most frequently in the course of proceedings for judicial review. It points out that the Scotland Act 1998 has been supplemented by the Scotland Acts 2012 and 2016, which have added to the devolved powers, including the powers to tax, of the Scottish Parliament. The treatment of judicial review concerning Wales is also brief since, while devolution has created some special features, it has not had the same legal or practical significance as in Scotland.

JUDICIAL REVIEW IN SCOTLAND

1.21 Finally, the substantive law of judicial review in Scotland is described in CHAPTER 22. There are very substantial overlaps between the law of England and Wales and the law of Scotland which ensure that much of the rest of the contents of this book has equal relevance to both jurisdictions. On the other hand, there are also some important differences and the main aim of this chapter is to explain those differences. This is done by beginning with a description of the application for judicial review in Scotland, the supervisory jurisdiction of the Court of Session and the scope of judicial review. Alternative statutory remedies and the exclusion of judicial review are then discussed, followed by title and interest to sue. Mora, taciturnity and acquiescence are explained. There is then a discussion of the general powers of the court, the grounds of judicial review, remedies in judicial review, and procedure; the chapter covers the important change to Scottish practice in respect of the rules on standing made by the Supreme Court in *AXA General Insurance Ltd v Lord Advocate (Scotland)*.[1]

It also covers the Courts Reform (Scotland) Act 2014, which introduces new rules on standing, a time limit for the commencement of proceedings and a new permission stage in applications for judicial review. As the chapter explains that when the time came for the implementation of these changes by amendment of the Rules of Court, the opportunity was taken for a complete revision of Chapter 58 (Judicial Review).

[1] 2012 SC (UKSC) 122, 2011 SLT 1061.

Chapter 2

JUDICIAL REVIEW: THE HISTORICAL BACKGROUND

INTRODUCTION

2.1 The writer of a current textbook on administrative law observes that, 'the origins of judicial review are complex, and are interwoven with the intricacies of the prerogative writs'.[1] Writing six decades previously, another pair of commentators had suggested, in similar vein, that, 'the structure of judicial review derives from two sources: the prerogative writs (particularly certiorari and mandamus) and actions for damages'.[2]

[1]   P P Craig, *Administrative Law* (8th edn, 2016) p 4.
[2]   Louis L Jaffe and Edith G Henderson, 'Judicial Review and the Rule of Law' (1956).

2.2 Tackling this complex subject from one perspective, the history of judicial review can indeed be traced through an examination of the development of legal remedies. The modern procedures relating to judicial review of administrative action have evolved through the gradual adaptation to changing social and constitutional circumstances of the ancient writs of certiorari, prohibition and mandamus, allied with the subsequent development, in public law contexts, of other remedies, notably declaratory orders and injunctions. The major reforms of judicial review from the 1970s and 1980s onwards, outlined later in this chapter, involved the rationalisation of this disparate cluster of antique remedies under the procedural umbrella of a unified application for judicial review.

2.3 The medieval origins of the prerogative writs; the various constitutional and jurisdictional struggles of the seventeenth century; the adaptation of the early writs to changing circumstances by, in particular, famous eighteenth century jurists like Holt, Blackstone and Mansfield – all these aspects are part of the chequered history of judicial review, and remain of interest, and even of some practical relevance, today. Ancient authorities are still sometimes cited as precedents in modern actions (examples will be found in the chapters that follow). Some of the nomenclature of antique procedural forms and remedies has survived modern judicial treatment and recent procedural reforms and still retains a place in the lexicon of administrative law even in the twenty-first century, although efforts have been made in recent years to replace some of the old terminology with language that is more akin to plain English. A sketch of the history of judicial remedies – full treatment of this immensely complicated subject would require a much larger canvas than is available here – must therefore be an indispensable part of any chapter on the historical origins of judicial review.

2.4 However, looking at the subject from another perspective, one quickly becomes aware that the early development of legal remedies belongs to the prehistory of a very modern area of jurisprudence. We are, after all, talking about judicial review of *administrative* action, and public administration and public bureaucracy are phenomena peculiar to modern developed societies. It is possible, by indulging in some imaginative contortions, to trace some of the organisational forms and practices of modern administrative practice back to the ancient polities of Egypt and Greece; the concept of a civil service is sometimes said to have originated in China during the Tang dynasty, of the seventh to the tenth centuries AD. But we can be reasonably certain that the rulers of those ancient civilisations would have blinked in amazement at the sheer scale and complexity of the governmental and bureaucratic arrangements of modern nation states.

2.5 In Britain, with its long timescale of constitutional evolution, the theory, practice and institutions of public administration are, relatively speaking, of very recent origin. The term 'civil servant' was first used towards the end of the eighteenth century to distinguish the covenanted civilian employees of the East India Company from military personnel.[1] The modern United Kingdom civil service began to emerge after the Northcote Trevelyan Report of 1854; but it has been pointed out that, until 1870, 'statesmen and leading administrators were reluctant to talk of the "Civil Service"; they used instead such terms as the "public offices" or the "public establishments"'.[2] Local government, in even an embryonic version of the form in which we see it today (leaving aside recurrent controversies and continuing pressures for reform), dates back only to the first half of the nineteenth century. Health authorities, the executive agencies of government departments, and so on, are even more recent manifestations.

[1]   Gavin Drewry and Tony Butcher, *The Civil Service Today* (2nd edn, 1991) p 13. See also
     Henry Parris, *Constitutional Bureaucracy* (1969). A succinct historical summary of the
     development of the administrative system can be found in Craig *Administrative Law*, CH 2.
[2]   R A Chapman and J R Greenaway, *The Dynamics of Administrative Reform* (1980) p 53.

2.6 Thus in 1885, when the first edition of Dicey's *Introduction to the Law of the Constitution* was published, the landscape of public administration was unrecognisably different to that which confronts us – and the courts in their exercise of their public law functions – today. The expression, public administration, is itself a product of the latter part of the nineteenth century.[1] The word 'bureaucracy', deployed so pejoratively in the 1920s by Lord Chief Justice Hewart in *The New Despotism*, was barely a recognisable item of English vocabulary in Dicey's day.[2] The expression 'civil servant' was only just gaining general currency.

[1]   Andrew Dunsire, *Administration – The Word and The Science* (1973) CH 1.
[2]   Martin Albrow, *Bureaucracy* (1970).

2.7 There were none of today's major public departments of (for instance) Health; Culture, Media and Sport; Transport; Education; Work and Pensions; and International Development – and there was nothing resembling a modern

Ministry of Justice. The Cabinet had no secretariat. Multi-purpose elected local authorities – the focus, as we shall see, for much of the modern development of judicial review – were just beginning to emerge, albeit with only a fraction of the range of responsibilities heaped on local government in the twentieth and twenty-first centuries. The National Health Service, now responsible for the employment of over a million people, was a thing of the distant future. The governance of Ireland remained a political issue, but devolution of power to Scotland and Wales – let alone the possibility of restoring Scottish Independence – was not even on the edge of the political agenda. Quangos and regulatory agencies were entities undreamed of – even in Dicey's most vivid collectivist nightmares. Public legislation – primary and secondary – was on a miniscule scale compared with today. Relations with neighbouring European countries were not, as has been increasingly the case in the last four decades, an integral part of the day-to-day context and content of domestic government. And the phrase 'human rights' would barely have been comprehensible to Dicey's contemporaries.

2.8 Despite moves by the Conservative administrations, which exercised political dominance in the period 1979 to 1997, to establish a smaller and less interventionist public sector – moves subsequently resumed by the post-2010 Coalition Government and its Conservative successor – we still live in an era of big government. Even given recent and continuing cutbacks in pubic spending, there can surely be no reversion to the Victorian State, founded upon economic *laissez faire* and limited notions of social regulation. The modern institutional structure of public administration has been transformed: collective consumption and the rule of market forces have become the basis of today's political-economic philosophy, pretty well as much under Tony Blair's and Gordon Brown's 'New' Labour' administrations and more recently under the Cameron-Clegg Coalition and Theresa May's Conservative Government, as it was in the era of Margaret Thatcher. It can be argued that many of the issues regarded as central to the debates about administrative law and redress of citizens' grievances against the state in the 1950s and 1960s, and forming the basis of the agenda of the JUSTICE-All Souls Review of Administrative Justice in the 1980s (see below), are no longer of much relevance to the constitutional and political landscape that confronts us today.[1] These facts are inescapably a part of the context in which the historical development of judicial review must be considered.

[1]   See Patrick McAuslan, 'Administrative Justice - A Necessary Report?' (1988) *Public Law*, pp 402–413.

2.9 We must remember, moreover, that the process of administrative change is unceasing. The development of judicial review from the 1980s onwards has taken place against a backcloth of massive institutional change: privatisation (in all its manifestations); the outsourcing of public services; market testing; continuing cuts in public sector manpower; the transferring of large areas of departmental service-delivery to semi-independent executive agencies; huge changes in the mechanisms and the substance of local government funding; the Citizen's Charter (and its evolutionary successors); major alterations to the management and funding of the National Health Service; the creation of new regulatory agencies; substantial developments in the European Union, including enlargement of its membership and the development of a new constitutional framework under the terms of the Lisbon Treaty. The catalogue of such recent and continuing changes is enormous. Recent volumes of the Statute Book and of statutory instruments and EU regulations bear eloquent, albeit incomplete, testimony to the cumulative magnitude of these changes. The inevitably transformative impact of the 2016 'Brexit' referendum and its aftermath is lying in wait, just over the horizon, as this chapter is being written.

2.10 Such developments have had a massive impact on the agenda of public law – not least because of the consequent blurring of the dividing line between what is 'public' and what is 'private'. But although in some respects the scope of public administration may have shrunk, *pari passu* with the contraction of the State (and has shrunk even further in response to continuing public spending cutbacks), judicial review of administrative action has apparently been something of a growth industry.[1] Accordingly, by the time the next edition of this book appears in print there can be little doubt that the landscape will have undergone further significant changes, to which the courts, and the practitioners of public law who appear before them, will have to respond.

[1]   The raw statistics must be interpreted with caution: see Maurice Sunkin, 'The Judicial Review Case-load, 1987–1989' (1991) *Public Law* pp 490–499 and Varda Bondy and Maurice Sunkin, 'The Use of Statistics in Proposing Reforms to the Public Funding of Judicial Review Litigation: A Critical View' (2009), vol 14 *Judicial Review* pp 372–379. Ministerial claims about the supposedly unacceptable increase in the incidence of judicial review cases was one of several contentious features of the Coalition Government's consultation exercise, referred to in section 2.55, below.

THE PRE-HISTORY OF JUDICIAL REVIEW: REMEDIES[1]

[1]   For further discussions of remedies, see CHAPTER 16 and CHAPTER 17.

2.11 In its 1976 *Report on Remedies in Administrative Law,*[2] published at a time when the scope and impact of administrative law had begun to grow substantially, the Law Commission critically examined the procedures governing the various remedies – the prerogative orders, declarations and injunctions – by which a litigant could obtain judicial review of the acts or omissions of public authorities. It concluded that the litigant is sometimes faced with a dilemma in that:

> 'The scope and procedural particularities of one remedy may suit one case except in one respect; but another remedy which is not deficient in this respect may well be unsatisfactory from other points of view; and to add to his difficulties he may not be able to apply for both remedies in one proceeding'.[3]

And, in further support of its diagnosis, the Commission went on to quote the late Professor S A de Smith, in his evidence to the Franks Committee on Administrative Tribunals and Enquiries in the mid-1950s:

> 'Until the Legislature intervenes, therefore, we shall continue to have two sets of remedies against the usurpation or abuse of power by administrative tribunals – remedies which overlap but do not coincide, and which must be sought in wholly distinct forms of proceedings, which are overlaid with technicalities and fine distinctions, but which would conjointly cover a very substantial area of the existing field of judicial control. This state of affairs bears a striking resemblance to that

which obtained when English civil procedure was still bedevilled by the old forms of action'.[4]

[2] Law Com No 73, Cmnd 6407, 1976.
[3] Law Com No 73, Cmnd 6407, 1976, paragraph 31.
[4] Law Com No 73, Cmnd 6407, 1976, paragraph 32; *Report of the Committee on Administrative Tribunals and Inquiries*, Cmnd 218, 1957, Minutes of Evidence, Appendix I, p 10.

2.12 Similarly, the 1988 Report of the JUSTICE-All Souls Review of Administrative Law,[1] having welcomed the major reforms that took place in the late 1970s and early 1980s and given a succinct summary of the *status quo ante*, concluded, with some understatement, that 'before the reform was introduced the law was in an untidy state'.[2] The actions which were taken to disentangle and modernise this confusion of antique remedies through the introduction of a unified application for judicial review will be described later.

[1] *Administrative Justice: Some Necessary Reforms*, Report of the Committee of the JUSTICE-All Souls Review of Administrative Law in the United Kingdom, Oxford, 1988.
[2] *Administrative Justice: Some Necessary Reforms*, paragraph 6.3.

2.13 Meanwhile, our main present purpose is to disentangle the long chain of events by which such remedies came to form the basis of judicial control of administrative action (bearing in mind what has already been said about the modernity of the term 'administrative' in this context). It will become apparent from the account that follows that the development and application of these remedies in an ever-growing variety of public law contexts was the product of many centuries of uncoordinated judicial activity, most of it directed at problems that have little parallel with those that come before the Administrative Court today – hence the tangle. Moreover, it took place without benefit of foresight about how a modern interventionist State might eventually look. We must of course remember that foreknowledge of the modern characteristics and requirements of a system of administrative law appropriate to an age of big and complex government, was not available to those who developed the remedies in earlier and quite different circumstances.

2.14 Edith Henderson sums up the unfolding of events as follows:

'The doctrine of limited judicial review was worked out in England during the seventeenth and early eighteenth centuries, in connection with the agencies of local government. Partly implicit in the older remedy of prohibition and in common-law damage suits, it was made explicit in the new remedies of certiorari and mandamus. In the eighteenth century the doctrine was part of the great compromise by which the Tory gentlemen of England did as they saw fit in the country while the Whigs controlled the central government. In later times, when the English and American social conscience began to catch up with technical organisation, it provided a means of regulating industrial life'.[1]

[1] Edith G Henderson, *Foundations of English Administrative Law*, Cambridge, Mass (1963) p 5.

2.15 The cluster of prerogative writs (re-named prerogative orders in 1938[1]) that became, via a long and disjointed succession of evolutionary stages, the core of judicial review in the guise we know it today, comprised the ancient writs of certiorari, prohibition and mandamus – albeit recently relabelled, in the interests of 'modernisation', with non-Latin names (see below).

¹ Administration of Justice (Miscellaneous Provisions) Act 1938 (repealed; see now the Senior Courts Act 1981, s 29).

2.16 Professor de Smith has explained¹ how these writs, alongside others, now more or less defunct, were originally associated exclusively with the King but were later issued selectively, to the King's subjects. The writ of certiorari, 'essentially a royal demand for information', was developed by the Court of King's Bench, mainly on the basis of its being increasingly recognised as an invaluable device for regulating the activities of justices of the peace, whose statutory powers were greatly extended in the years following the Restoration. Its origins lie in the thirteenth century. More than four hundred years later, we find Chief Justice Holt declaring, in *Groenvelt v Burwell*² (an action for false imprisonment, relating to actions taken by the College of Physicians, acting as a court of record) that: 'where any court is erected by statute, a certiorari lies to it'.

¹ S A de Smith, 'The Prerogative Writs' (1951) 11 CLR 40–56.
² (1700) 1 Ld Raym 454, 12 Mod Rep 386.

2.17 The ancient writ of prohibition, forbidding the commencement or continuance of proceedings in absence or excess of jurisdiction or contrary to law, was used originally to limit the jurisdiction of the ecclesiastical courts.

2.18 Mandamus, issued to compel performance of a public duty, began to assume its modern form in the sixteenth century, though its status was established by *James Bagg's Case*¹ in 1615. Herein the Court of King's Bench ordered the reinstatement of a dispossessed chief burgess of Plymouth to his 'freehold' of office. Chief Justice Coke asserted the scope of mandamus in sweeping terms:

> 'And in this case it was resolved, that to this Court of King's Bench belongs authority, not only to correct errors in judicial proceedings, but other errors and misdemeanours extra-judicial, tending to the breach of peace, or oppression of subjects, or to the raising of faction, controversy, debate or any manner of misgovernment: so that no wrong or injury, neither private nor public, can be done, but that it shall be here reformed or punished by due course of law'.²

¹ (1615) 11 Co Rep 93b.
² (1615) 11 Co Rep 94, 98.

2.19 The basis of the decision was that Bagg had been removed from office without notice or hearing, and the case is an early landmark in the evolutionary development of the *audi alterem partem* rule, one of the two principles of natural justice (the other being the rule against bias – *nemo judex in causa sua*). The rules of natural justice were, in effect, judge-made yardsticks of the minimum acceptable standards of procedural fairness.

2.20 We have already noted the fact that the history of judicial review is essentially bound up with the determination of the High Court to assert its power to superintend the conduct of local justice and local administration, and it comes as no surprise to discover that the earliest applications of the *audi alterem partem* rule were directed at the proceedings of justices of the peace.

The principles of natural justice – or, in the phrase commonly used nowadays, the duty to act fairly[1] – have evolved, via landmark cases like *Cooper v Wandsworth Board of Works*[2] in the nineteenth century and *Ridge v Baldwin*[3] in the twentieth – into important weapons in the armoury of judicial review today.

[1]   See CHAPTER 11 below at 11.44 et seq.
[2]   (1863) 14 CBNS 180.
[3]   [1964] AC 40, [1963] 2 All ER 66.

2.21 It has been noted that, in spite of Coke's sweeping language, which can perhaps best be interpreted as a defiant assertion of the powers of the common law courts as against the royal prerogative:

'seventeenth century lawyers were very cautious in extending the doctrine of *Bagg's Case* beyond its narrowest holding. For fifty years after that case much energy of counsel was spent on a search for authority for it (which was on the whole fruitless).'[1]

[1]   Jaffe and Henderson p 360.

2.22 More than a century later, Lord Mansfield averred that mandamus 'ought to be used for all occasions where the law has established no specific remedy, and where in justice and good government there ought to be one'.[1] And it was Lord Mansfield, in the middle of the eighteenth century, who first designated these writs collectively as 'prerogative writs', because of their intimate connections with the rights of the Crown, by which time, de Smith notes, 'each writ had developed piecemeal its own characteristics'.[2] And, according to the same writer:

'there can be no doubt that the absence in the common-law systems of a distinct body of public law, whereby proceedings against public authorities are instituted only before special administrative courts and are governed by a special body of rules, is directly traceable to the extensive use of prerogative writs by the Court of King's Bench'.[3]

[1]   *R v Barker* (1762) 3 Burr 1265.
[2]   S A de Smith, 'The Prerogative Writs' (1951) p 56.
[3]   de Smith, 'The Prerogative Writs' p 48.

2.23 As already noted, certiorari acquired a particularly important role in enabling the High Court to exercise supervision over justices of the peace. Throughout the eighteenth century, and for the early decades of the nineteenth century, the justices were responsible not only for summary judicial functions but also for the entire business of local government in the counties. In their use of the prerogative writs to supervise and correct these inferior courts the judges of the High Court made little distinction between the judicial and administrative functions of the justices: 'it is clear that many of the acts and proceedings of the Justices of the Peace were not "judicial", yet all of them were subject to review on certiorari and mandamus'.[1]

[1]   Jaffe and Henderson p 361.

2.24 But from the 1830s onwards a new system of local government gradually emerged, and with it a new role for the prerogative writs:

> 'Elected local government authorities and *ad hoc* bodies with extensive powers over persons and property were set up to administer the expanding functions of government. In some cases duties formerly discharged by the justices were transferred to them. Parliament often provided a statutory appeal by way of certiorari from acts and decisions of these bodies. It was natural that the courts should hold that common law certiorari would issue to the new bodies where Parliament had made no express provision for a method of challenge. Similarly, it was decided (though not without some hesitation) that acts of central government departments presided over by responsible ministers were amenable to certiorari and prohibition. No longer was the availability of the writs limited to courts *stricto sensu*, or even to bodies closely resembling courts. Accordingly, the question whether the writs would issue in a particular case came to be determined by reference to the character of the act or decision rather than by reference to the character of the body that had rendered it'.[1]

[1] S A de Smith, 'Wrongs and Remedies in Administrative Law' (1952), 15 MLR 189, at 191–192.

2.25 A line of important cases such as *Cooper v Wandsworth Board of Works*,[1] in which the Court of Common Pleas supplied 'the justice of the common law [to the] omission of the legislature', and held that a local authority intending to carry out a demolition order should have given notice to the property owner and an opportunity for him to be heard, marked the dawn of the modern era of judicial review. The role of the courts was set to expand *pari passu* with the translation of the Victorian night-watchman state into the modern era of large-scale and interventionist government.

[1] (1863) 14 CBNS 180.

2.26 In the last few decades of the twentieth century, local authorities, created by statute and subject (until recently) to a strict ultra vires rule, came to feature more and more prominently in the reports of judicial review proceedings – sometimes as respondents to the aggrieved citizen-applicant, sometimes in litigious dispute with another local authority (as in the *Fares Fair* case)[1] or with central government (as in the *Tameside* case).[2] We have noted how the origins of judicial review lie in the assertion of centralised judicial authority against inferior, local tribunals – meaning, until well into the nineteenth century, justices of the peace. Nowadays, local authorities are not only a frequent *target* for judicial proceedings initiated by the aggrieved citizen but may also behave as a species of interest group, ready to *use* judicial review for their own purposes, sometimes in circumstances that are politically highly charged.

[1] *Bromley London Borough Council v Greater London Council* [1983] 1 AC 768, [1982] 1 All ER 129.

[2] *Secretary of State for Education and Science v Tameside Metropolitan Borough Council* [1977] AC 1014, [1976] 3 All ER 665.

2.27 Before leaving the subject of public law remedies, we must note the development, alongside the prerogative writs, of another remedy, the declaratory judgment, commonly reinforced by the coercive relief of an injunction, destined in due course to find common shelter under the umbrella of the application for judicial review.

2.28 Zamir, the leading authority on the declaratory judgment, has written as follows of the prerogative orders:

'They were well established, respectable and respected. Each had, as might be expected, its particular ways, manners and caprices, which could be traced back to the days of their forefathers. Some of the rigid principles, it must be admitted, have been modified to suit modern times. But many others, though having no better reason to support them than their ancient origin, have been as unshakeable as those of any other society of noblemen. And although it did not escape their notice that here and there their manners were labelled extraordinary and outdated, they seemed to be quite content with themselves. They had reasonable ground to believe that they would pass the rest of their days conducting their business in safety and esteem, much as before. But, alas, into this quiet Victorian atmosphere the declaratory judgment has unexpectedly intruded'.[1]

---

[1]   I Zamir, *'The Declaratory Judgment v the Prerogative Orders'* (1958) Public Law p 341.

2.29 Yet, as Professor Harry Lawson (writing in the 1970s) pointed out, 'the declaratory judgment, unaccompanied by coercive relief, is in England not more than a hundred years old, though it had long been a regular remedy in Scotland under the name of "declarator"'.[1] There has been much discussion about the theoretical drawbacks of a non-coercive remedy. Lord Denning, who played a particularly prominent part in the development of the declaratory judgment as a major public law remedy in such leading cases of the 1950s as *Taylor v National Assistance Board*[2] and *Pyx Granite Co Ltd v Ministry of Housing and Local Government*,[3] gave characteristically robust support to this remedy in the first series of Hamlyn Lectures:

'Just as the pick and shovel are no longer suitable for the winning of coal, so also the procedures of mandamus, certiorari, and actions on the case are not suitable for the winning of freedom in the new age. They must be replaced by new and up-to-date machinery, by declarations, injunctions and actions for negligence'.[4]

---

[1]   F H Lawson, *Remedies of English Law* (1972) p 266.
[2]   [1957] P 101, [1957] 1 All ER 183.
[3]   [1958] 1 QB 554, [1958] 1 All ER 625.
[4]   Alfred Denning, *Freedom Under Law* (1949) p 126.

2.30 Thirteen years later, Sir William Wade confessed himself 'by no means sure that the old remedies are now as outmoded as this vivid comparison suggests', but agreed with Lord Denning that 'it is primarily for the courts rather than for Parliament to modernise the legal machinery for preventing the abuse of power'.[1] In the event, the old remedies were destined, some three decades after Lord Denning's pronouncement, not for replacement by but for amalgamation with the new – and it was through amendments to the rules of court, inspired by the Law Commission, that these changes were brought about, in circumstances described below.

---

[1]   H W R Wade, *Law, Opinion and Administration* (1962) p 13.

JUDICIAL REVIEW: THE DICEYAN LEGACY

2.31 The year 1885 saw publication of the first edition of A V Dicey's *Introduction to the Study of the Law of the Constitution,* in which he warned right-thinking Englishmen, and in particular his own Oxford undergraduates, that any attempt to introduce a separate system of administrative law, along the lines of the French *droit administratif,* administered by a separate administrative court, like the *Conseil d'Etat,* would contravene the rule of law. He had principally in mind that aspect of the rule of law which meant, in his words, 'equality before the law, or the equal subjection of all classes to the ordinary law of the land administered by the ordinary law courts'.[1] However, in the same decade, another distinguished professor, F W Maitland, was pointing out to his undergraduates, in the University of Cambridge, that:

> 'If you take up a modern volume of the reports of the Queen's Bench division, you will find that about half the cases reported have to do with rules of administrative law; I mean with such matters as local rating, the powers of local boards, the granting of licences for various trades and professions, the Public Health Acts, the Education Acts and so forth'.[2]

[1]   A V Dicey, *Introduction to the Study of the Law of the Constitution* (10th edn, 1961) p 193.
[2]   F W Maitland. *The Constitutional History of England* (1955) p 505.

2.32 Neglect of the existence of these matters, he warned, would lead to 'a false and antiquated notion of our constitution': an echo, perhaps, of the former Select Committee on Legal Education which had, as long ago as 1846, urged academic teachers of law to include in the university curriculum. 'Administrative Law, in its connection with magisterial and official duty'.[1]

[1]   Cited in Brian Abel-Smith and Robert Stevens, *Lawyers and the Courts* (1967) p 69.

2.33 A J P Taylor's ringing, though somewhat hyperbolic, affirmation that 'until August 1914 a sensible, law abiding Englishman could pass through life and hardly notice the existence of the state, beyond the post office and the policeman',[1] serves as a reminder of the novelty of interventionist government. But, as Maitland's statement makes clear, even by the 1880s both the law reports and the statute book already contained much evidence of the growing interest of governments and Parliament, and hence of the courts, in state regulation of the lives of citizens through the medium of law.

[1]   A J P Taylor, *English History 1914-45* Harmondsworth, 1970, p 25: but see Sir William Wade's comment on this passage, Wade & Forsyth *Administrative Law* (9th edn, 2004) p 3.

2.34 Dicey's doctrines, taught to successive generations of fledgling English lawyers, undoubtedly discouraged serious discussion of the need to respond to the imperatives of growing state intervention by developing, in a purposive and coherent way, a distinctive corpus of administrative law. Some commentators have depicted the *Arlidge* case,[1] decided by the House of Lords in 1915, as symptomatic of a conscious disengagement by the courts, operating in the shadow of Dicey, from any attempt to control the administrative procedures of central government departments. The Donoughmore Committee on Ministers' Powers,[2] set up in 1929 to refute the alarmist warnings of Lord Hewart against *The New Despotism,*[3] started life with (to quote the famous phrase of

Professor Robson) 'the dead hand of Dicey lying on its neck'.[4] The authors of
a comparative study of administrative law in Britain and the United States in
the 1960s observed that many leading British lawyers of the era of the Second
World War 'could say very little about administrative law except that they had
been taught at university that there was no such thing'.[5]

1   *Local Government Board v Arlidge* [1915] AC 120.
2   *Report of the Committee on Ministers' Powers*, Cmnd 4060, 1932; and see D G T Williams,
    'The Donoughmore Report in Retrospect' (1982) 60 *Public Administration* 273–292.
3   Rt Hon Lord Hewart of Bury, *The New Despotism* (1929).
4   W A Robson, *Justice and Administrative Law* (2nd edn, 1947) p 318.
5   Bernard Schwartz and H W R Wade, *Legal Control of Government* (1972) p 322.

2.35 But, of course, there *was* such a thing. Administrative law, Professor
David Williams once observed, 'is for the courts largely an exercise in statutory
interpretation',[1] and the steady growth of the functions and powers of
government throughout the nineteenth century, and the institutional diversi-
fication associated therewith, had been effected by and reflected in a huge
accumulation of new statute law. We have already noted the use of the
prerogative writs, from the 1830s onwards, as an instrument of judicial review,
particularly in relation to the new apparatus of local government. Maitland
recognised and publicly acknowledged this new statutory domain to be
'administrative law'. Dicey himself was acutely aware that 'the powers of
English Government have, during the last sixty years or so, been largely
increased'[2] and he proclaimed, as a central pillar of his conception of the
rule of law, the crucial role of the ordinary courts in checking abuses:

> 'Any official who exceeds the authority given him by the law incurs the common law
> responsibility for his wrongful act; he is amenable to the authority of the ordinary
> courts, and the ordinary courts have themselves jurisdiction to determine what is the
> extent of his legal power, and whether the orders under which he has acted were
> legal and valid. Hence the courts do in effect limit and interfere with the actions of
> the "administration", using that word in its widest sense.'[3]

1   D G T Williams. 'Statute Law and Administrative Law' (1984) Stat LR 157, at 159.
2   Dicey p 389.
3   Dicey p 389.

2.36 However, he extended his conception of the rule of law to exclude, not
merely the exercise of 'arbitrary power' but also 'wide discretionary authority'
– a view that looked back to an age of Victorian *laissez faire* and, by its lack
of foresight, gave currency to a cripplingly restricted view of public law which
failed to accommodate the looming reality of a twentieth-century interventionist State.

2.37 In rejecting William Robson's scheme for introducing a separate system
of administrative courts, the Donoughmore Report, published in 1932,
expressly invoked Diceyan arguments and went on to assert that the *droit
administratif* is incompatible with a 'flexible unwritten Constitution under
which there is no clear-cut separation of powers and the administration is
subject to the almost daily supervision of the Courts of Law, as every reader of
the daily law reports in *The Times* newspaper knows'.[1] Some readers of that
newspaper might have felt that 'almost daily supervision' was putting matters
a little too strongly. The point is, however, that while Diceyan doctrine had no

place for administrative law as something that sets the state and its function-aries in any way apart from the ordinary citizen, it *did* attach a great deal of importance to the supervisory role of the courts – to what nowadays we would call judicial review.

1   *Report of Committee on Ministers' Powers*, p 111.

TWENTIETH AND TWENTY-FIRST CENTURY DEVELOPMENTS

2.38 Even before the publication of the Donoughmore Report on Ministers' Powers, the writings of jurists like Sir Cecil Carr,[1] W A Robson[2] and F J Port[3] had begun to lay the intellectual foundations of the process by which administrative law gradually won its spurs as a distinctive and respectable area of legal theory and practice. This process accelerated after the Second World War, and the 1950s saw a major upsurge of interest in various aspects of the subject. The sixth series of Hamlyn Lectures, delivered in 1954 by C J Hamson,[4] did much to dispel residual Diceyan prejudices against the *Conseil d'Etat*. The Franks Report on Administrative Tribunals and Enquiries,[5] provided a significant focus for public debate about some aspects of the subject, and led to some notable reforms. However, it may be noted that the third edition of *Halsbury's Laws of England*, published in 1959, still had no separate entry for administrative law.[6]

1   C T Carr, *Delegated Legislation: Concerning English Administrative Law* (London, 1921).
2   W A Robson, *Justice and Administrative Law* (1928).
3   F J Port, *Administrative Law* (1929).
4   C J Hamson, *Executive Discretion and Judicial Control* (1954).
5   Published in 1957.
6   This omission was remedied in the subsequent editions of Halsbury: see, Volume 20 of the 5th edition, *Constitutional and Administrative Law*, Lexis Nexis, 2014, edited by Robert Blackburn.

2.39 It should also be remarked that although there was much debate about administrative law in the twenty years or so following the Second World War, those years were not particularly noted for activism and innovation on the part of the courts in their exercise of judicial review. Many instances could be cited (and generalisations are always hazardous): but perhaps one might single out for special mention *Associated Provincial Picture Houses v Wednes-bury Corpn*,[1] which narrowed down the test of 'reasonableness' on the part of a public authority to the cripplingly restrictive proposition that 'if a decision on a competent matter is such that no reasonable authority could ever have come to it, then [and, by implication, only then] the courts can interfere . . . '. Since then the courts' attempts to apply and develop the '*Wednesbury* unreasonableness' test has yielded such leading cases as *Tameside*[2] and *Lonrho*[3] – which are discussed in later chapters of this book.

1   [1948] 1 KB 223, [1947] 2 All ER 680. For further discussion of this case, see CHAPTER 8 below at **8.3.2** et seq.
2   [1977] AC 1014, [1976] 3 All ER 665.
3   *Lonrho plc v Secretary of State for Trade and Industry* [1989] 2 All ER 609.

2.40 There is of course much scope for legitimate debate about how active judges *should* be in intervening in the business of elected government (though some of the more intemperate media criticisms of the role of the courts in adjudicating upon aspects of the implementation of 'Brexit' have, arguably, crossed the boundary of what constitutes 'legitimate debate'). Some of those who have expressed scepticism about the desirability of encouraging judicial activism have remarked upon the social exclusivity of the judges and their perceived tendency to isolate themselves from the 'real' world, and upon the judges' non-accountability to the electorate. Some commentators have noted also the shortcomings of an adversarial, bi-polar judicial process as a means of resolving problems that need often to be considered in relation to wider considerations of public policy, considerations that lie beyond the narrow boundaries of particular litigation.[1] Such arguments have been thrown into sharper focus by the growing political impact of judicial decisions, particularly ones involving provisions of the Human Rights Act 1998.[2]

[1] See Gavin Drewry, 'Judicial Review – Quite Enough of a Fairly Good Thing?' (1990) 5 *Public Policy and Administration*, pp 20–32, and references cited therein.
[2] See CHAPTER 9 at 9.55.

2.41 Perhaps the non-interventionist attitude adopted by the courts in the 1940s and 1950s was a hangover from their understandable reluctance to impede the exercise of executive power in time of war: the much-discussed wartime cases of *Liversidge v Anderson*[1] and *Duncan v Cammell Laird & Co Ltd*[2] come particularly to mind in this context. Perhaps it also had something to do with the judges' anxiety to avoid seeming hostile to the radical measures of the Attlee Government: J A G Griffith once suggested that the judges of that period seemed sometimes 'to be leaning over backwards almost to the point of falling off the Bench to avoid the appearance of hostility'.[3] The House of Lords' decision in *Smith v East Elloe RDC*,[4] in the mid-1950s, has been cited by many commentators as being the high-water mark of judicial timidity in the exercise of judicial review during the period.

[1] [1942] AC 206, [1941] 3 All ER 338.
[2] [1942] AC 624, [1942] 1 All ER 587.
[3] In M Ginsberg (ad), *Law and Opinion in the Twentieth Century* (1959); cf Abel-Smith and Stevens, CH 11.
[4] [1956] AC 736, [1956] 1 All ER 855.

2.42 Another point to note is that the substance of debate in the 1940s and 1950s about the state of administrative law had relatively little to do with the role of the courts. True, there was debate in Parliament, mostly rather technical in flavour, about the Crown Proceedings Bill, enacted in 1947 – though this legislation was concerned with private law proceedings against the Crown rather than with judicial review *per se*. But much of the discussion that took place in this period had to do with non-judicial aspects of administrative law: with tribunals and inquiries (the subject of the Franks Report); and with the possibility of setting up an ombudsman to investigate complaints of maladministration by central government. The latter debate — details of which are well documented elsewhere[1] — culminated in the passing of the Parliamentary Commissioner Act 1967. The PCA operates within the constitutional framework of ministerial responsibility to Parliament, can receive complaints only via Members of Parliament (although this restriction has come in for growing criticism in recent years), and was always perceived as an adjunct to the traditional role of the MP in taking up constituents' grievances.[2]

[1]   Frank Stacey, *The British Ombudsman* (1971); Roy Gregory and Peter Hutchesson, *The Parliamentary Ombudsman* (1975); Roy Gregory and Philip Giddings, *The Ombudsman, The Citizen and Parliament* (2002).
[2]   Gavin Drewry and Carol Harlow. 'A "Cutting Edge"'? The Parliamentary Commissioner and MPs' (1990) 53 MLR 745–769.

2.43 It is a characteristic of administrative law in Britain, in contrast to other European countries, that at least as much importance is attached to political remedies, through the role of elected MPs in responding to the grievances of their constituents, as to strictly legal ones[1] — and this fact forms an important part of the context of our present discussion. It is arguable that the protracted debate in the 1950s and 1960s about the desirability of having some kind of ombudsman, as well as the attention given to Report of the narrowly-focused Franks Committee on Administrative Tribunals and Enquiries, distracted attention from more fundamental problems stemming from the chronic underdevelopment of administrative law.

[1]   F F Ridley, 'The Citizen Against Authority: British Approaches to the Redress of Grievances' (1984) 37 *Parliamentary Affairs* pp 1–32.

2.44 The 1960s saw what many commentators have described as a more 'activist' phase in the sphere of judicial review, coinciding both with the succession of Lord Reid to the position of senior law lord, formerly occupied by the deeply conservative Viscount Simonds, and with the appointment of Lord Denning as Master of the Rolls, to preside over the Court of Appeal. A turning point was the decision of the House of Lords in *Ridge v Baldwin*,[1] which initiated a line of subsequent cases, discussed later in this book,[2] extending the application of the rules of natural justice into a wide variety of administrative contexts.

[1]   [1964] AC 40, [1963] 2 All ER 66.
[2]   See CHAPTER 11 below at 11.38 et seq.

2.45 In July 1966 the Lord Chancellor issued a statement on behalf of himself and the Lords of Appeal in Ordinary to the effect that their Lordships proposed 'to modify their present practice and, while treating former decisions of this House as normally binding, to depart from a previous decision when it appears right to do so'.[1] Having loosened very slightly the self-imposed bonds of precedent, the House of Lords took an early opportunity, in *Conway v Rimmer*,[2] to modify the much-criticised 'Thetis' doctrine, relating to Crown Privilege (since replaced by the term Public Interest Immunity[3]), dating back to the wartime case of *Duncan v Cammell Laird & Co*.[4] Other particularly innovative public law decisions of the House of Lords during this important decade included *Burmah Oil Co (Burmah Trading) Ltd v Lord Advocate*;[5] *Padfield v Minister for Agriculture, Fisheries and Food*[6] and *Anisminic v Foreign Compensation Commission*.[7]

[1]   [1966] 1 WLR 1234.
[2]   [1968] AC 910, [1968] 2 All ER 304n.
[3]   *Rogers v Home Secretary* [1973] AC 388, per Lord Reid at 400.
[4]   [1942] AC 624, [1942] 1 All ER 587.
[5]   [1965] AC 75, [1964] 2 All ER 348.
[6]   [1968] AC 997, [1968] 1 All ER 694.

[7] [1969] 2 AC 147, [1969] 1 All ER 208.

2.46 Meanwhile, there was renewed debate about the possibility of more radical reforms, of a procedural and institutional character, transcending cautious changes of emphasis in the pattern of judicial decisions. Twenty-five years after the Donoughmore Committee on Ministers' Powers had rejected William Robson's call for a fully-fledged administrative court, the Franks Committee on Administrative Tribunals and Enquiries turned down his more modest proposal for a general administrative appeal tribunal.[1] Professor J D B Mitchell was a particularly eloquent and persistent advocate of radical reform of administrative law.[2] There were calls for a British administrative court, along the lines of the French *Conseil d'Etat*.[3] Proposals of a similar kind came also from the Inns of Court Conservative and Unionist Association.[4] In 1971. JUSTICE called for the establishment of an administrative division of the High Court, along with the promulgation of a general statement of 'Principles of Good Administration'.[5]

[1] Cmnd 218, paragraphs 120–123.
[2] For example 'Administrative Law and Parliamentary Control' (1967) 38 *Political Quarterly* 360–374; 'The Causes and Effects of the Absence of a System of Administrative Law in the United Kingdom' (1968) *Public Law* 95–118; 'Administrative Law and Policy Effectiveness', in J A G Griffith (ed) *From Policy to Administration* (1976).
[3] M H Smith, 'Thoughts on a British Conseil d'Etat' (1967) 45 *Public Administration*, pp 23–42.
[4] *Let Right be Done* (1966); *Proposal for an Administrative Court* (1970).
[5] JUSTICE, *Administration Under Law* (1971).

2.47 In 1979 the Law Commission called for a Royal Commission, or a body of similar standing, to inquire, inter alia, into the question 'how far should changes be made in the organisation and personnel of the courts in which proceedings may be brought against the administration?'[1] The then Labour Government rejected this proposal and, instead, directed the Law Commission itself 'to review the existing remedies for the judicial control of administrative acts and omissions with a view to evolving a simpler and more effective procedure'. The Commission published a Working Paper on the subject in 1971,[2] and a final report, *Remedies in Administrative Law* in 1976.[3] Two years later, JUSTICE, in association with All Souls College Oxford, set up an unofficial committee, chaired by Sir Patrick Neill, QC, to undertake a review of administrative law in the United Kingdom: it published a discussion paper in 1981[4] and a final report, *Administrative Justice: Some Necessary Reforms,*[5] in 1988.

[1] *Administrative Law*, Cmnd 4059, 1969.
[2] Working Paper No 40 of 1971.
[3] Law Com No 73, Cmnd 6407, 1976.
[4] Discussion Paper, April 1981.
[5] McAuslan, 'Administrative Justice – A Necessary Report?' (1988) *Public Law*.

2.48 In 1977,[1] following the Law Commission's Report (and in the wake of important reforms of administrative law procedures in Canada, Australia and New Zealand) Order 53 of the Rules of the Supreme Court was promulgated, effectively subsuming the disparate and confusing array of public law remedies relating to the exercise of administrative power under a common 'application for judicial review'. The litigant no longer had to decide irrevocably at the outset which kind of remedy to seek: it was now left to the Court to determine the appropriate remedy once judicial review has been granted.

[1]   The following account draws substantially upon Louis Blom-Cooper, 'The New Face of Judicial Review: Administrative Changes in Order 53' (1982) *Public Law* pp 250–261. See also Andrew Grubb, 'Two Steps Towards a Simplified Administrative Law Procedure' (1983) *Public Law* pp 190–202.

2.49 Meanwhile a substantial backlog, built up over a number of years, had accumulated in the Queen's Bench Divisional Court, the problem being exacerbated by the declining health of the then Lord Chief Justice, Lord Widgery. In 1980, his successor, Lord Lane, arranged for Lord Justice Donaldson (as he then was) to be seconded from the Court of Appeal to tackle the arrears. A new version of Order 53 was promulgated, coming into effect in January 1981, to streamline the procedures of the Divisional Court. As explained in later chapters, the governing provisions for judicial review are now found in the Supreme Court Act 1981 and in Pt 54 of the Civil Procedure Rules.

2.50 As explained in CHAPTER 19, applications for judicial review cannot proceed without the permission of the court. The application for permission is considered by a judge on the papers. If it is refused, the applicant will receive reasons for the refusal, and may renew the application at an oral hearing. There is provision for further appeal, subject to the granting of permission, to the Court of Appeal (an avenue that the Government tried unsuccessfully to block in the Administration of Justice Bill of the 1984–85 parliamentary session).

2.51 From July 1981 there was also a Crown Office List,[1] providing for the grouping together of judicial review cases with other categories of administrative law proceedings, such as appeals to the High Court from sundry administrative tribunals, and in town and country planning matters. Furthermore, in October 2000, an old Diceyan taboo was exorcised when the Crown Office List was replaced by an Administrative Court, still embedded in the Queen's Bench Division. There is now a cadre of 37 High Court judges (some from the Chancery and Family Divisions) nominated by the Lord Chief Justice to deal with cases in the Administrative Court, a development that marks a significant contribution to the development of more consistent and coherent principles in administrative law.

[1]   *Practice Direction (Trials in London)* [1981] 3 All ER 61, [1981] 1 WLR 1296.

2.52 The verdict, necessarily an interim one, on the new procedures reached by the JUSTICE-All Souls Review was that, while some procedural defects remained:

> 'the introduction of the application for judicial review appears to have had a dramatic effect on the flow of administrative law cases. Although the substantive law was not itself modified, the flexibility of the new procedure has made it much easier to use and hence more attractive to litigants'.[1]

As for more radical, institutional reforms, the Report – having earlier renewed the call by JUSTICE in 1971 for the formulation of a codified set of principles of good administration – went on:

'we do not support any proposal for the creation of a completely new Administrative Division of the High Court along the lines earlier proposed. There is nothing that such a division could achieve that cannot be achieved through existing machinery. In practice though not in name there is already a functional segregation of administrative law cases and they are generally tried by specialist judges. There seems to us to be no need to amend the Judicature Acts so as to replace the flexibility of the present system with the rigidity of a separate division . . . For much the same reasons we find ourselves opposed to the introduction of anything on the lines of a Conseil d'Etat. There are, however, some additional objections . . . '.[2]

[1] JUSTICE-All Souls Report, paragraph 6.12.
[2] JUSTICE-All Souls Report, paragraphs 7.3 and 7.4.

2.53 The Law Commission subsequently returned to the subject of judicial review procedure. In a report published in 1994[1] it recommended, inter alia, a more liberal approach to the controversial principle of 'exclusivity' enunciated by the House of Lords in *O'Reilly v Mackman*, and some relaxation of the rules relating to standing. It also recommended that the antique terms certiorari, mandamus and prohibition should be replaced by modern English equivalents – in line with some Commonwealth jurisdictions, where they have been susperseded 'by a modern review remedy to compel, prohibit or set aside the exercise of administrative power'.[2] Since 1 May 2004, orders of mandamus, prohibition and certiorari have been replaced by mandatory, prohibiting or quashing orders. Surely only the most sentimental of sentimentalists would resent this severance of the confusing linguistic linkage of judicial review of administrative action in the modern complex State to its remote origins in the medieval Court of King's Bench? The Law Commission has continued, in recent years, to be actively interested in the reform of administrative law procedures and remedies.[3]

[1] *Administrative Law: Judicial Review and Statutory Appeals,* Law Com No 226 (HC 669, 1993–94); see also the preceding Consultation Paper, No 126, issued in 1993.
[2] Law Com No 226, paragraph **8.2.**
[3] See in particular their more recent publications, *Monetary Remedies in Public Law: Discussion Paper* (October 2004); *Remedies Against Public Bodies: A Scoping Report* (October 2006); *Administrative Redress: Public Bodies and the Citizen. A Consultation Paper* (July 2008).

2.54 Mention should also be made of the continuing process of rationalisation of the tribunal system, following a report by Sir Andrew Leggatt in 2001[1], which led to the enactment of the Tribunals, Courts and Enforcement Act 2007. Tribunals, administered by the Tribunals Service (an executive agency of the Ministry of Justice, subsequently merged with the Courts Service to form a unified agency, HM Courts and Tribunals Service), have been more closely integrated into the mainstream of the judicial system. One manifestation of this, particularly relevant to the present work, is that the judicial review of decisions by first-tier tribunals has been transferred from the Administrative Court to the Administrative Appeals Chamber of the Upper Tribunal. In this and other contexts, discussion of administrative justice has placed a growing emphasis on the needs of the citizen and has increasingly stressed the complementarity of the respective roles of courts, tribunals and ombudsmen – and of less formal ADR mechanisms, such as mediation – in the redress of grievances against public bodies.

¹   *One System, One Service*, March 2001. See also Sir Robert Carnwath, 'Tribunal Justice – A New Start' [2009] PL, pp 48–69.

2.55 In December 2012, the government published a consultation paper, 'Judicial Review: Proposals for Reform', inviting comment on various measures intended to curb what it claimed (misleadingly, in the view of some critics) to be an unacceptable growth in the incidence of judicial review proceedings. Following the consultation, a number of changes – including the reduction of time limits and increases in court fees for some categories of judicial review proceedings – were implemented through changes to the Civil Procedure Rules in July 2013. Another consultation paper, 'Judicial Review: Proposals for Further Reform' led to further proposals being included in the Criminal Justice and Courts Bill, which received Royal Assent in February 2015.¹ It should be noted that the proposed changes were, from the outset, widely criticised² – and the government found itself obliged to water-down some of its proposals in the course of the two consultation exercises.

¹   The background to these changes is set out in a House of Commons Library Briefing Paper, *Judicial Review: Government Reforms in the 2010–15 Parliament*, No. 6616, 4 June 2015.
²   See, for instance, Alex Mills, 'Reforms to Judicial Review in the Criminal Justice and Courts Act 2015: Promoting Efficiency or Weakening the Rule of Law?' [2015] PL 583–595.

2.56 Meanwhile, the growth in the significance and impact of judicial review has weakened the validity of the late Professor de Smith's characterisation of it as having merely a 'sporadic and peripheral' influence on public administration.¹ Since the 1950s, when de Smith first coined that famous phrase, public law has become a prominent part of the landscape of UK public administration, and judicial review decisions have begun to have a significant impact on the day to day work of administrators.² The coming into force of the Human Rights Act 1998 reinforced that impact. The ghost of Dicey, which has rested hitherto in some semblance of tranquility, may now have some cause for unease – after all, the Administrative Court in London may not be the counterpart of the French *Conseil d'Etat*, but it *is*, authentically, an administrative court.

¹   S A de Smith, Lord Woolf and Jeffrey Jowell, *Judicial Review of Administrative Action* (5th edn, 1995) p 3: repeating the words used in earlier editions, the first of which was published in 1959.
²   One obvious sign of this is the issuing by the Cabinet Office of guidelines on judicial review for civil service administrators, prepared by the Treasury Solicitor's Department, *The Judge Over Your Shoulder*, the first edition of which appeared in 1987 and the second in 1994. A third edition appeared in March 2000, taking on board the implications of the Human Rights Act 1998. The current edition, published in July 2016 is available online at https://www.gov.uk/government/publications/judge-over-your-shoulder).

Chapter 3

JUDICIAL REVIEW: ITS PROVENANCE AND SCOPE

INTRODUCTION

3.1 Lord Devlin once observed that the British had no more wish to be governed by judges than they had to be judged by administrators. Although the burgeoning over recent years of a distinctively English style of public law might have caused Lord Devlin to add that the public has a desire nevertheless that administrators should not go unjudged by the courts, recent government reforms and judicial commentary suggest a move away from such activism, notwithstanding the uproar of the press when faced with a judgment perceived as unpopular.[1]

[1] The response of some newspapers after the judgment of the Divisional Court in *R (Miller) v Secretary of State for Exiting the European Union* [2017] 1 All ER 158 was nothing short of furious. See, for example, *'Enemies of the People'* – *Daily Mail*, 3 November 2016.

3.2 Thus the judicial quest basically has been to find the right balance between ministerial discretion to decide matters which are political in nature or issues of social policy, and therefore essentially not justiciable, and the need to remedy any unfairness in the exercise by administrators of executive power. The reality, on occasion, has been a judicial activism (not to say, creativity) over a wider range of decision-making in public administration. Such has been the breadth and rapidity of the development of public law in meeting the perceived demands of the citizen in the post-Second World War period, to curb the overweening and sometimes overwhelming power of Ministers and administrators in an increasingly complex society, that it was always likely that the enthusiasm for judicial supervision and control of administrative action would require the application of a judicial brake, if not a legislative one. The advent of the Human Rights Act 1998 displayed endorsement of nascent judicial activism plus encouragement to cement the contemporary English-style administrative law (Dicey would be suitably astonished!).[1]

[1] An account of the history leading to enactment of this statute will be found in CHAPTER 4.

3.3 A period of retrenchment, following a decade or more of judicial activism, that sometimes seemed to breach the Devlin axiom, was best expressed by Lord Scarman in *Nottinghamshire County Council v Secretary of State for the Environment*.[1] 'Judicial review', he proclaimed, 'is a great weapon in the hands of the judges; but the judges must observe the constitutional limits set by our parliamentary system upon the exercise of this beneficent power'. If anyone were prompted to dismiss this sage warning as a mere *obiter dictum* from a radical member of the higher judiciary of recent times, and therefore to be treated as an idiosyncratic aberration, it has received the endorsement of the Law Lords generally. The words of Lord Scarman were echoed by Lord Bridge of Harwich, speaking on behalf of the Judicial Committee of the Privy Council when reversing an interventionist decision of the New Zealand Court of Appeal in *Petrocorp Exploration Ltd v Minister of Energy*.[2] An observance of judicial restraint is nevertheless the mood, while the proper exercise of judicial power to rein in any unbridled executive functioning remains the new order of an old prerogative power exercisable by Her Majesty's judges. It is enhanced by the power to declare any legislative act incompatible with the European Convention on Human Rights without conferring a power to strike down legislation,[3] although European Union law may require that the courts disapply domestic legislation.[4] In the first appeal to the Supreme Court, the President (Lord Phillips of Worth Matravers) in the asset-freezing order case, *Ahmed v HM Treasury (No 2)*,[5] ended his judgment (at paragraph 157) decisively: 'Nobody should conclude that the result of this appeal . . . constitutes interference with the will of Parliament. On the contrary, it upholds the supremacy of Parliament in deciding whether or not measures should be imposed that affect the fundamental rights of those in this country.'

[1] [1986] AC 240 at 251.
[2] [1991] 1 NZLR 64.
[3] See Chapter 4.
[4] See 15.71 below.
[5] [2010] UKSC 5, [2010] 2 AC 534, [2010] 4 All ER 829.

3.4 The restraint has two contemporary manifestations. One is the ambit of judicial intervention; the other covers the scope of the court's ability to quash an administrative decision on its merits. Both restraints bear the hallmarks of the origins of judicial control over administrative action.

ORIGINS OF CPR PART 54

3.5 The prerogative orders were specifically designed in origin to invest the Crown – hence they are called 'prerogative' and became orders instead of writs only in 1938 – with the ability to ensure that public authorities carried out their duties lawfully, and that inferior tribunals kept within the bounds of their defined jurisdiction.[1] Certiorari, mandamus, and prohibition were the main remedies whereby the courts could maintain:

(1)   standards of efficiency in government administration; and
(2)   order in the hierarchy of courts and other manifestations of governmental administration, in particular local authorities and statutory bodies.

[1]   Prerogative remedies are discussed in detail in Chapter 16.

3.6 The Crown has, ever since the early days of such power, lent its legal prerogatives to its citizenry in order that the individual might collaborate to ensure good and lawful government. Today the form of the procedure in

Part 54 of CPR is a fiction redolent of its origins. Not too often is the Crown the applicant for judicial review. More often, it is the subject of a challenge by the aggrieved citizen. (Hence the citation adopts the individuality of the applicant: *R (A.N. Other) v Secretary of State et al*).

3.7 Now, subsumed under the single rubric of judicial review, the traditional remedies – supplemented by declaratory relief and the power to award damages in specific categories of case – remain as the outcrop of a successful application under Part 54 of the Civil Procedure Rules 1998 (CPR). Although confirmed by section 31 of the Supreme Court Act 1981, the judicial control over administrative action is, in essence, no more than an enhanced and modernised form of the prerogative orders. And there is no pretence about it: the prerogative orders are specifically declared to be part of Part 54, as itemised in Part 54.2 (following the wording of the amendments to the Supreme Court Act 1981).

PUBLIC LAW/PRIVATE LAW DICHOTOMY

3.8 The seminal decision of the House of Lords in 1982 in *O'Reilly v Mackman*[1] forced the judges operating the Crown Office list to compartmentalise the public law application from the private law action. Both before and after that decision there seemed to be no limit to the expansiveness of the High Court's reach into the realms of administration. Any activity which exemplified a direct interest of the public was swept up in the enveloping cloak of judicial review. The expansiveness of the judicial arm was amply demonstrated when the Court of Appeal held that the City's Panel on Take-overs and Mergers was deemed to be engaged in a public law activity, although the court indicated that its power to intervene by quashing a decision would be sparingly used.[2] A subsequent challenge to the Panel's procedures came within an ace of success. A refusal by the Panel to grant the Guinness company adjournment of an oral hearing was ultimately found not to be an infringement of a rule in the Panel's procedure. Since the Panel's decision had not in the event resulted in injustice, the Court of Appeal, with some hesitation, held that there had been no procedural irregularity.[3] There was no hesitation, however, about embracing within the compass of judicial review a self-regulatory body, exercising no statutory powers but only the powers conferred on it by the members of the Stock Exchange. The Panel is an unincorporated association whose members are appointed by, and represent many of the most influential associations and financial institutions in the City of London. It possesses no legal powers. Nor is it in contractual relations with those whose conduct is being supervised. Its function is to ensure compliance with the City Code, which does confer powers on the Panel, subject to the framework of the law relating to statutory powers of the Department of Trade and Industry, and subject to control, in the last resort, by the Competition Commission.

[1] [1983] 2 AC 237, [1982] 3 All ER 1124. See **5.50** and **6.8**.
[2] *R v Panel on Take-overs and Mergers, ex p Datafin* [1987] QB 815.
[3] *R v Panel on Take-overs and Mergers, ex p Guinness plc* [1990] 1 QB 146.

3.9 A similar approach was adopted by the High Court in a challenge to a decision of another self-regulatory body, the Advertising Standards Authority (ASA).[1] The Authority is a company limited by guarantee whose prime object is to promote the highest standards of advertising. To that end, since 1961, it has supervised the advertising industry through Codes of Practice. The main Code describes itself as the body of rules by which British advertisers have agreed among themselves to regulate their conduct. The overriding provision of the Code is that advertisements should be 'legal, decent, honest and truthful'.

[1]   *R v Advertising Standards Authority, ex p Insurance Service plc* (1989) 2 Admin LR 77.

3.10 The characteristics of the ASA are not very dissimilar to those of the Take-over Panel. The ASA too has no powers given to it by the common law or by statute. Nor does it have contractual relationships with advertisers. Its main activities are controlled by a Board of Management which consists of a Chairman unconnected with the advertising business, five independent members and five members of the advertising industry.

3.11 Not unnaturally the Court relied heavily on the earlier decision relating to the Take-over Panel. Other similar bodies have, or are likely to come within the scope of judicial review. PhonepayPlus, now known as the Phone-paid Services Authority, which operates a code to regulate the activities of the premium-rate service industry on the telecommunications network, has been subjected to judicial challenge. The Court of Appeal suggested in one case that the Press Complaints Commission (PCC), may be a candidate for judicial review, and the new official press oversight body, the Press Recognition Panel, is currently the subject of challenge.[1] With increasing privatisation, the residual public element in the denationalised bodies will certainly attract courts' supervisory powers. Despite the fact that these developments exhibit a lack of judicial restraint, it is still uncertain how far the courts will cross the borderline between public and private law. The decision in *Lonrho plc v Tebbitt and the Department of Trade and Industry*[2] in which the Vice-Chancellor declined to strike out a private law action in respect of a governmental delay in releasing Lonrho from its undertaking, restricting its ability to bid for shares in House of Fraser which owned Harrods department store, reflects an uncertainty about the duality or exclusivity of either the public law remedy or the private law action. A more positive sign of judicial restraint came, surprisingly, in the litigation over the Football Association's decision to form a premier league in defiance of opposition to the Football League's desire to maintain the exclusive administration of league football: *R v Football Association, ex p Football League Ltd.*[3] In deciding that the Football Association was not a body subject to judicial review. Rose J (later LJ) said that the application to the governing body of football (the national game in whose administration millions of people are indirectly interested) 'of a tool for controlling government organs would be something of a quantum leap'. Interestingly, the judge introduced a severely pragmatic reason for declining to envisage judicial control: 'It would also be a misapplication of judicial resources. It would bog down the courts and slow down the application in other cases of what ought to be a fast remedy.' The limitation, now seemingly being imposed on the exercise of judicial control, accurately reflects the origins of the prerogative order which was for the Crown to supervise public authorities (including inferior tribunals) and not engage in reviewing the actions of private organisations, however much they operated for the benefit of the public body beyond the organisations' members.

1   See the pre-action protocol correspondence in a proposed claim by the News Media Association, available online at: http://www.newsmediauk.org/write/MediaUploads/PDF%20 Docs/Letter_to_PRP_Dated_5_December_2016.pdf
2   Cf *Jain v Trent Strategic Health Authority* [2009] UKHL 4, [2009] AC 853, [2009] 1 All ER 957, and see Public Law (2009), p 195.
3   [1991] 4 All ER 973.

THE REASONABLENESS OF ADMINISTRATIVE DISCRETION

3.12 Much – indeed most – of what parades under the rubric of judicial review is about the form in which decision-making within government departments is couched, and not the substance of the decision. Procedural irregularity has been the prime instrument of challenge to administrative decisions. To encompass the fairness of the process of all decision-making would call for a prolonged study of the ways of civil servants. To penetrate the minds of lawyers and administrators in public service – 'the separate and the unequal' – might be exemplified by the behaviour of Sir Humphrey Appleby in *Yes, Prime Minister*, which led the Rt Hon James Hacker (or indeed his counterparts in real political life) to regard the English language not as a window into the ministerial mind, but as a curtain to draw against it. In short, judicial intervention into the process of administrative decision-making requires a piercing of the veil of bureaucratic practices and devices that can perplex even the penetrative judicial mind. The merits of any ministerial decision, however, are not so readily concealed under a morass of departmental documentation. They stand or fall by external criteria, Wednesburian or otherwise.

3.13 The predominant focus of judicial review has thus been what the Americans conveniently call due process, which is not overtly directed to confront the merits of ministerial or administrative decisions. The power to strike down those decisions which no reasonable Minister or administrator could properly have made is, in practice, the long-stop of judicial power. The principle propounded by Lord Greene MR in the *Associated Provincial Picture Houses Ltd v Wednesbury Corpn*[1] has been variously interpreted and applied. At one end of the spectrum of the unreasonableness test is Lord Diplock's irrationality (something bordering on the insane) to other judges' views, as less of mental disorder and more of a socially unacceptable verdict, on the basis of declared fact and public or professional opinion. Those judges who have attempted to broaden out the challenge to ministerial or administrative decision, ostensibly on the grounds that the decision is manifestly unjust to any reasonable outsider, have generally been roundly rebuffed by appellate courts.

1   [1948] 1 KB 223. For commentary on this decision, see **2.39** above and **8.4** et seq below.

3.14 Thus, in *Minister for Arts, Heritage and Environment v Peko-Wallsend Ltd*,[1] Brennan J in the High Court of Australia expostulated, arguendo:

'that seems to me to be as blatant an invitation for the courts to take over government as I have heard, and when you think of the nature of the problem that the Cabinet was addressing [a Cabinet decision to seek the inclusion of an area of national park located in the Northern Territory of Australia in the World Heritage Committee's list of properties forming part of a State's cultural and natural heritage pursuant to the World Heritage Convention 1972] and the nature of the submission that you make as your second basis, it is tantamount to that, is it not?'

[1]   (1987) 75 ALR 218.

3.15 An exchange between counsel for the companies, which held ministerial leases within the relevant area of that national park, and the Chief Justice makes the point even more vividly:

'Mason CJ: You are asking us to say that the Cabinet decision was irrational?

Mr Conti: Yes, because a decision which is manifestly unjust is irrational — irrationality is a synonym for manifestly unjust.

Mason CJ: A new era may open up if we are going to subject all Cabinet decisions to the test of irrationality?'

3.16 This Australian riposte mirrors the English judicial attitude. The powers of the court on judicial review are circumspect and do not function as an appeal. The court will not, and cannot, substitute its own opinion for the opinion resided statutorily or otherwise in, and formed by, the decision-maker – so long, of course, as the Minister or the administrator has applied the law correctly and has proceeded regularly. There is nothing new in all this. Questions of the balance between the efficiency of public administration and the resources available to public authorities have traditionally been left for answer by those politically accountable for the decisions. Courts properly fear to tread where the subject matter for decision is inextricably linked to political action. It would have been unthinkable for judges of any earlier generation to contemplate a power over ministerial discretion, which had been made according to proper procedures. *Liversidge v Anderson*[1] is a classic example.

[1]   [1942] AC 206. See also Blom-Cooper, Dickson and Drewry (eds), *The Judicial House of Lords 1876-2009*, OUP 2009, Chapter 11.

3.17 In recent years, however, there has been a move towards closer review of executive decision-making on proportionality, rather than rationality, grounds, particularly where fundamental common law or human rights are engaged. This suggests that a flexible approach to judicial review should be adopted with appropriate weight afforded to the claimant's status as a victim of a human rights breach and to the nature of the challenge. This approach requires there to be greater scrutiny by the Court of the reasonableness of the defendant's decision to refuse to adjourn. This approach has been endorsed by the Supreme Court.[1]

[1]   *Pham v Secretary of State for the Home Department* [2015] 1 WLR 1591, per Lord Carnwath, at paragraph 60, and *Kennedy v Information Commissioner* [2015] A.C. 455, per Lord Mance, at paragraphs 51–55.

3.18 It is the covert intervention by courts that leads one to conclude, with some circumspection, that judges will not leave untouched by judicial hand the action advised upon by Sir Humphrey. Under the guise of Lord Diplock's 'procedural impropriety' there lurks a multitude of maladministrative actions which provide the court, suspicious of the merits (or rather the demerits) of the substantive decision, with the power of intervention.[1] The fact that the court in judicial review supplies only the remedy of striking down the impugned decision, on the grounds of illegality or procedural irregularity, with a second, unflawed stab at getting the decision right, is on the face of it evidence of only a procedural safeguard and not a substitution of judicial decision in preference to the expression of political will. But this also is merely a disguise. A court that has a distinct dislike for an administrative decision, because it appears to be manifestly wrong or unjust, can easily transpose the decision itself with a flawed process of decision-making. The courts' willingness to challenge government decision-making through procedural irregularity may be one reason for the introduction of a new test, whereby permission for judicial review (and relief following a judicial review hearing), can be refused if it appears to the court to be highly likely that the outcome for the applicant would not have been substantially different if the conduct complained of had not occurred.[2]

1 Review for procedural impropriety is discussed in CHAPTERS 10, 11 and 12.
2 Senior Courts Act 1981, s 31(3).

3.19 The court can be, and sometimes is, assiduous to find a procedural irregularity. The decision-maker has, for example, failed to consult a party affected by a projected decision (eg, the *GCHQ* case); an opportunity has not been afforded to someone to make prior oral or written representation to a Minister invested with a discretionary power; there has been a failure to give proper, adequate and intelligible reasons for the decision, although the English courts have yet to adopt the broad principle enunciated by Kirby P in the Court of Appeal in New South Wales, and rejected, unfortunately, by the High Court of Australia in *Public Service Board of New South Wales v Osmond*.[1] These examples of potential procedural irregularities are not exhaustive. A neat example of the court's approach to such questions is provided by the case of *R v Secretary of State for the Environment, ex p Greenwich London Borough Council*.[2] A leaflet on the community charge (pejoratively described as the poll-tax) was issued by a government department in which it failed to make any reference to the joint liability of spouses or people living together. The High Court decided that, since the selection of information to be included in a document explanatory of legislation was for the relevant government department, the omission about the position of co-habitees did not render the leaflet inaccurate or misleading to its readers. One could envisage another court deciding that the statutory provisions might be better interpreted for the ordinary citizen in précis form by Parliament itself.[3] A governmental explanation of Parliament's intention in the statute is inevitably partisan, so that any relevant omission to expound a statutory provision would render the document flawed.

1 (1986) 63 ALR 559, 60 ALR 209.
2 [1989] COD 530, (1989) Times, 17 May.
3 The innovation of 'notes on Sections of Acts' goes some way towards this.

3.20 Perhaps more easily manipulative in the hands of the courts is the determination of the proper ambit of the investigation made by the decision-maker. There is a clear legal duty on an administrator to inform himself properly and adequately before he can move to a position of making a decision. The principle is, almost catechismically, that the administrator shall take into account all those things that are relevant and discount all those things that are irrelevant. Even then, having correctly packaged the parcel of relevant facts, the administrator must ask himself the right questions, applying the relevant law. The case of *Secretary of State for Education and Science v Tameside Metropolitan Borough Council*[1] is an example of how the courts are provided with almost unlimited scope for discerning some slip in the administrator's tortuous path through the thickets of often complex law and complicated factual situations. Much of the court's ability to uncover the fault in the process depends on both the court's power to order disclosure of documents and for it to test the statements by Ministers and government officials. We still await the full application of what Lord Diplock said in *O'Reilly v Mackman*,[2] to the effect that the court's leave for disclosure and cross-examination in judicial review cases is governed by the same principles as in actions begun by writ or originating summons – namely, that 'it should be allowed whenever the justice of the particular case so requires'.[3] Practice reveals that the courts are hesitant about liberally implementing a power to examine documents, disclosable on the grounds of relevance, which is the test in an ordinary claim, although the Court has done so in some recent cases. 'Justice' in this context appears to have a limiting function. But it may not continue to be so limited. Experience has shown that skilful draughtsmanship of statements by those acting for government departments may not always protect the Executive from judicial scrutiny.[4] Orders for cross-examination may also be made where there are crucial factual disputes between the parties relating to the application of human rights principles.[5]

[1] [1977] AC 1014, [1976] 3 All ER 665, and see also *R (on the application of Binyam Mohamed) v Secretary of State for Foreign and Commonwealth Affairs* [2010] EWCA Civ 65.
[2] [1983] 2 AC 237, [1982] 3 All ER 1124.
[3] [1983] 2 AC 237 at 283A.
[4] Compare *R v Secretary of State for Social Services, ex p Lewisham, Lambeth and Southwark London Borough Council* (1980) Times, 26 February and *Council of Civil Service Unions v Minister for the Civil Service* [1985] AC 374, [1984] 3 All ER 935, HL.
[5] *R (Wilkinson) v Broadmoor Hospital* [2002] 1 WLR 419 and *R (Al-Sweady) v Secretary of State for Defence* [2009] EWHC 2387 (Admin) at para 19, [2010] HRLR 2, at para 19.

CONCLUSION

3.21 Activism in the courts, if unchecked, will invariably be seen by government as a voracious judicial appetite that goes beyond the bounds of acceptable regulation of public administration. But, in reality, it may be no more than an expression of willingness on the part of the judges to protect the desired public weal (and not just the challenge by one individual, whether aggrieved or not by any administrative decision) from *dirigisme*. Where the decision-maker is either a public body, outwith central or local government; or a governmental agency; or a local authority; or it is a decision palpably made by a civil servant and not personally made by a Minister — in all these instances the courts are not slow to use judicial review in all its aspects. It is only where the decision is ministerial, implementing the policy of government, that courts are understandably wary of being accused of substituting their own judgments, for which they are unaccountable other than in the appellate court structure. But recent events have disclosed a welcome shift towards judicial insistence on ministerial observance of the rule of law. The House of Lords on 14 December 2004[1] concluded that provisions in primary and secondary legislation conferring the power to detain without trial foreigners who were 'suspected international terrorists' did not rationally address the threat to security, constituted a disproportionate response, and were not strictly required by the exigencies of the situation. Accordingly, the secondary legislation was quashed and the primary legislation was declared incompatible with the European Convention on Human Rights. Lord Bingham's opinion in that case helpfully summarised the view of the House of Lords as to the relationship of the system of justice to the system of government:

> 'The more purely political (in a broad or narrow sense) a question is, the more appropriate it will be for political resolution and the less likely it is to be an appropriate matter for judicial decision . . . Conversely, the greater the legal content of any issue, the greater the potential role of the court, because under our constitution and subject to the sovereign power of Parliament it is the function of the courts and not of political bodies to resolve legal questions.'[2]

This decision reflected a judicial awakening to the fact that even in the context of national security – traditionally, a hands-off area, of which the *GCHQ* case in 1984[3] was a prime example – the courts have a responsibility to ensure ministerial compliance with the rule of law. Nevertheless, this responsibility only stretches so far. In November 2014, the Supreme Court emphasised that a court of review must not usurp the function of the decision-maker, even when human rights are engaged. As Lord Sumption put it:

> 'Ministers are politically responsible for the consequences of their decision. Judges are not. These considerations are particularly important in the context of decisions about national security on which . . . "the cost of failure can be high".'[4]

[1] *A v Secretary of State for the Home Department* [2004] UKHL 56, [2005] 2 AC 68.
[2] [Ibid], at para 29.
[3] *Council of Civil Service Unions v Minister for the Civil Service* [1985] AC 374.
[4] *R (Lord Carlile of Berriew and others) v Secretary of State for the Home Department* [2015] AC 945, per Lord Sumption at paragraph 32.

3.22 The extent to which courts will nevertheless seek to control even political decisions, under the guise of procedural impropriety or illegality, ebbs and flows depending on the contemporary political climate. At times when Government appears all-powerful and uncontrolled by Parliament, judges may incline to supplement parliamentary control. At other times, when the institutional checks and balances on unbridled political power are in place and fully operative, judges may be inclined to back off from using their ultimate weapon of judicial review. Recent years have borne witness to a government challenge to perceived judicial activism, which is manifested in critical press commentary on individual judicial decisions[1] and reforms that limit access to judicial review.[2]

[1] As described by Sir Stephen Sedley in *'Judicial Politics'* (London Review of Books, 23 February 2012, at p 16).
[2] Criminal Justice and Courts Act 2015, Part 4. For the background to these reforms, see the Ministry of Justice consultation response: *'Judicial Review – proposals for further reform: the Government response'* (Ministry of Justice, February 2014).

3.23 The democratic process is something more subtle than the postulation of rights and duties, powers and responsibilities. One of the niceties of judicial activism is the public sense that intervention by judges in the governmental process needs to be finely tuned to the particular situation. It too calls for judicial review of a different kind. It is not a question of whether Mr Justice Cocklecarrot or Sir Humphrey Appleby should make the final decision. Rather it is a matter of variable choice, according to the mood of the times and the circumstances of the topic under decision.

3.24 In the past, judges studiously avoided any association with public administration, because to show even the slightest awareness of how the executive operates might appear to destroy – or in fact destroy – the highly prized virtue of judicial independence. But, under the impact of the development of judicial review, courts and administrators do not always, any longer, keep their respective distances. They sensibly regard the executive and the judiciary, along with the legislature, as discrete parts of a unified system of government (with a small 'g') functioning in harmony, if not in harness. The fact that courts are independent adjudicators of administrative action against the citizen does not minimise the political reality that they are the arms of established government.[1] Courts do not, now at least, operate on the periphery of society, but are vital cogs in the wheels of a well-oiled vehicle of good and sound government. 'Judges', Lord Scarman wrote – perhaps on a note of self-fulfilling prophecy – in his Child Lecture in 1976, *The Laws in Transition* (p 12), 'always have been political animals. They have always had to act in the marketplace and in the political arena. They operate, of necessity, in a social, political, economic setting . . . The most important thing is that they act judicially'. And the Minister or administrator must act judiciously in his or her approach to the law in action. Some Ministers in recent times have not always observed that injunction. That duality of government in a modern setting can be upset, and cause unnecessary tension between the judicial and executive arms of government, if judges fail to observe restraint in their judgments. Twice in recent years a member of the higher judiciary has notably crossed the borderline with a statement that was certainly incautious, even injudicious. In the Belmarsh detainees case, Lord Hoffmann, one of the eight Law Lords in the majority, said:

> 'The real threat to *the life of the nation*, in the sense of a people living in accordance with its traditional laws and political values, *comes not from terrorism but from laws such as these*. That is the true measure of what terrorism may achieve. It is for Parliament to decide whether to give the terrorists such a victory'.[2]

---

[1] Joshua Rozenberg in his book, *Trial of Strength* (Richard Cohen Books, 1997), was, with respect, wrong to correct Will Hutton, then the editor of the Observer, who talked of the judiciary as the 'third branch of government' in *The State We're In*.

[2] *R v Secretary of State for the Home Department* [2004] UKHL 56, at para 97 (italics supplied).

3.25 And in a torture case in 2010, Lord Neuberger, the Master of the Rolls, wrote, in part of his draft judgment (withdrawn and later modified), as follows:[1]

> 'Fourthly, it is also germane that the SyS [security services] were making it clear in March 2005, through a report from the Intelligence and Security Committee that "they operated a culture that respected human rights and that coercive interrogation techniques were alien to the Services' general ethics, methodology and training" (*paragraph 9 of the first judgment*), indeed they "denied that [they] knew of any ill-treatment of detainees interviewed by them whilst detained by or on behalf of the

[US] Government" (*paragraph 44(ii) of the fourth judgment*). Yet that does not seem to be true: as the evidence in this case showed, at least *some SyS officials appear to have a dubious record when it comes to human rights and coercive techniques*, and indeed when it comes to frankness about the UK's involvement with the mistreatment of Mr Mohammed by US officials. I have in mind in particular witness B, but it appears likely that there were others. The good faith of the Foreign Secretary is not in question, but he prepared the certificates partly, possibly largely, on the basis of information and advice provided by SyS personnel. Regrettably, but inevitably, this must raise the question whether any statement in the certificates on an issue concerning such mistreatment can be relied on, especially when the issue is whether contemporaneous communications to the SyS about such mistreatment should be revealed publicly. *Not only is there an obvious reason for distrusting any UK Government assurance, based on SyS advice and information, because of previous "form", but the Foreign Office and the SyS have an interest in the suppression of such information'.*

---

¹ *R (on the application of Binyam Mohamed) v Secretary of State for Foreign and Commonwealth Affairs* [2010] EWCA Civ 65 (italics supplied).

3.26 In recent years, a perceived trend towards greater judicial activism has attracted considerable criticism from politicians and the senior judiciary alike. In a case about the detention and questioning of a journalist at Heathrow Airport, the Divisional Court demonstrated a distinct lack of willingness to interfere in questions of national security.[1]Addressing the claimant's proportionality argument, Laws LJ had '*real difficulty in distinguishing this from a political question to be decided by the elected arm of government*'. Laws LJ was also dismissive of those who, outside of government, seek to piece together the jigsaw of threats to national security.[2]

Lord Sumption has also argued strongly in favour of a less intrusive judiciary in two extra-judicial speeches, asking: '*How do we decide what is the "right" answer to a question about which people strongly disagree, without resorting to a political process to mediate that disagreement?*'[3] This analysis attracted a robust response.[4] Notwithstanding the comments of Lord Hoffmann and Lord Neuberger, above, the current trend therefore appears to point away from judicial activism.'

---

¹ *R (Miranda) v Secretary of State for the Home Department* [2014] EWHC 255 (Admin), [2014] 3 All ER 447.
² [Ibid], at paras 40, 58, and 71.
³ '*The Limits of Law*', the 27th Sultan Azlan Shah Lecture, 20 November 2013, at p 14; see also '*Judicial and Political Decision-Making – the Uncertain Boundary*', the F.A. Mann Lecture, 2011.
⁴ Sir Stephen Sedley '*Judicial Politics*' (*London Review of Books*, 23 February 2012, at pp 15–16).

3.27 No one case has summed up the concerns about an overactive judiciary more acutely than the recent 'Brexit' challenge, *R (Miller) v Secretary of State for Exiting the European Union* [2017] 2 WLR 583. The issue was whether the Government could 'trigger' the process for leaving the European Union without Parliamentary approval. When the Divisional Court found in favour of the claimant, the reaction was nothing short of furious, with newspapers suggesting that the Court was trying to interfere with a referendum result and with the judges being angrily described as, 'Enemies of the People', in one front-page story.[1] In giving judgment, the Supreme Court was therefore careful to explain that the question of law for it to determine was justiciable:

'It deserves emphasis at the outset that the court in these proceedings is only dealing with a pure question of law. Nothing we say has any bearing on the question of the merits or demerits of a withdrawal by the UK from the EU; nor does it have any bearing on government policy, because government policy is not law. The policy to be applied by the executive government and the merits or demerits of withdrawal are matters of political judgment to be resolved through the political process.'[2]

[1] *Daily Mail*, 3 November 2016.
[2] *R (Miller) v Secretary of State of Exiting the European Union* [2017] 2 WLR 583, per Lord Neuberger, at paragraphs 5.

Chapter 4

THE HUMAN RIGHTS ACT AND JUDICIAL REVIEW

THE BACKGROUND TO THE HUMAN RIGHTS ACT 1998

4.1 The legal structure of government and administration in England and Wales comprises three main elements:

(1)   the legislative supremacy of Parliament;
(2)   the powers and duties of central government (the Executive) and other public authorities charged with acting in the general interest;
(3)   the role of the courts in adjudicating upon the rights and duties, privileges and immunities, both of private individuals and public authorities.

4.2 In the absence of a written constitution, no 'higher law' limits the power of Parliament to legislate, and the courts may not review the validity of Acts of Parliament. But all legislation by Parliament is subject to being interpreted and applied by the courts.[1] Under the principle of the 'rule of law', the courts play an authoritative role in determining what the law for the time being requires both in relations between private persons, and in relations between private persons and the public authorities that exercise executive power. This latter function of the courts is, to a large extent, exercised through the process of judicial review. The foundations for the law of judicial review have been much debated.[2] While the powers and duties of public authorities are mainly the result of legislation, the most significant rules applied by the courts in judicial review do not derive directly from legislation but have been developed by the courts within their jurisdiction at common law. Yet the common law rules may be modified by statute and may be excluded from applying in particular situations.

[1] See AV Dicey, *Law of the Constitution* ECS Wade (ed) (10th edn, 1959), Ch 1 and pp 413–414. This traditional view is discussed in Chapter 6. For the special position of Acts passed under the Parliament Act 1911, see *R (Jackson) v A-G* [2005] UKHL 56, [2006] 1 AC 262, [2005] 4 All ER 1253.

[2] See Chapter 6 and, in particular, C Forsyth (ed), Judicial Review and the Constitution (2000) and M Elliott The Constitutional Foundations of Judicial Review (2001).

4.3 The royal assent is an essential formality before a Bill approved by both Houses becomes law, and the Crown has in principle no power to legislate without Parliament. However, the Crown, acting through its ministers, exercises many executive functions that derive from the royal prerogative at common law.[1] The prerogative includes the conduct of foreign relations, by which the Government enters into agreements with other states that bind the United Kingdom in international law. The treaty-making prerogative does not include power to alter the law in the United Kingdom, for which legislation by Parliament is required.[2] Thus British entry to the European Communities on 1 January 1973 took effect through:

(1)   the Government's adherence to the Treaty of Brussels; and
(2)   enactment of the European Communities Act 1972, giving effect in the United Kingdom to Community law.[3]

By contrast, exiting the European Union has been held to require the mandate of Parliament because this will alter the law in the United Kingdom.[4]

[1] See 4th Report, Public Administration Committee of the House of Commons (HC 422, 2003–04), 'Taming the Prerogative: Strengthening Ministerial Accountability to Parliament'. Orders in Council made under prerogative powers are in principle subject to judicial review: *R (Bancoult) v Secretary of State for Foreign and Commonwealth Affairs (No 2)* [2008] UKHL 61, [2009] AC 453, [2008] 4 All ER 1055; and see **5.35**.

[2] *R (Miller) v Secretary of State for Exiting the European Union* [2017] UKSC 5.

[3] For discussion of European Union law and its impact on judicial review, see Chapter **15**.

[4] *R (Miller) v Secretary of State for Exiting the European Union* [2017] UKSC 5.

4.4 The background to the Human Rights Act 1998 (HRA 1998) lies in a different application of the same fundamentals. The European Convention on Human Rights, signed in 1950, was one of the first regional treaties aimed at protecting human rights. In March 1951, the UK Government was the first signatory to ratify the Convention. However, in the absence of legislation by Parliament, ratification of the Convention did not enable rights guaranteed by the Convention to be protected in national law. It is often claimed that the substance of many Convention rights (for example, the individual's right to liberty and the right to freedom of expression) was recognised at common law,[1] but the common law rules had mainly evolved long before the Convention existed, and they could at any time be restricted by Acts of Parliament. For this reason, rights and liberties had a residual character, since in essence they consisted of the freedom to do whatever was not restricted by common law or by statute.

[1]   Other Convention rights were not — for example, the right to respect for an individual's privacy (ECHR, art 8): *Wainwright v Home Office* [2003] UKHL 53, [2004] 2 AC 406, [2003] 4 All ER 969. But rights based directly upon private property have long been protected: eg *Entick v Carrington* (1765) 2 Wils 275.

4.5 Nearly 50 years elapsed between British ratification of the Convention in 1951 and enactment of the HRA in 1998.[1] Unlike the European Community treaties, the Convention did not require direct effect in national law to be given to Convention rights. States that adhere to the Convention undertake to secure to everyone within their jurisdiction the Convention rights and freedoms (art 1), and to provide an effective remedy before a national authority (art 13), but how these duties should be performed is largely left to each state to decide,[2] subject to the jurisdiction of the European Court of Human Rights (the Strasbourg Court) to deal with alleged breaches of Convention rights. The Convention is often described as a 'living instrument', and the meaning of the rights that it protects is to be found in the decisions of the Strasbourg Court, as it has evolved in the light of changing circumstances.[3] In its origins, the Convention sought to ensure that minimum standards for protecting rights were observed across Europe. For many years after 1951, successive UK Governments took the view that the law in the UK complied with these minimum standards, and thus that it was unnecessary to incorporate the Convention rights in national law. Later, as many decisions of the Strasbourg Court showed that Convention rights were breached by UK law or practice, the Government's stance changed to emphasising its determination to comply with the court's decisions, and its willingness if necessary to change the law so that it would be consistent with the Convention. This policy was compatible with the Convention scheme for protecting the guaranteed rights, since (as we have seen) States are not required to give the Convention any particular status in national law.[4]

[1]   For an account of events between 1951 and 1998, see A Lester, D Pannick and J Herberg, *Human Rights Law and Practice* (3rd edn, 2009), Ch 1. For the UK's role in the making of the Convention, see AWB Simpson, *Human Rights and the End of Empire: Britain and the Genesis of the European Convention* (2004).
[2]   *Swedish Engine Drivers' Union v Sweden (Application 5614/72)* (1976) 1 EHRR 617, paragraph 50; *Ireland v United Kingdom (Application 5310/71)* (1978) 2 EHRR 25, paragraphs 236–240.
[3]   See, eg *Johnston v Ireland (Application 9697/82)* (1986) 9 EHRR 203, paragraph 53.
[4]   For the effect and status of the ECHR in 32 states, including the UK, see R Blackburn and J Polakiewicz (ed), *Fundamental Rights in Europe: The ECHR and its Member States, 1950–2000* (2001).

4.6 Having ratified the ECHR in 1951, the Government in 1966 accepted what at that time were optional features of the Convention system, namely:

(1)   the right of individuals to petition Strasbourg for relief under the Convention; and

(2)   the jurisdiction of the court to hear such petitions against the Govern-

ment.[1]

[1] See A Lester. 'Fundamental Rights: the United Kingdom isolated' [1984] *Public Law* 46; and 'UK Acceptance of the Strasbourg Jurisdiction: What Went on in Whitehall in 1963' [1998] *Public Law* 237.

4.7 The first decision by the Strasbourg Court involving the UK was made in 1975.[1] By 1990, some 30 substantive decisions involving the UK had been made by the court as well as many preliminary decisions dealing with petitions from Britain. By 1 March 2000, over 60 such decisions by the court had been made in which one or more violations of the Convention had been found.[2] Two significant early decisions may be mentioned. In *Sunday Times Ltd v United Kingdom (Application 6538/74)*,[3] the court held by a majority that a decision by the House of Lords applying the law on contempt of court had infringed the newspaper's freedom of expression under art 10. Thereafter, the national law was amended by the Contempt of Court Act 1981. In *Malone v United Kingdom (Application 8691/79)*, there was an even more striking divergence between English law and the Convention: the English High Court having held that the police did not have to show legal authority for telephone-tapping, the Strasbourg Court held that telephone-tapping without a proper legal basis infringed the Convention. Legislation on telephone-tapping was thereafter enacted.[4]

[1] *Golder v United Kingdom (Application 4451/70)* (1975) 1 EHRR 524.
[2] A list of these cases is in Blackburn and Polakiewicz (see **4.5** above), at pp 972–973.
[3] (1979) 2 EHRR 245, [1979] ECHR 6538/74.
[4] See *Malone v United Kingdom (Application 8691/79)* (1984) 7 EHRR 14; and the Interception of Communications Act 1985.

4.8 Inevitably some decisions by the Strasbourg Court have been unwelcome to the UK Government.[1] The strongest political criticism of this kind has been directed to the ruling of the Strasbourg Court in respect of the UK's blanket ban on the right of all convicted prisoners to vote.[2] Sections of the media and some politicians claim that the Court has enlarged the ambit of rights under the Convention to a point at which it is taking power from national parliaments to make decisions for which the latter should be democratically accountable.[3] Adherence to the Convention is obligatory for all members of the Council of Europe. Therefore, leaving the Convention (and the supervisory jurisdiction of the European Court of Human Rights) would require not only repeal of the HRA 1998, but also the UK's departure from the Council of Europe.

Within Europe, there has been emphasis on creating greater subsidiarity within the judicial process, most notably via the Izmir, Interlaken and Brighton declarations and the new Protocol 15 ECHR adopted in May 2013, but not yet in force.[4] Judges in the UK have emphasised that the Convention does not 'supersede the protection of human rights under the common law or statute'; rather, the general guarantees of the Convention are to be fulfilled through the more specific provisions of domestic law.[5] In addition, there has been considerable judicial comment emphasising the role of dialogue between the Strasbourg Court and the UK courts.[6] There is the prospect of the new draft Optional Protocol 16 ECHR, providing for increased advisory jurisdiction of the Strasbourg Court which has been opened for signature but is not yet in force, that may shift the balance in the approach of the Strasbourg Court.[7]

1   In particular, *McCann v United Kingdom (Application 18984/91)* (1995) 21 EHRR 97, [1995] ECHR 18984/91; *Chahal v United Kingdom (Application 22414/93)* (1996) 23 EHRR 413,(1996) Times, 28 November.

2   See *Hirst v United Kingdom (No 2) (Application 74035/01)* (2005) 42 EHRR 849, (2005) Times, 10 October; *Scoppola v Italy (No 3) (Application 126/05)* (2012) Times, 12 June, 33 BHRC 126and *R (Chester) v Secretary of State for Justice* [2013] UKSC 63, [2014] AC 271, [2014] 1 All ER 683.

3   See M Hunt, H Hooper and P Yowell (eds), *Parliaments and Human Rights: Redressing the Democratic Deficit* (2017). In response to the prisoner voting decision, the House of Commons passed a resolution on 10 February 2011 expressing the opinion that *'legislative decisions of this nature should be a matter for democratically elected lawmakers'* (HC Deb, 10 February 2011, col. 493). The Conservative Party's briefing paper in advance of the 2015 General Election 'Protecting Human Rights in the UK: The Conservatives' Proposals for Changing Britain's Human Rights Laws' contended that *'The European Court of Human Rights has developed "mission creep"'*.

4   Available on the ECHR website: www.echr.coe.int; accessed on 5 May 2014.

5   Lord Reed, *Osborn v Parole Board* [2013] UKSC 61 at paragraphs 55–57,[2014] 1 All ER 369 at paragraphs 55–57, [2013] 3 WLR 1020 at paragraphs 55–57. At paragraph [63] he noted that the appellants had wrongly supposed that 'because an issue falls within the ambit of a Convention guarantee, it follows that the legal analysis of the problem should begin and end with the Strasbourg case law'. This echoes Lord Reed's lecture 'The interrelationship of Strasbourg and UK Human Rights Law' to the Scottish Public Law Group, March 2011. And see *Kennedy v Charity Commission* [2014] UKSC 20, paragraphs 38 and 46,[2014] 2 All ER 847, paragraphs 38 and 46, (2014) Times, 02 April, paragraphs 38 and 46.

6   See for example, Sir Nicholas Bratza, 'The relationship between the UK courts and Strasbourg' [2011] EHRLR 505; Lord Phillips in *R. v Horncastle* [2009] UKSC 14 at paragraphs 11 and 108[2010] 2 AC 373 at paragraphs 11 and 108,[2010] 2 All ER 359 at paragraphs 11 and 108; and Sir Nicholas Bratza's concurring opinion in *Al-Khawaja and Tahery v United Kingdom (Applications 26766/05 and 22228/06)* (2012) 54 EHRR 23, [2012] Crim LR 375.

7   Although note Lord Judge's concern about Protocol 16 in evidence to the Joint Committee on Human Rights, HC 873(ii) 2010–12 on 15 November 2011, q 98.

The case for incorporation of Convention rights

4.9   As will be evident from other chapters,[1] the last quarter of the twentieth century saw rapid growth in judicial review of administrative action in English law. This was evidenced by a series of influential public law decisions made by the appellate courts and a succession of procedural reforms, including creation of the procedure of 'application for judicial review'.[2] In the same period, influential calls were made for the enactment of a new Bill of Rights to declare the rights and freedoms of the individual vis-à-vis the state and to limit the power of Parliament to infringe those rights and freedoms.[3] Some groups coupled with this a call for a written constitution for the United Kingdom.[4] Moreover, responding to the record of the UK before the Strasbourg Court, many (including senior judges)[5] argued for the incorporation of the ECHR, so that arguments based on the Convention might be made in judicial review proceedings.

1   See Chapters 2 and 3 and paragraph 11.38 et seq.

2   See Senior Courts Act 1981, s 31. And see Chapters 2 and 3.

3   See, eg Lord Scarman *English Law — the New Dimension* (1974).

4   See Institute for Public Policy Research, *The Constitution of the United Kingdom* (1991).

5   See eg Lord Browne-Wilkinson, 'The Infiltration of a Bill of Rights' [1992] *Public Law* 397; Sir T H Bingham, 'The ECHR: Time to Incorporate' (1993) 109 LQR 390; Lord Woolf, 'Droit

public: English Style' [1995] *Public Law* 57; Sir S Sedley, 'Human Rights: a 21st Century Agenda' [1995] *Public Law* 386.

4.10 The case for reform included the view that the absence of substantive public law rights in English law led to unsatisfactory judicial reasoning,[1] and that the scope of judicial review should be enlarged to protect rights guaranteed by the Convention.[2] Only in certain exceptional situations were the courts entitled to apply the Convention.[3] In *R v Secretary of State for the Home Department, ex p Brind*,[4] the House of Lords held, on an application for judicial review of a Minister's decision to restrict broadcasting of certain material in the public interest, that the courts could not, absent legislation giving effect to the Convention, apply art 10 (freedom of expression). The Minister's power to restrict the content of broadcasting was held to be broad but not ambiguous. Further, in *Brind* the applicants argued that decisions limiting freedom of expression should be subject to the test of proportionality, rather than the test in English law of *Wednesbury* unreasonableness, but it was held that proportionality was not part of national law.[5]

[1]   As in *Wheeler v Leicester City Council* [1985] AC 1054.
[2]   J Jowell and A Lester, 'Beyond *Wednesbury*: Substantive Principles of Administrative Law' [1987] *Public Law* 368.
[3]   See M Hunt, *Using Human Rights Law in English Courts* (1997). Two situations in which the courts were willing to apply the Convention were (a) where legislation was ambiguous and a Convention-compliant interpretation was possible, and (b) where the common law was developing and the court was able to develop the law in a manner that was Convention-compliant.
[4]   [1991] 1 AC 696, [1991] 2 WLR 588.
[5]   See CHAPTERS 8 and 9.

4.11 Despite the absence of legislation to incorporate the ECHR, English courts referred to the Convention and its case law in an increasing number of situations.[1] The indirect influence of the Convention was seen in many judicial review decisions developing the principles of administrative law: in particular, the traditional *Wednesbury* test of unreasonableness was modified in cases involving human rights.[2] The courts were increasingly referred to decisions concerning human rights in other jurisdictions,[3] including decisions under the Canadian Charter of Rights and Freedoms 1982 and the New Zealand Bill of Rights Act 1990. Yet all proposals for incorporating the Convention at this time were blocked by the Government.[4]

[1]   See note 3 to paragraph **4.10** above.
[2]   See CHAPTER 8 (which includes cross-references to the account of the law of Scotland in CHAPTER 21) and, in particular, *R v Ministry of Defence, ex p Smith* [1996] QB 517,[1996] 1 All ER 257 CA.
[3]   See, eg *Pratt v A-G of Jamaica* [1994] 2 AC 1, [1993] 4 All ER 769, PC.
[4]   See A Lester, 'The Mouse that Roared: the Human Rights Bill 1995' (1995) *Public Law* 198.

4.12 The campaign for incorporating the Convention received indirect support from the way in which the 'incoming tide' of Community law had been received into English law. The *Factortame* litigation established that even when the Westminster Parliament had legislated on a matter, a statutory provision could be disapplied if it was inconsistent with rights in Community law.[1] There was thus a sharp contrast between the power of the courts to review statutes where necessary to ensure conformity with Community law, and the uncertainties that faced a litigant who sought to rely on the ECHR.[2]

> [1] *R v Secretary of State for Transport, ex p Factortame Ltd (No 2)* [1991] 1 AC 603, [1990] 3 WLR 818, HL. See **15.73** et seq.
> [2] See note 3 paragraph **4.10** above.

4.13 In preparation for the 1997 general election, the Labour and Liberal Democrat parties adopted a common platform of constitutional reform that included incorporation of the ECHR. In October 1997, the Human Rights Bill was published, and the Human Rights Act 1998 (HRA 1998) was enacted a year later.[1] A duty to comply with Convention rights accompanied the devolution of powers to Scotland and Wales,[2] but the Act was brought into force only on 2 October 2000.

Since it came into force, the HRA has been of fundamental constitutional significance because of the increased role that it gives to the superior courts in reviewing the compatibility of primary legislation with the Convention. The decisions of the courts have had a particular impact in relation to national security and anti-terrorist measures.[3] Questions have been raised as to whether there should be a UK Bill of Rights to supplement the HRA 1998, and in 2012 the report of a commission appointed by the government set out an extensive range of options.[4] The Conservative Party published a briefing paper prior to the 2015 General Election proposing to repeal the HRA 1998 and replace it with a British Bill of Rights; that commitment was reiterated in the Queen's Speech 2016, but at the time of going to press no consultation document or draft Bill has been published.[5]

> [1] For the policy decisions behind the HRA, see the White Paper *'Rights Brought Home: the Human Rights Bill'* (Cm 3782, October 1997).
> [2] Scotland Act 1998, ss 29(2)(d), 57(2); Government of Wales Act 1998, s 107 (now Government of Wales Act 2006, s 81). See also Northern Ireland Act 1998, ss 6(2)(c), 24(1)(a). These provisions are discussed in Chapter **21**. As explained in that chapter, questions as to the compatibility with Convention rights of the exercise of devolved powers are treated as 'devolution issues', and significant cases concerning Convention rights (among them *Starrs v Ruxton (Procurator Fiscal Linlithgow)* (1999) Times, 17 November, 2000 SLT 42 and *Brown v Stott (Procurator Fiscal Dunfermline)* [2001] 2 LRC 612, [2003] 1 AC 681) have arisen in this form.
> [3] See further A Lester, D Pannick and J Herberg, *Human Rights Law and Practice* (3rd edn, 2009), 1.53–1.73.
> [4] The Commission on a Bill of Rights report, *A UK Bill of Rights? The Choice Before Us*, December 2012. See also M Elliott, 'A Damp Squib in the Long Grass' [2013] EHRLR 137.
> [5] 'Protecting Human Rights in the UK: The Conservatives' Proposals for Changing Britain's Human Rights Laws'.

THE STRUCTURE OF THE HRA 1998

4.14 Before the Act's implications for judicial review are discussed, the key provisions of the Human Rights Act 1998 must be outlined.[1] The stated purpose of the Act is 'to give further effect' to the rights and freedoms guaranteed by the Convention. The Act requires that all legislation must (so far as possible) be 'read and given effect' in a way that is compatible with Convention rights; the Act imposes a duty on all public authorities to act in a way which is compatible with those rights; and remedies are available in order that someone who claims that his or her Convention rights have been infringed may obtain a judicial decision on the matter.

[1]   And see A Lester, D Pannick and J Herberg *Human Rights Law and Practice* (3rd edn, 2009), Ch 2.

Convention rights – their definition and application

4.15   The term 'Convention rights' is defined (s 1(1)) as meaning the rights and freedoms set out in arts 2–12 and 14 of the Convention and in certain Protocols to the Convention,[1] all as read with arts 16–18 of the Convention. These articles 'are to have effect for the purposes of this Act', subject to any reservation or derogation from them that the UK may have made (s 1(2)). The House of Lords emphasised that there is a clear distinction between rights arising under the Convention and rights created by the Act by reference to the Convention.[2] In deciding questions that arise in connection with a Convention right, all courts and tribunals must take into account decisions of the European Court of Human Rights,[3] where these appear relevant to the proceedings in which the question has arisen (s 2). There has been much debate about what 'take into account' means.

Firstly, does this mean that the Supreme Court is bound by decisions of the Strasbourg Court? It is notable that Lord Phillips of Worth Matravers, then President of the Supreme Court, and Lord Judge, then LCJ, differed on this point in evidence to the Joint Committee on Human Rights in 2011.[4] Lord Phillips considered that Strasbourg would always 'win', whereas Lord Judge noted that perhaps Strasbourg 'should not win and does not need to win'.[5] Lord Irvine has been emphatic that s 2 of the HRA means that 'judges are not bound to follow the Strasbourg Court: they must decide the case for themselves'. He emphasised that s 2 used the language of 'take account of' not 'follow', 'give effect to' or 'be bound by'.[6]

The Supreme Court took this approach in *R v Horncastle*[7] regarding hearsay evidence by declining to follow the apparently clear Strasbourg decision in *Al -Khawaja v United Kingdom (Applications 26766/05 and 22228/06)*.[8] Lord Phillips explicitly set out why the Supreme Court disagreed with *Al -Khawaja* and that, having taken it into account, the court declined to follow it.[9] However there are limits to this process, particularly where the matter has already been referred to the Grand Chamber: 'It would have then to involve some truly fundamental principle of our law or some most egregious oversight or misunderstanding before it could be appropriate for this court to contemplate an outright refusal to follow Strasbourg authority at the Grand Chamber level'.[10]

The second question is whether the UK courts may go beyond decisions of the Strasbourg Court, particularly where that court has not yet considered a particular issue. Lord Bingham in *R (Ullah) v Special Adjudicator* stated that protection should be 'no more, but certainly no less'.[11] Lord Brown in *R (Al-Skeini) v Secretary of State for Defence* thought the protection should be 'no more' than that provided by Strasbourg.[12] However, in *Rabone v Pennine Care NHS Foundation Trust*[13] he stated that 'it would be absurd' to suggest that the domestic courts could not determine an issue because it had not been specifically resolved by Strasbourg jurisprudence.[14] Lord Hope in *P (adoption: unmarried couple), Re* considered that Strasbourg case law should not be treated as a straightjacket[15] but went on in *Ambrose v Harris (Procurator Fiscal Oban) (Scotland)*[16] to state that 'Parliament never intended to give the courts of this country the power to give a more generous scope to those rights than that which was to be found in the jurisprudence of the Strasbourg court'.[17] The Court of Appeal refused to use s 2 to go beyond Strasbourg jurisprudence in direct opposition of the will of Parliament.[18] However, in the Supreme Court, Lord Wilson has stated that he would welcome an opportunity for that court to consider whether 'it might now usefully do more than to shadow the ECtHR . . . '[19] and subsequently set out a timeline of cases showing 'retreat from the *Ullah* principle' which led him to conclude that 'protracted consideration over the last six years has led this court substantially to modify the *Ullah* principle', such that in the absence of a directly relevant decision of the ECtHR 'we can and must do more'.[20]

---

1. Articles 1–3 of the First Protocol, and arts 1 and 2 of the Sixth Protocol.
2. *McKerr, Re* [2004] UKHL 12, paragraph 25, [2004] NI 212, paragraph 25, [2004] 2 All ER 409, paragraph 25; *R (Al -Jedda) v Secretary of State for Defence* [2007] UKHL 58, paragraph 51, [2008] 3 LRC 718, paragraph 51, [2008] 3 All ER 28, paragraph 51. See also Lord Scott, *R (Animal Defenders International) v Secretary of State for Culture, Media and Sport* [2008] UKHL 15, paragraphs 42–46 [2008] 1 AC 1312, paragraphs 42–46, [2008] 3 All ER 193, paragraphs 42–46. This principle has been criticised by Beatson et al, *Human Rights: Judicial Protection in the UK* (2008).
3. And of the former European Commission on Human Rights.
4. Evidence to Joint Committee on Human Rights, HC 873(ii) 2010-12 on 15 November 2011. See in particular answers to questions 71 and 124.
5. See answers to questions 64, 70, 81 and 124.
6. Lord Irvine, 'A British Interpretation of Convention Rights' [2012] *Public Law* 237 at 239 and 241. See also P Sales, 'Strasbourg Jurisprudence and the Human Rights Act: a response to Lord Irvine' [2012] *Public Law* 253 and J. Sumption QC (as he then was), 'Judicial and political decision-making: the uncertain boundary' [2011] JR 301.
7. [2009] UKSC 14,[2010] 2 AC 373, [2010] 2 All ER 359.
8. (2009) 49 EHRR 1, [2009] Crim LR 352.
9. This led to the effective reversal of *Al -Khawaja* by the Grand Chamber (2012) 54 EHRR 23. In his concurring opinion, Sir Nicolas Bratza approved the Supreme Court's approach in *Horncastle*. Arguably he takes this further in his article (see **4.8** note 6) at 512, stating that 'I believe that it is right and healthy that national courts should continue to feel free to criticise Strasbourg judgments . . . '. See also *Manchester City Council v Pinnock* [2010] UKSC 45 at paragraph 48, [2011] 1 All ER 285 at paragraph 48, **[2011] 3 WLR 1441 at paragraph 48**, *R (Aguilar Quila) v Secretary of State for the Home Department* [2011] UKSC 45 at paragraph 43, **[2012] 1 AC 621 at paragraph 43**, [2012] 1 All ER 1011 at paragraph 43 and *R (Hicks) v Commissioner of Police of the Metropolis* [2014] EWCA Civ 3; [2014] 1 WLR 2152. Protocol 16 ECHR will enable the Supreme Court to seek an advisory opinion from the Strasbourg Court on questions of principle in relation to the interpretation of the Convention, see: www.echr.coe.int/Documents/Protocol_16_ENG.pdf.. However, this is not yet in force.
10. Lord Mance, *R (Chester) v Secretary of State for Justice* [2013] UKSC 63 at paragraph 27, [2014] AC 271 at paragraph 27, [2014] 1 All ER 683 at paragraph 27. In *R (Kaiyam) v Secretary of State for Justice* [2014] UKSC 66 at paragraph 21, [2015] AC 1344 at paragraph 21, Lord Mance clarified that 'the degree of constraint imposed or freedom allowed by the phrase "must take into account" is context specific', and the reference to 'some egregious oversight or misunderstanding' is no more than a 'general guideline'.
11. [2004] UKHL 26 at paragraph 20, [2004] 2 AC 323 at paragraph 20, [2004] 3 All ER 785 at paragraph 20.
12. [2007] UKHL 26 at paragraph 106, [2008] 1 AC 153 at paragraph 106, [2007] 3 All ER 685 at paragraph 106.
13. [2012] UKSC 2, [2012] 2 AC 72, [2012] 2 All ER 381.
14. At 112.
15. [2008] UKHL 38 at paragraph 50, [2008] NI 310 at paragraph 50, [2008] 2 FCR 366 at paragraph 50.
16. [2011] UKSC 43, [2011] 1 WLR 2435, [2011] 40 LS Gaz R 21.

[17] At paragraph 19. Lord Kerr dissented, stating that 'it is not open to courts of this country to adopt an attitude of agnosticism and refrain from recognizing such a right simply because Strasbourg has not spoken' (at paragraph 128). This was approved of, extra-judicially, by Lord Irvine, at note 6 above, at 250. See similarly Lady Hale, '*Argentoratum Locutum:* Is Strasbourg or the Supreme Court Supreme?' [2012] 12 HRLR 65 at 76.

[18] *R (Nicklinson) v Ministry of Justice* [2013] EWCA Civ 961 at paragraph 112, [2014] 2 ALL ER 32 at paragraph 112, [2014] 3 WLR 200 at paragraph 112. When the case reached the Supreme Court, Lord Neuberger commented that this was 'not the occasion to address the question whether, and if so how far, the principle enunciated by Lord Bingham in Ullah's case, paragraph 20, should be modified or reconsidered': [2014] UKSC 38 at paragraph 70, [2015] AC 657 at paragraph 70.

[19] *Sugar v British Broadcasting Corpn* [2012] UKSC 4 at paragraph 59, [2012] 2 All ER 509 at paragraph 59, [2012] 1 WLR 439 at paragraph 59. This was echoed by Laws LJ in *R (The Children's Rights Alliance for England) v Secretary of State for Justice (The Equality and Human Rights Commission intervening)* [2013] EWCA Civ 34 at paragraphs 62–64, [2013] 1 WLR 3667 at paragraphs 62–64.

[20] *Moohan v Lord Advocate* [2014] UKSC 67 at paragraphs 104–105, [2015] AC 901 at paragraphs 104–105. Lord Wilson dissented as to the outcome of the appeal. This passage was cited by Lord Kerr in *Keyu v Secretary of State for Foreign and Commonwealth Affairs* [2015] UKSC 69 at paragraph 234; [2016] AC 1355 at paragraph 234. At paragraph 291 of *Keyu*, Baroness Hale further noted that 'we do not have slavishly to follow the Strasbourg jurisprudence.'

4.16 The geographical extent of the Convention has also proved contentious. A state's jurisdictional competence under Article 1 of the Convention is primarily territorial,[1] and extra-territorial jurisdiction will arise only in exceptional cases in which the power of a state has been exercised outside its borders.[2] "Exceptional" is not an especially high threshold.[3] The list of exceptional cases is not closed and includes state agent authority and control; where a state has effective control over an area; and the Convention legal space.[4] The indivisibility of the entire Convention rights is no longer a relevant consideration.[5]

[1] *Bancovic v Belgium (Application 52207/99)* (2001) 11 BHRC 435.

[2] *Al-Skeini v United Kingdom* (2011) 53 EHRR 589 at paragraph 131, (2011) Times, 13 July at paragraph 131. See also *R (Sandiford) v Secretary of State for Foreign and Commonwealth Affairs* [2014] UKSC 44; [2014] 1 WLR 2697.

[3] *Smith v Ministry of Defence* [2013] UKSC 41 at paragraph 30, [2014] AC 52 at paragraph 30, [2013] 4 All ER 794 at paragraph 30.

[4] *Al Skeini v UK* (2011) 53 EHRR 18 at paragraphs 133–137. The first category includes members of the armed forces operating in Iraq: *Smith v Ministry of Defence*, above overturning *R (Smith) v Secretary of State for Defence* [2010] UKSC 29, [2011] 1 AC 1, [2010] 3 All ER 1067. See also *Keyu v Secretary of State for Foreign and Commonwealth Affairs* [2015] UKSC 69; [2016] AC 1355.

[5] *Smith v Ministry of Defence* at paragraph 49.

4.17 Section 3(1) is of central importance to the Act. It provides:

> 'So far as it is possible to do so, primary legislation and subordinate legislation[1] must be read and given effect in a way which is compatible with the Convention rights.'

[1] For definition of 'primary legislation' and 'subordinate legislation', see HRA 1998, s 22(1); and see **4.37** below.

4.18 This duty binds all courts and tribunals, as well as all other decision-makers concerned with the operation of legislation. The duty expressly applies to all primary and subordinate legislation whenever enacted (s 3(2)(a)). But the duty does not affect the validity and continuing operation of primary legislation (s 3(2)(b)); nor does it affect the validity and continuing operation of incompatible subordinate legislation if primary legislation prevents removal of the incompatibility (s 3(2)(c)). The broad effect of this duty is that, 'so far as it is possible to do so', all legislation must be *interpreted and applied* in a manner which is Convention compliant, even when (apart from the new duty) the effect of the legislation would be inconsistent with a Convention right.[1]

1   See **4.29** below.

Incompatibility with a Convention right

4.19 Where a superior court (that is, the High Court or a higher court) holds that a provision in primary legislation is incompatible with a Convention right, and it is not possible to read and give effect to it in a way which is compatible with Convention rights, the court *may* make a declaration of that incompatibility (s 4(2), (5)).[1] The power to make a declaration of incompatibility may be applied to a provision of subordinate legislation where the primary legislation in question prevents removal of the incompatibility (s 4(4)).[2] Such a declaration of incompatibility is a novel power of the court that differs from the declaratory remedies that have long been available. The declaration does not affect the validity or continuing operation of the statutory provision in question, nor is it binding on the parties to the proceedings in which it is made (s 4(6)). Before a court may make a declaration of incompatibility, the Crown is entitled to notice of the proceedings that give rise to the possibility of a declaration, and the Crown may choose to be joined as a party to those proceedings (s 5(1), (2)).

1   See *R (Chester) v Secretary of State for Justice* [2013] UKSC 63,[2014] AC 271,[2014] 1 All ER 683 where the Supreme Court declined to make a declaration despite finding the legislation to be incompatible. See similarly *R (GC) v Metropolitan Police Comr* [2011] UKSC 21, [2011] 3 All ER 859, [2011] Cr App Rep 206.
2   For a list of declarations of incompatibility, see www.lse.ac.uk/humanrights. See also the annual Ministry of Justice report, '*Responding to human rights judgments*', made to the Joint Committee on Human Rights.

4.20 Another key provision of the HRA 1998 is s 6(1):[1]

'It is unlawful for a public authority to act in a way which is incompatible with a Convention right.'

1   See **4.47** below.

4.21 This provision does not apply if, because of primary legislation, the public authority could not have acted differently; nor does it apply if the authority was acting to give effect to provisions of, or made under, primary legislation which cannot be read or given effect in a way which is compatible with a Convention right (s 6(2)). 'Public authority' includes a court or tribunal, but it does not include either House of Parliament, nor a person exercising functions in connection with proceedings in Parliament (s 6(3)). The term 'public authority' includes any person whose functions include functions of a public nature as well as those of a private nature, but the duty under s 6(1) does not apply to the act of such a person 'if the nature of the act is private' (s 6(5)).[1] Section 6(1) applies both to an action and to a failure to act; but it does not apply to a failure to introduce in Parliament a proposal for legislation, nor to a failure to make any primary legislation (s 6(6)).

[1]   See **4.52** below.

Remedies for breach of Convention rights

4.22 Where it is claimed that a public authority has acted, or is proposing to act, in a manner which is made unlawful by s 6(1), someone who is or would be a victim of the unlawful act (within the meaning of 'victim' in the case law of the Strasbourg Court)[1] may either bring proceedings against the authority in an appropriate court or tribunal, or rely on the Convention right in any legal proceedings (s 7(1)). If the proceedings take the form of judicial review, the applicant is to be taken as having a sufficient interest in relation to the unlawful act only if he is, or would be, a victim of the unlawful act (within the Strasbourg Court's case law) (s 7(3)). Subject to any rule imposing a shorter time limit (for example, the time limit on applying for judicial review),[2] proceedings against the public authority must be brought within one year of the act complained of.

[1]   See **4.63**(1) below.
[2]   CPR 54.5. And see **4.63**(3) below.

4.23 When a court or tribunal finds that the act of a public authority was unlawful within the meaning of s 6(1), it may grant such relief or remedy within its powers as it considers just and appropriate (s 8(1)). However, damages may be awarded only:

(1)   by a court with power to award damages or compensation in civil proceedings (s 8(2)); and
(2)   if such an award is 'necessary to afford just satisfaction', to the victim of the unlawful act (s 8(3)).

4.24 Any award of damages must take into account the principles applied by the Strasbourg Court in the award of compensation under art 41 of the ECHR (s 8(4)).[1]

[1]   See **4.64** below.

4.25 Courts and tribunals are declared to be public authorities (s 6(3)(a)).[1] It follows that all courts and tribunals are subject to the duty to act compatibly with Convention rights under s 6(1). However, proceedings taken in respect of a 'judicial act', as will be necessary if it is claimed that a court or tribunal has breached s 6(1), must in general be taken either by appeal or by application for judicial review (s 9(1)). Subject to the right of someone who has been unlawfully detained to recover compensation under art 5(5) of the ECHR, no damages are to be awarded for a judicial act that has been done in good faith (s 9(3)).

[1]   Section 6(4) declared the House of Lords to be a public authority when acting in its judicial capacity. This was repealed by the Constitutional Reform Act 2005 Sch 18 Pt 5 upon the creation of the Supreme Court which falls within the definition in s 6(3).

4.26 We have seen that under the Act a superior court may make a declaration of incompatibility when it is impossible to interpret and apply primary legislation in a way that is compatible with a Convention right. When such a declaration has been made, or when there has been a decision by the Strasbourg Court in a case against the UK indicating that a statute is incompatible with the Convention, a government minister may take remedial action. The purpose of this action is to authorise a ministerial order to make such amendments to the legislation in question as are necessary to remove the incompatibility (s 10, Sch 2). Except in a case of urgency, a ministerial order made for this purpose must first have been laid in draft in Parliament and the draft must have been approved by resolution of each House.

Other provisions

4.27 Other provisions in the HRA 1998 include s 11, by which reliance on a Convention right does not affect any other rights that an individual may have in national law. Section 12 governs matters that must be taken into account when a court is considering whether to grant relief that might affect the Convention right to freedom of expression. Sections 14–17 deal with the effect of derogations or reservations that the UK Government may have made to the Convention or its protocols.[1] By s 19, a minister in charge of a Bill in either House of Parliament must, before second reading of the Bill, state that in his or her view the Bill is compatible with the Convention rights, or (if such a statement cannot be made) that the Government in any event wishes the Bill to proceed. Section 22(4) gives limited retrospective effect to the operation of the Act: where proceedings are brought by a public authority against an individual (for example, to enforce a decision by the authority) the individual may rely on his Convention rights in the proceedings, whatever the date of the act of the public authority.[2]

[1] For judicial review of a derogation from art 5, see *A v Secretary of State for the Home Department* [2004] UKHL 56, [2005] 2 AC 68, [2005] 3 All ER 169 but note *A v United Kingdom (Application 3455/05)* (2009) 49 EHRR 29, (2009) Times, 20 February; **4.104** below.

[2] On the HRA's retrospectivity in civil matters, see *Wilson v First County Trust Ltd* [2003] UKHL 40, [2004] 1 AC 816, [2003] 4 All ER 97. Also *R (Hurst) v London Northern District Coroner* [2005] All ER (D) 316 (Jul). On its retrospectivity in criminal matters, see *R v Lambert* [2001] UKHL 37, [2002] 2 AC 545; and *R v Kansal (No 2)* [2001] UKHL 62, [2002] 2 AC 69, [2002] 1 All ER 257. For a general discussion of retrospectivity and the HRA 1998 see *Keyu v Secretary of State for Foreign and Commonwealth Affairs* [2015] UKSC 69; [2016] AC 1355.

Joint Committee on Human Rights

4.28 Although the HRA 1998 does not mention this, among the reforms proposed by the Government in October 1997 was the creation of a new parliamentary committee concerned with human rights.[1] There has since 2001 been established the Joint Committee on Human Rights, with members drawn from both Houses. The functions of the Joint Committee are, firstly, to consider matters relating to human rights in the UK (but excluding consideration of individual cases); and, second, to consider remedial orders and draft remedial orders made or to be made under HRA 1998, s 10 and to consider whether the special attention of Parliament should be drawn to them. The Committee regularly reports to Parliament on the human rights implications of pending Bills, and it also examines the statements made by Ministers under s 19 of the Act.[2]

1   See the Government's White Paper (note 2 paragraph **4.12** above), paragraphs 3.6, 3.7.
2   See D Feldman, 'Parliamentary Scrutiny of Legislation and Human Rights' [2002] *Public Law* 323. The Committee's reports may all be read on www.parliament.uk.

IMPLICATIONS OF THE HRA 1998 FOR JUDICIAL REVIEW

Interpretative power of the courts under HRA 1998, s 3

4.29 The HRA 1998 was hailed as an ingenious and well-crafted compromise between conflicting constitutional doctrines.[1] While it conferred new jurisdiction on the courts to protect Convention rights, it does not enable them to strike down a provision in a statute that is incompatible with Convention rights. Although the superior courts are expressly empowered to review primary legislation for compatibility with Convention rights, no court or tribunal may set aside or disapply primary legislation on this ground.[2] We have seen that where a court makes a declaration of incompatibility, a remedial order may be made under HRA 1998, s 10 to remove the incompatibility. Thus, subject to the approval of each House, ministers may amend primary legislation to protect Convention rights. While the Act did not make a frontal attack on the legislative supremacy of Parliament, it authorises statutes to be reviewed by the courts and, if necessary, modified by delegated legislation. In practice, it may well be difficult for the executive to enforce a provision that a superior court has declared to be incompatible with a Convention right, since anyone who is adversely affected by it will have ready-made grounds on which to apply to the European Court of Human Rights. In that event, the Strasbourg Court will make its own decision on whether the applicant's Convention rights have been breached, and it will not be bound by the view of the national court that the legislation in question did breach those rights. However, the Strasbourg Court will surely take into account the national decisions already made, and this will not assist the Government in defending the legislation.

1   See *R v DPP, ex p Kebilene* [2000] 2 AC 326, 367 ('It is crystal clear that the carefully and subtly drafted 1998 Act preserves the principle of parliamentary sovereignty', Lord Steyn); *Wilson v First County Trust Ltd* [2003] UKHL 40, paragraph 79, [2004] 1 AC 816, paragraph 179, [2003] 4 All ER 97, paragraph 179 ('The 1998 Act is beautifully drafted. Its structure is tight and elegant . . . ', Lord Rodger of Earlsferry); and *Ahmed v HM Treasury (No 2)* [2010] UKSC 5, paragraph 115, [2010] 2 AC 534, paragraph 115, [2010] 4 All ER 829, paragraph 115(judicial consideration 'accords to s 3 a role of constitutional importance', Lord Phillips).
2   'It may on another occasion be appropriate to examine whether the sovereignty of Parliament empowers it to dispense with or divest itself of its own or any part of its sovereignty, but so far as the 1998 Act is concerned, this question simply does not arise. Neither [the Court of Appeal] nor any other court is empowered to repeal or amend, ignore or act contrary to any single statute, or any part of any statute. To the contrary: the Act is carefully drafted to ensure that the court cannot and must not strike down or dispense with any single item of primary legislation': *K (a child) (secure accommodation order: right to liberty), Re* [2001] Fam 377, paragraph 121, [2001] 2 All ER 719 at paragraph 121(Judge LJ), CA.

4.30 Nevertheless, declarations of incompatibility have been relatively rare.[1] This is mainly because of HRA 1998, s 3 which requires all legislation, so far as is possible, to be 'read and given effect' in a way that is compatible with Convention rights. In *Ghaidan v Mendoza*,Lord Steyn said that 'interpretation under s 3(1) is the prime remedial remedy, and . . . resort to s 4 must always be an exceptional course'.[2] The duty under HRA 1998, s 3(1) is especially significant in administrative law, since many judicial review cases raise issues as to the *vires* of the decision under review, and these issues often involve questions of the interpretation and/or effect that is to be given to the legislation.[3] As s 3 applies to all legislation whenever enacted, courts and tribunals may need to re-visit their pre-HRA 1998 decisions interpreting or applying legislation, to consider whether a new outcome is possible that will be compatible with Convention rights.

[1] See paragraph **4.19**.
[2] [2004] UKHL 30, [2004] 3 All ER 411, [2005] 1 LRC 449.
[3] The importance of both parts of the s 3(1) duty (to read and give effect) was stressed by Lord Rodger in *Ghaidan v Mendoza* [2004] UKHL 30, [2004] 3 All ER 411 at paragraph 107.

4.31 The interpretative duty under HRA 1998, s 3 is consistent with, but goes considerably further than, the previous emphasis that the courts laid on the importance of protecting 'constitutional rights' against their being repealed by implication.[1] Under s 3, the duty of deciding whether a Convention-compliant interpretation of a statute is possible arises whether or not the legislation in question is ambiguous. In the leading decision, *Ghaidan v Mendoza*,[2] decided in 2004, the House of Lords held that, where a statutory tenant under the Rent Act 1977 had been one of a cohabiting homosexual couple before his death, the surviving member was entitled to succeed to the statutory tenancy of the couple's home. It was held, applying HRA 1998, s 3, that it was possible to read the Rent Act 1977 in a way that treated the surviving partner of a same-sex couple as if he were the surviving spouse of the deceased tenant. This reading of the Act was necessary to avoid a breach of the survivor's Convention right (under art 8, read with art 14) not to be discriminated against in his right to respect for his home and family life by reason of his sexual orientation. It was said that HRA 1998, s 3 might require legislation to be given a meaning which departed from the unambiguous meaning that it would otherwise have, and that the operation of s 3 did not depend on the precise language used in the statute. However, said Lord Nicholls of Birkenhead:

'Parliament . . . cannot have intended that in the discharge of this extended interpretative function the courts should adopt a meaning inconsistent with a fundamental feature of legislation. That would be to cross the constitutional boundary s 3 seeks to demarcate and preserve. Parliament has retained the right to enact legislation in terms which are not Convention-compliant. The meaning imported by application of s 3 must be compatible with the underlying thrust of the legislation being construed.'[3]

[1] See in particular *R v Secretary of State for the Home Department, ex p Pierson* [1998] AC 539, [1997] 3 All ER 577, *HL* and *R (Daly) v Secretary of State for the Home Department* [2001] UKHL 26, [2001] 2 AC 532, [2001] 3 All ER 433.
[2] [2004] UKHL 30, [2004] 3 All ER 411, [2005] 1 LRC 449.
[3] As above, paragraph **33**. Similarly s 3 is a 'powerful tool to enable [the court] to interpret legislation and give effect to it. But it does not enable the court to change the substance of a provision from one where it says one thing into one that says the opposite' (Lord Hope, *Doherty v Birmingham City Council (Secretary of State for Communities and Local*

Government intervening) [2008] UKHL 57 [2009] AC 367, paragraph 49, [2009] 1 All ER 653). See also the summary of the extent of the section 3 HRA 1998 power at *Re Z (A Child)* [2015] EWFC 73 paragraphs 25–34, [2015] 1 WLR 4993 paragraphs 25–34. See also the summary of the extent of the section 3 HRA 1998 power at *Re Z (A Child)* [2015] EWFC 73 paragraphs 25–34, [2015] 1 WLR 4993 paragraphs 25–34. On the boundary between s 3 and s 4, see *Secretary of State for the Home Department v MB* [2007] UKHL 46, paragraph 44,[2008] 1 AC 440, paragraph 44, [2008] 1 All ER 657, at paragraph 44 (Lord Bingham) and more recently *R (Boots Management Services Ltd) v Central Arbitration Committee* [2014] EWHC 65 (Admin), [2014] IRLR 278.

4.32 Drawing an analogy with decisions in which legislation has been given an effect consistent with Community law,[1] Lord Rodger of Earslferry in *Ghaidan v Mendoza* said that the courts could:

'supply by implication words that are appropriate to ensure that legislation is read in a way which is compatible with Convention rights. When the court spells out the words that are to be implied, it may look as if it is "amending" the legislation, but that is not the case. If the court implies words that are consistent with the scheme of the legislation but necessary to make it compatible with Convention rights, it is simply performing the duty which Parliament has imposed on it and on others. It is reading the legislation in a way that draws out the full implications of its terms and of the Convention rights. And, by its very nature, an implication will go with the grain of the legislation. By contrast, using a Convention right to read in words that are inconsistent with the scheme of the legislation or with its essential principles as disclosed by its provisions does not involve any form of interpretation, by implication or otherwise. It falls on the wrong side of the boundary between interpretation and amendment of the statute.'[2]

[1] In particular, *Pickstone v Freemans plc* [1989] AC 66 and *Litster v Forth Dry Dock and Engineering Co Ltd* [1990] 1 AC 546, [1989] 1 All ER 1134, HL.
[2] [2004] UKHL 30, [2004] 3 All ER 411, [2005] 1 LRC 449.

4.33 On whether a Convention-compliant interpretation is possible, Lord Steyn said:

'What is necessary . . . is to emphasise that interpretation under s 3(1) is the prime remedial remedy and that resort to s 4 must always be an exceptional course. In practical effect there is a strong rebuttable presumption in favour of an interpretation consistent with Convention rights.'[1]

[1] As above, paragraph [50]. Where an individual's Convention right has been breached by the act of a public authority under legislation that is capable of being applied compatibly with the right, this does not justify recourse to interpretation under HRA 1998, s 3 to provide a remedy for the breach: *R (Nunn) v First Secretary of State (Leeds City Council, interested parties)* [2005] EWCA Civ 101, [2005] 2 All ER 987, [2006] LGR 224.

4.34 The decision in *Ghaidan v Mendoza* did not solve all difficulties arising at this sensitive boundary,[1] but these statements of principle should resolve differences of approach that had developed in earlier decisions.[2]

[1] Lord Millett dissented, taking the view that it was for Parliament to decide the question of social policy raised by the case: 'In my view s 3 does not entitle the court to supply words which are inconsistent with a fundamental feature of the legislative scheme; nor to repeal, delete, or contradict the language of the offending statute': as above, paragraph 68.
[2] These decisions were reviewed in *Ghaidan v Mendoza* [2004] UKHL 30, [2004] 3 All ER 411, [2005] 1 LRC 449, and an annotated table of them is appended to Lord Steyn's speech. They include *R (Anderson) v Secretary of State for the Home Department* [2002] UKHL 46, [2003] 1 AC 837, [2002] 4 All ER 1089 (declaration of incompatibility made); *R v A* [2001] UKHL

25, [2002] 1 AC 45, [2001] 3 All ER 1 (interpretation based on HRA 1998, s 3 upheld); and *S (Minors) (Care Order: Implementation of Care Plan), Re* [2002] UKHL 10, [2002] 2 AC 291, [2002] 2 All ER 192 (imposition of additional procedure not upheld, as amounting to amendment of the legislation).

4.35 If a judicial review case raises an issue of interpretation, and we have seen that this does not depend on there being an ambiguity in the statutory text, the court will first decide that issue without reference to the s 3 duty,[1] before deciding whether s 3 may make a material difference. Where a Convention-compliant interpretation is not possible, the High Court or above has a discretion to make a declaration of incompatibility under the HRA 1998. Such a declaration provides no practical relief to the claimant but, given the possibility of a remedial order under HRA 1998, s 10, it may lead to an amendment of the law that would benefit all persons who are in the same position as the claimant. If a remedial order is not made, the claimant's only recourse may be to apply to the European Court of Human Rights.

[1] *Poplar Housing and Regeneration Community Association Ltd v Donoghue* [2001] EWCA Civ 595 at paragraph 75, point (a), [2002] QB 48 at paragraph 75, point (a), [2001] 4 All ER 604 at paragraph 75, point (a). This approach was approved by the Supreme Court in *Kennedy v Information Commissioner* [2014] UKSC 20 at paragraph 225, [2015] AC 455 at paragraph 225.

4.36 This discussion has emphasised the significance for the superior courts of the interpretative duty imposed by HRA 1998, s 3, because it is they who may as an alternative remedy make a declaration of incompatibility under s 4. While the authoritative interpretation of legislation is a function of the superior courts, s 3 is drafted to apply to all courts and tribunals, and indeed to all public authorities who make decisions giving effect to legislation. Accordingly, when a Convention-compliant interpretation is possible and a public authority does not apply s 3, that decision is itself subject to judicial review for error of law, and for breach of duty under s 6(1).[1]

[1] See CHAPTER 7, where cross-references are given to the account of the law of Scotland in CHAPTER 22.

Distinction between primary and subordinate legislation

4.37 Although all legislation whenever enacted is subject to the interpretative duty under HRA 1998, s 3, the power of the superior courts to make a declaration of incompatibility applies only to primary legislation as defined for the purposes of the Act. *Primary legislation* means: any Act of Parliament; measures of the Church Assembly and the General Synod of the Church of England; certain Orders in Council, including orders made under the royal prerogative;[1] and also an order or other instrument made under primary legislation 'to the extent to which it operates to bring one or more provisions of that legislation into force or amends any primary legislation'.[2] Accordingly, an Order in Council or statutory instrument made under a Henry VIII clause (power to amend an Act in Parliament by delegated legislation) is to be treated as primary legislation.

[1] HRA 1998, s 22(1). See, also, P Billings and B Pontin, 'Prerogative orders and the Human Rights Act: elevating the status of Orders in Council' (2001) *Public Law* 21.

2   HRA 1998, s 22(1). But excluded are instruments made under devolved powers in Scotland, Wales or Northern Ireland.

4.38 *Subordinate legislation* is defined by the HRA 1998 as meaning: Orders in Council other than those that are treated as primary legislation:[1] Acts of the Scottish Parliament or of a Northern Ireland legislature; other instruments relating to devolved powers (including those made by a devolved government in exercise of prerogative or other executive powers of the Crown); and also a very wide range of instruments made under primary legislation, except to the extent to which they bring primary legislation into force or amend any primary legislation.

1   HRA 1998, s 22(1). These will be Orders in Council made under statutory authority and classed as statutory instruments, except for Orders in Council that amend primary legislation or bring an Act into force: see **4.37** above.

4.39 This particular classification of legislation into primary and subordinate legislation was created for the purposes of the HRA 1998. There is a case to be made on constitutional grounds for limiting the power of the courts in respect of Acts of Parliament to making declarations of incompatibility that do not affect the validity of the legislation. Consequently, giving effect to that domestic legislation cannot be held to be unlawful.[1] But that constitutional case does not apply to certain forms of legislation by the Government that the HRA 1998 brings within the class of 'primary legislation'. And other executive measures may be brought within the category 'primary legislation' by later Acts.[2]

1   See *Doherty v Birmingham City Council (Secretary of State for Communities and Local Government intervening)* [2009] AC 367 at 400.
2   The Civil Contingencies Bill (2003–04) initially provided for emergency regulations to be treated as primary legislation under the HRA 1998, but this provision was dropped in response to criticism from, inter alia, the Joint Committee on Human Rights. See Civil Contingencies Act 2004, s 30(2).

Review of subordinate legislation under HRA 1998

4.40 We have seen that the HRA 1998 does not permit primary legislation, as there defined, to be set aside or disapplied by the courts. The reasons for this limitation do not apply to subordinate legislation, and the courts have long exercised the power of setting aside such legislation which is ultra vires.[1] As was said in the White Paper, 'Rights Brought Home':

'The courts can already strike down or set aside secondary legislation when they consider it to be outside the powers conferred by the statute under which it is made, and it is right that they should be able to do so when it is incompatible with the Convention rights and could have been framed differently.'[2]

1   See, eg *Boddington v British Transport Police* [1999] 2 AC 143, [1998] 2 All ER 203, HL.
2   Cm 3782, paragraph 2.15.

4.41 Possibly because this power has long been exercised by the courts, the HRA 1998 does not expressly set out the policy on secondary legislation contained in 'Rights Brought Home'. As the Act is drafted, the power of the courts to set aside subordinate legislation that is not Convention-compliant must largely be inferred from the HRA 1998 read against existing principles of administrative law. When may it be necessary for the courts to exercise this power?

4.42 Where the power to make subordinate legislation is found in general words of delegation within the parent Act, those words must, under the HRA 1998, s 3(1), be interpreted, 'so far as it is possible to do so', so as to exclude the delegation of power to make regulations that are incompatible with Convention rights.[1] However, this will not always be possible: for instance, when the parent Act delegates powers to make regulations, the terms of delegation may expressly state a purpose that *must* or *may* be achieved by the regulations. In such cases, the making of a regulation to achieve that purpose may be said to be 'mandated' by Act of Parliament.[2] The HRA 1998, s 3(3)–(4) gives such subordinate legislation the same protection that it gives to primary legislation, namely, that the court may not set it aside or disapply it. However, a superior court may, under s 4(4), declare the subordinate legislation to be incompatible with a Convention right.

[1]   *R (Bono) v Harlow District Council* [2002] EWHC 423 (Admin), [2002] 1 WLR 2475, [2002] HRLR 38 (regulations made under general power which did not require regulations to be made in breach of ECHR, art 6(1)).

[2]   The word 'mandated' is wholly appropriate when the parent Act states that the minister shall make a regulation whose effect is necessarily incompatible with a Convention right. But the word 'mandated' is less appropriate when the parent Act states that the Minister may make a regulation with such an effect. In the first case, the Minister is left no choice by the Act. In the second case, the Minister is left with the choice of making or not making such a regulation. However, in deciding whether primary legislation prevents removal of the incompatibility, the court must disregard 'any possibility of revocation': HRA 1998, s 3(2)(c); see also s 4(b). The duty to disregard the possibility of revocation appears to dissolve the distinction between an express duty to make a regulation with a non-compliant effect, and an express power to make such a regulation. On this basis, the decisive matter is the express provision in the parent Act dealing with the content of the regulation.

4.43 Accordingly, under s 3, the following sequence of decisions may need to be made by a court when a litigant claims that subordinate legislation is incompatible with a Convention right:

(1)   is it possible to interpret or give effect to the subordinate legislation in a manner that is Convention compliant? If so, no further question arises under the HRA 1998. If this is not possible, then—

(2)   are the terms of the parent Act mandatory, in that they expressly oblige or empower the rule-maker to make subordinate legislation infringing the Convention right? In answering this question, the court must apply the interpretative duty under HRA 1998, s 3 to the terms of the parent Act. If having done so, the only possible conclusion is that the terms of the parent Act are mandatory, a superior court may make a declaration of incompatibility. If however, having applied s 3, the terms of the parent Act are not mandatory, then—

(3)   the parent Act must be interpreted as delegating power limited to making subordinate legislation that *is* compatible with the Convention right. If the subordinate legislation in question is not so compatible (and the court will already have found that it is not: see (1) above), it must be held to be ultra vires of the parent Act (as interpreted under the

HRA).[1]

[1] See, eg *R (Bono) v Harlow District Council* [2002] EWHC 423 (Admin), [2002] 1 WLR 2475, [2002] HRLR 38.

4.44 Except in the case of subordinate legislation that is protected as if it were primary legislation because its content is 'mandated' by Act of Parliament, and thus can be the subject of a declaration of incompatibility, the function of deciding whether subordinate legislation should be set aside because it is incompatible with a Convention right may be exercised by all courts and tribunals, and not merely by the superior courts.[1] In practice, lower courts and tribunals that exercise this function know that their decisions will be subject to appeal or judicial review on these issues of law.

[1] See *Boddington v British Transport Police* [1999] 2 AC 143, [1998] 2 All ER 203, HL and cf *Chief Adjudication Officer v Foster* [1993] AC 754, [1993] 1 All ER 705, HL.

4.45 To what extent, if at all, does the validity of subordinate legislation under the HRA 1998 depend on the date at which the subordinate legislation was enacted? Three broad possibilities exist:

(1) the parent Act and the subordinate legislation were both enacted before the HRA 1998 came into force (2 October 2000);

(2) the parent Act pre-dates 2 October 2000, and the subordinate legislation is made on or after that date;

(3) both parent Act and subordinate legislation are enacted after 2 October 2000.[1]

[1] The date of 2 October 2000 in this analysis is not material to the protection for Convention rights given by the devolution legislation in respect of powers devolved to Northern Ireland, Scotland and Wales.

4.46 Since the interpretative duty introduced by the HRA 1998 applies to 'primary legislation and subordinate legislation *whenever enacted*' (s 3(2)(a)), it is submitted that the same outcome should be achieved regardless of these three possible sequences of dates. Certainly, in situation (1) above the subordinate legislation was valid when made, and it will continue to be so unless and until a judicial decision is made on its compliance with the Convention. However, the fact that it was valid when made does not necessarily mean that it will continue in force unaffected by the HRA 1998. In general, the Act does not have a retrospective effect upon action taken before 2 October 2000 and (at least in civil proceedings) does not reopen decisions made before that date.[1] It is submitted that where the legal effect of events occurring after that date has to be determined, the impact of the HRA on pre-existing legislation cannot be regarded as retrospective. Further, if subordinate legislation that was valid before 2 October 2000 cannot at a later date be held invalid by reason of the HRA, a gap in the judicial protection of Convention rights may exist, in that HRA 1998, s 4 does not empower the superior courts to grant a declaration of incompatibility regarding subordinate legislation that has not been mandated by the parent Act.[2] In situation (2) above (where the parent Act pre-dates 2 October 2000, and the subordinate legislation is made on or after that date) and situation (3) (where both parent Act and subordinate legislation are enacted after 2 October 2000), no question of retrospection arises. An extra element arises in situation (3), where the parent Act is made after the HRA 1998 came into force: in this case, it may be relevant to consider whether a ministerial statement was made under HRA 1998, s 19 to the effect that the Bill that became the parent Act was compatible with the Convention. If so, it would be difficult for the public authority to argue that the Act mandated the making of subordinate legislation that was incompatible with a Convention right.

[1]   On the retrospective effect of the HRA 1998 in civil proceedings, see *Wilson v First County Trust Ltd* [2003] UKHL 40, [2004] 1 AC 816, [2003] 4 All ER 97, holding that the rights of parties to a transaction that took place before 2 October 2000 must be decided in accordance with the law prevailing at the date of the transaction. On retrospectivity, see *McKerr', Re* [2004] UKHL 12, [2004] NI 212, [2004] 2 All ER 409 and *Keyu v Secretary of State for Foreign and Commonwealth Affairs* [2015] UKSC 69; [2016] AC 1355. See also Lord Rodger of Earlsferry, 'A Time for Everything under the Law: Some Reflections on Retrospectivity' (2005) 121 LQR 57. For the effect of the HRA 1998 on secondary legislation, see D Squires. 'Challenging Subordinate Legislation under the HRA' [2000] EHRLR 116 and A W Bradley, R Allen and P Sales, 'The impact of the HRA 1998 upon subordinate legislation promulgated before October 2, 2000' [2000] *Public Law* 358. Failure to make subordinate legislation is not an 'act' for the purposes of HRA 1998, s 6: see, applying s 6(6)(a), *R (Smith) v Secretary of State for Defence* [2004] EWHC 1797 (Admin), [2005] 1 FLR 97, [2004] Fam Law 868.

[2]   However, a court could in this situation give a declaratory judgment of the traditional kind, as opposed to a declaration of incompatibility under the HRA 1998.

The duty of public authorities to act compatibly with Convention rights

4.47 We have seen that by HRA 1998, s 6(1) it is unlawful for a public authority to act in a way that is incompatible with a Convention right, except where primary legislation (or secondary legislation that has been mandated by primary legislation) does not permit the authority to act differently.[1] The duty under s 6(1) is imposed on all public authorities (including courts and tribunals), with wide implications for administrative law. The HRA does not spell out all the consequences of a breach of the duty, and the meaning of the word 'unlawful' is not defined. Nothing in the Act creates a criminal offence (s 7(8)), but in the context of judicial review we can accept that at least the same consequences follow as for an administrative decision that is held ultra vires.[2] Certainly, HRA 1998, s 6(1) has added a significant new element to the existing grounds on which administrative action may be held ultra vires.[3]

[1]   The obligation is not to *act* in a way that is incompatible with a Convention right. This does not import a requirement to make a decision in a particular way. The court must decide whether the outcome of the decision is a breach of a Convention right: *R (SB) v Governors of Denbigh High School* [2007] 1 AC 100 at 126B and *Miss Behavin' Ltd v Belfast City Council* [2007] UKHL 19 at paragraph 13, [2007] NI 89 at paragraph 13, [2007] 3 All ER 1007 at paragraph 13.

[2]   Another consequence of the illegality is that damages may be payable by way of compensation: see 4.64 below and CHAPTER 17.

[3]   Human rights considerations are now inextricably 'woven into the fabric of public law': *Doherty v Birmingham City Council (Secretary of State for Communities and Local Government intervening)* [2009] AC 367 at 432E–433A.

4.48 In the well-known *GCHQ* case,[1] Lord Diplock adopted a threefold classification of these grounds, namely:

(1)   illegality;
(2)   irrationality; and
(3)   procedural impropriety,

and he left open the possible development of a fourth ground, proportionality, which he observed was already recognised in the administrative law of some members of the European Community. It is not necessary here to set out a new classification of the grounds of judicial review, but for a public authority to act incompatibly with a Convention right (in breach of the duty in s 6(1)) is certainly now a ground for judicial review. Whether such a breach has occurred will very often depend on a decision as to the proportionality of action taken that limits or restricts a Convention right.[2] This does not mean a move to a merits review, rather that the intensity of review is greater where Convention rights are involved.[3] In terms of Lord Diplock's classification in the *GCHQ* case, breach of the s 6(1) duty would, in general, be an instance of illegality; but in some circumstances the breach might be a form of procedural impropriety (where it concerns the right to a fair hearing under ECHR, art 6(1)).[4] Proportionality in the Convention context is for several reasons to be distinguished from the test of irrationality in English law.[5] There has been a recent move towards incorporating a standard of scrutiny akin to proportionality in judicial review, depending on the circumstances of the case.[6] However, apart from its place under the ECHR and within European Community law, the test of proportionality has not yet been received into the general principles of English administrative law.[7]

[1] *Council of Civil Service Unions v Minister for the Civil Service* [1985] AC 374, 410.
[2] See Chapter 9. Also M Fordham and T de la Mare, 'Identifying the principles of proportionality', in (ed) J Jowell and J Cooper, *Understanding Human Rights Principles* (2001), pp 27–89; and A Lester, D Pannick and J Herberg, *Human Rights Law and Practice* (3rd edn, 2009), pp 115–116.
[3] Lord Bingham, *R (SB) v Governors of Denbigh High School* [2007] 1 AC 100 at 116C.
[4] See Chapters 7, 11 and 12, where cross-references are given to discussion of the law of Scotland in Chapter 22.
[5] Chapters 8 and 9. Also see M Elliott, 'The Human Rights Act 1998 and the standard of substantive review', [2001] *Camb Law Jl* 301.
[6] *Kennedy v Information Commissioner (Secretary of State for Justice intervening)* [2014] UKSC 20 at paragraphs 51, 54, [2015] AC 455 at paragraphs 51, 54; *Pham v Secretary of State for the Home Department (Open Society Justice Initiative intervening)* [2015] UKSC 19 at paragraphs 96, 113, 115 [2015] 1 WLR 1591 at paragraphs 96, 113, 115.
[7] *Keyu v Secretary of State for Foreign and Commonwealth Affairs* [2015] UKSC 69 at paragraphs 131–134; [2016] AC 1355 at paragraphs 131–134. Lord Kerr commented at paragraph 271, 'I suspect that this question will have to be frankly addressed by this court sooner rather than later'; his view was that 'the very notion that one must choose between proportionality and irrationality may be misplaced'.

4.49 Another important consequence of s 6(1) is its effect on the role of damages as a remedy in administrative law. A remedy in damages is now available for the breach of a Convention right, although that remedy does not lie for an act that is merely ultra vires.[1]

[1] See **4.64** below and Chapter 17.

4.50 Accordingly, the remedies for breach of the duty under s 6(1) include:

(1)   the quashing of a decision by way of judicial review;
(2)   the award of damages;
(3)   an appeal, in the case of a decision by a court or tribunal.[1]

[1] See **4.62** below.

4.51 When the breach is relevant to existing proceedings (such as a claim in an employment tribunal for unfair dismissal), the breach may affect the outcome of those proceedings (s 7(l)(b)).

Meaning of 'public authority'

4.52 Since the aim of the HRA 1998 is to enable litigants to rely on Convention rights in national courts without going to the European Court of Human Rights, it must be remembered that, at Strasbourg, Her Majesty's Government is responsible for breaches of an individual's Convention rights within the jurisdiction of the UK, whether these have arisen through acts or omissions of the legislature, the executive or the judiciary.[1] The UK's responsibility under international law extends beyond central government to include local authorities and bodies with devolved powers, such as the Scottish Executive, as well as the effects of legislative and judicial decisions. The Convention therefore has what may be termed a 'vertical' effect since it concerns the relationship between the state and the individual. By the same reasoning, it is not in general directly concerned with 'horizontal' relationships that arise between a private individual and other private persons or corporations.[2] However, the Convention imposes certain duties on organs of the state to protect individuals against breach of their Convention rights. Such a duty may arise where an individual has been harmed by another individual, and this may affect judicial proceedings that arise between them.[3] Performance of the duty may be affected by legislation.

[1] The independence of the judiciary, which is protected by ECHR, art 6, does not prevent liability arising for a national government where a judicial decision has breached Convention rights. On the territorial scope of Convention rights, and the meaning of 'jurisdiction' in art 1 ECHR, see **4.16** above.
[2] On the horizontal effect of some Convention rights, see **4.59** below.
[3] *Costello-Roberts v United Kingdom* (Application 13134/87) (1993) 19 EHRR 112, [1994] 1 FCR 65; *A v United Kingdom (Human Rights: Punishment of Child)* (Application 25599/94)(1998) 27 EHRR 611, [1998] 3 FCR 597. For instances of actions between private persons being affected by the HRA 1998, see *Campbell v MGN Ltd* [2004] UKHL 22, [2004] 2 AC 457, [2004] 2 All ER 995; and *Ghaidan v Mendoza* [2004] UKHL 30, [2004] 3 All ER 411, [2005] 1 LRC 449. Neither decision turned on the duty of public authorities under HRA 1998, s 6(1).

4.53 Under the HRA 1998, proceedings are directed, not against the UK Government, but against the 'public authority' responsible for the act, decision or omission in question. There is no comprehensive definition of the term 'public authority' in the HRA 1998. However, the Act provides that:

(1) 'public authority' includes all courts and tribunals (s 6(3)(a));
(2) 'public authority' includes 'any person certain of whose functions are functions of a public nature' (s 6(3)(b)); such persons, who therefore also exercise functions of a private nature, are not to be regarded as a 'public authority' in relation to a particular act, if the nature of the act is private (s 6(5));
(3) 'public authority' does not include either House of Parliament or a person exercising functions in connection with proceedings in Parliament (s 6(3)); but, as we have just seen, this exclusion does not apply to the House of Lords in its judicial capacity.

4.54 The definition of 'public authority' has given rise to difficult litigation.[1] The category of 'core' public authority (or 'pure', 'standard' or 'ordinary' public authority)[2] consists of government departments, local authorities, the armed forces, the police, courts and tribunals, and other bodies created to carry out public functions.[3] These bodies are within the HRA 1998 as public authorities while exercising *all* their functions, even though these functions involve acts (for example, buying goods, employing staff or exercising property rights) which are essentially similar to functions that are undertaken by private persons.[4] A second category of 'public authority' comprises persons whose functions include some of a public nature and others of a private nature. They come within HRA 1998, s 6(1) only in relation to those of their acts which are of a public nature: they have been referred to as hybrid authorities, or 'functional authorities'.[5] Under the scheme of the Act, a 'core' public authority is subject to the Act even when it is carrying out acts of a private nature such as the placing of a commercial contract. But a 'functional' authority is not subject to the HRA 1998 in respect of such private acts, even though the funds to pay for the contract or other act have come from a public source.

[1] Including *Poplar Housing and Regeneration Community Association Ltd v Donoghue* [2001] EWCA Civ 595, [2002] QB 48, [2001] 4 All ER 604; *Aston Cantlow and Wilmcote with Billesley Parochial Church Council v Wallbank* [2003] UKHL 37, [2004] 1 AC 546, [2003] 3 All ER 1213; *YL v Birmingham City Council* [2007] UKHL 27, [2008] 1 AC 95, [2007] 3 All ER 957; and *R (Weaver) v London and Quadrant Housing Trust (Equality and Human Rights Commission intervening)* [2009] EWCA Civ 587, [2009] 4 All ER 865, [2010] 1 WLR 363. See D Oliver. 'The Frontiers of the State: Public Authorities and Public Functions under the HRA' [2000] *Public Law* 476; and 'Functions of a Public Nature under the HRA' [2004] *Public Law* 329. Also *R (West) v Lloyds of London* [2004] EWCA Civ 506, [2004] 3 All ER 251, [2004] 2 All ER (Comm) 1.

[2] See the 7th Report of the Joint Committee on Human Rights, 2003–04 (HL 39, HC 382), paragraphs 3–7, discussed by M Sunkin 'Pushing Forward the Frontiers of Human Rights Protection: the meaning of "public authority" under the HRA' [2004] *Public Law* 643.

[3] A list of Non-Departmental Public Bodies is regularly issued by the Cabinet Office; all such bodies would appear to be 'core' public authorities.

[4] *R (Weaver) v London and Quadrant Housing Trust (Equality and Human Rights Commission intervening)* [2009] EWCA Civ 587, [2009] 4 All ER 865, [2010] 1 WLR 363; *R (Bevan & Clarke LLP) v Neath Port Talbot CBC* [2012] EWHC 236 (Admin) at paragraphs 46–48, [2012] BLGR 728 at paragraphs 46–48. It is likely that in relation to many acts of a private nature carried out by 'core' public authorities (such as placing contracts for the purchase of goods or services), the scope for operation of the HRA 1998 will be very restricted, compared to the scope for Convention rights to be engaged when powers are exercised that impinge on the rights and duties of private persons.

[5] See note 2 above. For example, in *Hampshire CC v Beer (t/a Hammer Trout Farm)* [2003] EWCA Civ 1056; [2004] 1 WLR 233 a limited company with the power to grant licences to stall-holders in a farmer's market was a public authority.

4.55 Difficulties have arisen when tasks that could be carried out directly by public authorities are entrusted to private persons or to charitable organisations. A housing association (with the status of a registered social landlord) was held not to be a 'core' public authority; however, it was regarded as a 'hybrid' or 'functional' public authority because its functions were 'enmeshed' in the activities of the local authority and its housing stock had come to it from the local authority; and its action in suing in the county court to recover possession of its property from an unsatisfactory tenant was held to be an act of a public nature.[1] By contrast, where a charitable foundation provided residential accommodation for disabled persons, some of whom were paid for from public funds by social service authorities or the NHS, it was held not to be performing any public functions; the services that it provided were considered to be of a private nature.[2] In very different circumstances, a parochial church council set up by measures of the Church of England was in *Aston Cantlow PCC v Wallbank* held by the House of Lords to be neither a core nor a hybrid public authority; the matter that was in dispute (its decision to impose a charge on the owner of private property to pay for repairs to the chancel of the parish church) was held (Lord Scott dissenting) to be of a private nature, since the charge was regarded as an instance of a private law obligation.[3] But the governors of a Church of England primary school, who exercise functions under the Education Acts in the state sector of education, will be regarded as a public authority, at least in regard to their statutory functions.[4]

[1] *Poplar Housing and Regeneration Community Association Ltd v Donoghue* [2001] EWCA Civ 595, [2002] QB 48, [2001] 4 All ER 604. Cf *R (Weaver) v London and Quadrant Housing Trust (Equality and Human Rights Commission intervening)* [2009] EWCA Civ 587, [2009] 4 All ER 865, [2010] 1 WLR 363.

[2] *R (Heather) v Leonard Cheshire Foundation* [2002] EWCA Civ 366, [2002] 2 All ER 936, [2002] HLR 893. Similarly see *YL v Birmingham City Council* [2007] UKHL 27, [2008] 1 AC 95, [2007] 3 All ER 957: a private care home taking local authority residents was not performing a public function. This decision was reversed by the Health and Social Care Act 2008, s 145 (provision of accommodation and care in such circumstances to be a function of a public nature.); that provision can now be found in the Care Act 2014 at s 73.

[3] *Aston Cantlow and Wilmcote with Billesley Parochial Church Council v Wallbank* [2003] UKHL 37, [2004] 1 AC 546, [2003] 3 All ER 1213. See also V Sachdeva, 'The Scope of Hybrid Public Authorities within the HRA 1998' (2004) *Judicial Review* 43.

[4] Cf *A v Head Teacher of Lord Grey School* [2004] EWCA Civ 382 at paragraphs [36]–[38], [2004] QB 1231 at paragraphs [36]–[38], [2004] 4 All ER 628 at paragraphs [36]–[38] (court in no doubt that governing body of a maintained school was a public authority). The House of Lords allowed the appeal but on grounds such that the question of whether the school was a public authority did not have to be considered: [2006] UKHL 14.

4.56 In the *Aston Cantlow* case, Lord Nicholls of Birkenhead said that the broad purpose of HRA 1998, s 6(1) is:

> 'that those bodies for whose acts the state is answerable before the European Court of Human Rights shall in future be subject to a domestic law obligation not to act incompatibly with Convention right.'

4.57 The phrase 'public authority' in s 6(1) was 'essentially a reference to a body whose nature is governmental in a broad sense of that expression'.[1] Lord Nicholls observed that a body that is to be regarded as a public authority in respect of all its acts, regardless of their 'nature', could not be regarded as a 'non-governmental organisation' for the purposes of art 34 of the ECHR, and would thus be incapable of claiming to be a victim of an infringement of Convention rights.[2] Further, that there is no single test of universal application for deciding whether a function or act of a hybrid authority is to be regarded as of a public nature.[3] Factors to be taken into account in deciding whether a function is of a public character include:

'the extent to which in carrying out the relevant function a body is publicly funded, or is exercising statutory powers, or is taking the place of central government or local authorities, or is providing a public service.'[4]

1 *Aston Cantlow and Wilmcote with Billesley Parochial Church Council v Wallbank* [2003] UKHL 37 at paragraphs 6 and 7, [2004] 1 AC 546 at paragraphs 6 and 7, [2003] 3 All ER 1213 at paragraphs 6 and 7.
2 *Aston Cantlow PCC v Wallbank*, at paragraph 8.
3 *Aston Cantlow PCC v Wallbank*, at paragraph 12.
4 *Aston Cantlow PCC v Wallbank*, at paragraph **12.**

4.58 Two other points emerge from the *Aston Cantlow* judgments. The case law that deals with whether particular entities are subject to judicial review is not determinative of whether a body is a 'core' or a 'hybrid' public authority under the HRA 1998.[1] Nor is the approach under the Act to be found by analogy from the case law governing the definition of a public authority in Community law as regards the direct effect of directives.[2] Lord Scott in *YL v Birmingham City Council* emphasised that it is not enough merely to consider the activities that are carried out; it is also necessary to consider why the person in question is carrying out those activities, in particular whether this is being done pursuant to public law obligations or private law contractual obligations.[3]

The principles for determining whether a particular function of a hybrid public authority fall within the Act were summarised by Elias LJ in *R (Weaver) v London and Quadrant Housing Trust (Equality and Human Rights Commission intervening)*[4]

'First the source of the power will be a relevant factor in determining whether the act in question is in the nature of a private act or not. Second, that will not be decisive however since the nature of the activities in issue in the proceedings is also important. This leads on to the third and related proposition, which is that the character of an act is likely to take its colour from the character of the function of which it forms part.'

1 *Aston Cantlow PCC v Wallbank*, paragraph 52 (Lord Hope). In *Hampshire County Council v Beer* [2003] EWCA Civ 1056, paragraph 28, [2004] 1 WLR 233, paragraph 28, [2004] UKHRR 727, paragraph 28, it was observed that national case law on amenability to judicial review could be very helpful, but must if necessary yield to relevant Strasbourg jurisprudence. See, also, CHAPTER 5.
2 The *Aston Cantlow* case, paragraphs 53–55, referring to *Foster v British Gas plc*: Case C-188/89 [1991] 1 QB 405, [1990] 3 All ER 897, ECJ.
3 [2007] UKHL 27, paragraph 31, [2008] 1 AC 95, paragraph 31, [2007] 3 All ER 957, paragraph 31. This is criticised by A Lester, D Pannick and J Herberg, *Human Rights Law and Practice* (3rd edn, 2009) at paragraph 1.49.
4 [2009] EWCA Civ 587, paragraph 41, [2009] 4 All ER 865, paragraph 41, [2010] 1 WLR 363, paragraph 41.

Horizontality

4.59 The HRA 1998 is unusual among legislation in having potential implications across the whole field of law.[1] Although the primary effect of rights under the European Convention is on the 'vertical' relationship between a private individual and organs of the state, the question of whether the Convention affects the 'horizontal' relationship between one private individual and another has been much discussed.[2] In some circumstances, such an effect certainly does occur: for instance, when the Strasbourg Court has had to consider whether national courts in determining defamation cases between private parties have made decisions that are consistent with the freedom of expression guaranteed by ECHR, art 10.[3] The Convention also imposes duties on a state to secure the rights of individuals, if necessary by taking positive steps to protect them against other individuals;[4] failure to do so may give rise to state responsibility.[5] Since, under HRA 1998, s 6(1), courts and tribunals are 'public authorities', it appears that in any proceedings between private parties to which the question of a possible infringement of a Convention right is relevant and is raised by the party concerned, the court or tribunal must decide the question. But civil proceedings are adversarial and such an issue ought not to be raised by the court on its own initiative.[6] If the issue involves the effect of legislation, the interpretative duty under s 3 comes into play in any event[7] and may cause the court or tribunal to re-visit earlier interpretations of the legislation, even if s 6(1) does not apply. Where litigation between two private parties affects their Convention rights and turns on rules of the common law, the courts as 'public authorities' are required by s 6(1) to have regard to the requirements of the Convention in developing the common law.[8] In *Campbell v MGN Ltd*, the House of Lords applied arts 8 and 10 of the ECHR in holding that a newspaper had published material that infringed the claimant's right to respect for her private life.[9] Lord Nicholls of Birkenhead said:

> 'The time has come to recognise that the values enshrined in articles 8 and 10 are now part of the cause of action of breach of confidence . . . The values embodied in articles 8 and 10 are as much applicable in disputes between individuals or between an individual and a non-governmental body such as a newspaper as they are in disputes between individuals and a public authority.'[10]

---

[1]   *Wilson v First County Trust Ltd* [2003] UKHL 40 at paragraph 182, [2004] 1 AC 816 at paragraph 182, [2003] 4 All ER 97 at paragraph 182(Lord Rodger of Earlsferry).

[2]   The many articles include M Hunt. 'The "Horizontal Effect" of the HRA' [1998] *Public Law* 423 and HWR Wade, 'Horizons of Horizontality' (2000) 116 LQR 217. And see M Hunt, 'The "horizontal effect" of the HRA: moving beyond the public-private distinction' in J Jowell and J Cooper, *Understanding Human Rights Principles* (2001) 161–178. See also Mummery LJ, *X v Y* [2004] EWCA Civ 662, paragraph 45, [2004] ICR 1634, paragraph 45, [2004] IRLR 625, paragraph 45. J Wright, *A damp squib? The impact of section 6 HRA on the common law: horizontal effect and beyond* [2014] *Public Law* 289 highlights the disparity between the extensive academic commentary on horizontality and its practical impact.

[3]   See *Tolstoy Miloslavsky v United Kingdom* (Application 18139/91)(1995) 20 EHRR 442, [1995] ECHR 18139/91 and *Bladet Tromso and Stensaasv Norway* (Application 21980/93)(1999) 29 EHRR 125, 6 BHRC 599.

[4]   See A R Mowbray, *The Development of Positive Obligations under the ECHR by the European Court of Human Rights* (2004).

[5]   See *A v United Kingdom (Human Rights: Punishment of Child)* (Application 25599/94)(1998) 27 EHRR 611, [1998] 3 FCR 597.

[6]   In *Wilson v First County Trust Ltd* [2003] UKHL 40, [2004] 1 AC 816 it was held that the Court of Appeal had been wrong to decide on its own initiative that the outcome of a dispute concerning a loan regulated by the Consumer Credit Act 1974 breached the lender's Convention rights.

[7]   4.29 above. Also see *X v Y* [2004] EWCA Civ 662, [2004] IRLR 625 (duty of employment tribunal to read and give effect to Employment Rights Act 1996, s 98 in manner compatible with ECHR, arts 8 and 14, thus enabling the art 8 right to be blended with existing law on unfair dismissal).

[8]   The process of having regard to the Convention requires care: see *Flood v Times Newspapers Ltd* [2012] UKSC 11, paras 44–47 (Lord Phillips) and paras 138–146 (Lord Mance),

[2012] 2 AC 273, [2012] 4 All ER 913. Also see *Osborn v Parole Board*, noted in **4.8** above, paras 54-63 (Lord Reed).

9   [2004] UKHL 22, [2004] 2 AC 457, [2004] 2 All ER 995. See, also, on the right to privacy, *Wainwright v Home Office* [2003] UKHL 53, [2004] 2 AC 406 and *Douglas v Hello! Ltd* [2001] QB 967, [2001] 2 All ER 289, CA.

10   *Campbell v MGN Ltd*, at paragraph 17.

4.60 Questions of horizontality are unlikely to arise in cases of judicial review, since the defendant in those proceedings will generally be a core 'public authority' within the meaning of the HRA 1998. However, we have already seen that the boundaries of judicial review do not coincide exactly with the duty under s 6(1), so it is possible that:

(1)   a claim for judicial review may concern an act that is not the act of a public authority within s 6; and conversely

(2)   a decision by a 'core' public authority (for instance, relating to a commercial contract) may by its nature fall outside the scope of judicial review.[1]

1   See **4.63**(2) below.

4.61 In these situations, the general principle expressed by Lord Nicholls in *Campbell v MGN Ltd* and quoted above is material, since the court may have to decide whether a discretionary decision affecting an individual was properly made. For this reason, it is unsafe to assume that the HRA 1998 has no relevance to an issue in dispute, whether the case in which the issue arises is one of judicial review or the exercise of statutory rights of appeal, or has the form of civil litigation between private parties.

Remedies

4.62 The policy behind the HRA 1998 is that where someone claims that his or her Convention rights have been infringed by a public authority, he or she should be able to raise this claim in proceedings before any court or tribunal to which that claim is relevant.[1] Although the Act does not state this in terms, it may be inferred from ss 7–9 that an individual who claims that his or her Convention rights have been infringed by a public authority will often have a remedy in the form of an application for judicial review. This is subject to the possibility discussed below[2] that the s 6(1) duty of 'public authorities' may arise in situations that would otherwise fall outside the scope of judicial review. Moreover, if there are ongoing proceedings to which the alleged breach of Convention rights is relevant, the individual will be expected to raise the claim before the court or tribunal seised of those proceedings, and in any related appellate proceedings. The principle that the Administrative Court will not generally permit an application to be made for judicial review where an alternative remedy will apply, along with other discretionary bars to relief.[3]

1   And see 'Rights Brought Home: the Human Rights Bill' (Cm 3782, 1997), paragraph 2.4.
2   See **4.63**.
3   See CHAPTER **18**.

4.63 Although a claim for judicial review is often the appropriate means of bringing an alleged breach of Convention rights into court, the scope and procedure of (i) judicial review, and (ii) the remedy under the HRA 1998, do not coincide.

(1)   First, if a claim for judicial review is brought to enforce the duty under HRA 1998, s 6(1), the applicant for review must be taken as having a sufficient interest in relation to the unlawful act only if he or she is or would be a victim of the act for the purposes of art 34 ECHR.[1] Accordingly, in some cases of judicial review involving the public interest, an applicant with 'sufficient interest' for the purposes of judicial review may be unable to rely on the claimed breach of Convention rights under s 6(1).[2] Thus a trade union is unable to take proceedings concerning infringement of the Convention rights of its members,[3] but may do so to protect the union's own Convention rights. And, as a governmental organisation within the meaning of art 34, 'core' or 'pure' public authorities such as a local council are excluded from the category of potential victims: hence a local authority cannot, in a claim for judicial review against a government department or another public body, rely on the Convention rights of local residents.[4] The inconvenience of this is to an extent mitigated by the fact that in any judicial proceedings to which statutory interpretation is relevant, the interpretative duty under HRA 1998, s 3 applies, whether or not a party to the proceeding would satisfy the 'victim' test. Thus a party with standing for the purpose of judicial review will be able to assert that legislation should be construed compatibly with Convention rights, and in the alternative to seek a declaration of incompatibility.

(2)   As we have seen in considering the meaning of 'public authority',[5] the duty under HRA 1998, s 6(1) applies to 'core' public authorities in respect of all their acts, including acts of a public and acts of a private nature. In the case of the latter acts (for instance, dismissal of an employee or a dispute over a contract for the sale of goods), the appropriate remedy will, in these instances, be a claim made to an employment tribunal or to the county court.[6] Conversely, it is possible that judicial review may lie concerning the acts of a 'hybrid' public authority, even though those acts are held to be of a private nature for the purposes of s 6.

(3)   An application for judicial review must be made promptly and in any event within three months of the grounds for judicial review having arisen, but the Administrative Court has a discretion to extend the time.[7] Under HRA 1998, s 7(4), proceedings concerning the breach of a public authority's duty under s 6(1) must be brought before the end of one year, beginning with the date of the act complained of, and a court or tribunal has a discretion to extend the period.[8] The burden is on the claimant to establish that there are circumstances where it would be equitable to extend time.[9] Since this limit is subject to any rule imposing a stricter time limit for a particular procedure, the ordinary rules for judicial review will generally apply where that is the appropriate remedy. Where an individual affected by a public authority's decision discovers only after the three-month period that the decision was made in breach of his or her Convention rights, this could be a reason for the Administrative Court to extend the time for claiming.

(4)   The Strasbourg court may only deal with matters once domestic remedies have been exhausted and within six months of the 'final decision'.[10] Article 4 of the draft Protocol No 15 will shorten this period to four months but this awaits the signature and ratification of the Protocol by all member states.[11]

[1]   HRA 1998, s 7(3) (English law); s 7(4) (Scots law). By ECHR, art 34, the Strasbourg Court 'may receive applications from any person, non-governmental organisation or group of individuals claiming to be the victim of a violation' of the Convention rights. 'Victim' status is not lost by accepting a settlement for a separate negligence claim: *Rabone v Pennine Care NHS Trust* [2012] UKSC 2, [2012] 2 All ER 381.

[2]   Standing for the purposes of judicial review is discussed in Chapter 18, where cross-references are given to discussion of the law of Scotland in Chapter 22. For the position of the non-victim in relation to substantive review, see Elliott. 'The Human Rights Act 1998 and the standard of substantive review', (2001) *Camb Law Jl* 301, pp 323–334.

[3]   See the admissibility decision of the Commission in *Ahmed v United Kingdom* (1995) 20 EHRR CD 72, 77–78.

[4]   On the meaning of 'non-governmental organisations', see *Holy Monasteries v Greece* (1994) 20 EHRR 1, paragraph 49; on local authorities, see *Austria Municipalities v Austria* (1974) 17 Yearbook 338 and *Rothenthurm Commune v Switzerland* (1988) 59 DR 251. This exclusion from the category of potential victims does not apply to the many organisations (such as church bodies) that in principle enjoy Convention rights (cf HRA 1998, s 13); they do not lose their non-governmental status merely because a particular act of the organisation (eg under the Education Acts) is of a public nature for the purposes of HRA 1998, s 6(5): see **4.52** above.

[5]   See **4.52** above.

[6]   It is doubtful whether s 7(3) and (4) provide a sufficient basis in English and Scots law respectively for re-drawing the boundaries of the judicial review jurisdiction. For the jurisdiction of the Court of Session, see Chapter 22.

[7]   In relation to planning matters the time limit is now six weeks: see CPR r 54.5(5). See also Chapter 18, where the question of compatibility of the time limit with the Convention is discussed, and where cross-references are given to discussion of the law of Scotland in Chapter 22.

[8]   Although the issue did not need to be decided, the House of Lords indicated that where the complaint related to a 'true continuing act', time runs from the date the act ceased: Lord Hope, *Somerville v Scottish Ministers (HM A-G for Scotland intervening)* [2007] UKHL 44, [2007] 1 WLR 2734, 2008 SC (HL) 45. See also *O'Connor v Bar Standards Board* [2016] EWCA Civ 775, [2016] 1 WLR 4085 (appeal outstanding at the time of going to press).

[9]   Sir Michael Turner, *Cameron v Network Rail Infrastructure Ltd* [2006] EWHC 1133 (QB), paragraph 47, [2007] 3 All ER 241, paragraph 47, [2007] 1 WLR 163, paragraph 47. However, Lord Kerr has commented that 'few cases of this type lend themselves to a ready resolution by the application of a burden of proof'; he preferred 'to approach the question . . . by an open ended examination of the factors that weigh on either side of the argument': *A v Essex County Council (National Autistic Society intervening)* [2010] UKSC 33 at paragraph 33, [2011] 1 AC 280 at paragraph 33.

[10]   Article 35.

[11]   As at 14 February 2017, 43 states had signed the Protocol and 33 had ratified it: https://www.conventions.coe.int/Treaty/Commun/ChercheSig.asp?NT=213&CM=8&DF=&CL=ENG.

Compensation[1]

[1]   English law on this topic is discussed generally in Chapter 17, where cross-references are given to discussion of the law of Scotland in Chapter 22.

4.64 The Administrative Court may order damages to be paid in judicial review proceedings, although a claim for judicial review may not seek damages alone.[2] However, in English law damages are not payable just because a decision that adversely affects the claimant is quashed as ultra vires. For a claim of damages to succeed, the claimant must show that the defendant's conduct amounted to a tort.[3] Where the individual complains of having suffered maladministration at the hands of a public authority, he or she may not even have grounds for judicial review; in such a case, the sole recourse is a complaint to the relevant Ombudsman, who will have power to recommend the payment of compensation should the complaint of maladministration be upheld.[4]

[2]   Senior Courts Act 1981, s 31(4); and CPR 54.3(2).
[3]   See, eg *Dunlop v Woollahra Municipal Council* [1982] AC 158, [1981] 1 All ER 1202, PC; and CHAPTER 17.
[4]   Parliamentary Commissioner Act 1967, s 10(3); Local Government Act 1974, s 31(2B), (3).

4.65 By art 41 of the ECHR, the Strasbourg Court shall, 'if necessary', afford 'just satisfaction' to someone whose rights have been infringed and full reparation has not been made in national law.[1] Just satisfaction does not include exemplary damages.[2] In only one specific situation does the Convention require compensation to be paid to someone whose rights have been infringed, namely when he or she has been the victim of arrest or detention in breach of the right under art 5 to liberty and security of person.[3]

[1]   See J Varuhas, *Damages and Human Rights* (2016). See also A R Mowbray, 'The European Court of Human Rights' Approach to Just Satisfaction' [1997] *Public Law* 647; A Lester, D Pannick and J Herberg, *Human Rights Law and Practice* (3rd edn, 2009), pp 74–79; Law Commission, *Damages under the Human Rights Act 1998* (Law Com no 266; Cm 4853, 2000); D Scorey and T Eicke, *Human Rights Damages: Principles and Practice* (2002): J Hartshorne, 'The HRA 1998 and Damages for non-pecuniary loss' (2004) EHRLR 660. See Harris, O'Boyle and Warbrick, *Law of the European Convention on Human Rights* (3rd edn, 2013), pp 155–162 for detail on recent case law regarding just satisfaction.
[2]   *Watkins v Secretary of State for the Home Department* [2006] UKHL 17, [2006] 2 AC 395, [2006] 2 All ER 353.
[3]   ECHR, art 5(5).

4.66 These Convention provisions are reflected in the HRA 1998. By virtue of s 8(1), a court or tribunal which finds that an act of a public authority has been unlawful (ie in breach of s 6(1)) may award damages to the victim if it considers that such a remedy would be 'just and appropriate'. But this power may be exercised only by a court or tribunal with power in civil proceedings to order the payment of damages or compensation (s 8(2)); such a court or tribunal in using this power must take into account the principles applied by the Strasbourg Court in relation to the award of compensation under art 41 of the ECHR (s 8(4)). Limited provision is made for damages to be awarded in respect of a judicial act.[1] What is the effect of these provisions on proceedings for judicial review?

[1]   See 4.70 below.

4.67 The power to award compensation for breaches of Convention rights raises difficult questions, both about principles of liability and issues of quantum. In *R (Greenfield) v Secretary of State for the Home Department*,[1] the House of Lords strongly discouraged litigation that sought to recover compensation from public authorities for every infringement of Convention rights. It declared that there is no general rule under the HRA that an individual has a right to recover compensation whenever a public authority has infringed a Convention right. In *Greenfield*, a convicted prisoner had been required under prison disciplinary rules to serve additional days of imprisonment for a drug offence, but the hearing of the charge against him did not comply with his right to a fair hearing under ECHR, art 6(1). In rejecting his claim for compensation, the House observed that earlier decisions of the English courts had concerned different Convention rights, but applied the following principles.

(1)   National courts under the HRA 1998 must follow the approach of the Strasbourg Court in holding that the focus of the Convention is the protection of human rights, not the award of compensation. In the great majority of cases, including Greenfield's claim, the finding of a breach of Convention rights will be 'just satisfaction' within ECHR, art 41. The Strasbourg Court is prepared to depart from this approach and award compensation for non-pecuniary loss (the equivalent of general damages in English law) only where it finds a causal connection between the breach of the Convention right and the loss suffered by the claimant. Thus, non-pecuniary loss for a breach of the right to a fair hearing may attract compensation only where compliance with the right would or might very well have been more favourable to the claimant; and the court is reluctant to speculate about such matters.

(2)   The Strasbourg Court has been very sparing in making awards for non-pecuniary loss based on anxiety and frustration caused by a violation of art 6(1). In particular, the ordinary practice of the court is not to make an award in cases involving structural bias.

(3)   Even where awards are made, the amounts are modest. In awarding damages under HRA 1998, s 8, national courts should not apply domestic scales of damages.[2] The HRA 1998 is not a tort statute. The aim of the Act was to make it easier for claimants to get remedies to which they were entitled under the Convention, not to give them a better remedy. National courts must seek to make awards that they judge to be fair in the individual case, and these should be broadly the same in amount as awards at Strasbourg.

[1]   [2005] UKHL 14, [2005] 2 All ER 240, [2005] 1 WLR 673. And see R Clayton, 'Damage limitation: the courts and HRA damages' [2005] *Public Law* 429.
[2]   In *R (Faulkner) v Secretary of State for Justice* [2013] UKSC 23 at paragraph 13, [2013] 2 AC 254 at paragraph 13, [2013] 2 All ER 1013 at paragraph 13, it was noted that awards should broadly reflect those of the Strasbourg court.

4.68 In important respects, these principles departed from the earlier approach taken in the Court of Appeal in a group of cases involving the right under ECHR, art 8 to respect for private and family life,[1] and in a case concerning the right to education under art 1, First Protocol.[2] One emphasis made in the former group of cases is not affected by *Greenfield*, namely that, where there was a claim to compensation, the costs of adversary litigation were likely to be disproportionate to the amount of any award; the court would encourage any procedure, including alternative dispute resolution, that would keep down the costs; if other relief could be sought as well as damages, the claim should be brought by way of judicial review, but it should otherwise be brought as an ordinary claim in the Administrative Court.

[1]   *Anufrijeva v Southwark London Borough Council* [2003] EWCA Civ 1406, [2004] QB 1124, [2004] 1 All ER 833 (failure by local authority to provide accommodation to meet special

needs, and delays by Home Office in dealing with asylum-seekers). The House in *Greenfield* also disapproved dicta in *R (Bernard) v Enfield London Borough Council* [2002] EWHC 2282 (Admin), [2003] LGR 423, [2003] HRLR 111 and *R (KB) v Mental Health Review Tribunal* [2003] EWHC 193 (Admin), [2004] QB 936, [2003] 2 All ER 209.

2 *A v Head Teacher of Lord Grey School* [2004] EWCA Civ 382, [2004] QB 1231, [2004] 4 All ER 628. The House of Lords allowed the appeal, holding that no question of compensation arose since on the facts A's Convention right to education had not been breached: [2006] UKHL 14.

4.69 In *Greenfield*, the House of Lords warned of the 'risk of error if Strasbourg decisions given in relation to one article of the Convention are read across as applicable to another',[1] observing that the court had wisely refrained from laying down hard and fast rules 'in a field which pre-eminently calls for a case-by-case judgment'.[2] *Greenfield* has been applied in several contexts and relevant guidance provided. The issue of prisoner's rights was addressed both in *R (Walker) v Secretary of State for Justice*[3] and in *R (Faulkner) v Secretary of State for Justice*,[4] where the Supreme Court confirmed that damages could be awarded for the frustration and anxiety caused by a delay in determination by the Parole Board, even where it was not established that the prisoner would have been released earlier. The victim must however establish that the effects of the breach were sufficiently grave to merit compensation.[5] No award was made for the loss of the chance of earlier release.[6] In relation to Article 2, the Supreme Court noted the relevance of the closeness of the family ties and the fact of the expressed anxiety of the family materialising in a case of the failure of the operational duty.[7] Where the breach of Article 8 is both substantive and procedural, or where there would have been a different outcome but for the breach, then a higher award of compensation may be appropriate.[8] A failure by the police to investigate, resulting in breaches of Article 3 and Article 4, has been held to merit pecuniary compensation for additional distress and frustration suffered on account of that failure.[9]

1 *R (Greenfield) v Secretary of State for the Home Department* [2005] UKHL 14, paragraph 7, [2005] 2 All ER 240, paragraph 7, [2005] 1 WLR 673, paragraph 7.

2 *R (Greenfield) v Secretary of State for the Home Department*, paragraph 15.

3 [2009] UKHL 22, [2010] 1 AC 553, [2009] 4 All ER 255.

4 [2013] UKSC 23, [2013] 2 AC 254, [2013] 2 All ER 1013.

5 *Lee-Hirons v Secretary of State for Justice* [2016] UKSC 46 at paragraph 46, [2017] AC 52 at paragraph 46.

6 See particularly paragraph **13** of Faulkner, above. However, damages for loss of opportunity in other circumstances have been made by the ECtHR; see eg *Hooper v United Kingdom (42317/98)* (2005) 41 EHRR 1. Damages for loss of chance were awarded in *Van Colle v Chief Constable of Hertfordshire* [2007] EWCA Civ 325, [2007] 1 WLR 1821 (a decision reversed by the House of Lords on other grounds).

7 *Rabone v Penine Care NHS Foundation Trust* [2012] UKSC 2, at paragraph 87, [2012] 2 AC 72, at paragraph 87, [2012] 2 All ER 381 at paragraph 87.

8 *R (DL) v Newham London Borough Council* [2011] EWHC 1890 (Admin), [2012] 1 FLR 1, [2011] Fam Law 1324.

9 *O v Commissioner of Police of the Metropolis* [2011] EWHC 1246 (QB), [2011] HRLR 29.

Compensation in respect of a judicial act

4.70 Where the breach of a Convention right results from a judicial act,[1] under HRA 1998, s 9(3), an award of damages may be made in only two situations:

(1)   where the act is not done in good faith; or
(2)   where an award is necessary under art 5(5) of the ECHR to compensate someone who has been detained in breach of his or her rights under art 5 (the right to liberty and security).

[1]   Defined in HRA 1998, s 9(5) as a 'judicial act of a court and includes an act done on the instructions, or on behalf of, a judge'. Also by s 9(5), 'court' includes a tribunal, and 'judge' includes a member of a tribunal.

4.71 In proceedings for compensation in respect of a judicial act, the award must be sought against the Crown; and the minister responsible for the court or tribunal concerned (or person or department nominated by him) must be joined as a party to the proceedings (s 9(4)). Unlike the common law rules on liability for judicial acts, these provisions do not distinguish between the acts of superior courts, which have in the past enjoyed complete immunity from liability, and the acts of inferior courts and tribunals.[1]

[1]   See A W Bradley. 'The Constitutional Position of the Judiciary' in D Feldman (ed) *English Public Law* (2nd edn, 2009), ch 6, pp 309–313. Also see *Sirros v Moore* [1975] QB 118, [1974] 3 All ER 776, CA, and A Olowofoyeku, *Suing Judges: a Study of Judicial Immunity* (1993).

ASPECTS OF EUROPEAN CONVENTION LAW

4.72 The consequences for judicial review of the effect of particular Convention rights are dealt with as necessary in other chapters.[1] Here, it is proposed to deal with three general aspects of Convention law that are often relevant to judicial review of administrative decisions. These are:

(1)   the Convention right to a hearing in matters of civil right (ECHR, art 6(1));
(2)   the requirement in the Convention for the acts of public authorities to be 'prescribed by law'; and
(3)   the margin of appreciation, discretionary decisions and the discretionary area of judgment.

[1]   See, in particular, the account of proportionality and its relation to *Wednesbury* unreasonableness in CHAPTER 8 and the effect of ECHR, art 6(1) on the common law rules of fairness and bias in CHAPTERS 10 and 11.

The right to a hearing in matters of civil rights[1]

[1]   English law on this topic is discussed in CHAPTER 17, where cross-references are given to aspects of the law of Scotland in CHAPTER 22.

4.73 A complex area of Convention case law lies behind the challenges based on ECHR, art 6(1) that have been made to methods of decision-making that have long been accepted in the public law of the UK.[2] Article 6(1) (the right to a fair trial) provides in part as follows:

'In the determination of his civil rights and obligations or of any criminal charge against him, everyone is entitled to a fair and public hearing within a reasonable time by an independent and impartial tribunal established by law. Judgment shall be pronounced publicly but the press and public may be excluded from all or part of the trial . . . .'[3]

[2]   See J Herberg, A Le Sueur and J Mulcahy, 'Determining Civil Rights and Obligations', in J Jowell and J Cooper (ed), *Understanding Human Rights Principles* (2001) pp 91–137. The leading House of Lords' decisions discussed below are *R (Alconbury Developments Ltd) v Secretary of State for the Environment, Transport and the Regions* [2001] UKHL 23, [2003] 2 AC 295, [2001] 2 All ER 929 and *Runa Begum v Tower Hamlets London Borough Council* [2003] UKHL 5, [2003] 2 AC 430, [2003] 1 All ER 731.

[3]   In the French text, the first sentence reads: 'Toute personne a droit à ce que sa cause soit entendue équitablement, publiquement et dans un délai raisonnable, par un tribunal indépendant et impartial, établi par la loi, qui décidera, soit des contestations sur ses droits et obligations de caractère civil, soit du bien-fondé de toute accusation en matière pénale dirigeé contre elle'. The article applies to all adjudicating bodies, whether these are styled courts or tribunals.

4.74 When the Convention was being drafted, the aim behind art 6(1) was to guarantee the integrity of national systems of civil and criminal justice, since it is on the observance of 'due process' in the machinery of justice that the rule of law and the rights of individuals depend. In numerous decisions under art 6(1), the Strasbourg Court has applied minimum standards of fair adjudication to the proceedings of national courts, dealing with such matters as the rule that a hearing must take place publicly and within a reasonable time, the use of hearsay evidence,[1] the rule that the court or tribunal must be 'independent and impartial', and the distinction between civil and criminal charges. One series of cases[2] brought about reforms in the system of courts-martial in the armed forces; more recently, other important cases have concerned various anti-terrorist measures.[3] The question that we now consider is whether art 6(1) applies to all decision-making by public authorities.[4] To what extent, if at all, should all public authorities be required to adopt structures and procedures modelled on those of the courts'? This is not a new question in administrative law, and it underlies much case law on the rules of natural justice at common law.[5] But the HRA 1998 made it necessary to re-assess the case law and related legislation, in conformity with the Strasbourg jurisprudence. From this, it appears that for art 6(1) to apply, the claimant must establish that there is an existing dispute (in French, *contestation*) that has led to proceedings that may be determinative of what are properly claimed to be his or her civil rights or obligations.[6] Particular difficulties arise as to the meaning of the term 'civil rights and obligations' and the following paragraphs concentrate on this issue.

[1]   See, eg *Horncastle v United Kingdom* (Application 4184/10) (2015) 60 EHRR 31).

[2]   See, eg *Findlay v United Kingdom* (Application 22107/93) (1997) 24 EHRR 221, [1997] ECHR 22107/93.

[3]   *A v United Kingdom* (Application No 3455/05 (2009) 49 EHRR 625, (2009) Times, 20 February. Domestic cases regarding the use of closed material and related procedure include *CF v Security Service* [2013] EWHC 3402 (QB), [2014] 2 All ER 378, [2014] 1 WLR 1699; *AT v Secretary of State for the Home Department* [2012] EWCA Civ 42, [2012] All ER (D) 57 (Feb); *Al-Rawi v Security Service* [2011] UKSC 34, [2012] 1 AC 531, [2012] 1 All ER 1; *Home Office v Tariq* [2011] UKSC 35, [2012] 1 AC 452, [2012] 1 All ER 58; *Kiani v Secretary of State for the Home Department* [2015] EWCA Civ 776; [2016] QB 595. And see Justice and Security Act 2013.

[4]   See Lester, Pannick and Herberg, ss 4.6.23–25 (pp 298–391); P Craig, 'The HRA, art 6 and Procedural Rights' [2003] *Public Law* 753 and Herberg, Le Sueur and Mulcahy, 'Determining Civil Rights and Obligations' (as above).

[5]   From *Local Government Board v Arlidge* [1915] AC 120, 12 LGR 1109, HL onwards.

6   Herberg, Le Sueur and Mulcahy, 'Determining Civil Rights and Obligations' at 91. For instances of planning decisions that were held not to affect the claimant's civil rights, see *R v Camden London Borough Council, ex p Cummins* [2001] EWHC 1116 (Admin) (Ouseley J: permission for development of planning authority's land) and *Bovis Homes Ltd v New Forest DC* [2002] EWHC 483 (Admin) (Ouseley J: adoption of local plan). Contrast the clear breach of art 6(1) in *R (Nunn) v First Secretary of State (Leeds City Council, interested parties)* [2005] EWCA Civ 101, [2005] 2 All ER 987, [2006] LGR 224. By contrast in *R (Wright) v Secretary of State for Health* [2009] UKHL 3; [2009] 1 AC 739, placing an individual on a list under s 82(4)(b) of the Care Standards Act 2000 that prevented her from working with vulnerable adults was held to amount to a determination of her civil right.

4.75 It is reasonably clear from the *travaux préparatoires* that the framers of art 6(1) did not intend to require court-like procedures to be adopted whenever action was 'taken by administrative organs exercising discretionary power conferred on them by law'.[1] Both English and French texts of the Convention are of equal authority in the Strasbourg Court.[2] On the question of how far, if at all, art 6(1) applies to executive decision-making, the meaning of 'civil rights and obligations' is crucial. A common lawyer readily assumes that any decisions made about someone's rights and duties that do not involve a criminal charge affect their 'civil rights and obligations', and thus that decisions subject to administrative law are included. However, in a civil law system, as in France or Germany, the term *droits et obligations de caractére civil* may be assumed to refer to matters governed by *droit civil* (private law) and not to matters of administrative law (public law).[3]

1   Quoting the Danish jurist, Max Sorensen, during the debate on the draft Convention. This passage was cited by the minority of the court in *Feldbrugge v Netherlands* (Application 8562/79)(1986) 8 EHRR 425, 445. Cf FC Newman, 'Natural Justice, Due Process and the New International Covenants on Human Rights' [1967] *Public Law* 274.

2   For the French text, see note 2 paragraph **4.73** above.

3   For an outline of the Strasbourg case law, see *R (Alconbury Developments Ltd) v Secretary of State for the Environment, Transport and the Regions* [2001] UKHL 23 at paragraphs 77–88, [2003] 2 AC 295 at paragraphs 77–88, [2001] 2 All ER 929 at paragraphs 77–88(Lord Hoffmann). See also Lester, Pannick and Herberg, pp 283–287. On the meaning of criminal proceedings, the UK case law includes *R (McCann) v Crown Court at Manchester* [2002] UKHL 39, [2003] 1 AC 787, [2002] 4 All ER 593; *R (Smith) v Parole Board* [2005] UKHL 1, [2005] 1 All ER 755, [2005] 1 WLR 350; *R (R) v Durham Constabulary* [2005] UKHL 21, [2005] 2 All ER 369, [2005] 1 WLR 1184; *R (Tangney) v Governor of Elmley Prison* [2005] EWCA Civ 1009, (2005) Times, 30 August; and *Secretary of State for the Home Department v MB* [2007] UKHL 46, [2008] 1 AC 440, [2008] 1 All ER 657, particularly paragraph 24. And see *Ezeh v United Kingdom (Application 39665/98)* (2003) 39 EHRR 1, [2004] Crim LR 472; *Black v United Kingdom (Application 56745/00)* (2007) 45 EHRR 619; and *Young v United Kingdom (Application 60682/00)* (2007) 45 EHRR 689, [2007] ECHR 60682/00.

The interpretation of art 6(1)

4.76 Whatever may have been the original intention behind ECHR, art 6(1), the long-established approach of the Strasbourg Court is that the Convention is a 'living instrument'[1] and its interpretation does not depend on the original intention of its framers.[2] Key concepts in the Convention are given an 'autonomous' interpretation by the Strasbourg Court, that is, one that does not depend on meanings given to them in national legal systems. As regards art 6(1). Lord Hoffmann said:

'The court has not simply said . . . that one can have a "civil right" to a lawful decision by an administrator. Instead, the court has accepted that "civil rights" mean only rights in private law and has applied article 6(1) to administrative decisions on the ground that they can determine or affect rights in private law.'[3]

[1] See, eg *Johnston v Ireland (Application 9697/82)* (1986) 9 EHRR 203, paragraph 53. And note the broad interpretation of art 6(1) in *Golder v United Kingdom (Application 4451/70)* (1975) 1 EHRR 524. See also Sir Nicolas Bratza, 'Living instrument or Dead letter — the future of the European Convention on Human Rights' [2014] EHRLR 116.

[2] This view is not without its critics, most notably Lord Sumption, see eg. '*The Limits of Law*', 27th Sultan Azlan Shah Lecture, Kuala Lumpur, 20 November 2013, which lecture provided the jumping-off point for N Barber, R Ekins and P Yowell (eds), *Lord Sumption and the Limits of the Law* (2016).

[3] *R (Alconbury Developments Ltd) v Secretary of State for the Environment, Transport and the Regions* (as above) at 79.

4.77 Thus the Strasbourg Court has held that the right to a fair hearing under art 6(1) applies to the granting of an official permit before a disposition of land can take effect,[1] to decisions regulating the right to practise a profession,[2] to decisions with an economic impact on civil rights, such as the licensing of trade in certain goods, the sale of alcohol and transport services,[3] and to the control of land use.[4] Also within art 6(1) are decisions concerning the award to individuals of benefits under occupational health insurance and industrial injury schemes[5] and public sector pensions.[6]

[1] *Ringeisen v Austria (Application 2614/65)* (1971) 1 EHRR 455.

[2] *Albert and Le Compte v Belgium (Applications 7299/75 and 7496/76)* (1983) 5 EHRR 533; *De Moor v Belgium (Application 16997/90)* (1994) 18 EHRR 372.

[3] Respectively *Benthem v Netherlands (Application 8848/80)* (1985) 8 EHRR 1; *Tre Traktörer Aktiebolag v Sweden (Application 1087/84)* (1989) 13 EHRR 309; and *Pudas v Sweden(Application 10426/83)* (1987) 10 EHRR 380, [1987] ECHR 10426/83.

[4] *Sporrong and Lönnroth v Sweden (Applications 7151/75 and 7152/75)* (1982) 5 EHRR 35, [1982] ECHR 7151/75.

[5] *Feldbrugge v Netherlands* (Application 8562/79)(1986) 8 EHRR 425 and *Deumeland v Germany* (Application 9384/81)(1986) 8 EHRR 448. Article 6(1) was later held to apply to other social insurance and welfare benefits in *Salesi v Italy* (Application 13023/87)(1993) 26 EHRR 187 (delayed payment of non-contributory disability pension) and *Shuler-Zgraggen v Switzerland* (Application 14518/89)(1993) 16 EHRR 405, [1994] 1 FCR 453(withdrawal of invalidity pension). See also *Schouten and Meldrum v Netherlands* (Applications 19005/91 and 19006/91)(1994) 19 EHRR 432 (employer's contribution to social welfare plan). In *R (Hamid Ali Husain) v Asylum Support Adjudicator* [2001] EWHC 852 (Admin), [2002] ACD 10, (2001) Times, 15 November, the asylum support scheme was held to create rights under art 6(1).

[6] *Massa v Italy* (Application 14399/88) (1993) 18 EHRR 266. But see **4.88** below in relation to disputes arising from public sector employment.

4.78 These are all matters on which primary decision-making is entrusted by national law not to courts but to officials, regulators, disciplinary boards, and other public bodies.[1] These first-instance decision-makers are very unlikely to meet the criteria required for the status of an 'independent and impartial court or tribunal'. But their decisions are often subject to rights of appeal or review. An appeal may lie to a judicial body such as the High Court or to a specialised tribunal, and the scope of the appeal is generally determined by legislation. Such decisions are generally also subject to judicial review, although this is not available where there is an effective alternative remedy.[2]

[1] It was thought that internal disciplinary proceedings regarding allegations that could result in the employee being barred from a profession or included in a statutory register preventing them from working with children might engage Article 6. However this was subsequently rejected in UK courts: *Mattu v University Hospitals of Coventry and Warwickshire NHS Trust*

[2012] EWCA Civ 641, [2012] 4 All ER 359, [2012] IRLR 661; and *R (G) v Governors of X School* [2011] UKSC 30, [2012] 1 AC 167, [2011]4 All ER 625. The test is whether the internal disciplinary procedure will either be decisive or alternatively have a 'substantial influence or effect' on the subsequent determination of the civil right by the relevant regulatory body: *R (G) v Governors of X School* at paragraph 69. Circumstances in which the test is satisfied are likely to arise only rarely. Homeless persons' claims to be rehoused (*Ali v Birmingham Council* [2010] UKSC 8, [2010] 2 AC 39, [2010] 2 All ER 175), variations of bail conditions (*R (BB) v Special Immigration Appeals Commission* [2012] EWCA Civ 1499, [2013] 2 All ER 419, [2013] 1 WLR 1568), and prisoners' segregation board decisions (*R (King) v Secretary of State for Justice* [2012] EWCA Civ 376, [2012] 4 All ER 44, [2012] 1 WLR 3602) have all been held not to engage Article 6. (However, the latter was subsequently held to be unlawful under the common law: [2015] UKSC 54; [2016] AC 384.)

[2] See Chapter 18.

The test of 'full jurisdiction'

4.79 In an early case concerning disciplinary proceedings in the Belgian medical profession, the Strasbourg Court held that:

(1) the initial proceedings did not take place before an independent and impartial tribunal; and

(2) review proceedings in the civil court of appeal *(cour de cassation)* did not remedy earlier defects because the court, while being an independent and impartial tribunal, was not competent to deal with the merits of the decision.

4.80 The Court laid down the principle that:

'the Convention calls at least for one of the two following systems: either the jurisdictional organs themselves comply with . . . article 6(1), or they do not so comply but are subject to subsequent control *by a judicial body that has full jurisdiction* and does provide the guarantees of article 6(1).'[1]

[1] *Albert and Le Compte v Belgium* (Applications 7299/75 and 7496/76) (1983) 5 EHRR 533 at paragraph 29 (emphasis supplied).

4.81 In deciding the impact of art 6(1) on administrative decisions, the Strasbourg Court is thus prepared to take into account both the initial decision-making procedure and any subsequent rights of access to a court or tribunal by way of appeal or review. In some cases, the art 6(1) guarantees are satisfied at the appellate or review level. This approach underlines the need for an effective system of judicial review, since this can provide guarantees of due process that are not found at the primary stage of decision-making.[1] What has caused difficulty is the question whether the jurisdiction exercised by way of judicial review is sufficiently extensive to compensate for shortcomings (from an art 6(1) viewpoint) at the primary stage. The passage quoted above refers to the opportunity for subsequent control of a decision by a judicial body *'that has full jurisdiction'*. Does this require the reviewing court to have full power to decide all questions of law, fact, merits and discretion? If so, this would go well beyond the limits of judicial review in the UK and in many European legal systems. However, in 1993 the Strasbourg Court referred to the 'respect which must be afforded to decisions taken by administrative authorities on grounds of expediency', and held that, on a compulsory purchase of land in Austria, it was not necessary for the Administrative Court to be able to review the merits of a policy decision.[2]

1 See, eg *Zander v Sweden* (Application 14282/88) (1993) 18 EHRR 175.
2 *Zumtobel v Austria* (Application 12235/86) (1993) 17 EHRR 116 at paragraph 32, [1993] ECHR 12235/86.

4.82 Questions of this kind have arisen concerning the use of public inquiries in Britain in the control of land use. In *Bryan v United Kingdom (Application 19178/91)*,[1] where a planning inspector had rejected an appeal against an enforcement notice served for breach of development control, the Strasbourg Court held that there was no breach of art 6(1). Two elements were stressed by the court:

(1) the appeal proceedings had been conducted in a quasi-judicial and fair manner, but the inspector was not 'independent and impartial' for purposes of art 6(1), since he was a salaried employee of the Secretary of State:

(2) judicial review by the Administrative Court of the inspector's decision was a 'sufficiently full jurisdiction' to comply with art 6(1), account being taken both of the safeguards dealing with the appeal hearing and of the court's ability to intervene when the inspector's findings of fact were shown to be perverse or irrational.

1 (1995) 21 EHRR 342, [1996] 1 PLR 47, discussed by Lord Hoffmann in *R (Alconbury Developments Ltd) v Secretary of State for the Environment, Transport and the Regions* [2001] UKHL 23 at paragraphs 77–88, [2003] 2 AC 295 at paragraphs 77–88, [2001] 2 All ER 929 at paragraphs 77–88. See also *Chapman v United Kingdom (Application 27238/95)* (2001) 33 EHRR 18, 10 BHRC 48.

4.83 In the *Alconbury* case, brought under the HRA 1998, several decisions relating to the development and purchase of land had been 'called in' by the Secretary of State to enable the decisions to be made by him and not by the planning inspectorate. The Divisional Court held that, despite the availability of judicial review, the call-in procedures breached art 6(1), for the reason (by contrast with *Bryan v United Kingdom*) that the decisions had been made by the Secretary of State, and not by a planning inspector; the legislation authorising the call-in procedure was accordingly declared to be incompatible with art 6(1). Reversing this decision, the House of Lords held that art 6(1) had not been breached, since it did not require the called-in decisions to be made by an independent and impartial tribunal, but that there must be a sufficient means of ensuring judicial review of the legality of the decisions and of the procedures. Lord Clyde said:

'We are concerned with an administrative process and an administrative decision. Planning is a matter for the formation and application of policy. The policy is not matter for the courts but for the executive.'[1]

1 The *Alconbury* case, (see note 1 paragraph **4.82** above), paragraph 139.

4.84 Lord Hoffmann said of the term 'full jurisdiction' that it 'does not mean full decision-making powers. It means full jurisdiction *to deal with the case as the nature of the decision requires*'.[1]

1 The *Alconbury* case, paragraph 87 (emphasis supplied). In *Kingsley v United Kingdom* (2002) 35 EHRR 177, a decision by the Gaming Board that the claimant was unfit to take part

in the gaming industry was held to breach art 6(1) where the reviewing court lacked power to quash the decision affected by bias. *Alconbury* was applied in *R (McLellan) v Bracknell Forest Borough Council* [2001] EWCA Civ 1510, [2002] QB 1129, [2002] 1 All ER 899(judicial review of notices served by housing authorities for termination of introductory tenancies); *R v Department for the Environment, Food and Rural Affairs, ex p Langton* [2001] EWHC 1047 (Admin), [2002] Env LR 20, [2002] EHLR 9(works for disposal of animal by-products); *R (Whitmey) v Commons Comrs* [2004] EWCA Civ 951, [2005] QB 282, [2004] 3 WLR 1342(statutory review of registration of a village green). See also *R v English Nature, ex p Aggregate Industries Ltd* [2002] EWHC 908 (Admin), [2003] Env LR 3, [2002] ACD 67 (land notified as site of special scientific interest). For the impact of art 6 on planning decisions, see J Maurici, 'Planning and Article 6: where are we now?' [2003] *Judicial Review* 21;.and on homelessness decisions, I Loveland. 'Does Homelessness Decision-Making engage Article 6(1) ECHR?' (2003) EHRLR 176.

The test of 'full jurisdiction' qualified

4.85 In *Runa Begum v Tower Hamlets London Borough Council*,[1] the House of Lords made a further inroad into the principle that the reviewing court must have 'full jurisdiction' when the first-instance decision does not comply with art 6(1). Under the homelessness legislation, a housing authority's senior review officer decided that the claimant had unreasonably refused an offer of housing, with the consequence that the council did not need to make a further offer to her. This decision was upheld on appeal to the county court. Making the assumption (but not deciding) that the claimant's right under the legislation was a matter of 'civil right', the House held that: (a) the senior review officer was not an 'independent and impartial tribunal' within art 6(1); but (b) the jurisdiction of the county court, which in essence was a statutory power of judicial review, was sufficient to comply with art 6(1), even though the court did not have jurisdiction to make its own decision as to the facts. Lord Bingham said that the case exposed the importance of the inter-relation within art 6(1) between the concept of 'civil rights' and the requirement of an 'independent and impartial tribunal':

> 'The narrower the interpretation given to "civil rights", the greater the need to insist on review by a judicial tribunal exercising full powers. Conversely, the more elastic the interpretation given to "civil rights", the more flexible must be the approach to the requirement of independent and impartial review if the emasculation (by over-judicialisation) of administrative welfare schemes is to be avoided.'[2]

However, the Strasbourg Court in *Tsfayo v United Kingdom (Application 60860/00)* held that the existence of judicial review was insufficient to remedy breaches of art 6 by a local housing benefit review board that was 'deciding a simple question of fact'.[3] The board had to determine whether there was 'good cause' for the delay in the applicant's application for benefits and based their decision primarily on a view of her credibility. In these circumstances judicial review was too limited to have the necessary 'full jurisdiction'. The earlier decision, *Runa Begum*, could be distinguished because it involved issues requiring professional knowledge or experience and the exercise of administrative discretion pursuant to wider policy aims.

In *R (Wright) v Secretary of State for Health*, Baroness Hale reviewed the above decisions and gave the following guidance:

'What amounts to "full jurisdiction" varies according to the nature of the decision being made. It does not always require access to a court or tribunal even for the determination of disputed issues of fact. Much depends upon the subject matter of the decision and the quality of the initial decision-making process. If there is a "classic exercise of administrative discretion", even though determinative of civil rights and obligations, and there are a number of safeguards to ensure that the procedure is in fact both fair and impartial, then judicial review may be adequate to supply the necessary access to a court, even if there is no jurisdiction to examine the factual merits of the case'.[4]

---

1   [2003] UKHL 5, [2003] 2 AC 430, [2003] 1 All ER 731, not approving observations made in *Adan v Newham London Borough Council* [2001] EWCA Civ 1916, [2002] 1 All ER 931, [2002] 1 WLR 2120. See R Clayton and V Sachdeva, 'The Role of Judicial Review in Curing Breaches of Article 6' (2003) Judicial Review 90 and P Craig, 'The HRA, Article 6 and Procedural Rights', [2003] Public Law 753.

2   *Runa Begum v Tower Hamlets London Borough Council*, paragraph 5. At paragraph 34, Lord Hoffmann said: ' . . . looking at the matter as an English lawyer, it seems to me . . . that an extension of the scope of article 6 into administrative decision-making must be linked to a willingness to accept by way of compliance something less than full review of the administrator's decision'.

3   (2006) 48 EHRR 457, [2007] LGR 1.

4   [2009] UKHL 3 at paragraph 23, [2009] 1 AC 739 at paragraph 23. See also *R (Bourgass) v Secretary of State for Justice* [2015] UKSC 54; [2016] AC 384 and *R (XH) v Secretary of State for the Home Department* [2017] EWCA Civ 41.

4.86 In *Runa Begum*, Lord Bingham observed that it was very far from certain that the Strasbourg Court would hold that the right enjoyed by Runa Begum under the homelessness legislation was a 'civil right' within art 6(1).[1] Subsequently the Supreme Court held that offers of accommodation under s 193 Housing Act 1996 do not engage art 6, as the making of evaluative judgements of how the applicant's need should be met did not involve the determination of a 'civil right'.[2] While the Strasbourg Court has, over several decades, extended the scope of art 6(1), many decisions taken by public authorities, although subject to judicial review, are not regarded by it as concerning matters of 'civil right' under art 6(1). In *Ferrazzini v Italy (Application 44759/98)*,[3] a complaint of excessive delay in the handling of tax assessments by Revenue authorities was held by the court (by 11-6) to be outside art 6(1), since the claimant's rights and obligations in tax law were not regarded as being 'civil' in character:

> 'The Court considers that tax matters still form part of the hard core of public-authority prerogatives, with the public nature of the relationship between the taxpayer and the tax authority remaining predominant'.[4]

---

1   See similarly *R (M) v Lambeth London Borough Council* [2009] UKSC 8, [2010] 1 All ER 469, [2009] 1 WLR 2557.

2   *Ali v Birmingham City Council* [2010] UKSC 8, [2010] 2 AC 39, [2010] 2 All ER 175.

3   (2002) 34 EHRR 45, [2003] BTC 157. And see Craig, 'The HRA, Article 6 and Procedural Rights', [2003] *Public Law* at 756–759.

4   (2002) 34 EHRR 45, at paragraph 29. Note the important qualification made in the concurring judgment of Ress J.

4.87 The majority in *Ferrazzini* held that it was not possible to read art 6(1) as if it did not contain the word 'civil'. Taking a different approach, the minority accepted that 'civil rights' did not mean any rights that were not criminal, but emphasised the effect of taxation on the individual's pecuniary interests[1] and that tax law was not based on the exercise of discretionary powers by the administration. It will be evident that the approach of the majority in *Ferrazzini* is wholly opposed to the customary approach in the UK taken towards matters of taxation: the decision has not been followed in respect of VAT by the VAT and Duties Tribunal.[2]

1   Citing *Editions Périscope v France (Application 11760/85)* (1992) 14 EHRR 597.
2   VAT penalties and surcharges were held to be matters of 'civil right' within art 6(1): *Ali and Begum (t/a Shapla Tandoori Restaurant) v Customs and Excise Comrs* [2002] V&DR 71, [2004] STI 1302, VAT and Duties Tribunal, 30 May 2002. The tribunal held that the taxpayer's pecuniary interests were central to the appeal; in this context, there was no place in the UK for a 'public law' relationship distinct from 'civil rights and obligations'. See also D Oliver, 'English Law and Convention Concepts', in (ed) P Craig and R Rawlings, *Law and Administration in Europe* (2003), ch 5, pp 88–94. By HRA 1998, s 2(1), national courts and tribunals must take the Strasbourg case law into account but are not required to apply that case law in every circumstance: see **4.15** above.

Public law decisions excluded from art 6(1)

4.88 The Strasbourg Court has held that art 6(1) does not apply to disputes over the exercise of political rights, such as the right to stand for election, even if matters of pecuniary interest are affected.[1] Also excluded from art 6(1) are disputes involving the entry, stay and deportation of aliens.[2] Another excluded category applies to certain disputes arising from public sector employment:[3] this reflects the tradition in France and in other European legal systems by which these disputes are within the jurisdiction of the administrative courts, as they raise questions of public law and are outside *le droit civil*. In 2001, the excluded category was given a much narrower 'functional' formulation by the Strasbourg Court.[4] This was intended to create a 'workable concept' for ascertaining whether the particular applicant exercised 'functions which could be characterised as falling within the exercise of public power'.[5] However, the Strasbourg Court in *Eskelinen (Vilho)* noted that the case law showed that this could lead to anomalous results.[6] Consequently the Court developed the *Pellegrin* approach and further narrowed the excluded category. In effect it is presumed that art 6 will apply and it is for the Government to demonstrate that it does not.[7] To do this, they must show not only that there is a 'special bond of trust and loyalty' between the civil servant and the State, as employer, but that 'the subject matter of the dispute in issue is related to the exercise of the state power or it has called into question the special bond'.[8] Therefore there is no justification for the exclusion from art 6(1) of 'ordinary' labour disputes.

1   *Pierre-Bloch v France (Application 24194/94)* (1998) 26 EHRR 202.
2   *Maaouia v France (Application 39652/98)* (2001) 33 EHRR 42, 9 BHRC 205. And see *R (G) v Immigration Appeal Tribunal* [2004] EWHC 588 (Admin), [2004] 3 All ER 286, [2004] 1 WLR 2953; affirmed in (the same) [2004] EWCA Civ 1731, [2005] 2 All ER 165. In *R (BB (Algeria)) v Special Immigration Appeals Commission* [2012] EWCA Civ 1499, [2013] 2 All ER 419, [2013] 1 WLR 1568 the Court of Appeal held that following Maaouia, the ancillary decision as to the grant of bail pending deportation did not fall within Article 6(1) either.
3   See, eg *Huber v France* (Application 26637/95)(1998) 26 EHRR 457, [1998] HRCD 263 and *Neigel v France* (Application 18725/91)(2000) 30 EHRR 310, [1997] ECHR 18725/91.
4   *Pellegrin v France* (2001) 31 EHRR 26.
5   *Eskelinen (Vilho) v Finland (Application 43803/98)* (2007) 45 EHRR 43, paragraph 47, 24 BHRC 327, paragraph 47.
6   In *Eskelinen (Vilho)*, the Court said that *Pellegrin* would put police officers outside the protection of art 6 but not the office assistant, despite both groups being involved in the same dispute over the payment of an allowance. In addition the Court noted the difficulty of ascertaining the nature and status of the applicant's functions, paragraph 49.
7   Ibid, paragraph 59.

4.89 The exclusion of many public law decisions from art 6(1) remains contentious, and it has been argued that procedural rights under the article should extend to all cases in which a public authority's decisions affect the legal position of an individual.[1] In fact, serious difficulties would arise if a court-like hearing complying with the full requirements of art 6(1) had to be held whenever a public authority made a decision affecting individuals' rights and interests. The existing Strasbourg case law on the scope of 'civil rights and obligations' is difficult to justify, but the impact of its complexities on public law in the United Kingdom is mitigated by two factors. First, so far as art 6(1) protects the fairness of decision-making, that concept is already well-developed in administrative law, and it applies generally to all functions of government.[2] Second, by constitutional practice that goes back to the Franks Report on tribunals and inquiries in 1957, many specialised tribunals adjudicate independently of the public authorities responsible for the areas of policy concerned. Under the Tribunals, Courts and Enforcement Act 2007, a unified tribunal system is established for many key areas,[3] and this has made for significantly greater consistency. The statutory framework, together with the rules of procedure made for the chambers of the First-tier Tribunal and the Upper Tribunal, means that these tribunals have no difficulty in meeting the standard of 'independence and impartiality' required by art 6(1).[4] Article 6(1) continues to have a significant effect on access to administrative justice: governments are sometimes tempted for short-term reasons to abolish or curtail the jurisdiction of tribunals, and art 6(1) should serve as a disincentive to the adoption of such policies.

[1]   P van Dijk and van Hoof, *Theory and Practice of the ECHR* (4th edn, 2006) p 538. See also P Craig, 'The HRA, Article 6 and Procedural Rights' [2003] *Public Law* 753.
[2]   See Chapters **11** and **12**. And see, eg *R (Al-Hasan) v Secretary of State for the Home Department* [2005] UKHL 13, at paragraph 45, [2005] 1 All ER 927, at paragraph 45, (2005) *Times*, 18 February, at paragraph 45.
[3]   Including war pensions, social security, criminal injuries compensation, mental health review, social care, special educational needs, taxation and land valuation. On the status of the Upper Tribunal and its susceptibility to judicial review, see *R (Cart) v Upper Tribunal* [2011] UKSC 28, [2012] 1 AC 663, [2011] 4 All ER 127and *Eba v Advocate General for Scotland* [2011] UKSC 29, [2012] AC 710, [2011] STC 1705.
[4]   The HRA 1998 has had the effect of improving practices in regard to the appointment of part-time judges and tribunal members: see *Starrs v Ruxton (Procurator Fiscal Linlithgow)* (1999) Times, 17 November, 2000 SLT 42 (appointment of part-time sheriffs in Scotland): *Millar v Dickson (Procurator Fiscal, Elgin)* [2001] UKPC D4, [2002] 3 All ER 1041, [2002] 1 WLR 1615; *R (Chief Constable of Lancashire) v Crown Court at Preston and Gosling*; *R (Smith) v Lincoln Crown Court* [2001] EWHC 928 (Admin), [2002] 1 WLR 1332 (composition of Crown Court for hearing licensing appeals); *Scanfuture UK Ltd v Secretary of State for the Department of Trade and Industry* [2001] ICR 1096, [2001] IRLR 416, EAT(appointment of employment tribunal members by Secretary of State for proceedings to which Secretary of State a party); *In matter of Charanjit Singh (application for judicial review)* (Outer House, Court of Session, 10 October 2001, Lord Mackay).

Acts of public authorities must be 'prescribed by law'

4.90 Some Convention rights (for instance, the right not to be tortured, art 3) are absolute, but most rights are qualified in that they may, where it is necessary to do so, be restricted for certain purposes that override the individual's right. A recurrent theme in the Convention is the need for there to be lawful authority if such restrictions are to be justifiable. Thus by art 5(1), no one shall be deprived of his or her liberty except for stated purposes and in accordance with a procedure 'prescribed by law'. In the case of other rights, such as the right to respect for private and family life (art 8) and freedom of expression (art 10), each article specifies the purposes for which the right in question may be restricted or qualified, and requires that the restrictions shall be 'in accordance with the law' (or 'prescribed by law'), and that they shall be 'necessary in a democratic society'.[1]

[1]   See H Mountfield, 'The Concept of a Lawful Interference with Fundamental Rights', in J Jowell and J Cooper (ed), *Understanding Human Rights Principles*, pp 5–25. See also Lester, Pannick and Herberg, note 1 paragraph **4.4** above, pp 118–122.

4.91 The requirement that a restriction shall be 'prescribed by law' is interpreted as governing both form and substance. The formal aspect is that the interference with a Convention right must have been authorised by the legislature or must have another recognised source of legal authority. In 1979, when the question of the legality of telephone-tapping by the police came before the High Court, Megarry V-C held that the police were not required in English law to show authority for intercepting telephone conversations, since (in his view) the practice did not involve the commission of a tort:

'If the tapping of telephones by the Post Office at the request of the police can be carried out without any breach of the law, it does not require any statutory or common law power to justify it: it can lawfully be done simply because there is nothing to make it unlawful'.[1]

[1]   *Malone v Metropolitan Police Commissioner* [1979] Ch 344, 367.

4.92 The Strasbourg Court took an opposite view: in the absence of clear legal authority for police telephone-tapping, the minimum degree of protection against arbitrary action to which citizens were entitled under the rule of law was lacking.[1] Moreover, the phrase 'in accordance with the law':

'does not merely refer back to domestic law but also relates to the quality of the law, requiring it to be compatible with the rule of law, which is expressly mentioned in the preamble to the Convention'.[2]

[1]   *Malone v United Kingdom* (1984) 7 EHRR 14.
[2]   *Malone v United Kingdom* (1984) 7 EHRR 14 at paragraph 67. And see P Craig, 'Formal and Substantive Conceptions of the Rule of Law: an Analytical Framework' [1997] *Public Law* 467.

4.93 The Court held that the law:

'must be sufficiently clear in its terms to give citizens an adequate indication as to the circumstances in which and the conditions on which public authorities are empowered to resort to this secret and potentially dangerous interference with the right to respect for private life and correspondence'.[1]

[1]   *Malone v United Kingdom* (1984) 7 EHRR 14 at paragraph 67.

4.94 As regards the legal position of telephone-tapping in the UK:

'it cannot be said with reasonable certainty what elements of the powers to intercept are incorporated in legal rules and what elements remain within the discretion of the executive'.[1]

> [1] *Malone v United Kingdom* (1984) 7 EHRR 14 at paragraph 80. The Interception of Communications Act 1985 subsequently authorised telephone-tapping by the police subject to the conditions stipulated. This did not authorise interception of internal phones within the police service: *Halford v United Kingdom*(Application 20605/92)(1997) 24 EHRR 523, [1997] IRLR 471.

4.95 By contrast, in *Sunday Times Ltd v United Kingdom*,[1] the court held (by a majority) that the common law rules on contempt of court met the test of being 'prescribed by law' in that they were sufficiently 'accessible' (so that an individual had an adequate indication of the rules) and were formulated with sufficient precision to enable the individual to regulate his or her conduct. In neither the *Malone* nor the *Sunday Times* cases had Parliament legislated on the subject-matter. In *Silver v United Kingdom (Application 20605/92)*,[2] dealing with the censorship of prisoners' letters, there was both primary legislation (the Prisons Act 1952) and delegated legislation (the Prison Rules), but the operative rules of censorship were found in unpublished instructions to prison officers. The court re-affirmed that the law must be sufficiently accessible and formulated with sufficient precision to enable the individual to foresee the consequences of a given action. Although the unpublished directions lacked the force of law, they could be taken into account 'to the admittedly limited extent to which [the prisoners] were made sufficiently aware of their contents'.[3] The court thus did not go so far as to hold that the detailed rules of censorship must be contained in the Act or Prison Rules, and it found that many but not all of the rules satisfied the test of foreseeability. This is reflected in *R (Purdy) v DPP* where Lord Phillips noted that 'the word "law" in this context is to be understood in its substantive sense, not its formal one . . . law for this purpose goes beyond the mere words of the statute'.[4] This is significant in view of the widespread practice of government in relying on 'soft law' (circulars, guidance, codes of practice, internal instructions and the like), rather than giving the force of law to the detailed rules on which it relies. A crucial factor in such situations is the extent to which the content of rules has been made known to those who are directly affected.[5]

> [1] (1979) 2 EHRR 245. The court, by 11-9, held that the ban on publishing articles about the thalidomide litigation was not 'necessary in a democratic society for maintaining the authority and impartiality of the judiciary'. Judges Zekia. O'Donoghue and Erigenis disagreed with the majority on the 'prescribed by law' issue.
> [2] (1983) 5 EHRR 347, [1983] ECHR 5947/72.
> [3] (1983) 5 EHRR 347 at paragraph 88.
> [4] [2009] UKHL 45, paragraph 41, [2009] 4 All ER 1147,, paragraph 41, [2009] 3 WLR 403, paragraph 41. Therefore for the purposes of art 8(2), provisions of the Code for Crown Prosecutors were 'prescribed by law'. See also *R (Munjaz) v Mersey Care NHS Trust* [2005] UKHL 58, paragraph 34, [2006] 2 AC 148, paragraph 34, [2006] 4 All ER 736, paragraph 34 (Lord Bingham).
> [5] See *Christian Institute v Lord Advocate* [2016] UKSC 51; 2016 SLT 805. And see Lord Bingham, *R (Gillan) v Metropolitan Police Comr* [2006] UKHL 12, paragraph 34, [2006] 2 AC 307, paragraph 34, [2006] 4 All ER 1041, paragraph 34:
>
>> 'The lawfulness requirement in the Convention addresses supremely important features of the rule of law. The exercise of power by public officials . . . must be governed by clear and publicly accessible rules of law. The public must not be vulnerable to interference by public officials acting on any personal whim, caprice, malice, predilection or purpose other

than that for which the power was conferred. This is what . . . is meant by arbitrariness, which is the antithesis of legality.'

On the duty of government departments to comply with published policies, and on the distinction between policies and rules, decisions of the Supreme Court include *R (Lumba) v Secretary of State for the Home Department* [2011] UKSC 12, [2012] 1 AC 245, [2011] 4 All ER 1; *R (Davies) v Revenue and Customs Comrs* [2011] UKSC 47, [2012] 1 All ER 1048, [2011] 1 WLR 2625and *R (Alvi) v Secretary of State for the Home Department* [2012] UKSC 33, [2012] 4 All ER 1041, [2012] 1 WLR 2208.

4.96 Other cases have concerned the ancient power of magistrates to bind over persons to be of good conduct. In *Steel v United Kingdom*[1] the power was held to be 'in accordance with a procedure prescribed by law' and capable of being applied to someone who had committed a breach of the peace (involving harm to others or the provocation of violence). But in an art 10 case, *Hashman and Harrup v United Kingdom (Application 25594/94)*,[2] the power to bind over to be of good behaviour a non-violent hunt protester who was considered to have acted *contra bonos mores*[3] was held not to be 'prescribed by law' since it had a 'purely prospective effect',[4] was imprecise and gave little guidance as to the type of conduct that would amount to a breach of the peace.

The test of foreseeability was further developed in the art 8 case of *MM v United Kingdom (Application 24029/07)*.[5] MM was not offered a job after a disclosure by the Northern Ireland police to her prospective employer of a caution, which she had accepted some years previously. The Strasbourg Court held that the retention and disclosure of adult cautions (originally under a common law power, later pursuant to the Police Act 1997) was not 'in accordance with the law' because of the lack of sufficient safeguards to prevent arbitrary treatment in violation of art 8. The court relied on the *cumulative* effect of various shortcomings, including the lack of clarity regarding collection and storage of data, absence of an independent review mechanism, and failure to make distinctions based on the nature of offence, disposal, time elapsed, or type of employment sought.

MM was relied upon by the Supreme Court in *R (T) v Chief Constable of Greater Manchester*.[6] A statutory scheme for disclosing spent criminal warnings and convictions to prospective employers was held not to be 'in accordance with the law' due to the cumulative effect of 'the failure to draw any distinction on the basis of the nature of the offence, the disposal in the case, the time which has elapsed since the offence took place or the relevance of the data to the employment sought, and the absence of any mechanism for independent review'. (However, Lord Wilson considered that these factors should properly be taken into account with regards to necessity or proportionality rather than legality.)

By contrast, in *R (Roberts) v Commissioner of Police of the Metropolis*[7] the Supreme Court held that a police power to stop and search in a designated area, without grounds for suspicion, under s 60 of the Criminal Justice and Public Order Act 1994 was 'in accordance with the law' for the purpose of art 8(1) because there were sufficient safeguards which enabled the proportionality of any art 8 interference to be adequately examined.

[1] (1998) 28 EHRR 603, [1998] Crim LR 893.
[2] (1999) 30 EHRR 241, [2000] Crim LR 185.
[3] That is, 'conduct which is wrong rather than right in the judgment of the majority of contemporary citizens': (1999) 30 EHRR 241 at paragraph 13.

⁴   (1999) 30 EHRR 241 at paragraph 35. See also *R (Laporte) v Chief Constable of Gloucestershire Constabulary (Chief Constable of Thames Valley Police, interested parties)* [2006] UKHL 55, [2007] 2 AC 105, [2007] 2 All ER 529 as to breaches of the peace.
⁵   *The Times*, 16 January 2013.
⁶   *R (T) v Chief Constable of Greater Manchester* [2014] UKSC 35; [2015] AC 49. See the concluding paragraph 119, Lord Reed's discussion of MM at paragraphs 113–116 and Lord Wilson's dissenting remarks at paragraphs 35–38.
⁷   [2015] UKSC 79; [2016] 1 WLR 210.

4.97 The fact that legislation has been enacted on a subject does not resolve the question of whether a particular restriction is prescribed by law. The Contempt of Court Act 1981 was held sufficient to meet the Convention test in *Goodwin v United Kingdom (Application 17488/90)*,¹ but a Swiss law on the interception of communications was held not to do so, when it did not provide proper safeguards against abuse of the power.²

In *Christian Institute v Lord Advocate*,³ the Supreme Court held that the legislative scheme for data-sharing contained in part 4 of the Children and Young People (Scotland) Act 2014 was not sufficiently accessible to those affected to be 'in accordance with the law'. The scheme was held to be incompatible with art 8. As Baroness Hale, Lord Reed and Lord Hodge explained in their joint judgment, to be 'in accordance with the law' requires not only that a measure must have some basis in domestic law, but also that it must be 'accessible to the person concerned' and 'foreseeable as to its effects':

> 'These qualitative requirements of accessibility and foreseeability have two elements. First, a rule must be formulated with sufficient precision to enable any individual — if need be with appropriate advice — to regulate his or her conduct . . . Secondly, it must be sufficiently precise to give legal protection against arbitrariness . . .'⁴

¹   (1996) 22 EHRR 123, (1996) Times, 28 March. See also *R (Kent Pharmaceuticals Ltd) v Director of the Serious Fraud Office* [2004] EWCA Civ 1494, [2005] 1 All ER 449, [2005] 1 WLR 1302 and *R (Gillan) v Metropolitan Police Comr* [2006] UKHL 12, paragraph 34, [2006] 2 AC 307, paragraph 34, [2006] 4 All ER 1041, paragraph 34.
²   *Amann v Switzerland* (Application 27798/95)(2000) 30 EHRR 843, [2000] ECHR 27798/95.
³   [2016] UKSC 51; 2016 SLT 805.
⁴   *Christian Institute v Lord Advocate* at paragraph 79; see further paragraphs 80–85.

4.98 In *R v Somerset County Council, ex p Fewings*,¹ it was confirmed that any action taken by local authorities, as statutory bodies, must be justified by positive law. But the Crown has sometimes established that it has the ordinary capacity of a private person to act, even when the context and effect of its acts are of an essentially governmental nature.² One consequence of the Convention is that where acts inconsistent with a Convention right have occurred, the public authority concerned (including the Crown) will have to show positive legal justification for the conduct; it will be unable to claim that it has full power to act except where specific conduct is prohibited.³

¹   [1995] 3 All ER 20, 25, confirming the statement by Laws J at [1995] 1 All ER 513, 524.
²   *R v Secretary of State for Health, ex p C* [2001] 1 FLR 658 (non-statutory list of persons considered unsuitable to work with children); *Shrewsbury and Atcham Borough Council v Secretary of State for Communities and Local Government* [2008] EWCA Civ 148, [2008] 3 All ER 548, (2008) Times, 12 March. But cf 13th report, HL Committee on the Constitution, 'The Pre-Emption of Parliament' (HL paper 165, 2012–13), chap 3. And see A Lester and M Weait, 'The use of ministerial powers without parliamentary authority: the Ram doctrine' [2003] Public Law 415.

³ *Malone v Metropolitan Police Comr* (1984) 7 EHRR 14.

Margin of appreciation and the discretionary area of judgment

4.99 A fundamental feature of judicial review of administrative action is that review does not provide a right of appeal against the merits of every official decision. Particularly in respect of discretionary decisions, the principle of legality does not require a reviewing court to decide that only one correct decision was possible in a given case.¹ In English law, the doctrine of irrationality (or *Wednesbury* unreasonableness)² expressed, however imperfectly,³ an approach that sought to identify the boundaries of administrative discretion, while leaving it to the decision-maker to decide what action to take from the range of solutions legally available. Adoption of the test of proportionality rather than irrationality has inevitably occurred under the HRA 1998, but the test does not 'mean that there has been a shift to merits review'.⁴ Under the European Convention, the Strasbourg Court reviews for compliance with the Convention action taken by national governments, legislatures and judiciaries. This process involves complex judgments to be made of the balance between competing Convention rights, of the balance between collective interests and the individual's rights, as to whether restrictions have been imposed for a legitimate purpose and, if so, whether those restrictions are 'necessary in a democratic society'. Although not found in the Convention's text, the doctrine of 'margin of appreciation' was developed by the court to signify 'the latitude which signatory states are permitted in their observance of the Convention'.⁵ On this basis, in many situations a measure of choice is exercised by national authorities, and a violation of the Convention will be found only if the decision has been made outside the range of permissible courses of action in those situations.

¹ However, in a case which turns on an issue of jurisdictional fact, the reviewing court must be satisfied that the issue was determined correctly (as in *Khawaja v Secretary of State for the Home Department* [1984] AC 74, [1983] 1 All ER 765, HL). This principle was applied in *R (A) v Croydon London Borough Council* [2009] UKSC 8, [2010] 1 All ER 469, [2009] 1 WLR 2557.

² See CHAPTERS 8, 9.

³ See *R (Daly) v Secretary of State for the Home Department* [2001] UKHL 26, paragraph 32, [2001] 2 AC 532, paragraph 32, [2001] 3 All ER 433, paragraph 32 (Lord Cooke of Thorndon). Even when modified to take fuller account of the protection of human rights, as explained by Lord Steyn in *Daly* at paragraphs 27–28, the Wednesbury doctrine set too high a threshold for national courts to be able to enter into issues of judgment that arose under the ECHR: see *Smith and Grady v United Kingdom (Applications 33985/96 and 33986/96)* (1999) 29 EHRR 493, 543.

⁴ Lord Steyn, in *Daly* at paragraph 28.

⁵ T H Jones, 'The Devaluation of Human Rights under the European Convention' [1995] *Public Law* 430, 431.

4.100 In developing this doctrine, the court has been criticised for devaluing rights protected by the Convention and for showing excessive deference to national decision-makers. More recently, criticism has been levelled at the Court for failing to give due deference to national sovereignty and applying a wide enough margin of appreciation.¹ But the doctrine has never permitted a State to exercise unlimited discretion. The Court has emphasised that 'the domestic margin of appreciation is . . . accompanied by a European supervision'.[2] The doctrine has been applied with varying degrees of emphasis to different Convention rights. Thus, member states enjoy a wider margin of appreciation in respect of matters that involve the protection of morals and freedom of artistic expression,[3] than in the case of a ban on publishing articles imposed to protect the authority of the judiciary.[4] The margin of appreciation is particularly wide in questions of the right to life and the regulation of IVF treatment and consent.[5] Moreover, there are Convention rights (such as art 3, prohibition of torture) for which no margin of appreciation would be justified.[6]

1   See 4.8. This tension was reflected in the Brighton Declaration at paragraphs 10–12: hub.coe. int/20120419-brighton-declaration and forms the basis for Article 1, Draft Protocol 15, see note 11, 4.63.

2   *Brannigan and McBride v United Kingdom(Application 14553/89)* (1993) 17 EHRR 539, 569.

3   See eg *Handyside v United Kingdom (Application 5493/72)* (1976) 1 EHRR 737, [1976] ECHR 5493/72; *Muller v Switzerland (Application 10737/84)* (1988) 13 EHRR 212.

4   *Sunday Times Ltd v United Kingdom(Application 6538/74)* (1979) 2 EHRR 245, [1979] ECHR 6538/74.

5   On the right to life and assisted suicide, see *Pretty v United Kingdom (Application 2346/02)* (2002) 35 EHRR 1, [2002] 2 FCR 97 and *Nicklinson v United Kingdom (Admissibility) (Application 2478/15)* (2015) 61 EHRR SE7). On reproductive rights, see *Evans v United Kingdom (Application 6339/05)* (2008) 46 EHRR 34, [2007] 2 FCR 5. See also *A v Ireland (25579/05)* (2011) 53 EHRR 13, [2011] 3 FCR 244; the Grand Chamber held that Ireland's prohibition of abortion fell within the margin of appreciation.

6   The margin of appreciation is particularly wide when matters involve sensitive social and political issues: *RMT v United Kingdom* (8 April 2014, unreported) at paragraph 86. For an extensive study, see D Spielmann, *Allowing the Right Margin. The European Court of Human Rights and the national margin of appreciation doctrine: Waiver or subsidiarity of European review?* CELS Working Paper, February 2012.

4.101 One justification for the court's recognition of a margin of appreciation is that the ECHR seeks to ensure that minimum standards of human rights are recognised, not to harmonise law and practice across Europe. But a State with a policy or practice that diverges far from the consensus in Europe is at risk of being condemned for this reason.[1] Another reason advanced at an international level for recognising a margin of appreciation is that on some matters (for instance, as to what would be best policy in the planning sphere):

'the national authorities are in principle better placed than an international court to evaluate local needs and conditions when applying European-wide standards to national circumstances'.[2]

1   Consider, eg *Campbell and Cosans v United Kingdom (Application 7511/76)* (1982) 4 EHRR 293; and *Dudgeon v United Kingdom (Application 7525/76)* (1981) 4 EHRR 149, [1981] ECHR 7525/76. Cf *Goodwin v United Kingdom (Application 28957/95)* (2002) 35 EHRR 447 at paragraphs 84–85, [2002] IRLR 664 at paragraphs 84–85 (no evidence of a common European approach, but 'clear and uncontested evidence of a continuing international trend').

2   *Buckley v United Kingdom (Application 20348/92)* (1996) 23 EHRR 101 at paragraph 75, (1996) Times, 9 October at paragraph 75.

4.102 Whatever the justification for the margin at the European level, the need for a 'margin of appreciation' in upholding Convention rights in national law must take a different form.[1] In discussion of HRA 1998, this has been termed 'the discretionary area of judgment'. Lord Bingham of Cornhill stated:

'While a national court does not accord the margin of appreciation recognised by the European Court as a supra-national court, it will give weight to the decisions of a representative legislature and a democratic government within the discretionary area of judgment accorded to those bodies'.[2]

Lord Hope of Craighead has said that in national courts:

'the Convention should be seen as an expression of fundamental principles rather than as a set of mere rules. The questions which the courts will have to decide in the application of these principles will involve questions of balance between competing interests and issues of proportionality'.[3]

[1] See R Singh, M Hunt and M Demetriou, 'Is there a role for the "margin of appreciation" in national law after the HRA?' [1999] EHRLR 15. Beatson et al argue that the concept of margin of appreciation 'is beginning to creep back into domestic law' *Human Rights: Judicial Protection in the UK* (2008) paragraph 3–188.

[2] *Brown v Stott (Procurator Fiscal, Dunfermline)* [2003] 1 AC 681, at 703.

[3] *R v DPP, ex p Kebilene* [2000] 2 AC 326 at 380–381. On subsequent case law, see A Lester, D Pannick and J Herberg (ed), *Human Rights Law and Practice* (3rd edn, 2009), pp 122–129.

4.103 In their jurisdiction under the HRA 1998, the courts must review decisions already made by public authorities, and (continued Lord Hope):

'In some circumstances it will be appropriate for the courts to recognise that there is an area of judgment within which the judiciary will defer, on democratic grounds, to the considered opinion of the elected body or person whose act or decision is said to be incompatible with the Convention'.[1]

Where a public authority's decision involves balancing competing rights and they have made no attempt to do so, then the court has no alternative but to strike the balance itself 'giving due weight to the judgements made by those who are in much closer touch with the people and the places involved that the court could ever be'.[2] However, where the legislation itself is intended to strike that balance, then the court should be slow to intervene and the applicant should challenge the legislation rather than the act of the public authority.[3]

[1] *R v DPP, ex p Kebilene*. See also *Brown v Stott (Procurator Fiscal, Dunfermline)* [2003] 1 AC 681, 710–711 (Lord Steyn) and *Nicklinson v Ministry of Justice* [2014] UKSC 38; [2015] AC 657.

[2] Lady Hale, *Miss Behavin' Ltd v Belfast City Council* [2007] UKHL 19, paragraph 37, [2007] NI 89, paragraph 37, [2007] 3 All ER 1007, paragraph 37.

[3] *Kay v Lambeth London Borough Council* [2006] UKHL 10, [2006] 2 AC 465, [2006] 4 All ER 128. But this is only where the legislation 'may truly be said to represent a considered democratic compromise': Lord Bingham, *Huang v Secretary of State for the Home Department* [2007] UKHL 11, paragraph 17, [2007] 2 AC 67, paragraph 17, [2007] 4 All ER 15, paragraph 17.

4.104 Many decisions on the violation of Convention rights turn on whether a particular restriction of a right is 'proportional' to the public interest that the restriction serves.[1] In making such decisions, a court ought to take into account limitations that exist upon its own capacity to reach a fully informed decision on the matters in issue, and also constitutional principles (such as the democratic accountability of the executive and Parliament) that govern the powers entrusted to the main branches of the state. As Lord Bingham, in *A v Secretary of State for the Home Department* noted 'The more purely political (in a broad or narrow sense) a question is, the more appropriate it will be for political resolution and the less likely it is to be an appropriate matter for judicial decision'.[2] It is not possible here to explore in depth the extent to which, if at all, judicial 'deference' to legislative and executive decisions is appropriate under the HRA 1998.[3] Certainly, the HRA 1998 has extended the functions of the courts in reviewing the compatibility of legislation with the Convention and in assessing the proportionality of executive and legislative decisions that affect Convention rights. The impact of the HRA 1998 is to be seen on a daily basis in many decisions made on claims for judicial review.[4] But this does not mean that the courts are required wholly to ignore established constitutional practice in carrying out their enlarged functions.[5] Inevitably there exist executive powers, the most obvious being in regard to national security, in respect of which the courts have in the past been likely to hold that primary responsibility for decisions must be borne by the executive, accountable through the democratic process for those decisions.[6] Nevertheless, in a very significant decision that would have been impossible apart from the HRA 1998, it was held after a hearing before nine Law Lords that the power of the Secretary of State (under the Anti-terrorism, Crime and Security Act 2001, s 23) to detain without trial and without limit of time foreign citizens who were suspected of involvement in terrorism but who could not be deported, was in breach of their Convention rights.[7] Lord Bingham of Cornhill accepted that great weight should be given to the judgment of the Home Secretary and of Parliament on detention without trial, 'because they were called on to exercise a pre-eminently political judgment'.[8] But he was in no doubt that the HRA 1998 required the courts to review, on proportionality grounds, the compatibility with the ECHR of the power to detain without trial; and the courts were not precluded by any doctrine of deference from scrutinising the issues raised.[9]

Domestic courts will also be reluctant to interfere in matters of socio-economic policy;[10] although a more scrupulous review may be called for where the government defends a measure on socio-economic grounds not in the mind of the decision-maker at the time.[11]

[1] See CHAPTER 9.
[2] [2004] UKHL 56, at paragraph 29, [2005] 2 AC 68, at paragraph 29, [2005] 3 All ER 169, at paragraph 29.
[3] See R Edwards, 'Judicial Deference under the HRA' (2002) 65 MLR 859 and F Klug, 'Judicial Deference under the HRA' (2003) EHRLR 125. In *R (ProLife Alliance) v British Broadcasting Corpn* [2003] UKHL 23, at paragraphs 74–77, [2004] 1AC 185, at paragraphs 74–77 [2003] 2 All ER 977, at paragraphs 74–77 Lord Hoffmann argued that questions as to the extent to which the courts were prepared to recognise the decision-making powers of the legislature and executive turned on questions of law, and that talk of deference and courtesy was wholly misplaced. Similarly see Lord Bingham in *Huang v Secretary of State for the Home Department* [2007] UKHL 11, paragraph 16. See J Jowell, 'Judicial deference: servility, civility or institutional capacity?' [2003] *Public Law* 592 and (same author) 'Judicial Deference and Human Rights: a Question of Competence', in P Craig and R Rawlings (ed). *Law and Administration in Europe* (2003) Ch 4. See also R Ekins, 'Judicial Supremacy and the Rule of Law' (2003) 119 LQR 127: R Clayton. 'Judicial deference and "democratic dialogue": the legitimacy of judicial intervention under the HRA 1998' [2004] *Public Law 33*; Lord Steyn 'Deference: a Tangled Story' [2005] *Public Law* 346 and Lord Justice Dyson 'Some thoughts on Judicial Deference' [2006] *Judicial Review* 103.
[4] See V Bondy, 'The Impact of the HRA on Judicial Review' [2003] *Judicial Review* 149 and T de la Mare and D Pievsky. 'Impact of the HRA 1998 on Judicial Review' [2003] *Judicial Review* 221.
[5] In *Wilson v First County Trust Ltd* [2003] UKHL 40, [2004] 1 AC 816[2003] 4 All ER 97. Lord Nicholls recognised the new role of the court in reviewing primary legislation but stressed that it is a 'cardinal constitutional principle that the will of Parliament is expressed in the language used by it in its enactments' (paragraph 67). And Lord Hope has referred to 'the

familiar question' of where the margin lies between matters for the democratically elected assembly and those where the court can legitimately intervene: *R (Countryside Alliance) v A-G* [2007] UKHL 52, paragraph 76, [2008] 1 AC 719, paragraph 76, [2008] 2 All ER 95, paragraph 76.

6 See *Rehman v Secretary of State for the Home Department* [2001] UKHL 47, [2003] 1 AC 153, [2002] 1 All ER 122(especially Lord Hoffmann at paragraph 62).

7 *A v Secretary of State for the Home Department* [2004] UKHL 56, [2005] 3 All ER 169. For comment, see A Tomkins [2005] *Public Law* 259 and a short symposium of articles in (2005) 68 MLR 654–680.

8 *A v Secretary of State for the Home Department* at paragraph 29.

9 *A v Secretary of State for the Home Department* at paragraph 42.

10 *Brewster's Application for Judicial Review, Re* [2017] UKSC 8 at paragraph 49. This reflects the wider margin of appreciation allowed to member states by the Strasbourg Court in relation to social or economic strategy: *Stec v United Kingdom (65731/01)* (2006) 43 EHRR 47; 20 BHRC 348. The test formulated in Stec (at paragraph 52) is whether the measure under scrutiny is 'manifestly without reasonable foundation'. This test has subsequently been adopted in the domestic context: see *Humphreys v Revenue and Customs Comrs* [2012] UKSC 18, [2012] 1 WLR 1545 at paragraph 19; *R (SG) v Secretary of State for Work and Pensions* [2015] UKSC 16, [2015] 1 WLR 1449 at paragraph 11; and Brewster at paragraph 55.

11 *Brewster's Application for Judicial Review*, Re at paragraph 50.

Chapter 5

THE AMBIT OF JUDICIAL REVIEW

WHEN IS JUDICIAL REVIEW AVAILABLE?

5.1 Two concepts must be distinguished at the outset. These are the grounds on which judicial review is available, and the types of decision which are amenable to judicial review. The first topic is considered in Chapters 6–13. This chapter deals with the second.

5.2 Although it is easy to see why judicial review is available in a straightforward case, it is impossible to formulate a succinct definition of the classes of case in which judicial review will be available. This is because its availability depends on a combination of two factors: the source of the decision-maker's power to make the decision in question, and the nature of that decision.[1] An easy case at one end of the spectrum is a decision-maker exercising statutory powers who makes a decision with an obvious public law content: say, a decision by an immigration officer to refuse leave to enter, or to detain a person.[2] A less obvious case is a decision by a statutory body in a commercial context (a local authority selling land, or Lloyd's regulating the affairs of its members) or in an employment context (an NHS trust, or perhaps a fire authority, disciplining or dismissing an officer or employee). A less obvious case still is a decision by a non-statutory body, apparently private in nature, not to grant a licence to someone which affects that person's ability to earn a living. As the cases show, some decisions of a statutory body will not be amenable to judicial review; and some decisions of an apparently private body will be.

---

[1]   The word 'decision' is used as a convenient shorthand for the matter which the claimant seeks to have reviewed. For further discussion, see 5.5.

2   Note, however, that in some cases with obvious public law content, a statutory appeal may be an appropriate remedy; see CHAPTER 18.

5.3 The question in any particular case is not whether the decision-maker is, in general terms, amenable to judicial review, but whether a particular decision is.[1] A focus on the nature of the decision is found both in the common law and in the Human Rights Act 1998. As explained in CHAPTER 4,[2] s 6(1) of the Act makes it unlawful for a public body to act in a way which is incompatible with a Convention right. Section 6(3)–(5) defines 'public authority'.[3] These provisions make clear that a body may be a public authority for some purposes,[4] and in relation to those purposes subject to the duty to respect the rights set out in Sch 1 to the 1998 Act, but not for others.

1   An insight which comes from the decision of the Court of Appeal in *R v Panel on Take-overs and Mergers, ex p Datafin* [1987] QB 815 at pp 847C and 848C–848D per Lloyd LJ, with whom Nicholls LJ agreed.
2   See **4.20** above.
3   In *Aston Cantlow and Wilmcote with Billesley Parochial Church Council v Wallbank* [2004] 1 AC 546, the House of Lords made it clear that amenability to judicial review is not determinative of a body's status under the Human Rights Act 1998, s 6 (see **4.58** above). However, if in relation to a particular matter a body falls within s 6, it is highly likely to be amenable to judicial review in relation to that matter. See also *YL v Birmingham City Council* [2007] UKHL 27; [2008] 1 AC 95.
4   Ie a 'hybrid authority'.

5.4 There is another aspect which calls for consideration. This is whether the matter which the claimant seeks to have reviewed has reached a stage where review is appropriate. This is discussed in the next section of this chapter.

PREMATURITY

5.5 While it can be convenient to refer to the matter which the claimant seeks to have reviewed as a 'decision', this can be misleading. The availability of judicial review does not necessarily require a decision.[1] Further, the mere fact that a decision of some nature has been taken does not necessarily mean that the matter has reached a stage at which judicial review is appropriate.[2] There will often be no doubt at all that there has been a decision and that it is of a kind which is susceptible to judicial review. Occasionally, however, the position may be less clear. Two situations can arise which illustrate this problem. The first is when a body issues a general statement or policy, with which a would-be claimant disagrees strongly, but which has not yet been applied to him, or had any impact on him. The second is when there is an issue between a would-be claimant and an authority, and the question is considered on successive occasions by that authority, in the light of a series of representations made by the potential claimant.

1   See CHAPTERS 16 and 17.
2   Questions which arise in this regard may have strong link with questions of standing and the discretionary nature of the relief: these issues are discussed in CHAPTER 18.

5.6 The courts have not been wholly consistent in their approach to the first type of case. In *R v Secretary of State for Health, ex p Imperial Tobacco*,[1] a tobacco company applied for judicial review of a report on passive smoking by the Scientific Committee on Tobacco and Health ('the Committee'). The judge held that the report was not unlawful and had been part of a continuing process of consultation. But, in any event, he also held, advice given to government in the shape of a report given by the Committee should not be, and in this case was not, susceptible to judicial review. However, judicial review may be available in principle in respect of guidance (whether statutory or non-statutory), even if nothing unlawful has yet been done in reliance on it. This conclusion is implicit in the approach of the Court of Appeal in *R (ISPSEA Limited) v Secretary of State for Education and Skills.*[2] This was an unsuccessful challenge to the lawfulness of the SEN Toolkit, a publication produced by the Department of Education and Skills, which summarised the obligations of local education authorities in relation to special educational needs. The judge refused permission to apply, and the Court of Appeal upheld that decision. However, this was on the basis that there was nothing unlawful in the Toolkit, rather than that it was not in principle amenable to judicial review. Finally, the decision of Munby J in *R (Burke) v GMC*[3] is significant in this context. He quashed as unlawful guidance of the GMC dealing with the withdrawal of artificial feeding. The claimant was not yet in the position of needing such assistance, but suffered from a degenerative condition which meant that in due course he would. The Court of Appeal allowed an appeal against Munby J's decision.[4] While differing from his view about the lawfulness of the guidance on the facts, they did not quarrel with the principle that guidance could be amenable to judicial review in an appropriate, albeit rare, case.[5] In *R (Purdy) v DPP*[6] the House of Lords went further, and required the DPP to publish offence-specific guidance on aiding and abetting suicide.

[1]   Unreported, QBD (Crown Office List) (Hidden J) 21/12/1999.
[2]   [2003] ELR 393. See also *YA v Secretary of State for Health* [2009] EWCA Civ 225, [2010] 1 WLR 279, where unlawful parts of non-statutory guidance were quashed, even though the claimant was not at that stage the victim of any unlawful conduct.
[3]   [2004] EWHC 1879 (Admin), (2004) 7 CCLR 609.
[4]   [2005] EWCA Civ 1003, [2006] Q.B. 273.
[5]   Judgment, paragraphs 21 and 41–47.
[6]   [2009] UKHL 45; [2009] 3 WLR 403.

5.7 The second situation creates a quandary for a claimant. If the claimant does not identify the 'right' decision to challenge and waits too long, he may be faced with a delay argument which defeats his challenge altogether. Equally, if he applies too soon, he may be met with an argument that his application is premature.[1] Sometimes a defendant who has reconsidered a case for tactical reasons (perhaps because the first consideration was vulnerable to challenge) will have no interest in taking a delay point. However, there will be cases in which a defendant will be only too pleased to take a delay or a prematurity point.[2] The safest course for a claimant in such a case may be to issue proceedings to protect his position once it looks as though something resembling a decision has been made, but to apply for a stay while any negotiations or re-consideration continue. A slightly different situation was considered in *R v Secretary of State for Education, ex p Bandtock*.[3] In that case there was a two-tier decision-making process involving a local education authority (LEA) and the Secretary of State. Collins J observed, differing from the Divisional Court in *R v Secretary of State for Education and Science, ex p Threapleton*,[4] that the better view was that if the decision of the LEA was fatally flawed and could not be cured by the decision of the Secretary of State, a claimant who delayed until after the Secretary of State's decision would not act promptly. In that case, the initial decision was fatally flawed. However, he was bound by *Threapleton*, and had to acknowledge, that technically, therefore, it was open to the claimant to challenge the later decision of the Secretary of State. None the less, he relied on both *Threapleton* and *Nichol v Gateshead Metropolitan Borough Council*[5] to refuse relief in his discretion.

1   See Chapter **18**.
2   See, for example, *Burkett v Hammersmith and Fulham London Borough Council* [2002] 1 WLR 1593 at paras 42, 43 and 45, per Lord Steyn and *R (Breckland DC) v Electoral Commission Boundary Committee for England* [2009] EWCA Civ 239; [2009] BLGR 589 at paras 101–111.
3   [2001] ELR 333.
4   Unreported, 12 May 1988.
5   (1988) 87 LGR 435.

WHO, OR WHAT, IS AMENABLE TO JUDICIAL REVIEW?

5.8   The cases show that the mere fact that the body whose decision it is sought to challenge does not derive its powers from statute or the prerogative[1] is not decisive of the question, either, whether one of its decisions is amenable to judicial review, or whether it is, in relation to a particular function, a public authority for the purposes of the Human Rights Act 1998. In part at least, this is nothing new: it was established as long ago as the *Datafin* case, in relation to the Takeover Panel,[2] that its decisions could be susceptible to judicial review even though it had, at that stage,[3] no statutory underpinning at all, because of the quasi-governmental functions it performed in the public interest. However, some private bodies, despite the fact that they have a quasi-monopoly over activities which the Government might well regulate if they did not exist, have escaped the tentacles of judicial review. The most notorious example is the Jockey Club, which has eluded several challenges.[4] The essential reason for this is that the foundation of the club's jurisdiction is a contract,[5] and the courts' sense that the functions it performs are not governmental. In a similar way, an arbitrator who derives his authority from an arbitration clause in a contract is not amenable to judicial review.[6]

1   See below, and see Chapter **3** at 3.8 et seq. For Scots law on this question, see **22.11**.
2   *R v Panel on Take-overs and Mergers, ex p Datafin* [1987] QB 815. For further discussion of this case, see Chapter **3** above. See, also, *R (on the application of Beer (t/a Hammer Trout Farm)) v Hampshire Farmers Markets Ltd* [2003] EWCA Civ 1056; [2004] 1 W.L.R. 233; *R v Advertising Standards Authority ex p Insurance Services plc* [1990] COD 42.
3   The Takeover Panel has since been given a statutory basis: see Chapter **1** of Part 28 of the Companies Act 2006.
4   Despite the fact that it is created under the prerogative by royal charter: *R v Disciplinary Committee of the Jockey Club, ex p Massingberd-Mundy* [1993] 2 All ER 207; *R v Jockey Club, ex p RAM Racecourses Limited* [1993] 2 All ER 225; *R v Disciplinary Committee of the Jockey Club, ex p His Highness the Aga Khan* [1993] 1 WLR 909; and *R (Mullins) v The Appeal Board of the Jockey Club* [2005] EWHC 2197 (Admin). A similar conclusion has been reached about the football league: *R v Football Association, ex p Football League Limited* [1993] 2 All ER 833.
5   The relationship between parents and a private school is also governed by contract; and for this reason judicial review of exclusion decisions is held to be unavailable: *R v Muntham House School, ex p R*, (unreported, 29 October 1999). The contract may provide, expressly or impliedly, for an element of procedural fairness before an exclusion decision is taken: *Gray v Marlborough College* [2006] E.L.R. 516.
6   Though subject to the limited supervision of the court via the Arbitration Act 1996.

5.9 The Society of Lloyd's is an interesting case, and the authorities appear to illustrate a nuanced approach of the courts to the question of amenability to judicial review. Lloyd's is a statutory body established by private Act of Parliament. Lloyd's has been judicially reviewed in relation to disciplinary decisions.[1] However, it has successfully resisted judicial review of its decisions about the working out of the contractual arrangements between its members and their agents. Two reasons have been given: such decisions are concerned solely with a commercial relationship, and Lloyd's is itself subject to external government regulation.[2] The Court of Appeal has held, for similar reasons, that Lloyd's cannot be guilty of the tort of misfeasance in public office.[3]

[1]   *R v Committee of Lloyd's, ex p Posgate* (1983) Times, 12 January, *R v Committee of Lloyd's, ex p Moran* (1983) Times, 24 June and *R v Chairman of the Regulatory Board of Lloyd's, ex p MacMilllan* [1995] LRLR 485.
[2]   *R v Corporation of Lloyd's, ex p Briggs* [1993] 1 Lloyd's Rep 176 and *R (West) v Lloyd's of London* [2004] EWCA Civ 506 [2004] 3 All ER 251 at paragraphs 31–32. For criticism, see Jordan, [2004] Judicial Review 286. The latter case also decided that Lloyd's was not a public authority for the purposes of the Human Rights Act 1998 in relation to the working out of contractual arrangements between its members and their agents. The fact that the acts in question were supervised by a public regulatory body was insufficient to make Lloyd's a public body in relation to those activities. Contrast the position of other bodies, usually regulatory in nature, which have been seen by the courts as having (or have conceded they have) a more public dimension, thus making some of their decisions amenable to judicial review: *R v Code of Practice Committee of the British Pharmaceutical Industry, ex p Professional Counselling Aids Limited* (1991) 3 Admin LR 697; *R v Life Insurance and Unit Trust Regulatory Organisation, ex p Ross* [1992] 1 All E.R. 422 and *R v Financial Intermediaries Managers and Brokers Regulatory Association, ex p Cochrane* [1990] COD 33 (in the last two cases the point was conceded).
[3]   *Society of Lloyd's v Henderson* [2007] EWCA Civ 930; [2008] 1 WLR 2255.

5.10 In *R (Beer trading as Hammer Trout Farm) v Hampshire Farmers' Market Limited*,[1] the Court of Appeal held that unless the source of the power of a decision-maker originating from statute or prerogative clearly provided the answer, the question whether a decision was amenable to judicial review required careful consideration of the nature of the power and function to be exercised to see whether the decision had a sufficient public element, flavour or character to bring it within the purview of public law.

[1]   [2004] 1 WLR 233.

5.11 *Beer* concerned a company limited by guarantee and set up by a local authority to operate a farmers' markets on a not-for-profit basis. Initially the market was set up by a local authority under the Local Government and Housing Act 1989. Applications to join the market were dealt with by an employee of the authority. In due course the authority decided to hand the market over to its stallholders, and set up the company for that purpose. The company's registered address was initially the authority's offices. The council provided some finance and administrative assistance to the company. The company secretary was a council employee who became the company's business development manager and one of its directors.

5.12 The claimant applied to join the company's 2002 programme. His application for a licence was refused, and he applied for judicial review of the decision. The council appeared as an interested party at the application. The judge granted the application. He held that the company was a public authority under the functional test contained in s 6 of the Human Rights Act 1998.

5.13 The Court of Appeal distinguished those cases where a statutory or prerogative source of power provided a clear answer from those in which it was necessary to analyse closely the nature of the function being exercised to see if the decision had a sufficiently public element to make it amenable to judicial review. On a close look, the court held, a number of factors pointed to a sufficient public element in this case. Of special importance was the fact that the power was being exercised to control the right of access to a public market held on publicly owned land; but also of importance was the relationship between the company and the local authority; in particular, the fact the company had been created by, and 'stepped into the shoes of', the local authority, and had been materially assisted by the local authority.

5.14 Dyson LJ cited the reasoning of Lord Woolf CJ in *Poplar Housing and Regeneration Community Association v Donoghue*.[1] Among significant factors in that case were that the defendant (which had received a transfer of housing stock from a local housing authority) had no primary public law duties of its own; the activity in question (providing housing for rent) was not intrinsically a public function; the fact that the body in question was a charity was not decisive; a function which was intrinsically a private one can only become a public one if 'a feature or combination of features' imposes 'a public character or stamp on the act'. Statutory authority can help to mark an act as public; but oversight by a public regulatory body will not. In the end what tipped the balance in that case was the close relationship between the body and the local housing authority which had created it, and the court's wish that the claimant (who had been a tenant of both bodies) should not be disadvantaged by the transfer of housing stock between the two bodies. Lord Woolf went on to say that in a borderline case, the question is very much one of fact and degree.

[1]   [2002] QB 48. This was another case about the s 6(3) HRA 1998 question.

5.15 The analysis in *Beer* was followed by the Divisional Court in the recent challenge to the GCSE English grading decision in the summer of 2011: *R (Lewisham London Borough Council) v Assessment and Qualifications Alliance (AQA), and Pearson Education Ltd (Edexcel)*.[1] The claimant local authorities, schools and pupils affected by the marking challenged the decision making of the examination boards. Although the examination boards were private bodies, and had entered into contractual arrangements with schools, the Divisional Court held that the decisions in question plainly had a 'public element, flavour and character' to them, adopting the language in Beer. The court acknowledged that the determination of GCSE grades, taken by students across the country, was a matter of 'very significant public importance potentially affecting the life chances of those who are candidates for the examination'; and that this was a classic case of contracting out of a public function.

[1]   [2013] EWHC 211 (Admin).

5.16 Two key cases which went the other way are *YL v Birmingham City Council*[1] and *R (Heather) v Leonard Cheshire Foundation*[2]. Both cases concerned care homes that were independent of local authorities but provided accommodation for residents who were publicly funded. This element of public funding made no difference. The House of Lords in *YL v Birmingham City Council* held that the fact the care home was a private, profit-making company pointed against treating it as a body with functions of a public nature. The actual provision, as opposed to the arrangement, of care and accommodation for those unable to arrange it themselves was not an inherently governmental function. The mere possession of special powers conferred by Parliament did not of itself mean that a body had functions of a public nature. Another persuasive factor appears to have been the fact that it was not desirable for residents at the same care home to be afforded different levels of protection under the law depending on whether they were publicly or privately funded.

[1]   [2007] UKHL 27; [2008] 1 AC 95.
[2]   [2001] EWHC Admin 429; 4 CCLR 211; [2002] EWCA Civ 366; [2002] 2 All ER 936, CA. In *R v Servite Houses, ex p Goldsmith* [2001] LGR 55, a similar result was reached at common law, before the Human Rights Act 1998 came into force.

5.17 By contrast, in *R (Weaver) v London & Quadrant Housing Trust*,[1] the majority of the Court of Appeal considered that the fact that a registered social landlord received substantial public funding was an important factor: the provision of subsidised housing was a governmental function. This weighed in favour of the Court's decision that, in terminating a tenancy agreement, the registered social landlord was performing a public function for the purposes of the Human Rights Act 1998, and was amenable to judicial review. Although amenability to judicial review will not always decide whether a body is subject to section 6, in *Weaver* the two conclusions were closely linked. *Weaver* was applied in *R (Macleod) v Peabody Trust Governors*:[2] a case concerning a tenancy agreement with a charity housing association that was held not to be exercising a public function. It was relevant that public funds had not been used to purchase the property and the tenancy was not subject to the same level of statutory regulation as social housing.

[1]   [2009] EWCA Civ 587; [2010] 1 WLR 363.
[2]   [2016] EWHC 737 (Admin); [2016] H.L.R. 27. Factors weighing for and against the conclusion are discussed at paragraphs 20–22.

5.18 In *R (A) v Partnerships in Care Ltd*[1] a patient challenged a decision of the managers of the private psychiatric hospital in which she was detained under s 3(1) of the Mental Health Act 1983 ('the 1983 Act') to change the nature of the treatment provided in the ward in which she was detained. The hospital was registered under the Registered Homes Act 1984 ('the 1984 Act'). The challenge was brought under arts 3 and 8 of the European Convention on Human Rights, and also on the grounds that the decision was irrational. Keith J held that the decision was one made 'in relation to the exercise of a public function' within the meaning of CPR 54.1(2)(a)(ii) and that the managers were a functional public authority for the purposes of s 6 of the Human Rights Act 1998. There were three basic reasons: regulations made under the 1984 Act imposed a duty on the managers as the registered person in relation to the hospital to provide adequate professional staff and adequate treatment facilities, there was a public interest in patients receiving care and treatment which might enable them to live in the community again, and patients admitted under s 3 of the 1983 Act were detained compulsorily. He therefore decided the preliminary question (whether the patient could challenge the decision by judicial review) in her favour.

¹   [2002] 1 WLR 2610.

5.19 Thus at common law there is no neat dichotomy between the bodies that are, or are not, amenable to judicial review, because (as the examples given above suggest that they might), the cases show that a body may be amenable in respect of some types of decision, but not others. The picture is not even as clear-cut as that: some categories of decision will sometimes have a sufficient stamp of public law about them, and sometimes not. Two examples can be given: employment by public bodies, and land and other commercial transactions by public bodies. These are discussed below,¹ together with areas which have been treated in the cases as more, or less, off-limits: certain exercises of the prerogative, policy decisions, and national security. There is then a short discussion of other particular matters affecting the court's jurisdiction, and a brief consideration of the approach of the courts of Northern Ireland.

¹   See 5.20 and 5.23 below

EMPLOYMENT¹

¹   For Scots law on this aspect, sec **22.17** et seq.

5.20 Generally, a decision affecting the employment of a public employee will not, without more, be amenable to judicial review, even though the power to employ and dismiss may be conferred by statute or by the prerogative. Thus, for example, civil servants, teachers and other local government employees are not usually entitled to challenge disciplinary action and dismissal by judicial review.² There are two underlying reasons for this: the private, contractual character of the decisions, and the availability of the remedy of unfair dismissal to a wide range of employees and officials. Thus in *R v Civil Service Appeal Board, ex p Bruce*³ the Divisional Court held that the civil service appeal board was in theory amenable to judicial review, because, in the absence (as the court thought) of a contract of employment, it was performing a judicial function which had a sufficient public law element to mean that in an appropriate case the supervision of the court might be required. However, leave to apply for judicial review should only be granted in very exceptional cases, because of the availability of the alternative remedy of unfair dismissal.⁴

²   See, eg *R v East Berkshire Health Authority, ex p Walsh* [1985] QB 152 (where the court considered whether the role had sufficient 'statutory underpinning' to justify judicial review), and *R v Derbyshire County Council, ex p Noble* [1990] ICR 808.
³   [1988] ICR 649, affirmed by the Court of Appeal [1989] 2 All E. R. 907 on the grounds that the decision of the Divisional Court (which was, in effect, to withhold relief in the exercise of its discretion) was not plainly wrong.
⁴   At 660E.

5.21 *McClaren v The Home Office*¹ was a private law claim brought by a prison officer alleging breach of a collective agreement which he claimed was incorporated in his contract of employment. The Home Office applied to strike the action out on the grounds that the plaintiff's only remedy was to apply for judicial review. The Judge struck the action out, but the Court of Appeal reinstated it, holding that it was arguable that the plaintiff had a contract of employment and that his claim raised questions of private, not public, law.[2] Woolf LJ summarised the position in some detail. He said that: 'In relation to his personal claims against an employer, an employee of a public body is normally in exactly the same situation as other employees'. Such claims can be vindicated by an ordinary action. However, there can be situations in which some additional factor means that he can seek judicial review, unlike an ordinary employee, for example, if the employment is regulated by a disciplinary or other body established under statute or the prerogative.[3] Further, he may be adversely affected by a decision of his employer which applies generally and which he contends is flawed on public law grounds.[4] There may also be cases where a disciplinary procedure does not have a sufficient public law content to render decisions made pursuant to it amenable to judicial review, but where, none the less, a public employee may be entitled not merely to damages for breach of the procedure, but a declaration or injunction to enforce its provisions.

[1]   [1990] ICR 824.
[2]   In passing, Dillon LJ noted (at p 830B) that the court had heard argument the previous week in a case about a prison officer which plainly did raise a question of public law and was appropriately litigated by an application for judicial review: *R v the Secretary of State for the Home Department, ex p Attard* [1990] COD 261. This concerned the interpretation of the code of discipline for prison officers, which was made under the prison rules, and had statutory force.
[3]   See, eg *R v Hampshire County Council, ex p Ellerton* [1985] 1 All ER 599 and *R (Dunbar and others) v Hampshire Fire and Rescue Service* [2004] EWHC 431 (Admin), [2004] ACD 38, [2004] All ER (D) 431 (Mar): two cases concerning the fire services discipline code, a statutory instrument made under the Fire Services Act 1947, s 17. The Fire and Rescue Services Act 2004 repealed this machinery. *R v the Secretary of State for the Home Department, ex p Attard* [1990] COD 261 and in *R v Civil Service Appeal Board, ex p Bruce* [1988] ICR 649 are other examples. *Malloch v Aberdeen Corporation (No.1)* [1971] 1 WLR 1578 is another: the pursuer benefited from a statutory procedural protection in relation to dismissal.
[4]   He gave *Council for Civil Service Unions v Minister for the Civil Service* [1985] AC 374 as an example. In that ('the GCHQ case') the respondent gave an instruction that in the interests of national security, civil servants working at GCHQ should no longer be allowed to belong to trade unions.

5.22 In *R (Shoesmith) v Ofsted*,[1] the Court of Appeal considered the availability of judicial review for the former Director of Children's Services at the London Borough of Haringey. There was no doubt that the claimant was entitled to pursue a judicial review claim against the Secretary of State for Children's Services who had directed the local authority to remove Ms Shoesmith from her statutory position. There was a question mark over whether she was entitled to claim judicial review against the local authority who dismissed her following her removal from the statutory post, or whether she could only pursue her remedy of unfair dismissal in the employment tribunals. Maurice Kay LJ explained that a distinction had to be drawn between the issues of amenability to judicial review and alternative remedy. In the great majority of cases, proceedings in the employment tribunal would be the better, if not the only, remedy. However, there were cases which were amenable to judicial review and where the remedy in the employment tribunal would be inappropriate or less appropriate, due for example to the inadequacy of compensation that can be paid or the superimposition of wider issues than those which are the subject of inquiry at the employment tribunal. In the instant case, it was necessary to look at the statutory context: every children's services authority was required to appoint a Director to carry out particular statutory functions, and the authority must have regard to guidance which includes the roles to be performed by the Director. The Director was the person with 'ultimate executive responsibility and accountability for children's services'. The position of Director was 'created, required and defined by and under statute'. It therefore had the necessary 'statutory underpinning' for judicial review to be available.

There is conflicting authority as to whether judicial review is available for non-disciplinary decisions. In *R (Tucker) v Director General of the National Crime Squad*[2], the claimant complained of a decision to terminate his secondment to the national crime squad without notice and without giving reasons. The decision had been made for operational reasons, essentially because the claimant's superiors had lost confidence in him. The Court of Appeal, differing from the judge, held that this decision was not amenable to judicial review, essentially because of the private character of the decision, and its managerial background.[3] Doubt has, however, been cast on this decision by the Privy Council in *Ramjohn v Permanent Secretary, Ministry of Foreign Affairs; Kissoon v Manning*.[4] The decision in *Tucker* has also been distinguished in other scenarios. In *R (Simpson) v Chief Constable of Greater Manchester Police*,[5] the court held that judicial review would lie against a decision of the Chief Constable to dissolve the pool of police officers awaiting a suitable promotion vacancy. Unlike in *Tucker* where the decision only affected the claimant, the *Simpson* case affected a number of officers who had been selected for promotion; the decision had been taken on 'policy' considerations; and, unlike in *Tucker*, the decision affected the status of the claimants.

[1]   [2011] EWCA Civ 642.
[2]   [2003] EWCA Civ 57, [2003] ICR 599.
[3]   The court was not persuaded that his lack of a private law remedy was a sufficient reason to make judicial review available.
[4]   [2011] UKPC 20.
[5]   [2013] EWHC 1858 (Admin).

LAND AND COMMERCIAL TRANSACTIONS

5.23 The effect of the cases about commercial transactions is similar.[1] In general terms, the attitude of the courts has been to require, either, a public law element in the decision which goes beyond the exercise of a public body's private rights to dispose of, and manage its assets and/or enter into contracts, or an arguable claim of abuse of power, before permitting judicial review of decisions about disposals of land and other commercial matters.[2] Four examples may be given to illustrate the types of abuse of power which will prompt the court's intervention.

[1]   In *Supportways Community Services Ltd v Hampshire County Council* [2006] EWCA Civ 1035 Lord Justice Neuberger said that the mere fact that the party alleged to be in breach of contract is a public body plainly cannot, on its own, transform what would otherwise be a private law claim into a public law claim: 'Where the claim is fundamentally contractual in nature, and involves no allegation of fraud or improper motive or the like against the public

body, it would, at least in the absence of very unusual circumstances, be right, as a matter of principle, to limit a claimant to private law remedies.'

2   See, for example, *R (Menai Collect Ltd) v Department for Constitutional Affairs* [2006] EWHC 724 (Admin) and *R (Gamesa Energy UK Ltd) v National Assembly for Wales* [2006] EWHC 2167 (Admin). This account, of course, ignores the duties which public bodies may owe under the EU and domestic procurement regimes, which are outside the scope of this chapter. Challenges based on EU procurement arguments were raised in *R (Chandler) v Secretary of State for Children, Schools and Families* [2009] EWCA Civ 1011; [2010] 1 CMLR 1 (unsuccessfully) and in *R (Law Society) v Legal Services Commission* [2007] EWCA Civ 1264; [2008] QB 737 (successfully). An area in which the courts have intervened is in sales of land by local authorities at an undervalue: again, this is because s 123 of the Local Government Act 1972 imposes a duty generally not to dispose of land for a consideration which is less than the best which can reasonably be obtained. The structure of the section means that such decisions have elements which are more than purely commercial, and there is scope for legal error: see, eg *R (Lemon Land Ltd) v Hackney London Borough Council,* [2001] EWHC 336 (Admin), and more recently *R (London Jewish Girls High Ltd) v Barnet London Borough Council* [2013] EWHC 523 (Admin).

5.24 The first is *Wheeler v Leicester City Council.*[1] In that case a local authority banned a rugby club from a recreation ground for a year. The justification advanced for this was the authority's statutory duty to promote good race relations. The club had refused to condemn an England rugby tour to South Africa, in which three of its members had taken part. The evidence showed that the real reason for the decision was to punish the club for refusing to support the authority's policy about the tour. The House of Lords held that the decision was unlawful. Three distinct grounds were given for the decision. The most persuasive are that the decision was *Wednesbury* unreasonable and/or taken for an improper purpose: that is, to punish the club when it had done nothing wrong, but merely disagreed, for legitimate reasons, with the local authority's policy.

1   [1985] AC 1054.

5.25 The second is *R v Ealing London Borough Council, ex p Times Newspapers Limited.*[1] The local authority in that case decided not to buy newspapers published by the applicant. The reason had nothing to do with the content or characteristics of the newspapers, and everything to do with the authority's disapproval of the applicant's conduct in the Wapping dispute. The decision was quashed. This is again best analysed as an example of a decision taken for an improper purpose.

1   (1986) 85 LGR 316.

5.26 The third is *Birmingham City Council v Qasim.*[1] In that case, an employee of the local authority had knowingly let accommodation belonging to the authority to tenants in breach of the authority's mandatory statutory allocation scheme. The authority then sought possession of the accommodation on the grounds that the tenancies were ultra vires and void. The Judge dismissed the claim, and the Court of Appeal upheld his decision. The court held that allocation and letting were distinct activities, and that the fact that a failure to allocate property in accordance with the statutory allocation scheme might have been susceptible to judicial review did not make the subsequent letting ultra vires; valid secure tenancies had been created, despite the failure to follow the allocation scheme.

¹ [2009] EWCA Civ 1080; [2010] BGLR 253.

5.27 The approach in this case sits rather uneasily with the approach in *Weaver v London and Quadrant Housing Trust*¹ in which the Court of Appeal endorsed the view that in terminating a tenancy a registered social landlord was both exercising a public function within s 6 of the Human Rights Act 1998 and was amenable to judicial review. It also sits uneasily with the developing jurisprudence on the protection accorded by public law and art 8 to the tenants and licensees of local authorities.² The explanation may be that there is slightly more judicial scepticism in the face of a local housing authority's attempt to rely on a public law argument to undermine a tenant's private law rights than there is towards reliance by a tenant on public law or human rights arguments to negative a public authority's private law rights.

¹ [2009] EWCA Civ 587, [2010] 1 WLR 363.
² See *Kay v Lambeth LBC* [2006] UKHL 10, [2006] 2 AC 465; *Doherty v Birmingham City Council* [2008] UKHL 57, [2009] 1 AC 367; *Doran v Liverpool City Council* [2009] EWCA Civ 146, [2009] 1 WLR 2365; and *Taylor v Central Bedfordshire Council* [2009] EWCA Civ 613, [2010] 1 WLR 446; *Holley v Hillingdon LBC* [2016] EWCA 1052.

5.28 It may be that the courts are slower to detect a public law element in cases where the claimant's challenge is based on a commercial interest in a transaction or proposed transaction. There is a contrast here, in the context of land transactions, between *R v Bolsover District Council, ex p Pepper*¹ and *Wandsworth London Borough Council v A.*² In the first case, the claimant owned a landlocked parcel of undeveloped land for which he obtained planning permission. Its only potential means of access to a street was via a recreation ground owned by the local authority. The local authority refused to sell him part of the ground which would have enabled him to gain access to that street, although there had been negotiations between him and the authority. Those, however, had been expressly subject to contract. He sought judicial review of that decision. The judge refused the application. He held that the mere fact that the authority was refusing to exercise a statutory power³ did not make the question one of public law: there was no additional element which made it any different from an exercise by a private landowner of his rights over his land. The existence of the negotiations, which were expressed to be subject to contract (and thus founding no private rights) could not form the basis of a legitimate expectation in public law.

¹ [2001] BLGR 43.
² [2000] 1 WLR 1246. See also *R (Montgomery) v Hertfordshire CC* [2005] EWHC 2026 (Admin); *R v Broxtowe BC, ex p Bradford* [2000] IRLR 329.
³ Local Government Act 1972, s 123.

5.29 The *Wandsworth* case also concerned the exercise by a public landowner of the rights incidental to ownership. In that case, a school withdrew a licence given to a parent to enter school premises. However there was an extra element which transformed the decision into one which was governed by public law. There was no evidence about the terms of the licence by which parents were generally allowed to enter the school, but the Court of Appeal was unwilling to assume that they were as restricted as those applying to ordinary callers at the school. The parent was at the school not casually, but because of the local education authority's duty to educate her son, and her duty to ensure that he went to school. As a result, the court held, the school could not exclude a parent as casually as a textbook seller or a milkman.[1] The relationship was not governed purely by private law, but also by public law. In the context the requirements of public law were not onerous: the defendant should have been given an opportunity to make representations before the decision to exclude her was made. A letter asking for comments and giving a short time for reply would have been enough. No prolonged formal investigation was necessary. Indeed, a warning, without demur from the defendant, would have been enough. However, because she had not been consulted, the decision was invalid, and could not be relied on as a basis for seeking an injunction to exclude the defendant from the school.

1   At p 1253 per Buxton LJ.

5.30 The fourth example involves the setting by local authorities of care home fees, where the potential for abusing power has been recognised by the Courts. There have been a series of challenges in recent years to the setting of care home fees, and the Courts have accepted that this decision is susceptible to judicial review. In *R (Bevan & Clarke LLP) v Neath Port Talbot County Borough Council*[1], the court explained that the wider context of providing care or making arrangements for others to provide care to those who need it was a public function. Furthermore, the local authority did not have the freedom that a private party would have to use its bargaining power to drive down the price as far as possible. In other words, there was an intrinsic constraint on the local authority's power in the marketplace, which needed to be checked. The court also explained that the decision was not purely incidental or supplementary to the function of making arrangements for the provision of care, and the mere fact that the complained about decision concerned the setting of a fee under contract did not mean that it was a 'private act'.[2]

1   [2012] EWHC 236 (Admin).
2   See also *R (Redcar & Cleveland Independent Providers Association) v Redcar and Cleveland Borough Council* [2013] EWHC 4 (Admin); *R (Members of the Committee of Care North East Northumberland) v Northumberland CC* [2013] EWCA Civ 1740.

POLICY DECISIONS

5.31 The reasoning in *Tucker*[1] shades into another aspect of public administration which the court is reluctant to investigate: pure questions of policy.[2] Of course, this reluctance is not here based on the fact that the claimant's argument is essentially based on private, contractual rights which are best vindicated by action, but rather on a recognition that this is an area which falls wholly outside the court's competence to supervise.[3] As Lord Bingham put it in *A v the Secretary of State for the Home Department*:[4]

'. . . great weight should be given to the Home Secretary, his colleagues and Parliament on this question, because they were called upon to exercise a pre-eminently political judgment . . . Any prediction about the future behaviour of human beings (as opposed to the phases of the moon or high water at London Bridge) is necessarily problematical. Reasonable and informed minds may differ, and a judgment is not shown to be wrong or unreasonable if because that which is thought likely to happen does not happen . . . It is perhaps better to approach this question as one of demarcation of functions or what Liberty in its written case calls "relative institutional competence". The more purely political (in a broad or a narrow sense) a question is, the more appropriate it will be for political resolution and the less likely it is to be an appropriate matter for judicial decision. The smaller, therefore, will be the potential role for the court. It is the function of political and not judicial bodies to resolve political questions . . . The present question seems to me to be very much at the political end of the spectrum'.

1   [2003] EWCA Civ 57. See **5.22** above.
2   And see, eg *Nottinghamshire County Council v the Secretary of State for the Environment* [1986] AC 240: expenditure targets set by the Secretary of State in a rate support grant report: and *R v Secretary of State for the Environment, ex p Hammersmith and Fulham LBC* [1991] 1 AC 521. The reader is also referred to the fuller discussion at **7.32** below of the question whether there are unreviewable discretions. There is inevitably a degree of overlap between that discussion and this, which is necessarily rather brief.
3   As Laws LJ put it in a somewhat different context, 'We cannot don the mantle of the statute's practical administrators' (dissenting in *R (Tesema and Limbuela) v the Secretary of State for the Home Department* [2004] EWCA Civ 540, [2004] 3 WLR 561 at paragraph 41).
4   [2004] UKHL 56, [2005] 2 AC 68 at paragraph 29. The case, in fact, concerned national security, as to which see **5.34** below.

5.32 A specialised, and unusual, type of decision which will not be scrutinised, on, effectively, policy grounds, is the prerogative power to legislate for a ceded territory. Such a power is to legislate for 'the peace order and good government' of the territory. In *R (Bancoult) v Secretary of State for Foreign and Commonwealth Affairs (No 2)*[1] the House of Lords, by a majority, held that the power might be exercised in the wider interests of the United Kingdom, and that it was not open to the courts to strike it down on the basis that it was not conducive to those stated objectives. Moreover, the decision of the majority shows that while the exercise of that power was reviewable by the court, if the purposes pursued by the enactment of the legislation were wide, political objectives, it would be difficult to show that the legislation was unlawful.

1   [2008] UKHL 61; [2009] 1 AC 453; distinguished in *R (Barclay) v Secretary of State for Justice* [2014] UKSC 54.

5.33 This approach is similar to that adopted by the courts in relation to qualified rights under the Human Rights Act 1998.[1] The courts have recognised in a wide range of different types of case the necessity of deference to decisions of the executive about such matters as the allocation of scarce resources.[2]

1   See CHAPTER 12.
2   See, eg, in relation to justification under art 14, *Carson and Reynolds v the Secretary of State for Work and Pensions* [2003] EWCA Civ 797, [2003] 3 All ER 577, paragraphs 68 and 73. That decision was upheld by the House of Lords, and paragraph **73** cited with approval by Lord Walker of Gestingthorpe (with whom Lords Nicholls and Rodger of Earlsferry agreed): *R (Carson) v Work and Pensions Secretary* [2005] UKHL 37, [2005] 2 WLR 1369 at paragraph 79. While the decision of the House of Lords in *R (Alconbury Developments Limited) v the Secretary of State for the Environment Transport and the Regions* [2003] 2 AC 295 concerned art 6, which is not a qualified right, a good deal of the discussion of deference recalls the sort of approach taken in cases concerning qualified rights.

NATIONAL SECURITY

5.34 The role of the court in cases involving national security is discussed in CHAPTER 7 below.[1]

[1]   See 7.34(6).

THE PREROGATIVE

5.35 It used to be thought that action taken under the royal prerogative was never amenable to judicial review.[1] The Court of Appeal suggested that this was not the case in *R v Criminal Injuries Compensation Board, ex p Lain*,[2] holding that a decision of the Criminal Injuries Compensation Board (CICB), a non-statutory body set up under prerogative powers, was amenable to judicial review. Although this view was strictly obiter, the majority of the House of Lords later held that the exercise of prerogative powers was in some circumstances reviewable.[3] A number of different aspects of the exercise of prerogative powers have been considered by the courts: the issue of a passport,[4] the prerogative of mercy,[5] the (former) prerogative power to issue warrants to monitor telephone calls,[6] an ex gratia compensation scheme for those formerly interned by the Japanese,[7] the prerogative power to make legislation for a ceded territory,[8] the grant of a Royal Charter,[9] the Government's intention to give notice under an EU treaty,[10] and the refusal to fund legal expenses for British nationals in foreign criminal proceedings, even in death penalty cases.[11] Not all such decisions will be justiciable.[12]

> 'The question is simply whether the nature and subject matter of the decision is amenable to judicial process. Are the courts qualified to deal with the matter, or does the decision involve such questions of policy that they should not intrude because they are ill-equipped to do so?'[13]

Thus in *ex p Bentley* the Divisional Court thought that the formulation, under the prerogative, of the criteria for granting a pardon was probably not susceptible to judicial review.[14] Nevertheless, a decision not to grant a pardon which was based on flawed reasoning was.

[1]   This topic is discussed at 7.33 below.
[2]   [1967] 2 QB 864.
[3]   *Council of Civil Service Unions v Minister for the Civil Service* [1985] AC 374. That case concerned a direction given by the Minister under provisions of an Order in Council, not the direct exercise of a prerogative power.
[4]   *R v Secretary of State for Foreign and Commonwealth Affairs, ex p Everett* [1989] QB 811.
[5]   *R v Secretary of State for the Home Department, ex p Bentley* [1994] QB 349.
[6]   *R v Secretary of State for the Home Department, ex p Ruddock* [1987] 1 WLR 1482. Following adverse decisions in Strasbourg the matter was regulated by statute.
[7]   *R (ABCIFER) v the Secretary of State for Defence* [2003] QB 1397.
[8]   *R (Bancoult) v Secretary of State for Foreign and Commonwealth Affairs (No 2)* [2008] UKHL 61; [2009] 1 AC 453.
[9]   *R (Project Management Institute) v Minister for the Cabinet Office* [2016] EWCA Civ 21.
[10] *R (Miller) v Secretary of State for Exiting the European Union* [2017] UKSC 5.
[11] *R (Sandiford) v Secretary of State for Foreign and Commonwealth Affairs* [2013] EWCA Civ 581, [2013] 1 WLR 2938.
[12] In the *CCSU* case Lord Roskill gave a number of examples of the exercises of prerogative powers which would not be justiciable: the making of treaties, the defence of the realm, the prerogative of mercy, the grant of honours, the dissolution of Parliament and the appointment of ministers. However, as to the un-making of EU treaties, see *R (Miller) v Secretary of State for Exiting the European Union* [2017] UKSC 5.

¹³ Per Watkins LJ in Bentley at p 363B. He gave the example of a person refused a pardon on the grounds of his sex, race or religion. In such a case, he said, ' . . . the courts would be expected to interfere and, in our judgment, would be entitled to do so'.

¹⁴ At p 363F.

5.36 Sections 108 to 117 of, and Schs 6 and 7 to, the Criminal Justice Act 1988 ('the 1988 Act') contained a statutory scheme closely modelled on the CICB. Those provisions were never brought into force. On 9 March 1994 the Secretary of State published a decision to implement a tariff scheme to replace the CICB. This would have resulted in smaller payments of compensation to victims of crime than the existing scheme, or its proposed statutory equivalent. In *R v the Secretary of State for the Home Department, ex p Fire Brigades Union*,[1] the House of Lords considered the interaction of the statutory power of the Home Secretary to make a commencement order bringing provisions of the 1988 Act into force (section 171) with his prerogative power to introduce a scheme replacing the CICB scheme. The majority held that although the statutory power conferred a wide discretion on the Secretary of State whether, and if so when, to bring the relevant provisions of the 1988 Act into force, he could not validly bind himself never to bring them into force. Moreover, so long as the statute remained unrepealed, its shadowy existence prevented him from any exercise of the prerogative which was inconsistent with the will of Parliament as expressed in the 1988 Act. As Lord Browne-Wilkinson put it ' . . . it would be most surprising if, in the present day, prerogative powers could be validly exercised by the executive so as to frustrate the will of Parliament expressed in a statute . . . ',[2] even though the statute was not in force.

[1] [1995] 2 AC 513.
[2] At p 552D.

5.37 This apparently clear principle has not always been closely followed, however. In *Shrewsbury and Atcham BC v Secretary of State for Communities and Local Government*[1] the Secretary of State had adopted a procedure for reforming local government which was inconsistent with the existing statutory framework. The Court of Appeal, perhaps surprisingly, held that he had a common law power to do this, and that this had been retrospectively validated by new legislation. The court followed *R v Secretary of State for Health ex p C*,[2] in which the Court of Appeal had held that it was lawful for the Secretary of State for Health to keep an extra-statutory 'consultancy service index' of people whose suitability to work with children was in doubt, because the Crown has all the powers of a natural person, and such a list could be maintained by such a person. It is suggested that where Parliament has legislated specifically, as in the *Shrewsbury* and *Miller* cases, it is doubtful that the Crown can assert that there are co-existing common law powers which enable it to do something different.[3]

[1] [2008] EWCA Civ 148; [2008] 3 All ER 548.
[2] [2000] 1 FLR 627.
[3] *R (Miller) v Secretary of State for Exiting the European Union* [2017] UKSC 5. See further, 'What the Crown May Do' (John Howell QC), Judicial Review, Vol 15, issue 1, p 36.

PARTICULAR MATTERS AFFECTING JURISDICTION

5.38 Particular matters affecting the court's jurisdiction are discussed in the following paragraphs.

The visitor

5.39 The House of Lords has held that charitable foundations which would otherwise be amenable to judicial review may not be where a complainant may apply to a visitor under the rules governing the foundation. Such a complainant must first apply to the visitor, who is only subject to judicial review for acting outside jurisdiction (in the narrow sense of entering upon a proceeding when not empowered to do so), for abuse of power or for breach of natural justice.[1] This decision mainly affects those who seek to challenge action or inaction by colleges and universities. For many such institutions, however, it has been overtaken by section 46 of the Higher Education Act 2004 (the 2004 Act) (as respects employment disputes relating to academic staff of qualifying institutions) and by s 20 of the 2004 Act (as respects complaints about admissions, and by students and former students of qualifying institutions. 'Qualifying institutions' are defined in s 11 of the 2004 Act.

[1]   *R v Hull University Visitor, ex p Page* [1993] AC 682.

Territorial scope

5.40 Questions concerning action or inaction outside England and Wales may raise issues of law as to territorial jurisdiction. These are discussed elsewhere.[1]

[1]   See **16.35.**

Judicial review of the Crown

5.41 Discussion of judicial review of the Crown in its various capacities will be found later in this book.[1]

[1]   See CHAPTERS **13, 16** and **17** below.

No control of superior courts

5.42 In certain circumstances the Crown Court may be subject to an application for judicial review. These circumstances, and the general rule that superior courts are not subject to judicial review, are discussed elsewhere.[1]

[1]   See **16.56** below. The identification of a superior court may itself be a tricky exercise, as *R (Cart) v Upper Tribunal* [2009] EWHC 3052 (QB) shows. In that case the Divisional Court held that a non-appealable decision of a tribunal which had been designated a 'superior court of record' was amenable to judicial review, albeit on narrow grounds, because its jurisdiction was limited and it was not an 'alter ego' of the High Court. That decision was upheld by the Court of Appeal: [2010] EWCA Civ 859, [2011] Q.B. 120, and the Supreme Court [2011] UKSC 28; [2012] 1 AC 663. CPR Part 54 has now been amended to incorporate a new CPR 54.7A which governs judicial review of decisions of the Upper Tribunal.

Proceedings in Parliament

5.43 The Bill of Rights 1688 precludes the court from impeaching or questioning proceedings in Parliament. This protection has been held to extend to the Parliamentary Commissioner for Standards.[1] It was one of several reasons for rejecting a challenge to the Government's failure to hold a referendum on the Lisbon Treaty.[2]

[1] *R v Parliamentary Commissioner for Standards, ex p Al Fayed* [1998] 1 All ER 93.
[2] *R (Wheeler) v Office of the Prime Minister* [2008] EWHC 1409 (Admin); [2008] ACD 70. See also *Office of Government Commerce v Information Commissioner* [2008] EWHC 774 (Admin); [2010] QB 98; *R (Bradley) v Secretary of State for Work and Pensions* [2007] EWHC 242 (Admin), [2007] Pens LR 87; and *R (Federation of Tour Operators) v HM Treasury* [2007] EWHC 2062 (Admin); [2008] STC 547.

Other unreviewable discretions

5.44 Questions concerning other unreviewable discretions are discussed in CHAPTER 7.[1]

[1] See 7.34.

A PERSPECTIVE FROM NORTHERN IRELAND

5.45 It is of some interest to see the approach which has been adopted to these questions in Northern Ireland. Three cases can be mentioned. In the first. *Re Phillip's Application*,[1] Carswell LJ stated[2] that he considered it 'preferable to consider the nature of the issue itself and whether it has characteristics which import an element of public law rather than to focus on the classification of the civil servant's employment or office'. In *Re McBride's Application*[3] Kerr J said an issue is one of public law where it involves a matter of public interest in the sense that it has an impact on the public generally and not merely on an individual or group. However:

> 'That is not to say that an issue becomes one of public law simply because it generates interest or concern in the minds of the public. It must affect the public rather than merely engage its interest to qualify as a public law issue. It seems to me equally clear that a matter may be one of public law while having a specific impact on an individual in his personal capacity.'

[1] [1995] NI 322.
[2] At p 322.
[3] [1999] NI 299, approved when the same applicant came before the Court of Appeal on a second application, [2003] NI CA 23 — see the judgment of Carswell LCJ at paragraph 25.

5.46 Carswell LJ applied this approach in *Re Kirkpatrick's Application for Judicial Review*,[1] holding that fishing rights on Lough Neagh, the largest inland waterway in the UK, while privately owned, were matters of legitimate public concern, and their grant or refusal was amenable to judicial review. The application was refused, not on grounds of lack of jurisdiction, but because there was an alternative remedy. This suggests that the Jockey Club cases might have been decided differently.

¹ [2003] NI QB 49. This decision was followed in *Re Wylie's Application for Judicial Review* [2005] N.I. 359 (a decision of Weatherup J concerning the refusal by the defendant fishing cooperative to issue the claimant with a boat owner's licence to fish for eels on Lough Neagh).

THE RELATIONSHIP OF JUDICIAL REVIEW WITH ORDINARY ACTIONS

5.47 The procedure in CPR Pt 54 differs in two main respects from that which applies in ordinary actions. The procedure cannot be invoked as of right, because the court's permission is needed: and there is a much shorter limitation period (subject to discretionary extension). These requirements are necessary to protect public authorities from claims which can readily be seen to have no merit, and to preserve the expectations of those who have acted on the basis of apparently valid decisions. Although it must be clear from the limited discussion earlier in this chapter that, at the margins, it is sometimes not absolutely obvious whether a decision is amenable to judicial review or not, it is equally clear that if these procedural safeguards are to work, the court must be careful to ensure that they are not evaded.¹

¹ See CHAPTERS 6, 7 and 16.

5.48 If a challenge is started by an application for judicial review, and it then emerges that the application has no sufficient connection with public law, there is usually little difficulty (provided that a private cause of action exists) in permitting the challenge to proceed as an ordinary claim. In such a situation, the claimant has obtained no unfair procedural advantage by starting with the wrong procedure, and it is pointless to require him to incur extra costs by commencing a completely new set of proceedings. CPR 54.20 makes express provision for this situation, by enabling the court to permit a case which has been started by an application for judicial review to proceed as an ordinary claim.¹ There may also be cases which are rightly started as an application for judicial review, but in which the initial application is made academic by a new decision, yet an underlying common law for damages claim survives. An example is an unlawful detention, which is properly challenged by an application for judicial review. The defendant may decide, or be ordered by the court, to release the claimant, and the court may decide (or the defendant may concede) that the detention was unlawful. Here too, the court can then order the claimant's outstanding claim for damages to proceed as if it were an ordinary action.²

¹ Judicial review is a remedy of last resort. This means that there may be claims, which, while they possess a public law element, should normally be pursued by ordinary claim rather than judicial review: see, eg *R (McIntyre) v Gentoo Group Ltd* [2010] EWHC 5 (Admin). There is a useful discussion of the relationship between public and private law in paragraphs **28–37** of the judgment.

² In *BA v Home Office* [2011] EWHC 1446 (QB), the court permitted an asylum seeker to proceed with a private law action in damages for false imprisonment arising from her unlawful detention at an immigration centre. A related issue is the proper forum for litigation about the welfare of children or of incompetent adults. If a decision of a public authority is involved, then the challenge is properly brought by an application for judicial review, preferably to be listed before a nominated judge of the Administrative Court who is also a judge of the Family Division. On the other hand, cases about the best interests of children or of incompetent

adults, even if they involve some issue of public law, should be litigated in, and before judges of, the Family Division: per Munby J in *A v a Health Authority* [2002] Fam 213. The crucial issue is the identity of the decision-maker and the nature of the substantive issue before the judge. In *Westminster City Council v C* [2008] EWCA Civ 198, [2009] 2 WLR 185, the Court of Appeal held that the inherent jurisdiction of the High Court to safeguard the welfare of incompetent adults survived, and was reinforced by, the enactment of the Mental Capacity Act 2005.

5.49 The difficult issue is whether, and if so, to what extent, a litigant may properly raise issues of public law in an ordinary action (or, a connected point) in litigation other than an application for judicial review. Just as it is obvious that it is desirable that issues of public law should be decided in a specialist forum subject to the procedural safeguards for defendants provided by judicial review, it should be plain that it would be very unjust if a litigant were in all circumstances prevented from raising public law challenges in other litigation. The tension between these two axioms probably generated more decisions of the House of Lords in a shorter space of time than any other procedural issue. However, after a period of intense satellite litigation about procedural points, the approach of the court has become significantly less technical and more pragmatic.[1]

[1] Some of the cases are discussed in 'Procedural Exclusivity: What Happened to Clark?' by Rachel Bateson in [2004] Judicial Review 140.

5.50 The starting point is *O'Reilly v Mackman.*[1] This was the first case in which the House of Lords explored the relationship between the (then relatively new) procedure under RSC Ord 53 and ordinary actions. Although he recognised that nothing in Ord 53 said in terms that it was an exclusive procedure. Lord Diplock's reasoning was that the *quid pro quo* for the new benefits conferred by Ord 53 on applicants for judicial review was that they should be required to use that procedure if they wished to advance a public law challenge. He said this:

' . . . it would in my view as a general rule be contrary to public policy, and as such an abuse of the process of the court, to permit a person seeking to establish that a decision of a public authority infringes rights to which he was entitled to protection under public law to proceed by way of ordinary action and by this means to evade the provisions of Order 53 for the protection of such authorities . . . I am content to rely on the express and the inherent power of the High Court, exercised on a case by case basis, to prevent abuse of its process whatever might be the form taken by that abuse.'[2]

He recognised that there might be exceptions:

' . . . particularly where the invalidity of the decision arises as a collateral issue in a claim for infringement of a right of the plaintiff arising under private law, or where none of the parties objects to the adoption of the procedure by writ or originating summons.'[3]

He went on to say:

'Whether there should be other exceptions should, in my view, at this stage, in the development of procedural public law, be left to be decided on a case by case basis.'[4]

[1] [1983] 2 AC 237.
[2] The decision in *O'Reilly v. Mackman* was followed by the Court of Appeal in *Trim v North Dorset District Council of Nordon* [2010] EWCA Civ 1446, [2011] 1 WLR 1901. In that case

a landowner had issued proceedings seeking declarations in respect of a breach of condition notice promulgated by the local authority. The court held that once a breach of condition notice was served, if the landowner wished to regularise his planning permission, he could seek judicial review promptly to challenge the validity of the notice or apply to discharge the condition. The service of a breach of condition notice was a purely public law act. There is a strong public interest in its validity, if in issue, being established promptly, both because of its significance to the planning of the area, and because it turns what was merely unlawful into criminal conduct. It was an 'abuse of process' to seek to challenge it otherwise than by judicial review.

3 This, it seems, is the only coherent explanation why *Gillick v West Norfolk and Wisbech Area Health Authority* [1986] AC 112 got as far as it did.

4 At p 285.

5.51 The House of Lords rapidly acknowledged that there should be exceptions to the rule beyond those expressly recognised in *O'Reilly v Mackman* itself.[1] As Lord Steyn repeated in *Boddington v British Transport Commission*,[2] the express purpose of the rule is to prevent abuse of process, and that purpose must underly any consideration of the scope of the rule. Decisions after *O'Reilly* explained that the rule governed situations in which the litigant's sole aim was to challenge a decision. It does not therefore apply in civil cases where the litigant seeks to establish a private right which cannot be established without a consideration of the validity of a public law decision.[3] Nor does it apply when a defendant in a civil case defends himself by impugning the validity of the decision on which the claimant's claim is based.[4]

1 In *Cocks v Thanet District Council* [1983] 2 AC 286, unlike O'Reilly, the issues were not purely questions of public law: the House of Lords decided that where private rights depended on prior public law decisions they too must ordinarily be litigated by judicial review. That this could not be a universal rule became clear almost immediately, and it is doubtful to what extent it now represents the law.

2 [1999] 2 AC 143 at p 172F.

3 *Roy v Kensington Family Practitioner Committee* [1992] 1 AC 624; *Chief Adjudication Officer v Foster* [1993] AC 754. The second of these cases also establishes the narrower point that on an appeal on a point of law (where that right is conferred by a statutory adjudication scheme) the relevant adjudicatory body (there the social security commissioner) has jurisdiction to declare a statutory instrument ultra vires. See, also, *Mercury Communications Limited v Director General of Telecommunications* [1996] 1 WLR 48. This case stresses the importance of retaining a degree of flexibility in decisions about whether judicial review should have been used rather than, eg the originating summons procedure, bearing in mind that the purpose of the rule is to prevent abuse of process, and that the boundaries between public and private law are still being worked out. The issue was the construction of a licence granted by the Secretary of State to BT and then, on Mercury's case, misinterpreted by the Director General in a determination which substituted a new clause in an agreement between BT and Mercury. The Director General was acting pursuant to statutory powers. The House of Lords held that the originating summons procedure (now CPR Pt 8) was at least as convenient as judicial review.

4 *Wandsworth London Borough Council v Winder* [1985] AC 461. In *Bunney v Burns Anderson Plc* [2007] EWHC 1240 (Ch); [2007] 4 All ER 246 Lewison J pointed out that there is a strong presumption, based on the rule of law, that in enacting statutory decision-making machinery, Parliament does not intend that the only permissible way of challenging a decision should be by judicial review. There has been much litigation in which tenants and licensees of public bodies have relied on article 8 of the ECHR as a defence to possession proceedings, and the courts have been gradually teasing out the extent to which such a defence should be recognised. See, eg *Manchester City Council v Pinnock* [2010] UKSC 45. See further, paragraph 5.47.

5.52 Two cases about claims based on public law questions can be used to illustrate the courts' approach to such claims. In *Gough v Local Sunday Newspapers (North) Limited*[1] the claimant, who had been a returning officer in a local election, sued a newspaper for libel, for suggesting that his conduct of the election had been incompetent. The claim involved a detailed consideration of electoral law, but there was no suggestion that it was an abuse of process for the claimant to raise such questions in a libel claim.[2] Similarly, in *Richards v Worcestershire CC*,[3] a claim was made for restitution against a local authority for failing to provide after-care services they had considered should be supplied under the Mental Health Act 1983, s 117. It was held that the claimant was asserting a private law claim and so was not required to pursue the case by way of judicial review.

[1] [2003] 1 WLR 1836.
[2] A related type of claim is a negligence claim against a public authority when the allegations of breach of duty of care involve scrutinising public law decisions or the performance of public law powers and duties: *Dart v Isle of Wight Council* (14 February 2002, unreported) (Gross J, claim alleging negligence in the handling of a footpath modification order not struck out) and *Douce v Staffordshire County Council* [2002] EWCA Civ 506, (2002) 5 CCL Rep 347 (claim alleging negligence of registration authority in the setting of staff levels for a care home not struck out). However, there may in many cases be policy reasons for deciding that in the context of a particular statutory regime, no duty of care is owed by the public authority. A striking example of this approach is *Jain v Trent Strategic Health Authority* [2009] UKHL 4; [2009] 1 AC 853. A registration authority applied ex p for a closure order after a slipshod investigation. The appellants appealed successfully against the order, but suffered significant economic loss while it remained in force. The House of Lords decided that they had no cause of action against the registration authority; suggesting, obiter, that the position might have been different had the Human Rights Act 1998 been in force at the material time.
[3] [2016] EWHC 1954 (Ch).

5.53 *Clark v University of Lincolnshire and Humberside*[1] is only slightly less straightforward. In that case the claimant wanted to claim that the defendant's conduct in marking her final examination was a breach of the contract evidenced by the defendant's student regulations. The defendant argued that the claim was an abuse of process and should be struck out, on the grounds that the proper remedy was an application for judicial review and the time for making such an application had long passed. Lord Woolf MR indicated that post CPR the courts would be flexible in their approach.[2] The availability of an application for summary judgment under CPR Pt 24, and the court's ability to stay proceedings for abuse of process mean that a public body can be protected from ordinary claims made very late which should have been made if at all by an application for judicial review.[3] He suggested that the nature of the claim could be relevant to the question whether there was abuse of process: a claim for some sort of review, or for a discretionary remedy, is different from a claim for a sum of money due under a contract. The court will be stricter if what is being claimed could affect the public generally and not just the parties. Where, however, as in that case, a claim in contract was made which 'could more appropriately have been made' by judicial review, the court would not strike out the claim solely on the basis that the wrong procedure had been used; but only if, having regard to all the circumstances, including any delay, the use of the wrong procedure was abusive. Lord Woolf stressed that the aim of the CPR is to 'harmonise procedures as far as possible and to avoid barren procedural disputes which generate satellite litigation'.

[1] [2000] 1 WLR 1988. See, also, *R v Chief Constable of Warwickshire, ex p Fitzpatrick* [1998] 1 All ER 65.
[2] This echoes his approach pre-CPR in *Trustees of the Dennis Rye Pension Fund v Sheffield City Council* [1998] 1 WLR 840. The Court of Appeal held that it was not an abuse of process to bring an ordinary action to claim a housing improvement grant which had been approved

in principle but the payment of which had been withheld on the grounds that the local housing authority was not satisfied that the conditions for payment of the grant had been fulfilled. This decision is at first sight a bit too pragmatic, since under the relevant statutory scheme, payment of the grant was conditional on the works being completed to the satisfaction of the authority. Nevertheless, for the reasons given by Lord Woolf MR, the issues were probably largely factual ones which the Administrative Court might be ill-equipped to resolve.

3   Judgment, paragraphs 27 and 33–37. *Ford-Camber Ltd v Deanminster Ltd* [2007] EWCA Civ 458; (2007) 151 SJLB 713 is a case in which an abuse of process argument succeeded so as to prevent a claimant from amending his claim in order to rely on an argument that an earlier decision of a public body (which was not a party to the proceedings) was invalid.

5.54 Even before the CPR, the position about defending proceedings was apparently more generous to the litigant who wished to raise a public law defence to an ordinary claim. Thus in *Wandsworth London Borough Council v Winder*, a council tenant was sued in the county court for arrears of rent. He sought to challenge the decision of the local housing authority to increase the rents charged to their tenants: and he sought to do it in the county court proceedings. He wanted to argue that the decision to increase rents was ultra vires (and therefore void) because it was *Wednesbury* unreasonable. The local authority applied to have his defence struck out. The House of Lords held that he was entitled as of right to rely on that defence. In the language of Lord Fraser of Tullybelton, the defence was based on 'the ordinary rights of private citizens to defend themselves against unfounded claims'.[1]

1   At p 509. *Wandsworth London Borough Council v A* [2000] 1 WLR 1246 is another example of such a case. A parent who had been excluded from school premises in a manner which was flawed on public law grounds could rely on those flaws as a defence to a claim for an injunction preventing her from entering the premises. In *A* the Court of Appeal acknowledged (at p 1256H) that it was bound by *Winder*. It distinguished *Hackney London Borough Council v Lambourne* (1992) 25 HLR 172 and *Tower Hamlets London Borough Council v Abdi* (1993) 25 HLR 80 (both decisions of the Court of Appeal in homelessness cases) on the basis that the defendants in those cases had no rights in private law at all, so that their attempts to rely on supposed public law right to be housed as a defence to possession proceedings were an abuse of process. In this case, the defendant's private law right to be on the land, a mere licence at will, was a right which, 'however fragile', sufficed to bring her within the principle in *Winder*. See also footnote [4], paragraph **5.51**, above.

5.55 *Rhondda Cynon Taff County Borough Council v Watkins*[1] is a decision of the Court of Appeal dealing with the same point. In that case a local authority confirmed a compulsory purchase order (CPO) in respect of the defendant's land in 1965. The purpose of the CPO was to use the land as a public open space. Shortly after the service of the authority's notice to treat and entry on the land (in 1966), the former owner re-entered, and occupied the land. A reference was made to the lands tribunal in 1968, which assessed the value of the land (in 1977). The authority lodged that sum in the High Court in 1987 and in 1988 executed a deed poll vesting the land in itself. It issued possession proceedings in 2000. The defence was that the defendant had been in possession adverse to the authority since 1965, and that the deed poll was ineffective because the local authority no longer intended to use the land as a public open space. The Court of Appeal, reversing the judge, held that the defendant was entitled to raise the validity of the deed poll in his defence to the possession proceedings, even though that involved issues of public law, and despite the long period which had elapsed between the execution of the deed and the challenge to it. This represents an extension of the reasoning in *Winder*. An important difference between that case and this is that the defendant here was seeking to challenge a public law decision which affected only him. What seems to have swayed the court was the long periods which elapsed both between the defendant's wrongful entry on the land and the execution of the deed and between that event and the possession proceedings, during which his possession was not challenged by the authority.

¹   [2003] 1 WLR 1864.

5.56 *Boddington v British Transport Commission*¹ establishes that a defendant may rely on a public law defence to a criminal prosecution. In that case, the appellant had been convicted of smoking on a train, contrary to a byelaw made by the respondent. He was prosecuted in the magistrates' court, and challenged the validity of the byelaw as part of his defence. On his appeal to the Divisional Court, that court held that issues of the substantive and procedural validity of byelaws were outside the jurisdiction of a criminal court. The appellant appealed to the House of Lords. The appeal was dismissed, on the grounds that the byelaw was valid, but their Lordships held that a defendant was entitled to challenge the validity of a byelaw as a defence to a criminal prosecution.²

¹   [1999] 2 AC 143.
²   A related question is the relationship between the jurisdiction of the criminal courts and of the Administrative Court in the context of the powers of the Director of Public Prosecutions. In *R (Pretty) v DPP* [2002] 1 AC 800 the claimant applied for judicial review of a refusal by the DPP to undertake that he would not enforce s 2(1) of the Suicide Act 1961 should the claimant's husband help her to commit suicide. Lord Steyn stated (at paragraph 67) that if the DPP refuses consent to a prosecution, the only remedy is judicial review.
On a connected point, in *R (Purdy) v DPP* [2009] UKHL 45; [2009] 3 WLR 403 the House of Lords required the DPP to produce an offence-specific policy setting out the factors he would take into account in deciding whether to initiate a prosecution for aiding or abetting a suicide.
If the complaint is that the DPP has given his consent to a prosecution, then following *R v DPP, ex p Kebeline* [2000] 2 AC 326, the matter can only be tested by judicial review, if there is 'dishonesty, mala fides or an exceptional circumstance'. Any other complaint about the consent must therefore be ventilated in the process of the criminal trial (and any appeal).

5.57 They rejected the heresy, promoted by the Divisional Court in *Bugg v DPP*,¹ that a subordinate instrument such as a byelaw is effective until formally quashed, unless it is plainly invalid on its face, or patently unreasonable. This had led the Court in *Bugg* to hold that the invalidity of a byelaw cannot be relied on as defence if its invalidity can only be established by calling evidence about it. They did sound one cautionary note. They made it clear that some statutory provisions may be drafted in such a way as to preclude, expressly or by implication, challenge by any other than a prescribed route. An example given by Lord Irvine of Lairg LC² was an enforcement notice: the Town and Country Planning Act 1990 is an elaborate statutory code, which includes a right of appeal against such notices. That context excluded necessarily a right to challenge the validity of an enforcement notice in a prosecution based on its alleged breach.³ Nevertheless, it would require clear words to exclude the jurisdiction of the courts.⁴

¹   [1993] QB 473; overruled in *Boddington v British Transport Commission* [1999] 2 AC 143.
²   At p 160D: the example is drawn from the decision in *R v Wicks* [1998] AC 92. In that case the appellant had appealed unsuccessfully against an enforcement notice, still failed to comply with it, and then attempted to defend the subsequent criminal proceedings on the basis that the enforcement notice was ultra vires.

[3] There is a further point in that context, which is that, unlike a byelaw, an enforcement notice has an immediate effect on the rights of a very small class of persons (usually one) and, barring mishaps, is brought to the attention of that person very soon after it is made: see per Lord Irvine of Lairg LC at page 161G–162C.
[4] Ibid at p 161D.

5.58 The lesson to be learnt from the cases is that if there is a genuine doubt whether a particular challenge raises issues of public law or not, the claimant is best advised to issue an application for judicial review as soon as possible in order to protect his position. Nevertheless, there will be cases in which, despite the lack of a prompt challenge to a public law decision, a litigant will not be prevented from questioning it in subsequent litigation. This is likely to be so if the litigant is not affected personally by the decision at the time it was made, and it has an impact on a private right which he wishes to assert in that litigation (or it founds a prosecution brought against him). In some exceptional cases, a litigant will not be prevented from raising a public law defence even when the decision in question affects only him. Under the CPR, it can be expected that the courts will be flexible and will take into account the overriding objective in their application of the doctrine of abuse of process.

5.59 Another aspect of abuse of process was considered by Collins J in *R (G and M) v IAT*.[1] That case concerned the relationship between judicial review and statutory review (by a High Court judge) of decisions of the Immigration Appeal Tribunal (IAT) refusing permission to appeal from a decision of an adjudicator to the IAT. The judge held that it would be an abuse of process for a claimant who had applied for a statutory review of a decision, and failed, then to apply, on the same grounds, for judicial review of that decision of the IAT. He did not consider at any length whether the doctrine of *res judicata* applies in such a context. However, it is suggested that despite some dicta that the doctrine does not apply in judicial review, the doctrine is perfectly apt in an adjudicative context such as that at issue in *G and M*.[2] *G and M* was followed by the Court of Appeal in relation to the later appellate regime in *R (F (Mongolia)) v Asylum and Immigration Tribunal*.[3]

[1] [2004] EWHC 588 (Admin) [2004] 3 All ER 286, upheld by the Court of Appeal [2004] EWCA Civ 1731, [2005] 2 All ER 165.
[2] See the discussion of this point by Lightman J in *Westminster City Council v Haywood (No 2)* [2000] BLGR 526 at paragraph 20, citing *Thrasyvoulou v the Secretary of State for the Environment* [1990] 2 AC 273 at p 289. Compare, however, the analysis at **18.65** below.
[3] [2007] EWCA Civ 769; [2007] 1 WLR 2523. Compare *R (AM (Cameroon)) v Asylum and Immigration Tribunal* [2008] EWCA Civ 100; [2008] 1 WLR 2062.

OUSTER OF JUDICIAL REVIEW

5.60 The starting point is *Anisminic v Foreign Compensation Commission*,[1] which is authority for the proposition that Parliament can oust the supervisory jurisdiction of the court, provided it does so in clear terms, but the courts will presume against ouster save in the clearest cases.[2] Legislation which ousts the High Court's supervisory jurisdiction gives rise to the issues discussed in CHAPTER 6.[3] There has been much debate on the question whether the High Court's supervisory jurisdiction over inferior tribunals can be ousted.[4]

[1] [1969] 2 AC 147.

2   *R (Privacy International) v Investigatory Powers Tribunal* [2017] EWHC 114 (Admin) is an
    example of an ouster clause which was upheld by the High Court.
3   See **6.7** et seq.
4   See Fordham, [2004] JR 86, and contributions by others at [2004] 9 JR 95–121.

5.61 There are fundamental objections to an ouster clause which apparently makes an inferior tribunal the final judge of the legal questions which fall to it for decision. It does not follow, if clear language is used, that there is any such objection to a provision which preserves the jurisdiction of the High Court over an inferior tribunal, but accords to the person who wishes to challenge that tribunal a limited right of recourse: for example, one which is subject to a stricter time limit than judicial review, and at the same time excludes judicial review. This emerges from a number of cases in which the courts have considered the effect of express restrictions on the right to apply for judicial review in the context of a substituted statutory right of access to the High Court.[1] Cases where Parliament confers a right and a limited remedy for breach of that right (which excludes judicial review), in the same statutory scheme are not subject to the same objections as ouster clauses, which restrict existing remedies.[2]

1   *Smith v East Elloe Rural District Council* [1956] 1 All ER 855. (compulsory purchase order);
    R v the Secretary of State for the Environment, ex p Ostler [1976] 3 All ER 90 (compulsory
    purchase order); *R v Cornwall County Council, ex p Huntingdon* [1994] 1 All ER 694
    (interim variation of definitive map); *R (Deutsch) v Hackney London Borough Council* [2003]
    EWHC 2692 (Admin), [2004] ACD 11 (order designating controlled parking zone).
2   See *Barraclough v Brown* [1897] AC 615 and *R (A) v Director of Establishments of the
    Security Service* [2009] UKSC 12; [2010] 2 WLR.

5.62 A further question is whether judicial review can ever be excluded by implication. Two situations should be distinguished: the case in which the an implied ouster (if effective) would leave an unsupervised inferior tribunal, and that in which Parliament has provided an alternative route to High Court from the decision of the inferior tribunal, albeit one which differs from judicial review in some respect.

5.63 The first kind of case was considered by the Court of Appeal in *R (Sivasubramanian) v Wandsworth County Court*.[1] The claimant applied for judicial review of a decision of a circuit judge refusing him leave to appeal from a decision of another circuit judge and of a district judge. The Lord Chancellor's Department intervened in the proceedings and argued that the court's judicial review jurisdiction was by implication excluded by the existence of a statutory code governing appeals within and from the county court. That argument was rejected in reliance on *R v Medical Appeal Tribunal, ex p Gilmore*.[2] However, the court indicated that as a matter of discretion, any such application would, save in very exceptional circumstances,[3] be summarily dismissed on the basis that (if the claimant had not sought leave to appeal under the statute) he had an alternative remedy, or (if he had sought leave to appeal and been refused) on the basis that 'Parliament has put in place an adequate system for reviewing the merits of decisions by district judges and it is not appropriate that there should be a further review of these by the High Court'. It is significant that the reason why the judicial review jurisdiction exists, in the second class of case is that ' . . . as a matter of jurisprudential theory . . . the judge in question has a limited statutory jurisdiction and that it must be open to the High Court to review whether that jurisdiction has been exceeded.'[4]

[1] [2003] 1 WLR 475; followed in *Strickson v Preston County Court* [2007] EWCA Civ 1132, and recently in *R (Tummond) v Reading County Court* [2014] EWHC 1039 (Admin).

[2] [1957] 1 QB 574 at p 583 per Denning LJ: 'The remedy of certiorari is never to be taken away by any statute except by the most clear and explicit words'.

[3] ' . . . and we find it hard to envisage what these could be' (at paragraph 48, per Lord Phillips of Worth Matravers MR).

[4] At paragraph 54. *Sivasubramaniam* was distinguished by the Court of Appeal, in the context of refusals of permission to appeal by social security commissioners in *R (Wiles) v Social Security Commissioners* [2010] EWCA Civ 258. The Court of Appeal held that judicial review was available on conventional grounds, but that given the special expertise of the Commissioners, the reviewing court would not be astute to detect error.

5.64 There is authority that if there is no express preclusive clause, a statutory right of recourse to the High Court and the right to apply for judicial review co-exist.[1] This is no doubt based on the strong dicta in *Anisminic* and *Gilmore* to the effect that clear language is required to oust the jurisdiction of the High Court, and the wide statement in *Sivasubramanian* that the High Court's jurisdiction cannot be ousted by implication. However, it is suggested that these authorities may overlook the fact that those dicta and that statement were all made in cases in which, had the argument for ouster succeeded, the outcome would have been an inferior tribunal with an unsupervised power to determine in its own jurisdiction.[2] But where Parliament has provided a means of access to the High Court from an inferior tribunal, such as the statutory review procedure which was the subject of the decision in *G and M*, it is not obvious, on policy grounds, why the court should make judicial review available even in theory, even if that procedure does not correspond in every respect with judicial review.[3]

[1] *R (G and M) v IAT* [2004] EWHC 588 (Admin); [2004] 3 All ER 286; *R (Cheltenham Builders Limited) v South Gloucestershire District Council* [2003] EWHC 2803 (Admin), [2004] JPL 975.

[2] The passage from paragraph 54 of *R (Sivasubramanian) v Wandsworth County Court* [2003] 1 WLR 475 cited above makes this obvious.

[3] Cf *Re Racal Communications Limited* [1981] AC 374. This concerned s 441 of the Companies Act 1948 which empowered a High Court judge to make an order for the inspection of a company's books in certain circumstances. The statute provided that the judge's decision was to be final. The DPP applied unsuccessfully for such an order and then appealed to the Court of Appeal, which allowed the appeal on the grounds that the judge had made an error of law which went to his jurisdiction. The House of Lords held that the Court of Appeal had no jurisdiction to entertain the appeal: when Parliament conferred a power on a court of law, rather than an inferior tribunal, to decide a question, there was no presumption that Parliament did not intend to confer on it a power to determine questions of law going to jurisdiction as well as questions of fact, and judicial review was not available to correct any error of law made by it. Counsel for the company is recorded as submitting (at p 378): 'A judge might have a brainstorm or make an error or go to sleep but, where the jurisdiction is denied by statute, hardship does not bestow it'.

5.65 Where a statutory right of review is given, a question may arise whether the statutory review body can re-open its decision. In *Taylor v Lawrence*,[1] the Court of Appeal (which has a statutory jurisdiction) held that it has an inherent power to re-open its own decisions in very exceptional cases where the interests of justice require it.[2] The reasoning of the court was based in large part on the fact that, for practical purposes, that court is a court of last resort, because of the limited circumstances in which the House of Lords will grant leave to appeal.[3] The scope of this decision is not entirely clear. The Court of

Appeal has extended it to cases in which the High Court's decision on an appeal is final.[4] The Employment Appeal Tribunal, on the other hand, has held in *Asda Stores Limited v Thompson*[5] that it has no such power. This is because it is not a court of last resort, and also in the interests of speed and finality. It seems unlikely that *Taylor v Lawrence* can apply to an inferior tribunal (or a superior court of record) from which there is a further, realistic, right of appeal, for the reasons given by the Employment Appeal Tribunal in the *Asda* case. However, in any case where the High Court, sitting as a court of final appeal, does have this jurisdiction, then if an exceptional injustice came to light even after the High Court had made a 'final' decision, there would arguably be a mechanism for putting it right. In such a case there would be no need to retain a residual right of judicial review.

[1]   [2003] QB 528.
[2]   In *R (Nicholas) v Upper Tribunal (Administrative Appeals Chamber)* [2013] EWCA Civ 799, the Court of Appeal explained that the *Taylor v Lawrence* jurisdiction was 'invented by this court in 2002 to cater for glaring injustice'. It did not apply to mere lawyers' mistakes.
[3]   Compare the approach of the House of Lords in *R v Metropolitan Stipendiary Magistrate ex p Pinochet Ugarte No 2* [2000] 1 AC 119.
[4]   *Seray-Wurie v Hackney London Borough Council* [2003] 1 WLR 257.
[5]   [2004] IRLR 598.

Chapter 6

ILLEGALITY: THE PROBLEM OF JURISDICTION

INTRODUCTION

6.1 The scope of this chapter is the nature of the supervisory jurisdiction of the High Court exercised by way of judicial review. 'Jurisdiction', like 'reasonableness', is a protean word. Its easiest application is the case where a body has express but limited powers conferred on it by another body: so if it acts outside those powers, it exceeds its jurisdiction. But the superior courts in England are not constituted on any such basis. The extent of their power is not determined by Parliament. The judges have, in the last analysis, the power they say they have. The Senior Courts Act 1981 regulates the jurisdiction of the Senior Courts, but does so by providing (as regards the High Court) that it is to exercise:

'(a) all such jurisdiction (whether civil or criminal) as is conferred by this or any other Act; and

(b) all such other jurisdiction (whether civil or criminal) as was exercisable by it immediately before the commencement of this Act . . . ' (s 19(2)).'

6.2 There is an effectively identical provision relating to the Court of Appeal contained in s 15, and in substance, these measures replicate earlier legislation. It is true that the Court of Appeal is a creature of statute, as is the Supreme Court (under ss 23–60 of the Constitutional Reform Act 2005). The arrangements for rights of appeal against High Court decisions have changed over time, as has the designation of the High Court itself. Further, the Human Rights Act 1998 has added significantly to the bases on which the courts can review the actions of public authorities. But the ancient jurisdiction of the Queen's Bench to call up the decisions of inferior bodies for review was never conferred by Parliament; all Parliament has done is to confirm its existence, and from time to time regulate the manner of its exercise and the substantive principles of law upon which such review may proceed. Even the doctrine of Parliamentary sovereignty exemplifies this position. The reason why the court cannot strike down main legislation is not that Parliament has so decreed. It is because that position has been vouchsafed by the court. Indeed, Parliament could not invest itself with sovereign power: that would be to assume the very authority which falls to be conferred.[1]

[1]   See Wade, 'The Basis of Legal Sovereignty', [1955] CLJ 172; Bradley, 'The Sovereignty of Parliament – in Perpetuity?', Ch 4 of 'The Changing Constitution' (3rd edn, 1994), ed Jowell and Oliver. In his essay on Sovereignty (*Essays in Constitutional Law*, Stevens), R F V Heuston supports the proposition that the courts have power to question the validity of an Act of Parliament on the ground that the relevant rules prescribing the composition or procedure of the sovereign legislature have not been observed. He takes issue with Wade's view, expressed in the 1955 article, that there is a sacrosanct rule of the common law that the courts will enforce statutes and that this rule cannot itself be altered by statute. He says (p 24): 'this seems to miss the point that the argument turns upon whether the measure which the courts are called upon to enforce is a *statute* . . . The issue . . . is one of manner and form, and not of area of power'. But assuming Heuston to be correct, his analysis does not touch the proposition that Parliament cannot confer sovereign power on itself: it must be, as it has been, mediated through the courts.

6.3   The term 'jurisdiction' in public law denotes both the authority of the reviewing court and the extent of the powers possessed by the inferior body which is subject to review (whether minister, lower court, tribunal, or any other). In the former sense it is a *dynamic* concept: responsive to the conditions of the times, and to the judges' perceptions of the requirements of the supervisory power. In the latter sense, however, it is on the face of it a *static* concept: no reviewable body has the lawful power to fix the reach of its own jurisdiction; its jurisdiction is conferred *aliunde* (from elsewhere), usually by statute.

6.4   This, however, gives an inadequate account of the way in which the court's power is brought to bear upon inferior bodies. In modern administrative law the court does not merely enquire whether the express limits of the respondent's legal remit have been exceeded, as, for example, would be the case where a licensing authority granted a licence subject to conditions when the enabling statute only empowered it to grant or refuse a licence *simpliciter*. A statute may confer a discretion without any apparent limits on its exercise: but the court will not merely ascertain whether the act done is within the express words of the statute. It will strike an act down at common law if it is done in breach of the well-established principles of fairness (as they fall to be applied in the context of the case[1]), reasonableness (in the *Wednesbury*[2] sense), or so as to run counter to the policy and objects of the Act (*Padfield v Minister of Agriculture, Fisheries and Food*[3]). All these principles have been developed by the judges, not created by Parliament, and are now elementary tenets in our public law jurisprudence. So while it may truly be said that an inferior body has no *jurisdiction* to breach these principles, this is only so because the jurisdiction of the courts has been shaped to enable them to demand compliance with them. Thus the jurisdiction of the inferior body is in part a function of the jurisdiction of the High Court: breach of express statutory limits apart (including such limits as are imposed by the Human Rights Act 1998), the former only has power to act as the latter permits it to act.

[1]   See CHAPTERS 10, 11 and 12.
[2]   *Associated Provincial Picture Houses Ltd v Wednesbury Corporation* [1948] 1 KB 223; see CHAPTER 8.
[3]   [1968] AC 997; see CHAPTER 7.

6.5 Such an account of the foundation of judicial review, which identifies the common law as the ultimate source of public law principles, is consistent with the manner in which the courts' judicial review jurisdiction expanded in the latter half of the last century. This significant period of expansion was neither driven nor endorsed by any Act of Parliament. Rather, as would be expected under a common law account, it was the product of vigorous and creative judicial consideration and the gradual accretion of precedent. By way of example, in *A v Secretary of State for the Home Department*,[1] Lord Bingham expressed the 'abhorrence' of the common law for torture and confirmed that this could not be overridden by 'a statute and procedural rule which make no mention of torture'.

[1] [2006] 2 AC 221 at [51].

6.6 Further, an important aspect of this expansion of judicial review has been the recognition that, in certain circumstances, the courts can supervise powers exercised in the absence of any statutory underpinning. Thus, it is established that judicial review will in certain circumstances lie against the exercise of a prerogative power.[1] Further, non-statutory bodies may also be subject to judicial review[2] and, in cases such as *Royal College of Nursing v Department of Health and Social Security*[3] and *Gillick v West Norfolk Area Health Authority*,[4] the courts accepted jurisdiction to rule on the lawfulness of departmental guidance even though that guidance had not been issued pursuant to any statutory power.[5] The common law account of the foundations of judicial review that is set out above provides a straightforward means of explaining how it is that the courts may review acts taken without any direct statutory authority. Under the common law theory, a court is in principle performing the same function – scrutinising the lawfulness of a given exercise of power by reference to common law principles – irrespective of the source of the power at issue.

[1] See, for instance, *R v Secretary of State for Foreign and Commonwealth Affairs, ex p Everett* [1989] QB 811 and *R v Secretary of State for the Home Department, ex p Bentley* [1994] QB 349. These cases confirm the earlier obiter view of the majority of their Lordships in *R v Minister for the Civil Service, ex p Council of Civil Service Unions* [1985] AC 374 that, in a proper case, judicial review would lie against the exercise of prerogative power. Further discussion is in Chapter 5 at **5.35** and Chapter 8 at **8.30**.

[2] See *R v Panel on Take-overs and Mergers, ex p Datafin Plc* [1987] QB 815, where the Court of Appeal held that the Take-over Panel could be judicially reviewed even though it performed its functions, in the words of Sir John Donaldson MR at p 824H, 'without visible means of legal support'. Further discussion is in Chapter 5 at **5.8** et seq and Chapter 8 at **8.23**.

[3] [1981] AC 800.

[4] [1986] AC 112.

[5] Further discussion is in Chapter 5 at **5.8** et seq.

THE ULTRA VIRES THEORY AND *ANISMINIC*

6.7 The traditional account of the basis of judicial review is, however, different from that advanced above. That traditional account, known as the 'ultra vires theory', sought to locate the source of the courts' powers to intervene in the intention of Parliament. Such an approach had obvious content when the court's power to intervene turned on a distinction between errors of law said to be *within* the jurisdiction of the deciding body and errors

123

of law said to be *outside* its jurisdiction. Aside from the now obsolete jurisdiction to review decisions for error on the face of the record, the court only reviewed the latter form of errors of law. But this distinction between different forms of errors of law was in effect laid to rest by the House of Lords in *Anisminic*.[1] The House had to consider s 4(4) of the Foreign Compensation Act 1950:

'The determination by the commission of any application made to them under this Act shall not be called in question in any court of law'.

[1]   *Anisminic Limited v Foreign Compensation Commission* [1969] 2 AC 147.

6.8 The claimant company brought an action for a declaration (since the *O'Reilly*[1] case, this would be a claim for judicial review) that a provisional determination by the commission was a nullity in that the determination had proceeded upon a misconstruction of a statutory instrument made under the Act. The defendants contended that the court lacked jurisdiction to entertain the claim, by reason of s 4(4). The House held by a majority (Lord Morris dissenting) that a purported determination which proceeded on a misconstruction of the statutory instrument was not a determination at all, so that s 4(4) did not operate to preclude the court from inquiring whether it was a nullity; and the declaration sought was granted. Lord Reid said (at 171B–E):

'I have come without hesitation to the conclusion that in this case we are not prevented from inquiring whether the order of the commission was a nullity. It has sometimes been said that it is only where a tribunal acts without jurisdiction that its decision is a nullity. But in such cases the word "jurisdiction" has been used in a very wide sense, and I have come to the conclusion that it is better not to use the term except in the narrow and original sense of the tribunal being entitled to enter on the inquiry in question. But there are many cases where, although the tribunal had jurisdiction to enter on the inquiry, it has done or failed to do something in the course of the inquiry which is of such a nature that its decision is a nullity. It may have given its decision in bad faith. It may have made a decision which it had no power to make. It may have failed in the course of the inquiry to comply with the requirements of natural justice. It may in perfect good faith have misconstrued the provisions giving it power to act so that it failed to deal with the question remitted to it and decided some question which was not remitted to it. It may have refused to take into account something which it was required to take into account. Or it may have based its decision on some matter which, under the provisions setting it up, it had no right to take into account. I do not intend this list to be exhaustive. But if it decides a question remitted to it for decision without committing any of these errors it is as much entitled to decide that question wrongly as it is to decide it rightly'.

[1]   *O'Reilly v Mackman* [1983] 2 AC 237; see Chapter 5 at 5.50.

6.9 Their other Lordships (save Lord Morris) agreed in the result arrived at by Lord Reid, and their reasoning is nowhere inconsistent with his. Although there were some initial doubts as to whether *Anisminic* had truly laid to rest the distinction between errors within and without jurisdiction, Lord Diplock roundly acknowledged it to be so in the later cases of *Re Racal Communications Ltd*[1] and *O'Reilly*.[2]

[1]   [1981] AC 374, 383B–383D.
[2]   [1983] 2 AC 237, 278C–278D.

6.10 Thus the distinction between errors within and errors without juris-diction should be regarded as having passed into history, and the ultra vires rule as having lost much of its utility. The rule remains unobjectionable if it is merely used in its narrow sense to cover the illegality ground of review described by Lord Diplock in *CCSU*.[1] But, of course, the grounds of review extend beyond illegality, and any attempt to use the ultra vires rule to explain the general basis of judicial review is unhelpful and confusing: the rule pur-ports to refer to the reach or extent of the powers of the body reviewed, but in fact can be no more than a label for the degree of intervention which the reviewing court will, on different and developing grounds, contemplate. The position now is, on the best view of the law, as set out above: the powers of the body reviewed are themselves a function of the power of the reviewing court.[2]

[1]   [1985] AC 374; see Chapter 7. See *R (Queen Mary University of London) v HEFCE* [2008] EWHC 1472 for an example of this narrow approach to jurisdiction.

[2]   In *Cakabay v Secretary of State for the Home Department (No 2)* [1999] Imm AR 176 Schiemann LJ endorsed the view expressed in the second edition of this work that there are significant problems with seeking to distinguish between errors within jurisdiction and errors outside it.

6.11 The supporters of the ultra vires theory have not, however, remained idle. They recognise that the various grounds of judicial review (aside, presumably, from those grounds that derive from the Human Rights Act 1998) cannot in any obvious sense be said to derive from the will of Parliament. They have therefore modified the theory in an effort to take account of the role played by the courts in shaping the contours of judicial review. The result, which is generally known as the 'modified' ultra vires theory, may be summarised in the following terms:

'Unless Parliament clearly indicates otherwise, it is presumed to intend that decision-makers must apply the principles of good administration drawn from the common law as developed by the judges in making their decisions'.[1]

[1]   Forsyth, 'Heat and Light: A Plea for Reconciliation'. Ch 18 of 'Judicial Review and the Constitution' (2000) Hart Publishing, p 396.

6.12 It is difficult to believe that such an intention is generally present when Parliament passes statutes. Indeed, where such an approach is used in an effort to legitimate the court's attitude towards ouster clauses, the position becomes absurd: Parliament is presumed to have intended a result that flies in the face of its express intention as enshrined in the ouster clause itself. The premise of the modified ultra vires theory is thus on its face a rather artificial one, as indeed its supporters recognise.[1] Further, the modified ultra vires theory lacks the explanatory force of the common law model as regards the ability of the courts judicially to review powers that are exercised without any statutory underpinning. In such circumstances, supporters of the modified theory must resort to the common law to explain and justify the court's powers of intervention.[2] To see whether, despite these flaws, the modified ultra vires theory ought nevertheless to be accepted it is necessary to look in greater detail at some of the criticisms that have been made of the common law account in the academic literature.

[1]   Wade & Forsyth, *Administrative Law* (10th edn, 2009) Oxford, p 31.

2   'Of Fig Leaves and Fairy Tales: The *Ultra Vires* Doctrine, the Sovereignty of Parliament and Judicial Review'. Vol 55 [1996] CLJ 122, p 124.

CRITICISMS OF THE COMMON LAW POSITION

6.13 Supporters of the modified ultra vires theory advance three main criticisms of the common law account in an effort to suggest that the modified ultra vires theory should be embraced, despite its artificial air. They argue, first, that the common law model necessarily leads to a rejection of Parliamentary sovereignty; second, that its adoption undermines the judiciary's ability to resist ouster clauses and (at least implicitly), third, that it prevents the courts from being able to entertain collateral challenges to decisions that are unlawful in a public law sense. In addition to these three arguments that are advanced from the standpoint of principle, the supporters of the modified ultra vires theory also claim that their theory is the one that has, as a matter of fact, been accepted as authoritative by the courts.

Parliamentary sovereignty

6.14 In an early and important article on the modified ultra vires theory,[1] Dr Christopher Forsyth identifies what he terms 'weak' and 'strong' criticisms of the ultra vires position. The 'weak' criticism consists in the proposition, for which he cites[2] a passage in an article by, that the developed doctrines of modern administrative law – *Wednesbury, Padfield* and the requirements of fairness and proper procedure:

> '. . . are, categorically, judicial creations. They owe neither their existence nor their acceptance to the will of the legislature. They have nothing to do with the intention of Parliament, save as a fig-leaf to cover their true origins. We do not need the fig-leaf any more'.[3]

1   '. . . Of Fig Leaves and Fairy Tales: The *Ultra Vires* Doctrine, the Sovereignty of Parliament and Judicial Review', Vol 55 [1996] CLJ 122.
2   'Of Fig Leaves and Fairy Tales: The *Ultra Vires* Doctrine, the Sovereignty of Parliament and Judicial Review', Vol 55 [1996] CLJ 122, p 127.
3   Sir John Laws, 'Law and Democracy' [1995] Public Law 72, p 79.

6.15 In essence, the weak critics' position is the common law account set out above. Forsyth proceeds to categorise the 'strong' critics as those who argue that 'the judges may in appropriate circumstances pronounce upon the validity of Acts of Parliament'.[1]

1   'Of Fig Leaves and Fairy Tales: The *Ultra Vires* Doctrine, the Sovereignty of Parliament and Judicial Review', Vol 55 [1996] CLJ 122, p 127.

6.16 He cites Lord Woolf's extra-judicial statement:[1]

> 'if Parliament did the unthinkable [and undermined substantially the role of the High Court on judicial review], then I would say that the courts would also be required to act in a manner which would be without precedent . . . I myself would consider that there were advantages in making it clear that there are even limits on the supremacy of Parliament which it is the courts' inalienable responsi-

bility to identify and uphold . . . [These limits] are no more than are necessary to enable the rule of law to be preserved'.

¹ [1995] Public Law 57 at p 69.

6.17 It is no part of our purpose in this chapter to mount any assault on the doctrine of Parliamentary sovereignty, which remains the plainest constitutional fundamental at the present time; see for example *R (Jackson) v Attorney General*,¹ ruling on the validity of the Hunting Act, with the House of Lords reaffirming 'the supremacy of the Crown in Parliament'. See also *R (Hooper) v Secretary of State for Work and Pensions*² per Lord Scott; 'There are not, under English domestic law, any fundamental constitutional rights that are immune from legislative change'. A departure from Parliamentary sovereignty will only happen, in the tranquil development of the common law, with a gradual re-ordering of our constitutional priorities to bring alive the nascent idea that a democratic legislature cannot be above the law.³ Rather, under this heading, we are concerned to refute Forsyth's argument that 'weak' criticism is, like it or not, 'strong' criticism in disguise.⁴ This is how Forsyth's theoretical argument is put:⁵

> 'Suppose that a Minister in the apparent exercise of a statutory power to make regulations, makes certain regulations which are clearly so vague that their meaning cannot be determined with sufficient certainty. Classic theory tell us that Parliament never intends to grant the power to make vague regulations – this seems an entirely reasonable and realistic intention to impute to Parliament – and thus the vague regulations are ultra vires and void . . . But classic theory has been abandoned: the grounds of review derive, not from the implied intent of the legislature, but from the common law. It follows that although the regulations are *intra vires* the minister's powers, they are none the less invalid because they are vague.
>
> The analytical difficulty is this: what an all powerful Parliament does not prohibit, it must authorise either expressly or impliedly. Likewise if Parliament grants a power to a minister, that minister either acts within those powers or outside those powers. There is no grey area between authorisation and prohibition or between empowerment and the denial of power. Thus, if the making of the vague regulations is within the powers granted by a sovereign Parliament, on what basis may the courts challenge Parliament's will and hold that the regulations are invalid? If Parliament has authorised vague regulations, those regulations cannot be challenged without challenging Parliament's authority to authorise such regulations'.

¹ [2006] 1 AC 262 at [9].
² [2005] 1 WLR 1681 at [92].
³ But see 'Law and Democracy' [1995] Public Law 72, pp 81–93, for the personal view of Sir John Laws. See also Fordham [2004] JR 86, and further discussion by other contributors at [2004] JR 95–121. These approaches are reflected in the speech of Lord Steyn in *Jackson* at [102]; 'the supremacy of Parliament is . . . a construct of the common law'. See also Lord Hope at [107]; 'the Courts have a part to play in defining the limits of Parliament's legislative sovereignty'.
⁴ Although it is to be noted that Forsyth's own position as regards Parliamentary sovereignty is not entirely free from difficulty. In Forsyth's view, the courts' policy as regards ouster clauses is one of 'total disobedience to Parliament': p 616 of Wade & Forsyth (10th edn, 2009). However, Forsyth does not seek to criticise the attitude of the courts towards ouster clauses – indeed, as explained at **6.25** below, Forsyth's second criticism of the common law account is that its acceptance might *prevent* the courts from resisting such provisions. There is thus an obvious tension between Forsyth's stance on ouster clauses and his argument that the common law account is deficient as it amounts to a challenge to the sovereignty of Parliament.

[5] 'Of Fig Leaves and Fairy Tales: The *Ultra Vires* Doctrine, the Sovereignty of Parliament and Judicial Review', Vol 55 [1996] CLJ 122, pp 133 ff.

6.18 Forsyth's reasoning as to the 'analytical consequences' of the abandonment of ultra vires is unsound. It is simply not correct to assert that 'there is no grey area between authorisation and prohibition'. The clearest analysis of the flaw in this aspect of Forsyth's reasoning is that of Andrew Halpin.[1] As Halpin points out, the logical principle that underlies the issue is the law of the excluded middle, which asserts that a given proposition must be either true or false, and cannot be something in between.[2] The crucial point is that one can assert that there is something in between authorisation and prohibition without denying the law of the excluded middle. This is because the negation of the proposition X prohibits Y is not X *authorises* Y but X *does not prohibit* Y. It is, as a matter of logic, quite possible for Parliament neither to authorise nor to prohibit a particular act. Such a situation would arise where, as regards a particular issue, Parliament has expressed no intention one way or the other.

[1] 'The Theoretical Controversy Concerning Judicial Review' [2001] MLR 500.
[2] 'The Theoretical Controversy Concerning Judicial Review' [2001] MLR 500, p 502.

6.19 The fact that Parliament is all powerful does not affect this conclusion. The sovereignty of Parliament means that, through expressions of its intent in statutory form, Parliament can lay down any legal rule that it chooses. It is, however, simply a *non sequitur* to say that therefore every legal rule must be derived (whether expressly or impliedly) from such expressions of intent. Thus, Forsyth is wrong to claim that 'what an all powerful Parliament does not prohibit, it must authorise either expressly or impliedly'. The fact that Parliament has power to prohibit any particular act does not render it necessary to conclude that, unless and until such power is exercised, Parliament must be taken to have expressly or impliedly authorised the act.

6.20 In a later article, Forsyth restates his argument as follows:[1]

'The concepts of ultra vires and intra vires are mutually exclusive: a decision-maker either acts within or outside his or her powers, there is no middle ground. It is like pregnancy, you are either pregnant or you are not, or like a light switch which is either on or off. If, say, a decision-maker, in denying a hearing in certain circumstances, acts within the powers granted by Parliament the common law cannot impose a duty of fairness upon that decision-maker without challenging Parliament's power to allow him or her to make valid decisions without a hearing. Otherwise you have the position where every requirement for validity laid down expressly or impliedly by Parliament is satisfied yet the common law is imposing an additional requirement for validity. That is a challenge to Parliamentary supremacy. And "weak critics" become "strong critics"'.

[1] Forsyth (2000), p 402 (see **6.11** above).

6.21 It seems, from the reference to an individual being either pregnant or not and to a light switch being either on or off, that Forsyth is here attempting to suggest that his position is a consequence of the law of the excluded middle. But, on closer examination, it is apparent that Forsyth's argument begs the question. It must, of course, be accepted that the concepts of ultra vires and intra vires are mutually exclusive. However, before that proposition can have any impact on the debate, it is necessary to ascertain what is covered by the term 'vires'. Forsyth simply assumes that vires means power *as granted by Parliament*. But that is precisely what is at issue between him and those who support the common law account of judicial review. Thus, Forsyth's argument fails as he has to assume the very conclusion that he sets out to prove. Further, Forsyth cannot seek to make good that omission by relying on the argument cited at **6.17** above, as, for the reasons already given, that argument is unsound.

6.22 One further argument needs to be considered. It has been claimed that those who support the common law account must necessarily assert that Parliament is indifferent to whether a power granted by it is exercised fairly, and that such an assertion is 'self-evidently unrealistic'.[1] However, supporters of the common law account are not in this predicament. What separates the two camps is not what Parliament may or may not have considered or intended in any particular context, but what is *necessary* before an exercise of public power may be struck down by the courts as unlawful. Forsyth's position is that in all such cases, it is necessary at least formally to identify an intention on Parliament's behalf that legitimises the intervention of the courts. Those who support the common law account need not assert that no such Parliamentary intention will ever exist: they merely assert that its existence is not required before the courts may intervene. Thus, those who support the common law account are free to accept that there may well be particular statutory contexts in which there is a discernible Parliamentary intention that a certain judge-made public law principle (or set of such principles) should apply.

[1]   Forsyth (2000), p 401. See also Elliott, 'The Ultra Vires Doctrine in a Constitutional Setting: Still the Central Principle of Administrative Law' [1999] CLJ 129, pp 145 ff.

6.23 The true position is clear. Forsyth is wrong to claim that the position of the 'weak' critics of the ultra vires doctrine collapses into that of the 'strong' critics. It is perfectly consistent both to assert that Parliament is supreme – in that it can make or unmake any law – and to assert that there is at present within the common law a body of judge-made rules against which the lawfulness of any exercise of public power may fall to be considered. All that is necessary is for the courts to be satisfied that Parliament has not sought, whether expressly or by implication, to alter or overturn those common law rules. Forsyth's example of the decision-maker who refuses to hold a hearing may be used to illustrate the point. The eventual decision may well be within the express terms of the relevant statutory provisions. However, it may also be the case that there is no clear Parliamentary intent to the effect that the common law principles of natural justice should be excluded from the relevant decision-making process. Such a conclusion by the court would not be to deny that Parliament is all powerful, it would merely be a consequence of the fact that an all-powerful Parliament had not expressed itself one way or the other on the matter. Thus, in such a situation, the court could declare the decision to be unlawful in reliance on the common law rules of natural justice without impugning the sovereignty of Parliament. What Parliamentary sovereignty means in this context is that, in principle, Parliament is free to confer a decision-making function on an individual and to provide that the common law rules of natural justice should not apply to that individual in the exercise of that function.

6.24 There is, of course, nothing unusual in this analysis of the relationship between legislation and the common law. The same relationship exists in private law fields such as contract and tort, where common law rules co-exist alongside specific legislative interventions from Parliament. Indeed, where civil liability is imposed on public bodies, the analogy becomes very close indeed. In such circumstances, the courts are not in general concerned to inquire whether it was Parliament's intention that a given public body should be subject to the common law principles of contract, tort, etc in the exercise of their statutory powers. Rather, the courts apply these common principles because Parliament has not itself expressed any particular intention on the subject.[1]

[1]   See Craig, 'Competing Models of Judicial Review', [1999] Public Law 428, pp 432 ff.

Ouster clauses and the ultra vires theory

6.25 Forsyth's second challenge to the common law theory lies in the claim that the abandonment of ultra vires will, or may, actually 'eviscerate' the judicial review jurisdiction.[1] In developing this argument he draws on the jurisprudence of South Africa (in which he is a distinguished expert). In *Staatspresident v United Democratic Front*[2] the issue was the validity of certain emergency regulations, severely restricting press freedom, made by the State President purportedly acting under powers granted by main legislation. It was said that the regulations were so vague as to be null and void. But on the face of it they were protected by an ouster clause in the enabling Act: 'no court shall be competent to enquire into or to give judgment on the validity of any . . . proclamation' made under the relevant section. If the regulations fell to be regarded as ultra vires, then on *Anisminic* principles they were not made under the section and the court's power to strike them down could not be excluded by the ouster provision. However, the Supreme Court, by a majority, upheld the regulations: while the Roman-Dutch common law might presume against vague regulations, nevertheless, the regulations were made under the Act (intra vires) and so protected by the ouster clause. Dicta from Rabie A C J and Hefer J A cited by Forsyth show that this conclusion was arrived at by a rejection of the conventional ultra vires approach, so that *Anisminic* principles had no application. Thus, in short, Forsyth argues[3] that abandonment of ultra vires unwrites the *Anisminic* doctrine and deprives the courts of their best weapon to ensure that unfair or irrational decisions are not protected by ouster clauses.[4]

[1]   'Of Fig Leaves and Fairy Tales: The *Ultra Vires* Doctrine, the Sovereignty of Parliament and Judicial Review', Vol 55 [1996] CLJ 122, pp 129 ff.
[2]   1988(4) SA 830(A).
[3]   'Of Fig Leaves and Fairy Tales: The *Ultra Vires* Doctrine, the Sovereignty of Parliament and Judicial Review', Vol 55 [1996] CLJ 122, pp 131–132.
[4]   Further discussion of ouster clauses is in Chapter 5 at 5.60.

6.26 There is on its face something rather peculiar about this aspect of the ultra vires debate. Supporters of the ultra vires theory supposedly accept the doctrine of Parliamentary sovereignty. Indeed, this doctrine plays a central role in the first form of criticism of the common law account discussed above. But if the supporters of the ultra vires theory are truly committed to the notion of Parliamentary sovereignty then surely they must also accept that an ouster clause could in principle be drafted that would successfully oust the review jurisdiction of the High Court. Thus, in effect, the debate between the two camps is really only about *how hard* Parliament must try before it is successful. This reflects the approach of the courts in practice, as exemplified by the judgment of the Court of Appeal in *R (G) v Immigration Appeal Tribunal*:[1]

> 'The common law power . . . to review the legality of administrative action is a cornerstone of the rule of law in this country . . . If Parliament attempts by legislation to remove that power, the rule of law is threatened. The courts will not readily accept that legislation achieves that end'.[2]

[1] [2005] 1 WLR 1445 at [13].
[2] Leave to appeal the Court of Appeal judgment to the House of Lords was refused on 28 July 2005; [2005] 1 WLR 2857. See however *R (Hilali) v Governor of Whitemoor Prison* [2008] 1 AC 805 for the exclusion of habeas corpus by clear statutory words. See also *A v B* [2010] 1 All ER 1149 and *Farley v Secretary of State for Work and Pensions* [2006] 1 WLR 1817 for the acceptability of ouster clauses where an effective means of challenging a decision is provided elsewhere, for instance through a specialist tribunal.

6.27 But even in this more restricted context, Forsyth's concerns are misplaced: the courts may properly subject ouster clauses to searching scrutiny without having to rely on the ultra vires doctrine.[1] It is useful to begin the analysis by considering the position of inferior courts.

[1] We leave aside the possible impact of art 6 of the European Convention on Human Rights on ouster clauses, as this has no direct bearing on the theoretical merits of Forsyth's criticism of the common law account.

Ouster clauses and inferior courts

6.28 In *Pearlman v Harrow School*,[1] the county court had refused to make a declaration as to the rateable value of a house for the purposes of the Leasehold Reform Act 1967. By paragraph 2(2) of Sch 8 to the Housing Act 1974, the judge's determination was made 'final and conclusive'. Section 107 of the County Courts Act 1959 provided that:

> 'no judgment or order of any judge of county courts . . . shall be removed by . . . certiorari or otherwise . . . except in the manner and according to the provisions in this Act mentioned'.

[1] [1979] QB 56.

6.29 The Court of Appeal held by a majority that certiorari would lie. A passage in Lord Denning's judgment (at 69E–70F) is a ringing affirmation of the barrenness of the distinction between errors of law within and without jurisdiction. But it is not clear whether Eveleigh LJ, who concurred with Lord Denning in the result, took quite the same view. Geoffrey Lane LJ, dissenting, held that the County Courts Act 1959 abolished certiorari as a means of attacking a county court judgment or order for error on the face of the record, and that, because the judge's error was within jurisdiction, certiorari was not available.

6.30 *Pearlman* received attention in two later authorities, decided respectively by the Privy Council and the House of Lords, within ten days of each other in

1980. In *South East Asia Fire Bricks*,[1] the Privy Council was concerned with the Malaysian Industrial Relations Act 1967, s 29(3)(a) which provided:

' . . . an award of the [Industrial] Court shall be final and conclusive, and no award shall be challenged, appealed against, reviewed, quashed or called in question in any court of law'.

[1]   [1981] AC 363.

6.31 The Judicial Committee, having cited *Anisminic*, said (at 370D–E):

'But if the inferior tribunal has merely made an error of law which does not affect its jurisdiction, and if its decision is not a nullity for some reason such as breach of the rules of natural justice, then the ouster will be effective'.

6.32 The Committee repudiated Lord Denning's suggestion in *Pearlman* that the distinction between errors of law within and without jurisdiction should be discarded and agreed with the dissenting judgment in that case of Geoffrey Lane LJ.

6.33 On its face, this authority runs against the view that has been put forward above, although there is no analysis of the *nature* of the difference between errors on the face and nullities in the developed state of the law. However, if it is contended that the reasoning in it shows, as a matter of general principle, that the concept of nullity remains a touchstone for the reach and extent of the judicial review jurisdiction, it has to be looked at in light of the House of Lords' reasoning (nine days later!) in *Re Racal Communications Ltd*.[1] That case concerned an application under s 441 of the Companies Act 1948 to the High Court to authorise the inspection of books etc belonging to or under the control of a named company. Section 441(3) provided:

'The decision of a judge of the High Court . . . on an application under this section shall not be appealable'.

[1]   [1981] AC 374.

6.34 The Court of Appeal had held, notwithstanding this, that it had jurisdiction to overturn the judge's decision on the application because he had made an error of law which went to his jurisdiction. The House allowed an appeal: the Court of Appeal had no power to entertain what was in effect a judicial review of the High Court Judge's decision, and could not entertain an appeal against it because of the terms of s 441(3). Lord Diplock, while still adhering to the language of nullity, said this of *Anisminic* (at 383B–D):

'The break-through made by *Anisminic* [1969] 2 AC 147, [1969] 1 All ER 208, was that, as respects administrative tribunals and authorities, the old distinction between errors of law that went to jurisdiction and errors of law that did not was for practical purposes abolished. Any error of law that could be shown to have been made by them in the course of reaching their decision on matters of fact or of administrative policy would result in their having asked themselves the wrong question with the result that the decision they reached would be a nullity'.

6.35 Lord Keith agreed in terms with Lord Diplock's speech and there is nothing in the other reasoned speeches that disagrees with it. It is important to note that Lord Diplock attached significance to the distinction between a case where a court of law makes a legal error, and one where such an error was made by an administrative authority. He pointed out that *Anisminic* was only concerned with the latter. He said (at 383E):

'But there is no presumption that where a decision-making power is conferred by statute upon a court of law, Parliament did not intend to confer upon it power to decide questions of law as well as questions of fact . . . '.

6.36 *Racal* itself, of course, was concerned with a High Court decision. But Lord Diplock continued:

'In the case of inferior courts where the decision of the court is made final and conclusive by the statute, this may involve the survival of those subtle distinctions formerly drawn between errors of law which go to jurisdiction and errors of law which do not that did so much to confuse English administrative law before *Anisminic*'.

6.37 And he agreed that *Pearlman* was wrongly decided, because (at 383G):

' . . . the superior court conducting the review should not be astute to hold that Parliament did not intend the inferior court to have jurisdiction to decide for itself the meaning of ordinary words used in the statute to define the question which it has to decide. This, in my view, is the error into which the majority of the Court of Appeal fell in *Pearlman* . . . '.

6.38 Here, again, the language of Parliamentary intention (and thus impliedly of ultra vires) is used. But behind it we can discern the essence of an important judicial policy. It is one thing for Parliament, through the medium of an ouster provision, to consign the making of a final decision *as to what the law is* to a court. It is quite another for such a decision to be given to a body which is not a court at all. So far as Lord Diplock's speech in *Racal* contemplates a limited survival (in relation to statutory provisions giving the final word to an inferior court) of the old distinction between errors of law within and without jurisdiction, it is by no means a litmus test for the general nature of the High Court's review power. Rather it reflects two factors. One is the sense that there is nothing inevitably repugnant to the rule of law in the notion that an inferior *court* may have questions of law remitted to it for decision, upon which it has the last word. The other is that the rule of law is, however, infringed if any body other than the High Court is seemingly given the right to determine the reach of its own power; so that an inferior court must be kept within the bounds of its statutory remit. Accordingly, there may be occasions where an ouster provision has to be construed so as to make space for these two dimensions of the rule of law. However, these factors will generally only arise in a single matrix where the body whose decisions are sought to be protected by the ouster clause is an inferior court. If it is an administrative body or tribunal, the first factor will be absent and *Anisminic* will run its full length. If it is the High Court (in its capacity as such), the second factor will be absent, judicial review is unavailable ouster clause or no, and the only effect of the ouster provision will be to deny what would otherwise be the purely statutory right to go to the Court of Appeal.[1]

---

[1] In fact, *Racal* cannot be taken as indicating that inferior courts generally will be immune from review for errors of law committed within the scope of the subject-matter remitted to them provided that Parliament has enacted an ouster clause. In *O'Reilly v Mackman* [1983] 2 AC 237 Lord Diplock himself (at 278) contemplated that the *Anisminic* principle ran to inferior courts. See the discussion in de Smith, Woolf and Jowell *Judicial Review of Administrative Action* (7th edn, 2013) Sweet & Maxwell, at pp 215-217, citing (among other materials)

O'Reilly; R v Greater Manchester Coroner, ex p Tal [1985] QB 67, and *R v Lord President of the Privy Council, ex p Page* [1993] AC 682.

Ouster clauses and the rule of law

6.39 These reflections about ouster clauses and courts point the way to a clearer view of the true relationship between Parliament and the judges, which is illuminated by a deeper consideration of ouster clauses generally. An ouster clause is not sufficiently described by the mere proposition that it limits, indeed excludes, the High Court's jurisdiction; the real position is that by such a clause Parliament, in some circumstances at least, would be setting the decision-maker above the law. The premise upon which any such provision must necessarily be approached is that prima facie the commitment of a final decision as to what the law is to any body other than the High Court is an infringement of the rule of law itself. The position may be relaxed, as we have seen, where an inferior court is given the last word upon the law relating to matters within its remit, and is relaxed in the case of a body such as the university visitor who administers a private internal law,[1] but otherwise, it is an affront to the rule of law for an institution other than the High Court to be empowered to reach final determinations as to the state or content of the law of England.

[1] *R v Lord President of the Privy Council, ex p Page* [1993] AC 682.

6.40 Thus the rigour of the court's approach to ouster clauses is a function of the rule of law; the vindication of the rule of law is the constitutional right of every citizen. So if it is to be breached by Parliament or with Parliament's permission, the High Court will require express words to be used.[1] Here is the true place of the idea of legislative intention. Parliament may override the rule of law, but only where it is shown, on the face of the statute, that it *actually* intended to do so. In other words, the statute would have to provide that the decision of the body in question could not be reviewed for any failure to comply with the principles of public law; it would be tantamount to a provision to the effect that the decision-maker was not obliged to be reasonable, or to be fair, or to act within the confines of the Act's purpose, or according to its correct construction, and so forth.

[1] Compare the principle of legality and the attitude of the courts to fundamental rights under the common law: *R v Secretary of State for the Home Department, ex p Simms and O'Brien* [2000] 2 AC 115, per Lord Hoffmann at p 131E–G.

6.41 The constitutional principle for which we have contended can be seen at work through the cases, notwithstanding their use of the language of nullity and ultra vires. *Anisminic* is itself an early instance. It is necessary to examine the true extent of the difference between the expressed reasoning in *Anisminic*, with its references to nullity, and the analysis that might be given of the same case upon the premise that the only question was whether s 4(4) of the Foreign Compensation Act 1950 on its true construction was effective to permit the commission to act beyond its legal remit, and thus breach the rule of law. After citing s 4(4), Lord Reid said (at 169Hff):

'The respondent maintains that these are plain words only capable of having one meaning. Here is a determination which is apparently valid . . . If it is a nullity, that could only be established by raising some kind of proceedings in court. But that would be calling the determination in question, and that is expressly prohibited by the statute. The appellants maintain that that is not the meaning of the words of this provision. They say that "determination" means a real determination and does not include an apparent or purported determination which in the eyes of the law has no existence because it is a nullity . . . It is one thing to question a determination which does exist: it is quite another thing to say that there is nothing to be questioned . . . It is a well-established principle that a provision ousting the ordinary jurisdiction of the court must be construed strictly – meaning I think, that if such a provision is reasonably capable of having two meanings, that meaning shall be taken which preserves the ordinary jurisdiction of the court'.

6.42 Lord Pearce said (at 194F):

'Such [inferior] tribunals must, however, confine themselves within the powers specially committed to them on a true construction of the relevant Acts of Parliament':

and at 199F–200A (after citing s 4(4)):

'It has been argued that Your Lordships should construe "determination" as meaning anything which is on its face a determination of the commission including even a purported determination which has no jurisdiction . . . A more reasonable and logical construction is that by "determination" Parliament meant a real determination, not a purported determination. On the assumption, however, that either meaning is a possible construction and that therefore the word "determination" is ambiguous, the latter meaning would accord with a long established line of cases which adopted that construction'.

6.43 Of particular interest is Lord Wilberforce's observation (at 207H–208B):

'It is sometimes said, the argument was presented in these terms, that the preclusive clause does not operate on decisions outside the permitted field because they are a nullity. There are dangers in the use of this word if it draws with it the difficult distinction between what is void and what is voidable, and I certainly do not wish to be taken to recognise that this distinction exists or to analyse it if it does. But it may be convenient so long as it is used to describe a decision made outside the permitted field, in other words, as a word of description rather than as in itself a touchstone'.

6.44 The above passages emphasise how important was the construction of the particular subsection. It is clear that the term 'nullity' is used to do no more than describe a decision which lay outside the legal remit vouchsafed to the commission by the statute; and the question was whether s 4(4) operated to prevent the court from confining the commission within that remit. The House did not hold that there existed a legal principle which disabled Parliament from legislating so as to exclude the court's jurisdiction to examine a decision of an inferior tribunal once it was shown that the decision was something which the law categorised as a 'nullity'; manifestly, such a putative rule would be repugnant to the sovereignty of the legislature. Since, then, the legislature *could* have enacted an ouster clause which would have been effective to prevent review of 'null' decisions, the only question was whether it had done so in the instant case. The metaphysical overtones of 'nullity' add nothing. There was, of course, no question but that the commission had as a matter of fact done the act complained of; and Lord Reid's words, already set out, that 'it is quite another thing to say that there is nothing to be questioned' contradict none of this. The wealth of authority cited in particular by Lord Pearce at 196E–200H presses with undiminished force. The presumption that the court's jurisdiction is not ousted is untouched. That presumption's strength rests, no doubt, upon the consideration that but for its operation the rule of law is made more fragile, as we have sought to explain; but the muscular protection which the courts will afford to the rule of law, whose only guardians, in the last analysis, they are, is rendered no stronger by conceptions such as nullity, and certainly no weaker because it rests on the application of constitutional principle rather than a fiction about the intention of the legislature.

6.45 Their Lordships' reasoning is thus consistent with the existence of the constitutional principle for which we have argued. It is true that there is no recognition in terms of the proposition that Parliament can only abrogate the rule of law by an express measure to that effect. Clearly, however, the thrust of the case is that the inferior body will not be permitted to exceed its proper remit unless the court is driven by the statute to allow such a thing.

6.46 Indeed, such an analysis of *Anisminic* was expressly advanced by the Court of Appeal in *R (G) v Immigration Appeal Tribunal*.[1] The two claimants in *G* had been refused asylum by special adjudicators. Subsequent applications for permission to appeal had also been refused by the Immigration Appeal Tribunal. Each claimant then applied unsuccessfully to the High Court for a review of the Immigration Appeal Tribunal's decision in their case under s 101(2) of the Nationality, Immigration and Asylum Act 2002. The question for the Court of Appeal was whether the claimants should be permitted in these circumstances to bring a judicial review so as to mount a further challenge to the Immigration Appeal Tribunal's refusal of permission to appeal. It was not argued before the Court of Appeal that s 101 of the 2002 Act ousted the court's jurisdiction to entertain such judicial reviews and thus the issue was merely whether such claims should ordinarily be refused as a matter of the court's discretion. Nevertheless, the court made some important remarks about the relationship between the rule of law and the ability of Parliament to oust the judicial review jurisdiction of the courts. The crucial passages, for our purposes, are to be found in paragraphs 12 and 13 of the Court of Appeal's judgment:

'It is the role of the judges to preserve the rule of law. The importance of that role has long been recognised by Parliament. It is a constitutional norm recognised by statutory provisions that protect the independence of the judiciary, such as sections 11 and 12 of the Supreme Court Act 1981. It is recognised by statutory provisions that define the jurisdiction of the judges, such as section 15 of the Supreme Court Act 1981. It is recognised by a large number of statutory provisions which confer on the citizen the right to appeal to a court against decisions of tribunals.

These rights are additional to the common law right of the citizen to have access to the courts. In particular, they are additional to the right of the citizen, subject to the permission of the court, to seek judicial review by the High Court of administrative decisions. *The common law power of the judges to review the legality of administrative action is a cornerstone of the rule of law in this country and one that the judges guard jealously.* If Parliament attempts by legislation to remove that power, the rule of law is threatened. The courts will not readily accept that legislation achieves that end: see *Anisminic* . . . ' [emphasis added].

¹ [2005] 1 WLR 1445.

6.47 The principle for which we contend can also be seen at work in a second Court of Appeal case: *R (Sivasubramaniam) v Wandsworth County Council.*¹ *Sivasubramaniam* concerned how the judicial review jurisdiction of the courts should be reconciled with the new procedural regime governing appeals in civil cases that had been introduced under the Access to Justice Act 1999. The Act did not expressly seek to oust that jurisdiction. Nevertheless, it was argued on behalf of the Lord Chancellor's Department that it was *implicit* in the Act that the decision of an appeal court refusing permission to appeal was not susceptible to judicial review challenge. This argument was however confidently rejected by the Court of Appeal on the following basis:

> 'Nearly 50 years ago Denning LJ stated in *R v Medical Appeal Tribunal, ex p Gilmore* [1957] 1 QB 574, 583 that "the remedy by certiorari is never to be taken away by any statute except by the most clear and explicit words". All the authorities to which we have been referred indicate that this remains true today. The weight of authority makes it impossible to accept that the jurisdiction to subject a decision to judicial review can be removed by statutory *implication*'.

¹ [2003] 1 WLR 475.

6.48 The principle also lies behind the cases concerned with inferior courts, which are discussed above. The distinction between inferior courts and administrative tribunals, whereby the court may construe an ouster provision to allow greater latitude to the former, cannot surely be attributed to anything save a concern with the rule of law.

6.49 Our analysis is also borne out by the attitude of the courts towards those provisions in the planning Acts and similar legislation that limit rather than exclude the jurisdiction of the courts to review the exercise of public power. Such provisions repay somewhat deeper scrutiny, because here the courts have held that the measures in question *do* constitute a successful ouster of judicial review as a common law remedy.

6.50 Section 284 of the Town and Country Planning Act 1990 provides in part:

> '(1) Except in so far as may be provided by this Part, the validity of:
>
> . . .
>
> (f) any such action on the part of the Secretary of State as is mentioned in subsection (3), shall not be questioned in any legal proceedings whatsoever.
>
> . . .
>
> (3) The action referred to in subsection (1)(f) is action on the part of the Secretary of State and of the following descriptions
>
> . . .
>
> (b) any decision given on an appeal under section 78 . . . '.

6.51 Section 78 empowers appeals to the Secretary of State against refusal of planning permission, or grant of permission subject to conditions. Section 288 provides in part:

> '(1)   If any person:
> (b)   is aggrieved by any action on the part of the Secretary of State to which this section applies and wishes to question the validity of that action, on the grounds:
> (i)   that the action is not within the powers of this Act, or
> (ii)   that any of the relevant requirements have not been complied with in relation to that action, he may make an application to the High Court under this section'.

6.52 Section 288(3) provides that such an application must be made within six weeks from the date on which the action is taken, and subsection (4) applies the section to actions mentioned in s 284(3), thus including decisions on s 78 appeals.

6.53 Section 288 creates (or, more accurately, continues) a form of statutory judicial review. But the jurisdiction which it confers can only be exercised if an application is brought within the six-week time limit. That limit is not a mere procedural bar which can be lifted in the court's discretion: the court has no power to entertain a late application.[1] *R v Secretary of State for the Environment, ex p Kent*[2] shows that even though, because of the fault of the local planning authority, an applicant was wholly unaware that an appeal had been brought and a decision made until after expiry of the six-week period, still time would run against him from the date of the decision. Against this background, s 284 is effective to exclude the operation of common law judicial review upon a s 78 appeal: see, again, *East Elloe* and *Ostler*. *East Elloe*, in fact, was a case of an action brought, after the six-week period, to assault a compulsory purchase order by means of injunction and declaration; and the claim included allegations of fraud. *Ostler* was an application for certiorari. Both claims fell on the ground that the court was prevented from entertaining them by reason of the statutory bar in the legislation, which was a precise equivalent of s 284 of the Act of 1990. In *Ostler*, Lord Denning MR said (at 135B–D):

> 'I think that *Smith v East Elloe Rural District Council* must still be regarded as good and binding on this court. It is readily to be distinguished from the *Anisminic* case . . . The points of difference are these:
>
> > "First, in the *Anisminic* case the Act ousted the jurisdiction of the court altogether. It precluded the court from entertaining any complaint at any time about the determination. Whereas in the *East Elloe* case the statutory provision has given the court jurisdiction to inquire into complaints so long as the applicant comes within six weeks. The provision is more in the nature of a limitation period than of a complete ouster".'

---

[1]   For example. *Smith v East Elloe* [1956] AC 736, [1956] 1 All ER 855; *ex p Ostler* [1977] QB 122, [1976] 3 All ER 90 (these were cases under the compulsory purchase legislation, but the statutory scheme is the same).
[2]   (1988) 57 P & CR 431.

6.54 Thus, applying this reasoning to the relevant sections of the Act of 1990, the true construction of s 284(1) is critically affected by the existence of s 288.

The decision in *Ostler* involves a judicial perception to the effect that the ouster may be allowed to run because s 288 means that the rule of law is not abrogated. The very statute which actually or purportedly excludes jurisdiction, in a different breath confers it. The common law allows Parliament to regulate the rule of law's policing. We can be very sure that were it not for s 288 a different approach would be taken to the construction of s 284.

6.55 In summary, then, judges may accept the common law account of judicial review without losing their ability to subject ouster clauses to searching scrutiny. Forsyth is thus wrong to contend that the adoption of the common law account would risk undermining the judiciary's ability to resist such clauses.

Collateral challenges

6.56 Public law acts or decisions may be subjected to collateral challenge outside of the confines of judicial review.[1] In *Wandsworth London Borough Council v Winder*,[2] the local authority brought proceedings against a council tenant for arrears of rent. Mr Winder's defence was that the resolution setting the rents was ultra vires. The House of Lords held that such defences could be raised, and if raised must be adjudicated upon, in the proceedings in which the defendants were taken to court, notwithstanding that they were not judicial review proceedings. More recently, in *Boddington v British Transport Police*.[3] the House of Lords unanimously confirmed that a defendant who was charged with an offence under a byelaw could raise as a defence a contention that the relevant byelaw was unlawful.

[1] Further discussion is in Chapter 5 at 5.47 and Chapter 16.
[2] [1985] AC 461.
[3] [1999] 2 AC 143.

6.57 Forsyth argues that the ultra vires theory is required in order to ensure that such collateral challenges may be brought in criminal proceedings.[1] Thus, in a case such as *Boddington*, the suggestion is that the ultra vires theory is necessary in order to permit the magistrates' court properly to consider a defence that the byelaw in question was invalid. The argument is put by Forsyth as follows:

> 'Now the magistrates' court before which the invalidity of a byelaw might be raised as a defence has no power to issue *certiorari* and quash an invalid byelaw. Thus the success of such a collateral (or defensive) challenge depends upon the invalid byelaw being void, not voidable (for otherwise the byelaw would still exist in law and have to be applied by the court). And an act done beyond the legal power of the actor (ie an ultra vires act) is non-existent in law or void. Thus the rule of law requires that collateral challenges should be generally available, which requires that unlawful acts should be void not voidable which requires that they should be ultra vires'.

[1] Forsyth (2000), p 407.

6.58 However, the fact that, in collateral challenge cases, the court will give effect to its conclusion that a decision is unlawful by refusing relief to a claimant or prosecutor who seeks to rely on the decision confers no utility on the void/voidable distinction in the judicial review context. It merely serves to demonstrate that, as a matter of judicial policy, the courts have recognised a class of case *outside* judicial review in which they will refuse to uphold a bad decision. In short, unlawful decisions are always at risk: and the courts have decided to take two approaches to them:

(1)   first, that in judicial review cases the risk is subject to the court's discretion to give relief; and

(2)   second, that an unlawful decision will not be allowed to prevail when its unlawfulness is raised by way of defence against a public law body which brings proceedings in reliance on it.

6.59 None of this requires recourse to be had to the metaphysic of nullity. Indeed to suggest otherwise is to beg the true question: Forsyth's argument must be that since a bad decision is, in the collateral cases, denied legal effect *without* its being quashed, the decision has to be categorised as void because otherwise the court would be bound to uphold it. This assumes, however, what must be demonstrated, namely that the label of nullity must be attached to a decision before the court can, absent a quashing order, refuse to give effect to it. But this is a false assumption: in the collateral case the court is faced with a defendant who correctly asserts that the decision prayed in aid against him was unlawfully made; the court's response to such a state of affairs is then a matter of judicial policy, and the clear policy of the courts is to allow such a defence to prevail.

6.60 While for these reasons the collateral cases do not generate a requirement for the void/voidable distinction to be maintained as a useful or necessary concept in public law, it has nevertheless to be recognised that they give rise to serious difficulties. In the first of the 1989 Hamlyn Lectures,[1] Lord Woolf says at pp 30–31:

> 'I would, however, have expected there to have been some indication by the House of Lords [in *Winder*] that the right to rely on the defence would be subject to the court exercising its discretion in the same way as it would on an application for judicial review, and therefore that it would be preferable for the case to be transferred to the High Court so that it could be heard by one of the nominated judges who would have heard the application for judicial review. I am, however, appalled that a situation should be able to arise where Mr Winder would not succeed on an application for judicial review because the court would not exercise discretion in his favour but he could still succeed on the same facts as a defence and for the purposes of obtaining a declaration by way of counterclaim. It appears that for no good reason we now have as a result of the *Winder* case not only an understandable exception to the *O'Reilly v Mackman* principle but also have accepted that different standards will apply where the invalidity of a council decision is relied on as a defence from those which will apply when it is relied on as the grounds for an application for judicial review . . .

> The problem may be related to the fact that the courts have yet to establish clearly the effect of a decision being void'.

[1]   *'Protection of the Public* – A New Challenge' (1990) Stevens & Sons.

6.61 The principal difficulty here is that first identified by Lord Woolf: in allowing public law points to be taken by way of defence in private law proceedings or criminal prosecutions, the courts have not made any room for the exercise of discretion in deciding whether or not the defence should prevail.

Accordingly, a defendant in such a case is in a better position than an applicant for judicial review who raises precisely the same public law complaint. And this problem is incapable of being resolved by any appeal to the notion of voidness; in judicial review cases a successful assertion that the impugned decision is 'void' does not guarantee relief to the applicant. The court may as much refuse relief as in a case where the decision is not characterised as 'void'.

6.62 It may be said that a defendant should have larger rights than a judicial review applicant precisely because he is a defendant: it is not his choice that he is in court; unless his defence, good as it is on its legal merits, is allowed to prevail, he will be subjected to a civil judgment or criminal penalty. But there are cases daily heard in the Administrative Court List in which, unless the claimant succeeds, he will be adversely affected by the decision in question as surely as if the defendant public authority had made the first move and sought to enforce it against him by proceedings.

6.63 On analysis, therefore, the collateral cases are incapable of underpinning a theory which rests public law jurisdiction on the 'ultra vires' doctrine. At most, they disclose an anomaly arising from the dislocation between the discretionary nature of judicial review remedies and the non-discretionary nature of defences in private law or criminal proceedings.

The position of the courts

6.64 In claiming that the courts have accepted the ultra vires theory as being the proper articulation of the basis for judicial review, Forsyth points, understandably, to the decisions of the House of Lords in *R v Lord President of the Privy Council, ex p Page*[1] and *Boddington*.[2] In *Page*, Lord Browne-Wilkinson said this at 701C–E:

> 'The fundamental principle [of judicial review] is that the courts will intervene to ensure that the powers of public decision-making bodies are exercised lawfully. In all cases, save possibly one, this intervention by way of prohibition or certiorari is based on the proposition that such powers have been conferred on the decision-maker on the underlying assumption that the powers are to be exercised only within the jurisdiction conferred, in accordance with fair procedures and, in a *Wednesbury* sense . . . reasonably. If the decision-maker exercises his powers outside the jurisdiction conferred, in a manner which is procedurally irregular or is *Wednesbury* unreasonable, he is acting ultra vires his powers and therefore unlawfully . . . .'.

[1] [1993] AC 682.
[2] See Forsyth, 'Collateral Challenge and the Foundation of Judicial Review: Orthodoxy Vindicated and Procedural Exclusivity Rejected' [1998] PL 364 and 'Of Fig Leaves and Fairy Tales: The *Ultra Vires* Doctrine, the Sovereignty of Parliament and Judicial Review', Vol 55 [1996] CLJ 122, p 135.

6.65 There then follows at 701F–G a passage in Lord Browne-Wilkinson's speech that undoubtedly bears strong similarities to the modified ultra vires position:

> 'In my judgment the decision in *Anisminic* . . . rendered obsolete the distinction between errors of law on the face of the record and other errors of law by extending the doctrine of ultra vires. Thenceforward it was to be taken that Parliament had

only conferred the decision-making power on the basis that it was to be exercised on the correct legal basis: a misdirection in law in making the decision therefore rendered the decision ultra vires'.

6.66 In the more recent case of *Boddington*, Lord Browne-Wilkinson stated in a brief speech that he adhered to his view 'that the juristic basis of judicial review is the doctrine of ultra vires' (164B). Further, Lord Steyn, who cited Lord Browne-Wilkinson in *Page* with approval, stated (at 171F–G):

'Leaving to one side the separate topic of judicial review of non-legal powers exercised by non statutory bodies, I see no reason to depart from the orthodox view that ultra vires is "the central principle of administrative law" as *Wade and Forsyth* . . . described it'.[1]

---

[1] See also Lord Irvine LC at 154B–154D and 158E–158F.

6.67 However, in our respectful view, these dicta are not sufficient to establish that the ultra vires theory has, in fact, been generally taken by the courts to be the true basis for judicial review. Indeed, as Forsyth seems compelled to admit, Lord Steyn's approval of the proposition that ultra vires is the central principle of administrative law was made 'without consideration of the constitutional questions'.[1] Thus, for instance, there is no debate in the speeches in *Page* or *Boddington* of whether the rejection of the ultra vires theory and the adoption of a common law account of judicial review would amount to an assault on Parliamentary sovereignty. It cannot therefore be assumed that their Lordships were addressing their minds to the deeper constitutional issues that have been discussed in this chapter. Indeed, there is nothing to indicate that any of the judges in these two cases considered that an adoption of the common law account of judicial review would have prevented them from making precisely the same rulings as were in fact made.

---

[1] Wade & Forsyth (2009), p 30 at fn 61.

6.68 Further, *Boddington* has not been taken by the courts to have authoritatively established that the ultra vires theory is the true basis for judicial review. Thus, in the more recent case of *G* (in which *Boddington* was cited in argument), a unanimous Court of Appeal took the power of the judges to review the legality of administrative action to be a *common law* power.[1]

---

[1] See the passage cited at **6.46** above.

6.69 Further, as Jeffrey Jowell has pointed out, 'the very general statement that ultra vires is the foundation of judicial review massively begs the question of what we mean by *vires*'.[1] In *Page* itself, Lord Browne-Wilkinson's statement that a tribunal or inferior court acts ultra vires if it reaches its conclusion on a basis erroneous under what was referred to as the 'general law of the land' arguably suggests that he was concerned with a notion of vires that went beyond the intent of Parliament and included principles derived solely from the common law. Further, Jowell himself notes that the speeches of both Lord Steyn and Lord Browne-Wilkinson in *R v Secretary of State for the Home Department, ex p Pierson*[2] can be seen to support a wider notion of vires that permits the courts to look beyond the implied intention of Parliament and engage directly with constitutional principle.[3]

1   Jeffrey Jowell, 'Of Vires and Vacuums: The Constitutional Context of Judicial Review'. Ch 15 of 'Judicial Review and the Constitution' (2000) Hart Publishing, ed Forsyth, p 337.
2   [1998] AC 539.
3   Jeffrey Jowell (2000), p 337.

6.70 In seeking to determine the attitude of the courts to the competing models of judicial review it is, we think, useful also to consider the reasoning in those cases where the courts have contemplated extending the scope of judicial review into areas where public power is exercised without direct statutory authority. In particular, the two rival accounts of the foundation of judicial review that we have been considering should result in very different forms of judicial reasoning in such cases. Under the common law account, as has already been noted, the basis for intervention – the common law – is the same whether what is at issue is a statutory power or a power that lacks statutory underpinning such as a prerogative power. Those who support some form of the ultra vires theory claim that the implied intention of Parliament justifies judicial review in the ordinary case, but they are compelled to accept that, where the decision under review lacks any statutory underpinning, the justification for judicial intervention is to be found in a quite separate source – the common law.

6.71 Thus, if judges were truly committed to the ultra vires theory of judicial review, then we would expect the court's reasoning, in any case where an extension of judicial review beyond its traditional limits was being contemplated, to contain clear and express recognition of the fact that such an extension would lead the court to enter into a form of review that was wholly distinct, in terms of its juridical foundation, from that which had gone before. But, of course, there is no such indication in the relevant cases. Thus, for instance, there is no suggestion in *CCSU* – a true milestone in the courts' articulation of the judicial review jurisdiction – that reviewing a prerogative power would be an exercise that required some distinct and separate justification from that which legitimised the intervention of the courts in ordinary judicial review claims. On the contrary, their Lordships expressly rejected the notion that the availability of judicial review should turn on the source of the power the exercise of which was at issue. As Lord Diplock said in his celebrated speech in that case:

> 'I see no reason why simply because a decision-making power is derived from a common law and not a statutory source, it should *for that reason only* be immune from judicial review'.[1]

1   At 410C–410D. See, also, to similar effect, Lord Scarman at 407F–407G and Lord Roskill at 417G–417H.

6.72 Further, Lord Diplock's famous tripartite account of the grounds of judicial review, which immediately follow this statement, is expressed in general terms without regard to the source of the power at issue.

6.73 *Datafin* provides a further telling illustration of the point. It is clear that no member of the Court of Appeal in that case considered that a review of a decision of the Take-over Panel would be a form of judicial scrutiny that was entirely distinct, in terms of its foundations, from a review of an exercise of statutory power. The court was again more concerned with the nature of the power at issue, than its source. As Lloyd LJ said (at 845F–G):

'The panel wields enormous power. It has a giant's strength. The fact that it is self-regulating, which means, presumably, that it is not subject to regulation by others, and in particular by the Department of Trade and Industry, makes it not less but more appropriate that it should be subject to judicial review by the courts'.

6.74 And, in the same vein, Lloyd LJ remarked at 846C–D:

'So long as there is a possibility, however remote, of the panel abusing its great powers, then it would be wrong for the courts to abdicate responsibility. The courts must remain ready, willing and able to hear a legitimate complaint in this as in any other field of our national life'.

6.75 In the light of the above, it cannot be said that the courts have conclusively adopted the modified ultra vires theory as the true basis for judicial review. Indeed, a number of important authorities offer clear support for the common law position that has been set out.[1]

---

[1]   For further support for the proposition that the justification for the courts' judicial review lies not in the intention of Parliament, but rather in the common law's promotion of the rule of law, see the recent case of *R (Cart) v Upper Tribunal (Secretary of State for Justice, interested party) (Public Law Project intervening)* [2010] EWCA Civ 859 at para 28 [2011] QB 120, at para 28,[2010] 4 All ER 714 at para 28 per Sedley LJ, and in the Supreme Court ([2011] UKSC 28 [2012] 1 AC 663), at paras 32 and 37, per Lady Hale JSC.

THE SIGNIFICANCE OF THE DEBATE

6.76 The advent of the Human Rights Act 1998 has lessened the significance of the debate between those who support some form of ultra vires theory and those who advocate the common law position. Prior to the 1998 Act, the extent to which human rights jurisprudence could have an influence in the domestic context was in large part dependent upon the degree to which the courts considered themselves free – in the absence of legislation incorporating the Convention into domestic law – to refashion the traditional principles of judicial review so as to achieve that end. In this context, the question of precisely what justified the courts' powers of review assumed a particular importance. Now that the 1998 Act has brought Convention law principles into our domestic law, the position has changed. Judges are bound to review decisions on the basis of human rights law principles and, in so doing, they are unquestionably putting into effect Parliament's express will. There is no longer any need for supporters of human rights law principles to articulate an account of judicial review's foundations that would permit reliance to be placed on such principles in the domestic courts: Parliament has itself taken the necessary steps by enacting the Human Rights Act 1998. This is made clear by Lord Bingham's speech in *R (Baiai) v Secretary of State for the Home Department*[1]

'The court cannot abdicate its function of deciding whether as a matter of law the scheme, as promulgated and operated, violates the respondents' right to marry guaranteed by article 12'.

---

[1]   [2008] 3 WLR 549 at [25].

6.77 Furthermore, on the face of it, the position we take does not look very different from Forsyth's 'reconciliation' of the 'weak' criticisms with what he regards as orthodoxy. We agree that Parliament may at any stage legislate so as to change, curtail, or qualify the common law doctrines of rationality and the rest. In addition, as argued above, the common law account of judicial review renders the courts no less able to resist ouster clauses or to allow collateral challenges than the ultra vires theory. Thus, it is difficult to see how the outcome of any individual case would turn on whether the court adopted the common law account or, its rival, the ultra vires theory.

6.78 What, then, is the value of the debate? First, in the authors' opinion, there is simply an intrinsic value in determining the precise theoretical basis for judicial review, not least given the vital place of that jurisdiction in the overall constitutional order. But, second, there is a merit in preferring the common law account over the ultra vires theory as the former is likely to be more conducive to the principled development of the law.

6.79 Unlike the ultra vires theory, the common law account does not need to introduce any artificial distinctions between cases where the exercise of a statutory power is under challenge and those where the courts are reviewing public power wielded without such statutory authority. Under the common law account the court tests the lawfulness of the exercise of power by reference to the same common law principles regardless of whether what is under review is a statutory power, a prerogative power or a common law power of a non-statutory body. Such an approach can only be of assistance in ensuring a coherent development of public law.

6.80 More fundamentally, the common law account allows for a more coherent development of the law generally. In the sphere of private law, there are numerous means, such as the doctrine of unlawful restraint of trade, by which the courts can protect individuals from the abuse of power. In many instances, the principles that are applied bear strong similarities to their counterparts in public law. Thus, as Dawn Oliver has cogently argued, the court's equitable jurisdiction in trusts resembles in many aspects the common law jurisdiction in judicial review:

> 'Public decision-makers and trustees must act in accordance with the intention of the body from whom their power derives – respectively Parliament (normally) or the settlor. Neither public decision-makers nor trustees must act capriciously or "*Wednesbury* unreasonably", nor must they act for ulterior or improper purposes. Both must take account of relevant considerations, and not be influenced by irrelevant considerations. They may take into account ethical considerations, as long as they do not allow these to run counter to the overall purpose of their functions. They must exercise discretions with an open mind. They may not delegate their discretions to others, or fetter their discretion'.[1]

---

[1]   Oliver, 'Review of (Non-statutory) Discretions', Ch 14 of 'Judicial Review and the Constitution' (2000) Hart Publishing, ed Forsyth, p 311.

6.81 Further examples include the duties imposed on membership associations and regulatory bodies to act towards, respectively, their members and those they regulate with due respect for procedural propriety[1] and the duty, in employment law, to exercise ostensibly unfettered contractual discretions within the bounds of rationality.[2]

1   See Oliver (2000), pp 317 and 318.
2   *Clark v Nomura International plc* [2000] IRLR 766.

6.82 Freeing judicial review from the need to be grounded in Parliamentary intent – as the common law account does – permits and encourages a greater dialogue to be had between those different branches of the law in which the courts scrutinise the exercise of power. In a precedent-based system where past wisdom often provides the source and inspiration for fresh developments in the common law, such increased dialogue is to be welcomed. Further, as has been noted in the academic literature, this process brings with it the promise of a more principled and unified account of how the courts can provide redress for the abuse of power, whatever its source.[1]

1   See Oliver, (2000) and Sir Stephen Sedley, 'Public Power and Private Power'. Ch 13 of 'Judicial Review and the Constitution'.

CONCLUSIONS

6.83 It is submitted that nothing of substance has been found in Forsyth's account of the ultra vires rule save that whatever it is it must be (and be no more than) some form of self-denying ordinance. He and Wade say that:

> 'the simple proposition that a public authority may not act outside its powers (ultra vires) might fitly be called the central principle of administrative law'.[1]

1   Wade & Forsyth (2009), p 30.

6.84 But the proposition has no force as a description of the court's jurisdiction unless the authority's powers are defined by a body other than the court. Otherwise, it tells us no more than that public bodies must obey the law. Everyone committed to the rule of law will no doubt agree with that; it is, as the philosophers say, true but uninteresting. It says nothing about the nature or source of a decision-maker's power, nor does it offer any analysis of the constitutional quality of the courts' authority.

6.85 Forsyth's discussion of ultra vires seems to show that he has in mind only that the judges are bound to apply Parliament's law, given in main legislation. Thus, he argues:

> 'they have no constitutional right to interfere with action which is within the powers granted (intra vires): if it is within jurisdiction, and therefore authorised by Parliament, the court has no right to treat it as unlawful . . . Having no written constitution on which he can fall back, the judge must in every case be able to demonstrate that he is carrying out the will of Parliament as expressed in the statute conferring the power. He is on safe ground only where he can show that the offending act is outside the power'.[1]

1   Wade & Forsyth (2009), p 31.

6.86 But the court's obedience to Parliament is, as we have indicated, a *judge-made* rule. It is important to recognise that this is a necessary, not merely a contingent truth. We have said that Parliament cannot confer power on itself.[1] More tightly, Parliament cannot create any duty of obedience to its dictates. But this is merely an example of a deeper reality, which lies outside the law: the fact that X issues a command is never *of itself* a reason to obey X. In moral philosophy it is expressed in Hume's Law, that is, the principle of logic that you cannot derive an *ought* from an *is*. The proposition that you ought to obey X cannot be inferred or deduced from the fact only that X tells you to do so, and this is true whatever the identity of X (even if X is God). There must always be a higher premise, to the effect that if X issues command Y, there arises a duty (whether upon an individual, a group, or the whole of society) to obey Y. The higher premise cannot consist in Y, and X cannot be the source of it.

[1]   See note 1, **6.2**.

6.87 In our constitution, the duty to obey Parliament is given by the common law. The common law is the higher premise. However, it may at once be objected upon our own reasoning that any obligation to abide by the common law itself requires a higher premise no less than does the duty to obey Parliament. So far as it goes, this is true. But the common law represents the historical consensus of community, ultimately the fact of organised society itself, the rejection of anarchy. It marks in concrete form the will of the people, which confers its authority, and so constitutes the necessary major premise. Here the will of the people means something quite different from the democratic voice that elects Parliament. In the latter case the phrase is, in essence at least, a shorthand for the moral legitimacy conferred on government by democratic elections. In the former it does not refer to any particular form of executive rule. It is shorthand of a different kind. It represents a collection of fundamental civic aspirations which in one form or another are a necessary reflection of our nature as rational beings, possessed of free will, living in community with others of our kind: justice, freedom and order. The common law has to give effect to these aspirations, because they are its *fons et origo*. If the judges were to deny them, they would not merely act unwisely; they would contradict the very basis of their own existence, and we would not recognise what they do as law. It is not, of course, to say that bad decisions are never made; plainly from time to time they are. Nor is it to say that the content of these core values is static. The judges of a hundred (and less) years ago would, for example, be astonished by their modern successors' views about such matters as equal treatment without respect to class, sex, or race.

6.88 The content of the common law, therefore, is by necessity limited. Its substance is by very definition bound to consist in an articulation of these aspirations, justice, freedom and order. Their reach, their colour, and their bite may alter across generations; and in difficult cases they will cut and clash against each other. But they remain the inevitable fundamentals of the law.

6.89 However, Parliament's law is not so confined. Indeed, it is not confined at all. On conventional doctrine Parliament may pass any law it likes, upon any subject-matter. As our constitutional arrangements are presently understood, the potential content of Parliament's law has no limits whatever.[1] Accordingly, it is a matter of contingent good fortune if Parliament does good things. This is a function of the very fact, and the heavy burden, of its absolute power. Its power being absolute, it is of necessity morally neutral, for it is a condition of any morality that the actor in question recognises supervening limits on his freedom of action: they define him as a moral being. But Parliament is not constrained by any definition of itself.[2] Its virtue is its democratic credentials and accountability to the electorate. It is constrained by the ballot-box, the conscience and wisdom of its members, and by the traditions of British Government. Given all these considerations, we may see that Wade and Forsyth's description of the ultra vires rule as the foundation of the court's constitutional function puts the cart before the horse. The common law is logically prior to statute. The common law's obedience to Parliament is neither a defining limitation of it nor an axiom on which its jurisdiction proceeds.

[1] Our membership of the European Union (ongoing until 'Brexit' occurs) constitutes no exception to this, since as a matter of law it is open to Parliament to repeal the European Communities Act 1972. For the special position of Acts passed under the Parliament Act 1911, see *R (Jackson) v Attorney General* [2006] 1 AC 262.

[2] Save as regards established rules relating to the form of primary legislation.

Chapter 7

DISCRETION AND DUTY: THE LIMITS OF LEGALITY

INTRODUCTION

7.1 This chapter is concerned with discretions and duties. In that context it examines the first ground of review identified by Lord Diplock in *Council of Civil Service Unions v Minister for the Civil Service ('CCSU')*:[1] the decision-maker must understand correctly the law that regulates the decision-making power and must give effect to it.[2]

[1] [1985] AC 374; [1984] 3 WLR 1174; [1984] 3 All ER 935.

2   For Scots law on this topic, see **22.60** et seq.

7.2 It is important to keep in mind the place of judicial review within the overall framework of legal and political control of the actions of public bodies. Although with respect to certain types of decisions the courts have been more willing to come closer to considering the merits of that decision, the statement that 'Judicial review is concerned, not with the decision, but with the decision making process' remains apt.[1] Decisions taken in the exercise of discretionary powers may be open to appeal; depending on the available ranges of grounds of appeal in a particular case this may offer greater opportunity to re-open the exercise of discretion on its merits.[2] Alternative means of seeking redress, such as resort to the Parliamentary Commissioner for Administration or Commissioner for Local Administration, or to one of the increasing number of regulatory or watchdog authorities, may also, on occasion, be more convenient and effective. Judicial review is a remedy of last, rather than first, resort, albeit that its importance in enabling the courts to set down general principles of administrative legality is a central feature of the maintenance of government according to law. In relation to judicial review of discretionary decisions, it should also be remembered that grounds of review include those which are not special to discretion, in particular, those concerned with procedural propriety, and the existence or non-existence of the preconditions to a body having jurisdiction.

1   Per Lord Brightman in *Chief Constable of North Wales Police v Evans* [1982] 1 WLR 1155; [1982] 3 All ER 141 at 1173.
2   Judicial review remedies are themselves discretionary. The existence of a right of appeal may also be a reason for refusal, as a matter of judicial practice or discretion as to relief, to intervene by way of a remedy on judicial review. This is especially so where the matter giving rise to the application for review could have formed a ground of appeal.

7.3 In the context of discretionary powers, the role of judicial review is also affected by the nature of the remedies available. The court's concern is legality, not, as such, merits, and it will therefore be rare for the court to be willing to require a discretion to be exercised in a particular way.[1] The more usual form of mandatory relief is to consider and determine the matter in accordance with law, including whatever conclusions as to the meaning of relevant law the court may give in its judgment. Unless the only discretion vested in the decision-taker is whether to do a particular act, the court cannot determine (although it may influence) the outcome of exercising a discretionary power.

1   *Padfield v Minister of Agriculture, Fisheries and Food* [1968] AC 997; [1968] 2 WLR 924; [1968] 1 All ER 694 is an example; see **7.8** below.

DISCRETION AND DUTY

7.4 The distinction between a discretion and a duty is superficially, but deceptively, simple. It is succinctly stated in the (Northern Ireland) Interpretation Act 1954, s 38 thus: ' . . . the expression "shall" shall be construed as imperative and the expression "may" as permissive and empowering'. This understanding of the meaning of the words 'shall' and 'may' has been cited in numerous cases, where it has been emphasised that 'may' denotes an executive discretion whereas 'shall' is to be interpreted as connoting a mandatory provision.[1]

In reality matters are far from simple: a power may confer any of a number of degrees of distinction on a continuum from the virtual imposition of a duty to act to an almost unrestricted discretion. The nature of a power in each case depends heavily on statutory construction.[2] As Lord Wilberforce has noted,[3] 'there is no universal rule as to the principles on which the exercise of a discretion may be reviewed: each statute or type of statute must be individually looked at'. Moreover it is not just the wording of the enabling provision, important though that is, which requires examination. The purpose of the conferment of power must also be considered, and to this end the rest of the statute may need to be taken into account as disclosing the overall Parliamentary intention and the context within which the power was conferred.[4] It will be apparent that the opportunity for the courts to restrict or enlarge the ambit of discretionary powers for reasons of general policy lies just beneath the surface of this, as of many aspects of statutory construction. In particular the views of judges as to the desirability, by reference to general considerations of public policy, of strictly controlling certain repositories and categories of power can be put into effect in this way.[5] Moreover, the influence of the context and purpose of the Act may be of greater importance than the mere wording of the power, as the following case illustrates.

[1] For example see *London & Clydeside Estates Ltd v Aberdeen District Council* [1980] 1 WLR 182; [1979] 3 All ER 876 at 201H, where it was said that

'the word "shall" . . . is normally to be interpreted as connoting a mandatory provision, meaning that what is thereby enjoined is not merely desired to be done but must be done' and *Holgate-Mohammed v Duke* [1984] AC 437 [1984] 2 WLR 660; [1984] 1 All ER 1054 at 443.

[2] Or analysis of case law where the power is part of the royal prerogative.

[3] *Secretary of State for Education and Science v Tameside Metropolitan Borough Council* [1977] AC 1014; [1976] 3 WLR 641; [1976] 3 All ER 665 at 1047.

[4] Cf Lord Reid in *Padfield* at 1030C: 'Parliament must have conferred the discretion with the intention that it should be used to promote the policy and objects of the Act; the policy and objects of the Act must be determined by construing the Act as a whole and construction is always a matter of law for the court'. Cf also the conclusion of the House of Lords in *R v Soneji* [2005] UKHL 49; [2006] 1 AC 340; [2005] 3 WLR 303 that the correct approach to the legal consequences of a failure to comply with a procedural precondition to the exercise of a power is to ask whether it was a purpose of the legislature that an act done in breach of that provision should be invalid; and see further CHAPTER 10 at 10.1–10.5 below.

[5] This also reflects changes in judicial attitudes over a period of time. The mushrooming of Administrative Law in the 1970s and since suggests that earlier cases disclosing reluctance to intervene need to be approached with caution as guides to even closely similar wording. (But there are plenty of examples of earlier judicial activism also). The policy emphasis has also been intensified by the additional dimension in an increasing number of cases of EU law (see CHAPTER 15); an example is *Sita UK Ltd v Greater Manchester Waste Disposal Authority* [2011] EWCA Civ 156; [2012] PTSR 645 at 651, where the Court of Appeal held that the EU principle of effectiveness may convert the court's discretion to extend time into a duty. As to the impact of Convention Rights and the Human Rights Act 1998, see further at 7.26 below; CHAPTER 4 and CHAPTER 9.

7.5 In *R v Mitchell, ex parte Livesey*,[1] a statute provided that a person charged under the Act 'may . . . declare that he objects to being tried for such offence by a court of summary jurisdiction, and thereupon the court of summary jurisdiction *may* [emphasis added] deal with the case in all respects as if the accused were charged with an indictable offence'.[2] This was construed by the Divisional Court as conferring a right to jury trial and therefore imposing an obligation on the court to accede to the accused's objection. In this context, as Lord Coleridge CJ put it, 'the word "may" is compulsory and not discretionary'.[3] Here, the context and purpose of the statutory provision clearly established a duty, a conclusion perhaps facilitated by the suitability of the issue for judicial review. In other contexts apparently mandatory language may be construed to create no more than a discretion: alternatively the various stages within a particular statutory power may be interpreted as subject to differing degrees of mandatory status.[4]

[1] [1913] 1 KB 561.

[2] Conspiracy, and Protection of Property Act 1875, s 9 (now repealed), relating to offences under s 7 (now re-enacted in the Trade Union and Labour Relations (Consolidation) Act 1992, s 241).

[3] Loc cit at p 571. The headnote offers the proposition that 'the word "may" is an enabling word empowering the court to give effect to the right of the accused, which accordingly that court is bound to do'. See, also, *Sheffield Corpn v Luxford* [1929] 2 KB 180. In *Singh (Pargan) v Secretary of State for the Home Department* [1992] 1 WLR 1052; [1992] 4 All ER 673 the House of Lords held that the word 'may' in a provision relating to the making of regulations by the Secretary of State in an immigration context, did not mean he had a discretion whether or not to make the regulations. Lord Jauncey stated at 1056 F–G:

> 'In my view Parliament intended that the Secretary of State should be required to make regulations which would ensure, so far as practicable, that persons upon whom the rights of appeal had been conferred should be enabled effectively to exercise those rights. It follows that the Secretary of State does not have a discretion as to whether or not he shall make regulations'

[4] Compare the reluctance of the courts to construe the duty of chief constables to enforce the law as excluding a considerable measure of operational discretion: *R v Metropolitan Police Comr, ex parte Blackburn* [1968] 2 QB 118, [1968] 1 All ER 763; *R v Metropolitan Police Comr, ex parte Blackburn (No 3)* [1973] QB 241, [1973] 1 All ER 324; *R v Chief Constable of Devon and Cornwall, ex parte Central Electricity Generating Board* [1982] QB 458, [1981] 3 All ER 826; *R v Chief Constable of Sussex, ex parte International Trader's Ferry Ltd* [1999] 2 AC 418; [1998] 3 WLR 1260; [1999] 1 All ER 129. Cf also *Vince v Chief Constable of the Dorset Police* [1993] 1 WLR 415; [1993] 2 All ER 321 (duty to appoint sufficient custody officers subject to discretion as to deployment of officers).

7.6 It would be impossible to list exhaustively the categories of discretion that may arise under an ostensibly discretionary statutory power. The range can be illustrated by identifying a number of broad categories across a spectrum from an effective duty to an apparently open discretion. The categories overlap and examples given can readily be multiplied.

Categories of discretion and duty[1]

[1] See also the discussion of the mandatory/directory classification in CHAPTER 10 at 10.5.

Duty to act couched in discretionary language

7.7 Apart from the type of situations illustrated in *R v Mitchell, ex parte Livesey* and *Singh (Pargan) v Secretary of State for the Home Department*[1] (where the fact that a discretion is conferred to enable another's legal rights to be effected necessitates that the 'discretion' is compulsory), a bare duty to act will rarely be deduced from permissive language. The purely formal carrying out of an act required by statute is sometimes classified as a ministerial act. Such acts may well feature as adjuncts to a substantive discretion. For instance, an authority may have a discretion whether or not to grant a licence to applicants satisfying certain criteria. There may then be a duty to record the issue of the licence in a public register. The latter duty can only arise on the granting of a licence and is a separate but subordinate ministerial act; but compression of drafting may make it less than obvious that it is non-discretionary.

¹   [1992] 1 WLR 1052; [1992] 4 All ER 673.

Duty to exercise a power expressed in discretionary terms

7.8 The context of the power may persuade a court that there is a duty to exercise it. The leading case is *Padfield v Minister of Agriculture, Fisheries and Food*.¹ The Agricultural Marketing Act 1958 created, inter alia, a Milk Marketing Board, with producer representatives from each of 12 regions making up the majority of its membership. Section 19 of the Act created a standing committee of investigation charged with the duty 'if the Minister in any case so directs' of considering and reporting on complaints about the operation of the milk marketing scheme. Its reports were to be published and the Minister was empowered to take action, including the amendment or revocation of the scheme, if he thought fit after considering the report. Producers in the South East region had a long-standing grievance about inter-regional price differentials which the Minister refused to refer to the committee. The House of Lords directed that mandamus should issue to require him to refer the complaint.²

¹   [1968] AC 997; [1968] 2 WLR 924; [1968] 1 All ER 694.
²   Lord Morris of Borth-y-Gest dissenting. The Divisional Court had initially granted mandamus; the Court of Appeal (Lord Denning MR dissenting) had allowed the Minister's appeal.

7.9 It will be apparent that the Minister's power offered only two options, to refer or not to refer. The order to refer should not therefore be taken as authority for any more general power to direct that a discretion be exercised in a particular way. Their Lordships concluded from the context and purposes of the Act as a whole that its policy was that bona fide and non-trivial complaints which could not be resolved within the Marketing Board structure should be dealt with through the committee of investigation. Any discretion conferred on the Minister was exercisable to promote the policy and objectives of the Act. It followed that there was a duty to refer whenever the promotion of the policy of the Act so required, and in the absence of a good reason for not referring.¹

¹   It was also stated that if the circumstances indicated that a reference was required and the Minister gave no reason for not referring the complaint, the court should infer that he had no legitimate reason. See, eg Lord Pearce, *loc cit* at 1053G–1054A. However since reasons had been given, this point is strictly obiter.

7.10 *Padfield* is widely and rightly regarded as a landmark in administrative law, but the case is not authority for the extinction of any distinction between a duty and discretion. It will be rare that the policy of any Act requires something to be done in all cases yet is couched in permissive language. In *Padfield* itself their Lordships left a measure of discretion to the Minister: to decide whether a complaint was substantial, and whether it could more conveniently be dealt with through other channels. The duty identified by their

Lordships was to exercise the power in a manner consistent with the policy of the Act,[1] which would in the particular case necessitate exercising it in a particular way; it was not a duty to exercise the power in that way as such.

> [1]   See further *R (Electoral Commission) v Westminster Magistrates' Court* [2010] UKSC 40; [2011] 1 AC 496; [2010] 3 WLR 705 at 508G–H per Lord Phillips; *R (GC) v Commissioner of Police of the Metropolis* [2011] UKSC 21; [2011] 1 WLR 1230; [2011] 3 All ER 859 at 1253F–H per Lord Kerr.

7.11   Within this category of discretionary powers, therefore, there will be a considerable range of judicial control, according to the interrelationship between the ostensible discretion and the general statutory framework. This type of situation was described by Lord Hodson in *Padfield* as 'a power coupled with a duty'.[1] This is perhaps a somewhat insufficient description; it would be more accurate to describe it as a discretionary power governed by a conditional duty.

Padfield has been used as authority for the proposition that a public body in exercising its discretion cannot do so in a manner which will frustrate Parliament's intention.[2] In *R (Webster) v Swindon Local Safeguarding Children Board* [2009] EWHC 2755 (Admin) a local authority children's board failed to conduct a serious case review in a timely manner in circumstances where a child had been the victim of a serious racially aggravated assault. Referring to *Padfield* Kenneth Parker J held that the Board had been required, but had failed to provide a 'compelling reason that was well-formulated and properly substantiated' why it had not carried out the review.

The *Padfield* principle also applies to a failure to exercise a power. In *M v Scottish Ministers* [2012] UKSC 58; [2012] 1 WLR 3386, the Mental Health (Care and Treatment) (Scotland) Act 2003 provided for certain terms to be defined in ministerial regulations, which were to come into force no later than 1 May 2006. No regulations were made. The Supreme Court found that the ministers' failure to make the necessary regulations had thwarted the intention of the Scottish Parliament and was therefore unlawful. The ministers were under an obligation to exercise that power by the specified date: [43], [47] per Lord Reed.

> [1]   *Loc cit* at 1045C, citing *Julius v Bishop of Oxford* (1880) 5 App Cas 214. For a recent application, see *R (Rights of Women) v Lord Chancellor* [2016] EWCA Civ 91; [2016] 1 WLR 2543, where the Civil Legal Aid (Procedure) Regulations 2012, reg 33, which specified the supporting evidence to be provided by a legal aid applicant who claimed to be the victim of domestic violence, were found not to be ultra vires the Legal Aid, Sentencing and Punishment of Offenders Act 2012. However, the regulation frustrated the purposes of the Act (per *Padfield*) and was invalid insofar as it required that the verification of domestic violence had to be dated within a period of 24 months before a legal aid application and insofar as it made no provision for victims of financial abuse. The purpose of the Act was partly to withdraw civil legal services from certain categories of case in order to save money, but also to make such services available to the great majority of persons in the most deserving categories: [41].
> [2]   See also *R v Tower Hamlets London Borough Council, ex p Chetnik Developments Ltd* [1988] AC 858; [1988] 2 WLR 654; [1988] 1 All ER 961 at 872B–F per Lord Bridge, stating that: 'Statutory power conferred for public purposes is conferred as it were upon trust, not absolutely – that is to say, it can validly be used only in the right and proper way which Parliament when conferring it is presumed to have intended.'

Duty to determine with discretion as to the determination

7.12 A discretionary power may encompass elements both of duty and of discretion. An example is the power to license. A body may be charged with the discretion to grant or refuse a licence, on the application of a prospective licensee. The court will readily imply a *duty* to entertain and determine the application, leaving a *discretion* (which may be more or less structured and reviewable according to the context, purpose or wording of the statute) as to the substance of the decision. Were the licensing body under no duty even to consider the application, the purpose of the statute of allocating the licensing function to it would be undermined.[1]

> [1] Among examples of this duality are the classification powers conferred by the Video Recordings Act 1984, s 4. See, also, *Besterly v Secretary of State for the Environment* [2001] 2 AC 603; [2000] 3 WLR 420; [2000] 3 All ER 897 (duty of Secretary of State in considering whether to approve a called-in planning application to *consider* whether application fell within categories for which an environmental assessment was required under applicable statutory provisions). A problem which may arise is the time within which a determination must be reached. On this see *R v Secretary of State for the Home Department, ex parte Phansopkar* [1976] QB 606; [1975] 3 WLR 322; [1975] 3 All ER 497 (unreasonable delay in issuing certificate of patriality); *R (Kobir) v Secretary of State for the Home Department* [2011] EWHC 2515 (Admin) (delay in deciding leave to remain as conspicuous unfairness); *R (MK (Iran)) v Secretary of State for the Home Department* [2010] EWCA Civ 115; [2010] 1 WLR 2059 (public law duty to decide asylum application within a reasonable time).

Duty to act dependent on exercise of discretion

7.13 A duty or power to act may be dependent on circumstances or conditions the existence of which must first be established. The process of deciding whether the necessary conditions exist may in itself entail an exercise of discretion or judgment, which the repository of the duty or power may be required to undertake but the exercise of which is only open to challenge on the usual grounds for judicial review. To that extent a measure of discretion may be attached to the primary duty. The following cases illustrate this. In *R v South Hams District Council, ex parte Gibb*[1] the duty was to provide accommodation for gypsies.[2] The Court of Appeal held that this necessarily imported a power to determine whether applicants seeking accommodation *were* gypsies. The Council's determination was a matter for it, subject to the possibility of review. In the second case, *R v Monopolies and Mergers Commission, ex parte South Yorkshire Transport*,[3] the power of the Commission to accept a reference from the Secretary of State depended on whether South Yorkshire was 'a substantial part of the United Kingdom'; the House of Lords held that this was a matter for determination by the Commission in the light of the circumstances and the proper construction of the phrase quoted.[4] More recently in *R (G) v London Borough of Southwark* the House of Lords considered the duty to provide a 'child in need' with accommodation pursuant to a local authority's duty under s 20 of the Children Act 1989. Baroness Hale held that s 20 entailed a series of judgments but that if those were assessed in the applicant's favour then a duty to accommodate arose.[5] These examples are, in effect, the converse of the cases involving the existence of a precondition the existence of which is a matter for the court, discussed at **7.17** below.

> [1] [1995] QB 158.

² Under the Caravan Sites Act 1968, s 8 (since repealed by the Criminal Justice and Public Order Act 1994, s 80(1)).

³ [1993] 1 WLR 23; [1993] 1 All ER 289.

⁴ See, also, *R v Radio Authority, ex parte Bull* [1996] QB 169 (determination whether advertisement 'mainly of a political character' (which the Radio Authority was under a duty to prohibit); held 'a large measure of discretion must be left to the regulatory authority'); this decision was upheld on appeal ([1998] QB 294) with the caveat that a restriction on freedom of political expression should be restrictively applied, but leaving 'a reasonable degree of tolerance' to the Authority. See further *R v Broadcasting Standards Commission, ex parte BBC* [2001] QB 885, CA, adopting an equally reticent approach to the Commission's discretion.

⁵ [2009] 1 WLR 1299.

Duty to achieve a result with discretion as to how

7.14 Many duties imposed on public authorities are cast in wide and general terms which necessarily confer discretion as to the way in which the result is to be achieved. These duties have been labelled as 'target' or 'general' duties. Examples include the duty of local education authorities to secure the availability in their area of sufficient schools,¹ the duty upon local authorities to safeguard and promote the welfare of children in need within their area,² and the duty on a statutory agency to make children's guardians available in care proceedings.³ The nature and ambit of the discretion in such instances is derived from the interplay of the nature of the duty and the terms in which it is expressed, together with whatever detailed framework may be prescribed for the function. A target or general duty is generally regarded as unsuitable for judicial enforcement and may differ little in its effect as a regulator of discretion from the statutory policy and purposes, deduced by the court from the general framework of an Act. However, a target duty may crystallise into an enforceable duty in certain circumstances.⁴

¹ Education Act 1996, s 14(1) (re-enacting Education Act 1944, s 8). Interestingly, the marginal note to s 14 refers to 'functions' rather than duties, but the statutory provision itself uses 'shall'. See in this respect *R v Inner London Education Authority, ex parte Ali* (1990) 2 Admin LR 822.

² As set out in s 17(1) of the Children Act 1989 and considered by the House of Lords in *R (G) v Barnet London Borough Council* [2003] UKHL 57; [2004] 2 AC 208.

³ As set out in s 12 of the Criminal Justice and Court Services Act 2000 and considered by the Court of Appeal in *R (R) v Child and Family Court Advisory and Support Service* [2012] EWCA Civ 853.

⁴ Woolf et al (eds), *De Smith's Judicial Review* (7th edn, 2013), paragraph 5–069; see eg *R (West) v Rhondda Cynon Taff CBC* [2014] EWHC 2134; *(Admin)* [2015] ACD 9, where Supperstone J found that a local authority's decision to withdraw funding for the full-time nursery education of three-year-olds failed to have regard to its duties under the Children Act 1989, s 17(1) and s 18 to provide care for children in need, to its duty to secure nursery education, and to its duty to secure sufficient childcare for working parents.

Discretion whether to act at all but duty to act in a particular manner if discretion exercised

7.15 This category is best illustrated by *R v Greater London Council, ex parte Blackburn.*¹ The Council was the licensing authority for cinemas within its area. The Cinematograph Act 1909, as amended, empowered it to issue licences 'on such terms and conditions and under such restrictions as . . . the Council may . . . determine'.² The conditions contained in the Council's standard licences included a prohibition on showing films not either certified by the British Board of Film Censors or permitted by the Council, and on the showing of films the effect of which would be to tend to deprave and corrupt. The Court of Appeal held that it was a matter for the discretion of the GLC whether to impose conditions as to the content or prior approval of films at all, but that if they did so it was their duty to adopt criteria for content and approval consistent with the general law applicable to the public screening of films, namely that the showing of films which outraged public decency was an offence.[3] The extent to which the structuring of a discretion in this way approximates it to a duty will vary according to all the relevant circumstances.

[1] [1976] 3 All ER 184; [1976] 1 WLR 550.

[2] Section 2(1), as amended by the Cinematograph Act 1952, Sch. The 1952 Act added a duty to impose conditions restricting the admission of children to unsuitable films, which inferentially reinforces the lack of any duty to impose such conditions for exhibitions to adult audiences. Section 2(1) of the 1909 Act was replaced by the Cinemas Act 1985, s 1(2), which still applies in Scotland, but has in turn been replaced in England and Wales by the Licensing Act 2003, Part 3.

[3] *Knuller (Publishing, Printing and Promotions) Ltd v DPP* [1973] AC 435; [1972] 2 All ER 898; see now Criminal Law Act 1977, s 53 and Obscene Publications Act 1959, s 2(4).

7.16 This category is also appropriate for those cases where a discretion must be exercised, if at all, in accordance with a general legal obligation of the body concerned independent of the discretionary power, but to a greater or lesser extent regulating its exercise. The best example is the cases in which local authorities in exercising their powers to fix levels of pay for employees, or fares for transport services provided by them, have been held to be under a duty to their ratepayers, sometimes described as fiduciary, which circumscribed the apparently unfettered discretion conferred on them.[1] A closely analogous restriction on the exercise of discretionary powers arises from the provisions of the Human Rights Act 1998, discussed at **7.25** below.

[1] *Roberts v Hopwood* [1925] AC 578; *Prescott v Birmingham Corpn* [1955] Ch 210; [1954] 3 WLR 990; [1954] 3 All ER 698; *Bromley London Borough Council v Greater London Council* [1983] 1 AC 768; [1982] 2 WLR 92; [1982] 1 All ER 153. In the last mentioned case only Lord Diplock decided the matter squarely on the failure in the exercise of a discretion to have regard to fiduciary duties; the majority view was that the statutory powers on their true construction did not in any event confer the power to reduce fares in the manner adopted by the GLC. See also *Rose Gibb v Maidstone and Tunbridge Wells NHS Trust* [2009] EWHC 862 (QB) in which the court held that a compromise agreement awarding a former NHS Trust's chief executive substantial compensation, was irrationally generous and a decision reached outside the Trust's powers.

A discretion may be dependent on satisfaction of a precondition as to its exercise

7.17 It is possible to analyse almost all discretionary powers as being subject to one or more preconditions – for instance, that the body seeking to exercise the discretion *is* the body upon which the discretion is conferred and is duly constituted to act in that capacity. More generally, conditions precedent may range from the almost entirely subjective 'if it thinks fit' to the existence of a circumstance the existence of which is a matter of objective fact. Thus the discretion to grant or refuse planning consent can only be exercised in respect of land within the area of the planning authority. Issues of fact relating to preconditions to the exercise of discretion may be subject to the court's interpretation and application of statutory wording, as in *White and Collins v Minister of Health*,[1] where a power of compulsory purchase granted by a statute was subject to a provision that 'nothing in this Act shall authorise the compulsory purchase . . . of any land . . . which forms part . . . of any park'.[2] In *Tan Te Lam v Superintendent of Tai A Chau Detention Centre*,[3] a case which concerned a statutory power to detain illegal immigrants pending removal from Hong Kong, the Judicial Committee of the Privy Council held it was limited to cases where removal was possible within a reasonable time. The question whether that was so (and hence whether the power of detention was available) was for the court, not the immigration authorities, to determine, since it was a matter precedent to jurisdiction and not merely 'incidental to the exercise of discretionary powers' delegated to the authorities.[4] More recently in *R (A) v London Borough of Croydon* the Supreme Court held that, in circumstances involving a local authority's power to provide services to children under the Children Act 1989, it was a question of jurisdictional fact whether a young person was in fact a child, and therefore entitled to services under the Act.[5]

[1] [1939] 2 KB 838, [1939] 3 All ER 548.
[2] Housing Act 1936, s 75; the power was contained in s 74. This case is the converse of *R v South Hams DC, ex parte Gibb* [1995] QB 158 and *R v Monopolies and Mergers Commission, ex parte South Yorkshire Transport Ltd* [1993] 1 WLR 23; [1993] 1 All E.R. 289 – see **7.13** above.
[3] [1997] AC 97; [1996] 2 WLR 863; [1996] 4 All ER 256.
[4] Ibid at *112C–112F*; following *R v Secretary of State for the Home Department, ex parte Khawaja* [1984] AC 74; [1983] 2 WLR 321; [1983] 1 All ER 765, the burden was on the authorities to show the existence of the conditions justifying detention. Compare *R v Personal Investment Authority and PIA Ombudsman, ex parte Burns-Anderson Independent Network plc* (1998) 10 Admin LR 57 (question whether time-share scheme was investment business (and so within jurisdiction of Ombudsman), question of fact to be determined by Ombudsman).
[5] [2009] UKSC 8; [2009] 1 WLR 2557; [2010] 1 All ER 469. This case was applied in *R (FZ acting by his ligation friend Parivash Ghanipour) v Croydon London Borough Council* [2011] EWCA Div 59, [2011] PTSR 748.

7.18 Much of the discussion appropriate to this aspect of classification of discretion belongs with a discussion of jurisdiction.[1] Here it is sufficient to note that even subjectively expressed preconditions to the exercise of a power may provide a separate target for judicial review that avoids the need to impugn the merits or rationality of the exercise of the power as such. Indeed, in many cases they are the primary target: a provision that 'if the Minister is satisfied that X, he may do Y' may well in its context not only create a virtual duty to do Y if the condition of satisfaction is present, but also leave considerable room for challenge as to the rationality of the satisfaction or non-satisfaction or the procedural propriety of the manner in which it was reached.[2]

[1] See CHAPTER 6, and, on Scots law, CHAPTER 22 para **22.65** et seq. See, also, the discussion of the relationship between irrationality and illegality in CHAPTER 8.
[2] See, eg *Secretary of State for Education and Science v Tameside Metropolitan Borough Council* [1977] AC 1014; [1976] 3 WLR 641; [1976] 3 All ER 665 at 1047, 1065–1066, 1072. See also *Office of Fair Trading v IBA Healthcare Ltd* [2004] EWCA Civ 142 (statutory phrase 'is satisfied' means court must inquire as to whether belief was 'reasonable and objectively justified by relevant facts': [45]).

Pure discretion

7.19 Can a discretionary power be regarded as conferring a pure discretion unfettered by constraints of substantive law? The concept of a pure discretion is distinguishable from the question whether a discretionary power is unreviewable, which involves consideration both of the limits developed by the courts to the range of bodies and types of decision which fall within the ambit of judicial review, and of judicial abstention from matters of particularly sensitive policy. Moreover conceptually, the fact that a power is purely discretionary is not incompatible with review of its exercise, particularly on procedural grounds.

7.20 In the context of a public authority, having been created by statute, for purposes specified explicitly or implicitly by Parliament and with powers deriving from statute, it is difficult to conceive of any discretionary power, save perhaps purely internal to the authority, devoid of preconditions or framework for its existence.[1] Wade and Forsyth,[2] in a passage approved by the House of Lords in 1988,[3] rejected the possibility of an unfettered discretion in unequivocal terms: 'It is only where powers are given for the personal benefit of the person empowered that the discretion is absolute. Plainly this can have no application in public law'.

[1]   A trivial example would be a decision by a local authority to prohibit smoking during committee meetings.
[2]   *Administrative Law* (11th edn, 2014) p 296.
[3]   The passage was approved (as it appeared in a previous edition) in *R v Tower Hamlets London Borough Council, ex parte Chetnik Developments Ltd* [1988] AC 858; [1988] 2 WLR 654; [1988] 1 All ER 961 at 872, applied in *R (Electoral Commission) v City of Westminster Magistrates' Court* [2010] UKSC 40; [2011] 1 AC 496. There are numerous cases in which the courts have stated that statutory powers are not unlimited. For two recent examples see the comments of Lord Hope in *Ahmed v HM Treasury* [2010] UKSC 2; [2010] 2 AC 534 at [45] and the comments of Lord Bingham in *R (Corner House Research) v Director of the Serious Fraud Office* [2008] UKHL 60; [2009] 1 AC 756; [2008] 3 WLR 568 at [32].

7.21 But despite this judicially endorsed view, the control of some discretionary powers, particularly of the Government acting under the prerogative in international affairs, is political not judicial. To debate whether, for instance, the power to make a treaty is a pure discretion may serve little practical purpose given clear authority that the courts cannot review the exercise of the power.[1] Contrast the position where the power is not used merely to make (or un-make) treaties, but is used to alter domestic law. In *R (Miller) v Secretary of State for Exiting the European Union* [2017] UKSC 5; [2017] 2 WLR 583; [2017] 1 All ER 593, the Supreme Court held that prerogative powers could not be used to change domestic law; ministers could not serve notice of the UK's withdrawal from the EU under Article 50 of the Treaty of European Union without statutory authorisation (see further **7.33** below).

[1]   *R v Secretary of State for Foreign and Commonwealth Affairs, ex parte Rees-Mogg* [1994] QB 552; [1994] 2 WLR 115; [1994] 1 All ER 457 (the Maastricht Treaty of Union). But cf *R (Wheeler) v Office of the Prime Minister* [2008] EWHC 1409 (Admin) at [55] (on the Lisbon Treaty; see further **7.22** below), where the Divisional Court held in obiter:

> 'One issue is the extent to which a decision to ratify a treaty is amenable to judicial review at all. That such a decision is not altogether outside the scope of judicial review is illustrated by the fact that s 12 of the European Parliamentary Elections Act 2002 makes statutory approval a condition precedent to the ratification of any treaty which provides for an increase in the powers of the European Parliament: . . . a decision to ratify without such

approval would be amenable to review. . . . Nevertheless it seems to us that the limits of reviewability should be determined on a case by case basis if and when the need arises.'
Cf also *Blackburn v Attorney General* [1971] 1 WLR 1037; [1971] 2 All ER 1380 (on the Treaty of Accession to the EEC).

7.22 One example of what had previously been regarded as an institution immune from review and, in effect, possessed of a pure discretion is the office of the Parliamentary Commissioner for Administration. The authority for this view, *Re Fletcher's Application*,[1] related to the refusal of the Divisional Court and the Court of Appeal to order the Commissioner to investigate a complaint. The complainant's petition to the House of Lords Appeal Committee for leave to appeal further was rejected on the reasoning that there was no jurisdiction to order an investigation since the statute[2] conferred a discretion whether to investigate or not. However, the Divisional Court has more recently, albeit obiter, roundly rejected the notion that the Commissioner had a discretion for the exercise of which he was answerable only to Parliament, even in relation to a decision whether to investigate a complaint;[3] and in *R v Parliamentary Commissioner for Administration, ex parte Balchin*,[4] the court actually quashed a Report of the Commissioner for self-misdirection and failure to consider a relevant factor in reaching his conclusion.[5] However, the Court of Appeal in *R v Parliamentary Commissioner for Standards, ex parte Al Fayed*[6] held that decisions of the Commissioner for Standards were not amenable to judicial review; the Commissioner is concerned with matters directly related to what happens in Parliament and is answerable to Parliament; the analogy with the Parliamentary Commissioner was therefore false. In *R (Wheeler) v Office of the Prime Minister* the claimant sought to challenge the Government's decision not to hold a referendum in respect of the Lisbon Treaty. As one of the grounds for dismissing the claim the Divisional Court (Richards LJ and Mackay J) relied upon *ex parte Al Fayed* in holding that if the claim were to succeed it would involve an unjustifiable interference by the courts with proceedings in Parliament.[7] These cases do effectively create an area of unreviewable discretion but are perhaps better seen as examples of judicial respect for the autonomy and self-regulation of Parliament than any broader exception to the Courts' general approach.

[1] [1970] 2 All ER 527.
[2] Parliamentary Commissioner Act 1967, s 5.
[3] *R v Parliamentary Commissioner for Administration, ex parte Dyer* [1994] 1 WLR 621; [1994] 1 All ER 375 at 625C–626H: the application to review the Commissioner's refusal to reopen an investigation was rejected on the merits.
[4] [1997] COD 146.
[5] The courts have shown a willingness in principle to intervene by way of judicial review in the process of investigation conducted by statutory ombudsmen and similar bodies, but have acknowledged reasons for caution in making such interventions. See, eg *R v Broadcasting Complaints Commission, ex parte Owen* [1985] QB 1153; [1985] 2 WLR 1025 (relief refused by Court of Appeal as a matter of discretion).
[6] [1998] 1 WLR 669; [1998] 1 All ER 93.
[7] [2008] EWHC 1409 (Admin); [2008] ACD 70.

7.23 The categorisation given above deals with the interaction between discretion and duty. One other classification of discretion should be noted. Discretion is often conferred on courts and tribunals in apparently unrestricted language. It is likely to be characterised as a judicial discretion, that is, a discretion to be exercised in accordance with principles of consistency and established judicial practice. The general discretion of the High Court as to costs,[1] which is required to be exercised in accordance with well-established principles and practice, is an example.[2] Where a power conferred on a subordinate court or tribunal is classified as a judicial discretion its exercise is more amenable to review.[3] The process of so classifying it may well form an integral step in the assertion of a wider power of review. Judicial discretion is also of very considerable importance in relation to remedies in judicial review proceedings, and to some extent overlaps with substantive issues of review-ability: marginal cases may be dealt with under either the substance of vires or the discretion not to grant relief. Development of this point is more appropriately considered in the context of remedies generally.[4]

[1] CPR Part 44. See also *M v Croydon London Borough Council* [2012] EWCA Civ 595, [2012] 1 WLR 2607 at [1].
[2] A further helpful example is provided by *Thomas v Metropolitan Police Commissioner* [1997] QB 813; [1997] 2 WLR 593; [1997] 1 All ER 747 (on the discretion under the Rehabilitation of Offenders Act 1974, s 7(3) to admit evidence of spent convictions in civil proceedings); see particularly the analysis of the discretion by Scott V-C, dissenting, at 597H–598B.
[3] See, eg *R v Manchester Legal Aid Committee, ex parte Brand & Co Ltd* [1952] 2 QB 413, [1952] 1 All ER 480.
[4] See CHAPTERS 16–18.

7.24 The gradations of duty and discretion outlined here can be conveniently drawn together in the following passage from the speech of Lord Penzance in *Julius v Lord Bishop of Oxford*,[1] quoted with approval by Lord Pearce in *Padfield* at 1053:

> 'The words "it shall be lawful" are distinctly words of permission only – they are enabling and empowering words. They confer a legislative right and power on the individual named to do a particular thing, and the true question is not whether they mean something different, but whether, regard being had to the person so enabled – to the subject matter, to the general objects of the statute and to the person or class of persons for whose benefit the power may be intended to have been conferred – they do, or do not, create a duty in the person upon whom it has been conferred, to exercise it.'

[1] (1880) 4 App Cas 214.

THE HUMAN RIGHTS ACT 1998

7.25 The effect on discretionary powers of the Human Rights Act 1998 is both complex and highly significant.[1] The impact of the Act depends on the presence of a number of factors, the most obvious of which is that the exercise of the discretion in question in a particular way has, or might have, the effect of infringing one of the Convention rights incorporated into domestic law through Schedule 1 to the Act, of a person affected by the action concerned.

[1] For a more general discussion see CHAPTER 4.

7.26 If the repository of a discretionary power is a public authority, its exercise of the power is subject to s 6(1) of the Act, which renders it unlawful for a public authority to act in a way which is incompatible with a Convention right, subject to the other provisions of s 6. These:

(1)   limit the application of the section, in the case of 'hybrid' public authorities, by excluding those acts the nature of which is private (s 6(5));[1]

(2)   exclude Parliament from the ambit of s 6 (by s 6(4)):

(3)   disapply s 6(1) where as the result of one or more provisions of primary legislation, the authority could not have acted differently (s 6(2)(a)); and

(4)   disapply s 6(1) where a provision of, or made under, primary legislation cannot be read or given effect in a way which is compatible with the Convention rights.[2]

[1]   As noted in CHAPTER 4 above, the question whether a hybrid authority is in a particular case performing a public function (or indeed whether a body is a public authority) is not the same question as whether the exercise of the function is amenable to judicial review, albeit the answer will in the great majority of cases be the same; the essential requirement for s 6 to be engaged is that the function is one for the exercise of which the United Kingdom would be answerable under the Convention in the European Court of Human Rights. This necessitates consideration of the jurisprudence of the Strasbourg Court as well as that on the ambit of judicial review: *Aston Cantlow and Wilmcote with Billesley Parochial Church Council v Wallbank* [2003] UKHL 37; [2004] 1 AC 546; [2003] 3 WLR 283. For a review of the authorities on the applicability of s 6 and when a body is exercising public functions see *R (YL) v Birmingham City Council* [2007] UKHL 27; [2008] 1 AC 95; [2007] 3 WLR 112; see further *R (Holmcroft Properties Limited) v KPMG LLP and the Financial Conduct Authority* [2016] EWHC 323 (Admin), which was a claim for judicial review of KPMG LLP, having been appointed as a 'skilled person' under the Financial Services and Markets Act 2000. The Divisional Court found that there was no direct public law element in KPMG's role and it was not amenable to judicial review.

[2]   In that event, the court may have to consider whether a declaration of incompatibility should be issued (in the case of primary legislation) or the offending legislative provision declared invalid (in the case of secondary legislation).

7.27 These provisions need to be read together with s 3 of the Act, which requires that both primary and subordinate legislation, whenever enacted, must so far as possible be read and given effect in a way which is compatible with the Convention rights. Section 6 must also be considered in the context of the duty it imposes on courts and tribunals, which are themselves 'public authorities' for the purposes of the duties imposed on such authorities by s 6.

7.28 The effect of these provisions is threefold, in a case where a person's Convention rights are, or may, be affected by the exercise of a discretionary power. First, the power must be so construed, if that is considered possible by the construing court, that the discretion can only be exercised in ways compatible with any relevant Convention right. That may have the effect of narrowing the apparent breadth of the discretion. Secondly, if the repository of the power is a public authority (which will nearly always, if not necessarily in every case, be so for a body or person amenable to judicial review), it may not exercise the discretion in a way that is incompatible with a Convention right enjoyed by a person who will be affected by the decision taken, unless it cannot lawfully do otherwise. By the nature of a discretion, that will rarely be the case. Thirdly, the reviewing court must, in determining the lawfulness of the exercise of discretion under review, refrain from reaching a decision incompatible with a Convention right, unless compelled to do so by the terms of the governing legislation.

7.29 The third of these effects has led to a more interventionist approach to judicial review by the courts in cases with a Convention element.[1] The latter feature is, of course, a condition precedent to any of the provisions of the Act affecting the reviewability or scope of a discretion: it is necessary to show that a particular course of action or decision would entail an infringement of a right safeguarded by the Convention. Whilst Convention rights are widely expressed and, in some cases, wide ranging, nearly all are subject to significant qualifications or reservations, and experience since the coming into force of the Act has been that breaches of the Convention are asserted far more frequently than they are established. However, in those areas where they are established, there is a clear ring of constraints imposed on the discretionary powers of public authorities.

1   The degree of interventionism will depend on the nature of the power and the circumstances of its exercise as well as the rights affected. The court's approach to national security is considered in *A v Secretary of State for the Home Department* [2004] UKHL 56, [2005] 2 AC 68; [2005] 2 WLR 87; see **3.21, 5.31, 5.34, 8.30** and CHAPTER 9. More recently, Lord Carnwath explained in *R (Naik) v Secretary of State for the Home Department* [2011] EWCA Civ 1546 at [48]:

> 'Ministers, accountable to Parliament, are responsible for national security; judges are not. However, even in that context, judges have a duty, also entrusted by Parliament, to examine Ministerial decisions or actions in accordance with the ordinary tests of rationality, legality, and procedural regularity, and, where Convention rights are in play, proportionality. In this exercise great weight will be given to the assessment of the responsible Minister.'

For earlier cases, see also *Secretary of State for the Home Department v Rehman* [2001] UKHL 47; [2003] 1 AC 153 at 57–62 per Lord Hoffmann and *R(Q) v Secretary of State for the Home Department* [2002] EWCA Civ 1502; [2002] QB 355. A proportionality approach has more recently been taken in relation to common law rights in *Kennedy v Information Commissioner* [2014] UKSC 20; [2015] AC 455; [2014] 2 WLR 808 at [54]per Lord Mance; see further below at **7.38**.

7.30 A further way in which the Human Rights Act 1998 has an impact on the review of discretionary decisions arises where the decision amounts to a determination of the civil rights or obligations of a person affected thereby, and the decision-taker is not an 'independent and impartial tribunal' for the purposes of Art 6(1) of the Convention. If, in these circumstances, there is no right of appeal to a court, recourse to judicial review may provide the remedy required by art 6(1), but only if the scrutiny provided by way of judicial review is sufficiently rigorous to meet the requirements of art 6 in the circumstances of the case.[1] This opens the way to a more comprehensive scrutiny of the legality of the exercise of power under review, but it does not require that the Court should review the merits of a policy decision taken by a minister of the Crown answerable to Parliament.[2]

1   *R (Alconbury Developments Ltd) v Secretary of State for the Environment, Transport and the Regions* [2001] UKHL 23; [2003] 2 AC 295; [2001] 2 WLR 1389. The House of Lords held that the Secretary of State, in exercising powers to grant or refuse planning applications, was determining the civil rights and obligations of affected landowners; that he was not an 'independent and impartial tribunal' within art 6(1); but that the conferment of powers on the Secretary of State was compatible with art 6(1) because of the availability of judicial review, provided that this affords a 'sufficient review' of the legality of decisions and of the procedures followed (Lord Slynn at [49]). This decision was followed by the House of Lords' judgment in *Runa Begum v Tower Hamlets LBC* [2003] UKHL 5; [2003] 2 AC 430; [2003] 2 WLR 388, in which it was held that the right of appeal pursuant to s 204 of the Housing Act 1996, with respect to a Housing Authority's offer of homelessness accommodation, was sufficient to comply with the requirements of Article 6(1) ECHR. Contrast these decisions with *Tsfayo v UK* (2009) 48 EHRR 18 in which the European Court of Human Rights held that a claim for housing benefit constituted a determination of a civil right for the purposes of art 6 ECHR and that a local authority housing benefit review board did not constitute an independent and impartial tribunal. This was because its members, who included councillors, were directly

connected to one of the parties in the dispute (the local authority) and this might affect the board's judgment when reaching primary findings of facts which were necessary for the applicant's application for back-dated housing benefit to be determined.

2   See, eg Lord Slynn at paragraphs 50–54, Lord Hoffmann at paragraphs 69–74. There have however been more recent judicial pronouncements stating that where fundamental rights are involved the courts will be prepared to delve into the merits of the impugned decision – see *R (JB) v Haddock (Responsible Medical Officer)* [2006] EWCA Civ 961; [2006] HRLR 40 referring to the earlier decision of the Court of Appeal in *R (Wilkinson) v Broadmoor Hospital* [2001] EWCA Civ 1545; [2002] 1 WLR 419 where it was held that in the context of a detained patient challenging forcible medical treatment, engaging arts 2, 3 and 8 ECHR, it was necessary for the court to reach its own view on the merits of the medical decision.

7.31 The substantive issues of the application of Convention rights are outside the scope of this chapter, as are the general issues of statutory interpretation raised by the courts' obligations under s 3, and the equivalent obligations arising in the reconciliation of domestic legislation with EU law. It should also be noted that there are specific provisions enabling victims of the acts of public authorities which infringe Convention rights to bring proceedings before appropriate courts, including proceedings by way of judicial review (s 7(2), (3)).

ARE THERE UNREVIEWABLE DISCRETIONS?[1]

1   For a general discussion, see CHAPTER 5 at 5.31 et seq. On the status of decisions relating to national security, see Woolf et al (eds), *De Smith's Judicial Review* (7th edn, 2013), paragraph 1–041. See further Fordham, *Judicial Review Handbook* (6th edn, 2012), Ch 34; see particularly Fordham on 'Special "non-justiciable" (prerogative?) functions', id, [34.4.5] and see further 7.34 below.

7.32 It is not yet possible to give a short, negative answer to this question, despite the continuing growth of judicial review and the evolution of grounds for judicial intervention. The question is not the same as whether a power confers a 'pure discretion'. The discretion so conferred may be subject to evident limitations on, or criteria as to, its exercise but nevertheless be judged to be of a nature such that the exercise of the discretion is not appropriate for judicial scrutiny. It is also a question less important in practice than in theory, since a court which is unwilling to interfere with a challenged exercise of discretion can more readily dispose of the matter by reference to the lawfulness of the particular decision than by attributing a general principle of sanctity to the power. It is alien to the judicial instinct to concede an area to be outside the supervisory jurisdiction of the courts, and by parity of reasoning with the courts' strict construction of legislative attempts to exclude review, a self-imposed exclusion will not be readily adopted.

7.33 The major category of supposedly unreviewable powers, those derived from the Royal Prerogative, has been shown not to be a separate category after all. In the landmark House of Lords decision in *CCSU*,[1] their Lordships unanimously affirmed that a power conferred on the Minister for the Civil Service by a prerogative Order was not immune from review. Lords Scarman, Diplock and Roskill were prepared to say that the exercise of a prerogative power as such, as well as a power derived from the prerogative, was justiciable,[2] Lords Fraser of Tullybelton and Brightman reserving their position on the point. Although the broader basis of the majority's approach was strictly obiter, it has since been adopted by the Courts. The basis on which reviewability is to be assessed can now be summarised thus: 'the controlling factor in determining whether the exercise of prerogative power is subject to judicial review is not its source but its subject matter'.[3] *Miller*, cited above at 7.21, affirmed that prerogative powers only went so far (see [92]); they could not be used to cut off a source of domestic law and of fundamental rights and thereby effect major constitutional change; this required an Act of Parliament: [101].

[1] *(CCSU)* [1985] AC 374, [1984] 3 All ER 935
[2] The decision under challenge was an oral instruction by the Minister to ban trade union membership amongst crown servants employed in GCHQ, which she was empowered to issue by Article 4 of the Civil Service Order in Council 1982, a prerogative order. See further below 7.34(2) and the authorities cited there.
[3] [1985] AC 374, [1984] 3 All ER 935 at 407F.

7.34 The repositioning of the basis of judicial review by the House of Lords in *CCSU*[1] enables us to offer a relatively simple approach to the question of unreviewable discretion. Lord Diplock could see 'no *a priori* reason to rule out irrationality as a ground for judicial review of a ministerial decision taken in the exercise of "prerogative" powers'[2] (albeit his Lordship understandably had great difficulty in envisaging a successful instance).[3] This leaves only one substantial ground of unreviewability: that the subject matter of the power is not justiciable because its policy content renders it unsuitable for adjudication. This may apply to statutory as well as to common law prerogative powers, and the ambit of the area of unreviewability is an issue better addressed in relation to judicial review as a whole. Here it is sufficient to make a number of brief general points.[4]

(1)   As noted earlier, the remedy of judicial review is a remedy of last resort, and may be refused where a better alternative remedy is available. This might be thought to be relevant also to the question whether powers are reviewable at all. However, in the one area where this is likely to arise as a live issue, where a power is subject to Parliamentary control or the repository of the power is answerable to Parliament, judicial deference to that institution has been overcome in recognition of the uncertain effectiveness of Parliamentary controls. The proposition that the Parliamentary Commissioner for Administration is answerable only to Parliament and therefore not answerable to judicial review has been 'unhesitatingly' rejected by the Divisional Court.[5]

(2)   Areas of prerogative powers that by virtue of their content might have been regarded as unreviewable and subject only to Parliamentary control on the basis of dicta in *CCSU*[6] have since been accepted as reviewable. In particular, the courts have intervened, in areas hitherto regarded as having too high a policy content: over the refusal to issue a passport, the refusal by the Home Secretary to recommend a posthumous pardon for a man hanged for murder, and with respect to an Order in Council displacing the inhabitants of the Chagos Islands.[7] In relation to statutory powers of Ministers with a high international policy content, an increased readiness by the court to intervene was strikingly demonstrated by the granting of a declaration that the Foreign Secretary had acted unlawfully in approving a foreign aid grant for the Pergau Dam project in Malaysia.[8] In *R (Abbasi) v Secretary of State for Foreign and Commonwealth Affairs* the Court of Appeal

refused relief to the claimant who was a detainee at Guantanomo Bay and who sought to argue that the British government had acted in unlawfully by failing to make representations on his behalf to the American government. However, the Court held that the proposition that there was no scope to review a refusal to render diplomatic assistance to a British subject who was suffering violation of a fundamental human right as the result of the conduct of the authorities of a foreign state was flawed.[9]

(3) On the other hand it is clear that certain areas of the powers of the Central Government remain immune from review. Traditionally, one such is the making of treaties,[10] which is not justiciable both because it raises no issue of domestic law (a treaty having no legal status in domestic law unless incorporated by statute) and because of the nature of the act of ratification. However, more recently in *R (Wheeler) v Office of the Prime Minister*,[11] the Divisional Court held that whether the decision to ratify a treaty is amenable to judicial review should be determined case by case. It can also no longer be assumed, following the decision of the House of Lords in *A v Secretary of State for the Home Department*[12] that the court will defer to the Executive in matters of national security, particularly where the decision under review involves an interference with rights protected by the European Convention on Human Rights.

(4) Any attempt to rationalise the categories of power which are and are not amenable to review is difficult. Some have simply never arisen directly for consideration in the UK (although there is a substantial body of authority in Commonwealth jurisdictions)[13] and the factors taken into account in decided cases show, as might be expected, a balancing of conflicting considerations. Factors in favour of judicial intervention include the absence of alternative effective redress, impact on the individual applicant and the extent to which the factors to be considered by the decision-taker are susceptible to judicial assessment. Factors pointing towards non-reviewability include a high (particularly foreign) policy content and the inappropriateness of factors considered for judicial assessment. But it will be clear from the examples given that these factors alone do not provide a sufficient basis to predict accurately how the courts are likely to assess particular situations.

(5) An illustration of the last point is the powers of the Attorney-General. Dicta of the House of Lords in *Gouriet v Union of Post Office Workers*[14] that decisions of the Attorney-General whether to consent to relator proceedings are not justiciable were not dependent on the categorisation of his powers as part of the prerogative, and the dicta were therefore not in terms affected by the decision in *CCSU*.[15] The refusal to permit review of decisions by the Attorney-General may appear anomalous in the face of the courts' general readiness to intervene by judicial review in the area of the administration of justice, but a number of cases since *Gouriet* have affirmed the non-reviewability of other classes of decision of the Attorney-General, in acknowledgement of his role as guardian of the public interest and the sensitive policy content of his decisions.[16]

(6) It is a statement of the obvious that courts will be more reluctant to intervene in situations of emergency or where issues of national security are involved,[17] but even here a greater willingness in principle to intervene can be seen in a number of cases,[18] and the House of Lords has twice held that a plea of national security unsupported by evidence does not preclude judicial intervention in relation to the exercise of a discretionary power.[19] More recently, the House of Lords has confirmed that the exercise of the power to derogate from the European Convention on Human Rights 'in time of war or other public emergency threatening the life of the nation' (art 15) is subject to review, although such an assessment being pre-eminently political in character, to be made by the Executive and Parliament, great weight was to be accorded by the courts to their judgment.[20]

(7) At a practical level, the reviewability of discretionary powers which do not entail interference with the rights or legitimate expectations of particular individuals will depend on the availability of a person or body accepted as having standing to apply for judicial review. The trend of recent decisions on standing has been to accept a wider range of legitimate interest in significant policy decisions where there are substantial grounds for review, and if an individual or group with a bona fide interest in a matter is prepared to apply for leave, the question of standing is unlikely to be regarded as a barrier to the court's intervention if intervention would otherwise be appropriate.[21] Nevertheless, whether such individuals or groups come forward in a particular case may be fortuitous.

(8) Not all powers of public bodies have a sufficient public law content to be amenable to judicial review, and many decisions taken by public bodies in the exercise of their powers have a sufficient effect on the private law rights of individuals for the appropriate remedy to be in private law rather than by way of judicial review.[22] Disciplinary action taken by public bodies against employees has generated the most case law on this issue in recent years, but it also applies to purely commercial decisions by public bodies such as decisions by public utilities as to contracts of supply with particular customers.[23] In one sense decisions of these types may be regarded as unreviewable; it can equally be said that they are subject to legal control in a different legal arena. In two senses there may in these areas be genuinely unreviewable discretions. First, parties other than the party whose private law rights have been affected are unlikely to have standing to apply for judicial review even if the decision in issue also has a public law dimension.[24] Second, there may be decisions which have no sufficient public law element and at the same time do not infringe any individual's rights in private law.[25]

(9) There is no single dividing line between reviewable and unreviewable powers. Review of a decision involving sensitive policy issues is more likely to be possible on grounds of procedural unfairness than of irrationality or taking into account irrelevant considerations. This reflects both the natural reluctance of judges to impugn the motives of Ministers of the Crown and the breadth of discretion conferred by the prerogative and by many statutory powers operating in the areas formerly part of the prerogative.[26] More generally, the courts have repeatedly indicated that a less interventionist approach to review of the

substance of decisions is appropriate where the power concerned either is subject to Parliamentary control or has a high policy content not readily capable of judicial analysis.[27] The converse is that decisions having a particularly direct effect on individual liberty, in an area with which the court is more naturally familiar, a greater 'intensity of review', as it has been described, is possible.[28]

(10) The fact that a decision made in the exercise of a discretionary power has been endorsed by affirmative resolution of both Houses of Parliament does not render it unreviewable. It was so held by the Court of Appeal in *R (Asif Javed) v Secretary of State for the Home Department*[29] in relation to the designation of Pakistan as a 'safe country' for the purpose of the statutory regime for the return of unsuccessful applicants for asylum; the designation was by way of an Order made under the Asylum and Immigration Act 1996 which had been laid in draft before both Houses and approved after debates in each House. The Order was nevertheless quashed by the Court of Appeal as an irrational exercise of the enabling power in the light of the evidence available to the Secretary of State as to the risks of persecution of returned asylum seekers.

---

[1] [1985] AC 374; [1984] 3 All ER 935.

[2] Ibid at 411D.

[3] But in relation to those powers which remain within the prerogative by historical accident and are not intrinsically different from statutory powers, such a possibility is surely real. Cf *R v Home Secretary, ex parte Cox* [1991] Times, 10 September, Popplewell J (order to person released on licence from sentence of life imprisonment to return to a secure prison on conviction of minor offences quashed as irrational).

[4] For a fuller discussion, see CHAPTERS 8 and 9.

[5] *R v Parliamentary Commissioner for Administration, ex parte Dyer* [1994] 1 WLR 621; [1994] 1 All ER 375, 625 (Simon Brown LJ). See, also, *R v Criminal Injuries Compensation Board, ex parte P* [1995] 1 WLR 845; [1995] 1 All ER 870 (decisions of Home Secretary as to the terms of the former (prerogative) Criminal Injuries Compensation Scheme reviewable to ensure the fair distribution of the funds voted by Parliament for the Scheme).

[6] See particularly Lord Roskill at 418B: 'Prerogative powers such as those relating to the making of treaties, the defence of the realm, the prerogative of mercy, the grant of honours, the dissolution of Parliament and the appointment of ministers as well as others'. See also Fordham, *Judicial Review Handbook* (6th edn, 2012), on 'Special "non-justiciable" (prerogative?) functions' at [34.4.5].

[7] *R v Secretary of State for the Home Department, ex parte Bentley* [1994] QB 349; *R (Bancoult) v Secretary of State for Foreign and Commonwealth Affairs (No.2)* [2008] UKHL 61; [2009] 1 AC 453; [2008] 3 WLR 955; affirmed in *R (Bancoult) v Secretary of State for Foreign and Commonwealth Affairs (No 4)* [2016] UKSC 35; [2016] 3 WLR 157; [2016] All ER (D) 173 (Jun). See further *R (on the application of Barclay) v Lord Chancellor (No 2)* [2014] UKSC 54; [2015] AC 276; [2015] 1 All ER 429, in which the Supreme Court affirmed that the courts of England and Wales in certain circumstances had jurisdiction to review Orders in Council giving royal assent to Channel Islands legislation.

[8] *R v Secretary of State for Foreign and Commonwealth Affairs, ex parte World Development Movement* [1995] 1 WLR 386; [1995] 1 All ER 611. See, also, *Williams Construction Ltd v Blackman* [1995] 1 WLR 102: fact that statutory power conferred on the cabinet (of the Bahamas) no bar to judicial review, since it was the nature of the power (in this case the award of a construction contract) rather than the repository of it that determined the availability of review.

[9] [2002] EWCA Civ 1598; [2003] UKHRR 76, especially at [99], [106], [107]. For application of *Abbasi* and arguments on similar points, see *R (Al-Haq) v Secretary of State for Foreign and Commonwealth Affairs* [2009] EWHC 1910 (Admin) (it was beyond the court's competence to declare or direct what action the government of the United Kingdom was to take upon the assumed breach of international law by Israel; *Abbasi* was distinguished); *R (Al-Rawi) v Secretary of State for Foreign and Commonwealth Affairs* [2006] EWCA Civ 1279; [2008] QB 289; [2007] 2 WLR 1219 (per *Abbasi*, the only legitimate expectation that Guantanamo Bay

detainees had was that the Secretary of State would consider a British national's request that representations be made on their behalf; see also *R (Sandiford) v Secretary of State for Foreign and Commonwealth Affairs* [2014] UKSC 44; [2014] 1 WLR 2697; [2014] 4 All ER 843, where it was held that the Government's blanket policy of refusing to provide funding for legal representation for British nationals facing criminal proceedings abroad was lawful in a death penalty case overseas.

10   *R v Secretary of State for the Home Department, ex parte Bentley* [1994] QB 349; [1994] 2 WLR 101, which was distinguished but not disapproved by the Judicial Committee in *Reckley v Minister of Public Safety and Immigration* [1996] AC 527; [1996] 2 WLR 281; [1996] 1 All ER 562.

11   [2009] EWHC 1409 (Admin) at [55].

12   [2004] UKHL 56, [2005] 2 AC 68. See for the position prior to this case *Rehman v Secretary of State for the Home Department* [2001] UKHL 47; [2003] 1 AC 153 at 57–62 per Lord Hoffmann.

13   See *Patriotic Front-ZAPU v Minister of Justice, Legal and Parliamentary Affairs* 1986 (I) SA 532 (Zimbabwe Supreme Court); *Operation Dismantle v R* (1985) 18 DLR (4th) 481 (Supreme Court of Canada); *Walker* [1987] Pub Law 62.

14   [1978] AC 435; [1977] 3 WLR 300; [1977] 3 All ER 70.

15   [1985] AC 374, [1984] 3 All ER 935.

16   *R v A-G, ex parte Ferrante* [1995] COD 18 (refusal to consent to application for a fresh inquest under the Coroners Act 1988, s 13): *R v Solicitor-General, ex parte Taylor* (1995) 8 Admin LR 206 (decision whether to institute proceedings for contempt of court): *Mohit v Director of Public Prosecutions of Mauritius* (PC) in which Lord Bingham made clear that the current position in English law remained that the Attorney General's decisions remain immune from judicial review: [2006] 1 WLR 3343. See, also, *Turner v DPP* (1978) 68 Crim App Rep 70 (grant of immunity to witness by DPP not justiciable): *R v Chief Constable of Kent, ex parte L* [1993] 1 All ER 756 (DPP's discretion to discontinue criminal proceedings reviewable) and *R(B) v DPP* [2009] 1 WLR 2072 in which the claimant successfully established that the decision to discontinue a prosecution was irrational and involved a misapplication of the code for Crown Prosecutors.

17   *R v Secretary of State for the Home Department, ex parte Hosenball* [1977] 1 WLR 766; [1977] 3 All ER 452; *R v Secretary of State for the Home Department, ex parte Cheblak* [1991] 1 WLR 890; [1991] 2 All ER 319 (a decision on deportation on grounds of national security during the Gulf crisis); *Balfour v Foreign and Commonwealth Office* [1994] 1 WLR 681; [1994] 2 All ER 588; [1994] ICR 277 (refusal to go behind Public Interest Immunity certificate issued on grounds of national security); *R v Secretary of State for the Home Department, ex parte Chahal* [1995] 1 WLR 526; [1995] 1 All ER 658 (court could not review evidence relied on by the Home Secretary to order deportation on grounds of national security and hence could not overturn decision).

18   For example, *R (Cart) v Upper Tribunal* [2010] EWCA Civ 859; [2011] QB 120 (decisions of the Special Immigration Appeals Commission were held to be reviewable); see further [2011] UKSC 28; [2012] 1 AC 663 at [30]-[31]; *Secretary of State for Defence v Guardian Newspapers Ltd* [1985] AC 339 [1984] 3 WLR 986; *CCSU*, above; *R v Secretary of State for the Home Department, ex parte Ruddock* [1987] 1 WLR 1482 (national security considerations did not preclude judicial review of decision to authorise tapping of applicant's telephone).

19   *R v Secretary of State for the Home Department, ex parte Khawaja* [1984] AC 74 [1983] 2 WLR 321; *Bugdaycay v Secretary of State for the Home Department* [1987] AC 514; [1987] 2 WLR 606.

20   *A v Secretary of State for the Home Department* [2004] UKHL 56, [2005] 2 AC 68.

21   See, particularly, *R v Inspectorate of Pollution, ex parte Greenpeace Ltd (No 2)* [1994] 4 All ER 329; *R v Secretary of State for Foreign and Commonwealth Affairs, ex parte World Development Movement Ltd* [1995] 1 WLR 386; [1995] 1 All ER 611; *R v Secretary of State for Employment, ex parte Equal Opportunities Commission* [1995] 1 AC 1; [1994] 2 WLR 409 (on the standing of the Commission) and more recently *R (Quintavalle) v Human Fertilisation and Embryology Authority* [2005] 2 AC 561; [2005] 2 WLR 1061, where the representative of an organisation committed to fostering debate on ethical issues surrounding human reproduction, sought to challenge the Authority's decision to permit tissue typing.

22   The leading case remains *R v East Berkshire Health Authority, ex parte Walsh* [1985] QB 152; [1984] 3 WLR 818.

23   *Mercury Energy Ltd v Electricity Corpn of New Zealand* [1994] 1 WLR 521. The possibility of a public law challenge for *Wednesbury* unreasonableness was not ruled out, but the

Judicial Committee considered that such a challenge would in practice only be possible on grounds of fraud, corruption or bad faith (at 529). This principle was restated by Wyn Williams J in *R (Birmingham Solihull Taxi Association) v Birmingham International Airport Limited)* [2009] EWHC 1913 (Admin) at [67], a case in which the claimant challenged the defendant's decision to terminate an exclusive licence agreement with it.

24   As envisaged in *Mercury Energy*, above.

25   Eg a decision not to pay a purely *ex gratia* severance payment to a dismissed employee, having met any statutory or contractual liabilities.

26   See per Lord Diplock in *CCSU at 411.* Cf also *R v Lord President of the Privy Council, ex parte Page* [1993] AC 682; [1992] 3 WLR 1112.

27   *Nottinghamshire County Council v Secretary of State for the Environment* [1986] AC 240; [1986] 2 WLR 1; [1986] 1 All ER 1986; *R v Secretary of State for the Environment, ex parte Hammersmith and Fulham London Borough Council* [1991] 1 AC 521; [1990] 3 WLR 898; [1990] 3 All ER 589. In the latter case, a challenge to the Minister's exercise of a power to designate local authorities whose expenditure was in the Minister's opinion excessive, there was much emphasis on the political nature of a judgment as to what level of expenditure was 'excessive' as a reason for not interfering with the Minister's exercise of the power (*at 593E–594B*). See, also, *R v Parliamentary Commissioner for Administration, ex parte Dyer* [1994] 1 WLR 621. A further example of the boundaries of reviewability occurred in *Nicklinson v Ministry of Justice* [2014] UKSC; [2015] AC 657; [2014] 3 WLR 200, where the Supreme Court held that it was one thing for the court to decide that the DPP must publish a policy concerning the facts and circumstances that he would take into account in deciding whether to consent to a prosecution under s 2(1) of the Suicide Act 1961, but it was another to dictate what should be the content of that policy; reversing the Court of Appeal's judgment on this point: [2013] EWCA Civ 961.

28   *R v Minister of Defence, ex parte Smith* [1996] QB 517; [1996] 2 WLR 305 [1996] 1 All ER 257; see particularly per Sir Thomas Bingham MR at 336c–338c, explaining why the human rights considerations (arising from a policy of discharging homosexuals from the armed services) prevailed over the considerations in the authorities at note 23 above in determining the power of the court to intervene. The duty to be imposed on public authorities by the Human Rights Act 1998 to give effect to the rights safeguarded by the European Convention on Human Rights has added to the possibilities for this interventionism. The phrase quoted in the text derives from 1(1) *Halsbury's Laws of England* (4th edn, reissue) paragraph 89.

29   [2001] EWCA Civ 789, [2002] QB 129.

POTENTIAL GROUNDS OF CHALLENGE TO THE EXERCISE OF DISCRETIONARY POWERS

7.35   Lord Diplock's classic restatement of the potential grounds for judicial review under the heads of illegality, irrationality and procedural impropriety[1] provides a natural starting point for a consideration of the more specific grounds of challenge available in relation to discretionary powers. Illegality in Lord Diplock's usage is not confined to the obvious instances of a body purporting to exercise a power it does not possess. It covers equally the ostensible exercise of a discretionary power in circumstances open to challenge on a number of other distinct grounds, other than the unreasonableness of the act itself and defects in the procedures adopted. Such a challenge may raise more than one of the recognised grounds; in practice, this may simply involve the same point formulated in different ways. Often such grounds of challenge are closely interlinked with assertions of irrationality, and the latter is in practice rarely successful on its own.[2] (Conversely, an allegation of irrationality may be added to allegations of various kinds of illegality to buttress a challenge to the exercise of a discretionary power.)

1   In *CCSU* [1985] AC 374; [1984] 3 All ER 935 at 410D.

2   See Chapters 8 and 9.

7.36 The principal categories within the heading of illegality discussed in this chapter are as follows.

(1) *Unlawful sub-delegation or divestment of the decision-making power.* This covers conduct sometimes categorised as acting under the dictation of a third party, and allowing the participation of an extraneous party in decision-making. There are special rules and considerations for the allocation and delegation of power within a government department (or the Government as a whole), and within local authorities. The common feature of illegality in these situations is that all involve a fettering of the decision-taker's power by parting with authority: what may be described as 'fettering by divestment'.

(2) *Fettering of discretion in the sense of imposing limits on the decision-taker's future freedom of action – 'temporal fettering'.* Under this category we examine the extent to which a policy can be adopted to regulate the future exercise of a discretion: the limits of the doctrine of estoppel as a bar to the exercise of powers in a particular way; and the extent to which the creation of a legitimate expectation can require a discretionary power to be fettered.

(3) *Relevant and irrelevant considerations*, including the distinction between the identification of those considerations to which regard must be had and the relative weight to be attached to each consideration, and the purposes for which a power may or may not be exercised, including the concept of bad faith.

7.37 As a general comment it should be stressed that while in most cases the criteria applied by the court under these heads will be statute based, in those areas where a discretionary power not derived from statute is nevertheless judicially reviewable[1] the criteria will have to be taken from whatever material is available to establish the framework for the exercise of the power. In the former situation the court is much more likely to be able to base any finding of illegality on the statutory limits of power, leaving irrationality as a residual line of attack. In the latter, however, there may be much less to go on and the court's power to intervene is more likely to depend on a vigorous approach to irrationality.[2]

[1] Such as the powers of the City Panel on Take-overs and Mergers, the Advertising Standards Authority or certain trade associations: *R v Panel on Take-overs and Mergers, ex parte Datafin plc* [1987] QB 815; [1987] 1 All ER 564; *R v Panel on Take-overs and Mergers, ex parte Guinness plc* [1990] 1 QB 146; [1989] 1 All ER 509; *R v Advertising Standards Authority Ltd, ex parte Insurance Services plc* [1990] COD 42; 2 Admin LR 77; *R v Code of Practice Committee of the British Pharmaceutical Industry, ex parte Professional Counselling Aids Ltd* (1990) 3 Admin LR 697. A case to the contrary is *R (West) v Lloyd's of London* [2004] EWCA Civ 506; [2004] 3 All ER 251. See, also, *R v Chief Rabbi, ex parte Wachmann* [1992] 1 WLR 1036 and *R v Disciplinary Committee of the Jockey Club, ex parte Aga Khan* [1993] 1 WLR 909 (both cases where the person or body challenged was held not to be amenable to review). See, generally, CHAPTER 5.

[2] Less so in the other main area of non-statutory powers, those derived from the prerogative; see 7.32 above.

7.38 The jurisprudence of the Human Rights Act 1998, and of the application of principles of EU law, has led to an increasing focus on proportionality as a criterion for determining the lawfulness of the exercise of a discretionary power. In *R (Association of British Civilian Internees: Far East Region) v Secretary of State for Defence*, the Court of Appeal affirmed that proportionality as a test of legality has not displaced the *Wednesbury* test of unreasonableness or irrationality where a challenge to a decision does not raise any human rights or Community law issues.[1] In *Keyu v Secretary of State for Foreign and Commonwealth Affairs*,[2] a majority of the Supreme Court held that it would be inappropriate for a five-judge panel of the Court to consider replacing *Wednesbury* reasonableness with a test of proportionality, but in any event the decision under review – whether the UK was obliged to hold a public inquiry into the deaths of 24 civilians killed by British soldiers in colonial Malaya in 1948 – was not disproportionate. In *Kennedy v Charity Commission*,[3] Lord Mance suggested that domestic judicial review should incorporate a form of proportionality analysis 'even outside the scope of Convention and EU law'.[4] In *Pham v Secretary of State for the Home Department*,[5] the Supreme Court declined to express a view on whether deprivation of Mr Pham's UK citizenship also deprived him of EU citizenship and thereby altered the standard of review from *Wednesbury* reasonableness to proportionality, but the majority endorsed a flexible approach to the standard of review particularly in cases affecting fundamental rights, noting that proportionality is an important tool: *[60], [98]*. See further *R (Lumsdon) v Legal Services Board*,[6] where the Supreme Court reviewed in detail the nature and applicability of the proportionality principle in EU and national law: at [33]–[82].

[1]   [2003] EWCA Civ 473; [2003] QB 1397 (rejecting a claim in relation to the claimants' exclusion from a scheme to pay ex gratia compensation to former World War II internees). See, generally, CHAPTERS 8 and 9.
[2]   [2015] UKSC 69; [2015] 3 WLR 1665.
[3]   [2014] UKSC 20; [2015] AC 455; [2014] 2 WLR 808.
[4]   Ibid at [54]. De Smith notes that 'Although the English courts have yet to embrace this form of review outside the fields of European Union Law and Convention rights, the approach is having a growing influence on the common law in purely domestic cases': Woolf et al (eds), De Smith's *Judicial Review* (7th edn, 2013), paragraph 11-009. See further P. Craig, 'Proportionality, Rationality and Review' [2010] N.Z.L.Rev 265; T. Hickman, 'Problems and Proportionality' [2010] N.Z.L. Rev 303.
[5]   [2015] UKSC 19; [2015] 1 WLR 1591; [2015] 3 All ER 1015.
[6]   [2015] UKSC 41; [2016] AC 697; [2015] 3 WLR 121.

UNLAWFUL SUB-DELEGATION: FETTERING BY DIVESTMENT[1]

[1]   See Smith, Woolf and Jowell, *Judicial Review* (6th edn, 2007) paragraphs 5–138—5–161.

7.39 There is no absolute rule of law prohibiting the repository of a discretion from delegating the power conferred on it to another. However, there is a strong presumption that the repository of the power must exercise it personally (or in the case of a body, corporately). The maxim *delegatus non potest delegare* (the delegate is not permitted to delegate) has aptly been described as a rule of statutory construction,[2] and whether it applies in a particular context therefore depends on the construction of the statute and whatever indications of a contrary intent can be deduced from the wording, objects and context. The presumption is strongest in the area of judicial and analogous powers, and here the indications needed to establish a contrary intention must be exceptionally strong. Where sub-delegation of a power is permissible, it is also necessary to show sub-delegation in fact; this may need to be formally sanctioned, but in some limited cases may be implied. The mischief of the presumption against sub-delegation is the loss by the delegate of the power to decide conferred on it by the enabling power; lawful sub-delegation, on the other hand, normally results in a decision treated as that of the principal. This distinction also makes it clearer why sub-delegation of investigation and recommendation, reserving the final decision to the principal, is more likely to be accepted by the courts.[3]

[2] See John Willis, 'Delegatus non potest delegare', (1943) 21 Can Bar Rev 257.

[3] See *R v Commission for Racial Equality, ex parte Cottrell and Rothon* [1980] 3 All ER 265, [1980] 1 WLR 1580, following *R v Race Relations Board, ex parte Selvarajan* [1975] 1 WLR 1686.

Judicial and similar proceedings

7.40 The presumption that the repository of a discretion must exercise it personally is strongest where power is given to a judge in a court of law. It is only slightly less strong in the context of tribunals, whether statutory or not, exercising powers of a judicial nature, including disciplinary powers.[1] The use of the term 'judicial' here is not intended to invoke a technical classification of powers; it is as likely to be used to explain a strict insistence on the personal exercise of a power as to require it. The presumption is not against sub-delegation only. The person or body entrusted with the decision, and nobody else, should take it. Thus the participation of persons not within the ambit of the delegation of authority in the decision under challenge will normally be fatal;[2] mere presence of a third party during the deliberations is, however, not as such a valid reason for challenge on the ground of improper divestment,[3] although it may, of course, be relevant to a challenge for procedural impropriety. An exception to the general rule is the practice permitting justices' clerks to advise the justices on the law applicable to their deliberations.[4]

[1] For example *Re S (a Barrister)* [1970] 1 QB 160; [1969] 1 All ER 949 (disciplinary jurisdiction of Inns of Court over Barristers); *Leary v National Union of Vehicle Builders* [1971] Ch 34; [1970] 2 All ER 713 (expulsion from trade union); *Ward v Bradford Corpn* (1971) 70 LGR 27 (expulsion of student from college).

[2] As in *Leary* above; in *Ward*, above, the court in its discretion declined to intervene.

[3] See *Leary*, above, at 53–54. Cf also the comments of Megarry J at 55B on *Lane v Norman* (1891) 66 LT 83.

[4] *Practice Direction* [1953] 2 All ER 1306n; [1953] 1 WLR 1416; *R v East Kerrier Justices, ex parte Mundy* [1952] 2 QB 719; [1952] 2 All ER 144.

7.41 Delegation within a judicial body or tribunal, for instance to its chairman, may also raise problems. Many statutes provide for certain of the functions of a tribunal to be exercisable by its chairman alone,[1] or by a quorum smaller than the full tribunal. In the absence of such a provision, the validity of a decision taken by only some of the members of the tribunal will depend on whether the statutory definition of the tribunal is broad enough for the deciding group to be validly constituted as a tribunal: if it is, no question of improper sub-delegation arises.[2]

[1] For example, for Employment Tribunals, powers are conferred on a tribunal consisting only of a Chairman to hear certain categories of claim: Employment Tribunals Act 1996, s 4(2), (3).

[2] *Howard v Borneman (No 2)* [1976] AC 301; [1975] 2 All ER 418 (tribunal constituted under the Finance Act 1960, s 28(7); s 28(7) required only that the tribunal consist of a Chairman and two or more members appointed by the Lord Chancellor. Decision taken by Chairman and four out of the five appointed members held valid). See, also, *R v Solicitors' Complaints Bureau, ex parte Curtin* (1993) 6 Admin LR 657 (delegation by Law Society of disciplinary

sanction expressly authorised by statute). See also the converse: in *R (Bridgerow Ltd) v Cheshire West and Cheshire Borough Council* [2014] EWHC 1187 (Admin); [2015] PTSR 91, power to renew licences had been sub-delegated to a panel 'comprising' three members of the licensing committee; because 'comprising' was a prescriptive term, it was unlawful for the full licensing committee of 12 to purport to make the determination.

Delegation and agency

7.42 There is considerable similarity between concepts applicable to the limits of delegation of discretionary power and the rules of agency. An agent may not further delegate or transfer his authority to another agent without the authority of the principal; the agent's acts are treated as those of the principal: and the principal does not by appointing an agent divest himself of the power to act. Likewise, the presumption against sub-delegation precludes further delegation by the repository through delegation of a power. Generally, any lawful further delegation by the repository of power does not divest that person or body of responsibility for the acts of the delegate; nor does the repository relinquish the right to exercise the power notwithstanding the delegation.[1] Despite these analogies it is suggested that the comparison adds little to a clear understanding of the problems of delegation of power. Clearly, a public authority may, like any other person, appoint agents to act for it. This does not answer the question whether a particular task may lawfully be delegated. A better approach is to consider the questions functionally. Executive and administrative functions may be delegated, but not decision-taking or the exercise of the core of the power vested in the principal.

[1]   Cf *Blackpool Corpn v Locker* [1948] 1 KB 349; [1948] 1 All ER 85 and the discussion in Woolf et al (eds), De Smith's *Judicial Review* (7th edn, 2013), paragraph 5–156.

7.43 This line of distinction can be illustrated by several cases of permitted delegation where it was not the core power which was relinquished. In *Horder v Scott*[1] an inspector was empowered to procure samples for analysis. Sending his assistant to buy a sample was held to be lawful; no discretion was transferred. A succession of cases before[2] and since[3] of investigations being undertaken by officers or a committee of the body charged with deciding the matter can be cited in support of the proposition that so long as the court is willing to conclude that the decision-taking power has been reserved, there is no improper delegation. In a case involving the authorisation on behalf of a trade union of a strike following a successful ballot, where the statute required the person named on the ballot paper to authorise the action, the General Secretary (who was the person named) was held to be acting lawfully in giving authority to call the strike to the Regional Officer, if negotiations failed to resolve the dispute. There was no delegation of the operative decision in this case, which was that a strike should be called if it proved necessary.[4]

[1]   (1880) 5 QBD 552.
[2]   *Osgoode v Nelson* (1872) LR 5 HL 636.
[3]   *R v Race Relations Board, ex parte Selvarajan* [1975] 1 WLR 1686; [1976] 1 All ER 12; *R v Commission for Racial Equality, ex parte Cottrell and Rothon* [1980] 3 All ER 265, [1980] 1 WLR 1580. The basis for holding that the final decision is that of the original repository is sometimes rather exiguous, as in *Osgoode v Nelson*, above, and *Re S (a Barrister)* [1970] 1 QB 160; [1969] 1 All ER 949.
[4]   *Tanks and Drums Ltd v Transport and General Workers' Union* [1992] ICR 1.

Delegation and divestment

7.44 At the heart of the presumption against sub-delegation are the cases illustrating situations in which sub-delegation was held to invalidate a decision. These, however, do not provide a formula or test, and it would be almost impossible to construct one suitable for the range of statutory contexts in which the issue may arise. Generally, divestment of decision-taking will be unlawful unless expressly or implicitly permitted, but the borderline between what is, and is not, a divestment is problematic, especially where part of a process of decision-taking has been conferred on a subordinate body or person. More recent case law relevant to this point focuses on 'contracting-out' by local authorities; for example, the practice adopted by some local authorities of contracting out to a company the conduct of reviews under s 202 of the Housing Act 1996 of the suitability of temporary accommodation provided by the local authority or of the refusal of homelessness applications: this was found to be lawful in *De Winter Heald v Brent LBC* [2009] EWCA Civ 930; [2010] 1 WLR 990; cf concerns expressed about this practice in *Runa Begum v Tower Hamlets LBC* [2003] UKHL 5; [2003] 2 AC 430; [2003] 2 WLR 388, eg at [46] per Lord Hoffman. Some earlier authorities are offered as examples of cases where a sub-delegation rendered a decision unlawful, and which may indicate categories of situations likely to produce such a finding, as follows:

(1) *Allingham v Minister of Agriculture and Fisheries*[1] – the Minister had validly delegated to a war agricultural executive committee power to give directions to landowners as to the cultivation of land. The committee, having decided that a landowner should be directed to grow certain crops, left it to an officer to determine and direct the specific distribution of crops to particular fields. The officer's directions were held to be ultra vires.

(2) *Barnard v National Dock Labour Board*[2] – the statutory dock labour scheme constituted a joint committee of employer and employee representatives, and empowered it to exercise disciplinary powers of suspension. These were delegated to the port manager who suspended the plaintiff. His suspension was declared unlawful.

(3) *Ellis v Dubowski*[3] – local authorities were empowered to impose conditions on the grant of licences for cinemas. The local authority concerned purported to impose a condition that (subject to immaterial qualifications) no film should be shown which had not been approved for unrestricted screening by the British Board of Film Censors (a non-statutory body established by the film industry). This condition was held to be unlawful but with a broad hint that if the condition was made subject to the overriding authority of the licensor to permit a film to be shown, it would be valid.

(4) *Mills v LCC*[4] – this was the sequel to *Ellis* in which the same condition, but with the addition 'without the consent of the Council', was held to be lawful.

---

[1]   [1948] 1 All ER 780.
[2]   [1953] 2 QB 18, [1953] 1 All ER 1113. See, also, *Vine v National Dock Labour Board* [1957] AC 488, [1956] 3 All ER 939.
[3]   [1921] 3 KB 621.

⁴ [1925] 1 KB 213.

7.45 *Ellis*¹ is, in many ways, a case that could equally be regarded as one of acting under the dictation of a third party, an aspect of illegality considered in more detail below.² For present purposes, however, it and the following case of *Mills*³ serve to show very clearly the distinction between a complete divestment of the power to decide which films should be shown, and the retention of a right to override the decisions of the third party (albeit in one direction only). Both *Ellis*⁴ and *Allingham*⁵ were concerned with the implementation of a policy decided by the principal, and in all three of the successful challenges the operative, disputed decision was left to the subordinate or third party.⁶ In such cases, unless there is statutory power to delegate in the manner complained of, or a power to delegate can be implied (which as the foregoing discussion indicates will be rare), the divestment will render the exercise of discretion by the sub-delegate liable to successful challenge.

¹ [1921] 3 KB 621.
² See **7.46** below.
³ [1925] 1 KB 213.
⁴ [1921] 3 KB 621.
⁵ [1948] 1 All ER 780.
⁶ The farmer in *Allingham* was being prosecuted for growing the sugar beet in the wrong field. The defendants in *Ellis* and *Mills* had been prosecuted for showing films, in breach of the licence conditions, which had not been approved for universal exhibition by the Board of Film Censors.

Acting under dictation

7.46 A variant on the complaint that the decision-making power has been delegated unlawfully to X is the argument that the repository of the power takes decisions in accordance with the dictates of X. In practice the two tests are likely to produce the same result. A body which has regard to the views of X, however vigorously expressed, is neither acting under dictation nor delegating its function of deciding to X.¹ If X's views are decisive, the decision will be open to challenge on both grounds. Similarly there is a considerable overlap between acting under the dictation of a third party and fettering the exercise of a discretion by agreeing in advance to decide subject to the view or policy of a third party. In *H Lavender & Son Ltd v Minister of Housing and Local Government*² Willis J explicitly rested his decision on both grounds (in a case where the Minister had refused planning permission for gravel extraction in accordance with a policy of refusal unless the Minister of Agriculture was not opposed to the development). Cases of discretionary decisions being successfully impugned solely on the ground of acting under dictation are therefore inherently unlikely,³ and it is suggested that this is best seen as an alternative formulation to reinforce other grounds of challenge; in particular, it is a refinement of, rather than a separate point from, improper sub-delegation.

¹ There may still be an issue as to whether X's views are a relevant consideration in the particular decision.
² [1970] 3 All ER 871, [1970] 1 WLR 1231. Compare, on the question when pursuit of policy becomes an unlawful fettering of discretion. *Stringer v Minister of Housing and Local Government* [1971] 1 All ER 65, [1970] 1 WLR 1281.

3   There appears to be no reported decision relying solely on this point. However, see *R (S) v Secretary of State for the Home Department* [2007] Imm Ar 781 in which Carnwath LJ held that the Home Office had acted under dictation/fettered its discretion by postponing its decision on the respondent's asylum claim solely to meet the requirements of a "public service agreement" agreed between the Home Office and Treasury, which had the effect of prioritising new rather than existing asylum claims.

7.47 Examples of cases where acting under dictation has been successfully relied on reinforce the point that the effective divestment of a power of decision-making is the touchstone of illegality in this area. In *Simms Motor Units Ltd v Minister of Labour and National Service*[1] a national service officer on whom powers to direct reinstatement of essential workers had been personally conferred adopted a policy of following the directions of the Minister as to the exercise of his discretion. This could equally be seen as a delegation to another of the effective decision: the fact that the other was hierarchically his superior would appear irrelevant since the discretion was vested in the officer not the Minister. Again, in *R v Police Complaints Board, ex parte Madden*,[2] the Board adopted a policy of not instituting disciplinary proceedings where the Director of Public Prosecutions had determined not to prosecute on the same facts. This transferred the operative decision to the DPP as well as involving acting under his 'dictation' (a harsh description since the DPP was exercising an autonomous discretion and not purporting to dictate anything, but such an intention does not appear to be a necessary feature of the other party's offence of abdicating discretion). The Board's decision was accordingly quashed.[3] This can be contrasted with the decision of the Court of Appeal in *R (Ealing London Borough Council) v Audit Commission*,[4] rejecting a challenge to the policy of the Audit Commission, in awarding performance ratings to local authorities, automatically to award a 'poor' rating if the Commission for Social Care Inspection (the body with statutory responsibility for inspecting the authority's social services functions) had awarded a score of zero; that rating would itself have been open to challenge by the aggrieved authority, and its consequences for the Audit Commission's rating were, in the court's view, still determined by that body.

1   [1946] 2 All ER 201.
2   [1983] 2 All ER 353; [1983] 1 WLR 447, decided under the Police Act 1976.
3   See *R v Chief Constable of Thames Valley Police, ex parte Police Complaints Authority* [1996] COD 324 (refusal to proceed with internal disciplinary proceedings where DPP had said insufficient evidence to prosecute on same matter). See, further, *R v Waltham Forest London Borough Council, ex parte Baxter* [1988] QB 419; [1987] 3 All ER 671, CA (councillors voting for a rate must not vote in blind obedience to party instruction but may give full weight to view of their party). Sir John Donaldson MR was emphatic that a decision of a local authority could be invalidated even if some councillors voted solely in obedience to a party Whip imposed by the party caucus of councillors – a pure fettering of discretion – as well as if they acted on the instructions of a Borough Party Committee whose membership was not confined to councillors, which could therefore be seen as a third party. Where the person on whose instructions the repository of a discretion purports to act has improper motives these may taint the repository's exercise of power with the impropriety. But see the recent case of *R (Lewis) v Redcar and Cleveland Borough* [2009] 1 WLR 83. Here the Court of Appeal made plain that councillors determining a planning application were not in a judicial or quasi judicial position, but were democratically accountable decision-takers who had been elected to provide and pursue policies entitled to be predisposed to determine the application in accordance with their political views and policies, provided they had given fair consideration to all relevant points. See also *Ronacarelli v Duplessis* (1959) 16 DLR (2nd) 689 (revocation of licence of active supporter of Jehovah's Witnesses in accordance with instruction or policy of Prime Minister of Province founded on hostility to Jehovah's Witnesses).

⁴   [2005] EWCA Civ 556; (2005) Times, 26 May.

7.48 An interesting example of a challenge by the holder of the delegated power to the third party seeking to dictate the manner of exercise of delegated powers is *R v Cornwall County Council, ex parte Cornwall and Isles of Scilly Guardians ad Litem*,[1] where an instruction to guardians ad litem who were appointed by the court from a panel maintained by a Council that they must not devote more than a stated number of hours to each case was quashed as an abuse of power by the Council.

¹   [1992] 1 WLR 427.

Government departments

7.49 The normal principles applicable to the delegation of discretionary powers are substantially modified in the case of powers conferred by statute on Ministers of the Crown. Such powers rarely confer express authority to delegate decision-making to officials. However, the realities of public administration have long necessitated that the great majority of such powers are, in fact, exercised by officials and not by the Minister in person. The constitutional principles necessary to accommodate this have consistently received the endorsement of the courts, and are discussed in Chapter 14 below.

Local authorities

7.50 The principles developed for ministers and government departments have been applied by the Divisional Court to powers conferred on chief constables.[1] They may well be capable of application more generally to hierarchical organisations where it can be inferred that Parliament conferred power on an office holder not because of that person's personal qualifications, but because that person would take responsibility for what was done by appropriately qualified individuals in the hierarchy. Local government calls for special mention, however, as an area where elaborate statutory provisions on delegation are in place and there may be limited room for any application of the *Carltona* principles.[2]

¹   See *R (Chief Constable of West Midlands) v Birmingham Magistrates Court* [2002] EWHC 1087 (Admin); [2003], Prim LR 37, see also **14.29**.
²   But cf *R (Essex County Council) v Secretary of State for Education* [2012] EWHC 1460 (Admin) at [42] (*Carltona* applicable to 'non-delegable' equality due regard duties).

7.51 Statutory powers within the local government sphere are almost invariably conferred on local authorities as such. Clearly, the taking of decisions by the full local authority on all the many day-to-day matters that even a small authority must decide would be impracticable. Sections 101 and 102 of the Local Government Act 1972 (as amended by the Localism Act 2011) contain the current statutory powers to delegate. Detailed discussion of these provisions is beyond the scope of this work.[1] Briefly, a local authority is empowered to delegate any function, not specifically excluded from the general power, either to a committee or sub-committee or to an officer.[2] A committee charged with a function by its parent authority may in turn delegate the power to act to a sub-committee or an officer, and a subcommittee so charged may delegate to an officer.[3] Additional provisions allow for delegation of joint functions to committees or officers. Three further points about the legislative scheme should be noted: first, there is express power to create committees and sub-committees where membership includes persons other than elected members of the authority.[4] Second, the local authority is not precluded by delegation from exercising the powers itself.[5] Third, a decision taken under delegated authority is treated as a decision of the authority.[6]

[1] For a detailed commentary see *Butterworths Local Government Law* (Tottel Publishing), Chs 6B and 6C.

[2] Local Government Act 1972, s 101(1). This does not permit the delegation of the power to determine the size and composition of committees: *R v Brent London Borough Council, ex parte Gladbaum and Woods* (1990) 2 Admin LR 634. The fact that delegation is possible does not remove the necessity for the authority to do so formally: *R v St Edmundsbury Borough Council, ex parte Walton* [1999] Env LR 879; (1999) Admin LR 648. However, if delegation has formally taken place under the wrong legal provision that does not make it unlawful if it was permissible under another legal provision (see R *(on the application of Raphael) v Highbury Corner Magistrates' Court* [2011] P.T.S.R. 152) where the Court held that although a licensing committee had purported to delegate functions under the Licensing Act 2003 (before the relevant provisions of the Act had come into force) it had properly delegated the same functions under the Local Government Act 1972, s 101.

[3] Local Government Act 1972, s 101(2), unless the local authority or committee or otherwise direct.

[4] Local Government Act 1972, s 102(3), excluding finance committees. Persons disqualified under Part V of the Act from membership of or election to the authority may not be members of a committee or sub-committee, with certain exceptions in the educational field: s 104(1), (2); however those disqualified from membership or election under the Local Government and Housing Act 1989, Pt 1 may be co-opted members of committees.

[5] Local Government Act 1972, s 101(4).

[6] *Battelley v Finsbury Borough Council* (1958) 56 LGR 165. This has the consequence that the deliberations of the delegate are treated as those of the authority (a point of considerable relevance where questions arise as to whether all relevant considerations have been taken into account). See *Goddard v Minister of Housing and Local Government* [1958] 1 WLR 1151; [1958] 3 All ER 482.

7.52 The governance of local authorities has been significantly rationalised by the provisions of the Local Government Act 2000 (as amended by the Localism Act 2011 in England). These require local authorities in England to adopt executive arrangements in accordance with one of two options[1] set out in the Act, referred to respectively as a 'mayor and cabinet executive' and a 'leader and cabinet executive'. By s 9D of the Act (s 13 for Wales), functions of the authority conferred by statute are to be the responsibility of the executive, other than those prescribed by the Secretary of State by regulations. There are parallel provisions for delegation of executive functions to the mayor or leader, to committees or members of the executive and to officers.[2]

[1] Local Government Act 2000, s 9C(1), (2), (3).

[2] By ss 9E, 14, 15 and 16, in each case without prejudice to the exercise of a particular power being undertaken by the original repository in place of the delegate.

7.53 While the statutory framework of delegation thus created is extensive, it is important to stress its limits. Formal resolutions creating and defining the composition of committees and sub-committees, and delegating specific functions to them, are necessary for the statutory provisions to apply.[1] Unless this is specifically provided for by the relevant legislation, there is no room for committees comprising members (especially co-opted individuals who are not elected members) other than those appointed by the authority, or for committees acting out with the scope of their express delegation. However, the case law shows that the courts permit some flexibility beyond the formal statutory framework. Thus, within certain limitations, the decision of an officer taken without prior delegated power can be ratified by the authority (eg a decision to institute legal proceedings).[2] However, subsequent ratification cannot cure a decision which at the time was ultra vires the authority, even if the decision could validly have been made by the authority, at the time of the purported ratification.[3] Neither can subsequent ratification validate the purported act of a sub-delegate to whom there is no power to delegate, as noted earlier.[4] Flexibility within local government arises from the existence of such extensive powers to delegate.[5]

[1] *Western Fish Products Ltd v Penwith District Council* [1981] 2 All ER 204, at 219g, per Megaw LJ.
[2] *Warwick RDC v Miller-Mead* [1962] Ch 441; [1962] 1 All ER 212 (on the Public Health Act 1936, s 100), followed in *Stoke on Trent City Council v B & Q (Retail) Ltd* [1984] Ch 1; [1983] 3 WLR 78; [1984] 2 All ER 787 (application for injunction to restrain illegal Sunday trading); *R v Southwark London Borough Council, ex parte Bannerman* (1990) 2 Admin. L.R. 381; [1990] COD 115.
[3] *A-G (ex rel Co-operative Retail Services Ltd) v Taff-Ely Borough Council* (1981) 42 P & CR 1. Cf *R v Rochester Upon Medway City Council, ex parte Hobday* (1989) 58 P & CR 424.
[4] *Barnard v National Dock Labour Board* [1953] 2 QB 18; [1953] 1 All ER 1113, above, note 117. It should be noted that s 101 of the 1972 Act also allows for delegation of decisions to committees subject to ratification. In such cases ratification is necessary because of the conditional nature of the delegation of power. Cf the avoidance of this problem in *R v Southwark London Borough Council, ex parte Bannerman* (1990) 2 Admin. L.R. 381; [1990] COD 115 (request to institute proceedings signed by subordinate officer on behalf of the designated officer, held a matter of internal organisation not sub-delegation).
[5] An example outside local government of delegation expressly authorised by the statute is *R v Solicitors' Complaints Bureau, ex parte Curtin* (1993) 6 Admin LR 657; [1993] COD 467 (delegation by Law Society of powers to impose conditions on solicitors' practising certificates).

7.54 The cases referred to in the previous paragraph were concerned with challenges by those subject to or adversely affected by decisions. A different line of authority deals with the existence and scope of a right to rely on decisions, assurances or representations made on behalf of a local authority by an officer acting outside the scope of his or her delegated authority. The balance between the protection of individual rights where the claimant has relied on the decision or representation to his or her detriment, and the public interest in not fettering the discretion of the true repository of the statutory power, has proved controversial. The courts have confined the ambit of estoppel in this area narrowly.[1] This is discussed below in the context of the fettering of discretion but see also the principles relating to legitimate expectations, which are dealt with at **7.64 to 7.73**.[2]

[1] *Western Fish Products Ltd v Penwith District Council* [1981] 2 All ER 204, restricting the application of *Lever Finance Ltd v Westminster (City) London Borough Council* [1971] 1 QB 222; [1970] 3 All ER 496. For more recent consideration of the availability of estoppel in public law, see *R (Capital Care Services (UK) Ltd) v Secretary of State for the Home Department* [2012] EWCA Civ 1151 and *R (Butt) v Secretary of State for the Home Department* [2013] EWHC 1793 (Admin), in which Michael Kent QC (sitting as a Deputy High Court Judge) held: 'There is a continuing debate about the extent to which the doctrine of estoppel has any application in the public law context but it is at least clear that where it does it is simply another way of saying that it would be unfair and amount to an abuse in all the circumstances for the public authority to rely upon the point in dispute. That is simply an

aspect of the requirement of good administration.' For the requirement of detriment, see also *Norfolk County Council v Secretary of State for the Environment* [1973] 3 All ER 673; [1973] 1 WLR 1400. The restricted form of estoppel arising in planning cases within the *Lever* principle is to be distinguished from the application of issue estoppel to planning appeal proceedings: *Thrasy-voulou v Secretary of State for the Environment* [1988] QB 809; [1988] 2 All ER 781; *Downderry Construction Ltd v Secretary of State for Local Government, Transport and the Regions* [2002] EWHC 2 (Admin); [2002] ACD 62 at [19].

2   As to the enforceability of contracts with local authorities certified by an authorised officer of the authority, see the Local Government (Contracts) Act 1997, ss 2–5.

FETTERING DISCRETION[1]

1   See, generally, Woolf et al (eds), *De Smith's Judicial Review* (7th edn, 2013), Ch 9 (where the matter is dealt with as an issue of procedural fairness rather than a substantive ground of review: the overlap in relation to legitimate expectation makes either categorisation equally tenable).

7.55 In respect of this heading the most usual ground of challenge arises from the *application* of the fetter in relation to an individual case. This may involve an argument that a policy adopted by the public body is an irrelevant consideration, so that having regard to it is an improper and unlawful manner of exercise of the discretion,[2] or the policy may be so applied that the discretion vested in the body is not in reality exercised at all in the particular case. This section is concerned primarily with the latter argument,[3] but we must also consider the ways in which it may be argued that a valid restriction on the ambit of a discretionary power may come into existence.

2   For example, a licensing authority adopting a policy that it will not entertain applications from people with red hair (cf *Short v Poole Corpn* [1926] Ch 66 at 91, per Warrington LJ).
3   For a discussion of irrelevant considerations, see **7.81**.

7.56 A public body charged with a discretionary function will often find it expedient to adopt a policy towards the exercise of its functions. This may assist its officers in making recommendations in individual cases, and applicants assessing the prospects of a successful application for the exercise of the power in their favour. Much of the structure of administrative discretion is constructed on the assumption that policy will guide the detailed exercise of discretionary powers. Policy may assist the promotion of the objects of the Act conferring the power.[1] Similar considerations may support a general adherence by a public authority to the policy of the government of the day, where relevant. A failure to follow an established policy may give grounds for judicial review;[2] this is closely linked to the doctrine of legitimate expectation, discussed below.[3]

1   As in *R v Port of London Authority, ex parte Kynoch Ltd* [1919] 1 KB 176.
2   For the modern authoritative statement of this principle see *R (Lumba) v Secretary of State for the Home Department* [2011] UKSC 12; [2012] 1 AC 245; [2011] 2 WLR 671 at [35] where Dyson JSC held: 'The individual has a basic public law right to have his or her case considered under whatever policy the executive sees fit to adopt provided that the adopted policy is a lawful exercise of the discretion conferred by the statute'. See also the decision of the Supreme Court in *R (Kambadzi) v Secretary of State for the Home Department* [2011] UKSC 23; [2011] 1 WLR 1299; [2011] 4 All ER 975.
3   See **7.64**.

7.57 There is a fine line between legitimate adherence to a general policy and the view, affirmed in numerous cases, that it is unlawful for a body to bind itself or divest itself of any discretion by adopting a blanket policy or adhering over-rigidly to its policy. The courts have found the identification of the line difficult both in individual cases and in expressing the principle more specifically than at this fairly general level. See for a recent example of a case where a bright-line rule or blanket policy was regarded in part as disproportionate by a majority of the Supreme Court: *R (Tigere) v Secretary of State for Business, Innovation and Skills* [2015] UKSC 57; [2015] 1 WLR 3820; [2016] 1 All ER 191 (requirement that an applicant for a student loan be 'settled' in the UK).

7.58 The general position is illustrated by the leading case, *British Oxygen Co Ltd v Minister of Technology*.[1] The Board of Trade was empowered[2] to make grants towards capital expenditure for plant and equipment. It declined to make grants in respect of oxygen cylinders purchased by the appellants costing about £20 each, in pursuance of a policy not to make grants where individual items of equipment cost less than £25. The House of Lords, in refusing to declare the policy unlawful, indicated that the adoption of such a policy was justifiable and desirable. Moreover, there was, in their Lordships' view, no real difference between a policy and a rule:

> 'What the authority must not do is to refuse to listen at all. But a Ministry or large authority may have had to deal already with a multitude of similar applications and then they will almost certainly have evolved a policy so precise that it could well be considered a rule. There can be no objection to that, provided the authority is always willing to listen to anyone with something new to say – of course I do not mean to say that there need be an oral hearing'.[3]

---

[1] [1971] AC 610; [1970] 3 All ER 165. See the recent decision of the High Court in *R (Rowe) v Revenue and Customs Commissioners* [2015] EWHC 2293 (Admin); [2015] BTC 27, in which it applied the *British Oxygen* case to hold that a policy governing the use of the statutory scheme for the giving of partner payment notices by HMRC, requiring accelerated payment of tax, was lawful, as the policy did not preclude HMRC departing from it in exceptional cases.

[2] Under the Industrial Development Act 1966.

[3] [1971] AC 610 at 625D–625E, per Lord Reid. See, also, Viscount Dilhorne, at 631A, to the same effect.

7.59 A case the other side of the line is *R v Secretary of State for the Home Department, ex parte Venables*,[1] where the Home Secretary was found by the House of Lords to have adopted an unlawful policy in fixing a tariff period of detention for young offenders sentenced to be detained at Her Majesty's pleasure which would in no circumstances be varied by reason of matters occurring during the tariff period.

---

[1] [1998] AC 403. Cf also *R v Secretary of State for the Home Department, ex parte Hindley* [1998] QB 751, affd [2001] 1 AC 410; *R (Smith) v Secretary of State for the Home Department* [2005] UKHL 51; [2005] 3 WLR 410 (Secretary of State's policy of not reviewing tariff periodically once set not unlawful); and *R (F) v Secretary of State for the Home Department* [2009] EWCA Civ 792; [2010] 1 WLR 76; [2010] 1 All ER 1024 (decision by the Court of Appeal that the Sexual Offences Act 2003 s 82 was incompatible with the European Convention on Human Rights 1950 art 8 in subjecting certain sex offenders to notification requirements indefinitely without the opportunity for review); and *R (T and others) v Chief Constable of Greater Manchester and Secretary of State for the Department* [2014] UKSC 35; [2015] AC 49 (a decision that the blanket statutory regime for issuing

criminal records certificates and requiring the disclosure of spent warnings to a potential employer was unlawful). See also *R (Mayaya) v Secretary of State for the Home Department* [2011] EWHC 3088 (Admin), [2012] 1 All ER 1491 at [46], [53] (discretionary leave policy not an unlawful fetter on the basis that it used length of sentence as a criterion of seriousness of offending, but policy unlawfully fettered by barring consideration before the passage of 10 years).

7.60 Thus a policy or rule may be adopted which effectively decides 'normal' cases, *provided* that the policy or rule is itself proper, and that the deciding authority retains a willingness to consider each case. The last point may appear at first sight to be procedural formalism carried to excess, but it serves two important purposes: to allow an opportunity for the cases which are *not* 'normal' to identify themselves, and to allow applicants the hope of persuading the deciding authority to reconsider the policy in the light of a new consideration. The twin themes of liberty to discharge a discretionary power by policy-making and the duty to deal with each case individually are reiterated with nuances of emphasis in numerous cases;[1] the courts are constrained by the nature of the question to adopt a case-by-case consideration of which side of the line a decision-taking process falls. The great majority of cases involve a refusal to exercise a discretion, but the same considerations apply to a policy of automatically exercising a discretion without hearing a person whose interests would be adversely affected thereby.[2] It would appear that the making of a policy by informal decision is no less valid if the policy could have been made formally by statutory instrument.[3]

[1] See, eg, *R (Alvi) v Secretary of State for the Home Department* [2012] UKSC 33; [2012] 1 WLR 2208; [2012] 4 All ER 1041 at [111] per Lord Walker; *R v Ministry for Agriculture Fisheries and Food, ex p Hamble (Offshore) Fisheries Ltd* [1995] 2 All ER 714 at 722a-c per Sedley J. See, eg (cases where decision upheld) *R v Port of London Authority, ex parte Kynoch Ltd* [1919] 1 KB 176; *British Oxygen Co Ltd v Minister of Technology* [1971] AC 610; [1970] 3 All ER 165; *Stringer v Minister of Housing and Local Government* [1971] 1 All ER 65; [1970] 1 WLR 1281; *Re Findlay* [1985] AC 318; [1984] 3 All ER 801 (a case on formulation of policy); *Smith v Inner London Education Authority* [1978] 1 All ER 411; *R v Secretary of State for the Home Department, ex parte McCallion* [1993] COD 148 (refusal to adopt policy of automatic reference of criminal convictions to Court of Appeal when new points of law raised); and (cases where decision successfully challenged) *R v Flintshire County Council County Licensing (Stage Plays) Committee, ex parte Barrett* [1957] 1 QB 350; [1957] 1 All ER 112 (condition imposed to preserve consistency; this case could equally be regarded as an example of taking an irrelevant consideration into account): *R v Secretary of State for the Environment, ex parte Brent London Borough Council* [1982] QB 593; [1983] 3 All ER 321 (express refusal to hear affected authority before exercising discretionary power in accordance with announced policy); *R v Chief Constable of South Wales, ex parte Merrick* [1994] 1 WLR 663 (policy of not allowing prisoners in cells at a magistrates' court access to legal advisers after 10am, applied without regard to circumstances of request for access). Two examples involving a policy of never awarding discretionary student grants, or never finding the special circumstances required to meet the council's criteria for awarding a grant, are *R v London Borough of Bexley, ex parte Jones* [1995] ELR 42 and *R v Warwickshire County Council, ex parte Collymore* [1995] ELR 217. Cf *R v Warwickshire County Council, ex parte Williams* [1995] ELR 326, where the Council's policy, modified to meet the decision in *ex parte Collymore*, was upheld.

[2] As in *R v Paddington and St Marylebone Rent Tribunal, ex parte Bell London and Provincial Properties Ltd* [1949] 1 KB 666; [1949] 1 All ER 720 (automatic referral of lettings to Rent Tribunal if two successful references in same block of flats).

[3] *Kilmarnock Magistrates v Secretary of State for Scotland* 1961 SC 350 (Secretary of State's policy on qualification of appointee to post of chief constable). See, also, *R (Lumba) v Secretary of State for the Home Department* [2011] UKSC 12; [2012] 1 AC 245; [2011] 2 WLR 671.

Tribunals and licensing bodies

7.61 There is no difference of principle between tribunals and licensing bodies on the one hand, and other public authorities. However, the nature, and circumstances of exercise, of their powers and functions have led to a considerable body of case law on the question of fettering discretion. In the exercise of its discretion a tribunal must act in accordance with the law, and apply the law. It is, of course, bound to follow the construction of the law adopted by the superior courts. This is not a fettering of its discretion but part of the framework which identifies and delimits the discretion. It may be artificial to say that a tribunal can or cannot bind itself as to the law, since it is not the final arbiter of the matter. Consistency of treatment of like cases would suggest that tribunals should follow each other's conclusions on points of statutory construction (and indeed common law) unless and until a court takes a different view, but in general tribunals are not bound by their own decisions on points of law.[1] Necessarily, a tribunal exercising a function of a judicial nature must make findings of fact based on the evidence in each case, and would act ultra vires if it applied findings of fact derived from one dispute to an adjudication between other parties.[2]

[1] Even the Employment Appeal Tribunal, which is presided over by a High Court or Court of Session judge. See, also, *Merchandise Transport Ltd v British Transport Commission* [1962] 2 QB 173; [1961] 3 All ER 495 (Transport Tribunal). The position in respect of tribunals is similar to that of the High Court: see *R v Greater Manchester Coroner, ex parte Tal* [1985] QB 67; [1984] 3 WLR 643, where it was held that departure from a prior Court decision should be rare and in circumstances when it was considered that the earlier decision was clearly wrong).

[2] Compare the factual background to *Pearlman v Keepers and Governors of Harrow School* [1979] QB 56; [1979] 1 All ER 365. A finding of an employment tribunal can create an issue estoppel between the parties even in subsequent High Court proceedings: *O'Laoire v Jackel International (No 2)* [1991] IRLR 170. See also in the immigration context the decision in *Devaseelan v Secretary of State for the Home Department* [2002] UKIAT 30702 (approved by the Court of Appeal most recently in *R(on the application of AM (Iran) v Secretary of State for the Home Department)* [2016] EWCA Civ 667), which establishes that a second tribunal should take the first tribunal's findings as a starting point and should be cautious of allowing matters determined by the first tribunal to be re-litigated on the same evidence.

7.62 But it is not in the context of tribunals discharging an adjudicative function, however informally, that the question of fettering discretion most frequently arises; rather it is in relation to those bodies, whether tribunals, justices or a local or public authority or minister, charged with a licensing power embodying a discretion as to the decision to license. It is most often in this context that a body with judicial or quasi-judicial functions is also vested with a discretion containing a considerable policy element. Licensing authorities may vary substantially in the extent to which policy issues are delegated to them or spelt out in the statutory enabling framework: the very fact of conferring on a locally constituted body the regulation of the licensed activity is apt to suggest that the evaluation and application of local circumstances is to be undertaken.[1] The courts will not allow a tribunal to 'pursue consistency at the expense of the merits of individual cases',[2] but subject to that and to a willingness to consider each case on its facts, the adoption and application of a policy[3] is perfectly proper, even for a body, such as licensing justices, whose constitution might suggest a higher standard of judicial neutrality.[4] As with other discretionary powers, however, the repository must not divest itself of any discretion by adopting a policy that precludes any consideration of applications, such as by announcing in advance that it will refuse all applications or all within a particular category.[5] The only exceptions are the rare cases where the enabling legislation expressly permits such a policy decision.[6]

[1] See, eg *Boyle v Wilson* [1907] AC 45 and *R v Torquay Licensing Justices, ex parte Brockman* [1951] 2 KB 784; [1951] 2 All ER 656.

[2] *Merchandise Transport Ltd v British Transport Commission* [1962] 2 QB 173 at 192 (Devlin LJ, citing Jenkins LJ in *R v Flintshire County Council County Licensing (Stage Plays) Committee, ex parte Barrett* [1957] 1 QB 350 at p 367). Devlin LJ also emphasised the value of the tribunal (the Transport Tribunal) disclosing the general principles on which it proceeded, by way of reasoned decisions. See further *R v Criminal Injuries Compensation Board, ex parte Ince* [1973] 3 All ER 808; [1973] 1 WLR 1334.

[3] Eg giving priority to those applicants (for a limited number of street-trading licences) who do not already have a licence: *R v Tower Hamlets London Borough Council, ex parte Kayne-Levenson* [1975] QB 431 at 444, 448 and 453 (Lord Diplock and Lawton LJ).

[4] See, eg the cases cited at note 1 above. The higher standard of procedural fairness expected of licensing justices, as compared say to the Board of Trade in the circumstances of the *British Oxygen* case (cf Lord Reid's comment cited at **7.58** note 3 above), may make the pursuit of policy considerations a less dominant element in individual decisions.

[5] Eg *R v LCC, ex parte Corrie* [1918] 1 KB 68 (refusal of permit to sell pamphlets in parks, following resolution that no permits would be issued): *R v Tower Hamlets London Borough Council, ex parte Kayne-Levenson*, [1975] QB 431 (refusal to determine application by existing licensee for an additional licence in accordance with policy that licences should be issued only to persons without one).

[6] See the Local Government (Miscellaneous Provisions) Act 1982, Sch 3, paragraph 12(3)(c) and (4) (refusal of licence for sex establishment on ground that number of such establishments equals or exceeds number considered appropriate, which may be nil). Cf *R v Herrod, ex parte Leeds City District Council* [1976] QB 540, [1974] 3 All ER 362.

Other situations

7.63 The same diffuse principles govern a wide range of other situations in which discretionary powers arise. The case law scarcely admits of analysis, but illustrations serve the purpose of indicating the type of situation in which the court may be more, or less, favourably disposed to allow a wide latitude in prior policy formulation effectively circumscribing discretion. Unsurprisingly, powers entrusted to ministers with a high policy content[1] and powers in areas such as planning where formal machinery for considering the representations of interested parties must be used[2] are areas where the courts are less ready to intervene. But even discretions generally regarded as relatively unsuited to judicial supervision, such as the discretion to prosecute, are not immune from challenge if the discretion is fettered to the point of extinction.[3] In the context of a decision-making process which attracts a relatively strict standard of procedural fairness such as a tribunal, a policy which inhibits the deciding body's capacity to fulfil the requirements of procedural fairness is particularly vulnerable to challenge.[4] The challenge may, in substance, be for procedural impropriety but its origin lies in the adoption of a fettering policy. Indeed, for two reasons the requirements of procedural fairness may be made stricter where the decision-taker is acting under the constraint of a self-imposed policy: because the policy may require the showing of special circumstances to secure exemption, or because the policy creates a legitimate expectation for those meeting the criteria, which can only be denied after a fair hearing.[5] Among the wide range of other discretionary powers that have resulted in litigation on allegations of improper fettering, cases of interest as examples of the judicial approach are noted below.[6]

1   For example, *Schmidt v Secretary of State for Home Affairs* [1969] 2 Ch 149; [1969] 1 All ER 904 (policy of excluding alien Scientologists from the UK); *British Oxygen Co Ltd v Minister of Technology* [1971] AC 610; [1970] 3 All ER 165 (grants for industrial plant and equipment).

2   *Franklin v Minister of Town and Country Planning* [1948] AC 87; [1947] 2 All ER 289 (designation of New Town); *Stringer v Minister of Housing and Local Government* [1971] 1 All ER 65; [1970] 1 WLR 1281 (policy to disallow development interfering with Jodrell Bank telescope).

3   *R v Metropolitan Police Comr, ex parte Blackburn* [1968] 2 QB 118; [1968] 1 All ER 763. For various applications, see *R v DPP, ex p Jones (Timothy)* [2000] Crim LR 858; *R (Joseph) v DPP* [2001] Crim LR 489; *R (Dennis) v DPP* [2006] EWHC 3211 (Admin); and *R (Waxman) v CPS* [2012] EWHC 133 (Admin); (2012) 176 J.P. 121.

4   For example, the cases on refusal of legal representation to parties in accordance with a self-imposed policy: *Pett v Greyhound Racing Association* [1969] 1 QB 125, [1968] 2 All ER 545; *Enderby Town Football Club Ltd v Football Association Ltd* [1971] Ch 591, [1971] 1 All ER 215; and especially *R v Secretary of State for the Home Department, ex parte Tarrant* [1985] QB 251, [1984] 1 All ER 799. See also *R. (on the application of Medical Justice) v Secretary of State for the Home Department* [2010] EWHC 1925 (Admin)), as was approved by the Court of Appeal: [2011] EWCA Civ 1710, that the provisions of a policy should be declared unlawful if there was 'an unacceptable risk or a "serious possibility" that the right of access to justice . . . will be or is curtailed.'

5   On legitimate expectation in this context creating a duty to act fairly see below at notes 7.70–7.71 below.

6   See *Smith v Inner London Education Authority* [1978] 1 All ER 411 (policy in discharge of duty under the Education Act 1944, s 8 of not maintaining selective schools); *Bromley London Borough Council v Greater London Council* [1983] 1 AC 768; [1982] 1 All ER 129 (discretion in issuing directions to London Transport as to levels of fares); *R v Secretary of State for the Environment, ex parte Brent London Borough Council* [1982] QB 593; [1983] 3 All ER 321 (imposition of reduction in rate support grant); *R v Secretary of State for Transport, ex parte Sherriff & Sons Ltd* (1986) Times, 18 December (policy of refusal to make grants for projects commenced before application made; *R (S) v Chief Constable of South Yorkshire* [2004] 1 WLR 2196 (blanket policy to retain DNA and fingerprint samples considered lawful by the House of Lords, a decision subsequently criticised by the European Court of Human Rights in *S and Marper v UK* (2009) 48 EHRR 50 who found the policy to be contrary to Article 8 ECHR. For cases where a misconstruction of its powers led an authority to act or decline to act without considering how it should exercise the discretion in law vested in it, see *R v St Pancras Vestry* (1890) 24 QBD 371 (applied in *R (Tromans) v Cannock Chase DC* [2004] EWCA Civ 1036, [2004] BLGR 735 (see Chapter 8 at 8.26; see, also, *Perilly v Tower Hamlets London Borough Council* [1973] 1 QB 9; [1972] 3 All ER 513.

Contract, estoppel and legitimate expectation

7.64 A person of normal contractual capacity is free to contract so as to prevent him or herself from exercising at some time in the future a power or freedom. This may be done expressly or by an implied term necessary to give business efficacy to the contract, for instance, by securing that the consideration cannot subsequently be negatived. The future freedom of the individual is, within the limits imposed by public policy,[1] a saleable commodity. Public authorities, and those invested with statutory powers, are in a different situation. The contractual capacity of a body created by statute, including a local authority,[2] is itself statutory, and a contract made by such a body outside its statutory powers is ultra vires and cannot be enforced against it.[3] More fundamentally, if a public body can by contract prevent or restrict itself from exercising a statutory power, then public rights and expectations would also be saleable commodities. On the other hand an inability to make long-term commitments may inhibit the effective contemporaneous use of powers in favour of their preservation for a future use that would be equally inhibited. And the non-fettering of one power may only be achievable at the expense of the non-exercise of another.

1   For example, the policy against unreasonable restraint of trade agreements.
2   *Hazell v Hammersmith and Fulham London Borough Council* [1992] AC 1; [1991] 1 All ER 545: rule applicable to a local authority created by Royal Charter.
3   As in *Hazell*, above. This is now subject to the application of the Local Government (Contracts) Act 1997, s 2 of which validates contracts certified by an authorised officer of the authority under the Act, but subject to the preservation of limited powers of challenge to the vires of the contract by judicial review (s 5).

7.65 The courts' approach to this, as to many other aspects of Administrative Law spanning a vast range of powers and circumstances, has been to evolve a general approach based on compromise between the conflicting considerations but without any precise and consistent definition of the dividing line. The tide of judicial restrictiveness has moved some way back from the high water mark reached in *Ayr Harbour Trustees v Oswald*,[1] where the Harbour Trustees were held to be acting unlawfully in offering an undertaking, on the compulsory acquisition of certain land, not to develop part of it. The statutory purpose of the Trustees was the development of the land, and their undertaking was likened in a later case to renouncing a part of their statutory birthright.[2] The case was unusual in that the Trustees had only one purpose, part of which they would be disabled from executing by the undertaking. Nevertheless, the apparent effect of the decision was to prevent the trustees from exercising a judgment as to their need for development land and minimising the cost of acquiring it.

1   (1883) 8 App Cas 623.
2   *Birkdale District Electric Supply Co Ltd v Southport Corpn* [1926] AC 355 at 372, per Lord Sumner.

7.66 Cases since *Oswald* suggest a less rigorous general approach. The leading case is *Birkdale District Electric Supply Co v Southport Corpn*,[1] the source of the dictum that 'a public body . . . cannot enter into any contract or take any action incompatible with the due exercise of their powers or duties'. But the House of Lords upheld an undertaking by a statutory utility, empowered to make such charges as it saw fit up to a prescribed limit for electricity, to agree not to charge more than a neighbouring municipal supplier.[2] The undertaking did not prevent the company from discharging its statutory function; nor was it a fetter on the Corporation, which could release the company if so minded. The lack of centrality to the powers conferred by statute was the key distinction enabling *Oswald*[3] not to be applied. Cases since the *Birkdale* case continue the more liberal approach; they can be grouped into a number of broad principles, none being totally inflexible.

(1)   A contract not to exercise a statutory discretion will be invalid, as will an undertaking independent of contract. An agreement to refuse planning permission is a clear example.[4]

(2)   An express term of a contract which has the effect of restricting the exercise of a statutory power is not necessarily unlawful.[5] It is more likely to be lawful if the restriction is merely incidental to the contract,

and the contract is otherwise a proper exercise of the power of the public body.[6] An ambiguous term may be interpreted so as to avoid the problem by the application of a presumption against an unlawful fetter on discretion.

(3)   Whether a term will be implied in a contract made by a public body which would restrict some other statutory power will depend on the circumstances, but the authorities generally indicate that such a fetter will not readily be implied.[7]

(4)   A term normally implied into an agreement, such as a covenant for quiet enjoyment in a lease, may be overridden to the extent that it would fetter the exercise of a statutory or prerogative power of the public authority granting the lease.[8]

[1]   [1926] AC 355.

[2]   The undertaking was contained in an agreement collateral to the agreement vesting the power of supplying electricity in the company under statutory powers.

[3]   (1883) 8 App Cas 623.

[4]   For example, *Ransom and Luck Ltd v Surbiton Borough Council* [1949] Ch 180; [1949] 1 All ER 185. A policy of refusing permission, subject to individual representations, is capable of being lawful: *Stringer v Minister of Housing and Local Government* [1971] 1 All ER 65, [1970] 1 WLR 1281.

[5]   See, eg *Dowty Boulton Paul Ltd v Wolverhampton Corpn* [1971] 2 All ER 277; [1971] 1 WLR 204 (undertaking on sale of land to maintain airfield and grant access to purchaser for 99 years overrode power to designate land for housing development); *British Transport Commission v Westmorland County Council* [1958] AC 126; [1957] 2 All ER 353 (grant of easement to cross railway line valid despite fettering of power to demolish bridge carrying right of way); *R v Hammersmith and Fulham London Borough Council, ex parte Beddowes* [1987] QB 1050; [1987] 1 All ER 369 (sale of block of rented flats with covenants as to basis of future lettings of other flats retained by Council held not an unlawful fetter on future housing policy). Contrast *ex parte Beddowes* with *R (Kilby) v Basildon District Council* [2007] HLR 39 in which the Court of Appeal held that it was impermissible for a housing authority to bind itself to only varying the terms of secure tenancies if a majority of a tenant's representative committee agreed, because this was inconsistent with the local authority's statutory power (s 103 of the Housing Act 1985) to vary such tenancies unilaterally.

[6]   For example, a contract to sell an asset of the public body such as a council house: *Storer v Manchester City Council* [1974] 3 All ER 824; [1974] 1 WLR 1403.

[7]   *William Cory & Son Ltd v London Corpn* [1951] 2 KB 476; [1951] 2 All ER 85 (power to make byelaws that would render continuing waste disposal contract unprofitable not restricted): *Windsor and Maidenhead Royal Borough Council v Brandrose Investments Ltd* [1983] 1 All ER 818; [1983] 1 WLR 509 (power to designate a conservation area not restricted by planning agreement).

[8]   *Crown Lands Comrs v Page* [1960] 2 QB 274; [1960] 2 All ER 726 (requisitioning of land leased by Crown not an infringement of tenant's right to quiet enjoyment of property). Cf *Board of Trade v Temperley Steam Shipping Co Ltd* (1926) 26 Ll L Rep 76 at 78 (a similar point in relation to a charterparty).

7.67 The leading authority in relation to the last category also illustrates a difficult point. The Crown as landlord granted a tenancy; the Crown as repository of the defence prerogative requisitioned the premises. The Crown's defence raised the point that it did not act as landlord, but this was not the basis of the decision in its favour. Rather the case was based on the principle that the Crown (and other public bodies) in entering into private contracts, does not undertake to fetter itself in the use of those powers.[1] Despite this, it is at first sight tempting to rationalise this and some of the other cases as explicable by reference to the different capacities in which public authorities act when making contracts and when exercising discretionary powers in the public interest. The fallacy in this argument is the assumption that making a contract is not the exercise of a discretionary power in the public interest. Moreover, the dual capacity approach is difficult to reconcile with the case law of the Court of Justice of the European Union, holding any body which is in EU law an 'emanation of the state' to be subject to the horizontal direct effect of EU Directives regardless of the capacity in which its actions the subject of the claim were undertaken.[2]

1   *Crown Lands Comrs v Page* [1960] 2 QB 274 at 291 (Devlin LJ).
2   *Marshall v Southampton and South West Hampshire Area Health Authority (Teaching)*: C-152/84 [1986] QB 401, ECJ (emanation of the state acting as employer precluded from relying on the state's failure to implement an EC Directive to avoid liability for breach of the Directive (which would as against a private employer not be directly enforceable)); and see *Foster v British Gas plc*; C-188/89 [1991] 1 QB 405, ECJ; apld [1991] 2 AC 306, HL.

7.68   Another specific aspect of the authorities on the effect of contracts with the Crown is the rule that the Crown cannot be under any contractual restriction against dismissing its servants at pleasure.[1] The rationale of this rule has been undermined by statute,[2] by the evolution of a complex disciplinary system[3] and most recently by the acceptance by the courts that civil servants may be engaged under a contract of employment.[4] Nevertheless, the principle has not been expressly disavowed and it may require a decision of the House of Lords to do so.[5]

1   *Riordan v War Office* [1959] 3 All ER 552; [1959] 1 WLR 1046 (affirmed on another point [1960] 3 All ER 774n, [1961] 1 WLR 210): War Department Civilian Staff Regulations giving staff a right to a period of notice void insofar as they took away the right to dismiss at pleasure.
2   Employment Rights Act 1996, s 191 (a statutory re-enactment of legislation dating back to 1971), giving most civil servants (but not members of the Armed Forces) statutory protection against unfair dismissal; s 192, extending unfair dismissal protection to the Armed Forces.
3   Under the Civil Service Order in Council 1992 (a prerogative order). The Civil Service Appeal Board, which hears final appeals against disciplinary decisions, is amenable to judicial review and may be required to give reasons for its decisions: *R v Civil Service Appeal Board, ex parte Cunningham* [1991] 4 All ER 310, CA.
4   *R v Lord Chancellor's Department, ex parte Nangle* [1992] 1 All ER 897.
5   The decision in *CCSU* [1985] AC 374; [1984] 3 All ER 935 is a step towards such a conclusion. It would not be difficult to argue that dismissal of an established civil servant without some procedural safeguards was unlawful given the legitimate expectation created by the disciplinary procedures established under the Civil Service Order in Council. This is leaving aside potential challenges under the Human Rights Act 1998 and the European Convention on Human Rights.

7.69   Two related matters require mention. The first is the lack of any general right at common law to compensation when a party's apparent rights are overridden by the subsequent exercise of a discretionary power not validly fettered by the contract with, or undertaking given to, the party. The position may be different where a party is able to rely upon Article 1 of Protocol 1 of the European Convention on Human Rights – in claiming that it has a 'right to property', which is being violated by the State, consideration of which falls outside of the scope of this chapter. Not only is the common law's lack of remedy regrettable; it may also discourage courts from giving full effect to the statutory powers of public bodies where to do so would involve injustice to another party. To some extent this problem has been alleviated by the establishment of statutory complaints mechanisms and ombudsmen, particularly in local government and the health service, as well as the Parliamentary Commissioner for central government.

7.70 The second related matter is the creation of legitimate expectations by the giving of undertakings and assurances.[1] It is well-established law that a legitimate expectation may give rise to *procedural* rights, and corresponding obligations on the decision-taker.[2] In the seminal case of *R v North and East Devon Health Authority, ex parte Coughlan*,[3] the Court of Appeal considered the extent to which legitimate expectations may give rise to *substantive* rights as to the exercise of a discretionary power. A decision to close a home for severely disabled individuals was quashed because of promises given to residents, as an inducement to move to the home from a hospital which was closing, that they would be able to occupy the home for life.

[1]   Legitimate expectation is also discussed below in relation to review for unreasonableness (see CHAPTER 8) and procedural propriety (see CHAPTER 11).
[2]   See early authority: *R v Liverpool Corpn, ex parte Liverpool Taxi Fleet Operators' Association* [1972] 2 QB 299; [1972] 2 All ER 589; *A-G of Hong Kong v Ng Yuen Shiu* [1983] 2 AC 629; [1983] 2 All ER 346; *R v Secretary of State for the Home Department, ex parte Asif Mahmood Khan* [1985] 1 All ER 40; [1984] 1 WLR 1337; *CCSU* [1985] AC 374; *R v London Borough of Camden, ex parte Maughan* [1990] COD 390 (no legitimate expectation on facts); *R v Secretary of State for the Home Department, ex parte Golam Mowla* [1992] 1 WLR 70 (stamp on passport not creating legitimate expectation of re-admission to UK); *R v Secretary of State for the Home Department, ex parte Hargreaves* [1997] 1 WLR 906 (no legitimate expectation by prisoner of home visits remaining available in accordance with policy in operation at start of sentence). More recently, see *R (Cornwall Waste Forum St Denis Branch) v Secretary of State for Communities and Local Government* [2012] EWCA Civ 379; [2012] Env. L.R. 34 (whilst a promise had been made by a planning inspector to follow a particular procedure, circumstances had changed justifying a departure from that promise).
[3]   [2001] QB 213, at 238A–254D.

7.71 The approach adopted by the Court of Appeal in *Coughlan* was that where a promise had been made and relied on such as to create a legitimate expectation of a substantive benefit,[1] rather than merely procedural safeguards, a decision which overrode that expectation might be so unfair as to amount to an abuse of power;[2] in that event, the court could intervene to enforce the legitimate expectation. Factors which would be relevant to the decision whether there was an abuse of power included whether the promise was made to a small and identifiable group (or an individual) or to persons more generally, and what the consequences of the enforcement of the original promise for third parties or the wider public interest would be.[3] An overriding public interest could justify disregarding the promise, but not (as in the instant case) merely financial consequences.[4]

[1]   As to what amounts to a 'legitimate' expectation see *Re Findlay* [1985] AC 318, at 338 (Lord Scarman); *R v Secretary of State for Education and Employment, ex parte Begbie* [2000] 1 WLR 1115 (no legitimate expectation flowing from statements by opposition party before it was elected into office): *R v Uxbridge Magistrates' Court, ex parte Adimi* [2001] QB 667 (accession by the UK to the United Nations Convention on the Status of Refugees created legitimate expectation in minds of asylum seekers that an immunity conferred by the Convention would be applied to them; but see for the limits of such a principle *Thomas v Baptiste* [2000] 2 AC 1, PC). Knowledge of the policy, practice or decision on the part of the person relying on it is a necessary prerequisite to a legitimate expectation: *R v Minister of Defence, ex parte Walker* [2000] 1 WLR 806; *R v Secretary of State for the Home Department, ex parte Hindley* [1998] QB 751, affd [2001] 1 AC 410, though reliance per se is not essential: *R (Bancoult) v Secretary of State for Foreign & Commonwealth Affairs (No 2)* [2008] UKHL 61; [2009] AC 453 at [60] per Lord Hoffman. See, generally, CHAPTERS 8 and 11.
[2]   For a case where this threshold defeated a claim to rely on a legitimate expectation, see *R (Association of British Civilian Internees: Far East Region) v Secretary of State for Defence* [2003] EWCA Civ 473; [2003] QB 1397. For cases where it has been held that a substantive legitimate expectation was frustrated and therefore the relevant public body had acted

unlawfully see *R (Rashid) v Secretary of State for the Home Department* [2005] EWCA Civ 744 – Secretary of State's failure to apply an asylum policy to the claimant; and *R (BAPIO Action Ltd) v Secretary of State for the Home Department* [2008] 2 WLR 1073 – Department of Health guidance in effect preventing non British/EEA doctors from working in the UK.

3   An additional factor may arise by reference to the Human Rights Act 1998. Thus a legitimate expectation in relation to a person's interest in the enjoyment of property may be protected by art 1 of the First Protocol to the European Convention on Human Rights as a 'possession': *Rowland v Environment Agency* [2003] Ch 581.

4   However, it is not self-evident that financial considerations can be separated from wider considerations of the public interest in this way, especially where the funds available to the public body concerned are fixed: cf *R v Gloucestershire County Council, ex parte Barry* [1997] AC 584 and *R v East Sussex County Council, ex parte Tandy* [1998] AC 714.

7.72 In *R (S) v Secretary of State for the Home Department*[1] the Court of Appeal further considered the concept of an abuse of power in the context of the Home Office's delay in dealing with old asylum cases in order that it could meet a target to process new ones. In his judgment Carnwath LJ explained that an abuse of power was not a new category of judicial review but a description of circumstances where a public body had effectively acted irrationally or with conspicuous unfairness.[2]

1   [2007] EWCA Civ 546; [2007] Imm AR 781. This decision was cited with approval and applied by the Supreme Court in *TN v Secretary of State for the Home Department* [2015] 1 WLR 3083.

2   See paragraphs [39]–[47].

7.73 It will be apparent that the conditions for a court to enforce a party's legitimate expectation substantively on the repository of a discretionary power are very similar to, if not the same as, those which would provide the basis for a successful plea of estoppel by representation in private law, save only for the added dimension of the public interest in the final equation. It is not entirely clear whether, or if so to what extent, the principles applying to estoppel by representation in the context of public authority can be outflanked by reliance instead on the doctrine of legitimate expectation, but it would be unsatisfactory to have two closely parallel lines of challenge to public authorities' decisions that would potentially produce a different outcome. To that extent *Coughlan* should be read as a clarification and qualification of the law on estoppel by representation rather than as a separate basis for challenge.

7.74 The general principles applicable in the public law context to estoppel by representation can be summarised as follows. The concept of estoppel by representation has developed as a rule of evidence preventing a party from asserting and proving some fact or matter where the party has made representations or given assurances to the contrary to the other party, and the latter has reasonably relied on them to his or her detriment.[1] Save to this extent, it is not a source of legal rights. However, its application to the conduct of public bodies would potentially compromise the exercise of statutory functions by such bodies. Against this must be balanced the detriment to those who have relied on representations if they cannot in the event use the representations as a shield. The same question of balance, therefore, arises as in relation to contracts fettering a public authority's powers; however, the principles developed by the courts are if anything more strongly protective of public authorities' freedom to discharge their powers unfettered. Although the case law is not free from difficulty, the following principles appear from the authorities.

(1) A public body cannot bind itself to act in a way that would be ultra vires. There can be no creation or enlargement of a power by estoppel or any analogous principle;[2] similarly, a tribunal's jurisdiction cannot be enlarged by estoppel.[3] Conversely, a power or jurisdiction is not lost by disuse or non-enforcement even in circumstances that would in private law give rise to an estoppel.[4]

(2) Statutory preconditions to the acquisition of a right cannot be overridden by the actions of the public body responsible for the matter. This is so *a fortiori* where an officer of the responsible body has assumed authority wrongfully.[5] Dicta of Denning J to the contrary[6] have been firmly disapproved by the House of Lords.[7] However, the position is no longer as clear as had been thought, in the light of *Gowa v A-G*.[8] The Court of Appeal, by a majority, held that the Crown was bound by an (incorrect) assurance that the applicants were citizens of the UK, on which their father had relied in discontinuing an application for registration which would have secured that status. The House of Lords affirmed the Court of Appeal's decision on a different point (of statutory construction) and expressly left open the correctness of the Court of Appeal's reasoning, but with fairly strong indications of doubt as to its correctness.[9]

(3) A failure to discharge a duty or exercise a discretion as a result of a mistake of fact cannot bind the authority not to discharge the duty or exercise its discretion when the mistake is realised.[10] Although the authorities deal with mistake of fact, a mistake of law would, it is submitted, fall *a fortiori* within the same principle.

(4) A representation may nevertheless have legal effect where an individual relies on a formal decision of a public authority taken by the authorised officers of the authority but in breach of their instructions or the authority's policy. Thus in *R v Secretary of State for the Home Department, ex parte Ku*[11] the applicants entered the UK on work permits ostensibly valid but issued by an official of the Department of Employment in breach of official instructions. The applicants were unaware of the irregularity. The Court of Appeal held that the applicants, having been granted leave to enter the UK, were not 'illegal entrants' under the immigration legislation and not liable to deportation.[12]

(5) In principle, the same rules apply in planning cases. Thus in *Norfolk County Council v Secretary of State for the Environment*[13] the Council's Planning Committee determined to refuse planning consent but by mistake a notification of a grant of permission was sent to the applicant. The mistake was realised and rectified within a short time. The Council was held not to be bound by the error; it would not have been so bound even if the applicant had suffered a detriment in reliance on the misinformation (which on the facts it was held had not been the case). However, the existence of wide statutory powers to delegate planning functions and to dispense with formal procedural requirements has contributed to a line of cases casting doubt on the general position.[14] These in turn have been construed as narrowly as possible in the leading case of *Western Fish Products Ltd v Penwith District Council*.[15] In that case the element of reliance was lacking on the facts, and so any general statement of principle was not strictly

necessary to the decision; however, it was a strong and unanimous Court of Appeal decision which it submitted now represents the law in this area. On this basis the position is:

(i)   assurances given by an officer of a council generally do not create an estoppel against enforcement of planning requirements[16] (similarly, assurances by an officer of a local authority as to what action the authority will take cannot create a legitimate expectation that the authority will take that action);[17]

(ii)   a local authority (but not, presumably, an officer, unless acting under delegated power) may waive a procedural irregularity by an applicant for planning consent;[18]

(iii)   where a matter is capable of delegation to an officer, the officer purports to decide or give an assurance and this is relied on by the applicant to his or her detriment, and there are special circumstances making it reasonable for the applicant to believe that the officer had delegated authority,[19] the council will be estopped from enforcing the planning legislation in breach of the decision or assurance.[20]

[1]   This concept must be distinguished from proprietary estoppel (as to which in this context see *Western Fish Products Ltd v Penwith District Council* [1981] 2 All ER 204, at 217–218) and issue estoppel (which in the same case Megaw LJ suggested was 'akin to' estoppel by representation (at 219j)). On the application of issue estoppel in the planning context see *Thrasyvoulou v Secretary of State for the Environment* [1988] QB 809; [1988] 2 All ER 781.

[2]   *Minister of Agriculture and Fisheries v Matthews* [1950] 1 KB 148; [1949] 2 All ER 724 (creation of unlawful tenancy by Crown); *A-G for Ceylon v Silva* [1953] AC 461, [1953] 2 WLR 1185 (unauthorised assertion of title to goods sold by crown servant did not bind Crown). It is worthy of note that the promise given by the Health Authority in *R v North and East Devon Health Authority, ex parte Coughlan* [2001] QB 213 at 244G, paragraph 66 was not ultra vires.

[3]   *Secretary of State for Employment v Globe Elastic Thread Ltd* [1980] AC 506; [1979] 2 All ER 1077, (estoppel between employer and employee could not confer additional statutory jurisdiction on industrial (now employment) tribunal). See also *Newbold v Coal Authority* [2012] UKUT 20 (LC) applying the decision in *Globe Elastic Thread*, to the effect that the tribunal could not be required to give effect to the Coal Mining Subsidence Act 1991, as if certain persons had a statutory right to claim damages, when in fact they did not.

[4]   Cf *Yabbicom v King* [1899] 1 QB 444 (enforcement of bye law); *Redbridge London Borough v Jaques* [1971] 1 All ER 260; [1970] 1 WLR 1604 (inaction by local authority no defence to prosecution for long-standing obstruction of highway: local authority has no power to license obstruction).

[5]   *Howell v Falmouth Boat Construction Ltd* [1951] AC 837; [1951] 2 All ER 278 (licence which by statute required written approval for modifications could not be varied to encompass subsequent oral approval given by licensing officer; case decided on another ground of statutory construction).

[6]   In *Robertson v Minister of Pensions* [1949] 1 KB 227; [1948] 2 All ER 767.

[7]   *Howell v Falmouth Boat Construction Ltd* [1951] AC 837, [1951] 2 All ER 278 at 845, per Lord Simonds: 'The illegality of an act is the same whether or not the actor has been misled by an assumption of authority on the part of a government officer . . . .'.

[8]   [1985] 1 WLR 1003. The decision of the Court of Appeal is reported in (1984) 129 Sol Jo 131.

[9]   Lord Roskill, [1985] 1 WLR at 1005G. The decision in *Gowa* was distinguished by the High Court in *R v Secretary of State for the Home Department*, ex p. Chaumun [1999] I.N.L.R. 479, where it was explained by Latham J (at page 487) '*Whilst there is no doubt that the doctrine of estoppel, now in the guise of legitimate expectation, plays an important part in the armoury of the court in exercising supervision and control over public bodies, its use to provide substantive as opposed to procedural rights must be very carefully exercised. In the field of statutory rights there are obvious problems if the courts are prepared to recognise the existence of statutory rights by virtue of estoppel or legitimate expectation, where the facts are not those upon which Parliament, by statute, has decreed that those rights should arise. For that would be the result of my acceding to the claimants' argument.*'

¹⁰ See, respectively, *Maritime Electric Co Ltd v General Dairies Ltd* [1937] AC 610; [1937] 1 All ER 748, PC (on statutory duties) and *Rootkin v Kent County Council* [1981] 2 All ER 227; [1981] 1 WLR 1186 (on discretionary powers).

¹¹ [1995] QB 364, [1995] 2 All ER 891.

¹² The decision does not consider the issue of estoppel or cases referred to in paragraph (2) above, but is confined to the proper construction of the relevant provisions of the Immigration Act 1971. However, the result is difficult to reconcile with *Howell* in particular.

¹³ [1973] 3 All ER 673, [1973] 1 WLR 1400.

¹⁴ *Wells v Minister of Housing and Local Government* [1967] 2 All ER 1041; [1967] 1 WLR 1000; *Lever (Finance) Ltd v Westminster (City) London Borough Council* [1971] 1 QB 222. Both cases were decided by the Court of Appeal under Lord Denning MR.

¹⁵ [1981] 2 All ER 204 (decided in 1978). The single judgment of the court given by Megaw LJ is the most thorough recent judicial pronouncement on this subject.

¹⁶ *Southend-on-Sea Corpn v Hodgson (Wickford) Ltd* [1962] 1 QB 416; [1961] 2 All ER 46.

¹⁷ *R v London Borough of Tower Hamlets, ex parte Tower Hamlets Combined Traders Association* [1994] COD 325, at 327.

¹⁸ *Wells v Minister of Housing and Local Government* [1967] 2 All ER 1041; [1967] 1 WLR 1000.

¹⁹ The reference to special circumstances is the limitation placed on *Lever (Finance) Ltd v Westminster (City) London Borough Council* [1971] 1 QB 222, by *Western Fish Products Ltd v Penwith District Council* [1981] 2 All ER 204 at 220h: 'For an estoppel to arise there must be some evidence justifying the person dealing with the planning officer for thinking that what the officer said would bind the planning authority. Holding an office, however senior, cannot, in our judgment, be enough by itself'.

²⁰ The authority may, of course, adopt an assurance or decision (provided it would have been lawful if competently made), and may also exercise its discretion not to enforce a planning requirement where the applicant has been misled. Usually it will do so (it is a nice question whether forbearance to act could then be challenged for reliance on an irrelevant consideration). The interests of those prejudiced by lack of compliance with the procedure must, however, also be respected. Reliance and detriment are required in any event. Cases where no such detriment was found include *Norfolk County Council v Secretary of State for the Environment* [1973] 3 All ER 673, [1973] 1 WLR 1400, *Rootkin v Kent County Council* [1981] 2 All ER 227, [1981] 1 WLR 1186 and *Western Fish Products Ltd v Penwith District Council* [1981] 2 All ER 204.

7.75 The position is now reasonably clear. It is, however, far from fully satisfactory. The applicant who is misled by assurances which turn out to be worthless has a legitimate grievance but no right, at common law, to compensation. The possibility of bringing a claim under the HRA and complaints of maladministration to the Commissioner for Local Administration reduces somewhat the harshness of that situation, and it may be noted that Lord Denning's attempts to redress injustice to applicants occurred before the creation of these alternative remedies.[1] Nevertheless, in this area the lack of a fully developed system of public law can only perpetuate an element of uncertainty as to how the courts may react to marginal cases.

¹ By the Local Government Act 1974. The wider questions of damages and other remedies for maladministration are outside the scope of this chapter.

RELEVANT/IRRELEVANT CONSIDERATIONS AND PROPER/IMPROPER PURPOSES[1]

¹ See Woolf et al (eds), *De Smith's Judicial Review* (7th edn, 2013), at paragraphs 5–082 to 5–119 and 5–120 and 5–144, dealing respectively with improper purposes and irrelevant considerations.

7.76 It is difficult to deal with these aspects of the ambit of judicial review of discretion at a level which extends beyond platitudes. It is almost self-evident that the repository of a discretion must, in deciding whether or how to exercise its power, take into account all the considerations that the law categorises as relevant, and not be influenced by those considerations categorised as irrelevant.[2] Equally, it must act only for purposes acknowledged as proper for the particular power by relevant law, and must not be motivated by improper purposes or act in bad faith. Each of these formulations entirely begs the questions what considerations are relevant and irrelevant and for what purposes the power may lawfully be exercised. The answer can only be fully enunciated on a case-by-case basis, ranging over a massive array of powers many of which have never been illuminated by judicial exegesis. Dealing first with relevance of considerations, the considerations that are relevant may need to be extracted from any or all of the following.

(1)   *Express provisions in the enabling statute.* Many licensing statutes, for instance, itemise matters to which the licensing authority may or must[3] have regard. The interpretation of these express provisions will frequently be the key issue in determining whether the matters are, on the correct interpretation of the statute, the relevant matters, and no others have been taken into account, and an erroneous construction of the statute will not – of course – excuse a deviation from the limits of the permissible or a neglect of the obligatory.

(2)   *Provisions elsewhere in the statute or in other legislation.* Local authorities, in particular, have been entrusted with a number of general powers and duties,[4] and subjected to a number of statutory restrictions of a general character on their powers.[5] These may be relevant considerations in the exercise of quite separate statutory discretions; but whether a particular provision is relevant will depend on the interplay of all the statutory provisions and other relevant factors.

(3)   *The general common law and relevant principles of EU law.* The common law liberties of individuals may be a consideration relevant in the exercise of a discretionary power in a way that would interfere with individuals' exercise of their liberties.[6] There is an obligation on EU Member States to ensure fulfilment of the obligations of EU membership arising from the Treaty of Rome, and to abstain from measures that could jeopardise attainment of the objectives of the Treaty.[7] 'Member States' would encompass not only the Crown but local authorities[8] and most other public authorities as, in EU parlance, emanations of the state.[9] A privatised water company has been held by the High Court to be an emanation of the state.[10]

(4)   *Rights conferred by the European Convention on Human Rights may be a relevant, or even decisive, consideration.* Relevance is dependent in the first instance on whether the exercise of a discretionary power would, in the particular circumstances of the case, entail an interference with a Convention right of any person likely to be affected by the decision.[11] If so, it would be necessary to determine whether such interference is permitted by the Convention itself: most of the substantive rights under the Convention are subject to permissible interference by a public authority. If a decision by a public authority would involve an impermissible interference with a Convention right, s 6(1) of the Human Rights Act 1998 prohibits the exercise of the power in that way

unless the authority is required to act in that way by legislation (construed so far as possible to be compliant with the Convention).[12] In such cases there may effectively be no discretion to act in a way other than in accordance with the Convention. Accordingly, Convention rights are always a relevant consideration to the extent that it is necessary to consider whether they may be engaged by the decision to be taken; whether they are a relevant consideration beyond that stage in the exercise of a discretionary power depends on the conclusion reached at the first stage.[13]

(5)   *Specifically, the duty of a local authority to have regard to the interests of its council tax payers.* Whether or not it is technically correct to describe the duty as fiduciary, it is clear that an otherwise lawful exercise of a discretion involving expenditure of local authority funds may be unlawful by virtue of the authority's failure to have regard to the burden on council tax payers[14] or to give this consideration sufficient weight.[15]

---

2   Cf the formulation given by Lord Greene MR in *Associated Provincial Picture Houses Ltd v Wednesbury Corpn* [1948] 1 KB 223 at 229. 'The law' is used deliberately to indicate that relevance may be derived not just from the enabling statute, or indeed other relevant statutes, but also general legal principles which may enlarge or confine the range of relevant criteria.

3   The distinction between the mandatory and the permissive is important but not exhaustive, as the degree of liberty to disregard a 'may' consideration will vary considerably according to the circumstances. Cf *Yorkshire Copper Works Ltd v Trade Marks Registrar* [1954] 1 All ER 570; [1954] 1 WLR 554.

4   An example is the duties imposed on local authorities (and other public bodies) under s 149 of the Equality Act 2010. See also the duty imposed by the Race Relations Act 1976, s 71 (as originally enacted; the duty was significantly enlarged by the Race Relations (Amendment) Act 2000) to make appropriate arrangements with a view to securing that the functions of the authority are carried out with due regard to the need to eliminate unlawful racial discrimination and promote good race relations. For the use of this section as then in force as a relevant consideration see *Wheeler v Leicester City Council* [1985] AC 1054; [1985] 2 All ER 151 and *R v Lewisham London Borough Council, ex parte Shell UK Ltd* [1988] 1 All ER 938 (s 71 a relevant consideration in deciding to boycott products of applicant: decision unlawful on other grounds). The Human Rights Act 1998 imposes a general statutory obligation to act in conformity with the European Convention on Human Rights on all public authorities, and this will be a relevant consideration in any case where a Convention right is in issue; see **7.76**(4).

5   See, eg the Local Government Act 1986, s 2 (prohibition of publication of material promoting a political party). As to the relevance of s 2 see *R v Barnet London Borough Council, ex parte Johnson and Jacobs* (1991) 3 Admin LR 149.

6   *Wheeler v Leicester City Council* [1985] AC 1054; [1985] 2 All ER 151 (requirement to express opposition to sporting links with South Africa under pain of loss of permission to use council-owned sports facilities).

7   Article 5. See *Marleasing SA v La Comercial Internacional de Alimentacion SA*; C-106/89, [1992] 1 CMLR 305. The Treaty of Amsterdam 1997 added to the objectives of the Treaty the elimination of discrimination on grounds of sex, race, age and other socially unacceptable grounds; see now art 13 of the Consolidated Treaty, and Directive 2000/78/EC establishing a general framework for equal treatment in employment and occupation.

8   *Fratelli Costanze SpA v Comune di Milano* [1990] 3 CMLR 239, ECJ. See, also, *National Union of Teachers v Governing Body of St Mary's Church of England (Aided) Junior School* [1997] IRLR 242, holding that the governors of a voluntary aided school are an emanation of the state for these purposes.

9   See generally *Foster v British Gas plc* [1991] 1 QB 405; [1991] 2 AC 306, HL. See, also, *Doughty v Rolls-Royce plc* [1992] IRLR 126, CA.

10   *Griffin v South West Water Services Ltd* [1995] IRLR 15.

11   There are many examples of the exercise of a discretionary power affecting an individual's Article 5 rights. See, for an example, *R (Q) v Secretary of State for the Home Department* [2003] EWCA Civ 364; [2004] QB 36 and the decision in *R (Lumba)*.

12   On the application of s 6, see **7.25** above.

¹³ If the decision-taker incorrectly concludes that a particular decision is not incompatible with the Convention rights of persons affected by it, or that it cannot act differently because of a statutory obligation, the court can intervene; the basis for its intervention would not be limited to considerations of rationality, since compliance with s 6 requires that the authority does not act in a way incompatible with a Convention right, not that it does not act in a way it believes to be incompatible with such a right.

¹⁴ The case law predates the abolition of domestic rates and the introduction of a uniform, nationally prescribed business rate. It may be arguable that the fiduciary duty formerly owed to business as well as domestic ratepayers has been diluted by the ending of any direct link between an authority's spending and the level of the business rate. The point is probably academic since the duty, initially to those paying the community charge, and since 1993 to council tax payers, clearly remains. See now the Local Government Finance Act 1992.

¹⁵ See especially *Roberts v Hopwood* [1925] AC 578; *Prescott v Birmingham Corpn* [1955] Ch 210; [1954] 3 All ER 698; *Bromley London Borough Council v Greater London Council* [1983] 1 AC 768, [1982] 1 All ER 129.

7.77 Relevance of considerations may operate on two planes. Where a body has taken a matter into account, the question is whether it was permissible to do so. Where it has not, the rather different question arises whether it was obliged to do so. In either case there may be a further question of the relative importance inter se of material considerations. It is possible to act unlawfully by giving too much, as well as too little, or no, weight, to a consideration[1] although the court may be more reluctant to judge such questions, particularly where there is a high policy content in the decision.[2] On the other hand, a decision may be reached after having taken into consideration a factor which is legally irrelevant, yet the decision may be lawful either because it was not in fact influenced by the irrelevant matter,[3] or, more controversially, because the decision is intrinsically proper and reasonable.[4] Failure to observe trivial requirements as to the matters relevant to a decision will not normally provide grounds for judicial intervention; the court is likely to reject any challenge, either on the issue of substance or by exercising discretion as to remedy.

¹ *South Oxfordshire District Council v Secretary of State for the Environment* [1981] 1 All ER 954; [1981] 1 WLR 1092 (previous planning decision a 'vitally material consideration'). See, also, *Bath Society v Secretary of State for the Environment* [1992] 1 All ER 28; [1991] 1 WLR 1303 (duty to pay special attention to the desirability of preservation or enhancement of conservation area 'the first consideration'). However there are a number of cases in which it has been stressed that weight is, in the first instance, a matter for the decision maker, only reviewable if the weight attributed is unreasonable, one of the most oft-cited being *Tesco Stores Ltd v Secretary of State for the Environment* [1995] 1 WLR 759, which itself was cited with approval by the Court of Appeal in *C v London Borough of Lewisham* [2003] EWCA Civ 927. See also *Secretary of State for the Home Department v AP (No.1)* [2011] 2 AC 1 per Lord Brown at [12]. In this regard, see also the summary of relevant cases provided by Morris J in the recent case of *R (Luke Davey) v Oxfordshire County Council and the Equality and Human Rights Commission* [2017] EWHC 354 (Admin) at paragraphs [50] and [51].

² *R v Secretary of State for Transport, ex parte Richmond upon Thames London Borough Council (No 4)* [1996] 1 WLR 1460.

³ *Hanks v Minister of Housing and Local Government* [1963] 1 QB 999 at 1020 (Megaw J).

⁴ *Re Walker's Decision* [1944] 1 KB 644, CA (local authority having regard in fixing wage levels to living expenses of employees with children; consideration irrelevant but since wage levels fair and reasonable, no illegality). Cf *R v Barnet and Camden Rent Tribunal, ex parte Frey Investments Ltd* [1972] 2 QB 342 at 368–369, per Stamp LJ. *Quaere* whether a court would now be as reluctant to look at the reasons as well as the result. See, also, *R v Broadcasting Complaints Commission, ex parte Owen* [1985] QB 1153, [1985] 2 All ER 522; *R (UNISON) v First Secretary of State* [2006] EWHC 2373 (Admin); [2006] IRLR 926 and *R (FDA and others) v Secretary of State for Work and Pensions* [2013] 1 WLR 444 per Lord Neuberger MR at paragraphs [67] to [68].

7.78 It is also possible that a consideration is one which it is open to the decision-taker to take into account or not, as he judges appropriate, that decision not being open to challenge on other than procedural or *Wednesbury*, grounds. Such considerations could be described as *potentially* material. However, it is not enough to entitle the court to strike down a decision that the decision-maker has failed to take into account a consideration that may properly be taken into account, or even one which many people, including the court, would have taken into account, if the enabling power, properly construed, does not require that it be taken into account.[1] However, a factor may, whilst not being one that the decision-taker is formally required by the relevant statutory provision to take into account, be so material to the issue to be determined that anything short of direct consideration of it would not be compatible with the decision-maker's obligations.[2]

[1] *CREEDNZ Inc v Governor General* [1981] 1 NZLR 172, at 183, per Cooke J, a passage approved by Lord Scarman in *Re Findlay* [1985] AC 318 at 333–334. See also *R (Aldard) v Secretary of State for the Environment, Transport and the Regions* [2002] EWCA Civ 735; [2002] 1 WLR 2515, at 39–41, per Simon Brown LJ, and *R (Khatun) v Newham London Borough Council* [2004] EWCA Civ 55; [2005] QB 37, at 34–35, per Laws LJ. For more recent application, see *R (ICO Satellite Ltd) v Office of Communications* [2011] EWCA Civ 1121 at [49]; *Badger Trust v Welsh Ministers* [2010] EWCA Civ 807 at [50]; *R (Hurst) v Northern District of London Coroner* [2007] UKHL 13; [2007] 2 AC 189 at [57].

[2] As in *R (Coghlan) v Chief Constable of the Greater Manchester Police* [2004] EWHC 2801 (Admin); [2005] 2 All ER 890 (failure to refer to guidance issued by Home Office in exercise by Chief Constable of power to permit a senior officer to retire whilst under investigation for potential disciplinary offence, held to invalidate decision notwithstanding that the guidance covered a matter outside the ambit for which there was statutory authority to issue guidance (to which the Chief Constable would have been required by the statute to have regard).

7.79 It is difficult to distinguish effectively between relevancy of considerations and propriety of purposes, and all that has been said about the range of sources from which relevant considerations and their weight may be deduced applies equally to questions of proper purposes. Effectively, the two concepts represent different perspectives on the central question of judicial review, the manner in which a power is exercised.[1] A further perspective is that the public body's exercise of discretion is an abuse of power. These concepts also have particular importance in their close interaction with irrationality, since a court which regards a decision as based on an improper use / abuse of power may find it easier to express a conclusion to that effect on the grounds of a failure correctly to follow the legal framework for reaching the decision than to attribute perversity to the decision-taker. However, these concepts have an independent existence and significance; courts can and do make findings that decisions were tainted by improper purposes or failure to take into account all relevant considerations and no others, without any supporting reliance on irrationality.[2]

[1] See Lord Brightman in *Chief Constable of the North Wales Police v Evans* [1982] 1 WLR 1155 at 1174G. See further, for a helpful discussion of the application of the tests of irrelevant considerations and improper purposes in the context of the exercise of a legislative power *In the Matter of Kelly and Shiels* [2001] NI 103, NICA.

[2] See further on the relationship between illegality and unreasonableness in Chapter 8.

7.80 In the light of the necessarily very specific factual, and usually also statutory, basis for most of the decisions on relevancy of considerations and propriety of purposes, little value is to be gained from an exhaustive review of the case law. Different degrees of willingness to intervene can be detected which it would be difficult to ascribe only to the appropriateness of the power for judicial review, and relatively indiscriminate use of terminology is apparent in judgments. Many, if not most, of the cases could serve as illustrations of both grounds of review. A small selection of cases has been taken to illustrate the types of situation in which courts have been asked to intervene, successfully and unsuccessfully, more for reference than analysis. It may be noted that a significant number of the cases cited involve planning, where the relatively detailed prescription of the administrative context for individual planning decisions has helped to encourage a relatively high level of readiness to intervene (perhaps assisted historically by the traditional importance of the protection of private property).[1]

---

[1] Cf Wade and Forsyth, *Administrative Law* (11th edn, 2014), p 328, fn 288, comparing the court's readiness to intervene in this area with the US doctrine of 'hard look review'.

Relevant and irrelevant considerations

7.81 Examples of successful challenges have included cases where a local authority failed to take account of a destitute overstayer's extant immigration application for leave to remain in the country, in refusing support to her and her children under the Children Act 1989,[1] a refusal by a local authority to accommodate and support a vulnerable adult,[2] where the Home Secretary[3] and the Immigration Appeal Tribunal[4] were found to have failed to consider factors relevant to an immigrant's claim to admission, and where a local authority failed to have regard to the implicit policy of a statutory provision governing the refunding of overpaid rates.[5] As an example of a relevant factor properly considered, the House of Lords has held a local authority's future road-widening plans to be relevant to a decision to refuse planning permission for a development that would be affected by the widening, although this relieved it of the need to pay compensation to the intending developer;[6] the House of Lords has also held that alleviating hardship to tenants was a relevant factor to take into account in exercising a statutory power to limit permitted increases in regulated rents under s 31 of the Landlord and Tenant Act 1985, although the primary purpose of the section was to counter general inflation.[7]

---

[1] *R (Clue) v Birmingham City Council* [2010] EWCA Civ 460; [2011] 1 WLR 99 at [77] and [78].

[2] *R (GS) v Camden London Borough Council* [2016] EWHC 1762 (Admin), [2017] P.T.S.R. 140.

[3] *Bugdaycay v Secretary of State for the Home Department* [1987] AC 514; [1987] 1 All ER 940 (danger to refugee of persecution in home state).

[4] *R v Immigration Appeal Tribunal, ex parte Bakhtaur Singh* [1986] 1 WLR 910 (value of skills of proposed deportee to Sikh community in UK).

[5] *R v Tower Hamlets London Borough Council, ex parte Chetnik Developments Ltd* [1988] AC 858; [1988] 1 All ER 961 (under the General Rate Act 1967, s 9(1)). For other examples, see *R v Secretary of State for Education and Science, ex parte Inner London Education Authority* (1985) 84 LGR 454 (resources of boroughs contributing to further education funds irrelevant to level of contributions) and *Landau v Secretary of State for the Environment* [1992] COD 6 (financial status of applicant for compulsory purchase order irrelevant).

[6] *Westminster Bank Ltd v Minister of Housing and Local Government* [1971] AC 508; [1970] 1 All ER 734. This case is authority for a general proposition that a power may lawfully be

exercised by a public authority despite the existence of an overlapping power which it would be more financially advantageous to the party affected to use, but the proposition is not immune to exceptions.

7 *R v Secretary of State for the Environment, Transport and the Regions, ex parte Spath Holme Ltd* [2001] 2 AC 349; the Court of Appeal ([2000] 3 WLR 141) had quashed the statutory instrument concerned for improper purpose.

7.82 Examples of irrelevant considerations abound, but most are equally or more appropriately to be regarded as examples of improper purposes (so far as the distinction can be drawn) and are dealt with as such below. A good example of a case turning specifically on what considerations were relevant is *R v Secretary of State for the Home Department, ex parte Venables.*[1] The Home Secretary was empowered[2] to fix a 'tariff' or minimum period of detention to be served by the applicants, who had been convicted of murder as juveniles and sentenced to detention during Her Majesty's pleasure. He fixed minimum periods of 15 years (in excess of the recommendations of the trial judge and the Lord Chief Justice), taking into account both that the sentence should be punitive as well as reformative and petitions and representations from members of the public pressing for a longer minimum sentence. The Court of Appeal[3] held that on a proper construction of the legislation there was a punitive element in the sentence, which the Home Secretary was entitled to regard as a relevant consideration, but that public pressure was not a relevant consideration and taking it into account vitiated his decision, which was quashed. The House of Lords affirmed the decision on the latter point but reversed the Court of Appeal's decision on the former, on the different but related point that the fixing of a minimum sentence which could not be reconsidered was an unlawful fettering of his discretion to reconsider the applicants' possible release if circumstances so warranted, and thus an unlawful policy.[4]

A further recent example of an irrelevant consideration also relating to government policy occurred in *R (Clue) v Birmingham City Council (Shelter intervening).*[5] In that case, it was held that a local authority was wrong to take into account the Home Secretary's policy on removal of children from the UK in the course of deciding whether to exercise its powers under s 17 of the Children Act 1989 to provide support for a mother and children pending their application for indefinite leave to remain.

1 [1998] AC 407. This case contains considerable helpful analysis of relevance of factors in a complex situation. For subsequent proceedings see *V v UK* (1999) 30 EHRR 121 and *R (Bulger) v Secretary of State for the Home Department* [2001] 3 All ER 449.
2 By the Criminal Justice Act 1991, s 35, as applied by ss 43 and 51.
3 [1998] AC at 413.
4 On this aspect of the decision see 7.50 and note 4, 7.53 above.
5 [2010] EWCA Civ 460; [2011] 1 WLR 99.

7.83 As a further example of irrelevant considerations, the Court of Appeal in *R (Crown Prosecution Service) v Registrar General of Births, Deaths and Marriages*[1] held that it was not a consideration relevant to the exercise of his discretion by a prison governor whether to permit a prisoner to marry in his prison that the marriage would make the prisoner's intended wife a non-compellable witness at his forthcoming trial. The Court of Appeal has also held that the opposition on moral grounds to stag hunting is an irrelevant consideration for a local authority making decisions concerning the use and management of its land (the decision being to prohibit stag hunting).[2]

1   [2002] EWCA Civ 1661; [2003] QB 1222.
2   *R v Somerset County Council, ex parte Fewings* [1995] 1 WLR 1037. As to the pursuit of
    political or electoral advantage as an irrelevant consideration see *Porter v Magill* [2001]
    UKHL 67; [2002] 2 AC 357 (at **7.88** below).

7.84 A striking example of a consideration held to be relevant was the
decision of the House of Lords in *R v Gloucestershire County Council, ex
parte Barry*[1] that a local authority, in assessing the needs of an elderly resident
under s 2(1) of the Chronically Sick and Disabled Persons Act 1970 for social
services, was entitled to have regard to the availability of its own resources,
and to withdraw services previously provided when its allocation of funds was
reduced.[2] The reviewability of resource allocation decisions depended on
numerous factors, including whether the relevant duty was an absolute duty or
a target duty, and bearing in mind the court's lack of competence to decide
policy or polycentric matters.[3]

In other cases, factors considered and accepted by the courts as relevant have
included planning as well as housing considerations in a compulsory purchase
case,[4] and a previous, lapsed planning consent in deciding a subsequent
planning application.[5] The fees paid to prosecuting counsel were held to be a
relevant consideration for a taxing master taxing defence counsel's fees under
the Legal Aid Act in *Lord Chancellor v Wright*.[6] In the *Wednesbury* case itself,[7]
the welfare of children was held to be a relevant consideration in determining
conditions to be attached to cinema licences.

1   [1997] AC 584 (Lords Lloyd and Steyn dissenting). *ex parte Barry* was followed by the Court
    of Appeal's decision in *R (Spink) v Wandsworth Borough Council* [2005] 1 WLR 2884 that
    a local authority was entitled to take into account the means of the parents of a disabled child
    in determining whether to exercise a power to fund adaptations to the child's home.
2   Reversing on this point the Court of Appeal [1996] 4 All ER 421. Contrast the decision in *R
    v East Sussex County Council, ex parte Tandy* [1998] AC 714 (on provision for a child with
    special educational needs).
3   See *R (G) v Barnet London Borough Council* [2003] UKHL 57; [2004] 2 AC 208.
4   *Hanks v Minister of Housing and Local Government* [1963] 1 QB 999; [1963] 1 All ER 47.
5   *South Oxfordshire District Council v Secretary of State for the Environment* [1981] 1 All ER
    954; [1981] 1 WLR 1092; but the decision was quashed because the factor had been accorded
    excessive weight.
6   [1993] 1 WLR 1561.
7   [1948] 1 KB 223; [1947] 2 All ER 680.

7.85 Although not obviously linked to the question of relevancy of considerations, the question of what rules of evidence a decision-maker must apply
may arise in this context. The reason is that by applying evidential criteria
other than those required by the empowering statutory provisions, the
decision-maker may exclude relevant, or admit irrelevant, factors into the
equation. It is, of course, primarily in the decision-making processes of bodies
exercising judicial functions that restrictions on the admissibility of evidence
will arise, but this does not necessarily confine the point to the decisions of
judicial bodies.[1]

1   See, eg *R v Nat Bell Liquors* [1922] 2 AC 128 PC, per Lord Sumner at 144; *R v Bedwellty
    Justices, ex parte Williams* [1997] AC 225.

Improper purposes

7.86 Improper purpose in the exercise of a power or duty automatically renders that exercise invalid. Under this heading, examples show a wide range of impropriety, from the technical, arising from a misconstruction of a statutory power, to collateral or ulterior purposes clothed thinly with the veil of the statutory purpose. The former include planning cases in which the protection of tenants was held to be an improper purpose in the licensing of a caravan site,[1] and a requirement to construct a road as a condition of planning permission was held to be an unlawful collateral obligation.[2] The 'misplaced philanthropy' cases involving payment of improperly generous wages[3] and subsidising public transport[4] are also examples of intrinsically legitimate objects that simply lacked statutory authority.[5]

[1]   *Chertsey UDC v Mixnam's Properties Ltd* [1965] AC 735; [1964] 2 All ER 627.
[2]   *Hall & Co Ltd v Shoreham-by-Sea UDC* [1964] 1 All ER 1; [1964] 1 WLR 240. See for the subsequent history of planning agreements (under the Town and County Planning Act 1971, s 52; now the Town and County Planning Act 1990, s 106), *Tesco Stores Ltd v Secretary of State for the Environment* [1995] 1 WLR 759, HL.
[3]   *Roberts v Hopwood* [1925] AC 578; *Re Walker's Decision* [1944] 1 KB 644.
[4]   *Prescott v Birmingham Corpn* [1955] Ch 210; [1954] 3 All ER 698; *Bromley London Borough Council v Greater London Council* [1983] 1 AC 768; [1982] 1 All ER 129.
[5]   In the case of *Re Walker's Decision* [1944] 1 KB 644, the wage levels fixed were lawful, and the 'improper' purpose of assisting employees with dependent children did not invalidate them.

7.87 Many cases involve the pursuit of purposes at variance with the policy of the relevant legislation or directly opposed to it. Examples include: a decision by the government to impose a 'residence test' for individuals seeking legal aid funding;[1] a decision by the government to not pay for work done on an application for permission to apply for judicial review where permission was subsequently refused;[2] a refusal to raise rents;[3] and an allocation of a local authority's entire required rent increase to a single unoccupied house;[4] in order to avoid the requirements of legislation authorising or requiring increased rents for the authority's properties generally;[5] the exercise of a prerogative power to remove the designation of an airline under a bilateral international agreement in order to defeat the purpose of the regulatory statute;[6] use of a prerogative power to introduce a new scheme for criminal injuries compensation inconsistent with a scheme enacted by Parliament but which had not been brought into effect by a commencement order;[7] refusal to exercise a discretion to refer a dispute to a committee of investigation to avoid political embarrassment;[8] fixing high overtime rates for shop workers to force shops to close earlier in the evening;[9] and removing local authority-appointed school governors to secure compliance with the authority's policy for the school.[10] An example of an ulterior purpose, albeit benign, is the leading case of *Webb v Minister of Housing and Local Government*,[11] where a power of compulsory purchase for coastal protection was used ostensibly for the permitted purpose but, in reality (as inferred, amongst other things, from the width of the strip of land acquired), was to enable the construction of a promenade. Improper political purposes occasionally feature in successful challenges, as in two cases involving opposition to Mr Rupert Murdoch's activities.[12] Use of a broad discretionary licensing power to enforce the payment of money to the Crown without Parliamentary sanction has also been held to involve an unlawful purpose.[13] On the other hand, the House of Lords.[14] overruling the Court of Appeal, has upheld the use of a power of compulsory purchase in a way designed to create price control over development land.[15]

[1]   *R (Public Law Project) v Lord Chancellor (Office of the Children's Commissioner Intervening* [2016] UKSC 39; [2016] AC 1531.

[2]   *R (Ben Hoare Bell Solicitors and others v Lord Chancellor)* [2015] EWHC 523 (Admin); [2015] 1 WLR 4175.

[3]   *Taylor v Munrow* [1960] 1 All ER 455; [1960] 1 WLR 151.

[4]   *Backhouse v Lambeth London Borough Council* (1972) 116 Sol Jo 802. The rent was increased from £7 to £18,000 a week.

[5]   Respectively under the Rent Act 1957 and the Housing Finance Act 1972. In the former case the local authority was held to have incurred unlawful expenditure in paying extra compensation to the private landlords who were prevented from increasing rents as permitted by the Act.

[6]   *Laker Airways Ltd v Department of Trade* [1977] QB 643; [1976] 3 WLR 537, a rare example of use of a prerogative power for an improper purpose.

[7]   *R v Secretary of State for the Home Department, ex parte Fire Brigades Union* [1995] 2 AC 513: the Home Secretary's action was also characterised as an unlawful fettering of his discretion whether to make the commencement order (to bring into force the Criminal Justice Act 1988, ss 108–117).

[8]   *Padfield v Minister of Agriculture, Fisheries and Food* [1968] AC 997.

[9]   *Brownells Ltd v Ironmongers' Wages Board* (1950) 81 CLR 108.

[10]   *Brunyate v Inner London Education Authority* [1989] 2 All ER 417; this was described by Lord Bridge as a 'usurpation' of the independent authority of the governors (of a voluntary school); see, also, *R v Warwickshire County Council, ex parte Dill-Russell* (1990) 89 LGR 640 (removal not unlawful) and *R v Greenwich London Borough Council, ex parte Lovelace (No 2)* [1992] QB 155; [1992] 1 All ER 679 (removal of councillors from committee for failure to follow party line not unlawful).

[11]   [1965] 2 All ER 193; [1965] 1 WLR 755. Contrast *R (Fisher) v English Nature* [2004] EWCA Civ 663; [2005] 1 WLR 147, CA (decision to designate land as a Site of Special Scientific Interest not made for ulterior purpose of underpinning proposal for designation of the land under an EU Directive to protect migrant bird habitat).

[12]   *R v Ealing London Borough Council, ex parte Times Newspapers Ltd* (1986) 85 LGR 316 (refusal to stock newspapers in local libraries because of opposition to proprietor's conduct of industrial dispute); *R v Derbyshire County Council, ex parte Times Supplements Ltd* (1991) 3 Admin LR 241 (refusal to advertise vacancies in newspapers after attack on council's conduct published in other newspapers owned by same group). See, also, *R v Lewisham London Borough Council, ex parte Shell UK Ltd* [1988] 1 All ER 938 (refusal to buy company's products for purpose of pressurising it to disengage from South Africa: improper purpose). On the imposition of discriminatory conditions in a local authority permit being outside the statutory purposes see *R v Barnet London Borough Council, ex parte Johnson and Jacobs* (1991) 3 Admin LR 149 (restrictions on political activities at festival). Adoption of a policy of selecting employees of a local authority for redundancy in a way that indirectly discriminates contrary to the Sex Discrimination Act 1975 or the Race Relations Act 1976 is amenable to judicial review; *R v London Borough of Hammersmith and Fulham, ex parte NALGO* [1991] IRLR 249.

[13]   *Congreve v Home Office* [1976] QB 629; [1976] 1 All ER 697 (cancellation of otherwise valid television licences to compel licence holders to comply retrospectively with an increase in licence fees).

[14]   *Earl Fitzwilliam's Wentworth Estates Co v Minister of Town and Country Planning* [1951] 2 KB 284; [1951] 1 All ER 982.

[15]   The Divisional Court in *R v Elmbridge District Council, ex parte Active Office Ltd* (1998) 10 Admin LR 561 went further in concluding that the principles summarised here have no application in relation to a challenge to a local authority's decision to prosecute a landowner for breach of a listed building enforcement order.

7.88 An extreme example of an ulterior purpose vitiating an otherwise ostensibly lawful exercise of a discretionary power was the subject of the House of Lords' decision in *Porter v Magill*.[1] Westminster City Council had been found by the District Auditor to have used its powers to increase the numbers of owner-occupiers, who the Council's leaders believed were more likely to vote Conservative, in marginal wards, for the purpose of increasing the prospects of the re-election of the Conservative Party as the majority party in future Council elections. In upholding the decision of the Auditor that this was both an unlawful purpose and wilful misconduct (with the result that the Leader of the Council was subjected to a surcharge of the money lost to the Council by this policy), their Lordships reaffirmed as basic principles of public law that powers conferred on a public authority can only lawfully be used for the public purpose for which they were conferred, and may not be used to promote the electoral advantage of a political party.[2]

1   [2001] UKHL 67; [2002] 2 AC 357.
2   Ibid. See, eg Lord Bingham *at 463–465, [19]*.

Duality of purpose

7.89 De Smith[1] has described as a 'legal porcupine' the body of law dealing with the identification of the purpose to be addressed by the court where a body acts for mixed purposes. The case law can be used to support a number of different formulations of the law. The first is that of dominant purpose: if a body exercises a discretion for multiple purposes one of which would be improper, the decision is open to challenge if the improper purpose was the dominant or principal one, but not if it merely arose incidentally as a collateral benefit of the decision. Thus in the old but still helpful case of *Westminster Corpn v London and North Western Rly Co*,[2] the corporation was empowered to construct public conveniences and chose to construct one beneath Whitehall at the entrance to Parliament Square, accessible by subway from both sides of the street. The two parts of the subway could be used to cross under the street, but on a finding that that was an incidental benefit and not the primary purpose of the form of construction, the work was held to be lawful. Other cases supporting the dominant purpose approach include *Webb*,[3] and, more arguably, *R v Governor of Brixton Prison, ex parte Soblen*[4] and *HXA v The Home Office*.[5] The claimant succeeded in establishing that his immigration detention was unlawful because, following the Court determining the Secretary of State's true purpose in making a deportation order, which was pivotal to determining the lawfulness of the detention, it was apparent detention had continued to achieve a purpose not provided for under the Immigration Act 1971.

1   Woolf et al (eds), De Smith's Judicial Review (7th edn, 2013), paragraph 5–109.
2   [1905] AC 426.
3   *Webb v Minister of Housing and Local Government* [1965] 2 All ER 193; [1965] 1 WLR 755. See Danckwerts LJ at 778H.
4   [1963] 2 QB 243; [1962] 3 All ER 641. This case is one where the court looked for the true purpose of the Home Secretary's deportation order, but the challenge to it fell for lack of evidence of the alleged improper motive (of disguised extradition for a political offence).
5   [2010] EWHC 1177 (QB).

7.90 A full review of the law is set out in *R v Inner London Education Authority, ex parte Westminster City Council*,[1] which concerned expenditure by the ILEA on publishing literature with the dual purposes of information and political persuasion. Glidewell J, after referring to other authorities supporting the dominant purpose test, adopted two tests distilled by de Smith[2] from the authorities, namely: what was the true purpose; and whether any unauthorised purpose had materially influenced the actor's conduct. His Lordship also adopted the analysis of the problem given by Megaw J in *Hanks v Minister of Housing and Local Government*,[3] which concluded that it was simplest to view the whole of this area of law as a matter of relevant and irrelevant considerations. Clearly applying a test of the *materiality* to a decision of an irrelevant consideration or improper purpose may offer a lower threshold of illegality than the requirement that an improper purpose was the *true or dominant* purpose.[4] The actual decision in the *ILEA* case was that the improper political purpose was 'a, if not the, major purpose of the decision',[5] which was accordingly quashed. It is submitted that in a case where the decision turned on whether dominant purpose or material influence was the correct test a court would be free to decide which to follow. A slight variation on the material influence approach, supported by Australian authority[6] but not directly by English authority, is whether the impugned purpose is a substantial purpose, in the sense that but for its impetus the offending decision would not have been taken. This 'causation' test may well be an attractive compromise resolution to the problem. A slightly more recent, and helpful, review of the tests was undertaken by Lord Carswell CJ in *In the matter of Kelly and Shiels*.[7] The case concerned the validity of regulations made by the Law Society of Northern Ireland prescribing the conditions for admission to the profession of solicitor in the Province, which included a requirement to have been accepted on a particular postgraduate training course, places on which were limited. The court accepted that the permitted legislative purposes did not include restricting the numbers of those admitted to the profession, but went on to hold that although that was a consequence of the regulation, it was not the Law Society's dominant purpose in making it, which was to secure a proper level of professional training, which was only available in the Province through the specified course. Lord Carswell CJ's conclusion was that the 'true or dominant purpose' test and the test that an irrelevant consideration or purpose 'demonstrably exerted a substantial influence' on the result were useful alternatives, both being an application of the 'basic principle that the donee of a power must act within the limits of the discretion conferred on him'.[8]

[1] [1986] 1 All ER 19; [1986] 1 WLR 28. See also *R (Hicks) v Metropolitan Commissioner* [2012] EWHC 1947 (Admin) at [231], referring to the speech of Lord Hutton in *R v Southwark Crown Court*, ex p. Bowles [1998] 2 WLR 715; [1998] 1 AC 641.
[2] (4th edn) pp 330–332. The authorities cited were *Westminster Corpn v London and North Western Rly Co* [1905] AC 426 and Denning LJ in *Earl Fitzwilliam's Wentworth Estates Co v Minister of Town and Country Planning* [1951] 2 KB 284, 307; [1951] 1 All ER 982.
[3] [1963] 1 QB 999; [1963] 1 All ER 47.
[4] But see also *In the matter of Kelly and Shiels*, discussed below.
[5] [1986] 1 WLR at 49H.
[6] *Thompson v Randwick Corpn* (1950) 81 CLR 87 at 106.
[7] [2001] NI 103.
[8] [2001] NI 103, paragraph 37.

7.91 The discussion above deals with purpose and can equally be applied to motive, in the sense synonymous with purpose. An improper motive in the wider sense, as where a decision taken is motivated by personal animosity towards the subject of the decision, should certainly justify invalidating the decision, and not only in the context of proceedings of a judicial character.[1] Conduct of such a kind may reasonably be categorised as 'bad faith'. Unfortunately this term has on occasion been more widely used as the converse of a concept of good faith which is little more than synonymous with acting within the legal limits of a power. In that sense bad faith is really no more than a pejorative description of grounds of illegality. The Court of Appeal has deprecated such usage in clear terms:

' . . . in some authorities and textbooks the phrase "bad faith" is used to describe cases in which a statutory authority has, in what would ordinarily be called good faith, made a mistake as to the extent of its powers or without any dishonesty or malice, acted in a way that was not permitted by its powers and in a way that infringed someone's legal rights. We regret that there should be that debasement of the currency of language. It is not fair to a public authority or its members or its servants that the public, not versed in the technical jargon, should read that a court has held them to be guilty of "bad faith" when they have made an honest mistake'.[2]

[1] Cases of actual bias are happily extremely rare. An example is *Catalina SS (Owners) v Norma* (1938) 61 Ll L Rep 360 where an arbitrator categorised the entire racial group (Portuguese) to which one party's witnesses belonged as liars. See further on bias in Chapter 12, and on bad faith, see Chapter 13.

[2] *Western Fish Products Ltd v Penwith District Council* [1981] 2 All ER 204 at 215h (judgment of the court, given by Megaw LJ). See, also, *Cannock Chase District Council v Kelly* [1978] 1 All ER 152; [1978] 1 WLR 1, CA.

7.92 In the light of this it is suggested that 'bad faith' as a concept should be, and properly is, limited to cases of malicious or deliberately ulterior motives or knowingly ultra vires actions. Authority is not needed for the proposition that a court may intervene when a public body's decisions are shown to be tainted by such factors.[1]

[1] Bad faith, in this sense, like fraud, must be pleaded if an allegation is to be relied on.

Evidence of purposes

7.93 Some problems may arise of establishing the considerations taken, or not taken, into account in reaching a decision, or the dominant or substantial purposes of the deciding body. This is likely to be particularly so of a body whose decisions are taken by a group of individuals such as the members of a local authority committee; here the further question arises of what consequences flow from the decision of some or even one of the group being affected by irrelevant considerations or motivated by improper purposes. A number of points may be made as follows.

(1)   Where the body acts within the ostensible limits of its powers it is for the person alleging that the decision is nevertheless ultra vires to demonstrate this: 'It is for those who assert that the local authority has contravened the law to establish that proposition'.[1]

(2)   In a body exercising a power of a kind in respect of which a court would be likely to attach a high degree of importance to the need for a demonstrably fair procedure, it is more likely that irrelevant considerations influencing a single member of the body will be fatal. In a case where an administrative decision is reached by, say, a local authority, and the errant views of the member were probably not determinative of the decision, the decision may survive challenge.[2]

(3)   A failure by the body concerned to give reasons for its decision may lead to the inference that it lacked good reasons, or that its motive or purpose was legally improper.[3] Increasingly, the giving of reasons is seen as a facet of the obligation to deal fairly with the parties.[4] In the absence of a general duty to give reasons for decisions, the ambit of this point must be uncertain. A body which is not asked for reasons is in a stronger position than one which is but refuses the request.

(4)   In practice it is common that reasoned decisions are given, and the reasons given may then be subjected to scrutiny which on occasions nears that given to a statute.[5] How far it is appropriate to dissect statements of reasons must depend, at least in part, on how far the body giving the reasons is able to call on professional advisers to draft them.

(5)   Where a body takes decisions on formal documents, as is usual for a local authority, the documents before the body will provide clear evidence of what considerations were drawn to its attention (and, by inference, presumed to have been taken into account). This may help to establish the taking into account of irrelevant matters in particular. The increasingly common practice of minutes or resolutions of local authorities formally recording the matters taken into account in reaching a decision, no doubt a reaction to the increasing frequency of applications for judicial review, is also of assistance in overcoming evidential obstacles.[6]

---

[1]   *Associated Provincial Picture Houses Ltd v Wednesbury Corpn* [1948] 1 KB 223 at 228, per Lord Greene MR.

[2]   See, eg *R v Waltham Forest London Borough Council, ex parte Baxter* [1988] QB 419; [1987] 3 All ER 671 where the impugned decision to set a rate had been approved by 31 votes to 26 and it was alleged that some members of the majority party had acted under the dictation of a local political committee. Sir John Donaldson MR said that had this allegation been sustained (involving six or seven councillors) the decision would have been invalid (at 422H), but in relation to one councillor in particular his Lordship left open whether had his vote been so influenced the court would have exercised a discretion not to quash, since the vote was not decisive (at 426F). Stocker LJ appeared to regard one councillor's improper motives as sufficient to invalidate the decision, while Russell LJ said that 'his [the Councillor's] vote can be impugned and any resolution supported by his vote *potentially flawed*' (at 428H, emphasis added). Cf *Smith v Hayle Town Council* [1978] ICR 996 (dismissal of clerk by vote of six-five, one of six admitting to anti-trade union prejudice as reason for vote: held not sufficient to establish that union membership was 'principal reason' for dismissal).

[3]   *Padfield v Minister of Agriculture, Fisheries and Food* [1968] AC 997 at 1053G–1054A, per Lord Pearce (obiter, since reasons had in fact been given); *R v Civil Service Appeal Board, ex parte Cunningham* [1991] 4 All ER 310; [1991] IRLR 297.

[4]   See the decision of the Court of Appeal in *Oakley v South Cambridgeshire District Council* [2017] EWCA Civ 71 at [29] where Elias LJ explained:
'29 It is firmly established that there is no general obligation to give reasons at common law, as confirmed by Lord Mustill in the ex parte *Doody* case. However, the tendency increasingly is to require them rather than not. Indeed, almost twenty years ago, when giving judgment in *Stefan v General Medical Council (no.1)* [1999] 1 WLR 1293, 1300, Lord Clyde observed: "There is certainly a strong argument for the view that what was once seen as exceptions to a rule may now be becoming examples of the norm, and the cases where reasons are not required may be taking on the appearance of exceptions." In view of this, it may be more accurate to say that the common law is moving to the position whilst there is no universal obligation to give reasons in all circumstances, in general they should be given unless there is a proper justification for not doing so.'

[5]   For example, *Lavender & Son Ltd v Minister of Housing and Local Government* [1970] 3 All ER 871; [1970] 1 WLR 1231 and *South Oxfordshire District Council v Secretary of State for the Environment* [1981] 1 All ER 954; [1981] 1 WLR 1092, both planning cases which turned on the interpretation of a phrase in a decision letter.

[6] In *Telstra Corporation v Hurstville City Council* [2002] FCAFC 92, the Full Court of the Federal Court of Australia, having referred to this sub-paragraph in the previous edition of this book, approved the proposition that where a local authority adopted a recommendation put before it 'without more, it can . . . properly be inferred that the "intentions, beliefs, motives and state of mind" of the Council (as a collegiate body) are as disclosed in the reports and other documents brought into existence by its officers' (at paragraph 50).

Chapter 8

UNREASONABLENESS

INTRODUCTION

Scope of this chapter

8.1 This chapter is concerned with the circumstances in which a court may review a decision in the field of public law on grounds of unreasonableness, sometimes described as 'irrationality'. Under this head of review a decision is unlawful if it falls outside the range of reasonable responses open to the decision maker. This standard is commonly applied to decisions of fact, or of how to exercise a discretionary power. However, there is no longer a consistent test as to what makes a decision unreasonable. The intensity of review now depends on the context, such as on the importance of the rights affected by the decision. Unreasonableness is a common law concept and, as a consequence, evolves to reflect changing legal norms; thus, the introduction of a concept of fundamental rights to the jurisprudence of the domestic courts (whether as human rights or as rights derived from EU law) has necessitated a revision of the suitability of unreasonableness to subject decisions to a sufficient degree of scrutiny.[1] Review for lack of proportionality is a concept developed initially by continental jurists. It now forms part of English law in areas governed by European Union law or where the European Convention on Human Rights comes into play.[2] Drawing on observations by Lord Steyn that the criteria of proportionality are more precise and sophisticated, the Court of Appeal has suggested that the House of Lords may take the step of replacing reasonableness with proportionality as the criterion for common law review.[3] Proportionality as a concept is discussed in CHAPTER 9. This chapter begins with an overview of the development of the modern principles of review on the grounds of reasonableness, before turning to general questions of terminology, the time at which, and evidence with which, a decision is to be tested, and the consequences of a finding of unreasonableness. The next section examines the relationship of the principle of reasonableness with the principles governing review based on illegality, procedural impropriety and other grounds. The third section discusses circumstances where the principle of reasonableness has been said to be inapplicable, or modified in its application. The fourth section surveys aspects of the principle of reasonableness in operation.

[1] See *Burgdaycay v Secretary of State for the Home Department* [1987] AC 514; *R v Ministry of Agriculture, Fisheries and Food, ex p. First City Trading Limited* [1997] 1 CMLR 250, QBD.

[2] See *R (Association of British Civilian Internees: Far East Region) v Secretary of State for Defence* [2003] QB 1397, esp paragraphs 34 ff, p 1413. The observations by Lord Steyn are in *R (Daly) v Secretary of State for the Home Department* [2001] 2 AC 532, 547–548, paragraph 27. The Court of Appeal also referred to remarks found in paragraph 51 of the speech of Lord Slynn of Hadley in *R (Alconbury Developments Ltd) v Secretary of State for the Environment, Transport and the Regions* [2003] 2 AC 295, 320–321, and by Lord Cooke of Thorndon in the *Daly* case, at pp 548–549, paragraph 32. For a general discussion, see CHAPTER 9.

[3] For Scots law on these topics, see **22.69–22.74**.

Overview of unreasonableness as a ground of review

8.2 The courts have long asserted that those exercising what would now be described as public law powers must act within the confines of what is reasonable. Lord Coke CJ in *Rooke's Case*,[1] a private law action of replevin against Commissioners of Sewers, held the Commissioners' actions unlawful and said that the Commissioners' discretion was 'bound with the rule of reason'. In *R v Askew*[2] Lord Mansfield considered whether mandamus should be granted against the College of Physicians, and summarised what would now be described as public law principles – including the requirement that discretion should not be exercised in an arbitrary or capricious way – in two sentences which have value more than two centuries later:

> 'It is true, that the judgment and discretion of determining upon this skill, ability, learning and sufficiency to exercise and practise this profession is trusted to the College of Physicians: and this court will not take it from them, nor interrupt them in the due and proper exercise of it. But their conduct in the exercise of this trust thus committed to them ought to be fair, candid, and unprejudiced: not arbitrary, capricious, or biased; much less, warped by resentment, or personal dislike'.[3]

---

[1] (1598) 5 Co Rep 99b.
[2] (1768) 4 Burr 2186.
[3] (1768) 4 Burr 2186, p 2188.

Review of a decision outside the limits of reason

8.3 The assertion of a claim to examine the reasonableness of what had been done by a public authority inevitably led to differences of judicial opinion as to the circumstances in which the court should intervene. These differences of opinion were resolved in two landmark cases which confined the circumstances for intervention to narrow limits. In *Kruse v Johnson*[1] a specially constituted divisional court[2] had to consider the validity of a byelaw made by a local authority. In the leading judgment of Lord Russell of Killowen CJ, the approach to be adopted by the court was set out.[3] Such byelaws ought to be 'benevolently' interpreted, and credit ought to be given to those who have to administer them that they would be reasonably administered. They could be held invalid if unreasonable: where, for instance, byelaws were found to be partial and unequal in their operation as between different classes, if they were manifestly unjust, if they disclosed bad faith, or if they involved such oppressive or gratuitous interference with the rights of citizens as could find no justification in the minds of reasonable men. Lord Russell emphasised[4] that a byelaw is not unreasonable just because particular judges might think it went further than was prudent or necessary or convenient.

---

[1] [1898] 2 QB 91.
[2] There were seven judges, one of whom dissented.
[3] [1898] 2 QB 91 at 99.
[4] [1898] 2 QB 91 at 100. See also the comment of Kennedy LJ in *R (Mahmood) v Royal Pharmaceutical Society of Great Britain* [2002] 1 WLR 879 at paragraph 35, p 889: 'It is a high test'.

8.4 In 1947 the Court of Appeal discussed the review of executive discretion generally in *Associated Provincial Picture Houses Ltd v Wednesbury Corpn*.[1] This case was concerned with a complaint by the owners of a cinema in Wednesbury that it was unreasonable of the local authority to licence performances on Sunday only subject to a condition that 'no children under the age of 15 years shall be admitted to any entertainment whether accompanied by an adult or not'. In an extempore judgment, Lord Green MR drew attention to the fact that the word 'unreasonable' had often been used in a sense which comprehended different grounds of review.[2] He summarised the principles as follows:[3]

'The court is entitled to investigate the action of the local authority with a view to seeing whether or not they have taken into account matters which they ought not to have taken into account, or, conversely, have refused to take into account or neglected to take into account matters which they ought to take into account.[4] Once that question is answered in favour of the local authority, it may still be possible to say that, although the local authority had kept within the four corners of the matters which they ought to consider, they have nevertheless come to a conclusion so unreasonable that no reasonable authority could ever have come to it. In such a case, again, I think the court can interfere. The power of the court to interfere in each case is not as an appellate authority to override a decision of the local authority, but as a judicial authority which is concerned, and concerned only, to see whether the local authority has contravened the law by acting in excess of the power which Parliament has confided in them'.

[1]   [1948] 1 KB 223, [1947] 2 All ER 680. For the background to the case, see Sir Robert Carnwath. 'The Reasonable Limits of Local Authority Power' [1996] PL 244.

[2]   [1948] 1 KB 233 at 229, where it is said that the dismissal of a teacher for having red hair (cited by Warrington LJ in *Short v Poole Corpn* [1926] Ch 66, 91, as an example of a 'frivolous and foolish reason') was, in another sense, taking into consideration extraneous matters, and might be so unreasonable that it could almost be described as being done in bad faith: see, also, *R v Tower Hamlets London Borough Council, ex p Chetnik Developments Ltd* [1988] AC 858 at 873.

[3]   At page 233; these principles are the same as those applicable to the review of bye-laws: see per Lord Denning in *Fawcett Properties v Buckingham County Council* [1961] AC 636 at 639, applied by Diplock LJ in *Mixnam's Properties Ltd v Chertsey UDC* [1964] 1 QB 214 (upheld on appeal [1965] AC 735). Lord Greene's approach was applied to byelaws by the Northern Ireland Court of Appeal in *Belfast Corpn v Daly* [1963] NI 78. See, also, *Percy v Hall* [1996] 4 All ER 523, [1997] 3 WLR 573.

[4]   This would now be regarded primarily as part of the investigation of the legality of the authority's approach: see per Lord Bridge in *R v Secretary of State for the Environment, ex p Hammersmith and Fulham London Borough Council* [1991] 1 AC 521 at 597 (although review for unreasonableness may still have a part in relation to the identification of relevant and irrelevant matters; see **8.53** below).

8.5 This summary by Lord Greene has been applied in countless subsequent cases. The grounds of review that it describes are not confined to unreasonableness, but Lord Greene's criterion of 'a conclusion so unreasonable that no reasonable authority could ever have come to it' was so frequently cited that this head of review came to be known as '*Wednesbury* unreasonableness'.

8.6 The narrowness of the limits within which the court can intervene was stressed by Lord Diplock, who gave this head of review a new name – 'irrationality' – when expounding his tripartite classification of the grounds of review in *Council of Civil Service Unions v Minister for the Civil Service*.[1]

Elaborating on this aspect of Lord Greene's exposition, Lord Diplock[2] said of this head of review:

'By "irrationality" I mean what can now be succinctly referred to as "*Wednesbury* unreasonableness" (*Associated Provincial Picture Houses v Wednesbury Corpn* [1948] 1 KB 223). It applies to a decision which is so outrageous in its defiance of logic or of accepted moral standards that no sensible person who had applied his mind to the question to be decided could have arrived at it'.

[1] [1985] AC 374 at 410.
[2] Described as 'classical', but not exhaustive by Lord Scarman in *Nottingham-shire County Council v Secretary of State for the Environment* [1986] AC 240 at 249.

8.7 Lord Diplock's statement of principle underlines the crucial feature that the court is *not* concerned with what it regards as the appropriate decision, but rather with the quite different test of whether sensible decision-makers, properly directed in law and properly applying their minds to the matter, could have regarded the conclusion under review as a permissible one.[1] Adopting the words of Cooke P in the New Zealand case of *Webster v Auckland Harbour Board*,[2] what is required before the court may intervene on this ground is that the decision is one outside the limits of reason.[3]

[1] For an affirmation of this principle, see *R v Secretary of State for Trade and Industry, ex p Lonhro plc* [1989] 1 WLR 525, 535. (However, see also the discussion of mistake of fact in Chapter 13 at **13.16** below.)
[2] [1987] 2 NZLR 129, 131.
[3] In this regard it may be unfortunate that Lord Greene's words have become an 'incantation': see Lord Cooke of Throndon's speeches in *R v Chief Constable of Sussex, ex p International Trader's Ferry Ltd* [1999] 2 AC 418, 452 and *R v Secretary of State for the Home Department, ex p Daly* [2001] 2 AC 532 at paragraph 32.

8.8 Moreover, the test is stringent:[1] the court is not concerned with peccadilloes. Reasonable people may differ about moral standards, and about the rigour with which logic must be applied. An assertion that a decision is illogical or fails to meet moral imperatives must be weighed against the needs of good administration, recognising that administrators will sometimes find themselves confronted with a Gordian knot, and must not shirk from applying a common sense solution. Only if the solution strays so far from logic or accepted moral standards that no reasonable administrator could have thought it right will it be condemned as irrational. This involves a value judgment by the court: but it is a judgment of a very limited kind.

[1] This is sometimes underlined by the use of emphatic expressions when describing the test: eg 'acting perversely' and 'verging on absurdity' (*Puhlhofer v Hillingdon London Borough Council* [1986] AC 484 at 518), 'totally unreasonable' (*Champion v Chief Constable of the Gwent Constabulary* [1990] 1 WLR 1 at 5). Andrew Le Sueur has questioned whether the court in practice applies a high threshold: 'The Rise and Ruin of Unreasonableness?' [2005] JR 32.

8.9 There is a concern, however, that Lord Diplock's analysis may have put the test too high.[1] *Wednesbury* unreasonableness affords a decision-maker a wide margin of appreciation. Within a very short time it was observed that Lord Diplock's statement of the principle was not to be construed as if it were a statute.[2] Criticisms followed in academic journals and texts.[3] The boundaries of judicial review were extended when it was held that, in certain limited circumstances, the court could intervene where discretionary powers had been exercised on a false basis of fact.[3] The narrowness of this approach – and the capcity for challenge which it afforded – became the subject of concern, in particular following the introduction of the Human Rights Act 1998 and the concept of what have been referred to as 'fundamental rights' cases, which necessitated a degree of 'anxious scrutiny' which went beyond conventional *Wednesbury*.[4] Thus in R *(Mahmood) v Secretary of State for the Home Department*,[5] Laws LJ found that, in additional to the traditional *Wednesbury* test, in fundamental rights cases, a court could 'insist that that fact be respected by the decision-maker, who is accordingly required to demonstrate either that his proposed action does not in truth interfere with the right, or, if it does, that there exist considerations which may reasonably be accepted as amounting to a substantial objective justification for the interference' and could also adopt a yet further approach in cases challenging rights under the European Convention.

The Court of Appeal explicitly recognised in R *(Q) v Secretary of State for the Home Department* that the law has moved on:[5]

'The common law of judicial review in England and Wales has not stood still in recent years. Starting from the received checklist of justiciable errors set out by Lord Diplock in *Council of Civil Service Unions v Minister for the Civil Service* [1985] AC 374, the courts, as Lord Diplock himself anticipated they would, have developed an issue-sensitive scale of intervention to enable them to perform their constitutional function in an increasingly complex polity. They continue to abstain from merits review – in effect, retaking the decision on the facts – but in appropriate classes of case they will today look very closely at the process by which facts have been ascertained and at the logic of the inferences drawn from them'.[6]

[1]   See note 1, 8.8 above, and R *v Panel on Take-overs and Mergers, ex p Guinness plc* [1990] 1 QB 146 at p 160; see also Lord Scarman [1990] PL 490.
[2]   See, eg Sir Robert Carnwath, 'The Reasonable Limits of Local Authority Power' [1996] PL 244; Walker, 'What's Wrong With Irrationality?' [1995] PL 556 (where a discussion of the 'logic' and 'moral standards' elements in Lord Diplock's test will be found).
[3]   See CHAPTER 13.
[4]   See CHAPTER 9, below, and cf. *Burgdaycay v Secretary of State for the Home Department* [1987] AC 514, and *Vilvarajah v United Kingdom* (1991) 14 EHRR 248, ECHR
[5]   [2001] 1 WLR 840, CA.
[6]   [2004] QB 36, paragraph 112, p 81. For the court's additional remarks about human rights review now involving questions of illegality, see 4.47 above. Further judicial recognition that the strictness of the test has been relaxed will be found in R *(Association of British Civilian Internees: Far East Region) v Secretary of State for Defence* [2003] QB 1397, paragraph 34, p 1413. See also the discussion of proportionality, CHAPTER 9.

8.10 It can be seen from the fourth section of this chapter (at **8.38** below) that courts have, in fact long applied the test of unreasonableness in a flexible way which has taken account of changes in values.

The current contextual approach to reasonableness

8.11 The common law no longer insists on the uniform application of the rigid test of irrationality once thought applicable under the so-called *Wednesbury* principle. The nature of judicial review in every case depends upon the context, and on factors including the gravity of the issue which the decision determines.

It is inappropriate to treat all cases of judicial review together under a general but vague principle of reasonableness, and preferable to look for the underlying tenet or principle which indicates the basis on which the court should approach any administrative law challenge in a particular situation. Reasonableness review involves considerations of weight and balance, with the intensity of the scrutiny and the weight to be given to any primary decision maker's view depending on the context.[1]

1   *Kennedy v Charity Commission* [2014] 2 WLR 808, 51–56, citing Paul Craig 'The Nature of Reasonableness' (2013) 66 CLP 131.

8.12 Some categories will require the court to subject an administrative decision to the more rigorous examination. Examples of such categories are those decisions which are particularly oppressive, or where a common law right or constitutional principle is in issue, such as liberty, the right of access to a court, open justice, accountability, transparency, consistency,[1] or citizenship.[2] At the other end of the scale a lower intensity of review is applied to decisions depending essentially on political judgment, such as decisions about public expenditure or the allocation of resources, or to issues with which judges are less well equipped to deal, for example because they lack the requisite experience or knowledge.[3] The intensity of review may be influenced by the respective constitutional roles of the court and decision maker, because some decisions may be entrusted to a particular decision maker or to a court; by the legislative and administrative scheme behind the discretionary power.[4] A statutory discretion should not be exercised in a way which frustrates the policy and objects of the relevant legislation:[5] and the subject matter of the decision. The courts have a particular constitutional capacity to protect the rule of law.[6]

1   See, for example, *R (Aguilar Quila) v Secretary of State for the Home Department* [2012] 1 AC 621.
2   *Pham v Secretary of State for the Home Department* [2015] 1 W.L.R. 1591.
3   *Kennedy v Charity Commission* [2014] 2 WLR 808, 51–56.
4   Ibid.
5   *Padfield v Minister of Agriculture, Fisheries and Food* [1968] AC 997; *R (Ben Hoare Bell and Others) v Lord Chancellor* [2015] 1 W.L.R. 4175
6   *R (Jackson) v A-G* [2005] UKHL 56, [2006] 1 AC 262 at 107.

8.13 Common law discretions have been modeled to meet the needs of Convention articles, and to ensure that Convention rights apply to the relationships between private parties if necessary,[1] and there is an increasing enthusiasm to develop the common law so that it reflects Convention rights.[2] In such cases, a proportionality approach equivalent to that applied by the Strasbourg Court will often be applied. The advantage of the terminology of proportionality is that it introduces an element of structure into the exercise, by directing attention to factors such as suitability or appropriateness, necessity and the balance or imbalance of benefits and disadvantages. There seems no reason why such factors should not be relevant in judicial review even outside the scope of Convention and EU law.[3]

1   *Kennedy v Charity Commission* [2014] 2 WLR 808 at 38.
2   *Osborn v Parole Board* [2013] UKSC 61, [2013] 3 WLR 1020 at 62.
3   *Kennedy v Charity Commission* [2014] 2 WLR 808 at 54.

8.14 There are differing views of exactly what test should be applied. At one end of the scale, reasonableness review may be equivalent to proportionality. A decision may be unlawful unless the public body puts forward an adequate justification. The courts may anxiously scrutinize the decision-making process to ensure that the public body has properly and carefully explored and summarized the relevant factors.[1] At the other end of the scale, the courts will not intervene unless a high threshold is met, such as that the decision is arbitrary or perverse.[2]

[1]   *Huang v Secretary of State for the Home Department* [2007] 2 AC 167 at 15; and *De Smith's Judicial Review* (7th edn) Woolf, Jowell, et al, 11–102.
[2]   For example, *Hayes v Willoughby* [2013] 1 WLR 935.

8.15 The remainder of this chapter, in particular some of the older cases, should be read with the current shift towards a more contextual approach to unreasonableness in mind.

Terminology

8.16 Lord Diplock, in *Council of Civil Service Unions v Minister for the Civil Service*, introduced the term 'irrationality' to describe this ground of review, and earlier in his speech said that the word 'reasonable' bore different meanings according to whether the context in which it was being used was that of private law or of public law.[1] However, 'irrationality' is an unsatisfactory label for the circumstances in which a court quashes a decision on grounds of unreasonableness. It wrongly casts doubt on the mental capacity of the decision-maker;[2] moreover, it wrongly suggests that the test is logicality (whereas not all departures from logic will ground review), it ignores the important role of moral values, and the use of a term redolent of severe criticism carries with it the danger that a court may not intervene in a case where intervention is needed.[3]

[1]   [1985] AC 374, 409, where the expression 'reasonable expectation' is rejected in favour of 'legitimate expectation'; the term 'irrationality' is introduced at 410 without any express reference back to the discussion at 409, but it may be surmised that this reasoning underlay Lord Diplock's abandonment of the terminology of reasonableness in this context.
[2]   See de Smith, Woolf and Jowell *Judicial Review of Administrative Action* (5th edn, 1995) p 550, citing Lord Donaldson MR in *Devon County Council v George* [1989] AC 573, 577; see, also, Sir John Laws in [1996] JR at p 50.
[3]   These points are discussed in Walker. 'What's Wrong With Irrationality?' [1995] PL 556, 566–571. See, also, Thomas J in *Waitakere City Council v Lovelock* [1997] 2 NZLR 385.

8.17 For these reasons the term 'unreasonableness' will generally be used in this chapter to describe the head of review now under consideration, and 'unreasonable' will be used to describe decisions which warrant review under that head.

Time at which the decision is to be tested

8.18 The lawfulness of an administrative decision generally falls to be judged as of the date of that decision,[1] and accordingly, in general, a challenge for unreasonableness will be determined by reference to the circumstances at that time.[2] But the position may be different in a case concerning the liberty of the individual. In *R v Secretary of State for the Home Department, ex p Launder*, the Secretary of State had considered whether it would be unjust, oppressive or wrong to permit the applicant's extradition to Hong Kong, and decided both initially and on reconsideration that it would not. Lord Hope (with whom other members of the House agreed) said:[3]

> 'Although we are concerned primarily with the reasonableness of the decisions at the time when they are taken we cannot ignore [subsequent] developments. We are dealing in this case with concerns which have been expressed about human rights and the risks to the applicant's life and liberty. If the expectations which the Secretary of State had when he took his decisions have not been borne out by events or are at risk of not being satisfied by the date of the applicant's proposed return to Hong Kong, it would be your Lordships' duty to set aside the decisions so that the matter may be reconsidered in the light of the changed circumstances'.

[1] Provisions for internal review may give rise to a question of construction whether the reviewer should proceed only by reference to what is known at the date of the decision under review: see *Mohamed v Hammersmith and Fulham LBC* [2001] UKHL 57, [2002] 1 AC 547.

[2] *R v Secretary of State for the Environment, ex p Knowsley MBC* ((1991) *The Independent*, 25 September, transcript pp 25, 54–55; *R v Ministry of Defence, ex p Smith* [1996] QB 517 (Sir Thomas Bingham MR at pp 554, 558; Henry LJ at p 563; Thorpe LJ at 566). It was accepted in *Secretary of State for Education and Science v Tameside Borough Council* [1977] AC 1014 (see 1038, 1052, and 1056) that the reasonableness of the council's proposals, and the lawfulness of the Secretary of State's conclusion that they were unreasonable, had to be judged at the date of that conclusion.

[3] [1997] 1 WLR 839, 860–861. By contrast in *E v Secretary of State for the Home Department* [2004] 2 WLR 123, CA, the only issue was whether the tribunal erred in law in finding that the claimants were not entitled to asylum as refugees. That issue fell to be determined on the evidence before the tribunal. The Court of Appeal said that later evidence of the wife's current mental condition might found an application that her removal would be contrary to the Human Rights Act 1998, or that she should be granted exceptional leave to remain, but those matters were not before the court.

8.19 In *Re Brewster*,[1] Lord Kerr, giving the judgment of the Supreme Court, stated that reasons not relied upon at the time of the decision-making could supplement the decision, but that they would be subject to more intense scrutiny.

[1] [2017] 1 W.L.R. 519 at [64].

Evidence with which the decision is to be tested

8.20 In general, a challenge for unreasonableness will be determined by reference to the evidence known to the decision-maker at the time of the decision (unless the exception described at **8.18** above applies).[1] It is not uncommon for other evidence to be adduced by the parties on an application for judicial review on grounds other than unreasonableness. Applying what was said by Orr LJ in *R v West Sussex Quarter Sessions, ex p Albert and Maud Johnson Trust Ltd*, fresh evidence is admitted at the hearing of an application for judicial review as a mode of proving some defect or irregularity which would constitute a ground for judicial review.[2] This will now be particularly important in cases of review for mistake of fact.[3] In so far as the ground of challenge is unreasonableness, and absent an assertion of failure to investigate or to take account of relevant material, new opinion evidence can seldom help to demonstrate that an evaluation by the decision-maker was unreasonable.[4] Expert evidence advancing an opinion that a decision was irrational is usurping the function of the court and will not be allowed. However, in order to carry out its function, the court must be able to understand the material put before it. Accordingly, in a truly technical field, where the significance of a particular process is in issue, expert evidence can be admitted to explain the process and its significance.[5] Similarly, where the subject is complex the court will commonly receive evidence explaining the context in which the issues arise.[6]

One consequence of the breadth of *Wednesbury* is that it leaves little if any scope for analysis of fact. The usual procedure in judicial review cases is first for there to be no oral evidence and second, in so far as there are factual disputes between the parties, the court is ordinarily obliged to resolve them in favour of the defendant.[7] That said, the courts have drawn a distinction between 'a broad judgment whose outcome could be overruled only on grounds of irrationality' and 'a hard-edged question [where t]here is no room for legitimate disagreement'.[8] In case of 'hard-edged' questions of fact, it may be necessary to allow oral evidence and cross-examination and, in cases where there are crucial factual disputes between the parties relating to jurisdiction of the ECHR and the engagement of its Articles, such evidence may become commonplace.[9]

---

[1] See, eg *R v Ministry of Defence, ex p Smith* [1996] QB 517. Thus Lord Russell of Killowen in *Secretary of State for Education and Science v Tameside Borough Council* [1977] AC 1014, 1056, was not willing to accept that facts subsequently brought forward as existing at the date of a decision by the Secretary of State could be relied on in support of the decision unless those facts were of such a character that they could be taken to be within the knowledge of the department (see also *R v Secretary of State for the Environment, ex p Powis* [1981] 1 WLR 584, [1981] 1 All ER 788, at pp 596–597). For authorities which establish a similar position in planning cases, see *Ashbridge Investments Ltd v Minister of Housing and Local Government* [1965] 1 WLR 1320, [1965] 3 All ER 371; *Green v Minister of Housing and Local Government* [1967] 2 QB 606; *Glover v Secretary of State for the Environment* (1980) 44 P&CR 359; *Sears Blok v Secretary of State for the Environment and London Borough of Southwark* [1982] JPL 248; *Chris Fashionware (West End) Ltd v Secretary of State for the Environment* [1980] JPL 678.

[2] [1974] QB 24 per Orr LJ at 39. Presumably fresh evidence is also admissible to rebut such an allegation. Where questions of jurisdiction or procedure arise fresh evidence may often be admitted (see *Green v Minister of Housing and Local Government* [1967] 2 QB 606; *R v Secretary of State for the Home Department, ex p Muse* [1992] Imm AR 282); similarly if the decision-maker failed to investigate the matter there may be a separate ground of challenge (see 8.27 below). Notwithstanding the limited statement of exceptions in *R v Secretary of State for the Environment, ex p Powis* [1981] 1 WLR 584, 595–596, [1981] 1 All ER 788, judicial review hearings generally proceed on the basis that the court should have before it such evidence as may be relevant to the issues which properly arise from the parties' affidavits and arguments. For discussion of discovery of fresh evidence as a ground of review, see 13.16 below. Cases where evidence not before the inspector may be introduced in planning matters are discussed in *Encyclopaedia of Planning Law and Practice* Vol II, paragraph 288.13. The circumstances in which reasons given for a decision may be supplemented by affidavit (when resisting legal challenge) are discussed by Richard McManus in 'The Timing of Statutory Reasons' [1996] JR 156. On this and other questions concerning admissibility of evidence at the hearing, see generally Chapter 19 below.

[3] See 13.16 below.

[4] See *Roussel Uclaf Australia Pty Ltd v Pharmaceutical Management Agency Ltd* [1997] 1 NZLR 650, 658–659. However, later events may bear out the wisdom (or lack thereof) of a decision. It was said in *R v Secretary of State for the Environment, ex p Powis* [1981] 1 WLR 584, [1981] 1 All ER 788 at 597 that the converse of Lord Russell's proposition (note 35 above) is that fresh evidence may be admitted of facts within the knowledge of the department though unknown to the Secretary of State at the time of his decision.

5   *R (Lynch) v General Dental Council* [2004] 1 All ER 1159 at paragraphs 24 to 25, where Collins J added that such cases will be very rare, and that on a challenge to a decision of an expert body, or a body advised by an expert assessor, it will be virtually impossible to justify the submission of expert evidence which goes beyond explanation of technical terms since a challenge to the factual conclusions and judgment of an expert is inappropriate for a reviewing court.

6   See eg *Nottinghamshire County Council v Secretary of State for the Environment* [1986] AC 240, [1986] 1 All ER 199. The topic of expert evidence in judicial review is discussed generally by Lidbetter, [2004] JR 194.

7   *R v Board of Visitors of Hull Prison ex p St Germain (No 2)* [1979] 1 WLR 1401, 1410 H *per* Geoffrey Lane LJ.

8   *R v Monopolies & Mergers Commission ex p South Yorkshire Transport Ltd* [1993] 1 WLR 23, 32 D–F.

9   R (Al-Sweady and Others) v the Secretary of State for Defence [2009] EWHC 2387 (Admin); *R (N) v M and others* [2003] 1 WLR 562 at 574; *R (Wilkinson) v Broadmoor Special Hospital Authority* [2002] 1 WLR 419.

Consequences of a finding of unreasonableness

8.21 In concluding this introductory section on review for unreasonableness, mention should be made of the consequences of a finding of unreasonableness. General principles as to the appropriateness of quashing orders, mandatory orders, prohibiting orders, declarations and injunctions will come into play, as will general principles concerned with the grant of discretionary relief: these are dealt with elsewhere.[1] Also relevant may be general principles dealing with the circumstances in which a flawed part of a determination may be severed, and the remainder of the determination saved or recast so as not to be invalidated.[2] In general, where a decision is quashed it is elementary that the decision may (and often must) be reconsidered by the decision-maker. While it is doubtful that the doctrine of issue estoppel may be relied on in judicial review,[3] in the absence of new information it may be expected that the decision-maker will not repeat an unreasonable decision. Thus in *West Glamorgan County Council v Rafferty*[4] Ralph Gibson LJ, referring to the fact that circumstances would continue to change, declined to make a declaration formulating any plan as to what would be reasonable. If, exceptionally, there is no possibility of change of relevant circumstances, then a finding of unreasonable failure to exercise a power will amount to a public law duty to act,[5] and, if a coercive order is needed, this may be imposed under Part 54 Rule 54.19 CPR by directions when the court remits the matter, or by mandatory or prohibition orders.[6]

1   See Chapters **16, 17** and **18.**, and s 31 of the Senior Courts Act 1981 as amended by s 141 of the Tribunals, Courts and Enforcement Act 2007.

2   An example of severance of an unreasonable qualification upon a benefit, leaving the remaining criteria intact, is *R v Immigration Appeal Tribunal, ex p Manshoora* [1986] Imm AR 385.

3   See **18.65** below.

4   [1987] 1 WLR 457, 478.

5   See *Stovin v Wise* [1996] AC 923 at 953 (Lord Hoffmann); at 936 Lord Nicholls adopts a similar approach (although dissenting on the issues concerning common law duty of care). In *Cocks v Thanet District Council* [1983] 2 AC 286 Lord Bridge, at p 295, recognised that a finding of unreasonableness on undisputed primary facts may effectively determine the issue. See also *R v Ealing LBC, ex p Parkinson* (1995) 8 Admin LR 281, 287; *R v Inner London North District Coroner, ex p Linnane* [1989] 1 WLR 395, 403.

6   See Senior Courts Act 1981, sections 29ff and Chapter **16.**

RELATIONSHIP BETWEEN 'UNREASONABLENESS' AND 'ILLEGALITY'

Unreasonableness and 'jurisdictional' illegality

8.22 When granting public law powers to a body, Parliament may stipulate that certain precedent (or 'jurisdictional') facts must exist before the body may exercise the jurisdiction conferred upon it.[1] The question whether such precedent facts exist is a matter for the court. They are to be contrasted with findings of fact (and judgments of policy) which are entrusted by Parliament to the body in question: here the court may only intervene on public law grounds. The matter may be complicated, however, where a body is given a statutory jurisdiction dependent only upon a subjective assessment by the body in question; thus, for example, many statutes confer powers upon decision-making bodies where certain circumstances 'appear to' that body to exist. In such cases the court will recognise that Parliament has conferred upon the decision-maker the power to decide whether the facts giving jurisdiction have arisen: but the determination by the decision-maker of that question may be reviewed on reasonableness grounds.[2]

---

[1] See, generally, CHAPTER 6 and CHAPTER 7.
[2] See *Secretary of State for Employment v Associated Society of Locomotive Engineers and Firemen (No 2)* [1972] 2 QB 455 (the *ASLEF* case), especially per Roskill LJ at pp 510–511; *R v Chief Registrar of Friendly Societies, ex p New Cross Building Society* [1984] QB 227, per Slade LJ at pp 272–273; *Bugdaycay v Secretary of State for the Home Department* [1987] AC 514. For circumstances in which review may be limited, see **8.29** below. As to the whether such a determination may be reviewed on the ground of mistake of fact, see **13.16** below.

8.23 The application of this principle is more difficult in the context of non-statutory bodies.[1] These are bodies whose jurisdiction does not derive from Parliament. Such bodies may not act in breach of the general law,[2] and it will be for the court to determine whether the law has been broken. As to whether or not facts exist which entitle the body to exercise its powers, it is submitted that this will be a matter for the body in question to decide, subject only to review on public law grounds. It has been suggested by Lord Donaldson MR[3] that there are particular difficulties in the case of a body like the Panel on Take-overs and Mergers, which is itself charged with the duty of making a judgment on what is and what is not relevant. In these circumstances Lord Donaldson suggested that, given the unique nature of the Panel, it may be preferable to eschew any formal categorisation of the grounds for review in favour of consideration of an 'innominate ground': whether something had gone wrong of a nature and degree which required the intervention of the court.

---

[1] See, eg *R v Criminal Injuries Compensation Board, ex p Lain* [1967] 2 QB 864, [1967] 2 All ER 770; *R v Panel on Take-overs and Mergers, ex p Datafin plc* [1987] QB 815, [1987] 1 All ER 564; *R v Panel on Take-overs and Mergers, ex p Guinness plc* [1990] 1 QB 146, [1989] 1 All ER 509; *R v Advertising Standards Authority Ltd, ex p The Insurance Service plc* (1990) 9 Tr LR 169.
[2] See *R v Panel on Take-overs and Mergers, ex p Guinness plc* [1990] 1 QB 146, per Lord Donaldson MR at 159.
[3] In *R v Panel on Take-overs and Mergers, ex p Guinness plc* [1990] 1 QB 146 at 159.

Unreasonableness and illegality as grounds of review

8.24 The head of review, which Lord Diplock in *CCSU* called 'illegality', requires that the decision-maker must understand correctly the law that regulates the decision-making power and must give effect to it. This head of review will generally call for consideration before turning to unreasonableness, for two reasons. The first is that a conclusion which appears unreasonable may well have been reached because the law governing the power in question was misunderstood.[1] If that is shown to be the case, then there may be no need to go on to consider unreasonableness.[2] Second, considerations as to what is within the bounds of reason will generally be guided by an understanding of the law governing the power in question.

---

[1] The law governing the power in question may include rules of evidence as to findings of fact; see **8.43** below and see, also, CHAPTER 7.

[2] A common example is where it seems unreasonable to have given overwhelming weight to a particular factor. As discussed at **8.43** below, the weight to be given to particular factors may be a matter of legality.

8.25 Prior to *CCSU*, there had been eminent judicial support for the argument that an unreasonable result led to the inference that there had been a misdirection in law. Lord Radcliffe had said in *Edwards v Bairstow and Harrison*[1] that where the facts found were such that no person acting judicially and properly instructed as to the relevant law could have come to the determination in question, the court had no option but to assume that there had been some misconception of the law and that this had been responsible for the determination. This approach was the subject of comment by Lord Diplock. He said[2] that it was no longer necessary to justify the courts' intervention by ascribing irrationality to an inferred, though unidentifiable, mistake of law, as had been done in *Edwards v Bairstow*: 'irrationality' could now stand upon its own feet as an accepted ground on which a decision may be attacked by judicial review. It is plain from Lord Diplock's analysis that even where a decision-maker has properly understood the law that regulates the decision-making power, and given effect to that law when exercising the power, nevertheless, the court will not rule out the possibility that the decision-maker has reached a decision which goes beyond reasonable limits – and, in such circumstances, the decision will be open to review. Such circumstances have been rare. In the great majority of cases where a finding of unreasonableness has been made, the court has either expressly or implicitly coupled this finding with an alternative conclusion that the body under review had misdirected itself in law. Plainly, it will only be in the most exceptional case that a body which has directed itself properly in law will nevertheless act unreasonably. But however rare such circumstances may be, it is nevertheless salutary to remember that they may exist, and that a decision reached in those circumstances is unlawful.

---

[1] [1956] AC 14 at p 36, [1955] 3 All ER 48; see also *Champion v Chief Constable of the Gwent Constabulary* [1990] 1 All ER 116, [1990] 1 WLR 1, where Lord Lowry at 17 adopted Lord Radcliffe's 'conclusion that a misconception of the relevant law can sometimes be inferred even though the mistake does not appear on the surface'. In *R (ProLife Alliance) v BBC* [2004] 1 AC 185, the claimant argued that undisputed facts were sufficient in themselves to show that decision-makers must have made some unspecified error of law. The argument failed (see Lord Hoffmann at paragraphs 78–80, pp 240–241).

² [1985] AC at 419; Lord Diplock added that whether a decision was irrational was a question that judges by their training and experience should be well equipped to answer, or else there would be something badly wrong with our judicial system.

UNREASONABLENESS AND PROCEDURAL IMPROPRIETY

8.26 The requirements of procedural propriety, frequently described as the rules of natural justice, have been developed and determined by the courts.¹ Here it is not sufficient for a decision-maker merely to say of the procedure he adopted that it fell within the range of procedures which might be regarded as reasonable. On the contrary, it is for the court to consider whether the principles of procedural fairness have been infringed, although it will, depending on the context, give appropriate weight to the tribunal's own view of what is fair.²

¹ See Chapters 10 and 11.
² *R v Take-over Panel, ex p Guinness plc* [1990] 1 QB 146 per Lloyd LJ at 183–184. For criticism of this approach, see Lord Irvine, 'Judges and Decision-makers: the Theory and Practice of Judicial Review' [1996] PL 556. See, also, *R v Monopolies and Mergers Commission, ex p Matthew Brown plc* [1987] 1 WLR 1235 per Macpherson J at pp 1238–1241. Of course, there may be facts where a failure to act fairly (in the legal sense of complying with the requirement of procedural propriety) will entail a failure to have acted reasonably: see eg *R (Tromans) v Cannock Chase DC* [2004] EWCA Civ 1036, [2004] BLGR 735.

8.27 Reasonableness may nevertheless have a part to play in review for procedural impropriety.¹ There is a further procedural element where reasonableness may have a part to play. It is the duty of persons exercising discretionary power to take 'reasonable steps to acquaint [themselves] with the relevant information'.² This duty of investigation was considered by the Court of Appeal in *R v Panel on Take-overs and Mergers, ex p Guinness plc*,³ where it was said by Lord Donaldson MR⁴ that in this regard the conduct of the tribunal had to be judged in the light of the position as it saw it, provided always that its assessment was a reasonable one. This is a classic adoption of the *Wednesbury* approach. However, Lloyd and Woolf LJJ appear to have adopted a different approach, forming their own view of whether the criticisms of the Panel's investigation were such as to result in injustice, although Woolf LJ⁵ recognised that in considering whether the Panel should have taken advantage of its ability to bring pressure to bear on those operating in the City of London it must be for the Panel and the Panel alone to decide whether, and if so how, it should use such a power.

¹ Apart from the example given in the text which follows, it may be noted that in *Mahon v Air New Zealand Ltd* [1984] AC 808, [1984] 3 All ER 201, Lord Diplock, delivering the advice of the Privy Council, said that the first rule of natural justice required that a finding must be based upon some material that tends logically to show the existence of facts consistent with the finding and that the reasoning supportive of the finding, if it be disclosed, is not logically self-contradictory. These two elements, however, do not seem properly to be described as requirements of procedural propriety, but rather constitute two well-recognised aspects of reasonableness; see **8.44** below. Another occasion on which the expression 'natural justice' was used in this sense was *R v Deputy Industrial Injuries Comr, ex p Moore* [1965] 1 QB 456, 488, 490 (and see also per Willmer LJ at 476).
² *Secretary of State for Education and Science v Tameside Metropolitan Borough Council* [1977] AC 1014 per Lord Diplock at 1065 (compare Scarman LJ at p 1030 in relation to ignorance of an established and relevant fact); *Prest v Secretary of State for Wales* (1982) 81 LGR 193. In *Taiaroa v Minister of Justice* [1995] 1 NZLR 411, where a statutory power was

to be exercised 'as soon as practicable' was nevertheless implicitly required that reasonable steps be taken to publicise the proposed action. A statutory requirement that a decision-maker be satisfied that it had 'adequate information' was considered by the New Zealand Supreme Court in *Discount Brands Ltd v Westfield (New Zealand) Ltd* [2005] 2 NZLR 597. See also Braier. 'Judicial Review for Material Unfairly Presented to the Decision-Maker' [2005] JR 156.

3 [1990] 1 QB 146, [1989] 1 All ER 509.

4 [1990] 1 QB 146 at 179; a similar approach was taken by the Court of Appeal in *R v Westminster City Council, ex p Monahan* [1990] 1 QB 87 at 117–119.

5 At 197; he also commented at 194 that, as long as the party affected by its decision was given a reasonable opportunity to put forward any facts it wished, it would normally be a matter for the judgment of the panel as to what steps it should take.

UNREASONABLENESS AND OTHER GROUNDS OF REVIEW

8.28 Grounds of review other than illegality, procedural impropriety, unreasonableness and lack of proportionality also call for consideration. These include mistake of fact and vagueness, where there is likely to be considerable overlap with review for unreasonableness. This overlap, and the relationship between unreasonableness and remaining possible grounds of review – bad faith, procedural fraud or other mishap, breach of fiduciary duty and the suggested 'innominate' ground – are discussed in CHAPTER 13.

QUALIFICATIONS ON APPLICABILITY OF THE PRINCIPLE

8.29 In confirming the status of unreasonableness as a separate ground for judicial review, the House of Lords in the *CCSU* case[1] did not suggest that it was subject to any *a priori* qualifications not applicable to other grounds of review. Nevertheless, there are circumstances where some qualification upon its applicability calls for consideration.[2]

1 See [1985] AC 374 at 410 (Lord Diplock) and 414 (Lord Roskill).

2 For general discussion of matters which may not be susceptible of judicial review, discretionary powers which may be unreviewable, and limitations on review of procedural fairness, see Chapters 5, 7 and 10.

Prerogative powers[1]

1 See Squires, 'Judicial Review of the Prerogative after the Human Rights Act' (2000) 116 LQR 572., and *R (Elias) v. Secretary of State for Defence* [2006] 1 WLR 3213 at 194.

8.30 It was established by *CCSU* that an instruction given in the exercise of a delegated power conferred by the sovereign under the royal prerogative may be the subject of judicial review under the normal principles.[2] Where the decision is justiciable, an unreasonable exercise of the prerogative will be unlawful. In *CCSU* Lord Roskill added that the right of challenge could not be unqualified, stating that prerogative powers such as those relating to the making of treaties,[3] the defence of the realm,[4] the prerogative of mercy, the grant of honours, the dissolution of Parliament and the appointment of ministers as well as others were not susceptible to judicial review because their nature and subject matter were not amenable to the judicial process.[5] Since that case was decided, some of the fields mentioned by Lord Roskill have been regarded as potentially justiciable.[6] Questions of national security are not necessarily exempt from review for unreasonableness: if a factual basis is established by evidence so that the court is satisfied that national security is a relevant factor, the court will accept the opinion of the Crown or its responsible officer as to what is required to meet it 'unless it is possible to show that the opinion was one which no reasonable minister advising the Crown could in the circumstances reasonably have held'.[7]

[2]   [1985] AC 374 at 400 and 423–424. Review of exercise of the prerogative is more fully discussed in CHAPTER 5 above.

[3]   See *Laker Airways v Department of Trade* [1977] QB 643, [1977] 2 All ER 182 and compare in the field of foreign relations *British Airways Board v Laker Airways* [1985] AC 58 at 92; the grant of a passport was held open to review in *R v Secretary of State for Foreign Affairs, ex p Everett* [1989] QB 811, [1989] 1 All ER 655.

[4]   However, in *R v Attorney-General for England and Wales* [2004] 2 NZLR 577, 587, a soldier gave a contractual undertaking to the Ministry of Defence that he would not publish information about the SAS without consent; the Privy Council thought that a refusal of consent by the Ministry of Defence could have been the subject of challenge by judicial review.

[5]   [1985] AC at 418.

[6]   *R (Bancoult) v Secretary of State for Foreign and Commonwealth Affairs* [2008] QB 365 at 46.

[7]   Per Lord Diplock in CCSU at p 406; see also *R v Secretary of State for the Home Department, ex p Cheblak* [1991] 2 All ER 319, [1991] 1 WLR 890, and *R v Ministry of Defence, ex p Smith* [1996] QB 517, 556 per Sir Thomas Bingham MR. For a case concerning the armed forces where national security was not involved, but the absence of legal right or duty was held to preclude judicial review, see *R v Secretary of State for Defence, ex p Sancto* (1992) 5 Admin LR 673. In *R v Secretary of State for the Home Department, ex p McQuillan* [1995] 4 All ER 400 it was deposed on behalf of the respondent that reasons for the making of an exclusion order under the Prevention of Terrorism (Temporary Provisions) Act 1989 could not be given because to do so might well lead to the discovery of sources of information available, and so possibly compromise police operations and/or put at risk the lives of informants, or their families. Sedley J followed earlier authorities which held that this assertion was sufficient to preclude further enquiry by the court into the legitimacy of the Secretary of State's conclusion that an exclusion order was expedient; however, in the absence of such authorities he would have been prepared to assess, with proper safeguards, the national security issues against the importance of the other rights involved. In *Secretary of State for Home Department v Rehman* [2001] UKHL 47, [2003] 1 AC 153, HL(E) Lord Steyn at paragraph 31, [2003] 1 AC 187 said it was well established that issues of national security did not fall beyond the competence of the courts and that, while national courts must give great weight to the views of the executive on matters of national security, not all the observations in *Chandler v DPP* [1964] AC 763 can be regarded as authoritative in respect of the current statutory position. Compare Lord Hoffmann at paragraph 54 (p 193). The position under the Human Rights Act 1998 is examined in *A v Secretary of State for the Home Department, ex p A* [2004] UKHL 56, [2005] 2 AC 68; see Sayeed, 'Beyond the language of deference' [2005] JR 111.

8.31 Generally, in those cases where exercise of the prerogative is reviewable, the nature of the relevant prerogative, and the subject matter, will be an important element in the assessment of any allegation of unreasonableness. If a prerogative decision fails to have regard to a factor that the law states regard must be had to, or interferes with a constitutional right, it ought to be subject to review. It has been said that where a decision under review concerns international relations between the United Kingdom and a foreign sovereign state, the courts would often be unwilling to intervene.[1] Similarly, in a case concerning the policy for ex gratia compensation for prisoners whose convictions were overturned, Stuart-Smith LJ rejected assertions that the Home Secretary had acted unreasonably and added:[2]

'It is an exercise of the royal prerogative. He is not obliged to have such a policy. He has in fact laid down such a policy for himself and it seems to me that it would be highly undesirable for this court to indicate conditions or the manner in which he should seek to exercise it'.

---

[1] *British Airways Board v Laker Airways* [1985] AC 58; see also *R v Secretary of State for the Home Department, ex p Launder* [1997] 1 WLR 839, 854. The State immunity' or 'Act of State' doctrines may mean a decision cannot be challenged. But it is important not to exclude from review those cases in which the 'judicial taboo of foreign relations is a red herring': *R (Carson) v Secretary of State for Work and Pensions* [2003] EWCA Civ 797, [2003] 3 All ER 577 at §66.

[2] *R v Secretary of State for the Home Department, ex p Harrison* [1988] 3 All ER 86, 93. See also *R v Secretary of State for the Home Department, ex p Atlantic Commercial Ltd* [1997] BCC 692 Popplewell J, and *R (Elias) v Secretary of State for Defence* [2006] EWCA Civ 1293, [2006] 1 WLR 3213 at §192.

Can the court review the rationality of political judgment?

8.32 If a decision depends essentially on political judgment, such as decisions about public expenditure or the allocation of resources, that will favour broad latitude being given to the decision. It is important to distinguish here between the adoption of a policy, as in statutory guidance or some other written procedure for the exercise of a power, and matters of political judgment. Courts should give a decision maker latitude in the latter context, but not as a matter of principle in the former.[1] As indicated in *CCSU*,[2] examination of the reasons for government policy taking one course rather than another will normally involve questions for which the judicial process is not apt. This has not, however, prevented review on rationality grounds of the implementation of policy decisions, particularly where this has arisen in the exercise of statutory powers.[3] In general, the greater the policy content of a decision, and the more remote the subject matter of a decision from ordinary judicial experience, the more hesitant the court must necessarily be in holding a decision to be unreasonable.[4] However, other relevant contextual factors should be considered in deciding the intensity of review, such as whether a constitutional right is involved in the decision.[5]

---

[1] *R (Munjaz) v Mersey Care NHS Trust* [2006] 2 AC 148 at [69].

[2] [1985] AC at p 411.

[3] See, eg *R v Secretary of State for Transport, ex p Greater London Council* [1986] QB 556, [1985] 3 All ER 300; *R v Immigration Appeal Tribunal, ex p Manshoora Begum* [1986] Imm AR 385; in *R v HM Treasury, ex p Smedley* [1985] QB 657, [1985] 1 All ER 589, the Court of Appeal considered whether the Minister could reasonably have regarded an undertaking as 'ancillary to' Community treaties and concluded that he could.

[4] *R v Ministry of Defence, ex p Smith* [1996] QB 517, 556 per Sir Thomas Bingham MR, who added. 'Where decisions of a policy-laden, esoteric or security-based nature are in issue even greater caution than normal must be shown in applying the test, but the test itself is sufficiently flexible to cover all situations'. See also Hare, [1996] CLJ 179, *R v Lord Chancellor, ex p Maxwell* [1997] 1 WLR 104, 112 and *R v Secretary of State for the Home Department, ex p Launder* [1997] 1 WLR 839, 854. In *R v Criminal Injuries Compensation Board, ex p P* [1995] 1 WLR 845 the Court of Appeal were unanimous in holding that there was jurisdiction to hear a challenge on grounds of unreasonableness to the making of ex gratia payments by the Board; Evans and Peter Gibson LJJ determined the issue of unreasonableness against the applicants on the merits, while Neill LJ regarded the allocation of resources as a 'polycentric' question which was non-justiciable. See 8.78 below. Andrew Le Sueur has described cases of this kind a 'light-touch' review: 'The Rise and Ruin of Unreasonableness?' [2005] JR 32.

Review for unreasonableness of decisions which have been, or must be, considered by Parliament

8.33 It would not be unnatural for the courts to be reluctant to impeach the reasonableness of decisions which have been approved, or cannot have effect unless approved, by the House of Commons. Until 1985 it had generally been thought that there was nevertheless no legal bar to such a challenge.[1] The constitutional propriety of such a challenge was considered by the House of Lords in *Nottinghamshire County Council v Secretary of State for the Environment*.[2] The applicants in that case challenged guidance for the expenditure of local authorities issued by the Secretary of State under the Local Government. Planning and Land Act 1980, s 59 as amended by the Local Government Finance Act 1982. The purpose of issuing the guidance was so that the Secretary of State would have power, in those cases where the guidance requirements had not been met, to reduce the grant payable to the Local Authorities in question: but such power would only be exercised if he reported to and obtained the approval of the House of Commons. Lord Scarman, with whom the other members of the Appellate Committee agreed, commented that a challenge to the guidance as irrational raised an important question as to the limits of judicial review in the field of public financial administration. He said that only in very exceptional circumstances would it be constitutionally appropriate for the court to intervene in matters of political judgment.[3]

'I refuse in this case to examine the detail of the guidance or its consequences. My reasons are these. Such an examination by a court would be justified only if a prima facie case were to be shown for holding that the Secretary of State had acted in bad faith, or for an improper motive, or that the consequences of his guidance were so absurd that he must have taken leave of his senses . . . If, as your Lordships are holding, the guidance was based on principles applicable to all authorities, the principles would either have to be a pattern of perversity or an absurdity of such proportions that the guidance could not have been framed by a bona fide exercise of political judgment on the part of the Secretary of State. And it would be necessary to find as a fact that the House of Commons had been misled: for their approval was necessary and was obtained to the action that he proposed to take to implement the guidance'.

[1] *Hoffmann La-Roche & Co AG v Secretary of State for Trade and Industry* [1975] AC 295, [1973] 3 All ER 945; *R v Secretary of State for the Environment, ex p Greater London Council* (3 April 1985, unreported). Divisional Court cited by Himsworth [1986] PL 374 at 380.
[2] [1986] AC 240, [1986] 1 All ER 199. For Scots law on this question, see **22.73** below.
[3] [1986] AC 240 at 247.

8.34 In a later passage,[1] Lord Scarman summarised the point in these terms:

'But if, as in this case, effect cannot be given to the Secretary of State's determination without the consent of the House of Commons and the House of Commons has consented, it is not open to the courts to intervene unless the Minister and the House must have misconstrued the statute or the Minister has – to put it bluntly – deceived the House . . . If the action proposed complies with the terms of the statute . . . it is not for the judges to say that the action has such unreasonable consequences that the guidance upon which the action is based and upon which the House of Commons had notice was perverse and must be set aside. For that is a question of policy for the Minister and the Commons, unless there has been bad faith or misconduct by the Minister'.

¹ [1986] AC 240 at 250.

8.35 These passages were interpreted by the Divisional Court in *R v Secretary of State for the Environment, ex p Hammersmith and Fulham London Borough Council*¹ as precluding examination of the reasonableness of an exercise of statutory power which had to be approved by the House of Commons in order to take effect. The Court of Appeal disagreed, concluding² that Lord Scarman was merely warning of the narrowness of review for unreasonableness. The issue was dealt with in the speech of Lord Bridge in the House of Lords:³

> 'The restriction which the Nottinghamshire case imposes on the scope of judicial review operates only when the court has determined that the ministerial action in question does not contravene the requirements of the statute, whether express or implied, and only then declares that, since the statute has conferred a power on the Secretary of State which involves the formulation and the implementation of national economic policy and which can only take effect with the approval of the House of Commons, it is not open to challenge on the grounds of irrationality short of the extremes of bad faith, improper motive or manifest absurdity'.

¹ [1991] 1 AC 521 at 545.
² [1991] 1 AC 521 at 561–564.
³ [1991] 1 AC 521 at 597.

8.36 The first 'extreme' identified in the last sentence is a ground of review in itself, while the second would lead to review for illegality. The remaining 'extreme' is manifest absurdity. In earlier editions of this book it was suggested that, Lord Bridge intended this to mean something more than such irrationality as would ordinarily justify review: by confining it to 'manifest absurdity' he, like Lord Scarman in the earlier of the two passages cited above from the *Nottinghamshire* case, was prohibiting an examination of the detail of the Secretary of State's decision in the absence of a prima facie case that its consequences were 'so absurd that he must have taken leave of his senses'.¹ This can be contrasted with an ordinary challenge, where the applicant is not limited to the consequences of the decision and may instead seek to demonstrate that the decision-maker's underlying approach was unreasonable.² Now, however, this suggested limitation on review for unreasonableness has been re-examined by the Court of Appeal in *R (Javed) v Secretary of State for the Home Department*.³ This case concerned questions of asylum and human rights, far removed from the questions of financial policy which arose in *Nottinghamshire* and *Hammersmith and Fulham*. The Court of Appeal quashed an Order designating Pakistan as a country in which there was in general no serious risk of persecution, and said that the extent to which a statutory power was open to judicial review on the ground of irrationality depended critically on the nature and purpose of the enabling legislation.⁴

¹ In this sense the requirement which was struck down in *R v Immigration Appeal Tribunal, ex p Manshoora Begum* (see **8.75** below) could be regarded as an example of manifest absurdity. See, generally, Himsworth, 'Poll Tax Capping and Judicial Review' [1991] PL 76. For the

position in Scotland, see the discussion in Chapter 21 below of *Edinburgh City District Council v Secretary of State for Scotland* 1985 SLT 551 and subsequent cases.

2 See **8.41–8.57** below.

3 [2002] QB 129. See also *R. (D) v Secretary of State for the Home Department* [2010] EWHC 880 (Admin).

4 The court was able to conclude that the applicants challenge was to the legality rather than to the rationality of the 1996 Order, in that the empowering legislation only entitled the Secretary of State to designate countries in respect of which the evidence available to him enabled him rationally to conclude that there was in general no serious risk of persecution. At p 147 the court noted that in *R v Secretary of State for the Environment, ex p Greater London Council* (3 April 1985, unreported) Mustill LJ recorded with approval concessions made on behalf of the Secretary of State. In fact, the same concessions were made by the Secretary of State in *Nottinghamshire*, and a copy of the judgment of Mustill LJ was made available to the House of Lords, although no mention was made of this by Lord Scarman.

8.37 The limitations envisaged in *Nottinghamshire* have not often prevented the court from applying the ordinary principles of review for unreasonableness.[1] In a case where review for unreasonableness failed on ordinary principles, it was said to be very doubtful whether, save perhaps in exceptional cases, the principle of legitimate expectation could be invoked to invalidate either primary or secondary legislation which was put before Parliament.[2] An attempt to extend *Nottinghamshire* so as to preclude review of government policy in certain circumstances failed in *R v Ministry of Defence, ex p Smith*.[3]

1 In addition to *Hammersmith and Fulham*, cases where the *Nottinghamshire* limitation was applied include *R v Secretary of State for the Environment, ex p Islington LBC* (Webster J 26.3.86, CO/287/86, holding that the limitation covered questions as to the matters to be, or not to be, taken into account), *R v Secretary of State for the Environment, ex p West Yorkshire Police Authority* (McCowan J 1.7.86, CO/325/86 adopting and applying the reasoning of Webster J), *R v Secretary of State for the Environment, ex p Derbyshire County Council* (CA 26.6.89, CO/301/88) and *R v Secretary of State for the Environment, ex p Cambridge City Council* (Auld J 28.2.91, CO/278/91). In *R v Secretary of State for the Environment, ex p British Telecommunications plc* (Auld J 26.7.91, CO/503/90) a question as to relevancy was held to constitute a challenge based on illegality, and hence not within the *Nottinghamshire* limitation.

2 *R v Secretary of State for the Environment, ex p National and Local Government Officers' Association* (1992) 5 Admin LR 785, 804. For discussion of legitimate expectations, see **8.81** below.

3 [1996] QB 517; see **8.32** above. The circumstances relied on to justify the extension were that the policy: (1) touched on issues of national security and defence which are essentially for debate and decision through the political process, and (2) had been recently reaffirmed by Parliament (see 549–540).

THE PRINCIPLE IN OPERATION

8.38 It will be seen from the foregoing that the concept of reasonableness may involve the assessment of a decision-maker's exercise of power against a judgment by the court as to the width of the limits to that exercise. The precise location of those limits will depend on the circumstances of each case.

8.39 What may be seen from the cases is that the limits of what is reasonable are dependent upon the subject-matter and nature of the decision. The determination of those limits is usually a task which the court does not need to perform with any precision:[1] for in the great majority of cases where reasonableness is an issue, the court is able to say that what was done was well within the limits of reason. In the difficult cases, where the line has to be drawn, the task of identifying a point which goes beyond the limits of reason requires the court to identify and apply the fundamental values of our society.[2] Those values are not immutable: to take an extreme example, no court today would adopt the view of the Court of Appeal in 1925 that a council could reasonably regard a policy of dismissing married women teachers as one which would be a benefit to the cause of education generally in their district.[3] Such fundamental values can be identified not only from statute and authority, but also from other acceptable sources of law or principle.[4] It may be seen from cases which show the principle of reasonableness in operation that the modern willingness of judges to give overt recognition to the courts' role in identifying fundamental values provides an increasingly principled approach to review for unreasonableness.[5] This is not to assert that acting contrary to such fundamental values is of itself a ground of review: instead it is to suggest that the now extensive case law dealing with review for unreasonableness offers a useful guide to the approach of the courts in future cases and to the role which fundamental values are likely to play.[6]

[1] Henry LJ said in *R v Lord Chancellor, ex p Maxwell* [1997] 1 WLR 104, 109: 'Decisions so unreasonable as to warrant interference jump off the page at you'. Moreover, in cases where action appears at first sight to be unreasonable, the decision-maker will often be found to have misinterpreted the relevant law with the result that the decision is quashed for illegality and the question of unreasonableness does not arise.

[2] See Walker, 'What's Wrong with Irrationality?' [1995] PL 556, 571–576.

[3] *Short v Poole Corpn* [1926] Ch 66. A more modern approach is seen in *Van Gorkom v A-G* [1978] 2 NZLR 387. Sir Stephen Sedley has described extra-judicially his perception of changes in our 'moral economy' which have rendered the legitimacy of government heavily contested, and have conferred legitimacy upon the court's willingness to adapt and expand old principles to new and different administrative structures: 'The moral economy of judicial review' in Wilson (ed) *Frontiers of Legal Scholarship* (1995).

[4] *R (Buckinghamshire County Council) v Secretary of State for Transport* [2014] UKSC 3, [2014] 1WLR 342 per Lord Neuberger and Lord Mance at § 207. They include respect for human dignity: *Osborn v Parole Board* [2013] UKSC 61, [2013] 3 WLR 1020 at 68; respect for the right to life: *Bugdaycay v Secretary of State for the Home Department*, [1987] AC 514 at 531G; access to effective legal representation and equality of arms: A-G's Reference (No 82a of 2000) [2002] EWCA Crim 215, [2002] 2 Cr App Rep 342 per Lord Woolf at § 14; and the right of access to a court: *R v Secretary of State for the Home Department, ex p Simms and O'Brien* [2000] 2 AC 115 at 131.

[5] Particularly striking examples are the judgments of the House of Lords in *Wheeler v Leicester City Council* [1985] AC 1054, and Simon Brown LJ in *R v Coventry City Council, ex p Phoenix Aviation Ltd* [1995] 3 All ER 37. In *Wheeler* Lord Templeman, applying *Congreve v Home Office* [1976] QB 629, affirmed that a local authority cannot punish where there has been no wrongdoing; see Chapter 9.

[6] An important and influential discussion of substantive principles of review will be found in Jowell and Lester, 'Beyond *Wednesbury*: Substantive Principles of Administrative Law' [1987] PL 368. In de Smith, Woolf and Jowell *Judicial Review of Administrative Action* (5th edn, 1995), Ch 13 gives an exposition based upon a tripartite categorisation: material defects in the decision-making process, violation of common law or constitutional principles, and oppressive decisions.

8.40 Accordingly, in the following paragraphs, examples are given of the operation of the principle of reasonableness by reference to particular features of the decision in question. These examples are not intended to limit what must always be a flexible test which may require sensitivity to all the circumstances of the case:[1] as Arden LJ has observed 'facts and facts again are decisive'.[2]

[1] See paragraph **8.11** above. In *R v IRC, ex p Unilever plc* [1996] STC 681 Simon Brown LJ stressed (at 694–695) that the 'flexibility necessarily inherent' in this guiding principle 'should not be sacrificed on the altar of legal certainty'. See also Thomas J in *Waitakere City Council*

v Lovelock [1997] 2 NZLR 385: 'The list of grounds . . . in determining that a decision is unreasonable is . . . probably limitless . . . '.
2   *Ahmed v Leicester City Council* [2007] EWCA Civ 843; [2008] HLR 6, at [28].

A decision which is imperfect need not be unreasonable

8.41 In *Fawcett Properties Ltd v Buckingham County Council*,[1] a property owner sought permission to build a pair of cottages for farm workers. The proposed site was in the green belt, and the local authority imposed a condition in somewhat complicated terms, the purpose of which was to seek to ensure that the houses were occupied by persons connected with agriculture. The House of Lords upheld the condition, even though it could be demonstrated that in certain circumstances the condition would fail to achieve its object. Lord Jenkins[2] said that the condition, no doubt, fell short of perfection, but so far as it went in practice, it might reasonably be expected to carry out the local authority's planning policy.

1   [1961] AC 636. Another example of a decision where anomalous consequences were not sufficient to demonstrate unreasonableness is *R v LAUTRO Ltd, ex p Kendall* [1994] COD 169. In *Taiaroa v Minister of Justice* [1995] 1 NZLR 411 the Minister acknowledged that mistakes were made in the course of an exercise seeking to publicise an electoral option; the New Zealand Court of Appeal accepted that they did not vitiate the exercise, the test being reasonableness rather than perfection.
2   [1961] AC 636 at 687.

A determination may be invalid for lack of clarity

8.42 Review for unreasonableness should be distinguished from review for vagueness: the *Fawcett* case establishes that a public authority must not insert a condition in a licence if that condition is so unclear as to be void for uncertainty.[1] In these instances, the test put forward is not one of reasonableness: rather it is for the court to resolve whether the words used are too vague. It may be unreasonable to lay down a condition which gives no clear indication to those affected of the circumstances when it operates,[2] and such unreasonableness could exist even though an ambiguity might ultimately be resolved through legal proceedings. Nevertheless, for certain purposes it may be appropriate to identify a criterion which is broad enough to call for the exercise of judgment rather than an exact quantitative measurement.[3]

1   See **12.9** below.
2   *R v Bradford MBC, ex p Ali* (1994) 6 Admin LR 589, [1994] ELR 299; *R v Blackpool Borough Council, ex p Red Cab Taxis Ltd* [1994] COD 513; *R v Newcastle-upon-Tyne City Council, ex p Dixon* (1993) 92 LGR 168. For the principle of legal certainty in European law, see Chapter 15 below.
3   This was held to have been the effect of certain statutory provisions in *R v Monopolies and Mergers Commission, ex p South Yorkshire Transport Ltd* [1993] 1 WLR 23 at 32. In *R v Institute of Chartered Accountants, ex p Nawaz* (CA, 25.4.97) the court rejected an argument that a byelaw giving power to delegate was too broad: the postulated unlawful delegations were impossible because those delegating were constrained by a duty not to exercise the power unreasonably.

The reasoning of the decision-maker may be examined in appropriate cases

8.43 There are several factors which call for special mention here. First, it is by no means a foregone conclusion that the applicant will have the benefit of a statement of the decision-maker's reasons.[1] The absence of reasons where there is no duty to give them will not of itself provide any support for a contention that the decision is unreasonable.[2] Second, the reasoning of the decision-maker may be examined for purposes which are, in principle, quite separate from those of reasonableness: in particular, in order to determine whether the decision-maker has directed himself properly in law.[3] Thus, a statute may expressly require that a particular reasoning process be adopted.[4] Similarly, in certain classes of case, a true construction of the decision-maker's powers may require that certain rules of evidence be applied,[5] or that greater or lesser regard be paid to particular factors, and a decision may be quashed for illegality if the decision-maker does not comply with such requirements.[6] Third, when considering a reasonableness challenge, the limitations described at **8.29** et seq above should be borne in mind: a decision-maker's reasoning on broad questions of policy will usually be unsuitable for judicial examination, and review may be restricted where parliamentary approval is envisaged. In general, however, it may be said that where the decision involves matters which are apt for judicial examination, the court has been willing to examine the internal logic of the decision, the reasonableness of the findings of fact on which the decision is based, the reasonableness of any decision that a particular aspect of the matter is relevant or irrelevant, and the reasonableness of the decision-maker's evaluation of the matter as a whole in reaching a conclusion. Examples of such examination are set out below.

[1] This may depend upon the construction of the statute in question (as in *R v Secretary of State for the Environment, ex p Hammersmith and Fulham London Borough Council* [1991] 1 AC 521) in which event the particularity of such reasons may also depend on the interpretation of the statute; it may also depend on the requirements of fairness; see **9.12** et seq and **10.16** et seq below. If special circumstances exist, it is conceivable that a court may compel the provision of reasons because it would be unreasonable to fail to provide reasons, see **8.77** below.

[2] *R v Secretary of State for Trade and Industry, ex p Lonrho plc* [1989] 1 WLR 525 (see also *Cannock Chase District Council v Kelly* [1978] 1 WLR 1 per Megaw LJ at 6); however, if all other known facts and circumstances appear to point overwhelmingly in favour of a different decision a decision-maker who has given no reasons cannot complain if the court draws the inference that he had no rational reason for his decision (*ex p Lonrho*, 539–540, citing *Padfield v Minister for Agriculture, Fisheries and Food* [1968] AC 997, [1968] 1 All ER 694); see also *R v Secretary of State for the Home Department, ex p Sinclair* [1992] Imm AR 293 and *R v Civil Service Appeal Board, ex p Cunningham* [1991] 4 All ER 310, CA. Consider also the comments of Lord Clyde in *Stefan v GMC* [1999] 1 WLR 1293, that situations where reasons are not required are – in the light of art 6, European Convention, 'taking on the appearance of exceptions'. A challenge on the basis that there is a general right to reasons is, however, more likely to be seen as an aspect of fairness, rather than irrationality: *R v Higher Education Funding Council, ex p Institute of Dental Surgery* [1994] 1 WLR 242, QBD.

[3] See, generally, Chapter 7.

[4] For example, Local Government Amendment Act (No 3) 1996 (NZ).

[5] *R v Nat Bell Liquors Ltd* [1922] 2 AC 128 per Lord Sumner at 144; *R v Bedwellty Justices, ex p Williams* [1997] AC 225. In *Secretary of State for the Home Department v Rehman* [2001] UKHL 47, [2003] 1 AC 153, HL(E) it was held that when the Secretary of State considered what was conducive to the public good under the Immigration Act 1971 any specific facts on which the Secretary of State relied should be proved on the ordinary civil balance of probability, but no particular standard of proof was appropriate to the formation of his executive judgment or assessment whether it was conducive to the public good that a person should be deported, which was simply a matter of reasonable and proportionate judgment on the material before him.

[6]   See **8.11** to **8.15** above. See also *London Rent Assessment Committee v St George's Court Ltd* (1984) 48 P & CR 230; *R v Secretary of State for the Home Department, ex p Dinesh* [1987] Imm AR 131. In general questions of weight will be exclusively for the fact-finding body (see *R v Immigration Appeal Tribunal, ex p Naushad Kandiya* [1989] Imm AR 491), but this is subject to the limits identified in *West Glamorgan County Council v Rafferty* [1987] 1 WLR 457 (see **8.11** above and **8.56** below) and a decision may be quashed for illegality when it is apparent that no weight has been given to a consideration forming part of the statutory purpose: *Champion v Chief Constable of the Gwent Constabulary* [1990] 1 All ER 116, [1990] 1 WLR 1. Conversely, in *N (Kenya) v Secretary of State for the Home Department* [2004] EWCA Civ 1094 Judge LJ held that an adjudicator erred in wrongly treating one particular factor as a 'paramount consideration'.

Deficiencies of logic may render a decision unreasonable

8.44 It was observed earlier[1] that not every departure from logic will be unreasonable.[2] *Fawcett Properties*[3] is an example of a licence condition whose logical flaws could easily be demonstrated. Nevertheless, those flaws were not so great, in the context of a planning decision, as to render the condition invalid. By contrast, in the *Mahon* case[4] one of the Commissioner's findings (about low flying) was held invalid because it was based upon an illogical conclusion that untruthfulness on the part of the individual witnesses had stemmed from a concerted plan of deception, while another finding (about the intentional adoption of a new waypoint) suffered the same fate because it was self-contradictory.[5] The context was quite different from that of *Fawcett*, and it is plainly the case that fundamental values require the highest standards of reasoning to be applied before inferring fraud.

[1]   See **8.3** above. A fuller discussion will be found in Walker. 'What's Wrong With Irrationality?' [1995] PL 445.

[2]   As to whether there is a departure from logic, the Court of Appeal in *R (Association of British Civilian Internees: Far East Region) v Secretary of State for Defence* [2003] QB 1397 at paragraph 40, p 1415 identified a governing criterion in a non-statutory scheme and accepted that it was permissible to admit an exception to this governing criterion where there is a justification for doing so which is rational and does not destroy the very foundation of the scheme. Such an exception satisfied the test that measures designed to further the relevant objective must be rationally connected to it: see Lord Steyn in the Daly case [2001] 2 AC 532, 547B, quoting with approval the test propounded by Lord Clyde in *de Freitas v Permanent Secretary of Ministry of Agriculture, Fisheries, Lands and Housing* [1999] 1 AC 69, 80.

[3]   See **8.42** above.

[4]   See **8.26** above.

[5]   The finding on low flying is dealt with at [1984] 1 AC 823–825; the finding on intentional adoption of a new waypoint is dealt with at [1984] 1 AC 831–836 (this finding was also found to be unsupported by evidence, as to which see **8.49** below).

8.45 While such high standards may not be required for all purposes, an action or omission wholly inconsistent with the internal logic of an activity undertaken by a public authority may be held to be unreasonable. Thus, in *R v Securities & Investment Board, ex p Independent Financial Advisers Association*,[1] the Securities & Investment Board gave guidance in a statement to self-regulatory organisations on action which it considered appropriate to ensure that independent financial advisers (IFAs) addressed the problem of mis-selling of personal pensions. The main ground of challenge – that the SIB had asserted a power to enforce the statement – failed; but in one respect the court intervened:[2]

'In our judgment the statement ought to say that notwithstanding paragraphs 41 and 42. IFAs are not to be required to take any step which will invalidate their insurance cover without their insurers' consent. To the extent that it does not say that, the statement is wholly irrational'.

[1]   [1995] 2 BCLC 76.
[2]   [1995] 2 BCLC 76 at 90.

8.46 Here a vital practical aspect of the provision of compensation for investors was that, in the case of many smaller IFAs, their professional indemnity insurers remained 'the one source of funding which could be relied upon to provide compensation for investors'. Taking a realistic and common sense view, there was a paramount need to ensure that insurance cover was not invalidated: no reasonable supervisor could fail to give priority to this when giving guidance to regulatory organisations.[1]

[1]   Similarly, in *R v Director General of Electricity Supply, ex p Scottish Power plc* [1997] CLY 4949 (3 February 1997, CA), it was held that a refusal to propose a modification to a licence could not be justified by the reasons advanced; the decision is remarkable in that the English Court of Appeal (absent any contention by the parties to the contrary) assumed jurisdiction to decide the validity of action taken by a regulator which had effect only in Scotland (see **16.35**). In *R (National Association of Colliery Overmen Deputies and Shotfirers) v Secretary of State for Work and Pensions* [2004] ACD 14, the claimant succeeded on judicial review because the defendant's written guidance to diagnosis of industrial injury was out of line with its avowed aim.

8.47 By contrast, in *R (Association of British Civilian Internees: Far East Region) v Secretary of State for Defence*,[1] the Court of Appeal was concerned with a non-statutory ex-gratia compensation scheme for British civilians interned by the Japanese. The scheme denied compensation to individuals where neither they nor their parents or grandparents were born in the UK. The court affirmed the requirement of internal logic:

'Just as in satisfying the requirements of proportionality, so too in meeting the *Wednesbury* test, the measures designed to further the objective must be rationally connected to it: see Lord Steyn in the *Daly* case [2001] 2 AC 532, 547B, quoting with approval the test propounded by Lord Clyde in *de Freitas v Permanent Secretary of Ministry of Agriculture, Fisheries, Lands and Housing* [1999] 1 AC 69, 80'.

[1]   [2003] QB 1397 at 1415, paragraph 40.

8.48 Applying this principle the court concluded:[1]

'The basic criterion of a close connection with the UK at the time of internment remains as the factor which controls the scheme. It is permissible to admit an exception to this governing criterion where there is a justification for doing so which is rational and does not destroy the very foundation of the scheme. It was plainly rational to exclude from the scheme (without destroying its essential character) those who are, or may be, eligible for compensation under a different scheme administered by another country with which claimants currently have a closer connection than with the UK. But in our view, it does not follow from the fact that the Government has excluded such claimants that the whole scheme is irrational on the grounds that it has also excluded some of those who currently have a close connection with the UK. There are perfectly rational, but different, reasons for excluding both those who are currently entitled to receive compensation from other countries, and those who currently have a close connection with the UK, but who did not have such a connection at the time of their internment'.

¹   [2003] QB 1397 at 1416, paragraph 46. See, in a different context, *R (Stamford Chamber of Trade and Commerce) v Secretary of State for Communities and Local Government* [2009] EWHC 719 (Admin), [2009] 2 P & CR 19.

A material finding of fact is unreasonable if made in the absence of evidence capable of warranting such a finding

8.49 It is well established that the court will examine a decision to see if it is based upon an express or implicit finding of fact, and will quash the decision if there was no evidence at all to warrant such a finding.¹ A clear error of uncontentious and objectively verifiable fact is a ground for review.² Further, there have been several cases where there was some evidence which pointed towards the finding in question, but the court has quashed the decision because no reasonable tribunal could have regarded it as sufficient to warrant such a finding.³ This does not mean, however, that the court will permit a party to adduce evidence not known to the decision-maker⁴ (although if the decision-maker failed to investigate the matter there may be a separate ground of challenge).⁵

¹   For example, *R v Board of Education* [1910] 2 KB 165, *Williams v Giddy* [19111 AC 381; *Penwith District Council v Secretary of State for the Environment* (1977) 34 P & CR 269; *Philglow Ltd v Secretary of State for the Environment and the London Borough of Hillingdon* (1984) 51 P & CR 1; *R v Hillingdon London Borough, ex p Thomas* (1987) 19 HLR 196, 200; see also **8.22** above, and Jones [1990] PL 507, Years. 'Findings of Fact' in Richardson and Genn (eds) Administrative Law and Government Action (1994) and Demetriou and House-man [1997] JR 27; see further the analysis of *A-G for New South Wales v Quin* (1990) 170 CLR 1 by Craig (1992) 108 LQR 79.

²   *E v Secretary of State for the Home Department* [2004] QB 1044 at 66.

³   For example, *R v Ealing London Borough, ex p Richardson* (1982) 4 HLR 125; the court will, if necessary, go behind the account of the facts given by the decision-maker for this purpose: *East Hampshire District Council v Secretary of State for the Environment* [1978] JPL 182; affd [1979] JPL 533; *Forkhurst v Secretary of State for the Environment and Brentwood District Council* (1982) 46 P & CR 89; *R (McNally) v Secretary of State for Education* [2002] ICR 15. This may be subject to the exception suggested at **8.33** above.

⁴   *Glover v Secretary of State for the Environment* [1981] JPL 110; *Sears Blok v Secretary of State for the Environment and London Borough of Southwark* [1982] JPL 248; *Chris Fashionware (West End) Ltd v Secretary of State for the Environment* [1980] JPL 678. See **8.20** and **12.14** above for discussion of this principle and for the position concerning fresh evidence which could not have been found with due diligence before the hearing.

⁵   See **8.26** above.

8.50 Moreover, the flawed finding must be material to the decision-maker's reasoning: if the court is satisfied that the decision-maker would have reached the same conclusion without regard to the flawed finding, the decision will not be invalid.¹ The position is *a fortiori* if the flawed finding appears only in an advisory paper, and was not an integral part of the decision. As was said by Lord Goff in *R v Independent Television Commission, ex p Television South West*:²

'Advisory papers . . . may well place emphasis on points which are considered important and may well tend towards a certain conclusion. But those who draft advisory papers are not decision-makers, nor are they performing a judicial or quasi-judicial role . . . In the circumstances, even if there had been significant errors [in the advisory paper] there is no basis for assuming that those errors would have infected the reasoning of the Commission which formed its own independent judgment and did not simply follow the recommendations of its staff'.

Likewise, Lord Neuberger commented in *Holmes-Moorhouse v Richmond-upon Thames LBC*:[3]

'a decision can often survive despite the existence of an error in the reasoning advanced to support it. For example, sometimes the error is irrelevant to the outcome; sometimes it is too trivial (objectively, or in the eyes of the decision-maker) to affect the outcome; sometimes it is obvious from the rest of the reasoning, read as a whole, that the decision would have been the same notwithstanding the error; sometimes, there is more than one reason for the conclusion, and the error only undermines one of the reasons; sometimes, the decision is the only one which could rationally have been reached. In all such cases, the error should not (save, perhaps, in wholly exceptional circumstances) justify the decision being quashed'.

[1] *Simplex G E (Holdings) Ltd v Secretary of State for the Environment and the City and District of St Albans District Council* (1988) 57 P & CR 306 and cases there cited, and see, also, *Mason v Secretary of State for the Environment* [1984] JPL 332. See also *R v Independent Television Commission, ex p Television South West* [1996] JR 185, [1996] EMLR 291 (HL, 1992) per Lord Templeman at 191–192: Lord Templeman's speech contains robust warnings of the danger of allowing judicial review to become an appeal on the merits.
[2] [1996] JR 185 (HL, 1992) at 198.
[3] [2009] UKHL 7; [2009] 1 WLR 413 at [51].

8.51 Examples of decisions where a finding of fact was held to be unreasonable[1] are cases where an immigration appeal tribunal had miscalculated an applicant's period of absence,[2] or where a planning inspector proceeded upon the basis that a proposed development would only partially affect the view from the applicant's window, whereas he could only reasonably have concluded that the view would be completely obstructed.[3] It is to be stressed that, in accordance with the principle in *R v Nat Bell Liquors Ltd*,[4] in all these cases the court is concerned only to consider whether the finding of fact is one which has no reasonable basis, and is not interfering with the decision-maker's function of resolving disputed matters of fact falling within jurisdiction.[5] Similar principles will apply where the task of the decision-maker is to ascertain whether there is sufficient evidence to warrant a further hearing.[6] It may also be noted that evidence of scrupulous care and a meticulous approach on the part of decision-makers will render it unlikely that they have reached a view of the facts not reasonably open on the basis of the material before them.[7]

[1] In addition to those cited in the first sentence of the preceding note, and to *Mahon v Air New Zealand Ltd* [1984] AC 808, [1984] 3 All ER 201 (discussed at **8.44** above).
[2] *R v Immigration Appeal Tribunal, ex p Muhammad Safiullah* [1986] Imm AR 424.
[3] *Jagendorf v Secretary of State* [1987] JPL 771.
[4] [1922] 2 AC 128 (under which it is enough to justify the decision that there is some evidence supporting it: compare *R v Bedwellty Justices, ex p Williams* [1997] AC 225, 232–233). See also *New Zealand Fishing Industry Association Ltd v Minister of Agriculture* [1988] 1 NZLR 544, cited by Jones [1990] PL 507 at 514. For a case in which a finding of fact was held to have a reasonable basis, but procedural fairness required consideration of the holding of an inquiry, see *R v Secretary of State for Wales, ex p Emery* [1996] 4 All ER 1. In *R v Secretary of State for the Home Department, ex p Abdi* [1996] 1 WLR 298 letters from the Secretary of State were produced stating that from unparticularised knowledge and experience the Secretary of State had no reason to believe that Spain would not comply with the Geneva convention: the majority of the House of Lords held that the letters constituted *some* evidence, and as this evidence had not been challenged and no issue raised on the point, it was sufficient to entitle special adjudicators to make findings of primary fact.

[5] In *R v London Residuary Body, ex p Inner London Education Authority* (1987) Times, 24 July, Watkins LJ rejected a contention that a decision-maker's mistake of fact was a separate ground of challenge.

[6] Committal by examining justices who had before them no admissible evidence of the defendant's guilt was described both as 'error of law' and as 'a material substantive error' leading to quashing of the committal in *R v Bedwellty Justices, ex p Williams* [1997] AC 225, 234: in his speech Lord Cooke of Thorndon observes, at 237, that in *Neill v North Antrim Magistrates' Court* [1992] 1 WLR 1220 a committal was quashed where inadmissible evidence much influenced the justices, and it could not be assumed that the remaining admissible evidence would have led them to commit. The 'error of law' in such cases is presumably that identified at p 163, text at fn 13.

[7] *R v Independent Television Commission, ex p Virgin Television Ltd* [1996] EMLR 318; see Herberg [1996] JR 123, Marsden [1997] Nottingham Law Journal 86.

8.52 The decision-maker may have a role in determining whether there is, or is not, admissible evidence on a question of fact. Decisions as to admissibility of evidence may themselves be reviewed for reasonableness.[1]

[1] *Re Proulx* [2001] 1 All ER 57 DC: provided that a magistrate had correctly directed himself on the law, the Divisional Court held that it would only interfere with his findings of fact and assessment of their significance when ruling on the admissibility of evidence in relation to extradition if they were outside the range of conclusions open to a reasonable magistrate.

Assessments of relevancy must be within the limits of reason

8.53 The first stage in identifying relevant and irrelevant factors must be a consideration of relevant statutory provisions. As has been said by Lord Bridge:[1]

' . . . if there are matters which, on the true construction of the statute conferring discretion, the person exercising the discretion must take into account and others which [that person] may not take into account, disregard of those legally relevant matters or regard of those legally irrelevant matters will lay the decision open to review on the ground of illegality'.

[1] *R v Secretary of State for the Environment, ex p Hammersmith and Fulham LBC* [1991] 1 AC 521, 597.

8.54 How is this to be reconciled with the observation by Lord Donaldson in *R v Panel on Take-overs, ex p Guinness plc*[1] to the effect that review for unreasonableness may be available where a decision-maker has taken a view on the relevancy of a particular matter which no reasonable decision-maker could have thought right? The answer lies in the recognition that, as was observed by Laws J in *R v Secretary of State for Transport, ex p Richmond LBC*:[2]

' . . . in a case where the statute itself does not specify the considerations to be taken into account in arriving at a discretionary decision, it will be for the decision-making body to decide what is and what is not a relevant consideration, and this decision will itself only be subject to review on Wednesbury grounds'.

[1] [1990] 1 QB 146, 159.
[2] [1994] 1 WLR 74, 95, founding on the observations of Cooke J in *CREEDNZ v Governor-General* [1981] 1 NZLR 172, as endorsed by Lord Scarman in *Re Findlay* [1985] AC 318, 333–334. See also *R (Association of British Civilian Internees: Far East Region) v Secretary of State for Defence* [2003] QB 1397 at p 1416, paragraph 40: 'Just as in satisfying the

requirements of proportionality, so too in meeting the *Wednesbury* test, the measures designed to further the objective must be rationally connected to it: see Lord Steyn in the *Daly* case [2001] 2 AC 532, 547B, quoting with approval the test propounded by Lord Clyde in *de Freitas v Permanent Secretary of Ministry of Agriculture, Fisheries, Lands and Housing* [1999] 1 AC 69, 80'.

8.55 By parity of reasoning, where the decision-maker has had regard to those matters which the law requires consideration of,[1] there will remain a range of considerations which the decision-maker may decide to take into account or to ignore, provided only that this decision is within the limits of reason.[2] A decision which went beyond the limits of reason in this sense was quashed in *R v Secretary of State for the Home Department, ex p Mehari:*[3] a special adjudicator had (reasonably) disbelieved an applicant's account of events, but had then unreasonably treated this as relevant to the question whether the applicant could be safely returned to France.

[1] For example, the UN Convention on the Rights of the Child: *R v Secretary of State for the Home Department, ex p Venables and Thompson* [1998] AC 407 per Lord Browne-Wilkinson in *Venables* at 499F–G.

[2] Note that the statute itself may prescribe that regard be had to material considerations: *Tesco Stores Ltd v Secretary of State for the Environment* [1995] 1 WLR 759. In this context Lord Hoffmann said (at 784) that it will be open to the decision-maker, on rational planning grounds, to give such a consideration no weight.

[3] [1994] QB 474, 492.

The decision-maker's evaluation of the matter may be reviewed

8.56 The court will intervene where the facts found taken as a whole could not reasonably warrant the conclusion of the decision-maker. While the question of weight as between competing considerations is normally a matter for the decision-maker rather than the court, the court may assess weight and balance depending on the context.[1] If the weight of facts pointing to one course of action is overwhelming, then a decision the other way cannot be upheld.[2] Thus, in *Emma Hotels Ltd v Secretary of the State for the Environment,*[3] the Secretary of State referred to a number of factors which led him to the conclusion that a non-residents' bar in a hotel was operated in such a way that the bar was not an incident of the hotel use for planning purposes, but constituted a separate use. The Divisional Court analysed the factors which led the Secretary of State to that conclusion and, having done so, set it aside. Donaldson LJ said[4] that he could not see on what basis the Secretary of State had reached his conclusion. Similarly, in *R v Sheffield City Council, ex p Chadwick,*[5] the Court of Appeal considered whether the facts known to a local authority could reasonably warrant the conclusion that budget proposals should not be disclosed to an elected member of the authority. Similarly, in *N (Kenya) v Secretary of State for the Home Department,*[6] a majority of the Court of Appeal (Judge and May LJJ) held that factors relied upon by an adjudicator, when set against countervailing factors, could not reasonably justify his decision. The stringency of this examination will depend upon the nature of the function under review. Thus a decision merely to lay charges in a disciplinary matter need not be reviewed with the same intensity as other decisions concerning quasi-criminal proceedings.[7] Other examples of examination for unreasonableness of the evaluation made by the decision-maker appear in the remainder of this section.

1   See paragraphs **8.11** to **8.15** above.
2   *West Glamorgan County Council v Rafferty* [1987] 1 All ER 1005, [1987] 1 WLR 457 (see
     8.11 above); *R v Secretary of State for the Home Department, ex p Hickey (No 2)* [1995] 1
     WLR 734, 757 (failure to recognise the force of new material in the case of Davis). For
     commonwealth authority to the same effect, see *Minister for Aboriginal Affairs v Peko-
     Wallsend Ltd* (1986) 66 ALR 299, 309–310 (High Court of Australia) and *Isaac v Minister
     of Consumer Affairs* [1990] 2 NZLR 632 (New Zealand High Court).
3   (1980) 41 P & CR 255.
4   (1980) 41 P&CR 255 at 259–260.
5   (1985) 84 LGR 563. Evaluations of factors for and against granting anonymity to a witness
     were considered in *R (A) v Lord Saville of Newdigate* [2002] 1 WLR 1249 and *R (A) v
     HM Coroner for Inner London South* [2005] ACD 3.
6   [2004] EWCA Civ 1094; note, however, the strong dissent by Sedley LJ.
7   *B v Canterbury District Law Society* [2005] 2 NZLR 753 (NZCA). For consideration of a
     decision not to lay charges, see *R v General Council of the Bar, ex p Percival* [1991] QB 212
     (DC), *Singh v Auckland District Law Society* [2000] 2 NZLR 605 (NZ High Court).

It may be unreasonable to require that which cannot lawfully be done

8.57 In *Arlidge v Islington Corpn*,[1] the local authority had power to make
byelaws under a Public Health Statute. It made a byelaw requiring the landlord
of a lodging house to cause every part of the premises to be cleansed in the
month of April, May or June in every year; and a penalty was imposed for
breach of the byelaw, although proceedings were not to be taken against the
landlord until the landlord had failed, after notice, to comply with it. The
divisional court held the byelaw invalid, because it would require the landlord
who may not have a right of entry to trespass. It was not possible to save the
byelaw by relying upon the council only to enforce it in those cases where it
would be reasonable to do so. By contrast, however, it is not necessarily
unreasonable for a decision-maker to conclude that he should not confer a
benefit unless the applicant is able to procure a state of affairs which is not
necessarily within his power: this must depend upon the circumstances.[2]

1   [1909] 2 KB 127.
2   *Grampian Regional Council v City of Aberdeen District Council* (1983) 47 P & CR 633;
     British Railways Board v Secretary of State for the Environment [1994] JPL 32.

8.58 The impact of an individual's financial resources was considered by the
New Zealand High Court in *Isaac v Minister of Consumer Affairs*,[1] where the
Minister directed Mr Isaac to recall a large quantity of bicycles which he had
sold and to refund the price, despite Mr Isaac's contention that such an
obligation would bankrupt him. Tipping J rejected a challenge for unreasonableness, holding that, while at first sight it might appear odd for the Minister
to have ordered something which Mr Isaac could not do, there were tenable
reasons for her to have done so:[2] if a recall for refund was otherwise justified,
Mr Isaac's financial position did not render an otherwise reasonable course
unreasonable.

1   [1990] 2 NZLR 606. See also *R v Hackney LBC, ex p Adebir* (1997) Times, 5 November.
2   [1990] 2 NZLR 606 at 632; among such reasons were the fact that a recall for refund might
     have some utility for purchasers, and the undesirability of distinguishing between solvent and
     insolvent suppliers.

Evaluation of interference with human rights

8.59 The first question in any case where breach of human rights is alleged must be whether or not the court has power itself to determine on the facts that such a breach has occurred, with the consequence that the impugned action is unlawful. Thus a statutory provision affecting the liberty of immigrants was held to require that the court determine whether the person concerned was an illegal immigrant.[1] Many human rights are expressly recognised by English statute and common law: and unless the legislature has conferred power to override those rights, it will be the duty of the English court to enforce them.[2] In doing so the courts ensure that decision-makers comply with the principle of legality.

---

[1]   *R v Secretary of State for the Home Department, ex p Khawaja* [1984] AC 74, endorsing the dissenting judgment of Lord Atkin in *Liversidge v Anderson* [1942] AC 206.

[2]   For recent examples, see *R v Customs and Excise Comrs, ex p Kay & Co* [1996] STC 1500 (at 1520–1521, taking account of the Bill of Rights 1688) and *R v Lord Chancellor, ex p Witham* [1997] 2 All ER 779. The question whether English common law includes principles of customary international law for this purpose was left open in *R (European Roma Rights Centre) v Immigration Officer at Prague Airport* [2004] UKHL 55.

8.60 As discussed in CHAPTER 4 above, the Human Rights Act 1998 gives important effect in English law, subject to any reservation or derogation that the United Kingdom may have made, to the rights and freedoms set out in arts 2–12 and 14 of the European Convention on Human Rights and in certain Protocols to the Convention,[1] all as read with arts 16–18 of the Convention.[2] The result is that a failure by the state to act compatibly with relevant articles of the Convention and Protocols will constitute an error of law, unless the public body is compelled to Act differently by primary legislation.[3]

---

[1]   Articles 1–3 of the First Protocol, and arts 1 and 2 of the Sixth Schedule.

[2]   An overview of relevant legal principles is given in CHAPTER 4. For detailed analysis of the Convention (which is beyond the scope of this work) reference should be made to texts on human rights law.

[3]   Sections 2, 3 and 6 of the Human Rights Act 1998; *R (Q) v Secretary of State for the Home Department* [2004] QB 36, paragraph 112, p 81.

8.61 Prior to the 1998 Act the courts developed a sophisticated framework for reviewing the reasonableness of decisions where human rights questions arose. In most human rights cases this will no longer be needed, although the courts recently emphasised that the effect of the 1998 Act was not to render common law principles 'ossuary'.[1] As is the case more generally, if error of law is established, there will be no need for an analysis in terms of reasonableness. More specifically in relation to human rights issues, if the Convention tests are met it will be highly unlikely that the decision-maker will have acted unreasonably. Nevertheless, there may be cases involving human rights where the 1998 Act does not apply, and there may be other cases where grave issues involving other international conventions arise.[2] For these reasons the following paragraphs describe the framework developed by the courts.

---

[1]   *Kennedy v The Charity Commission* [2014] 2 WLR 808, at [133].

[2]   See Geiringer. '*Tavita* and All That' (2004) 21 NZ Universities Law Review 66: Fatima *Using International Law in Domestic Courts* (2005), Hart Publishing.

8.62 The modern starting point for development of the framework was *R v Secretary of State for the Home Department, ex p Brind*.[1] Drawing on the well-established principle that, in appropriate circumstances, an international convention may be used to interpret ambiguous legislation, an attempt was made to persuade the court that a statutory conferral of administrative discretion carried with it the implication that the discretionary power could not be used in a manner which contravened the Convention. This attempt failed on the ground that such an implication would be a judicial usurpation of the legislative function.[2]

---

[1]   [1991] 1 AC 696. For discussion of this case, see Hunt;, *Using Human Rights Law in English Courts* (1993).

[2]   Per Lord Bridge at 748; see also Lords Roskill (749, agreeing with Lord Bridge), Templeman (expressing a contrary view at 751), Ackner (759–762) and Lowry (763, agreeing with Lord Ackner). Contrast the position in Australia, where compliance with an international treaty has been held to constitute an enforceable legitimate expectation (*Minister for Immigration and Ethnic Affairs v Teoh* (1995) 183 CLR 273; see Allars (1995) 17 Syd L Rev 204. Taggart (1996) 112 LQR 50). The New Zealand Court of Appeal in *Ashby v Minister of Immigration* [1981] 1 NZLR 222 contemplated that some international obligations might be so important that no reasonable minister could fail to take them into account, a question further discussed by that court in *Tavita v Minister of Immigration* [1994] 2 NZLR 257. *Puli'uvea v Removal Review Authority* (1996) 14 FRNZ 322; *Rajan v Minister of Immigration and NZ Airline Pilots Association v A-G* (CA 300/96, 16.6.97); see also *Elika v Minister of Immigration* [1996] 1 NZLR 741. *Patel v Chief Executive, Department of Labour* [1997] 1 NZLR 102 and *Patel v Minister of Immigration* [1997] 1 NZLR 252 (and compare *R v Ministry of Defence, ex p Smith* [1996] QB 517 per Sir Thomas Bingham MR at 558).

8.63 It does not follow from this, however, that an allegation of breach of human rights was irrelevant to review for unreasonableness. Thus, in *Bugday-cay v Secretary of State for the Home Department*,[1] Lord Bridge, having held that the resolution of any issue of fact and the exercise of any discretion in relation to an application for asylum as a refugee lay exclusively within the jurisdiction of the Secretary of State subject only to the court's power of review, continued:

> 'The limitations on the scope of that power are well known and need not be restated here. Within those limitations the court must, I think, be entitled to subject an administrative decision to the more rigorous examination, to ensure that it is in no way flawed, according to the gravity of the issue which the decision determines. The most fundamental of all human rights is the individual's right to life and when an administrative decision under challenge is said to be one which may put the applicant's life at risk, the basis of the decision must call for the most anxious scrutiny'.

---

[1]   [1987] AC 514, 531; see also Lord Templeman at 537 ('where the result of a flawed decision may imperil life or liberty a special responsibility lies on the court in the examination of the decision-making process'). In *R v Secretary of State for the Home Department, ex p Launder* [1997] 1 WLR 839 Lord Hope, having quoted these observations, described other aspects of the issue in that case (whether the People's Republic of China could be trusted to implement its treaty obligations) which would require great caution to be exercised, despite the need for anxious scrutiny, before holding that the decision was unreasonable.

8.64 Anxious scrutiny by the House of Lords of the relevant decisions led to the conclusion that they should be quashed: the Secretary of State's confidence that Kenya would not knowingly return Ugandan refugees to Uganda had been shown to be (at least to some extent) misplaced, and the decisions in question had not taken into account the fact that Kenya had in the past been in breach of the Geneva Convention.

8.65 Similarly, in *R (Yogathas) v Secretary of State for the Home Department*[1] on a challenge to a certificate that an allegation of a breach of human rights[2] was manifestly unfounded, it was held that the court should subject the Secretary of State's decision to the most anxious scrutiny by way of rigorous examination.[3]

---

[1]   [2003] UKHL 36, [2003] 1 AC 920 HL(E).
[2]   Made on an appeal under s 65 of the Immigration and Asylum Act 1999.
[3]   See paragraphs 9 (Lord Bingham), 58–59 (Lord Hope), 74 (Lord Hutton), 77 (Lord Millett), 121 (Lord Scott).

8.66 Other cases have concerned interference with rights of property. Thus in a case at the beginning of the last century,[1] the Court of Appeal held that it was unreasonable to prohibit alterations to property where no good object could be served by doing so. It may be unreasonable to take a course which deprives a landowner of property without compensation. In *Hall & Co Ltd v Shoreham-by-Sea UDC*,[2] the local authority imposed a condition on planning permission requiring the site owner to construct an ancillary road at its own expense. Had the procedure under the Highways Act been adopted, the site owner would have received compensation for the land used in constructing the road. The Court of Appeal held the condition invalid. The view of Lord Justice Willmer[3] was that it was unreasonable to have taken the course which deprived the owner of compensation. It should be noted, however, that Harman and Pearson LJJ[4] treated the case as one of illegality, where the Council had contravened the general law relating to highways. There is no general principle that a body exercising statutory powers may not deprive a property owner of his rights without compensation: this is a question of construction of the statute.[5] But there will remain some moral imperatives: thus the Court of Appeal has pointed out that no reasonable Secretary of State would confirm a compulsory purchase order if the landowner was willing to sell other land which would serve equally well.[6]

---

[1]   In *Repton School Governors v Repton RDC* [1918] 2 KB 133.
[2]   [1964] 1 All ER 1, [1964] 1 WLR 240.
[3]   At 251; the Court of Appeal has subsequently adopted a similar approach in *Bradford City Metropolitan Council v Secretary of State for the Environment* (1986) 53 P & CR 55. A full account of the background to, and consequences of, the decision, and observations on its relevance to planning cases today, will be found in the speech of Lord Hoffmann in *Tesco Stores Ltd v Secretary of State for the Environment* [1995] 1 WLR 759. See also Sir Robert Carnwath, 'The reasonable limits of local authority powers' [1996] PL 244, 260–261.
[4]   At 256 and 261.
[5]   *Westminster Bank v Minister of Housing and Local Government* [1971] AC 508; *Kingston-upon-Thames Royal London Borough Council v Secretary of State for the Environment* [1974] 1 All ER 193, [1973] 1 WLR 1549, disapproving the reasoning of Glyn-Jones J in *Allnatt London Properties Ltd v Middlesex County Council* (1964) 62 LGR 304.
[6]   *R v Secretary of State for Transport, ex p de Rothschild* [1989] 1 All ER 933 at 942.

8.67 In *Brind* itself, Lord Ackner observed[1] that in a case involving a fundamental human right, close scrutiny must be given to the reasons provided as justification for the interference with that right, and the House of Lords examined whether restrictions on the freedom of speech imposed by the Home

Secretary could reasonably be regarded as warranted by the public interest of combating terrorism. Lord Bridge indicated[2] that the court was entitled to start from the premise that any restriction of the right to freedom of expression requires to be justified and that nothing less than an important competing public interest will be sufficient to justify it. A suggestion, however, that these statements lowered the threshold of a challenge for unreasonableness was rejected by Neill LJ in *R v Secretary of State for the Environment, ex p National and Local Government Officers' Association.*[3] Similarly, in *R v Cambridge Health Authority, ex p B*[4] the Court of Appeal, differing from the judge below, held that where an authority was under challenge for failure to fund expensive treatment which might save the life of a 10-year-old child, even though the case was one of the greatest seriousness to which the court gave 'the most critical, anxious consideration', the court could not require the authority to demonstrate that if the treatment were provided then another patient would have to go without.

[1] [1991] 1 AC 696, 757, where his Lordship discusses the observations of Slade LJ in *R v Secretary of State for Transport, ex p de Rothschild* [1989] 1 All ER 933.
[2] [1991] 1 AC 696, 748–749. In his 1992 Administrative Law Bar Association Lecture ('Is the High Court the Guardian of Fundamental Constitutional Rights?' [1993] PL 59, 70–71) Laws J deployed this passage in support of an argument that where the subject matter of a decision engaged fundamental rights, any decision adverse to the citizen should only survive judicial scrutiny if it were found to rest on a distinct and positive justification in the public interest.
[3] (1992) 5 Admin LR 785, 798.
[4] [1995] 1 WLR 898.

8.68 There is a link here with the doctrine of legitimate expectation[1] and also with international law. An international instrument will be binding in domestic law if it is incorporated into a statute. However, that is not the only way international law is relevant. But international law may be influential in other ways. There is a presumption that domestic law, including the common law, will accord with the United Kingdom's international law obligations.[2] However, a treaty does not automatically have binding force in this country.[3]

[1] Discussed below at **8.80** et seq.
[2] *Assange v Swedish Prosecution Authority* [2012] 2 WLR 1275 at 10, 98, 112 and 122, and *A v Secretary of State for the Home Department (No 2)* [2006] 2 AC 221 at 27.
[3] *Ahmed v HM Treasury (No 2)* [2010] 2 AC 534 at 109. See the differing views of the Justices in *R (SG and others) v Secretary of State for Work and Pensions (Child Poverty Action Group and another intervening)* [2015] 1 W.L.R. 1449 as to the impact of unincorporated treaties in the human rights context.

8.69 The more substantial the interference, the more the court will require by way of justification before it is satisfied that the decision is reasonable.[1] In adopting this approach, the courts have attached importance to the recognition by the European Court of Human Rights of the role of judicial review in satisfying the requirement in Article 13 of the European Convention that there should be a national remedy to enforce the substance of the Convention rights and freedoms.[2]

[1] *See paragraphs* **8.11–8.15** above. R v Ministry of Defence, ex p Smith [1996] QB 517, CA, applied in *R v Secretary of State for Transport, ex p Richmond LBC (No 4)* [1996] 1 WLR 1460, CA. See Hare, [1996] CLJ 179. For a more expansionist approach, see Fordham 'Anxious Scrutiny' [1996] JR 81. In *R v Secretary of State for the Home Department, ex p McQuillan* [1995] 4 All ER 400 Sedley J at 423 envisaged that the court would measure rationality by, among other things, asking whether in the light of its impact the executive

action challenged could reasonably be considered an expedient response by a Home Secretary who has given proper weight to the fundamental right thereby put at risk.

2   *R v Ministry of Defence, ex p Smith* [1996] QB 517 per Lord Bingham CJ at 555, and *R v Secretary of State for the Home Department, ex p Launder* [1997] 1 WLR 839, 867.

8.70 What is a basic human right in this context? This has been touched upon above, in paragraph **8.39**, footnote 4. In *Runa Begum v Tower Hamlets LBC*[1] Lord Bingham said,[2] in relation to a decision that accommodation offered to a homeless person had been reasonable, that he saw no warrant in that context for applying notions of 'anxious scrutiny'. Many of the cases identifying basic human rights have been concerned with rights recognised by the European Convention on Human Rights and its accompanying Protocols.[3] However, the European Convention is not the sole register of human rights, and differs in its content from other international statements.[4] Moreover, the English common law has itself long recognised and given effect to certain human rights[5] and the courts should develop the common law to arrive at a result which is compliant with the Convention.[6] In *R v Secretary of State for the Home Department, ex p Moon*,[7] Sedley J summarised the principle of close scrutiny and concluded:

> 'The law of close scrutiny . . . amounts today to a doctrine that the court will demand clear justification for an executive decision which interferes with an important right; not, however, so as to persuade the court to agree with the executive view, but simply to demonstrate that there was a sufficient basis on which the view could sensibly be reached'.

1   [2003] UKHL 5, [2003] 2 AC 430, HL (E).
2   At paragraph 7 ([2003] 2 AC at p 439).
3   In a case governed by the law of the EU, the assertion of a right (which may include a right under the Convention) will be examined by reference to the jurisprudence of the EU: see CHAPTER 15.
4   See Harris, O'Boyle and Warbrick *Law of the European Convention on Human Rights* (1995) pp 1–5. Thus the Court of Appeal said in *R (Q) v Secretary of State for the Home Department* [2004] QB 36, paragraph 115, p 82: 'We should make it clear in this connection that we do not regard the proposition in *R v Ministry of Defence, ex p Smith* as confined to rights set out in the European Convention on Human Rights. In view especially of its date, it is apt in our judgment to apply to the right to seek asylum, which is not only the subject of a separate international convention but is expressly recognised by article 14 of the Universal Declaration of Human Rights (1948) (Cmd 7662)'.
5   Among which are included the right of access to the courts: eg in the context of review for illegality, *R v Lord Chancellor, ex p Witham* [1997] 2 All ER 779. For a full discussion by Lord Lester of Herne Hill QC and Professor Dawn Oliver of case law concerning fundamental freedoms, see 'Constitutional Law and Human Rights' 8(2) *Halbury's Laws* (4th edn, reissue).
6   *Osborn v Parole Board* [2013] UKSC 61, [2013] 3 WLR 1020 at 62.
7   (1995) 8 Admin LR 477.

8.71 It is consistent with established principle to hold that the court must examine whether the interference in question *could* be regarded as a sensible exercise of power; the corollary (which has yet to emerge clearly from the case law) is that, in determining that the right in question is so important as to demand clear justification, the court is in truth making an assessment that no decision-maker could reasonably have proceeded on any other basis.[1]

1   Compare Lord Irvine of Lairg QC, [1996] PL 59, 64: 'Consistent with *Wednesbury*, however, the court can only require . . . a decision-making process in this form where the fundamental right is unquestioned, representing an undoubted value of our society'. For

further discussion of difficulties with the 'anxious scrutiny' approach, see Andrew Le Sueur. 'The Rise and Ruin of Unreasonableness?' [2005] JR 32.

It may be unreasonable to make a decision which reserves to the decision-maker the exercise of arbitrary power in the future

8.72 Difficult questions can arise where a decision-maker has power to impose conditions, and uses that power to restrict further action without the decision-maker's consent. An initial question will be whether the statute permits the imposition of such conditions.[1] If it does, the question may nevertheless arise whether the use of the power in this way is unreasonable. Thus, in *Parker v Bournemouth Corpn*,[2] the local authority made a byelaw prohibiting certain types of commercial activity on the beach except in pursuance of an agreement to be made with itself. The byelaw was held by the Divisional Court to be bad: it sought to put it in the power of the local authority to make any agreement it liked, and, if valid, would have prevented the reasonableness of its actions from being reviewed.[3] In *Mixnam's Properties Ltd v Chertsey UDC* a number of conditions affecting a caravan site owner's freedom of contract were imposed, one of which stated that the site rents were to be agreed with the Council. In the Court of Appeal[4] Willmer LJ held that this was unreasonable in the sense explained by Lord Russell of Killowen CJ in *Kruse v Johnson*[5] as it would enable the local authority to behave in a completely arbitrary manner, and could indeed be used to render the site licence virtually valueless to the licensee.[6] In the House of Lords,[7] as in the Court of Appeal, the conditions were struck down on the general ground that they were not within the scope of the relevant statute. On the question whether they were reasonable, Lord Reid[8] was prepared to proceed upon the basis that the Council did not act unreasonably in seeking to impose such a condition. Lord Upjohn, however, would have struck down the condition as to rent, together with other conditions relating to security of tenure and the control of premium as oppressive, while the remaining conditions limiting the site owner's freedom of contract with his tenants were, in his view, a gratuitous interference with the rights of the occupier and wholly unnecessary for the good governance of the site.[9] It is, of course, common for a decision-maker to take a complex decision in stages; there can be no objection to this, provided that each stage will be open to review.

[1] A licence modification imposing a condition of this kind was held to be permitted under the Telecommunications Act 1984 only when the licensee had consented to the modification: *R v Director-General of Telecommunications, ex p British Telecommunications plc* (Divisional Court, 20.12.96, CO 3596/96, transcript pp 29–32).

[2] (1902) 66 JP 440.

[3] Similarly, in *Bugg v DPP* [1993] QB 473, 503, the Divisional Court held that byelaws could not validly leave it up to the Secretary of State at some later date to fix the boundaries of prohibited land. By contrast, in a case where the Secretary of State had statutory power to deprive a local authority totally of certain functions, this was held to permit the imposition by the Secretary of State of a condition that his approval be obtained before the functions were performed – any concerns that the approval might be withheld arbitrarily being removed by assurances given by the Secretary of State: *R v Secretary of State for the Environment, ex p Knowsley MBC* (31 July 1991, unreported) CA, transcript pp 35–44, 69, 76.

[4] [1964] 1 QB 214, [1963] 2 All ER 787.

[5] [1898] 2 QB 91, 99.

[6] [1964] 1 QB 214 at 229.

[7] [1965] AC 735.

8   [1965] AC 735, at 747.
9   [1965] AC 735 at 765.

The important role of the rule of law

8.73 Lord Bridge said in *Bennett v Horseferry Road Magistrates' Court*[1] that there was no principle more basic to any proper system of law than the maintenance of the rule of law itself. The House of Lords in that case was concerned to ensure that the Divisional Court exercises a supervisory role to prevent abuse of process in criminal proceedings. The importance of legal certainty[2] is reflected in the cases concerned with the arbitrary reservation of power, discussed at **8.72** above, in the principles upon which the court deals with uncertainty in regulations and conditions (discussed at **8.42** above and **13.11** below), and in the recognition that review is available in cases of abuse of power (which may, in certain circumstances, arise out of the non-fulfilment of legitimate expectations and in other ways; see **8.87** et seq below). The rule of law, however, does not require the transposition into public law of principles applicable to private bodies. For example, the doctrine of restraint of trade does not operate so as to render restrictions by a regulatory authority prima facie contrary to public policy: instead, the validity of such restrictions is to be determined by the test of unreasonableness, taking account of the fact that the restriction in question is in restraint of trade.[3] Questions of particular difficulty may arise when public authorities have to consider how to cope with sustained campaigns of illegal protest. In *R v Coventry City Council, ex p Phoenix Aviation Ltd*[4] public authorities administering air and sea ports which had been subject to disruption by animal rights protesters were held to have no discretion to refuse cargoes of livestock; but even if they had possessed such a discretion the Divisional Court said that the importance of the rule of law was such that the cargoes could not be banned. The court's judgment noted that a variation or short-term suspension of services might be justified, and continued:[5]

> 'But it is one thing to respond to unlawful threats, quite another to submit to them . . . Tempting though it may sometimes be for public authorities to yield too readily to threats of disruption, they must expect the courts to review any such decision with particular rigour – this is not an area where they can be permitted a wide measure of discretion. As when fundamental human rights are in play, the courts will adopt a more interventionist role'.

1   [1994] 1 AC 42, 67, [1993] 3 All ER 138, 155.
2   The principle of legal certainty is well recognised in European law; see Chapter **15**.
3   *R v General Medical Council, ex p Colman* [1990] 1 All ER 489; *R v LAUTRO, ex p Kendall* [1994] COD 169. As to the impact of public law concepts in cases governed by private law, see *Stevenage Borough Football Club Ltd v Football League Ltd* (1997) 9 Admin LT 109, (1996) Times, 1 August (Carnwath J) and 9 August (CA).
4   [1995] 3 All ER 37.
5   [1995] 3 All ER at p 62.

8.74 The need for a public authority to uphold the rule of law must nevertheless be set in the context of the authority's general powers and duties. Accordingly, in a subsequent case where protection of convoys of lorries from animal rights protesters had required the deployment of substantial numbers of police officers five days a week and there was no prospect of obtaining significant extra resources, it was not unreasonable for the police to limit protection to two days a week.[1]

[1] *R v Chief Constable of Sussex, ex p International Trader's Ferry Ltd* [1999] 2 AC 418.

It is unreasonable to impose conditions upon a benefit which are manifestly unjust

8.75 An example of this arose where immigration rules made provision for a dependent parent to be admitted to the United Kingdom in the most exceptional compassionate circumstances, and appeared to require that, as one of such circumstances, the parent should have a standard of living substantially below that of his or her own country. Simon Brown J held that the rules on their true construction did indeed make such a requirement, and struck it down as invalid in *R v Immigration Appeal Tribunal, ex p Manshoora Begum*[1], saying that he could see no possible basis in sense or justice for a requirement which would automatically disqualify from admission under the rule virtually all those from the poorer countries of the world, and yet allow most dependents from the more affluent countries to be considered on general compassionate grounds.[2]

[1] [1986] Imm AR 385. See also *Zohra Begum v Immigration Appeal Tribunal* [1994] Imm AR 381.
[2] At 394. At the other extreme, it may not be unreasonable for the monetary effects of financial services regulation to operate harshly: see *R v Securities and Investments Board, ex p Sun Life Assurance Society plc* [1996] 2 BCLC 150.

Delay

8.76 Inordinate or manifestly unreasonable delay has been held to be unlawful.[1] In *Niarchos (London) Ltd v Secretary of State for the Environment and Westminster City Council (No 2)*,[2] the Court of Appeal examined the reasons given by the Secretary of State for proposing that an inquiry should be re-opened before he reached a decision, concluded that none provided any rational justification for such a delay, and directed him to determine the matter without further inquiry or delay.[3]

[1] Such as in *R (HA (Nigeria)) v Secretary of State for the Home Department* [2012] EWHC 979 (Admin).
[2] (1980) 79 LGR 264; see also *R v Secretary of State for the Environment, ex p Fielder Estates (Convey) Ltd* (1988) 57 P & CR 424, art 6 of the European Convention on Human Rights, and c 29 of Magna Carta 1215.
[3] Sir Robert Carnwath, [1996] PL 244, 261, suggests that this case ought to have been decided not on principles of reasonableness, but by a determination of the court as to whether there had been procedural impropriety (see **8.26** above). For cases on the need for unreasonable delay before the court can intervene, see **16.53** below.

The court may consider whether information ought to be provided

8.77 As mentioned at **8.43** above, there may be a statutory requirement to supply reasons for a decision, or procedural fairness may require that reasons be provided. Independently of these obligations, however, in appropriate circumstances a refusal to supply information may be condemned as unreasonable. Thus in one case a decision of the Secretary of State for Defence not to release the findings of an Army Board of Inquiry (there being no issue of national security) was held to have been 'outrageous'.[1]

[1] *R v Secretary of State for Defence, ex p Sancto* (1992) 5 Admin LR 673, [1993] COD 44, DC: the court, however, held that no relief could be granted because the applicants had no legal rights and were owed no legal duty. See also *R v Sheffield City Council, ex p Chadwick* (1985) 84 LGR 563 (at **8.56** above).

Allocation of scarce resources

8.78 Questions as to the priorities in allocating scarce resources are par excellence questions for the decision-making body rather than the court. This does not mean that the mere fact that resources are limited will preclude review for unreasonableness, assuming that resources are relevant to the issue being decided.[1] Thus, in *R v Criminal Injuries Compensation Board, ex p P*,[2] the Court of Appeal unanimously dismissed a suggestion that the allocation of funds under the ex gratia scheme for payments to victims of crime could not be the subject of judicial review; and the majority rejected a suggestion that the allocation was not justiciable.[3] But although the allocation was reviewable, the court had little difficulty in concluding in that case that it was not unreasonable. Applicants who assert that very substantial sums should be spent on a particular project will inevitably face great difficulties in attempting to persuade a court that an authority's decision not to give preference to them was unreasonable.[4]

[1] *Cf. Holmes-Moorhouse v Richmond RLBC* [2009] UKHL 7; [2009] 1 WLR 413, where it was held that the fact that social housing was a scare resource could be taken into account when determining priority for such housing, but not to the point where it inhibited the discharge of statutory functions.
[2] [1995] 1 WLR 845.
[3] The dissentient on this point was Neill LJ; see note 3, **8.32** above.
[4] *R v Cambridge Health Authority, ex p B* [1995] 1 WLR 898, [1995] 2 All ER 129; *R v Chief Constable of Sussex, ex p International Trader's Ferry Ltd* [1999] 2 AC 418. See, also, *R (Bibi) v Newham LBC* [2002] 1 WLR 237 at paragraph 64, p 252: 'In an area such as the provision of housing at public expense where decisions are informed by social and political value judgments as to priorities of expenditure the court will start with a recognition that such invidious choices are essentially political rather than judicial. In our judgment the appropriate body to make that choice in the context of the present case is the authority. However, it must do so in the light of the legitimate expectations of the respondents'.

Considering exceptions to policy

8.79 As stated above, a discretionary public law power may not be exercised arbitrarily or with partiality as between individuals or classes potentially affected by its use; nevertheless it is also impermissible to apply a policy for the exercise of such a discretion with a rigidity which excludes consideration of possible departure in individual cases.[1] It was observed by Sedley J in *R v Ministry of Agriculture Fisheries and Food, ex p Hamble (Offshore) Fisheries Ltd*[2] that the line between individual consideration and inconsistency, slender enough in theory, can be imperceptible in practice. In that case, it was held that while the framer of a policy for the exercise of a governmental discretion must be prepared to consider making exceptions where these are merited, the inclusion of thought-out exceptions in the policy itself may well be exhaustive of the obligation: while any further candidates for exemption must be considered, it will always be a legitimate consideration that to make one such exception may well set up an unanswerable case of partiality or arbitrariness.

1 See Chapter 7. For the position where a public authority departs from policy to the detriment of the claimant, see the discussion of legitimate expectation at **8.80–8.87** below, and the discussion of even-handedness at **8.97** below.

2 [1995] 2 All ER 714, 722–733; this part of the judgment is unaffected by the decision in *R v Secretary of State for the Home Department, ex p Hargreaves* [1997] 1 WLR 906, [1997] 1 All ER 397.

Legitimate expectations and unfairness generally

8.80 Courts often confront an apparent dilemma between the importance of preserving a public body's freedom lawfully to exercise statutory powers without restraint and the undesirability of allowing the body in its dealings with private citizens to exercise its powers in a way which would be impermissible if the body were itself a private citizen.[1] One method of resolving the dilemma has been to hold that in certain circumstances the public body may make a binding contract as to the exercise of its discretionary powers, may irrevocably waive an irregularity, or may be estopped from going back on an assurance. These matters are discussed in Chapter 7 above. A second method of resolving the dilemma was to have resort to a doctrine of legitimate expectations which, although originally concerned with the procedure adopted by the decision-maker, now has a role to play as to the substantive content of the decision.[2] A third method (sometimes but not always linked to the second method) has been to develop the concept of intervention by the court where there has been an unfair abuse of power. Just as rational individuals may differ about what is reasonable, so they may differ about what is fair. Sometimes, of course, a degree of unfairness may, as a matter of practical reality, be unavoidable when carrying out the requirements of statute. Plainly there may be review on reasonableness grounds where a decision has been taken which is so unfair that no reasonable decision-maker could have regarded it as appropriate. So far as procedural fairness is concerned, this will generally be a matter for assessment by the court.[3] But what of substantive unfairness? Is this a separate ground of review, so that the court may intervene (albeit in limited circumstances) even though the decision in question has survived challenge for unreasonableness?[4] Or is an allegation of substantive unfairness merely an assertion which brings into play the principles of review for unreasonableness, so that the court only intervenes if no reasonable decision-maker could have regarded the decision as appropriate?[5] In the succeeding paragraphs the current English law on 'legitimate expectations' (in so far as relevant to the substance of a decision) is described, a number of cases on unfairness are examined, and an attempt is made to answer these questions.[6]

1 In the Hong Kong case of *Chu Pitt-Wing v A-G* [1984] HKLR 411 (cited by Staughton LJ in *R v Croydon Justices, ex p Dean* [1993] QB 769, 778). McMullen V-P said that there was a

strong public interest to be observed in holding officials of the state to promises made by them in full understanding of what is entailed by the bargain.

2   At one stage the development of this doctrine was thought to have been arrested: *R v Secretary of State for the Home Department, ex p Hargreaves* [1997] 1 WLR 906, [1997] 1 All ER 397, see **8.84** below].

3   See **8.26** above.

4   See per Cooke P in *Thames Valley Electric Power Board v NZFP Pulp & Paper Ltd* [1994] 2 NZLR 641, 652–653; compare, however, the cautionary remarks of McKay J (654) and Fisher J (654). For an excellent discussion of the leading New Zealand cases, and a prescient analysis of English case law, see Poole, 'Legitimate Expectation and Substantive Fairness: Beyond the Limits of Procedural Propriety' [1995] NZ Law Review 426.

5   See Lord Roskill in *Council of Civil Service Unions v Minister for the Civil Service* [1985] AC 374, 414–415: 'It is not for the courts to determine whether a particular policy or particular decisions taken in fulfilment of that policy are fair'.

6   For further discussion, see Schonberg *Legitimate Expectations in Administrative Law* (2000). OUP; Clayton, 'Legitimate Expectations, Policy and the Principle of Consistency' (2003) 62 CLJ 93; Sales and Steyn, 'Legitimate Expectations in English Public Law: An Analysis' [2004] PL 564; Blundell, '*Ultra Vires* Legitimate Expectations' [2005] JR 147.

Legitimate expectations and the substance of a decision

See, further, CHAPTER **11** at **11.88** and **11.89** below, *Steele 'Substantive Legitimate Expectations: Striking the Right Balance?'* (2005) 121 LQR 300, *Christopher Forsyth* [2011] JR 429, and Daniel Kolinsky [2012] JR 161.

8.81 The concept of legitimate expectations was initially developed by the courts as part of the process of identifying those individuals who would be protected by procedural safeguards. This development is discussed in CHAPTER **11** below: as a matter of procedural fairness the courts insisted that if a decision-maker had encouraged a legitimate expectation that a benefit would be conferred (or continued) then the benefit should not be withheld without a hearing and, similarly, that in the case of a legitimate expectation that a particular procedure would be followed, the court could hold the decision-maker to that procedure.

8.82 From this developed the suggestion that where a decision-maker could be said to have encouraged a legitimate expectation of a particular substantive result then the court might (in appropriate circumstances) require the decision-maker to fulfil that expectation.[1] In *R v Secretary of State for the Home Department, ex p Khan*[2] Parker LJ held that the Secretary of State should not be able to resile from an undertaking to allow persons (who met certain conditions) into the country 'without affording interested persons a hearing and then only if the overriding public interest demands it'. Dunn LJ went further, holding that by acting outside the published criteria the Secretary of State had misdirected himself and acted unreasonably.

1   See Elias, 'Legitimate Expectation and Judicial Review' in Jowell and Oliver (eds) *New Directions in Judicial Review* (1988) especially pp 45–49; Craig, 'Substantive Legitimate Expectations in Domestic and Community Law' [1996] CLJ 289; Singh and Steyn, [1996] JR 17, [1997] JR 33. For the EU principle of legal certainty, see CHAPTER **15**.

2   [1984] 1 WLR 1337.

8.83 Citing the *Khan* decision, Taylor J in *R v Secretary of State for the Home Department, ex p Ruddock*[1] said that although most of the cases on legitimate expectation were concerned with a right to be heard, he did not think that the doctrine was so confined. This led[2] to a divergence of judicial opinion between the (now elevated) counsel for the protagonists in *Ruddock*. Laws J (who had been counsel for the respondent in that case) held in *R v Secretary of State for Transport, ex p Richmond LBC*[3] that *Ruddock* demonstrated no more than that there may be circumstances in which it will be unfair to change a policy adhered to over time without giving those affected a right to be heard. His view was that the reference by Parker LJ in *Khan* to the overriding public interest meant simply that a reasonable public authority, having regard only to relevant considerations, will not alter its policy unless it concludes that the public will be better served by the change (which was to assert no more than that the change in policy must not transgress *Wednesbury* principles). This analysis of *Ruddock* was itself the subject of a critique by Sedley J (who had been counsel for the applicants in that case) in *R v Ministry of Agriculture Fisheries and Food, ex p Hamble (Offshore) Fisheries Ltd*[4] where, drawing in part on the jurisprudence of the European Court of Justice, it was held that the same principle of fairness governed the question whether a decision-maker could frustrate a legitimate expectation that something would or would not be done as governed the question whether the decision-maker could frustrate a legitimate expectation that the applicant would be heard before a particular step was taken.[5]

[1]   [1987] 1 WLR 1482, 1496–1497.
[2]   In the meantime, there were a number of cases where the effect of alleged 'legitimate expectations' did not need to be explored because the legitimacy of the expectation was not established. For example, in *R v Independent Television Commission, ex p TSW Broadcasting Ltd* [1996] JR 185 (HL, 1992) an assertion that by identifying certain tests a decision-maker has precluded itself from adopting other tests was rejected on the facts as 'preposterous', Lord Goff adding that any substance which the argument might have possessed was dissolved by the fact that the applicant had made enquiries of the decision-maker designed to identify the criteria it would apply, and the decision-maker had failed to respond to those enquiries (see p 199). A claim based on legitimate expectation as to the content of regulations was rejected by Neill LJ in *R v Secretary of State for the Environment, ex p National and Local Government Officers' Association* (1993) 5 Admin LR 785, 804 because the alleged assurance was given at a time when legislation and the regulations were still being considered, because interested parties were consulted prior to the final draft of the regulations, and because it was very doubtful whether, save perhaps in exceptional cases, the principle of legitimate expectation could be invoked to invalidate either primary or secondary legislation which was put before Parliament (see **8.33** above).
[3]   [1994] 1 WLR 74, 92–94.
[4]   [1995] 2 All ER 714, 723–732.
[5]   Legitimacy here was held to be a relative concept, to be gauged proportionately to the legal and policy implications of the expectation, which was why it had proved easier to establish a legitimate expectation that an applicant will be heard than that a particular outcome will be arrived at by the decision-maker ([1995] 2 All ER 714 at 724). This analysis was said by Lord Irvine of Lairg QC ([1996] PL 59, 73) to be part right, part wrong: it was for the court to decide whether a legitimate expectation existed and what it required, but only on grounds of reasonableness could the court review whether a decision-maker (who had properly recognised a legitimate expectation) could decide that there was a public interest which should override the substantive expectation.

8.84   At one stage it seemed that the divergence of view had been resolved by the Court of Appeal in *R v Secretary of State for the Home Department, ex p Hargreaves*,[1] overruling the reasoning of Sedley J and holding that a clear distinction must be maintained between review by the court of matters of substance and review of procedure: a legitimate expectation did not entitle the court to judge the fairness of a decision of substance. On the basis of this decision, in English law[2] a legitimate expectation would confer a right to be heard before any change of policy or practice, but in relation to review of the substance of the decision would not constitute anything more than a factor to be taken into account when evaluating a challenge for unreasonableness.

[1] [1997] 1 WLR 906, [1997] 1 All ER 397. See Himsworth [1996] PL 590.

[2] For the position in Australia, see *Minister for Immigration and Ethnic Affairs v Teoh* (1995) 69 ALJR 423. In New Zealand, see *Northern Roller Milling Co Ltd v Commerce Commission* [1994] 2 NZLR 747, criticised by Poole, 'Legitimate Expectation and Substantive Fairness: Beyond the Limits of Procedural Propriety' [1995] NZ Law Review 426. As to whether a doctrine of legitimate expectation assists domestic protection of human rights, see Hunt. *Using Human Rights in English Courts* (1997), pp 253–259.

8.85 However, the Court of Appeal in *R v North and East Devon Health Authority, ex p Coughlan*[1] held that the principle, apparently earlier embraced in *Hargreaves*, to the effect that the court would only enforce expectations as to procedure as opposed to expectations of a substantive benefit, was wrongly framed. The health authority provided specialist accommodation for the severely disabled at Mardon House, where the applicant was resident. It published eligibility criteria as to when long-term 'specialist' nursing services should be provided by the health authority as opposed to 'general' nursing care which should be purchased by local authorities. Purporting to apply those criteria, it decided to close Mardon House and to transfer the long-term general nursing care of the applicant to the local authority, although no alternative placement for her was identified. Hidden J quashed the decision to close Mardon House, holding among other things that the applicant and other patients had been given a clear promise that Mardon House would be their home for life and the health authority had not established an overriding public interest which justified it in breaking that promise. The Court of Appeal held that the closure decision was unlawful because it depended on a misinterpretation by the health authority of its responsibilities. It also held that if a public body exercising a statutory function made a promise as to how it would behave in the future which induced a legitimate expectation of a benefit which was substantive, rather than merely procedural, to frustrate that expectation could be so unfair that it would amount to an abuse of power; that, in such circumstances, the court had to determine whether there was a sufficient overriding interest to justify a departure from what had previously been promised; that in view of the importance of the promise to the applicant, the fact that it was limited to a few individuals and that the consequences to the health authority of honouring it were likely to be financial only, the applicant had a legitimate expectation that the health authority would not resile from its promise unless there was an overreaching justification for doing so; and that, in the circumstances, including the fact that the quality of the alternative accommodation to be offered to the applicant was not known, the closure decision was an unjustified breach of that promise which constituted unfairness amounting to an abuse of power.

[1] [2001] QB 213.

8.86 In recognising that a breach of promise may be so unfair as to constitute a reviewable abuse of power, the court in *Coughlan* was following a well-trodden path, discussed below. In that context it has given an enhanced role to the concept of legitimate expectation, and it is convenient to examine this as part of a more general discussion of unfair departure from promises, assurances or representations.

Unfair departure from promises, assurances or representations

8.87 In *Preston v IRC*[1] it was affirmed by Lord Scarman that the unfairness of administrative action could be relevant in determining whether what was done was ultra vires or unlawful.[2] Lord Templeman indicated[3] that there may be unfairness amounting to an abuse of power if the conduct of the body in question would amount to a breach of contract or estoppel by representation. The circumstances which might amount to such an abuse were explored in subsequent cases, most of which involved the Inland Revenue Commissioners, and the general trend of which has been to loosen rather than strengthen any direct link to contract or estoppel.[4] It was held not to be an abuse to revoke an authorisation when further matters had come to notice which led to doubts about whether it had been right to give the authorisation.[5] Bingham LJ has said[6] that generally a statement formally published by the Inland Revenue to the world may safely be regarded as binding, subject to its terms, in any case falling clearly within them;[7] while in a case where the approach to the Revenue is of a less formal nature a more detailed inquiry is necessary, and certain conditions must be fulfilled if a taxpayer is to succeed in saying that the Inland Revenue has agreed or represented that it will forgo tax which might arguably be payable. First, taxpayers must 'put all [their] cards face upwards on the table'.[8] Second, it is necessary that the ruling or statement relied upon be clear, unambiguous and devoid of relevant qualification.[9] Judge J, in the same case, stated:[10]

> 'Abuse of power may take the form of unfairness. This is not mere "unfairness" in the general sense. Even if "unfair", efficient performance of the statutory obligations imposed on the Revenue will not, of itself, amount to an abuse of power'.

---

[1] [1985] AC 835.

[2] [1985] AC 835 at 852; see, also, the statement of Lord Mustill in *R v IRC, ex p Matrix-Securities Ltd* [1994] 1 WLR 334 at 358 that the spirit of fair dealing 'should inspire the whole of public life'.

[3] [1985] AC 835 at 866, referring to *HTV Ltd v Price Commission* [1976] ICR 170 and the authorities there cited.

[4] Vitally important, of course, will be the statutory context. An argument that the giving of assurances on behalf of the Commissioners was contrary to their statutory duty was rejected in *R v IRC, ex p MFK Underwriting Agencies Ltd* [1990] 1 WLR 1545.

[5] *R v IRC, ex p Camacq Corpn* [1990] 1 WLR 191.

[6] In *R v IRC, ex p MFK Underwriting Agencies Ltd* [1990] 1 WLR 1545.

[7] A claim was made in *R v IRC, ex p S G Warburg & Co Ltd* [1994] STC 518 that a change in valuation policy fell within a statement of practice: the court rejected an assertion that failure by the revenue to apply the statement of practice was an abuse of power, holding instead that the revenue decision (that the new basis of valuation was outside the statement) was not unreasonable and therefore was not open to challenge.

[8] This means ([1990] 1 WLR 1545 at 1569) giving full details of the specific transaction (unless identical to an earlier transaction on which a ruling has been given), indicating the ruling sought (distinguishing between seeking agreement as to a view of the law and asking whether the revenue will forgo any claim to tax on any other basis), making plain that a fully considered ruling is sought, indicating the use intended to be made of any ruling given (in particular because knowledge that a ruling is to be publicised in a particular market could affect the person by whom and the level at which a problem is considered, and whether it is

appropriate to give a ruling at all). Other cases where full disclosure has been emphasised include *Re Preston* [1985] AC 835 and *R v IRC, ex p Matrix-Securities Ltd* [1994] 1 WLR 334.

9   *R v IRC, ex p MFK Underwriting Agencies Ltd* [1990] 1 WLR 1545, 1569. See, also, *R v Jockey Club, ex p RAM Racecourses Ltd* [1993] 2 All ER 225, where the Divisional Court held that in the circumstances of that case, in addition to the need for a clear and unambiguous representation, the applicant must be within a class of persons entitled to rely on it (or at any rate show that it was reasonable to rely on it without more), must have relied on it, and must have done so to its detriment; if these hurdles were surmounted by the applicant, the respondent could nevertheless deprive the applicant of success by showing that there was an overriding interest arising from its duties and responsibilities which entitled it to change its policy to the detriment of the applicant. In *R v O'Kane and Clarke, ex p Northern Bank* [1996] STC 1249 it was held that representations made by the Revenue were not assurances about the way in which a particular statutory provision would be operated, with the result that no legitimate expectation arose; as to the judge's conclusions on the true construction of the statutory provisions, see *R v IRC, ex p Ulster Bank Ltd* [1997] STC 832, CA. In *R v IRC, ex p Allen* [1997] STC 1141, the applicant's accountant had previously been employed by the Revenue: the court held that his knowledge of unpublished internal policy derived from that employment could not represent the touchstone of conduct between the Inland Revenue and a taxpayer. In *R (Niazi) v Secretary of State for the Home Department* [2008] EWCA Civ 75, the fact that a code of practice governing consultations existed meant that meant that it was to apply whenever it was decided as a matter of policy to have a public consultation, not that public consultation was a required prelude to every decision made. In *AA (Pakistan) v Secretary of State for the Home Department* [2009] UKAIT 3, the claimant's argued that the introduction of a Highly Skilled Migrant Workers programme as a control on immigration breached their legitimate expectation that the rules current when they first applied for entry to the UK would continue to apply to them. Dismissing that argument, the need for a promise or represenation was reiterated, but the Trinunal stated that, in deciding what, if any, promise or representation was made, an objective approach was required, *i.e.* reading the documents on which the expectation was said to be based not in an excessively self-serving way and having regard to its context.

10   *R v IRC, ex p MFK Underwriting Agencies Ltd* [1990] 1 WLR 1545 at 1573.

8.88 In a subsequent case which reached the House of Lords, a claim that the Inland Revenue was bound by an assurance given by an inspector of taxes failed (among other reasons) on the ground that the taxpayer knew that the assurance should have been sought from a specialist division.[1] The Commissioner of Inland Revenue in Hong Kong was held by the Privy Council in relation to one company not to have made any representation by an alleged failure to assess and collect tax when due, and in relation to another company not to be bound by an exemption given in specific circumstances which that company erroneously assumed would continue to apply in different circumstances.[2] The Commissioners of Customs and Excise were held not to be entitled to resile without notice and with immediate effect from an assurance that the deadline for certain claims would not take effect until a future date: and this was so despite the Government's intention to introduce legislation to alter the deadline.[3] By contrast, where there has been a change in the law, or a new judicial interpretation of the law, then the Commissioners were not bound by assurances given in different circumstances based on a different view of the law which has been held to be mistaken.[4] It is to be emphasised, moreover, that the statement of a policy does not of itself preclude a later change in that policy, provided always that the adopted policy is a lawful exercise of the relevant discretion.[5]

1   *R v IRC, ex p Matrix-Securities Ltd* [1994] 1 WLR 334 at 346, 356–357 (per Lords Griffiths and Browne-Wilkinson) and 355 (per Lord Jauncey of Tullichettle, holding that it would not be unfair to revoke a clearance which 'did not bear to have been given with the authority of' the specialist division). Lord Jauncey decided the case primarily on the ground that there had

not been full disclosure (355–356), Lord Templeman (346) held that the taxpayer's disclosure had been inaccurate and misleading, and Lord Mustill (358) approached the matter on a broader front, taking into account all aspects of the exchanges between the parties, including their timing, the level of communication, the complexity of the scheme and its documentation, and the guarded terms of the letters.

2   *Harley Development Inc v IRC* [1996] 1 WLR 727.

3   *R v Customs and Excise Comrs, ex p Kay & Co* [1996] STC 1500 at 1522–1528.

4   *R v Customs and Excise Comrs, ex p Littlewoods Home Shopping Group Ltd* [1997] STC 317.

5   *Re Findlay* [1985] AC 318 at 338 (Lord Scarman); *R v Secretary of State for the Home Department, ex p Ruddock* [1987] 1 WLR 1482 at 1487; *R v Secretary of State for Health, ex p US Tobacco* [1992] QB 353, where it was held that a moral commitment to a single company could not prevail over the public interest; *R v Secretary of State for the Home Department, ex p Hargreaves* [1997] 1 All ER 397; *R v Customs and Excise Comrs, ex p Littlewoods Home Shopping Group Ltd* [1997] STC 317. Similarly, it was accepted in *R v Secretary of State for the Home Department, ex p Moon* (1995) 8 Admin LR 477 at 484 that in deciding that exclusion of a person from the United Kingdom would be conducive to the public good the Secretary of State is entitled to take the view that an earlier finding by an adjudicator has been overtaken by events. In *R (Fisher) v English Nature* [2004] 1 WLR 503, Lightman J held that statutory provisions concerning sites of special scientific interest conferred no discretion but required English Nature to decide whether certain criteria were met in accordance with its expert judgement. It followed that the decision-maker's duty could not be qualified by its own past practice or guidelines, which could not constrain (but might inform) the decision-maker in reaching its judgement. In *R (Mullen) v Secretary of State for the Home Department* [2005] 1 AC 1 the Secretary of State was held entitled to depart from policy, having first given the claimant the opportunity to argue against this course.

8.89 Much less emphasis is now being placed upon the private law concepts which were identified by Lord Templeman in *Preston*.[1] More recently, Lord Hoffman in *R (Reprotech (Pebsham) Ltd) v East Sussex County Council* said[2] that in this area, 'public law has already absorbed whatever is useful from the moral values which underlie the private law concept of estoppel and the time has come for it to stand upon its own two feet'. Lord Hoffmann had earlier discussed the relevant public law principles in this way:[3]

'There is of course an analogy between a private law estoppel and the public law concept of a legitimate expectation created by a public authority, the denial of which may amount to an abuse of power: see *R v North and East Devon Health Authority, ex p Coughlan* [2001] QB 213. But it is no more than an analogy because remedies against public authorities also have to take into account the interests of the general public which the authority exists to promote. Public law can also take into account the hierarchy of individual rights which exist under the Human Rights Act 1998, so that, for example, the individual's right to a home is accorded a high degree of protection (see *Coughlan's* case, at pp 254–255) while ordinary property rights are in general far more limited by considerations of public interest: see *R (Alconbury Developments Ltd) v Secretary of State for the Environment, Transport and the Regions* [2001] 2 WLR 1389'.

1   See *Preston v IRC* [1985] AC 835.

2   [2003] 1 WLR 348 at paragraph 35, p 358; Lords Nicholls, Mackay, Hope and Scott agreed with Lord Hoffmann, Lord Mackay commenting at paragraph 6, p 351, that if 'public law in this area . . . stand[s] upon its own two feet . . . greater clarity will result than if it is treated as standing upon some less discrete base'.

3   At paragraph 34, p 358.

8.90 In the *Reprotech* case the claimant failed on its legitimate expectation claim because the resolution it relied upon was not a representation that any determination had been made, it could not have been a representation that it was, and the parties had not acted on the basis of any agreed assumption. This conclusion reflects the nature of the claimant's arguments, which focused on estoppel, and should not be regarded as a decision that one or other of these features must be present in order to found a case based on abuse of power in public law. Keene LJ commented in *South Bucks DC v Flanagan*[1] that in *Reprotech* the House saw the earlier cases where estoppel had been applied in planning law as an attempt to achieve justice at a time when the concepts of legitimate expectation and abuse of power had scarcely made their appearance in public law. Now that those concepts are recognised, there was no longer a place for the private law doctrine of estoppel in public law or for the attendant problems which it brings with it.[2]

[1]   [2002] 1 WLR 2601 at 2607, paragraph 16.
[2]   However, estoppel is the basis of the doctrine of ostensible authority, and thus may still have a part to play on the question whether a representation gives rise to a legitimate expectation, as discussed in the text which follows.

8.91 Building on the decision in *Coughlan*, the Court of Appeal in *R (Bibi) v Newham LBC*[1] analysed legitimate expectation cases generally. It was said that whether review was substantive or procedural, three practical questions arise. The first question was, 'To what has the public authority, whether by practice or by promise, committed itself?' The second was whether the authority had acted or proposed to act unlawfully in relation to its commitment. The third is what the court should do. (These questions are dealt with in the procedural context in CHAPTER 11.) In the following paragraphs these three questions are examined.

[1]   [2002] 1 WLR 237. The analysis was preceded by two observations (paragraph 18, p 244): 'The case law is replete with words such as "legitimate" and "fair", "abuse of power" and "inconsistent with good administration". When reading the judgments care needs to be taken to distinguish analytical tools from conclusions which encapsulate value judgments but do not give any indication of the route to those conclusions'.

8.92 On the first question it was said that it was generally appropriate to consider the issue of legitimacy in this context. In other words, if the public body had done nothing and said nothing which could legitimately have generated the expectation that is advanced to the court, the case would end there.[1] It seemed likely that a representation made without lawful power would be in this class.[2] It may be noted here that in *R (Association of British Civilian Internees: Far East Region) v Secretary of State for Defence* the Court of Appeal commented:[3]

'It will be only in an exceptional case that a claim that a legitimate expectation has been defeated will succeed in the absence of a clear and unequivocal representation. That is because it will only be in a rare case where, absent such a representation, it can be said that a decision-maker will have acted with conspicuous unfairness such as to amount to an abuse of power. In the *Unilever* case, the taxpayer had, in effect, been lulled into a false sense of security, and had regulated its tax affairs in reliance on the Revenue's course of conduct, and thereby acted to its detriment. In those circumstances, and in the light of the Revenue's acceptance of its duty to act fairly and in accordance with the highest public standards, it is not surprising that the court felt able to treat this as a wholly exceptional case'.

[1]   Cf. *AA (Pakistan) v Secretary of State for the Home Department* [2009] UKAIT 3, it was said that the correct approach when determining whether a statement had given rise to a legitimate

expectation (on the facts, guidance by the Secretary of State) was: 'to ask "'what would a reasonable reader of the guidance understand was being said?" That reader will not approach the guidance in a pedantic, overly analytical way but will read it sensibly and not in an excessively self-serving way necessarily ignoring or resolving ambiguities in their own favour. In addition, the reasonable reader will bear in mind the context in which the guidance is issued. It should be readily apparent to anyone that immigration policy reflects the Government and Parliament's current view of the public interest.'

2   *Bibi* at paragraph 21, p 244. In *South Bucks DC v Flanagan* [2002] 1 WLR 2601 it was conceded that a legitimate expectation based on a representation allegedly made on behalf of a public body can only arise if the person making the representation as to that body's future conduct has actual or ostensible authority to make it on its behalf.

3   [2003] QB 1397 at 1423, paragraph 72.

8.93 The court in *Bibi*[1] said that to a degree the answer to the second question depended on the approach one took to the first. As Laws LJ pointed out in *R v Secretary of State for Education and Employment, ex p Begbie*:[2]

'The more the decision challenged lies in what may inelegantly be called the macro-political field, the less intrusive will be the court's supervision. More than this: in that field, true abuse of power is less likely to be found, since within it changes of policy, fuelled by broad conceptions of the public interest, may more readily be accepted as taking precedence over the interests of groups which enjoyed expectations generated by an earlier policy'.

1   Paragraph 23, p 244.
2   [2000] 1 WLR 1115, 1131.

8.94 When considering (for the purposes of this second question) whether the authority has acted unlawfully, the court in *Bibi*[1] noted attempts to find a formulation which will provide a test for all cases. It warned that history showed that wide-ranging formulations, while capable of producing a just result in the individual case, were seen later to have needlessly constricted the development of the law. The *Begbie* case indicated that reliance, though potentially relevant in most cases, is not essential. In that case a letter sent to the parents of one child affected by legislative and policy changes concerning assisted school places came to the knowledge of another child's parent, who relied on it in judicial review proceedings.[2] The court added that where one is dealing with a promise made by an authority, a major part of the problem is that it is often not adequate to look at the situation purely from the point of view of the disappointed promisee who comes to the court with a perfectly natural grievance. Sometimes many promises have been made to many different persons each of which has induced a reasonable expectation of a substantive benefit for that person but all of which promises cannot be fulfilled. On any view, if an authority, without even considering the fact that it is in breach of a promise which had given rise to a legitimate expectation that it would be honoured, made a decision to adopt a course of action at variance with that promise then the authority was abusing its powers.[3]

1   Paragraphs 25–28, p 245.
2   The court at paragraph 32, p 246 also cited *R (Zeqiri) v Secretary of State for the Home Department* [2001] 1 EWCA Civ 342; [2002] Imm AR 42 as a case where the court proceeded on the basis that Zeqiri had a legitimate expectation that, in the events as they had turned out in relation to the test case, his application for asylum would be determined in this country and concluded that change of position or reliance on the part of Zequiri did not need to be shown. At paragraph 53ff, p 250, the court added that the fact that someone has not changed his position after a promise has been made to him does not mean that he has not relied on the

promise. An actor in a play where another actor points a gun at him may refrain from changing his position just because he has been given a promise that the gun only contains blanks. *Bibi* itself was seen as a case of reliance with moral, but not concrete, detriment. The moral detriment mattered because, among other things, to disregard the legitimate expectation because no concrete detriment can be shown would be to place the weakest in society at a particular disadvantage.

3   Paragraphs 35–36 and 39, pp 247–248.

8.95 As to the functions of the court on the second and third questions, the court in *Bibi* said[1] it was a mistake to isolate from the rest of administrative law cases those which turn on representations made by authorities. The same constitutional principles applied to the exercise by the court of each of these two functions. On the third question it commented:

> 'The court, even where it finds that the applicant has a legitimate expectation of some benefit, will not order the authority to honour its promise where to do so would be to assume the powers of the executive. Once the court has established such an abuse it may ask the decision taker to take the legitimate expectation properly into account in the decision making process'.

1   Paragraphs 40–41, p 248.

8.96 Overall on the third question the court said that while in some cases there could be only one lawful ultimate answer to the question whether the authority should honour its promise, at any rate in cases involving a legitimate expectation of a substantive benefit, this would not invariably be the case.[1] Relevant factors included the possibility of monetary compensation or assistance. At issue in *Bibi* was the allocation of secure housing, and the defendant pressed the court with the effect on others on the housing list of giving the present applicants special preference. The court commented that, while this was ostensibly powerful, it faced the obstacle that nothing unlawful would necessarily be involved in allocating secure housing to the applicants.

1   Paragraph 43, p 248.

Unfair treatment inconsistent with that afforded to others

8.97 There are a number of laws which prohibit discrimination in certain contexts and on certain grounds.[1] Those laws are supplemented to some extent by the common law. It was said by Lord Russell of Killowen CJ in *Kruse v Johnson*[2] that a decision is unreasonable if it is partial and unequal in its operation as between different classes. This example has a nineteenth-century ring, but it is reflected in more modern times by the principle of equality in European law.[3] It has been applied by the Divisional Court in striking down a condition imposed by a local authority which prohibited participation by those affiliated with political parties at events to be held in the authority's parks.[4] The principle was also applied by Simon Brown J in the *Manshoora* case.[5] Plainly, in many cases it will be the duty of a decision-maker to discriminate between those who are, and those who are not, entitled to benefit from the exercise of statutory powers. The vice exists where the discrimination

257

is 'partial and unequal' or arbitrary in the sense that it is not founded upon any rational distinction between the classes in question. Thus, here too, the court is concerned to examine for unreasonableness the evaluation made by the decision-maker.[6]

[1]   In particular, the Equality Act 2010, Article 14 of the ECHR, and the EU principle of equality.

[2]   [1898] 2 QB 91.

[3]   See CHAPTER 15 below.

[4]   *R v Barnet London Borough Council, ex p Johnson* (1989) 88 LGR 73, where Parker LJ added at p 84 that the condition was thus outside the statutory purpose. The decision was upheld on appeal (1990) 89 LGR 581, where it was stressed that the Divisional Court had not held that any political condition would be discriminatory.

[5]   [1986] Imm AR 385; this case, and the *Barnet* case (note 3 above), demonstrate that the word 'classes' refers to any division in society.

[6]   *R (E) v Nottinghamshire Healthcare NHS Trust (Equality and Human Rights Commission intervening)* [2010] PTSR 674 at 90. In *R (Mahmood) v Royal Pharmaceutical Society of Great Britain* [2002] 1 WLR 879, the Court of Appeal was concerned with byelaws as to the registration of pharmacists, which in some cases but not others required that an examination be passed at the third attempt; an assertion of arbitrary discrimination failed because the distinction giving rise to the requirement was not irrational. See, also, *R v Ministry of Agriculture Fisheries and Food, ex p Humble (Offshore) Fisheries Ltd* and cases on even-handedness (discussed below).

8.98 In more modern times it has often been stated to be a principle of public law that an authority charged with the duty of exercising its discretion must do so fairly and consistently.[1] However, this does not mandate any rigid approach, for the decision-maker must be entitled (while recognising the importance of acting even-handedly) to take account of the differences in individual cases, and each case will need to be considered in the light of its own facts.[2] Thus when an assertion was made that the Inland Revenue could only lawfully decide to prosecute some, but not all, of those involved in criminal tax evasion if there were distinguishing features which made the cases of those prosecuted more serious than the others, the assertion failed: it was inconsistent with the Inland Revenue's policy of selective prosecution, and it was impracticable.[3] Similarly unsuccessful was an attempt to extend the duty of fairness so that when the Inland Revenue published a Statement of Practice it was obliged retrospectively to assist those taxpayers who took decisions which would have been different if they had known of the statement: the taxpayer had taken a considered decision and to hold otherwise would be to discourage the Inland Revenue from publishing any helpful statement of clarification.[4] In another case the court stated that in the absence of reliance by the applicant on a consistent practice on the part of the Inland Revenue, the existence of such a practice would not provide a ground in public law for other taxpayers to assert that the practice should be repeated in their favour.[5]

[1]   *HTV Ltd v Price Commission* [1976] ICR 170 at 185–186, 191–192; *Re Preston* [1985] AC 835 at 864–867, [1985] 2 All ER 327 at 329–341; *IRC v National Federation of Self-Employed and Small Businesses Ltd* [1982] AC 617 at 651, [1981] 2 All ER 93, 112; *R v IRC, ex p Mead* [1993] 1 All ER 772 at 783. See the discussion of exceptions to policy at **8.79–8.81** above; also Steyn, 'Consistency – A Principle of Public Law?' [1997] JR 22. In *R (Rashid) v Secretary of State for the Home Department* [2005] EWCA Civ 744, [2005] Imm AR 608, a failure to apply the correct policy led to the quashing of the relevant decision for unfairness. See *FH (Bangladesh) v Secretary of State for the Home Department* [2009] EWCA Civ 385; [2010] Imm AR 3, where 'culpable and undue delay' by the Secretary of State had led to unfairness; see also *R (Matembera) v Secretary of State for the Home Department* [2007] EWHC 2334 (Admin).

2   *Isaac v Minister of Consumer Affairs* [1990] 2 NZLR 606; *R v IRC, ex p Mead* [1993]
    1 All ER 772 at 783. In *R v Secretary of State for Education, ex p C* [1996] ELR 93 Schiemann
    J said that in a borderline case, it was not irrational even for the same person to make different
    assessments of the same facts as different times.
3   *R v IRC, ex p Mead* [1993] 1 All ER 772, per Stuart-Smith LJ at 783 and per Popplewell J at
    785 (agreeing that on the facts the application should be dismissed).
4   *R v IRC, ex p Kaye* [1992] STC 581 at 589.
5   *R v IRC, ex p S G Warburg & Co Ltd* [1994] STC 518 at 541–542. In fact the court held that
    no such practice had been shown to exist. The argument on the part of the Inland Revenue
    asserting the necessity for reliance was based on the assertion that the relevant analogy from
    private law was estoppel by representation (p 535): compare, however, Simon
    Brown LJ's warning about analogies from private law in *R v IRC, ex p Unilever plc* [1996]
    STC 681 at 695.

8.99 If one of the relevant articles of the European Convention on Human
Rights is in play then an issue of law may arise under the Human Rights Act
1998 as to whether the decision has contravened the prohibition on discrimination in art 14.[1] More generally, there may be scope to argue that the broader
provisions found in the International Covenant on Civil and Political Rights
can be relied on.[2]

1   See the discussion at **8.59** above. In *R (Association of British Civilian Internees: Far East
    Region) v Secretary of State for Defence* [2003] QB 1397, it was common ground that freedom
    from discrimination under art 14 was not free-standing: the question at issue must fall within
    the scope of one or more of the substantive provisions of the Convention before art 14 can be
    engaged. In this context, the Court of Appeal went on to hold at p 1426, paragraph 82, that
    claims which have been held to be without foundation cannot be possessions which are linked
    to, or within the scope of, art 1 of the First Protocol.
2   See the paragraphs cited in note 1 above, and the decision of the Privy Council in *Matadeen
    v Pointu* [1999] 1 AC 98 at 115–116, holding that the power to quash the Minister's decision
    as unreasonable would have been entirely adequate to secure compliance with the equal
    treatment provisions of art 26 of the Covenant. Lord Hoffmann, in that case, said at p 108 that
    the fact that equality of treatment is a general principle of rational behaviour does not entail
    that it should necessarily be a justiciable principle – that it should always be the judges who
    have the last word on whether the principle has been observed. In *R (Association of British
    Civilian Internees: Far East Region) v Secretary of State for Defence* [2003] QB 1397,
    the Court of Appeal doubted whether Lord Hoffmann envisaged a free-standing principle
    separate from the requirement of reasonableness, and added (p 1427, paragraph 86) that if a
    free-standing principle of equality were to be applied, it would have to be on the basis that the
    court would give the Minister a margin of appreciation to determine what was a valid reason
    for treating internees differently.

Other unfair abuses of power

8.100 The cases dealt with in the preceding paragraphs are not the only
circumstances in which unfairness may amount to an abuse of power. In *R v
IRC, ex p Unilever plc*,[1] both the taxpayer and the Inland Revenue had, for
many years, shared an honest error as to the applicability of a time limit. When
the Inland Revenue, without notice, sought to rely on the time limit in
circumstances where it had suffered no prejudice, the Court of Appeal held
that reliance on the time limit was an abuse of power. Sir Thomas Bingham MR said:[2]

'the categories of unfairness are not closed, and precedent should act as a guide not
a cage. Each case must be judged on its own facts, bearing in mind the Rev-

enue's unqualified acceptance of a duty to act fairly and in accordance with the highest public standards".'

1 [1996] STC 681. See Bamforth, (1997) 56 CLJ 1.
2 [1996] STC 681 at 690. See, also, *R (Bibi) v Newham LBC* [2002] 1 WLR 237 at paragraph 27, p 245.

Substantive unfairness: a separate ground of review?

8.101 The principles developed by the courts concerning abuse of power, in the sense analysed above, can readily be placed under the umbrella of review for unreasonableness. Those cases where abuse of power of this kind has been shown to exist are *a fortiori* cases where the decision-maker has gone beyond the limits of reason. Conversely, those cases where allegations of abuse of power have failed have involved decisions falling within the limits of reason. In this way 'abuse of power' can be seen as an example of unreasonableness. Thus, in *R v IRC, ex p Unilever plc*, Sir Thomas Bingham MR,[1] having found in favour of the applicant that there had been an unfair abuse of power, thought that a claim based on unreasonableness did not in truth raise any new point. In the same case Simon Brown LJ said:

> '"unfairness amounting to abuse of power" as envisaged in Preston and the other Revenue cases is unlawful not because it involves conduct such as would offend some equivalent private law principle, not principally indeed because it breaches a legitimate expectation that some different substantive decision will be taken, but rather because it is illogical or immoral or both for a public authority to act with conspicuous unfairness and in that sense abuse its power'.

1 [1996] STC 681, 692.

8.102 It is consistent with these remarks to conclude that the line of cases which has developed since *Preston* is no more than a development of review for unreasonableness as analysed in *CCSU*. Sir Thomas Bingham's statement that precedent should act as a guide not a cage has validity, not only in cases involving allegations of unfair abuse of power, but also in relation generally to the principles upon which the court approaches review for unreasonableness. Those principles will enable the courts to determine in any particular case whether an unfair abuse of power has been shown to exist. Matters such as the extent of reliance by, and detriment to, the claimant, and willingness on the part of the defendant to compensate for particular types of loss suffered by the claimant)[1] may form part of the evaluation of reasonableness.

1 This aspect was mentioned by Lord Griffiths in *R v IRC, ex p Matrix-Securities* [1994] 1 WLR 334, 346–347.

Chapter 9

PROPORTIONALITY

INTRODUCTION

Scope of this chapter

9.1 This chapter addresses the role and application of the principle of
proportionality in the context of judicial review. Proportionality is a concept
that has become increasingly important in British public law over recent years,
although initially it was incorporated into domestic adjudication only grudg-
ingly, and often because European obligations required it.1 Judicial review
jurisprudence toyed with the idea of adopting it as a general principle,2 but
proportionality first really took hold in areas heavily influenced by European
Union law, such as indirect discrimination.3 However, the Human Rights Act
1998 (HRA) has made proportionality a much more common doctrine in
judicial review cases. This chapter examines how far proportionality has come
and where it currently stands. It first explains the genesis of the principle in
European law, as well as its place in the legal regimes of the European Union
(EU) and the European Convention on Human Rights (ECHR). It then sets out
the various 'tests' of proportionality, their logic, and the structure of the

proportionality analysis in its most refined form. The chapter next explores in more detail where these tests fit within domestic judicial review, first with regard to the application of EU law and then, through the HRA, the ECHR jurisprudence of the European Court of Human Rights (ECtHR). A final section considers the progress of proportionality as a free—standing ground for review in the UK. First, however, this Introduction provides an overview of the nature of the principle of proportionality, the different uses to which it is put, and terminology that is required to discuss it.[1] Judicial review jurisprudence toyed with the idea of adopting it as a general principle,[2] but proportionality first really took hold in areas heavily influenced by European Union law, such as indirect discrimination.[3] However, the Human Rights Act 1998 (HRA) has made proportionality a much more common doctrine in judicial review cases. This chapter examines how far proportionality has come and where it currently stands. It first explains the genesis of the principle in European law, as well as its place in the legal regimes of the European Union (EU) and the European Convention on Human Rights (ECHR). It then sets out the various 'tests' of proportionality, their logic, and the structure of the proportionality analysis in its most refined form. The chapter next explores in more detail where these tests fit within domestic judicial review, first with regard to the application of EU law and then, through the HRA, the ECHR jurisprudence of the European Court of Human Rights (ECtHR). A final section considers the progress of proportionality as a free–standing ground for review in the UK. First, however, this Introduction provides an overview of the nature of the principle of proportionality, the different uses to which it is put, and terminology that is required to discuss it.

[1] *R (Daly) v. Home Secretary* [2001] UKHL 26, [26], [27], [32]; *R (Brind) v Home Secretary* [1991] 1 AC 696, 766–767; Hunt, Using Human Rights Law in English Courts (1998).

[2] *R (Pegasus Holdings (London) Ltd) v Transport Secretary* [1988] 1 WLR 990.

[3] *Allonby v Accrington and Rossendale College* [2001] IRLR 364, [23]–[29]; Ellis, 'Proportionality in European Community Sex Discrimination Law' in Ellis (ed) *The Principle of Proportionality in the Laws of Europe* (1999), 170–172.

Overview of proportionality as a principle

9.2 Proportionality in the judicial review context is largely concerned with controlling invasions of rights. The principle also arises in deciding the propriety of penalties[1] or the permissibility of disappointing a legitimate expectation.[2] However, for the purposes of this chapter proportionality should be understood as a test of when, and to what extent, the state may encroach on a protected right. In this role proportionality defines the content of rights: the extent and contours of the protection afforded by the ECHR or EU Treaty against state interference. In its simplest sense, proportionality is the principle that the harms of a state measure, in terms of its invasion of a right or its impact on the right holder, must not outweigh the importance of the measure in terms of the aim it pursues and its efficacy in pursuing it.[3] Put another way, a measure must not be disproportionate to its impacts, requiring that there be a balance between the state's need for the measure and its effects. In practice proportionality is not always applied in this simple way. Courts have developed multi-step tests, ostensibly designed to ensure that rights receive an appropriate weight in the balancing exercise.

1   *R (Smith) v Ministry of Defence* [1995] 1 All ER 256; Craig 'Unreasonableness and Proportionality in UK Law,' in Ellis (ed) *The Principle of Proportionality in the Laws of Europe* (1999).

2   *R (MFK Underwriting Agents) v Inland Revenue Commissioners* [1990] 1 WLR 1545; *R (Unilever) v Inland Revenue Commissioners* (1996) 68 Tax Cases 205.

3   *Bank Mellat v Her Majesty's Treasury (No 2)* [2013] UKSC 39 [74]; A and Ors v Home Secretary [2004] UKHL 56, [50]; Ghaidan v Godin-Mendoza [2004] UKHL 30, [19]–[20]; National Union of Belgian Police v Belgium 1 EHRR 578, [49] (1975).

9.3 Proportionality comes to European jurisprudence through German law,[1] which developed a doctrine of proportionality requiring that state acts or measures be (1) suitable to achieve a legitimate purpose, (2) necessary to achieve that purpose, and (3) proportional in the narrower sense: they must not impose burdens or 'cause harms to other legitimate interests' that outweigh the objectives achieved.[2] 'Proportionality in the narrower sense' (proportionality *stricto sensu*), became the foundation of the ECHR analysis in the Belgian Linguistics case, which was the first mention of the doctrine of proportionality by the ECtHR.[3] This basic European principle of proportionality requires that invasions of a right impose no greater restrictions on the right (or on 'rights interests') than can be balanced out by the need of the state to invade the right; the state's 'need' refers not only to the importance of the objective but to the 'need' for the particular means employed to achieve it. This principle is now slightly more refined than pure proportionality stricto sensu, while more complicated formulations are essentially structured analyses intended to ensure the observation of the principle.

1   British decisions frequently refer to Canadian jurisprudence as the source of the proportionality test used by British courts, but that test, as well as the jurisprudence which predominantly requires its application, adopted proportionality from German law. See *Bank Mellat v Her Majesty's Treasury (No 2)* [2013] UKSC 39 [68]–[74]. R (MFK Underwriting Agents) v Inland Revenue Commissioners [1990] 1 WLR 1545 Bank Mellat v Her Majesty's Treasury (No 2) [2013] UKSC 39 [74].

2   Lord Hoffmann, '*The Influence of the European Principle of Proportionality upon UK Law*' in Ellis (ed) *The Principle of Proportionality in the Laws of Europe* (1999), 107.

3   *Belgian Linguistics* (1968) 1 EHRR 252 [10]; Eissen, 'The Principle of Proportionality in the Case Law of the European Court of Human Rights,' in Macdonald, Matscher & Petzold (eds) *The European System for the Protection of Human Rights* (1993), 140.

9.4 Proportionality *stricto sensu* is also included in the CJEU understanding of proportionality, but is sometimes far less emphasised, depending on the area of law concerned. In the context of indirect discrimination, for example, the CJEU adopts a structured analysis involving 'real need' and necessity.[1] Such a test rests on a presumption that invasion of a right has substantial weight in the balancing exercise. A justification cannot outweigh this impact unless at least

(a)   the state has a real need to achieve a particular aim, and
(b)   the measure it employs to achieve it is necessary, in the sense of representing the least restrictive alternative.

Thus the CJEU approach guarantees proportionality by requiring a level of scrutiny that goes beyond striking an ad hoc balance, in effect giving rights a presumptively high weight by approving as justified only means necessary to meet a real need of the state. The CJEU test in the context of competition law has been set out in even more exacting detail, such that to satisfy proportionality

> 'the measure:
> (1)   must be effective to achieve the legitimate aim in question (appropriate),
> (2)   must be no more onerous than is required to achieve that aim (necessary),
> (3)   must be the least onerous, if there is a choice of equally effective measures, and
> (4)   in any event must not produce adverse effects which are disproportionate to the aim pursued.'[2]

[1]   *Cadman v Health and Safety Executive* [2006] ICR 1623, 1635–1639, 1647; see also Green, 'Proportionality and the Sovereignty of Parliament in the UK', in Ellis (ed) *The Principle of Proportionality in the Laws of Europe* (1999), 146.

[2]   *BAA Ltd v Competition Commission* [2009] CAT 35 [137]. See *R v Minister of Agriculture, Fisheries and Food, ex p Fedesa (Case C-331/88) EU:C:1990:391*, [1990] ECR I–4023 for a similar test in the context of agricultural policy.

9.5 The UK judiciary approved a detailed four-step test, in 2007, which has since become firmly established. The pre-HRA case of *de Freitas v Secretary of Agriculture*[1] set out a test of proportionality that courts had been applying throughout the life of the HRA, and it asks, whether:

(i)   the legislative objective is sufficiently important to justify limiting a fundamental right;

(ii)   the measures designed to meet the legislative objective are rationally connected to it; and

(iii) the means used to impair the right or freedom are no more than is necessary to accomplish the objective.[2]

The House of Lords recognised the need for a fourth step recently in *Huang v Home Secretary*,[3] where de Freitas was expressly found wanting to the tune of proportionality *stricto sensu*, with the admonition that 'if, as counsel suggest, insufficient attention has been paid to this requirement, the failure should be made good'.[4] This added a fourth step to the test, which was confirmed in *Bank Mellat* as asking:

> (1) whether the objective of the measure is sufficiently important to justify the limitation of a protected right; (2) whether the measure is rationally connected to the objective; (3) whether a less intrusive measure could have been used without unacceptably compromising the achievement of the objective; and (4) whether, balancing the severity of the measure's effects on the rights of the persons to whom it applies against the importance of the objective, to the extent that the measure will contribute to its achievement, the former outweighs the latter.[5]

This clarity has substantially improved the application of proportionality in UK courts, where previously decisions often used only pieces of the test, or resorted to a broad-brush balancing that roughly resembles proportionality *stricto sensu*. As will be seen below, however, there remains a strong judicial tendency to resist the full effect of the proportionality test.

[1]   [1999] 1 AC 69.
[2]   *de Freitas* [1999] 1 AC 69 at 80.
[3]   [2007] UKHL 11.
[4]   *Huang v Home Secretary* [2007] UKHL 11, [19].

⁵ *Bank Mellat v Her Majesty's Treasury (No 2)* [2013] UKSC 39 [68]–[74].

Overview of the distinct functions for which the principle is employed

9.6 One of the most enduring difficulties in understanding the place of proportionality in judicial review is that it can and has been used for all of the following purposes:

(1)   as an element of reasonableness,[1]
(2)   as a standard of review,[2]
(3)   as principle of good government,[3]
(4)   as an aspect of the definition of a right,[4] and
(5)   as a general tool for assessing the propriety of penalties, conditions, or other aspects of public and private relationships.

This chapter is not concerned with (5), because in those cases proportionality is simply a generic principle made relevant by the factual setting, and not a principle of judicial review. However, (1) through (4) all apply in judicial review cases, and the different purposes for invoking proportionality affect its application. For example, the function and application of proportionality are different at the ECtHR from what they would be before a domestic court. In any court, the stringency of the test can depend on subject matter, such that the application of proportionality looks different in cases relating to social benefit rules as compared to those involving school dress codes.[5] As a result, this chapter considers several different settings in which proportionality is applied and even expressed distinctly: proportionality as used by European courts, EC proportionality in domestic courts, proportionality under the HRA, and proportionality as a part of domestic judicial review generally.

¹   *AAS v Secretary of State for the Home Department* [2010] CSIH 10, [14]–[20].
²   *The Sunday Times Case* (1979–1980) 2 EHRR 245; *Lingens v Austria* (1986) 8 EHRR 407.
³   *R (L) v Commissioner of Police of the Metropolis* [2009] UKSC 3, [39]–[46]; Craig, note 1, 9.2 above at 99–100.
⁴   *R (SB) v Governors of Denbigh High School* [2006] UKHL 15, [29]–[32].
⁵   *Humphreys v Revenue and Customs Commissioners* [2012] UKSC 18 [16]21]].

9.7 Although these issues are discussed in greater detail in sections **9.51–9.68** below, what is most important for understanding these different functions of proportionality is the distinction between proportionality as a standard of review, like *Wednesbury* unreasonableness, and proportionality as a standard for decision, such as when it forms part of the definition of a right. Unreasonableness, for example, can be seen as serving both functions. We expect decision makers to make reasonable decisions, so in that sense the standard for decision is reasonableness. However, *Wednesbury* reasonableness is a standard of review, requiring that the court keep a certain distance from the decision, and look only for a decision that no reasonable decision-maker could make. These different functions are emphasised in cases requiring 'anxious scrutiny.'[1] The standard for decision in such a case is raised beyond day-to-day reasonableness: the decision-maker must conclude that there is a competing interest sufficiently strong to warrant an interference with a fundamental right.[2] The standard of review, however, does not change: the court should not disturb the decision under review unless no reasonable decision-maker could reach that conclusion. The standard of review constrains the reviewing court, limiting how intensely it can scrutinise the decision. The standard for decision defines the requirements placed on the original decision-–maker.[3] The standard for decision can affect how carefully the reviewing court scrutinises the decision—a more demanding standard for decision necessarily constrains the options of the original decision-maker, which makes the scrutiny appear more invasive—but the standard for decision is not aimed at defining the role of the reviewing court.

[1] See **8.59** above.
[2] *R (Brind) v Secretary of State for the Home Department* [1991] 1 AC 696 at pp 749–751, 757–758, 765 (applied by Popplewell J in *R (Cox) v Secretary of State for the Home Department* [1992] COD 72).
[3] See, eg, *Pham v Secretary of State for the Home Department* [2015] UKSC 19; [2015] 3 All ER 1015 [95]116]– [115],[96]]; *R (Lord Carlile of Berriew) v Secretary of State for the Home Department* [2014] UKSC 60; [2015] 2 All ER 453 [22]34]]; *Caroopen v Secretary of State for the Home Department* [2016] EWCA Civ 1307 [81]–[83].

9.8 This distinction comes into its own with proportionality, because it is openly employed as both a standard of review and a standard for decision. Indeed, it could be argued that it has no pedigree as a standard of review, and is only treated as one because

(1) judicial review in the UK is built around the idea of constraints on the intensity of review and
(2) the UK legal community learned proportionality from the CJEU and ECtHR, where the 'margin of appreciation' doctrine forces proportionality to behave like a standard of review.[1]

Be that as it may, where proportionality features because of a rights challenge under the HRA or a challenge to an EU measure, it begins by serving the function of a standard for decision. The EU has adopted proportionality as the standard for when certain measures, such as rules of the Common Agricultural Policy, are improper limitations on, for example, the free movement of goods. This is not a rule for how far courts may explore the issue, it is a rule for what counts as improper: it is a standard for decision. Similarly, the ECtHR has used proportionality as the test for whether restrictions on the so-called qualified rights — represented by arts 8 through 11 — are 'necessary in a democratic society.' If the restriction is not proportionate, the right has been violated; proportionality does not here seek to answer the question of how intensely a reviewing court will scrutinise the decision that resulted in the restriction.

[1] Sottiaux, *Terrorism and the Limitation of Rights: the ECHR and the US Constitution* (2008), 54; Clayton and Tomlinson, *The Law of Human Rights* (2000), 274; Feldman, 'Proportionality and the HRA 1998' in Ellis (ed) *The Principle of Proportionality in the Laws of Europe* (1999), 127.

9.9 The foregoing observations notwithstanding, domestic courts have often treated proportionality as a standard of review.[1] Because proportionality can take different forms, and be applied with varying degrees of intensity (and because, again, experience with the 'margin of appreciation' has set the tone for it), courts have used the way they apply the test as their standard of review. This is not inevitable. Courts can, and sometimes do, view their standard of review — in the sense of a constraint on the intensity of their review — as something they do within the proportionality analysis, calling it deference or an 'area of discretionary judgment' allowed to the decision-maker.[2] However, until recently it has been just as common for courts to soften the test, according to their sense of how much distance they should maintain from the decision, by leaving out more hard-edged aspects of the test, like 'necessity',[3] or by suggesting that, in the circumstances, proportionality requires no more than reasonableness.[4] In the last few years the Supreme Court has been making it clearer that proportionality is a substantive test, which the test does not change, and that context only changes the weight given to various justifications and impacts.[5] In EU and HRA cases, as will be seen below, it is properly viewed as a standard for decision first and foremost. The courts are increasingly coming to see that the standard of review admits of no other constraint than deference to expertise or democratic legitimacy, and even there only to those parts of the state's side of the balance that attract it.[6]

1   R (Sosancy) v GMC [2009]EWHC 2814 (Admin); R (Assn of British Civilian Internees: Far East Region) v Secretary of State for Defence [2003] QB 1397; R (CCSU) v Minister of Civil Services (GCHQ Case) [1985] AC 374; R (Hargreaves) v Secretary of State for the Home Department [1997] 1 All ER 397.

2   R (P & Q) v Secretary of State for the Home Department [2001] EWCA Civ 1151; R (Samaroo) v Secretary of State for the Home Department [2001] UKHRR 1622; Huang v Home Secretary [2007] UKHL 11.

3   R (Boroumand) v Secretary of State for the Home Department [2010] EWHC 225 (Admin); SM (JM) v Advocate General [2010] CSOH 15.

4   R (Carson) v Secretary of State for Work and Pensions [2005] UKHL 37; SM (JM) v Advocate General [2010] CSOH 15.

5   Pham v Secretary of State for the Home Department [2015] UKSC 19; [2015] 3 All ER 1015 [95]–[96], [115]–[116]; R (Lord Carlile of Berriew) v Secretary of State for the Home Department [2014] UKSC 60; [2015] 2 All ER 453 [22]–[34]; Bank Mellat v Her Majesty's Treasury (No 2) [2013] UKSC 39.

6   Ibid; R (SB) v Governors of Denbigh High School [2006] UKHL 15; A and Ors v Home Secretary [2004] UKHL 56; Ghaidan v Godin–Mendoza, [2004] UKHL 30.

Terminology

9.10 Much of the key terminology of proportionality has been used in the sections above, but it is useful to explain the terms systematically here. The term proportionality refers to the basic principle itself, and should not be confused with proportionality *stricto sensu*. The latter refers to a final check, in a structured proportionality analysis, that the negative impacts of a measure do not outweigh its advantages. The former, broader term encompasses all of the manifestations of proportionality, including broad-brush balancing, the ECHR formulation ('a reasonable relationship of proportionality between the means employed and the aim sought to be realized'[1]), and structured proportionality. 'Broad-brush balancing' refers to the, until recently, common practice among UK courts of treating proportionality as a simple utilitarian weighing of the interests of the individual against those of the community. 'Structured proportionality' refers to EU-style and de Freitas-style three- or four-part analyses, which include steps requiring 'suitability' and 'necessity'. 'Suitability' requires that the challenged measure actually advance the stated objective, and can be used to reject under-inclusive measures, while necessity generally means that there must be no alternative course of action that would be less intrusive than the one chosen, making that measure 'necessary'. This last understanding is not universal: some courts treat necessity as requiring only that there is a strong need for the measure.

¹ *Belgian Linguistics* (1968) 1 EHRR 252, [10].

9.11 Section **9.6** already explained the different meanings of 'standard of review' and 'standard for decision' which are themselves better understood by reference to 'the margin of appreciation' and 'deference'. The margin of appreciation is a classic standard of review. It is a doctrine used by the ECtHR to give effect to its status as a supervisory court operating as a check on very different national systems. This is explained further in section **9.59**, but essentially it means that the Strasbourg Court will defer to the proportionality balance struck by the national authorities in certain fields (such as public morals, economic and social rights) unless the decision is clearly disproportionate or inconsistent with an established consensus of the signatory states. It is like a supranational *Wednesbury* test, except that the standard *for decision* is often more demanding than 'reasonableness'. The 'margin' standard of review varies according to the centrality of the right at issue and the subject matter of the national decision. It is not applicable in domestic courts, but is often replaced by deference. Commentators have offered myriad views on what the term 'deference' conveys,¹ but it has been used by courts as a standard of review (eg, a refusal to question executive decisions made in certain areas of expertise or democratic responsibility) or as a consideration to inform the assignment of weight to reasons given in support of a measure in a proportionality balancing (where proportionality is accepted as the standard for decision). This issue receives more attention at section **9.62** below.

¹ See King, '*Institutional Approaches to Judicial Restraint*' (2008) 28 OLJS 409 for a helpful discussion of the various models for deference put forward by commentators.

THE LOGIC OF PROPORTIONALITY IN COMPARATIVE PERSPECTIVE

9.12 It has been observed that comparative law frequently proves its worth through significant contributions to specific, novel and difficult problems, and that the stimulus for comparative investigation is often a problem that one's home system does not handle very well.¹ The importance attached to a consideration of foreign legal concepts has been noted by a number of writers.² In the field of administrative law, the creative law-making and decision-making of the European Court of Justice have been highly instrumental in this process, to the point where a cross-cultural perspective and the search for similarities and differences in the resolution of administrative law problems within the European legal system has become a practical necessity.³ It is now common for UK courts to consider comparative materials to assist in fine-tuning the application of proportionality.⁴ For all these reasons it is highly instructive to examine how proportionality is applied in other legal systems; at the same time, it is necessary to have firmly in mind some important cautionary notes. Each legal system has its own methods for handling legal materials, procedures for resolving disputes, and roles for those engaged in the law: one of the leading texts stresses that it is only by discovering how the relevant rules have been created and developed by the legislature or the courts and ascertaining the practical context in which they are applied that one can understand why a particular legal system resolves a given problem the way it does and not otherwise.[5] This section first considers some of the differences in how proportionality is applied in different countries. The next two sections look at how the Court of Justice of the European Union (CJEU) and the European Court of Human Rights (ECtHR) apply proportionality. Later sections will address what CJEU and ECtHR jurisprudence means for how domestic courts should apply proportionality; these sections simply treat them as examples for comparison and attempt, where possible, to avoid generalisations and to set cases in their context.[6]

[1]   Glendon, Gordon and Osakwe *Comparative Legal Traditions* (2nd edn, 1994), 10.
[2]   See, in particular, the contributions in Markesenis (ed) *The Gradual Convergence: Foreign Ideas, Foreign Influences and English Law on the Eve of the 21st Century* (1994).
[3]   Schwarze *European Administrative Law* (1992), 4; for a comparative study devoted to proportionality, see Emiliou *The Principles of Proportionality in European Law: A Comparative Study* (1996).
[4]   *Beghal v Director of Public Prosecutions* [2015] UKSC 49; [2016] AC 88 [40]; *Main v Scottish Ministers* [2015] CSIH 41 [40]; *R (Animal Defenders International) v Secretary of State for Culture, Media and Sport* [2008] UKHL 15; [2008] 1 AC 1312 [35].
[5]   Zweigert and Kötz *An Introduction to Comparative Law* (3rd edn, 1998), 5.
[6]   See Kahn-Freund. 'On uses and misuses of comparative law' (1974) 37 MLR 1; Markesenis, Comparative Law — a subject in search of an audience' (1990) 53 MLR 1.

9.13 The German principle of *Verhältnismäßigkeit* means 'proportionality', and has both a broad and a narrow sense. The broad sense developed from late nineteenth-century decisions of the Prussian Supreme Administrative Court which limited the discretionary powers of the police.[1] Prior to the 1939–45 war, two aspects of the principle had been developed, which would be applied after a preliminary finding that the aim of the state was legitimate: 'suitability' and 'necessity'.[2] The first of these limited the administrative authorities, when enforcing a law, to such means as were capable of the accomplishment of the purpose of that law. This capability was to be decided objectively. Thus measures which were contrary to the purpose of law were 'unsuitable', as were measures which were legally or factually impossible to be carried out.[3] Control of administrative measures in this way appears akin to controls which in English law traditionally flowed from review for illegality and unreasonableness. But control on 'suitability' alone was not found sufficient to prevent unnecessary injury to the individual, and this led to the development of the second aspect, generally called the principle of 'necessity', which requires that the administration must have no other mechanism at its disposal which is less restrictive of freedom. It has been said that it is not the method used which has to be necessary, but 'the excessive restriction of freedom involved in the choice of method'.[4] Singh, who observes that the principle of necessity might also be called 'the principle of mildest means', adds that for the principle to apply there must be several suitable means to achieve the end of the law: thus in a case where that end could only be achieved by the withdrawal of a licence from unsuitable drivers, insistence upon a partial withdrawal of the licence was of no avail.[5]

[1]   Singh, *German Administrative Law in Common Law Perspective* (2001), 160. One of the most celebrated was the *Kreuzberg* decision (14 June 1882, 9 PrOVGE 353) which held that police functions were confined to the maintenance of public security and did not extend to public welfare at large (Singh at 22; see, also, Schwarze at 685, who says of this decision that it saw the adoption by the courts of the notion that the state requires special permission whenever it infringes the citizen's civil liberties).

² Singh at 160.
³ Singh at 163 and 164; Emiliou at 26–29.
⁴ Schwarze at 687, citing G Haverkate *Rechtsfragen des Leistungsstaats* (1983) at 29.
⁵ Singh at 164, citing decision of 12 January 1962, 13 BVerwGE 288: Emiliou at 29–31.

9.14 Following the 1939–45 war, an additional aspect was developed which came to be known as proportionality in the strict sense (referred to in this Chapter as proportionality *stricto sensu*), or the principle of *Verhält-nismäßigkeit* in the narrow sense: this requires a proper balancing to ensure that the disadvantages to the individual are not disproportionate to the advantages to the community.[1] Thus decisions refusing permission to continue to stay in Germany were held invalid because they were founded on minor traffic violations during a long period of stay, whereas 'in considering the proportionality of the disadvantages associated with the refusal and the aimed consequences the authorities must examine the circumstances of each case in terms of length of stay, economic and social integration of the person, his economic standing, his contacts with his native land, his overall behaviour, etc'.[2] Singh describes the approach of the courts on this aspect as follows:[3]

> 'In determining this proportionality courts normally give weight to the administrative decision and would interfere only when a clear case of disproportionality is made out. Thus the court refused to interfere with the decision of the city authorities merely because in imposing fee[s] on the plaintiff for putting up hoardings they had failed to establish an exact equivalence between the burden on the plaintiff and the benefit to the community'.

¹ Schwarze at 686; Singh at 160 and 165: Emiliou at 32–37.
² Singh at 166, citing decisions of 13 November 1979, 59 BVerwGE 105 and 112.
³ Singh at 165, citing decisions of 14 April 1967, 26 BVerwGE 305, 309 and of 16 December 1971, 39 BVerwGE 190, 195.

9.15 Schwarze observes that the proportionality principle is generally accepted as governing both the law-making process (including a constitutional dimension) and the application of the law, and it has a significant role as a tool of interpretation.[1] He adds that wide-ranging and far-reaching criticisms have been levelled at the proportionality principle, and that the charge is constantly made that the principle has been stretched beyond acceptable limits (in particular, by moving the principle from the administrative law level to that of constitutional law).[2] A comparison with English law would suggest that the German approach resembles the four-part structured proportionality test that is increasingly articulated in UK courts, except that German courts are far more likely to apply their second step—the third step of structured proportionality: necessity.[3] Moreover, they are more likely to apply it in the rigorous way that actually requires that the means be the least intrusive available (that could advance the aim to the same degree).[4] Finally, notwithstanding that necessity is regularly applied, most cases are resolved by applying the final step, to establish whether the objectives of the state (and the extent to which the chosen means advance that objective) are sufficiently weighty to counterbalance the degree and kind of disadvantage or intrusion.[5] This is almost certainly because, as with British courts, German courts only require a 'legitimate' aim, and do not assess the importance of the state's aim at all until applying proportionality *stricto sensu.*

¹ Schwarze at 689–691. On the constitutional dimension, see, also, Singh at 160–163, and Foster *German Legal System and Laws* (2nd edn 1996), 158.
² Schwarze at 691.
³ Emiliou discusses the German notion of reasonableness at 37–40. See also Lübbe-Wolff, 'The Principle of Proportionality in the Case–Law of the German Federal Constitutional Court' (2014) 34 HRLJ 12.
⁴ Grimm, 'Proportionality in Canadian and German Constitutional Jurisprudence' (2007) 57 U Toronto Law Journal 383, 390-393.
⁵ Ibid., at 393–395.

9.16 The German approach represents a telling contrast to the Canadian jurisprudence. Canada applies a nearly identical test to that of Germany, in that there are ultimately four steps: (1) sufficient aim, (2) suitability, (3) necessity, and (4) proportionality *stricto sensu.*[1] It has been suggested that the similarity is no accident, and that Canada borrowed the principle fully developed. However, the Canadian courts do much more of the heavy lifting in the sufficient aim and necessity parts of the test than the German or British courts do.[2] In Canada, as in Britain, and by contrast with Germany, proportionality is not used as a general principle of administrative law, but as a test for the extent to which the state may invade a fundamental right. For this reason Canadian proportionality requires a preliminary assessment of whether the state's legitimate aim is sufficiently important to justify invading a fundamental right. However, in practice this is usually an easy hurdle to clear—in most cases an aim that is legitimate is deemed capable of justifying the invasion of a right—but then the matter becomes important again in connection with necessity. The Canadian necessity inquiry is prepared to look not only at whether the achievement of the state's objective could be achieved with less intrusion, but at whether (a) the aim is important enough and (b) the means sufficiently advances the aim, to justify the degree of intrusion.[3] Put another way, Canadian necessity does not simply accept the degree of legitimate-aim-achievement targeted by the state: it is prepared to find that either the means does not achieve enough or that less achievement must be accepted. It is no surprise, then, that many more cases are resolved on grounds of necessity than proportionality *stricto sensu.* It is interesting that courts in the UK have yet to adopt either the Canadian practice of calling for a 'sufficient,' as opposed to a 'legitimate', aim, nor the German practice of consistently applying necessity before moving on to the striking of a balance.

¹ *R v Oakes* [1986] 1 S.C.R.103.
² Grimm, 'Proportionality in Canadian and German Constitutional Jurisprudence' (2007) 57 U Toronto Law Journal 383, 387–393.
³ Ibid., at 390–393.

9.17 Finally, a comparative glance at Ireland, which does not boast a counterpart to the HRA, is instructive. Until 2010 Ireland applied a reasonableness standard, much like *Wednesbury*, even in cases involving fundamental or ECHR rights. Although courts from time to time considered proportionality relevant, there was no firm doctrine within Irish law calling for its application.[1] In 2010 the Irish Supreme Court held that proportionality should be adopted as a strand of unreasonableness review in cases involving fundamental rights.[2] Biehler and Donnelly argue that four years later the incorporation of proportionality into unreasonableness has not enhanced unreasonableness, but weakened proportionality.[3] It appears that, in effect, some members of the Irish judiciary have applied the proportionality *standard for decision* within the constraints of the unreasonableness *standard of review.* The predictable result is that most cases treat the balance struck by the decision-maker as one of many different reasonable responses, without making a fresh assessment of proportionality. Moreover, Biehler and Donnelly suggest that part of the reason for this is that the *Meadows* decision itself featured conflicting visions of deference, disagreeing about whether deference happens *within* proportionality, or whether it decides 'spatially' where proportionality can apply and where it cannot.[4] In comparative law context colours everything, so there might be no lesson here of relevance to the UK. However, the stance in Ireland seems clearly to illustrate the fundamental inconsistency between proportionality, as a standard for decision, and a standard of review that affords the state areas within which the judiciary must defer to it.

[1]   Biehler and Donnelly, 'Proportionality in the Irish courts: the need for guidance' [2014] EHRLR 272, 277.
[2]   *Meadows v Minister for Justice, Equality and Law Reform* [2010] 2 I.R. 701.
[3]   Biehler and Donnelly, n 1 above.
[4]   Ibid. at 273–274.

Proportionality in the European Court of Justice

9.18   A discussion of the general principles of the law of the European Union will be found in CHAPTER 16, where it is explained that the principle of proportionality as applied by the European Court of Justice denotes that the means used to attain a given end should be no more than is appropriate and necessary for attaining that end. The principle of proportionality is one of a number of such general principles: among others are the principles of equality, legal certainty, legitimate expectations and subsidiarity.

9.19   Lord Diplock expressed the thinking behind the principle as developed by the European Court of Justice very simply in *R v Goldstein*[1] by saying, 'You must not use a steam hammer to crack a nut'. But the matter is more complicated than this, for two different types of test are deployed by the European Court of Justice. Brealey and Hoskins[2] describe a 'narrow principle of proportionality' which governs the legality of Community legislation where the act complained of arises from the exercise of a discretionary power involving economic or political responsibilities. An example is *R v Minister for Agriculture, Fisheries and Food, ex p FEDESA*[3] where a directive banned the administration of certain hormone substances to livestock. After reciting the principle of proportionality in its 'wide' form (discussed below), the court continued:

> '14. However, with regard to judicial review of compliance with those conditions it must be stated that in matters concerning the common agricultural policy the Community legislature has a discretionary power which corresponds to the political responsibilities given to it by Articles 40 and 43 of the Treaty. Consequently, the legality of a measure adopted in that sphere can be affected only if the measure is manifestly inappropriate having regard to the objective which the competent institution is seeking to pursue'.

[1]   [1983] 1 WLR 151, 155.

2   *Remedies in EC Law* (1998), 116–120; see, also, Schwarze at 854–864, Nolte at 192–194 and 205–212, Vaughan *Law of the European Communities* 2 [1242], Schermers and Waelbroeck *Judicial Protection in the European Communities* (5th edn, 1992) [129], Craig and de Burca *European Community Law: Text, Cases and Materials* (3rd edn. 2002), 71–379, and *Emiliou* at 134ff.

3   C-331/88; [1990] ECR 1–4023. See also *Jippes v Minister van Landbouw, Natuurbeheer en Visserij (Case C-189/01) EU:C:2001:420,* [2001] ECR I-5689 [83]; *R v Minister for Agriculture, Fisheries and Food, ex p National Farmers' Union: C-354/95* [1997] ECR 1–4559.

9.20 It is apparent that this 'narrow' principle is a standard of review more than a standard for decision, and is very similar to the English concept of review for unreasonableness. Indeed, the use of the word 'manifest' indicates that review is to be conducted on a basis akin to the limited examination which the Supreme Court (and previously the House of Lords) has held appropriate to decisions involving national economic policy approved by the House of Commons. An example of a case involving the exercise of legislative power by the Commission in relation to the common agricultural policy is *R v Intervention Board for Agricultural Produce, ex p E D & F Man (Sugar) Ltd*: 181/84.[1] Article 6(3) of Commission Regulation 1880/83 provided for forfeiture of a deposit (paid by intending sugar exporters) if application for a licence was not made within a limited time. The applicants' deposit was forfeited even though they were only a few hours late. The European Court of Justice closely analysed the legislative framework, explaining that the primary obligation secured by the deposit was that successful tenderers should export the quantity of sugar concerned. The need for an export licence was secondary to this. The court held[2] that it followed that the automatic forfeiture of the entire security, in the event of an infringement significantly less serious than the failure to fulfil the primary obligation, which the security itself is intended to guarantee, must be considered too drastic a penalty in relation to the export licence's function of ensuring the sound management of the market in question. If this question had been governed by English domestic law, and the automatic forfeiture had been prescribed by a body which had correctly directed itself in law, the case appears an obvious example of manifest unreasonableness: automatic forfeiture, on the face of the matter, seems to make no sense in the context of the relevant legal provisions. The key point is that the proportionality questions are still asked: 'manifestly inappropriate' describes how wrong the answers must be.[3]

1   [181/84; [1986] 2 All ER 115.
2   See paragraph **29** of the court's judgment, [1986] 2 All ER at 126. The point is developed further at paragraph 30 of the judgment.
3   *R (Lumsdon) v Legal Services Board* [2015] UKSC 41; [2016] 1 *All ER* 391 [42]–[46] .

9.21 In other spheres, when applying the 'wide' test of proportionality, the court asks first whether the measures in question are appropriate and necessary, and next whether the disadvantages caused are disproportionate to the aims pursued.[1] This goes beyond merely considering whether a decision-maker could reasonably have thought that an appropriate balance had been achieved.[2] Indeed, this requirement to go beyond traditional judicial review principles was unavoidably imposed on British courts by s 3(1) of the European Communities Act 1972, and only such statutory instructions would have overcome early resistance. The EU proportionality requirement calls for the court (either European or national) to make a judgment on the merits beyond the limited value judgment inherent in review for unreasonableness. But a number of observations may be made.

(1)   The extent to which the judgment of proportionality under European Union law is to go beyond an assessment of the reasonableness of the decision under review will vary. In the first case to come before the European Court on a reference from the House of Lords, Advocate-General Warner suggested that the proportionality requirement (in the context of a prohibition on imports said to be justified on grounds of public morality) was the same as, or at least an aspect of, the concept of reasonableness.[3] Factors which influence the question of whether and how rigorously to examine a measure for proportionality include not just the subject matter of the dispute and the nature of the interests concerned, but also matters relating to the limits of the judicial role and the judicial process, as well as the relationship between the interests of the European Community and those of the Member States.[4]

(2)   It is for the national court, in the light of answers given by the European Court to any questions which it may have posed, to assess the compatibility of national legislation with European law. But in a clear case the European Court will state its view on this question. One such case was *Stoke-on-Trent City Council v B & Q plc.*[5]

(3)   In practice the result, in some cases, may not be different from that which a challenge for unreasonableness would produce.[6] Thus in *R v Chief Constable of Sussex, ex p International Trader's Ferry Ltd*[7] Kennedy LJ, having held that the respondent's deployment of officers to protect convoys of export lorries was not unreasonable, continued in relation to art 36 of the EEC Treaty:

> 'Proportionality requires the court to judge the necessity of the action taken as well as whether it was in the range of courses that could reasonably be followed. Proportionality can therefore be a more exacting test in some circumstances . . . but . . . in the context of this case and allowing for differences in terminology, each test will in practice yield the same result. To borrow a phrase from Lord Hoffmann's recent lecture. "A Sense of Proportion" (14 November 1996) it is not possible to see daylight between them'.

(4)   The European Court's analysis of proportionality often includes elements which in domestic administrative law would have been addressed by review for illegality. For example, in *R v Intervention Board for Agricultural Produce, ex p E D & F Man (Sugar) Ltd*: 181/84[8] the Court held that the Commission wrongly treated the obligation to apply for an export licence as a primary obligation, whereas the relevant legislation did not have that effect.[9] This seems to be a case where the Commission had misdirected itself in law. Similarly, decisions by the European Court of Justice holding prohibitions on entry by immigrants and importation of articles invalid, where the court conducted its own examination of the necessity for the prohibitions, have been explained as cases where the court's judgment contained suggestions that the primary aim of the prohibition was to target non-national migrants and imports respectively.[10] Again, such a ground of review would fall within the English concept of review for illegality.

(5)   Finally, the task of determining the width of the principle of propor-
        tionality in the context of a power conferred by legislation has many
        similarities for an English administrative lawyer with the task of
        construing the legislation and ascertaining the statutory purpose in the
        context of review for illegality: considerations of the kind described by
        de Burca (subject matter, nature of the interests concerned, limits of the
        judicial role and the judicial process, and the relationship between the
        interests of the European Community and those of the Member States)
        would be relevant to both tasks.

[1]   See Advocate-General Van Gerven in *Stoke-on-Trent City Council v B & Q plc* C–169/91;
        [1993] AC 900, 941–942. For analysis by the Supreme Court of Ireland of review under EU
        law for 'manifest error', see *SIAC Construction Ltd v Mayo County Council* [2002] 3 IR 148.
[2]   See, eg *R v Goldstein* [1983] 1 All ER 434, [1983] 1 WLR 151; *Torfaen Borough Council v
        B & Q plc* C–145/88 [1990] 2 QB 19, 53; *R v Ministry of Agriculture, ex p Roberts*
        [1991] 1 CMLR 555 at 579.
[3]   *Henn and Derby v DPP* [1981] AC 850, 879. The court did not refer to this point in its
        judgment.
[4]   Grainne de Burca, 'The Principle of Proportionality and its Application in EC Law' [1993]
        Yearbook of European Law 105, 105106.
[5]   C-169/91; [1993] AC 900.
[6]   See *Pham v Secretary of State for the Home Department* [2015] UKSC 19; [2015] 3 All ER
        1015, *discussed further below at section* 9.51et seq.
[7]   [1997] 2 All ER 65, 80; on appeal, [1999] 2 AC 418.
[8]   181/84; [1986] 2 All ER 115.
[9]   See paragraphs 22–28 of the judgment, [1986] 2 All ER 115, 125.
[10]   See Grainne de Burca, 'The Principle of Proportionality and its Application in EC Law' [1993]
        Yearbook of European Law 105, 130–132, discussing *Adoui and Cornuaille v Belgian State:*
        115/81 and 116/81 [1982] ECR 1665 and *Conegate Ltd v Customs and Excise Comrs* 121/85
        [1986] ECR 1007.

9.22 The application of the principle of proportionality in the law of the
European Union is a task which is undertaken with increasing frequency by
English courts. On occasion, that review performs a function which is no more
extensive than review for unreasonableness. More commonly the principle
requires the identification of precedent facts, and an assessment by the court as
to whether the challenged decision was in fact proportionate. How courts in
the UK should apply EU proportionality is addressed further in section **9.51**
below. Before the European Court of justice, the determination of where — on
the spectrum of intensity — review in relation to a particular measure should
lie will depend on the subject matter, nature of the interests concerned, the
limits of the judicial role and the judicial process, and the relationship between
the interests of the European Union and those of the Member States.

Proportionality and the European Convention on Human Rights

9.23 The approach of English courts to questions involving human rights
following enactment of the Human Rights Act 1998 is discussed in CHAPTER 4.
Reference should be made to that chapter on the subject of human rights
generally. How domestic courts should handle proportionality under the HRA
is addressed beginning at **9.55**. The discussion below gives a brief description
of the development and application of proportionality before the ECtHR.

9.24 By art 3 of the Statute of the Council of Europe 1949, a Member State
of the Council must accept the principles of the rule of law and of the

enjoyment by all persons within its jurisdiction of human rights and fundamental freedoms. These rights and freedoms are described in the European Convention on Human Rights, which was adopted in 1950 and came into force in 1953. The Convention established the European Court of Human Rights (ECtHR) to decide whether breaches of the Convention had occurred. The United Kingdom, as a member of the Council of Europe, is party to the Convention, has given its citizens the right of individual petition to the ECtHR, and has incorporated those rights into UK law through the HRA. Inherent in the Convention is a search for a fair balance between the demands of the general interest of the community and the requirements of the protection of the individual's fundamental rights.[1] This balance was described in the principles adopted by the Committee of Ministers of the Council of Europe in 1980:[2]

> 'Proportionality. An appropriate balance must be maintained between the adverse effects which an administrative authority's decision may have on the rights, liberties, or interests of the person concerned and the purpose which the authority is seeking to pursue'.

[1] *Soering v United Kingdom* (1989) 11 EHRR 439, ECtHR, [89].
[2] Recommendation No R(80)2, 11 March 1980.

9.25 Four years earlier the European Court of Human Rights had held[1] that permission granted in articles 8 to 11 of the Convention to restrict rights to the extent 'necessary in a democratic society' required the court to examine whether the restriction was 'proportionate to the legitimate aim pursued'. The court has similarly examined the proportionality of State action in relation to other articles of the Convention.[2] Thus the court gives the final ruling on whether a restriction is reconcilable with a protected freedom, but in doing so it recognises a 'domestic margin of appreciation'.[3] The degree of discretion afforded by this margin to states is not uniform, and has been described as follows:[4]

> 'A state is allowed a considerable discretion in cases of public emergency arising under Article 15, in some national security cases and in the protection of public morals and generally when "there is little common ground" between the contracting parties. At the other extreme, the margin of appreciation is reduced almost to vanishing point in certain areas, as where the justification for a restriction is the protection of the authority of the judiciary . . . The margin of appreciation doctrine serves as a mechanism by which a tight or slack rein is kept on state conduct, depending on the context . . . The difficulty with the doctrine lies not so much in allowing it as in deciding precisely when and how to apply it on the facts of particular cases.'

[1] *Handyside v United Kingdom* (1976) 1 EHRR 737, [49].
[2] See Harris, O'Boyle and Warbrick *Law of the European Convention on Human Rights* (1995), 11–12.
[3] See *Handyside* (above) at [48]–[49]; *Markt Intern and Beerman v Germany* (1989) 12 EHRR 161, 174; *Informationsverein Lentia v Austria* (1993) 17 EHRR 93, 112. The width accorded to the margin of appreciation in *Markt Intern* caused unease; see Eissen. 'The Principle of Proportionality in the Case-law of the European Court of Human Rights' at 145–146 of McDonald, Petzold and Matscher (eds) *The European System for the Protection of Human Rights* (1993).

⁴ Harris, O'Boyle and Warbrick, *Law of the European Convention on Human Rights* (1995), 14–15.

9.26 It is tempting for an English lawyer to equate the doctrine of the 'domestic margin of appreciation' with the fundamental English doctrine that there may be a range of reasonable responses open to a decision-maker under domestic principles of judicial review. Both are standards of review, but their logic and application are distinct. The 'domestic margin of appreciation' is permitted because State authorities, through their 'direct and continuous contact with the vital forces of their countries' are better placed to assess, for example, public morality or budgetary constraints, and the need for restrictions to meet them.[1] In a case where the Strasbourg Court permits a domestic margin of appreciation, this amounts to a self-imposed limitation by the court when it determines whether the Convention has been complied with. By contrast, the recognition by an English court on judicial review that there may be a range of reasonable responses is an inevitable application of the principles on which judicial review is founded. It is not a standard of review to determine the rigour with which proportionality will be applied, but an attitude to assessing justifications for decisions *within* the proportionality analysis. As explained in **9.68** below, recognition by the domestic courts that the Convention should be seen as an expression of fundamental principles rather than mere rules has led to the development of a concept of a 'discretionary area of judgment' afforded to the executive in the application of the Human Rights Act 1998.[2]

[1] See *Handyside* (above) at [48].
[2] It is in this context that the notion of 'deference' by the court to the executive has arisen, a concept which may carry inappropriate overtones and which is not to be regarded as precluding scrutiny of relevant issues: *A v Secretary of State for the Home Department* [2005] 2 AC 68, discussed in Sayeed, 'Beyond the language of deference' [2005] JR 111.

9.27 Prior to the enactment of the Human Rights Act 1998 it could be said that a close link had been identified between the approach of the English courts to allegations of unreasonable interference with human rights and the doctrines of proportionality and 'domestic margin of appreciation' developed (in the supra-national context described above) by the European Court of Human Rights in Strasbourg. Thus, the House of Lords in *R v Secretary of State for the Home Department, ex p Launder*[1] said that if the applicant were to have an effective remedy in a case where the decision-maker says that the Convention was taken into account, it must surely be right to examine the substance of the argument, and this was permitted by ordinary principles of judicial review because the argument was directed to the rationality and legality of the decisions in question. The link could also be seen in the explanation of English domestic law given by Sedley J in *R v Secretary of State for the Home Department, ex p Moon*.[2] If the executive provides justification for its view that interference with an important right was justified, and an English court determines that the justification is clear enough to demonstrate that there was a sufficient basis on which that view could sensibly be held, then the English court is holding that the infringement is one which could reasonably be regarded as proportionate to the aim pursued.[3] Factors which are relied on by the English court in this regard may well be factors which could play a part in

a decision by the Strasbourg Court to hold that the restriction was proportionate to the legitimate aim pursued, or that the matter fell within the
domestic margin of appreciation.[4]

1   [1997] 1 WLR 839, 865 (Lord Hope of Craighead).
2   (1995) 8 Admin LR 477.
3   See, generally, **8.59** above.
4   Note, however, that in a case where the English court was not in possession of relevant
    national security evidence (*R v Secretary of State for the Home Department, ex p Chahal*
    [1995] 1 WLR 526) the European Court of Human Rights held that there were violations of
    arts 5(4) and 13 (*Chahal v United Kingdom* (1997) 23 EHRR 413). The decision gives added
    force to criticisms of the courts' approach to national security issues by Sedley J in *R v
    Secretary of State for the Home Department, ex p McQuillan* [1995] 4 All ER 400. Note, also,
    the deployment of the Convention by the European Court of Justice; see *Johnston v
    Chief Constable of the Royal Ulster Constabulary*: 222/84 [1987] QB 129, [1986] 3 All ER
    135, discussed by Koopmans 'European Public Law: Reality and Prospects' [1991] PL 53;
    Grief, '*The Domestic Impact of the European Convention on Human Rights as mediated
    through Community Law*' [1991] PL 555.

9.28 Since the coming into force of the Human Rights Act 1998, there has
been a succession of cases where the limits of the discretionary area of
judgment have been explored in relation to particular articles of the Convention. This is discussed in further detail in **9.68** below,[1] but the current position
may be briefly illustrated by taking two contrasting decisions of the House of
Lords. In *R(Hooper) v Secretary of State for Work and Pensions*[2] complaint
was made of the United Kingdom's failure to make provision for the paying of
widow's pension to men. The House of Lords held that the Convention
jurisprudence showed that Member States were allowed to treat groups
unequally in order to correct factual inequalities between them. Such decisions
were usually recognised by the courts as being matters for the elected
representatives of the people. Accordingly, the courts were not in a position to
say that the decisions taken by Parliament in relation to widow's pension were
inescapably right or wrong or should have been taken earlier or later: they
were matters of legislative judgment. By contrast, in *A v Secretary of State for
the Home Department*[3] ('the Belmarsh Prisoners case') the House of Lords,
while paying due regard to the role of government in matters of policy and of
national security, nevertheless concluded that provisions in primary and
secondary legislation conferring the power to detain without trial foreigners
who were 'suspected international terrorists' did not rationally address the
threat to security, constituted a disproportionate response, and were not
strictly required by the exigencies of the situation. Accordingly the secondary
legislation was quashed and the primary legislation was declared incompatible
with the European Convention on Human Rights. The trend at the time of
writing has been moving away from Hooper in the direction of the Belmarsh
Prisoners case, but divergent views persist.[4] The current state of development
is best evidenced in the *Bank Mellat*[5] and *Lord Carlile*[6] cases, discussed more
fully at **9.59** and **9.62**.

1   See also **4.99** above.
2   [2005] 1 WLR 1681. For further discussion of proportionality review, see *R v Shayler* [2003]
    1 AC 247, especially Lord Hope at [61].
3   [2005] 2 AC 68. On national security and 'deference' see Sayeed, 'Beyond the language of
    deference' [2005] JR 111.
4   Vaughn, 'Minimum Interference Versus Rationality: The New Battleground in HRA Propor-
    tionality?' [2013] JR 416.
5   *Bank Mellat v Her Majesty's Treasury (No 2)* [2013] UKSC 39.

THE STRUCTURE OF PROPORTIONALITY AS A TEST

9.29 Proportionality can, as we have seen, be expressed as a principle or as a structured analysis. The ECtHR does not always treat proportionality as a structured test. It most often uses proportionality to establish whether an encroachment on one of the qualified rights, in arts 8–11, is 'necessary in a democratic society.' This will be so where the measure pursues a legitimate aim, and there is 'a reasonable relationship of proportionality between the means employed and the aim sought to be realized.'[1] In practice this formulation will always require an objective sufficient to justify limiting a right, because the express terms of the qualified articles enumerate the proper objects. The CJEU, by contrast, does call for an assessment of proportionality according to a structured analysis, sometimes consisting of two steps, sometimes of three. The two step formulation asks whether the means employed to achieve an objective correspond to the importance of that objective, and whether the means are necessary for the achievement of that objective.[2] This assumes that the objective is a legitimate one. The three-part test requires suitability, necessity, and proportionality *stricto sensu*. The CJEU almost always means by 'necessity' that the measure is the least invasive measure available to the decision-maker; this is not always so when the ECtHR considers necessity. UK courts applying the CJEU test have recently taken to expressing it in this way: 'the measure: (1) must be effective to achieve the legitimate aim in question (appropriate), (2) must be no more onerous than is required to achieve that aim (necessary), (3) must be the least onerous, if there is a choice of equally effective measures, and (4) in any event must not produce adverse effects which are disproportionate to the aim pursued.'[3]

1   *Belgian Linguistics* (1968) 1 EHRR 252, [10].
2   Case C-319/06 *European Commission v Luxembourg* EU:C:2008:350, [2009] All ER (EC) 1049, [2008] ECR I-4323; Case 66/82 *Fromancais SA v Fonds d'Orientation et de Regularisation des Marches Agricoles* [1983] ECR 395, [8]; Van Gerven, AG, in Case C-159/90 *Society for the Protection of Unborn Children Ireland Ltd v Grogan* [1991] ECR I-4685, [27].
3   *BAA Ltd v Competition Commission* [2009] CAT 35 [137].

9.30 Until 2007, the proportionality formulation under the HRA, considering ECHR rights in UK courts, was the so-called *de Freitas*[1] three stage test, adopted by the House of Lords in *Daly*.[2] There the Lords said that restrictions on protected rights can only stand if the court finds that:

(i)   the legislative objective is sufficiently important to justify limiting a fundamental right;
(ii)   the measures designed to meet the legislative objective are rationally connected to it; and
(iii) the means used to impair the right or freedom are no more than is necessary to accomplish the objective.

This lacks an element found in the four-stage test which is used by the German courts, and which also correlates with that used by the Canadian courts in Charter adjudication under *R v Oakes*.[3] The first three stages of these formulations correspond with *de Freitas*, but the fourth adds a key (some might say essential) element: 'Finally, the court must establish whether the measure is proportionate in the strict sense, namely whether it strikes a proper balance between the purpose and the individuals' rights in question.'[4] This fourth stage, proportionality *stricto sensu*, also appears in *Oakes*: 'There must be a proportionality between the effects of the measures which are responsible for limiting the . . . right or freedom and the objective which has been identified as of "sufficient importance"'.[5] By the time it reaches proportionality *stricto sensu* the court has accepted that the measure pursues an important aim and is suitable and necessary for attaining it; it is at this stage that judgments become more openly normative. The courts essentially ask whether the benefits of the measure — already acknowledged in the first three steps — justify the extent of the invasion or impairment of the right in question. The need to add the fourth element was finally recognised in *Huang v Secretary of State for the Home Department*,[6] and has been firmly established in subsequent UK Supreme Court decisions.[7]

1   From the decision of the Privy Council in *de Freitas v Permanent Secretary of Ministry of Agriculture, Fisheries, Lands and Housing* [1999] 1 AC 69, 80.
2   *R (Daly) v Secretary of State for the Home Department* [2001] 2 WLR 1622.
3   [1986] 1 SCR 103 at 137, 138:

   'First, the objective, which the measures responsible for a limit on a Charter right or freedom are designed to serve, must be of 'sufficient importance to warrant overriding a constitutionally protected right or freedom' . . . . The standard must be high in order to ensure that objectives which are trivial or discordant with the principles integral to a free and democratic society do not gain . . . protection. It is necessary, at a minimum, that the objective relate to concerns which are pressing and substantial in a free and democratic society before it can be characterised as sufficiently important.'

4   Goold, Lazarus, and Swiney, *Public Protection, Proportionality, and the Search for Balance* (2007), 2.
5   1 SCR 103, 138.
6   [2007] UKHL 11.
7   *R (Aguilar Quila) v Secretary of State for the Home Department* [2011] UKSC 45; *Bank Mellat v Her Majesty's Treasury (No 2)* [2013] UKSC 39.

9.31 Domestic courts have shown a tendency not to employ any kind of recognisable structure in their proportionality inquiry, adopting instead a broad–brush balancing between state or community interests and rights interests.[1] This tends to happen when the court considers that the challenged measure does not invade a fundamental right[2] (or aspect of a right[3]) or where it decides that the prerogative of the decision-maker deserves extensive deference. Broad-brush balancing can work for the claimant, such as when a measure intentionally discriminates on the basis of nationality and detailed investigation of the reasons appears beside the point, but usually the broad-brush approach presages a capitulation to the state. Possibly some confusion arises owing to the apparent similarity between broad-brush balancing and proportionality *stricto sensu*. If — it might be argued — the ultimate question proportionality seeks to answer is whether the needs of the state are sufficiently strong to outweigh a measure's negative impacts on rights, then what is so wrong with proceeding straight to that question, without the preliminaries? Or perhaps the de Freitas formulation is an alternative to proportionality *stricto sensu*: surely a measure that satisfies tests of sufficient importance, rational connection, and necessity must perforce justify any effects on rights interests? As an empirical or historical matter, of course, neither of these suggestions would be correct. As discussed in **9.12** above, proportionality began with the simple principles of suitability and necessity, but the idea of proportionality *stricto sensu* has been a part of the seminal German proportionality formulation for half a century. The ECHR conception of proportionality was based on this foundation, although the ECtHR formulation resembles *stricto sensu* overlaid with the language of necessity in a democratic society. So clearly proportionality *stricto sensu* is meant always to be present, and the other steps, other than least-intrusive-method necessity, are implied by the language of arts 8–11.

1   *Main v Scottish Ministers* [2015] CSIH 41, [43]–[49] (Lord Drummond Young defends at
     length a broad-brush approach, showing particular resistance to the least onerous means test);
     see also the approach of Lord Carswell in *Secretary of State for the Home Department v MB*
     [2007] 3 WLR 681MB, at [83]: "In the present case one has to balance two interests, that of
     the controlee and the public interest." See also Goold et al at 2.
2   *Lithgow v United Kingdom* (1986) 8 EHRR 329.
3   Fenwick and Phillipson, *Media Freedom under the Human Rights Act* (2006) 56–60, 80–81,
     410–422.

9.32 However, four-stage structured proportionality deserves defending on more substantive grounds. The first, and perhaps obvious, reason judges should not skip ahead to the fourth stage — or engage in mere broad–brush balancing — is that the first three steps serve to calibrate the balancing in a way that gives appropriate weight to rights interests. It should be remembered that proportionality, in the ECHR context, represents a kind of affirmative defence: a right has been prima facie infringed, but the state seeks to invoke an exception or justification. A structured proportionality test reflects a presumption in favour of prohibiting the encroachment, rebuttable if the government purpose is sufficiently important, and the measure rationally connected to it and necessary. Broad-brush balancing tends to lead judges to under-value the right.[1] The most obvious way in which this happens is through failure to apply the powerful least–onerous–means test. The first three steps of structured proportionality must apply in each case to ensure that rights receive at least some protection that cannot be balanced away. Neither the ECtHR nor domestic courts always do this, however, and whether a structured approach applies tends to depend on whether the judges find the rights claim compelling or not.[2] Judges generally do not articulate their reasoning in those terms, preferring to attribute their light touch or broad–brush review to deference[3] or a margin of appreciation,[4] or by observing that the rights interest infringed was not central (eg, invoking distinctions between political and other speech,[5] or between the core of privacy and more peripheral aspects of the concept[6]). It is to be hoped that this practice will become less common after the Supreme Court made it clear in recent cases that deference cannot change the four-step proportionality test, but can only inform the weight to be given to certain considerations within it.[7] The individual steps of the test are discussed in turn below.

1   Goold et al at 48–51.
2   *Ibid*; Sottiaux at 44–45; *R (Lord Carlile of Berriew)) v Secretary of State for the Home
     Department* [2013] EWCA Civ 199; *M's Guardian v Advocate General for Scotland* [2010]
     CSOH 15.
3   *R (Lord Carlile of Berriew) v Secretary of State for the Home Department* [2013] EWCA Civ
     199 [64]–[73]; *R (Huitson) v Revenue and Customs Comrs* [2010] EWHC 97 (Admin); *R
     (Gurung) v Ministry of Defence* [2008] EWHC 1496 (Admin).
4   *Leander v Sweden* (1987) 9 EHRR 433 [59]; Sottiaux at 54–55.
5   *The Sunday Times Case* (1979–1980) 2 EHRR 245; Feldman at 138.

[6]   *Dudgeon v United Kingdom* (1981) 4 EHRR 149, [52].
[7]   *Pham v Secretary of State for the Home Department* [2015] UKSC 19; [2015] 3 All ER 1015 [[95][115]–[116]96]; *R (Lord Carlile of Berriew) v Secretary of State for the Home Department* [2014] UKSC 60; [2015] 2 All ER 453 [22]–[34] ; *Bank Mellat v Her Majesty's Treasury (No 2)* [2013] UKSC 39.

Legitimate aim or pressing social need

9.33 In the context of Convention rights, the de *Freitas* first stage corresponds to the 'pressing social need' requirement read into the exceptions to articles 8 through 11. Although these articles catalogue specific grounds that can represent such social needs, Strasbourg has required more than that the stated objective fit within the list of acceptable grounds in a purely definitional sense. For example, art 8, protecting privacy and family life, identifies 'the protection of health or morals' as a legitimate reason for a limitation on the right. The ECtHR has not been satisfied that literally any purpose that fits that definition can justify limitation of the right to privacy, and therefore has insisted that the legitimate objective relied on by the state represent a 'pressing social need' before it can be seen as 'necessary in a democratic society'. Often the ultimate question of whether the need is sufficiently pressing is assumed by courts to involve some deference to the lawmaker or actor. Thus in the first step of structured proportionality a court faces initially the fairly uncontroversial task of interpreting the list of exception-justifying grounds — and precedent related to them — to determine whether the purpose is potentially sufficient, followed by the more controversial enterprise of deciding whether or not to accept the state's position on how pressing the need is.

9.34 When proportionality defines rights in non-convention contexts, such as EU rights or domestic anti–discrimination law (largely dependent on the EU conception), it often requires simply that an invasion be 'a proportionate means of achieving a legitimate aim'[1] or 'justified by a legitimate aim and . . . appropriate and necessary'.[2] In these contexts no list of authorised objectives assists the analysis of what counts as a legitimate aim. This creates a temptation, yielded to by many courts, to require nothing more than that the aim pursued be minimally legitimate. However, the CJEU has made it clear that these formulations of proportionality require that restrictions 'correspond to a real need' and are 'necessary.'[3] Thus legitimate aim really means 'an aim that is legitimate and that corresponds to a real need of the state.' However, domestic courts tended to ignore this 'real need' aspect of the analysis until the Supreme Court emphasised the requirement in *Homer*.[4]

[1]   Equality Act 2010 s19(2)(d).
[2]   Council Directive 2000/78 establishing a general framework for equal treatment in employment and occupation.
[3]   Case-83/14 *CHEZ Razpredelenie Bulgaria AD v Komisia za zashtita ot diskriminatsia* [2016] 1 CMLR 14 (CJEU (Grand Chamber)); *Bilka-Kaufhaus* Case C-170/84 [1987] ICR 110, 126.
[4]   *Homer v Chief Constable of West Yorkshire Police* [2012] IRLR 601.

9.35 An example of this phenomenon, albeit not from the judicial review context, is *Allen v GMB*.[1] That case involved a situation where a planned job evaluation scheme would demonstrate that several women workers had been underpaid for years, and several other employees, mostly men, had been overpaid. In other words, some women would wind up reclassified upward, and have Equal Pay Act 1970 claims for past underpayment, while several men (a much greater proportion of the GMB union's membership) would be reclassified down, and face pay cuts. The GMB pressured female union members to take risible settlements of their equal pay claims, in order to leave the employer enough money to grant better concessions to protect the pay of those reclassified downward. The Employment Tribunal (ET) found the union's bargaining policy indirectly discriminatory against women, and applied a justification test that called for the policy to pursue a legitimate aim through proportionate means.[2] Because it did not follow the requirements of a 'real need' for the challenged policy, the ET found the aim of the policy — 'to avoid or minimise "losers"' in the pay reclassification — legitimate. Nevertheless the ET found that the means — failing to push the equal pay claims harder and using 'spin' to get women to agree to the settlements — were not proportionate. This conclusion rested on the assumption that it could never be proportionate for the union 'to procure the acceptance or acquiescence of the claimants by a marked economy of truth in what it says and writes to them.'[3] On appeal the Employment Appeal Tribunal (EAT) found the discrimination justified, and did not replace the ET's 'legitimate aim' test with a 'real need' requirement. It is doubtful whether it could ever be a legitimate objective intentionally to favour, in collective bargaining, the interests of mostly male reclassified employees over the interests of exclusively, and not accidentally, female employees, but the tribunal below had conceded the legitimacy of this aim as an issue of fact. The EAT could hardly fail to have reached a different result had GMB been required to prove a real need for its discriminatory bargaining position. Although the Court of Appeal subsequently rejected the EAT ruling and reinstated that of the ET on the ground that dishonesty could not be proportionate, no effort was made to correct or strengthen the analysis used.[4] It left in place a test that (1) does not require a 'real need' for the discriminatory policy and (2) fails to acknowledge that not all 'legitimate aims' are created equal.

[1]   [2007] IRLR 752.
[2]   *Allen v GMB* [2007] IRLR 752, 760.
[3]   Ibid.
[4]   *Allen v GMB* [2008] EWCA Civ 810, [18]–[34].

9.36 *GMB v Allen* does not represent all decisions on the EU-based formulation of proportionality. Better examples include *Allonby v Accrington and Rossendale College*[1] and *R(Elias) v Secretary of State for Defence*.[2] Following CJEU guidance *Allonby* held that the decision of the tribunal below, that 'sound business reasons' amounted to a justification, could not stand. The court held that justification required 'a critical evaluation of whether the [employer's] reasons demonstrated a real need . . . ; if there was such a need, consideration of the seriousness of the disparate impact . . . on women including the applicant; and an evaluation of whether the former were sufficient to outweigh the latter.'[3] *Elias*, a judicial review case applying the Race Relations Act definition of indirect discrimination, adopted the *de Freitas* formulation, requiring that the legitimate aim be 'sufficiently important to justify limiting a fundamental right.'[4] This formulation appears to have come to its full maturity in *Homer v Chief Constable of West Yorkshire Police*, in which the Supreme Court not only emphasised both the 'real need' and 'sufficiently important' language, (both of which it viewed as serving the same basic purpose), but explained their significance in the later balancing exercise, calling for 'a comparison of the impact of that criterion upon the affected group as against the importance of the aim to the employer'.[5] Indeed, all of the remaining steps of structured proportionality depend for their acuity on a proper assessment of the degree to which the 'legitimate aim' represents a 'real need' or is 'sufficiently important'.

[1]   [2001] ICR 1189.
[2]   [2006] EWCA Civ 1293.
[3]   *Allonby v Accrington and Rossingdale College* [2001] ICR 1189, 1201.
[4]   [2006] EWCA Civ 1293 [165].
[5]   [2012] UKSC 15, [2024].

Suitability

9.37 The question of whether the means employed to pursue a legitimate aim are suitable to that aim (according to the German formulation) or rationally connected to it (according to the *de Freitas* formulation) is essentially a straightforward inquiry into whether the measure appears calculated to advance the aim. This kind of question gets asked regardless of whether the court adopts a structured analysis. Even broad-brush balancing will find that the interest of the state in an intervention that in reality does little to accomplish its stated objective is unlikely to outweigh substantial rights interests. In unstructured analyses, where typically the question is viewed merely as whether the state action was 'proportionate to a legitimate aim', courts have employed a suitability inquiry, without labelling it as such, to find that the stated aim was not legitimate, or that the challenged measure was not proportionate owing to under-inclusiveness. So, for example, in *Ghaidan* the House of Lords found incompatible with the Convention a provision of the Rent Act 1977 that permitted a surviving spouse or unmarried cohabiting heterosexual partner to inherit the statutory tenancy of a deceased statutory tenant.[1] According to Lord Nicholls, the case fell 'at the first hurdle: the absence of a legitimate aim,' because it failed to advance the stated aim of preserving the traditional family.[2] Although it was accepted that homosexual couples were less likely to have children, there was nothing in the Rent Act that required heterosexual couples, married or otherwise, to have children, so the distinction on sexuality grounds in no way advanced the alleged aim. This was not treated as a separate 'suitability' step in the analysis, but as an obvious question to ask with regard to any claim that a challenged measure pursues a legitimate aim.

[1]   *Ghaidan v Godin–Mendoza* [2004] UKHL 30, [4]–[5].
[2]   [2004] UKHL 30, [16]–[18].

9.38 Similarly, in the *Belmarsh Prisoners* case, Lord Bingham found that detention of foreign national suspected terrorists, under s 23 of the Anti-terrorism, Crime and Security Act 2001, was disproportionate because it was under-inclusive.[1] In essence, the measure could not be proportionate because it detained non-UK suspected terrorists on the ground that their detention was necessary to public safety, while it did not detain UK suspected terrorists, who according to the record represented at least as great a threat.[2] This point was treated as involving the necessity of the measure, in the sense that it could hardly be necessary to intern non–UK nationals when it was evidently not necessary to detain UK nationals. However, this is analytically incorrect, because it does not prove one way or the other whether detention was necessary; instead, it shows that *if* detention of terrorist suspects was necessary, the challenged measure was not suitable to achieve that objective. This analytical distinction is important, because confusion on the issue could have anomalous results. In the *Belmarsh* case the government argued that the limitation to non-UK nationals was what made the measure the least restrictive alternative available: the distinction, the government claimed, imposed no greater impacts on rights interests than was necessary because its effect was restricted to those with no right of abode in the UK.[3] This argument persuaded the Court of Appeal, which did not ask the suitability question. This suggests that a failure to investigate suitability can leave the necessity question open to mishandling. Put another way, if a court does not address itself to the question of whether a measure sufficiently advances the objective relied upon, it can conclude that the measure is necessary in that it imposes no more negative impacts than it must, without confronting the issue of whether it accomplishes enough to justify those impacts.

[1] *A v Secretary of State for the Home Department* [2004] UKHL 56.
[2] [2004] UKHL 56 [43].
[3] [2004] UKHL 56 [52], [67].

Necessity

9.39 The third stage of structured proportionality tends in CJEU jurisprudence and in the *de Freitas* formulation to equate with a least-intrusive-means test. This appears obvious, in the sense that one can hardly call a measure necessary to accomplishing an aim when another measure with less negative impact can advance the objective to the same degree. This form of necessity makes clear the importance of a proper suitability inquiry, in that the comparison of alternatives in terms of their ability to advance the legitimate aim assumes an assessment of how far the challenged measure meets its objectives. A measure could not be said to 'fail' the least intrusive means test because there existed an alternative that would impose a lesser burden on rights interests, if the alternative would not advance the legitimate aim as far as the challenged measure would. However, this least intrusive means approach does not appear in all Strasbourg or domestic cases. Indeed, the presence or absence of this test often signals the difference between intense scrutiny and deferential scrutiny.[1]

[1] Fenwick, *Civil Liberties and Human Rights*, 5th edn (2016) ch 4; Arai–Takahashi, *The Margin of Appreciation Doctrine and the Principle of Proportionality in the Jurisprudence of the ECHR* (2002), 14, 193. Also, compare *SS (Nigeria) v Secretary of State for the Home Department* [2013] EWCA Civ 550, [38]–[47] to *R (Lord Carlile of Berriew) v Secretary of State for the Home Department* [2013] EWCA Civ 199, [64]-[73].

9.40 In domestic cases, the least intrusive means requirement is often resisted even where it clearly applies. How the UK judiciary responded to *Enderby v Frenchay Health Authority* furnishes an example.[1] The CJEU in *Enderby* rejected the EAT's approach to justification in an Equal Pay Act 1970 case —

the EAT had found an entire pay differential justified, but only a proportion of the differential was actually necessitated by market forces — because it allowed some discriminatory impact that could have been avoided, and was not therefore shown to be necessary. In short, the result reiterated that 'necessary' meant that no justification would succeed where a less discriminatory alternative was available. In reaching this result, the CJEU reminded the UK courts that they must apply the principle of proportionality in UK law. It was this reminder that Lord Nicholls, in the leading House of Lords speech in *Barry v Midland Bank*, relied on to claim that *Enderby* stood for the following proposition:

> '[T]he ground relied upon as justification must be of sufficient importance for the national court to regard this as overriding the disparate impact of the difference in treatment, either in whole or in part. The more serious the disparate impact on women or men, as the case may be, the more cogent must be the objective justification.'[2]

Lord Nicholls essentially 'complied' with *Enderby* by adopting broad-brush balancing, and went on to opine that once the employer's objective had been found 'legitimate', the policy in question was justified so long as it was 'needed' in order to achieve the objective: he rejected the idea that a policy could be challenged on the ground that it did not correspond to the needs, as opposed to the convenience, of the business.[3] Thus no least intrusive means test was required despite a clear steer on the matter from the CJEU.

[1]   *Enderby v Frenchay Health Authority* Case C-127/92 [1994] ICR 112, 129–130, 163.
[2]   *Barry v Midland Bank plc* [1999] ICR 859, 870–872.
[3]   Ibid. See also *Main v Scottish Ministers* [2015] CSIH 41, [43]–[49] (Lord Drummond Young defends at length a broad-brush approach, showing particular resistance to the least onerous means test).

9.41 *Barry* notwithstanding, it is generally clear that when applying EU law courts are expected to require that a challenged measure be the least intrusive means available.[1] This is less clear with regard to cases involving Convention rights. Although the *de Freitas* steps are used in HRA cases, the courts often followhave at times followed the Strasbourg practice of using the least intrusive alternative test (and hence *de Freitas*) only where the invasion of rights is seen as substantial, or where the rights interest at stake is seen as 'core' or 'fundamental'.[2] The test was ignored, for instance, in *R (Begum) v Headteacher and Governors of Denbigh High School* where, although the claimant invoked the right to freedom of religion (article 9 ECHR), the restriction in question was viewed as not sufficiently intrusive to require a least intrusive means test.[3] The claimant was prohibited from wearing a jilbab — a full-body covering designed to hide the female form — to school, where other schools in the area allowed the jilbab, and the Denbigh school allowed a shalwar kameeze, consisting of a smock-like dress and loose trousers tapered at the ankles. The rule was found proportionate, based on reasoning that focused on the availability to the claimant of other options (attending other schools, the shalwar kameeze) and on the prerogative of the school governors to make determinations relating to school dress. A consideration of less intrusive options would almost certainly have produced a different result, given that the legitimate objective was the protection of the rights and freedoms of others. It is difficult to see how people offended by the jilbab would not be offended by the shalwar kameeze, and the apparent ability of other schools to maintain public order in the face of the jilbab would make it difficult to argue that the jilbab and the jilbab alone was the key to ensuring social tranquillity.

1   *Barclays Bank plc v Competition Commission* [2009] CAT 27, [19]–[20]; *R (Age UK) v Secretary of State for Business, Innovation & Skills* [2009] EWHC 2336 [39]–[40](Admin).
2   *R (Samaroo) v Secretary of State for the Home Department* [2001] UKHRR 1622; *Lough v First Secretary of State* [2004] EWCA Civ 905, [2004] 1 WLR 2557, (2004) Times, 29 July.
3   [2006] UKHL 15.

9.42 Be that as it may, there is something to the idea that not every application of proportionality must involve the least intrusive alternative test. As discussed in section **9.29** above, structured proportionality, and especially the suitability and necessity tests, are methods of weighting the proportionality balancing in favour of rights interests. However, just as not all legitimate aims are created equal, neither are all rights interests. Not every case that properly arises under the HRA, for example, poses such a threat to core convention interests that the state should be called upon to employ only the least intrusive means available. Rightly or wrongly, the Lords in *Denbigh* almost certainly skirted the test because it would skew the balancing too far in favour of the interests of a claimant who, in their eyes, had other options and was not entitled to dictate the dress code of her school. In a less controversial decision, the Court of Appeal in *Lough* expressly rejected a least restrictive means test in favour of broad-brush balancing because 'the process outlined in *Samaroo*, while appropriate where there is direct interference with Article 8 rights by a public body, cannot be applied without adaptation in a situation where the essential conflict is between two or more groups of private interests. In such a situation, a balancing exercise . . . is sufficient to meet any requirement of proportionality.'[1] It is difficult to argue with the conclusion that when the rights of two private parties clash, the test for a claim by one of the parties should *not* require that the decision in favour of the other was the least intrusive means possible, as this would pre–judge the relative claims of the parties. Some courts have identified what they call 'second category cases' where the encroachment on core rights interests is so small that while a proportionality justification is required, it need not impose the necessity standard.[2] Strasbourg appears to provide support for the selective disapplication of the least intrusive means test simply by failing, without explanation, to apply it where it deems the margin of appreciation extensive or the rights interests at stake unworthy of vigorous protection.[3] It is submitted that this selective disapplication can be justified in certain cases, but should be done openly, noting the test as a normal part of structured proportionality and justifying departures on a case by case basis.However, the Supreme Court has made it clear that the test should not be disapplied, but applied with a 'margin of discretion' in mind, just as the ECtHR appears to ignore the test only when it deems the choice of means to fall entirely with the 'margin of appreciation'. 'The question is whether a less intrusive measure could have been used without unacceptably compromising the objective' opined the majority in *Bank Mellat*, explaining that respect for the expertise and democratic legitimacy of the executive decision-maker should render the court hesitant to re-make the decision, not to skip a key part of the proportionality analysis.[4]

1   *Lough v First Secretary of State* [2004] EWCA Civ 905, [2004] 1 WLR 2557, (2004) Times, 29 July (Keene, LJ).

² *M's Guardian v Advocate General for Scotland* [2010] CSOH 15; *R (Carson) v Secretary of State for Work and Pensions* [2005] UKHL 37.

³ *Carson v United Kingdom* Application 42184/05 (16 March 2010) (Grand Chamber)(2008) 48 EHRR 941, (2008) Times, 20 November; compare with *Campbell v United Kingdom* (Application 13590/88) (1992) 15 EHRR 137, [1992] ECHR 13590/88 Judgment of 25 March 1992, A 233 [48] and *Peck v United Kingdom* (Application 44647/98)(2003) 36 EHRR 719, [2003] IP & T 320, both of which applied the least intrusive means test.

⁴ *Bank Mellat v Her Majesty's Treasury (No 2)* [2013] UKSC 39 [20]–[21] (the Court here found that the challenged measure failed the least-onerous-means test despite having afforded the Secretary of State a wide margin of discretion).

9.43 An argument has emerged in recent years to the effect that the necessity test should be dispensed with in cases where the ECtHR would afford the broadest margin of appreciation.[1] This claim was rejected by the Supreme Court in *Lord Carlile*[2] and *Bank Mellat*, but it is worth explaining why the claim *should* fail. Firstly, it is based, in terms of authority, on the fact that the ECtHR frequently does not apply the least-intrusive–means test when it affords a member state a broad margin. As will be explained more fully in a subsequent section, the margin of appreciation doctrine does not apply to domestic decisions, so the fact that Strasbourg feels it is unable, at a distance, to assess what is the least intrusive means available sheds no light on how a domestic court should approach the task when evidence, parties, and institutional setting are familiar and close at hand. Second, the view grows out of a conflation of the language 'necessary in a democratic society' with the necessity test that forms a part of the orthodox proportionality test around the world. The words 'necessary in a democratic society' come from the Convention itself; the ECtHR has decided that the best way to assess this is through the application of the principle of proportionality. Therefore, the test that falls to be applied is proportionality. A court cannot, as Lady Arden in *Lord Carlile (CA)* sought to, avoid the meaning of proportionality by saying that 'necessary in a democratic society' does not necessarily entail a least restrictive means test: according to Strasbourg it *does* necessarily entail proportionality, so dispensing with an element of that test requires an independent justification. Finally, the substance of Lady Arden's justification in *Lord Carlile (CA)* was that with regard to certain matters, proportionality becomes *Wednesbury* reasonableness: 'In the context of national security and foreign policy, this is achieved as the Divisional Court held by a review of the Secretary of State's decisions for rationality, legality and procedural irregularity, not by the substitution by the court of its own judgment on the merits.'[3] This verges on a retreat to non-justiciability. If the relevant law calls for the application of proportionality as a standard for decision (as it did in *Lord Carlile*) judges must not simply declare that categories of subject matter are excluded from the application of proportionality.[4] If the special expertise or institutional legitimacy of a particular decision maker justify affording their views deference, this is properly recognised *within* the application of proportionality, not through replacing it with a test (*Wednesbury*) that has no more connection with the adjudication of human rights than that it is a comfort blanket for daunted judges. There are reasons for a court to restrain itself in applying the necessity test; however, as is explained below, these must have either to do with the limited importance of the rights interests at stake, or with the factual inability of the court to reliably challenge the executive determination. Fortunately, much of the domestic judiciary recognise the important role that the necessity element plays in proportionality, and recognise deference as something to afford within the proportionality analysis, not as an excuse to ignore proportionality altogether.[5] In *Lord Carlile (SCt)* the arguments above carried the day, as the Court noted that notwithstanding all of the grounds for exercising deference, 'the legal principle is clear enough . . . The court must consider whether some less onerous alternative would have been available without unreasonably impairing the objective.'[6]

1.   *R (Lord Carlile of Berriew) v Secretary of State for the Home Department* [2013] EWCA Civ 199, [6473]; ('Lord Carlile (CA)'); Monaghan, 'Judicial Discretion, Parliament and Executive Accountability in the Twenty-first Century: *R (Lord Carlile of Berriew and others) v Secretary of State for the Home Department*' [2013] JR 388.

2.   *R (Lord Carlile of Berriew) v Secretary of State for the Home Department* [2014] UKSC 60; [2015] 2 All ER 453 [22]34]] *('Lord Carlile (SCt)')*.

3.   *Lord Carlile* at [7(iii)].

4.   Kavanagh, 'Reasoning about proportionality under the Human Rights Act 1998: outcomes, substance and process' (2014) 130 LQR 235, 254.

5.   *R (T) v Secretary of State for the Home Department* [2014] UKSC 35, [50]; *SS (Nigeria) v Secretary of State for the Home Department* [2013] EWCA Civ 550, [3847].

6.   *R (Lord Carlile of Berriew) v Secretary of State for the Home Department* [2014] UKSC 60; [2015] 2 All ER 453 [34].

9.44 It has also been argued that the least intrusive means test assesses 'relative proportionality' as opposed to overall proportionality, and as such represents a problem or anomaly in the proportionality analysis.[1] This is based on the fact that courts have (a) required less restrictive alternatives that achieve less advancement of the aim than the challenged measure and (b) resorted to defining the legitimate aim so narrowly as to preclude the identification of any alternative to the measure under scrutiny.[2] However, these are simply judicial mistakes, not anomalies in the principle. Both of these circumstances are properly addressed by proportionality *stricto sensu*. If a challenged measure is the least intrusive means available to advance the objective to the degree the measure advances it, it should not be rejected by the least intrusive means test merely because there exists another hypothetical measure that would be less intrusive *but would advance the objective less effectively*. On the other hand, a court applying *stricto sensu* can properly find that a measure that is the least intrusive effective option nevertheless imposes an unacceptable degree of impact on rights interests. Such a finding would compel the conclusion that a less effective, less intrusive measure would be more appropriate.[3] A finding of disproportionate impact under *stricto sensu* would also smoke out attempts to circumscribe the legitimate aim in a way that would allow no less restrictive alternative (because the aim is identical with the measure). In sum, there is nothing problematic about either 'catching' those cases where a narrow legitimate aim compels a given measure (the narrow aim might not attract sufficient weight to justify the measure according to proportionality *stricto sensu*) or explaining those cases where the measure preferred by the court is less effective than the one proposed by the state (the measure proposed causes unacceptable impacts according to *stricto sensu*). However, what is problematic, from the standpoint of coherence, is the case where a court declines to ask whether the measure in question is the least intrusive one available to the decision-maker. Is this acceptable or not? Does proportionality as a principle require that all measures be the least intrusive? The answer turns on whether the principle is understood as consisting of each of the component questions of the structured analysis, or if those elements are merely instrumental in ensuring that the ultimate principle is observed.

[1] Hickman, '*The Substance and Structure of Proportionality*' [2008] PL 694, 701–711.
[2] *R (Clays Lane Housing Co-operative Ltd) v Housing Corpn* [2004] EWCA Civ 1658 [25]; *Smith v Secretary of State for Trade and Industry* [2007] EWHC 1013 (Admin) [50].
[3] See, eg, *Wallace v Secretary of State for Education* [2017] EWHC 109 (Admin).

9.45 In Germany there is a separate term for the necessity principle: 'Übermaßverbot', meaning 'prohibition of excess'.[1] This principle addresses the fact that there are cases where the least intrusive means test is indispensable in subjecting a measure to proper scrutiny, such as where the right is sufficiently core or fundamental that any excess is by definition a violation. But it is difficult to resist the idea that, in the absence of a clear requirement of 'Übermaßverbot', a court could, in tracing the extent and contours of a protected right, conclude that in a given case the right allows enough different options that the state might properly choose one that intrudes more than it needs to. UK courts and Strasbourg appear at times to take this view: that proportionality is about the ultimate balance, and that the least intrusive means test is at times superfluous because there is enough space in the right to allow for the challenged measure regardless of whether the same results could be achieved in a less intrusive way. Thus, for example, a limitation on advertising placards — commercial speech being deemed less fundamental than political speech — might properly be limited to any number of specific places in a town centre. If the local council decides to limit them to two locations when a limit of four would probably accomplish the objective of protecting the rights of others, is this inherently disproportionate because it goes further than it must? Assessed according to broad brush balancing the question would not be asked, yielding instead to the question of whether the negative impacts of the restriction outweighed the council's interest in imposing it. If not, then the 'excess', which would be forbidden by 'Übermaßverbot', is simply not proscribed by the proportionality principle. The only way to render this coherent is by seeing it as a reflection of deference. Sometimes the rights interests are sufficiently muted that the court must allow the decision-maker the freedom to choose an approach that is more intrusive than is necessary. This is consistent with the reasoning in *Lord Carlile (SCt)*.

[1] Goold et al at 12.

9.46 Robert Alexy has argued that this logic can only work because the state is often pursuing more than one interest.[1] Put more simplistically than Alexy puts it, if there is not at least some legitimate interest that justifies that part of the intrusion that is not strictly necessary, then that part of the intrusion must be viewed as lacking a legitimate aim, and must fail proportionality for that reason. The necessity test is, in short, implicit in rights whose contours are defined by proportionality, because they are guaranteed against intrusions without a legitimate aim. This supports the view that a necessity test must be applied, and the state must articulate the other objectives that explain the more intrusive choice (this would be consistent with the logic in *Lough*). Ultimately, UK courts and Strasbourg have not adequately answered this question: is it a central requirement of the principle of proportionality that the state should never impose more of a burden on a right that it must to achieve its objective? The case law is not clear, but enough cases ignore least-intrusive-means necessity to suggest that at least in practice the test is treated as merely instrumental to, rather than a fundamental aspect of, proportionality.

1   Alexy, *A Theory of Constitutional Rights* (translated by Rivers 2002) 399–401.

Proportionality stricto sensu

9.47 Proportionality *stricto sensu* means more than that the court must weigh the interests of the state against those of the claimant. It means that *even if* a challenged measure is important, suitable, and necessary, it *still* violates proportionality if it produces impacts that outweigh benefits actually achieved by the measure.[1] Keeping in mind that proportionality is usually invoked as a defence of state action that invades a right, the measure itself must pass muster, not merely its effect on the claimant, so 'impacts' means all of the impacts produced by the measure or policy. In other words, a state measure is not proportionate because its benefits outweigh its impacts on the claimant: its benefits must outweigh its impacts on rights interests generally.[2] However, this robust view of proportionality *stricto sensu* has not firmly taken hold in domestic jurisprudence. As we have seen, in *Huang v Secretary of State for the Home Department*[3] the House of Lords took an opportunity presented by an immigration case to point out a gap in the leading UK formulation of proportionality found in *De Freitas v Permanent Secretary of Ministry of Agriculture, Fisheries, Lands and Housing*.[4] This test required that:

(i)   the legislative objective is sufficiently important to justify limiting a fundamental right;

(ii)   the measures designed to meet the legislative objective are rationally connected to it; and

(iii) the means used to impair the right or freedom are no more than is necessary to accomplish the objective.[5]

This formulation of course assumes that if means are 'necessary to accomplish the objective,' then they satisfy proportionality, whatever their effects. UK courts had been citing *De Freitas* for years without appearing to notice the missing reference to, well, proportionality (proportionality *stricto sensu*). This of course must be set alongside the fact that UK courts have often eschewed any structured proportionality, opting instead for broad-brush balancing with its approximation of proportionality *stricto sensu*.[6] It leaves the impression that the judiciary had assumed that the choice is *either* broad-brush balancing, with its emphasis on weighing the competing interests *or* structured proportionality with its focus on scrutiny of the state's reasons for its action, but never both. Although *Huang* and *Bank Mellat* have on paper corrected this, it is worth bearing in mind the judicial tendency to resist the full structured test.

1   Ibid at 401–414; Goold et al at 2.
2   *Eweida and others v United Kingdom* [2013] ECHR 48420/10 [94];*A v Secretary of State for the Home Department* [2004] UKHL 56, [50]; *Ghaidan v Godin–Mendoza* [2004] UKHL 30, [19]–[20]; *National Union of Belgian Police v Belgium* (1976) 1 EHRR 578; Baker, 'Proportionality and Employment Discrimination in the UK' (2008) 37 ILJ 305, 319–323.
3   [2007] UKHL 11.
4   [1999] 1 AC 69.
5   *De Freitas* [1999] 1 AC 69 at 80.
6   Murray, 'Proportionality and Deference under the UK Human Rights Act: An institutionally Sensitive Approach (Book Review)' [2013] EHRLR 352, 354.

9.48 One reason for doubting the judicial commitment to the *stricto sensu* step is the lack of attention paid in most judgments to weighing the impacts of a challenged measure, as opposed to scrutinising the reasons for the measure. In *Huang*, while emphasising the need for the step, the House of Lords stopped short of providing guidance on what to weigh, how to assign values, and how to strike the balance.[1] In a case decided just before *Huang* the Lords made similar statements, striking the perfect note about proportionality, and then proceeding to apply it with little mention of the impacts of the measure at issue. In *Denbigh*,[2] the leading speech reminded courts that when they reached the proportionality part of the analysis, they must not merely examine whether the decision-maker performed the correct inquiry, they must perform it themselves:

> 'The domestic court must now make a value judgment, an evaluation, by reference to the circumstances prevailing at the relevant time. Proportionality must be judged objectively, by the court. As [Paul] Davies observed in his article cited above, "The retreat to procedure is of course a way of avoiding difficult questions". But it is in my view clear that the court must confront these questions, however difficult.'[3]

Having thus begun with an admonition for robust proportionality, Lord Bingham then proceeded to reject the Court of Appeal's finding of a violation of Article 9, based exclusively on the persuasiveness of the reasons in support of the challenged measure, as opposed to any analysis of its impacts.[4] As already noted, the three *De Freitas* steps are essentially scrutiny of the challenged measure and its reasons, while proportionality stricto sensu is the first place in the analysis where the effects of the measure take centre stage. It has also been noted that the Denbigh analysis avoided the structured proportionality tests of suitability and necessity, leaving very little to be considered other than how much thought the school put into the decision, and how many other options the claimant appeared to have. Although it could be argued that consideration of the options open to the claimant touches on impacts, it only does so if one finds the following syllogism persuasive:

(1) the only relevant impacts are those on the claimant alone, as opposed to the societal interest in protecting the manifestation of religion;

(2) if the claimant has other avenues for enjoyment of the right the impacts of the measure on her essentially disappear; and

(3) if something in the challenged policy makes the impacts less, then they must not be very bad.

The problem, of course, is that the options open to the claimant mean nothing if they are not set against a background of the overall effects of the measure; in short, they beg the question.[5] The Denbigh judgment makes no attempt to assess the impacts on rights interests (social inclusion, dignity, freedom of expression, freedom of religion) of a state-sanctioned policy that decides which religious clothing may be worn. It should be noted that this criticism of the reasoning employed does not in any way suggest that the decision reached in *Denbigh* was incorrect, only that despite a proper articulation of the proportionality analysis, the House of Lords failed actually to perform one.

[1] The case involved instructions to the Immigration Appeal Tribunal on how to review immigration decisions. The opinion urged the tribunal carefully to consider the petitioner's evidence, indicating that this could be decisive. However, the opinion offers no help on how to apply the principle of proportionality *stricto sensu*.

[2] [2006] UKHL 15.

3 Ibid at [30] (internal citations omitted).
4 Ibid at [30]–[34] (the other members of the majority followed suit).
5 *Eweida and others v United Kingdom* [2013] ECHR 48420/10 [94].

9.49 There is Strasbourg authority for the proposition that impacts on rights interests beyond those of the claimant must be weighed, and can outweigh even suitable, necessary measures in pursuit of important state aims.[1] In *Dudgeon v United Kingdom*[2] the ECtHR found unjustified a law in Northern Ireland that outlawed homosexual sex between consenting adults. In analysing whether the challenged measure satisfied proportionality under Article 8 (right to privacy), the Court noted that no less restrictive alternatives existed that would meet the state's objectives.[3] The Court then went on to hold that, 'on the issue of proportionality, the Court considers that such justifications as there are for retaining the law in force unamended are outweighed by the detrimental effects which the very existence of the legislative provisions in question can have on the life of a person of homosexual orientation like the applicant.'[4] Earlier in its opinion the Court had catalogued these effects and commented on the vast number of people affected and the sweeping extent of the effect in terms of the ability of those people to act according to their inclinations. The Court's analysis considered not only the effect of the law on the claimant, but on all homosexuals, and on society as a whole. Proportionality in Strasbourg routinely takes into account impacts not only on the claimant but on the claimant's group, upon society, and upon Convention interests in general.[5] The same analysis applies even where the rights at issue are not as 'fundamental' or 'core' as privacy.[6] The CJEU has also clarified that the final step of proportionality requires consideration of impacts well beyond the individual claimant. In the *Chez*[7] case the CJEU addressed an indirectly discriminatory[8] practice of placing electricity meters in a Roma neighbourhood, but not in other neighbourhoods, too high for easy access, because people in that neighbourhood were thought likely to vandalise them or steal electricity. In assessing whether the discrimination could be justified as proportionate, the Court found the first three steps satisfied, but strongly doubted whether *stricto sensu* proportionality could be satisfied in light of the broader impacts:

> '123 Furthermore, assuming that no other measure as effective as the practice at issue can be identified, the referring court will also have to determine whether the disadvantages caused by the practice at issue are disproportionate to the aims pursued and whether that practice unduly prejudices the legitimate interests of the persons inhabiting the district concerned (see to this effect, in particular, judgments in Ingeniørforeningen i Danmark, C-499/08, EU:C:2010:600, paragraphs 32 and 47, and Nelson and Others, C-581/10 and C-629/10, EU:C:2012:657, paragraph 76 et seq).
>
> 124 The referring court will, first, have to pay regard to the legitimate interest of the final consumers of electricity in having access to the supply of electricity in conditions which do not have an offensive or stigmatising effect.
>
> 125 It will also be incumbent upon it to take into consideration the binding, widespread and long-standing nature of the practice at issue which, as is common ground, and as has already been pointed out in paragraph 84 of the present judgment, is imposed without distinction and lastingly on all the inhabitants of the district concerned notwithstanding the fact — which is for the referring court to

verify — that no individual unlawful conduct is attributable to most of them and they cannot be held accountable for such acts caused by third parties either.

126 In its assessment, the referring court will, finally, have to take account of the legitimate interest of the final consumers inhabiting the district concerned in being able to check and monitor their electricity consumption effectively and regularly, an interest and monitoring which, as has already been pointed out in paragraph 44 of the present judgment, have been expressly recognised and encouraged by the EU legislature.

127 Although it seems that it necessarily follows from the taking into account of all the foregoing criteria that the practice at issue cannot be justified within the meaning of Article 2(2)(b) of Directive 2000/43 since the disadvantages caused by the practice appear disproportionate to the objectives pursued, in the context of proceedings concerning a preliminary reference made on the basis of Article 267 TFEU it is for the referring court to carry out the final assessments which are necessary in that regard.'[9]

It should be noted that the case involved a single claimant who was not herself Roma.

[1] *Dudgeon v United Kingdom* [1981] 4 EHRR 149; *Paulik v Slovakia* [2006] ECHR 10699/05.
[2] (1981) 4 EHRR 149.
[3] *Dudgeon v United Kingdom* (1981) 4 EHRR 149, [59].
[4] Ibid at [60].
[5] *Unal Takeli v Turkey* [2004] ECHR 29865/96, [59]–[69] (invoking the impact of a rule requiring wives to take on the names of their husbands on the European interest in advancing gender equality); *Smith v United Kingdom* [2000] ECHR 33985/96, [90]–[94] (cataloguing the impacts of sexual orientation discrimination on homosexuals in the military, including on job prospects); *Sidabras* [2004] ECHR 395, [51]–[61] (noting the long-term impacts of anti-former-KGB-agent ban on the careers and prospects of those affected by it).
[6] *Paulik v Slovakia* [2006] ECHR 10699/05.
[7] Case C-83/14 CHEZ *Razpredelenie Bulgaria AD v Komisia za zashtita ot diskriminatsia* [2016] 1 CMLR 14 (CJEU (Grand Chamber)).
[8] The analysis of the proportionality of indirect discrimination before the CJEU is typical of the analysis of any invasion of a fundamental right.
[9] Case C-83/14 CHEZ *Razpredelenie Bulgaria AD v Komisia za zashtita ot diskriminatsia* [2016] 1 CMLR 14 (CJEU (Grand Chamber)) [123]–[127].

9.50 Resistance to this kind of approach taking hold in the UK is rooted in judicial review. Judges accustomed to the traditional restraint and deference so inherent in the UK judicial review culture find it very difficult to accept that they must disapply, 'read down', or declare incompatible a measure that pursues an important state objective, in a way that is both suitable to achieving it and causes no more harm than is necessary to achieve it. Lord Justice Laws very recently summed up the domestic judicial attitude to the fourth step of structured proportionality thusly:

'I think it needs to be approached with some care. It appears to require the court, in a case where the impugned measure passes muster on points (i)–(iii), to decide whether the measure, though it has a justified purpose and is no more intrusive than necessary, is nevertheless offensive because it fails to strike the right balance between private right and public interest; and the court is the judge of where the balance should lie. I think there is real difficulty in distinguishing this from a political question to be decided by the elected arm of government. If it is properly within the judicial sphere, it must be on the footing that there is a plain case.'[1]

However, other recent cases have shown less discomfort with an explicit balancing exercise. In *R (Aguilar Quila) v Secretary of State for the Home*

Department[2] the Supreme Court upheld a challenge to a rule excluding spouses from receiving leave to remain by virtue of marriage to a UK citizen if they are under the age of 21 when they marry. The objective of the rule was to reduce forced marriages. The judgment carefully considered:

(1)   the impact of the policy as a whole;
(2)   the impact of the particular application of the policy to the claimant;
(3)   the respective weights of the interests at stake; and
(4)   the implications of a report by social scientists on the risk factors for forced marriages.

In *R (L) v Commissioner of Police of the Metropolis* [2009] UKSC 3 the new UK Supreme Court found a system for deciding what information would be contained on Enhanced Criminal Record Certificates disproportionate, because it elevated the rights of those protected by the scheme above the privacy rights of those subject to it.[3] This case likewise involved a careful consideration of empirical evidence of the impacts of the system, and a painstaking consideration of the relative weights given by the system to the rights of potential victims of crime and the rights of those accused, but never convicted, of crimes. These bright spots are not yet representative,[4] and most cases continue to be decided with at best perfunctory assessments of impacts. It is likely that this flows less from entrenched judicial attitudes than from the fact that advocates do not direct their arguments and proof at the weight of impacts.

[1]   *R (Miranda) v Secretary of State for the Home Department* [2014] EWHC 255 (Admin), [40].
[2]   [2011] UKSC 45.
[3]   [2009] UKSC 3.
[4]   Although their number is growing, and includes cases such as *Homer v Chief Constable of West Yorkshire Police* [2012] UKSC 15 and *R (T) v Secretary of State for the Home Department* [2014] UKSC 35.

EU PROPORTIONALITY IN DOMESTIC COURTS

The role of the reviewing court in EU proportionality cases

9.51 Previous sections have outlined the general approach of the CJEU to proportionality; this section is concerned with how UK courts should approach proportionality in cases involving EU law. The question involves the distinction between using proportionality as a standard for decision rather than a standard of review. Decisions of the CJEU itself will doubtless contain language which makes proportionality look like a standard of review, touching on issues of respect for national traditions and superior local knowledge.[1] Here the proportionality analysis not only serves to describe the scope of the right in question, but to achieve a certain distance from the original decision, and describe the deference due to national authorities. In the hands of the domestic judiciary, however, EU proportionality is exclusively a standard for decision. The European Communities Act 1972 places UK courts in a position where they may not stand back from the original decision in the way that *Wednesbury* implies. The domestic court must, in essence, certify that the decision was proportionate, not that the decision-maker could reasonably conclude that it was.[2] There are many EU rights and regulatory schemes that incorporate proportionality in some way, and proportionality is a general principle of EU law, so it is not possible to set out all of the sources of the principle here. Wherever the principle arises, however, the court must decide whether the challenged decision or rule is proportionate, and must gather evidence and establish factual findings where necessary to determine the merits of the proportionality question.[3] EU cases in particular have noted that full discovery must be required to assist the proportionality determination, even in a judicial review setting, because policy documents are often conflicting, the policy process ill-informed, and statements of policy themselves are insufficient to establish the true reasons for policies and their contemplated effects.[4]

[1]   *R (Age UK) v Secretary of State for Business, Innovation & Skills* [2009] EWHC 2336 [36] (Admin).
[2]   Green, 'Proportionality and the Sovereignty of Parliament in the UK', in Ellis (ed) *The Principle of Proportionality in the Laws of Europe* (1999), 148; *Stoke-on-Trent City Council v B & Q plc* [1993] AC 900. This is of course subject to the 'narrow' approach to some classes of case, with its 'manifestly inappropriate' standard, mentioned at **9.18**. This is discussed further below.
[3]   *R v Ministry of Agriculture, Fisheries and Food, ex p First City Trading Ltd* [1997] 1 CMLR 250, 278.
[4]   *R v Secretary of State for Transport, ex p Factortame Ltd* [1998] Eu LR 475 (DC); [1998] 3 CMLR 192 (CA).

9.52 The use of the hated word 'merits' above does not suggest that there is no detachment at all in the standard of review for EU cases. A proper application of proportionality should in most cases yield a range of activity that would not violate the right in question. Even a 'least intrusive means' requirement leaves room for several different approaches, so long as all of them roughly equally advance the stated aim and impose the same degree of restriction on rights. In short, judges can honour judicial review tradition by refusing to ask whether they would make the same decision, while at the same time arriving at an independent assessment of whether the decision at issue satisfied the proportionality standard for decision.[1] Moreover, deference can play as large a part in EU cases as in any other. ECJ articulations of the demands of proportionality have identified areas (eg, social policy) where national authorities are afforded a wide margin of appreciation. UK courts do not hesitate to pass the greater part of this margin on to Parliament and the executive. This has effect not so much in the form of a standard of review as in the weight to be given to state's reasons in the *stricto sensu* balancing.[2] Finally, as indicated at 9.18 above, there are some classes of cases where it is appropriate for a UK court to apply a 'manifestly inappropriate' standard of review when applying proportionality as an EU standard for decision. The CJEU applies this standard of review when considering acts and decisions of EU institutions, or of member state institutions implementing EU law by exercising a discretion granted by that law.[3] However, the standard does not apply in the majority of cases, which involve either (a) a member state imposing a burden on an EU or fundamental right or (b) a member state derogating from EU law.[4] Prior to the Supreme Court's decision in *Lumsden*, UK courts had tended to use the manifestly inappropriate standard in any EU case where it suited their views of its proper disposition, almost certainly because of the previously-noted judicial resistance to full-blooded proportionality. The Court found it necessary, therefore, to expound at length about (1) when that deferential standard should apply, and (2) what the standard means in practice. While clarifying that the standard had no place in cases alleging that the UK has infringed a right (except when exercising EU-granted discretion), the Court explained that the manifestly inappropriate standard was not an alternative to proportionality, but a calibration of how searchingly a court should apply each step of the test: 'the word 'manifestly' appears to describe the degree of obviousness with which the impugned measure fails the proportionality test.'[5]

[1]   Green at 154–155; *Barclays Bank plc v Competition Commission* [2009] CAT 27 [22]–[29].
[2]   *BAA Ltd v Competition Commission* [2009] CAT 35 [136]–[139].
[3]   *R (Lumsdon) v Legal Services Board* [2015] UKSC 41; [2016] 1 All ER 391 [40]–[49], [73].
[4]   Ibid [50]–[72], [74].
[5]   Ibid [42].

9.53 The role of the UK judge in relation to EU law—where the domestic judge applies EU proportionality essentially as a matter of first impression—differs meaningfully from the role of the UK judge applying the ECHR, which is discussed below. There is a suggestion, however, that this gap is closing and is likely to close further.[1] The EU continues to investigate accession directly to the ECHR, which could mean that soon the EU will itself be directly bound by Convention rights. Indeed, the CJEU has recently taken to conforming its judgments to Strasbourg principles without accession, whenever the EU Charter of Fundamental Rights applies and can be connected to an analogous provision in the ECHR. In *Case C-400/10PPU, J McB v LE*, the CJEU held that in such a case the Court of Justice should follow any clear and constant jurisprudence of the European Court of Human Rights, adding:

> 'It is clear that the said Article 7 [of the Charter] contains rights corresponding to those guaranteed by Article 8(1) of the ECHR. Article 7 of the Charter must therefore be given the same meaning and the same scope as Article 8(1) of the ECHR, as interpreted by the case-law of the European Court of Human Rights(see, by analogy, Case C-450/06 Varec [2008] ECR I-581, paragraph 48).'[2]

It should be kept in mind, therefore, that already, and increasingly, EU cases can open the door to consideration of ECHR rights and Strasbourg teaching. This will almost certainly mean that ECtHR jurisprudence will dictate where proportionality is required to define the contours of a right, while EU requirements with regard to the attitude of the domestic court will dictate how proportionality is applied.

[1]   O'Neill, 'How the CJEU Uses the Charter of Fundamental Rights' [2012] JR 203.
[2]   [2011] 3 WLR 699, [53].

The structure of the EU law test

9.54 The structure of the proportionality test in EU law is variable, as it is in ECHR law, but the structure tends to follow either a two-part or three-part formulation.[1] The language most often used in EU instruments and the Treaty is that measures must be 'appropriate and necessary to a legitimate aim'. As we have seen, this can even be refined to a test that identifies four specific principles. For example the judgment of the CJEU in *R v Minister of Agriculture, Fisheries and Food and the Secretary of State for Health, ex p Fedesa* said of proportionality, '[b]y virtue of that principle, the lawfulness of the prohibition of an economic activity is subject to the condition that the prohibitory measures are appropriate and necessary in order to achieve the objectives legitimately pursued by the legislation in question; when there is a choice between several appropriate measures recourse must be had to the least onerous, and the disadvantages caused must not be disproportionate to the aims pursued.'[2]

Domestic courts have teased this out into the following formulation:

'[a challenged] measure: (1) must be effective to achieve the legitimate aim in question (appropriate), (2) must be no more onerous than is required to achieve that aim (necessary), (3) must be the least onerous, if there is a choice of equally effective measures, and (4) in any event must not produce adverse effects which are disproportionate to the aim pursued.'[3]

In this test step 3, or least-intrusive-means necessity, must be seen as a fundamental part of what is meant by proportionality, and not to be dispensed with in the way courts sometimes do in ECHR cases.

[1]   Green at 146.
[2]   Case C-331/88 [1990] ECR I-4023 [13].
[3]   *BAA Ltd v Competition Commission* [2009] CAT 35 [137].

PROPORTIONALITY UNDER THE HRA 1998

Proportionality as part of the definition of rights

9.55 ECHR jurisprudence under the HRA requires proportionality not because this is the standard of review, but because it has been adopted by the ECtHR as part of the definition of certain rights. Most obviously, arts 8–11 have limitation clauses which specify that the rights (to privacy, religion, expression, and association) can be qualified or restricted in pursuit of enumerated interests, where to do so is 'prescribed by law and necessary in a democratic society.' The Strasbourg court has employed proportionality to define what counts as 'necessary in a democratic society.' This means that the actual content of these rights — the extent and contours of the protection afforded by the Convention against state interference — is defined as, for example, the right not to have your expression restricted except in a way that is proportionate and prescribed by law. Article 6, protecting the right to a fair trial, also depends on proportionality to define the right of access to a court.[1] Here the standard requires that restrictions on access:

(1)   not impair the 'essence of the right';
(2)   pursue a legitimate aim; and
(3)   are proportionate to that aim.

Steps (2) and (3) are the familiar Strasbourg formulation of the test. Although art 6 is not qualified in the way arts 8–11 are, the definition of the implied right of access to a court depends on proportionality for its content. Thus proportionality comes before a domestic court applying the HRA not as a general principle to help govern the review of administrative decisions, but as a substantive standard for defining the content of the rights at issue.

[1]   *Tinnelly & Sons Ltd v United Kingdom (Application 20390/92); McElduff v United Kingdom (Application 21322/93)* (1998) 27 EHRR 249.

9.56 Proportionality also plays a part in defining the rights that do not have qualifications, or those with qualifications that do not incorporate the phrase 'necessary in a democratic society.' Article 5, setting out the right to liberty and security of person, allows for limitations of that right on grounds much more constricted than 'necessary in a democratic society.' There is clear authority to the effect that art 5 has no inherent proportionality requirement,[1] but this same authority requires that detention not be arbitrary, which is tested by way of proportionality. Domestic cases have found proportionality relevant to the time period of detention in mental health[2] and immigration[3] cases, and that domestic law authorising detention not be arbitrary or disproportionate.[4] Finally, the House of Lords recently found that whether crowd control measures which constrain freedom of movement constitute deprivations of liberty depends on the proportionality of the crowd control measures.[5] This leaves little doubt that proportionality plays a part in defining the contours of the right to liberty, but only around the margins. Proportionality plays a similar role in determining the scope of the unqualified rights to life and to be free from torture, in arts 2 and 3 respectively. A kind of 'strict necessity' proportionality is used to define what uses of force — that lead to unintended killings — are acceptable in the application of the art 2(2) exceptions.[6] The ECtHR has used a form or proportionality to assess whether certain kinds of treatment amount to 'inhuman or degrading treatment,' by considering whether the anguish imposed on a death row inmate was disproportionate to the gravity of the crime committed.[7] In all of these cases, however, the 'proportionality' used must be distinguished from the general test of proportionality with which this chapter is concerned. The point in discussing them here is to emphasise that where proportionality applies under the HRA, it does so because the ECtHR, and domestic courts following its lead, have incorporated it into the meaning of ECHR rights.

[1]   *Winterwerp v Netherlands* (1979) 2 EHRR 387 at [39] and *Ashingdane v United kKingdom* (1985) 7 EHRR 528, [1985] ECHR 8225/78.

[2]   *R (H) v London North and East Region Mental Health Review Tribunal (Secretary of State intervening)* [2001] EWCA Civ 415,[2002] QB 1 at [33], applied in *R (Secretary of State for the Home Department) v Mental Health Tribunal* [2002] EWHC 1128 (Admin) at [24] ('in determining whether it is appropriate to detain a patient in hospital, the interests of the patient have to be weighed against those of the public, and the tribunal has to determine whether the detention is proportional to the risks involved').

[3]   *ID v Home Office* [2005] EWCA Civ 1554 [2005] INLR 278 [100].

[4]   *R (Saadi) v Secretary of State for the Home Department* [2002] UKHL 41, [2002] 1 WLR 3131 at [43] and *R v Governor of Brockhill Prison, ex p Evans (No 2)* [2001] 2 AC 19 at 32.

[5]   *Austin v Metropolitan Police Comr* [2009] UKHL 5 [34].

[6]   Fenwick, *Civil Liberties and Human Rights*, 4th edn (2007) 43–45.

[7]   *Soering v United Kingdom* (1989) 11 EHRR 439 [104].

Section 6(1) HRA and the standard of review

9.57 Section 6 HRA makes it 'unlawful for a [court] to act in a way which is incompatible with a Convention Right,' without express authority from Parliament. This prohibition applies to other state entities as well. It means that presumably all legislative and executive acts have been issued subject to this requirement, but institutionally the courts have the final word, because they have the last chance to prevent Convention-incompatible state actions, and the duty to do so.[1] The courts are bound to apply Parliamentary statutes, but s 3(1) HRA requires judges, 'so far as it is possible to do so' to read and 'give effect' to legislation, regulations, or decisions in a way compatible with Convention rights, even where a natural reading of the law would violate the Convention. Where a measure cannot be read in a Convention-compatible way without going against the manifest intent of Parliament, s 4 HRA requires that the court issue a 'declaration of incompatibility,' meaning that the court will apply the statute as written, but substantial political pressure will exist for Parliament to amend the offending statute (although it is not obligated to do so). This means that the courts are empowered essentially to change the effects of measures—amend them from what they would have been upon a natural reading—unless the offending effects were consciously intended by Parliament, in which case they are to tell Parliament if they think it struck the balance incorrectly.[2]

[1] See, eg, Klug, '*The Human Rights Act—A "Third Way" or "Third Wave" Bill of Rights*,' [2001] EHRLR 361; Leigh, '*Taking Rights Proportionately: Judicial Review, the Human Rights Act and Strasbourg*', [2002] PL 265, 282–286; Jowell, *Beyond the Rule of Law: Towards Constitutional Judicial Review*, [2000] PL 671; Elliott, '*The HRA 1998 and the Standard of Substantive Review*,' 60 CLJ 301 (2001); Craig, *Administrative Law* (4th edn, 1999) 546, 556–557, 561.

[2] Kavanagh, '*The Elusive Divide between Interpretation and Legislation under the Human Rights Act 1998*,' (2004) 24 OJLS 259, 274–277.

9.58 This means that judges have been expressly instructed to make a determination as to whether Convention rights *have been violated*, not whether Parliament or an executive decision-maker reasonably thought they were acting consistently with Convention rights. This is how Lord Steyn in *R (Daly) v Secretary of State for the Home Department* put it:

'First, the doctrine of proportionality may require the reviewing court to assess the balance which the decision maker has struck, not merely whether it is within the range of rational or reasonable decisions. Secondly, the proportionality test may go further than the traditional grounds of review inasmuch as it may require attention to be directed to the relative weight accorded to interests and considerations.[1]'

This was further clarified in *Denbigh* to require that courts ask not whether the original decision-maker properly performed a proportionality analysis, but whether the decision was or was not proportionate: 'The domestic court must . . . make a value judgment, an evaluation, by reference to the circumstances prevailing at the relevant time; [p]roportionality must be judged objectively, by the court.'[2] Courts have been at pains to say that this is not 'merits' review, observing that the role of judge and decision-maker are distinct.[3] How this is fleshed out is addressed in more detail in **9.62** below, but the general approach of domestic courts is to give deference to decision-makers in areas of their explicit expertise or based on democratic legitimacy. Nevertheless, courts in HRA cases do carefully review the facts and assign weights to the respective sides of the balance, according to their own view of the evidence and their own assessment of the interests at stake.[4] Moreover, in judicial review cases UK courts are frequently willing to accept new evidence and make specific factual findings to support their proportionality determinations:

'In the minority of judicial review applications in which the precise facts are significant, procedures exist . . . for disclosure of specific documents to be sought and ordered. Such applications are likely to increase in frequency, since human rights decisions under the Convention tend to be very fact-specific and any judgment on the proportionality of a public authority's interference with a protected Convention right is likely to call for a careful and accurate evaluation of the facts.[5]'

Thus, while the standard of review might not amount to merits review, it bears little resemblance to *Wednesbury*.[6]

[1]   [2001] UKHL 26 [27].
[2]   [2006] UKHL 15 [29] (citations omitted).
[3]   *Daly* [2001] UKHL 26 [28].
[4]   *R (Boroumand) v Secretary of State for the Home Department* [2010] EWHC 225 (Admin); *R(L) v Metropolitan Police Comr* [2009] UKSC 3; *R (Quila) v Secretary of State for the Home Department* [2009] EWHC 3189 (Admin).
[5]   *Tweed v Parades Commission for Northern Ireland* [2006] UKHL 53 [3].
[6]   Kavanagh, 'Reasoning about proportionality under the Human Rights Act 1998: outcomes, substance and process' (2014) 130 LQR 235, 254.

The inapplicability of the margin of appreciation

9.59   The ECtHR applies proportionality, of course, from the perspective of a supranational Court whose job is to supervise the compliance of several sovereign states with an international treaty. One cannot understand the Strasbourg approach to proportionality without understanding the 'margin of appreciation'. An underlying principle of the ECHR is that Strasbourg determines the standard to which human rights must be protected, but the Contracting Parties decide how to deliver this level of protection. In other words, the mode of protection of Convention rights is not expected to be the same throughout Europe. From this principle has emerged the doctrine of the margin of appreciation, which refers to an area within which Strasbourg defers to the prerogative of the signatory state to strike its own characteristic balance when human rights must give way to overriding state interests. This does not mean that the ECtHR does not impose limits, it simply means that states are allowed to reach different outcomes when applying proportionality, as long as the outcomes are not outside the margin of appreciation.[1] The ECtHR loosens or constricts the margin of appreciation according to the kinds of rights at stake or the kind of public interest behind the challenged measure.[2] This has led the Court at times to give Convention rights unnecessarily constricted protection.[3] However, the Strasbourg Court does not really 'do' proportionality beyond what is necessary to determine whether the balance struck by the signatory state exceeds the margin of appreciation. In doing so the Court often takes its own view of the weights to be attributed to the state's reasons for its action and the impacts of that action, including individual, group, or broader societal impacts.[4] The actual mechanics of proportionality, however, have always been for the Contracting Parties to sort out, and it is for the state to decide whether the legislature, the judiciary, the executive, or some combination thereof, ultimately strikes the balance.[5]

[1]   Fleshing out the contours of Strasbourg's margin of appreciation falls outside the scope of this chapter. For a thorough discussion, see Arai–Takahashi, *The Margin of Appreciation Doctrine and the Principle of Proportionality in the Jurisprudence of the ECHR* (2002).
[2]   For a full discussion of the variation of proportionality intensity, see generally Rivers, 'Proportionality and Variable Intensity of Review' (2006) 65(1) CLJ 174–207.
[3]   See Generally Fenwick, *Civil Liberties and Human Rights, 4th edn* (2007) ch 4; Arai-Takahashi, *The Margin of Appreciation Doctrine and the Principle of Proportionality in the*

Jurisprudence of the ECHR (2002), Letsas, *A Theory of Interpretation of the European Convention on Human Rights* (2007), 84–92.

4   *Belgian Linguistics* (1968) 1 EHRR 252, 283.

5   See, eg, *Unison v United Kingdom* [2002] IRLR 497; *Schmidt and Dahlstrom v Sweden* (1976) 1 EHRR 632, [34]–[36] (1976).

9.60 The margin of appreciation itself has no application in domestic adjudication, where courts do not need to consider divergent cultural contexts. There have been arguments, however, to the effect that the margin of appreciation defines the substantive scope of Convention rights.[1] This logic has it that Strasbourg uses the margin to describe the area of activity within which the state is free to operate, in essence saying that the Convention rights have no purchase in this area. If this were so, then domestic courts would be right to treat any activity within the margin, as identified by ECtHR decisions, as within the prerogative of the state. However, Strasbourg does not in fact use this logic to defend the margin of appreciation. It is true that the Court often focuses on the indeterminacy of some rights issues, relying on the absence of a clear consensus among the Contracting Parties to justify allowing a given state wide discretion.[2] The contemporary understanding, however, is that the margin is a creature of subsidiarity, the principle that decisions should be taken at the level closest to the relevant interests.[3] The Court consistently links the margin with the fact that national authorities are in a better position to judge what counts as a compelling state interest, local understandings of the content of rights, and local impacts.[4] Thus the consideration of varying practices among Contracting parties reflects not indeterminacy or a range of discretion, but the recognition that what proportionality requires depends on context. Remember that proportionality defines the qualified rights as a guarantee against invasion of the protected rights interests except by measures that are suitable and necessary to achieve a sufficiently important state interest without imposing impacts disproportionate to that interest. Therefore the extent and contours of the right in any given case depend on the reasons for the interference, their necessity, and their impacts. These contours thus depend on local circumstances much more appropriately assessed by national authorities. The lesson of the margin of appreciation, then, is that where the ECtHR might find that a particular state action falls within the margin, it does so only because from Strasbourg the area within the margin is a 'grey area,' impenetrable from afar, but which local courts have no excuse not to clarify.

1   See, eg, Letsas, at 84–92, for an insightful discussion of this argument, although it should be noted that Letsas does not argue that this is the correct conception.

2   *S and Marper v United Kingdom* (Applications 30562/04 and 30566/04) (Grand Chamber 2008)(2008) 48 EHRR 1169, [2009] Crim LR 355.

3   Feldman at 138, Sottiaux at 54.

4   *Handyside v United Kingdom* (1976) 1 EHRR 737, [48]–[49]; Sottiaux at 53.

9.61 The clarity of the foregoing logic makes it particularly difficult to swallow a recent line of jurisprudence that has emerged around cases involving the discriminatory denial of state benefits. The current understanding is that where a general (ie not directly discriminatory) rule about entitlement to a state benefit is found to be indirectly discriminatory, in that it places members of a certain status group at a disadvantage, it can be justified without satisfying proportionality, so long as it is not 'manifestly without reasonable foundation'.[1] This line of authority has evolved from *Stec v UK*,[2] in which the ECtHR explained that with Article 14 discrimination claims in benefits cases it would afford member states great latitude:

'The scope of this margin will vary according to the circumstances, the subject-matter and the background. As a general rule, very weighty reasons would have to be put forward before the Court could regard a difference in treatment based exclusively on the ground of sex as compatible with the Convention. On the other hand, a wide margin is usually allowed to the State under the Convention when it comes to general measures of economic or social strategy. Because of their direct knowledge of their society and its needs, the national authorities are in principle better placed than the international judge to appreciate what is in the public interest on social or economic grounds, and the Court will generally respect the legislature's policy choice unless it is 'manifestly without reasonable foundation.'

The domestic decisions in *R (RJM (FC)) v Secretary of State for Work and Pensions*[3] and later *Humphreys* converted this directly into a principle that the test for justification of indirect discrimination *in benefits cases only* would be 'manifestly without reasonable foundation' instead of proportionality, which applies in all other cases of discrimination under ECHR Article 14. Because in other cases the UK courts have clearly evidenced their understanding that the margin of appreciation is not a domestically relevant doctrine, this line of jurisprudence seems wilfully obtuse. As we have seen already with sensitive areas like foreign policy and national security, indirect discrimination in benefits appears to be an area where UK judges will snatch at whatever excuse Strasbourg dictum offers to avoid subjecting government policy to the scrutiny of a proportionality test. As it began with the House of Lords and has been confirmed by the Supreme Court, this special test is probably here for a while.[4] In terms of doctrinal coherence, however, it stands outside the general rule that where the contours of an ECHR right fall to be defined according to proportionality, the fact that the ECtHR used the margin of appreciation to explain its failure to apply rigorous proportionality does not excuse domestic courts from their responsibility to do so. The test is also applied without the respect for proportionality evidenced in Lumsden's[5] approach to the 'manifestly inappropriate standard' in EU law, as well as flying in the face of more general statements about how deference must occur within the proportionality assessment in *Bank Mellat*[6] and *Lord Carlile*[7] (SCt).

[1]   *Humphreys v Revenue and Customs Comrs* [2012] UKSC 18, [15]–[21].
[2]   (2006) 43 EHRR 1017, [52].
[3]   [2008] UKHL 63. This approach was subsequently taken again in *R (SG) v Secretary of State for Work and Pensions (Child Poverty Action Group intervening)* [2015] UKSC 16.
[4]   It has, however, been questioned, and not applied in the case of student loans even though they were accepted to be a kind of state benefit: *Hunter v Student Awards Agency for Scotland* [2016] CSOH 71 [39]–[50].
[5]   *R (Lumsdon) v Legal Services Board* [2015] UKSC 41; [2016] 1 All ER 391 [42].
[6]   *Bank Mellat v Her Majesty's Treasury (No 2)* [2013] UKSC 39 [20]–[21].
[7]   *R (Lord Carlile of Berriew) v Secretary of State for the Home Department* [2014] UKSC 60 [34].

Deference and the area of discretionary judgment

9.62 However, some of the reasons behind Strasbourg's application and adjustment of the margin of appreciation bear on the domestic application of proportionality. Courts in the UK have sought to translate the margin of appreciation into a domestic 'area of discretionary judgment'. The logic here is that where the ECtHR would leave certain determinations to local authorities, courts should leave them to executive decision-makers and Parliament. On its face, of course, this begs the question of why these decisions should be left only to these representatives of the 'national authorities' deferred to by Strasbourg using the margin of appreciation; the judiciary surely count as part of the national authorities. The implication of the margin is that the local authorities must not only make the decisions left to them by the margin, but that they must decide which authorities make which parts of the decision. This means that if there is to be a domestic analogue to the margin, it must be freshly worked out and not simply passed on to the arms of the state most sensitive to majority opinion. However, UK courts have often used the margin as authority to defer to executive or legislative decisions that fall within the area that the ECtHR would have left to the national authorities generally. Most House of Lords or UK Supreme Court decisions have avoided treating the area of discretionary judgment as coterminous with the margin of appreciation, using instead the language of 'deference'.[1] The prevailing account has courts defining the area of discretion afforded to the 'democratic' branches of government according to many of the observations made by the ECtHR in respect of the margin of appreciation, but distinguishing those aspects that do not fall within the special expertise of those organs of the state, or that do not call for the articulation of majority preference.[2] However, many decisions appear simply to pass the margin of appreciation in its entirety on to the executive and Parliament.[3] For example, the case of *R (Smith) v Secretary of State for Defence*[4] involved a claim of sex and age discrimination under arts 8 and 14 of the Convention, complaining that the law on pension sharing for divorced spouses allowed a man to receive his share of the pension, if payable under its terms, before he reached 60, but required his ex-spouse to wait until the age of 60 before receiving her share. The Court of Appeal, Dyson, LJ, found *prima facie* sex discrimination, and had this to say about the proportionality justification:

> 'It seems to me to be important to bear in mind that the justification put forward in the present case is in the area of social and economic policy. It is well established that the court will accord to government a substantial margin of appreciation in relation to judgments in the field of social and economic policy — that is for the simple reason that the court is ill–equipped to form judgments in that area, less well equipped than it is in areas such as those of justice, for example. Conversely, the court acknowledges that it is precisely in the areas of social and economic policy that government is peculiarly well equipped to form judgments. It is clearly the considered view of government that the impugned provision is necessary in order to promote and assist in the achievement of the aim of encouraging ex–spouses to work until the age of 60.'

That was all the court had to say on the matter. No specific findings were made about the government's reasons for the rule or impact of the provision, either on the claimant or on divorced wives in general (nor had there been in the Administrative Court below). The provision was proportionate because the decision was one properly within the government's margin of appreciation.

[1] *R (L) v Metropolitan Police Comr* [2009] UKSC 3; *Huang* [2007] UKHL 11 at [16]; *R v Lichniak* [2002] UKHL 47 [14].
[2] Hickman at 697 and fn 14.

3   See, eg, *Humphreys v Revenue and Customs Comrs* [2012] UKSC 18; *R (RJM (FC)) v Secretary of State for Work and Pensions* [2008] UKHL 63; *R (Lord Carlile of Berriew) v Secretary of State for the Home Department* [2013] EWCA Civ 199; *R (Marper) v Chief Constable of South Yorkshire* [2004] 1 WLR 2196, 2212–13; *R (Gillan) v Metropolitan Police Comr* [2006] UKHL 12, [29]–[30], [63]–[64]; *R (Farrakhan) v Secretary of State for the Home Department* [2002] EWCA Civ 606.
4   [2004] EWCA Civ 1664 [11].

9.63 Fortunately this has not been the dominant view of the area of discretionary judgment. The better cases view the area as limited to those parts of the proportionality assessment that fall within the particular expertise of the executive decision-maker, or within the category of judgments courts view as 'democratic'.[1] The preferred account of the 'area' is that it reflects deference to the prerogatives of the other branches, honouring *Daly's* insistence that the role of court and decision-maker must remain distinct. A great deal of academic debate has swirled around this subject, from the (very persuasive) claim that deference is an indefensible abdication of the court's obligation to determine the content of rights protection,[2] to the view that deference is essentially justiciability by another name,[3] to the argument that deference is the only principle that keeps courts from simply substituting their moral preferences for that of the other arms of government.[4] The most reliable statement thus far of how domestic courts will handle deference (or the area of discretionary judgment) is found in Lord Carlile (SCt). There it was made clear that no aspect of the proportionality test was off limits to courts owing to any constitutional deference concerns, and that 'The court is the ultimate arbiter of the appropriate balance between two incommensurate values: the convention rights engaged and the interests of the community relied upon to justify interfering with it.'[5] However, each step of the proportionality test must be assessed with the following prudential considerations in mind:

> In the first place, although the Human Rights Act requires the courts to treat as relevant many questions which would previously have been immune from scrutiny, including on occasions the international implications of an executive decision, they remain questions of fact. The executive's assessment of the implications of the facts is not conclusive, but may be entitled to great weight, depending on the nature of the decision and the expertise and sources of information of the decision-maker or those who advise her.
>
> Secondly, rationality is a minimum condition of proportionality, but is not the whole test. Nonetheless, there are cases where the rationality of a decision is the only criterion which is capable of judicial assessment. This is particularly likely to be true of predictive and other judgmental assessments, especially those of a political nature. Such cases often involve a judgment or prediction of a kind whose rationality can be assessed but whose correctness cannot in the nature of things be tested empirically.
>
> Thirdly, where the justification for a decision depends upon a judgment about the future impact of alternative courses of action, there is not necessarily a single 'right' answer. There may be a range of judgments which could be made with equal propriety, in which case the law is satisfied if the judgment under review lies within that range .
>
> Fourthly, although a recognition of the relative institutional competence of the executive and the courts in this field is a pragmatic judgment and not a constitutional limitation, it is consistent with the democratic values which are at the heart of the convention, because it reflects an expectation that in a democracy a person

charged with making assessments of this kind should be politically responsible for them.[6]

While this sets out clearly the position the courts tend to take, it begs several questions, not the least of which is why the UK judiciary insists on excluding itself from the category of 'democratic powers'. The intention is clearly to distinguish the courts' democratic role in protecting minority and individual rights from the roles of the other branches of government in giving effect to the will of the majority. However, the distinction is not very helpful in fleshing out the respective functions of the branches in the proportionality balancing, because, as we have seen, the ultimate point of proportionality is to define the limits of rights, and describe the boundary beyond which the state, implementing the will of the majority, may not pass. Surely the majoritarian branches are no better suited to this task.

[1]   *R (Lord Carlile of Berriew) v Secretary of State for the Home Department* [2014] UKSC 60; *R (L) v Metropolitan Police Comr* [2009] UKSC 3; *Huang* [2007] UKHL 11 at [16]; *R v Lichniak* [2002] UKHL 47 [14]; *International Transport Roth GmbH v Secretary of State for the Home Department* [2002] EWCA Civ 158 [85]; *Rehman v Secretary of State for the Home Department* [2001] UKHL 47 [50].

[2]   See generally Allan, 'Human Rights and Judicial Review: A critique of "Due Deference"' (2006) 65 CLJ 671.

[3]   Allan at 689; Feldman at 131; Hunt, 'Sovereignty's Blight: Why Contemporary Public Law Needs the Concept of "Due Deference"' in Bamforth and Leyland (eds) *Public Law in a Multi-Layered Constitution* (2003) 339, 346–348; King at 420–422.

[4]   Kavanagh, 'Judging the Judges under the Human Rights Act: Deference, Disillusionment and the "War on terror"' [2009] PL 287, 299–302.

[5]   *R (Lord Carlile of Berriew) v Secretary of State for the Home Department* [2014] UKSC 60 [34].

[6]   Ibid at [32].

9.64 Regardless of whether one is persuaded by the view that representatives of the majority, directly answerable to the voters for their decisions, somehow boast greater legitimacy with regard to the question of the limits of majority power, it represents the approach domestic courts generally take, and requires some consideration of where in the proportionality analysis these considerations should come into play. Again, the practice of courts in this area is not consistent. The key question is whether deference applies to the balance to be struck (proportionality *stricto sensu*) or merely to aspects of that balance, specifically those that relate to the reasons for the challenged interference. In theory, courts should defer only to the assertions of public bodies in relation to:

(1)   what constitutes the public (majority) interest,
(2)   what measures are likely to be most effective, and
(3)   which public interests are more pressing than others.

The model then would have the court placing its own judgments of the impacts of the measure and the importance of the right in question on one side of the balance, and then assessing the other side of the balance (legitimate aim, suitability, necessity) with deference to the state's views on how pressing is the social need for the legitimate aim, what is the most effective way of pursuing that aim, and whether lesser means would accomplish the aim. This deference would not be absolute, but would accord the decision-maker's representations a due degree of deference in light of the particular expertise and majoritarian sensitivity of the agent in question. Again, in theory, this would mean that the court could disagree with, for example, the decision-maker's assessment of the effectiveness of the challenged measure, but only if there was cogent evidence to contradict the 'expert' view of the decision-maker. In this model, deference amounts essentially to a willingness to be persuaded by the other organs of the state, or a presumption that what they decide is right, rebuttable by cogent evidence or by an obvious lack of actual expertise on the part of the original decision-maker[1] There are several leading cases where this model is in fact followed,[2] and it is submitted that this is the only arguably valid role for deference. However, there are enough cases that do not follow this model to make it misleading to suggest that this is the 'law' on deference. A sizable weight of authority treats deference as something that cocoons the proportionality balancing altogether—the *Humphreys* rule on applying only the 'manifestly without foundation' standard in benefits cases has not been overruled. According to this model, once a court finds that the subject matter of a decision falls into the particular area of responsibility of the decision-maker (eg, national security and the Home Office, or economic and social policy and Parliament) the court is bound to defer almost the entire balancing exercise to the relevant decision-maker.[3] This latter model finds no support in theory or Strasbourg precedent, and falls foul of extensive dicta in *Lord Carlile* (SCt), but must be recognised as a fact of judicial review practice. Better informed courts will use deference to assist the assignment of weight to the state's side of certain aspects of the proportionality analysis, but many courts will use it to abstain from the proportionality assessment altogether.

[1]   Allan at 687–693. *See Caroopen v Secretary of State for the Home Department* [2016] EWCA Civ 1307 [81], differentiating between the deference to be accorded to the Secretary of State and that to be accorded to a Home Office caseworker.

[2]   *Homer v Chief Constable of West Yorkshire Police* [2012] UKSC 15; *R (T) v Secretary of State for the Home Department* [2014] UKSC 35; *(R (Aguilar Quila) v Secretary of State for the Home Department* [2011] UKSC 45; *R v DPP, ex p Kebilene* [2000] 2 AC 326, 381]; *International Transport Roth GmbH v Secretary of State for the Home Department* [2002] EWCA Civ 158 [85]; *Huang* [2007] UKHL 11 at [16]; *R (Begum) v Headteacher and Governors of Denbigh High School* [2006] UKHL 15.

[3]   See, eg, *Humphreys v Revenue and Customs Comrs* [2012] UKSC 18; *R (RJM (FC)) v Secretary of State for Work and Pensions* [2008] UKHL 63; *R (Lord Carlile of Berriew) v Secretary of State for the Home Department* [2013] EWCA Civ 199; *R (Farrakhan) v Secretary of State for the Home Department* [2002] EWCA Civ 606; *R (Carson) v Secretary of State for Work and Pensions* [2005] UKHL 37; *R (ProLife Alliance) v British Broadcasting Corpn* [2004] 1 AC 185.

9.65 The foregoing focuses on the paradigm of deference to, for example, a Secretary of State. Another issue has attracted attention of late: what kind of deference should apply to the deliberations of a local authority? The question, which first came to prominence in connection with the *Denbigh*[1] case, concerns itself not merely, or even mostly, with the difference in level of authority and expertise between, say, a Local Education Authority and a Secretary of State. It involves also the question whether it makes any difference if the relevant authority conducted something like a proportionality assessment of its own. There has been some suggestion that *Denbigh* stood for the proposition that on judicial review, courts should be concerned only with whether the ultimate decision was proportionate, not with the process used to reach the decision, and that this tells local authorities—and indeed any state authority—not to bother trying to make a proportionality assessment. A careful reading of *Denbigh* and similar authorities does not bear this out. As

Aileen Kavanagh has explained, the implications of *Denbigh* are much more complex, and can be summed up as follows:

'1.   The question of proportionality is a question for the court to answer; the court must determine whether Convention rights have been violated.

2.   However, this does not mean that the court will show no deference to the public body. On the contrary, the court will 'treat with appropriate respect' the views of the public authority on how to proceed.

3.   If a public authority has conscientiously paid proper attention to the human rights considerations when making its decision, the task of the challenger is harder and there will be a greater likelihood that the authority's decision will be regarded as proportionate.

4.   Where the public authority has not paid this kind of attention to Convention rights, that, in itself, will not necessarily be fatal to its decision. But it may lead the court to pay less deference to the decision. Unassisted, the court strikes its own balance.

5.   Public authorities do not have to follow a legally prescribed decision-making structure or make a decision concerning human rights 'in the structured way in which a judge might have done'.[2]

---

[1]   *R (SB) v Governors of Denbigh High School* [2006] UKHL 15.
[2]   Kavanagh, 'Reasoning about proportionality under the Human Rights Act 1998: outcomes, substance and process' (2014) 130 LQR 235, 254-255 (footnotes omitted).

Variable intensity of review

9.66   We have seen that courts will apply proportionality using different tests — such as broad-brush balancing versus structured proportionality — and that each test will be applied using distinct degrees of deference or areas of discretionary judgment. Judges and commentators disagree about whether these differences should exist at all, whether they should result exclusively from calibrations of deference in the context of a single test as opposed to through the use of separate tests, and whether the differences should follow the lead of Strasbourg or flow from home-grown principles applicable only under the HRA. It is not the purpose of this Chapter to resolve these debates.[1] What must be grasped by the student or practitioner of the law of judicial review is that these differences in the intensity of proportionality review do exist, and will continue to do so. Despite the non-applicability of the margin of appreciation to the domestic context, ECtHR jurisprudence — which cannot be ignored by domestic courts according to s 2 HRA — clearly treats some Convention rights, or aspects of rights, as requiring greater protection, and some state or majority interests as having more compelling weight than others. Indeed, the HRA adds to this complexity by elevating freedom of expression above other rights in section 12(4). It is possible to construct an approach to proportionality that gives effect to this teaching without incoherence and without a multiplicity of tests or conceptions of deference. However, no such model is in place. Julian Rivers has attempted a less ambitious model in which all variations of the intensity of review begin with the degree of intrusion of the right in question, and adjust on that basis the amount of evidence and argument a court will require to be convinced of the proportionality of the measure at issue.[2] While Rivers' approach and his discussion in support of it are immensely helpful, they cannot change the fact that courts continue to (1) adjust discretion or deference according to the right at issue, the state interest at issue, or both, (2) use different formulations of proportionality depending on their sense of the importance either of the state interests or rights interests at stake (or both), and (3) make inconsistent adjustments to their intensity of review in the same case, for example by noting that the rights interest calls for more intense scrutiny, while the state prerogative in issue calls for greater deference, leaving the resulting level of scrutiny unclear.

[1] For an in-depth discussion of the debates and their optimal resolution, see Baker, *Proportionality beyond the UK Human Rights Act* (forthcoming, Hart, 2017).
[2] Rivers, '*Proportionality and Variable Intensity of Review*' (2006) 65 CLJ 202–207.

9.67 In light of the foregoing, the most useful observations that can be made about these variations in the intensity of review relate to what effects particular interests have on the level of scrutiny, regardless of whether these effects manifest themselves through the kind of test applied or the degree of deference observed. For example, we have already seen that judges will require less justification from the state when expertise or democratic legitimacy call for deference to the executive or Parliament. However, Strasbourg has articulated and UK courts have tended to adopt discrete categories of state expertise or authority that call for more or less scrutiny. Specifically, national authorities tend to receive the widest margin of appreciation from the ECtHR when they act on matters of national security or public order, and a slightly less wide, but still wide, margin on matters of public morality or broad social or economic issues; domestic courts tend to pass this leeway on to Parliament and the executive.[1] It should also be remembered that arts 8–11 specify different state interests that can justify limiting the right — for example art 8(2) lists economic well-being while art 10(2) does not — so one would not expect a court to grant the state a wide area of discretion when it pursues an interest not specified in the limitation clause for the right in question.[2] On the other side of the balance, rights interests also tend to fall into a loose hierarchy, where some rights call for more intense scrutiny than others. The unqualified rights — such as arts 2 and 3, which in theory do not involve proportionality at all — require the most careful scrutiny any time balancing comes into play, followed closely by arts 6 and 5 (fair trial and liberty respectively), and then the qualified rights, with political expression at the top of the qualified hierarchy and property (article 1 of protocol 1) at the bottom.[3] Even within this ranking the degree of intensity can be fine-tuned according to how closely the invasion of the right links to the right-holder's life, dignity, or political participation.[4] The main point to keep in mind is that the actual intensity of review in a given case, or the degree of rigour of the proportionality test, will depend upon a combination of the rough ranking of the state's legitimate aim, the rough ranking of the rights interests, and whether the court is minded in the circumstances to defer to the decision-maker on grounds of expertise or democratic responsibility.

[1] Feldman, 'Proportionality and the HRA 1998' in Ellis (ed) *The Principle of Proportionality in the Laws of Europe* (1999), 127 at 138.
[2] Rivers, '*Proportionality and Variable Intensity of Review*, (2006) 65 CLJ 202–207 at 195.
[3] Feldman at 138; Rivers at 195.
[4] Feldman at 138.

Evidence to inform the proportionality balancing

9.68 An aspect of proportionality with which the domestic culture of judicial review struggles is the fact that in many cases the proportionality assessment requires the collection of fresh evidence and the finding of facts. Clear instructions from the CJEU in the EU law context have helped courts get past their initial discomfort with the merits-like feel of making their own factual findings in judicial review cases.[1] Guidance from Strasbourg has been less clear (and would be less dispositive in any event), so judges still need periodic reminders to perform their own proportionality analysis with new evidence where necessary.[2] However, often these reminders beg the question of what evidence a court should be prepared to consider. The obvious bread-and-butter of judicial review are the statements of decision-makers and the documents that evidence their bases for adopting a challenged measure. Courts appear less comfortable, however, with evidence of the impacts of the impugned measure on rights interests.[3] However, it is in assessing impacts, as opposed to questioning the wisdom of executive or Parliamentary decisions, that courts have the most obvious institutional legitimacy. Indeed, there should be no limits on how far a court may enquire into impacts other than that it must restrict itself to finding judicial, rather than legislative, facts. 'Judicial facts' refers to retrospective facts –those that relate to what has actually happened or what is now clearly likely to happen — received in a forum where both sides of the debate have an equal procedural standing, regardless of the number of people that support each side. Judicial facts need not, however, relate exclusively to the individual complainant or to a specific group of complainants. It is true that at first, when a court faces the question whether a claimant has suffered a *prima facie* invasion of a right, it should consider only the facts germane to the claimant's situation. However, once a *prima facie* engagement of the right has been found, and the state claims that its measure satisfies a limitation clause (essentially an affirmative defence), the question shifts to whether the decision-maker, in adopting the challenged measure to meet a stated objective, acted proportionately. The burden of this inquiry rests on the state, and the answer depends upon whether the measure produces harms to rights interests disproportionate to the degree to which it advances a legitimate aim.[4] Nothing requires or even supports restricting these rights interests to those of the claimant or claimants. As has already been noted, proportionality in Strasbourg routinely takes into account impacts not only on the claimant but on the claimant's group, upon society, and upon rights interests generally.[5] Whether a measure is 'proportionate' depends on *the measure's* benefits compared to *the measure's* impacts, not merely to those impacts that happened to be felt by the claimant.[6] Ample precedent exists in which UK courts receive and consider evidence of the wider impacts of regulatory schemes,[7] and some have assumed that ECHR cases would require this kind of evidence.[8] As discussed in **9.49** above, the CJEU has recently clearly endorsed a broad scope for the consideration of impacts.[9]

---

[1] *R v Ministry of Agriculture, Fisheries and Food, ex p First City Trading Ltd* [1997] 1 CMLR 250, 278; *R v Secretary of State for Transport, ex p Factortame Ltd* [1998] Eu LR 475 (DC); [1998] 3 CMLR 192 (CA).

[2] *Denbigh* [2006] UKHL 15 [29]; *Tweed v Parades Commission for Northern Ireland* [2006] UKHL 53 [3].

[3] See Baker, **9.47**, n 2 above at 310–315.

⁴ *Allonby v Accrington and Rossendale College* [2001] ICR 1189; *A v Secretary of State for the Home Department* [2004] UKHL 56, [50]; *Ghaidan v Godin–Mendoza* [2004] UKHL 30, [19]–[20]; *National Union of Belgian Police v Belgium* (1976) 1 EHRR 578.

⁵ *Dudgeon v United Kingdom* (1981) 4 EHRR 149, [59]–[60] (citing the impact, of a law against homosexual acts between consenting adults, on the ability of all homosexuals in society to live according to their inclinations); *Ünal Tekeli v Turkey* [2004] ECHR 29865/96, [59]–[69] (invoking the impact of a rule requiring wives to take on the names of their husbands on the European interest in advancing gender equality); *Smith v United Kingdom* [1999] ECHR 33985/96, [90]–[94] (cataloguing the impacts of sexual orientation discrimination on homosexuals in the military, including on job prospects); *Sidabras* [2004] ECHR 395, [51]–[61] (noting the long-term impacts of anti-former-KGB–agent ban on the careers and prospects of everyone affected by it).

⁶ *Homer v Chief Constable of West Yorkshire Police* [2012] UKSC 15; *R (T) v Secretary of State for the Home Department* [2014] UKSC 35; *(R (Aguilar Quila) v Secretary of State for the Home Department* [2011] UKSC 45.

⁷ *R v Lord Chancellor, ex p Witham* [1997] 2 All ER 779 (court swayed by evidence offered by NGO *amicus* about wider public implications of challenged order); *R v Preston Supplementary Benefits Appeal Tribunal, ex p Moore* [1975] 1 WLR 624 (evidence of actual workings of benefits scheme received).

⁸ *R v Ministry of Defence, ex p Smith* [1996] QB 517, 564 (in dicta, Henry, LJ opined that a domestically incorporated ECHR would require a 'Brandeis Brief' to deal with difficult cases).

⁹ *Case C-83/14 CHEZ Razpredelenie Bulgaria AD v Komisia za zashtita ot diskriminatsia* [2016] 1 CMLR 14 (CJEU (Grand Chamber)) [123]–[127].

9.69 What this means, of course, is that courts in performing judicial review functions under the HRA must be prepared to receive expert opinion or reports from social scientists. For example, impacts could be proved by evidence of the economic and psychological impacts of discrimination, such as the imposition of a 'racial tax.'¹ Ample evidence exists that people subject to unfairness suffer stress-related health problems that impose a societal cost that must be weighed against the benefits of the policy in question.² Courts do deal with this kind of evidence, and the rarity of it probably results more from the failure of advocates to present these kinds of evidence than from an unwillingness of courts to consider it. For example, the ECtHR recently rejected s 44 of the Terrorism Act 2000, which allowed police to conduct random searches in specified areas, on the ground that it violated privacy under art 8 and was not 'prescribed by law'. In reaching this conclusion the Court relied on extensive social sciences data:

'84. In this connection the Court is struck by the statistical and other evidence showing the extent to which resort is had by police officers to the powers of stop and search under section 44 of the Act. The Ministry of Justice recorded a total of 33,177 searches in 2004/5, 44,545 in 2005/6, 37,000 in 2006/7 and 117,278 in 2007/8 (see paragraphs 44–46 above). In his Report into the operation of the Act in 2007, Lord Carlile noted that while arrests for other crimes had followed searches under section 44, none of the many thousands of searches had ever related to a terrorism offence; in his 2008 Report Lord Carlile noted that examples of poor and unnecessary use of section 44 abounded, there being evidence of cases where the person stopped was so obviously far from any known terrorism profile that, realistically, there was not the slightest possibility of him/her being a terrorist, and no other feature to justify the stop.

85. In the Court's view, there is a clear risk of arbitrariness in the grant of such a broad discretion to the police officer. While the present cases do not concern black applicants or those of Asian origin, the risks of the discriminatory use of the powers against such persons is a very real consideration . . . [t]he available statistics show that black and Asian persons are disproportionately affected by the powers, although the Independent Reviewer has also noted, in his most recent report, that

there has also been a practice of stopping and searching white people purely to produce greater racial balance in the statistics . . . [3]

The domestic High Court in *Quila* (which culminated in the Supreme Court's decision in *(R (Aguilar Quila) v Secretary of State for the Home Department)* likewise carefully considered a social sciences report, on which the applicant claimed the state should have relied to adopt a policy different from the one under challenge.[4] The court considered all of the reasons the state offered for not relying on the report, and agreed that there were grounds for doubting its usefulness as a basis for policy (this was subsequently reversed). Interestingly, in both *Gillan* and *Quila* the reports in question were prepared at the behest of the government. In both cases the courts demonstrated no discomfort with considering the weight or persuasiveness of the material. This suggests that there is nothing inherently problematic about a judge deciding the weight to be assigned to evidence in support or condemnation of a policy, and somewhat calls into question one of the main justifications for deference to government expertise. Be that as it may, courts are clearly institutionally suited to the retrospective fact finding necessary to determine the actual impact of a measure, and to consider the persuasiveness of statistics and reports that purport to shed light on that issue.[5]

[1] Kennedy, *Race, Crime, and the Law* (1997), 159.
[2] See, eg, DeVogli, Ferrie, Chandola, Kivimaki, and Marmot, 'Unfairness and Health: Evidence from the Whitehall II Study' 61 (2007) *Journal of Epidemiology & Community Health* 513; Mays, Cochran, and Barnes, 'Race, Race-Based Discrimination, and Health Outcomes Among African Americans,' (2007) 58 *Annual Review of Psychology* 201–225.
[3] *Gillan and Quinton v United Kingdom* [2009] ECHR 28 (12 January 2010).
[4] *R (Quila) v Secretary of State for the Home Department* [2009] EWHC 3189 (Admin) [22]–[26]. See also *R (L) v Metropolitan Police Comr* [2009] UKSC 3.
[5] See, eg, Fiss, 'Forms of Justice,' (1979) 93 *Harvard Law Review* 1, regarding the institutional suitability of courts to the task of weighing public policy concerns against individual rights; *but see* Leigh and Lustgarten, 'Making Rights Real: the Courts, Remedies, and the Human Rights Act,' (1999) 58 CLJ 509, 522–526, arguing that judicial review procedures in the UK at the time of the enactment of the HRA were not up to the task of coping with the kind of justification inquiry called for by the HRA.

PROPORTIONALITY AS A FREE-STANDING GROUND OF REVIEW

9.70 In the light of 'Brexit' (the referendum vote advising that the UK should withdraw from the EU) and debates about a possible replacement for the Human Rights Act 1998, the question of whether proportionality has become a part of British law takes on a certain degree of urgency. It is of course by no means new to ask whether domestic administrative law should extend the categories of review in order to include a free-standing principle of proportionality, an issue which has excited the interest of academics and practitioners[1] shortly after Lord Diplock first mooted the possibility. A claim for judicial review expressly seeking to rely upon the principle of proportionality outside the field of European Community law was considered in 1991 by the House of Lords in *R v Secretary of State for the Home Department, ex p Brind*.[2] The House was unanimous in rejecting the claim in the particular case in question. Lord Ackner[3] drew attention to the fact that a total lack of proportionality would lead to a decision which no reasonable administrator could make, and thus qualify for review on *Wednesbury* grounds; but short of this the application of the proportionality test would involve an inquiry into the merits (albeit allowing the administrator a 'margin of appreciation') for which there was at present no basis in English law. Lord Lowry agreed,[4] drawing attention to the danger of extending the judges' supervisory jurisdiction into fields which had been entrusted to politicians and for which judicial experience and training was not apt, leading to increased uncertainty and greater demands on court time. Lords Bridge and Roskill did not go this far, although both were agreed that application of the doctrine of proportionality would not advance the applicants' case.[5] Lord Roskill added that, in the present case, the principle could not be applied because this would be incompatible with Parliament having entrusted the judgment in question to the Secretary of State, but this did not exclude possible future development of the law in this respect.[6] Lord Templeman in a characteristically concise judgment referred to the doctrine of proportionality and the margin of appreciation and concluded that, applying those principles, there had been no abuse of power.[7] In short, the idea was rejected either because (a) it would make no difference, or (b) it would have judges going into areas the law did not permit them to go. It should be clear from the foregoing sections that the latter, more dispositive consideration, no longer applies.

[1] See, especially, Jowell and Lester in 'New Directions in Judicial Review' (1988), 51–72; *R v Secretary of State for Transport, ex p Pegasus Holdings (London) Ltd* [1989] 2 All ER 481, [1988] 1 WLR 990.
[2] [1991] 1 AC 696.
[3] At 762.
[4] At 763.
[5] At 749 and 750.
[6] At 750.
[7] At 751.

9.71 Meanwhile, the question of whether it would make a difference remains a live one. Drawing on observations by Lord Steyn that the criteria of proportionality are more precise and sophisticated, the Court of Appeal subsequently suggested that the House of Lords might take the step of replacing reasonableness with proportionality as the criterion for common law review.[1] The speeches of Lords Bridge, Roskill and Templeman in *Brind*[2] demonstrated that the door was not finally closed on possible recognition of proportionality as an independent ground of review. The implications of such a course continued to be canvassed in academic journals,[3] and in curial observations both in England[4] and in other jurisdictions.[5] An invigorating constitutional discussion by (then) Sir John Laws in 1993[6] suggested that despite *Brind* the High Court could not only use the European Convention as a text to inform the common law, but also deploy proportionality as a ground of review where a decision overrides a fundamental right without sufficient objective justification.[7] This suggestion was noted by Sedley J in *R v Secretary of State for the Home Department, ex p McQuillan*[8] who continued:

'Once it is accepted that the standards articulated in the Convention are standards which both march with those of the common law and inform the jurisprudence of the European Union, it becomes unreal and potentially unjust to continue to develop English public law without reference to them. Accordingly . . . the legal standards by which the decisions of public bodies are supervised can and should differentiate between those rights which are recognised as fundamental and those which, though known to the law, do not enjoy such a pre-eminent status. Once this point is reached, the standard of justification of infringements of rights and freedoms by executive decision must vary in proportion to the significance of the right which is at issue. Such an approach is indeed already enjoined by Ex parte Bugdacay in relation to a predominant value of the common law — the right to life — which, as it happens, the Convention reflects. Whether this is in itself a doctrine of proportionality I do not now pause to ask; if it is, the House of Lords has long since contemplated its arrival with equanimity.'

1 See *R (Association of British Civilian Internees: Far East Region) v Secretary of State for Defence* [2003] QB 1397, [34]ff, p 1413. The Court of Appeal also referred to remarks found in [51] of the speech of Lord Slynn of Hadley in *R (Alconbury Developments Ltd) v Secretary of State for the Environment, Transport and the Regions* [2003] 2 AC 295, 320–321, and by Lord Cooke of Thorndon in the *Daly* case, at 548–549, [32].

2 [1991] 1 AC 696, [1990] 1 All ER 469. Herberg, Jowell and Le Sueur (1992) 45 CLP Part 1 Annual Review have pointed out that the headnotes at [1990] 1 All ER 469 and [1991] 2 WLR 588 are inaccurate in this respect.

3 See, for example, Lord Irvine of Lairg QC, 'Judges and Decision–makers: the Theory and Practice of *Wednesbury* Review' [1996] PL 59; Jowell, 'Is Proportionality an Alien Concept?' [1996] European Public Law 401; Jowell, 'In the Shadow of *Wednesbury*' [1997] JR 75.

4 Examples are *R v Secretary of State for Health, ex p United States Tobacco International Inc* [1992] QB 353, (especially at 366), *R v Plymouth City Council, ex p Plymouth & South Devon Co–operative Society Ltd* [1993] 2 PLR 75, 88; *R v Secretary of State for the Environment, ex p National and Local Government Officers' Association* (1992) 5 Admin LR 785, 789–801. As to the suggestion in the latter case of a possible special status for decisions of government ministers, see Le Sueur and Sunkin, [1997] PL 580.

5 The Supreme Court of Northern Ireland has been reluctant to accept proportionality as a ground of review, 'even where an administrative decision involves matters with which a judge may be supposed to be familiar'; see Hadfield [1996] JR 170, 172. In Canada, see *Edwards Books and Art Ltd v R* (1986) 35 DLR (4th) 1. In New Zealand, proportionality was held by Tipping J in *Isaac v Minister of Consumer Affairs* [1990] 2 NZLR 606 to be nothing other than a criterion when considering whether a decision was unreasonable; other judges have spoken in favour of a North American 'hard look' doctrine (see *New Zealand Public Service Association v Hamilton City Council* [1997] 1 NZLR 30, 34–35). The majority of the High Court of Australia in *South Australia v Tanner* (1989) 166 CLR 161 tested delegated legislation by asking whether it was capable of being considered reasonably proportional to the pursuit of the enabling purpose, but added, 'it is not enough that the court thinks the regulation inexpedient or misguided. It must be so lacking in reasonable proportionality as not to be a real exercise of power'. See, also, Chaper 8 above; Smyth, 'The Principle of Proportionality Ten Years after GCHQ' (1995) 2 AJAL 189; McEvoy (1997) 4 AJAL 216.

6 'Is the High Court the Guardian of Fundamental Constitutional Rights?' [1993] PL 59, 71–75. The analysis is taken further in '*Law and Democracy*' [1995] PL 72, arguing for the notion of a higher order law to which even Parliament is subject, and in 'The Constitution: Morals and Rights' [1996] PL 622, asserting among other things that the idea of justice involves a requirement of proportionality, ie a reasonable relationship between the severity of legal sanctions and the aim which in any particular case the sanctions seek to achieve. Responses by Lord Irvine of Lairg QC to these suggestions are at [1996] PL 59 and 636.

7 Sir John Laws opposed categorising these cases in *Wednesbury* terms because, despite their primacy, fundamental rights may occupy different places in the hearts of reasonable people. But this may be queried: if it is accepted that respect for human rights is a fundamental value of our society, then the courts rightly draw the limits of reasonableness so that interference with such rights is permitted only where the importance of the right in question can sensibly be regarded as outweighed by the interest protected by the interference.

8 [1995] 4 All ER 400.

9.72 The perceived danger of proportionality as a ground of review is that it may lead to courts assessing (rather than reviewing) substantive merits, taking decisions themselves and offering in effect an appeal from the decision of the administrator. Prior to the Human Rights Act 1998, Jeffrey Jowell responded that this would happen only if proportionality 'lowers the margin of appreciation to the decision-maker'. In essence he was noting the distinction between a standard of review and a standard for decision. Nothing about adopting proportionality as a standard of decision — owing to its precision and sophistication — requires changing the standard of review. The standard of review in HRA cases is different from the traditional judicial review standard because the HRA makes it so, but this need not be the case in the non-Convention and non-EU context. Jowell's analysis was that proportionality offered the advantages of:[1]

'(a) intelligibility — being more explicit about why a decision is unreasonable;

(b) coherence — common standard for directly effective EC law and purely domestic law;

(c) improvement of the quality of decision-making by:

(i) encouraging the consideration of alternatives;

(ii) heightening sensitivity to the impact of the decision upon individual rights and interests;

(iii) focusing on the relationship between legitimate ends and appropriate means.'

---

[1]   Jowell, [1997] JR 75, 80. See, also, Emiliou at 267–274.

9.73 The Supreme Court has recently dropped extensive hints that it could soon take the step of applying proportionality as a general tool of judicial review.[1] It has become increasingly common to see courts discussing the similarities and differences between *Wednesbury* unreasonableness and proportionality, and considering whether proportionality might have a place at common law.[2] Although none of these cases has taken the step of declaring proportionality a principle of common law judicial review, all suggest that:

(1)   each aspect of the proportionality test is either implicit in or can be derived from the idea of reasonableness;

(2)   the part of proportionality that has always been threatening to the common law mindset is really about the standard of review, or the margin of discretion, which can remain distinct between HRA cases and common law ones; and

(3)   recent Supreme Court authorities have made it clear that even where courts are applying proportionality with the ultimate authority to decide on the correct balance, this is not the same thing as merits review, or re-making the original decision.

Put more simply, if resistance to accepting proportionality was based on a fear of shifting decision-making authority to the courts, that is not what is happening even in human rights cases, and where the common law setting requires something like a perversity standard of review, that is already present in standards like 'manifestly inappropriate'. Because these arguments are compelling and growing in acceptance, by both courts and commentators, there is a very good chance that neither Brexit nor the advent of a UK Bill of Rights will diminish the role of proportionality in UK courts.

---

[1]   *Pham v Secretary of State for the Home Department* [2015] UKSC 19; [2015] 3 All ER 1015 [94]–[96], [115]116]]; *Kennedy v The Charity Commission* [2014] UKSC 20; [2015] 1 AC 455 [54]–[55].

[2]   *Caroopen v Secretary of State for the Home Department* [2016] EWCA Civ 1307 [83]; *R (SA) v Secretary of State for the Home Department* [2015] UKUT 00536 (IAC) [30]; *Whittier v the Commissioners for Her Majesty's Revenue and Customs* [2016] EWCA Civ 1160.

9.74 In the final analysis, the question will probably be decided more by practice than by Brexit or by replacement of the HRA. As noted in section **9.53** above, accession of the EU to the ECHR, as well as the increasing practice of the CJEU following Strasbourg guidance with regard to fundamental rights, all suggest a growing convergence regarding the role of proportionality in cases involving such rights. Both supranational courts recognise the importance of harmonising their rights practice where possible. A UK Bill of Rights is unlikely to go so far as to withdraw from the ECHR altogether, so proportionality will not go away in human rights cases. It seems unlikely that judges using proportionality in that context will long resist the tendency, demonstrated nearly everywhere but the United States, to incorporate the principles into other administrative law contexts.[1] This analysis suggests that the preferable course may be to recognise that review for unreasonableness will ultimately involve an examination of proportionality. This is consistent with the principles identified by Lord Steyn and Lord Cooke in *Daly*.[2] The stringency of that examination will be dependent on the subject matter and purpose of the power or duty in question. Where statutory powers and duties are concerned, the proper interpretation of the statute is likely to determine the court's role, as it does under the HRA.

---

[1] Schlink, 'Proportionality in constitutional law: why everywhere but here?' (2012) 22 *Duke Journal of Comparative & International Law* 291.

[2] See *R (Daly) v Secretary of State for the Home Department* [2001] 2 AC 532, 547–548, [27] and [32].

Chapter 10

PROCEDURAL RULES
AND CONSULTATION

INTRODUCTION

10.1 In *Council of Civil Service Unions v Minister for the Civil Service* (the *'GCHQ* case'), Lord Diplock identified, as the third of the grounds upon which a decision of a public authority or officer could be susceptible to 'judicial review', 'procedural impropriety'. He said:[1]

> "I have described the third head as "procedural impropriety" rather than failure to observe basic rules of natural justice or failure to act with procedural fairness towards the person who will be affected by the decision. This is because susceptibility to judicial review under this head covers also failure by an administrative tribunal to observe procedural rules that are expressly laid down in the legislative instrument by which its jurisdiction is conferred, even where such failure does not involve any denial of natural justice'.

The development of appropriate administrative procedures is fundamental to any proper system of administrative law in the interests of orderliness, openness, timeousness and justice.

[1]   [1985] AC 374 at 411.

10.2 Procedural requirements are frequently imposed by Parliament, either directly in the form of legislation, or indirectly as delegated legislation. The advantage of procedures being imposed in this way is that they can be specifically tailored to meet the requirements of the particular body under consideration. In addition, however, statutory and other bodies frequently exercise powers which may impinge upon individuals but in relation to which no, or only limited, specific procedural requirements have been laid down in legislation. In these circumstances, the courts will have a pivotal role in determining which safeguards are required. These are imposed under the rubric of natural justice or, as is now more common, the duty to act fairly. These principles are discussed in detail in the following chapters.

10.3 In this chapter we shall consider statutory procedural safeguards. We start by looking at the consequences of failure to comply with legislative procedural requirements, both generally and as to time, before turning to the relationship between statutory procedures and the common law concepts of natural justice and the duty to act fairly. In later sections of the chapter we discuss statutory obligations to consult, to make 'due inquiry', and to give reasons.[1]

[1] For Scots law on topics discussed in this chapter, see **22.75** et seq below.

STATUTORY PROCEDURES

10.4 Statutory procedures take a wide variety of forms and regulate a wide range of decisions. They may regulate the conduct of inquiries, investigations and disciplinary decisions; or impose the service of notices or consultation or due inquiry before decisions are reached. They may require that decisions be taken within a particular time limit, or that any decision made shall be accompanied by a statement of the grounds upon which it was made or a statement of the reasons for it. The particular instances are legion and it is beyond the scope of a book of this (or any) kind to list or identify them all. It is necessary always in considering the propriety or otherwise of an act or decision which it is sought to challenge to consider with care what procedural requirements have been imposed by the particular legislative regime. However, two issues of general importance arise in relation to statutory procedures. The first is the effect of a failure to comply with a procedural provision. Will it inevitably render the decision ultra vires? The second is the question whether statutory procedures are exhaustive or whether they may be supplemented by additional common law procedural safeguards.

FAILURE TO COMPLY: GENERAL

10.5 When the courts are seeking to determine the consequences of non-compliance with an express procedural requirements laid down in legislation, they are theoretically at least undertaking an exercise in statutory construction; did Parliament intend that a breach of a provision should result in a decision being invalid?[1]

[1] In this section we have considered the general approach of the courts to determining the consequences of a failure to comply with statutory procedures. The application of this approach in the specific situations of failures to comply with time limits, to consult and to give reasons is discussed below at **10.11**, **10.53** and **10.66** respectively.

10.6 In the past, the courts frequently distinguished between what are termed mandatory and directory provisions.[1] In *O'Reilly v Mackman*,[2] Lord Diplock summarised the significance of the distinction as follows:

> "it is a question of construction of the relevant legislation, to be decided by the court in which the decision is challenged, whether a particular procedural provision is mandatory, so that its non-observance in the process of reaching the decision makes the decision itself a nullity, or whether it is merely directory, so that the statutory tribunal has a discretion not to comply with it if, in its opinion, the exceptional circumstances of a particular case justify departing from it'.

The classic approach which the courts adopted for differentiating between the two was laid down by Lord Penzance in *Howard v Boddington*.[3] He said that in making the appropriate classification it is necessary for the court to have regard to the whole purpose of the enactment, as well as the importance of the provision which has been disregarded and its relation to the general object to be secured by the Act. However, the House of Lords began to slowly move away from the distinction in a series of cases between 1980 and 2000, finding the mandatory or directory classification to be an unhelpful distraction from the legislative intention.[4]

[1] The more general question of whether a decision maker is under a duty or has a discretion is discussed in CHAPTER 7 at **7.4** above.
[2] [1983] 2 AC 237, 275–6.
[3] (1877) 2 PD 203, 211.
[4] *London and Clydesdale Estates v Aberdeen District Council* [1980] 1 WLR 182; *Wang v Commissioner of Inland Revenue* [1994] 1 WLR 1286; *A-G's Reference (No 3 of 1999)* [2001] 2 AC 91.

10.7 The historic case law was reviewed by Lord Steyn in his speech in *R v Soneji*, which is now the leading authority on this issue.[1] Lord Steyn also analysed a number of decisions from overseas jurisdictions which have also cast doubts upon the utility of the mandatory/directory distinction. In particular, he approved the following passage from the judgment of the High Court of Australia in *Project Blue Sky Inc v Australian Broadcasting Authority*.[2] In the joint judgment of McHugh, Gummow, Kirby and Hayne JJ, the court concluded, at paragraph 93:

> 'In our opinion, the Court of Appeal of New South Wales was correct in *Tasker v Fullwood* in criticising the continued use of the "elusive distinction between directory and mandatory requirements" and the division of directory acts into those which have substantially complied with a statutory command and those which have not. They are classifications that have outlived their usefulness because they deflect attention from the real issue which is whether an act done in breach of the legislative provision is invalid. The classification of a statutory provision as mandatory or directory records a result which has been reached on other grounds. The classification is the end of the inquiry, not the beginning. That being so, a court, determining the validity of an act done in breach of a statutory provision, may easily focus on the wrong factors if it asks itself whether compliance with the provision is mandatory or directory and, if directory, whether there has been substantial compliance with the provision. A better test for determining the issue of validity is to ask whether it was a purpose of the legislation that an act done in breach of the provision should be invalid. This has been the preferred approach of courts in this country in recent years, particularly in New South Wales. In determining the question of purpose, regard must be had to "the language of the relevant provision and the scope and object of the whole statute.'

Lord Steyn referred to this as an "improved analytical framework" for examining these questions. He concluded:[3]

> 'Having reviewed the issue in some detail I am in respectful agreement with the Australian High Court that the rigid mandatory and directory distinction, and its many artificial refinements, have outlived their usefulness. Instead, as held in *Attorney General's Reference (No 3 of 1999)*, the emphasis ought to be on the consequences of non-compliance, and posing the question whether Parliament can fairly be taken to have intended total invalidity. That is how I would approach what is ultimately a question of statutory construction.'

[1] [2005] UKHL 49, [2006] 1 AC 340.
[2] (1998) 194 CLR 355.
[3] [2005] UKHL 49, [2006] 1 AC 340, at paragraph 23. In *R v Soneji*, Lord Carswell was not willing to give the traditional classification its final quietus, observing that there was still some value in the approach, particularly in the case of substantial compliance (paragraph 63). But it is suggested that it will never be more than a first step in any analysis.

10.8 In practical terms the likely effect of the approach in *R v Soneji* is to make it relatively rare for the courts to treat a provision as being mandatory such that any departure from it renders a decision a nullity. Lord Woolf made this point in *R v Immigration Appeal Tribunal, ex p Jeyeanthan* when he said:[1]

> 'Because of what can be the very undesirable consequences of a procedural requirement which is made so fundamental that any departure from the requirement makes everything that happens thereafter irreversibly a nullity it is to be hoped that provisions intended to have this effect will be few and far between. In the majority of cases, whether the requirement is categorised as directory or mandatory, the tribunal before whom the defect is properly raised has the task of determining what are to be the consequences of failing to comply with the requirement in the context of all the facts and circumstances of the case in which the issue arises. In such a situation the tribunal's task will be to seek to do what is just in all the circumstances'.

He repeated these observations in *Mckay v First Secretary of State and High Wycombe District Council*.[2]

[1] [2000] 1 WLR 354 at 359B–359D.
[2] [2005] EWCA Civ 774, [2006] 1 P & CR 363 at paragraph 16.

10.9 However, this will not always be the case. Although the courts seek to do justice, the starting point must still be that the courts should "try to get at the real intention of the legislature by carefully attending to the whole scope of the statute to be construed". (see Lord Woolf LCJ in *R v Sekhon*[1]). If it is plain from the legislation that a failure to comply renders a determination a nullity, the courts must, of course, give effect to that however inconvenient or unjust that may appear to be. The language may compel a conclusion which appears to the court to be undesirable, as the House of Lords has made clear. In *Seal v Chief Constable of South Wales Police*[2] the claimant sought to bring proceedings against the police for wrongful use of their powers under s 136 of the Mental Health Act 1983. By s 139(2) no proceedings in respect of actions pursuant to the Act could be brought without the consent of the court. That permission had not been obtained. The House of Lords (by a majority) concluded that the wording of the provision compelled the conclusion that proceedings commenced without consent were a nullity. Similarly, in *R v Clarke*[3] the House of Lords determined that Parliament intended that a bill of indictment would not become an indictment unless and until it had been signed by a proper officer. Lord Bingham commented that:[4]

'The decisions in *R v Sekhon* [2003] 1 WLR 1655 and *R v Soneji* [2006] 1 AC 340 are valuable and salutary, but the effect of the sea change which they wrought has been exaggerated and they do not warrant a wholesale jettisoning of all rules affecting procedure irrespective of their legal effect.'

[1] [2002] EWCA Crim 2954, [2003] 1 WLR 1655 at paragraph 25.
[2] [2007] UKHL 31, [2007] 1 WLR 1910.
[3] [2008] UKHL 8, [2008] 1 WLR 338.
[4] [2008] UKHL 8, [2008] 1 WLR 338, at paragraph 20.

10.10 Finally, as is implicit in Lord Woolf's observations in the *Jeyeanthan* case quoted above, in doing justice the courts must have regard not only to the question whether in principle the breach creates a nullity or not, but also to the question whether the court in its discretion ought to grant relief.[1] Accordingly, breach of the same statutory provision could, in some circumstances, justify the court invalidating a decision – because, for example, the breach was deliberate or the prejudice significant – but not in others where these factors were not present.

[1] General principles about the discretionary nature of relief are discussed in CHAPTER 18 at **18.45** et seq.

FAILURE TO COMPLY: TIME LIMITS

10.11 An illustration of the flexible approach of the courts and the importance of considering the particular consequences of breach are reflected in their approach to statutory time limits. Sometimes, such as where statute sets limitation periods for taking proceedings, they are treated as binding. It can readily be inferred that Parliament meant that proceedings should not be valid if taken out of time. This is particularly so where it is important for the parties to be able to assume that a decision can be relied upon, such as in the field of planning and compulsory purchase. In such case the courts tend to take a very strict view for the need for compliance.[1]

[1] See, eg *Smith v East Elloe Rural District Council* [1956] AC 736 and *R v Secretary of State for the Environment, ex parte Ostler* [1977] QB 122.

10.12 In other contexts, however, acts have been held valid even if done after a statutory time limit has expired. In *Charles v Judicial and Legal Service Commission*[1] where the failure involved infringing time limits imposed in the course of carrying out an investigation, the court noted that "if a complaint is made about the non-fulfilment of a time limit the giving of relief will usually be discretionary". In that case the applicant was not materially prejudiced and the court considered that it would be inimical to the disciplinary regime to allow delays to prevent disciplinary proceedings being taken at all.

[1] [2002] UKPC 34, [2003] 2 LRC 422.

10.13 In *Soneji* the question was whether the statutory obligation to consider confiscation orders against someone found guilty of a criminal offence could still be exercised even though the time limit for making the order had been exceeded. This was a case which directly and significantly affected the individual, and in a criminal context. The Court of Appeal held that the confiscation proceedings were invalid but that decision was reversed unanimously by the House of Lords. Again, they held that the intention could not have been that a failure to comply prevented this important function being exercised. The question arises why the time limit is specified at all. Lord Rodger expressed the view that "presumably, Parliament was concerned that in the absence of a time limit, matters might tend to drift". This does not, however, mean that such time limits are entirely open-ended or of no materiality. As their Lordships pointed out, undue delay may give rise to an abuse of process argument, although Lord Carswell thought that Parliament could not have intended that the time limit could be extended indefinitely but provided there was substantial observance of the time limit, that would suffice.[1] Here there was: the breach was minor and no prejudice or injustice resulted.

[1]   [2005] UKHL 49, [2006] 1 AC 340 at paragraph 67.

STATUTORY PROCEDURES AND THE COMMON LAW

10.14 When will statutory procedures be supplemented by common law requirements and when will they be considered exhaustive of procedural rights? The courts have not adopted a clear principle on this issue which inevitably depends on the particular statutory context. There is a general presumption, at least in cases affecting individuals, that Parliament intends to act fairly and that accordingly judges can, where appropriate, import additional safeguards over and above those provided by statute. In *Lloyd v McMahon*[1] Lord Bridge said:[2]

> 'it is well established that when a statute has conferred on any body the power to make decisions affecting individuals, the court will not only require the procedure prescribed by the statute to be followed, but will readily imply so much and no more to be introduced by way of additional procedural safeguards as will ensure the attainment of fairness'.

[1]   [1987] AC 625.
[2]   [1987] AC 625 at 702–703. See also *Cooper v Wandsworth Board of Works* (1863) 14 CB (NS) 180 and *R v Secretary of State for the Home Department, ex p Doody* [1994] 1 AC 531, 560 per Lord Mustill: 'where an Act of Parliament confers an administrative power there is a presumption that it will be exercised in a manner which is fair in all the circumstances'.

10.15 Lord Bridge appears to accept that it is the function of the courts to determine what is fair. But will the courts start by assuming that what Parliament has enacted is fair unless that is manifestly not so? In *Wiseman v Borneman*[1] Lord Reid treated the statutory procedures as minimum rather than maximum requirements and was apparently not prepared to make that assumption. He adopted a similar approach in *Malloch v Aberdeen Corpn*[2] in connection with a right to be heard 'where a statutory form of protection would be less effective if it did not carry with it a right to be heard, I would not find it difficult to imply this right'.[3] The long-standing, if simplistic, principle was articulated by Byles J in *Cooper v Wandsworth Board of Works* that 'the justice of the common law will supply the omission of legislature'.[4]

1   [1971] AC 297.
2   [1971] 1 WLR 1578, HL.
3   [1971] 1 WLR 1578 at 1582.
4   (1863) 14 CBNS 180, 143 ER 414, 420.

10.16 In *Pearlberg v Varty*,[1] both Lords Pearson and Viscount Dilhorne accepted that there was a presumption that Parliament intends to act fairly, but they reached different conclusions as to the implications of this. Lord Pearson held that since Parliament intends to act fairly the courts could in suitable cases (and perhaps always) imply an obligation to act with fairness. In other words, it should be assumed that Parliament, in formulating procedural safeguards, was intending that the courts should supplement them to give effect to the judicial perception of fairness. By contrast, Viscount Dilhorne held that the effect of the presumption was that what Parliament had enacted should be considered to embody what was fair until the contrary was shown. It is submitted that the former more accurately reflects the law. This is particularly so where the specified procedures are limited, for as Lord Mustill pointed out in *R v Secretary of State for the Home Department, ex parte Doody*,[2] it could not be assumed that Parliament intended to exclude other aspects of fair treatment. This is also reflected in the conclusion in *R v Secretary of State for Health, ex parte Kamal*[3] that a decision maker has an inherent power to ensure that a decision is taken in accordance with natural justice. Another implication of the principles of natural justice is that, where a statute confers a discretion in relation to the procedure to be adopted, the decision maker will be expected to exercise that discretion in accordance with those principles.[4]

1   [1972] 1 WLR 534, HL.
2   [1994] 1 AC 531 at 562.
3   (1992) 4 Admin LR 730.
4   See, for example, *R (on the application of McNally) v Secretary of State for Education* [2002] ICR 15 in which a school governing body was considering the dismissal of a teacher. Under the statutory procedure the chief education officer was entitled, but was not required, to advise the governing body at the disciplinary hearing. Kennedy LJ concluded that, on the facts of the case, it would have been contrary to natural justice to exercise that entitlement in the absence of the teacher who was the subject of disciplinary action because the teacher could reasonably have regarded the chief education officer as being part of the "prosecution team".

10.17 Ultimately the question is what Parliament must have intended. In many cases this is not clear. For example, in *Furnell v Whangarei High Schools Board*[1] the applicant was a teacher who had been suspended without pay, and without a hearing, in the course of investigations into his conduct. The statutory provisions had been fully complied with but he contended that nonetheless these should be supplemented by a right to a hearing. The Privy Council, by a majority of three to two, dismissed his appeal. Lord Morris, giving judgment for the majority, distinguished two sets of statutory provisions: those which gave scope for unfairness and where the court, in the interests of fairness, must supplement the provisions; and those which set down an exhaustive and fair code. In the circumstances the majority held that the procedures fell into the latter category so that no further implication was permissible. The minority (Lord Reid and Viscount Dilhorne) disagreed, concluding that the code, although detailed, was not exhaustive and should be supplemented to make it fair. Strictly, once the majority had construed that it was exhaustive it was irrelevant to decide whether or not it was fair; but their perception that it was fair no doubt significantly influenced their conclusion that it was intended to be exhaustive. However, Lord Bingham expressly doubted, in *R (West) v Parole Board*, that the principle of statutory construction expressed in the maxim *expressio unius exclusio alterius* could operate to exclude so basic a right as fairness.[2]

¹ [1973] AC 660, [1973] 1 All ER 400, PC.
² [2005] UKHL 1, [2005] 1 WLR 350, paragraph 29. See also: *Bank Mellat v Her Majesty's Treasury (No 2)* [2013] UKSC 39, [2014] AC 700, paragraph 35 and *R (Plantagenet Alliance Ltd) v Secretary of State for Justice* [2014] EWHC 1662 (Admin), paragraph 92.

10.18 Nonetheless, it should not be assumed that the courts will always readily imply additional safeguards. In *Lloyd v McMahon* Lord Bridge made it clear that whilst there was a presumption that the courts would supplement statutory procedures where individual rights were in issue, no such presumption applied to other administrative decisions. This will be so if the court takes the view that the legislative code is intended to be comprehensive, or if the imposition of further requirements would frustrate the statutory purpose: see, for example, *R v Secretary of State for the Home Department, ex parte Abdi*[1] in which a specific duty to disclose specific documents was held to be inconsistent with a general duty, implied at common law, to disclose all relevant documents. Similarly, in *R v Secretary of State for the Environment, ex p Hammersmith and Fulham London Borough Council*,[2] the minister was empowered to designate local authorities which in his opinion had set excessive budgets. The House of Lords refused to imply any duty of consultation, or giving reasons, or disclosing documents. Lord Bridge emphasised that it was not akin to a case where the rights or reputation of citizens were affected, nor was it being alleged that councillors either individually or collectively had acted unlawfully or discreditably. He doubted whether it was in principle appropriate for the courts in such a case to supplement the procedures laid down by Parliament, but in any event a statutory procedure was established and no further implication was legitimate.[3] As to the question of disclosure, it would frustrate Parliament's intention because it would delay what was plainly a process intended to operate with great expedition.[4]

¹ [1996] 1 WLR 298.
² [1991] 1 AC 521.
³ [1991] 1 AC 521 at p 599.
⁴ [1991] 1 AC 521 at p 601. See also *R (Khatun) v Newham London Borough Council* [2004] EWCA Civ 55, [2005] QB 37, paragraph 30, per Laws LJ.

10.19 In *Bank Mellat v Her Majesty's Treasury (No 2)*[1] the Supreme Court considered the procedural fairness of the Treasury having made an Order under Sch 7 to the Counter-Terrorism Act 2008 prohibiting all persons in the United Kingdom entering into any business relationship or transaction with Bank Mellat, an Iranian bank suspected of having links to the Iranian nuclear weapons programme. The Order had been made without any opportunity having been given to the Bank to make representations. Lord Sumption declined to accept an argument that the provision of a right to appeal the designation, impliedly excluded any common law duty of fairness imposed on the Treasury. Consultation with the affected party would not cut across the statutory scheme, and the right of appeal only guaranteed the Bank's existing rights, which could be (or had been) adversely affected by the length of time a statutory appeal took. *Bank Mellat* was, of course, a classic case of individual rights, albeit of a financial institution. Just as importantly, Lord Sumption also rejected the argument that no common law duty of fairness could apply to the legality of secondary legislation which is subject to an affirmative resolution of Parliament. The relevance of the distinction between legislation subject to affirmative and negative resolutions was doubted and Lord Sumption held that an Order which targeted individuals would not allow the affected party to argue its case during the course of the Parliamentary proceedings. The duty of fairness was, held Lord Sumption, a limitation on the discretion of the decision-maker which is implied into the statute. By a majority of 6-3 the Supreme Court held the Order to be unlawful on procedural grounds.

[1]   [2013] UKSC 39, [2014] AC 700.

10.20 In some cases Parliament requires a procedure protecting certain safeguards to be followed but gives no indication how precisely it should be adhered to. In such circumstances the court will assume that the intention is to permit the person carrying out the procedure to decide how it should be done.[1] That decision is, however, subject to normal principles of judicial review. See, for example, the cases concerning the proper procedure in inquiries, *Bushell v Secretary of State for the Environment*;[2] *B Johnson & Co v Minister of Health*;[3] *R v Westminster City Council, ex parte L*.[4]

[1]   This can be contrasted to statutes which require the decision-maker to make 'due inquiry' before a decision is taken; see **10.59** below.
[2]   [1981] AC 75, per Lord Diplock at 94–95.
[3]   [1947] 2 All ER 395, 399–400.
[4]   [1992] 1 WLR 253, 259.

10.21 We now consider three specific requirements which are frequently imposed by statute. The first is a duty to consult, the second is an obligation that a decision be taken only after 'due inquiry', and the third is a duty to give reasons.

CONSULTATION

10.22 It is generally accepted good administrative practice for those directly affected by administrative decisions to be consulted before the final decision is made. The precise jurisprudential basis of this was not entirely resolved by the Supreme Court in *R (Moseley) v Haringey London Borough Council*, in which Lord Wilson (and Lord Kerr) anchored the duty in a general requirement of procedural fairness, while Lord Reed prioritised the particular statutory context of the duty in that case (concerning council tax reduction schemes).[1] Lord Reed purported to agree with Lord Wilson;[2] Lady Hale and Lord Clarke purported to agree with both while clearly favouring the analysis of Lord Reed.[3] There will be occasions upon which the debate may matter, although probably relatively few. However, as Dillon LJ stated in *R v Devon CC, ex parte Baker*,[4] 'judicial review is not granted for a mere failure to follow best practice' and there remains no general duty to consult in all cases.[5] There must be a failure of some legal obligation, whether imposed by statute or common law.

1   [2014] UKSC 56, [2014] 1 WLR 3947, paragraphs 23 and 37 (per Lord Wilson and Lord Reed respectively).
2   [2014] UKSC 56, [2014] 1 WLR 3947, paragraph 34.
3   [2014] UKSC 56, [2014] 1 WLR 3947, paragraph 44.
4   [1995] 1 All ER 73, 85.
5   *R (BAPIO Action Ltd) v Secretary of State for the Home Department* [2007] EWCA Civ 1139. For example, no duty to consult was found in relation to a decision to place surface-to-air missiles on a tower block during the London 2012 Olympics: *R (Harrow Community Support Ltd) v Secretary of State for Defence* [2012] EWHC 1921 (Admin), [2012] NLJR 962.

10.23 A duty to consult may be imposed by statute. There are many situations where such a duty arises in the public sphere, including such areas as planning, school closures, and the development of 'best value' criteria under the Local Government Act 1999. The duty also arises sometimes in the private sphere, such as under the very detailed procedures requiring consultation by employers in connection with making collective redundancies or transferring businesses. Moreover, consultation is a crucial part of central government decision making. It improves the information and understanding of the decision-maker, and therefore leads to better administration. In addition, it is an important aspect of democracy; those affected by decisions are able through the consultative process to have some influence on that decision. Much consultation by central government is undertaken voluntarily; there are official Consultation Principles which set out certain consultation criteria which are generally to be treated as binding on government departments and agencies. A statutory obligation to consult frequently arises in the context of the procedure to be followed in making subordinate legislation. There is no general duty to consult where delegated legislation is made which is an expression of legislative policy and is applicable generally, rather than targeted at particular persons.[1] Where secondary legislation is targeted at particular persons then the duty to consult is closely analogous to the principle of natural justice that an affected person should have the opportunity to make representations.[2] Nevertheless, in practice, central government does generally consult before making delegated legislation. Moreover, the courts have left open the possibility that a duty to consult in relation to delegated legislation could be found to have arisen in an appropriate case.[3]

1   *R (BAPIO Action Ltd) v Secretary of State for the Home Department* [2007] EWCA Civ 1139.
2   *Bank Mellat v Her Majesty's Treasury (No 2)* [2013] UKSC 39, [2014] AC 700.
3   *R (BAPIO Action Ltd) v Secretary of State for the Home Department* [2007] EWCA Civ 1139.

10.24 Statutory provisions regulating consultation differ significantly in their detail. For example, the procedures applicable to employers consulting workers' representatives in connection with redundancies are very fully set out. Such detail is rare, however, and often the courts have been required to give flesh to the statutory bones in determining such questions as what consultation requires,[1] who should be consulted and when the duty to consult is satisfied.

1   *Rollo v Minister of Town and Country Planning* [1948] 1 All ER 13; *Union of Whippingham and East Cowes Benefices, St James, Re, Derham v Church Comrs for England* [1954] AC 245, PC; *Port Louis Corpn v A-G of Mauritius* [1965] AC 1111, PC; *Sinfield v London Transport Executive* [1970] Ch 550, CA; *Agricultural, Horticultural and Forestry Industry*

Training Board v Aylesbury Mushrooms Ltd [1972] 1 WLR 190; *R v Secretary of State for Social Services, ex p Association of Metropolitan Authorities* [1986] 1 WLR 1; *R v Rochdale Health Authority, ex parte Rochdale Metropolitan Borough Council* (1992) 8 BMLR 137; cf: for the USA: The Administrative Procedure Act 1946, s 4 for a more generalised and formal approach to consultation on rule-making.

10.25 The courts have also in some circumstances imposed a duty to consult as an element of fairness even where no statutory obligation arises. For example, it is now well recognised that even where there is no statutory requirement to consult, there may be a legitimate expectation of consultation. Such an expectation may be engendered because of the importance of the rights in issue, a past practice of consultation or a representation that a party will be consulted.[1] However, in *Re Westminster City Council*,[2] Lord Bridge stated that although a duty to consult might arise out of a legitimate expectation, such an expectation would not arise simply from the scale or context of an administrative decision otherwise:

'the duty . . . would be entirely open ended and no public authority could tell with any confidence in what circumstances a duty of consultation was cast upon them'.

Similarly, the view has been expressed that where Parliament has not imposed the duty, the courts should not do so.[3] Nonetheless, in exceptional circumstances, a duty to consult may be found at common law where it would be conspicuously unfair not to do so.[4]

[1] The Court of Appeal analysed procedural legitimate expectations of this nature most thoroughly in *R (Niazi) v Secretary of State for the Home Department* [2008] EWCA Civ 755. and that analysis was applied by the Supreme Court in *R (Davies & Gaines-Cooper) v HMRC* [2011] UKSC 47, [2011] 1 WLR 2625. See also: *R (Luton Borough Council) v Secretary of State for Education* [2011] EWHC 217 (Admin), [2011] LGR 553 and *R (Dudley Metropolitan Borough Council) v Secretary of State for Communities and Local Government* [2012] EWHC 1729 (Admin), [2013] LGR 68.
[2] [1986] AC 668.
[3] *R (London Borough of Hillingdon) v The Lord Chancellor* [2008] EWHC 2683 (Admin), [2009] LGR 554.
[4] *R (Cheshire East Borough Council) v. Secretary of State for Environment, Food and Rural Affairs* [2011] EWHC 1975 (Admin), paragraph 81.

10.26 Although the extent of consultation (which is considered in more detail at **10.27** *et seq* below) may vary from case to case, the same broad principles are applicable whether the duty to consult arises from statute or from the common law.[1] Furthermore, where a public body has decided to consult (regardless of whether it was subject to a statutory or common law obligation to do so) it will be obliged to conduct the consultation fairly.[2] Of course, it remains possible that statutory procedures may be treated as exhaustive and to that extent provide fewer procedural safeguards than would be afforded if common law principles were applicable.[3]

In the next part of this chapter, we focus on the principles governing how consultation ought to be carried out.

[1] See *R (Partingdale Lane Residents' Association) v Barnet London Borough Council* [2003] EWHC 947 (Admin), paragraph 45; cf *R v Secretary of State for Education and Employment, ex p M* [1996] ELR 162, CA, 208.
[2] See *R v North and East Devon Health Authority, ex parte Coughlan* [2001] QB 213, paragraph 108.

³   For a comprehensive restatement of the principles relating to the situations in which a duty to consult may arise, and the nature of that duty, see *R (Plantagenet Alliance Ltd) v Secretary of State for Justice* [2014] EWHC 1662 (Admin), [2015] 3 All ER 261, paragraph 98.

Who Should Be Consulted?

10.27 Sometimes statute will define the consultees expressly. Where this is so, a claim by other bodies that they are entitled to be consulted is likely to be rejected on the basis of the maxim *'expressio facit cessare tacitum'*.¹ For example, in *R (Hillingdon London Borough Council) v Lord Chancellor* a three-man Divisional Court held at first instance that the Lord Chancellor was not under any obligation to consult with local authorities prior to implementing a substantial rise in court fees in public law family proceedings.² Dyson LJ indicated that:

> 'In my judgment, the fact that, when conferring on the Lord Chancellor the power to prescribe court fees, Parliament decided whom he should consult before doing so militates strongly against the idea that there should co-exist a common law duty to consult more widely (in the absence of a clear promise by the Lord Chancellor that there would be wider consultation and in the absence of any clear established practice of wider consultation).'³

¹   See, eg, *Bates v Lord Hailsham of St Marylebone* [1972] 1 WLR 1373; *R v Secretary of State for Education and Employment, ex parte Morris* (1995) Times, 15 December.
²   [2008] EWHC 2683 (Admin), [2009] LGR 554.
³   [2008] EWHC 2683 (Admin), [2009] LGR 554, paragraph 38.

10.28 Sometimes the statute confers a power to consult on the body concerned in subjective terms, for example, such bodies as appear to it to be representative, or as appear to be appropriate. In such cases the discretion as to whom to consult is initially for the consulting body but reviewable on *Wednesbury* principles.¹ In *Agricultural, Horticultural and Forestry Industry Training Board v Aylesbury Mushrooms*,² the fact that the Mushroom Growers Association (the applicants) had, in fact, been sent information by the Minister was treated as evidence that it was a body which 'appeared to the Minister to be representative of substantial numbers of employers engaged in the activities concerned' under the relevant statutory provision. Further, the Minister's affidavit did not deny that it should be consulted, and this was held to be decisive, even though the court considered that, given its small membership, the Minister could properly have concluded that the Mushroom Growers Association was not, in fact, sufficiently representative.

¹   See, eg, *Gallagher v Post Office; Rollo v Minister of Town and Country Planning* [1948] 1 All ER 13 and *R (Liverpool City Council) v Secretary of State for Health* [2003] EWHC 1975 (Admin).
²   [1972] 1 WLR 190.

10.29 Sometimes the courts will have to construe the statutory language to determine precisely who should be consulted. For example, in *Grunwick Processing Laboratories v ACAS*,¹ which concerned a statutory obligation placed on employers to recognise trade unions, ACAS was obliged to ascertain the opinions of 'workers to whom the issue relates'. The House of Lords held that this did not require consultation with each worker but that ACAS must at least ascertain the opinions of every group of workers of significant size. This conclusion was supported, in the view of the court, by the omission of the definite article before the word 'workers'.

¹   [1978] AC 655.

10.30 Where the duty to consult arises from a legitimate expectation rather than from a statutory provision, the parties to be consulted will obviously be those who can satisfy the court that they have the legitimate expectation. Again, however, it is unlikely to be necessary to consult each individual who might be affected by a particular decision. Meetings where views can be expressed are likely to suffice, or hearing representations through an appropriate support group: see *R v Devon County Council, ex parte Baker*,¹ a case concerning the closure of a residential home. However, where a specific premises – such as a day care centre – is to be closed, consultation which is generalised and not also specific with the users of the particular premises may be unfair.²

¹   [1995] 1 All ER 73, per Dillon LJ.
²   *R (LH) v Shropshire Council* [2014] EWCA Civ 404, [2014] PTSR 1052.

10.31 However, where there is a duty to consult, it is not for the consultor to impose conditions on the right of the consultee to make representations. In *Nelligan v Comrs for Lambeth, Southwark and Lewisham Health Area*,¹ the Commissioners consulted members of the Community Health Council on the proposed transfer of in-patient services but stipulated that any objection to the proposals must, inter alia, incorporate alternative proposals for making equivalent savings. Woolf J held that it was unlawful to impose such a condition. This is probably best understood as an aspect of the requirement to consult with an open mind.

¹   13 November 1979, unreported, QBD.

The nature of consultation

10.32 Statutes which impose a duty to consult generally do so in terms. Sometimes other language is used, such as a duty 'to seek the views' of groups or individuals. This requires more than simply taking into account any representations which a body chooses to make. Rather it involves actively seeking such representations.

10.33 A comprehensive statement of what the duty to consult necessarily entails in all cases would be a chimera. Indeed, in *Port Louis Corpn v A-G of Mauritius*,¹ Lord Morris held that the nature and object of consultation must be related to the particular circumstances in which it is required. However, the courts have attempted to provide general guidance as to the requirements of consultation. A useful dictum is that of Bucknill LJ in the Court of Appeal in *Rollo v Minister of Town and Country Planning*² where, approving a dictum of Morris J at first instance, he said:

'The holding of consultation with such local authorities as appear to the Minister to be concerned is, in my judgment, an important statutory obligation. The Minister, with receptive mind, must by such consultation seek and welcome the aid and advice which those with local knowledge may be in a position to proffer in regard to a plan which the Minister has tentatively evolved. For the reasons which I have given, I consider that on the facts of this particular case, consultation did take place so as to be a compliance with the statute'.

1 [1965] AC 1111, PC.
2 [1948] 1 All ER 13.

10.34 It is now clearly established that the nature of the duty of consultation, in whatever form, is most helpfully set out in what are usually known as the *Gunning* principles:

(1) consultations when the proposals are still at a formative stage;
(2) adequate information on which to respond;
(3) adequate time in which to respond; and
(4) conscientious consideration by an authority of the response to consultation.[1]

It is helpful to analyse the duty by reference to these four elements, although the precise requirements, and how they apply, may vary from case to case. These principles have been repeatedly approved in the lower courts and were, for the first time, explicitly adopted by the Supreme Court in *R (Moseley) v Haringey London Borough Council*.[2]

However, it is important to remember that the essence of these requirements is fairness,[3] and that the *Gunning* principles are applied because they are a 'prescription for fairness'.[4]

1 See Hodgson J in *R v Brent London Borough Council, ex p Gunning* (1985) 84 LGR 168. The formula was one originally advanced by Stephen Sedley QC and was approved by the Court of Appeal in *R v Haberdashers' Aske's Hatcham School Governors, ex p Inner London Education Authority* [1989] COD 435 (Woolf LJ).
2 [2014] UKSC 56, [2014] 1 WLR 3947, paragraph 25. See too: *R v North and East Devon Health Authority, ex p Coughlan* [2001] QB 213, paragraph 108.
3 *R (Moseley) v Haringey London Borough Council* [2014] UKSC 56, [2014] 1 WLR 3947, paragraphs 23 and 37 (per Lords Wilson and Reed respectively, in slightly different senses). See further, the decision of Maurice Kay J in *R (Medway Council) v Secretary of State for Transport* [2002] EWHC 2516 (Admin), [2003] JPL 583, paragraph 28; the decision of the Court of Appeal in *R (Edwards) v Environment Agency* [2006] EWCA Civ 877, paragraphs 90-94 and 102-106; the decision of Sullivan J in *R (Greenpeace) v Secretary of State for Trade and Industry* [2007] EWHC 311 (Admin), [2007] Env LR 29, particularly paragraphs 59–63; and, finally, the comments on *Greenpeace* made by Carnwarth LJ in *R (Hillingdon London Borough Council) v Secretary of State for Transport (Transport for London, interested party)* [2010] EWHC 626 (Admin).
4 *R (Royal Brompton and Harefield NHS Foundation Trust) v Joint Committee of Primary Care Trusts* [2012] EWCA Civ 472, paragraph 9.

When should consultation begin and on what?

10.35 The first and fourth elements listed at **10.34** above are really interrelated. There must be some specific proposal on which to consult, otherwise there would be no focus for the representations from the consultees. That, of course, presupposes that the authority will have formed at least a tentative view as to what it wants to do. An authority may properly consult on a 'preferred option'.[1] But plainly the authority should not have closed its mind to any changes otherwise there could be no scope genuinely to consider the representations made. A decision made 'in principle' may not amount to consultation at a formative stage.

In *R (Sardar) v Watford Borough Council*, Wilkie J commented as follows:[2]

> ' . . . The description "a formative stage" may be apt to describe a number of different situations. A council may only have reached the stage of identifying a number of options when it decides to consult. On the other hand it may be gone beyond that and have identified a preferred option upon which it may wish to consult. In other circumstances it may have formed a provisional view as to the cause to be adopted or may "be minded" to take a particular course subject to the outcome of consultations. In each of these cases what the council is doing is consulting in advance of the decision being consulted about being made. It is, no doubt, right that, if the council has a preferred option, or has formed a provisional view, those being consulted should be informed of this so as better to focus their responses . . . In my judgment, however, it is a difference in kind for it to have made a decision in principle to adopt a policy and, thereafter, to be concerned only with the timing of its implementation and other matters of detail. Whilst a consultation on the timing and manner of implementation may be a proper one on these issues it cannot, in my judgment, be said that such a consultation, insofar as it touches upon the question of principle, is conducted at a point at which policy on that issue is at a formative stage.'

---

[1] See *Nichol v Gateshead Metropolitan Borough Council* (1988) 87 LGR 435 as approved in *Chandler v Secretary of State for Children, Schools and Families* [2009] EWHC 219 (Admin), paragraph 55. See too: *R (Westminster City Council) v Mayor of London* [2002] EWHC 2440 (Admin), [2003] LGR 611, paragraph 27.
[2] [2006] EWHC 1590 (Admin), paragraph 29.

10.36 Prior to the decision of the Supreme Court in *R (Moseley) v Haringey London Borough Council*,[1] it had generally been taken to be the law that there was no legal obligation on a decision-maker to consult on all conceivable solutions, or solutions which it had no intention of pursuing, or discarded options.[2] *Moseley* concerned a consultation exercise carried out by a local authority in relation to a proposed council tax reduction scheme, which it was required by statute to carry out. The proposal set out for consultation was to pass on the shortfall in central government funding to recipients of council tax benefit; it did not consult on alternative methods of addressing the shortfall, such as making savings in other parts of the budget. The Supreme Court held that it had been unfair for the local authority not to refer in its consultation document to alternative options and the reasons for their rejection, as well as finding that the consultation document was misleading in suggesting that there was no choice but to pass on the shortfall. The analysis of Lord Wilson focused on the procedural unfairness in the consultation, which he considered meant in the context that interested persons be consulted upon discarded but arguable alternatives. The analysis of Lord Reed emphasised the particular statutory context as requiring consultation on alternatives, with less indication that such an approach would apply in other, different, contexts. The Supreme Court did not give clear guidance as to the circumstances in which consultation on alternatives would be required as a matter of common law or statutory fairness. Lord Wilson indicated that fairness might involve a sliding scale, influenced by the degree to which the eventual decision would deprive people of benefits as opposed to considering the conditions for a future benefit.[3] Lord Reed indicated that the test hinged on whether, in the circumstances, a meaningful view could be expressed on the proposal.[4]

[1]   [2014] UKSC 56, [2014] 1 WLR 3947.
[2]   *R (National Association of Health Stores) v Secretary of State for Health* [2003] EWHC 3133 (Admin), paragraph 83. See also, for example, *R (Enfield Borough Council) v Secretary of State for Health* [2009] EWHC 743 (Admin), paragraph 17; *Vale of Glamorgan Council v Lord Chancellor and Secretary of State for Justice* [2011] EWHC 1532 (Admin), paragraph 24; and *R (United Co Rusal) v London Metal Exchange* [2014] EWCA Civ 1271, [2015] 1 WLR 1375.
[3]   [2014] UKSC 56, [2014] 1 WLR 3947, paragraph 26.
[4]   [2014] UKSC 56, [2014] 1 WLR 3947, paragraph 40.

10.37 Unsurprisingly, the aftermath of *Moseley* has seen a considerable number of High Court and Court of Appeal decisions considering the extent to which the outcome on the facts of *Moseley* extends as a legal requirement in other sorts of consultation exercises in other sorts of cases. The Court of Appeal has taken a clear approach to the effect that *Moseley* amounted to nothing more than an endorsement of the general principles of consultation, and the application of them on the facts of a particular case.[1] It has declined to treat *Moseley* as generating a general principle of universal application. The High Court has followed suit in a range of cases also concerning budget cuts.[2] The clear trend has been to isolate *Moseley* and emphasise the reasoning of Lord Reed that the outcome derived from the particular statutory context of that case.

[1]   *R (Robson) v Salford City Council* [2015] EWCA Civ 6, [2015] LGR 150 (closure of passenger transport units for disabled adults) and *R (Sumpter) v Secretary of State for Work and Pensions* [2015] EWCA Civ 1033 (replacement of Disability Living Allowance).
[2]   *R (L & P) v Warwickshire County Council* [2015] EWHC 203 (Admin), [2015] ELR 271; *R (T) v Trafford Metropolitan Borough Council* [2015] EWHC 369 (Admin); *R (Morris) v Rhondda Cynon Taf County Borough Council* [2015] EWHC 1403 (Admin), (2015) 18 CCL Rep 550; *R (Tilley) v Vale of Glamorgan Council* [2015] EWHC 3194 (Admin); *R (Plant) v Lambeth London Borough Council* [2016] EWHC 3324 (Admin).

10.38 Although the scope of consultation is generally for the consultor to define, the decision as to the scope of the matter being consulted about is not an unfettered discretion. It may also be unlawful for a body to exclude certain areas from the scope of consultation if it is acting *Wednesbury* unreasonably in so doing or if it prevents a proper consideration of the matter in issue. This is a harder test to satisfy than that adopted in *Moseley*, but it can be met. So, for example, in *R (Medway Council) v Secretary of State for Transport*,[1] Maurice Kay J held that it was procedurally unfair for the Secretary of State to exclude consideration of expansion at Gatwick airport in a consultation document on the future development of air transport in the United Kingdom. The Minister's reasons for so doing were irrational. Again, in *R v Lambeth Borough Council, ex p N*,[2] the court held that consultation over a school closure was inadequate where it failed to deal with the proposed timetable and alternative proposals. In *R (Montpeliers and Trevors Association) v Westminster City Council*, Munby J held that a consultation carried out by Westminster City Council was unlawful because the Council had excluded particular options.[3] It will inevitably be the case that some of the older authorities which pre-date Moseley will require reassessment in the light of the Supreme Court's approach.

¹   [2002] EWHC 2516 (Admin); [2003] JPL 583.
²   [1996] ELR 299.
³   [2005] EWHC 16 (Admin); [2006] LGR 304, paragraphs 21–29. See also *R (Parents for Legal Action Ltd) v Northumberland County Council* [2006] EWHC 1081 (Admin), [2006] LGR 646, paragraphs 33–39.

Providing appropriate information

10.39 Statute rarely states what information is to be provided in the course of a consultation; the courts have to divine the nature of that information from the statutory context.¹ Accordingly, only the most general statement can be made about the information to be supplied, as it will vary depending upon the issue under consideration.

Certain guidelines can be identified in the authorities. In *R v Secretary of State for Social Services, ex p Association of Metropolitan Authorities*,² Webster J said that the consultee in that case should be given:

'sufficiently informed and considered information or advice about aspects of the form or substance of the proposals, or their implications for the consulted party, being aspects material to the implementation of the proposals as to which the [consultor] might not be fully informed or advised, and as to which the party consulted might have relevant information or advice to offer.'

Similarly, in *Coughlan* the Court of Appeal stated:

'It has to be remembered that consultation is not litigation: the consulting authority is not required to publicise every submission it receives or (absent some statutory obligation) to disclose all its advice. Its obligation is to let those who have a potential interest in the subject matter know in clear terms what the proposal is and exactly why it is under positive consideration, telling them enough (which may be a good deal) to enable them to make an intelligent response. The obligation, although it may be quite onerous, goes no further than this'.³

¹   See, eg *Rollo v Minister of Town and Country Planning* [1948] 1 All ER 13 and *Powley v ACAS* [1978] ICR 123. Contrast, however, the provisions of TUPE discussed, inter alia, in *Institution of Professional Civil Servants v Secretary of State for Defence* [1987] 3 CMLR 35.
²   [1986] 1 WLR 1.
³   [2001] QB 213 at paragraph 112.

10.40 In *R (Capenhurst) v Leicester City Council*,¹ Silber J referred to *Coughlan* and also the comments of Lord Mustill in *R v Secretary of State for the Home Department, ex parte Doody*² and concluded that a consultee must be made aware of the basis upon which a proposal will be considered so that the consultee is able to give intelligent consideration to the proposals and the consultor can then give an intelligent response. On the facts of *Capenhurst* (which involved the withdrawal of council funding from six local voluntary organisations) this required that the council informed the consultees of the criteria which would be adopted and the factors which would be considered decisive or of substantial importance in deciding whether to withdraw funding. As the council had failed to provide this information, its consultation had been unfair and Silber J quashed the decisions. Of course, if the information fails to give the true reasons for the proposal, it must follow that the process is flawed: see *R (Madden) v Bury Metropolitan Borough Council.*[3] *In R (Save our Surgery Ltd) v Joint Committee of Primary Care Trusts*, Nicola Davies J found that a consultation process relating to a proposed reduction in paediatric cardiac surgery centres was unlawful where respondees had not been provided with sub-scores given to each centre by an independent assessment panel, which fed into a final score. The final score was disclosed. She held that even if the decision-maker did not look at the information specifically, it was still unfair that consultees could not see it.[4]

[1]   [2004] EWHC 2124 (Admin); (2004) 7 CCL Rep 557 at paragraphs 40–47.
[2]   [1994] 1 AC 531 at 550. See too: *Bushell v Secretary of State for the Environment* [1981] AC 75, 96 per Lord Clyde.
[3]   [2002] EWHC 1882 (Admin); (2002) 5 CCL Rep 622, paragraphs 58 and 62; *R (Lloyd) v Barking and Dagenham London Borough Council* [2001] EWCA Civ 533, [2001] 2 FLR 763, paragraph 13.
[4]   [2013] EWHC 439 (Admin). For a contrasting result, see *R (London Borough of Islington) v Mayor of London & London Fire and Emergency Planning Authority* [2013] EWHC 4142 (Admin).

10.41 The extent of disclosure required is inevitably context-specific. The information supplied must be sufficiently clear to enable an intelligent response.[1] In some cases, the information supplied must not merely state the proposed action and the factual information on which it is based, but also the reasons or assumptions underlying the proposals.[2] The information should be comprehensible and materially accurate.[3]

The court is, however, entitled to take account of background information which consultees will already have and the consultation paper itself need not be drafted (depending on the context) as if all readers were coming to the issue afresh.[4]

In *R (Eisai Limited) v National Institute for Health and Clinical Excellence* the Court of Appeal held that NICE's failure to disclose a fully-executable version of an excel model to pharmaceutical companies was a breach of procedural fairness, despite the fact that NICE had disclosed a read-only version of the model and despite the fact that Eisai had in fact made 'an intelligent response' without having received such a fully-executable model.[5] Commenting upon the authorities, Richards LJ indicated:[6]

'The mere fact that information is "significant" does not mean that fairness necessarily requires its disclosure to consultees. In *Coughlan* itself, for example, it was held that there was no need to disclose to the claimant a report which had been received from a third party in response to the consultation exercise, even though that report was plainly significant. . . . Nevertheless the degree of significance of the undisclosed material is obviously a highly material factor.'

'What fairness requires depends on the context and the particular circumstances: see, for example, *R v Secretary of State for Education, ex parte M* [1996] ELR 162, at pp 206–207, where Simon Brown LJ emphasised the need to avoid a mechanistic approach to the requirements of consultation. . . . '

The Court of Appeal has reiterated the importance of context in determining what fair consultation requires in *R (easyJet Airline co) v Civil Aviation Authority.*[7] Dyson LJ commented that:

' . . . the principles of fairness should not be applied "by rote" (per Lord Mustill in *Doody*) or by adopting a "mechanistic approach" (per Simon Brown LJ in *ex parte M*). What fairness requires depends on the facts and context of the particular case and on a consideration of all the circumstances of the case.'

On the facts of *easyJet*, the Court of Appeal held that there had been no procedural unfairness when they were not granted an opportunity to comment on a late submission made by another party. The *Eisai* case could be distinguished. Eisai had consistently asked for access to the fully-executable model; easyJet had not. The governing statutory schemes were very different. In contrast, in *R (London Criminal Courts Solicitors Association) v Lord Chancellor*[8] the court was prepared to apply *Eisai* and require the disclosure — and re-consultation — of externally prepared reports relied upon by the Lord Chancellor when consulting on the number of criminal legal aid contracts set by reference to those reports. The reports were of central importance to a consultation exercise which would have very significant impacts on the affected profession.

[1] See *R (Greenpeace) v Secretary of State for Trade and Industry* [2007] EWHC 311(Admin); [2007] Env LR 29.
[2] See *R v Brent LBC, ex p Gunning* 84 LGR 168, and *R v Sutton London Borough Council, ex parte Hamlet*, (unreported decision of Webster J dated 26 March 1986). In both cases the courts held that the information provided had been wholly inadequate. Moreover, in the latter case the judge said that the information must be provided in readily intelligible form.
[3] *R (Royal Brompton and Harefield NHS Foundation Trust) v Joint Committee of Primary Care Trusts* [2012] EWCA Civ 472; *R (Stirling) v Haringey London Borough Council* [2013] EWCA Civ 116, [2013] PTSR 1285; *R (Breckland District Council) v Boundary Committee* [2009] EWCA Civ 239.
[4] *R (United Co Rusal) v London Metal Exchange* [2014] EWCA Civ 1271, [2015] 1 WLR 1375.
[5] [2008] EWCA Civ 438. Context is everything: *Eisai* was distinguished by the Administrative Court in *R (Bristol-Myers Squibb Pharmaceuticals Ltd) v National Institute for Health and Clinical Excellence* [2009] EWHC 2722 (Admin) and in *R (H) v Birmingham City Council* [2010] EWHC 3754 (Admin).
[6] [2008] EWCA Civ 438, paragraphs 26–27.
[7] [2009] EWCA Civ 1361.
[8] [2014] EWHC 3020 (Admin). See too: *British Dental Association v General Dental Council* [2014] EWHC 4311 (Admin).

10.42 However, in *R (Beale) v London Borough of Camden*,[1] Munby J suggested that proper consultation did not require 'sufficient information to be given about any objections to the proposals to enable those consulted to give intelligent consideration and an intelligent response to the *objections*'. In other words, it is not generally incumbent on a consultor to summarise the arguments against a particular proposal. Nor is it necessary for the responses to the consultation themselves to be the subject of further consultation. That would make the obligation never ending. For the same reason it will not normally be necessary to disclose internal documents, or internal response documents produced following consultation by way of a further consultation exercise.[2]

[1] [2004] EWHC 6 (Admin); [2004] HLR 48 at paragraph 19.
[2] *Bushell v Secretary of State for the Environment* [1981] AC 75, 102 per Lord Diplock; *R (Edwards) v Environment Agency* [2008] UKHL 22, [2008] 1 WLR 1587, paragraph 44.

Giving adequate time for response

10.43 In general, statutory consultation procedures do not set down time limits and therefore the courts have to decide whether the consultee has been given adequate time to consider, research and produce his response. In the *Port Louis* case the Privy Council indicated that eleven days was insufficient for a local authority to comment on a proposal to enlarge its boundaries, at least in the absence of any need for urgency, although on the facts it found that a longer period had been given and relief was refused. The Board also rejected the application because the consultee had not asked for any extension of time.[1] In *Lee v Secretary of State for Education and Science*,[2] four days were given for a response to the proposed change to the Articles of a school introducing comprehensive education. Not surprisingly, Donaldson J held this to be insufficient and indicated that the minimum period should have been four weeks. Claims that the time allowed was insufficient were also upheld in the *ex parte Gunning* and *ex parte Hamlet* cases, even though in neither was any extension of time specifically requested. Both these cases were education cases, where the parents were the consultees, and it may be that a failure to seek an extension will not jeopardise the applicant's case in a situation of that kind, whereas it may do so where, as in *Port Louis*, the number of consultees is small. In the *Building Schools for the Future* litigation, the court accepted the need for urgency but still held that a short consultation period for the affected parties, perhaps only of three weeks, was required.[3] In many cases, in line with the Cabinet Office Code of Practice on Consultation, a practice has grown up of a twelve week consultation period.

1   *Port Louis Corpn v A-G of Mauritius* [1965] AC 1111, PC.
2   (1967) 111 Sol Jo 756.
3   *R (Luton Borough Council) v Secretary of State for Education* [2011] EWHC 217 (Admin), [2011] LGR 553, paragraph 94.

10.44 The courts are likely to require the applicant for judicial review to adduce evidence demonstrating that it could not reasonably respond in time. This is supported by dicta of Mustill LJ in *R v Secretary of State, ex p Greater London Council and Inner London Education Authority*.[1] In that case the court also indicated that if information had been provided over a period of time, this would influence the determination of what was a reasonable period to respond once the full information had been provided. Here, the applicants had been in possession of the basic information for months. The more complicated the information provided as part of the consultation, the longer the time will need to be to respond. By contrast, the more information which has been in the public domain, the less time will be required.[2]

1   CO/237/85, CO/252/8 (1985), unreported.
2   *R v Secretary of State for Education and Employment, ex p M* [1996] ELR 162, CA.

Genuinely considering representations

10.45 Consultation requires that the consultor must give careful consideration to the representations made, though obviously he is not bound to follow them.[1] In practice, it will be difficult to show that representations have *not* been taken into consideration.[2] Nonetheless, the consultor must grapple with the main issues which have been raised by the consultees.[3]

1   See *Fletcher v Minister of Town and Country Planning* [1947] 2 All ER 496.
2   For an unsuccessful attempt see: *R (London Criminal Courts Solicitors Association) v Lord Chancellor* [2015] EWHC 295 (Admin).

3 *R (Morris) v Newport City Council* [2009] EWHC 3051 (Admin), paragraph 38; *R (Mackenzie) v Secretary of State for Justice* [2009] EWCA Civ 669, paragraph 34.

10.46 If the consultation takes place very close to the taking of the final decision that will be some evidence at least that the consultation process was not genuine. As O'Connor LJ pointed out in *Nichol v Gateshead MBC*,[1] if consultation takes place at a point when the work has been done and there is a timescale set for the making of the final decision, this will inevitably colour the approach of the authority to any representations. There will almost inevitably be a reluctance to go back to the drawing board and disrupt the time scale. If the consultation is to be genuine, there must be a real willingness to alter or even reject the proposals in the light of the consultation. A decision following consultation must extend beyond the mere repetition of assertion.[2] Nonetheless, in the *Rollo* case, the Minister had gone so far as to publish a draft order before consulting, but this was still treated by Bucknill LJ in the Court of Appeal as a tentative proposal.

Furthermore, in *R v Hillingdon Health Authority, ex parte Goodwin*,[3] Woolf LJ indicated that it was proper for a consultor to decide what course he wished to adopt if he was unpersuaded by the representations made in the consultation process. Indeed, once it is accepted that a proposal may be formulated before consultation begins, this conclusion is inevitable. Moreover, in a context where many decisions are taken in the political arena, it would be wholly unrealistic for the law to say that it would be wrong or unlawful for the consultor to have a predisposition to a particular solution.

1 (1988) 87 BLGR 435 at 455.
2 *R v Ealing London Borough Council, ex p C (2000) 3 CCL Rep 122*
3 [1984] ICR 800.

10.47 In practice, it is difficult for the courts to conclude that there has been a failure genuinely to consider the representations if the consultor deposes to the contrary in a witness statement and is not cross-examined.[1] In *Nelligan*,[2] a substantial reorganisation of health services was carried out on the day representations were received, but the judge accepted the respondent's affidavit that the representations had been considered.

1 *R (Liverpool City Council) v Secretary of State for Health* [2003] EWHC 1975 (Admin).
2 *Nelligan v Comrs for Lambeth, Southwark and Lewisham Health Area* (13 November 1979, unreported. QBD).

10.48 It is important, however, to emphasise that unless the statutory provisions indicate to the contrary, there is in general no obligation on the consultor to respond to the representations. The obligation is merely to take those representations into consideration. Sometimes statute does require more. For example, in the field of employment law, consultations are required prior to the employer making staff redundant and also in relation to transfers of an undertaking. In such cases the obligation, in line with EU law, is to consult 'with a view to reaching agreement'. Clearly this does require a response to representations made and comes close to imposing a duty to negotiate in good faith. Similarly, it has been held that where the duty is to 'consult with' potentially affected persons, this involves more than simply receiving and considering such observations as they may make: see *R v Camden London*

Borough Council, ex parte Cran.[1]

[1]   (1995) 94 BLGR 8.

10.49 Nonetheless, the duty to consult will not include a duty to obtain the consensus or agreement of all consultees: see *R (Smith) v East Kent Hospital NHS Trust.*[1] Nor is it necessary to circulate the consultation responses to other consultees: *R (Robin Murray & Co) v Lord Chancellor.*[2]

[1]   [2002] EWHC 2640 (Admin), (2003) 6 CCL Rep 251, paragraph 61.
[2]   [2011] EWHC 1528 (Admin).

Amending proposals: the implications for consultation

10.50 A practical problem which frequently arises is whether consultation should take place not merely in relation to the original proposals but also in relation to any amended proposals — amendments which will frequently have been made as a result of the initial consultations. As Schiemann J pointed out in *R v Shropshire Health Authority, ex parte Duffus,*[1] if the courts are too liberal in their use of the power to require consultation, there is a danger that the process will inhibit change, either because the consultor will be disinclined to make amendments to proposals because of the repeated consultation processes that might result, or because the consultation process itself will drag on interminably. The solution which the courts have adopted to this conundrum is that if the proposals had been amended so fundamentally as to make them fresh proposals, then further consultation will be necessary unless the statute indicates to the contrary, but otherwise it will not. In *Legg v Inner London Education Authority,*[2] Megarry J indicated that this was very much a matter of impression. The fact that different opinions may be formed on this different question is reflected by the decision of the House of Lords in the case of *Re Westminster City Council*[3] where the court held by a bare majority that the GLC had so amended certain original proposals that the new determination constituted new proposals requiring fresh consultation. It seems that the distinction lies between cases where the consultation demonstrates that the original proposals require major reformation, and those where they are merely amended as a result of the consultation process itself: see *R v Islington London Borough Council, ex parte East.*[4] Where a new factor emerges during the course of consultation the test is not whether there has been a fundamental change, but whether the new factor is of such significance that in all the circumstances fairness demands that it must be drawn to the attention of the consultee: *R (Stirling) v Haringey London Borough Council.*[5]

[1]   [1990] COD 131.
[2]   [1972] 1 WLR 1245.
[3]   [1986] AC 668.
[4]   [1996] ELR 74.
[5]   [2013] EWCA Civ 116, [2013] PTSR 1285, paragraphs 23-24.

10.51 An interesting and difficult point in the application of this principle arose in the *Duffus* case. The Shropshire Health Authority was making a vast number of proposed changes and consulted over one hundred organisations. Subsequently it made alterations relating to one specific hospital, and those affected by that change alleged that fresh consultation should take place. Is the test in such circumstances to be judged by the whole of the original proposal or merely that part impinging upon the applicant consultee? Schiemann J did not have to decide the point since he held that the changes did not constitute a fresh proposal even in relation to the latter. However, unless it is possible to treat the proposals as severable, it is submitted that the comparison should be between the original proposals taken as a whole and any amendments, otherwise the spectre of indefinite consultation would become a reality.

10.52 *Duffus* and *East* were followed in *R (Smith) v East Kent Hospital NHS Trust*[1] in which Silber J concluded that the interests of fairness did not create a duty to 'reconsult' because the differences between the proposal and the option consulted on were not fundamental.[2] In the *Smith* case four options had been consulted upon and a fifth option was then proceeded with which incorporated elements from the options consulted upon. The decision, and the test of fundamental difference, has been followed in a number of recent decisions,[3] adopted so as to 'illustrate the very high order of the significance of any difference which would warrant re-consultation'.[4] The ultimate test is one of fairness and whether something has gone 'clearly and radically wrong'.[5]

[1]   [2002] EWHC 2640 (Admin), (2003) 6 CCL Rep 251. See, in particular, paragraphs 43–45.
[2]   For a case in which the Secretary of State allowed a further period of consultation, but the time allowed was held by the court to be inadequate, see *R v Secretary of State for Education and Employment ex p National Union of Teachers* [2000] Ed CR 603.
[3]   *Smith* was applied in *R (London Borough of Wandsworth) v Secretary of State for Transport* [2005] EWHC 20 (Admin). See also the comments made in *R (Edwards) v Environment Agency* [2006] EWCA Civ 877, paragraph 103, and *R (Elphinstone) v City of Westminster Council* [2008] EWCA Civ 1069, [2009] BLGR 158, paragraph 62
[4]   *Keep Wythenshawe Special Ltd v University Hospital of South Manchester NHS Foundation Trust* [2016] EWHC 17 (Admin), paragraph 75.
[5]   *R (Royal Brompton and Harefield NHS Foundation Trust) v Joint Committee of Primary Care Trusts* [2012] EWCA Civ 472, paragraph 13.

Consequences of failure to consult

10.53 Historically, the duty to consult has been treated as mandatory. Although an approach based on the classification of obligations as mandatory or directory has virtually been eliminated, failure to consult is still a significant breach and, in general, a complete failure to consult will lead to the resulting decision being quashed.[1] An illustration of the seriousness with which the courts have historically regarded a failure to consult is given in *Bradbury v London Borough of Enfield*,[2] where persons were not consulted as required in relation to educational reorganisation. The council had successfully argued before Goff J that no relief should be granted because chaos would result. However, the Court of Appeal reversed his decision, with Lord Denning declaiming that 'even if chaos should result, still the law must be obeyed'.

[1]   The consequences of a failure to comply with statutory procedures, both generally and in relation to time limits, are discussed at **10.3** and **10.4** above. The consequences of a failure to give reasons when required by statute to do so are considered at **10.18** below.
[2]   [1967] 1 WLR 1311.

10.54 A similarly robust approach was taken recently by Munby J in *R (Montpeliers and Trevors Association) v Westminster City Council*.[1] Munby J quashed a traffic order made by Westminster which authorised the installation of barriers which limited vehicle access to two residential squares. He also granted a mandatory order requiring the Council to conduct an adequate public consultation.

¹   [2005] EWHC 16 (Admin), [2006] LGR 304.

10.55 Nonetheless, the courts will sometimes adopt a more pragmatic approach. On a pragmatic approach, provided that the essential objective is complied with, it will often not matter that specific procedures, designed to secure that objective, have not been strictly honoured.¹ For example, in *R v Secretary of State for Social Services, ex p Association of Metropolitan Authorities*² Webster J declined to quash regulations made in absence of mandatory consultation with the applicants.

¹   See, eg *Coney v Choyce* [1975] 1 WLR 422.
²   [1986] 1 WLR 1.

10.56 In *Edwards*, the Court of Appeal accepted that it would be pointless to quash a permit to enable consultation on data which had become out-of-date.¹ Similarly, in *R (LH) v Shropshire Council* the Court of Appeal declined to quash a decision to close a day care centre where the council had conducted a very wide consultation exercise, but unfairly not sufficiently specific.² The centre had closed, staff had dispersed and it would have been over-legalistic to undo the decision. These cases provide an illustration of the pragmatic approach of the court to procedural irregularity even where it constitutes what might be regarded as the breach of a mandatory provision. In *R (Hunt) v North Somerset Council* the Supreme Court³ upheld the decision of the Court of Appeal to grant no relief — not even declaratory relief — following a procedural failure but where quashing would have nullified a local authority annual budget for a financial year since ended, and where a declaration had not been sought. The Supreme Court did, however, indicate that the grant of no relief at all would not be the ordinary course.

However, whilst Silber J recognised in *Capenhurst*⁴ that if there has been inadequate consultation, there will be cases in which it would not be unfair not to quash the subsequent decision, he endorsed the comments of Bingham LJ in *R v Chief Constable of the Thames Valley Police, ex p Cotton*⁵ that these cases would be "of great rarity". He quashed the council's decision to withdraw funding from six voluntary organisations on the grounds of inadequate consultation.⁶

¹   [2006] EWCA Civ 877, paragraphs 121–132, particularly paragraph 126.
²   [2014] EWCA Civ 404.
³   [2015] UKSC 51, [2015] 1 WLR 3575.
⁴   [2004] EWHC 2124 (Admin); (2004) 7 CCL Rep 557, paragraph 58.
⁵   [1990] IRLR 344.
⁶   See also, in the context of delegated legislation, the decision of the Court of Appeal in *R (C) v Secretary of State for Justice* [2008] EWCA Civ 882, [2009] QB 657, overturning the decision of the Divisional Court not to quash regulations made without lawful consultation and without the production of a Race Equality Impact Assessment. C.f. *R (Hurley and Moore) v Secretary of State for Business, Innovation and Skills* [2012] EWHC 201 (Admin), [2012] HRLR 13.

10.57 In exceptional cases a decision may be treated as invalid merely in relation to the party not consulted. This was the result of the *Aylesbury*

Mushrooms case.[1] The order in question was held not to be valid as against the Mushroom Growers Association, who had not been consulted (the Minister had sought to consult them but the letter had gone astray), though it remained valid and effective against others. Obviously, in some – perhaps most – cases, a solution involving partial invalidity will not be possible.

---

[1] *Agricultural, Horticultural and Forestry Industry Training Board v Aylesbury Mushrooms Ltd* [1972] 1 WLR 190.

10.58 As with all forms of procedural complaint, a judicial review challenge for breach of the duty to consult is particularly susceptible to the use of s 31(3C) of the Senior Courts Act 1981, which requires the court to consider whether permission should be granted and refuse permission where it is highly likely that the outcome for the applicant would not have been substantially different had the conduct complained of not occurred. Similarly, relief must be refused on the same basis: s 31(2A). Both tests are subject to an exceptional public interest carve-out, but are quite deliberately designed to reduce the number of purely procedural complaints which, it can be suggested, would have made little or no difference. Reliance on the 'no substantial difference' test can, however, pose tactical problems for a defendant public authority: if it is asserted that running a consultation would have made no substantial difference, but the claim is successful, it will be hard for the defendant to avoid complaints that it did not have an open mind. There can, however, be presentational ways around this.[1]

---

[1] For an example, see *R (London Criminal Courts Solicitors Association) v Lord Chancellor* [2014] EWHC 3020 (Admin), paragraph 46.

'DUE INQUIRY'

10.59 Statutes sometimes require that a decision be taken only after 'due inquiry'.[1] This has been equated to a duty to act fairly. In *General Medical Council v Spackman*,[2] a decision to remove a doctor from the medical register on grounds of alleged adultery was quashed after he had been denied an opportunity to call evidence rebutting the charge. Lord Wright said that the Council has to make due inquiry and,[3] that 'the medical practitioner who is impugned should be given a full and fair opportunity of being heard'.[4]

---

[1] By contrast, in some cases Parliament gives no indication of how a specific safeguard should be achieved. In such circumstances the decision-maker may be afforded a wider discretion; see 10.20 above.
[2] [1943] AC 627.
[3] At 644.
[4] See also *R v Secretary of State for Transport, ex parte Philippine Airlines* (1984) 1 S & B Av R IV/31, CA; *Majora v Kurivana Bus Service Pty Ltd* (1990) (1) ZLR 87 (SC).

10.60 Another facet of the duty to make due inquiry is that a public authority must take reasonable steps to acquaint itself with the relevant information, in order to properly perform its statutory functions. As Lord Diplock pointed out in *Secretary of State for Education and Science v Tameside Metropolitan Borough Council*,[1] this is an aspect of the requirement to take account of relevant considerations. Compliance is assessed on the *Wednesbury* standard, on the basis that where the statute does not prescribe the relevant considerations, relevancy is for the decision-maker.[2] However, it is important that the *Tameside* duty is not used to introduce a requirement of consultation by the backdoor nor used as a proxy for a process challenge. The duty to make due inquiry is a substantive obligation assessed by reference to rationality, not a procedural matter for the court to determine.[3] The content of the duty is, however, context-specific. It may require more careful inquiry depending on the complexity of the issues or the degree of impact of the decision.[4]

[1]   [1977] AC 1014, 1065. See too: *R London Criminal Courts Solicitors Association) v Lord Chancellor* [2015] EWHC 295 (Admin). For a collection of the principles applicable to such cases, see *R (Plantagenet Alliance Ltd) v Secretary of State for Justice* [2014] EWHC 1662 (Admin), [2015] 3 All ER 215, paragraph 100.

[2]   *CREEDNZ Inc v Governor General* [1981] 1 NZLR 173, 183; *Re Findlay* [1985] AC 318; *R (Khatun) v Newham London Borough Council* [2004] EWCA Civ 55, [2005] QB 37; *R (Khatib) v Secretary of State for Justice* [2015] EWHC 606 (Admin).

[3]   *R (Plantagenet Alliance Ltd) v Secretary of State for Justice* [2014] EWHC 1662 (Admin), [2015] 3 All ER 215, paragraphs 137-139.

[4]   *R (Refugee Action) v Secretary of State for the Home Department* [2014] EWHC 1033 (Admin); *R (Shaffi) v Secretary of State for Justice* [2011] EWHC 3113 (Admin).

REASONS

10.61 In *R v Home Secretary, ex parte Doody*,[1] Lord Mustill stated that 'the law does not at present recognise a general duty to give reasons for an administrative decision'. This remains the position in principle, as the Court of Appeal has confirmed in *Hasan v Secretary of State for Trade and Industry*[2] and *R (Lee-Hirons) v Secretary of State for Justice*.[3] Nonetheless, a duty to give reasons will be implied in appropriate circumstances in accordance with the principles of natural justice. In addition, many statutory powers expressly require a decision-maker to give reasons for a decision. It is also important for practitioners to have in mind art 6 of the European Convention on Human Rights, which will require the giving of reasons in certain contexts.[4] This section focuses on the statutory duty to give reasons. The relationship between reasons and natural justice is explored in CHAPTER 11. Other issues which may arise when a decision-maker gives or refuses reasons are discussed in CHAPTER 8.[5]

[1]   [1994] 1 AC 531 at 564E.

[2]   [2008] EWCA Civ 1311, [2009] 3 All ER 539, paragraph 8.

[3]   [2014] EWCA Civ 553, [2015] QB 385. The Supreme Court judgment did not address the existence or otherwise of a general common law duty, which was unnecessary given the application on the facts of a policy which promised the giving of reasons: [2016] UKSC 46, [2016] 3 WLR 590.

[4]   Consideration of the authorities under art 6 is beyond the scope of this chapter

[5]   See **8.43** above.

Purpose and adequacy of reasons

10.62 In the Privy Council decision, *Stefan v General Medical Council*,[1] Lord Clyde, delivering the judgment of the Committee, said:

'The advantages of the provision of reasons have been often rehearsed. They relate to the decision-making process, in strengthening that process itself, in increasing the public confidence in it, and in the desirability of the disclosure of error where error exists. They relate also to the parties immediately affected by the decision, in enabling them to know the strengths and weaknesses of their respective cases, and to facilitate appeal where that course is appropriate.'

1   [1999] 1 WLR 1293,1300. See also, for example, the discussion of the value of providing reasons in a particularly statutory context in the case of *Cullen v Chief Constable of the Royal Ulster Constabulary* [2003] UKHL 39, [2003] 1 WLR 1763, paragraphs 7 and 56. See more generally: M. Elliott, 'Has the Common Law Duty to Give Reasons Come of Age Yet?' [2011] PL 56.

10.63 As Lord Clyde makes clear in this passage from *Stefan*, the obligation to give reasons may serve a number of purposes. First, and most obviously, reasons explain the decision to interested parties and the general public. Reasons enable interested parties to appeal against or challenge the decision, where this avenue is available. Secondly, the obligation to give reasons may also be an integral part of the decision-making process, intended to concentrate the minds of the decision-makers and ensure that they take into account in a disciplined manner all issues relevant to their decision. There are therefore both normative and instrumental bases for reason-giving. Taken together, these purposes contribute to individual and public confidence in the decision-making process. In addition, in *Cullen v Chief Constable of the Royal Ulster Constabulary*, Lords Bingham and Steyn commented that the provision of reasons assists the courts in performing their supervisory function if judicial review proceedings are launched.[1]

1   [2003] UKHL 39, [2003] 1 WLR 1763, paragraph 7.

10.64 The leading authority on what amounts to adequate reasons is the judgment of Lord Brown in *South Buckinghamshire District Council v Porter (No.2)*,[1] in which he said that:

'The reasons for a decision must be intelligible and they must be adequate. They must enable the reader to understand why the matter was decided as it was and what conclusions were reached on the "principal important controversial issues", disclosing how any issue of law or fact was resolved. Reasons can be briefly stated, the degree of particularity required depending entirely on the nature of the issues falling for decision. The reasoning must not give rise to a substantial doubt as to whether the decision-maker erred in law, for example by misunderstanding some relevant policy or some other important matter or by failing to reach a rational decision on relevant grounds. But such adverse inference will not readily be drawn. The reasons need refer only to the main issues in the dispute, not to every material consideration. They should enable disappointed developers to assess their prospects of obtaining some alternative development permission, or, as the case may be, their unsuccessful opponents to understand how the policy or approach underlying the grant of permission may impact upon future such applications. Decision letters must be read in a straightforward manner, recognising that they are addressed to parties well aware of the issues involved and the arguments advanced. A reasons challenge will only succeed if the party aggrieved can satisfy the court that he has genuinely been substantially prejudiced by the failure to provide an adequately reasoned decision.'

1   [2004] UKHL 33, [2004] 1 WLR 1953, paragraph 36. See too: *Nzolameso v Westminster City Council* [2015] UKSC 22, [2015] 3 All ER 942.

10.65 Other issues which may arise when a decision-maker gives or refuses reasons are discussed in CHAPTER 11.[1]

[1]   See **11.238–11.241** below.

Consequences of failure to give reasons

10.66 Where a public authority has failed to give reasons (or adequate reasons) when statutorily required to do so, there are two potential remedies.[1] The first remedy is to allow the authority another opportunity to provide reasons. This may be achieved either by permitting further evidence of the reasons to be adduced at the judicial review hearing or granting a mandatory order requiring that reasons are provided. The second possible remedy is to quash the decision and require the decision-maker to reconsider the matter and take the decision afresh.

[1]   The consequences of a failure to comply with statutory procedures, both generally and in relation to time limits and the failure to consult, are discussed above at **10.5, 10.11** and **10.53** respectively.

10.67 Public bodies seeking a second chance to give reasons might claim support for their position from the comment of Lord Keith in *London and Clydeside Estates Ltd v Aberdeen District Council*[1] that:

> '[the] consequences of failure to state reasons in writing . . . can always be put right at a later date without anything more serious than some inconvenience'.

However, this comment was obiter. The better view is that it was intended only to apply to the facts of that case rather than being of general application.[2] The ordinary course is that a failure to provide reasons in breach of a duty to do so will be that the decision is quashed and remitted.[3]

[1]   [1980] 1 WLR 182,201E.
[2]   See further the judgment of Lord Reed in *Chief Constable of Lothian and Borders Police v Lothian and Borders Police Board* [2005] CSOH 32, [2005] SLT 315, paragraph 44.
[3]   Which means re-taking the decision, not simply giving reasons for the quashed decision: *R v Westminster City Council, ex p Ermakov* [1996] 2 All ER 302, 315.

10.68 Furthermore, bearing in mind the purposes served by an obligation to give reasons, it is clear that a failure to give reasons will not always be cured by the provision of reasons at a later date. For example, subsequent reasons should not permit a decision-maker to adopt an ex post facto rationalisation of a decision originally taken for impermissible reasons. In addition, where the obligation to give reasons was intended to be a part of the decision-making process, the subsequent provision of reasons will not cure the decision-maker's default.

10.69 To a large degree, the case law has been illustrative rather than normative: the authorities have often been decided based upon the subject matter of the case rather than any detailed analysis of the underlying principles which ought to be applied. So, for example, there are certain areas such as housing, planning and licensing where the courts have traditionally treated the failure to give reasons as a basis for quashing the whole decision and requiring that the decision be taken afresh. On the other hand, there have been many cases supporting the view that a mere failure to give proper reasons, even if statutorily required, does not of itself entitle a court to hold that there is an error of law justifying quashing the decision.[1] In such cases an order to provide full reasons will suffice (although the reasons there disclosed may demonstrate further grounds for challenge). Unfortunately, there is no very convincing basis for distinguishing these different situations. These differing decisions illustrate the importance of considering the factual and statutory context in each case. This was explained by Richards J in *R (Richardson) v North Yorkshire County Council*:[2]

'The consequences of a failure to comply with a requirement to give reasons depend very much on statutory context and the particular circumstances of the case. The authorities cited by counsel cover a range of different situations . . . There is no substitute for a careful examination of the particular statutory context and the precise nature of the requirement to state reasons in each case.'

[1] See, eg *R v Criminal Injuries Compensation Board, ex p Cook* [1996] 1 WLR 1037; *Mountview Court Properties Ltd v Devlin* (1970) 21 P & CR 689; *Crake v Supplementary Benefits Commission* [1982] 1 All ER 498.
[2] [2003] EWHC 764 (Admin), [2004] Env LR 13 at 47–48; upheld on appeal: [2003] EWCA Civ 1860, [2004] 1 WLR 1980.

10.70 One of the complicating factors in analysing the authorities on this issue is that a number of cases dealing with a failure to give adequate reasons have focussed on whether it is appropriate and permissible for a decision-maker to adduce further evidence of the reasons for the decision at the judicial review hearing. Therefore, these issues have been dealt with as a question of admissibility of evidence as well as being a question which goes to the remedy for breach. In principle the factors to be taken into account when deciding whether to allow such evidence ought to be similar to those which are taken into account when determining whether to grant a mandatory order requiring that reasons are provided. Logically, however, these are separate questions.

10.71 The Court of Appeal considered the scope for a public body to adduce further evidence of its reasons at a judicial review hearing in *R v Westminster City Council, ex p Ermakov*.[1] The local housing authority had decided that the applicant was intentionally homeless. Pursuant to s 64(4) of the Housing Act 1985, the authority was required to notify the applicant that they were satisfied that he became homeless intentionally and, at the same time, to give him the reasons for that decision. The Court of Appeal concluded that the authority was not entitled to rely on evidence of its reasons at the judicial review hearing, largely influenced by the statutory requirement that the decision and reasons were given at the same time. However, the court noted that there could be exceptions to this approach. Hutchison LJ stated:

'The court can and, in appropriate cases, should admit evidence to elucidate or, exceptionally, correct or add to the reasons; but should, consistently with Steyn LJ's observations in *ex parte Graham*, be very cautious about doing so. I have in mind cases where, for example, an error has been made in transcription or expression, or a word or words inadvertently omitted, or where the language used may be in some way lacking in clarity. These examples are not intended to be exhaustive, but rather to reflect my view that the function of such evidence should generally be elucidation not fundamental alteration, confirmation not contradiction. Certainly there seems to me to be no warrant for receiving and relying on as validating the decision evidence – as in this case – which indicates that the real reasons were wholly different from the stated reasons.'[2]

[1] [1996] 2 All ER 302, CA. See also *R v Northamptonshire County Council ex p W* [1998] ELR 291, per Laws J, and the decision of the Court of Appeal *Hijazi v Kensington and Chelsea Royal London Borough Council* [2003] EWCA Civ 692, [2003] HLR 1113.

[2] At 315H.

10.72 When considering whether to allow evidence of reasons to be adduced, it is, of course, important that any such evidence should be directed towards the reasons actually relied upon at the time the decision was made; see *Re L.*[1] Plainly in such cases the court must be alert to the dangers of ex post facto rationalisation. One of the risks of such ex post facto rationalisation is that there may be a natural temptation for decision-makers to support their original decision. The court will therefore require considerable comfort that, notwithstanding a failure to give adequate reasons at the time of the decision, the decision-maker would still have reached the same conclusion. This is illustrated by the decision in *R (Lynch) v General Dental Council*[2] which concerned an appeal decision to reject the claimant's application to join the General Dental Council's specialist panel of orthodontists. The appeal panel gave inadequate reasons for its decision and one of the reasons appeared to reflect a misunderstanding of the evidence. Collins J stated that:

> 'where there are inadequate reasons and particularly where an important reason can be shown to have been based on a possible misunderstanding, the court will intervene if persuaded that the result might have been 'different'.

Given that the appeal panel may have come to a different conclusion if they had correctly understood the facts, their decision was quashed.

[1] [1994] ELR 16. It is important to consider the judgment in *Ermakov* (above).

[2] [2003] EWHC 2987 (Admin), [2004] 1 All ER 1159, paragraph 32.

10.73 Ultimately, the application of the principles in *Ermakov* will depend on the statutory context and facts of the case at hand. For example, the general principle that supplementary evidence should not contradict reasons already given was applied by the Court of Appeal in *R (Richards) v Pembrokeshire County Council*[1] in determining that the local authority would not be permitted to rely on additional reasons for a decision when its original stated reasons were ultra vires.

[1] [2004] EWCA Civ 1000, [2005] LGR 105. This decision also illustrates that where the reasons identified show that the decision-maker has acted for an improper purpose or otherwise unlawfully, the decision will be quashed.

10.74 By contrast, in *R (Jackson) v Parole Board,*[1] Richards J concluded that the Secretary of State was not bound by his original, erroneous statement of reasons for recalling the claimant to prison following release on parole and was allowed to rely on the correct reasons for the recall, which had been set out in a contemporaneous document. Richards J distinguished *Ermakov* on several grounds including the fact that on the facts of *Jackson* there was no statutory duty to give reasons to the claimant at the same time as the recall decision (unlike in *Ermakov*). Rather the statutory requirement was that reasons were to be given later and for the purpose of enabling the recalled prisoner to make representations to the Parole Board. It was the duty of the Parole Board to consider the matter on the basis of the material available to it at the time of its decision, and it was not restricted to the reasons of (and material available to) the Secretary of State.[2]

1   [2003] EWHC 2437 (Admin); [2004] Prison LR 1, paragraphs 24–25.
2   *R (Gulliver) v Parole Board* [2007] EWCA Civ 1386, [2008] 1 WLR 1116.

10.75 Bearing in mind the extent to which factual and statutory contexts will vary, it is perhaps not surprising that the development of overarching principles has been somewhat slow. Nevertheless, in *R (Nash) v Chelsea College of Art and Design*[1] Stanley Burnton J reviewed the decision in *Ermakov* (along with other authorities) and distilled the following propositions:

'(i)   Where there is a statutory duty to give reasons as part of the notification of the decision, so that "the adequacy of the reasons is itself made a condition of the legality of the decision", only in exceptional circumstances if at all will the court accept subsequent evidence of the reasons.[2]

(ii)   In other cases, the court will be cautious about accepting late reasons. The relevant considerations include the following, which to a significant degree overlap:

(a)   Whether the new reasons are consistent with the original reasons.

(b)   Whether it is clear that the new reasons are indeed the original reasons of the whole committee.

(c)   Whether there is a real risk that the later reasons have been composed subsequently in order to support the tribunal's decision, or are a retrospective justification of the original decision. This consideration is really an aspect of (b).

(d)   The delay before the later reasons were put forward.

(e)   The circumstances in which the later reasons were put forward. In particular, reasons put forward after the commencement of proceedings must be treated especially carefully. Conversely, reasons put forward during correspondence in which the parties are seeking to elucidate the decision should be approached more tolerantly.'

1   [2001] EWHC 538 (Admin), paragraph 34. This list of relevant factors is not exhaustive: see the decision of Silber J in *R (Leung) v Imperial College of Science, Technology and Medicine* [2002] EWHC 1358 (Admin), [2002] ELR 653, paragraphs 29–30 and see *R (London Fire and Emergency Planning Authority) v Secretary of State for Communities and Local Government* [2007] EWHC 1176 (Admin), [2007] LGR 591, paragraph 65.
2   This strict approach is, however, subject to the general exception, set out in *Ermakov*, permitting the admission of evidence that merely elucidates the original written reasons: see the comments of Stanley Burnton J in *R (Ashworth Hospital Authority) v Mental Health Review Tribunal for West Midlands and Northwest Region* [2001] EWHC 901, Admin, (2002) 5 CCL Rep 78; *R (London Fire and Emergency Planning Authority) v Secretary of State for Communities and Local Government* [2007] EWHC 1176 (Admin), [2007] BLGR 591, paragraph 65; and *R (KVP Ent Ltd) v South Bucks District Council* [2013] EWHC 926 (Admin). For an example which fell on the other side of the line, see *R (Moore) v Chief Constable of Merseyside* [2015] EWHC 1430 (Admin).

10.76 This analysis draws a clear distinction between cases where the obligation to provide reasons is part of the decision-making process and those where the obligation is to provide reasons to explain the decision. In the former case, Stanley Burnton J suggests that the courts will be extremely circumspect when allowing further evidence, particularly where the initial reasons were grossly inadequate.

In addition, Stanley Burnton J also suggested two further factors which might be relevant when considering whether to have regard to late reasons. The first was the subject matter of the decision; he suggested that the courts would apply particular scrutiny to subsequent reasons where the subject matter concerned important human rights. The second was the qualifications and experience of the decision-maker; comprehensiveness and clarity might be required from lawyers and those who regularly sit on administrative tribunals but would not be required to the same degree from occasional non-lawyer tribunal chairmen and members.[1]

[1]   [2001] EWHC 538 (Admin) at paragraphs 35 and 36. See, too, *R (Leung) v Imperial College of Science, Technology and Medicine* [2002] EWHC 1358 (Admin), [2002] ELR 653 at paragraphs 29 and 30 where Silber J suggested that, in determining the consequences of a failure to give reasons, a court should also take into account whether the decision maker would have been expected to state the reasons subsequently raised at the time the decision was made and also whether it would be just in all the circumstances to refuse to admit those subsequent reasons.

10.77 An example of the distinction between reasons required as part of the decision, and reasons which subsequently capture the decision, can be seen in *R (Richardson) v North Yorkshire County Council*.[1] A local authority had decided to grant planning permission to extend a quarry. It was required by reg 21(1) of the Town and Country Planning (Environmental Impact Assessment) (England and Wales) Regulations 1999[1] 'to make available for public inspection a statement containing the main reasons and considerations' on which the decision to grant permission was based. It had failed to do so. In his decision at first instance, Richards J concluded:[2]

'49.   . . . regulation 21(1) looks to the position *after* the grant of planning permission. It is concerned with making information available to the public as to what has been decided and why it has been decided, rather than laying down requirements for the decision-making process itself . . . '

'50.   The fact that the requirement focuses on the availability of information for public inspection after the decision has been made, rather than on the decision-making process, leads me to the view that a breach of regulation 21(1) ought not to lead necessarily to the quashing of the decision itself. A breach should be capable in principle of being remedied, and the legislative purpose achieved, by a mandatory order requiring the authority to make available a statement at the place, and containing the information, specified in the regulation.'[3]

[1]   [2003] EWHC 764 (Admin), [2004] Env LR 13.
[2]   SI 1999/293.
[3]   [2003] EWHC 764 (Admin), [2004] Env LR 13, paragraphs 49–50.

10.78 It is clear that in reaching this conclusion, Richards J was guided by the fact that regulation 21(1) required that reasons be given simply as an explanation of the decision. It was not a case where the requirement was intended actually to influence the decision-making process. The judgment was upheld and approved by the Court of Appeal.[1]

1   [2003] EWCA Civ 1860, [2004] 1 WLR 1920. See also, for example, *R (Wembley Field Ltd) v Brent London Borough Council* [2005] EWHC 2978 (Admin), [2006] Env LR 34.

10.79 In the Scottish case of *Chief Constable of Lothian and Borders Police v Lothian and Borders Police Board*,[1] Lord Reed considered the decision in *Richardson* along with a number of other authorities. He distilled a number of 'general propositions':

(1)   The stringency with which the court requires compliance with a statutory duty to give reasons will depend on the court's view of the intention of the particular statute. In that regard, one relevant question will be whether the purpose of the duty is solely to provide information about the reasons for the decision, or whether it has other purposes, such as to affect the decision-making process, or to maintain public confidence in that process.

(2)   Where there is a statutory duty to provide reasons as part of the notification of the decision to the parties, the court will normally interpret the legislation as having made the provision of adequate reasons with the decision a condition of the decision's validity.

(3)   In other cases the court may, in principle, be willing to regard the provision of late reasons (either voluntarily, or in response to an order) as sufficient compliance with the statutory duty, and will not therefore, in such a case, necessarily quash a decision by reason of the earlier failure in compliance. In such a case, however, the court will be cautious about accepting late reasons, and will take account of a number of overlapping factors, including whether the late reasons are consistent with any earlier reasons, whether it is clear that the late reasons are indeed the genuine reasons, whether there is a real risk that the late reasons are a retrospective justification of the decision, and the delay before the late reasons were put forward. In a case of this kind, if the court cannot be satisfied that substantial compliance with the statutory duty can be secured by the provision of late reasons, then whether the failure in compliance will invalidate the decision will again depend on the construction of the legislation in question.

(4)   Since a remedy is discretionary, the court may decline to quash a decision by reason of a failure to comply with a duty to give reasons.

(5)   Where the court quashes a decision, the matter must be reconsidered. Depending on the context, the matter may have to be reconsidered by the original decision-maker, or the court may have a discretion to direct that the matter should be dealt with by a differently constituted body.

1   [2005] CSOH 32, 2005 SLT 315, paragraph 70. Scots law is considered in Chapter 21. See also the summary of the relevant principles following the *Lothian and Borders* case given by the High Court of Northern Ireland in *Re X, Judicial Review* [2008] NIQB 22.

10.80 In summary, although the courts have been somewhat slow in developing guiding principles in this area, there have more recently been efforts to do so. Nonetheless, since the statutory and factual context will be so important in each case, and given that judicial review remedies are discretionary, it remains somewhat difficult to predict with certainty the judicial response to a failure to give reasons.

Contrast with appeals of judicial decisions

10.81 It is clear that the remedy for a failure to give reasons when required to do so by statute will depend on the statutory and factual context. However, in the *Richardson* case, Richards J stated that:[1]

> 'it is also important to bear in mind that there has been, as it seems to me, a tendency in recent years to adopt a stricter approach to the requirement to give reasons and to be readier to quash a decision for failure to give reasons and less ready to allow a deficiency of reasons to be cured by the provision of reasons or supplemental reasons at a later stage.'

[1] *R (Richardson) v North Yorkshire County Council* [2003] EWHC 764 (Admin), [2004] Env LR 13 at paragraph 47.

10.82 It is interesting to note that at a time when the courts appear to be reducing the scope for administrative decision-makers to support their decisions by providing subsequent reasons, the appellate courts have moved in the opposite direction in relation to appeals from first instance courts and tribunals. For example, in *English v Emery Reimbold & Strick Ltd*,[1] Lord Phillips MR, giving the judgment of the court, concluded that where there is an appeal on the ground that the trial judge failed to give reasons for his decision or part of it, it is appropriate to give the trial judge the opportunity to provide additional reasons for the decision or, where appropriate, a specific finding or findings. It was clear that he regarded this as the lesser of two evils, stating that:

> 'We are not greatly attracted by the suggestion that a judge who has given inadequate reasons should be invited to have a second bite at the cherry. But we are much less attracted at the prospect of expensive appellate proceedings on the ground of lack of reasons . . . while an appeal followed by a rehearing will involve a hideous waste of costs.'

[1] [2002] EWCA Civ 605, [2002] 1 WLR 2409, paragraphs 25–26.

10.83 The same approach has been adopted in relation to 'reasons' appeals against decisions of the Employment Tribunals: see *Barke v SEETEC Business Technology Centre Ltd*[1] which endorsed the Employment Appeal Tribunal's approach in *Burns v Royal Mail Group*.[2] In *Barke*, Dyson LJ giving the judgment of the court stated[3] that 'there is no true analogy between a judicial body like a court or an employment tribunal and other statutory bodies whose decisions are susceptible to judicial review'. He went on to note that:[4]

> 'the effect of taking into account subsequent reasons put forward by a decision-maker in judicial review proceedings is likely to be quite different from the effect of an appellate court or tribunal asking the lower court or tribunal for further reasons.'

[1] [2005] EWCA Civ 578, [2005] ICR 1373.
[2] [2004] ICR 1103.
[3] [2005] EWCA Civ 578, [2005] ICR 1373, paragraph 37.
[4] At paragraph 40.

10.84 The jurisprudence does not, however, speak with one voice. The statutory scheme for some tribunals has been interpreted to preclude remission.[1] Although there may continue to be a difference in the approach to an alleged failure to give adequate reasons according to whether the challenge is to a decision of a judicial body on the one hand, or an administrative decision-maker on the other, there is no clear rule to that effect. The *English* line of authority has not confronted the case law on subsequent evidence as to reasons, or sought to reconcile them. The statutory context will remain the determinative factor.

[1]   *VK v Norfolk County Council* [2004] EWHC 2912 (Admin), [2005] ELR 342.

Chapter 11

NATURAL JUSTICE AND FAIRNESS: THE AUDI ALTERAM PARTEM RULE

INTRODUCTION

11.1 The rules of natural justice are minimum standards of fair decision-making imposed by the common law.[1] There are two accepted rules of natural justice: *nemo judex in causa sua* (nobody is allowed to be a judge in his own cause); and *audi alteram partem* (hear the other side),[2] although other rules have been referred to (eg the need for probative evidence, the avoidance of material mistake of fact) without achieving general recognition at any rate under this rubric. This chapter deals with the second of the accepted rules. CHAPTER 12 deals with the first. These two accepted rules are conceptually distinct,[3] although denial of a fair hearing may provide evidence of actual or apparent bias. The purposes underlying the rule are threefold. It is conducive to arrival at the correct answer. It recognises the inherent interests and dignity of the individual affected. It enhances confidence in the decision reached. In *AF No 3*:[4] Lord Phillips saw no clear distinction between *'procedural fairness'* and *'procedure that produces a fair result.'*

1   The major monographs are: Jackson Natural Justice (2nd edn, 1979); Marshall Natural
Justice. Cʜ 15; Flick Natural Justice; Howard Natural Justice. Galligan. Due Process and Fair
Procedures (1996) Clarendon Press. See, also, Wade and Forsyth Administrative Law (10th
edn, 2009) ('Wade'), Cʜs 12 and 14; de Smith, Woolf and Jowell Judicial Review of
Administrative Action, Ch 4 (7th edn, 2013) ('De Smith'); Craig Administrative Law (7th edn,
2012) Chs 12–14; Garner Administrative Law (8th edn) pp 250–281; Harris Disciplinary and
Regulatory Proceedings (6th edn) Ch2; Gordon: Jaffé Judicial Review and Crown Office
Practice, paragraphs 3–185–3–209; Halsbury Laws (4th edn) pp 147–195; Fordham Judicial
Review Handbook (6th edn, 2012) Hart, pp 95–97, 618–636; Feldman (ed) English Public
Law (2009) OUP 2nd edn, Ch 15; CP Seepersal 'Fairness and audi alteram partem', pp
242–258 [1975] PL; Churches Justice and Executive Discretion in Australia [1980] PL, pp
397–430, 1; De Santi Natural Justice in Italy [1986] PL, pp 115–128, 744; Zellick 'Natural
Justice The Reason Why (1970) 120 NLJ; Chongwe: 'Limitation on the Principles of Natural
Justice: an African Perspective' CLB April 89, 620–626, 1987; Jain & Jain Principles of
Administrative Law (India. 4th edn) Cʜs 7 and 8; Sykes, Lanham, Tracey General Principles
of Administrative Law: (Australia) Cʜs 15, 16, 18, 19; Garner & Brown French Administrative
Law (3rd edn) p 143; Judicial Control of Administrative Action (USA) Ch 14; Hogan and
Morgan Administrative Law — Ireland (1986) pp 259–296; Kelly Fundamental Rights in the
Irish Law and Constitution, pp 313–314; Anderson Dansk Forvaltningsret Denmark, p 327ff;
Forsthoff: Lehrbuch de Verwal-tungs rechts (Germany) (10th edn) pp 235ff; Schwarze
European Administrative Law (1992) Sweet & Maxwell; Sorabjee 'Obliging Government
to Control itself. Recent Developments in Indian Administrative Law' [1994] PL 39–50; D
Galligan Due Process and Fair Procedure (1996) OUP; Beloff In Israel Among the Nations
(Kellerman, Siohr and Einhorn (eds)); Old Law: New Land: A Comparative Analysis of the
Public Law of the United Kingdom and Israel. Kluwer Int (1998) p 45; For Scotland, see —
Cʜᴀᴘᴛᴇʀ 22 and 'Judicial Review' Clyde and Edwards (2001) Edinburgh. For Singapore:
Halsbury's Laws of Singapore: 10, 5D pp 43–47;

2   *Kanda (B Surinder Singh) v Government of the Federation of Malaysia* [1962] AC 322 at 337;
Abraham v GMC 2008 EWHC 183 (Admin) at (4).

3   *Amec Capital Projects Ltd v Whitefriars City Estates Ltd* [2005] 1 All ER 723.

4   [2009] UKHL 28, [2009] 3 WLR 74.

11.2 The rules are judicially allied to, and sometimes co-extensive with,
procedural requirements imposed by statutes.[1] Breach of them is, in Lord
Diplock's categorisation in *Council of Civil Service Unions v Minister for the
Civil Service*[2] ('the *GCHQ* case') a form of 'procedural impropriety'. As
explained in Cʜᴀᴘᴛᴇʀ 4, the Human Rights Act 1998 (HRA 1998) imposes a
statutory obligation in many cases to afford a fair hearing compliant with art 6
of the European Convention on Human Rights (ECHR).[3] This, along with
specific domestic legislation as to procedure, means that judicial review for
procedural impropriety often also involves review for illegality. Reference will
be made below to some of the ECHR jurisprudence, and a fuller discussion of
the impact of HRA 1998 will be found at **11.319** below.

1   Legislative procedural requirements are discussed in Cʜᴀᴘᴛᴇʀ 10 above. In Australia the
Administrative Decisions (Judicial Review) Act 1977 makes 'breach of the rules of natural
justice' an express ground of judicial review: see Aronson, Dyer and Groves *Administrative
Law* (3rd edn, 2004) p 370.

2   *Neill v North Antrim Magistrates Court* 1992 1 WLR 1220, 1230D–E.

3   The relationship of domestic law and convention rights is set out in *Osborn v Parole Board SC*
[2013] 3 WLR 1020 at [54]–[63], Philip Murray CLJ 2014 5-8; see too the EU Charter of
Fundamental Rights Act 41 (the right to good administration). The status of this Charter in
English domestic law is controversial: *NS v Secretary of State for Home Department (Amnesty
International Ltd and the AIRE Centre (Advice on Individual Rights in Europe) (UK))*:
C-411/10 [2013] QB 102. *Rugby Football Union v Consolidated Information Services
(formerly Viagogo Ltd)* [2012] UKSC 55, [2012] 1 WLR 333. *Benkharbouche v Embassy of*

the Republic of Sudan (UKEAT/040/12) [2014] 1 CMLR 1088, [2013] 1 IRLR 918 G6 A Sanger CLJ 2014 1–4.

11.3 The rules were first applied to proceedings in courts of justice but transplanted to various public and, indeed, private law contexts.[1] It is now conventional to judge the validity of an administrative law decision challenged on such procedural grounds by reference to a test of fairness rather than of the rules of natural justice.[2] The concept of fairness has the advantage of emphasising the flexibility of the principle, whose content will vary depending upon the circumstances of the case. But it remains in its original form an essentially procedural concept; it is an aspect of adjectival, not of substantive law and should not be confused with natural law: the Americanism 'due process' is an appropriate synonym.[3] The questions 'Was the decision reached fairly?' and 'Was the decision a fair one?' remain separate questions. The test is not, 'has an unjust result been reached?' but, 'Was there an opportunity afforded for injustice to be done?'

[1]   The rules applied in court proceedings are not necessarily identical in content to those discussed below; however, texts on civil and criminal procedure will often provide helpful background.
[2]   See, for example, Re Reilly's Application for Judicial Review [2013] UKSC 61'the common law duty to act fairly'; *Secretary of State for Communities and Local Government v Hopkins Developments* [2014] EWCA Civ 470 at 85 'it does not generally matter whether what is at issue is characterised as "natural justice" or 'procedural fairness"'.
[3]   *Barrs v British Wool Marketing Board* 1957 SLT 153 per Lord Clyde.

11.4 Whether the decision is a fair one was, on the traditional view, only rarely, and within strict limits, a proper question in proceedings in judicial review. Courts have increasingly elided the two questions, and have regarded fairness, as distinct from rationality (or proportionality) as the touchstone of the validity of an administrative decision.[1] Moreover, built into the rules of natural justice is the assumption that, absent fair procedures, a decision is unlikely itself to be fair.

> 'The common law has thus shown its instinctive wisdom: it recognises that the ultimate decision is one for which the user can be held responsible only at the bar of public opinion, but that he will be more likely than not to arrive at a correct conclusion if he first of all observes this outward procedural pattern'.[2]

Although in theory a court, when confronted with a challenge on procedural grounds, should not have concerned itself with the merits[3] there have been in the past cases where the court has modified the requirements of fairness, or even ignored them, because of a lack of sympathy with the merits of the case, notoriously *Ward v Bradford Corpn*[4] (the student teacher expelled for having a man in her room) — an approach which attracted considerable concern; but is explicable as being of its time.

The reforms to judicial review introduced by the Criminal Justice and Courts Act 2015[5] have moved further away from the traditional view and require the Courts to consider, both when granting leave[6] and granting relief,[7] whether a decision would have been substantially different if a decision had been reached fairly. If it would not then leave or relief must be refused, save where it is appropriate not to do so due to "exceptional public interest".[8] These new provisions fundamentally modify the test and require the courts to consider not only whether there was an opportunity for injustice to be done, but whether it was in fact done. If the result would have been substantially the same then it follows that there was no injustice and the courts should not seek to remedy it.[9]

1 Eg *R (Rashid) v Secretary of State for Home Department* TLR 12.7.2005.
2 Heuston: Essays in Constitutional Law (2nd edn) p 184.
3 *Chief Constable of the North Wales Police v Evans* [1982] 1 WLR 1155) (discussed Grubb, 1983 CLJ 13).
4 (1971) 70 LGR 27.
5 2015 c.2
6 CCJA 2015, s 84(1)
7 CCJA 2015, s 84(2)
8 Ibid.
9 For further discussion of the reforms see A Samuels *Judicial review: The new law: The Criminal Justice and Courts Act 2015* Chapter 2 [2015] J.P.L. p 754–758 and A Mills *Reforms to Judicial Review in the Criminal Justice and Courts Act 2015: Promoting Efficiency or Weakening the Rule of Law?* [2015] P.L. 583.

11.5 There is one major respect in which a challenge on natural justice or fairness principles is unlike other judicial review challenges. When applying the *Wednesbury* principles, or otherwise reviewing the exercise of discretion, the courts have made it clear that it is not their function to substitute their view for that of the decision-maker. Where fairness is in issue (at least where it is being used as a procedural concept), the courts jealously guard their right to determine what the principle requires in any particular context[1] they do not simply review the procedural steps taken to decide whether a reasonable person might have considered them sufficient.[2] The point was put forcefully and unequivocally in the following dictum of Lloyd LJ in *R v Panel on Take-overs and Mergers, ex p Guinness plc*:[3]

'In the first place the question whether we are entitled to intervene at all is not to be answered, as Mr Buckley argued, by reference to *Wednesbury* unreasonableness: see *Associated Provincial Picture Houses Ltd v Wednesbury Corpn* [1948] 1 KB 223. It is not a question whether, in the language of Lord Diplock, quoted by Watkins LJ in the Divisional Court, the decision to hold the hearing on 2 September was so outrageous in its defiance of logic or of accepted moral standards that no sensible person who had applied his mind to the question to be decided could have arrived at it': see *Council of Civil Service Unions v Minister for the Civil Service* [1985] AC 374, 411.

Rather, the question has to be decided in accordance with the principles of fair procedure which have been developed over the years, and of which the courts are the author and sole judge. These principles, which apply as well to administrative as judicial tribunals, are known compendiously, if misleadingly, as the rules of natural justice.

Mr Buckley argued that the correct test is *Wednesbury* unreasonableness, because there could, he said, be no criticism of the way in which the panel reached its decision on 25 August. It is the substance of that decision, viz, the decision not to adjourn the hearing fixed for 2 September, which is in issue. I cannot accept that argument. It confuses substance and procedure. If a tribunal adopts a procedure which is unfair, then the court may, in the exercise of its discretion, seldom withheld, quash the resulting decision by applying the rules of natural justice. The test cannot be different, just because the tribunal decides to adopt a procedure which is unfair. Of course the court will give great weight to the tribunal's own view of what is fair, and will not lightly decide that a tribunal has adopted a procedure which is unfair, especially so distinguished and experienced a tribunal as the panel.'

1 See for example, *Re Reilly's Application for Judicial Review* [2013] UKSC 61 the court does not merely 'review the reasonableness of the decision-maker's judgement of what fairness required'; *R (LH) v Shropshire Council* [2014] EWCA Civ 404 at [29]'fairness is a matter for the Court . . . to decide'; *R(Flatley) v Hywel Dda University Local Health Board* [2014] EWHC 2258(Admin) at [88]'it is a matter for the court to decide whether a fair procedure was followed'.

2 See now *Gillies v Secretary of State for Work and Pensions (Scotland)* [2006] 1 WLR 781 at [6]; *Osborn v Parole Board* [2013] 3 WLR 1020 at [65].

3 [1990] 1 QB 146 at 183–184.

11.6 Lord Donaldson MR and Woolf LJ expressed similar sentiments, Lord Donaldson MR said:[1]

'As I have already indicated, I think that, at least in the circumstances of this appeal, it is more appropriate to consider whether something has gone wrong of a nature and degree which require the intervention of the court, rather than to approach the matter on the basis of separate heads of *Wednesbury* unreasonableness and unfairness or breach of the rules of natural justice: see *Associated Provincial Picture Houses Ltd v Wednesbury Corpn* [1948] 1 KB 223. In passing I would, however accept that whether the rules of natural justice have been transgressed is not to be determined by a *Wednesbury* test: "Could any reasonable tribunal be so unfair?" On the other hand, fairness must depend in part on the tribunal's view of the general situation and a *Wednesbury* approach to that view may well be justified. If the tribunal's view should be accepted, then fairness or unfairness falls to be judged on the basis of that view rather than the court's view of the general situation'.

1 [1990] 1 QB 146 at 178–179.

11.7 Woolf LJ said:[1]

'On the application for judicial review it is appropriate for the court to focus on the activities of the panel as a whole and ask with regard to those activities, in the words of Lord Donaldson of Lymington "whether something has gone wrong" in nature and degree which requires the intervention of the courts. Nowadays it is more common to test decisions of the sort reached by the panel in this case by a standard of what is called "fairness". I venture to suggest that in the present circumstances in answering the question which Lord Donaldson of Lymington MR has posed it is more appropriate to use the term which has fallen from favour of "natural justice". In particular in considering whether something has gone wrong the court is concerned as to whether what has happened has resulted in real injustice. If it has, then the court has to intervene, since the panel is not entitled to confer on itself the power to inflict injustice on those who operate in the market which it supervises'.

1 [1990] 1 QB 146 at 193–194.

11.8 This approach was followed in *R v Monopolies and Mergers Commission, ex p Stagecoach Holdings*[1] where the court held that while due deference should be given to the tribunal's own view of what was fair, ultimately the court was the arbiter of fairness.[2] This is not to say that the courts can substitute their preferred version of procedure for the decision-maker's; they must rather determine whether the procedures already chosen are fair. A similar attitude has been adopted by the courts in cases where the issue has been whether in fairness proceedings ought to have been adjourned: see, eg, *R v Panel on Take-overs and Mergers, ex p Fayed*,[3] when Neill LJ commented that there should be intervention only where there was a 'real risk of serious prejudice'; and *R v Institute of Chartered Accountants in England and Wales, ex p Brindle*.[4]

[1] TLR 23.7.1996.
[2] See, too, *R v Secretary of State for Wales, ex p Emery* [1996] 4 All ER 1.
[3] [1992] BCC 524.
[4] [1994] BCC 297, CA.

11.9 This approach is surely right and to be preferred to that of Ewbank J in *R v Hertfordshire County Council, ex p B*.[1] In that case where a local authority proposed to return a child to its natural parents but changed its mind after receipt of unsubstantiated allegations, the judge held, more austerely, that its failure to allow the parents to put forward their side of the story was *so unreasonable that no reasonable Council could adopt that approach*.

[1] TLR 19.8.1986.

11.10 Judges have an expertise in determining what procedures are appropriate: they ought not to defer to decision makers on this key question, and it would seriously undermine the great advances made in administrative law if they were to do so. Furthermore, the purpose of procedural fairness is to impose the quality of decision-making to avoid a sense of injustice by the victim of unfair process and to reflect the rule of law.[1] It is not a usurpation of the function of administrators to pass judgement on the manner in which their decisions should be made; on the contrary, it ought to enhance the standard of that decision-making. Yet, as Megarry VC observed in *McInnes v Onslow Fane*:[2]

> 'Justice is far from being a "natural" concept. The closer one goes to a state of nature, the less justice does one find'.

The phrase 'fundamental justice' might more aptly reflect the importance of the concept without creating the illusion that it was a product of nature rather than of the judicial art.

[1] *Osborn v Parole Board* [2013] 3 WLR 1020 at [66]–[71].
[2] [1978] 1 WLR 1520 at 1530.

11.11 It was once the position that it was only where fairness is being challenged on traditional procedural grounds — where the courts have expertise and will not be usurping the administrative function — that they will intervene so readily. For example, the Court of Appeal held in *R v Secretary of State for the Home Department, ex p Hargreaves*[1] that where the issue relates to the fairness of a change of policy (a matter of substance) as distinct from the fairness of a hearing (a matter of procedure), the standard of review remained the *Wednesbury* standard. Hirst LJ described the contrary view of Sedley J in *R v MAAF, ex p Hamble* as 'heresy'.[2] However, the same court *in R v North Devon Health Authority, ex p Coughlan*[3] (of which Sedley LJ was now a member) innovatively reviewed the area and decided that where the legitimate expectation was of a substantive benefit it is for the court to decide whether weighing the public interest in the balance it is fair for the expectation not to be fulfilled.[4] This is now the orthodox view[5] but it is not strictly speaking about procedure.

1   [1997] 1 WLR 906.
2   At p 921 adopting the submission of the first named author. See, also, Himsworth. 'Legitimately Expecting Proportionality' [1996] PL.
3   [2001] 1 QB 213 at 215, paragraphs 81–82.
4   See, for critique of *Hargreaves*, Craig: 'Substantive legitimate expectations and principles of judicial review' in 'English Public Law and the Common Law of Europe', ed M Andenas (1998). S Foster, 'Legitimate Expectation and Prisoners' Rights' 1997 60 MLR 727.
5   *R (Bancoult) v secretary of State for Foreign and Commonwealth Affairs (No 2)* [2009] AC 453, Lord Carswell at p 514; *R (Moseley) v Haringey LBC* [2014] UKSC 56 Lord Wilson at [23].

Right to notice and opportunity to be heard

11.12 The rule that no man shall be condemned unless he has been given prior notice of the allegations against him and a fair opportunity to be heard is a cardinal principle of justice. It has been stated to reflect God's treatment of Adam, before the expulsion from Eden;[1] and indeed to be an aspect of natural law in the sense of 'the laws of God and man'[2] (but see **11.10** above on the doubtfulness of this proposition). It embodies a principle which would be universally perceived as inherent in the concept of fair treatment.

1   *Bentley's case, R v University of Cambridge* (1723) 1 Stra 557 (Fortescue J).
2   See *Bentley's* case (above). It is certainly one of the 'general principles of law' applied by the Court of Arbitration for Sport's Ad Hoc Panel at successive Olympic games. But see Alder *How fundamental is Natural Justice? Fundamental Duties* (1980) Pergamon.

11.13 The *audi alteram partem* rule was recognised in the Statement of Principles of Good Administration (Administration Under Law, Justice 1971):

'Before making any decision, an authority shall take all reasonable steps to ensure that all persons who will be particularly and materially affected by such decision have been informed in sufficient time of its intention to make the decision and shall afford to all such persons a reasonable opportunity of making representations to the authority with respect thereto',

and was part of Resolution (77) 31: on the Protection of the Individual in Relation to the Acts of Administrative Authorities (adopted by the Committee of Ministers on 28 September 1977, Council of Europe):

'I.   Right to be heard
1.   In respect of any administrative act of such nature as is likely to affect adversely his rights, liberties or interests, the person concerned may put forward facts and arguments and, in appropriate cases, call evidence which will be taken into account by the administrative authority.
2.   In appropriate cases the person concerned is informed, in due time and in a manner appropriate to the case, of the rights stated in the preceding paragraph'.

11.14 It is embodied, indeed embedded, in the laws of many states[1] and is recognised in art 6(1) of the European Convention of Human Rights, domesticated by the Human Rights Act 1998 with effect from 2 October 2000.

1   *Transocean Marine Paint Association v EC Commission* 17/74 [1974] 2 CMLR 459 at 477. See also 'Judicial safeguards in Administrative Proceedings' N P Verlag Passim (1989) Austrian

Human Rights Institute. Schwarze *European Administrative Law* (1992) Sweet & Maxwell (cf Canada: Canadian Bill of Rights 1960 (s 2(c)). Canadian Charter of Rights and Freedoms 1982, s 7 (enacted as part of the Constitution Act 1982 by the Canada Act 1982. USA Constitution of the United States: 4th and 15th Amendments (due process)).

Co-extensive operation with the rules against bias

11.15 Normally, if one rule of natural justice applies, both do. They are associated in art 6(1) of the European Convention of Human Rights.

11.16 However, in certain circumstances there may be a right to an unbiased tribunal but no right to a hearing.[1] In *McInnes v Onslow Fane*,[2] it was held that the British Board of Boxing Control, a non-statutory body without whose licence it is in practice impossible to be a recognised boxing promoter, trainer or manager, must deal with applications for licences honestly and without bias or caprice, but with no obligation to disclose information held against the applicant or to give him any hearing. Indeed, it is easier to envisage justice being done by an impartial tribunal without any hearing, than after a hearing by a biased tribunal. Megarry J's view, however, that an absence of bias sufficed when grant of some benefit only was at stake may have been obsolete when he expressed it and is certainly so now (see below **11.19**). By contrast, inspectors investigating the affairs of a company are required to be fair, but may be biased.[3] because the relevant legislation envisaged that they may be both 'prosecutor' and judge. This is an instance of a rule of natural justice yielding to necessity: see **12.120** below.

[1] *R v Aston University Senate, ex p Roffey* [1969] 2 QB 538 per Donaldson J at p 552; *Hounslow London Borough Council v Twickenham Garden Developments* [1971] Ch 233, per Megarry J at 259; *Leary v National Union of Vehicle Builders* [1971] Ch 34 per Megarry J. 52.
[2] [1978] 1 WLR 1520.
[3] *R v Secretary of State for Trade, ex p Perestrello* [1981] QB 19.

DEVELOPMENT OF THE AUDI ALTERAM PARTEM RULE[1]
[1] Wade, Chapter 14.

The early case law

11.17 The story of natural justice is one of ebb and flow *'Whether it can be traced to Magna Carta itself is debatable, but the principle certainly finds expression in statutes from the 14th century'*.[1] The enthusiasm with which the courts have adopted and applied the principles has varied historically at different periods of time. The early case law can be divided broadly into three categories:

(1) *Proceedings before justices*
     One line of cases in which the rule was rigorously applied concerned summary proceedings before justices. The service of a summons upon a party was made a condition of the validity of such proceedings. Justices of the Peace were also in the seventeenth and eighteenth centuries the

principal administrative authorities. According to Wade[2] they were 'so habituated to formal hearings that they do not seem to have offended in this respect', which may be a partial, if sanguine explanation.

(2) *Deprivation of office*

A second line of cases concerned the deprivation of offices and other dignities. Two famous early cases were *Bagg's Case*[3] (disenfranchisement of Chief Burgess of Plymouth for unbecoming conduct), and *Bentley's Case*[4] (removal of academic degrees of Dr Bentley from the University of Cambridge). It became established that removal from office had to be preceded by notice and hearing if the office was a freehold or was to be forfeited only for cause, but not if there was a discretionary power to remove the office holder at pleasure. The principle extended even to dismissal of schoolmasters and parish clerks.

(3) *Ecclesiastical affairs*

A third line of cases concerned the regulation of ecclesiastical affairs. A leading case was *Capel v Child*[5] in which a bishop was empowered by statute to order a vicar to appoint a curate (to be paid by the vicar) when satisfied, either from his own knowledge or by affidavit, that the vicar had neglected his duties. The bishop was held to be under an absolute duty to give a vicar notice and opportunity to be heard before making the order.

[1] Oxford Public Law: 2nd edn, Chapter 15 paragraph 15.01.
[2] 7th edn (1994) Ch 15.
[3] (1615) 11 Co Rep 93b. On historical development: Craig *Administrative Law* (5th edn, 2003) Sweet & Maxwell, Ch 13, pp 407–408.
[4] *R v University of Cambridge* (1723) 1 Stra 557.
[5] (1832) 2 Cr & J 558.

The Victorian era

11.18 These pre-Victorian decisions confirmed that the courts would apply the principles of natural justice to cases of an administrative character. In the nineteenth century it was established further that the *audi alteram partem* rule governed the conduct of arbitrators, professional bodies and voluntary associations in the exercise of their disciplinary functions and like cases. In the case of societies and clubs, it was held to be an implied term of each member's contract of membership that he could not be expelled without a fair hearing, and the tendency was for the courts to treat a rule expressly purporting to exclude natural justice as void. Many of the great cases of natural justice were decided in this, the so-called golden age of the English common law. They were unfortunately forgotten in the next half-century: and only rediscovered by the House of Lords in *Ridge v Baldwin*.[1] Were it not for the wealth of contemporary jurisprudence, resort could still be had to the classic jurisprudence of this time for basic principle, if not for detailed elaboration.

[1] [1964] AC 40.

Growth of interventionist government

11.19 With the extension of the franchise and the decline of the doctrine of *laissez-faire* in the latter half of the nineteenth century, came a vast increase in the regulatory functions of public authorities, especially in the fields of housing and public health, discussed notably by Dicey in *Law and Public Opinion in Victorian England*[1] and by Maitland in *The Constitutional History of England*.[2] The courts applied the same standards as had been applied to these authorities' administrative predecessors, the Justices of the Peace. Where a statute authorising interference with property rights was silent on the question of notice and hearing, the court invoked 'the justice of the common law' to supply 'the omission of the legislature': *Cooper v Wandsworth BC*.[3] In that case a local board of works demolished a house built without first giving notice, although in conformity with express statutory procedures. The court held that the action constituted an unlawful act and was a trespass. Willes J said:[4]

> 'I apprehend that a Tribunal which is by law invested with the power to affect the property of our Her Majesty's subjects is bound to give such subject an opportunity of being heard before it proceeds: and that the rule is of universal application, and founded on the plainest principles of justice'.

The breach of natural justice rendered the subsequent conduct illegal.

[1] MacMillan (8th edn, 1915).
[2] CUP (1919).
[3] (1863) 14CB NS 180, Byles J at 194.
[4] (1863) 14CB NS 180 at 190.

The courts' reaction to regulatory functions

11.20 The judges recognised that the government departments which made institutional decisions could not be expected to follow the procedures of courts of justice; but they nevertheless superimposed upon their statutory responsibility the duty to act judicially, in certain situations, in the manner prescribed by the rules of natural justice. In *Board of Education v Rice*,[1] a decision on the appellate functions of a government department (ie the Board of Education), Lord Loreburn said:

> 'Comparatively recent statutes have extended, if they have not originated, the practice imposing upon departments of offices of state the duty of deciding or determining questions of various kinds. In the present instance, as in many others, what comes for determination is a matter to be settled by discretion, involving no law. It will, I suppose, usually be of an administrative kind; but sometimes it will involve matter of law as well as matter of fact, or even depend upon matters of law alone. In such cases the Board of Education will have to ascertain the law and also ascertain the facts. I need not add that in doing either they must act in good faith and listen fairly to both sides, for that is a duty lying upon everyone who decides anything. But I do not think that they are bound to treat such a question as though it were a trial. They have no power to administer an oath, and need not examine witnesses. They can obtain information in any way they think best, always giving a fair opportunity to those who are parties in the controversy for correcting or contradicting anything prejudicial to their view'.[2]

This case (not itself concerned with procedure) expressed the amplitude of the principle but also the limitations upon it. Principle and pragmatism came into crescent conflict.

¹ [1911] AC 179.
² At p 182.

11.21 As the role of central government expanded, so developed the statutory procedures of inquiry whereby the government department was to hear objections to some scheme. How far were the principles of natural justice to be grafted onto the inquiry procedure? The courts' response was that they should be, but only to a limited extent. In the case of *Local Government Board v Arlidge*,¹ it was held that a government department determining a housing appeal against a closing order, was not obliged to divulge one of its inspector's reports to the appellant, even though the report might well have contained relevant statements prejudicial to his case which he might have wished to controvert. The report was to be treated like any other internal government departmental document. Viscount Haldane commented that the Board's functions were akin to those of a government department and where Parliament entrusts it with official duties:

'Parliament must be taken, in the absence of any declaration to the contrary, to have intended it to follow the procedure which is its own, and is necessary if it is to be capable of doing its work efficiently'.²

¹ [1915] AC 120.
² [1915] AC 120 at 132.

11.22 In the same year Dicey expressed his optimism that:

'In some form or other the English Courts will always find the means for correcting the injustice, if demonstrated by any exercise by a Government department of judicial or quasi-judicial authority'.¹

This optimism was misplaced, and his omission of any reference to the exercise of *administrative* authority ominous.

¹ LQR (1915) p 151.

11.23 The decision in the *Arlidge* case marked the beginning of partial retreat by the English courts which was not reversed until the 1960s and, in particular, until the seminal decision of the House of Lords in *Ridge v Baldwin*.¹ (Even then it required administrative reforms following the report of the Franks Committee in 1957² to reverse the particular decision in *Arlidge* concerning the disclosure of the inspector's report.) Lord Hewart CJ could speak and write in 1929 of *The New Despotism*,³ but the courts tended, like Achilles, to sulk in their tents rather than combat any perceived erosion of individual liberties.

¹ [1964] AC 40.
² Cmnd 218.
³ Ernest Benn Ltd.

11.24 Another line of cases in the housing field dealt with the question of how far a government department could retain its normal administrative freedom while at the same time performing its quasi-judicial function of deciding a contested issue. The problem arose because the Minister had to decide whether to approve a scheme proposed by a local authority to which objections had been made, in circumstances where the department and the local authority would have been in close communication over the development of the scheme.

'The solution devised by the courts was that the minister's freedom was unfettered up to the point where the scheme is published and objection is lodged. From that point onwards there was an issue, a lis, between the local authority and the objectors, and the minister is no longer free to deal with one party without due consideration of the other'.[1]

Once the Minister's quasi-judicial duty began. Once it had begun, both the inspector holding the inquiry and the Minister considering whether to confirm the order were held to be performing quasi-judicial functions and required to observe the principles of natural justice, in the light of which the statutory procedure was interpreted.

[1] See, particularly, *Marriott v Minister of Health* (1935) 105 LJKB 125, 52 TLR 63; *Fredman v Minister of Health* (1935) 154 LT 240, and *William Denby & Sons Ltd v Minister of Health* [1936] 1 KB 337 for an example of a complaint which failed because it related to a period before the *lis* began.

11.25 In the Court of Appeal's decision on the Jarrow clearance order, *Errington v Minister of Health*,[1] a public inquiry had been held but after receiving the inspector's report, the Ministry sought to persuade the Jarrow Corporation to accept a less expensive scheme. An official of the Ministry and the inspector who had held the inquiry visited Jarrow and conferred with the Corporation on the site, after which it submitted further material to the Ministry. The Minister confirmed the order, but the objectors successfully impugned it, on the ground that these dealings between the Corporation and the Ministry after the public inquiry had been closed were a breach of natural justice in that the Minister had failed to be even-handed between the authority and the objectors.

'In accordance with the doctrine of the "lis", however, complainants uniformly failed where they took exception only to events which had happened *before* their objections were lodged and the lis arose. The court refused to set aside orders on the ground that the ministry advised the local authority before they published their proposals,[2] or because the ministry encouraged them to suppose that their order would be likely to be confirmed.[3] Nor did natural justice require that the minister should disclose documents or advice available in his department before issue was joined, and on which his decision was based'.[4]

[1] [1935] 1 KB 249.
[2] *Frost v Minister of Health* [1935] 1 KB 286.
[3] *Offer v Minister of Health* [1936] 1 KB 40, CA.
[4] Wade, p 485; *Miller v Minister of* Health [1946] KB 626; *Price v Minister of Health* [1947] 1 All ER 47; *Summers v Minister of Health* [1947] 1 All ER 184; *B Johnson & Co (Builders) Ltd v Minister of Health* [1947] 2 All ER 395. The judgment of Lord Greene MR was described by Lord Diplock as 'neglected, but luminous' in *Bushell v Environment Secretary* [1981] AC 75 ('Bushell'): see note 3, **11.27** below.

11.26 The word 'lis' refers to an issue which has crystallised and is to be decided in favour of one party or another. A defect of the 'lis' concept was that it could operate only in a triangular situation, where the minister was regarded as a kind of judge between some other public authority, the proposer of the scheme and the objector, but not where the minister was himself the originator of the scheme (as was sometimes the case). In the Kingston bypass case, *Re Trunk Roads Act 1936*,[1] at a public inquiry about a compulsory purchase order a ministry official read a statement of the proposals and produced documents and plans; but he called no witnesses, and engaged in no debate with the objectors. The court declined nevertheless to intervene.

[1] [1939] 2 KB 515.

11.27 The decision of the House of Lords in the *Stevenage New Town* case[1] implied not merely that natural justice had no part to play in a case where the minister was himself the originating authority: but that a minister confirming a scheme after an inquiry had no legal duty other than to follow the procedure prescribed by the Act and genuinely to consider objections in good faith. It was so interpreted by Denning J in *Freedom Under the Law*:[2]

> 'so long as the statutory procedure is complied with and the Minister genuinely considers the matter, the courts will not interfere'.

It was reasoned that the minister's function being 'purely administrative' was in no way quasi-judicial, and accordingly did not attract the rules of natural justice at all. Even in the interventionist 1980s Lord Diplock could still refer in the context of inquiries to the 'essentially administrative nature of the Minister's functions attracting only a constitutional duty to perform it honestly and fairly'.[3]

[1] *Franklin v Minister of Town and Country Planning* [1948] AC 87. See 1948 MLR 314, 1950 MLR 111.
[2] Stevens 'The Hamlyn Lectures' (1947) 1st Series.
[3] *Bushell v Environment Secretary* [1981] AC 75 at 95 and 102.

The primrose path of deviation

11.28 The retreat from natural justice was the result of various interrelated factors, some of which were expressly referred to by Lord Reid in *Ridge v Baldwin*.[1]

[1] [1964] AC 40.

11.29 First, in the First (and then the Second) World War, when enormous powers over persons and property were vested in the government, the courts showed a reluctance to scrutinise the exercise of essential powers in such a way as to make it more difficult for the government to govern in a situation of national emergency; unfortunately these cases were not for many years treated by the courts as exceptional — as they manifestly should have been.

11.30 Second, wide policy discretions were vested in a minister responsible to Parliament. This was thought to dictate not only the exclusion from judicial review of the merits of a particular decision on which the minister was answerable to the legislature, but also abstinence from setting minimum procedural standards to be observed in the course of reaching or executing such decisions.

11.31 Third, there was an implicit assumption that the attitude of the court in relation to administrative process should be one of rigorous self-restraint on grounds that such process was unfamiliar terrain.

11.32 Fourth, the characterisation of the Secretary of State's functions as executive and non-judicial was understood to exclude any implied obligation on his part to act in accordance with natural justice despite the impact of his decisions on individual rights. The reason for adopting the term 'quasi-judicial' had been to identify powers which, although administrative, would attract the doctrine of natural justice. But it had the reverse effect. As Wade pointed out:

> 'the judges seemed to forget that . . . it was essentially to administrative acts that the epithets judicial and "quasi-judicial" had been applied in order to impute the legal standard of fair procedure on judicial and administrative conduct alike'.[1]

Moreover, as Lord Reid observed in *Ridge v Baldwin*, they had been unduly influenced by a dictum of Atkin LJ in *R v Electricity Comrs, ex p London Electricity Joint Committee Co (1920) Ltd*[2] where he said that the prerogative writs applied to a body which had the duty to act judicially. As Lord Reid commented, this was misconstrued and treated by the courts as if there had to be some super added duty to act judicially before natural justice would apply.[3]

[1] See, generally, Wade, 'Quasi-Judicial and its Background' (1949).
[2] CLJ 216. [1924] 1 KB 171, 205.
[3] [1964] AC 40 at 72–75.

11.33 Fifth, in cases where the basic audi alteram partem principle was embodied in statutory form, this was thought to make unnecessary in the administrative area the nineteenth century approach of implying supportive principles.

11.34 Sixth, the courts may have shrunk — at any rate in the immediate aftermath of the Second World War — from appearing to be in active collision with the old Labour Government of the day.

The era of abdication

11.35 Judicial self-denial between 1935 and 1947 led to the failure of challenges alleging breach of natural justice by ministers confirming compulsory purchase orders and clearance orders. Where the ministers both initiated the proposal and confirmed the order, the courts showed an even stronger disinclination to review the discharge of statutory duties in terms of judicial standards (eg as in the *Franklin* case referred to at **11.27** above). Even where there was a 'triangular' situation and the courts could identify a 'lis' between the initiating authority and the objectors, the duty to comply with natural justice was held to apply only once proposals were published. These housing and town planning cases achieved so much prominence that older cases establishing a right to notice and hearing, despite the absence of a lis inter partes or express procedural requirement were overlooked. Decisions in the 1940s and 1950s showed a tendency to substitute for the presumption of the audi alteram partem principle, conditioning the exercise of powers in relation to persons and property (most strikingly in *Cooper v Wandsworth Board of Works*[1]), a presumption that if no statutory procedure was prescribed, then no rule of natural justice was to be implied. For example, in *Nakkuda Ali v Jayaratne*,[2] the controller of textiles in Ceylon cancelled a textile dealer's licence in pursuance of power to revoke a licence when he had 'reasonable grounds' of believing its holder to be unfit to continue as a dealer. The Privy Council held (obiter) that the controller, although obliged to act on reasonable grounds, was under no duty to act judicially. He was not determining a question affecting the rights of a subject, he was merely 'taking executive action to withdraw a privilege'. It was said that the power 'stands by itself on the bare words of the regulation'.[3] The contrast with *Cooper* could hardly be more stark. The future Lord Cooke of Thorndon wrote elegiacly of 'the twilight of natural justice'.[4]

[1] (1863) 14 CB NS.
[2] [1951] AC 66, (1950) LQR 422; (1951) LQR 103; Wade (1951) CLJ 71.
[3] See, also, *R v Metropolitan Police Comr, ex p Parker* [1953] 1 WLR 1150, (1953) LQR 203, (1953) MLR 507.
[4] (1954) CLJ 14.

11.36 Professor William Robson in *Justice and Administrative Law* identified 'the decline of judicial control' and detected in:

> 'some judicial utterances a certain lack of self-confidence in the ability of the court to intervene effectively in the administrative process, a readiness on the part of judges to leave public and administration to be regulated by Parliament and public authorities, a fear of intruding on the province of elected authorities or responsible Ministers in questions of policy'.[1]

[1] 1951 Stevens (3rd edn, p 242).

11.37 In the self-consciously named pamphlet 'The Rule of Law' (1955), The Inns of Court Conservative and Unionist Society had to *recommend* that the rules of natural justice should apply to a discretionary decision,[1] it being obviously assumed that such was not the current law.

[1] At p 35.

The Swinging Sixties

11.38 However, in the 1960s, the rule *audi alteram partem* recovered much of its former vitality. Again there was a variety of interwoven factors.

11.39 First, the enactment of the Tribunal and Inquiries Act 1958, in the wake of the publication of the Franks Report (Cmnd 218), made the climate more receptive to judicial activism.

11.40 Second, decisions in other jurisdictions, in the United States of America, but also the Commonwealth countries, Australia, New Zealand, Canada and Ceylon, retained the essence of the principle and refused to follow more restrictive English decisions: the new worlds could be called in to redress the balance of the old.

11.41 Third, in 1963 came the leading modern English case. The House of Lords in *Ridge v Baldwin*[1] held by a majority that a Chief Constable, dismissible only for cause prescribed by statute, was impliedly entitled to prior notice of the charge against him, and a proper opportunity for meeting it before any decision to dismiss was taken. As indicated above. Lord Reid repudiated the notions that the rules of natural justice applied only to the exercise of those functions which were analytically judicial, or that a 'super-added' duty to act judicially had to be visible before an obligation to observe natural justice could arise in the exercise of a statutory function affecting the rights of an individual. He emphasised that the duty to act in conformity with natural justice would prima facie arise wherever there was the exercise of a power to affect a person's rights or interests.[2] *Cooper v Wandsworth* was restored to its pedestal — and C K Allen could aptly describe *Ridge* in *Laws and Orders*[3] as 'The Magna Carta of natural justice'. The impact of the decision has been reviewed from a comparative American perspective by Schwarz in 'Ridge and Baldwin — the Right to be Heard' in *Lions over the Throne: The Judicial Revolution in Administrative Law*.[4]

[1]   [1964] AC 40 (discussed Goodhart [1964] LQR 105, *Bradley* (1964) CLJ 3).
[2]   Lord Reid at 114; see also Lord Hodson at 130.
[3]   Stevens (3rd edn) at p 242.
[4]   New York University Press (1987).

11.42 Thereafter, the rule, *audi alteram partem*, was extended to a wide variety of situations;[1] the distinction between judicial, quasi-judicial and administrative was eroded; less attention was paid to the distinction between a right and a privilege; and in certain circumstances even the grant of benefits was held to be within the ambit of the rule.[2] The rule extended its reach to decisions taken under prerogative powers as well as under statute.[3]

[1]   See discussion in (1980) Sol Jo 434.
[2]   *R v Gaming Board for Great Britain, ex p Benaim and Khaida* [1970] 2 QB 417.
[3]   *Council of Civil Services Unions v Minister for the Civil Service* ('the GCHQ case') [1985] AC 374 (discussed Lee (1985) PL 186–193, esp 190–2 and (1987).

11.43 Further, where the courts were reluctant to commit themselves to the proposition that there was an implied duty to observe the audi alteram partem rule, they insisted on the observance of a more loosely formulated procedural duty not to act 'unfairly'. It follows that Lord Diplock's classic dictum, 'any judicial statements on matters of public law if made before 1950 are likely to be a misleading guide to what the law is today'[1] is apposite in the area of natural justice — at any rate if confined to the first half of the twentieth century.

[1]   *IRC v National Federation of Self-Employed and Small Businesses* [1982] AC 617 at 640A.

Fairness

11.44 Fairness as a development of natural justice first found modern expression in *Re HK*[1] where an immigration officer at Heathrow had refused to admit a boy from Pakistan on the ground that he appeared to be well over the age of 16 — the maximum age for admission as a dependent. Lord Parker LJ held that even if an immigration officer was not acting in a judicial or quasi-judicial capacity, he must nevertheless act fairly.[2] The concept had its roots, however, in *Board of Education v Rice*[3] which is the origin of the statement 'the duty to act fairly . . . lies upon everyone who decides anything', and *Local Government Board v Arlidge:*[4] there the phrase seems to have been used to indicate a duty to act in a way which in some sense fell short of the traditional concept of natural justice.

On the one hand, the concepts appear to be equated, as when natural justice was described as 'fair play in action'.[5] In *O'Reilly v Mackman,*[6] Lord Diplock said:

> '[it] had acted out with its powers [including] . . . failure to observe the rules of natural justice: which means no more than to act fairly towards [the complainant] in carrying out [that body's] decision-making process, and I prefer so to put it'.

---

[1] [1967] 2 QB 617.

[2] See, further, *R v Gaming Board for Great Britain, ex p Benaim and Khaida* [1970] 2 QB 417 at 430; *Re Pergamon Press* [1971] Ch 388 at 399.

[3] [1911] AC 179.

[4] [1915] AC 120, per Viscount Haldane. LC, 133.

[5] *Wiseman v Borneman* [1971] AC 297, 309 per Lord Morris; *Edwards v Society of Graphical and Allied Trades* [1971] Ch 357 per Sachs LJ at 367.

[6] [1983] 2 AC 237 at 275. Other judges have adopted as analogous the transatlantic concept of due process: eg *R v Secretary of State for the Environment, ex p Kirkstall Valley Campaign Ltd* [1996] 3 All ER 304, 324f.

11.45 On the other hand, there are dicta which suggest that natural justice is the standard of procedure appropriate to judicial functions, while fairness is a lesser standard applicable to the performance of non-judicial functions[1] or that there is a continuum from natural justice to fairness, and from judicial to administrative functions.[2] Cases such as *Re HK* cited at **11.44** above and, *ex p Benaim and Khaida* cited at **11.87** below certainly support the proposition that fairness describes a lesser set of procedural requirements than does natural justice. In *AMEC Civil Engineering Ltd v Secretary of State for Transport*[3] it was held that an engineer deciding a dispute or difference between parties had a duty to act independently, honestly and fairly, but that did not encompass the rules of natural justice: he was not subject to the same procedural rules as someone acting judicially. But it is now generally recognised that it is not helpful conceptually to distinguish natural justice and fairness as two distinct concepts applicable to different kinds of functions. The preferred view is that natural justice and fairness are two names for a single doctrine whose content is variable, even if there is still an, albeit declining, preference by some judges to refer to the principles as principles of fairness where they wish to emphasise that the procedures applicable are not those applicable in a court of law.[4]

---

[1] *Pearlberg v Varty* [1972] 1 WLR 534, 547 per Lord Pearson; cf *B Johnson & Co (Builders) Ltd v Minister of Health* [1947] 2 All ER 395, 398–400 per Lord Greene, MR.

[2] *McInnes v Onslow Fane* [1978] 1 WLR 1520 at 1530. (See discussion in 'Fairness in Natural Justice — Distinct Concepts or Mere Semantics?' D Taylor (1977) 3 Monash University Law Review 191, Gravells (1976) MLR 342–347).

[3] TLR 22.3.05.

[4] See Lord Diplock in *Bushell v Environment Secretary* [1981] AC 75 at 95 for an earlier example.

The duty to be fair

11.46 The transformation of the traditional formula — a duty to obey the rules of natural justice — into its modern derivation, a duty to be fair, nonetheless indicates and reflects an alteration in the approach as well as the vocabulary of the courts[1].

[1] See *'Perspectives on Process: Common Law Statutory and Political'*: Craig Public law April 2010 275 at p 280–287.

11.47 First, it enlarges the number of bodies which are amenable to the court's supervisory jurisdiction on procedural grounds. It has enabled courts to exercise some degree of control over procedure in cases where they would not formerly have done so (eg immigration officers, *Re HK*;[1] the Gaming Board in *Benaim v Khaida*;[2] Companies' Act inspectors in *Re Pergamon Press*;[3] and *Maxwell v Department of Trade and Industry*;[4] the Independent Television Commission's allocation of TV franchises, *R v Independent Television Commission, ex p TSW Broadcasting Ltd*).[5] Systems, as well as decisions can be unfair.[6]

[1] [1967] 2 QB 617.
[2] [1970] 2 QB 617.
[3] [1971] Ch 388.
[4] [1974] QB 523.
[5] [1996] EMLR 291, HL.
[6] *R (Refugee Legal Centre) v Secretary of State for Home Department* [2005] 1 WLR 2219 at [6].

11.48 Second, it sets a different, usually lower, standard of procedural propriety for such bodies to attain. It has enabled courts to evade the full implications of Lord Reid's dictum in *Ridge v Baldwin*, namely that anyone having the power to make decisions affecting rights must comply with the requirements of natural justice, by holding that some lesser 'rights' deserve lesser procedural protection than that afforded by the traditional natural justice principles. In short, more breadth, less depth.

11.49 Third, because it is a more flexible concept than natural justice, it permits a review on the basis of a form of procedural fairness which may not be neatly fitted into the conventional mould of the traditional rules, but focuses upon the overall circumstances of the particular case.[1]

[1] For example, issues that fairness requires to be heard separately must be heard and decided separately: *Raja v GMC* [2003] 1 WLR 1052.

11.50 It has always been recognised that the requirements of natural justice vary according to the facts, but cases have traditionally been divided into classes or types according to their features (eg according to the type of function being performed, or the type of interest at stake). Fairness, on the other hand, is seen, on this view, as still more closely dependent on the detailed facts which has generally had the result that the requirement of a hearing has been given a truncated meaning, or has been subordinated to the idea of substantive fairness. For example, in *Machin v Football Association*[1] it was held that while a domestic tribunal must give a 'defendant' an opportunity of knowing the case against him and of dealing with it, and must come to a fair conclusion, it need *not* go further and copy the procedures of criminal courts.

[1]   TLR 21.7.1973.

11.51 Fourth, it breaks the spell cast by the concept of the judicial or quasi-judicial as the sole magnet for the rules of natural justice; 'fairness' can be applied to administrative decisions, the content of that concept reflecting the particular characteristics of the decision. In *R (Wandsworth LBC) v Secretary of State for Transport*[1] Sullivan J applied it to the decision-making process which led to the adoption of policies in part of a White Paper dealing with airports' policy in South East England.

[1]   [2005] EWHC 314 (Admin), TLR 22.2.2005.

11.52 Fifth, the courts now seem to feel free to develop in the name of fairness a new charter of procedural (and to some extent substantive) rights, without being constrained by the classic forms of natural justice, for example, to consider whether the delay in instructing disciplinary proceedings is so extreme as to defeat justice. In *R v Chief Constable of Mersey side Police, ex p Calverley*[1] a disciplinary hearing was held before the Chief Constable of the respondent police authority in relation to five police officers more than three years after the making of the complaints against them. The complaints were found proved against all five police officers, who were dismissed or compelled to resign. The substantive ground of their application for judicial review was breach both of relevant regulations and of the rules of natural justice. May LJ[2] said:

> 'Unnecessary delay . . . does occur [but] should not tempt one to resort to judicial review where no real abuse or breach of natural justice can be shown. That said, I think that abuse can be shown in the instant case'.

[1]   [1986] QB 424.
[2]   [1986] QB 424 at 439.

11.53 This equation of gross delay and unfairness was also recognised in *R v United Kingdom Central Council for Nursing, Midwifery and Health Visiting, ex p Thompson, Machin and Wood*[1] where, however, it was held that an adjournment of disciplinary proceedings for several months after their commencement did not lead to such delay in resuming the hearing as was sufficient to amount to a breach of the principles of natural justice or, indeed, an abuse of process.[2]

[1]   [1991] COD 275.
[2]   See, also, *R v Pharmaceutical Service Committee, ex p Conway* (1970) 114 Sol Jo 935, 1996.

11.54 Three cases may be cited to demonstrate the courts' fertility of approach and willingness to expand the boundaries of fairness. *R v Portsmouth City Council, ex p Gregory and Moss*[1] involved disciplinary proceedings by the council based on allegations of breaches of the National Code of Local Government Conduct. It was there held that justice requires that proceedings do not go on for too long each day. The overwhelming impression, said the court, was that too much emphasis had been placed on speed and too little on fairness, with the result that justice may have suffered. The claimant in *R v Independent Television Commission, ex p TSW Broadcasting Ltd*[2] succeeded in the Court of Appeal only to fail in the House of Lords. Nevertheless, the reasoning in the Court of Appeal contains an important recognition that unfairness could be constituted by the misleading of applicants for TV franchises as to the criteria of application. In *R v Chief Constable of West Midlands Police, ex p Carroll*[3] the court held that it was unfair to refuse to give a disciplinary hearing to a probationary constable whose services had been dispensed with in circumstances where the impression given was that he had been suspected of an offence.[4]

[1] (1990) 89 LGR 478, 1990 2 Admin LR 681.
[2] TLR 7.2.1992. The House of Lords dealt with the case robustly [1996] JR 60; [1996] EMLR 291, HL. See **11.236** and **11.286**.
[3] (1995) 7 Admin LR 45.
[4] Despite this expansion it is necessary to bear in mind that unfairness is not established by mere departure from best practice: *R v Secretary of State for Home Department ex p Doody* [1994] 1 AC 531 at 560 . It has been said in the context of consultation that the true test is whether the process is '*so unfair as to be unlawful*': *Vale of Glamorgan Council v Lord Chancellor and Secretary of State for Justice* [2011] EWHC 1532 (Admin) at [24].

11.55 In *ex p Guinness plc*, which concerned the Take-over Panel, the Court of Appeal imaginatively amalgamated the traditional heads of judicial review into a single test. Lord Donaldson MR, said:[1]

'*The jurisdiction of the court*

The court's jurisdiction and limitations on its exercise are established in *R v Panel on Take-overs and Mergers, ex p Datafin plc* [1987] QB 815. However the present appeal calls for a further review and, in particular, consideration of whether the separate grounds for granting relief: illegality, irrationality, procedural impropriety and, possibly, proportionality, are appropriate in all situations . . . And similar problems arise with procedural impropriety in the narrow sense of failing to follow accepted procedures, given the nature of the panel and of its functions and the lack of any statutory or other guidance as to its procedures which are intended to be of its own devising. Similarly, in the broad sense of breach of the rules of natural justice, what is or is not fair may depend on underlying value judgments by the panel as to the time scale which is appropriate for decision, the consequences of delay and matters of that kind. Approaching the problem on the basis of separate grounds for relief may at once bring several interlocking and mutually inconsistent considerations into play — were the underlying judgments tainted by illegality or irrationality? If not, accepting those judgments, was the action unfair? If the underlying judgments were so tainted, was the action unfair on the basis of judgments which might reasonably have been made? The permutations, if not endless, are considerable and confusing. It may be that the true view is that in the context of a body whose constitution, functions and powers are sui generis, the court should review the panel's acts and omissions more in the round than might otherwise be the case and, whilst basing its decision on familiar concepts, should eschew any formal categorisation. It was Lord Diplock who in *Council of Civil Service Unions v Minister for the Civil Service* [1985] AC 374, formulated the currently accepted categorisations in an attempt to rid the courts of shackles bred of the technicalities surrounding the old prerogative writs. But he added, at p 410, that further development on a case by case basis might add further grounds. In the context of the present appeal he might have considered an innominate ground formed of an amalgam of his own grounds with perhaps added elements, reflecting the unique nature of the panel, its powers and duties and the environment in which it operates, for he would surely have joined in deploring any use of his own categorisation as a fetter on the continuous development of the new "public law court". In relation to such an innominate ground the ultimate question would, as always, be whether something had gone wrong of a nature and degree which required the intervention of the court and, if so, what form that intervention should take'.

Here a generalised and elastic concept of fairness is being used as a basis for judicial review.

[1]   [1990] 1 QB 146 at 159–160.

Scope and application of the principles of natural justice

11.56 The rules of natural justice — or of fairness — are not cut and dried. They vary infinitely[1] — and not merely in their content but in their application. In *Lloyd v McMahon*[2] Lord Bridge said:

'The so-called rules of natural justice are not engraved on tablets of stone. To use the phrase which better expressed the underlying concept, what the requirements of fairness demand when any body, domestic, administrative or judicial, has to make a decision which will affect the rights of individuals depends on the character of the decision-making body, the kind of decision it has to make and the statutory or other framework in which it operates:

This enjoins a triple test.'[3]

[1]   *R v Secretary of State for the Home Department, ex p Santillo* [1981] QB 778 Lord Denning MR at p.795.
[2]   [1987] AC 625 at p.702.
[3]   See also **11.81** below.

11.57 All therefore depends upon the circumstances of the case — such as the nature of the inquiry, the rules under which the Tribunal is acting, the subject matter to be dealt with, and the potential sanction that might be imposed.[1] Lord Mustill, in *R v Secretary of State for the Home Department, ex p Doody*,[2] said that what fairness requires is 'essentially an intuitive judgment', in *R (Roberts) v Parole Board*,[3] Lord Woolf LCJ said:

'Under well-established principles of administrative law the requirement of fairness was not fixed: its content depended on the circumstances and in particular the nature of the decision to be made'.

Since whether those rules apply and the extent of the duty to apply them depend upon the particular type of case concerned, it is often difficult to predict with confidence what fairness will be considered to require in any particular context. However, the courts have on occasions tried to formulate some general guidelines to provide some indication at least of the characteristic features which will assist in determining both what principles should apply and when they will apply.

[1]   *Russell v Duke of Norfolk* [1949] 1 All ER 109 per Tucker LJ at 118. See also *Durayappah v Fernando* [1967] 2 AC 337 at 349 (Lord Upjohn); *Fairmount Investments v Secretary of State for the Environment* [1976] 1 WLR 1255; *R v Secretary of State for the Home Department, ex p Moon* (1995) 8 Admin LR 477; *R v Commission for Racial Equality, ex p Cottrell and Rothon* [1980] 3 All ER 265 per Lord Lane CJ at 271; *Mobil Oil Australia (Pty) Ltd v Federal Comr of Taxation* (1963) 113 CLR 475 at 504; *R v Mental Health Review Tribunal, ex p Gillespie* [1985] 2 Qd R 527.
[2]   [1994] 1 AC 531 at p 560.

11.58 As to the latter, the courts have emphasised that the normal assumption is that the rules will apply:

'The tendency of the courts at present is to apply the rules of natural justice to a very wide range of decision-making processes'.[1]

They have been stated indeed to apply:

'to all powers of decision unless the circumstances suffice to exclude them. These circumstances may be found in the person or body making the decision, the nature of the decision to be made, the gravity of the matter in issue, the terms of any contract or other provision governing the powers to decide and so on'.[2]

1   Jackson, p 101 (see note 1 above).
2   Per Megarry J in *Gaiman v National Association for Mental Health* [1971] Ch 317 at 333. It has long been clear that protection is not limited to those whose legal rights were at stake: see Lord Denning's seminal (dissenting) judgment in *Breen v AEU* [1971] 2 QB 175.

11.59 Where individuals are adversely affected by a decision, the presumption is very strong. It has long been clear that protection is not limited to those whose legal rights[1] were at stake. As Lord Reid noted in *Ridge v Baldwin*, the right to a fair hearing is 'a rule of universal application'[2] in the case of decisions affecting rights.[3] Similarly, the courts tend to require the principles of fairness to be applied before decisions are made which affect an individual's interests or expectations, though the content of the principles will generally be less stringent than when rights strictly so-called are in issue. Accordingly, a duty to act in accordance with natural justice will arise in the exercise of a power to deprive a person of his livelihood or of his legal status where that status is not merely terminable at pleasure;[4] or to deprive a person of liberty[5] or property rights[6] or of another legitimate interest or expectation;[7] or to impose a penalty on him[8] or to damage his reputation.[9] Where the body concerned has procedures derived from, even though not equivalent to, those of a court of law, the presumption in favour of the duty is particularly strong.[10]

1   See Lord Denning MR's seminal dissenting judgment in *Breen v AEU* [1971] 2 QB 175.
2   [1964] AC 100 at 69.
3   Compare again the similar sentiment expressed by Lord Loreburn LC in *Board of Education v Rice* [1911] AC 179 at 182 when he described the duty 'to act in good faith and fairly listen to both sides' as being 'a duty lying upon anyone who decides anything'. See Denny, 'Procedural Fairness in Competitions' (2003) JR 228. Where the rights involved are of fundamental importance, eg the right to life, the court adopts a more to the facts invasive approach: see Fordham: 'What is Anxious Scrutiny?' (1996) JR 81.
4   Eg *R v BBC ex p Lavelle* [1983] 1 WLR 22 (BBC employee); *R v Chief Constable of North Wales Police ex p Evans* [1982] 1 WLR 1155 (police officer); *McLaughlin v Governor of Cayman Islands* [2007] UKPC 50 (salary arrears payable in case of unlawful dismissal from office).
5   Eg *R v Secretary of State for Home Department* [1994] 1 AC 531 (access to parole).
6   Eg *Cooper v Wandsworth Board of Works* (1863) 14 CB.
7   *Breen v AEU* [1971] 2 QB 175 per Lord Denning MR at p 190.
8   *O'Reilly v Mackman* [1982] 2 AC 237 at 276B–C.
9   *R v Norfolk CC Social Services Dept: ex p M* [1998] QB 619 (entry on child abuse register).
10   On natural justice in administrative tribunals, see Ganz *Administrative Procedures* (1974) Sweet & Maxwell, pp 32–35.

11.60 By contrast the conferment of a wide discretionary power exercisable in the public interest may be indicative of, if not the absence of an obligation so to act, at least a variation in the manner of its exercise.[1] In a Canadian context a Board of Education resolved *in camera* to reorganise three schools because of declining enrolments and confirmed the decision at a public meeting without notice to the public: it was held that it was doubtful whether the principles of procedural fairness applied to an elected public body such as the Board, which, in good faith and within the jurisdiction assigned to it by legislation, resolved to reallocate the student body within its school district.[2] Where the SFO intended to give copies of documents it had seized to other government departments discharging functions on behalf of the Crown, it should normally give notice to the owners of those documents in time for them to make representations, but the court recognised that in some sensitive cases it might not be appropriate do so: *R (Kent Pharmaceuticals Ltd) v Director of SFO*.[3] A presumption that natural justice must be observed will, however, arise more readily where there is an express duty to decide only after conducting a hearing or inquiry,[4] or where the decision is one entailing the determination of disputed questions of law and fact.

1   *Gaiman v National Association for Mental Health* [1971] Ch 317 (expulsion of scientologists from company limited by guarantee). There is no obligation to receive representations on foreign policy issues by persons affected by them *R(Quark Fishing Limited) v FCO* [2002] Civ 1409 at (57).
2   *Vanderkloet v Leeds and Grenville County Board of Education* (1985) 51 OR (2d) 577 (CA).
3   [2005] 1 WLR 1302, [2005] 1 All ER 449.
4   *General Medical Council v Spackman* [1943] AC 627, 'due inquiry'.

11.61 It is not necessary to identify fault to establish unfairness. It is sufficient that objectively there was unfairness.[1]

1   *R v CICB ex p A* [1999] 2 AC 330 per Lord Slynn at 345C–D. See eg *R(Ford) v Leashold Valuation Tribunal* [2005] EWHC 503 at 45–46.

Implication into statute

11.62 *Cooper's* case does not provide *carte blanche* for implying the *audi alteram partem* rule into any statutory context. Lord Reid, in his statement of the principle in *Wiseman v Borneman*,[1] noted that there were two preconditions:

> 'For a long time the courts have, without objection from Parliament, supplemented procedure laid down in legislation where they have found that to be necessary for this purpose. But before this unusual kind of power is exercised it must be clear that the statutory procedure is insufficient to achieve justice and that to require additional steps would not frustrate the apparent purpose of the legislation'.[2]

1   [1971] AC 297 at 308. See also *Lloyds v McMahon* [1987] AC 625 per Lord Bridge at pp 702–703. *R v Secretary of State for the Environment, ex p Hammersmith and Fulham London Borough Council* [1991] AC 521 at 598, D–G implication of fairness into statutory powers. *R (Lumba) Secretary of State for the Home Department* [2011] UKSC 12, [2012] 1 AC 245. The constitutionally debatable view is that the process of supplementing statutory procedures is one not of implication of the legislative intent but of judicial imposition of fair process eg *R (Khatum) v London Borough of Newham* [2004] EWCA Civ 55, [2005] QB 37 at (30) per Laws LJ.

11.63 The modern statement of overarching principle is contained in the speech of Lord Browne-Wilkinson in *Pierson v Secretary of State for the Home Department*:[1]

> 'I consider first whether there is any principle of construction which requires the court, in certain cases, to construe general words contained in the statute as being impliedly limited. In my judgment there is such a principle. It is well established that Parliament does not legislate in a vacuum: statutes are drafted on the basis that the ordinary rules and principles of the common law will apply to the express statutory provisions: see Cross on Statutory Interpretation (3rd Edn, 1995) pp 165–166, Bennion on Statutory Interpretation (2nd Edn, 1992), p 727 and Maxwell on Interpretation of Statutes (12th edn, 1969) p 116. As a result, Parliament is presumed not to have intended to change the common law unless it has clearly indicated such intention either expressly or by necessary implication: Cross p 166, Bennion p 718 and Maxwell p 116. This presumption has been applied in many different fields including the construction of statutory provisions conferring wide powers on the executive. Where wide powers of decision-making are conferred by statute, it is presumed that Parliament implicitly requires the decision to be made in accordance with the rules of natural justice: Bennion p 737. However widely the power is expressed in the statute, it does not authorise that power to be exercised otherwise than in accordance with fair procedures'.[2]

¹ [1998] AC 539 at p 573–574.
² Cited in the judgment of Dyson LJ in *M v Secretary of State for Education* [2001] EWCA Civ 332 at 38, [2001] 2 FCR 11 at 38. *Belfast City CC v Misbehaving Ltd* [2007] UKHL 19, [2007] L WLR 1420 at (8) (discretion to consider late objections added to statutory scheme).

11.64 This principle had earlier been applied in *R v Birmingham City Council, ex p Ferrero Ltd*.[1] The applicant's assertion that it should have been heard before a suspension order on safety grounds was made against its products (chocolate eggs containing plastic animals) under the Consumer Protection Act 1987 was tested against both *Wiseman* conditions, and found wanting. The Act gave a right of appeal: and delay would militate against the utility of such orders. *ex p Ferrero* is also authority for the important proposition that if the *audi alteram partem* rule is to be implied, the implication must be for all cases or for none. Taylor LJ said:

> 'If the supposed duty to consult were to depend upon the facts and urgency of each case, enforcement authorities would be faced with a serious dilemma. What amounts to urgency is incapable of precise definition, and would be open in many cases to honest and reasonable differences of opinion. There would be a danger that although the authority reasonably suspected goods were dangerous, they would feel bound to delay serving a notice until they consulted the trader, whereas, without a duty to consult, they would have served forthwith. Valuable time would be lost and danger could result'.[2]

¹ [1993] 1 All ER 530, CA.
² At p 542. See now *Swiss Security Bank Trust Ltd v Francis* [2006] UKPC 11.

11.65 The result was that even if in the particular case, the court acknowledged that the local authority could properly have heard the applicants before making the order, it was under no duty to do so when in other cases which might arise and engaged safety considerations, the need for urgency would be paramount.

11.66 Another example of the courts' refusal to supplement a statutory procedure is provided by the charge-capping cases. There the analysis was that the statutory procedure was fair and, therefore, exhaustive.[1] Section 100(4) of the Local Government Finance Act 1988 empowered the Secretary of State for the Environment to set a limit to the level at which individual councils could set the charge for their respective areas. A challenge was made, inter alia, on the ground of 'procedural impropriety'. Lord Bridge said[2] he did not think it possible:

> 'to imply terms in the statute derived from the doctrine of audi alteram partem. But it is unnecessary to consider this point further because, at the only point in the process leading to "capping" at which it might be appropriate to insist that, as a matter of fair procedure, authorities should have the opportunity to be heard in opposition to the Secretary of State's proposed "cap" and to make a reasoned case in support of an alternative and less restrictive maximum for their budget, the Act itself by ss 102(5)(a) and 104 expressly prescribes a procedure precisely to this effect. This procedure was duly followed, and in addition all the authorities [concerned] . . . were given the opportunity to make representations orally . . . [to two junior ministers]'.

[1] *R v Secretary of State for the Environment, ex p Hammersmith and Fulham London Borough Council* [1991] 1 AC 521.
[2] [1991] 1 AC 521 at 599. In *R (Forest Heath District Council) v Electoral Commission, Boundary Committee for England* [2009] EWCA Civ 1296 when the statute provided expressly for consultation on draft proposals for boundary changes the Court of Appeal refused to graft an obligation [to consult] on an obligation to consult with local authorities at an earlier stage.

11.67 A yet further illustration of such refusal came in a case concerned with morals, not money. In *R (X) v Chief Constable of the West Midlands*,[1] there was a decision by the police, in exercising statutory powers, to disclose to a prospective employer details of discontinued criminal charges brought against a prospective employee. It was held that the prospective employee need not have been given an opportunity to comment.

[1] [2005] 1 WLR 65, [2005] 1 All ER 611.

11.68 In *R (WB and KA) v Leeds School Organisation Committee*[1] the Divisional Court ruled that a School Organisation Committee, when considering closure of a school, does not have to grant a hearing to objectors as the time for making objections comes earlier in the statutory consultation process. It is therefore up to the School Organisation Committee to consider whether to do it by reference to the position in each case. This again shows that a statutory procedure already informed by a right to be heard does not require, although it may permit, supplementation.

[1] [2002] EWHC 1927, [2003] ELR 67.

11.69 By contrast, a striking example of the courts' grafting of fair procedures into an unparticularised statutory scheme is *R v Secretary of State for the Home Department, ex p Fayed*[1] where the Secretary of State was held to have acted unfairly in declining to ventilate his concerns about the applicants before refusing their application for naturalisation. In the face of an express statutory exclusion, the Court of Appeal declined to order the Secretary of State to supply reasons for his decision after the event, thus establishing that the right to a fair hearing and the right to reasons are not umbilically linked; and that the absence of the latter is no basis for the absence of the former.[2] Lord Woolf MR nonetheless said:

> 'English law has long attached the greatest importance to the need for fairness to be observed prior to the exercise of a statutory discretion. However, English law, at least until recently, has not been so sensitive to the need for reasons to be given for a decision after it has been reached. So to exclude the need for fairness before a decision is reached because it might give an indication of what the reasons for the decision could be is to reverse the actual position. It involves frustrating the achievement of the more important objective of fairness in reaching a decision in an attempt to protect a lesser objective of possibly disclosing what will be the reasons for the decision'.[3]

[1] [1997] 1 All ER 228, [1998] 1 WLR 763.
[2] See, further, *A-G v Ryan* [1980] AC 718; *R v Gaming Board, ex p Benaim and Khaida* [1970] 2 QB 417.
[3] [1997] All ER 228 at 238.

The reach of the principles

11.70 However, subject to the provisos mentioned in **11.80** and **11.144** below, the tendency to apply the rules to all decision-making functions means that there are now virtually no areas where individuals are affected where the courts have held that it is inappropriate to apply any procedural safeguards at all. The fact that decisions are administrative or disciplinary is no longer a justification for excluding the rules, as the courts have recognised in *Ridge v Baldwin*,[1] in *Buckoke v Greater London Council*[2] and in *R v Board of Visitors of Hull Prison, ex p St Germain*.[3] Indeed the fact that someone is subjected to a detriment by an adjudicatory body is a ground for engaging rather than disengaging the rule.[4]

[1] [1964] AC 40.
[2] [1971] 1 Ch 655.
[3] [1978] QB 678. *R (on the Application of Ali) v Director of High Security Prisons*: 2009 EWHC 1732 (Admin). The duty applied to an escape risk classification decision.
[4] *O'Reilly v Mackman* [1983] 2 AC 237 at 276B–C.

11.71 Only rare traces of the old view distinguishing between rights and interests, quasi-judicial and administrative acts persist. For example, in *R v Tower Hamlets London Borough Council, ex p Thrasyvalou*.[1] Kennedy J held that there was no entitlement to be heard for applicant hoteliers where a local authority took decisions to their commercial detriment to withdraw all homeless families from hotels graded below a certain level. The authority was not carrying out any judicial or quasi-judicial act. The applicants were not office holders who were being deprived of office. The proposed resolution was not directed against them; it was based upon information which was apparently reliable, and it was intended to improve the lot of the homeless. There was no other special circumstance giving rise to a right to be heard.

[1]   [1991] COD 123, [1991] 23 HLR 38.

11.72 But the courts no longer accept, as they once did, that certain groups should not because of their status enjoy the protection afforded by natural justice. In *Leech v Parkhurst Prison Deputy Governor*,[1] the House of Lords finally overruled earlier authorities to the effect that a prison governor (as opposed to a board of prison visitors) was not subject to judicial review in exercising his disciplinary functions over prisoners — a stance which had effectively relieved the governor from any duty to comply with natural justice.

[1]   [1988] AC 533.

11.73 While the principles still do not apply to the exercise by public bodies of their contractual right to terminate the contracts of employment of their staff (in the absence of any express or implied terms), the position may be different if there is some office or status over and above the mere status of employee). Moreover, statute has now intervened, in the form of protection from unfair dismissal, and will often require similar or more precise procedural safeguards to those afforded by natural justice itself. (See further as to discipline and employment at **11.77** and **11.79** et seq below.)

11.74 The principles do not merely apply where individuals or other private bodies are affected. The principles may equally operate in favour of public authorities where they are adversely affected by the powers of central government. Thus a municipal council in Ceylon dissolved by the minister under his default powers was entitled to a fair hearing before the minister could legally make the order.[1] In *R v Secretary of State for the Environment, ex p Brent LBC*[2] it was held that before reducing a local authority's rate support grant the Secretary of State ought to have been willing to receive last-minute representations. Where a mental health review tribunal discharged a patient without notifying the Secretary of State, so that the Minister had no opportunity to be heard, the tribunal's order was set aside in 'a classic case of a failure of natural justice'.[3]

[1]   *Durayappah v Fernando* [1967] 2 AC 337.
[2]   [1982] QB 593.
[3]   *R v Oxford Regional Mental Health Review Tribunal, ex p Home Secretary* [1986] 1 WLR 1180; affd sub nom *Campbell v Secretary of State for the Home Department* [1988] AC 120.

11.75 The examples of the application of the rule in the modern context are legion and are scattered throughout this chapter. They include the finding of a Royal Commission (at the suit of the object of the damaging findings);[1] the finding of a Commission of Inquiry into Health Department;[2] an Exclusion Order from property usually open to the public;[3] the Secretary of State's refusal to issue a passport;[4] the disqualification of company director under Companies Act 1985, s 300;[5] the making of an interim care order in respect of a child (at suit of parents);[6] the transfer of application for revocation of maintenance ordered by one bench to another bench (at suit of the recipient of the maintenance);[7] the removal from Council's list of foster parents;[8] the refusal of political asylum;[9] the removal of contractor by local authority from list of approved contractors;[10] the placement on a register of child abusers;[11] mandatory destruction of a dog;[12] the exclusion from a private school;[13] and an embargo on legal aid[14] complementing the legal aid regulations which specifically provide the assisted person with the opportunity to make representations with respect to a discharge. Fairness requires that mandatory life sentence prisoners[15] and discretionary life sentence prisoners[16] have the right to make representations before the tariff period is fixed.[17] Similarly, high security 'Category A' prisoners may make representations before any review of security classifications.[18] A prisoner has a right to procedural fairness before a decision is taken by the parole board not to recommend his release or transfer to open conditions.[19] However, decisions involving resource allocation, delegated legislation or its equivalent, engage lesser, if any, obligations of fairness.[20]

[1] *Mahon v Air New Zealand Ltd* [1984] AC 808. For Tribunals of Enquiry, see Royal Commission on Tribunals of Enquiry 1966 (Cmnd 312); Reports of Crown Agents Tribunal (1982) HC 364, pp 3–7, 569–575. The Rt Hon The Lord Howe of Aberavon CH, QC at [1996] PL, pp 445–460; L Blom-Cooper QC, 'Procedure at Scott Inquiry: Witnesses before Public Inquiries: An Example of Unfairness?' [1966] PL pp 11 and 12; Scott VC (1995) LQR Vol 111, pp 596–616, 'Procedures at Inquiries — The Duty to be Fair'.

[2] *Vermaulen v A-G Western Samoa* SC, 2 May 1985 (1986 CLB 46).

[3] *R v London Borough of Brent, ex p Assegai* [1987] COD 291, (1987) Times, 18 June.

[4] *R v Secretary of State for Foreign and Commonwealth Affairs, ex p Everett* [1989] QB per O'Connor LJ at 818: 'It seems to me that the Secretary of State in the fair exercise of his discretion, was entitled to refuse the passport but obliged to give his reason for so doing . . . .'.

[5] *Re Lo-Line Electric Motors Ltd* [1988] 2 All ER 692.

[6] *R v Birmingham City Juvenile Court, ex p Birmingham County Council* [1988] 1 All ER 683, [1988] 1 WLR 337, CA. Note though that judicial review procedures do not apply to sports bodies even if judicial review principles do.

[7] *R v Wareham Magistrates' Court, ex p Seldon* [1988] 1 All ER 746, DC.

[8] *R v London Borough of Wandsworth, ex p P* [1989] 1 FLR 387 per Ewbank J: 'If a foster parent is removed from the approved list for specific misbehaviour or for suspicion of serious abuse of the child or a criminal act towards the child, the foster parent is entitled to know what grounds are alleged, in sufficient detail for her to meet them and to be heard in reply. There may be some cases where the bare allegations will be sufficient, but in a case of sexual abuse of a child, where material mostly comes from the child, it must be rare indeed that the bare allegations will be sufficient for a foster mother to meet the case'.

[9] *Gaima v Secretary of State for Home Department* [1989] Imm AR 205, CA.

[10] *R v Enfield London Borough Council, ex p TF Unwin (Roydon) Ltd* (1989) 46 BLR 1, DC.

[11] *R v Hampshire County Council, ex p K* [1990] 2 QB 71, [1990] 2 All ER 129.

[12] *R v Ealing Magistrates' Court, ex p Fanneran* (1995) 160 JP 409.

[13] *R v Campbell Manor School, ex p Brown* (1993) 5 Admin LR 159.

[14] *Brenda Oakes v Legal Services Commission* [2003] EWHR 1948 (Admin).

[15] *R v Secretary of State for the Home Department, ex p Doody* [1994] 1 AC 531.

[16] *R v Secretary of State for the Home Department, ex p McCartney* (1994) 6 Admin LR 629; *R v Secretary of State for the Home Department, ex p Chapman* (1994) 138 Sol Jo LB 216.

[17] For an important case in the context of tariffs, see *R v Secretary of State for the Home Department, ex p Venables* [1997] 3 WLR 23.

[18] *R v Secretary of State for the Home Department, ex p Duggan* [1994] 3 All ER 277. In *R v Secretary of State for the Home Department, ex p McAvoy* [1998] 1 WLR 790 it was held that in deciding whether the procedure adopted on a review of a prisoner's security categorisation was fair, consideration was to be given not only to the position of the prisoner but to the proper running of a prison. It was sufficient to supply the prison with the gist of reports about him; full reports were not required. However, a prison Governor is not obliged to hear representations from a prisoner, who was not a life sentence prisoner, before changing his prison categorisation. All that fairness required was that he had an opportunity to appeal under a prison service order: *R (Palmer) v Secretary of State for the Home Department* TLR 13.9.04; *R v Secretary of State for the Home Department, ex p Allen* TLR 21.3.04.

[19] See *R (Osborn) v Parole Board* [2013] UKSC 61, [2013] 3 WLR 1020, for a useful summary of the requirements of fairness in this context see [2].

[20] *De Smith* 7–024—7–039.

Private law bodies

11.76 The rules of fairness may also apply in the sphere of private law reflecting a wider tendency to equate the obligations of powerful private bodies with those of public authorities and to focus on the reality rather than the form of power.[1] As Lord Denning MR said in *Breen v AEU:*[2]

'Take first statutory bodies. It is now well settled that a statutory body, which is entrusted by statute with a discretion, must act fairly. It does not matter whether its functions are described as judicial or quasi-judicial on the one hand, or as administrative on the other hand, or what you will. Still it must act fairly. It must, in a proper case, give a party a chance to be heard: see *Re H K (An Infant)* [1967] 2 QB 617, 630 by Lord Parker CJ in relation to immigration officers; and *R v Gaming Board for Great Britain, ex p Benaim and Khaida* [1970] 2 QB 417, 430 by us in relation to the gaming board . . .

Does all this apply also to a domestic body? I think it does, at any rate when it is a body set up by one of the powerful associations which we see nowadays. Instances are readily to be found in the books, notably the Stock Exchange, the Jockey Club, the Football Association, and innumerable trade unions. All these delegate power to committees. These committees are domestic bodies which control the destinies of thousands. They have quite as much power as the statutory bodies of which I have been speaking. They can make or mar a man by their decisions. Not only by expelling him from membership, but also by refusing to admit him as a member; or, it may be, by refusal to grant a licence or to give their approval . . . They are not above the law, but subject to it. Their rules are said to be a contract between the members and the union. So be it. If they are a contract, then it is an implied term that the discretion should be exercised fairly. But the rules are in reality more than a contract. They are a legislative code laid down by the council of the union to be obeyed by the members. This code should be subject to control by the courts just as much as a code laid down by Parliament itself. If the rules set up a domestic body and give it a discretion, it is to be implied that that body must exercise its discretion fairly. Even though its functions are not judicial or quasi-judicial, but only administrative, still it must act fairly. Should it not do so, the courts can review its decision, just as it can review the decision of a statutory body. The courts cannot grant the prerogative writs such as certiorari and mandamus against domestic bodies, but they can grant declarations and injunctions which are the modern machinery for enforcing administrative law.

Then comes the problem: ought such a body, statutory or domestic, to give reasons for its decision or to give the person concerned a chance of being heard? Not always, but sometimes. It all depends on what is fair in the circumstances. If a man seeks a privilege to which he has no particular claim — such as an appointment to some post or other — then he can be turned away without a word. He need not be heard. No explanation need be given: see the cases cited in *Schmidt v Secretary of State for Home Affairs* [1969] 2 Ch 149, 170–171. But if he is a man whose property is at stake, or who is being deprived of his livelihood, then reasons should be given why he is being turned down, and he should be given a chance to be heard. I go further. If he is a man who has some right or interest, or some legitimate expectation, of which it would not be fair to deprive him without a hearing, or reasons given, then these should be afforded him, according as the case may demand. The giving of reasons is one of the fundamentals of good administration'.

---

[1] For example, private monopoly powers. For a generous view of what constitutes a reviewable authority for this purpose: *R v Panel on Take-overs and Mergers, ex p Datafin plc* [1985] QB 815.

² [1971] 2 QB 175 at 190–191.

11.77 Therefore, the principles apply to the exercise of disciplinary functions by trade unions;[1] by professional sporting bodies,[2] but not in amateur sport;[3] by medical bodies;[4] by clubs;[5] by other voluntary associations;[6] by the Take-over Panel;[7] by political parties;[8] by universities;[9] by schools — at any rate in an expulsion case.[10]

[1] *Leary v National Union of Vehicle Builders* [1971] Ch 34.
[2] Beloff, 'Pitch, Pool, Rink — Court? Judicial review in the sporting world: Public Law, 1989. Beloff, 'Natural Justice and Sports Bodies'. IAAF Symposium, Monte Carlo (1991). In *Jones v Welsh Rugby Football Union* TLR 6.3.1997, Ebsworth J held that it was arguable that a failure by a rugby union's disciplinary committee either to allow a player to challenge by question or evidence the factual basis of the allegation against him or to vary its procedures for reviewing video evidence without good reason was unfair. A player challenging such unfair treatment should not be suspended from playing pending resolution of the issue. Cf: TLR 19.12.1997 (CA).
[3] *Currie v Barton* (1987) Times, 12 February, CA.
[4] *R v General Medical Council, ex p Gee* [1987] 1 All ER 1204, [1986] 1 WLR 226.
[5] *Young v Ladies Imperial Club Ltd* [1920] 2 KB 523.
[6] See J F Garner, *Voluntary Associations and Natural Justice* (1965) 109 SJ, pp 524–526. 'The Law of Domestic Private Tribunals' (1982) Ch IV (1950) MLR 281; (1952) MLR 413 (1958) MLR 661 (1963) MLR 412 (all by Lloyd) Lloyd: *The Law of Unincorporated Associations* 127–130. Samuels: 'Some problems as with Domestic Tribunals' (2003) JR 54.
[7] *R v Panel on Take-overs and Mergers, ex p Datafin plc* [1987] QB 815.
[8] *Walsh v McLuskie* (1982) Times, 16 December. See also *Fountaine v Chesterton* (1968) 112 Sol Jo 690.
[9] *Glynn v University of Keele* [1971] 1 WLR 487.
[10] *R v Governors of London Oratory School, ex p Regis* [1989] Fam Law 67; *R v Campbell Manor School, ex p Brown* (1993) 5 Admin LR 159.

11.78 When such bodies exercise disciplinary and analogous functions, natural justice must be complied with even though their rules may not oblige them to act in the same way as courts of law. While the public law remedies are not always available to regulate such bodies,[1] but even where they are not, appropriate private law remedies have been successfully sought.[2]

[1] See Chapter 5.
[2] See *Breen* at **11.76** above.

11.79 Moreover, it seems that it will be contrary to public policy for a body to seek to exclude principles of natural justice which the courts would otherwise hold to be applicable. Lord Denning in particular expressed this view in a number of cases, eg *Lee v Showmens Guild*[1] and *Edwards v SOGAT*,[2] and has been followed by Bingham J at first instance in *Cheall v APEX*.[3] This approach is preferable to the contrary view which had been adopted in some earlier cases to the effect that in bodies such as clubs and trade unions, natural justice would only operate if there was an express or implied term requiring it.[4]

[1] [1952] 2 QB 329.
[2] [1971] Ch 354.
[3] [1982] 3 All ER 855.
[4] See, eg *Russell v Duke of Norfolk* [1949] 1 All ER 109, (1949) LQR 293, where other cases in support of this proposition are cited. *Maclean v Workers Union* [1929] 1 Ch 602 at 603; Citrine. *Trade Union Law* (3rd edn) p 278. Note too that the courts may be reluctant to give to an applicant more by way of procedure than he expressly bargained for, see, eg *University*

of *Ceylon v Fernando* [1960] 1 WLR 223 at 233; *Hamlet v GMBATU* [1987] 1 WLR 449 at 456B.

Some exemptions and limitations

11.80 However, cases have fallen on the other side of the line. Axiomatically a complaint of breach of natural justice cannot be entertained where the adjudicator had not been properly appointed and his decision was nullity for want of jurisdiction: *Amec Capital Projects Ltd v Whitefriars City Estate Ltd.*[1] There is no right in a condemned person to insist on an oral hearing before the President in presentation of a petition for a pardon;[2] or for an applicant for a permit to print a magazine under the Printing Powers and Publications Act 1984 (Malaysia).[3] In a case involving the legitimacy of the institutional decision of the Minister of Labour in resolving statutorily a trade union recognition dispute it was held that, in the absence of any lis, all that was required was a fair and reasonable decision, and there was no provision or need for any particular form of enquiry.[4] It was held too that there was no unfairness where the Secretary of State had not disclosed all the applicable criteria to a prisoner whose conviction was quashed and sought an *ex gratia* payment.[5] Natural justice was unsuccessfully sought to be applied to a dethronement of a chief.[6] More acceptably, in *North Yorkshire Family Health Service, ex p Wilson*,[7] it was held that principles of natural justice are not breached where a party is denied an opportunity to present an argument which is based on an irrelevant consideration.

[1]   [2005] 1 All ER 723.
[2]   *Kehor Singh v Union of India AIR* (1989) 653 SC. Cf *R v Secretary of State for the Home Department, ex p Bentley* [1994] QB 349. In *Reckley v Minister of Public Safety and Immigration* [1996] 1 AC 527, the Privy Council held that the petitioner's execution would not be unconstitutional by reason of a denial of natural justice during the process leading to the refusal by the Governor-General to exercise the prerogative of mercy in his favour since no rights may be ascribed on the basis of fairness when a person is essentially in mercy. [Criticised by Gelber in 'Reckley No 2 and the Prerogative of Mercy: Act of Grace or Constitutional Safeguard' (1997) MLR, p 572, esp pp 579–582.]
[3]   *Minister of Home Affairs v Persatman Ahran Keseduran Begara* (1990) 1 Malaysian CLJ 699 (SC).
[4]   *Tanjong Jaga Son Bhd v Ministry of Labour and Manpower* 27 August 1986 (Civil Appeal: No 132 of 1985 (Malaysia), SC.
[5]   *R v Secretary of State for the Home Department, ex p Harrison* [1988] 3 All ER 86.
[6]   *Ghana Republic v Togbe Agbona II, ex p Togbe Kwasi Dch III* (Civil Appeal No 32 of 1984 Ghana).
[7]   (1996) 8 Admin LR 613.

Overlap between scope and content

11.81 It is easier to determine when some principles will apply than to formulate what they will be in any particular context. The courts have emphasised the need for flexibility in the application of the principles — an objective facilitated by the utilisation of the duty to act fairly. But touchstones have been identified. In *Durayappah v Fernando*,[1] Lord Upjohn, giving judgment for the Privy Council, made reference to three matters which the court considered were relevant to the question where natural justice applied, but are no less apposite to the question of what the principles might be in any particular context. These considerations were the nature of the interest at stake; the precise terms of the statutory power to intervene; and the sanction involved.[2]

[1] [1967] 2 AC 337 at 349. See also **11.56** above.

[2] Wade, at p 495, said of another aspect of this case that it savoured of palm tree justice (as distinct, it may be, from natural justice).

11.82 In *McInnes v Onslow Fane*,[1] Megarry VC drew a distinction between three types of situations which reflect the different interests which individuals may have in their relations with public bodies.

[1] [1978] 3 All ER 211, [1978] 1 WLR 1520.

11.83 In the 'forfeiture' cases the applicant is deprived of some right or position which he already holds such as where he is expelled from a club, union or office. In such cases the applicant is entitled to the full panoply of procedural protection afforded by the rules of natural justice.[1]

[1] The same principles apply to corporate bodies: *R v Secretary of State for Transport, ex p Sherriff & Sons Ltd* (1986) Times, 18 December (breach of natural justice to revoke discretionary grant without a hearing) (discussed: *Bradley* Public Law [1987] 141–146). On removal of licence see *R (London Reading College Ltd) v Secretary of State for the Home Department* [2010] EWHC 2561(Admin), [2010] ELR 809 at p 42–48.

11.84 In 'legitimate expectation cases' the applicant seeks the renewal or confirmation of some licence, or membership, or office which he already holds; in such cases, apparently, because the applicant can normally legitimately expect the benefit to continue unless there is good reason to the contrary, the applicant would be entitled to be told before being refused renewal or confirmation, why it is proposed to reject his application so that he can say something in his defence[1]

[1] Even voluntary consultation must be fair. The concept of an intermediate case was identified in *Naidike v AG of Trinidad and Tobago* [2004] UKPC 49, [2005] 1 AC 538 [24].

11.85 In the pure 'application cases', the applicant merely seeks a licence, membership or office which he has not previously held. Here, according to Megarry J, the decision-maker's only obligation is to act 'fairly' which, in this context, means reaching its decision honestly and without bias or caprice (that is, without abusing its decision-making power). But provided it does so, it is under no duty to tell the applicant even the gist of the reasons for its refusal of his application, or to give him a chance to address it.

11.86 The triple categorisation provides a useful framework for initial analysis, even if the later jurisprudence suggests a higher obligation in relation to the first category. The *McInnes* approach vis à vis that category has not been wholeheartedly followed in Commonwealth jurisdictions, eg *Stininato v Auckland Boxing Association Inc*,[1] and is now all but eroded.[2]

[1] [1978] 1 NZLR 1 (NZCA).

[2] See *Ramjohn v Permanant Secretary, Ministry of Foreign Affairs; Kisson v Manning* [2011] UKPC 20 at [46] [48] when it was held 'clearly unfair' to veto an application without providing a reason. An applicant for a licence for coal mining was entitled to be told about

licensor's concerns about its case, but not to be told about its competitor *Abbey Mine Ltd v Coal Authority* [2008] EWCA Civ 353.

11.87 Indeed, a higher procedural standard was even before *McInnes* required for an 'application' case in *R v Gaming Board for Great Britain, ex p Benaim and Khaida*.[1] The applicants sought to challenge the refusal of a certificate necessary to support an application for a licence to run a gaming establishment. Lord Denning said that since the applicants are seeking a privilege rather than to enforce a right, the Board had no duty to give them detailed reasons for the refusal of the certificate, but need only tell them their impressions and give them a chance to disabuse the Board in advance if the impression was wrong. At least the rudiments of the opportunity to state a case was afforded to them, which is surely desirable since the grant of the certificate was essential to the applicants' ability to earn their living by running a lawful casino. Indeed, in these circumstances it can be argued that further safeguards were required. An effects test, assessing the effect of the decision, would be a better touchstone for deciding the principles applicable, whatever the technical nature of his interest. Where reputation or livelihood are at stake, it requires a cogent reason to deny him a hearing: *a fortiori* where both may be affected by the decision.

[1] [1970] 2 QB 417.

Right, interest and legitimate expectation

11.88 It is now fully recognised that procedural safeguards apply to protect not merely rights but also interests and — a category which may but need not overlap with interests — legitimate expectations.[1] For example, an individual may have an interest in having some benefit or privilege conferred upon him because of its significance, eg a licence. He does not have a right to such a benefit and in many cases cannot ever claim a legitimate expectation. Sometimes, however, his interest may be described as a right, though strictly that is a misnomer, such as where the concept of 'the right to work' is used to require a monopoly body to give a hearing to an applicant before refusing him membership: the applicant has no right to membership nor does he have any right to work in any legal sense. However, the courts will nonetheless protect such interests: see eg *Nagle v Feilden*[2] and *McInnes v Onslow Fane*.[3] Similarly, the Australian High Court has imposed on a racecourse control body an obligation to give a hearing before issuing a warning-off notice prohibiting a person from entering racecourses owned by a third party.[4]

[1] See, generally C Forsyth. 'Protection of Legitimate Expectations' (1988) CLJ 238: Ganz *Legitimate Expectation Public Law and Politics* (ed Harlow, 1986) p 145; Elias, 'Legitimate Expectations and Judicial Review' in *New Directions in Judicial Review* (ed Jowell and Oliver, 1988), pp 37–50; Craig 'Legitimate Expectations: a Conceptual Analysis' (1992) LQR, p 79; Roberts, 'Public Law Representations and Substantive Legitimate Expectations' (2001) MLR, p 112; Schonberg 'Legitimate Expectations in Administrative Law' (2000) OUP — a survey of English, French and EC Law. Harini Iyengar: 'Legitimate Expectation: Promise by a Different Public Authority (2003) JR 2. C Forsyth 'Legitimate Expectation revisited' JR 2011 429.

[2] [1966] 2 QB 633.

[3] [1978] 3 All ER 211, [1978] 1 WLR 1520.

[4] *Heatley v Tasmanian Racing and Gaming Commission* (1977) 137 CLR 487; *Forbes v NSW Trotting Club* (1979) 143 CLR 242.

Legitimate expectation

11.89 The concept of legitimate expectation, a construct of civilian law, used in contrast to rights and interests, was first developed by Lord Denning MR in *Schmidt v Secretary of State for Home Affairs*.[1] Schmidt was an alien who had been given leave to enter the United Kingdom and study scientology for a limited period. On expiry of that period the Home Secretary refused Schmidt an extension without hearing any representations he had to make. Schmidt sought a declaration that he should have been given a hearing. This was rejected by the Court of Appeal, but Lord Denning enunciated a general principle in the following terms:

'The speeches in *Ridge v Baldwin* [1964] AC 40 show that an administrative body may, in a proper case, be bound to give a person who is offered by their decision an opportunity of making representations. It all depends upon whether he has some right or interest or, I would add, some legitimate expectation, of which it would not be fair to deprive him without hearing what he has to say'.

On the facts of the case it was held that Schmidt had no legitimate expectation since the original period had expired; but it would have been otherwise if he had been deported before that time had expired.

[1] [1969] 2 Ch 149.

11.90 The concept of legitimate expectation has since been adopted widely, both in English courts and Commonwealth jurisdictions. The House of Lords recognised, both in *O'Reilly v Mackman*[1] and in *Re Findlay*,[2] that legitimate expectation would provide an applicant with standing in judicial review proceedings as well as a ground itself for review.

[1] [1983] 2 AC 237.
[2] [1985] AC 318.

11.91 In the case of *Council of Civil Service Unions v Minister for the Civil Service*[1] ('the GCHQ case'), Lord Diplock considered the concept on broader canvas when seeking to define the ambit of judicial review as follows:

'The decision must affect some other person either:
(a)   by altering rights or obligations of that person which are enforceable by or against him in private law; or
(b)   by depriving him of some benefit or advantage which either:
(i)   he had been permitted by the decision maker to enjoy and which he can legitimately expect to be permitted to continue to do unless there has been communicated to him some rational grounds for withdrawing it on which he has been given an opportunity to comment; or
(ii)   he has received assurance from the decision maker will not be withdrawn without giving him first an opportunity of advancing reasons for contending that they should not be withdrawn'.

[1] [1985] AC 374.

11.92 Lord Scarman described this analysis as exemplary but not exhaustive in *Nottinghamshire County Council v Secretary of State for the Environment*.[1] In one sense it is too narrow. The contrast drawn by Lord Diplock between rights and legitimate expectations, fails to recognise the fact that sometimes the law will protect interests which constitute neither rights nor legitimate expectations as defined. However, this analysis does bring out the fact that the legitimate expectation may refer either to an expectation that the benefit, privilege or other advantage will be conferred or (more likely) continued, and that accordingly it should not be denied save on rational grounds after a hearing; or it refers to an expectation arising out of some assurance that there will be consultation before a benefit or advantage is withdrawn. Indeed, in principle there is no reason to limit the latter situation to cases where a benefit is being withdrawn; it ought to be equally unfair to frustrate the expectation of a hearing where a benefit is being bestowed.

[1]   [1986] AC 240 at 249.

11.93 In *R v Devon County Council, ex p Baker*[1] Simon Brown LJ identified four categories of legitimate expectation, including the two referred to by Lord Diplock, ie the expectation resulting from the nature of the interests, and the special procedural safeguards resulting from assurances or past practice. The other two were cases where the expectation conferred substantive rights and cases where (superfluously and arguably unhelpfully) the term was used merely to refer to the basic interest which a claimant has to be treated fairly.[2]

[1]   [1995] 1 All ER 73. See now the analysis of Laws LJ in *R (on the application of Bhatt Murphy (a firm) v Independent Assessor* [2008] EWCA Civ 755.
[2]   See *R (Mosely) v Haringey LBC* [2014] 1 WLR 3947 at [23]'the search for the demands of fairness in this context is often illuminated by the doctrine of legitimate expectation'.

11.94 An example of the case where the nature of the interest gives rise to the expectation, ie that a substantive benefit will be conferred or continued, is provided by *O'Reilly v Mackman*.[1] In that case, Lord Diplock treated the expectation of a prisoner that in normal circumstances he would be entitled to a remission of one third of his sentence for good behaviour as a 'legitimate expectation'; it was a well-established policy even though falling short of a right as such. Accordingly it is unlawful to deprive a prisoner of the remission without good reason and after a hearing. Another is where a local authority changed its policy of providing free transport: *R v Rochdale MBC, ex p Schemet*.[2]

[1]   [1983] 2 AC 237. See also *Walsh v Secretary of State for Scotland* 1990 SLT 526; *Rea v Parole Board for Scotland* 1993 SLT 1074.
[2]   (1993) 91 LGR 425.

11.95 A number of cases illustrate the expectation, in the sense of the assurance of a hearing. Sometimes this is an express assurance and sometimes it is implied: it may in other words arise from promise or practice.[1] Examples of the express assurance include a case where the Liverpool Council gave an undertaking that they would hear representations from existing drivers before seeking to increase the number of cabs in the city, but then purported to effect the increase without such opportunity being offered;[2] and *A-G of Hong Kong v Ng Yuen Shiu*,[3] where the Government of Hong Kong promised that illegal immigrants, liable to be deported, would be interviewed individually but subsequently sought to deport without honouring this promise. It was held obliged to comply with the undertaking. Lord Fraser there explained "legitimate expectations" as justifiably arising on the footing that:

'when a public authority has promised to follow a certain procedure, it is in the interest of good administration that it should act fairly and should implement its promise, so long as implementation does not interfere with its statutory duty'.[4]

¹   [1985] AC 374 per Lord Fraser at 400–401. *R v Campbell Manor School, ex p Brown* (1993) 5 Admin LR 159.
²   *R v Liverpool Corpn, ex p Liverpool Taxi Fleet Operators Association* [1972] 2 QB 299 (discussed: (Evans) 1973 MLR S89), (Jackson) 1983 LQR 499; *R v Lord Chancellor, ex p Law Society* (1994) 6 Admin LR 333 (Law Society had prima facie legitimate expectation of consultation in legal aid matter in light, inter alia, of assurances given)).
³   [1983] 2 AC 629. Contrast, however, *Ng Sin Tun v Director of Immigration* (2002) 1 HK LRD 561.
⁴   [1983] 2 AC 629 at 638. Self-employed guardians had legitimate expectations based on the defendant's conduct and statements that they would be consulted before changes were made in their terms of engagement: *R (Application of National Association of Guardians v CAFCAS Services* (2002) 1 FLR 255. *R (on the application of Greenpeace Ltd) v Secretary of State for Trade and Industry* [2007] EWHC 311 (Admin) (promise of fullest public consultation on energy policy).

11.96 An example of an implied undertaking was the *GCHQ* case itself.[1] In that case, the Minister issued instructions varying the terms and conditions of civil servants working at the government's communication headquarters without first consulting with trade unions, contrary to a very long-established practice.

The House of Lords accepted that this invariable practice of consultation did create a legitimate expectation that such consultation would take place in normal circumstances, but on the particular facts it was held that interests of national security outweighed considerations of fairness.

¹   [1985] AC 374.

11.97 An area where the doctrine of legitimate expectation has been of particular importance is education. Grafted onto the statutory procedure which requires consultation after a local authority has presented a proposal to the Secretary of State for an individual school closure has been a common law procedure of requiring consultation by the local authority in formulating its proposal. It was also held obiter, that there could be a duty to consult with parents before a general reorganisation was proceeded with.[1]

¹   *Nichol v Gateshead Metropolitan Borough Council* (1988) 87 LGR 435. See, generally, on case law and Meredith, 'Legitimate Expectations and School Closures' [1988] PL p 4. Note, too, *R v Secretary of State for Trade and Industry, ex p Vardy* [1993] ICR 720 where past practice of consultation about redundancies gave rise to legitimate expectation.

11.98 Some caution should, however, temper deployment of the doctrine. In *Lloyd v McMahon*[1] Lord Templeman observed that one of the arguments for the appellant councillors was based on 'legitimate expectation' and continued with characteristic trenchancy:

'Counsel for the appellants . . . submits that a legitimate expectation of being invited to an oral hearing is an objective fundamental right which, if not afforded, results in a breach of law or breach of natural justice which invalidates any decision based on written material. This extravagant language does not tempt me to elevate a catchphrase into a principle'.[2]

Despite this, the doctrine has extended beyond the traditional restraint of requiring a promise or practice, to being engaged by a policy to consult[3] or even by general fairness.[4]

Similarly, in *R v ITC, ex p TSW*[5] Lord Donaldson MR said it 'was not a magic password'.

[1]   [1987] AC 625.
[2]   [1987] AC 625 at 714.
[3]   *R (Bhatt Murphy (a firm)) v Independent Assessor* [2008] EWCA Civ 755.,On the four triggers of the duty to consult: *R (Harrow Community Support Unit) v Secretary of State for Defence* [2012] EWHC 1921 (Admin). On the indicia of fair consultation: *R (Royal Brompton and Harefield NHS Foundation Trust) v Joint Committee of Primary Care Trusts* [2012] EWCA Civ 472, 126 BMLR 134 per Arden LJ at [8]–[14]. C. Sheldon 'Consultation: Revisiting the basic principles', J.R. 2012 152.
[4]   *R (Dudley Metropolitan Borough Council) v Secretary of State for Communities and Local Government* [2012] EWHC 1729 (Admin).
[5]   (1992) Times, 7 February, CA: see note 2, **11.54** above. The doctrine was criticised by the High Court of Australia. Nor can it be stretched too far: *Annetts v McCann* (1991) 47 ALR 177. In *R v Home Secretary, ex p Hindley* [2001] 1 AC 440 it was held that a mandatory life prisoner had no expectation that the Home Secretary would not impose a whole life tariff since she was unaware of the provisional decision to that effect.

11.99 Where consultation does take place, it itself has to be fair even if voluntary.[1]

[1]   *R (Eisai Ltd) v National Institute for Health and Clinical Excellence* [2008] EWCA Civ 438 at [24]. *R (Medway Council) v Secretary of State for Transport* [2002] EWHC 2516 (Admin) (consultation on development of Air Transport in S.E. England) [27]–[28].

Fairness as a substantive concept

11.100 The discussion so far principally examines the way in which the concept of legitimate expectation has been used as a basis for importing the requirement of natural justice into the decision-making process. If an assurance is given that a hearing will be given, that assurance must be honoured. Can the concept extend beyond the procedural area, so that if an assurance is given that a discretion will be exercised in a particular way, or in accordance with certain principles, the courts will say that fairness requires that the assurance should be honoured? The courts have held that in appropriate circumstances such an assurance or promise must indeed be respected. This is particularly important because government frequently distributes circulars or other statements of policy in which at least guidelines are given as to the way in which discretions will be exercised. If fairness requires discretion to be exercised in accordance with the guidelines, this will severely restrict the scope of the discretion.[1]

[1]   For further discussion, see **11.93** above Chapter 8 on *R (on the application of Nadarajah) v Secretary of State for the Home Department* [2005] EWCA Civ 1363 and *Paponette v A-G of Trinidad & Tobago* [2012] 1 AC 1.

11.101 The first case in which fairness was applied to constrain the substantive exercise of discretion was *R v Secretary of State for the Home Department, ex p Khan*.[1] In that case a Home Office circular specified the circumstances in which the Home Secretary would exercise his discretion to allow a child to be brought into the United Kingdom for adoption. The circular indicated that such permission would be granted if four conditions were satisfied, but the child was refused entry for an entirely different reason. The Court of Appeal, by a majority, held that the Home Secretary had acted unfairly. Parker LJ held that:

> 'the Secretary of State, if he undertakes to allow in persons if certain conditions are satisfied, should not in my view be able to resile from that undertaking without affording interested persons a hearing and then only if the overriding public interest demands it'.[2]

Moreover, it is important to note in this case that the circular was directed to the public at large, and not the applicant specifically, and there was no detrimental reliance on the circular. Dunn LJ adopted a slightly different approach. He held that the circular effectively circumscribed the range of relevant considerations so that it was unfair to take into account other factors.[3]

[1]   [1984] 1 WLR 1337.
[2]   At 1344.
[3]   At 1352.

11.102 The principles in *Khan* were applied in *R v Secretary of State for the Home Department, ex p Ruddock*,[1] a case in which it was alleged that the Home Secretary had approved the telephone-tapping of an active member of the Campaign for Nuclear Disarmament contrary to published criteria. Taylor J concluded that the doctrine of legitimate expectation was not merely a procedural concept and required the minister to keep his promise or undertaking as to how he would exercise his power, provided that exercise would not be inconsistent with his statutory duty or, as in *Ruddock* itself, his duty under the prerogative. On the facts, however, no unfairness was established.[2]

[1]   [1987] 1 WLR 1482.
[2]   In *Minister for Immigration v Teoh* (1995) 128 ALR 353, it was held by the High Court of Australia that an unincorporated convention (on the Rights of the Child) gave rise to a legitimate expectation that assessment of whether or not to deport someone, thereby breaking up his family, would be informed by the principles laid down in the Convention, ie that the best interests of the child were the primary consideration. See, also, *R v Secretary of State for Home Department, ex p Ahmed* (1999) Imm AR 73; *R v DPP, ex p Kebilene* [2002] 2 AC 326; *Rayment* 'What Does Kebilene Decide?' (2000) JR 52; *R v Uxbridge Magistrates Court, ex p Adimi*; *Higgs v Minister of National Security* [2002] 2 AC 228.

11.103 Two further important cases applying the principles concern the Inland Revenue. In *Re Preston*, the House of Lords held that an authority would be guilty of unfairness amounting to an abuse of power if they resiled from acting on representations in a way which would, in the field of private law, constitute a breach of contract or create an estoppel by representation. As Lord Templeman, giving the leading judgment, indicated,[1] such conduct would not always generally be an abuse of power. An exception would appear to be appropriate, for example, where compliance would be inconsistent with the performance of the body's statutory duty.

[1]   [1985] AC 835 at 866–867.

11.104 *Preston* was followed by the Divisional Court in *R v IRC, ex p MFK Underwriting*.[1] In that case a taxpayer was seeking to rely upon what he claimed was an undertaking by the Inland Revenue not to enforce full tax liability in certain circumstances. Bingham LJ accepted[2] that it would be compatible in certain circumstances with the Inland Revenue's statutory duty for it to give assurances, in the course of administering the tax system, that it would not seek to enforce the full liability. However, he held that normally two conditions need to be satisfied. The first is that the taxpayer must have made full disclosure to the Inland Revenue; and the second, that any ruling or statement relied upon should be clear, unambiguous and devoid of relevant qualification.[3]

¹ [1990] 1 WLR 1545. A representation must be clear and unequivocal in order to generate a procedural legitimate expectation: *(R) Falmouth-Truro Port Health Authority, ex p South West Water Limited* [2001] QB 445 at p 458–460; *R (Galligan) v Chancellors Masters and Scholars of the University of Oxford* [2002] ACD 33; *Rowland v Environment Agency* [2005] Ch 1.
² [1990] 1 WLR 1545 at 1569.
³ Also *R v ITC, ex p TSW*, (1992) Times, 7 February, CA. Lord Donaldson MR commenting on the Revenue cases.

11.105 In *R (Association of British Civilian Internees — Far East Region) v Secretary of State for Defence*,[1] the appellant organisation represented individuals interned by the Japanese during the Second World War as British civilians, but refused a £10,000 ex-gratia compensation payment made by the respondent. The appellant unsuccessfully alleged that the refusal was a breach of a legitimate expectation created by an earlier Ministerial announcement of 7 November 2000.

¹ [2003] EWCA QB 1397.

11.106 The Court of Appeal held that only in an exceptional case will a claim be sustained that a legitimate expectation has been defeated in the absence of a clear and unequivocal representation, since it will only be a rare case where, absent such a representation, a decision-maker will have acted with conspicuous unfairness such as to amount to an abuse of power. On the facts, no such unfairness was detected.

11.107 Such a rare case was however identified *R v IRC, ex p Unilever*[1] where it was held that there was an 'unfair' abuse of power by the IRC in disallowing a claim for loss relief outside a two-year limitation period in view of the IRC's past practice in regard to such claims, from which they were purporting to resile.[2]

¹ [1996] STC 681.
² See (1996) JR 178 Forsyth, (1997) PL 375. And note *R v IRC, ex p Kaye* [1992] STC 581. Contrast *R v Panel of Take-overs and Mergers, ex p Fayed* [1992] BCLC 938, CA where it was held that there was no legitimate expectation based on alleged past practice of panel to adjourn panel proceedings because of concurrent legal proceedings.

11.108 The equation of the substantive doctrine of legitimate expectation with estoppel introduced in *Preston* was taken a stage further by the Divisional Court in *R v Jockey Club, ex p RAM Racecourses Ltd*.[1] In that case the applicants were racecourse owners who alleged that they had a legitimate expectation that they should be allocated race meetings in accordance with a report on this subject provided by the Jockey Club. The action failed. The court was divided on the question whether judicial review applied to decisions of this kind by the Jockey Club. However, both Stuart Smith LJ and Simon

Brown J agreed that in any event the application failed on substantive grounds. Stuart Smith LJ, in whose judgment Simon Brown J concurred, held that in circumstances of this kind there were five conditions that needed to be complied with before an application based on legitimate expectation could be successful. These conditions were:

(1)   a clear and unambiguous representation (following Bingham LJ in the *MFK* case);
(2)   that the applicant was within the class of persons entitled to rely on the report, or at least that it was reasonable to rely upon it:
(3)   that he did rely on it;
(4)   that this was to his detriment; and
(5)   that there was no overriding public interest which entitled the Jockey Club to change its policies to the detriment of the applicant.

The court also held that the burden of proving the first four points — essentially an unequivocal representation which it was at least reasonable for the applicant to rely upon and which he did rely upon to his detriment — was upon the applicant, whereas the burden on the fifth point was on the respondent.

¹   [1993] 2 All ER 225, (1991) 5 Admin LR 265.

11.109 It has now been recognised that estoppel is of limited applicability in public law.¹ To the extent that they equated legitimate expectation and estoppel, the authorities cited above introduced an emphasis on reliance — a feature not apparently considered necessary in the *Khan* or the *MFK* case. Indeed, if *Khan* can properly be construed as a case where the range of relevant considerations was circumscribed by the circular, reliance would be irrelevant (and it will often be irrelevant where the legitimate expectation merely had procedural consequences).² But even on the wider approach adopted in *Khan*, two restrictions would appear to apply. First, prima facie the decision-maker need not adhere to any representations if that is inconsistent with his statutory duty, though the *MFK* case shows that it will not be difficult for a court to find that there is no inconsistency between the undertaking and the performance of the statutory duty.³ Second, whilst it may be difficult to justify exceptions to the policy, there can be no complaint if the policy itself is changed.

¹   See 18.65.
²   See *R v Secretary of State for Home Department, ex p Jaramillo-Silva* (1995) 7 Admin LR 445, CA. Commented on by Bamforth JR (1998). See further on the relevance or irrelevance of reliance: *R v MAFF, ex p Hamble* (1995) 2 All ER 714; *R v DEES* [2001] 1 WLR 1115; *Rowland v Environment Agency* [2005] Ch 1 at 46–51. Also see *R v RC, ex p Matrix Securities* [1994] 1 WLR 334.
³   See now discussion by Blundell in *Judicial Review* (2005) 147 'Ultra Vires Legitimate Expectation', commenting on *Rowland v The Environment Agency* [2005] Ch 1 and *Stretch v UK* (2004) 38 EHRR 12. See, also, Elliott, 'Unlawful Representations, Legitimate Expectations, and Estoppel in Public Law' (2003) JR 71.

11.110 This was recognised in *Re Findlay*.¹ In that case the Home Office altered the policy relating to the remission of sentences for certain categories of prisoner. A prisoner adversely affected alleged that he had a legitimate expectation that he would benefit from the policy and at least should have been consulted prior to the change. The House of Lords rejected this construction on the grounds that the legitimate expectation for any prisoner was that his case would be considered in accordance with whatever policy the Home Secretary thought fit to adopt, not a specific policy in force at any particular time. (This does not necessarily preclude the need to consult prior to any change of policy, but that obligation will not relate to every prisoner adversely affected by the policy change). *Re Findlay* was applied in *R v Secretary of State for the Home Department, ex p Hargreaves*[2] where prisoners unsuccessfully argued that they had a legitimate expectation to enjoy home leave after serving a particular period of their sentence, which expectation had been denied them by the Secretary of State's tightening up of the home leave policy.[3]

[1] [1985] AC 318.
[2] [1997] 1 All ER 397; for criticism of this case, see note 2, **11.112** below.
[3] See also *R v Council of Legal Education, ex p Eddis* (1995) 7 Admin LR 357 (no legitimate expectation that selection process for Bar School would remain unaltered).

11.111 The same approach informed the Court of Appeal in *R v Torbay Borough Council, ex p Cleasby*.[1] In the context of a local authority's system for licensing pleasure boats there was a decision to change from rota, and it was held where, as in the instant case the legitimate expectation relied on (ie that the rota system would continue until 1992) is derived from a local authority's policy, all that can be legitimately expected is that, in default of any private rights, the policy for the time being will be fairly applied. No such expectation can be relied on to prevent or interfere with a change of policy fairly carried out.

[1] [1991] COD 142.

11.112 Notwithstanding the cases in support of the view that the concept of legitimate expectation may extend beyond purely procedural parameters, Laws J anachronistically declined to treat it as a substantive concept in *R v Secretary of State for Transport, ex p Richmond upon Thames BC*.[1] However, the Court of Appeal took a great leap forward in *R v North and East Devon Health Authority, ex p Coughlan* where a painstaking analysis of the previous jurisprudence was carried out[2] and ruled that the court will, indeed, recognise a substantive legitimate expectation: that any decision which frustrates it will be judged by the touchstone of fairness, not rationality, that such decision can only be justified on grounds of overriding public interest; and the courts will judge whether it is, in all the circumstances, including the statutory context, fair to override it.[3] In this rapidly developing field the last case is often the best, and a modern review is to be found in the judgment of Mance LJ in *Rowland v Environment Agency*.[4]

[1] [1994] 1 All ER 577.
[2] [2001] 1 QB 213, paragraphs 55–82, pp 241–250. See also *R v Secretary of State for Education and Employment, ex p Begbie* [2001] 1 WLR 1115.
[3] See now: Forsyth, 'The Wednesbury Protection of Substantive Legitimate Expectation' [1997] PL 375; Allen, 'Procedural Substance in Judicial Review' [1997] CLT 246; 'Public Law: Legitimate Expectations' CLJ July 2004 261; Elliott, 'Legitimate Expectations: The Substantive Discussion' CLJ Nov 2000 421: Elliott, 'Fairness and Legitimate Expectation': CLJ March 1997, 1; Bamforth, 'Legitimate Expectation in English Public Law', CLJ Autumn 2002, 52: Sales and Steyn, 'Unlawful Regulations, Legitimate Expectations and Estoppel in Public Law'; Elliott (2003) JR p 71; Steyn, 'Substantive Legitimate Expectation' JR (2001) p 244; Havers and Sheldon, 'Politicians, Promises and the Abuse of Power' (2000) JR p 96; Fordham, 'Legitimate Expectation Domestic Principles' (2000) JR p 188; Bamforth, 'Legitimate Expectation and Estoppel' (1998) JR p 196.

⁴   [2005] Ch 1 at 46–51.

Excluding or modifying natural justice

11.113 There are a variety of circumstances in which the courts have held in principle that the principles of natural justice will either be wholly excluded or will apply only in a truncated form.

National Security

11.114 Exceptional considerations of national security will entitle the Government not to consult or give a hearing in circumstances where, absent these considerations, they would be required to do so. Accordingly, in the *GCHQ* case[1] it was held that not only was the Government permitted to ban the right of workers at GCHQ from belonging to a trade union, but further it was justified in not consulting with the trade unions before imposing the ban, despite the fact that this contravened a very well-established practice of consultation. However, as the court made clear in the *GCHQ* case itself, the mere assertion of national security is not enough. The Government must at least adduce sufficient evidence to demonstrate that considerations of national security do arise, though once the matter is put in issue there are, as Lord Scarman indicated, common sense limitations as to what is justiciable. It would have to be shown that the decision of the minister that national security should take precedence over natural justice was perverse.[2]

¹   [1985] AC 374.
²   At 406–407.

11.115 This case was followed in *R v Secretary of State for the Home Department, ex p Ruddock*[1] when the court did not accept that it should refuse even to consider an application for judicial review once the issue of national security was raised. However, in *R v Secretary of State for the Home Department, ex p Hosenball*[2] the court held that the Secretary of State was justified in not giving reasons for his decision to deport the applicant. Whilst the minister did permit representations to be made, these were clearly of limited value when the applicant did not know the case he had to meet, but national security was successfully relied upon to justify this truncation of the normal requirements of natural justice.

¹   [1987] 2 All ER 518, [1987] 1 WLR 1482.
²   [1977] 3 All ER 452, [1977] 1 WLR 766.

11.116 In *R v Secretary of State for the Home Department, ex p Cheblak*[1] it was held, consistently, that an immigrant was not entitled to full particulars of the case against him or to legal representation before the advisory panel where his deportation was stated by the Home Secretary to be conducive to the public good for reasons of national security.

¹   [1991] 1 WLR 890.

11.117 Lord Donaldson MR said:[1]

'Nevertheless the exercise of the jurisdiction of the courts in cases involving national security is necessarily restricted, not by any unwillingness to act in protection of the rights of individuals or any lack of independence of the executives, but by the nature of the subject matter. National Security is the exclusive responsibility of the executive and, as Lord Diplock said in *Council of Civil Service Unions v Minister for the Civil Service* [1985] AC 374, HL: "It is par excellence a non justiciable question".

That the prospective detainee is not entitled to be given the fullest particulars of what is alleged against him would, in other circumstances be objectionable as constituting a denial of natural justice. But natural justice has to take account of realities and something which would otherwise constitute a breach is not to be considered if it is unavoidable'.

[1] [1991] 1 WLR 890 at 902 and 907–908. The Master of the Rolls also had no doubt that the advisory panel was susceptible of judicial review if, for example, it could be shown to have acted unfairly within its terms of reference.
See, also, *R v Secretary of State, ex p Chahal* [1995] 1 All ER 658, CA (national security). See, generally, Daniels 141 NLJ 1338 Judicial Review and National Security. In *Jammat E Islami Hind v Union of India* [1995] 3 LRC 583 it was held that where an independent tribunal had to assess the lawfulness vel non by the Supreme Court of India of an association, and the state claimed proper privilege for certain material in their possession, the tribunal was empowered to devise a procedure suitably modifying the requirements of natural justice by which it could satisfy itself of the credibility of the material without disclosing it to the association. See, too, *R v Secretary of State for the Home Department, ex p Jahromi* (1996) Admin LR 197 (national security and giving of reasons).

11.118 However, there are indications of a more robust judicial attitude. While it had been held no obligation to give reasons for the exclusion orders made under the earlier prevention of terrorism legislation,[1] the compatibility with the elaborate statutory scheme of the Anti-Terrorism Crime and Security Act 2001 with the Human Rights Act 1998 was trenchantly disputed by the House of Lords on the ground that it allowed detention without charge (or trial), even though a detainee had an opportunity, albeit severely circumscribed, to make representations to a special body (SIAC).[2] This case may presage a less deferential approach to national security executive cases.[3] An overseas illustration of a firm refusal by the court to treat the invocation of national security as conclusive is provided by the Supreme Court of Malaysia where the cancellation of a foreign journalist's employment pass on alleged security grounds was quashed on grounds of denial of opportunity to make representations.[4]

[1] *R v Secretary of State for the Home Department, ex p Stitt* (1987) Times, 3 February (see also cases cited in Bonner Emergency Powers in Peacetime (1985) p 71).
[2] [2005] 3 All ER 169 and see now *Secretary of State for the Home Department v AF (No.3)* [2009] UKHL 28, [2009] 3 WLR 74: There is a need for disclosure of case against two suspected terrorists upon whom control orders were imposed [Elliott 495–8 CLJ Nov 09]. For its sequel (flawed control orders quashed with effect from their making), *Secretary of State for the Home Department v AF (No 4)* (CA) TLR, 1st September 2010. Note the influence of *A v United Kingdom* [2009] ECHR 3455/05: (2009 CLJ 245) cf: *Secretary of State for Home Department* [2007] UKHL 46, [2007] 3 WLR 681 disclosure to special advocate could suffice: CLJ 2008 1–4 Forsyth. *U v XC* [2009] EWHC 3052 (person cannot be refused bail solely on the basis of secret evidence). However disclosure of the grounds upon which the Government accepted assurances about the treatment of someone liable to deportation from the receiving state was held unnecessary on the basis that the putative deportee could make no real contribution on the strength of the assurances. *RB (Algeria) v Secretary of State for Home Department*: [2009] UKHL 10, [2009] 2 WLR 512 (en route to Strasbourg). *W (Algeria) v Secretary of State for the Home Department* [2010] EWCA Civ 898. There is no irreducible

minimum of information that had to be provided to appellant in proceedings before SIAC about the risk they posed to national security. Furthermore the appellants were not entitled to any procedural protection akin to the 'closed material' procedure available to the Secretary of States' witnesses. See *Bank Mellat v Her Majesty's Treasury (No 1)* [2013] UKSC 38 where Treasury order directed those in the financial sector to refuse to participate in transactions concerning the Bank. It disclosed evidence relied on under closed material procedure ('CMP') to court but not to the Bank itself. This was upheld: CLJ 2013 491-4. K Hughes 'Judicial Review and Closed material procedure in the Supreme Court'. *Home Office v Tariq* [2010] EWCA Civ 462 closed material procedure for national security cases in the Employment Tribunals (Construction and Rules of Procedure) Regulations 2004 was not inherently unlawful by reference to EU law or Art 6 ECHR. However the claimant was entitled to be provided with the allegations made against him in sufficient detail to enable him to give instructions to his legal representatives so that those allegations could be effectively challenged. National security: *Secretary of State for Home Department v MB* [2007] UKHL 46, [2008] 1 AC 440 at (72): a judge in control order proceedings could refuse disclosure of evidence to defendant but not where it would be incompatible with a fair trial. Closed material procedure. Fordham 'Secrecy Security and Fair Trials' 2012 JR 187. *Home Department v F* [2009] UKHL 28 (control orders).

3   See Lord Steyn '*Deference a Tangled Story*' (2005) PL 346.
4   *John Peter Berthelsen v DG of Immigration* (1986) 2 CLJ 409 (SC).

11.119 Only Parliament could introduce a closed material procedure as a substitute for or supplement to public interest immunity.[1]

1   *Al Rawi v Security Service* [2011] UKSC 34, [2012] 1 AC 531, [2012] 1 All ER 1.

Urgency

11.120 In *Durayappah v Fernando*[1] Lord Upjohn expressed the view that:

' . . . whilst great urgency may tightly limit such opportunity timeously, perhaps severely, there can never be a denial of that opportunity if the principles of natural justice are applicable'.

But on another occasion the Privy Council has recognised that the principles may be excluded in circumstances of severe emergency.[2] In particular, decisions may have to be taken in the case of health and safety with great urgency, as in *R v Davey*[3] where an order was made to remove a person with an infectious disease to hospital. Even in these cases, however, it will normally be possible to permit a hearing at a later stage and to reverse the original decision if it is shown to have been wrongly taken. Speedy justice may mean rough justice, but it ought not to mean no justice.

1   [1967] 2 AC 337, 345. Interim orders can be made *ex p R (Kenny) v Leeds Magistrates Court* [2003] EWHC 2963 2004 1 All ER 1333 at (3) Owen J.
2   *De Verteuil v Knaggs* [1918] AC 557.
3   [1899] 2 QB 301.

11.121 In *R v Birmingham City Council, ex p Ferrero*,[1] it was held that there was no legal requirement to receive representations from a manufacturer whose goods were subsequently made subject to a suspension notice under the Consumer Protection Act 1987, where the local authority took the view that the goods in question breached the general safety standard. The Act, however, provided a limited right of appeal to magistrates. So in *Lewis v Heffer*[2] it was held that the National Executive Council of the Labour Party did not have to comply with the rules of national justice in deciding temporarily to suspend the officers of the constituency party as a matter of urgency, pending an investigation into the officers of the branch. But this was a holding operation and natural justice was complied with before any final determination was made.[3]

1   [1993] 1 All ER 530 (CA).
2   [1978] 3 All ER 354, [1978] 1 WLR 1061.
3   See also *Gaiman v National Association for Mental Health* [1971] Ch 317 where Megarry J accepted that a factor justifying not applying the principles of natural justice to mass expulsions was the need for speed — in that case a fear by the members of the Association that it was being taken over by scientologists.

11.122 In *R v LAUTRO, ex p Ross*[1] it was held that a self-regulating organisation under the Financial Services Act 1986 was entitled to suspend an insurance company without notice. The court commented on the need not to trammel unnecessarily regulatory organisations of that kind.[2] Again, in *R v Secretary of State for Transport, ex p Pegasus Holdings (London) Ltd*,[3] judicial review was refused in regard to a decision made by the Secretary of State under the Air Navigation Order 1985,[4] summarily but provisionally to suspend certain permits relating to the operation by certain Romanian pilots of charter aircraft. Schiemann J noted that this reaction was based on a prima facie opinion; but observed that if fuller investigation showed it to be unfounded then, though only then, the suspension could be lifted. As to the contention that the suspension was so quickly applied that the applicants had no chance to be heard in their own defence, and were thus denied natural justice and fairness, the judge held that suspension of permission is the very least safeguard applicable in the circumstances, given the risk to passengers' lives if planes are being flown by incompetent pilots. Furthermore, subsequent representations, capable of being made promptly with the object of persuading the authorities to lift the suspension, were in no way precluded.[5]

1   [1993] QB 17.
2   *See also A v B Bank* (1993) QB 311 at 329.
3   [1989] 2 All ER 481, [1988] 1 WLR 990.
4   SI 1985/1643.
5   In *R v Lautro, ex p Ross* [1993] QB 17 it was held, if for reasons of urgency such a hearing cannot be given before action is taken, there is no reason why it should not be given as soon as possible afterwards.

11.123 In an analogous process of reasoning in *Calvin v Carr*[1] the Privy Council held that the fact that stewards running horseracing may have to take urgent decisions where there may be no time for procedural refinements, whilst not justifying an exclusion of natural justice, did at least justify the inference that individuals must be aware of this circumstance and would be taken to have accepted that any such defects could be cured on appeal. In *Re Davey* an order was held to have been validly made in the Court of Protection directing execution of a will without hearing an affected husband because the wife was at death's door.[2]

1   [1980] AC 574, [1979] 2 All ER 440.
2   [1981] 1 WLR 164.

11.124 However, in *R v Secretary of State for Social Services, ex p AMA*[1] it was held that exception to the duty to consult in cases of urgency does not apply to the case of self-induced urgency. Furthermore, in *R v Secretary of State, ex p Moon*,[2] it was held that fairness requires that an applicant refused admission to visit the UK should know why it was considered, unlike on previous occasions, that it was contrary to the public interest to let him visit even if the application was made only shortly before the date of the proposed visit.

¹ [1980] 3 All ER 342, [1981] 1 WLR 164. Discussed Jackson [1981] LQR p 371.
² (1995) 8 Admin LR 477.

Practicability

11.125 Sometimes it is simply not practicable to give an oral hearing because of the numbers involved. This does not mean that no procedural safeguards are applicable, but the administrative pressures will inevitably modify the vigour with which they will be applied. For example, in *R v Aston University Senate, ex p Roffey*,¹ Donaldson J accepted that a university could not be expected to interview all of its applicants for admission, though, of course, it will have information submitted by them on their behalf. Even here, however, there may be exceptions if the course which the applicant seeks to do is vital to the student's career.² Again, in *Re HK* the court accepted that an immigration officer dealing with immigrants could not be expected to mount a full hearing in the physical surroundings of an airport, given the volume of entrants to be processed. But the essential elements of fairness had to be met even in this situation.³

¹ [1969] 2 QB 538.
² As in *Central Council for Education and Training in Social Work v Edwards* (1978) Times, 5 May.
³ [1967] 2 QB 617. The problems of doing justice to objectors in major public inquiries are discussed in Purdue, Kemp and O'Riordan, 'The Layfield Report on the Sizewell B Inquiry' [1987] PL p 162.

Preliminary determinations

11.126 Where the courts are dealing with preliminary determinations, ie decisions which do not finally determine the rights or obligations of individuals, even though they may adversely affect individuals, being a stage in the process involving a determination of such rights or obligations, the principles of natural justice or fairness will often be truncated, and indeed may be excluded altogether. The rationale behind this approach is that natural justice is not guaranteed at all stages of the decision-making process, and provided the individual has a full opportunity to make proper representations before a decision affecting his rights has ultimately been made, its requirements of fairness will be met. At the same time, depending upon the nature of the process in issue, certain procedural safeguards may be required not merely having regard to the sequence of steps taken as a whole, but also in relation to particular individual steps in the process.

11.127 The classic example of an important preliminary decision which does not attract any procedural safeguards is the decision to prosecute. Obviously the prosecuting authority must determine that there is a prima facie case, but as Lord Reid pointed out in *Wiseman v Borneman*,¹ the accused has no right to be heard or consulted before any such decision is made. He will, of course, have a right to make full representations at his trial, and it is this which secures the safeguards of natural justice. Likewise there is no need to accord a suspect in a criminal investigation a hearing as a condition precedent to a Crown Court making an order granting access to special procedure material.[2] In *Wiseman* itself,[3] the issue concerned the exercise of power by the tax authorities. They were empowered to take a taxpayer before a tribunal who had to determine whether the object of certain transactions was the illegal avoidance of tax. However, they first had to satisfy the tribunal that there was a prima facie case. The question in issue was whether the taxpayer was entitled to see the material put before the tribunal at this preliminary stage and to make representations upon it. The House of Lords held that he was not; the opportunity to state a case was given at a later stage if and when the tribunal decided to embark upon a full hearing. However, their Lordships were not willing to accept that natural justice was always excluded where preliminary determinations were in issue: on the contrary, as Lord Wilberforce pointed out, there are many kinds of preliminary determinations, and the requirements of fairness will vary from one to another.

[1] [1971] AC 297.
[2] *R v Crown Court at Leicester, ex p DPP* [1987] 3 All ER 654, [1987] 1 WLR 1371.
[3] Discussed in de Smith (1970) CLJ 19.

11.128 Similarly, in *Norwest Hoist Ltd v Secretary of State for Trade*,[1] the Court of Appeal held that the Secretary of State was under no obligation to give an opportunity to a company to state its case before appointing inspectors to investigate its officers pursuant to a specific power in the Companies Act. Ormrod LJ[2] treated the situation as being precisely analogous to the decision to prosecute; and Geoffrey Lane LJ pointed out that the chance to make representations would occur during the inquiry itself.[3]

[1] [1978] Ch 201 (where the application was for summary judgment but the claim was struck out!). Discussed — Denning *Due Process of Law* (1980) Butterworths, pp 74–76.
[2] At 227.
[3] At 229.

11.129 An equivalent conclusion was reached in a different situation in *Herring v Templeman*.[1] In that case a student was held by the Court of Appeal not to be entitled to a hearing before an academic board which made a recommendation of his expulsion to the college's governing body, on the grounds that the recommendation had no final consequences and he was entitled to a hearing before the governing body itself. In the particular circumstances of the case, this conclusion is, however, open to criticism since as the Court of Appeal recognised, the governing body was not itself an expert body, and indeed the purpose of the hearing before the governing body was, in the words of Russell LJ 'to give the student a fair chance to show why the recommendations should not be accepted'. Clearly, therefore, the recommendations were going to be extremely influential: they did not merely establish the existence of a case against the student but raised what was in effect a 'rebuttable presumption' as to the appropriate sanction. Where the initial determination has such significance it is submitted that fairness does require that the student has the opportunity to comment upon the material against him at that initial stage.

[1] [1973] 3 All ER 565. Discussed Christie (1974) MLR 324; de Smith (1974) CLJ 23.

11.130 By contrast, in *Giles v Law Society*[1] it was held that rules of natural justice do not apply to the giving of a notice of intervention by the Law Society, on the ground of suspected dishonesty of a solicitor, since the solicitor is entitled to judicial consideration of the notice itself: hence there is no requirement that particulars of dishonesty or the reasons for suspecting it be given.

[1] (1995) 139 Sol Jo LB 218, CA.

Investigations and inquiries

11.131 One particular kind of preliminary conclusion which has raised difficult issues for the courts arises where adverse comments or conclusions relating to individuals are made following an investigation or inquiry. Are all individuals subject to adverse comment entitled to procedural safeguards before the report is produced? Clearly in a large inquiry an investigation giving individuals protection akin to that afforded to defendants in a court of law would significantly lengthen the proceedings, add to the cost and could create an unacceptable delay in the inquiry. Conversely, however, it is unacceptable to subject individuals to adverse criticism when they have no chance to answer those criticisms and to protect their good name. Moreover, adverse comments made in the report of an inquiry, eg an investigation under the Companies Act, may be the precursor to later legal proceedings.

11.132 The courts have tried to strike a balance between these conflicting interests. This is best illustrated by the approach to investigations under the Companies Act. An inspector's report of itself has no adverse legal consequences, though matters highlighted in the report may cause the prosecuting authorities to initiate legal proceedings. In *Re Pergamon Press Ltd*[1] two companies were under investigation, and certain directors refused to respond to questions unless they were informed of the chapter and verse of each allegation and given an opportunity to comment upon them. The inspectors refused to do this and the directors claimed a breach of natural justice. In effect they were seeking to impose upon the inspectors proceedings of an adjudicatory nature. The Court of Appeal rejected their claim. They held that whilst the inspectors must act fairly, this was achieved by putting the gist of any criticisms to the directors and giving them an opportunity to comment upon them. The preliminary nature of the proceedings combined with the need to respect the confidentiality of informants and to ensure that the investigation could be conducted efficiently and speedily, were important factors in reaching that conclusion. If further legal proceedings were initiated, individuals would of course be able to make appropriate representations at that stage.[2] In another case, the Court of Appeal held that in conducting investigations the Commission for Racial Equality must act fairly but that this was achieved if an individual was told in broad terms the case against him and given a fair opportunity of answering it. As Lord Denning commented, this is a fundamental right that should be afforded to a person whenever:

> '[he] may be subjected to pains or penalties, or be exposed to prosecution or proceedings, or deprived of remedies or redress, or in some such way adversely affected by the investigation and report'.[3]

As noted above, the entitlement to a hearing applied to the proceedings of a Royal Commission in the form of an inquiry into the Mount Erebus aeroplane crash disaster.[4]

1   [1971] Ch 388.
2   See also *Maxwell v DTI* [1974] QB 523; DTI Investigations Handbook (1990) HMSO, p 50. Salies 'Accountability of Government via Public Inquiries' (2004) JR 173 at p 180–181.
3   *R v Race Relations Board, ex p Selvarajan* [1975] 1 WLR 1686 at 1694.
4   See *Mahon v Air New Zealand Ltd* [1984] AC 808 discussed 1985 LQR 5 (Notes) 'Natural Justice by a Royal Commissioner'.

11.133 It is not immediately obvious why there should be procedural safeguards where adverse comments are made in a report of an inquiry or investigation, and yet no such safeguards apply where a decision is made as to whether legal proceedings — even criminal proceedings — should be initiated. The latter may have far more serious consequences for the individual than the former, particularly where the adverse comment is not in fact followed by subsequent legal proceedings. Paradoxically, however, the fact that there may be no such proceedings does of itself justify the distinction. If the matter goes no further, then the individual who is the subject of adverse comments may never have an opportunity satisfactorily to deal with them. The only effective safeguard may be the right to try to persuade the investigator that his criticisms are wrong before they are put into the report.

11.134 In the planning field it has been held that a minister need not offer a hearing to a local authority before calling in their local plan for his approval or consult them about objections to it received by him[1] nor to a potentially affected owner where he grants to a local authority an extension of time for submitting a compulsory purchase order in connection with a slum clearance scheme.[2] Further in resolving to adopt a slum-clearance scheme a local authority need not first give a hearing to an objecting landowner, since under the statutory procedure this resolution is the initial step and the Act provides amply for the hearing of objections at a statutory inquiry.[3] In the case of closing orders for individual houses there is a right to be heard at the initial stage.[4]

1   *R v Secretary of State for the Environment, ex p London Borough of Southwark* (1987) 54 P & CR 226.
2   *Aristides v Minister of Housing and Local Government* [1970] 1 All ER 195.
3   *Fredman v Minister of Health* (1935) 154 LT 240.
4   Housing Act 1985, s 264.

11.135 In some inquiries the paramount need to find facts in the public interest has been held implicitly to exclude those procedural guarantees which are natural to litigation. A cogent statement of the differences between an inquiry and litigation is to be found in the opening statement of Lord Scarman at the preliminary hearing of The Red Lion Square Inquiry 1974 held under section 32 of the Police Act 1964.[1]

1   All Souls/JUSTICE Report on Some Reforms of Administrative Law: App 13.

Suspensions pending investigations

11.136 A rather different form of preliminary determination arises where some form of action is taken pending investigation or inquiry. Frequently, for example, a person is suspended pending a disciplinary inquiry. This may be even before any decision has been taken to initiate disciplinary or other proceedings. Yet still the courts are reluctant to treat natural justice as applicable at this stage. However, it is important to distinguish between a suspension imposed as a sanction or penalty, and one imposed merely as an administrative act to aid the processes of investigation. In the former case, the principles of natural justice ought always to be applied, see the comments of Megarry J in *John v Rees*,[1] who treated such suspensions as akin to expulsion. By contrast, the latter do not attract any right to a hearing. In *Lewis v Heffer*[2] the Court of Appeal held that the Labour Party was entitled to suspend the officers of a faction ridden constituency party pending an inquiry without first hearing the officers. Lord Denning MR accepted that natural justice would apply where the suspension was inflicted by way of a punishment, but not where it was merely due by way of good administration.

[1]   [1970] Ch 345, [1969] 2 All ER 274. See *R v Lloyds, ex p Post gate* TLR 12.1.1983.
[2]   [1978] 3 All ER 354, [1978] 1 WLR 1061.

11.137 It is not always easy to determine into which category a particular suspension falls, however. For example, where a suspension of an employee is made without a salary being paid pending the determination of a disciplinary charge, there is clearly a direct and adverse pecuniary effect on the individual. Nevertheless in *Furnell v Whangarei High Schools Board*[1] the Privy Council determined by a majority (Lords Reid and Dilhorne dissenting) that the principles of natural justice did not apply where a teacher was suspended without pay pending investigations into his conduct. This is a questionable decision, however, and the decision was influenced by the particular statutory provisions. The majority concluded that although the suspension involved hardship, it was not intended as a penalty. The minority rejected this approach, Viscount Dilhorne commenting that the consequence was sufficiently serious to warrant a right to a hearing. The majority, therefore, focused upon the reasons for the adverse consequences, the minority focused on the fact that adverse consequences were in fact suffered. The latter would seem the preferable approach.

[1]   [1973] AC 660, [1973] 1 All ER 400, discussed [1973] MLR 439–444 [1973] PL 133.

11.138 There is more recent authority from the Commonwealth that there is a right to be heard in cases of suspension.[1] Likewise in Scotland: *Brentnall v Free Presbyterian Church of Scotland*,[2] and in *Balachardran Mahesan v K K Lum*[3] the Supreme Court of Malaysia declined to draw a distinction between suspension and expulsion from a club where a breach of the rules of natural justice invalidated the decision. Wade, says convincingly, 'in principle the arguments for a fair hearing are unanswerable'.[4]

[1]   See *Birss v Secretary for Justice* [1984] 1 NZLR 513 (NZ CA) and *Dixon v Commonwealth* (1981) 55 FLR 34 (Federal Court of Australia) which equate the requirements of natural justice in cases of suspension or expulsion.
[2]   1986 SLT 471, Inner House.
[3]   (1987) 1 CLR 525.

[4]   Wade, p 4643.

11.139 The Privy Council in *Rees v Crane*[1] accordingly quashed the suspension of a Judge by the Chief Justice of Trinidad and Tobago on the recommendation of the Judicial Services Commission where no notice or hearing was given to the Judge.

[1]   [1994] 2 AC 173.

Extradition

11.140 An allegation of denial of natural justice in relation to a conviction in respect of which extradition is sought is a matter for the Secretary of State, not the courts[1] — the consequence of the particular legislative regime. In *R v Secretary of State for the Home Department, ex p Sinclair*[2] it was held that the discretion under paragraph 8 of Sch 1 to the Extradition Act 1989 was:

'certainly broad enough to give ample scope to the Home Secretary to avoid a breach of natural justice when considering whether or not to order extradition of a person from this country'.

The law on extradition is now contained in the Extradition Act 2003.

[1]   *Royal Government of Greece v Governor of Brixton Prison* [1971] AC 250, sub nom *R v Governor of Brixton Prison, ex p Kotronis* [1969] 3 All ER 304; *Atkinson v Government of United States of America* [1971] AC 197.
[2]   [1992] Imm AR 293.

Prerogative

11.141 Although since the GCHQ case the courts have held that prerogative powers are in principle justiciable, there is still a reluctance to review them as fully as statutory powers. In *Reckley v Minister of Public Safety and Immigration (No 2)*,[1] the Privy Council in an appeal from the Bahamas held that the prerogative of mercy was not susceptible to judicial review.

[1]   [1996] AC 527.

Primary legislation

11.142 The rules of natural justice do not apply to the parliamentary process. Persons affected by legislation have no right to be heard before it is enacted.[1]

[1]   *Union of India v Cyanamid India Ltd AIR* 1987 1802 SC.

Delegated legislation

11.143 It was previously held that failure to comply with the rules of natural justice in the course of making delegated legislation does not usually invalidate the legislation.[1] The reasons for this are, first, that delegated legislation tends to affect large numbers of people, and if all had a right to be heard, the system of bringing it into force would be inoperable. Second, that the process making of delegated (as primary) legislation is seen as part of the political rather than of the judicial system. Unusually, in *R v Secretary of State for Health, ex p USTI*,[2] a manufacturer of oral snuff was held to be entitled, on the basis of fairness, to disclosure of a report of a committee which had influenced the Minister to introduce regulations banning sale of the product, and the regulations were accordingly set aside. This case[3] may be explained by the fact that the manufacturer was *uniquely* affected by the regulations so that as regards the manufacturer, the regulations had the substance, if not the form, of an executive order.[4] Primary legislation, however, often provides for a statutory consultation process prior to the making of delegated legislation.

A more recent view is that there is no such general principle: whether fairness required consultation prior to subordinate legislation depends on the context.[5]

[1] *Bates v Lord Hailsham of St Marylebone* [1972] 3 All ER 1019, [1972] 1 WLR 1373, cf: *R v Lord Chancellor, ex p The Law Society* [1994] 6 Admin LR 833: the Law Society had a legitimate expectation of consultation on legal aid regulations.

[2] [1992] QB 353.

[3] Criticised as inconsistent with principle in Analysis by Schwehr and Brown [1991] PL pp 163–170.

[4] But see *R v Lord Chancellor, ex p Law Society* (1994) 6 Admin LR 833, where the same analysis cannot be applied.

[5] *R (Bapio) v Secretary of State for Home Department* [2007] EWCA Civ 1139: 2008 ACD 7 per Sedley LJ at paragraphs [33]–[34] but not when Parliament has prescribed the negative resolution procedure unaccompanied by an express duty consult: Rimer LJ at [64]. There is no legitimate expectation of consultation prior to making of immigration rules ditto. *R (on application of 'C' v Secretary of State for Justice* [2008] EWHC 71 (Admin).

Exclusion by law[1]

[1] For further discussion of this question, see **10.14** et seq and **11.62** et seq.

11.144 The *audi alteram partem* rule can also be excluded by a provision of a Constitution[2] or by a statutory scheme of procedure[3] if compatible with ECHR. A specific ouster of the fair hearing rule is uncommon, although the statutory context may demonstrate that rights to object are catered for after, rather than prior to the decision.[4] The question which usually arises is whether the statutory scheme was intended to be exhaustive of the procedural rights of the applicant. In the absence of such express ouster (and substitution of the statutory procedures) the more detailed the statutory scheme the more likely it is that the rules of natural justice will not operate.[5] However a legislative procedural rule may be held unlawful if it creates an outcome that is inherently procedurally unfair.[6]

[2] *Union of India v Patel Air* 1985 SC 1416.

[3] *R v Herrod, ex p Leeds City District Council* [1976] QB 540 at 560. It can also be excluded when the procedure said to be unfair was bargained for: *Home Office v Tariq* [2011] UKSC 35, [2012] 1 AC 452 at [75] (closed process in an employment claim).

[4] *Hillbank Properties Ltd v Hackney London Borough Council* [1978] QB 998 at 1005.

[5] As to when it will be implied, see **11.62** above, and Jackson (1982) LQR 8 'Statutory Interpretation and Natural Justice'.

[6] *FP (Iran) v Secretary of State for Home Department* 2007 EWCA Civ 13.

11.145 In *R (Smith) v Parole Board* Lord Bingham said 'The maxim expressio unius exclusio alterius can rarely, if ever, be enough to exclude the common law rules of natural justice'.[1]

The court refused to apply the maxim to exclude a right to a hearing in a case involving entertainment licences[2]. In *R v Chichester Justices, ex p Collins*[3] it was held that just as clear statutory words are required to exclude the right to a hearing, so clear words are required to imply a second hearing. Accordingly where a person had a right to a hearing before a term of imprisonment was imposed for his failure to pay a fine, he was not entitled to a second hearing before a warrant of execution was issued.[4]

[1]   [2005] UKHL 1, [2005] 1 WLR 350 at paragraph 29.
[2]   *R v Huntingdon District Council, ex p Cowan* [1984] 1 All ER 58, [1984] 1 WLR 501, discussed Jackson (1984) LQR 367.
[3]   [1982] 1 All ER 1000, [1982] 1 WLR 334.
[4]   Cf *R v Poole Justices, ex p Fleet* [1983] 2 All ER 897, [1983] 1 WLR 974: warrant of commitment for non-payment of rates without a hearing held contrary to natural justice, discussed Jackson [1984] LQR p 21.

Fault other than that of the decision-maker

11.146 It has now been held by the House of Lords that the rules of natural justice are concerned solely with the propriety of the procedure adopted by the decision maker. Thus in *Al-Mehdawi v Secretary of State for the Home Department*[1] which concerned an appeal against the refusal of the Home Office to vary an immigrant's leave to stay in the United Kingdom, which was determined in the absence of the immigrant because his legal advisers failed to tell him the date of the hearing, the claim for certiorari was rejected by the House of Lords on the basis that there had been no irregularity in the conduct of the proceedings by the decision maker. It was stated that a person who fails through his own or his legal advisers refusal to avail himself of an opportunity to be heard cannot assert subsequently that any adverse decision is flawed because of lack of a hearing and that his remedy, if any, in the latter instance lies against his lawyers.

> 'A party to a dispute who has lost the opportunity to have his case heard through the default of his own advisers to whom he has entrusted the conduct of the dispute on his behalf cannot complain that he has been the victim of a procedural impropriety or that natural justice has been denied to him at all events when the subject matter of the dispute raises issues of private law between citizens. Is there any principle which can be invoked to lead to a different conclusion where the issue is one of public law and where the decision taken is of an administrative character rather than the resolution of a lis inter partes? I cannot discover any such principle and none has been suggested in the course of argument'.[2]

[1]   [1990] 1 AC 876. See, generally, Herberg [1990] PL 467–475 'The Right to A Hearing: Breach Without Fault', confirmed in *R (on application of Simla v GMC* [2008] EWHC 1732 (Admin) rejecting a submission that it was trumped by Article 6 of ECHR.
[2]   [1990] 1 AC 876 at 898. However the *Al-Melawi* principle is not universal (*Pomiechowski v District Court of Legnica, Poland* [2012] UKSC 20, [2012] 1 WLR 1604 at [36]). It does not stand easily in *ex p A* (see **11.149** below). *Haile v Immigration Appeal Tribunal* [2001] EWCA Civ 663, [2002] Imm AR 70 at [26] prioritising the 'wider interests of justice'.

11.147 However, there remains a stream of authority where relief has been granted in the absence of fault or even a mere error in the prosecution process. In *R v Leyland Justices, ex p Hawthorn*,[1] an applicant was convicted of a driving offence where the police had failed to disclose to him statements from two witnesses. This was identified by the Divisional Court as 'a clear denial of natural justice'.[2] In *Al-Mehdawi* (at **11.146** above), Lord Bridge questioned this classification, and preferred to analyse it as a case analogous to fraud, collusion and perjury.[3] Other instances of this discrete basis for impeaching a decision are *R v Crown Court at Knightsbridge, ex p Goonatilleke*;[4] *R v Kingston upon Thames Justices, ex p Khanna*;[5] *R v Crown Court at Liverpool, ex p Roberts*;[6] and *R v Bolton Justices, ex p Scally*[7] where guilty pleas were entered to charges of driving with excess blood alcohol concentration in the body where the police swabs were accidentally contaminated. It was held that a combination of the police and CPS activity objectively corrupted the process leading to conviction in a manner which was unfair.

[1] [1979] QB 283.
[2] [1979] QB 283 at 286.
[3] [1990] 1 AC 876 at 896. See, further. *Fisheries v Hughes* 1988 COD 281, proceedings held unfair where applicant represented by deaf person without aid of interpreter. Now see *R (Mathialagan v Southwark LBC* [2004] EWCA Civ 1689, (2004) Times, 21 December.
[4] [1986] QB 1, [1985] 2 All ER 498.
[5] [1986] RTR 364.
[6] [1986] Crim LR 622.
[7] [1991] 1 QB 537, [1991] 2 All ER 619.

11.148 The court observed that 'the overriding principle must surely be that justice should be done' and if it be demonstrated that another principle rigidly applied is, or would seem to be, the way of doing justice, the bounds of that principle require to be very critically examined in a modern light.[1]

[1] [1991] 1 QB 537 at p 555.

11.149 In *R v Criminal Injuries Compensation Board, ex p A*[1] the applicant's claim for compensation had been rejected by the Board, and she complained that the Board had proceeded without knowledge of the relevant police doctor's report and on the basis of incorrect evidence from a police officer. The House of Lords accepted her argument that the rejection was vitiated by unfairness, as the Board had in a crucial respect been led to proceed on wrong evidence and had not had the true facts before it.[2] Lord Slynn said:

'It does not seem to me to be necessary to find that anyone was at fault in order to arrive at this result. It is sufficient if objectively there is unfairness. Thus I would accept that it is in the ordinary way for the Applicant to produce the necessary evidence. There is no onus on the Board to go out to look for evidence, nor does the Board have a duty to adjourn the case for further enquiries if the Applicant does not ask for one . . . Nor is it necessarily the duty of the police to go out to look for evidence on a particular matter'.

Nonetheless, he considered that the police 'do have a special position in these cases', and he noted the evidence that the Board is 'very dependent on the assistance of and the co-operation of the police who have investigated these alleged crimes of violence'. He said:

'In the present case, the police and the Board knew that A had been taken by the police to see a police doctor. It was not sufficient for the police officer simply to give her oral statement without further inquiry when it was obvious that the doctor was likely to have made notes and probably a written report'.

He concluded:

'I consider therefore, on the special facts of this case and in the light of the importance of the role of the police in co-operating with the Board in the obtaining of the evidence, that there was unfairness in the failure to put the doctor's evidence before the board and if necessary to grant an adjournment for that purpose. I do not think it possible to say here that justice was done or seen to be done'.[3]

1   [1999] 2 AC 350.
2   On the question of duty to investigate, see the discussion at **8.27**.
3   [1999] 2 AC 350 at 345F–346B. For discussion of procedural mishap as a ground of review, see **13.6** below.

THE CONTENT OF NATURAL JUSTICE OR FAIRNESS

11.150 A variety of interrelated and overlapping procedural elements are embraced by the duty to be fair. To what extent (as well as whether) each applies depends, as noted, on:

'the character of the decision making body, the kind of decision it has to make and the statutory or other context in which it operates'.[1]

Court procedures are not the correct model for fair administrative procedures.[2] Equally a mere departure from best practice is not *ipso facto* unfair.[3]

1   Per Lord Bridge in *Lloyd v McMahon* [1987] AC 625 at 702. See *R (Forest Heath District Council) v Electoral Commission, Boundary Committee for England* [2009] EWCA Civ 1296 at [39].
2   *R v Secretary of State for Home Department ex p Venables* [1998] AC 407 at 503C–D.
3   *R v Secretary of State for Home Department ex p Doody* [1994] 1 AC 531, 560H & 561A: see *R (Thompson) v Law Society* [2004] EWCA Civ 167 [2004] 1 WLR 2522 at [50] up to F573 60.1.20.

11.151 Professor Garner put it this way:

'The question that needs to be considered is not the very general one "What does audi alteram partem require?" but rather "what in particular situations may audi alteram partem be held to require".'[1]

1   *Administrative Law* (7th edn) at 181.

11.152 What fairness requires is as context specific as whether fairness applies. In *R v Secretary of State for Home Department ex p Doody* Lord Mustill said:[1]

'What does fairness require in the present case? My Lords, I think it unnecessary to refer by name or to quote from, any of the often-cited authorities in which the courts have explained what is essentially an intuitive judgment. They are far too well known. From them, I derive that (1) where an Act of Parliament confers an administrative power there is a presumption that it will be exercised in a manner which is fair in all the circumstances. (2) The standards of fairness are not immutable. They may change with the passage of time, both in the general and in their application to decisions of a particular type. (3) The principles of fairness are not to be applied by rote identically in every situation. What fairness demands is dependent on the context of the decision, and this is to be taken into account in all its aspects. (4) An essential feature of the context is the statute which creates the discretion, as regards both its language and the shape of the legal and administrative system within which the decision is taken. (5) Fairness will very often require that a person who may be adversely affected by the decision will have an opportunity to make representations on his own behalf either before the decision is taken with a view to producing a favourable result; or after it is taken, with a view to procuring its modification; or both. (6) Since the person affected usually cannot make worthwhile representations without knowing what factors may weigh against his interests fairness will very often require that he is informed of the gist of the case which he has to answer.

My Lords, the Secretary of State properly accepts that whatever the position may have been in the past these principles apply in their generality to prisoners, including persons serving life sentences for murder, although their particular situation and the particular statutory regime under which they are detained may require the principles to be applied in a special way. Conversely, the respondents acknowledge that it is not enough for them to persuade the court that some procedure other than the one *561 adopted by the decision-maker would be better or more fair. Rather, they must show that the procedure is actually unfair. The court must constantly bear in mind that it is to the decision maker, not the court, that Parliament has entrusted not only the making of the decision but also the choice as to how the decision is made.'

¹   [1994] 1 AC 531 at p 560.

Technical rules, self-incrimination and privilege

11.153 The technical rules of evidence applicable to civil or criminal litigation form no part of the rules of natural justice[1] nor do other technical procedural rules. In *Gee v General Medical Council,*[2] the House of Lords held that the criminal law doctrine that a count which is duplicitous is bad does not apply to charges of professional misconduct which are being brought before a professional disciplinary body: however, it had been held by Mann[3] and upheld by the Court of Appeal that particulars of misconduct should be given.[4] The privilege against self-incrimination was considered in *R (Fleurose) v Securities and Futures Authority Ltd*[5] and held inapplicable to a financial investigatory process.[6]

¹   *Mahon v Air New Zealand* [1984] AC 808. See Comment (1984) Public Law (Notes) pp 143–144; (1985) LQR 166 and *R v Deputy Industrial Injuries Comr, ex p Moore* [1965] 1 QB 456; *Repatriation Commission v Smith* (1987) 74 ALR 537 (Administrative Appeals Tribunal).
²   [1987] 2 All ER 193, [1987] 1 WLR 564.
³   [1987] 1 All ER 1204, [1986] 1 WLR 226.
⁴   [1986] 1 WLR 1247.
⁵   [2001] 2 All ER (Comm) 481.
⁶   Analogous considerations may arise in relation to privilege. For discussion of public interest immunity, *R (Mohammed) v Secretary of State for Defence)* [2012] EWHC 3454 (Admin) ACD 2013 24: confidentiality ring lawful for PII. See Chapter 14.

11.154 In *Mahon v Air New Zealand*[1] and *ex p Moore*[2] it was, however, suggested that natural justice requires that a decision is based on some evidence of probative value, but this categorisation is doubtful. That principle is directed towards the merits of the decision rather than to the appropriate procedure to be adopted, and it is consequently confusing to treat it as an element of natural justice. The same point can be made about the more recent equation of unfairness and material mistake of fact: *E v Home Secretary.*[3]

¹   [1984] AC 808.

² [1965] 1 QB 456.
³ [2004] EWCA Civ 49, [2004] QB 1044. For discussion of mistake of fact as a ground of review, see **13.16** below.

Notification of the date, time and place of the hearing

11.155 It is obviously fundamental to fairness, at least where an oral hearing is given (and fairness will often, although not necessarily, require that it should be), that the potentially affected party should be aware of when and where it is to be held. In *Wilson v Secretary of State for the Environment*¹ a local resident was not notified of a planning appeal: the decision was quashed. Where written observations suffice, the procedure must be such that a full opportunity to make those observations exists prior to the decision being made.

¹ [1988] JPL 540. But if notice is given but not received because of failure of the designated recipient to update an email account, no procedural unfairness: *R (on the application of Peng Hu Sui)* [2008] EWHC 857 (Admin).

There must be notification of the case to be met

11.156 In *Kanda v Government of the Federation of Malaya*,¹ Lord Denning said:²

'If the right to be heard is a real right, which is worth anything, it must carry with it a right in the accused man to know the case which is made against him. He must know what evidence has been given and what statements have been made affecting him; and he must be given a fair opportunity to correct or contradict them. 'The right to know and effectively challenge the opposing case has long been recognized by the common law as a fundamental feature of the judicial process.'³

¹ [1962] AC 322.
² [1962] AC 322 at 337. See now the recent national security cases referred to at **11.114** above — especially *Secretary of State for the Home Department v AF* [2009] UKHL 28; *Secretary of State for the Home Department v MB* [2007] UKHL 46 and *Anufrieva* [2003] UKHL 36 at [26].
³ *Al Rawi v Security Service* [2011] UKSC 34, [2012] 1 AC 531 at [12]–[14]. The same principle *prima facie* applies to administration proceedings. See CLJ 2012 pp 21–23 'The Right to Know the case against you in civil claims', K Hughes on *Al Rawi*. See too *R (British Sky Broadcasting Ltd) v Central Criminal Court* [2011] EWHC 3451 (Admin), [2012] QB 785 at [28]. There is no need to flag up the obvious. See *Elhogiagou v SRS* [2013] EWHC 2444 ACD 1. There was no need in disciplinary proceedings to warn solicitor of risk of suspension being imposed.

11.157 This principle of criminal procedure has been applied in the administrative law context. In *Kanda* itself the Privy Council held that the dismissal of a police officer was void where the adjudicating officer was in possession of a report of a board of inquiry which made charges of misconduct and was not disclosed to the police officer.¹

¹ Cf a memorandum recommending dismissal for misconduct should have been shown to policeman prior to his dismissal for his comment: *Khan v A-G*, CA Civil App No 177 of 1985 (1986) HK Current Law CLP 1986: 548.

11.158 Again, in *Chief Constable of the North Wales Police v Evans*,[1] a probationary police officer was unlawfully required to resign because of allegations about his private life, on which he was not invited to comment.

[1]   [1982] 3 All ER 141, [1982] 1 WLR 1155, discussed McMullen (1984) MLR 234.

11.159 In *R v Hampshire County Council, ex p K*[1] a local authority brought care proceedings in respect of a handicapped and mentally retarded girl on the basis that she had been sexually abused. But the authority refused to disclose its medical evidence to the parents: the rules, as Watkins LJ put it, allowed the local authority:

> 'not only to keep its cards face down until the first court hearing but also to be as selective as it liked as to which cards were then to be turned up'.

[1]   [1990] 2 QB 71, [1990] 2 All ER 129.

11.160 It was noted that the local authority's decision was flawed, but the hearing before the justices was vitiated by failure to give the necessary disclosure. In *R v Enfield London Borough Council, ex p T F Unwin (Roydon) Ltd*[1] it was held that a local authority acted unfairly in removing the applicant's name from a list of approved contractors without informing them of the nature of the accusations and giving them a chance to answer, notwithstanding the fact that the police had advised that disclosure of names would hamper police investigations into the allegations.

[1]   (1989) 46 BLR 1, DC.

11.161 The degree of particularity required of the 'case against' is discussed in *Lloyd v McMahon*[1] and in *Bushell v Secretary of State for the Environment*.[2] There is a sliding scale as to what must be told to party affected as to factors telling against him. At one end of the scale a condemned prisoner is entitled to all relevant documents in respect of an application for prerogative of mercy, reflecting the paramountcy of the right to life *Lew's v AG of Jamaica* 2001 2 AC 50.

[1]   [1987] AC 625 per Lord Bridge at 707.
[2]   [1981] AC 75. See *R v Governors of St Gregory's RC Aided High School, ex p M* [1995] ELR 290 (no need for committee to hear direct evidence from witnesses where excluded pupil knew nature of case: but the pupil should have been allowed to give own account of incident leading to exclusion).

11.162 In *Interbrew SA v The Competition Commission*[1], a report of the Competition Commission that the takeover of a brewing company could be expected to operate against the public interest was challenged on grounds that the procedure adopted by the Commission was unfair. Moses J said at paragraph 69 that there could be no doubt but that the Commission owed a duty of fairness; and that the content of the duty would vary from case to case, but would generally require the decision-maker to identify in advance areas which were causing him concern in reaching the decision in question. Any person who might be adversely affected by a decision should be placed in a position where he may effectively make his views known, at least as regards the matters taken into account by the Commission as the basis for the decision.

¹   [2001] EWHC 367 (Admin).

11.163 In *Abbey Mine Ltd v Coal Authority*¹ the authority had decided under statutory power to offer an underground coal mining licence and demise of coal to one bidder rather than another. The unsuccessful bidder challenged the decision on grounds of unfairness because the authority had not disclosed the successful application to the unsuccessful bidder. Laws LJ concluded at paragraph 34 that the applicant was entitled to be told the decision-makers concern against his own case, but not the details of the rival's case. He had said at paragraph 32d that the decision-making body was concerned to arrive at a result in the public interest in conformity with the statutory obligations. If every applicant saws every other's bid and was entitled to comment and challenge and criticise, the resulting prolongation and complexity of the decision-making process could scarcely be exaggerated.

¹   [2008] EWCA Civ 353.

11.164 However, in *R v City of London Corpn, ex p Matson*,¹ it was held that election of an alderman did not attract the requirement of procedural fairness where absence of positive factors as well as presence of negative factors could have been responsible for the decision. This decision is, it is submitted, anomalous. First, there is no justification for denying someone the right to develop his own case as distinct from attacking the case against him. Second, the ex post facto reasoning is impermissibly based on hindsight. Third, it is peculiar that in the same case reasons after the event were required, particularly since the right to reasons is a less well-established right than the right to make representations.

¹   [1997] 1 WLR 765.

Opportunity to respond

11.165 The other side of the coin of notification is the ability to respond.¹ There must be a fair opportunity to correct or contradict the 'case against'. Such opportunity was held to be denied in *Tudor v Ellesmere Port & Neston Borough Council*² where the assertion that the applicant for a licence was not a fit and proper person was made only in the closing speech on behalf of the authority. Moreover, if there are two charges, the person against whom they are made should have an opportunity to answer both.³ In *R v JHCST, ex p Milner*⁴ the court held that opinions (as distinct from facts) in references need not be put to an applicant who seeks an approval from a professional body.

*R (Anufrijeva) v Secretary of State for Justice.*⁵ Lord Steyn at (3)) *'in our system of law surprise is considered the enemy of justice'.*

¹   See *Kanda* (note 1, **11.156** above). See now *Interbrew SA v Competition Commission and DM* (2001) EWHC Admin 367 discussed in Robertson 'The Interbrew Case' (2002) JR 88 and in the planning context, *Sabey v Secretary of State for the Environment* [1998] 1 All ER 586. There must be adequate time given to prepare eg *R v Secretary of State for Social Services, ex p AMA* [1986] 1 WLR 1 4E–H See *Application by 'JR17' for Judicial Review, an, In the Matter of* [2010] UKSC 27 at (5); *R (Shoesmith) v Ofsted* [2011] EWCA Civ 242, [2011] PSTR 1459 at (66); *R (Reilly) v Secretary of State for Work and Pensions* [2014] AC 453;

Ware Homes Limited v Secretary of State for Communities and Local Government [2016] EWHC 103(Admin); *R (B) v Westminster Magistrates' Court* [2015] AC 1195.
2 (1987) Times, 8 May.
3 *Maradana Mosque Board of Trustees v Mahmud* [1967] 1 AC 13, [1966] 1 All ER 545, PC.
4 (1994) 21 BMLR 11.
5 [2003] UKHL 36, [2004] 1 AC 604.

11.166 However, in *Public Disclosure Commission v Isaacs*,[1] (appeal from Bahamas) it was held that the rules of natural justice did not require the Commission to give the complainant opportunity of rebutting a finding that his complaint was not substantiated.

1 [1988] 1 WLR 1043, [1989] 1 All ER 137, PC.

11.167 But the process of giving an opportunity for a fair hearing must not be endless. Having heard a party's case the decision-maker is not then obliged to disclose his proposed decision so as to allow further commentary.[1]

1 *Hoffmann la Roche v DTI* [1975] AC 295 at p 369D–E per Lord Diplock.

Duty of decision-maker to assist?

11.168 Administrative bodies are not required to make someone's case for him. Thus, in *J Wattie Canneries Ltd v Hayes*,[1] it was held that natural justice did not require the Australian Customs Service to make further enquiries as requested by the appellant about whom a complaint of unlawful conduct had been made. But an applicant for public service promotion who was not advised of her rights by a departmental representative assigned to her was held to have been denied natural justice when, in consequence of such advice, she was not afforded an opportunity of being heard before an appeal board on matters vital to her.[2]

1 (1987) 74 ALR 202.
2 *R v Nutter, ex p McCubben* [1988] 2 Qd R 581.

11.169 Thus, there may be a duty to explain the law to a person affected by a decision to enable representations to be correctly focussed: *Dennis v UKCCN*.[1] This can be contrasted with *R v Bank of England, ex p Mellstrom* where the court held that there was no general need to draw the attention of a person to adverse factors not taken into account.[2]

1 (1993) 13 BMLR 146.
2 [1995] COD 163. See, generally, *Fordham* (see note 1, **11.1** above) paragraph 608, pp 1042–1043.

Adequate time to prepare one's case in answer

11.170 Disclosure of the case against must be made in reasonable time to allow the person affected to prepare his answer. In *R v Thames Magistrates' Court, ex p Polemis*[1] the conviction of a ship's captain was quashed because he had been served with a summons at 10:30 am returnable at 7:00 pm on the same day. The justices refused to grant an adjournment beyond 4:00 pm because the ship was sailing that evening. Lord Widgery LJ said:[2]

'If the court cannot conduct a trial in accordance with the rules of natural justice before the ship sails, the justices must adjourn the matter because the rules of natural justice are paramount'.

1   [1974] 2 All ER 1219. (Discussed [1976] PL: Comment 1–2).
2   [1974] 2 All ER 1219 at 1225 For adequate notice see in the planning context *Ashley v Secretary of State for Communities and Local Government* [2012] EWCA Civ 559, (2012) JPL 1235 at 42–53.

11.171 Wrongful refusal of an adjournment may accordingly amount to a failure to give a fair hearing.[1] It will either prevent the offended party from putting his case at all, or it may result in the party having insufficient time to put his case together as he would wish. In the latter case, however, the court will provide a remedy only if it considers that the applicant has been prejudiced by the refusal.[2] Moreover, not all refusals of applications for an adjournment will result in a breach of natural justice. In *Ostreicher v Secretary of State for the Environment*[3] a religious objection to the date of an inquiry was held properly to have been disregarded.

1   *Priddle v Fisher & Sons* [1968] 3 All ER 506, [1968] 1 WLR 1478; *Rose v Humbles* [1972] 1 All ER 314, [1972] 1 WLR 33; *Ottley v Morris* [1979] 1 All ER 65.
2   *R v Panel on Take-overs and Mergers, ex p Guinness plc* [1990] 1 QB 146, [1989] 1 All ER 509.
3   [1978] 3 All ER 82, [1978] 1 WLR 811.

11.172 In *Thorne v Sevenoaks General Comrs and IRC*,[1] the Commissioners refused to adjourn a hearing against a taxpayer designed to recover substantial penalties and interest on overdue tax from him when the taxpayer was ill and unable to attend. It was held that the Commissioners were at fault in regarding the doctors inability to say when the taxpayer would be fit as sufficient to justify refusal. They should have considered whether in all circumstances a refusal would give rise to injustice to him.

1   [1989] STC 560 (Morritt J).

11.173 In *R (Mahfouz) v Professional Conduct Committees of the General Medical Council*,[1] the court held that fairness, and the appearance of fairness, required that the Committee should have granted the limited adjournment requested to enable the applicant to take judicial review proceedings to challenge a medical disciplinary committee on grounds of bias.

Although, in general, it was preferable for proceedings to be allowed to take their course and a challenge to their validity to be taken by way of an appeal, consideration had also to be given to the difficulty of organising such proceedings in a complex case, and the potential inconvenience might be reluctant to repeat the experience. On the facts of the instant case, there should have been an adjournment to allow the application to be made to the High Court. The issue had arisen on the second day of a programmed eight-day hearing; it had been treated as an important issue, requiring detailed legal argument; and there had been an apparent difference of view between the committee and their legal adviser as to the correct test. The General Medical Council might well have wanted its own counsel to attend the application and be heard, particularly on the question of a stay.

1   [2004] EWCA Civ 233, [2004] All ER (D) 114, (2004) Lloyd's Rep Med 377.

11.174 In an application for renewal of a taxi cab licence it was held that the licensing board had a duty when the applicant was unable to attend the hearing to exercise his statutory opportunity to answer the results of any inquiries they had made to consider whether in the circumstances he ought to be given a further opportunity to present his views: *Jolly v Hamilton District Council*.[1]

1   (1992) SLT 28.

Staying proceedings

11.175 There is a right to a stay of pending related proceedings when the creation of one set of proceedings may prejudice the fairness of another. The situation has arisen not infrequently where accountants are faced both with professional disciplinary proceedings and with civil claims.[1]

1   *R v Panel on Take-overs and Mergers, ex p Fayed* [1992] BCC 524 at 531 discussed Beloff and Lewis 'Bringing Accountants to Book' PL (1994) Summer p 164; Houseman 'Staying Disciplinary Proceedings' (1999) JR p 60; 'Kerr a Reply' (1999) JR 188; *R v Executive Council of JDS, ex p Land* [2002] EWHC 2086.

Decision-makers must not rely on points not argued[1]

1   Lord Denning MR notoriously infringed this principle.

11.176 In *R v Vaccine Damage Tribunal, ex p Loveday*,[2] Nolan J held that a tribunal, when it heard a statement of facts not in dispute, had a duty either to accept it or make it clear that they did not and allow the applicant to adduce further evidence. (However, mandamus did not go because it was a medical question reflecting the court's traditional abstinence from interfering with technical decisions.)

2   TLR 20.4.1985.

11.177 Further, it has been held that where a tribunal desires to proceed on the basis of some point which has not been advanced before it by a party, the person whose case is being considered by the tribunal and any other persons represented at the hearing or enquiry should be alerted to the possibility of the tribunal taking the point concerned into account, so that all those affected by the decision have the opportunity to put forward any material which might persuade the tribunal differently on the point.[1]

1   *R v Mental Health Review Tribunal, ex p Clatworthy* [1985] 3 All ER 699, per Mann J at 704, following the observations of Lord Diplock in *Mahon v Air New Zealand Ltd* [1984] AC 808 at 821. This is so whether the point is one of fact or law: *Albion Hotel (Freshwater Ltd) v Maia E Silva* (2002) IRLR 200 at p 203.

11.178 But again the process of putting a case back for comment by the potentially affected party is not endless. As Lord Diplock said in *Hoffmann-La Roche & Co AG v Secretary of State for Trade and Industry*:[1]

> 'Even in judicial proceedings in a court of law once a fair hearing has been given to the rival cases presented by the parties the rules of natural justice do not require the decision maker to disclose what he is minded to decide so that the parties may have a further opportunity of criticising his mental processes before he reaches a final decision'.

[1]   [1975] AC 295 at 369.

11.179 In a application for refugee status in Australia it was held that failure to give the applicant a 'chance to comment on the view that he (the officer) had taken of it' (ie the claim) was not a breach of natural justice.[1] And in *Finegan v General Medical Council*,[2] it was held that the court was not obliged to discuss with counsel every possible type and length of sentence it may impose. The rules of natural justice were sufficiently observed where the Professional Conduct Committee of the GMC gave counsel for the doctor opportunity to put all the mitigation he wished before the Committee.

[1]   *Sinnathamby v Minister of Immigration and Ethnic Affairs* (1986) 66 ALR 502.
[2]   [1997] 1 WLR 121.

Decision-makers must take into account material submitted

11.180 Clearly, the principles of natural justice would be frustrated if there was no duty to consider fully representations made. Accordingly, in *R v Manchester Metropolitan University, ex p Nolan*[1] an examination board's disciplinary decision taken without reference to written testimonials and medical reports was quashed where the student did not appear and was 'entirely dependent' on what was placed before the Board.

[1]   [1990] ELR 380.

Disclosure of material available to the decision-maker

11.181 This is a general rule,[1] while capable of being overridden by considerations such as public interest immunity[2] or the need to keep confidential sensitive material relating to terrorists[3], it was held that there was no breach of natural justice by non-disclosure of a working party report after the conclusion of a planning inquiry but before decision.[4] It was held that a Minister was entitled to use information about general policy and:

> 'was under no obligation to disclose to the objectors and give them an opportunity of commenting on advice, expert or otherwise which he receives from his Department'.[5]

[1]   See *Crompton v General Medical Council* [1982] 1 All ER 35, PC, discussed Jackson 'Natural Justice and Professional Discipline' (1982) LQR 532; (1981) 131 NLJ at 913–914; Natural Justice — rules of application to medical practitioners Editorial Comment; *R v Department of*

Education and Science, ex p Kumar (1982) Times, 23 November, DC; *R v Secretary of State for Health, ex p USTI* [1992] QB 353, [1992] 1 All ER 212; *Ghandi* Admin LR (1990) 657 DC.

2   *R v Chief Constable of West Midlands Police ex p Wiley* [1995] 1 AC 274.
3   *R v Secretary of State for Home Department ex p McQuillan* [1995] 4 All ER 400.
4   *Rea v Minister of Transport* (1984) 48 P & CR 239, CA, applying *Bushell v Secretary of State for the Environment* [1981] AC 75, [1980] 2 All ER 608, HL.
5   Lord Diplock in *Bushell* at 102F. *R (Edwards) v Environmental Agency* [2006] EWCA Civ 877 at paragraphs [93], [94], [103].

11.182 In *R v Assistant Metropolitan Police Comr, ex p Howell*,[1] a cab driver's licence was refused on grounds of a medical report from a doctor of complainant's choice which was not shown to complainant. It was held that there had been no breach of natural justice and that, in the circumstances, the Assistant Commissioner was entitled to take reports at face value and not obliged to go beyond them.

1   [1985] RTR 181, Mann J.

11.183 In this context, distinctions are also drawn between policy considerations, and factual matters particular to the person affected. In *R v Bristol City Council, ex p Pearce*[1] Glidewell LJ considered that had the Council refused applications for street trading licences only on policy grounds as to the acceptable number of licences there would have been no need for a hearing: *aliter* if the refusal was based on the Council's view of the merits of the applicant's case.[2]

1   (1984) 83 LGR 711.
2   *Wickremansena v Griffin* (1990) 95 WLR 187. See, however, *ex p Chahal* (November 1991, unreported) DC, Popplewell J.

11.184 There was no need to put to an applicant for permanent resident status based upon alleged strong compassionate and humanitarian grounds a letter from a department of state upon the political situation in the applicant's country of origin.

'The application of the principle (ie that it is a denial of natural justice for the relevant body to act upon material put before it which is not disclosed to the other parties) depends upon the content of what is being put before the decision-maker.'

11.185 Again, distinction was drawn between material personal to the applicant, and general policy material.[1]

1   See, also, *IWA v Consolidated & Bathurst Packaging Ltd* (1990) 1 SLR 282, a case involving the Ontario Labour Relations Board.

11.186 The Parole Board could exceptionally withhold information relevant to a prisoner's parole review both from the prisoner and his representatives and instead disclose to a special advocate appointed to represent him in their absence at a closed hearing despite the absence of statutory provision to that effect: *R (Roberts) v Parole Board*.[1]

1   [2005] UKHL 45, TLR 8.7.2005, HL. The Parole Board could rely on hearsay evidence in a case in which a discretionary life prisoner's licence had been revoked: *R (Brooks) v Parole Board* [2004] All ER (D) 142.

11.187 However arrangements under which sensitive evidence is disclosed to a special advocate but not to the person represented may be insufficient to satisfy fairness.[1]

[1]   *Secretary of State for Home Department v MB* [2007] UKHL 46, [2008] 1 AC 440 (non-derogating control orders under the Prevention of Terrorism Act 2005. *Secretary of State for Home Department v AF* [2009] UKHL 28 (unfairness where case depends solely or decisively on closed materials).

11.188 The Court of Appeal made a significant advance in compelling disclosure.[1] In that instance, of the model informing NICE's economic calculations.

[1]   *R (Eisai Ltd) v National Institute for Health and Clinical Excellence)* [2008] EWCA Civ 438.

Decision-makers must not rely on their own private inquiries

11.189 In *Fairmont Investments Ltd v Secretary of State for the Environment*,[1] a compulsory purchase order was recommended by an inspector on the basis that foundations seen on a site visit were unsafe, without disclosure to an objector that the issue was different from that canvassed at the inquiry. It was held that the decision offended against the principles of natural justice, the applicant having had no opportunity to dispute the inspector's conclusions.

[1]   [1976] 1 WLR 1255.

11.190 It has been said that members of a tribunal can use their own experience to evaluate evidence but not to support or contradict a party's case unless it was intended that they would do so.[1]

[1]   Jackson (1982) LQR, p 192 'Expertise or Evidence'. See also Smillie 'The Problem of Official Notice' [1975] PL 164.

11.191 However there may be a duty on the decision-maker to make inquiries where this would assist the potentially adversely affected person.

'The individual interests at stake may be such as to require a proactive approach by the decision-maker to obtaining relevant information for the decision. Such interests include liberty, basic sustenance and social care'.[1]

This has a kinship with the principle in (*Thameside*[2]) on the duty on the decision-maker to take reasonable steps to acquaint himself of material matters.[3]

[1]   *R (MT) v Secretary of State for the Home Department* [2008] EWHC 1788 (Admin) at [36] per Cranston J.
[2]   [1971] AC 1014.
[3]   Per Lord Diplock at p 1065.

Access to material relevant to one's case

11.192 Prima facie all relevant evidence must be disclosed, but principle can be tempered by pragmatism and public policy. A broad obligation to disclose the substance, but not the detail of the case has been held to suffice in the case of immigration officers;[1] the Monopolies and Mergers Commission[2] and inspectors appointed under the Companies Act.[3]

1   *R v Secretary of State for the Home Department, ex p Mughal* [1974] QB 313, [1973] 3 All ER 796.
2   *R v MMC, ex p Matthew Brown plc* [1987] 1 WLR 1235; see, further, *R v MMC, ex p Elders IXL Ltd* [1987] 1 All ER 463, [1987] 1 WLR 1221.
3   *Re Pergamon Press Ltd* [1971] Ch 388.

11.193 A justification for this dilution of the standards sometimes advanced is that unacceptable delays would be caused in the process of administration if the person affected was entitled to comment on all the evidence impinging upon the matter in issue. In a case involving the London Borough of Newham[1] a petition signed by 1,302 local residents supporting grant-maintained status was sent to the Secretary of State and he determined to give grant-maintained status to the school and not to close it, as the local education authority wished. It was held that on the facts of the case, natural justice did not require the Secretary of State to disclose the existence of the petition to the LEA or other evidence of support to the LEA: it did not call for a response from the LEA since it stood as evidence in its own right. However, it was noted that there could be cases where letters of support would need to be notified to the opposing side and the same may be true of petitions. It was impossible to lay down a hard and fast line.

1   See *R v Secretary of State for Education and Science, ex p Newham London Borough* [1991] COD 279.

11.194 The *MMC* and *DTI Inspector* cases were distinguished in *R v Army Board of the Defence Council, ex p Anderson*[1] where a soldier complained to the Board that he had been the victim of racial discrimination. Taylor LJ said:

> 'In each of those cases, the function of the decision-making body was towards the administrative end of the spectrum. Because of the nature of the Army Board's function pursuant to the Race Relations Act, I consider that a soldier complainant under that Act should be shown all the material seen by the Board, apart from any documents for which public interest immunity can properly be claimed. The Board is not simply making an administrative decision requiring it to consult interested parties and hear their representations. It has a duty to adjudicate on a specific complaint of breach of a statutory right. Except where public interest immunity is established. I see no reason why on such an adjudication, the Board should consider material withheld from the complainant'.

1   [1992] QB 169, [1991] 3 All ER 375. See too, *Clayton v Army Board of the Defence Council* [2014] EWHC 1651 (Admin).

11.195 The public interest in maintaining the confidentiality of sources was however held to absolve the Gaming Board from the need to disclose the identity of objectors to applicants for gaming licences.[1]

1   *R v Gaming Board for Great Britain, ex p Benaim and Khaida* [1970] 2 QB 417. See, too, *R v Joint Higher Committee in Surgical Training, ex p Milner* (1994) 21 BMLR 11.

11.196 An example of balancing fairness to the individual with a wider public interest is provided by applications for judicial review regarding local authority use of Child Protection Registers (CPRs). The applicant argues that the decision to place his/her name on the CPR as a suspected child abuser had been reached unfairly. In *R v Norfolk County Council Social Services Department, ex p M*[1] the applicant succeeded in what Waite J described as an 'exceptional and extreme' case. Another application, made by a mother (Mrs D) suspected of having caused injury to her children, was refused at first instance by Anthony Lincoln J in *R v Harrow Borough, ex p D*.[2] Mrs D appealed against the refusal of her application by the London Borough of Harrow and the Court of Appeal dismissed her appeal.[3] The local authority had given the applicant an opportunity of making written submissions to the case conference and she had been permitted to make representations to the consultant paediatrician as to how certain injuries to the children had occurred. But she was not specifically informed of the allegation that she might be a child abuser. The applicant accepted that neither the parent nor anyone else has a right to attend a case conference — even though it may well be that the conference is the most important step in the decision-making process.

[1]   [1989] 2 All ER 359.
[2]   [1989] 2 FLR 51.
[3]   [1990] 3 All ER 12.

11.197 In seeking to justify this restrictive view of the scope of judicial review, the Court of Appeal placed reliance on the fact that in case conference decision-taking the relevant considerations are not limited to those affecting the individual who might be prejudiced or organisation being criticised; rather they are the welfare of the child. The court accepted that the interests of adults vitally affected by the outcome might have to yield to the need to protect the child:

'unlike other areas of judicial review the considerations are not limited to the individual who may have been prejudiced and the tribunal or organisation being criticised. In this field, unusually, there is a third component of enormous importance, the welfare of the child who is the purpose of the entry in the register'.[1]

The compromise is obviously a somewhat uneasy one; and the decision is all the more striking because of the current tendency to assert the importance of parental involvement in the taking of decisions relating to children.[2]

[1]   [1990] 3 All ER 12, per Butler-Sloss LJ at 17. This was criticised by Professor Cretney in the Family Law section of the All England Law Report Annual Review 1991 at 149.
[2]   See the decision of the European Court of Human Rights in *R v United Kingdom* [1988] 2 FLR 445, discussed in All ER Rev 1988, pp 154–155; the DHSS Guidance 'Working Together' (1988) paragraph 5.45. See, also, Le Sueur, 'Judicial Review Child Protection Registers' Journal of Child Law Vol 2, p 21; *R v Devon County Council, ex p L* [1991] FCR 599 (dissemination of belief by social workers that person a child sex abuser not vitiated by breach of natural justice in failure to tell him before).

Oral hearings and witnesses

11.198 Hearings will normally, but not necessarily, be oral. In *Lloyd v McMahon*,[1] it was held that an auditor had acted fairly towards councillors who were surcharged by him for wilful misconduct in failing to make a valid rate in offering to entertain representations in writing to his detailed complaints. It is to be noted however that the councillors had acted as a unit, and that none had asked for a hearing. If, however, material factual evidence is in dispute then it can only be properly resolved by cross-examination and that will require an oral hearing.[2] The decision-making body cannot rely upon disputed evidence to the prejudice of the individual unless it has been raised by cross-examination.[3]

[1] [1987] AC 625, discussed (Notes) [1987] LQR 317 for an example of where consideration of written representations was held sufficient. *R (Centro) v Secretary of State for Transport* [2007] EWHC 2729 (Admin) (Secretary of State's calculation of sums payable to bus operator in respect of transport concessions. Ditto *R (on the application of Ewing) v DCA* [2006] EWHC 504 (no right to oral hearing for vexations litigant seeking leave in statue proceedings: but one could be ordered if doubt as to factual basis of allegations.

[2] See *R v Hull Prison Visitors, ex p St Germain (No 2)* [1979] 3 All ER 545, [1979] 1 WLR 1401. In contrast see *R (Foster) v Secretary of State for Justice* [2015] EWCA Civ 281.

[3] *R v Blundeston Prison Board of Visitors, ex p Fox-Taylor* [1982] 1 All ER 646. 'If . . . at a hearing to determine the facts relevant to an issue under investigation, one of the parties is, without good reason denied the opportunity of questioning the witnesses put against him, of producing a material and available witness on his side, no-one would say that the dictates of natural justice had been observed' Lord McDermott: *Protection from Power* Hamlyn Lectures: Stevens (1957) pp 83–84.

11.199 A similar approach was adopted by the court in *R v Army Board of the Defence Council, ex p Anderson*[1] where it was held that the hearing does not necessarily have to be an oral hearing in all cases. There is ample authority that decision-making bodies other than courts and bodies whose procedures are laid down by statute, are masters of their own procedure. Provided that they achieve the degree of fairness appropriate to their task it is for them to decide how they will proceed and there is no rule that fairness always requires an oral hearing. Whether an oral hearing is necessary will depend upon the subject matter and circumstances of the particular case and upon the nature of the decision to be made. It will also depend upon whether there are substantial issues of fact which cannot be satisfactorily resolved on the available written evidence.

[1] [1992] QB 169, [1991] 3 All ER 375.

11.200 Taylor LJ held that in the particular case since the Board was dealing with fundamental statutory rights it should achieve a high standard of fairness. Whilst this did not necessarily require an oral hearing it would generally do so if there were central issues of fact to be determined. Although these would not inevitably have to be resolved by cross-examination, because, for example, one version may be inherently unlikely, cross-examination would be required save where the conflict was peripheral to the central issue. Generally, therefore, the need for an oral hearing and cross-examination could go together, though the Judge did recognise the possibility of an oral hearing merely to permit the individual to make submissions.[1]

[1] Comment [1991] PL at 317–325; *'Racial Discrimination v Public Sector' Anderson's* case, A W Bradley. See also McDermott: *Protection from Power* (1957) pp 83–84. In *R (Smith) v Secretary of State for the Home Department* [2004] 3 WLR 341, the Court of Appeal held that while art 6 normally required that a criminal sentence be determined at a public hearing, exceptional circumstances might render an oral hearing unnecessary, and that as the review of tariffs of young persons detained during HM pleasure was a routine task involving the consideration of progress reports and representations which could adequately be made in writing, and since delay would undoubtedly result from the introduction of oral hearings, the

procedure of reviewing without an oral hearing was in both the public interest and the interests of the individual detainees.

11.201 In *R (Smith) v Parole Board*,[1] the Court of Appeal considered and rejected a submission that the Parole Board should have held an oral hearing. Kennedy LJ approved (at pp 434–435) the following test.

'An oral hearing should be ordered where there is a disputed issue of fact which is central to the board's assessment and which cannot fairly be resolved without hearing oral evidence'.

[1] [2003] EWCA Civ 1269, [2004] 1 WLR 121.

11.202 Furthermore, in *R (West) v Parole Board*[1] the House of Lords held that in dealing with challenges by prisoners to revocation of their release on licence, the Parole Board had a duty at common law to adopt a procedure that fairly reflected the issues at stake for both the prisoner and society, which might well require an oral hearing, eg where material facts were in dispute or were open to explanation, mitigation or contextualisation.[2]

[1] [2005] UKHL 1, [2005] 1 WLR 350. *R (on application of H) v Secretary of State for Justice*: [2008] EWHC 2590 (Admin) [2009] ACD 44. Exceptional circumstances required an oral hearing of decision that prisoner should remain a category 'A' prisoner. *Roose v Parole Board* Times Law Report 1 September 2010, where a single member panel of the Parole Board had decided on paper that a prisoner was not suitable for release, the prisoner was not entitled as of right to an oral hearing. See now *Osborn v Parole Board* [2013] UKSC 61, [2013] 3 WLR 1020.

[2] But an oral hearing is not automatic. *R (on the application of O'Connor v Parole Board* [2007] EWHC 2591 (Admin), [2008] 1 WLR 979 cf: a case decided the other way *Campbell* 2008 SLT 231. *R (Flinders) v Director of High Security* [2011] EWHC 1630 (Admin), [2012] AACD 15: oral hearing was required for categorisation of prisoner and similarly in *R (Shaffi) v Secretary of State for the Home Department HC 3113* (Admin) but contrast with *R (Downs) v Secretary of State for Justice* [2011] EWCA Civ 1422 where an oral hearing was not deemed necessary. In relation to decisions relating to prisoners see generally Re Reilly's Application for Judicial Review [2014] AC 1115; *R (Whiston) v Secretary of State for Justice* [2015] AC 176; *R (King) v Secretary of State for Justice* [2015] UKSC 54.

11.203 It has been held that a statutory board, acting in an administrative capacity, may decide for itself whether to 'hear' an application orally or in writing.[1] In *Ghandi's* case[2] it was held that no oral hearing was required of a claim before the Secretary of State by a registered medical practitioner that he had been victim of race discrimination, although the applicant was entitled to all material relevant to presentation of his case.

[1] *R v Immigration Appeal Tribunal, ex p Jones* [1988] 2 All ER 65, [1988] 1 WLR 477.

[2] (1990) Admin LR 657, DC. *R v Parole Board, ex p Mansell* (1996) Times, 21 March (Parole Board — no necessity for oral hearing: [1996] PL p 539), but now see *R (West) v Parole Board* [2005] UKHL 1, [2005] 1 WLR 350. See, also, *R (G) v Immigration Appeal Tribunal, ex p G* (2005) 2 All ER 165, the rights of asylum seekers were given adequate and proportionate protection by a statutory review process (paper only).

11.204 In *Ayanlowo v IRC*[1] the Court of Appeal held that an absence of oral hearing was not a breach of natural justice: in the case of dismissal of a probationary unestablished tax officer. In *Brighton Corpn v Parry*[2] Willis J, held that the requirements of natural justice can be complied with without an oral hearing in the case of a student rusticated from college. It is doubtful if the same decision would be reached today when there are elaborate procedures in most institutions for higher and further education to accord procedural rights to students.[3]

¹ [1975] IRLR 253.
² (1972) 70 LGR 576.
³ Higher Education Act 2004, Pt 1.

11.205 A local government officer who was minded to find against an applicant asserting priority housing needs, despite an error in the decision making process, had to give the applicant notice of the grounds on which he intended to do so and provide an opportunity for written and, if requested, oral representations.[1]

¹ *Hall v Wandsworth London* TLR 7.1.2005, CA.

11.206 Furthermore, some statutory tribunals have power to dispense with oral hearings under their rules (eg immigration adjudicators), though this discretion should not be exercised in a manner inconsistent with natural justice. Conversely, there is no rule of natural justice that a litigant in person is entitled to conduct his case in any way he wishes, in particular by submitting written pleadings without attending the hearing.[1]

¹ *Banin v MacKinlay* [1985] 1 All ER 842, CA.

11.207 In *St Peter's, Draycott, Re*[1] the Chancellor articulated a series of relevant considerations in favour of oral distinct from written representation eg the need to test evidences by cross-examination or the presence of novel or difficult points of law.

¹ [2009] 3 WLR 248 Public and Third Sector Law Reports: (consistory Court).

Cross-examination

11.208 There may be the right to examine and cross-examine witnesses (including another party but it is not absolute[1]). Where a full oral hearing is given, it has been held that a tribunal must:

(1)   consider all relevant evidence which a party wishes to submit;
(2)   inform every party of all the evidence to be taken into account, whether derived from another party or independently;
(3)   allow witnesses to be questioned;
(4)   allow comment on the evidence and argument on the whole case.[2]

¹ *R (Bonhoeffer) v General Medical Council* [2011] EWHC 1585 Admin, [2011] ACD 315, concerned disciplinary proceeding of GMC and found no absolute right to cross examination of adverse witness. Laws LJ discussed material factors both at common law and under Article 6 ECHR. See also *R (Evans) v Chief Constable of Sussex* [2011] EWCA 2329 (Admin) and *R (Bancoult) v Secretary of State for Foreign and Commonwealth Affairs* [2012] EWHC 2115 (Admin).
² *R v Deputy Industrial Injuries Comr, ex p Moore* [1965] 1 QB 456 at 490. *Bushell v Secretary of State for the Environment* [1981] AC 75 and *Osgood v Nelson* (1872) LR 5 HL 636 for criminal law: see *R v Horncastle* [2009] UKSC 14.

11.209 Failure to allow rights (3) and (4) above, which include the right of cross-examination, has led to the quashing of punishments awarded by prison visitors in *R v Hull Prison Visitors, ex p St Germain (No 2).*[1] There the visitors refused to allow prisoners to call witnesses because of the administrative inconvenience of bringing them from distant prisons to which they had been dispersed after a riot, and for other inadequate reasons. However, the visitors would have been acting fairly if they had refused cross-examination and not relied upon the disputed evidence which the prisoners wished to contest. Failure to allow cross-examination by an objector at a statutory inquiry has led to the quashing of the Secretary of State's decision.[2]

[1]   [1979] 3 All ER 545, [1979] 1 WLR 1401.
[2]   *Nicholson v Secretary of State for Energy* (1978) 76 LGR 693.

11.210 On the other hand, there must be many administrative proceedings in which formal testimony and cross-examination are inappropriate, such as where the inquiry is informal, or where the interests of a potentially large group may be affected.[1] When offering a hearing after an investigation, the Commission for Racial Equality need not produce witnesses for cross-examination.[2] The decision whether to allow it will usually be inseparable from the decision whether to have an oral hearing.[3] The object of the latter will usually be to enable witnesses to be tested in cross-examination, although it would be possible to have an oral hearing simply to hear submissions.[4]

[1]   See *Re Pergamon Press Ltd* [1971] Ch 388 at 400.
[2]   *R v CRE, ex p Cottrell and Rothon* [1980] 3 All ER 265, [1980] 1 WLR 1580.
[3]   *R v Army Board of the Defence Council, ex p Anderson* [1992] QB 169, [1991] 3 All ER 375 discussed at **11.194** and **11.199** above.
[4]   *R v Army Board of the Defence Council, ex p Anderson* [1992] QB 169, [1991] 3 All ER 375.

11.211 In *Chilton v Saga Holidays plc*[1] which concerned the Small Claims Procedure, it was held that even where the procedure was informal, the rules of natural justice required that a party shall be entitled to cross-examine the other party, even if he is unrepresented. This, however, was in a court forum. Indeed it may even be right to adjourn a hearing to enable key witnesses to attend: see *R v CICB, ex p Cobb.*[2]

[1]   [1986] 1 All ER 841.
[2]   [1995] 1 PIQR 90, [1995] COD 126.

11.212 An abbreviated right to cross-examine only was recognised in *Bushell v Secretary of State for the Environment*[1] (road inquiry). See, in particular, Lord Diplock[2] ('It would be quite fallacious to suppose that at an inquiry of this kind the only fair way of ascertaining matters of fact and expert opinion is by the oral testimony of witnesses who are subjected to cross-examination on behalf of parties who disagree with what they have said . . . '). See also, *R v London Regional Passengers Committee, ex p Brent London Borough Council.*[3] Among factors which have been taken into account to limit the right is the stress which cross-examination would impose on civilian informants in the police disciplinary context.[4]

[1]   [1981] AC 75.
[2]   [1981] AC 75 at 97.
[3]   TLR 23.5.1985.

⁴   *O'Rourke v Miller* (1985) 59 ALJR 421.

11.213 In the case of an investigative tribunal (the stewards) when the evidence against the persons charged is represented by the observations and opinions of the tribunal, the members of the tribunal are not obliged to present themselves as witnesses to give evidence and to be cross-examined.¹

¹   *Justice v South Australian Trotting Control Board* (1989) 50 SASR 613.

11.214 In *R (B) v the Secretary of State for Education and Employment and others*¹ it was held that it was not the law that in all cases of exclusion from a school on grounds of assault where the facts were in dispute that it was necessary to call witnesses of fact so as to enable the excluded pupil's representative to question them. The fundamental principle, as laid down in *R v Head Teacher and Independent Appeal Committee of Dunraven School, ex p B*,² was that the pupil, through the pupil's parent, had the right to be heard. This entitled him or her to have access to witness statements and other relevant material, but did not include the right to question those witnesses, as was made clear by the Department of Education and Employment Guidance, contained in Circular 10/99. In this case, all the relevant material had been disclosed to T's mother before the hearing.

¹   [2001] EWHC Admin 229, (2002) ACD 15.
²   [2000] ELR 156.

11.215 In *R (D) v Secretary of State for the Home Department (Inquest intervening)*¹ (it was held that investigation into suicide of prisoners. Article 2 of ECHR did not require prisoners representatives to be able to cross-examine witness: person with conduct of inquiry should decide what fairness required.

¹   [2006] EWCA Civ 143.

Legal representation

11.216 In certain circumstances there may be a right to legal representation:¹ although often the decision-maker will have a discretion whether or not to permit it.²

¹   See, generally, Zellick, 'The Right to Legal Representation' (1971) 121 NLJ at pp 390–392; 'Right to Counsel/Solicitor' (1975) 125 NLJ at 1445.
²   See generally *R (Hone) v Board of Visitors of HM Prison The Maze* [1988] AC 379 at 392, per Lord Goff; Re BP's Application for Judicial Review [2015] NICA 20.

11.217 Many people who are affected by administrative decisions do not have the training or ability to put their case in its most convincing form. This is true whether the 'hearing' is oral or in the form of written submissions. Lawyers are trained to put (or to challenge) a case: and should, therefore, be able to provide useful assistance. However, the presence of lawyers is said to make proceedings more formal and legalistic, and is not always advantageous. Such philosophy was in part responsible for the creation and growth of the system of administrative tribunals, although lawyers have made a bridgehead in that forum too. In *R v Secretary of State for the Home Department, ex p Cheblak*,¹ Lord Donaldson MR commented (obiter):²

'the judicial system did not consist simply of the courts, but included a multitude of specialist tribunals and panels each with its own remit'.

¹ [1991] 1 1 WLR 890.
² [1991] 1 WLR 890 at 906.

11.218 That made sense, specialisation making for better, cheaper and quicker decision-making. Some hearings were open to the public, others involving intimate personal matters were not. Most permitted representation by lawyers, but it was not self-evident that that was an advantage.

11.219 Members of an experienced specialist tribunal or panel adopting a 'hands-on' approach might well be able to reach the right conclusion just as often, and much more cheaply and quickly, without as with such formal representation.¹

¹ The pros and cons of lawyers in this context are succinctly analysed by Hartley and Griffith in *Government and the Law* (2nd edn) p 340, but see for the pros: *R (G) v Governors of X School* [2010] EWCA Civ 1 per Laws J at [50].

11.220 The trend in the cases dealing with legal representation appears to be to deny that fairness imposes an obligation on any decision-maker, whether a domestic body the jurisdiction of which derives from contract, or a statutory body the procedure of which is regulated by statute or by regulations, to allow the applicant to be represented, whether by a legally qualified person or not. Whether to allow representation or not is a matter within the discretion of the body (but the discretion must be exercised reasonably).¹ It is likely to be contrary to the requirements of procedural fairness to refuse a party the right to be represented when the other party has such representation.² A contract, purporting to exclude entirely any right to legal representation, would probably not be held to be contrary to public policy.³

¹ See, eg *Tait v Central Radio Taxis (Tollcross) Ltd* 1987 SLT 506. *Kulkani v Milton Keynes Hospital NHS Trust* [2008] EWHC 1861 (QB) (no unfairness in refusal of legal representation at NHS disciplinary hearing). Contrast *R (on the application of G) v X School Governor* [2009] EWCA 504 (Admin) Schoolmaster entitled to legal representation at a disciplinary hearing given seriousness of allegation (breach of trust with a pupil) and consequences of a direction under s.142 of the Education Act 2002 (prohibition from working with children in educational establishment) Article 6(1) of ECHR was relied on. Upheld in the Court of Appeal ([2010] EWCA Civ 1).
² See for example *HM (Iraq) v Secretary of State for the Home Department* [2011] EWCA Civ 1536 in an immigration context.
³ *Pett v Greyhound Racing Association Ltd* [1969] 1 QB 125; *Same v Same (No 2)* [1970] 1 QB 46 discussed McKean (1977) CLJ 205; cf *Enderby Town Football Club v FA Ltd* [1971] Ch 591; *Maynard v Osmond* [1977] QB 240, discussed McKean (1977) CLJ 205; cf a police constable charged with disciplinary offences ought to be accorded legal representation in certain circumstances, *Prendergast v Comr of Police* Grand Courts of the Cayman Islands, 17 November 1989 (Cause No 244/89) CLB April 1990 p 479); nor are regulations which excluded such a right to be held for that reason to be unreasonable and ultra vires: *Maynard v Osmond*. The Court of Appeal have ruled in favour of a right of legal representation where a serious charge was made: *Pett v Greyhound Racing Association* [1969] 1 QB 125 but that was not followed at trial: *(No 2)* [1970] 1 QB 46 (Lyell J), discussed [1968] LQR p 451; (Hepple) (1969) CLJ 13.

11.221 A right to legal representation has been denied to a prisoner appearing before a Board of Prison Visitors Disciplinary Committee charged with a breach of prison discipline, on the ground that this would interfere with the smooth and speedy administration of discipline within the closed environment of a prison.[1] But it has been held that the Board of Visitors have a discretion to allow representation by a lawyer or some other person.[2] In *R v Board of Visitors of Swansea Prison, ex p McGrath,*[3] Forbes J held that a Board of Visitors was not bound to consider whether to grant legal representation to a prisoner unless the prisoner asks for it save in exceptional and unusual cases.

[1] *Fraser v Mudge* [1975] 3 All ER 78, [1975] 1 WLR 1132; upheld in *R v Board of Visitors of HM Prison, The Maze, ex p Hone* [1988] AC 379.
[2] *R v Secretary of State for the Home Department, ex p Tarrant* [1985] QB 251, discussed Jones (1984) MLR p 587; Livingston 1988 MLR p 525.
[3] TLR 21.11.1984.

11.222 By contrast, in *Manchanda v Medical Eye Centre Association*[1] it was held to be the duty of a domestic tribunal to allow legal representation where allegations of infamous conduct were made.[2]

[1] (1986) 131 Sol Jo 47, CA. *R (S) v Knowsley NHC PCT* ([2006] EWCH 26 (Admin) at 101 (trust should have allowed legal representation before deciding upon removal from NHS list) ditto oral evidence and cross-examination (91). *R (on the application of S) v Knowsley NHS Primary Care Trust* [2006] EWHC 26 (Admin) (removal from trusts lists of medical practitioners): Witnesses to be called when dispute of fact: cross-examination allowed for effective challenge: legal representation depended on the circumstances of each case particularly the complexity of allegations and evidence. *R (on application of Turner) v Highbury Corner Magistrates Court* [2005] EWHC 2568 (Admin): (Lack of legal representation constituted *"exceptional circumstances"* to justify adjournment of an application for a closure order under the Anti-Social Behaviour Act 2003.
[2] In *R (Fleurose) v Securities and Futures Authority Ltd* [2001] 2 All ER (Comm) 481 Morison J said at paragraph 62 that he doubted very much whether the Convention rights of access to the courts can simply be transposed to access to disciplinary tribunals which are outside the court system, albeit under the ultimate supervisory jurisdiction of the courts. See **11.319** below.

11.223 Lawyers, notoriously, cost money to hire — unless prepared to act pro bono. But there is no *right* to public funds for legal representation. Legal aid is available within statutory limits and subject to statutory conditions.[1] In *Perotti v Collyer-Bristow (a firm) and other applications,*[2] the claimant, a litigant in person, made a number of applications for permission to appeal in various sets of proceedings including orders that the Court of Appeal provide him with legal representation on the application for permission to appeal 'pursuant to the common law and/or [Convention]'. It was held the court had no power to grant legal representation in legal proceedings. The decision whether or not to fund legal services in civil proceedings was a matter for the discretion of the Legal Services Commission, although if the court were to indicate that legal representation was necessary in order to ensure a fair hearing, it would be likely that public funding would be made available, if the applicant qualified on financial grounds. The obligation on the state to provide legal aid in civil cases arose, under art 6(1) of the Convention, if the fact of presenting his own case could be said to prevent a claimant from having effective access to the courts. The test was whether a court was put in such a position that it could not do justice in the case because it had no confidence in its ability to grasp the facts and principles of the matter on which it had to decide. In such a case a litigant in person would be deprived of effective access because, although he could present his case, he could not do so in a way which would enable the court to fulfil its paramount function of reaching a just decision.

1   Access to Justice Act 1999. See, as to position under ECHR. *Granger v UK* (1990) 12 EHRR 469 discussed 139 NLJ 1514, legal aid as a human right.

2   [2003] EWCA Civ 1521, [2004] 2 All ER 189. By contrast an ophthalmic optician disqualified from certain lists of medical practitioners failed in an Article 6 claim based on fact that NHS Trust was represented by counsel and she was not. The test of indispensability of legal representation was not met. (*Martin v Greater Glasgow Primary Care NHS Trust* 2009 SLT 191).

11.224 As to art 6(1) of the Convention (now part of domestic law), in *Airey v Ireland*[1] the European Court of Human Rights said:

'The Convention is intended to guarantee not rights that are theoretical or illusory but rights that are practical and effective. This is particularly so of the right of access to the courts in view of the prominent place held in a democratic society by the right to a fair trial. It must therefore be ascertained whether Mrs Airey's appearance before the High Court without the assistance of a lawyer would be effective, in the sense of whether she would be able to present her case properly and satisfactorily'.

1   (1979) 2 EHRR 305 at pp 314–315 (paragraph 24). See Beloff and Hunt, 'The Legal Aid Green Paper' EHRR 1996 at 5. See for domestic consideration of it *Pascoe v First Secretary of State*: [2006] EWHC 2356 (Admin).

11.225 That may be contrasted with the position in relation to criminal proceedings, where the right is an absolute right. An unusual product of that right is that where an accused was remanded in custody and caught up in a dispute between the Government and the Bar, he could not sue the court over a four-month extension of his time in custody when the judge adjourned the hearing because he required legal representation: *R (Danes) v Nottingham Crown Court.*[1]

1   TLR 19.1.2005.

Assistance by friend

11.226 It is not decided whether a person has a right before an administrative body or tribunal to assistance from someone other than a lawyer. However, it is likely in the modern climate that such a right, even if defensible in certain circumstances, should be reorganised. In *R v Leicester City Justices, ex p Barrow*[1] it was held that, in the context of court proceedings, fairness dictated that a party of full capacity conducting the same should be afforded all reasonable facilities to enable him to exercise his rights of audience including the assistance of a friend to give advice and take notes unless in the interest of justice and exercising its powers to maintain order and regulate its procedure, the court ordered otherwise.

1   [1991] 2 QB 260, [1991] 3 All ER 935.

11.227 In *Re O (Children)*[1] it was held (in the context of family law cases) that where litigants in person applied to use the services of an unpaid adviser to assist, such applications should be considered favourably and only for compelling reasons could they be refused: such litigants in person and *Mckenzie* friends were entitled to disclosure of court information and documents relating to cases in which they were involved.

¹   TLR 22.6.2005.

He who decides should hear

11.228 The issue is whether the hearing be given by one body, eg a committee of the deciding authority, and the decision itself by another. The general principle is that any hearing should be attended by the decision-maker.

11.229 However, where the deciding authority is a minister or central government department, it must be assumed that Parliament intends the department to operate in its usual way, so that the minister's duties may be performed by subordinate officials.¹ This is often referred to as the *Carltona* principle after *Carltona Ltd v Works Comrs.*²

¹   See *Local Government Board v Arlidge* [1915] AC 120 and, more recently, *R v Secretary of State for the Home Department, ex p Oladehinde* [1991] 1 AC 254.
²   [1943] 2 All ER 560. See also Chapter **14**.

11.230 In many circumstances, particularly where large decision-making bodies are involved, it may be impracticable for all the members concerned to be involved in all the investigative or hearing stages especially where there is a lay component. However, there may be difficulties in delegating the decision making itself. In law decisions can be delegated only where there is an express or implied power to do so, and in the absence of an express power courts are slow to imply a power to delegate a judicial determination, such as a disciplinary decision.¹ As Denning LJ pointed out in the latter case, practical problems can often be bypassed by fixing a small quorum: this will achieve much the same effect as a delegation to a small committee.

¹   See *Vine v National Dock Labour Board* [1957] AC 488 and *Barnard v National Dock Labour Board* [1953] 2 QB 18.

11.231 Moreover, in appropriate cases the court will imply that Parliament must have intended that a small quorum alone should decide the matter, even if this is not expressly provided for. Thus in *R v Race Relations Board, ex p Selvarajan*¹ the Court of Appeal held that a race relations board committee exercising powers under the Race Relations Act could make a lawful determination even though only three members of the relevant body had access to all the relevant evidence and papers. Four other members merely had a brief report which contained a recommendation to the effect that it was a 'clearly predictable case'. The court held that these four would not have exercised an independent judgment, but that it was sufficient that the quorum of three had done so. Lord Denning indicated that this was permissible for administrative functions, though not for judicial ones. As the decision deprived Mr Selvarajan of his right to go to court — since, under the legislative regime then in force the Board alone could institute civil proceedings on behalf of an alleged victim of race discrimination. This was arguably a harsh decision.

¹   [1975] 1 WLR 1686.

11.232 However, even this technique of permitting a quorum to determine the matter may not always be available. In these circumstances whilst the courts have insisted on the duly authorised body making the final determination, they have in certain circumstances permitted some delegation, prior to the determination being made, of the investigative processes. So the Privy Council has held that a dairy board, making a determination affecting milk producers, need not have all the evidence and submissions itself but could appoint a third party to do this provided there was a full report back of the evidence and submissions.[1] In that case, however, no report of the evidence was made. In another case the refusal of a shop licence was quashed because neither the applicant's submissions nor the objections to them were reported to the relevant committee.[2]

[1]   *Jeffs v New Zealand Dairy Production and Marketing Board* [1967] 1 AC 551, discussed Keith (1968) 31 MLR 87.
[2]   *R v Preston Borough Council, ex p Quietlynn Ltd* (1984) 83 LGR 308. See, also, *R v Advertising Standards Authority, ex p Insurance Service plc* (1989) 133 Sol Jo 1545.

11.233 In *Telco v Telecom*,[1] Bermuda Court of Appeal, a decision of the Regulatory Authority refusing the company's application to raise its prices was set aside when members who took the decision included some who had been absent on the occasion when the company presented its case orally and had no sufficient record of what took place. Telford Georges J said:

'The principle that a decision maker should have available for consideration all the facts and submissions put forward by a party to a dispute which is being adjudicated is crucial. The records of the Commission should make that clear. They do not. It would not be necessary that every member of the Commission should attend every meeting but full notes (though not necessarily verbatim) of the evidence taken at each meeting should have been taken and circulated'.[2]

[1]   [1991] 43 WLR 90.
[2]   See, also, for the application of this principle to arbitrators, *European Grain and Shipping Ltd v Johnston* [1983] QB 520, [1982] 3 All ER 989, discussed Jackson [1983] LQR 173.

11.234 In *Anderson*, Taylor LJ said:[1]

'There must be a proper hearing of the complaint in the sense that the Board must consider, as a single adjudicating body, all the relevant evidence and contentions before reaching its conclusions. This means, in my view, that the members of the Board must meet. It is unsatisfactory that the members should consider the papers and reach their individual conclusions in isolation and, perhaps as here, having received the concluded views of another member. Since there are ten members of the Army Board and any two can exercise the Board's powers to consider a complaint of this kind, there should be no difficulty in achieving a meeting for the purpose'.

[1]   [1992] QB 169 at 187.

11.235 This right to delegate procedural stages can apply even to judicial functions, provided the decision-maker has sufficient detailed information properly to make the relevant decision. In *Osgood v Nelson*[1] the plaintiff was removed from his office as Registrar of the Sheriff's Court of the City of London by the Court of Common Council. The court had appointed a committee of its own members to investigate the matter, and a report was submitted to the Corporation. That report contained a detailed note of the evidence. The plaintiff was given a copy of the report and allowed to make submissions with respect to it before the court itself. In these circumstances the court held that there was no improper delegation.

¹   (1872) LR 5 HL 636.

11.236 Moreover, where a body reaches its decision after consideration of a staff paper, the mere fact that the paper is defective in certain respects will not of itself justify judicial review. It will be necessary to demonstrate that any errors were in turn relied upon by the body itself and were of a kind to justify judicial review, see *R v ITC, ex p TSW Broadcasting*.¹

¹   [1996] EMLR 291, HL.

Reasons

11.237 There may be a right to a reasoned decision which takes proper account of the evidence and answers one's case.¹ It can be argued that if the right to be heard is to have any real meaning, then it must entail a duty on the part of the decision-maker to take account of the applicant's arguments in reaching his decision and to address and either to accept or reject in a reasoned way the points he makes. Furthermore, unless a party is given reasons for the decision, he is deprived of a proper chance to challenge the decision if he thinks it is wrong. It is only if reasons are given that a party can know whether a decision-maker took account of some irrelevant consideration. Statute can, of course, include or exclude a right to reasons.²

¹   See, generally, G. Richardson, 'The Duty to Give Reasons: Potential and Practice' [1986] PL 437–469. 'The Duty to Give Reasons' is recommended in a powerful analysis by the Justice/All Souls Review Administrative Justice: Some Necessary Reforms, Cʜ 3 as part, however, of the lex ferenda, not the lex lata, (for a contrary view, see Carr, 'Concerning English Administrative Law' (1940) p 123). See, also, Bridge, 'The Duty to Give Reasons for Decisions as an Aspect of Natural Justice' in *Fundamental Duties* (1980) Pergamon; also Woolf: Protection of the Public — A New Challenge (1989) pp 92–97; Allen, 'Requiring Reasons for Reasons of Fairness and Reasonableness' (1994) 53 CLJ 207; Campbell, 'The duty to give reasons in Administrative Law' [1994] PL 184; Craig, 'The Common Law, Reasons and Administrative Justice' (1994) 53 CLJ 283. 'The Legal Duty to Give Reasons' A P Le Sueur *Current Legal Problems* (1999) identified three sources of obligation to give reasons: (i) The Code of Practice on Access to Government Information; (ii) The Common Law; (iii) Provisions in Acts of Parliament and delegated legislation on reason giving (p 156). 'The Duty to give Reasons: The Openness of Decision Making' Sir Patrick Neill QC, 161. The Golden Metwand and the Crooked Cord: Essays on public law in Honour of Sir William Wade QC (ed Forsyth and Hare, 1997). Toube, 'Requiring Reasons at Common Law' 1997 JR 69. Elliott 'Has the Common Law Duty to Give Reasons Come of Age Yet?' [2011] P.L. 56. See *R v Home Secretary ex p Doody*. In *R (on the application of Secretary of State for Birmingham CC Independent Appeal Panel* [2006] EWHC 2369 it was held that appeal panel in excluding pupils ought to have explained why it preferred schools policy to ministerial guidance.

²   *R v Home Secretary, ex p Fayed* [1997] 1 All ER 228 discussing British Nationality Act 1948, s 44(2).

11.238 According to the present law, if a body is under a statutory duty to give reasons for its decisions,¹ then those reasons must satisfy a minimum standard of clarity and explanatory force, and must deal with all the substantial points which have been raised. In *Re Poyser and Mills' Arbitration*[2] Megaw J, speaking of the duty to give reasons imposed by s 12 of the Tribunals and Inquiries Act 1958, said:[3]

> 'Parliament provided that reasons shall be given, and in my view that must be read as meaning that proper, adequate reasons must be given. The reasons that are set out must be reasons which will not only be intelligible, but which deal with the substantial points that have been raised'.

[1]   See, eg Tribunals and Injuries Act 1976, s 12.
[2]   [1964] 2 QB 467.
[3]   [1964] 2 QB 467 at 478.

11.239 In *Edwin H Bradley & Sons Ltd v Secretary of State for the Environment*[1] Glidewell J said, however, that reasons could be briefly stated. In *Save Britain's Heritage v Secretary of State for the Environment*,[2] Lord Bridge elaborated:

> 'The three criteria suggested in the dictum of Megaw J are that the reason should be proper, intelligible and adequate. If the reasons given are improper they will reveal some flaw in the decision-making process which will be open to challenge on some ground other than the failure to give reasons. If the reasons given are unintelligible, this will be equivalent to giving no reasons at all. The difficulty arises in determining whether the reasons given are adequate, whether, they deal with the substantial points that have been raised or enable the reader to know what conclusion the decision-maker has reached on the principal controversial issues. What degree of particularity is required? I do not think one can safely say more in general terms than that the degree of particularity required will depend entirely on the nature of the issues falling for decision.
>
> Whatever may be the position in any other legislative context, under the planning legislation, when it comes to deciding in any particular case whether the reasons given are deficient, the question is not to be answered in vacuo. The alleged deficiency will only afford a ground for quashing the decision if the court is satisfied that the interests of the applicant have been substantially prejudiced by it. It is for the applicant to satisfy the court that the lacuna in the stated reasons is such as to raise a substantial doubt as to whether the decision was based on relevant grounds and was otherwise free from any flaw in the decision-making process which would afford a ground for quashing the decision'.[3]

[1]   [1983] JPL 43.
[2]   [1991] 2 All ER 10, HL. Discussed Forsyth (1991) CLJ pp 379–381.
[3]   See, also, *Westminster City Council v Great Portland Estates* [1985] AC 661 at 773 per Lord Scarman; *Safeways Stores plc v National Appeal Panel* (1996) SLT 235 Inner House (adequacy of reasons in planning); *Bolton Metropolitan District Council v Secretary of State for Environment* [1996] 1 All ER 184, HL (Secretary of State's reasons for planning approval had to deal with important not peripheral points): *R v CICB, ex p Cook* [1996] 2 All ER 144, CA (reasons).

11.240 The locus classicus on the adequacy of reasons in a planning context is now *South Bucks DC v Porter*.[1] Where Lord Brown said at [36]:

> 'The reasons for a decision must be intelligible and they must be adequate. They must enable the reader to understand why the matter was decided as it was and what conclusions were reached on the "principle important controversial issues", disclosing how any issue of law or fact was resolved. Reasons can be briefly stated, the degree of particularly required depending entirely on the nature of the issues falling

for decision. The reasoning must not give rise to a substantial doubt as to whether the decision-maker erred in law, for example by misunderstanding some relevant policy or some other important matter or by failing to reach a rational decision on relevant grounds. But such adverse inference will not readily be drawn. The reasons need refer only to the main issues in the dispute, not to every material consideration. They should enable disappointed developers to assess their prospects of obtaining some alternative development permission, or, as the case may be, their unsuccessful opponents to understand how the policy or approach underlying the grant of permission may impact upon future such applications. Decision letters must be read in a straightforward manner, recognising that they are addressed to parties well aware of the issues involved and the arguments advanced. A reasons challenge will only succeed if the party aggrieved can satisfy the court that he has genuinely been substantially prejudiced by the failure to provide an adequately reasoned decision.'

1   [2004] 4 All ER 775 2004 UKHL 33. See now *R (on application of Davies) v SoS for Communities and Local Government* [2008] EWHC 2223 (Admin), 2009 ACD 12. Neither the Secretary of State nor Inspector required to respond to each and every point raised by parties at inquiry: only on the principal important controversial issue: *S Bucks v DC v Porter (No.2)* [2004] UKHL 33 followed. However see *T Mobile UK v Secretary of State*: [2004] EWHC 1713 (Admin) (inspector gave inadequate reasons for dismissing appeal against refusal to install telecommunications equipment).

11.241 In *Sudesh Madan v The General Medical Council*[1] the essential principle to emerge from the cases is that adequate reasons must be given to inform the recipient of the basis for the decision that he be removed from the register. A reason expressed as a conclusion will often not disclose the underlying basis for the decision.

1   [2001] EWHC Admin 322. *Threlfall v General Optical Council* ([2004] EWHC 2683 (Admin) (following Stefan [1999] 1 WLR 12930: duty to give reasons such that both parties and appellate court can understand why disciplinary committee reached its decision).

11.242 In *Asha Foundation v the Millennium Commission* [2003] EWCA Civ 88, the primary issue was the extent of The Millennium Commission's obligation to give reasons for its decision to refuse an application for a capital grant. Lord Woolf said this:

'28.   One of the issues that the Commission had to decide in this case was the question of eligibility. If the Commission had concluded that the application fell down because it did not meet the eligibility criteria then in my judgment it would be necessary for the Commission to point out in their decision why the application did not comply with the eligibility criteria. However, when considering the question of whether or not to grant an application which is eligible, differing situations can exist. There may be situations where the Commission conclude: "We reject the application, although it is eligible, on a particular ground." If that is the basis for the decision, then the Commission must say what the particular ground is. Certainly this is the case if they choose to make a promise, as was made in this case.

29.   But there are other kinds of decisions of the Commission where a realistic assessment of what is appropriate dictates a different conclusion. When the Commission is engaged in assessing the qualities of the different application which were before them in competition with each other, the difficulties which would be involved in giving detailed reasons become clear. First, the preference for a particular application may not be same in the case of each commissioner. Secondly, in order to evaluate any reasons that are given for preferring one application or another, the full nature and detail of

both applications has to be known. If the Commission were to be required to do what Mr Gordon submits was their obligation here, the Commission would have had to set out in detail each commissioner's views in relation to each of the applications and to provide the background material to Asha so that they could assess whether those conclusions were appropriate. This would be an undue burden upon any commission. It would make their task almost impossible. It certainly would be in my judgment impracticable as a matter of good administration.'

11.243 However, if there is no statutory duty, the common law still does not impose a duty in all cases.[1] Therefore, failure to give reasons, or the giving of inadequate reasons is not, at common law, by itself necessarily a public law wrong for which remedy can be given. (It was originally thought, for example, that reasons need not be given for refusal of parole.[2])

[1]   *Public Service Board of New South Wales v Osmond* (1986) 60 ALJ 209; *Crake v Supplementary Benefits Commission* [1982] 1 All ER 498; and *Lonrho plc v Secretary of State for Trade and Industry* [1989] 2 All ER 609, HL.
[2]   See, particularly, *Payne v Lord Harris of Greenwich* [1981] 2 All ER 842, [1981] 1 WLR 754; *R v Parole Board, ex p Bradley* [1990] 3 All ER 828. See now, however, *R v Parole Board, ex p Wilson* [1992] QB 740, [1991] 2 All ER 576, CA; *R v Secretary of State for the Home Department, ex p Pegg* [1994] 1 AC 531, (discussed at [1994] PL 646) illustrating a shift in judicial approach.

11.244 Although there is no general rule of law requiring the giving of reasons, an administrative authority may be unable to show that it has acted lawfully unless it explains itself. Thus where the Act empowered licensing justices to refuse a licence on one of several specified grounds, and they refused an application without stating any ground, mandamus was granted to make them state the ground even though they were not obliged to give their reasons for it.[1] In a series of cases it has been held that statutory tribunals whose decisions are subject to appeal must give satisfactory reasons in order that the losing party may know whether he should exercise his right of appeal on a point of law,[2] although in these cases there was a statutory duty to give reasons on request. The House of Lords has indicated that if a minister fails to explain a decision satisfactorily, it may be condemned as arbitrary and unreasonable.[3] However, this conclusion cannot be reached merely because of a failure to give reasons. There must be some other evidence justifying the inference that the decision may be unlawful.[4]

[1]   *R v Sykes* (1875) 1 QBD 52.
[2]   *Norton Tool Co Ltd v Tewson* [1973] 1 All ER 183, [1973] 1 WLR 45.
[3]   *Padfield v Minister of Agriculture Fisheries and Food* [1968] AC 997 (see now *ex p Chahal* (November 1991, unreported) Popplewell J (a political asylum case).
[4]   See *Lonrho plc v Secretary of State for Trade and Industry* [1989] 2 All ER 609, [1989] 1 WLR 525. See also *R v Secretary of State for the Home Department, ex p Sinclair* [1992] Imm AR 293.

11.245 In the case of *R v Lancashire CC ex p Huddleston*, where a local authority had refused to make a discretionary grant to a student,[1] Sir John Donaldson MR said that though reasons need not be given for such refusals, the position was quite different once leave to apply for judicial review had been given. It was then the duty of the authority 'to make full and fair disclosure', 'to explain fully what has occurred and why'. Accordingly once leave for judicial review is given, the decision-maker will have to disclose his hand 'with all cards face upwards on the table';[2] but, of course, without reasons, the potential applicant may not be able to establish that he has a case. This generous view may represent aspiration, not actuality. Parker LJ[3] put the matter more cautiously:

'I would not wish it to be thought that once an applicant has obtained leave he is entitled to demand from the authority a detailed account of every step in the process of reaching the challenged decision in the hope that something will be revealed which will enable him to advance some argument which has not previously occurred to him.'

1   [1986] 2 All ER 941.
2   [1986] 2 All ER 941 at 945. See also the discussion at **19.121**.
3   [1986] 2 All ER 941 at 947.

11.246 However, the *Huddleston* principle, as articulated by Sir John Donaldson MR, was more recently reiterated in *OFT v IBA Healthcare*.[1]

1   [2004] ICR 1364 per Carnwath LJ at paragraph 106. See also Coppel. 'Access to Information in Public Law Cases' (2004) JR 266.

11.247 Moreover, there are increasingly clear signs that the courts are developing, under the camouflage of the doctrine of fairness, a duty to give reasons. In *R v Civil Service Appeal Board, ex p Cunningham*,[1] it was held that the Board, a creature of the prerogative, should give reasons for its award to the applicant of compensation for unfair dismissal from the prison service. While Lord Donaldson MR accepted that:

'there was no general rule of common law or principle of natural justice that a public law authority should always or usually give reasons for its decisions . . . fairness required that the board should give outline reasons sufficient to show what it was directing its mind to and thereby indirectly showing not whether its decision was right or wrong which was solely a matter for it, but whether its decision was lawful'.[2]

11. Lord Justice McCowan said that:

'Not only was justice not seen to have been done, but there was no way in the absence of reasons in which it could be judged whether it was in fact done'.[3]

11. Lord Justice Leggatt said:

'The subject matter of a decision or the circumstances of an adjudication might be such that natural justice would necessitate the giving of reasons'.[4]

1   [1991] 4 All ER 311.
2   [1991] 4 All ER 311 at 316–320.
3   [1991] 4 All ER 311 at 322.
4   [1991] 4 All ER 311 at 325.

11.248 Subsequent cases have confirmed that whilst there is no general duty to give reasons (although certainly judges are under a general duty to give reasons — *Flanney v Halifax Estate Agencies Ltd*[1]), the duty will, in practice, readily be implied: see *R v Secretary of State for the Home Department, ex p Doody*;[2] *R v Kensington and Chelsea LBC, ex p Grillo*;[3] and *R v City of London Corpn, ex p Matson*.[4] Reasons will be required if statute so stipulates, or if there is a significant personal right or interest at stake in which case fairness may require the giving of reasons; sometimes a right of appeal is required which impliedly assumes that reasons will be provided; or if there is prima facie evidence that the decision is legally flawed and can only be challenged once reasons are given.[5] In *R v Higher Education Funding Council, ex p Institute of Dental Surgery*[6] the court said that reasons would be required

'(1) where the subject matters was an interest so highly regarded by the law, for example, personal liberty, that fairness required that reasons at least for the particular decision be given as of right. (2) Where the decision appeared aberrant.'

[1]   [2001] 1 WLR 377 at p 381.
[2]   [1994] 1 AC 531.
[3]   [1996] 28 HLR 94.
[4]   [1997] 1 WLR 765. See too *R (on the application of Wooder v Feggetter* (2003) QB 219 (reasons had to be given for imposing treatment on mental patient).
[5]   It was held to be impermissible that a life prisoner who had been recalled to detention because of breaches of the licence releasing him on parole should be told nothing of the reasons for that recall for eight days: *R (Hirst) v Secretary of State for the Home Department* TLR 4.7.2005. However, *R v Secretary of State for Transport, ex p Richmond* LBC [1996] 8 Admin LR 486 held that 'the law does not regard the giving of reasons as a necessary corollary of voluntary consultation'.
[6]   [1994] 1 WLR 241.

11.249 That the situation is one still of ebb and flow[1] is shown by *R v HEFCE, ex p Institute of Dental Surgery*[2] itself where a dental school was held not to be entitled to be given reasons for its research rating which would be critical in determining its grant entitlement from the Government. Fairness did not require that questions of academic judgment alone required reasons for decisions; although the court issued a caveat:

'It is necessary for public decision-making bodies to appreciate that there are already some circumstances (eg where unlawful sex or race discrimination is alleged) and more may well come, in which their legal position may well depend upon their ability to account intelligibly for their decisions by explaining not simply how but why they have reached them'.[3]

[1]   There is now a vast array of cases where the question of reasons has been considered. Recent cases include the following: *R v Secretary of State for the Home Department, ex p Cheorghia-des* [1993] ALR 437 (duty to give reasons for recall to prisoner on arrest 16 years after release on licence prior to his making an application to parole board); *R v Secretary of State for Social Security, ex p Richards* [1996] COD 507; *Evans v Secretary of State for Social Services* (1993) 16 BMLR 100; *R v Housing Benefits Review Board of South Tyneside MBC, ex p Tooley* [1996] COD 143; *R v Secretary of State for the Home Department, ex p Follen* [1995] COD 169; *R v Secretary of State for the Home Department, ex p Pegg* (discussed [1994] PL p 646). There is still, however, no general duty (*R (on the application of Hassan) v Secretary of State for Trade and Industry* [2008] EWCA Civ 1311.
[2]   [1994] 1 WLR 242.
[3]   At pp 262–263.

11.250 However, it has also been held that an academic body refusing admission should give reasons for its decision (*R (Nash) v Chelsea College of Art and Design*)[1] and, in *R (Wooder) v Fegetter*,[2] doubt was cast on the *HEFCE* decision. Sedley J in particular looked forward to further developments, 'the courts have to continue the process of working out and refining on a case-by-case basis the relevant principle of fairness'.[3] This is another area where, for the interested practitioner, the latest case is usually the best.[4]

[1]   (2001) EWHC Admin, (2001) TLR 25.7.2003.

2   [2003] QB 219.
3   [2003] QB 219 at paragraph 42.
4   There may be countervailing public interest factors to the giving of reasons *R (on the application of Trucker) v DG of NCS* [2003] ICR 599 (no need to give detailed reasons for termination of police officer's secondment to NCS).

11.251 Lord Clyde indeed has stated:[1]

'There is certainly a strong argument for the view that what one sees as exceptions to the general rule may now be becoming examples of the norm and the case where reasons were not required might be taking on the appearance of exceptions . . .

. . .

The provisions of Article 6(1) of the Convention . . . will require closer attention to be paid to the duty to give reasons, at least in relation to those cases where a person's civil rights and obligations are being determined. But it is in the context of the application of that Act that any wide-reaching review of the position at common law should take place . . .

. . .

In addition, however, to that narrow approach their Lordships are also persuaded that in all cases heard by the Health Committee there will be a common law obligation to give at least some brief statement of the reasons which form the basis for their decisions . . . '.

. . .

The extent and substance of the reasons must depend upon the circumstances. They need not be elaborate nor lengthy. But they should be such as to tell the parties in broad terms why the decision was reached. In many cases . . . a very few sentences should suffice to given such explanations as is appropriate to the particular situation'.

1   *Stefan v GMC* [1997] 1 WLR 1293 at 1301–1303.

11.252 English law may still lag behind European Law. Article 253 (formerly 190) of the Treaty of Rome imposes on community organs (Parliament, Council and Commission) a duty to state reasons for their binding acts. Whilst it is not expressly stated to apply to Member States' authorities, it may apply to public authorities in such States when they apply EC law.[1] Under art 6(1) of the European Convention of Human Rights, reasons are required so as to enable the effective party to decide whether to appeal.[2]

1   See also *UNECTEF v Heylens* Case 222/86 1987 ECR 4097 and **15.125** below.
2   *Hadjiamastaussiou v Greece* A 252 (paragraph 33) (1996) 393 222/86.

11.253 The advantages of the provision of reasons have often been rehearsed. They relate to the decision-making process, in strengthening that process, in increasing the public confidence in it, and in the desirability of the disclosure of error where error exists. They relate also to the parties immediately affected by the decision, in enabling them to know the strengths and weaknesses of their respective cases and to facilitate agreement where that course is appropriate. But there are also dangers in a universal requirement for reasons in that it may impose an undesirable legality into the process when a high degree of informality is appropriate, and may add to delay and expenses.[1]

[1] *Stefan v GMC* [1997] 1 WLR 1293 at p 1300.

Right of appeal

11.254 Natural justice does not require that there should be an appeal against a determination[1] — although specific procedures, statutory or domestic, may provide for one.

[1] *Ward v Bradford Corpn* (1971) 70 LGR 27.

11.255 If a properly conducted appellate hearing is given, this will usually remedy any defects at an earlier stage. If there is no right, either statutory or contractual, to an appeal but it is voluntarily given, there is a cogent case for saying that the appeal should be capable of putting right earlier errors. This will certainly be the case if the appeal is in effect a hearing *de novo*; the complainant is then being provided with the full hearing which is in any event all he would be entitled to if judicial review proceedings were successful.

11.256 However, where there is a statutory or contractual right of appeal it can be said with some force that the complainant is entitled to a right of appeal following a proper initial hearing, and not merely to one single properly conducted hearing. This analysis led Megarry J to hold, in the case of *Leary v National Union of Vehicle Builders*,[1] which concerned the expulsion of a person from a trade union, that as a general rule a failure of natural justice at the initial hearing is not cured on appeal.

[1] [1971] Ch 34.

11.257 However, in *Calvin v Carr*,[1] the Privy Council held that, stated as a general rule, this proposition was too broad. The court suggested that there were three different categories of case:

(1)   there were those where the rules provided for a rehearing by the initial body or some enlarged form of it, in which case it was possible to treat the appeal as superseding the initial hearing;

(2)   there were those where on an examination of the hearing structure in the context of a particular activity, there was a right to a fair hearing both at the initial and appeal stages;

(3)   there was an intermediate stage where the court was able to say that the parties must be deemed to have accepted that provided 'there has been a fair result achieved by fair methods', the court should not intervene.

[1] [1980] AC 574. Discussed Elliott [1980] MLR 66. See *Modahl v British Athletics Federation (No 2)* [2001] EWCA Civ 1447, [2002] 1 WLR 1192.

11.258 In effect, the Privy Council is saying that their expectations would not be that what the rules require would be complied with, but rather that the objectives which the rules are designed to achieve should be secured. It is, however, left extremely vague how to determine whether a particular case falls into the second or third category. The particular decision in the *Leary* case was approved on the grounds that in the case of trade unions the 'movement of solidarity and dislike of the rebel, or renegade' may make it difficult for appeals to be conducted with detached impartiality. But this tendency to support the initial determination will be strong in virtually all private organisations, and singling out trade unions is unconvincing.

11.259 *Calvin v Carr* was concerned with private organisations where the right of appeal is contractual. What is the position where the right is statutory? The point was considered by the House of Lords in *Lloyd v McMahon*[1] which concerned a right of appeal against a determination of the district auditor that certain councillors should be surcharged. In fact their Lordships held that there had been no breach of natural justice by the auditor. But even if there had been, it was cured by the appeal. As Lord Templeman emphasised, however, in that case, the appeal was in the form of a rehearing, the court determining the appeal on the basis of the evidence before it. No remedy in judicial review proceedings could lead to anything more than a proper rehearing in any event. Different considerations would apply if, as a matter of construction, the appeal was limited to points of law and the court had to accept determinations of fact found by the original tribunal. Clearly in such a case, it would rarely be possible for a court to be satisfied that a proper appeal would suffice to cure a effect in the original hearing.

[1] [1987] AC 625 at 1212.

11.260 The modern tendency is to assist a process overall by the touchstone of fairness rather than to analyse into its component parts. In *Mohdal v BAT*,[1] Latham LJ said:

> 'Where an apparently sensible appeal structure has been put in place (by consent) the parties should be taken to have agreed to accept what is in the end a fair decision'.

[1] [2002] 1 WLR 1192.

THIRD PARTY INTERESTS

11.261 The decision-maker is not obliged to accord a hearing to every person potentially affected by its decision. Prima facie the person accorded such right has to be the object of the decision. For example, if a licence holder is deprived of his licence, the decision may affect many persons: his family or those with whom he traded in exploitation of his licence: but, it is submitted, it would not be considered obligatory for the decision-maker to entertain representations from such persons in advance of the decision. In a case where a local authority proposed to increase the number of taxicab licences, contrary to the interests of the existing operators, the Court of Appeal held that the authorities, though acting purely on grounds of policy, must act fairly and afford a hearing to the operators' association.[1] This apparent exception can, however, be explained on the basis that there was a legitimate expectation created by a prior undertaking.

[1] *R v Liverpool Corpn ex p Liverpool Taxi Fleet Operators' Association* [1972] 2 QB 299.

11.262 The classic statement is that of Lord Diplock in *Cheall v APEX*.[1] He stated:[2]

'Decisions that resolve disputes between the parties to them, whether by litigation or some other adversarial dispute-resolving process, often have consequences which affect persons who are not parties to the dispute; but the legal concept of natural justice has never been extended to give such persons as well as the parties themselves rights to be heard by the decision-making tribunal before the decision is reached. If natural justice required that Cheall should be entitled to be heard, there could be no stopping there; any other member of either union who thought he would be adversely affected by the decision, if it went one way or the other, would have a similar right to be heard. To claim that this is a requirement of "fair play in action" (to borrow Sach LJ's description of natural justice in *Edwards v Society of Graphical and Allied Trades* [1971] Ch 354, 382) would be little short of ludicrous'.

¹ [1983] 2 AC 180. *R (Singapore) Medical Council v GMC* [2006] EWHC 3277 (Admin) (no duty to allow SMC to make representations before discontinuing against doctor complaints which SMC had previously upheld.

² [1983] 2 AC 180 at 190, HL. Discussed [1983] LQR 337.

11.263 Another example is provided by *R v International Stock Exchange, ex p Else*,¹ where the Court of Appeal held that shareholders whose company had been suspended from official listing on the Stock Exchange had no right to make representations under either EC or domestic law.

¹ [1993] QB 534.

11.264 This classic approach was reflected by the decision of the Divisional Court in *R v LAUTRO, ex p Ross*¹ where it was held that the Life Assurance Unit Trust Regulatory Organisation, a self-regulating organisation under the Financial Services Act 1986 which regulates the carrying on of investment business, does not have to hear representations from persons affected by its disciplinary decisions before it acts to protect investors. LAUTRO's suspension order against Norwich Union was based on the activities of their representatives, the Winchester Group of whom Ross was a member: the latter, although affected directly by the order, was not its object.

¹ [1993] QB 17.

11.265 Lord Justice Mann said that:

'if the law was to imply an obligation to hear representations then it must also specify with precision to whom that obligation was owed. If persons beyond the subject of decision were included then specificity became impossible.

A regulatory body should know with precision from whom (if anyone) it had to invite or receive representations without first having to form an impugnable judgment as to who those persons were'.¹

¹ At pp 31–32.

11.266 However, in the Court of Appeal Lord Justice Glidewell added a significant gloss:

'I accept that very frequently a decision made which directly affects one person or body will also affect, indirectly, a number of other persons or bodies, and that the law does not require the decision-making body to give an opportunity to every person who may be affected however remotely by its decision to make representations before the decision is reached. Such a principle would be unworkable in practice. On the other hand, it is my opinion that when a decision-making body is called upon to reach a decision which arises out of the relationship between two persons or firms, only one of whom is directly under the control of the decision-making body and it is apparent that the decision will be likely to affect the second person adversely, then as a general proposition the decision-making body does owe some duty of fairness to that second person, which, in appropriate circumstances, may well include a duty to allow him to make representations before reaching the decision. This will particularly be the case when the adverse effect is upon the livelihood or the ability to earn of the second person or body'.[1]

[1] At p 50.

11.267 Consequently, in *R v LAUTRO, ex p Tee*,[1] it was held that elementary reasons of fairness and justice required that a person who had been served with an intervention notice, on the basis that its contents might be prejudicial to that person, should have an effective opportunity to apply for its quashing, even though that person was not the object of the notice.

[1] (1995) Admin LR 289.

11.268 In other instances, the courts have enlarged the constituency of those to whom duties of fairness were owed. Objectors to a planning development, who in law enjoy no right of appeal, if the development is approved, have won a right to review of that approval on the grounds that they were not heard before it was granted.[1] A planning authority was held in breach of its duty to act fairly in not giving rival traders an opportunity to oppose a grant of permission for an amusement area and arcade.[2]

[1] See Hinds, 'Third Party Objection to Planning Applications: An Expectation of Fairness, (1988) JPL 742.
[2] *R v Great Yarmouth Borough Council, ex p Botton Bros Arcades Ltd* (1987) 56 P & CR 99. *R v RBKC, ex p Sloop* [1992] COD 87.

11.269 On occasion a claimant can rely upon a failure by the respondent to consult a third party see e.g. *R (C) v Secretary of State for Justice*[1] where the claimant relied on Minister's failure to consult children.

[1] [2008] EWCA Civ 882.

RESULTS OF BREACH

11.270 It is now generally accepted that a determination in breach of natural justice renders a decision void[1] or a nullity (the latter perhaps being a preferable term). This was the view of the majority of the House of Lords in *Ridge v Baldwin*.[2] However, after a full analysis of that decision the Privy Council in *Durayappah v Fernando*[3] took the view that a breach merely rendered the decision voidable. This was apparently because they were of the opinion that if the decision was void it could be challenged by anyone, and they felt that only someone adversely affected by the breach should be able to set it aside. This is a non sequitur; the fact that a decision is void does not mean that it is open to challenge by anyone. Even a void decision must be treated as valid and effective until set aside by someone with a sufficient interest to invoke the court's jurisdiction.[4]

[1]   See LQR Wade 'Unlawful Administration Acts — Void or voidable' (1967) pp 499–500: (1968) LQR, p 95.
[2]   [1964] AC 40.
[3]   [1967] 2 AC 337.
[4]   This case is discussed by Eekelaar (1967) MLR 701; Akehurst (1968) MLR 138; Garner (1967) PL 88. For discussion of nullities and the void/voidable distinction, see CHAPTERS 6 and 7.

11.271 In any event, in *O'Reilly v Mackman*,[1] Lord Diplock reaffirmed that a breach of the rules of natural justice should render a decision a nullity,[2] and the remainder of their Lordships agreed with his judgment. As Lord Bridge said in *Al Medhawi*:[3]

> 'It has traditionally been thought that a tribunal which denies natural justice to one of the parties before it deprives itself of jurisdiction. Whether this view is correct or not, a breach of the rules of natural justice is certainly a sufficiently grave matter to entitle the party who complains of it to a remedy ex debito justitiae'.[4]

[1]   [1983] 2 AC 237.
[2]   [1983] 2 AC 237 at 276. See also *Anisminic Ltd v FCC* [1969] 2 AC 147.
[3]   [1990] 1 AC 876.
[4]   [1990] 1 AC 876 at p 898.

Waiver of breach

11.272 It is sometimes assumed that if a determination in breach of natural justice is a nullity, it must follow that the principles of natural justice cannot be waived. This does not follow. There is indeed authority to support the proposition that a breach of natural justice can be waived and this is certainly so in the case of the rights to an independent tribunal — the second rule of natural justice.[1] This is a sensible principle reflecting the fact that no remedy should be given to a party who has with knowledge chosen not to complain of his rights. Indeed, it can be said with some force that in these circumstances there is no breach of natural justice at all, the individual having chosen not to insist upon his right to make representations. But although the latter argument is incorrect, there is no inconsistency in saying that even if a decision may be void, no remedy will be open even to the person affected if he has chosen to waive his right. The contrary argument that public confidence in the process would be undermined is of obvious weight.[2]

[1]   Eg *R v Comptroller-General of Patents, ex p Parke, Davies & Co* [1953] 1 All ER 862, and *R v BBC ex p Lavelle* [1983] 1 WLR 23, 39.
[2]   For general discussion of waiver, see **18.65**. Note, however, that in order to waive any right to an oral hearing the individual in question had to act in a way that clearly and unequivocally indicated that he was abandoning any such right. In *R (Smith) v Secretary of State for the Home Department* [2004] 3 WLR 341, although the issue of waiver did not strictly arise, the Court of Appeal addressed it. The claimant's original written submissions had sought an oral hearing. Eleven months later his solicitors wrote again expressing concern that there had been no decision for nearly a year and seeking a decision imminently. Six weeks later they were sent a large amount of material including prison reports and victims' family statements, accompanied by a request for comments within two months. The solicitors duly replied sending their comments. Differing from the Divisional Court, the Court of Appeal held that correspondence from the solicitors, given that the Lord Chief Justice had made it plain that he

was only seeking submissions in writing, did not amount to a clear and unequivocal waiver of their request for an oral hearing.

Remedies for breach

Remedies are discussed generally in Chapters 16 and 17.

11.273 An act or decision past or prospective, tainted by a breach of natural justice may be restrained by prohibition or an injunction, or set aside by a quashing order or, where legislation so provides, a statutory application to quash. Moreover, a declaration may be awarded that the act or decision is null and void.[1] In an appropriate case, a mandatory order unaccompanied by other relief may be directed to the decision to accord due process to the victim of breach. It may be possible to seek a re-hearing. It cannot be emphasised too strongly that after due process has been accorded, the adverse decision may recur — a matter of which litigants need to be reminded. If the act has involved an encroachment on private rights, a person aggrieved by it may be entitled to recover damages for trespass or another civil wrong. Where the breach is committed in the private sphere, the remedy will be a declaration that the decision challenged was unlawful coupled with an injunction to restrain the body concerned from acting upon it or damages. In *R v Lord Chancellor's Department, ex p Nangle*[2] Stuart Smith LJ said:[3]

'If the applicant can establish a breach of contract by failure to comply with the express or implied provisions of the disciplinary code which has resulted in loss, he can sue for damages for breach of contract'.

[1] In *R v Panel on Take-overs and Mergers, ex p Datafin plc* [1987] QB 815 when Sir John Donaldson MR suggested that declarations might be granted in respect of certain errors of the Take-over Panel, he reserved certiorari and mandamus for breaches of natural justice (p 842).
[2] [1991] ICR 743.
[3] [1991] ICR 743 at 752.

11.274 However damages will not be awarded for breach of national justice leading to economical loss where the breach was not itself tortuous.[1]

[1] *Trent Strategic Health Authority v Jain* [2009] UKHL4. Closure of 4 nursing homes. See criticism by Sir Lewis Blom-Cooper QC Public Law April 2009 195–198. See also Michael Fordham QC, Public Law January 2009 1–4 and Tom Croxford at p 70 commenting on Law Commission's Consultation Pager No 187. Administrative Public Bodies and the Citizen. See also Baroness Hale's Neill Lecture at All Souls 2011.

Discretion

Restrictions on remedies are discussed generally in Chapter 18.

11.275 The question arises in what circumstances, apart from waiver,[1] the courts might refuse relief to applicants where a breach of natural justice is established. Apart from general circumstances where relief might be refused in any judicial review case, eg delay,[2] failure to exhaust remedies, or lack of standing (see **11.273** above), or countervailing public interest,[3] there are two areas in particular where the courts have in their discretion refused a remedy, which are of particular significance in the field of natural justice. The first is where the conduct of the applicant is considered so unworthy as to preclude the right to relief. The second, which is often related, is where the court considers that in any event a hearing would have made no difference.

¹ *Fullbrook v Berkshire Magistrates' Court Committee* (1970) 69 LGR 75.
² Eg *R v Aston University Senate, ex p Roffey* [1969] 2 QB 538; *Heaton v Traffic Comr* (1988) SLT 82.
³ *Chief Constable of North Wales Police v Evans* [1982] 1 WLR 1155, discussed McMullen (1988) MLR 329.

11.276 As to the former, a number of authorities demonstrate the reluctance of the court to grant a remedy to the undeserving. In *ex p Fry*¹ a challenge to disciplinary action taken against a firm was refused on this ground. Even more strikingly, in *Cinnamond v British Airports Authority*² the Court of Appeal held that the conduct of the appellants (mini-cab drivers who were banned from using Heathrow allegedly in breach of natural justice) was such that with a record of past convictions they did not even have a legitimate expectation of a hearing at all. The concept of legitimate expectation was thus used negatively to deny a hearing that would otherwise occur. In this kind of case the conduct of the applicant does not merely impinge on the remedy which the court will give; it even determines whether the duty to comply with natural justice exists or not. These decisions permit merits to intrude upon procedural safeguards and are not justified.

¹ [1954] 1 WLR 730, discussed 1954 CLJ 154, 1954 MLR 375.
² [1980] 1 WLR 582, discussed Ward 1981 MLR 103, 1980 LQR 497 (Notes). Sec also *R v CICB, ex p Aston* [1994] COD 500.

11.277 A similar criticism can be mounted against cases in which the courts have held that no remedy should be granted unless a hearing might have made a difference. Lord Wilberforce adopted this approach in *Malloch v Aberdeen Corpn*¹ and it was likewise the reason that relief was refused to a student banned from the campus for sunbathing in the nude in *Glynn v Keele University*,² notwithstanding that the court accepted that natural justice had been denied. Where a decision is made for reasons wholly unconnected with the applicant, then this approach may be justified. In such a case there is really no breach of natural justice even though the applicant is adversely affected by the decision. Thus in *Cheall v APEX*³ a trade union member was expelled from his union because this was required by the Bridlington Agreement which regulates the poaching of members between unions. The expulsion was required automatically under the union's rules once a determination of the TUC Disputes' Committee, acting in pursuance of the agreement, had required this. In this exceptional case where there was no discretion and the conduct of the member was not in issue, it is submitted that the House of Lords was correct to say that it would have been a cruel deception to have afforded a hearing. However, where it might make a difference there is ample authority to support the principle that the courts should resist the temptation to speculate as to the outcome if a hearing had been given.⁴

¹ [1971] 1 WLR 1578, 1595 (discussed Farmer 1972 CLJ 30).
² [1971] 1 WLR 487.
³ [1983] 2 AC 180.
⁴ For example, *General Medical Council v Spackman* [1943] AC 627, 644; *R v Hull Prison Board of Visitors, ex p St Germain (No 2)* [1979] 1 WLR 1401, 1411–1412; and *John v Rees* [1970] Ch 345, where Megarry J delivered his oft quoted utterance that the path of the law is

strewn with unanswerable charges which were subsequently answered. See, generally, Clark, 'Natural Justice; Substance or Shadow' [1975] PL 27. However, note *Transkei Public Servants Association v Government of Republic of South Africa* [1996] 1 LRC 118 in which it was held that the association of public servants was not entitled to be heard by a Commission conducting an inquiry into the terms and conditions of employment in the public service, in the light of the narrowness of the enquiry and the fact that 'there was quite simply nothing of relevance that the applicant could have said in the course of the inquiry' that had not been said by others (at 128).

11.278 In *R v Chief Constable of the Thames Valley Police, ex p Cotton,*[1] Bingham LJ gave six reasons why the courts ought not to refuse relief in these circumstances:

'While cases may no doubt arise in which it can properly be held that denying the subject of a decision an adequate opportunity to put his case is not in all the circumstances unfair, I would expect these cases to be of great rarity. There are a number of reasons for this:

(1)   Unless the subject of the decision has had an opportunity to put his case it may not be easy to know what case he could or would have put if he had had the chance.

(2)   As memorably pointed out by Megarry J in *John v Rees,*[2] experience shows that that which is confidently expected is by no means always that which happens.

(3)   It is generally desirable that decision-makers should be reasonably receptive to argument, and it would therefore be unfortunate if the complainant's position became weaker as the decision-maker's mind became more closed.

(4)   In considering whether the complainant's representations would have made any difference to the outcome the court may unconsciously stray from its proper province of reviewing the propriety of the decision-making process into the forbidden territory of evaluating the substantial merits of a decision.

(5)   This is a field in which appearances are generally thought to matter.

(6)   Where a decision-maker is under a duty to act fairly the subject of the decision may properly be said to have a right to be heard, and rights are not to be lightly denied'.

In particular it is insufficient for the decision-maker to show that the decision would *'probably have been the same'.*[3]

[1]   [1990] IRLR 344. See, also, *R v Secretary of State for Home Department* [2003] 3 WLR 1169, HL at paragraph 52 (Lord Steyn).
[2]   [1970] Ch 345 at p 402.
[3]   *R (Smith) v North Eastern Derbyshire Primary Care Trust* [2006] EWCA Civ 1291, [2006] 1 WLR 3315.

11.279 The importance of 'appearances' as Bingham LJ described them, was also strongly emphasised by Lord Widgery in *R v Thames Magistrates' Court, ex p Polemis*[1] who glossed the classic dictum to the effect that it is 'absolutely basic to our system that justice must not only be done but must manifestly be seen to be done'. This has particular force where the decision-maker is in the public as opposed to the private sphere since appearances will affect the confidence in the decision-making system itself.

[1]   [1974] 1 WLR 1371.

11.280 Sometimes, of course, statute itself requires substantial compliance only[1] which focuses the court's attention on results, not form.

[1]   *Lake District Special Planning Board v Secretary of State for the Environment* (1975) 119 Sol Jo 187; *George v Secretary of State for the Environment* (1979) 38 P & CR 609.

SPECIAL SITUATIONS

Licences[1]

[1]   See Street, 'Justice in the Welfare State' Stevens (2nd edn, 1985) Hamlyn Lectures; Williams 'Control by Licensing' (1967) CLP 81.

11.281 Regulation of licence, issued for various reasons by both central and local authorities, is an increasingly significant phenomenon.[2] The ability to obtain and retain a licence may be fundamental in particular to enable a person fully to exercise his livelihood: this applies even to temporary licences.[3] As Megarry J's judgment in *McInnes v Onslow Fane*[4] demonstrates, the refusal or forfeiture of a licence may involve an interference with either rights or interests or expectations, depending upon the circumstances. There is little doubt that the revocation of a licence will almost always involve the full protection of natural justice.[5] (Indeed, in *R v Barnsley Metropolitan Borough Council, ex p Hook*,[6] the Court of Appeal was even willing to upset a decision to revoke a licence on the grounds that the sanction was wholly disproportionate to the offence, ie unfair in the substantive rather than the procedural sense only).

[2]   See Beloff and Mountfield 'Due Process in Licencing Applications, *Commercial Lawyer* Issue 13 (1997) p 71.
[3]   *Southampton Port Health Authority v Seahawk Marine Foods* [2002] EHLR 15 (the grant of a licence to where a vessel for Toothfishing in SGSSI waters was held to amount extremely valuable commodity thus generating the need for at least minimum standards of fairness). *R v Wear Valley District Council, ex p Binks* [1985] 2 All ER 699, discussed (Jackson) 1986 LQR 524; cf *William Hill (Scotland) Ltd v Kyle and Carrick District Licensing Board* 1991 SLT 559.
[4]   [1978] 1 WLR 1520.
[5]   See *Borroughs and the A-G of Katwando* (revocation of fire arms licence, CA (Trinidad and Tobago 1985; (1986) CLB 344).
[6]   [1976] 1 WLR 1052.

11.282 Similarly, as Megary J pointed out in *McInnes* where the licence is for a fixed term and an application is made for renewal, the individual will generally have a legitimate expectation that the licence will be reissued unless there is good reason not to do so, and the procedural safeguards should be akin to those which operate in the case of forfeiture. Indeed, in reality the effect is the same as forfeiture.[1]

[1]   [1978] 1 WLR 1520 at p 1530.

11.283 However, the same judge held that when an application was being made, the only duty on the licensor would be not to refuse the application for a capricious or arbitrary reason. This effectively denies any procedural safeguards at all, and it is difficult to justify the principle or to support with authority. It should, as already noted, be treated as obsolete.[1]

[1]   See Wade at 536–539. *R v Huntingdon District Council, ex p Cowan* [1984] 1 WLR 501.

11.284 De Smith[1] has further pointed out that this schematic analysis would, if strictly applied, lead to anomalies and injustice. While there are, in general, practical reasons why a hearing cannot be given to every applicant for a licence, but that situations can be imagined where the unfairness of the summary refusal of a licence, or the summary award of a licence to a competitor, will be so manifestly unfair that it would be right for a court to hold that the deciding body is under a duty to give the applicant an opportunity to make representations (whether in writing or orally) and of being appraised of all information on which the decision is founded. Any licence (or franchise) can confer considerable economic benefit: indeed may be a *sine qua non* of ability to pursue a business, trade or profession.

[1]   Paragraphs 7–014—7–023.

11.285 Slade J[1] has held that where a particular certificate was necessary to enable a social worker successfully to advance in his career, he should not be refused the opportunity to do the relevant course without an interview.

[1]   *Central Council for Education and Training in Social Work v Edwards* TLR 5.5.1978.

11.286 Again, in *R v Gaming Board for Great Britain, ex p Benaim and Khaida*,[1] the Court of Appeal accepted that the Gaming Board should indicate to a potential applicant for a gaming licence the gist of any matters they considered relevant to the question whether he should be certified as fit to hold such a licence, and give him the opportunity to comment on the impressions they had formed. But they did not have to disclose the source of their information because that could discourage potential informants coming forward, which would be against the public interest, nor did they have to give any reasons for their decisions. Where significant financial interests as well as the standing and reputation of individuals may be at stake (since the refusal to grant a licence may well cast doubts upon a person's fitness for the licence), the court was surely right to require compliance with basic procedural safeguards. In *Cinnamond v British Airports Authority*[2] Lord Denning MR said that there is no right to a hearing on the grant of industrial development certificates (now discontinued) or the award of television programme contracts, since there was no legitimate expectation of such. But in 1991 it appears to have been accepted that the allocation by the ITC of television franchises was susceptible to judicial review on, inter alia, grounds of unfairness.[3]

[1]   [1970] 2 QB 417 Discussed Birtles [1973] MLR 559.
[2]   [1980] 1 WLR 582 at 590.
[3]   See *R v ITC, ex p TSW* (1992) Times, 7 February, CA; affd [1996] EMLR 291, HL: see 'Jones Broadcasting Licences and Judicial Review' [1990] PL 156–161.

Discipline

11.287 Formerly the courts showed a reluctance to interfere in the disciplinary functions exercised by employers operating in an area where discipline was considered important for the efficiency of the operation, such as the police force and the fire service. Before *Ridge v Baldwin*, the courts held that natural justice was inapplicable in these areas on the grounds that such protection was afforded only to the exercise of judicial or quasi-judicial functions and discipline was neither.[1] In the former case which concerned the withdrawal of a taxi driver's licence on grounds of unfitness, Lord Goddard LCJ said that the Commissioner:

'was exercising what I may call a disciplinary authority, and where a person, whether he is a military officer, a police officer, or any other person whose duty it is to act in matters of discipline, is exercising disciplinary powers, it is most undesirable in my opinion that he should be fettered by threat of orders of *certiorari* and so forth, because that interferes with the free and proper exercise of the disciplinary powers which he has'.[2]

[1] See *R v Metropolitan Police Comr, ex p Parker* [1953] 1 WLR 1150 at 1155 and *ex p Fry* [1954] 1 WLR 730.
[2] See, also, Wade [1970] LQR.

11.288 Again, in the case of prisoners it was thought that natural justice would be inapplicable not only to the exercise of disciplinary powers by prison governors but also to such exercise by prison visitors. As to the former, Lord Denning expressed the view in *Becker v Home Office*[1] that 'if the courts were to entertain actions by disgruntled prisoners the life of the prison governor would be made intolerable'.

[1] [1972] 2 QB 407, 418.

11.289 Notwithstanding these dire prognostications, the courts have now made the disciplinary functions of both prison visitors and the prison governor subject to natural justice.[1] Given the gravity of the sanction imposed, and the severity of the sentences that may be imposed, the contrary view was quite unsustainable. As Shaw LJ indicated in the *St Germain* case, the rights of the citizen, however circumscribed by the penal process, ought always to be the concern of the courts save where Parliament had clearly indicated otherwise.[2]

[1] See *R v Board of Visitors of Hull Prison, ex p St Germain* [1979] QB 425, discussed Casey (1979) MLR 467, Jackson [1978] LQR 497: see Richardson. 'The House of Lords and Prison Discipline' [1985] PL 137 and *Leech v Deputy Governor of Parkhurst Prison* [1988] AC 533, discussed Grubb and Pearl (1988) CLJ 165. See, generally, Livingstone, Owen, McDonald *Prison Law* (3rd edn) Cн 9 'Prison Discipline'.
[2] See *Raymond v Honey* [1983] 1 AC 1; *R v Secretary of State for the Home Department ex p Wynne* [1992] QB 406, [1992] 2 All ER 301, CA: see, on prisoners' rights. Tetterborn [1980] PL pp 74–89; Zellick [1981] PL 435–442; [1990] PL 504–507, 1983 133 NLJ at 703–707.

11.290 *R (Gleaves) v Secretary of State for Home Department*[1] held that Prison Governors engaged in a disciplinary inquiry should set out in writing the essence of the case, the form of the inquiry, and, if the prisoner was found guilty, the reason why his defence was rejected, because the liberty of the prisoner was at issue. In *R (P) v Secretary of State for the Home Department*[2] it was held that a 17-year-old girl who was a remand prisoner in the young offender institution section of a prison had a right to make representations as to the making of a segregation order against her prior to the making of an order.[3] In serious cases legal representation before the Governor may be required: *Ezeh v UK*.[4]

[1] TLR 15.11.2004 at 455.
[2] TLR 21.1.2005.
[3] It is useful to note how a culture of procedural rights has invaded even unpromising territory, see Ghandi. 'Natural Justice in Prison' (1985) MLR 96–102.

⁴   [2004] 39 EHRR 1 15 BHRC 145.

11.291   The reluctance to interfere with the disciplinary decisions of universities was made manifest in a different way.[1] In that area the courts accepted that the principles of natural justice or fairness applied to such disciplinary actions, but would frequently find some reason not to grant relief whether because of undue delay[2] or on the grounds that a hearing would have made no difference.[3] The Higher Education Act 2004 has abolished the disciplinary jurisdiction of the university visitor[4] (who was subject to natural justice duties. *R v University of Hull, ex p Page*[5]) and provided in lieu an office of Independent Adjudication.[6]

1   See, generally, K Shrinivas Rao. 'University Discipline and the Principles of Natural Justice': An Indian View [1976] PL, pp 7–14.
2   *R v Aston University Senate, ex p Roffey* [1969] 2 QB 538, discussed Grunfeld 1969 MLR 680.
3   As in *Glynn v Keele University* [1971] 1 WLR 487 where the student was fined and excluded from the university campus for sunbathing in the nude, discussed Wade (1971) LQR 320: 'University Discipline and the Principles of Natural Justice, an Indian view' [1976] PL 7–14 Comment; and Wade 'Students Rights and Remedies' (1974) LQR 157. See also *Herring v Templeman* [1973] 3 All ER 569; *R v Oxford University, ex p Bolchover* TLR 7.11.1990.
4   Part I.
5   [1993] AC 682.
6   See Beloff and Bamforth, 'The University Visitor Academic Judgment and the ECHR' (2002) JR 221.

11.292   Disciplinary proceedings in the professions have attracted aspects of the rules of natural justice along with certain of the protections afforded by art 6 of the ECHR.[1]

1   See the discussion of suspension at **11.136** et seq and *R (Fleurose) v Securities and Futures Authority Ltd* [2001] 2 All ER (Comm) 481.

Trade unions

11.293   In contrast to these cases, now to be regarded as anachronistic, the courts have tended to take a very strict view of the need to comply with natural justice where trade unions were disciplining their members even where the 'closed shop' did not operate so their livelihood was not at stake.[1] Unlike the student and the prisoner, the union member has always been perceived as a person requiring the court's protection from the exercise of power by those in authority over him. But again, the precise requirements of fairness can be altered by particular circumstance.

1   See *Albert v Sullivan* [1952] 1 KR 189; eg *Annamunthodo v Oilfield Workers Trade Union* [1961] AC 945; *Lawlor v Union of Post Office Workers* [1965] Ch 712; and *Leary v National Union of Vehicle Builders* [1971] Ch 34; *Edwards v Sogat* [1971] Ch 354; *Breen v AEU* [1971] 2 QB 175.

11.294   In *Higgs v Northern Regional Health Authority*[1] Hutchison J held that where a hospital authority relied on extensive public enquiry before instituting disciplinary procedures, it was not required by rules of natural justice to hold a further enquiry into the employee's professional conduct.

[1]   [1989] 1 Med LR 1.

Aliens/Immigrants

11.295 Matters of immigration and deportation are subject to relatively detailed statutory procedures found principally in the Immigration Act 1971 and its successors.[1] In particular, these confer rights of appeal in many situations where a person is refused entry to, or is to be deported from, the United Kingdom. At common law the courts were traditionally reluctant to provide procedural safeguards for aliens; decisions relating to them were seen as executive and not judicial and therefore not subject to judicial review.[2] In *R v Governor of Brixton Prison, ex p Soblen*,[3] this approach was slightly modified, Lord Denning indicating that whilst no hearing was required before the deportation order was made, there may be circumstances where it should be accorded after the order was made but before it was executed. A further modification was seen in *Schmidt v Secretary of State for Home Affairs*.[4] There the Court of Appeal held that scientology students who had been given leave to study in Britain for a limited time had no right to a hearing when a request for an extension of their stay was refused, but the court indicated that such a hearing would have been required if the students had been deported before the time had expired: they would have had a legitimate expectation of being permitted to remain for that duration.

[1]   McDonald & Blake *Immigration Law* (5th edn) Butterworths.
[2]   See *R v Leman Street Police Station Inspector, ex p Venicoff* [1920] 3 KB 72 where the court held that the Secretary of State was not obliged to give a hearing to an individual being deported where his deportation was deemed to be conducive to the public good.
[3]   [1963] 2 QB 243.
[4]   [1969] 2 Ch 149, discussed Hopkins [1970] CLJ 9.

11.296 Nowadays the courts emphasise more simply the need for fairness in cases of this kind.[1] A general obligation for immigration officers to treat immigrants fairly, which involves putting any suspicions to the immigrant and giving him a real opportunity to deal with them, was laid down in the seminal case of *Re HK*.[2] In all cases the would-be entrant should be given a 'real opportunity' of satisfying the immigration officer that he or she should be admitted, and where immigration officers' suspicions are aroused they must make them known to the immigrant and give him or her a chance to explain.[3]

[1]   Macdonald and Blake *Immigration Law* (9th revised edn) Butterworths. Statute has provided some protection by way of appellate procedures: Immigration Act 1971, Pt II; Asylum and Immigration Act 1996; Nationality, Asylum and Immigration Act 2002; Immigration, Asylum and Nationality Act 2006. For protections of EU Law, see *Van Duyn v Home Office* (1975) 1 CM ER 1.
[2]   [1967] 2 QB 617.
[3]   *R v Secretary of State for the Home Department, ex p Mughal* [1974] QB 313. See also *R v Secretary of State, ex p Moon* [1996] Imm AR 477. Further, *R v Secretary of State for the Home Department, ex p Mowla* [1992] 1 WLR 70 (legitimate expectation and passport stamps).

11.297 In refugee cases, the Court of Appeal has, on more than one occasion, stressed that only the highest standards of fairness will suffice. In *Thirukumar* the court spoke of the opportunity to make representations and to attend interview. Bingham LJ said he was persuaded:[1]

'(i) that if an opportunity to make representations is to be meaningful the mind of the applicant must be directed to the considerations which will, as matters stand, defeat his application; and

(ii) that if an opportunity to supplement previous answers is to be meaningful the applicant must be reminded of or (preferably) shown the answers which he gave before; this is most obviously so where . . . a year had elapsed since the previous interview, but given the difficulties which can occur when questions are asked through an interpreter and the strain to which the applicant may well be subject at the time of the first interview I think it necessary even where the interval has been much shorter'.

---

[1] *Secretary of State for the Home Department v Thirukumar* [1989] Imm AR 270, CA; *Gaima v Secretary of State for the Home Department* [1989] Imm AR 205, CA. For natural justice in proceedings before appellate authorities, see Symes and Jorro *Asylum Law and Practice* London (2003) pp 675–83. *B (on the application of L) v Secretary of State for The Home Department* [2003] 1 All ER 1062, p 30; *R v Secretary of State for Home Office, ex p Awuku* (1987) TLR 3.11.1987.

11.298 In *R (Q) v Secretary of State for the Home Department*,[1] a system whereby support was withdrawn from asylum seekers who did not claim asylum as soon as reasonably practicable on arrival in UK was held to be unfair in so far as interviews were carried out without any clear statement as to its purpose: 'Fairness requires that the purpose of the interview should be more clearly explained to the Applicant'. Furthermore, the decision-maker was usually different from the interviewer so could not judge his credibility. The applicant should be told the case against him: 'the fact that the burden of proof rests on the applicant makes it more, not less, necessary'. In *R (Dirshe) v Secretary of State for the Home Department*,[2] it was held that a refusal to allow asylum seekers' solicitors to tape record an interview with immigration officers was procedurally unfair given the importance of the decision that had to be made.[3] Exceptionally, the doctrine of legitimate expectation may also assist an immigrant, as in *Oloniluyi v Secretary of State for the Home Department*[4] where an immigrant was assured that she would have no difficulty returning to the United Kingdom during the currency of a limited leave, and she was subsequently refused re-entry in breach of that assurance. The Court of Appeal held that this infringed her legitimate expectation and was unfair. The issue of what natural justice requires in the case of persons asserting a claim to refugee status was thoroughly explored in *Singh v Minister of Employment and Immigration*.[5] Immigration removal policy was held unlawful because insufficient time was allowed to seek legal advice.[6] Outline reasons to be given for decision to remove someone under Immigration and Asylum Act 1999, s 10.[7] SIAC could make order of non-disclosure prohibiting Secretary of State from revealing evidence or identity of witness called by appellant in a closed SIAC hearing.[8] Applicant for naturalisation entitled to be informed of matters adverse to his application.[9]

---

[1] [2003] EWCA Civ 364.
[2] [2005] EWCA Civ 421, [2005] 1 WLR 2685, CA.
[3] Contrast with the existing provisions relating to the recording of interviews in police stations contained in the Police and Criminal Evidence Act 1984, s 60.
[4] [1989] Imm AR 135.

[5] [1985] 1 SCR 177 (Canada). See further, *Gunaleela v Minister for Immigration and Ethnic Affairs* (1987) 74 ALR 252 doubting whether a decision-maker was subject to the rules of natural justice at all in such a situation.

[6] *R (Medical Justice) v Secretary of State for the Home Department* [2011] EWCR Civ 1710 at [24].

[7] *W (Algeria) v Secretary of State for the Home Department* [2012] UKSC 8, [2012] 2 All ER 699

[8] LQR 2014 511, 'The lesser of two evils;' Haley Hooper.

[9] *R (Thamby (Chockalingam)) v Secretary of State for Home Department* [2011] EWHC 1763 (Admin) 68–71. See too*R (Thapa) v Secretary of State for Home Department* [2014] EWHC 659 (Admin).

11.299 In Australia, standards in this area appear by contrast to have been somewhat diluted.

11.300 In *Daguio v Minister for Immigration and Ethnic Affairs*[1] it was held that it was not necessary to receive oral submissions before determining whether a non-citizen should be granted an entry permit.

[1] (1986) 71 ALR 173. See further. *Gunaleela v Minister for Immigration and Ethnic Affairs* (1987) 74 ALR 252 doubting whether a decision-maker was subject to the rules of natural justice at all in such a situation.

11.301 A proposal to prevent appellate immigration bodies from having their decision judicially reviewed even for breaches of natural justice was abandoned, thereby preventing a collision of judiciary and legislature.[1]

[1] Wade & Forsyth *Administrative Law* (9th edn) App 2.

Employment and office holders

11.302 Is a worker entitled to procedural safeguards before he is dismissed? The traditional answer, reaffirmed in *Ridge v Baldwin*,[1] is that he is not unless he holds an office[2] and even then not if that office can be terminated at pleasure.[3]

[1] [1964] AC 40.

[2] Garner 'Master & Servant. Dismissal of Public Servants' (1966) 110 SJ pp 45–46; see also *Pillai v City Council of Singapore* [1968] 1 WLR 1278, PC.

[3] See *R v Darlington School Governors* (1844) 6 QB 682, approved by Lord Reid in *Ridge's* case: *Pula Joaja v A-G* 1987 CLB 1217. Principles of natural justice did not require Governor General to hear public servant (dismissable at pleasure before dismissing him pursuant to advice of Civil Service Commission). *Shillingford Darnell v Public Service Commission and the A-G HCJ* (Suit No 38 of 1988).

11.303 However, before a public officer can be removed from office for whatever cause, the decision-maker must observe the rules of natural justice. The rule has proved particularly important in countries of the New Commonwealth.[1] This distinction between a worker subject to a contract of employment and an office holder (except one dismissible at pleasure) is now becoming blurred, for a number of interrelated reasons:

(1) *As a matter of contract employees increasingly have express contractual terms which require the employer to comply with certain procedures before they are dismissed.* Indeed, where the dismissal is for cause the courts have shown that they will be willing to imply the principles of

natural justice as did the Court of Appeal in *Stevenson v United Road Transport Union*.[2] More importantly, the courts have shown a willingness to grant injunctions to prevent an employer dismissing in breach of these procedures.[3] This effectively confers a right of natural justice — and indeed in some cases the procedural safeguards may be fuller than those which the traditional natural justice principles may afford (though query whether an injunction would be granted to restrain the employer from acting in breach of the letter of the procedures if the essence of natural justice was complied with). The old notion that an employee could be dismissed at will no longer accurately states even the common law.

(2)   *Employees are now entitled to claim for unfair dismissal provided they meet certain qualifying conditions.* This entitles them to a remedy if their dismissal was unfair even if the employer has dismissed strictly in accordance with the express terms of the contract. One of the remedies which an employment tribunal can grant is reinstatement, and though the employer can refuse to comply with such an order, he will have to pay additional compensation if he does so. An important element in many unfair dismissal cases will be whether the dismissal has been handled fairly. Fairness requires that in most cases employees should be entitled to make representations before they are dismissed and there are numerous examples where the failure to do so has rendered a dismissal unfair.[4] Since 1 October 2004, still more onerous procedural obligations have been imposed on employers.[5]

It should also be noted that the House of Lords has expressly rejected the contention that an otherwise unfair dismissal can be rendered fair if the tribunal is satisfied that the decision to dismiss would have been the same.[6]

(3)   *The courts have widened the concept of who constitutes an 'office holder' for this purpose.* In *Malloch v Aberdeen Corpn*,[7] Lord Wilberforce said that natural justice should apply in all save what he called 'pure master and servant' cases, which he described as cases where there is 'no element of public employment or service, no support by statute, nothing in the nature of an office or a status which is capable of protection'. He added that if any of these elements existed, then essential procedural safeguards should be observed. He criticised, in particular, an earlier case[8] where the Privy Council upheld the dismissal of a university lecturer in Ceylon in the absence of a hearing.[9]

1   *Akilisi Pohiva (Nuku' alofa) v Prime Minister of Tonga* SC 6 May 1988 (Civil Case No 7/86 (Tonga) CLB 1988 1249); *Shillingford Darnell v Public Services Commission High Court and Justices* Suit No 38 of 1988 (Dominica) CLB 1989 1168: *Muora & Madziwa v Minister for Home Affairs (Zambia) High Court*; 26 March 1986 CLB 1986 (Deputy Police Commissioner); *Shansiah Binti Ahmed Sham v PSC* (Malaysia) (1991) 1 Malaysian CLJ.
2   [1977] 2 All ER 941. See also *Marlborough Harbour Board v Goulden* [1985] 2 NZLR 378, NZ CA.
3   See *Irani v Southampton and South West Hampshire Health Authority* [1985] ICR 590; *R v BBC, ex p Lavelle* [1983] 1 All ER 241, [1982] IRLR 404, discussed Bowers, 1983 LQR p 22; Cripps, 1983 CLJ 180; *Jones v Lee* (1911) 106 LT 123 and *Robb v London Borough of Hammersmith and Fulham* [1991] ICR 514.
4   Eg *Earl v Slater & Wheeler (Airlyne) Ltd* [1973] 1 WLR 51, discussed Jackson (1973) MLR 433; *Budgen & Co v Thomas* [1976] ICR 344, (1975) 125 NLJ at pp 1201–1202; 'The

Procedural Aspects of Unfair Dismissal II — The right to a hearing'. Employments Rights Act
1996, Pt X.

⁵ Employment Act 2002.
⁶ *Polkey v AE Dayton Services Ltd* [1988] AC 344.
⁷ [1971] 1 WLR 1578, discussed (1972) MLR 94 (Jackson).
⁸ *Vidyodaya University of Ceylon v Silva* [1965] 1 WLR 77.
⁹ Discussed *SM Thio* (1965) MLR 475 551; *Bradley* (1965) CLJ 3.

11.304 *Malloch* represents the high watermark for the application of the
principles of natural justice in the employment context. Subsequent cases have
shown that at least as far as remedies are concerned, the courts are not willing
to permit public employees to obtain relief by way of judicial review where
their complaint is essentially for breach of the employment contract. In the
Walsh[1] case, Sir John Donaldson MR unconvincingly distinguished Lord
Wilberforce's analysis by saying that he had in mind only cases where there
were express statutory safeguards regulating the dismissal. Unfortunately the
questions of remedies and whether natural justice should apply have become
inextricably interlinked in the courts' eyes: the impression is that they are
reluctant to accept that natural justice may be derived from public law
principles precisely because it will lead to an increase in judicial review
applications. Nonetheless the current position is that unless a person is an
office holder in a strict sense[2] or is the subject of express statutory provisions
regulating those dismissals, no judicial review remedy will be available. In *R v
Lord Chancellor's Department, ex p Nangle*[3] it was held that the internal
disciplinary proceedings of the civil service were of a domestic nature and did
not have a sufficient public law element to make them susceptible to judicial
review.

¹ *R v East Berkshire Area Health Authority, ex p Walsh* [1984] ICR 743, discussed, (1985) CLJ
177 (Walsh) and *McClaren v Home Office* [1990] ICR 824 where there is a valuable
discussion by Woolf LJ as to when proceedings should be initiated by judicial review and when
by writ.
² Such as policemen: *Chief Constable of North Wales Police v Evans* [1982] 1 WLR 1155, or
prison officers: *R v Secretary of State for Home Department, ex p Benwell* [1985] QB 554,
discussed Cripps (1985) CLJ 177.
³ [1991] ICR 743.

11.305 Even in other contexts, however, this should not preclude a court from
implying as an element in the contract of employment that the right to natural
justice applies, as in the *Stevenson* case referred to at **11.303** above. Indeed, the
GCHQ case suggests it will be easy to imply even from past practice. This is
further reinforced by the comment of Woolf J in *Lavelle v BBC*[1] that the law
of unfair dismissal has dramatically changed the traditional distinction
between office holders and employees with a contract of employment. The
relative ease with which safeguards may be implied is further indicated by the
Malloch case itself. That case concerned the dismissal of a teacher whose terms
of service expressly stated that his position was held 'during the pleasure' of
the school board. Notwithstanding this, the House of Lords held that he was
entitled to a hearing before dismissal. The reason was that statute provided
three weeks' notice of intention to dismiss him, and the court held that the only
possible reason for this was to enable him to prepare a defence. By this device
the court managed to evade the operation of the rule that natural justice does
not apply to office holders dismissable at pleasure; it was held that Parliament
had impliedly stipulated to the contrary. Latterly, a school governor appointed

under statute by a local authority was held entitled to the opportunity to make representations in writing before being removed from his office.[2] There is arguably no reason to discriminate between offices held at pleasure and offices removable for cause since any office holder as distinct from a mere employee can be restored to post.[3]

[1] [1983] 1 WLR 23 1983 ICR 99, discussed Fredman and Morris [1991] PL, p 485.
[2] *R v Brent London Borough Council, ex p Assegai* (1987) Times, 18 June.
[3] The current state of flux is well represented in the academic commentary: Walsh, 'Judicial Review of Dismissal from Employment: Coherence or Confusion' [1989] PL 131–155; Sandra Freedland, 'Public or Private? State employer & judicial review; LQR 1991 at 10–14; Freedland, 'The Emerging Law of Public Employment' (1990) 1 LJ 199; Carty, 'Injunctions, Judicial Review and the Contract of Employment' (1990) Litigation pp 325–328; Carty, 'Aggrieved Public Sector Workers and Judicial Review' [1993] AC 682; Sir John Laws, 'Public Law and Employment Law: Abuse of Power' [1997] PL 455–466; Sir Stephen Sedley, 'Public Law and Contractual Employment' [1994] 23 Int LJ 201.

11.306 Certainly where reputation as well as livelihood is at stake the courts have extended the boundaries of the duty to act fairly.[1] In *R v Broxtowe Borough Council ex p Bradford*[2] an applicant coached children at a tennis club on council property and the council, having learned of a pupil's allegations of sexual abuse against the applicant, banned the applicant from coaching young people on council property without his having the opportunity to respond to allegations.

[1] See *Ridge v Baldwin* [1964] AC 40.
[2] [2000] LGR 381.

11.307 The Court of Appeal held that whilst the council had a duty to take all reasonable steps to protect children in their locality from the risk of molestation, they also had a responsibility not to use their position to interfere with an individual's right to earn his living without proper cause or without extending to him the basic requirements of fairness; that, except in the most exceptional situation, where serious allegations were being made against someone, that person should be given an opportunity to answer those allegations; that the applicant should not have been deprived of the opportunity to show that the council was acting under a misconception merely because it might have been difficult for him to show that he was not guilty of improper conduct; and that, accordingly, the council should reconsider the matter after giving the applicant the opportunity of a hearing.

Academic status

11.308 Senior and junior members of academic institutions are entitled to fairness — although, where the institutions have a visitor, the visitor's jurisdiction has hitherto been exclusive within its sphere.[1] The disciplinary role of the visitor, has been abrogated.[2] In any event the visitor's jurisdiction was concerned with the internal law of the institute.[3] If the issue was one of the public law, then the procedures for dismissal under the Education Reform Act 1988 take precedence.[4] University Commissioners now determine the procedural content of university statutes in relation to the dismissal of academic staff.[5] The requirements of natural justice in the context of a student charged before an Examination Committee with an examination offence (cheating) were fully explored in *Dolamanaga Lakshmi Chulasubhadra de Silva v University of Colombo.*[6] However in *R (Maxwell) v Office of the Independent Adjudicator for Higher Education,*[7] the court declined to impose upon an informed inquisitorial scheme an adversarial judicial process.

[1]   *Thomas v University of Bradford* [1987] AC 795; *R v University of Hull, ex p Page* [1991] 1 WLR 1277. See, generally: The NUS and NCCL Commission Academic Freedom and the Law (1970) Chs 1–4 and App 1; de Smith, 'Recent Cases involving Students and their College Authorities' [1960] MLR 228; 'The Abuse of Academic Disciplinary Power' (1994) NLJ 27 May; Zellick/CVCP. 'The Report of the Task Force on Student Disciplinary Procedures (1994); Farrington, 'Resolving Complaints by Students in High Education' *Public Law and the Individual*, March 1996, p 7; Beloff, 'Scholars, Students and Sanction' Dismissal and Discipline at the Modern University, Denning Law Journal (1998); Beloff and Bamforth, 'The University Visitor Academic Judgment and the ECHR' JR 2002 221; McManus *Education and the Courts* (2nd edn, 2004) Ch 8; 'Litigation and the University Student' Robertsons *'University Challenge'* (2000) JR 251.

[2]   The Education Reform Act 1988, ss 202–298: see for transitional provisions, *Pearce v University of Aston in Birmingham (No 1)* [1991] 2 All ER 461, *Pearce v University of Aston in Birmingham (No 2)* [1991] 2 All ER 469.

[3]   Education Act 2002, Pt I.

[4]   The Education Reform Act 1988, s 203(1)(b) and *Pearce v University of Aston in Birmingham (No 1)* [1991] 2 All ER 461.

[5]   Education Reform Act 1988, s 206(1)(b).

[6]   Supreme Court; SC No 52/88 (Sri Lanka).

[7]   [2011] EWCA Civ 1236 , [2012] PTSR 884 at [32]–[33].

Planning

11.309 The procedures relating to planning law are to a considerable extent codified and reference must be made to the Town and Country Planning Act 1990 and the rules made thereunder. However:

> 'Although much of the procedure governing decision making by inspectors and by the Secretary of State is now prescribed in some detail by the Inquiries Procedure Rules, the rules of natural justice are not automatically excluded. Not only do they extend to those types of decisions which are not regulated by the Rules (where in applying them the courts are closely influenced by the procedural model of the rules) but there are also some aspects of procedure which are touched on only in very general terms by the rules'.[1]

[1]   Grant *Urban Planning Law* (1982) p 64; see, also, *Hyndburn Borough Council v Secretary of State for the Environment* [1979] JPL 536.

11.310 The 'common law' rules applicable to planning appeals are now regarded as consisting of a general duty to act fairly.[1] However, where the statutory rules have not been breached, the courts have not been astute to detect unfairness.[2]

[1]   *Fairmount Investments Ltd v Secretary of State for the Environment* [1976] 1 WLR 1255.

[2]   *Rea v Minister of Transport* (1982) 47 P & CR 207; see, also, *R v Bickenhill Parish Council, ex p Secretary of State for the Environment* [1987] JPL 773.

11.311 Examples where such unfairness has been detected are:

(1)   *Performance Cars Ltd v Secretary of State for the Environment*[1] (applicant provided with documents containing authority's case only on morning of inquiry and offered only a long lunch break by inspector to consider them);

(2)   *Wilson v Secretary of State for the Environment*[2] (local residents not notified at all of planning appeal);

(3)   *Fairmount*[3] (inspector decided case on basis of observation at private site visit not put to affected party);

(4)   *Hambledon and Chiddingfold Parish Councils v Secretary of State for the Environment* (Secretary of State took into account information received after inquiry without communicating it to affected party);[4]

(5)   *Hibernian Property Co v Secretary of State for the Environment*[5] (information obtained by Inspector after close of inquiry in absence of objectors and to their prejudice).[6]

[1]   [1977] JPL 585.
[2]   [1988] JPL 540.
[3]   [1976] 1 WLR 1255R *(Tait) v Secretary of State for Communities and Local Government* [2012] EWHC 643 (Admin): it was unlawful for a planning inspector to carry out a site visit in the presence of the local authority representative but in the absence of the owner.
[4]   [1976] JPL 502.
[5]   (1973) 27 P&CR 197.
[6]   See now *EC Commission v Lisrestal C-32/95P* [1997] 2 CMLR 1, (1979) ECR 461. See also Purdue and Sauvain, 'Natural Justice and Post Inquiry Procedures' (1975) JPL 445, (1976) JPL 146; Hind. 'Third Party Objections to Planning Applications. An expectation of fairness' (1988) JPL 742; Thompson, 'Administrative Justice in Planning' (1989) JPL 5. See, generally, Telling and Duxbury *Planning Law and Procedure* (12th edn), pp 35–36 (public inquiries) pp 476–479 (right to a hearing). C-49/88; [1991] ECR I-3187, at paragraph 17.

Sport

11.312 Sports governing bodies are generally obliged to afford minimum standards of procedural protection to the individual, club or other constituent affected by their actions, and to act fairly. The content of the obligation to act fairly in a procedural sense is generally similar to that; and likewise, the extent of the obligation to act fairly in a procedural sense varies from case to case in the light of all the circumstances.[1]

[1]   Deloitte, Kevi, Demetrious, Beloff: 2nd edn. Hart 2012, 3.21–3.27, 7.101–7.138 Lewis and Taylor *Sports Law and Practice* 2ⁿᵈ edn (20014)Bloomsbury C.170: see, generally, Beloff, 'Pitch Pool, Rank . . . Court? *Judicial Review in the Sporting World* (2004) PL 1989, pp 95, 101–103; Beloff and Kerr. 'Judicial Control of Sporting Bodies: The Commonwealth Jurisprudence' (1996) *Sport and the Law Journal: Grayson Sport and the Law* (3rd edn. 2000) Butterworths; *Jones v Welsh RFU* TLR 18.12.1997. An obligation to be fair is one of the principles of the *lex sportiva* developed by the Courts of Arbitration for Sport: See three volumes of its case law (ed M Reeb) Kluwer International.

11.313 Sports governing bodies must afford the player, club and other participants a fair opportunity to put his, her or its case. What fairness requires depends in this context on the nature of the dispute and the severity of the consequences, and on whether the sports governing body is considering an application by the player, club or other participant to exercise its regulatory powers in some way, or is rather pursuing disciplinary proceedings against the player, club or other participant. The case put against the player, club or other participant must be fully disclosed: the respondent to disciplinary proceedings must know the details of the charge. The player, club or other participant must have an adequate opportunity to convey his, her or its case to the decision-making body. While it is possible that in some instances written submissions may be sufficient, the preferable view is that the player, club or other participant should have the option of a full oral hearing at which to present evidence and arguments. Whether legal representation must be allowed and whether the player, club or other participant must be permitted to call witnesses or to cross-examine the sports governing body's witnesses, and whether submissions must be allowed to take the particular form that the player, club or other participant wishes, will also depend on the circumstances.

11.314 It is not yet established that there is an obligation on sports governing bodies and their tribunals to give reasons for their decisions. That said, it is generally likely to be wiser for a sports governing body to provide the reasons for its decisions, particularly if there is an appeal process that involves something other than a complete re-hearing.

11.315 Most codes of sports governing bodies reflect the general principles of fairness, but not all do so.[1] The influence of art 6 of the European Convention on Human Rights may lead to the imposition of more rigorous standards and well as the adverse experience of litigation. Due process is one of the general principles of law applied by the Court of Arbitration for Sport at the Olympic Games.[2]

[1] See the preceding note.
[2] M J Beloff, 'Is there a Lex Sportiva?' 205 ISLR 3/05.

Regulators

11.316 There is a reluctance to impose obligations of fairness over and above those contained in the empowering statute on economic regulators. In *R (easyjet Airline Co) v Civil Aviation Authority*.[1] (CAA's decision as to price caps to be imposed on airlines by BAA at Gatwick, Maurice Kay LJ said:

'My starting point is that, in the words of Lord Mustill (paragraph 43, above) "what fairness demands is dependent on the context of the decision". The decision in the present case does not impact on personal liberty, a person's home, the use which a property owner may make of his property or the right to conduct a business. Its context is the regulation by a statutory body of one aspect of the prices charged by a private monopoly supplier to its customers. The duty imposed on the CAA by section 39(2) of the 1986 Act is to act "in the manner which it considers is best calculated (a) to further the reasonable interests of users of airports . . . ; (b) to promote the efficient, economic and profitable operation of airports; (c) to encourage investment in new facilities at airports . . . ; and (d) to impose the minimum restrictions that are consistent with the performance by the CAA of its functions". Essentially, the CAA is carrying out a balancing exercise. The airports need to charge the airlines for their service but the regulator has to ensure that they do not abuse their market power by overcharging. The "users" whose interests the CAA is required to further include both the airlines and their passengers (section 82). In the context of the present case, airlines and their passengers have an interest in the development of security measures and in protection against being overcharged for them. The ultimate issue is not the provision or non-provision of a service. It is simply the charge that may be levied by the airports per passenger.'

¹ [2009] EWCA Civ 1361.

Public Procurement Procedures

11.317 This is another area where the courts display reticence[1]. Judicial Review is available only for fraud, corruption or bad faith.

[1] See *Auckland LEU v Auckland D1&B* [2009] 1 NZLR 770 CA building on *Mercury Energy Ltd v Electricity Corp of NZ* [1994] 2 NZLR 385 PC. See generally SH Bailey 'Judicial Review of Contracting Decisions' 2007 Public Law 444.

COMMUNITY LAW[1]

[1] For discussion of EU law generally, see CHAPTER 15.

11.318 European Community law recognises the requirements of a due process of law, especially the right to be heard.[1] There is a significant body of jurisprudence to this effect. For example, in *Transocean Marine Paint Association v EC Commission*[2] the ECJ referred to 'the general rule that a person whose interests are perceptibly affected by a decision taken by a public authority must be given the opportunity to make his point of view known'. In *Hoffman La Roche*[3] it was specifically stated that the rule extended to administrative proceedings. In *Al Jubail Fertilizer Co v EC Council*,[4] an anti-dumping case, the ECJ stressed that the Commission must disclose to the challenged party information relevant to the defence of their interests. In *Solvay*[5] the CFI held that access to the file is a fundamental right of the defence in competition proceedings. The constitutionalisation of the rules of natural justice via the medium of EC law may strengthen its status in common law.[6] In addition the European Court of Justice takes account of the Convention of Human Rights as a source of law. The influence of general principle as distinct from specifically enforceable legal provisions of community law in the municipal courts of Member States has been recognised by many commentators.[7]

[1] See, also, Moore *Common Market Law Review* Vol 33, 353–369.
[2] See Case 17/74 *Transocean Marine Paint Association v EC Commission* [1974] ECR 1063, 1091.
[3] Case 85/76 *Hoffmann-La Roche & Co AG v EC Commission* [1979] ECR 461, 511; Case 136/79, *National Panasonic (UK) Ltd v EC Commission* [1980] ECR 2033, 2058 as well as the protection of legitimate expectations. See Case 111/63 *Lemmerz Werke v High Authority* [1965] ECR 677; Case 81/72 *EC Commission v EC Council* [1973] ECR 575, 584; Case 1/73 *Westzucker GmbH v Einfuhr-und Vorratsstelle Fur Zucker* [1973] ECR 723, 729, Case 74/74 *CNTA v EC Commission* [1975] ECR 533, 548.
[4] C-49/88; [1991] ECR 1–3187 at paragraph 17.
[5] Case 736/91.
[6] Nold (1974) CMLR 338 at 354; *Society for the Protection of Unborn Children (Ireland) Ltd v Grogan* C-159/90 [1991] 3 CMLR 849. The Decisions of the ECJ are binding on the United Kingdom under the European Communities Act 1972, see discussion (1980) 29 ICLQ 585 P J Duffy. Case 17/74; [1974] ECR 1063, at paragraph 15.
[7] Usher, 'The "Good Administration" of European Community Law'. Current Legal Problems (1985) pp 269–285; Jowell and Lester, 'Beyond Wednesbury: Substantive Principles of

Administrative Law', [1987] PL 368–382; Schwarze, 'Tendencies Towards a Common Administrative Law in Europe' [1991] PL; Laws 'Is the High Court of The Guardian of Fundamental Constitutional Rights?' [1979] PL; Bingham, 'There is a World Elsewhere': The Changing Perspectives of English Law (1992) 41 International and Comparative Law Quarterly. (Based on 1991 Mann Lecture) ('Bingham: ICLQ'); Bingham, 'The European Convention of Human Rights: Time to Incorporate' [1993] LQR 390–400; The European Community and The European Convention on Human Rights: Their Effect on National Law, Ch 5: The Gradual Convergence. Foreign Ideas, Foreign Influences and English Law on the Eve of the 21st Century (1994) Clarendon Press; Learning from Europe — With Emphasis on the European Convention on Human Rights, H G Schermers. Cripps, 'Some Effects of European Law on English Administrative Law Indiana Journal of Global Legal Studies' (1994) pp 213–231; Beloff, 'Judicial Review — 2001: A Prophetic Odyssey' [1995] MLR ('Beloff: 2001'); Plender, 'Redress in the European Community Courtts' Judicial Review Conference (1996); Beloff, 'Giving Effect to Community Law', ed Andenas 1991, 'Substantive Legitimate Expectations in Domestic and Community Law' (LJ) pp 289–312; Craig, 'Judicial Review in Transition: The Impact of Europe' ('Craig: Europe'), Judicial Review Conference (1995); Andenas, 'General Principles of EC Law', Ch 7: The Rights of Defence.

ECHR AND HRA 1998

11.319 CHAPTER 4 gives a general account of ECHR and HRA 1998. In considering whether there has been compliance with the rules of natural justice, attention should also be paid to the provisions of the ECHR and to cases decided thereunder. This was so even at common law.[1] Now, as explained in CHAPTER 4, under HRA 1998 the courts will seek to interpret English law in accordance with applicable articles of ECHR where possible.

[1] *R v Secretary of State for the Home Department, ex p Brind* [1991] 1 AC 696. See Grief, 'The Domestic Impact of the ECR on Human Rights as Mediated through Community law Public Law', December 1991, 501, Eg *R v Board of Visitors of HM Prison, The Maze, ex p Hone* [1988] AC 379 at 394 per Lord Goff. See, generally, the following: Lord Browne-Wilkinson, 'The Infiltration of a Bill of Rights' [1992] PL 397; Bingham, 'The European Convention of Human Rights: Time to Incorporate' [1993] LQR 390–400; Beloff and Mountfield, 'Unconventional Behaviour? Judicial Uses of the European Convention in England and Wales; European Human Rights Law Review' (1996) pp 467–495 ('Beloff/Mountfield'); Hunt, 'Using Human Rights Law in English Courts' (1997) Hart Publishing.

11.320 Article 6(1) of ECHR (which is subject to derogation in certain circumstances) provides:

'In the determination of his civil rights and obligations or of any criminal charge against him, everyone is entitled to a fair and public hearing within a reasonable time by an independent and impartial tribunal established by law. Judgment shall be pronounced publicly but the press and public may be excluded from all or part of the trial in the interest of morals, public order or national security in a democratic society, where the interests of juveniles or the protection of the private life of the parties so require, or to the extent strictly necessary in the opinion of the court in special circumstances where publicity would prejudice the interests of justice'.[1]

[1] P Craig *'The Human Rights Act, Article 6 and Procedural Rights'* (2003) PL 753. T Cross *'Is there a civil right under Article 6. 10 principles for public lawyers'* (2010) JR 366.

11.321 Article 6 rights are engaged only where there is a determination of civil rights and obligations or of a criminal charge. Each of these criteria have autonomous Strasbourg meanings. The jurisprudence of the European Court of Human Rights shows that in broad terms a 'determination' of an individual's civil rights and obligations arises only if the issue involves *private law* rights. *Lecompte, Van Leuven and De Meyer v Belgium*.[1] Thus, art 6(1) does not impose a general duty upon administrative bodies to provide a fair and impartial hearing to those affected by their decision. Convention rights can themselves equate the civil rights.[2]

[1]   C-49/88; [1991] ECR I-3187 at paragraph 17.
[2]   *Secretary of State for Home Department* [2010] 1 WLR 1542 (Admin) (A control order case).

11.322 'Civil rights and obligations' can, however, embrace 'administrative matters'. In *Weeks v United Kingdom*[1] the fact that the parole board in recommending that a paroled prisoner be released is not required to make full disclosure of all adverse evidence in its possessions was held to violate the prisoner's rights to a proper judicial decision. Judicial review (because it did not constitute an appeal on the merits) was held to be inadequate for this purpose.

[1]   *Lecompte, Van Leuven and De Meyer v Belgium* (1987) 10 EHRR 293.

11.323 The circumstances of each case must be investigated to see whether art 6(1) is engaged. The following are matters to which art 6(1) has been held by the Court or the Commission to be inapplicable on the ground that there is no determination of the applicant's civil rights and obligations: immigration and deportation, entitlement to tax benefits, the payment of discretionary grants, public employment and the procedures adopted by official investigations.[1]

[1]   Wadham, Mountfield, Prochaska, Desai Blackstone's Guide to *The Human Rights Act 1998* (7th edn) OUP Cʜᴀᴘᴛᴇʀ 7. On Social Security Benefits, *Bradley* 1987 PL 3. On immigration and deportation, including expulsion of aliens, see *R (G) v Immigration Appeal Tribunal* [2005] 2 All ER 165; *RB (Algeria) v Secretary of State for the Home Department* [2010] 2 AC 110; *BB v Secretary of State for the Home Department* [2015] EWCA Civ 9.

11.324 There are cases where administrative proceedings are considered to be 'decisive' of civil rights even where that is not their purpose. Where a contract for the sale of land was conditional upon the grant of permission by an administrative tribunal to use the land for non-agricultural purposes, art 6(1) was held to apply to the proceedings of that tribunal.[1] For similar reasons art 6(1) generally applies to matters directly regulating property rights and commercial activity through the grant of licences.

[1]   (1971) 1 EHRR 455 (which concerned the refusal of the Austrian Regional Real Property Transactions Commission to approve a contract for the sale of land); *Pudas v Sweden* (1987) 10 EHRR 380; *Boden v Sweden* (1988) 10 EHRR 367.

11.325 In matters affecting welfare benefits the Court has a tendency to extend the reach of the article in a manner not always consistent with its earlier decisions: *Bentham v Netherlands*;[1] *Tre Traktorer Aktiebolag v Sweden*.[2]

[1]   (1985) 8 EHRR.
[2]   (1989) 13 EHRR 309.

11.326 The general principle was stated thus by Lord Bingham in *Runa Begum v Tower Hamlets London BC*:[1]

'The importance of this case is that it exposes, more clearly than any earlier case has done, the interrelation between the art 6(1) concept of "civil rights" on the one hand and the art 6(1) requirement of "an independent and impartial Tribunal" on the other. The narrower the interpretation given to "civil rights", the greater the need to insist on review by a judicial Tribunal exercising full powers. Conversely, the more elastic the interpretation given to "civil rights", the more flexible must be the approach to the requirement of independent and impartial review if the emasculation (by over-judicialisation) of administrative welfare schemes is to be avoided. Once it is accepted that "full jurisdiction" means "full jurisdiction to deal with the case as the nature of the decision requires" (see *R (Alconbury Developments Ltd) v Secretary of Sate for the Environment, Transport and Regions* [2001] UKHL 23 at [87], [2001] 2 All ER 929 at [87], [2001] 2 WLR 1389), it must also be accepted that the decisions whether a right recognised in domestic law is also a "civil right" and whether the procedure provided to determine that right meets the requirements of art 6 are very closely bound up with each other. It is not entirely easy, in a case such as the present, to apply clear rules derived from the Strasbourg case law since, in a way that any common lawyer, would recognise and respect, the case law has developed and evolved as new cases have fallen for decision, testing the bounds set by those already decided'.[2]

[1]   [2003] 2 AC 430.
[2]   At paragraph 5. The last word on this subject remains to be said. See *Ali v Birmingham* CC [2010] UKSC 8.

11.327 So the duty to be fair extends to benefits in kind which required the exercise of a statutory discretion by the administrative authority after specific statutory criteria for the benefit had been fulfilled. It is undecided as to whether the same principles apply to purely discretionary benefits.

11.328 Lord Mackay of Drurnadoon, in the Court of Session in *Tehrani v UK Central Council for Nursing Midwifery and Health Visiting*,[1] summarised the position referable to disciplinary tribunals in this way.

'In my opinion as *Le Compte, Van Leuven and De Meyere* ((1982) 4 EHRR 1). *Albert and Le Compte* ((1983) 13 EHRR 415) and *Bryan* ((1996) 21 EHRR 342) establish that, as far such tribunals are concerned, no breach of the Convention arises if the tribunal is subject to control by a court that has full jurisdiction and itself complies with the requirements of Article 6(1).

In other words, when dealing with a disciplinary tribunal, such as the PCC, a right of appeal to a court of full jurisdiction does not purge a breach of the Convention. It prevents such a breach from occurring in the first place'.

[1]   [2001] IRLR 208 at 271, [2001] SLT 879 at 800.

11.329 In *R (Thompson) v Law Society*,[1] the court said:

'The courts have considered the application of art 6(1) in many different contexts and the correct approach in any particular case is likely to vary depending on the context. Thus in some cases compliance with it will require a full public and oral hearing at first instance with a full opportunity to cross-examine the relevant witnesses. In other cases, there will be compliance even though there was no public oral hearing and no cross-examination of witnesses at first instance, provided that when the process is considered as a whole there has been a fair and public hearing'.

1   [2004] EWCA Civ 167, [2004] 1 WLR 2522.

11.330 In *Thompson* the Court of Appeal said the key point of principle is that the question whether the procedure satisfies art 6(1), where there is a determination of civil rights and obligations, must be answered by reference to the whole process. The question in each case is whether the process involves a court or court having 'full jurisdiction to deal with the case as the nature of the decision requires'. There may be cases in which a public or oral hearing is required at first instance and other cases where it is not, just as there may be cases in which the potential availability of judicial review will not be sufficient to avoid a breach of art 6(1): *Fredin v Sweden (No 2)*[1] and *Jacobsson v Sweden (No 2)*.[2]

1   (1994) A283-A EctHR.
2   (1998) 32 EHRR 463

11.331 Article 6 was one of a number of articles of ECHR that were said by an alien to be engaged when asserting the fast-track procedures for his expulsion breached article 14. Without deciding the point, the Court of Appeal accepted that it was at least arguable that the facts of the case fell within the ambit of one or more Convention rights: *R (G) v Immigration Appeal Tribunal*.[1]

1   [2005] 1 WLR 1445.

11.332 The requirements of art 6 in criminal cases differ from those in civil cases.[1] In *Hooper v UK*,[2] the failure to give a defendant or his representative the opportunity to address the magistrate before the imposition of a binding over order was a violation of the Convention in that his right to a fair hearing and to legal assistance of his own choosing had not been respected contrary to art 6.

1   See also *R (Fleurose) v Securities and Futures Authority Ltd* [2001] 2 All ER (Comm) 481; *R (Mudie) v Dover Magistrates Court* [2003] QB 1238; *Gora v Customs and Excise Commissioners* [2004] QB 93.
2   (2005) 41 EHRR 1.

11.333 Article 6 does not require an appeal, but judicial review may, in appropriate circumstances, satisfy its conditions[1] since access to a court of 'full jurisdiction' may rectify non-compliance with art 6(1) by the decision-maker.

1   See the discussion in *R Alconbury Developments Ltd v Secretary of State for the Environment, Transport and the Regions* [2003] 2 AC 21. See, generally: A Boyle (1984) Public Law 89 'Administrative Justice, Judicial Review and the Right to a Fair Hearing under the ECHR': *Van Dijk* The interpretation of 'Civil Rights' and 'Obligations by the European Court of Human Rights — one more step to take' (in 'Protecting Human Rights: the European Dimension' (1985)); Bradley *Edinburgh Essays in Public Law* (1991) pp 200–203. Craig, 'The HRA. Article 6 and Procedural Rights' (2003) PL 753 and Cʜᴀᴘᴛᴇʀ 4 above. M Carrs-Frisk 'Rights to a Fair Hearing and Right to Property' 2000 JR 198. M Beloff and R Beloff. 'Judicial Review: Is it Sufficient for Arts 16 and 13 of the ECHR' JR 2001 154; Clayton and Sachdeva. 'The Role of Judicial Review in Curing Breaches of Article 6' (2003) JR 90. See, also. *W v UK*; *B v UK*; *R v UK*, Series A Vol 121 7 July 1987 (Child access cases): but see *Vilvarajah v United Kingdom* (1991) 14 EHRR 248, judicial review provides effective degree of control over

administrative decision in asylum case. There have been cases where the European Court of Human Rights Court has held that neither the Tribunal of first instance nor the reviewing court has provided a fair and public hearing within the meaning of art 6(1) (see, eg *W v UK* (1988) 10 EHRR 29 at 58 (paragraph 82), *Obermeier v Austria* (1990) 13 EHRR 290 at paragraphs 34, 35 and *Diennet v France* (1996) 21 EHRR 554).

11.334 It been argued that one emanation of the state has no obligation to ensure that other emanations of the state comply with their obligations under the Convention. In *R (Adlard) v Secretary of State for the Environment, Transport and the Regions*[1] it was said that the Secretary of State was not obliged to ensure that other public authorities acted compatibly with the Convention. However, the Court of Appeal in *R (Munjaz) v Mersey Care NHS Trust*[2] pointed out that this was in the context of an argument that the Secretary of State should have called in a planning application so as to avoid the risk that the local planning authority might act incompatibly with art 6. It may be that the decision in *Adlard* is best seen as an example of the principle that, where art 6(1) is engaged, there is no infringement of the right to a fair and public trial so long as the procedures, viewed as a whole, provide full jurisdiction to deal with the case as the nature of the decision requires.[3]

1 [2002] 1 WLR 2515.
2 [2004] QB 395, at paragraph 59.
3 See *R (Thompson) v Law Society* [2004] 1 WLR 2523 at paragraph 60 et seq.

11.335 Claims for breach of Article 6(1) may be made concurrently with claims for breach of common law fairness. As already noted, however, while there is overlap, there is not identity. The Convention applied only to decisions which determine civil rights and obligations or criminal charges: the common law has a wider speck: But where applicable, the right to a fair hearing has close affinity with the audi alterum partem rule: and is linked to it historically. Provisional inclusion in a list of persons precluded from working with vulnerable adults without a hearing breached fair trial rights under Article 6.[1]

1 *R (Wright) v Health Secretary* [2009] UKHL 3, [2009] AC 239 Moules 2009 CLJ 251–253. The curative principle under Article 6 will only cure procedural deficiencies if the initial decision-making body gave the individual a proper opportunity to be heard. *R (G) v Governors of X School 1291* [2009] EWHC 504 Admin. Dismissal of teacher for sexual impropriety with pupil: because of serious nature or charges and consequences (a s 142 direction under Education Act 2002 that he could not work with children), he was entitled to legal representation [paragraph 69] (Article 6).

11.336 Article 6 requires equality of arms: *Steel & Morris v United Kingdom*[1] (denial of legal aid to defendants in a complex defamation suit offended against the principle).

1 [2005] 41 EHRR 403.

INTERNATIONAL LAW

11.337 There are other provisions of public international law to the same effect as art 6 of the Convention, eg art 10: *Universal Declaration of Human Rights* (United Nations 1948),[1] and art 14: *Covenant on Civil and Political Rights* (CCPR) (1966).[2] These, however, lack legal force (as distinct from some legal influence) in domestic courts.

1   Discussed (1967) Public Law 267 (F C Newman). (See Bayne, 'Human Rights and Adminis-
    trative Law', (1991) LLB, esp pp 321–322 on the issue as to whether rights recognised in
    international human rights instruments attract rules of natural justice).
2   Discussed 'The Domestic Application of International Human Rights Norms' by Justice Lallah
    CLB April 1991, pp 671, 673–674.

Chapter 12

BIAS — INTEREST AND FAVOUR

INTRODUCTION

12.1 The second limb of natural justice (which, like the first, arises not only in the field of judicial review, but also in the fields of civil and criminal procedure) is the rule that in general no one should be a judge in what is to be regarded as his own cause, whether or not he is named as a party. The decision-maker must have no reasonably avoidable material interest (by way of gain or detriment) in the outcome of proceedings, save such as is candidly, fully and openly declared and objection to which is waived, expressly or by necessary implication. Interest may take many forms. It may be a personal interest. It may be a group interest. It may be pecuniary. It may not be. It may be direct. It may be indirect. It may arise from a personal relationship, or from a relationship with the subject matter; from a close relationship, or from a tenuous one. It may be apparent. It may be undisclosed. It may entail actual bias, ie a predisposition, based upon fear or favour affection or ill-will, to decide in a particular way rather than upon a proper and balanced consideration of the true merits of the issue. There may be no actual bias at all. A vitiating interest may even be non-existent or non-provable, but there may be sufficient of an appearance of it nonetheless, either because a reasonable outsider might think that there was a real possibility that the issue could not or would not be fairly determined on its merits, or because undue favour or partiality or antipathy was in the event manifested. There are a variety of interests which may infringe the rules of natural justice, but there are times when the interest will not constitute an infringement. The circumstances may enable the prospective decision-maker with an interest more or less readily to be excluded from the proceedings. The circumstances may be such that that is not reasonably practicable, or at least is not compatible with the construction of relevant legislative provisions. The interest may be substantial. It may be trivial. It may even be beneficial. It may be an interest of the entire decision-making body, or of only a part (influential or uninfluential) of it. It may be what is sometimes termed structural bias, built into the system, also described as institutional bias or systemic bias.

12.2 The rules that no one should be a judge in his own cause and that there should be no appearance of bias mean that as a matter of principle the decision-maker must be impartial. Not only must he not benefit himself, he must not favour one party or disfavour another.[1] In cases where art 6 of the European Convention on Human Rights (ECHR) applies, there is an allied principle that the decision-maker be independent.[2] Further, as a matter of principle, the decision-maker should not have such preconceived views as amount to an unlawful fettering of discretion.[3] All these principles, in cases where they apply, can be seen as manifestations of the general duty upon all public authorities to act fairly and to be seen to act fairly.

[1]   See '*Bias; the Judges and the Separation of Powers*': Sir David Williams QC DL [2000] PL 45. The position is summed up in the celebrated dictum of Lord Hewart LCJ in *R v Sussex JJ, ex p McCarthy* [1924] 1 KB 256 that justice should not only be done, 'but should manifestly and undoubtedly be seen to be done'.
[2]   See **12.4** below.
[3]   Fettering of discretion is discussed in CHAPTER 7.

12.3 It is unlawful for a public authority to act in a way which is incompatible with a Convention right: Section 6(1) of the Human Rights Act 1998. As explained in CHAPTER 4, Convention rights include art 6. Article 6(2) and (3) relate to criminal charges. Article 6(1) provides:

'In the determination of his civil rights and obligations or of any criminal charge against him, everyone is entitled to a fair and public hearing within a reasonable time by an *independent* and *impartial* tribunal established by law. Judgment shall be pronounced publicly but the press and public may be excluded from all or part of the trial in the interest of morals, public order or national security in a democratic society, where the interests of juveniles or the protection of the private life of the parties so require, or to the extent strictly necessary in the opinion of the court in special circumstances where publicity would prejudice the interests of justice' [emphasis added].'

12.4 Key elements therefore (in those cases where the decision in question is subject to the Human Rights Act 1998, discussed in CHAPTER 4 above) are whether there is a 'determination' of 'civil rights and obligations' (or of any 'criminal charge'), and what constitute a 'fair' and 'public' hearing, a 'reasonable time' and 'an independent and impartial tribunal established by law'.[1] The Convention rights to an independent and impartial tribunal are akin to the common law's aversion to incompatible functions, discussed at **12.57** below.[2]

[1]   As to the award of damages by way of just satisfaction for breaches of art 6, see *R (Greenfield) v Secretary of State for the Home Department* [2005] UKHL 14. The ordinary practice is not to make an award in cases of structural bias (at paragraph 19). The question of recovery of

costs from the State under the Human Rights Act 1998 in a case where there has been bias is dealt with by the Court of Appeal in *Re Medicaments and Related Classes of Goods (No 4)* [2002] 1 WLR 269.

2   The link between 'independent' and 'impartial' in art 6 of ECHR is discussed in *R (Alconbury Developments Ltd) v Secretary of State* [2001] AC 295, especially per Lord Slynn at paragraph 42, in *Runa Begum v Tower Hamlets LBC* [2003] 2 AC 430, especially per Lord Hoffmann at paragraphs 39–59 and per Lord Millett at paragraph 96 (concluding that the decision-maker in that case was 'impartial' but not 'independent'), and in *R (Anderson) v Secretary of State for the Home Department* [2003] 1 AC 837, *Alconbury* and subsequent developments are further discussed in CHAPTER 4 above, and the question whether a Secretary of State may be obliged to ensure that other public authorities act compatibly with art 6 of the Convention. Article 6 is discussed at **11.334**. In the event of a violation of art 6, there is the possibility of a damages claim. On the test for an 'independent and impartial' tribunal, see *San Leonard Band Club v Malta* (2006) 42 EHRR 23, *Pescador Valero v Spain* (2006) 42 EHRR 27, *Pabla Ky v Finland* (2006) 42 EHRR 34, *Tsfayo v UK* [2007] LGR 1, *Chmelir v Czech Republic* (2007) 44 EHRR 20, *Martin v UK* (2007) 44 EHRR 31, *Chronopost SA v UFEX* (2008) 3 CMLR 19 (participation in two hearings in same case) and *Elezi v Germany* (2008) 47 EHRR 53.

ACTUAL BIAS

12.5 Actual and conscious bias automatically disqualifies.[1] Any issue will be as to whether it exists. This is a question of fact. The allegation is seldom even made, because actual bias is mercifully rare and because it is very difficult to prove.[2]

1   *O'Reilly v Mackman* [1983] 2 AC 237; *R v Gough* [1993] AC 646; *Laker Airways Inc v FLS, Aerospace Ltd* [2000] 1 WLR 113. And may not be capable of waiver: *R v Home Secretary, ex p Fayed* [2001] Imm AR 134. On unconscious bias see *R v Barnsley Licensing Justices, ex p Barnsley and District Licensed Victuallers' Association* [1960] 2QB 167 per Devlin LJ at 187.
2   An example is referred to at **7.91** above.

12.6 Moreover, a mind having been made up does not mean that inevitably there is a bias. Even a concluded and firm view may be changed. As David Pannick QC stated in an article in the *Times* on 15 January 2009:

'There are many striking examples of judges changing their minds on legal issues before their courts. The principle is that stated by Baron Bramwell in 1872 when he was asked to follow an earlier decision of his own: "The matter does not appear to me now as it appears to have appeared to me then." In 1919 Chief Justice Lord Reading delivered the judgment of the Court of Criminal Appeal quashing a conviction for murder and substituting a verdict of manslaughter. The prosecution appealed. An eight-man Appellate Committee of the House of Lords heard and allowed an appeal, restoring the conviction for murder. Lord Reading was a member of the committee, concurring in the unanimous decision to reverse his own decision.

Sir Robert Megarry drew attention in A New Miscellany-at-Law to a very extreme case of judicial reconsideration. In 1845 Mr Justice Maule gave judgment for the plaintiff in a contractual dispute. The defendant asked the Court of Common Pleas to reverse the ruling. In 1846 three members of that court, including Chief Justice Tindal, dismissed the defendant's application, concluding that the ruling by Mr Justice Maule had been correct. One judge dissented, finding that Mr Justice Maule had been wrong in law. That judge was the same Mr Justice Maule.'

12.7 Further, as Rimer J, as he then was, observed in *Hackney LBC v Sagnia*, UKEAT/0600/03, there is a false logic in saying: 'I had a strong case, yet I lost, so the Court must have been biased against me.'

As Heddon-Cave J observed in R *(Allen) Parole Board* [2015] EWHC 2069 (Admin) a decision could be characterised as wrong, or even perverse, but that is different from alleging bias, whether actual or apparent, and such an allegation should be made only on a proper basis, which does not include disagreeing with the decision.

APPEARANCE OF BIAS

12.8 Almost all cases concern an allegation of appearance of bias. There are two classes of case in which it may be contended that a decision should be set aside on the ground that an adjudicator has an interest, real or perceived, in the outcome of proceedings, and an appearance of bias arises as a result. The first is where the adjudicator is in fact a party to the litigation or has a direct financial or proprietary interest in the outcome. In such a case, absent sufficient disclosure, disqualification is automatic.[1] There is no investigation into whether there is a real possibility of bias. This first class of case is sometimes described as 'presumptive' or 'presumed' bias. The second is where any financial or proprietary interest is indirect, or where there is no financial or proprietary interest at all, but nonetheless the surrounding circumstances give rise to a real possibility of lack of impartiality. In such a case disqualification is not automatic. The first class of case is discussed at **12.9–12.30** below, and the second at **12.41–12.57** below.

[1] See *'The Nemo Judex Rule: The Case Against Automatic Disqualification'*: Professor Olowo-foyeku [2000] PL 456, described as a 'powerful critical analysis' by Lord Phillips MR in *Re Medicaments and Related Classes of Goods (No 2)* [2001] 1 WLR 700, at paragraph 40.

Party to the cause

12.9 The modern leading case on this topic was one which arose in the context of extradition. *R v Bow Street Metropolitan Stipendiary Magistrate, ex p Pinochet Ugarte (No 2)*[1] ('*Pinochet (No 2)*') was concerned with the question of when a judge is to be treated as being a party to the action. *Pinochet (No 2)* was the second of three occasions when in quick succession the House of Lords dealt with litigation in relation to the extradition of Pinochet for human rights crimes in Chile. In *Pinochet (No 1)*[2] Lord Hoffmann sat. This led to the decision being set aside in *Pinochet (No 2)*, and there being a re-hearing, *Pinochet (No 3)*.[3] This was because Amnesty International (AI), having campaigned against Pinochet, had obtained leave to intervene in *Pinochet (No 1)*, and was represented by counsel to argue for a particular result. Lord Hoffmann was not a member of AI, but he was an unpaid director and chairman of Amnesty International Charity Limited (AICL), which was wholly controlled by AI, closely allied to AI and shared AI's objects.

[1] [2000] 1 AC 119.
[2] [2000] 1 AC 61.
[3] [2001] 1 AC147.

12.10 Lord Hoffmann had no financial or proprietary interest, nor did AI or AICL; but he was held to be automatically disqualified because a party to the proceedings (which included an intervener) embraces a member of the party or someone with a close connection with the party or its alter ego. The crucial point was that Lord Hoffmann was the director of a company wholly controlled by a party and carrying on much of its work as part of the same organisation promoting the same causes. This does not mean that judges are unable to sit on any cases of interest to charities in whose work they are involved. What disqualifies is being trustee or director of a charity closely allied to, and acting with, a party. Further, if the involvement of the judge is disclosed then waiver by the parties may bar any subsequent complaint. Waiver is discussed at **12.115** below.

12.11 Given that Lord Hoffmann was automatically disqualified because he was regarded as being so closely connected with a party to the proceedings that he was to be deemed to be acting in his own cause, it was unnecessary to go on to investigate whether there was a real possibility of unconscious bias. In a case where a plea of presumption of bias and automatic disqualification is rejected it will be necessary to go on to such an investigation into appearances. Moreover, automatic disqualification arising from a non-pecuniary interest may be peculiar to those exercising judicial functions.[1]

[1] See sections **12.30**, **12.50** and **12.61** below.

12.12 Post *Pinochet (No 2)* cases on whether an adjudicator is to be regarded as being a judge in his own cause on account of an arguably close connection with a party to the proceedings have concerned, amongst others, arbitrators,[1] deputy judges who are partners in a solicitors' firm,[2] judges who are former partners in a solicitors' firm,[3] acquaintanceship with a witness,[4] and the responsibilities of a Chief Constable in relation to police disciplinary proceedings.[5]

[1] *Laker Airways Inc v FLS Aerospace Ltd* [2000] 1 WLR 113; *AT&T Corporation v Saudi Cable Co* [2000] 2 Lloyd's Rep 127. See, also, as to a lay representative who was a member of the Professional Conduct and Complaints Committee of the Bar Council sitting as a panel member at a Visitors Tribunal Hearing, *P (A Barrister) v General Council of the Bar*, LTL 21/2/2005.
[2] *Locobail (UK) Ltd v Bayfield Properties Ltd* [2000] QB 451.
[3] *Bank of Credit and Commerce International SA (In Liquidation) v Ali (No.8)*, New Law Journal (2001) 151 NLJ 1852.
[4] *Man O'War Station Ltd v Auckland City Council* [2002] UKPC 28.
[5] *R (Bennion) v Chief Constable of Merseyside Police* [2002] ICR 136.

12.13 *Pinochet (No 2)* must now, however, be considered in the light of *Meerabux v Attorney General of Belize*[1] and *R (Kaur) v Institute of Legal Executives Appeal* Tribunal.[2] In *Meerabux*, Lord Hope of Craighead said (at paragraphs 21 and 24) that the decision in *Pinochet (No 2)* 'appears, in retrospect, to have been a highly technical one', and (at paragraph 22) that the circumstances of *Pinochet (No 2)* were 'striking and unusual'. In *Meerabux* it was held (at paragraph 24) that automatic disqualification does not follow from mere membership of an association by which proceedings are brought, but only where there is active involvement in the institution of the particular proceedings. In *Kaur* it was held that the Vice-President of the Institute of Legal Executives was disqualified from sitting on the Institute's Disciplinary or Appeal Tribunals. This was because of her leading role in the Institute, and, thereby, her interest in its policy of disciplinary regulation. This was, however, on the basis that it was possible to see the doctrine of automatic disqualification and the doctrine of apparent bias as two threads of an over-arching requirement that judges should not sit, or should face recusal or disqualification, where there is the 'real possibility', assessed by the 'fair minded and informed observer' that the judge objectively appeared to be or could be biased.

[1] [2005] UKPC 12, [2005] 2 AC 513.

² [2011] EWCA Civ 1168.

Pecuniary Interest

The general principle

12.14 Just as bias will be presumed where there is a close connection between the judge and a party to the proceedings, so too will bias be presumed if the judge[1] has a relevant economic interest, in general, a direct financial or proprietary interest.

¹ Or the judge's partner: *Jones v DAS Legal Expenses Insurance Co Ltd* [2004] IRLR 218; or other family member: *Locobail (UK) Ltd v Bayfield Properties Ltd* [2000] QB 451.

12.15 It has long been held by the courts, and is a very strictly applied maxim, that no man is qualified to adjudicate in any process (at any rate any judicial or quasi-judicial process) if he has a *direct* pecuniary interest in the outcome. Bias is conclusively presumed. In *Dimes v Grand Junction Canal*[1] the cause was heard before the Vice-Chancellor. He granted the relief sought by the company. On appeal by Dimes the Lord Chancellor simply affirmed the Vice-Chancellor's Order. The Lord Chancellor was, however, and had been for more than ten years, a large shareholder with a very considerable pecuniary interest in the company, partly in his own right and partly as trustee. This fact was, according to Dimes, unknown to him. The House of Lords held:

(1)   first, that the Lord Chancellor, by virtue of the shares he owned beneficially, was disqualified on the ground of measurable pecuniary interest, and that his decree was voidable and must be reversed;

(2)   second, that the Vice-Chancellor was a judge subordinate to, but not dependent on, the Lord Chancellor, and that, consequently, the disqualification of the Lord Chancellor did not affect him, but that his decree might be made the subject of appeal to the House of Lords;

(3)   third, that the act of enrolment by the Lord Chancellor of the decree made by the Vice-Chancellor, which enrolment was a condition precedent to appeal from the Vice-Chancellor, was, though performed by the Lord Chancellor, not affected by his disqualification, but was valid for the purpose of bringing up the appeal to the House of Lords;

(4)   fourth, that upon the merits the case was a very simple one and the decree of Vice-Chancellor was right and must be affirmed, unaffected by the orders and decrees, and the reversing of the orders and decrees, of the Lord Chancellor.

¹ (1852) 3 HL Cas 759.

12.16 Lord Campbell said:[1]

'No one can suppose that Lord Cottenham could be, in the remotest degree, influenced by the interest that he had in this concern; but, my Lords, it is of the last importance that the maxim that no man is to be a judge in his own cause should be held sacred. And that is not to be confined to a cause in which he is a party, but applies to a cause in which he has an interest. Since I have had the honour to be Chief Justice of the Court of Queen's Bench, we have again and again set aside proceedings in inferior tribunals because an individual, who had an interest in a cause, took a part in the decision. And it will have a most salutary influence on these tribunals when it is known that the High Court of last resort, in a case in which the Lord Chancellor of England had an interest, considered that his decree was on that account a decree not according to law, and was set aside. This will be a lesson to all inferior tribunals to take care not only that in their decrees they are not influenced by their personal interest, but to avoid the appearance of labouring under such an influence.'

[1]   At 793.

12.17 In *Leeson v General Council of Medical Education and Registration*,[1] which was concerned with the interest of members of a statutory professional disciplinary tribunal, Bowen LJ said:[2]

'nothing can be clearer than the principle of law that a person who has a judicial duty to perform disqualifies himself for performing it if he has a pecuniary interest in the decision which he is about to give, or a bias which renders him otherwise than an impartial judge . . . If he has a pecuniary interest . . . he must not be a judge. Where such a pecuniary interest exists, the law does not allow any further enquiry as to whether or not the mind was actually biased by the pecuniary interest. The fact is established from which the inference is drawn that he is interested in the decision, and he cannot act as a judge.'

[1]   (1889) 43 Ch D 366.
[2]   At 384. And see *R (Al-Hasan) v Secretary of State for the Home Department* [2005] UKHL 13, [2005] 1 WLR 688, at paragraphs 43 and 44: once proceedings have been successfully impugned for want of independence and impartiality on the part of the tribunal, the decision itself must necessarily be regarded as tainted by unfairness and so cannot be permitted to stand.

The quantum of the interest

12.18 If the interest is as a shareholder then it matters not that the shares are disposed of immediately before the decision.[1] No device to conceal the real nature of the situation will prevail.[2] Nor does it matter how small may be the number of shares or the proportion they bear to the total.[3]

[1]   *R v Hain, etc Licensing Justices* (1896) 12 TLR 373, cf *R v Devon and Cornwall Police Authority ex p Willis* (1984) 82 LGR 369.
[2]   *Norton v Taylor* [1906] AC 378.
[3]   *R v Hammond* (1863) 9 LT 423. And see *R v Secretary of State for Trade, ex p Anderson Strathclyde plc* [1983] 2 All ER 233, at p 237.

12.19 'The least pecuniary interest' disqualifies.[1] Even a pecuniary interest as a rate payer or taxpayer disqualifies (absent statutory relief).[2]

[1]   *R v Farrant* (1887) 20 QBD 58.
[2]   *R v Gaisford* [1892] 1 QB 381, where A L Smith J said, at 384: 'It is well-known law that the same person shall not act . . . as a judge in a case in the decision of which he has a pecuniary interest, unless relieved by statute, the fact that a man has even the slightest pecuniary interest operates to disqualify him from adjudicating upon a case'.

12.20 The rule regarding direct pecuniary interest was restated by Slade J in *R v Camborne Justices, ex p Pearce*:[1]

'It is of course clear that any direct pecuniary or proprietary interest in the subject matter of proceedings, however small, operates as an automatic disqualification. In such a case the law assumes bias.'

[1] [1955] 1 QB 41, [1954] 2 All ER 850.

12.21 Disqualification arises irrespective of the judge's state of knowledge as to his interest. There is however, a de minimis exception.[1]

[1] *Locobail (UK) Ltd v Bayfield Properties Ltd* [2000] QB 451; *Weatherill v Lloyds TSB Bank* [2000] CPLR 584.

Contrast with remote or contingent and non-beneficial interests

12.22 However, the interest must be 'direct and certain, and not remote or contingent' – per Mellor J in *R Manchester, Sheffield and Lincolnshire Rly Co*.[1]

[1] (1867) LR 2 QB 336 at 339. See, also, *Panel on Take-overs and Mergers v William Cheng Kai-Man* [1995] 4 LRC 369.

12.23 In *R v McKenzie*[1] the informant was a district superintendent of the Shipping Federation. The defendant was an officer of the National Amalgamated Seamen's and Firemen's Union. The summons arose out of disputes between the Federation and the Union. It was alleged that some of the convicting Sunderland justices had an interest, in that they held shares in ships which were insured by companies which were members of the Federation. It does not appear to have been suggested that they had a pecuniary interest. The court held that in order for it to be shown that the magistrates were disqualified on the ground of bias it must be apparent that they had some 'substantial interest'[2] in the result of the proceedings, and that there was no evidence of that. The court observed[3] that the position would have been very different if it could have been shown that the magistrates in question were by themselves or their agents the real prosecutors in the case, but that the facts were not nearly so strong as those in *Leeson*, where the Court of Appeal held that there was no bias.

[1] [1892] 2 QB 519.
[2] At 524.
[3] At 523.

12.24 In *R v Burton, ex p Young*,[1] one of two magistrates. Burton, was a practising solicitor (to the knowledge of Young) and an ordinary member of the Incorporated Law Society (which Young did not ascertain until after the hearing), though not a member of its Council. He sat and adjudicated on the hearing of a summons for falsely pretending to be a solicitor. The proceedings were taken by the Council of the Society. The Council controlled the proceedings of the Society. Ordinary members had no voice in them, and had no control over the institution or conduct of prosecutions. In prosecutions of this kind no part of any penalty that might be imposed was ever received by the Society. The court held that Burton was not disqualified by his membership of the Society, either as having a pecuniary interest in the proceedings, or as being a prosecutor, and therefore, he was justified in adjudicating, and that objection on the basis of his being a solicitor had been waived. His pecuniary interest was said to have arisen because if the Society were dissolved he would be entitled to a share of the assets and if the result of the prosecution was that the Society were condemned in costs, that these would be to some extent diminished. The court observed[2] that dissolution of the Society was 'a most unlikely contingency'. Collins J said:[3]

'As to the objection on the ground of pecuniary interest, though I agree that, however small the interest may be, if it exists it will disqualify, still it must not be a purely speculative chance, as it is here, depending on an event which could not with any probability happen in Mr Burton's lifetime, namely, the dissolution of the Incorporated Law Society, in which event it is urged that Mr Burton would come in for a smaller share of assets if the Society had to pay the costs of this prosecution.'

[1] [1897] 2 QB 468.
[2] At 472.
[3] At 474.

12.25 The court further held that the objection that he was in the position of prosecutor as well as judge must depend on his relation to the Society. Not only had he taken no part in directing the prosecution, he had no power with regard to the direction or management of the prosecution.

12.26 The question whether a trustee has a disqualifying pecuniary interest was considered in *R v Rand*.[1] Bradford Corporation were owners of waterworks. They were empowered to take the water of certain streams, but not those flowing into the Harden Beck without the assent of the mill-owners on that beck until it had been certified by justices that Doe Park Reservoir had been completed and filled with water, and of a given capacity. An application was made by the Corporation to justices and was opposed by the mill-owners. The justices granted the certificate. One of the justices in question was amongst the trustees of a friendly society and the other amongst the trustees of a hospital, and the friendly society and the hospital had, in the names of the trustees, invested part of their funds in bonds of the Bradford Corporation, charging the borough fund. Neither of them had, nor by any possibility could have, any pecuniary beneficial interest in these bonds. No doubt the security of their *cestui qui* trusts would be improved by anything improving the borough fund. Anything improving the waterworks would have that effect. The court held that this did not disqualify the justices from acting in what was certainly a judicial enquiry. Blackburn J said:[2]

'There is no doubt that any direct pecuniary interest, however small, in the subject of an inquiry, does disqualify a person from acting as a judge in the matter; and if by any possibility these gentlemen, though mere trustees, could have been liable to costs, or to other pecuniary loss or gain, in consequence of their being so, we should think the question different from what it is: for that might be held an interest. But the only way in which the facts could affect their impartiality would be that they might have a tendency to favour those for whom they were trustees; and that is an objection not in the nature of interest, but of a challenge to the favour.'

[1] (1866) LR 1 QB 230.
[2] At 232.

12.27 In *R v Mulvihill*,[1] it was held that a judge conducting a Crown Court criminal trial on indictment with a jury had no direct pecuniary or proprietary interest, and so the rules relating to automatic disqualification were not relevant, simply because he had shares in a bank or savings in a building society whose premises were the scenes of robberies. (Nor were there reasonable grounds for a suspicion that a fair trial was not possible.) The Court of Appeal said[2] that, in their view, a judge in a criminal trial is not, save possibly in some very exceptional circumstances, called upon to declare that he has some remote interest in premises which have become the scene of a crime.

1 [1990] 1 All ER 436, [1990] 1 WLR 438.
2 At 444G.

The effect of pecuniary interest

12.28 If one member of a decision-making body required to act *judicially* is disqualified by pecuniary interest then the decision cannot stand.[1]

1 *R v Hendon RDC, ex p Chorley* [1933] 2 KB 696, in which the decision of a local planning authority to grant permission for a development was quashed because one of the participating councillors was acting as estate agent for the owner of the land.

12.29 However, a party with an irresistible right to object to a judge hearing (or continuing to hear) a case might waive that right so long as he or she did so in clear and unequivocal terms and with full knowledge of the relevant facts.[1]

1 *Locobail (UK) Ltd v Bayfield Properties Ltd* [2000] QB 451.

Public authorities

12.30 The above principles apply with full force and effect in judicial and quasi-judicial contexts. In other contexts, the position is frequently governed by primary and secondary legislation relating to the registration and declaration of interests, and setting out the circumstances in which the interest will generally bar participation, and the procedures by which that bar may be removed by dispensation.

12.31 Local authorities are a case in point. Reference should be made to specialist works on local government law for the current statutory regimes in England and Wales respectively.[1] They are not in identical terms to the common law formulation of bias, but similar considerations apply.

1 See especially ss 29-34 inclusive of the Localism Act 2011 and the Relevant Authorities (Disclosable Pecuniary Interests) Regulations 2012, SI 2012/1464.

12.32 The purpose of the provisions is to prevent a conflict between private interest and public duty. They are intended to prevent members from being exposed to temptation, or even the semblance of temptation: see *Nutton v Wilson*[1] and *Barnacle v Clark*.[2]

1 (1889) 22 QBD 744 per Lord Esher MR at p 747, per Lindley LJ at 748 and per Lopes J at 749. And on the current regime, see *R (Richardson) v North Yorkshire County Council* [2003] EWCA Civ 1860, [2004] LGR 351.
2 [1900] 1 QB 279 at 282–284.

12.33 The prospect of an ultimate, but not too remote, pecuniary advantage, or disadvantage, has been regarded as enough under earlier legislation relating to pecuniary interests. The leading cases are *England v Inglis*,[1] *Brown v DPP*,[2] and *Rands v Oldroyd*.[3]

[1]   [1920] 2 KB 636 at 639/640.
[2]   [1956] 2 QB 369, [1956] 2 All ER 189.
[3]   [1959] 1 QB 204, [1958] 3 All ER 344 especially at 211–214.

12.34 In *Brown v DPP* the question was as to lodgers' allowances to be paid by tenants of council houses. Three of the councillors considering the matter were council house tenants, but did not have any lodgers. The court held that those councillors who were already tenants of council houses ('a potential income producing asset') did have a pecuniary interest in the terms of the contract of tenancy as to lodger charges, albeit that they did not have lodgers as yet and might never have lodgers. The court contrasted the position of those who might become tenants of a council house in the future but who as yet had not become tenants. Lord Goddard CJ referred to 'the very wide terms' of the statutory provision, having stated[1] that 'it is no doubt of the greatest possible importance that there should be a strict observance of the Act'.

[1]   At 374.

12.35 Donovan J said:

'The object of section 76(1) [of the Local Government Act 1933] is clearly to prevent councillors from voting on a matter which may affect their own pockets and which may therefore affect their judgement.'

12.36 In *Rands v Oldroyd* a member of a local authority who had a controlling interest in a building company was held to have an indirect pecuniary interest in the question whether the authority's direct labour force should be augmented, notwithstanding that the company had resolved that it would not in future tender for building contracts for the authority, so long as the company was a building company and could contract.

12.37 Like provisions to those applying to local authority members are to be found, for example in relation to public transport companies and school governors, for the purpose of prescribing the circumstances and cases in which a member shall be disqualified. See *Noble v ILEA*,[1] in which Stephenson LJ approved the statement of Nolan J as follows:

'The salary level is an important matter because of the clear purpose behind the bar . . . on voting by interested parties. Plainly it is designed to ensure that those who vote shall have no possibility of financial interest in the result.'

[1]   (1983) 82 LGR 291. Payment for attendance and travelling is, however, immaterial: *R (B) v Alperton Community School* [2001] ELR 359.

12.38 In *Bostock v Kay*[1] the Court of Appeal held that teacher-governors had a direct pecuniary interest in a proposal to convert voluntary aided schools into City Technology Colleges, because if the proposal were implemented (as to which there was a very real chance, even though there were a number of hurdles to be surmounted) they might well earn more (for longer hours) or receive a redundancy payment. Any teacher invited to vote on the proposal would understandably be tempted at the very least to ask how it would affect him financially. It mattered not that he could not necessarily know the answer to that, that there might be a number of imponderables still to be decided upon (by parties other than the governors) before he would be able to have an answer to that, that the proposal might in the end come to nothing.

[1]   (1988) 87 LGR 583.

12.39 In *R v Governors of Small Heath School, ex p Birmingham City Council*,[1] it was held that teacher-governors do not have a direct pecuniary interest in a proposal for the acquisition by the school of grant-maintained status; but that even if they had and should have disqualified themselves from voting the court would have declined to intervene on the grounds that:

(1)   the resolution was only a step in a procedure which resulted in the ballot and the fact that the governors employed at the school voted for the resolution did not have any direct effect on the result of the ballot;

(2)   the governors employed at the school could have disseminated their views outside the meeting;

(3)   had the governors employed at the school not taken part in the meeting, this would only have affected the size of the majority and the resolution would still have been passed;

(4)   the Council was represented at the meeting but at no time did it raise any objection to the governors employed at the school taking part; and

(5)   the result of quashing the ballot would have been to prevent the decision of the majority of parents in favour of a change in the status of the school being implemented in time for the next academic year.

[1]   (1990) 2 Admin LR 154.

12.40 So too in *R v Governors of Bacon's School, ex p ILEA*[1] it was held that, although the court would not ignore the long-term public interest in providing a sanction for breach of the rule prohibiting a school governor from voting in any matter in which he has a pecuniary interest, the rule should not be regarded as sacrosanct. Where governors passed an unlawful resolution involving a technical and inadvertent breach of the rule by a governor and then passed a second resolution, which did not infringe the rule, and which affirmed the first resolution, the court, having regard to the public interest in the children's future and in not frustrating the governors' clear wishes, exercised its discretion to refuse to declare the resolutions invalid.

[1]   [1990] COD 414.

Non-Pecuniary Interests

12.41 A sharp distinction is drawn between a pecuniary and any other kind of interest. When the prospective decision-maker has a non-pecuniary interest, when in the language of Blackburn J in *R v Rand* (see **12.22** above), there is a challenge to the favour, regard is had to the extent and nature of the interest and (absent proof, ie in practice expression, of actual bias) disqualification does not follow as a matter of course.

The test for bias

12.42 The reviewing court must first ascertain all the circumstances which have a bearing on the allegation of bias.[1] It must then ask itself whether the test for bias is satisfied. Bias does not mean a total absence of preconceptions and predispositions.

The test in *Porter v Magill* is consistent with the approach of the ECtHR to the requirement that a court be impartial, not only in fact, but from an objective viewpoint.[2] 'Bias' may have pejorative connotations, but it may also mean an absence of demonstrated independence or impartiality.[3] While the test of a 'real possibility of bias' is less rigorous than one of probability, it is nonetheless a test which is 'founded on reality', and is a test not of 'any possibility' but of a 'real possibility' of bias.[4] In *Gillies v SoS for Work and Pensions*[5] it was held by the House of Lords that the relationship of a medical member of the Disability Appeal Tribunal with the Benefits Agency was that of an independent expert adviser and there was no basis for finding that there was a reasonable apprehension of bias on the ground that she had a predisposition to favour its interests; that the fair-minded observer would understand that there was a crucial difference between the medical member approaching the issues that the tribunal had to decide with a predisposition to prefer the views of the examining medical practitioner to any contrary evidence, and drawing on her own medical knowledge and experience when testing those against the other evidence, and that he would have no reason to think that she was likely to be unconsciously biased in favour of those views. Lord Hope said, at paragraph 17:

> ' . . . the fair-minded and informed observer can be assumed to have access to all the facts that are capable of being known by members of the public generally, & It is to be assumed, . . . that the observer is neither complacent nor unduly sensitive or suspicious when he examines the facts that he can look at. It is to be assumed too that he is able to distinguish between what is relevant and what is irrelevant, and that he is able when exercising his judgment to decide what weight should be given to the facts that are relevant.'

But note Lord Mance in *R v Abdroikof*:[6]

> ' . . . the fair-minded and informed observer is him or herself in large measure the construct of the court. Individual members of the public, all of whom might claim this description, have widely differing characteristics, experience, attitudes and beliefs which could shape their answers on issues such as those before the court, without their being easily cast as unreasonable. The differences of view in the present case illustrate the difficulties of attributing to the fair-minded and informed observer the appropriate balance between on the one hand complacency and naivety and on the other cynicism and suspicion.'

---

[1] Each bias case must turn upon its own particular facts and the whole of the surrounding factual context must be considered: per Sullivan LJ in *R (Secretary of State for Communities and Local Government v Ortona Ltd* [2009] EWCA Civ 863.

[2] See *Findlay v UK* (1997) 24 EHRR 221, at paragraph 73; and *Yiacoub v R* (2014) UKPC 22, at paragraph 11.

[3] See *Millar v Dickson* [2002] 1 WLR 1615, at paragraph 63, and *Yiacoub*, above, at paragraph 12.

[4] See *Turner v SoS for CLG* (2015) EWCA Civ 582, at paragraph 9.

[5] (2006) 1 WLR 781.

6   (2007) 1 WLR 2679, at paragraph 81.

12.43 The test for bias is whether a fair-minded and well-informed observer might conclude from all the circumstances that there was a real possibility that the tribunal was biased: *Porter v Magill*.[1] The 'real danger' test in *R v Gough*[2] is no more. There is now no difference between the common law test of bias and the requirement under art 6 of the European Convention of Human Rights of an impartial tribunal.

1   [2002] 2 AC 357, at paragraphs 95–104: applied in *Taylor v Lawrence* [2003] QB 528.
2   See, however, 'Bias and the Informed Observer: A Call for a return to *Gough*', by Professor Abimbola A Olowofoyeku at (2009) CLJ 388.

12.44 A fair-minded and informed observer will adopt a balanced approach. A reasonable member of the public is neither complacent nor unduly sensitive or suspicious. Some practices, however, will fall prey to increasing sensitivity. What the public was content to accept many years ago is not necessarily acceptable in the world of today. The indispensable requirement of public confidence in the administration of justice, which is at the core of a democratic society, requires higher standards today than was the case even a decade or two ago. The informed observer of today may be aware of the relevant traditions and culture, but may not be wholly uncritical of the culture. The modern approach has been laid down by the House of Lords in *Lawal v Northern Spirit Limited*[1] and by the Privy Council in *A-G of Belize v Belize Bank Ltd*,[2] in which it was stated (at paragraph 36) that 'The notional observer must be presumed to have two characteristics: full knowledge of the material facts and fair-mindedness'; (at paragraph 38) that 'one needs to be alert to the danger of transforming the observer from his essential condition of disinterested yet informed neutrality to that of someone who, by dint of his engagement in the system that has generated the challenge, has acquired something of an insider's status'; (at paragraph 39) that 'it is necessary that the objectivity of the notional observer should not be compromised by being drawn too deeply into a familiarity with the procedures if that would make him too ready to overlook an appearance of bias'; (again at paragraph 39) that 'The phrase "capable of being known" . . . holds the key . . . This does not signify a need to restrict the material to that which is immediately in the public domain: it acknowledges that the observer must have such information as may be necessary for an informed member of the public without any particular, specialised knowledge or experience, to make a dispassionate judgment'; and (at paragraph 41) that 'The concept of apparent bias does not rest on impression based on an incomplete picture but on a fair and reasoned judgment formed as a result of composed and considered appraisal of the relevant facts'.

In *Yiacoub*, above, there was the appearance of a lack of independence and impartiality in relation to a process because the objective observer would have said of the process 'That surely cannot be right' (paragraph 15). Sufficient security of tenure is needed in order to demonstrate judicial independence, but that does not rule out ad hoc appointments.[3] The 'notional' fair-minded and informed observer is a 'legal construct' and a Court will be 'very cautious' about treating any particular person as the real personification of that observer.[4] The nature of the functions and responsibilities being discharged must be taken into account: ibid, at paragraph 17. Active management of a process, such as by a Planning Inspector, is not likely to give an appearance of bias[5] (ibid, at paragraph 18). In *Harb v Prince Aziz*[6] the Court of Appeal emphasised, obiter, at paragraph 69 that the opinion of the notional informed and fair-minded observer is not to be confused with the opinion of the litigant, who lacks the objectivity which is the hallmark of the fair-minded observer; and, at paragraph 72, that the informed and fair-minded observer is to be treated as knowing all the relevant circumstances, whether or not in the public domain, and that it is for the Court to make an assessment of these. In *R (Southwark LBC) v LFEPA*[7] a Divisional Court added that the fair-minded and informed observer is not someone directly concerned with the litigation. The test is objective. It assumes that the observer has considered and understood the relevant features of the decision to be taken. It is not to be derived from an instinctive or emotional perspective.

In *Broadview Energy Developments Ltd v SoS for CLG*[8] the Court of Appeal indicated, at paragraph 36, that a well-informed observer would know that it is the responsibility of a decision-maker to make what are often difficult decisions about controversial projects, such as on-shore windfarms, that sometimes such decisions are finely balanced, that the decision-maker has to make a decision one way or the other which the parties should accept, and that a decision in favour of a vocal body of local objectors supported by their MP does not show any bias against the promoter of a project. On the other hand, those making (planning) decisions should not allow themselves to be 'lobbied'.

1 [2003] ICR 856, especially at paragraphs 15 and 22. See, also, *R (PD) v West Midlands and North West Mental Health Review Tribunal* [2004] EWCA Civ 311, (2004) 148 SJLB (no appearance of bias where medical member of tribunal employed by NHS trust); *Starrs v Ruxton* 2000 SLT 42 (Scottish temporary sheriffs); *Scanfuture v Trade and Industry Secretary* [2001] IRLR 416 (employment tribunal members); and *R v Spear* [2003] 1 WLR 734 (court martials).
2 [2011] UKPC 36, upon which see Mark Elliott at (2012) CLJ, 71(2), 247–250. Note that the knowledge of the hypothetical fair-minded and informed observer used to determine apparent bias is not restricted to the information publicly available at the time of the decision in question: *Virdi v Law Society (Solicitors Disciplinary Tribunal intervening)* [2010] EWCA Civ 100 at paras 44–52.
3 *Misick v R* [2015] UKPC 31, (2015) 1 WLR 3215.
4 *Turner v SoS for CLG* [EWCA] Civ 582, at paragraph 16.
5 Ibid, at paragraph 18.
6 [2014] EWCA Civ 556.
7 (2016) EWHC 1701 (Advisor), at paragraph 61.
8 [2016] EWCA Civ 562.

12.45 Useful guidance may also be obtained from *Locobail (UK) Ltd v Bayfield Properties Ltd.*[1] Where apparent bias is asserted it is for the reviewing court, personifying the reasonable man with knowledge of the relevant circumstances and adopting a broad approach, to assess whether there is a real possibility of bias. In making that assessment the court might properly inquire whether the judge knew of the matter relied on as undermining his impartiality, since ignorance would preclude its having influenced his mind and dispel any such possibility; although the judge could not be cross-examined or required to give disclosure, the reviewing court might properly receive, but would not necessarily accept, a statement from him as to his state of knowledge, but not as to its effect on him since that issue was for the court, not the judge, to assess. In any case of personal embarrassment (or of automatic disqualification where the judge had knowledge of his interest) he should recuse himself before objection was raised and at the earliest possible stage; in any other case where he was, or became, aware of a matter which could arguably give rise to a real possibility of bias he should make disclosure to the parties in advance of any hearing so that where objection was taken he might consider and adjudicate on it. Where, following appropriate disclosure, no objection was taken to his hearing or continuing to hear a case no subsequent complaint of bias could be made in respect of the matter so disclosed. What constituted appropriate disclosure would largely depend on the stage reached in the proceedings so that where, in advance of the hearing, the judge became aware of a matter which might affect his fitness to sit he should inquire fully into it and make full disclosure, but where such a matter emerged during the hearing, the judge, while being required to disclose what he then knew, was not obliged to conduct any fuller inquiry. While members of the Bar would not ordinarily have any knowledge of or responsibility for the affairs of other members of chambers, since a solicitor who was a partner in a firm bore responsibility for his partners and owed a duty to their clients of whose affairs he might personally be ignorant, he should, prior to sitting in any assigned civil case, conduct a careful conflict search within the firm; where any association was discovered during the hearing it should be disclosed to the parties and addressed on the particular facts by reference to the test whether a real possibility of bias arose. Where, however, a conflict of interest, such as would prohibit the solicitor from acting for one of the parties under the solicitors' professional rules, emerged before or during the hearing he was not necessarily barred from hearing or continuing to hear the case nor was any judgment he had given necessarily to be set aside. *Locobail* also makes it clear that if in any case there is real ground for doubt that doubt should be resolved in favour of recusal; but, as Norris J observed in *Ghadami v Blomfield*[2] applications for recusal inevitably involve a tension between two principles: that justice be seen to be done and that litigants cannot choose their Judges.

1   [2000] QB 451. As to the relevance of the state of knowledge of the decision-maker, see, also *Deacons v White & Case LLP* [2003] 2 HKLR 840.
2   [2016] EWHC 1448 (Ch), at paragraph 16.

12.46 It is no doubt rare that an application of the 'real possibility' test yields a different result from the 'real danger' test. Nonetheless, cases where apparent bias was not found applying the 'real danger' test have now to be treated with care. This caveat applies to decisions in the period between *Gough [1993]* and *Re Medicaments and Related Classes of Goods (No 2) (2001)/Porter v Magill/Lawal v Northern Spirit Ltd.*

12.47 Moreover, *pre-Gough* cases should also be treated with care, both because it is by no means always clearly the case that they were applying the current test, and because of their relative antiquity – as to which see *Lawal*, above.

12.48 A prime example of the *Gough* test being satisfied is the decision of the Court of Appeal in *R v Inner West London Coroner, ex p Dallaglio*.[1] Fifty-one people were drowned when a dredger collided with a passenger launch, *MV Marchioness*, on the Thames. At the instance of relatives of victims, judicial review was granted on grounds of apparent bias, of decisions of the Coroner not to recuse himself and not to resume the inquest. He had told tabloid journalists that one of the applicants was 'unhinged'.

1   [1994] 4 All ER 139.

12.49 Other examples, where, even applying the 'real danger' test, or applying the 'real possibility' test, apparent bias has been found include:

(1)   *R v Wilson*[1] – a juror the wife of an officer at the prison where the accused had been on remand;

(2)   *R v Horseferry Road Magistrates' Court, ex p Bilhar Chima*[2] – racist comments;

(3)   *R v Highgate Justices, ex p Riley*[3] – indication of general readiness to accept police evidence;

(4)   *Locobail (UK) Ltd v Bayfield Properties Ltd*[4] – expression in intemperate terms in articles of pro-claimant views and criticisms of defendants and their insurers;

(5)   *R (Chief Constable of Lancashire v Preston Crown Court*[5] – Crown Court including members of same licensing committee from which appeal brought from a refusal to grant a licence;

(6)   *R v Abdroikov* — presence on jury of serving police officer or solicitor employed by prosecuting body.[6]

In *Meerabux* (see **12.9** above), the Privy Council said (at paragraph 22) that if the House of Lords had felt able *in Pinochet (No 2)* to apply the *Re Medicaments/ Porter v Magill/Lawal v Northern Spirit Ltd* test:

> 'it is unlikely that it would have found it necessary to find a solution to the problem that it was presented with by applying the automatic disqualification rule.'

[1]   (1996) 8 Admin LR 1, CA.
[2]   [1995] COD 317.
[3]   [1996] RTR 150. See, also, the Canadian case of *R v S (RD)* [1997] 3 SCR 484.
[4]   [2000] QB 451.
[5]   [2002] 1 WLR 1332.
[6]   [2007] 1 WLR 2679 (House of Lords). See especially per Lord Bingham at paragraphs 14–17, per Baroness Hale at paragraphs 48–50 and per Lord Mance at paragraphs 80–81.

Non-judicial bodies

12.50 The important issue as to whether non-judicial bodies, such as an urban development corporation, are governed by the common law test of bias, was addressed by Sedley J in *R v Secretary of State for the Environment, ex p Kirkstall Valley Campaign Ltd*.[1] He held that they are. The common law test of bias should be uniformly applied. What will differ from case to case is the significance of the interest and its degree of proximity or remoteness to the issue to be decided and whether, if it is not so insignificant or remote as to be discounted, the participation of the member in the decision violates the decision.

[1]   [1996] 3 All ER 304.

12.51 Certainly when, in the language of art 6 of the European Convention of Human Rights, the 'determination' of 'civil rights and obligations' is involved, the art 6/common law test of impartiality/bias (and the additional art 6 requirement of independence) must apply, subject to the provisos that a defect in this respect as regards the primary decision-maker may be cured by the availability of statutory appeal and/or judicial review, and that there must be flexibility to take account of different administrative contexts.

12.52 In *R v Secretary of State for the Environment, ex p Kirkstall Valley Campaign Ltd*,[1] Sedley J further held that a declaration of a conflicting interest followed by abstention from speaking and voting may not be enough. Withdrawal from the meeting whether held in public or private may be required.

[1] [1996] 3 All ER 304.

12.53 As with pecuniary interests, there are statutory codes (somewhat differing as between England and Wales) in relation to local authorities, school governors and other bodies relating to the registration and declaration of interests, and setting out the circumstances in which the interest will generally bar participation, and the procedures by which that bar may be removed by dispensation. As noted at **12.31** above, they are not in identical terms to the common law formulation of bias (and do not always distinguish between pecuniary and non-pecuniary interests), but similar considerations nonetheless apply. Moreover, procedural rules may be impliedly restricted by the overriding requirements of natural justice: see *R (McNally) v Secretary of State for Education*.[1]

[1] [2002] ICR 15.

12.54 An example of local authority members having a non-pecuniary interest is when Liverpool City Council was considering a planning proposal on behalf of Liverpool Football Club and they were season-ticket holders or regular attenders.[1]

[1] *R v Local Commissioner for Administration, ex p Liverpool City Council* (2001) 1 All ER 462, affirming (1999) 3 All ER 85. See, also, the important decision of the Court of Appeal in *R (Richardson) v North Yorkshire County Council* [2004] LGR 351 on 'prejudicial interests' within the meaning of the 'model code of conduct' adopted by local authorities under the regime contained in Part III of the Local Government Act 2000.

12.55 Examples relating to school governors include *Champion v Gwent Chief Constable*[1] and *R v Kirklees Council, ex p Beaumont*.[2]

[1] [1990] 1 All ER 116, [1990] 1 WLR 1, HL.
[2] (2001) LGR 187 (a decision on the now superseded National Code of Local Government Conduct).

Kinds of non-pecuniary interest

12.56 Non-pecuniary personal interests may take many forms, a number of instances of which occur in *Locobail (UK) Ltd v Bayfield Properties Ltd* (see **12.42** above), for example:

(1)   family connection: *University College of Swansea v Cornelius*;[1] *R v Wilson*,[2] *Roylance v GMC*;[3]

(2)   personal friendship or acquaintance or personal animosity: *Rees v Crane*[4], *Grant v Teachers Appeal Panel*:[5] it does not necessarily follow from personal knowledge of a witness that there will be prejudice in favour of (or against) that person's testimony: in each individual case it must be decided whether the familiarity in question is 'of such a nature

and degree' as to indicate lack of impartiality on the part of the decision-maker: *Armstrong v UK*,[6] and see *AWG Group Ltd v Morrison*;[7]

(3)   Active interest in an organisation: *Champion v Gwent Chief Constable*,[8] *Pillar v UK*,[9] *R (Port Regis School Ltd) v North Dorset DC*,[10] *Helow v Advocate General for Scotland*;[11] but previous experience may be a qualifying criterion rather than a basis for disqualification, *R (Sinn Fein) v SoS for Northern Ireland*[12] and *Laird v Tatum*;[13]

(4)   previous or dual involvement in the case: *Hamlet v GMBATU*,[14] *Jeyaretnam v Law Society of Singapore*,[15] and *R v Crown Court at Bristol, ex parte Cooper*,[16] with which contract *R (Chief Constable of Lancashire) v Preston Crown Court*,[17] *Nwabueze v GMC*,[18] and see in relation to adverse comments on a party in previous proceedings *Lodwick v Southwark LBC*,[19] in relation to consecutive advisory and judicial functions *Kleyn v Netherlands*,[20] and in relation to consecutive legislative and judicial functions *Davidson v Scottish Ministers*,[21] discussed in CHAPTER 22: generally previous decisions in the same case do not disqualify unless it can be shown that the later decision is likely to be reached by reference to extraneous matters or predilections or preferences: *Otkritic International Investment Management Ltd v Urumor*;[22]

(5)   previous relationships: *R v South Worcestershire JJs, ex parte Lilley*,[23] *ASMI Shipping Ltd of India v TTMI Ltd of England*,[24] *Smith v Kraemer Cementation Foundation Ltd*,[25] *Gillies v SoS for Work and Pensions*,[26] *R v Abdroikof*,[27] *Paul v Deputy Coroner of the Queen's Household*[28] and *Watts v Watts*;[29]

(6)   Contact during an adjournment or during the course of deliberations: *Marsh v SoS for the Environment*,[30] *R (McNally) v SoS for Education*,[31] *Joyce v Dorset County Council*,[32] *R (Opaka) v Principal of Southwark College*,[33] *Norbrook Laboratories v Tank*[34] and *R (Gardner) v Harrogate BC*;[35]

(7)   preconceived views, which may also amount to an unlawful fettering of discretion: *Ansar v Lloyds TSB*,[36] *Steadman-Byrne v Amjed*;[37]

(8)   previous adverse criticism, immoderate or intemperate use of language or excessive interruptions: *Berkeley Administration Inc v McClelland*,[38] *Cairnstores Ltd v Aktiebolaget Hassle*[39] and *Orange Telecommunications Ltd v Director of Telecommunications Regulations*.[40] An interim Report may contain such strongly worded allegations that a fair-minded and informed observer would conclude that the author had made up his mind and would not approach the remainder of the Inquiry with an open mind and would not produce an impartial Final Report: *Mitchell v Georges*.[41]

[1] [1988] ICR 735.
[2] (1996) 8 Admin LR 1, CA.
[3] [2000] AC 311.
[4] [1994] 2 AC 173.
[5] (2006) UKPC 59.
[6] ECtHR Judgment, 9 December 2014, Application No. 65282/09.
[7] [2006] 1 WLR 1163 (CA).
[8] (1990) 1 All ER 116, (1990) 1 WLR 1 (HL).
[9] (1996) 22 EHRR 391, ECtHR.
[10] (2006) EWHC 742 (Admin).
[11] (2008) UKHL 62, (2008) 1 WLR 2416.

[12] (2007) EWHC 12 *(Admin) (DC)*, especially at paragraphs **102/103**.
[13] 409 US 824.
[14] (1987) 1 All ER 631, (1987) 1 WLR 449.
[15] (1989) 2 AC 608, (1989) 2 All ER 193.
[16] (1990) 2 All ER 193, (1990), 1 WLR 103.
[17] (2002) 1 WLR 1332.
[18] (2000) 1 WLR 1760.
[19] (2004) EWCA Civ 306.
[20] (2004) 38 EHRR 14.
[21] (2004) HRLR 34.
[22] (2014) EWCA Civ 1315.
[23] (1993) 1 WLR 1595.
[24] (2005) EWHC 2238 (Comm).
[25] (2007) 1 WLR 370.
[26] (2006) 1 WLR 781 (HL).
[27] (2007) 1 WLR 2679.
[28] (2007) EWHC 408 (Admin).
[29] (2015) EWCA Civ 1297.
[30] (1995) 70 P&CR 637.
[31] (2002) ICR 15.
[32] (1997) ELR 26.
[33] (2003) 1 WLR 234.
[34] (2006) 2 Lloyd's Rep 485.
[35] (2008) EWHC 2942.
[36] (2007) IRLR 211 (CA).
[37] (2007) 1 WLR 2484 (CA).
[38] (1990) 2 QB 407, (1990) 1 All ER 958.
[39] (2003) FSR 23.
[40] (2000) 4 IR 159, especially Keane CJ.
[41] [2014] UKPC 43.

12.57 An active role in a prosecution or close connection with the prosecutor certainly will. An assumption of incompatible functions is bound to create an impression of unfairness. No two functions are inherently more incompatible than those of prosecutor and judge. *O'Neill v HM Advocate (Scotland)*[1] the Supreme Court held that the ECHR Article 6(1) requirement of a trial before an 'independent and impartial tribunal' was not infringed by a decision to proceed with a (murder) trial following adverse comments made by the trial judge regarding the character of the defendants, I and N. When the judge made his remarks he was addressing I and N in the performance of his judicial function. The fair-minded and informed observer would appreciate that he was a professional judge who had taken the judicial oath and had years of relevant training and experience. They would understand the context in which the remarks were made. They were made in open court while he was performing his duty as a judge at the trial. The informed observer would also appreciate that when the judge was presiding over the second trial he would be doing so in the performance of his duty and that, while the facts were a matter for the jury, the judge had functions to perform which required him to be impartial. It would only be if the judge expressed outspoken opinions that were entirely gratuitous regarding I and N's character, and only if he made them at a time when it was plainly outside the scope of the proper performance of his duties in conducting the trial, that his ability to perform those duties with an objective judicial mind would be doubted. The context indicated that that was not the position in the instant case. I and N had been entitled to be given some indication of likely sentence and the judge's comments were directly relevant to that issue. I and N and their legal representatives were present when the remarks were made and no objection was made then or at the start of the murder trial to the fact that the same judge was presiding. There was no basis for the suggestion that the judge was apparently biased. In *Igbalo v Solicitors Regulation Authority*[2] a Divisional Court held that no appearance of bias arose from the inclusion on the Solicitors Disciplinary Tribunal of a solicitor member who had previously acted for the SRA as an adjudicator in an unrelated case. A judge's previous employment history is not ordinarily relevant to the question of apparent bias. This contrasts with a continuing interest in an organisation.

In *Sanders v Airports Commission*[3] it was held that the presence on a commission set up to report on airport expansion of a commissioner who had been the chief executive of an airports group did not give rise to the appearance of apparent bias so as to taint the commission's activities and decisions. The other commissioners would not have given him undue deference and he had no disproportionate influence, and the commission had adopted a defensive strategy, in that the commissioner had absented himself from certain meetings before stepping down.

In *Roebuck v National Union of Mineworkers (Yorkshire Area)*[4] a libel action was brought by the union president against a newspaper. Members of the union made statements to the newspaper's solicitors and gave evidence. Disciplinary proceedings were taken by the union against the members, the machinery being set in motion by a complaint by the president expressing views of the members' guilt or culpability. The president sat as chairman of the disciplinary committee. On motions for interlocutory injunctions the court held that there was nothing in the union rules which made it essential for the president to sit as chairman of the area executive committee or of the area council if for some other reason he were disqualified from so doing. The ordinary rules of natural justice applied. The president, having in his complaint, expressed his views as to the guilt and culpability of those to be brought before the disciplinary tribunal, was disqualified from adjudicating upon the two cases on the grounds that he had acted as prosecutor and that he was a person who was biased. Justice had neither been done nor been seen to be done. The decisions of the executive committee and the area council were therefore void. Whether the president had a vote or not, or influenced the proceedings, mattered not one iota. The subsequent final judgment is to be found at *Roebuck v National Union of Mineworkers (Yorkshire Area) (No 2)*.[5]

1   (2013) UKSC 36.
2   (2013 EWHC 661 (Admin).
3   (2013) EWHC 3754 (Admin).
4   [1977] ICR 573.
5   [1978] ICR 676.

12.58 In *Haddow v ILEA*[1] the Employment Appeal Tribunal held that the fact that the education officer was the prosecutor at a teachers' disciplinary tribunal and was also required in accordance with the provisions of the staff code to be available for consultation by members of the tribunal did not involve a fundamental breach of the rules of natural justice because it was evident that the tribunal had acted fairly and justly. Moreover, there was no merit in the teachers' case. The evidence against them was overwhelming. *McNally*, (see **12.53** above), is to contrary effect, but *Haddow* does not appear to have been cited.

¹   [1979] ICR 202.

12.59 In *Re S (A Barrister)*,¹ the Committee of the General Council of the Bar preferred charges of misconduct against a barrister. The hearing took place before a disciplinary tribunal of the Senate of the Inns of Court and the Bar. The tribunal consisted of members of the Senate, practising barristers and a lay member. The Visitors to the Inner Temple held, dismissing an appeal, that the General Council of the Bar, although part of the Senate, acted as an autonomous body for the purposes of its separate powers and duties and under the regulations a member of its Professional Conduct Committee was precluded from being a member of the disciplinary tribunal. Since the regulations ensured that those who were responsible for investigating and prosecuting a complaint of misconduct did not adjudicate on the hearing of the complaint, there was no question of those who prosecuted being judges in the cause. Although lay members were now included as members of professional disciplinary tribunals in recognition of the public interest in ensuring that the investigation of the affairs of a profession was fair and impartial, it had always been recognised that professional men were peculiarly fitted to determine whether there had been a breach of the professional code of conduct and to judge the gravity of such breach. Therefore, a requirement that lay members should form a majority of a disciplinary tribunal was inconsistent with principle and authority. Accordingly, the members of the disciplinary tribunal could not be said to be biased because the majority of its members were also members of the profession.

¹   [1981] QB 683, [1981] 2 All ER 952.

12.60 *R v Secretary of State for the Environment, ex p Norwich City Council*¹ was concerned with the right to buy of council tenants. The question arose whether in order to state the price the council could employ the district valuer to make the initial valuation. He would sit on what was in effect an appeal from it to make the final valuation. The Court of Appeal (though with great anxiety on the part of Kerr LJ) approved the practice, on the basis that the initial valuation was done by a clerk in the district valuer's office, and the decision on appeal was made by the district valuer himself or his deputy.

Contrast, however, *Primary Health Investment Properties Ltd v Secretary of State for Health* [2009] EWHC 519 (Admin), in which apparent bias was found in the procedures adopted by the NHS for doctors claiming reimbursement of rent paid for surgery premises. The District Valuer (DV) was instructed to act on behalf of the NHS Trust. McCombe J held that the public perception would clearly be that the DV was acting in all senses as the agent of the Trust and as its expert adviser in the negotiation of the matter at its initial stages. It was also going to represent the Trust's presentation of its case on appeal. The adverse perceptions raised about the roles of the DV and the chief executive officer of the Valuation Office Agency could not be overcome by the fact that individual valuation office agency valuers strived to act professionally and, as far as they could do so, independently of each other, in their respective roles. The connections between the DV, acting for the Trust at all stages, and the chief executive's office of the Valuation Office Agency, advising the appeal unit as decision-maker in the dispute, were too close for justice to be seen to be done.

¹   [1982] QB 808.

THE AMBIT OF THE RULE AGAINST BIAS

12.61   The rule against pecuniary interests applies whether the decision-maker is performing a judicial or quasi-judicial role or is performing an administrative function. The rule against non-pecuniary interests, on the other hand, has traditionally had a much more limited ambit when applied in administrative rather than judicial or quasi-judicial contexts. This distinction is now, however, much eroded by art 6 of the European Convention of Human Rights, at any rate when the determination of civil rights and obligations is involved.

12.62   An instance of the contrast, or former contrast, is provided by *R v Secretary of State for Trade, ex p Perestrello*.¹ Under the Companies Act 1967, the Board of Trade was empowered to demand the production of certain papers from a company if it thought there was a good reason to do so. Considering a challenge to the exercise of this power on the grounds of bias, Woolf J, as he then was, said that he considered this was not an appropriate situation in which to apply the test for bias applied in the case of judicial or quasi-judicial functions. On looking at the functions of the Board of Trade Officers he found it wholly inappropriate to talk about them not being regarded as biased if they are performing their functions properly.

> 'They are acting in a policing role . . . it is wholly inappropriate for the case to be approached in the same way as one would approach a person performing a normal judicial role or quasi-judicial role; a situation where a person is making a determination.'

¹   [1981] QB 19, [1980] 3 All ER 28.

12.63   In this case the limits spelt out by Woolf J (not necessarily exhaustive, he said) were that the officers must not exceed or abuse the discretion given under the statute or use it for some ulterior purpose – although that much is required anyway, by the ultra vires doctrine.

12.64   In many administrative situations the possibility of bias is built into the system. Proposers of a scheme may have strong and carefully thought-out views on the subject, and yet may have guidelines to help them in their day-to-day application of legislation. In such situations the concept of a fair trial may be impossible and, indeed, undesirable to achieve. It has been pointed out (1932 (Cmd 4060))¹ that the more indifferent to the aim in view the less efficient is a Minister or civil servant likely to be. After all, it is his job to get things done. So, while the obvious prejudgment of an issue is not allowed, a challenge to a decision on the grounds of departmental bias is unlikely to succeed. It is a Minister's job to have a policy and to support it in public.²

¹   'Report of Committee on Ministers' Powers' at p 78.
²   This paragraph in a previous edition was cited in paragraph 84 of the judgment of the Divisional Court in *Alconbury* as well stating the undisputed position in domestic law (see paragraph 178 in the speech of Lord Hutton in the House of Lords).

12.65 Assistance on that question can be found in cases from New Zealand. Wild CJ said in *Turner v Allison*,[1] where members of a planning appeal board had expressed their views on the best use for the land in question:

'By the very nature of their work in a special field, the members of such a Board must acquire opinion about the type of questions they deal with.'

[1] [1971] NZLR 833.

12.66 Turner J said:

'It is not enough [to disqualify them] that the tribunal or some member of it has expressed a preconceived opinion, even one firmly held, on the matter to be tried . . . It must appear that the tribunal intends to adhere to the point of view which has been expressed, uninfluenced by further evidence or argument addressed to it.'

12.67 This being so, the case of *Franklin v Minister of Town and Country Planning*[1] may have been rightly decided, although not necessarily for the right reasons.[2] The House of Lords held that the Minister had a duty genuinely to consider objections to the inspector's report on the siting of a New Town but references to bias were out of place in the context: what was important was to follow the relevant procedure. The Court of Appeal, on the other hand, had held that the obligations of natural justice required the Minister to give an impartial consideration to the representations, and held that such consideration had been given, bearing in mind that impartiality cannot be the same in the context of a minister making such a decision as in the case of a magistrate hearing a case. The relevant question is whether the Minister, when he comes to make his decision, genuinely addresses himself to the questions with a mind which is open to persuasion. In *R (HS2 Action Alliance Ltd) v Secretary of State for Transport*[3] the Supreme Court (paragraph 103) approved *Franklin* on the basis that the Minister's decision-making function was not of a judicial or quasi-judicial character; the only question was whether he had genuinely considered the report and the objections when they were submitted to him; there is no universal rule requiring that decision-makers must possess the independence and impartiality required of a court or tribunal, and it is necessary to take account of the constitutional position of the decision-maker, and of the nature of the decision.

[1] [1948] AC 87, [1947] 2 All ER 289.
[2] See Aronson and Franklin *Review of Administrative Action* (1987) p 204.
[3] [2014] UKSC 3.

12.68 In *CREEDNZ Inc v Governor-General*,[1] where the making of a Development Order for an aluminium works was challenged on the ground that there was bias by reason of pre-determination of the issue, Cooke J said:

'Realistically, it was clear that the Government had decided that the project was to go ahead – but it was a fallacy to think that because the Government was highly likely to advise in favour of the Order, that they were disqualified from making a determination.'

[1] [1981] 1 NZLR 172. See, also, *Riverside Casino Ltd v Bishop of Waikato* [2001] NZCA 401.

12.69 To do the work that has been entrusted to them by Parliament, Ministers need to form and express opinions. To apply a test of impartiality would make the legislation unworkable. The relevant question is whether at the time of making the Order in Council the Ministers genuinely addressed themselves to the statutory criteria and were of the opinion that the criteria were satisfied (Cooke J). As Richards J said, the rule against bias must be tempered with realism.

12.70 There are many contexts where the test for bias applied in the case of judicial or quasi-judicial functions is inappropriate. The reasonable-man test cannot be applied rigidly in a situation where the reasonable man will always suspect bias, and nothing can be done about it. This has been much to the fore recently in cases concerning local planning authorities.[1] There is an obvious possibility of the appearance of bias in their dual role as developer of their own land and as planning authority.

[1] See 'Probity and Planning' by Charles George QC [1997] JPL 181; and note *In the Matter of Belfast Chamber of Commerce* [2001] NICA 6, a judgment of Carswell LCJ (as he then was) concerned with a ministerial planning decision, and an allegation of bias in respect of a very senior official adviser was made, and it was held that in such a situation the principles by which decisions of biased decision-makers are invalidated would apply (paragraph 75).

12.71 This does not mean that the decision of a planning authority cannot be held to be vitiated by bias.[1] In *Anderton v Auckland City Council*[2] the Supreme Court of New Zealand recognised that Parliament had made the Council judge in its own cause by vesting in that body the right to hear and determine objections to its own proposed scheme change; but held that the Council had become so closely associated with the development company's attempts to secure planning permission for its project over the six years preceding the hearing of its application that it had completely surrendered its powers of independent judgement and had determined in advance to allow the application. In consequence their decision was invalid.

[1] See Flick *Natural Justice* (2nd edn), p 165 and Aronson and Franklin *Review of Administrative Action* (1987), p 205.
[2] [1978] 1 NZLR 657.

12.72 Likewise in *Steeples v Derbyshire County Council*[1] – in 1972 the County Council had granted themselves outline planning permission to develop an area which became known as Shipley County Park. In 1979 they entered into a joint venture agreement with a company which provided that the County Council should take 'all reasonable steps to obtain the grant of outline planning permission for such parts of the development area as may be necessary to enable the development to proceed'. Thereafter the County Council purported to grant themselves planning permissions. Webster J quashed the grants.

[1] [1984] 3 All ER 468, [1985] 1 WLR 256.

12.73 The decision in *Steeples* was no doubt correct, but some of Webster J's observations have not survived subsequent judicial scrutiny. The sequel to *Steeples* is provided by *R v Amber Valley District Council, ex p Jackson*[1] which again concerned the Shipley County Park. The grounds upon which judicial review in the form of an order of prohibition was sought against the District Council were:

'Any decision by the Amber Valley District Council is likely to be biased and unfair and contrary to its statutory duty pursuant to section 29 of the Town and Country Planning Act 1971 in that important members of the Labour majority of the Amber

Valley District Council, including the leader of the Labour group and the Chairman of the Planning Committee, have by their conduct been shown to be likely to follow the decision of the Derbyshire County Council Labour group to the effect that planning permission should be granted and that decision was taken without any or any sufficient regard to the provisions of the said section 29 and when the persons making the said decision had an interest in the matter.'

1   [1984] 3 All ER 501, [1985] 1 WLR 298.

12.74 Woolf J held, dismissing the application, that the principles of natural justice applied to the consideration of an application for planning permission. Accordingly, in considering the company's application, the district council had a general duty to act fairly, as well as having a specific duty under s 29(2) of the Act of 1971 (now s 71(1) of the Town and County Planning Act 1990), to consider such representations as the applicant's which related to, and were made within a certain period of, the application. The political predisposition of the majority of council members in favour of the proposed development was not of itself a ground for disqualifying them from adjudicating on a planning application nor was it indicative of unfairness on their part. Accordingly, in the absence of any other evidence that the council would fail to consider the planning application and the representations thereto on their merits, there were no grounds for the court's intervention.

12.75 On the other hand, Woolf J stated that he would have difficulty in applying to an administrative decision of a planning committee the test applicable in the case of judicial or quasi-judicial functions. He said:[1]

'I fully accept, particularly having regard to the authorities to which I have referred, that there is an obligation upon the district council to deal fairly with the applications by KLF for planning permission and that in that sense the principles of natural justice apply to the consideration of an application for planning permission. Furthermore, I agree that this court has the right to intervene to prevent an application being dealt with in an unfair manner or contrary to the principles of natural justice by the district council. However, I cannot accept that Webster J's test can be applied in this situation. It is much easier for the court to interfere on the basis of procedural unfairness than on the basis of bias of the sort alleged in this case. It is to be noted that it is not alleged here that the district council had entered into any contract which precluded it from exercising an independent judgment as was alleged against the county council. Nor is it alleged that any individual district councillor has some personal financial interest. My conclusion as to what the evidence shows in this case is that it indicates that the majority of the district council can only be said to be "biased" in the sense that they are as the respondent's counsel contends "politically predisposed" in favour of the development in respect of which planning permission is sought. It had become the Labour group's policy to support the development. It is therefore likely that any Labour member of the planning committee will be more ready to grant planning permission than he would be if the Labour group had remained adverse to the development. But does this have the effect of disqualifying the Labour majority from considering the planning application? It would be a surprising result if it did since in the case of a development of this sort, I would have thought that it was almost inevitable, now that party politics play so large a part in local government, that the majority group on a council would decide on the party line in respect of the proposal. If this was to be regarded as disqualifying the district council from dealing with the planning application, then if that disqualification is to be avoided, the members of the planning committee at any rate will have to adopt standard of conduct which I suspect will be almost impossible to achieve in practice.

The rules of fairness or natural justice cannot be regarded as being rigid. They must alter in accordance with the context. Thus in the case of highways, the Department can be both the promoting authority and the determining authority. When this happens, of course any reasonable man would regard the department as being predisposed towards the outcome of the inquiry. The department is under an obligation to be fair and carefully to consider the evidence given before the inquiry but the fact that it has a policy in the matter does not entitle a court to intervene. So in this case I do not consider the fact that there is a declaration of policy by the majority group can disqualify a district council from adjudicating on a planning application. It may mean that the outcome of the planning application is likely to be favourable to an application and therefore unfavourable to objectors.

However, Parliament has seen fit to lay down that it is the local authority which has the power to make the decision and an applicant for planning permission in the normal way is entitled to have a decision from the local authority if the Secretary of State decides not to intervene. The legislation could have given a right of appeal to the objectors in the same way as this is given to applicants but this it has not done and they are dependent on the limited powers of this court to intervene by way of judicial review.

I do not say that the court can never intervene. Indeed I do not question Webster J's decision to do so in respect of the conduct of the county council. However in this case, while the Labour majority undoubtedly had a policy, there is no evidence before me on which it would be right to hold that they would not (despite the policy) consider the objections to the planning application on their merits. I would make it absolutely clear that they are under a duty to do so.'

---

[1]   At 307.

12.76 Woolf J's approach in Amber Valley has been followed by Glidewell J in *R v Sevenoaks District Council, ex p Terry*,[1] by Stocker J in *R v St Edmundsbury Borough Council, ex p Investors in Industry Commercial Properties Ltd*,[2] and by Macpherson J in *R v Carlisle City Council, ex p Cumbrian Co-operative Society Ltd*.[3] As to planning inspectors, *Bryan v United Kingdom*;[4] as to conduct of interviews to decide whether homelessness is intentional, *R v Tower Hamlets LBC, ex p Khatun*[5] and as to educational discipline, *R v Governors of the Sheffield Hallam University, ex p R*[6] illustrate the ambit of the rule against bias.

[1]   [1985] 3 All ER 226.
[2]   [1985] 3 All ER 234, [1985] 1 WLR 1157.
[3]   [1985] 2 EGLR 193. Bias was also not found in *R v Hereford and Worcester County Council, ex p Wellington Parish Council* (1995) 94 LGR 159, *R v Holderness Borough Council, ex p James Robert Developments Ltd* (1992) 66 P & CR 46, CA, and *R v Newport County Borough, ex p Avery* [1999] JPL 452 (applicant's father a member of the relevant planning committee); but contrast *Georgiou v Enfield LBC* [2004] LGR 497 (challenge to grant of planning permission for development of listed building succeeded where three members of the planning committee had previously been party to a decision of the council's conservation advisory group expressing unqualified support for the development); and *R (Ghadami) v Harlow DC* [2004] EWHC 1883 (Admin), [2005] LGR 24. See, also, *Bovis Homes Ltd v New Forest District Council* [2002] EWHC 483 (Admin). Ouseley J and *Kwan Kong Co v Town Planning Board* [1996] 2 HKLR 363.
[4]   (1996) 21 EHRR 342, ECt HR; see, also, [1996] JPL 359 and 386; *Jones v Secretary of State for Wales* (1995) 70 P & CR 211, CA (it may be appropriate to cross-examine); *R (Alconbury Developments Ltd) v Secretary of State* [2001] AC 295 (the role of the Secretary of State);

'Applying Alconbury: Article 6, third parties and development plans' by Timothy Corner QC and Paul Brown at [2002] JPL 661; 'Bias in planning decision-making' at [2002] JPL 783; and see, also, **4.76** above; *R (Friends Provident Life Office) v Secretary of State for the Environment* [2002] 1 WLR 1450 and *Ball v Secretary of State for Communities and Local Government* [2012] EWHC 3590 (Admin).

5 (1995) 27 HLR 465, CA.
6 [1994] COD 470.

12.77 There has always been a tension between the rule against bias and predetermination, and the fact that local authority members stand for office on the basis of stated policies which they are expected to implement once elected. This tension is addressed in the decision of Collins J in *R (on the application of Island Farm Development Ltd) v Bridgend County BC* [2007] LGR 60. The claimants had been granted planning permission to develop a site adjoining land belonging to the local authority. The development required that the local authority sell its land. Following elections, there was a change of control in the authority. The new administration was led by members of a party which had opposed the development in its manifesto. One cabinet member had been an active member of a pressure group devoted to opposing the development. A decision was subsequently taken not to sell the council's land to the claimants. The claimants challenged this decision on grounds of bias and predetermination. In a pragmatic judgment, Collins J refused the application. He noted (at [23]):

' . . . In principle, councillors must in making decisions consider all relevant matters and approach their task with no preconceptions. But they are entitled to have regard to and apply policies in which they believe, particularly if those policies have been part of their manifestos. The present regime believed that the development . . . was wrong and they had made it clear that that was their approach. In those circumstances, they were entitled to consider whether the development could lawfully be prevented . . . '

Collins J went on to doubt Richards J's dicta in *Georgiou v Enfield LBC* suggesting that no significant weight should be attached to members' own assertions that they approached a matter with an open mind, before commenting (at [30]):

' . . . Councillors will inevitably be bound to have views on and may well have expressed them about issues of public interest locally . . . It would be quite impossible for decisions to be made by the elected members whom the law requires to make them if their observations could disqualify them because it might appear that they had formed a view in advance . . . '

On the basis of the material before him that demonstrated that the members were prepared to and did consider the relevant arguments and were prepared to change their minds, Collins J accordingly dismissed the application. The decision in the *Island Farm Development* case recognises the realities of local politics in a manner which, it is to be hoped, will enhance the operation of local democracy.

In August 2007 the Standards Board for England issued an Occasional Paper, 'Predisposition, Predetermination or Bias, and the Code', accompanied by an Opinion, also on the Board's website, by Senior Treasury Council, Philip Sales QC, as he then was.

12.78 There is of course a vital distinction to be drawn between a legitimate predisposition towards a particular outcome and an illegitimate predetermination of the outcome. The former is consistent with a preparedness to consider and weigh relevant factors in reaching the final decision. The latter involves a mind that is closed to the consideration and weighing of relevant factors. It is to be noted that, even once a conclusion has been reached, there is not necessarily a predetermination in relation to reconsideration by the same person(s).[1] What is vital is that there are fairness and open-mindedness at the time of the final decision, whatever may have happened before.

[1] See *Grant v Teacher's Appeals Tribunal* [2006] UK PC 59 ('*Grant*') at paragraphs 30/31.

12.79 In determining whether there has been predetermination, it is necessary first to establish the actual facts. This means the totality of the circumstances as they appear from all the material available upon investigation, not just the facts known to the complainant, or available to a hypothetical observer, at the time of the decision.[1]

[1] See the decision of the Court of Appeal on 27 November 2006 in *Condron v National Assembly for Wales* [2006] EWCA Civ 1573,[2007] LGR 87 ('*Condron*'), at paragraphs 50 and 55 (Richards LJ), 114 and 117 (Wall LJ) and 121 and 122 (Ward LJ), overruling the first instance decision on precisely this point.

12.80 It is not the case that the participation of a single participant with a closed mind (but no personal and prejudicial interest) in a multi-member decision is necessarily fatal if it does not appear that the participation may have influenced the outcome. It is to be noted that in *Condron* significance was attached (eg at paragraph 5) to the facts that the individual in relation to whom there was concern was the Chair of the Committee, who might have had influence over the debate, that the Committee consisted of only four members, and that if there were an equality of votes he, as Chair, had a casting (as well as an original) vote. Also, in *Grant*, at paragraph 32, the Privy Council held that the admission of one invalid vote did not invalidate the decision, because of the size of the majority, and because it was not established that the other, valid, voters had been 'unduly swayed' by the invalid voter. See further *R (Berky) v Newport City Council*[1] where the Court of Appeal said (at paragraph 58) that 'there is really no reason at all to assume that the mere presence of one member who is biased or has made up his' mind in advance must automatically render a decision unlawful. Such a rule should certainly not be applied when, as in this case, the judge has made a specific finding of fact that the tainted member had no effect on the decision'.

In *ASM Shipping Ltd v Harris*[2] Andrew Smith J held that there is no invariable rule, nor is it necessarily the case, that where one member of a tribunal is tainted by apparent bias the whole tribunal is affected second-hand by apparent bias and should therefore recuse themselves or should be excluded from the proceedings. See to the same effect *R (Fraser) v National Institute for Health and Clinical Excellence*.[3]

[1] [2012] EWCA Civ 378.
[2] [2007] EWHC 1513 (Comm).
[3] [2009] EWHC 452 (Admin), 107 BMLR 178.

12.81 *Condron* is instructive. In *Condron* Lindsay J, relying on *Georgiou*, held that Carwen Jones AM, the Minister for Environment, Planning and Countryside of the Welsh Assembly Government, ('the WAG'), and Chair of the Planning Decision Committee ('the PDC'), had acted in a pre-determined manner when considering an application for planning permission where he had expressed an inclination to follow the Inspector's recommendation to grant planning permission. A fair minded observer would have concluded that there was a real possibility of bias in the decision of the PDC to grant planning permission and it had to be quashed.

12.82 The Court of Appeal unanimously overturned this decision. The leading Judgment was delivered by Richards LJ. The Court of Appeal approached the case on the basis that the day before the PDC Meeting the Chair remarked to an objector (Jennie Jones) that he was 'going to go with the Inspector's Report', which recommended approval of the planning application. There were only four members of the PDC.

12.83 Richards LJ observed (paragraph 38) that neither before Lindsay J nor before the Court of Appeal was there any disagreement as to the correct legal test. Applying that test Richards LJ concluded (paragraph 42), that:

' . . . when they are viewed objectively and in their context, the words appear to me to be consistent with the speaker having a predisposition to follow the inspector's report without necessarily having a closed mind on the subject.'

12.84 Richards LJ stated (paragraph 43) that the Court of Appeal had been referred to various cases in which the distinction has been drawn between:

(1)   A legitimate predisposition towards a particular outcome; and

(2)   An illegitimate predetermination of the outcome.

12.85 Richards LJ said:

'The former is consistent with a preparedness to consider and weigh relevant factors in reaching the final decision; the latter involves a mind that is closed to the consideration and weighing of relevant factors.'

12.86 At paragraph 44 Richards LJ referred to a submission that in some of the cases the Court had been influenced in its approach by a recognition that allowance needs to be made in order to reconcile the responsibilities of public authorities as decision-makers with the workings of the democratic process and the fact that declarations of policy are frequently made in the course of that process. Richards LJ responded:

'That may be so, but in my view it does not affect the validity of the distinction between predisposition and predetermination.'

12.87 At paragraph 45, Richards LJ stated that, in addition to the words themselves:

'It is necessary to bear in mind the context in which they were spoken.'

12.88 As regards their immediate context, these were a few words spoken towards the end of a short and rather tense conversation, following a chance encounter and without preparation or warning. Richards LJ observed:

'For my part, I think that a remark made in circumstances such as these needs to be treated with a considerable degree of caution. It is a case where the wider picture is particularly important in assessing the significance of the words used.'

12.89 At paragraph 47 Richards LJ stated that, in the light of the Inspector's Report, which Carwyn Jones had received as the responsible Minister:

'. . . there would be nothing surprising about his having a predisposition in favour of the grant of planning permission as recommended by the inspector.'

12.90 At paragraph 50, cited in *Turner v SoS for CLG*,[1] Richards LJ emphasised that Lindsay J's approach had been wrong, because:

'The court must look at all the circumstances as they appear from the material before it, not just at the facts known to the objectors or available to the hypothetical observer at the time of the decision.'

---

[1] [2015] EWCA Civ 582, at paragraph 16.

12.91 At paragraph 52 Richards LJ stated that the relevant matters included the qualifications for membership of the PDC. He stated:

'Even the most basic course of training in planning matters would bring home the importance of approaching decisions with an open mind and having regard to all relevant considerations. This would be reinforced by the requirements of the Code of Conduct . . . '

12.92 At paragraph 53 Richards LJ said:

'In the context of allegations of apparent bias against members of courts or tribunals, weight has been placed on the judicial oath of office and the fact that professional judges are trained to judge and to judge objectively and dispassionately:
. . . Whilst the position of members of a planning committee, even at the level of the Assembly, is of course very different from that of judicial office-holders, the fact that they have received relevant training and have agreed to be bound by a code of conduct is a consideration to which some weight can properly be attached when determining an issue of apparent bias.'

12.93 Richards LJ concluded, at paragraphs 55–57:

'the judge fell into error by disregarding relevant circumstances or in his assessment of their significance. He appears to have concentrated unduly on the encounter between Jennie Jones and Carwyn Jones on 2 February 2005 and how it would have appeared to an observer at the time, rather than taking into account the totality of circumstances apparent to the court upon investigation. . . . The conclusion I have reached is that a fair-minded and informed observer, having considered all the facts as they are now known, would *not* conclude that there was a real possibility that Carwyn Jones himself or the PDC as a whole was biased when reaching the decision to grant planning permission. Viewed in its wider context, the brief remark by Carwyn Jones that is at the centre of the case provides an insufficient basis for the suggestion that the decision was approached with a closed mind and without impartial consideration of all relevant planning issues.'

12.94 Wall LJ agreed (paragraph 114) that the test to be applied on the facts of the case is not what the fair-minded and informed observer would have concluded on the date of the encounter, but what the same observer would conclude having considered all the facts as they are known; and (paragraph 117) that Lindsay J's misapprehensions as to the correct test vitiates his conclusion on the apparent bias issue. It was thus open for the Court of Appeal to reach their own conclusion on the issue, and the allegation of apparent bias was not made out, for the reasons given by Richards LJ.

12.95 Ward LJ also agreed as to the test (paragraphs 121/122) and as to the application of the test to the relevant circumstances. These included the nature of the issue to be resolved. At paragraph 127 Ward LJ said:

'Here there had been a full inquiry held before the Inspector. The Merthyr Tydfil County Borough Council supported the application for planning permission. No substantive objection was offered by any of the statutory consultees. The opposition case was fully presented at the inquiry. The conclusion of the Inspector's thorough Report was to recommend the planning permission being granted. The officers of the Assembly's Planning Division accepted that conclusion subject to conditions. Of course it was open to the members of the PDC to come to a concluded view that the recommendation should not be accepted but they would need good planning grounds to do so and it would not come as a surprise to the fair-minded informed observer that a provisional view was in favour of endorsing the recommendation. It would perhaps be surprising if it were otherwise. In those circumstances, "I am going with the Inspector" is much more likely to mean, "On all I have read and all I know at the moment, but subject to further argument, I am going with the Inspector.'

12.96 Ward LJ added, at paragraphs 128 and 130:

'The observer who is neither complacent nor unduly sensitive or suspicious can, however, be taken to appreciate that, even though the members of the PDC are not judicial officers who have taken their judicial oath, nonetheless they had by the Standing Orders of the Assembly completed a course of relevant training, they had agreed to be bound by the current Code of Conduct and that required their "bringing an unbiased, properly directed and independent mind to their consideration of the matter". It would be a total abnegation of those duties to enter the Committee Room with a mind immovably made up. This was a highly sensitive decision to take and the fair-minded observer would assume that it would be taken fairly and justly.'

'Carwyn Jones' words were unwise, even injudicious, and hearing them might well have caused eyebrows to rise. But the informed observer would pause and stand back, then look at all the facts objectively. He would know that professional detachment and the trained ability to exercise independent judgment lie at the heart of the exercise of his function as a decision-maker especially in a case of such importance and sensitivity for the local community that it required the PDC to decide it. Bearing all matters in mind, the fair and informed observer would not, in my judgment, find that there was a real possibility that the Chairman of this Committee had predetermined the issue. The facts do not give rise to a real possibility of bias.'

12.97 The law is in an odd state. Transparency is regarded as essential in relation to interests, pecuniary or otherwise, but is sometimes regarded as undesirable in relation to predisposition. Moreover, the actuality of predisposition is liable to give rise to the appearance of predetermination. A 'firm view' is consistent with predisposition rather than predetermination. Indeed a 'strong predisposition' is not inimical to fairness. On the contrary, everyone being fully informed as to a predisposition will assist fairness by enabling responses to be focused. What is required is to 'keep an open mind' and be willing to be persuaded and change one's views.[1] Also, in *Singh v SSHD*[2] the Court of Appeal said, at paragraphs 30–38, that whereas the 'premature expression of a concluded view' or the 'manifesting of a closed mind' may amount to an appearance of bias, a 'strongly held view' could nonetheless be a 'provisional view', at any rate if expressed as such; there is no bar on 'robust expression', so long as it is not indicative of a closed mind, and sometimes robust expression may be 'positively necessary'.

[1] See *R (British Academy of Songwriters) v SoS for BIS* (2015) EWHC 1723 (Admin), paragraph 277, per Green J.
[2] [2016] EWCA Civ 492.

12.98 *R (Lewis) v Redcar & Cleveland BC* ('Lewis')[1] concerned the inevitable tension between, on the one hand the rule or rules against predetermination, partiality, lack of independence and the appearance of bias, and on the other hand the reality of the predisposition of elected local authority Members towards the implementation of policies with regard to which they are democratically accountable. This tension is one which the Courts have grappled with in a number of recent cases which are not easy to reconcile.

[1] [2008] LGR 781. Applied in *R (Chandler) v Camden LBC* (2009) EWHC 219 (Admin) at paragraphs 59–65.

12.99 They have been reviewed by the Court of Appeal in *Lewis*, which adopts a pragmatic approach. There is a vital distinction to be drawn between a legitimate predisposition towards a particular outcome and an illegitimate predetermination of outcome. The former is consistent with a preparedness to consider and weigh relevant factors in reaching the final decision. The latter involves a mind that is closed to the consideration and weighing of relevant factors. Even once a conclusion has been reached there is not necessarily a predetermination in relation to reconsideration. What is vital is that there are fairness and open-mindedness at the time of the final decision, whatever may have happened before.

12.100 In determining whether there has been predetermination, it is necessary first to establish the actual facts. This means the totality of the circumstances as they appear from all the material available upon investigation, not just the facts known to the complainant, or available to a hypothetical observer, at the time of the decision.

12.101 But what of the situation where there is no actual predetermination, but there is a clear predisposition? This is what produces the tension. The actuality of declared predisposition inevitably gives rise to an appearance of predetermination that would be unacceptable on the part of a Judge or Tribunal. The appearance of predetermination was the position in *Lewis* in relation to a planning decision made in a pre-election period in relation to land owned by the local planning authority. The Judge quashed the planning permission.

12.102 However, the Court of Appeal allowed the appeal. Pill LJ said:

'62   . . . The Committee which granted planning permission consisted of elected members who would be entitled, and indeed expected, to have, and to have expressed, views on planning issues. When taking a decision Councillors must have regard to material considerations and only to material considerations, and to give fair consideration to points raised, whether in an Officer's report to them or in representations made to them at a meeting of the Planning Committee. Sufficient attention to the contents of the proposal, which on occasions will involve consideration of detail, must be given. They are not, however, required to cast aside views on planning policy they will have formed when seeking election or when acting as Councillors. The test is a very different one from that to be applied to those in a judicial or quasi-judicial position.

63. Councillors are elected to implement, amongst other things, planning policies. They can properly take part in the debates which lead to planning applications made by the Council itself. It is common ground that in the case of some applications they are likely to have, and are entitled to have, a disposition in favour of granting permission. It is possible to infer a closed mind, or the real risk a mind was closed, from the circumstances and evidence. Given the role of Councillors, clear pointers are, in my view, required if that state of mind is to be held to have become a closed, or apparently closed, mind at the time of decision. . . .

71. It is for the court to assess whether Committee members did make the decision with closed minds or that the circumstances give rise to such a real risk of closed minds that the decision ought not in the public interest be upheld. The importance of appearances is, in my judgment, generally more limited in this context than in a judicial context.'

12.103 Rix LJ said:

'89. It is common ground that in the present planning context a distinction has to be made between mere predisposition, which is legitimate, and the predetermination which comes with a closed mind, which is illegitimate. However, there is a dispute between the parties as to the appropriate test to be applied for finding the illegitimate closed mind . . .

93. . . . In my judgment . . . it would be better if a single test applied to the whole spectrum of decision-making, as long as it is borne fully in mind that such a test has to be applied in very different circumstances, and that those circumstances must have an important and possibly decisive bearing on the outcome.

Thus, there is no escaping the fact that a decision-maker in the planning context is not acting in a judicial or quasi-judicial role but in a situation of democratic accountability. He or she will be subject to the full range of judicial review, but in terms of the concepts of independence and impartiality, which are at the root of the constitutional doctrine of bias, whether under the European Convention of Human Rights or at common law, there can be no pretence that such democratically accountable decision-makers are intended to be independent and impartial just as if they were judges or quasi-judges. They will have political allegiances, and their politics will involve policies, and these will be known. I refer to the dicta cited at paragraphs 43/52 above. To the extent, therefore, that in *Georgiou v Enfield London Borough Council* Richards J seems to have suggested (at paragraphs 30/31) that such decision-makers must be subject to a doctrine of apparent bias just as if they were like the auditor in *Porter v Magill* with an obligation therefore of both impartiality and the appearance of impartiality, I would, with respect, consider that he was stating the position in a way that went beyond previous authority and was not justified by *Porter v Magill*. . . .

95. The requirement made of such decision-makers is not, it seems to me, to be impartial, but to address the planning issues before them fairly and on their merits, even though they may approach them with a predisposition in favour of one side of the argument or the other. . . .

96. So the test would be whether there is an appearance of predetermination, in the sense of a mind closed to the planning merits of the decision in question. Evidence of political affiliation or of the adoption of policies towards a planning proposal will not for these purposes by itself amount to an appearance of the real possibility of predetermination, or what counts as bias for these purposes. Something more is required, something which goes

to the appearance of a predetermined, closed mind in the decision-making itself. I think that Collins J put it well in *R (on the application of Island Farm Development Ltd) v Bridgend County Borough Council* when he said (at paragraphs 31/32):

The reality is that councillors must be trusted to abide by the rules which the law lays down, namely that, whatever their views, they must approach their decision making with an open mind in the sense that they must have regard to all material considerations and be prepared to change their views if persuaded that they should . . . [U]nless there is positive evidence to show that there was indeed a closed mind, I do not think that prior observations or apparent favouring of a particular decision will suffice to persuade a court to quash the decision . . . It may be that, assuming the *Porter v Magill* test is applicable, the fair-minded and informed observer must be taken to appreciate that predisposition is not predetermination and that councillors can be assumed to be aware of their obligations.

In context I interpret Collins J's reference to "positive evidence to show that there was indeed a closed mind" as referring to such evidence as would suggest to the fair-minded and informed observer the real possibility that the councillor in question had abandoned his obligations, as so understood. Of course, the assessment has to be made by the court, assisted by evidence on both sides, but the test is put in terms of the observer to emphasise the view-point that the court is required to adopt. It need hardly be said that the view-point is not that of the complainant.

I think that Lord Justice Pill's conclusion at paragraph 71 above is to similar effect and also puts it well, if I may respectfully say so, when he says that the importance of appearances is generally more limited in this context than in a judicial context. . . .

12.104 Longmore LJ said:

102. The fundamental rule of natural justice that no one should be a judge in his own course has been the subject of considerable elaboration over the years. It is axiomatic that no person making a decision which is subject to judicial review should in fact be biased; in most cases it is axiomatic that there should also be no appearance of bias in the sense that a decision will be liable to be quashed if a fair-minded observer, knowing all the relevant facts, would think that there was a real possibility that the decision-maker would be biased. This latter proposition has, however, been qualified in cases in which allegations of what I may call institutional or structural bias are made. Then it is not open to a litigant to say that a person or body entrusted by Parliament to make a decision cannot be allowed to do so because there is a real possibility of bias, provided that there are sufficient safeguards in place to ensure that the decision is lawful, see *Alconbury v Secretary of State for the Environment* [2003] 2 AC 295.

106. It is clear from the authorities that the fact that members of a local planning authority are "predisposed" towards a particular outcome is not objectionable see e.g. *R v Amber Valley District Council* [1985] 1 WLR 298. That is because it would not be at all surprising that members of a planning authority in controversial and long-running cases will have a preliminary view as to a desirable outcome. That will be all the more so if there is an element of political controversy about any particular application, since planning authority members elected on a particular ticket would, other things being equal, be naturally predisposed to follow the party line. None of this is remotely objectionable.

107. What is objectionable, however, is "predetermination" in the sense I have already stated namely that a relevant decision-maker made up his or her mind finally at too early a stage. That is not to say that some arguments

cannot be regarded by any individual member of the planning authority as closed before (perhaps well before) the day of decision, provided that such arguments have been properly considered. But it is important that the minds of members be open to any new argument at all times up to the moment of decision.'

12.105 The foregoing is the state of the law on predetermination and predisposition both generally and with respect to local authorities in particular before the coming into force of s 25 of the Localism Act 2011 with respect to local authorities. Section 25 is headed: 'Prior indications of view of a matter not to amount to predetermination etc'. That was, as noted above, the previous state of the law.

12.106 Section 25(1) provides:

'Subsection (2) applies if —
(a) as a result of an allegation of bias or predetermination, or otherwise, there is an issue about the validity of a decision of a relevant authority, and
(b) it is relevant to that issue whether the decision-maker, or any of the decision-makers, had or appeared to have had a closed mind (to any extent) when making the decision.'

12.107 Section 25(2) provides:

'A decision-maker is not to be taken to have had, or to have appeared to have had, a closed mind when making the decision just because –
(a) the decision-maker had previously done anything that directly or indirectly indicated what view the decision-maker took, or would or might take, in relation to a matter, and
(b) the matter was relevant to the decision.

12.108 Section 25(3) states that sub-s (2) applies in relation to a decision-maker only if that decision-maker is a member or co-opted member of the relevant authority. Subsection (4) consists of definitions, including 'decision', 'member', 'co-opted member' and 'relevant authority'. Subsection (5) states:

'This section applies only to decisions made after this section comes into force, but the reference in subsection (2)(a) to anything previously done includes things done before this section comes into force.'

12.109 Section 25 does no more than to clarify the common law on unlawful predetermination. In effect it does this by attempting to highlight the important distinction between a closed mind and an empty mind. Although the common law has always regarded a closed mind to be a bad thing, it has never required decision-makers to undertake their work with empty minds. Hence the provisions of sub-s (2) of s 25, which do no more than to underline specific matters that are not of themselves to be determinative that there has been unlawful predetermination.

12.110 The limits of sub-s (2) are, however, important. The subsection does not require previous statements or actions to be disregarded. Rather it provides only that if such statements or actions have occurred, they are not of themselves to be treated as determinative of the case.

12.111 However, it remains virtually inevitable that a fact-specific claim, such as a claim of predetermination, is the sort of situation in which it will be difficult to predict with certainty how specific facts and context will be assessed by a court. Indeed the predetermination cases have led to an uncommonly high number of differences between first instance judges and the Court of Appeal.

12.112 Will s 25 mean that this element of unpredictability is removed or is diminished? The short answer is probably not:

(1)   Section 25 applies if there is an issue about the validity of a decision, as a result of an 'allegation of bias or pre-determination', or 'otherwise' and it is relevant to that issue whether the decision maker, or any of the decision makers, had or appeared to have had a closed mind (to any extent) when making the decision, thus it is drafted so as to catch as many cases as possible in which an allegation of predetermination might be made which might affect the validity of a decision, and catches allegations of actual, and apparent, predetermination (however tenuous);

(2)   The provision is also widely phrased in another sense: it applies to views not just about the subject matter of the decision in question, but to anything a member has done which might show, directly, or indirectly, what view he takes, or would take, or might take, about any matter which is relevant to the decision; and

(3)   The operative part is sub-s (2), which is to the effect that when making a decision, a decision-maker is not to be taken to have had, or to have appeared to have had, a closed mind (to any extent), '*just because*' he has previously done anything that directly or indirectly indicated what view he took, or would, or might take, in relation to 'a matter', and that matter was relevant to the decision.

12.113 '*Just because*' is interesting. It suggests that there is a line which can be crossed, but does not help to place it. Nevertheless, s 25 is a clear statement of comfort. It will no doubt be relied on by local authority members as an important statement of principle. However, it may achieve little in terms of dissuading committed claimants. In *IM Properties Development Ltd v Lichfield District* Council[1] Patterson J held that an email sent by a committee chairman to members of the same political party telling them to vote in a particular manner fell within s 25(2) of the Localism Act 2011 and was not to be taken as a predetermination. She found, at paragraph 86, that the tenor of the email was not 'so strident' as to remove the discretion on the part of the recipient as to how he or she would vote. Patterson J added: 'The debate shows a far-reaching discussion between members and displays no evidence of closed minds in relation to the decisions that had to be taken'; and 'A fair minded and reasonable observer in possession of all the facts would not be able to conclude on the basis of all the evidence that there was any real possibility of predetermination as a result of the e-mail . . . '. See also *EU Plants Ltd v Wokingham BC*.[2]

[1]   [2014] EWHC 2440 (Admin).
[2]   [2012] EWHC 3305 (Admin).

EXCEPTIONS TO THE RULE

12.114 The rules against interest and favour are subject to four areas of exception: waiver; contract; statute; and necessity.

Waiver[1]

[1] See *Eves (David) v Hambros Bank (Jersey) Ltd* [1996] 1 WLR 251 on whether the complainant has a legitimate concern; and *Locabail (UK) Ltd v Bayfield Properties Ltd* [2000] QB 451 on the need for waiver to be clear and unequivocal and based on full knowledge of all relevant facts. See also *Smith v Kvaerner Cementation Foundations Ltd (Bar Council intervening)* [2006] EWCA Civ 242,[2007] 1 WLR 370 and *Sumukan Ltd v Commonwealth Secretariat* [2007] EWHC 188 (Comm).

12.115 Waiver may be expressed or implied. However, some circumstances may not be capable of waiver.[1] Moreover, a waiver must be voluntary, informed and unequivocal.

[1] See **12.8** above.

12.116 Waiver will be implied if once a party or his representative has come to know of the facts that give rise to the disqualification no objection is taken, at least if the party or his representative is fully cognisant of the right to take objection.[1] For example, in *R v Nailsworth Licensing Justices, ex p Bird,*[2] the solicitor for an objector to an application for the grant of a licence discovered after the bench had retired that one of the justices had earlier signed a petition in favour of the licence being granted. Lord Goddard CJ said:[3]

> 'The solicitor did not take his objection then and it seems clear that he decided to let the matter go on, taking the view that this was a heaven-sent opportunity of getting the order quashed if the committee found in favour of the application. That would be sufficient ground for refusing this application . . . .'

[1] See *R v Essex Justices, ex p Perkins* [1927] 2 KB 475; *Fox v Secretary of State for the Environment and Dover District Council* [1993] JPL 448; and *Auckland Casino Ltd v Casino Control Authority* [1995] 1 NZLR 142 (NZ CA).
[2] [1953] 2 All ER 652, [1953] 1 WLR 1046.
[3] At 1048. See, also, *R v Altrincham Justices, ex p Pennington* [1975] QB 549 at 554 per Lord Widgery CJ; and *R v Home Secretary, ex p Fayed* [2001] Imm AR 134.

Contract

12.117 The parties may contract, as for example by membership of voluntary association, as to by whom and in what way disputes will be determined. The contract may have the effect of modifying the operation of the rules against interest and favour. Examples include *Jackson v Barry Rly Co;*[1] *Maclean v Workers Union;*[2] *Herring v Templeman;*[3] and *Hamlet v GMBATU;*[4] and as to arbitrators, *Tracomin SA v Nathaniel Gibbs (Canada) Ltd and Bridge.*[5]

[1] [1893] 1 Ch 238.
[2] [1929] 1 Ch 602.
[3] [1973] 3 All ER 569.
[4] [1987] 1 All ER 631, [1987] 1 WLR 449.
[5] [1985] 1 Lloyd's Rep 586.

12.118 Such contractual provisions will, however, be scrutinised as to whether they conform with public policy. See, for example, *Enderby Town Football Club Ltd v FA.*[1]

[1] [1971] Ch 591 at 605–607.

Statute

12.119 We have seen (at **12.61** above) how the operation of the rules against interest and bias may impliedly be modified by reference to the construction of statutory provisions, ie the scheme of an Act and common sense considerations of its practical operation. In *R (Bennion) v Chief Constable of the Merseyside Police*[1] it was held that the relevant statute envisaged that the Chief Constable's general interest in the outcome of disciplinary proceedings should not bar him from deciding those proceedings. In *Jeffs v New Zealand Dairy Production and Marketing Board*[2] the Privy Council held that a New Zealand Act required the Board to determine zoning applications, even though its pecuniary interests might be affected, and showed an intention to make an exception to the general rule that a person might not be made judge in his own cause. Accordingly, the Board's decision was not invalid on the ground of infringement of this rule of law. In addition, Parliament has mitigated the rule by creating (or giving the power to the Secretary of State of creating) express statutory exceptions. Such exceptions are, however, strictly construed. See, for example, *R v Lee, ex p Shaw*, (see **12.57** above and *R v Barnsley Licensing Justices, ex p Barnsley and District LVA*.[3] The exception may remove the disqualification, or it may validate the action notwithstanding the disqualification. Moreover, even if the disqualifying effect of a pecuniary interest has been removed by statute, it is, nonetheless, necessary to consider whether the nature of that interest gives rise to a likelihood of bias: see *R v Barnsley Licensing Justices*, above.

[1] [2002] ICR 136.
[2] [1967] 1 AC 551.
[3] [1960] 2 QB 167.

Necessity

12.120 The rules against interest and bias will yield to necessity. In order to prevent a failure of justice, an otherwise disqualified person may be allowed to adjudicate when no other qualified person is available. See *Dimes v Grand Junction Canal Co*,[1] *Phillips v Eyre*,[2] *R v Howard*,[3] *H Tolputt & Co Ltd v Mole*,[4] and 'Disqualified Adjudicators: the Doctrine of Necessity in Public Law'[5] illustrate this exception.

[1] (1852) 3 HL Cas 759.
[2] (1870) LR 6 QB 1.
[3] [1902] 2 KB 363.
[4] [1911] 1 KB 836.
[5] RRS Tracey at [1982] PL 628. See also 'Bias, Necessity and the Convention' at [2002] PL 407 (Professor Ian Leigh), an analysis based on *Kingsley v UK* (2001) 33 EHRR 288; and *Meerabux v Attorney General of Belize* [2005] UKPC 12; [2005] 2 WLR 1307.

12.121 The necessity doctrine will operate where:

(1)   the person's participation is authorised by statute;
(2)   no other adjudicator is available and the action is an administrative formality;
(3)   no other adjudicator is available and the conflict of interest is created by different statutes;

(4)   all available adjudicators are disqualified as a result of acts which were beyond their control.

12.122 The necessity doctrine will not operate where:

(1)   another qualified adjudicator is available, at least if the means exist under extant legislation for providing one;

(2)   (probably) no other adjudicator is available but the disqualifying act is voluntary;[1]

(3)   a provision as to constitution is construed as directory rather than mandatory.[2]

---

[1] See, eg, *Lower Hutt City Council v Bank* [1974] 1 NZLR 545.

[2] *Jeyaretnam v Law Society of Singapore* [1989] AC 608, [1989] 2 All ER 193. On the mandatory/directory distinction, see *R v Home Secretary, ex p Jeyeanthan* [2000] 1 WLR 354 at 360C.

12.123 In the case of multi-member tribunals with the requirement of a quorum when some, but not all, of the members are disqualified, the general principles outlined above will operate if so many members are disqualified that a quorum cannot be found, but if a quorum can be found after disqualified members have been excluded the disqualified members must absent themselves.[1]

---

[1] See, eg *Roebuck v NUM* [1977] ICR 573.

Chapter 13

OTHER GROUNDS OF REVIEW

INTRODUCTION

13.1 It remains convenient to analyse the grounds for judicial review under the three heads of illegality, irrationality and procedural impropriety, as identified by Lord Diplock in *Council of Civil Service Unions v Minister for the Civil Service* ('*CCSU*').[1]. However, in *CCSU* Lord Diplock was at pains not to exclude further development on a case-by-case basis, which might, in course of time, add further grounds. One possible further ground specifically identified by Lord Diplock was proportionality, the development of which is considered in CHAPTER 9. Furthermore, Lord Diplock's tripartite categorisation of grounds for judicial review struggles to incorporate comfortably certain well-recognised grounds of review, a number of which long pre-date the *CCSU* case. This chapter describes some of those grounds – bad faith, procedural fraud (and possibly procedural mishap generally), and vagueness – before turning to a more recently established ground, mistake of fact, and a rarely cited further ground – breach of fiduciary duty.

[1]   [1985] AC 374 at 410.

BAD FAITH

13.2 The expression 'bad faith' is frequently used but rarely defined. For the purposes of this chapter the expression 'bad faith' when referring to a decision-maker will be confined to cases where that person acts dishonestly, taking action which is known by the actor to be improper.[1] It is long established and uncontroversial that such action in the exercise of a public law power will vitiate that exercise of power.[2] In *Westminster Corpn v London & North Western Railway*[3] Lord Macnaghten said that the duty of a public body invested with statutory powers to act reasonably was 'involved in' its duty to act in good faith. Nevertheless, the two duties were analysed separately: and it was made clear that in order to establish lack of good faith it had to be shown that the Corporation was intent upon achieving an improper purpose 'under colour and pretence' of a proper purpose. The essential basis on which the court acts in the two cases is quite distinct: on the one hand, the most honest person can be quite unreasonable,[4] and on the other hand, when considering an allegation of bad faith it is not necessary for the court to find that no reasonable person could have thought the decision appropriate.

1   This formulation is based upon the well known exhortation of Megaw LJ in *Cannock Chase District Council v Kelly* [1978] 1 WLR 1. Megaw LJ recognised that an allegation of bad faith 'always involves a grave charge' and confirmed that public authorities accused of bad faith are entitled, like private individuals, to have the allegation properly particularised.

2   See, eg Lord Greene MR in *Associated Provincial Picture Houses Ltd v Wednesbury Corpn* [1948] 1 KB 223 at 229 (bad faith or dishonesty as stand alone examples of 'the sort of things that authorities must not do'), Lord Reid in *Anisminic Ltd v Foreign Compensation Commission* [1969] 2 AC 147, 171 (a decision in bad faith will be a nullity), and Lord Mustill in *R v Secretary of State for the Home Department, ex p Fire Brigades Union* [1995] 2 AC 513, 563–564.

3   [1905] AC 426, 430.

4   This point was made with force by Scrutton LJ in *R v Roberts, ex p Scurr* [1924] 2 KB 695, 719. For the decision of the House of Lords, see *Roberts v Hopwood* [1925] AC 578. The distinction between unreasonableness and bad faith is helpfully illustrated by the tort of malicious prosecution, which requires the claimant to prove both a lack of reasonable and probable cause for the prosecution and, additionally, malice or bad faith. Proof of one element does not, of itself, establish the other.

13.3 It is possible to analyse bad faith as involving illegality in the *CCSU* sense. Where a person is executing statutory power, it can be said that a decision-maker acting in bad faith has acted outwith and not given effect to the parliamentary intention — which can be assumed to be that the power is invariably to be exercised in good faith.[1] However, a decision-maker exercising a non-statutory power in bad faith falls less comfortably within the *CCSU* concept of illegality. It might be said that such a decision-maker has not given effect to the law governing that power, but only because the decision-maker has infringed the common law principles of judicial review — something which might equally be said in cases where procedural impropriety or unreasonableness have occurred.

1   See Chapter 7 at 7.36, 7.76 and 7.91 above.

13.4 It is alternatively possible to analyse good faith as an element of 'natural justice' — one of the prerequisites of a procedurally fair decision being that the tribunal or decision-maker should always act in good faith, regardless of the outcome of its decision.[1]

1   Harman J in *Byrne v Kinematograph Renters Society Ltd* [1958] 1 WLR 762 at 784. Taken up in the employment context in *Khanum v Mid Glamorgan Area Health Authority* [1979] ICR 40.

13.5 A fundamental principle which underlies bad faith as a ground of review, and warrants treating it separately from illegality, procedural impropriety and unreasonableness, is that fraud unravels everything.[1] Additionally, an important consequence of a finding of bad faith, not usually available merely because there has been illegality, procedural impropriety, or unreasonableness, is that the person acting in bad faith may be liable in damages.[2] This reinforces the case for treating bad faith as a separate ground of review, even though in those rare cases where it is shown to exist it may involve other defects so as to bring allegations of illegality, unreasonableness, or procedural impropriety into play.[3]

1   *Lazarus Estates Ltd v Beasley* [1956] 1 Q.B. 702 at 712, discussed recently in *Prest v Petrodel Resources Ltd* [2013] 2 AC 415 at 18. Here there is a link with review for procedural fraud

or mishap, discussed at **13.6** below: see Lord Bridge in *Al-Mehdawi v Secretary of State for the Home Department* [1990] 1 AC 876 at 895.

2   For this reason the House of Lords allowed in part the appeal in *Smith v East Elloe RDC* [1956] AC 736 (enabling the action for damages to proceed); and see, generally, *Clerk and Lindsell on Torts* (21st edn, 2014) which deals with claims for misfeasance in a public office at paragraphs 14–111ff, and discusses, at paragraphs 14–45ff, the circumstances in which unreasonable failure to exercise a statutory power may possibly be actionable in damages. In respect of damages as a remedy within administrative law proceedings, Senior Courts Act 1981, s 31(4) provides authority for the High Court to award damages in judicial review, see further CHAPTER **17**.

3   See the discussion of duality of purpose in CHAPTER **7** at **7.89** above; also de Smith *Judicial Review of Administrative Action* (7th edn, 2013) pp 289–305, where bad faith is considered as an example of illegality and *Kruse v Johnson* [1898] 2 QB 91, where bad faith is treated as an example of unreasonableness.

PROCEDURAL FRAUD OR MISHAP

13.6 Procedural unfairness may not be the fault of the tribunal or decision-maker. It is well established that fraud or perjury on the part of a party or witness may entitle the court to intervene by judicial review.[1] The position is less clear where there is some procedural mishap short of fraud or perjury. In *Khan (Bagga) v Secretary of State for the Home Department*[2] Bingham LJ said:

'If a procedural mishap occurs as a result of misunderstanding, confusion, failure of communication, or even perhaps inefficiency, and the result is to deny justice to an applicant, I should be very sorry to hold that the remedy of judicial review was not available'.

1   *R v Gillyard* (1848) 12 QB 527; *R v Leicester Recorder, ex p Wood* [1947] KB 726; *R (Burns) v Tyrone County Court Judge* [1961] NI 167. These cases were said by Lord Bridge, in *Al-Mehdawi v Secretary of State for the Home Department* [1990] 1 AC 876 at 895, to be examples of the principle that fraud unravels everything. In *R v Crown Court at Knights-bridge, ex p Goonatilleke* [1986] QB 1 at 13–14, the claimant sought certiorari in respect of his conviction which had been based on the evidence of a witness subsequently found to have been lying about his good character. Watkins LJ held that the claimant had to show (to a criminal standard) that the tribunal would have come to a different conclusion but for the fraud or perjury in question: but this seems inconsistent with the approach in cases of unreasonableness and error of law (eg *Neill v North Antrim Magistrates' Court* [1992] 1 WLR 1220 in which it was held that 'a really substantial error leading to a demonstrable injustice' would justify interference by the Divisional Court, followed in respect of England & Wales in *R v Bedwellty Justices, ex p Williams* [1997] AC 225 at 237.

2   [1987] Imm AR 543, 555, relied upon by way of 'analogy' in *Amao v Nursing and Midwifery Council* [2014] EWHC 147 (Admin).

13.7 Judicial review was granted by the Divisional Court in *R v Leyland Justices, ex p Hawthorn*[1] where there had been a failure on the part of a prosecutor to comply with the duty to inform the defendant of relevant evidence, it being said that such a failure preventing a fair trial should rank in the same category as fraud, collusion and perjury, and that there was 'a clear denial of natural justice'. This case was considered in the speech of Lord Bridge in *Al-Mehdawi v Secretary of State for the Home Department*,[2] who questioned the reference to natural justice: instead, the suppression of truth (albeit without dishonesty) had the same effect as an untruth in distorting and vitiating the process leading to conviction, so that in his view the analogy with fraud, collusion and perjury was the true principle on which the decision could be justified.

1   [1979] QB 283, followed in *R v Blundeston Prison Board of Visitors, ex p Fox-Taylor* [1982]
     1 All ER 646.
2   [1990] 1 AC 876 at 895–896. Applying Lord Bridge's analysis, Watkins LJ in *R v Bolton
     Justices, ex p Scally* [1991] 1 QB 537 at 551–556 held that failures by the police, in that case
     to ensure that samples were unadulterated and in other cases to check the probative value of
     evidence and to enter full details in a witness statement, were to be regarded as analogous to
     fraud, collusion or perjury — despite involving merely 'an ordinary lack of care'. *Scally* was
     followed by Munby J in *R (Marsh) v Lincoln District Magistrates' Court* [2003] EWHC 956
     (Admin) and applied by the Court of Appeal in *R (Harrison) v Birmingham Magistrates' Court*
     [2011] EWCA Civ 332 and the Divisional Court in*R (on the application of Wilmot) v Taunton
     Deane and West Somerset Magistrates' Court* [2013] EWHC 1399 (Admin).

13.8 Where the parallel with fraud, collusion or perjury is less obvious,
procedural mishap may still give rise to judicial review for breach of the
rules of natural justice or for material error of fact. This is established by *R v
Criminal Injuries Compensation Board, ex p A*.[1] The applicant's claim for
compensation had been rejected by the Board, and she complained that the
Board had proceeded without knowledge of a relevant police doctor's report
and on the basis of incorrect evidence from a police officer. The House of Lords
accepted her argument that the rejection was vitiated by unfairness, as the
Board had, in a crucial respect, been led to proceed on wrong evidence and had
not had the true facts before it. Lord Slynn noted that the applicant had asked
the House of Lords to find for her on the basis of a material error of fact. He
indicated that he would accept that there was jurisdiction to quash the decision
on that ground, but chose to decide the matter on the basis of a breach of
natural justice.[2] Insofar as there is any useful distinction between these
grounds, it appears likely that the applicant in *ex parte A* would today succeed
on grounds concerning mistake of fact (see below) or taking into account an
irrelevant consideration.[3] More recent dicta from the Court of Appeal shows
pure procedural mishap resulting in a claimant not being heard, rather than a
decision being taken on mistaken facts, continuing to be treated as a breach of
natural justice.[4]

1   [1999] 2 AC 330.
2   [1999] 2 AC 330 at 345–346.
3   In *Re Gracey's application for judicial review* [2014] NIQB 131the Northern Ireland
     Divisional Court relied upon *R v Criminal Injuries Comensation Board, ex p A* as part of the
     'well established authority to support the proposition that the court has jurisdiction to quash
     a decision reached on the basis of a material error of fact'. In the leading authority on mistake
     of fact, *E v Secretary of State for the Home Department* [2004] QB 1044, it was doubted
     whether there was any distinction between 'ignorance of fact' and 'unfairness' as grounds of
     review.
4   In *R (Harrison) v Birmingham Magistrates' Court* [2011] EWCA Civ 332 the claimant
     provided unchallenged evidence that she had had no notice of forfeiture proceedings, so the
     order against her was quashed. Munby LJ considered the case to involve a breach of the most
     elementary principle of natural justice, the right to be heard, and confirmed that 'the
     jurisdiction which is here invoked is exercisable even if the tribunal has behaved with complete
     propriety and even if there has been no misconduct or misbehaviour on the part of the
     prosecutor or complainant'. See also *Amao v Nursing and Midwifery Council* [2014] EWHC
     147 (Admin) in which a procedural mishap was recognised to have taken place, but it was
     concluded that no remedy was needed because it did not undermine the overall fairness of the
     fact-finding procedure.

13.9 Judicial review will not be available to a party who suffers as result of her
own procedural failing, but the position is less clear when the failure is by the

party's legal representative. In the *Al-Mehdawi*[1] case, the applicant's appeal against deportation was dismissed at a hearing which he did not attend, and it was held by the Court of Appeal[2] that, there being no actual fault on the part of the applicant, a failure by the applicant's solicitor to inform him of the date of the hearing was a breach of natural justice amounting to such a fundamental flaw in the decision-making process as would ground relief by judicial review. The Court of Appeal's decision was overturned by the House of Lords on the ground that in public law, as in private law, a party who has lost the opportunity to have his case heard through the default of his own advisers to whom he has entrusted the conduct of the dispute on his behalf cannot complain that he has been the victim of a procedural impropriety or that natural justice has been denied to him. However, this narrow ground cannot be absolute and must now be read, in cases where fundamental rights, including Convention rights, are brought into play, as subject to those rights — particularly where the potential breach of human rights could not be remedied adequately by a claim against the advisers. This has been recognised in immigration and asylum cases, where the consequences of an unfavourable decision may be stark.[3]

[1] [1990] 1 AC 876, 899–900.
[2] [1990] 1 AC 876, 880 to 887, applying the decision in *R v Diggines, ex p Rahmani* [1985] QB 1109.
[3] See *Haile v Immigration Appeal Tribunal* [2002] Imm. A.R. 170 at [26], in which it was held that *Al-Mehdawi* did not preclude a court from considering 'the wider interests of justice'; *R (Gungor) v Secretary of State for the Home Department* [2004] EWHC 2117 (Admin) at [17]; and *FP (Iran) and MB (Libya) v Secretary of State for the Home Department* [2007] Imm. A.R. 450 at [45] where it was held that "there is no general principle of law which fixes a party with the procedural errors of his or her representative'. See also *MM (Sudan) v SSHD* [2014] UKUT 105 (IAC) in which the Upper Tribunal considered it 'established that neither the rule in *Al-Mehdawi v SSHD* [1990] 1 AC 876 (that a procedural failure caused by an appellant's own representative did not lead to an appeal being in breach of the rules of natural justice) nor a failure to meet the first of the *Ladd v Marshall* principles, applies with full rigour in asylum and human rights appeals.' It may also be subject to a residual jurisdiction to enable the court to do justice in exceptional cases: see **13.16** below.

13.10 Nevertheless, after *Al-Mehdawi* it seems unlikely that inefficiency on the part of the applicant or the applicant's advisers will be ground for judicial review[1] — unless the protection of fundamental rights requires otherwise, or the case is in some other way exceptional. The circumstances in which misunderstanding, confusion, or failure of communication may or may not give rise to review remain to be authoritatively decided (as do the circumstances which constitute conduct analogous to fraud).[2] One matter that is clear is that an error by the claimant's legal representative does not fall within the established grounds for a claim based upon mistake of fact.[3]

[1] As acknowledged by Hughes J in *R (R) v Secretary of State for the Home Department* [2005] EWHC 520 (Admin) at [27]. 'if the error of legal representatives were to be a ground for judicial review, it would be open to every disappointed applicant to seek to re-argue his case, complaining that the advocacy in the court below had been insufficiently skilful.'
[2] It is noteworthy that Lord Bingham's general concern in *Bagga Khan* that a denial of justice should not go unremedied remains a justification for judicial intervention: see *Amao v Nursing and Midwifery Council* [2014] EWHC 147 (Admin). It is also noteworthy that, in the criminal sphere, the Divisional Court exercises a supervisory jurisdiction to prevent abuse of process in criminal proceedings: *R v Horseferry Road Magistrates' Court, ex p Bennett* [1994] 1 AC 42, [1993] 3 All ER 138. One possible approach would be to hold that judicial review lies where the responsibility for procedural impropriety can be attributed to a body exercising public authority (albeit not the body which made the decision under review): see Herberg [1990] PL

467, 474–475. However, this would not permit of review in, for example, exceptional cases where the responsibility for error lay with a legal representative, as considered in *FP (Iran) and MB (Libya) v Secretary of State for the Home Department* [2007] Imm. A.R. 450. A broader approach under which material misrepresentation would ground review was favoured by Fisher J in *Martin v Ryan* [1990] 2 NZLR 209 at 224 (New Zealand High Court; discussed by Liddell [1990] NZ Recent Law Review 279 and by Joseph *Constitutional and Administrative Law in New Zealand* (2007) p 948). But non-fraudulent misrepresentation is an everyday occurrence in administrative proceedings: it is hard to reconcile intervention by the court on such grounds alone with the constitutional imperative that Parliament has entrusted the finding of facts to the statutory decision-maker.

[3] See *E v Secretary of State for the Home Department* [2004] QB 1044 at [66].

VAGUENESS

13.11 Certainty is a fundamental principle of the common law.[1] Byelaws creating a criminal offence may be struck down by way of judicial review if they are too vague.[2] Similarly, *Fawcett Properties Ltd v Buckingham County Council*[3] established that a public authority must not insert a condition in a premises licence if that condition is so unclear as to be void for uncertainty.[4] Furthermore, Lord Diplock's terms of any prohibitory order rendering the subject liable to punishment for breach must be clear and unambiguous.[5] The cases do not contain any doctrinal statement that judicial review is generally available where there has been a lack of sufficient certainty. It can nevertheless be argued that the principles identified for byelaws, licences and prohibitory orders should be applied more generally, particularly where a decision or measure impacts on an individual's rights or freedoms. This would reflect the principle of certainty recognised in the common law, in European Union law and as an aspect of lawfulness under the European Convention on Human Rights.[6]

[1] See the discussion by LJ Judge in *R v Misra and Srivastava* [2004] EWCA Crim 2375; [2005] 1 Cr. App. Rep 328 (adopted by Lord Bingham in *R v Rimmington* [2006] 1 AC 459), which quotes from the 17th century writings of Francis Bacon:

> 'For if the trumpet give an uncertain sound, who shall prepare himself to the battle? So if the law give an uncertain sound, who shall prepare to obey it? It ought therefore to warn before it strikes . . . Let there be no authority to shed blood; nor let sentence be pronounced in any court upon cases, except according to a known and certain law . . . Nor should a man be deprived of his life, who did not first know that he was risking it.' (Quoted in *Coquillette*, Francis Bacon pp 244 and 248, from *Aphorism 8* and *Aphorism 39—A Treatise on Universal Justice*).'

[2] *McEldowney v Forde* [1971] AC 632, in which the majority of their Lordships considered the same principle applied to statutory instruments as well as byelaws; other authorities are reviewed in *Percy v Hall* [1996] 4 All ER 523, [1997] 3 WLR 573. The common law is now buttressed by the European Convention on Human Rights: Article 7 requires the criminal law to be sufficiently accessible and precise to enable an individual to know in advance what conduct is criminal: *Handyside v UK* (1976) 1 EHRR 737; and byelaws that infringe upon rights under the Convention will be unlawful if not sufficiently certain to be 'in accordance with the law': eg *Tabernacle v Secretary of State for Defence* [2008] EWHC 416 (Admin) (relying on *Gaweda v Poland* (2002) 12 BHRC 486).

[3] [1961] AC 636.

[4] See also Scott Baker LJ in *Crawley Borough Council v Attenborough* [2006] EWHC 1278 (Admin):

> 'The terms of a licence and its conditions may of course be the subject of enforcement. Breach carries criminal sanction. Everyone must know where they stand from the terms of the document. It must be apparent from reading the document what the licence and its conditions mean.'

This test for certainty of licence conditions is stricter than that applied to bye-laws because of the greater potential sanction on breach of the former: *R (on the application of the Mayor and the Citizens of Westminster City Council) v Metropolitan Stipendiary Magistrate* [2008] EWHC 1202 (Admin).

5   See Lord Bingham in *R (B) v Chief Constable of Avon & Somerset* [2001] All ER 5 (considering argument under the common law and the Convention):

> '[i]f anyone is the subject of a prohibitory court order for breach of which he is liable to severe punishment, that person is entitled to know, clearly and unambiguously, what conduct he must avoid to comply with the order . . . The order should be expressed in simple terms, easily understood even by those who, like the appellant, are not very bright.'

6   See CHAPTER 15 below. The overlap between lack of certainty as a ground of review, the requirement of lawfulness in the Convention and the common law principle of legality is apparent from the judgment of the Divisional Court in *R (Gul) v Secretary of State for Justice* [2014] EWHC 373 (Admin) at [53]–[58]. Both common law and Convention authorities were considered and the conclusion reached that 'a claimant who contends that a provision is insufficiently clear to satisfy common law requirements of certainty must overcome a high hurdle'. The court further concluded that no re-evaluation of the common law test was required in light of the equivalent test under the Convention.

13.12 In those instances which have come before the courts the test put forward is not one of the reasonableness of the dicta under scrutiny: rather it is for the court to resolve whether the words used are too vague or uncertain.[1] As noted in CHAPTER 8, however, it may be argued it is 'unreasonable' to lay down a condition which gives no clear indication to those affected of the circumstances when it operates.[2]

1   In cases involving prohibitory orders, emphasis is placed on the terms being sufficiently clear to be understood by the person subject to them (even if that person is 'not very bright' *(R (B) v Chief Constable of Avon & Somerset* [2001] All ER 5)) and to the party tasked with enforcing breach — eg *R v Boness; R v Bebbington* [2006] 1 Cr. App. Rep (S) 690. In *Percy v Hall* [1996] 4 All ER 523, [1997] 3 WLR 573, a case concerning the certainty of bye-laws, the test of 'a byelaw will be held void for uncertainty if it can be given no meaning or no sensible or ascertainable meaning' (Lord Denning in *Fawcett Properties Ltd v Buckingham County Council* [1961] AC 636) was preferred to the test of 'to be valid, a byelaw, carrying as this one does penalties for infringement, must be certain and clear in the sense that anyone engaged upon the otherwise lawful pursuit of hang gliding must know with reasonable certainty when he is breaking the law and when he is not breaking the law' (Lord Lane C.J. in *Staden v Tarjanyi (1980) 78 L.G.R. 614,* 623).

2   *R v Bradford MBC, ex p Ali* (1994) 6 Admin LR 589, [1994] ELR 299; *R v Blackpool Borough Council, ex p Red Cab Taxis Ltd* [1994] COD 513; *R v Newcastle upon Tyne City Council, ex p Dixon* (1993) 92 LGR 168.

13.13 As with bad faith, it might be possible to analyse vagueness as involving illegality in the *CCSU* sense. Where a person is executing statutory power, it can be said that a decision-maker who exercises power vaguely has not given effect to parliamentary intention – which can be assumed to be that the power is invariably to be exercised unambiguously. However, it is less clear that a decision-maker exercising a non-statutory power vaguely (on the assumption that this would give rise to judicial review) would properly be analysed as falling within the *CCSU* concept of illegality. As with review for bad faith, it might be said that such a decision-maker has not given effect to the law governing that power, but only because the decision-maker has infringed the common law principles of judicial review – something which might equally be said in cases where procedural impropriety or unreasonableness have occurred.[1]

1   The difficulty in categorising vagueness as a ground for judicial review was evident in *R (Grogan) v Bexley NHS Care Trust* [2006] EWHC 44 (Admin). A decision by the NHS Trust

was found to be unlawful because it had been based on policy criteria that failed to identify the proper test to be applied. Mr Justice Charles concluded, at paragraph 100, that it did 'not matter whether this is classified as a failure to set proper guidelines, or a failure to apply the correct approach at law, or a failure to give adequate reasons'.

13.14 Uncertainty may also be viewed from the perspective of the enabling statute on classic *ultra vires* grounds. In *Mixnam's Properties Ltd v Chertsey Urban District Council*[1] Diplock LJ made the following obiter remarks linking the validity of uncertain subordinate legislation to the powers conferred by statute:

'The various special grounds upon which subordinate legislation has sometimes been said to be void — for example, because it is unreasonable; because it is uncertain; because it is repugnant to the general law or to some other statute — can, I think, today be properly regarded as being particular applications of the general rule that subordinate legislation, to be valid, must be shown to be within the powers conferred by the statute . . . if the courts can declare subordinate legislation to be invalid for "uncertainty" as distinct from unenforceable, as in the case of a clause in a statute to which it is impossible to ascribe a meaning, this must be because Parliament is to be presumed not to have intended to authorise the subordinate legislation authority to make changes in the existing law which are uncertain . . . '.[2]

These dicta were relied upon by the Hong Kong Court of Final Appeal in *Noise Control Authority and Noise Control Appeal Board v Step In Limited*,[3] when, after a review of both English and Australian case law, it concluded that save for where 'the impugned instrument is . . . so uncertain in its terms as to be meaningless, uncertainty or unreasonableness in application or inconsistency with the general law are relevant to validity only insofar as they assist in answering the question whether the instrument falls within or without the power to make it'.[4]

[1] [1964] 1 QB 214 at 237–238, considered by the Court of Appeal in *Percy v Hall* [1996] 4 All ER 523, [1997] 3 WLR 573.
[2] It is noteworthy that Wilmer LJ disagreed with Diplock's analysis: 'Although I do not think it is strictly a question of vires, it must be accepted that a condition may be held void for uncertainty . . . '.
[3] [2005] HKCFA 20. See further discussion in Moules, 'Uncertainty as a Ground for Judicial Review' [2007] JR 104.
[4] Ibid., paragraph 40.

13.15 In other contexts, vagueness can appropriately be considered as an aspect of procedural fairness or natural justice. Vagueness in allegations of impropriety will undermine the ability of the person accused to exercise her opportunity to respond to the allegations.[1]

[1] See, for example, *R (Wheeler) v Metropolitan Police Assistant Comr* [2008] EWHC 439 (Admin) at 1.6: 'Vagueness is a ground for judicial review if it leads to unfairness in the proceedings, and the danger with a vague charge is that the parties, and in particular the respondent (now Mr Wheeler, the claimant), do not know with some precision what is alleged against them and therefore are not fully able to address those matters in the course of the hearing. Here what was alleged was, in my judgment, too vague and should have been clarified.' See also the general principle of tort that allegations of bad faith must be fully particularised.

MISTAKE OF FACT

13.16 The general principle is that judicial review proceedings deal with law, not fact.[1] This reflects the reality that the decision-maker will often be in a better position to evaluate the facts than the court reviewing the decision. One of the exceptions to this approach is that questions of fact are determined by the courts where they go to the decision-maker's jurisdiction — thus potentially rendering the decision *ultra vires*.[2] It is also now established that in certain limited circumstances a non-jurisdictional material error of fact is an independent ground upon which judicial review may be granted.

[1]   Of course the division between questions of fact and questions of law is not always straightforward. Indeed, in *Currie v IRC* [1921] 2 KB 332 at 339 Scrutton LJ noted that:

> 'there has been a very strong tendency, arising from the infirmities of human nature, in a judge to say, if he agrees with the decision of the Commissioners, that the question is one of fact, and if he disagrees with them that it is one of law, in order that he may express his own opinion the opposite way.'

[2]   'Jurisdictional' or 'precedent' fact. See CHAPTERS 6 and 7.

13.17 In the *ASLEF* case[1] it was said by Lord Denning — as regards non-jurisdictional errors — that the court could still intervene if the decision-maker 'plainly misdirects himself in fact'. This was taken up in *R (Alconbury Ltd) v Secretary of State for the Environment*[2] and in *Runa Begum v Tower Hamlets LBC*.[3] As explained above, a claimant who alleged a non-jurisdictional error of fact might succeed on judicial review because the defendant's factual conclusion was unreasonable. Where there is a 'plain misdirection' as to the facts on the basis of what is known to the decision-maker at the time of the decision (see **8.18** above) the principle identified in *ASLEF* can be seen as an example of review for unreasonableness. What was unclear was the extent to which the courts envisaged review for mistake of fact independently of review for unreasonableness.

[1]   *Secretary of State for Employment v Associated Society of Locomotive Engineers and Firemen (No 2)* [1972] 2 QB 455, 493, CA; approved in *Secretary of State for Education v Tameside Metropolitan Borough Council* [1977] AC 1014 at 1047.
[2]   [2003] 2 AC 295, HL(E): Lord Slynn at paragraph 53 (at p 321) reiterated the view he expressed in *R v Criminal Injuries Compensation Board ex p A* [1999] 2 AC 330, 344–345) that the court has jurisdiction to quash for a misunderstanding or ignorance of an established and relevant fact. Compare Lord Nolan at paragraph 62 (p 323), Lord Clyde at paragraph 169 (p 355).
[3]   [2003] 2 AC 430, where Lord Bingham at paragraph 7 (at p 439) cites Scarman LJ in *Secretary of State for Education and Science v Tameside MBC* [1977] AC 1014, 1030. Lord Bingham proceeds on the basis that on judicial review the court may quash the authority's decision if the decision-maker is shown to have misunderstood or been ignorant of an established and relevant fact. Lord Hope at paragraph 73 (p 457) and Lord Millett at paragraph 107 (p 464) agreed.

13.18 Some clarity was provided by the Court of Appeal's confirmation in *E v Secretary of State for the Home Department*[1] that mistake of fact giving rise to unfairness is a separate head of challenge on an appeal on a point of law, 'at least in those statutory contexts where the parties share an interest in co-operating to achieve the correct result'.[2] The court identified four requirements for this head of challenge to succeed. First, there must have been a mistake as to an existing fact, including a mistake as to the availability of evidence on a particular matter. Second, the fact or evidence must have been 'established' in the sense that it was uncontentious and objectively verifiable.

Third, the appellant (or his advisers) must not have been responsible for the mistake. Fourth, the mistake must have played a material (not necessarily decisive[3]) part in the Tribunal's reasoning. These are broadly similar to the principles which apply to the re-opening of civil proceedings.[4] The court recognised, however, that these principles might be departed from in exceptional circumstances where the interests of justice required.[5]

1. [2004] QB 1044 (cited approvingly by the Supreme Court in *IA (Iran) v Secretary of State for the Home Department* [2014] UKSC 6; [2014] 1 W.L.R. 384). See Craig, 'Judicial Review, Appeal and Factual Error' [2004] PL 788, Grekos [2004] JR 184 and Williams, 'When is an error not an error? Reform of jurisdictional review of error of law and fact' [2007] PL 793. For further discussion of mistake of fact in immigration cases, see *R (Iran) v Secretary of State for the Home Department* [2005] EWCA Civ 982, at paragraph 50.

2. This apparent limitation on the recognition of mistake of fact as a ground of judicial review is somewhat opaque, it being arguable that in every judicial review claim the interests of the claimant and the defendant should be to achieve the correct result (by holding the body amenable to judicial review to a lawful decision). See *R v Lancashire County Council, ex parte Huddleston* [1986] 2 All ER 941at 945c where Sir John Donaldson MR described judicial review as a 'a new relationship between the courts and those who derive their authority from the public law, one of partnership based on a common aim, namely the maintenance of the highest standards of public administration.' It is also unclear as a matter of principle why mistake of fact as a ground should be limited to statutory contexts. See 13.20 below for examples of the wide range of areas in which this ground has now been recognised.

3. For an example of a mistake that was considered 'neither decisive nor really material' see *R (Mitchell) v Secretary of State for the Home Department* [2008] EWHC 1370 (Admin). See also *R (Judith Watt) v London Borough of Hackney* [2016] EWHC 1978 (Admin), at paragraph 52 in which Gilbart J emphasised the relatively low hurdle this fourth requirement represents by holding that it should be applied 'by asking if it is possible to say that it did not' play a material part (drawing a parallel with the new statutory test in s 31(2A) of the Senior Courts Act 1981).

4. See 13.8 above. The Court of Appeal in *E* thus effectively concluded that the approach of Lord Denning in *R v West Sussex Quarter Sessions, ex p Albert and Maud Johnson Trust Ltd* [1974] QB 24 should prevail.

5. One way of interpreting *R (Haile) v IAT* [2001] EWCA Civ 663; [2002] INLR 283 is that it involved such exceptional circumstances: a critical witness was in fact a member of a totally different political party in Ethiopia to that which he was believed to support.

13.19 Applying E, the Court of Appeal in *Cabo Verde v Secretary of State for the Home Department*[1] held that the Secretary of State was entitled to an order re-opening a decision of the Immigration Appeal Tribunal. An asylum seeker had asserted that whilst in custody in Angola he had been subjected to torture and ill treatment. The tribunal had held on this basis that he was entitled to asylum. Subsequently the Portuguese government asserted that the asylum seeker had committed crimes in Portugal during the period when he had claimed to be in custody in Angola. The court remitted the case for reconsideration by the tribunal. In the subsequent case of *R (Iran) v Secretary of State for the Home Department*.[2] the Court of Appeal noted that in Cabo Verde the mistake of fact was a mistake as to the existence of evidence which put in issue the asylum-seeker's claim to have been in Angola at the relevant time. The mistake was 'established' within the second of the conditions in *E*; and that mistake led to a finding of unfairness.[3] In *IA (Iran) v Secretary of State for the Home Department*[4] the Supreme Court applied the test set down in *E* in the asylum context, concluding that the evidence of an interview of the claimant by the UNHCR could not be 'described as an uncontentious and objectively verifiable fact.'

1. [2004] EWCA Civ 1726.

[2] [2005] EWCA Civ 982, at paragraph 50. The limits on the mistake of fact jurisdiction in asylum proceedings are demonstrated in *Kaydanyuk v Secretary of State for the Home Department* [2006] EWCA Civ 368 and *XX (Ethiopia) v Secretary of State for the Home Department* [2013] QB 656.

[3] For further Court of Appeal recognition of this ground, see also *MT (Algeria) v Secretary of State for the Home Department* [2008] QB 533 at 112:

> ' . . . the issue that we have reviewed is different from the question of whether a mistake of law can occur when a tribunal proceeds in ignorance of, or by a mistaken understanding of, an existing and uncontentious fact: see the judgment of Carnwath LJ in E's case [2004] QB 1044, para 66. As our judgment indicates, we accept that that is now an established, if limited, category of error of law.'

[4] [2014] UKSC 6; [2014] 1 W.L.R. 384 at paragraphs 54–55.

13.20 It is now well established beyond the immigration context that an error of fact resulting in unfairness can be asserted as a separate ground of challenge on judicial review. In *Connolly & Havering LBC v Secretary of State for Communities & Local Government*[1] the Court of Appeal held (in an appeal under s 288 of the Town & Country Planning Act 1990) that a planning inspector's decision could be quashed on the basis of mistake of fact, where the local authority had failed to supply the inspector with material information about the planning history of the site – satisfying the four conditions in *E*. Looking beyond the planning context, in both *R (on the application of Assura Pharmacy Ltd) v NHS Litigation Authority*[2] and *R (Pharmacy Care Plus Ltd) v Family Health Services Appeals Unit*[3] the test in *E* was applied in the context of decisions on admission to the NHS Pharmaceutical List (permitting the provision of pharmaceutical services); in *Department of Education v Cunningham*[4] the test in *E* was applied in respect of a decision to close a primary school; and in *R (Gopikrishna) v Office of the Independent Adjudicator for Higher Education*[5] it was applied in respect of a challenge to a decision not to uphold the claimant's complaint about the termination of her university course.[6]

[1] [2009] EWCA Civ 1059.
[2] [2007] EWHC 289 (Admin).
[3] [2013] EWHC 824 (Admin).
[4] [2016] NICA 12.
[5] [2015] EWHC 207 (Admin); [2015] E.L.R. 190.
[6] Numerous other non-immigration cases have applied the test established in *E*: eg *Cox v Secretary of State for Communities and Local Government* [2010] EWHC 104 (Admin); *R (Chalfont St Peter Parish Council) v Chiltern District Council* [2013] EWHC 2073 (Admin); *Hiam v Secretary of State for Communities and Local Government* [2014] EWHC 4112 (Admin); *R (Judith Watt) v London Borough of Hackney* [2016] EWHC 1978 (Admin). In *The Manydown Company Ltd v Basingstoke* [2012] EWHC 977 (Admin) at [94]-[95] Lindblom J listed mistake of fact amongst other 'well known and uncontroversial principles of public law' applying to local authority decision-making. See also *R (March) v Secretary of State for Health* [2010] EWHC 765 (Admin) where it was agreed that:

> 'A public law decision may be quashed if the published reasons or reasoning of the government reveal a material error of fact in their reasoning process. But the claimant must demonstrate that (i) there is an error of fact; and (ii) it was material and that a different decision might have been made but for the error.'

13.21 The head of challenge identified in *E* does not mean that the court assumes the functions of the decision-maker. In order to found such a challenge it would have to be shown that the tribunal whose decision was under appeal had made a mistake as to an established fact which was uncontentious and objectively verifiable, including a mistake as to the availability of evidence on a particular matter, that the appellant or his advisers had not been responsible for the mistake, and that the mistake had played a material, though not decisive, part in the tribunal's reasoning. The head of challenge identified in *E* remains a relatively limited inroad into the decision-maker's role.

FIDUCIARY DUTY

13.22 A well-known (but rarely cited) line of authority beginning with *Roberts v Hopwood*[1] ('the *Poplar wages* case') has established that local authorities owe a fiduciary duty to council tax payers. Lord Atkinson stated in *Poplar wages* that, towards those from whom it collects its funds, a local authority 'stands somewhat in the position of trustees or managers of the property of others'. In *Bromley London Borough Council v Greater London Council ('Fares Fair')* Lord Wilberforce said that *Roberts v Hopwood* 'remains authoritative as to principle'.[2] The House of Lords in *Fares Fair* also said that the principle of *Prescott v Birmingham Corpn* remains valid. In *Prescott*, Jenkins LJ said that, whereas local authorities were not trustees for their ratepayers, they did owe 'an analogous fiduciary duty' to their ratepayers in relation to the application of funds contributed by them.[3] The Court of Appeal in *Charles Terence Estates Ltd v Cornwall CC*[4] has more recently confirmed that:

> 'this line of authority establishes that some decisions of local authorities will amount to a breach of fiduciary duty or of a duty analogous to a fiduciary duty and that, in public law proceedings at the suit of an interested party, the decision may be characterised as ultra vires and void.'

[1] [1925] AC 578 at 595–506. The line of authority is helpfully summarised in *Charles Terence Estates Ltd v Cornwall County Council* [2013] 1 WLR. 466 at paras 11–17.
[2] [1983] 1 AC 768 at 815C, [1982] 1 All ER 129. However, as to wages, see Re Walker's Decision [1944] 1 KB 644, [1944] 1 All ER 614, and on fares, see *R v Merseyside County Council, ex p Great Universal Stores Ltd* (1982) 80 LGR 639 and *R v London Transport Executive, ex p Greater London Council* [1983] QB 484.
[3] [1955] Ch 210, [1954] 3 All ER 698. Unsurprisingly, there have been major changes in local government finance since this decision: funding for local authorities comes in large part from central government, non-domestic rates are set and ultimately collected on a national basis and domestic rates have been abolished in favour of different forms of taxation (now council tax). See the Local Government Finance Acts 1988, 1992 and 2012.
[4] [2013] 1 W.L.R. 466 at 17.

13.23 In relation to this fiduciary duty Lord Diplock[1] in *Fares Fair* said that a local authority is not only under a duty not to expend monies 'thriftlessly': it is also under a positive duty 'to deploy the full financial resources available to it to the best advantage'. The courts have stressed, however, that the fiduciary duty must be balanced against duties owed to recipients of the Council's wide range of services, whose interests must also be taken into account.[2]

[1] *Bromley London Borough Council v Greater London Council* [1983] 1 AC 768 at 829H.
[2] See, eg *Simpsons Motor Sales (London) Ltd v Hendon Corpn* [1963] Ch 57 at 83; *R v Newcastle-upon-Tyne City Council, ex p Dixon* (1993) 17 BMLR 82; and the rent cases, notably *Taylor v Munrow* [1960] 1 All ER 455, [1960] 1 WLR 151; *Luby v Newcastle-under-Lyme Corpn* [1964] 2 QB 64, affd [1965] 1 QB 214, and *Hemsted v Lees and Norwich County Council* (1986) 18 HLR 424. In finding a breach of the fiduciary duty, Elias J in *R (Structadene Ltd) v Hackney London Borough Council* [2001] 2 All ER 225 recognised that 'it is possible for a council successfully to contend that there are social or other benefits to the

local community which outweigh the loss resulting from the failure to obtain the best price' but was unable to speculate what those benefits were in the absence of evidence.

13.24 In *Fares Fair* Lord Scarman added that relevant statutes must be 'construed in the light of the fiduciary duty'.[1] It follows that the fiduciary duty is a relevant consideration which, as a matter of statutory construction, local authorities must take into account when making decisions that involve incurring expenditure or levying charges. Particularly when the traditional judicial restraint in such areas is taken into account, a local authority which has properly understood the law relating to this statutory consideration, and has not gone beyond what is reasonable, will not be open to review merely because others, or even the court, would have assessed matters differently.[2] If so, the fiduciary duty would essentially be no more than an example of circumstances giving rise to review for illegality in the sense described by Lord Diplock in *CCSU*.

[1]   Lord Scarman in *Bromley London Borough Council v Greater London Council* [1983] 1 AC 768 at 838H.
[2]   See, as to expenditure. *Pickwell v Camden London Borough Council* [1983] QB 962, [1983] 1 All ER 602 and *R v Secretary of State for the Environment, ex p Hammersmith and Fulham London Borough Council* [1990] AC 521. As to the level of rate or charge levied, see *R v Greenwich London Borough Council, ex p Cedar Transport Group Ltd* [1983] RA 173. For the Scottish position, see Chapter 22 at **22.64** below.

Chapter 14

CROWN PROCEEDINGS

INTRODUCTION

14.1 The Crown, as the monarch, is usually regarded as a corporation sole,[1] who has the same ordinary common law powers as are available to any natural person (eg to make ex gratia payments, to enter into contracts), and also certain special prerogative powers. The Crown's common law and prerogative powers may be abrogated by statute by express words or necessary implication.

Common law powers are usually exercised by Ministers on the Crown's behalf, or on Ministers' advice. Judicial review proceedings to challenge the exercise of common law powers are brought against the relevant Minister or department.[2] The usual grounds of judicial review apply, These common law powers necessarily exist without reference to any specific statutory framework. That being so, the opportunity for successful challenge by reference to ordinary *Wednesbury* principles, of decisions taken in exercise of common law powers can often be low. Challenges contending that relevant matters have been left out of account, or that irrelevant matters have been considered will suffer from the absence of the sort of anchor points that will exist where the proper use of statutory powers is in issue.[3] Challenges are therefore more likely to succeed if they rely on inconsistency with some or other fixed legal standard, such as Convention rights, or anti-discrimination legislation.[4]

[1] Although sometimes the term, 'the Crown', is taken to be a reference to central government in the form of a corporation aggregate: see *Town Investments Ltd v Department of the Environment* [1978] AC 359.

[2] See, eg *M v Home Office* [1994] 1 AC 377, 416. The availability of judicial review in relation to the exercise of the royal prerogative was established in *Council of Civil Service Unions v Minister for the Civil Service* [1985] AC 374, and is discussed generally in CHAPTER 5. For cases concerning the administration of ex gratia payment schemes, see eg *R v Criminal Injuries Compensation Board, ex p P* [1995] 1 WLR 845; *R v Ministry of Defence, ex p Walker*

[2000] 1 WLR 806, HL; *R (Association of British Civilian Internees: Far East Region) v Secretary of State for Defence* [2003] QB 1397. For judicial review of the exercise of the royal prerogative of mercy, see *R v Secretary of State for the Home Department, ex p Bentley* [1994] QB 349. For practice in civil proceedings (other than judicial review) involving the Crown, see CPR Pt 66.

3   See, eg *R (Association of British Civilian Internees: Far East Region) v Secretary of State for Defence* [2003] QB 1397 at [39].

4   *A-G v De Keyser's Royal Hotel Ltd* [1920] AC 508; *R v Secretary of State for the Home Department, ex p Northumbria Police Authority* [1989] QB 26; *R v Secretary of State for the Home Department, ex p Fire Brigades Union* [1995] 2 AC 513; *R (Rottman) v Metropolitan Police Comr* [2002] 2 AC 692 at 75; *R (Hooper) v Secretary of State for Work and Pensions* [2005] 1 WLR 1681, HL.

14.2 'The Crown' is a term sometimes used to refer compendiously to the executive government of the day. Very many statutory powers are conferred upon Ministers, who exercise them by virtue of their public office. Ministers who exercise statutory powers are, for most practical purposes, in no different position from any other judicial review respondent when their decisions are challenged.

The distinction drawn between the Crown itself and Ministers of the Crown, is not without considerable difficulty. In *Town Investments Ltd v Department of Environment*[1] Lord Diplock referred to the fictional sense in which the expression 'the Crown' is used in English public law and considered it preferable to speak of 'the government', 'a term appropriate to embrace both collectively and individually all of the Ministers of the Crown and Parliamentary Secretaries under whose direction the administrative work of government is carried on by the civil servants employed in the various government departments'. Statute, too, draws no clear-cut distinction. The Interpretation Act 1978 defines the term 'Secretary of State' as meaning 'one of Her Majesty's Principal Secretaries of State'.[2] Thus, where statutory functions are conferred on the Secretary of State they may, in point of legal theory — and subject to secondary legislation distributing business between Ministers — be carried out by any Secretary of State.[3]

Similar considerations apply in relation to the prerogative. In Dicey's discussion of the prerogative he said: 'The prerogative is the name for the remaining portion of the Crown's original authority, and is therefore, as already pointed out, the name for the residue of discretionary power left at any moment in the hands of the Crown, whether such power be in fact exercised by the King himself or by his ministers'.[4] This was quoted with approval by the House of Lords in *A-G v De Keyser's Royal Hotel Ltd.*[5] This underlines the obvious legal fact, necessarily true in a constitutional monarchy, that for the purposes of measuring and controlling the power of the State, the Crown and its Ministers are one.

1   [1978] AC 359.
2   See at section 5 and Schedule 1.
3   See also *Hinchy v Secretary of State for Work and Pensions* [2005] 1 WLR 967, HL at 11.
4   Law of the Constitution (8th edn) p 421.
5   [1920] AC 508 at 526; see also *Council of Civil Service Unions v Minister for the Civil Service* [1985] AC 374 at 398D.

14.3 There are, however, several specific areas where special problems or questions have arisen, which are addressed below. These are as follows.

(1)   Crown immunity from process.
(2)   The *Carltona* principle, whereby functions vested in a Minister can be discharged by officials.
(3)   Modified disclosure procedures (public interest immunity against disclosure of documents in proceedings or the giving of reasons; and the closed material procedure under Part 2 of the Justice and Security Act 2013).
(4)   The role of the Crown where a declaration of incompatibility is sought under section 4 of the Human Rights Act 1998.
(5)   The liability of the Crown in damages for legislative or administrative measures in breach of EU law, or Convention rights under the Human Rights Act 1998.

THE CROWN'S IMMUNITY FROM PROCESS

14.4 The Sovereign in Her personal capacity is not subject to legal process.[1] Moreover, the Crown itself is immune from claims for mandatory orders, prohibiting orders and quashing orders (ie what were previously the prerogative writs of mandamus, prohibition and certiorari) 'both because there would be an incongruity in The Queen commanding herself to do an act, and also because the disobedience to a writ of mandamus is to be enforced by attachment'.[2] Yet it is commonplace for Ministers of the Crown to be judicially reviewed for acts done in their capacity as such, and although a mandatory order is rarely necessary (though frequently sought in the claim form), on the footing that the Minister will be loyal to the court's judgment without the need for a compulsory order, it has long been clear that the modern judicial review jurisdiction includes the power to issue a mandatory order against a Minister. As Lord Parker CJ said in *R v Customs and Excise Comrs, ex p Cooke and Stevenson (or ex p Cook)*:[3]

> 'Accordingly, one approaches this case on the basis, and I confess for my part an alarming basis, that the word of the minister is outweighing the law of the land. However, having said that, one moves on to the far more difficult question whether mandamus will lie. It is sometimes said as a general proposition that mandamus will not lie against the Crown or an officer or servant of the Crown. I think we all know in this day and age that that as a general proposition is quite untrue. There have been many cases, of which the most recent is *Padfield v Minister of Agriculture, Fisheries and Food* [1968] AC 997 in which a mandamus was issued to a minister. Indeed, that has always been the case . . . '.[4]

---

[1]   A question could have arisen in relation to the trial of Princess Diana's former butler, Paul Burrell, for theft whether the Queen should now be treated as a compellable witness, where Her evidence might be necessary to ensure a fair trial in compliance with the requirements of art 6 of the European Convention on Human Rights. The issue did not arise for decision, because in the event the prosecution was dropped.

[2]   See eg *R v Powell* (1841) 1 QB 352 at 361; *M v Home Office* [1994] 1 AC 377, 416.

[3]   [1970] 1 WLR 450, 455.

[4]   Lord Parker went on to refer to certain limits on the availability of mandamus against Ministers. For observations on how these limits have effectively fallen away, see per Lord Woolf in *M v Home Office* [1994] 1 AC 377 at 417.

14.5 It follows that a Minister is at least as amenable to a quashing order and declaratory relief. Relief by way of judicial review is granted against Ministers whenever the court holds that there has been unlawful action, unless there is a proper and compelling argument for the refusal of relief on discretionary grounds.[1]

[1] For discussion of discretionary bars to relief, see **17.28**.

14.6 The logical conclusion of this reasoning is that injunctions, either final or interlocutory, can also be granted against Ministers of the Crown in public law proceedings. This was recognised by the courts, but only in 1984, in *M v Home Office*.

Other remedies directed at securing interim relief in judicial review proceedings against Ministers of the Crown have also been considered but have become less important since injunctions became available.

It has also been established that, where a compulsory order is made against a Minister, breach of that order may give rise to liability in contempt, though the potential sanctions are more limited than in the case of a normal litigant. It is difficult to see how these developments, which are considered below, are to be squared with the continuing (and accepted) immunity of the Crown itself. Yet that question is of greater academic interest than practical significance.

INJUNCTIONS

14.7 By s 21 of the Crown Proceedings Act 1947 it is not open to a court in 'civil proceedings' to grant an injunction against the Crown. It follows that in such proceedings an injunction cannot be granted against a Minister where its effect would be to give relief against the Crown. However, by s 38(1), the interpretation section, 'civil proceedings', is defined so as not to include 'proceedings on the Crown side of the King's Bench Division': that is, judicial review proceedings. Thus the availability of an injunction in judicial review is not determined by the 1947 Act.

14.8 The accepted position now is that in judicial review proceedings injunctions can be granted against the Crown. However, the path to that conclusion was a winding path. In *Factortame Ltd v Secretary of State for Transport*,[1] the House of Lords concluded that s 21 of the 1947 Act did not itself determine whether or not injunctions were available in judicial review claims, but rather had the effect only of preserving the common law position. The House went on to state that there was no jurisdiction to grant injunctions against the Crown in judicial review proceedings. That clearly embraced the proposition that officers of the Crown, acting as such, were likewise immune.[2]

[1] [1990] 2 AC 85.
[2] See per Lord Bridge at [1990] 2 AC 145G–150H.

14.9 In *Factortame (No 2)* the decision in *Factortame (No 1)* was made subject to an important exception in cases where a claimant asserts directly effective rights under EU law. In *Factortame (No 2)* the CJEU concluded that where an interim injunction was required for the effective protection of EU rights then any rule of domestic law precluding the grant of such relief against a Minister must be set aside.[1] In that case in light of the ruling on the reference, the House of Lords went on to consider the principles to be applied in deciding whether to grant such an injunction; and, applying those principles to the facts of the case, held that an injunction should be granted, in effect dis-applying relevant provisions of the Merchant Shipping Act 1988 pending the determination of the substantive judicial review proceedings.

¹   [1991] 1 AC 603.

14.10 In *M v Home Office* the House of Lords reversed the decision in *Factortame (No 1)*, and accepted that injunctions could be granted against Ministers of the Crown.¹

M was a case, 'remarkable for the chapter of accidents, mistakes and misunderstandings' upon which it was based.² M, had unsuccessfully claimed political asylum, and had been returned by the Home Office to Zaire although it was said that an undertaking had been given by counsel to the court that he would not be so returned pending his application for leave to apply for judicial review by the court the next morning. The Home Office – lawyers and officials alike – did not believe that whatever was said to the judge (Garland J) amounted to an undertaking. When it was known that he was being returned to Zaire, his solicitor obtained ex parte, a mandatory order directed to the Home Secretary, requiring M to be brought back to the United Kingdom forthwith. The next day the Home Secretary, having been advised that there were doubts as to whether the judge possessed the power to make such an order, decided (subject to further advice, which was given, to the effect that this was legally proper) not immediately to bring M back, but first to apply to the judge to set aside the mandatory order. This application was successful. In the light of the judge's comments an attempt was nevertheless made, following the discharge of the mandatory order, to bring M back to the United Kingdom, but this proved impossible since by that time, contact with him had been lost.

¹   [1994] 1 AC 377.
²   Per Lord Donaldson MR in the Court of Appeal, [1992] QB 270 at 284.

14.11 Contempt proceedings were then launched against the Home Office and various named individuals, including by amendment the Home Secretary in person. The first instance judge (Simon Brown J) dismissed the application, concluding that the Crown was in law not amenable to the contempt jurisdiction, and neither was the Secretary of State qua Secretary of State.¹ The Court of Appeal concluded that neither the Crown nor the Home Office as an institution could be subject to contempt proceedings since such proceedings were personal and punitive in nature and could only be brought against natural persons or others with sufficient legal personality. But, said the Court of Appeal the jurisdiction did exist as against both Ministers of the Crown, and civil servants.²

¹   Had it been otherwise, he would have found the Home Office in contempt for failing to return the applicant from Paris where he landed on a stop-over to Zaire: this, in the judge's view, was a breach of the undertaking which by then had been communicated to the Home Office's Chief Immigration Officer by the applicant's solicitor.
²   [1992] QB 270.

14.12 On further appeal, the House of Lords considered both the position as to the availability of injunctions, and the position in respect of applications for contempt.

As to injunctions, the House of Lords concluded that the jurisdiction at s 31(2) of the Senior Courts Act 1981 included the jurisdiction to the court on applications for judicial review to grant injunctions or interim injunctions.

Section 31(2) of the 1981 Act is now in the following terms:

'(2) A declaration may be made or an injunction granted under this subsection in any case where an application for judicial review, seeking that relief, has been made and the High Court considers that, having regard to—

(a)   the nature of the matters in respect of which relief may be granted by mandatory, prohibiting or quashing orders;

(b)   the nature of the persons and bodies against whom relief may be granted by such orders; and

(c)   all the circumstances of the case,

it would be just and convenient for the declaration to be made or the injunction to be granted, as the case may be.'

Lord Woolf stated his conclusion in the following terms:

'I am, therefore, of the opinion that, the language of section 31 being unqualified in its terms, there is no warrant for restricting its application so that in respect of ministers and other officers of the Crown alone the remedy of an injunction, including an interim injunction, is not available. In my view the history of prerogative proceedings against officers of the Crown supports such a conclusion. So far as interim relief is concerned, which is the practical change which has been made, there is no justification for adopting a different approach to officers of the Crown from that adopted in relation to other respondents in the absence of clear language such as that contained in section 21(2) of the Act of 1947. The fact that in any event a stay could be granted against the Crown under Ord 53 r 3(10) emphasises the limits of the change in the situation which is involved. It would be most regrettable if an approach which is inconsistent with that which exists in Community law should be allowed to persist if this is not strictly necessary. The restriction provided for in section 21(2) of the Act of 1947 does, however, remain in relation to civil proceedings'.

14.13 So far as concerned the contempt jurisdiction, the House of Lords concluded that a finding of contempt could not be made against the Crown directly, but that a finding could be made against a government department, or against a Minister of the Crown in his official capacity — ie in circumstances in which the department for which he is responsible was guilty of contempt. The House observed that any finding of contempt ought ordinarily to be directed to the body against which the order breached had been made; and that in the context of judicial review proceedings that would ordinarily be the Minister of the Crown. The House also concluded that contempt proceedings could be brought against a Minister in his personal capacity, and that this would be appropriate where the contempt related to his own default.

14.14 The House of Lords also made an obvious (but none the less important) observation arising from the circumstances of that case: the order made by the Judge ought to have been approached on the basis that it was valid unless and until it was set aside. Thus it had been wrong for the department to act on the premise that the need to comply with the order would only arise if an application to set it aside had been made and had failed. The House of Lords stated that on the facts of that case the proper conclusion was that the Minister was in contempt in his official capacity; a finding of contempt was made on that basis.

14.15 The constitutional importance of this case is obvious. It goes to the heart of the relationship between the executive and the courts. Ministers of the Crown are subject to compulsory orders and the contempt jurisdiction of the courts for things done or not done in the execution of their office. The courts have asserted their ultimate power of control. The point was expressed most forcefully by Lord Templeman:

> 'My Lords, the argument that there is no power to enforce the law by injunction or contempt proceedings against a minister in his official capacity would, if upheld, establish the proposition that the executive obey the law as a matter of grace and not as a result of necessity, a proposition which would reverse the result of the Civil War.'[1]

---

[1]   [1994] 1 AC 377 at 395G–395H.

14.16 In his speech in *M v Home Office* Lord Woolf stated that the jurisdiction to grant injunctions should not be exercised 'except in the most limited circumstances'. His opinion was that in most instances a declaration would be sufficient in place of a final injunction; and he suggested that so far as interim proceedings were concerned, a practice of interim declarations would suffice (and would be appropriate). 'As has been the position in the past . . . ' he said ' . . . the Crown can be relied upon to co-operate fully with such declarations.' Although this sentiment was both then and is now, accurate, it is not one that is in tune with the instincts of the modern judiciary, in particular when it comes to applications for interim relief. Today, applications for interim relief in judicial review claims against Ministers are by no means uncommon. In practice, little if any thought is given to Lord Woolf's distinction between interim injunctions and interim declarations.

Applications for interim relief against the Crown are approached on almost the same basis as any other application for an interim injunction in judicial review proceedings. The starting point is the principle stated by Lord Diplock in *American Cyanamid*:[1] Is there a serious question to be tried? If there is, then a grant or refusal of interim relief depends on the court's assessment of the balance of convenience. The category of matters capable of weighing in the balance of convenience is not closed. As stated by Lord Diplock (also in American Cyanamid):

> 'It would be unwise to attempt even to list all the various matters which may need to be taken into consideration in deciding where the balance lies, let alone to suggest the relative weight to be attached to them. These will vary from case to case.'

However, in public law cases two distinctive matters arise. The first is that the inquiry as to whether damages would be an adequate remedy in lieu of interim relief is rarely the critical factor that it is in private law proceedings. The availability of damages claims against public authorities is restricted, and in any event (and in particular in claims against Ministers of the Crown) a claim for damages is not often a defining characteristic of the claim.

The second distinctive matter is that the public interest will always be a relevant consideration within the balance of convenience: how will any relevant public interest be affected by the grant or refusal of the interim relief claimed. This principle is summarised in the judgment of Cranston J in *R (Medical Justice) v Secretary of State for the Home Department*.[2] The notion of the wider public interest will include the risk of prejudice to third parties which may arise from a grant of interim relief. Where third party rights are affected, the claimant seeking the injunction may be required to give a cross-undertaking in damages extending to any loss incurred by the third party by reason of the injunction: see *R v Inspectorate of Pollution, ex p Greenpeace Ltd*[3] (see also *R v Secretary of State for the Environment, ex p RSPB*).[4]

However, the public interest that is relevant to the balance of convenience is not limited to instances of possible prejudice to identifiable third parties. It embraces any and all possible adverse consequences for public administration in the event that the injunction sought is granted.

In cases where an interim injunction is sought against a government department or Minister of the Crown, this wider public interest may have a particularly telling impact. For example, if the injunctive relief is aimed at suspending operation of a general policy adopted by a Minister the Court must consider and take into account the general public interest in maintaining that policy until the final hearing of the application for judicial review, notwithstanding the specific adverse effect that that policy may have on the claimant in the meantime. In many cases these competing interests will be capable of accommodation by framing any interim relief so that is directed only to the position of the claimant himself.

1   [1975] AC 396.
2   [2010] EWHC 1425 (Admin), see at §§6, 8, and **12**, **16**.
3   [1994] 1 WLR 570.
4   (1995) 7 Admin LR 434 at 443. See also Michael Fordham 'Interim Relief and the Cross-Undertaking' at [1997] JR 136.

14.17 One situation in which applications for interim injunctions have frequently arisen is where relief is sought pending a reference to the CJEU for a preliminary ruling on a question of EU law. In that situation the normal devices open in the course of national proceedings, such as an expedited hearing and a willingness on the part of the executive to stay its hand in the interim, are unavailable, and a delay measured in years rather than months pending the ruling is typical.

Yet such applications have not been conspicuously successful. True it is that an interim injunction was granted in *Factortame (No 2)*, where the basic ground rules were established by the House of Lords.[1] But subsequent attempts to secure interim relief pending such a reference have failed in a range of cases: see *R v Secretary of State for National Heritage, ex p Continental Television BV;*[2] *R v HM Treasury, ex p British Telecommunications plc;*[3] *R v Customs and Excise Comrs, ex p EMU Tabac Sarl (Imperial Tobacco Co Ltd intervening);*[4] *R v The Licensing Authority established by the Medicines Act 1968 (acting by Medicines Control Agency), ex p Generics (UK) Ltd and E R Squibb & Sons;*[5] *R v Ministry of Agriculture, Fisheries and Food, ex p Monsanto plc (Clayton Plant Protection Ltd intervener)*[6] and *R v Environment Agency, ex p Mayer Parry Recycling Ltd (No 2)*.[7]

The position for the party seeking the injunction is equally difficult in situations where the injunction is sought in aid of an anticipated direct claim before the Court of First Instance: see *R (Melli Bank plc) v HM Treasury.*[8]

It has been emphasised in those cases, notably in the judgment of Sir Thomas Bingham MR in *ex p British Telecommunications plc*, that there is no room for a formulaic approach to the balance of convenience. In practice, however, the courts can be expected in this context to place substantial weight both on the perceived strength of the applicant's case, to the extent that any view can sensibly be formed on it, and upon broad considerations of public interest (such as, in Continental TV, the public interest in protecting children from pornographic television programmes broadcast into the United Kingdom by satellite from another Member State). As to enforcement of injunctions granted in aid of EU law proceedings in the CJEU, see below at paragraph **14.20**.

[1] For the order made, see [1991] 1 AC 603 at 603; for the principles, at 671E–674D.
[2] [1993] 3 CMLR 387.
[3] [1994] 1 CMLR 621.
[4] (1995) Times, 10 August.
[5] [1997] 2 CMLR 201: affd on appeal (20 February 1997, unreported).
[6] [1999] QB 1161.
[7] [2001] Env LR 630.
[8] [2008] EWHC 1161 (Admin) per Moses LJ at paragraphs **44, 55** and **56**; and per Sullivan LJ at paragraph **86**.

Contempt of court

14.18 The decision of the House of Lords in *M v Home Office* is the key authority. The conclusions stated there in respect of liability to contempt proceedings are summarised above at paragraphs **14.13–14.14**. This applies not just to situations where there has been a breach of an injunction, but equally to breach of any other compulsory order of the court, such as a final mandatory or prohibitory order.

14.19 In the case of a finding of contempt, however, the normal remedies of fine, sequestration or imprisonment do not apply to a government department or Minister acting in his official capacity. In that context the remedy is not to be seen as personal or punitive. A finding of contempt should be sufficient by itself: it serves to demonstrate that a government department has interfered with the administration of justice, leaving it to Parliament to determine what should be the consequences of that finding. In judicial review proceedings the finding should normally be made against the respondent Minister in his official capacity, eg as 'Home Secretary', not against him personally as an individual.[1] To that may be added an order for costs. Similarly, contempt proceedings will not ordinarily be appropriate as against civil servants whose actions, by reason of the *Carltona* principle are the actions of the Minister.[2]

[1] Thus it was that in *M v Home Office* the personal finding of contempt by the Court of Appeal against Mr Kenneth Baker, who as Home Secretary had taken the decision not to comply immediately with the order of the court, was discharged by the House of Lords and replaced by a finding of contempt against 'the Home Secretary'.
[2] See *Beggs v Scottish Ministers* [2007] 1 WLR 455 per Lord Hope at paragraphs 8 – 11.

14.20 In holding that a finding of contempt can be made against a Minister, the House of Lords in *M v Home Office* has also solved a problem that could otherwise have arisen, at least in theory, in relation to the enforceability of an injunction granted for the protection of directly effective rights under EC law in accordance with the principles laid down in *Factortame (No 2).*[1] Such an injunction will now be enforceable in the same way as any other injunction granted against a Minister in his official capacity. There is no reason to believe that the protection afforded by such an injunction will be rendered ineffective by the fact that the remedy for breach is a 'mere' finding of contempt rather than a financial penalty or imprisonment. The House of Lords clearly (and justifiably) considered in *M v Home Office* that a finding of contempt alone would be a sufficient sanction to ensure compliance with compulsory orders of the court.

[1] It was suggested, for example, in the first edition of this book that, where an interim injunction was granted requiring the disapplication of a statute, it could be regarded as a stay properly so called; the relevant statutory provision is simply suspended.

Stays

14.21 For some time it seemed an important question whether a stay, as opposed to an injunction, could be granted against a Minister as a means of interim relief where a ministerial administrative decision was challenged in judicial review. In *R v Secretary of State for Education and Science, ex p Avon County Council*[1] the Court of Appeal concluded that such relief was available.[2]

However, since the judgment in *M v Home Office*, which established the jurisdiction to grant an interim injunction against a Minister in judicial review proceedings, the availability of a stay as a means of interim relief has assumed far less importance. The remaining question is not whether a stay is available at all,[3] but in what circumstances it is an appropriate form of relief.[4]

[1] [1991] 1 QB 558.
[2] A conclusion re-stated by the Court of Appeal in *R (Ashworth Hospital Authority) v Mental Health Review Tribunal for West Midlands and Northwest Region* [2003] 1 WLR 127 (paragraph 42), but at odds with prior authority of the Privy Council: see *Minister of Foreign Affairs, Trade and Industry v Vehicles and Suppliers Limited* [1991] 1 WLR 550 which identified a stay only as a means of halting proceedings before a court or tribunal.
[3] In *M v Home Office* [1994] 1 AC 377 at 422G Lord Woolf relied on 'the fact that in any event a stay could be granted against the Crown under RSC Ord 53, r 3(10)' as emphasising the limits of the change involved in the finding of jurisdiction to grant an injunction against a Minister.
[4] Where the question is whether or not a stay should be granted vis-à-vis the consequences of a court's judgment, pending appeal, an approach based on American Cyanamid principles has been applied, see *R(A) v Secretary of State for the Home Department* [2009] EWHC 3463 (Admin).

14.22 It was held in *Avon* that a ministerial administrative decision could be the subject of a stay because the term 'proceedings' in RSC Ord 53, r 3(10)(a) (which empowered the court to direct that the grant of leave to apply for judicial review shall operate as a 'stay of the proceedings to which the application relates'),[1] is wide enough to include administrative decisions of Ministers and not merely the proceedings of lower courts or tribunals.[2] Woolf and Taylor LJJ expressed the same view obiter in *R v Licensing Authority established under Medicines Act 1968, ex p Smith Kline & French Laboratories Ltd (No 2)*.[3]

That reasoning conflicted with the later decision of the Privy Council in *Minister of Foreign Affairs, Trade and Industry v Vehicles and Supplies Ltd*.[4] However, subsequent decisions have confirmed the wide meaning to be given to the term 'proceedings': it is not confined to proceedings before an inferior court or tribunal.[5]

It appears that a cross-undertaking in damages may be imposed as the condition for the grant of a stay.[6] Where a stay will, in practice, have the same effect as an interim injunction, the test for whether the stay should be granted should be the same as applies in relation to injunctive relief.

[1] See now CPR Pt 54.10(2).
[2] Per Glidewell LJ at 561F–562C.
[3] [1990] 1 QB 574.
[4] [1991] 1 WLR 550, see, especially, 566E–566H per Lord Oliver.
[5] See *M v Home Office* [1994] 1 AC 377, 419A–419B and 422G; *Scotia Pharmaceuticals International Ltd v Department of Health* [1997] EuLR 626, 646E–648C; *R (Ashworth Hospital Authority) v Mental Health Review Tribunal for West Midlands and Northwest Region* [2003] 1 WLR 127, esp, at 38 and 42.
[6] *R v Inspectorate of Pollution, ex p Greenpeace Ltd* [1994] 1 WLR 570, 577C.

Interim declaration

For general discussion of interim declarations, see **19.104**.

14.23 CPR 25.1(1)(b) permits the grant of an interim declaration. Declaratory relief is often of particular significance in relation to the Crown, since the Crown is trusted to act in accordance with any declaration of rights made by the court. Given the similarity in effect, in relation to the Crown, of an interim declaration and an interim injunction, the same balance of convenience test should usually be applied.[1]

In practice the availability of interim injunctions has meant that interim declarations are rarely sought. Any interim relief that is sought will in most cases be better and more appropriately formulated in terms of an interim injunction. Certainly, the approach that is applied to the grant or refusal of interim injunctions (and in particular, mandatory injunctions) cannot be side-stepped by characterising the relief sought in terms of a declaration.[2] Moreover, any invitation to a court to make an interim declaration that in any sense represents declaration of generically applicable legal principle is likely to be declined: the risk of adverse impact on third parties will be a known unknown, and will ordinarily be simply too great.

[1] See, eg *R v Environment Agency, ex p Mayer Parry Recycling Ltd (No 2)* [2001] Env. LR 630.
[2] Compare *R v Secretary of State for the Environment ex parte RSPB* (1995) 7 Admin LR 434.

14.24 In *R v Secretary of State for the Environment, ex p Royal Society for the Protection of Birds*[1] the House of Lords decided to refer a question of EC law to the ECJ and the RSPB then sought an interim declaration pending the outcome of the reference. The relief sought was refused on the ground that it was inappropriate in all the circumstances. It is interesting to note that one of the factors leading to that conclusion was the absence of a cross-undertaking in damages in circumstances where the objective was to prevent development by a third party pursuant to an existing planning permission, which could result in very large commercial loss:

> 'However, the RSPB were not prepared to give any cross undertaking in damages. Had they sought an interim injunction against the port authority or other developer proceeding further they would undoubtedly have been required to give such an undertaking as a condition of being granted relief. Instead, they are seeking to achieve the same result without the risk of incurring very substantial expenditure and thereby asking the House to adopt a most unusual course'.[2]

¹ (1995) 7 Admin LR 434.
² (1995) 7 Admin LR 434 at 443B.

14.25 It may well be the case that, as for an application for a stay, the giving of a cross-undertaking in damages could be imposed as the condition for the grant of an interim declaration in appropriate cases.

Interim habeas corpus

Habeas corpus, along with other prerogative remedies not dealt with by application for judicial review, is beyond the scope of this work: see CHAPTER 16 below where cross references to texts and cases on habeas corpus will be found.

14.26 In *R v Secretary of State for the Home Department, ex p Muboyayi*[1] the Court of Appeal took the view that habeas might issue against Crown servants such as Ministers. In that case the writ was issued as an interim protective measure to prevent an immigrant being removed before the court could give full consideration to the merits of the case. (Brooke J had issued the writ at first instance, counsel for the Home Office having quite properly – as was acknowledged in the Court of Appeal – declined to give an undertaking that the applicant would not be removed.) Such an approach was both novel and of doubtful validity, but the issue is unlikely to resurface in this form since the natural remedy is now an interlocutory injunction, and this is the course which the courts have adopted when the need for relief has arisen.

¹ [1992] QB 244.

THE *CARLTONA* PRINCIPLE

14.27 The business of government could not be carried on if every Minister or Secretary of State was obliged personally to take every decision which fell within his area of responsibility. The practical need for a devolution of his decision-making powers to an official of suitable seniority was recognised by the Court of Appeal in *Carltona Ltd v Works Comrs.*[1] In that case the issue before the court was the legality of an order made by the Commissioners of Works, requisitioning a factory. The requisition order had been signed by an official for and on behalf of the Commissioners. One of the grounds of challenge was that the decision was unlawful because the Commissioners' own minds had never been brought to bear on it. The Court of Appeal dismissed the challenge on that ground, and stated the following (per Lord Greene MR):

'In the administration of government of this country the functions which are given to ministers (and constitutionally properly given to ministers because they are constitutionally responsible) are functions so multifarious that no minister could ever personally attend to them. To take the example of the present case no doubt there have been thousands of requisitions in this country by individual ministries. It cannot be supposed that this regulation meant that in each case, the minister in person should direct his mind to the matter. The duties imposed upon ministers and the powers given to ministers are normally exercised under the authority of the ministers by responsible officials of the department. Public business could not be carried on if that were not the case. Constitutionally, the decision of such an official is, of course, the decision of the minister. The minister is responsible. It is he who must answer before Parliament for anything that his officials have done under his authority, and, if for an important matter he selected an official of such junior standing that he could not be expected competently to perform the work, the minister would have to answer for that in Parliament. The whole system of departmental organisation and administration is based on the view that ministers, being responsible to Parliament, will see that important duties are committed to experienced officials. If they do not do that, Parliament is the place where complaint must be made against them.'

Carltona has been treated as settled and uncontroversial law ever since it was decided. As was stated in *R v Secretary of State for the Home Department, ex p Oladehinde*:[2]

'It is well recognised that when a statute places a duty on a minister it may generally be exercised by a member of his department for whom he accepts responsibility: this is the Carltona principle'.

[1]   [1943] 2 All ER 560.
[2]   [1991] 1 AC 254 at 303B per Lord Griffiths.

14.28 The principle is a striking example of the pragmatism of the common law. It is also important to recognise that, as stated by the Court of Appeal in the *Carltona* judgment, the principle is neither a principle of delegation, nor a principle of statutory construction. Instead, it is a part of common law constitutional principle, underpinned by the further common law principle of ministerial responsibility to Parliament.

The *Carltona* principle is not a manifestation of the normal rule on delegation (that where a statute confers a function of decision upon X, it is X alone who is authorised to make the decision and it is unlawful for him to delegate the making of the decision to Y). *Carltona* must be viewed as an exception to the rule against delegation and, what is more, an exception which is admitted on purely practical (though undeniably compelling) grounds.[1] Nor is the *Carltona* principle a manifestation of any aspect of the principle of agency. The civil servant Y is entitled to make the decision for Minister X though he is not even the servant of Minister X; they are both servants of the Crown.

As is stated by Professor Forsyth, where *Carltona* applies, there is no true delegation:[2]

'Strictly speaking there is not even delegation in these cases. Delegation requires a distinct act by which the power is conferred upon some person not previously competent to exercise it. But the authority of officials to act in their ministers' names derives from a general rule of law and not from any particular act of delegation.'

He cites *Lewisham Metropolitan Borough and Town Clerk v Roberts*[3] and *R v Skinner*.[4]

Yet these cases, and the authorities more generally that seek to rely on the *Carltona* principle, have tended to mischaracterise the basis of the principle. For example, the judgments in *Lewisham* accept the language of delegation. In *Skinner*, the question was whether the decision could be regarded as having been made on the Minister's behalf. Lord Mustill in *ex p Doody* also used the language of delegation (although in *R v Secretary of State for the Home Department, ex p Oladehinde* the Court of Appeal treated the matter as one of 'devolution' rather than 'delegation', while Lord Griffiths referred to the Minister's power 'to devolve or delegate the decision').[5]

On these authorities, the underlying basis for the operation of the *Carltona* principle remains, in essence, one of delegation or proper authorisation of the official in question to take the decision;[6] it is just that there is not required to be an individual decision by the Minister to delegate to that particular official, as opposed to some settled practice of delegation or distribution of responsibility within the department.

¹ For general discussion of delegation, see **7.39** et seq.
² Wade & Forsyth *Administrative Law* (11th edn, 2014) p 266.
³ [1949] 2 KB 608.
⁴ [1968] 2 QB 700.
⁵ [1991] AC 254 at 283H–284A, CA, and 303C per Lord Griffiths.
⁶ See, also, *R (Chief Constable of the West Midlands Police) v Birmingham Justices* [2002] EWHC 1087 (Admin), [2003] Crim LR 37, at 9–10 per Sedley LJ: the *Carltona* principle is predicated on the proposition that the department head is responsible for things done under his authority; his implied power to delegate depends on: (i) the conferment of a power in terms which implicitly permits their delegation; and (ii) the existence of persons to whom he can delegate without imparting ultimate responsibility (although, having used the language of delegation, and again at 15, the court did express certain reservations about it at 12). The principle was in that case applied outside the context of a central government department, to cover delegation of his functions under s 1 of the Crime and Disorder Act 1998 by a chief constable. In that case, the court was not satisfied on the evidence that there had been a proper authorisation of, or delegation to, the officer who carried out one aspect of the chief constable's duty, and the matter was put back for further investigation. As to whether *Carltona* is really appropriate for extension to situations beyond those where there is Ministerial accountability and responsibility, see **14.29** to **14.30** below.

14.29 Yet further cases can be read as seeking to explain the *Carltona* principle, as a principle of statutory construction. Where Parliament confers a function on a Minister, it must be taken to intend to allow the function to be exercised by a member of his department for whom the Minister accepts responsibility — unless, as sometimes occurs, the statute makes clear that the function is required to be exercised by the Minister in person.[1] This is how it appears to have been treated by the House of Lords in *R v Secretary of State for the Home Department, ex p Doody*:[2]

'That the question whether statutory discretion is capable of delegation, and if so to what degree, principally depends upon the interpretation of the statute is beyond question . . . On the question whether the statute contemplates that the Home Secretary, with all his multifarious public duties, is required to exercise his particular discretion personally in every case, I agree with the reasons given by Staughton LJ[3] and wish to add nothing . . . Throughout the statute book there are innumerable instances where powers are conferred on a minister, and where it is perfectly obvious that Parliament contemplated a delegation. By contrast, there are very few instances in which a statute, or delegated legislation, refers to the Lord Chief Justice and in these instances it is equally obvious that the office-holder alone is to act . . . '.

In some cases, the analysis by reference to statutory construction is not likely to cause any distraction.[4] However, in some instances this analysis causes contortion and mis-application of the principle. The judgment in *Chief Constable of the West Midlands v Birmingham Justices*,[5] is a case in point. In that case there was a challenge to ASBO's issued by the *Chief Constable of the West Midlands Police*. The decisions had not been taken personally by the Chief Constable but by others identified by him for the purpose. It was accepted that the power was delegable; the issue for the court was whether the power of delegation extended to the persons who had actually taken the decisions to make the orders. Sedley LJ, concluded that the delegation had been lawful. He emphasised the difference between a conferral of powers upon the a person at the apex of an organisation itself composed of office-holders or otherwise hierarchically structured (where on his analysis, the *Carltona* principle would usually apply) and a conferral of powers on an office-holder because of the personal qualifications of the individual holder (where it may not). But the problem here is the application of *Carltona* at all. As explained by Lord Greene MR, the principle stems from the common law constitutional principle of ministerial responsibility to Parliament. The principle has no application to Chief Constables at all. The real issues in the Chief Constable of the West Midlands case was delegation. Inserting *Carltona* reasoning into such a context only serves to confuse.

[1] For an example, see ss 7(1)(g) and 8(6) of the Regulation of Investigatory Powers Act 2000, requiring certain warrants to be issued 'under the hand of the Secretary of State'.

[2] [1994] 1 AC 531, per Lord Mustill at 566F–567A. See also, *Edwards (John Michael) v United States of America* [2012] EWHC 3771 (Admin) per Collins J at paragraphs 11–17.

[3] See [1993] QB 157 at 194–196.

[4] For example, *R v Chief Constable of Greater Manchester, ex p Lainton* [2000] ICR 1324, 144 SJLB 203 and R (WH Smith Ltd) v Croydon Justices (6 November 2000, unreported).

[5] *R (Chief Constable of the West Midlands Police) v Birmingham Justices* [2002] EWHC 1087 (Admin), [2003] Crim LR 37, per Sedley LJ at 10, 13, and 14.

14.30 Thus the case law following *Carltona* largely assumes (or may have assumed, in some instances it is not clear) that the *Carltona* principle is either a matter of statutory construction, or delegation, or both. In most instances the adverse practical consequences of this analysis have been, and are likely to be, vanishingly small. Yet, the better analysis (and the one that better fits the statement of principle in *Carltona*) is that the starting point is a common law constitutional principle that decisions taken by officials are in law decisions of the Minister. One clear benefit of this as the starting point is that it provides a coherent explanation for the way in which the *Carltona* principle will apply to the exercise by ministers of common law powers.[1] A further benefit is that this approach provides a workable structure to consider the basis (in this regard) of decisions taken by executive agencies.[2] On this point, the judgment of the *Divisional Court in Castle v Wakefield and Pontefract Magistrates' Court* demonstrates a pragmatic approach, and a correct explanation of the basis for application of the *Carltona* principle.[3]

The question has been raised whether the *Carltona* principle can properly accommodate the devolution of powers to the executive agencies which have been created in recent years to exercise responsibilities in so many areas of government. Here, too, a pragmatic approach has been adopted and the validity of the exercise of the delegated powers has been accepted. Indeed, Parliament must have contemplated that many of the powers conferred on the Secretary of State would be exercised in practice by such agencies.

The next step is that application of the *Carltona* principle is capable of being displaced by the terms in which any specific statutory duty or power is formulated: if as a matter of construction the duty or power must be exercised personally by the minister, that requirement will prevail. This is no more than an instance of the usual principle that common law principle yields to specific requirement or provision in a statute.

The circumstances considered by the House of Lords in *R v Secretary of State for the Home Department, ex p Oladehinde* are readily explained on this basis. In that case the question was whether senior immigration officers might lawfully be required to take deportation decisions in the Secretary of State's name. This was argued to be objectionable on the footing that the Immigration Act 1971 allotted separate responsibilities to immigration officers and to the Secretary of State (as undoubtedly it does). This argument was accepted in the Divisional Court at first instance, but rejected in the Court of Appeal and the House of Lords. Perhaps the heart of the decision of the House of Lords is to be found in this passage from the speech of Lord Griffiths:[4]

> 'The immigration service is comprised of Home Office civil servants for whom the Secretary of State is responsible and I can for myself see no reason why he should not authorise members of that service to take decisions under the *Carltona* principle providing they do not conflict with or embarrass them in the discharge of their specific statutory duties under the Act and that the decisions are suitable to their grading and experience.'

In other words, the *Carltona* principle applied, but would give way in the face of different provision in the legislation itself.

Save for cases where the statute requires the decision to be taken personally by the minister, questions of the rule against delegation do not strictly arise.

[1]   The general statement of the principle in *Carltona* is in very wide terms: see [1943] 2 All ER 560 at 563A–563C, where reference is made to 'everything that [a Minister's] officials have done under his authority'; and the Court of Appeal in *R v Secretary of State for the Home Department, ex p Oladehinde* [1991] 1 AC 254 at 282, stated in terms that the principle applies not just to statutory powers, but also to the exercise of other powers of the Crown. The House of Lords did not call this statement into question.

[2]   See the discussion in Freedland, 'The rule against delegation and the Carltona doctrine in an agency context' [1996] PL 19; Freedland, 'The Crown and the Changing Nature of Government'. CHAPTER 5 in Sunkin and Payne (eds) *The Nature of the Crown: A Legal and Political Analysis* (1999); and Bradley and Ewing *Constitutional and Administrative Law* (13th edn) pp 274, 275.

[3]   [2014] 1 WLR 4279 per Pitchford LJ at paragraphs 15–24. See also *R v Secretary of State for Social Services, ex p Sherwin* (1996) 32 BMLR 1 (benefits agency). Compare the discussion of different forms of agencies in *R (National Association of Health Stores) v Secretary of State for Health* [2005] EWCA Civ 154, (2005) Times, 9 March at 41.

[4]   [1991] AC 254 at 303D–303F.

14.31 In *Carltona*, Lord Greene stated that a minister would be responsible to Parliament if he entrusted a decision to too junior or too inexperienced a civil servant. In practice, in such a case, the minister might be responsible to law too, but only if the allocation of the decision to the junior or inexperienced person amounted to an unlawful exercise of the substantive power by reference to ordinary *Wednesbury* principles. In *R v Secretary of State for the Home Department ex parte Oladehinde*, the Court of Appeal in the same case suggested that a decision to devolve a power of decision might be amenable to challenge on *Wednesbury* grounds, a point subsequently left open by the House of Lords in *ex p Doody*.[1]

---

[1] [1991] AC 254 at 284C–284D. On the facts of that case, since the decision had been taken in that case by a junior Minister and it was obvious that if delegation was possible at all, the power could properly be entrusted to such a person. In *R (Chief Constable of the West Midlands Police) v Birmingham Justices*, Sedley LJ observed that the delegation under the *Carltona* principle has to be to somebody suitable; and the determination of who is suitable is primarily for the officeholder (albeit subject to the possibility of review by the court on grounds of irrationality).

14.32 The *Carltona* principle governs the situation where a Minister leaves a decision to departmental officials, but there is no 'reverse *Carltona*', no complementary principle applicable where the question is whether a Minister who takes a decision personally should be treated as having sufficient information about matters relevant to his decision to be able to decide lawfully simply because those matters are within the knowledge of persons within his department.

In that context, a distinction is to be drawn. On the one hand there are matters which are centrally relevant to the decision ('the salient facts which give shape and substance to the matter'). These are matters that the Minister should inform himself of, or be informed by the officials advising him. On the other hand are other matters which, although relevant, are not centrally relevant and the detail of which it would be lawful for the Minister to be spared.[1] Ordinarily, it appears, there will be substantial scope within the relevant legal parameters for work by officials and others to digest the mass of material which may be relevant to a decision, and to summarise its effect for a Minister: the business of central government could not otherwise practically be discharged, save by the undesirable expedient of transferring still more decisions from Ministers to those officials who would have time personally to read and digest such underlying material.

The Court of Appeal in National Association of Health Stores stated that the relevant test for matters required to be brought to the attention of Ministers was equivalent to that given in *CREEDNZ Inc v Governor-General* between things which are so relevant that they must be taken into account, as distinct from matters which are relevant and may legitimately be taken into account but need not be.[2] The application of this approach depends upon construction of the relevant statutory decision-making power. It also seems plausible to suppose that Parliament will usually have intended that powers conferred upon Ministers should be practically capable of exercise by them across the full range of all their functions, and therefore will have intended that there should be considerable scope for work by officials lawfully to be carried out in digesting relevant material and summarising it for Ministers to take decisions.

1 *R (National Association of Health Stores) v Secretary of State for Health* [2005] EWCA 154, (2005) Times, 9 March, following the approach of the High Court of Australia in *Minister for Aboriginal Affairs v Peko-Wallsend Ltd* (1986) 162 CLR 24. As has been pointed out in the discussion of the Australian authorities by Aronson, Dyer and Groves Judicial Review of Administrative Action (3rd edn), p 315: 'The difficulty here is in predicting just how much of the fine detail needs to go into the brief [to the Minister]'. Moreover, the drafting of legislative provisions may modify the application of the imputation of the knowledge of officials to a Secretary of State as an abstract entity: see *Hinchy v Secretary of State for Work and Pensions* [2005] 1 WLR 967, HL.

2 [1981] 1 NZLR 172; and for application of the same approach in English law, see, eg *Re Findlay* [1985] AC 318, 333–334; *R (Adlard) v Secretary of State for the Environment, Transport and the Regions* [2002] 1 WLR 2515, CA at 41.

14.33 Where decisions are taken by Ministers or officials within a department, after calling on the expertise and experience available within the department to assist them, the legal requirement of adoption of a fair decision-making procedure will not usually require the decision-maker to give notice of the matters raised and issues discussed as part of the internal decision-making discussion. The decision-making process within a government department is usually treated as that of the collective entity, rather than that of the relevant Minister personally:

> 'Discretion in making administrative decisions is conferred upon a minister not as an individual but as the holder of an office in which he will have available to him in arriving at his decision the collective knowledge, experience and expertise of all those who serve the Crown in the department of which, for the time being, he is the political head. The collective knowledge, technical as well as factual, of the civil servants in the department and their collective expertise is to be treated as the minister's own knowledge, his own expertise'.[1]

1 *Bushell v Secretary of State for the Environment* [1981] AC 75, 95 (Lord Diplock). Also see *R v Secretary of State for Education, ex p S* [1995] ELR 71; *R (Alconbury Developments Ltd) v Secretary of State for the Environment, Transport and the Regions* [2003] 2 AC 295 at 126 and 127 per Lord Hoffmann ('the process of consultation within the department is simply the Secretary of State advising himself'); *R (National Association of Health Stores) v Secretary of State for Health* [2005] EWCA Civ 154, (2005) Times, 9 March.

MODIFIED DISCLOSURE: PUBLIC INTEREST IMMUNITY; CLOSED MATERIAL PROCEDURES

14.34 The public interest immunity rule is the means of reconciling two competing aspects of the public interest: first, the public interest in the administration of justice, which ordinarily requires that all relevant material is available to the parties to litigation; and secondly, the public interest in maintaining the confidentiality of certain documents or information the disclosure of which would be damaging. Claims to public interest immunity are not the sole prerogative of government departments, agencies and ministers. Claims to public interest immunity are often also made by police forces faced with civil claims, and in some instances by local authorities. However, regardless of the identity of the public authority making the claim, the principles applied are the same.

A successful assertion of public interest immunity will mean that documents or information otherwise discloseable in the judicial review proceedings, will not be disclosed; the claim serves to provide for modified disclosure in the proceedings concerned. The provisions of Part 2 of the Justice and Security Act 2013, are applicable to judicial review claims, and make different provision for modified disclosure — the so-called closed material procedure — if ordinary disclosure would entail disclosure of 'sensitive material' (defined as 'material the disclosure of which would be damaging to the interests of national security'). Use of a closed material procedure must be approved by the court. An application to use a closed material procedure is not the sole prerogative of government departments and ministers, but ministers are those who are most likely to seek to use these provisions. Where the 2013 Act is applied disclosure of the sensitive material is made to the court and to a Special Advocate appointed to represent the interests of the party who would otherwise receive the disclosure (ordinarily, the claimant). There is a specific link between PII applications and the application of Part 2 of the Justice and Security Act 2013. An application under the 2013 Act for a closed material procedure may only be made after consideration has been given to the possibility of claiming PII (see s 6(7) of the 2013 Act). This underlines that use of a closed material procedure is a matter of last resort.

Public interest immunity

14.35 There are situations in which the legal process has to be modified by the disapplication of the normal rules of disclosure or the exclusion of otherwise admissible evidence, because to require disclosure or to admit the evidence would cause damage to the public interest. For example, information about matters relating to national security must sometimes be withheld in the overall public interest, even if that information is central to issues in dispute in civil litigation.[1] The courts have recognised this and have developed principles to ensure that the public interest is protected. In earlier days this took the form of the concept of 'Crown privilege', whereby a Minister's certificate that the disclosure of certain material would damage the public service, or cause some identifiable danger, was accepted without question, so that the material in issue would be excluded from production: *Duncan v Cammell Laird & Co Ltd.*[2] This black and white approach changed with the House of Lords' decision in *Conway v Rimmer*,[3] which laid down that the courts in the last resort had the power and duty to decide whether the disclosure sought would, in fact, damage the public interest. Thereafter the terminology of Crown privilege' was replaced by the more accurate expression public interest immunity. This reflects the fact that the principle is not confined to the Crown and that the protection of material in the public interest was to be regarded as a duty rather than a privilege.[4]

---

[1]   There is a wealth of authority to this effect: see, eg *Conway v Rimmer* [1968] AC 910, 940C, 952A, 953G–954B, 954G–955B, 993E–F; *Council of Civil Service Unions v Minister for the Civil Service* [1985] AC 374, 402C–402F, 404E–404H, 406G–407A, 412E–412G, 420D–420G, 421A–421H; and *Balfour v Foreign and Commonwealth Office* [1994] 1 WLR 681. The leading decision of the House of Lords is now *R v Chief Constable of the West Midlands Police, ex p Wiley* [1995] 1 AC 274. Thus the courts have acknowledged that where the Crown, having the sole or predominant responsibility for the security of the State, asserts by evidence that a particular course of action was, or is, necessary for the safeguarding of

national security, the assertion will be accepted, for the courts are in no position themselves to decide such a question by the ordinary tools of adjudication; and the interests of security will prevail over the interests of parties to private litigation. This will be the position whether the question arises in the context of a duty of fairness, as in Council of Civil Service Unions, or where the Crown asserts a claim for public interest immunity in litigation between others. And these principles have, of course, been adumbrated not by the Government, which is not a source of law, but by the judges, who are.

2   [1942] AC 624.
3   [1968] AC 910.
4   See, eg *Rogers v Secretary of State for the Home Department* [1973] AC 388, 412; *Air Canada v Secretary of State for Trade* [1983] 2 AC 394, 446; *D v National Society for Prevention of Cruelty to Children* [1978] AC 171; and *ex p Wiley* [1995] 1 AC 274.

14.36 Consideration of issues of public interest immunity as it applies to disclosure of documents[1] involves three distinct questions:

(1)   Is the document disclosable on the normal criteria governing disclosure in the proceedings in question?

(2)   If so, does the document prima facie attract public interest immunity, having regard to the damage that would be done to the public interest by its disclosure?

(3)   If so, is the public interest in non-disclosure outweighed by the public interest in disclosure of the document for the purpose of doing justice in the proceedings?

1   The same principles apply to the giving of oral evidence but it is sufficient to focus here on the disclosure of documentary material. Nor is it necessary, in the context of this work, to consider public interest immunity in criminal proceedings.

14.37 The first stage is obvious, but on occasion is given insufficient attention. It is particularly important in judicial review proceedings, where there is no automatic disclosure and, on the application of normal principles, disclosure of documents is less rather than more often.[1] In judicial review proceedings, respondents have a duty of candour in presenting their evidence to the court.[2] As a corollary, the normal rule in judicial review proceedings is that the court will not usually order disclosure of documents so as to go behind the witness statements adduced by the respondent.[3] Disclosure will therefore not be ordered save where the witness statement adduced by the respondent in evidence is prima facie inaccurate or can be seen to be incomplete or inadequate.[4] The result is that it may rarely be necessary in this context to move on to consider the true issues of public interest immunity at the second and third stages. The usual position is simply that the defendant provides in evidence the gist of the information on which it acted, so far as that is possible without disclosing details (of informants etc.) which would be contrary to the public interest.[5]

However, in some situations consideration at the first stage will produce the conclusion that disclosure of the document is necessary (or, given the nature of the disclosure obligation in judicial review claims that reference to information that is subject to PII is necessary in the course of a witness statement). In such situations the second and third stages arise for consideration.

When it is necessary to consider the second and third questions that need to be addressed when any question of PII arises, it is open to the court to ask for the appointment of a special advocate for that purpose.[6] However, a request for a special advocate must be a matter of last resort.[7] It must be clear that there is a specific purpose that the special advocate can meet, and it must also be clear that that purpose cannot be met by other means.

[1] See generally, *Tweed v Parades Commission for Northern Ireland* [2007] 1 AC 650. In particular per Lord Bingham at paragraphs 3–4; Lord Carswell at paragraph 32; and Lord Brown at paragraphs 56–57. For general discussion of the principles governing disclosure and the duty of candour, see **19.47** and **19.116** et seq.

[2] See, eg *R v Lancashire County Council, ex p Huddleston* [1986] 2 All ER 941; *R (Quark Fishing Ltd) v Secretary of State for Foreign and Commonwealth Affairs* [2002] EWCA Civ1409; and *R (Al Sweady) v Secretary of State for Defence* [2009] EWHC 2387 (Admin)

[3] *R v Secretary of State for the Home Department, ex p Fayed* [1998] 1 WLR 763, 775B (Lord Woolf MR); and see also *Tweed v Parades Commission for Northern Ireland* [2007] 1 AC 950.

[4] *R v Secretary of State for the Environment, ex p Islington London Borough Council* (19 July 1991, unreported), CA; *R v Secretary of State for Foreign Affairs, ex p World Development Movement Ltd* [1995] 1 WLR 386; *R (Wiggins Group plc) v First Secretary of State* [2003] EWHC 680 (Admin).

[5] See, eg *Liversidge v Anderson* [1942] AC 206, 240–242 (Lord Atkin); *R v Secretary of State for the Home Department, ex p Hosenball* [1977] 1 WLR 766; *R v Gaming Board for Great Britain, ex p Benaim and Khaida* [1970] 2 QB 417; *NSH v Secretary of State for the Home Department* [1988] Imm AR 389; and compare *R v Secretary of State for the Home Department, ex p McAvoy* [1998] 1 WLR 790; *R (Sunder) v Secretary of State for the Home Department* [2001] EWHC 252 (Admin). This general approach to disclosure in judicial review proceedings was endorsed by the House of Lords in *Tweed v Parades Commission for Northern Ireland* [2007] 1 AC 950 subject to the proviso that where the court had to determine a question of proportionality under the Human Rights Act there could be situations in which the disclosure of key documents was required (as opposed to a description of the substance of such documents in a witness statement).

[6] Save where there is statutory authority, the court has no inherent power to modify its procedures to mimic a closed material procedure. See *Al Rawi v Security Service* [2012] 1 AC 531.

[7] See *R v H* [2004] 2 AC 134, HL. Availability of a special advocate procedure for this purpose was expressly endorsed by the Court of Appeal in *Al Rawi* [2010] 3 WLR 1069, per Lord Neuberger MR at paragraph 26; in the Supreme Court, this conclusion was not put in issue, see per Lord Clarke at paragraph 150.

14.38 At the second stage the established practice was formerly to consider whether disclosure of the document would damage the public interest either because of its 'contents' (eg disclosure of the identity of an informant who would thereby be placed at risk of retaliation) or because it fell into a 'class' of documents disclosure of which would be damaging (eg disclosure of confidential information in circumstances where sources of such information would tend to dry up if it became known that the information volunteered was liable to be made public). These classes overlap and had the same logical underpinning.

However, this categorisation and, indeed, the area of PII more generally became subject to growing criticism, most notably in the Scott Report into the Matrix Churchill affair. Following publication of that Report and a lengthy period of consultation, the Government announced in December 1996 the adoption of a new approach towards public interest immunity.[1] The essence of the matter was set out in the Attorney-General's statement to the House of Commons:

'Under the new approach, Ministers will focus directly on the damage that disclosure would cause. The former division into class and contents claims will no longer be applied. Ministers will claim public interest immunity only when it is believed that disclosure of a document would cause real damage or harm to the public interest.

The Government intend that the test shall be rigorously applied before any public interest immunity claim is made for any government documents. It is impossible in advance to describe such damage exhaustively. The damage may relate to the safety of an individual, such as an informant, or to a regulatory process; or it may be damage to international relations caused by the disclosure of confidential diplomatic communications. Normally it will be in the form of direct and immediate harm to, for example, the nation's economic interests or our relations with a foreign state. In some cases, it may be indirect or long-term damage to which the disclosure of the material would contribute, as in the case of damage to a regulatory process. In any event, the nature of the harm will be clearly explained'.

Now, there are no presumptions or assumptions; there are no fixed classes of immune documents. The decision to make a PII application should depend only on the assessment of harm to the public interest in the event of disclosure of the document in question. For these purposes, 'real damage or harm' is synonymous with serious damage or harm. If a Minister concludes that disclosure of a document would not cause real (or serious) harm to the public interest, no question of a claim for PII can arise. If, on the other hand, he considers that disclosure would cause real harm, it is necessary to move to the third stage.

1   Statements made on 18 December 1996 by the Lord Chancellor and the Attorney-General to the House of Lords and House of Commons respectively (Hansard cols 1507 (HL) and 949 (HC)) and Paper placed in the Library of both Houses. See Paul Walker and Tim Costigan, 'Public Interest Immunity: A New Approach' (1997) Judicial Review 35. The approach was affirmed by the incoming Labour administration in 1997.

14.39 The third stage requires the public interest in non-disclosure to be balanced against the public interest in disclosure for the purpose of doing justice in the proceedings, so as to determine whether the overall public interest favours non-disclosure or disclosure.

The need to carry out such a balancing exercise was laid down in *Conway*.[1] For a long time it was thought that the exercise was for the court rather than for a Minister, and that it was only in exceptional circumstances that a Minister could volunteer disclosure of documents that were prima facie subject to public interest immunity. However, in *R v Chief Constable of West Midlands Police, ex p Wiley*,[2] the House of Lords stated that in the case of government documents it is open to the responsible Minister to carry out the balancing exercise for himself and to volunteer disclosure if he concludes that it is in the overall public interest for the documents to be disclosed.

If however, the Minister concludes that the overall public interest favours non-disclosure, or if he is uncertain where the balance comes down (as, for example, where he is not sure how important the documents are for the litigation), the decision on disclosure will be made by the court, which remains the final arbiter in accordance with the principles laid down in *Conway*. In that event, the Minister must make a certificate explaining the reasons why he considers that disclosure would cause serious harm and the approach he has adopted towards the balancing exercise. In such a case the court ought, however, to attach significant weight to a reasoned conclusion stated in the certificate. The Attorney-General's statement to the House of Commons indicated that public interest immunity certificates would in future set out in greater detail than before, both what the document is and what damage its disclosure would be likely to do – unless to do so would itself cause the damage that the certificate aims to prevent.

1   *Conway v Rimmer* [1968] AC 910.
2   [1995] 1 AC 274.

14.40 In *R (Binyam Mohamed) v Secretary of State for Foreign and Commonwealth Affairs the Divisional Court,* acknowledged that the Minister (or senior official) is the expert on such matters, not the court.[1] This principle was upheld by the Court of Appeal.[2] This is relevant to the level of scrutiny applied by the court. In practice references to 'levels of scrutiny' are code for the extent to which judges will attach weight to evaluations made by Ministers and civil servants rather than simply deciding such matters for themselves. Inevitably this is an area of intense debate.

Previous editions of this work put the point as follows. Judges are now accustomed, on a daily basis, to dealing with challenges to the use of State power. Their independence and impartiality has not been called into question in the years in which this process has bloomed. So it is hardly surprising that, when it comes to public interest immunity, and the judge is asked to accept the Minister's opinion as to what the public interest demands, he should bring to the task a perception, created by his and his brethren's experience in judicial review, that government sometimes gets it wrong; and that it is or can be the court's role to confine the exercise of power by government within proper bounds, as much where a public interest immunity claim is asserted as where there is a substantive challenge to government action.

The risk, if the matter is put in such terms, is that the result is not a principled exercise. *Binyam Mohamed* does suggest a starting point that is principled – ie recognition that on many occasions the matters that are weighed in the balance may not be matters within the ordinary competence of the judiciary. None of this is to suggest any absence of judicial oversight; rather, it suggests oversight that is rigorous yet nevertheless recognises the appropriate limits of institutional competence.

1   [2009] EWHC 152 (Admin) [2009] 1 WLR 2653 at paragraph 64, having cited *Rehman v Secretary of State for the Home Department* [2003] 1 AC 153 and *R (Corner House Research) v Director of the Serious Fraud Office (BAE Systems plc, interested party)* [2009] AC 756
2   Judgment of Lord Neuberger MR at paragraphs **131–132**.

14.41 In this respect it is important to bear in mind that two distinct aspects of the public interest have to be weighed against each other under the *Wiley* balancing test. On the one hand, in relation to the sort of factors which are relevant to arguments of public interest tending against disclosure (such as the safety of informants, risk to national security and the like), Ministers will typically be best placed and qualified to assess what is at stake.[1] On the other hand, in relation to factors affecting the fairness of legal proceedings, the courts will typically be best placed and qualified to assess what is at stake. In relation to the former set of factors, when a Minister signs a public interest immunity certificate, he is making a decision about their importance in the public interest which is within his area of responsibility; he is also drawing on departmental expertise and experience in making the necessary judgment about that aspect of the public interest which falls within his remit. This is a decision in the public law arena as much as any other. It is his public duty to assert the public interest in such cases. It is difficult to see why the court should review the Minister's decision on those factors on any different basis from that which obtains on a review of any other decision he might make (ie on *Wednesbury* principles or, if Convention rights are in issue, by allowing a considerable margin of appreciation and respect for the judgment made by the Minister[2]). It is also true that the Minister will have expressed his own view in his certificate on how the balance should be struck between these factors and factors related to the fairness of the conduct of the proceedings, and since he (as well as the court) has a responsibility to act to promote the public interest overall and since his opinion on that balance inevitably involves consideration of matters on which his views are entitled to particular weight, it would seem correct in principle that his view about how the overall balance should be struck should be accorded a reasonable degree of respect by the courts. However, it is at that point that the court has its own constitutional remit to safeguard the fairness of legal proceedings. According to general principles of judicial review, the court has a wider role in relation to such matters than simple review of the decisions of others on a *Wednesbury* basis.[3] Ultimately, then, as *Wiley* indicates, the assessment is for the court, but should afford appropriate respect for the judgement expressed by the Minister.

[1]   In assessing difficult questions of national security etc, the courts recognise that a Minister will typically be better placed than a court to form judgments about how great the risks may be and about what steps should be taken to meet them: see, eg *Rehman v Secretary of State for the Home Department* [2003] 1 AC 153; *A v Secretary of State for the Home Department* [2005] 2 AC 68, at 29, 79, 112, 175 and 192.
[2]   See, eg *R v Shayler* [2003] 1 AC 247 at 76 and 77 (Lord Hope); *Leander v Sweden* (1987) 9 EHRR 433 at 49, 58 and 59; *Al-Nashif v Bulgaria* (2003) 36 EHRR 37 at 137.
[3]   See, in particular, *R v Panel on Take-overs and Mergers, ex p Guinness plc* [1990] 1 QB 146; also *R (A) v Lord Saville of Newdigate (No 2)* [2002] 1 WLR 1249. Also see generally **CHAPTER 11**.

14.42 The same public interest considerations which militate against disclosure in the context of litigation may also affect the content of the duty to act fairly in particular contexts[1] or the extent of any obligation to give reasons for a decision.[2] In a case where there is an obligation to give reasons, if there is some public interest consideration why full reasons cannot be given, that should be indicated on the face of the decision, so that the individual may have an opportunity of seeking to challenge the non-provision of such information.[3]

[1]   *Council of Civil Service Unions v Minister for the Civil Service* [1985] AC 374 is an example.
[2]   See *R v Secretary of State for the Home Department, ex p Fayed* [1998] 1 WLR 763. See further CHAPTERS **8**, **11**, **19** and **20**.
[3]   [1998] 1 WLR 763, 776–777.

14.43 The position at the third stage may also be affected by the Human Rights Act 1998. In some cases, eg where the life or safety of an informant might be at risk from disclosure of his identity, the Minister will have an obligation under s 6(1) of that Act to act compatibly with the Convention rights of the individual under arts 2, 3 and 8. The courts, as public authorities for the purposes of the Act, will also be under such an obligation.[1] In such cases, the level of judicial scrutiny of the certificate may well be more intense – ie the Court will decide any issue of compatibility with Convention rights for itself subject only to giving appropriate weight to the judgement of the Minister as set out in the certificate where that judgement is directed to matters outside the scope of the Court's institutional expertise.[2]

¹ Compare *R (A) v Lord Saville of Newdigate (No 2)* [2000] 1 WLR 1855; *R (A) v Lord Saville of Newdigate* [2002] 1 WLR 1249; and *Officer L, Re* [2007] 1 WLR 2135.
² See/compare *Tinnelly & Sons Ltd v United Kingdom*(Application 20390/92); *McElduff v United Kingdom* (Application 21322/93) (1999) 27 EHRR 249; *Chahal v United Kingdom* (1996) 23 EHRR 413, and *Rowe and Davis v United Kingdom* (2000) 30 EHRR 1.

14.44 A final matter that may arise at the third stage is whether it may be possible to devise some other approach short of excluding the documents from the proceedings, which would safeguard the relevant public interest but nevertheless permit some degree of disclosure to the claimant or his representatives. An option that is often raised is that of a 'confidentiality ring' under which disclosure of the relevant documents is given to the claimant's lawyers but not to the claimants themselves.[1] However, the arguments against such arrangements will ordinarily be compelling.[2]

¹ See *R (Mohammed) v Secretary of State for Defence* [2013] 2 All ER 897 per Moses LJ at paragraph 8–28.
² See *AHK v Secretary of State for the Home Department* [2013] EWHC 1426 (Admin) per Ouseley J at paragraphs 23–28. See also *Somerville v Scottish Ministers* [2007] 1 WLR 2734 at paragraphs 152–3 (Lord Rodger) and 203–204 (Lord Mance); and see *CF v Security Service* [2014] 1 WLR 1699

14.45 In judicial review proceedings, claims to PII by a defendant is best made at the ordinary time for service of evidence and documents.[1] In most instances this will be the earliest convenient time for the application to be made, and it is the sensible time since it will permit the court to consider the application for PII having sight of the context of the totality of the evidence relied on by the defendant in response to the substantive challenge. The claim for PII is usually made by certificate, made by a Minister (or senior permanent official), which will include a statement of reasons for the claim to PII. Strictly speaking it is open to the court to require cross-examination of the maker of the certificate.[2] However, the need for cross-examination is likely to arise only on rare occasions; in the vast majority of instances it will be unlikely that the reasons in support of the certificate will be illuminated or the ability of a court to assess them will be enhanced by cross-examination, rather than by submissions.

¹ The procedure for general civil proceedings is at CPR 31.19. No specific time for an application is specified.
² See *Re Grosvenor Hotel* [1964] Ch 464 (CA).

Closed material procedure

14.46 Part 2 of the Justice and Security Act 2013 permits a court to adopt a closed material procedure in cases in which a party to the proceedings would be required to disclose 'sensitive material' — defined by s 6(11) of the 2015 Act to mean material which if disclosed would be damaging to the interests of national security.[1] The difference between an application for PII and the application of a closed material procedure, is that the consequence of a successful PII application is that the relevant information ceases to play any part in the court's determination of the substantive issues in the case; whereas where a closed material procedure is used, the sensitive material remains in the proceedings and is taken into account by the court when it determines the substantive issues.

A closed material procedure may only be used in cases where a court has made a declaration under s 6 of the 2013 Act; and such a declaration may only be made if the court is satisfied both that sensitive material would be disclosable in the proceedings (see s 6(4) of the 2013 Act), and that 'it is in the interests of the fair and effective administration of justice in the proceedings' to make such a declaration (see s 6(5) of the 2013 Act). Thus the discretion is to be exercised by reference to the specific circumstances of the case in hand.[2]

1   Save where there is statutory authority, the court has no inherent power in judicial review proceedings to modify its procedures to mimic a closed material procedure. See *Al Rawi v Security Service* [2012] 1 AC 531.
2   For the approach required to the section 6 question, and an example of its application, see the decisions at first instance and in the Court of Appeal in *Sarkandi and others v Foreign Secretary* [2014] EWHC 2359 (Admin); and [2015] EWCA Civ 687, respectively.

14.47 If the court makes a section 6 declaration it is then for the party seeking to withhold disclosure of the sensitive material to apply to the court for permission to withhold disclosure of that material from the other party to the proceedings (see s 8 of the 2013 Act), and to ask the court to declare what parts of the sensitive material or what information pertaining to the sensitive material must in any event be disclosed to the other party so as to ensure that the proceedings remain consistent with the requirements of ECHR article 6. For this purpose, a Special Advocate will be appointed to represent the interests of the other party to the proceedings.[1] CPR Part 82 contains provisions for the Special Advocate to see the sensitive material. If the sensitive material is admitted into the proceedings (but not fully disclosed to the other party), the Special Advocate will continue to represent the interests of the other party in all parts of the proceedings at which the sensitive material is considered (known as the 'closed proceedings').

If the court has made a section 6 declaration, the court remains under an obligation to keep under review whether or not the declaration remains appropriate.[2] The court is required to revoke a section 6 declaration if it considers that maintaining it is no longer in the interests of the fair and effective administration of justice in the proceedings.

1   See s 9 of the Justice and Security Act 2013.
2   See s 7 of the Justice and Security Act 2013.

14.48 CPR Part 82 contains the procedural rules that apply both for the purpose of making an application for a declaration under s 6 of the 2013 Act, and thereafter if such a declaration is made. Two key features of CPR 82 should be noted. The first is that where any part of CPR 82 applies, the CPR Part 1 overriding obligation is modified such that the overriding obligation is given effect subject to the court's obligation ' . . . to ensure that information is not disclosed in a way which would be damaging to the interests of national security'.[1] The second is at CPR 82.14(9): this is to the effect that where a closed material procedure is in place, the party in possession of the sensitive material is always at liberty to withdraw that material from the proceedings rather than disclose sensitive material (or information derived from it) to the other party to the proceedings. If this does happen the situation is as if the material withdrawn had been the subject of a PII application: the litigation proceeds without reference being made to it; and the party who has withdrawn the material may not either advance any case based on that material, or advance any case inconsistent with that material.

¹ See CPR 82.2.

DECLARATIONS OF INCOMPATIBILITY

14.49 Under s 4 of the Human Rights Act 1998, a court may make a declaration of incompatibility in either of two situations. The first is where the court is satisfied that any provision in primary legislation is 'incompatible with a Convention right';¹ the second is where the provision in issue is in secondary legislation and the court is satisfied that it is incompatible with a Convention right and that the power in primary legislation under which the provision was made would not permit a different (compatible) provision, to be made.² Only specified courts may make declarations of incompatibility: the Supreme Court; the Privy Council; the Court of Appeal; and the High Court.³

¹ Human Rights Act 1998, s 4(2).
² Human Rights Act 1998, s 4(3)–(4).
³ These are the courts specified for England and Wales: see s 4(5). In Northern Ireland a declaration may be made by either the High Court or the Northern Ireland Court of Appeal. In Scotland declarations may be made either by the High Court of Justiciary (save where it is sitting as a trial court), or the Court of Session.

14.50 Section 5(1) of the Human Rights Act provides that where a court is considering whether to make a declaration of incompatibility, the Crown is entitled to notice of the proceedings.¹ By s 5(2), the Crown is then entitled, to be joined as a party to the proceedings. The Act thereby contemplates that the Crown has a special interest to be heard in such cases.²

CPR 19.4A sets out the applicable procedural rules.³ The section 5(1) notice is required to be served on the relevant person named in the list published under s 17 of the Crown Proceedings Act 1947.⁴ The Crown may, in such cases, defend the compatibility of the legislation (including, where appropriate, by argument by reference to s 3(1) of the Act)⁵ or may accept that it is incompatible. The court is not bound by the Crown's acceptance that a provision is incompatible; it must consider any argument by any other party to the proceedings as to the compatibility of the legislation.

¹ By CPR 19.4A(1) a court may not make a declaration of incompatibility unless 21 days' notice has been given.
² The Crown will ultimately have the burden of defending legislation and decisions in any proceedings alleged violation of Convention rights before the European Court of Human Rights in Strasbourg. The Crown does not have a statutory right to notice in cases where some novel or strained interpretation of a statutory provision is proposed under s 3(1) of the Act. However, it may be the case that the Crown will have a sufficient interest to be heard in relation to such cases (eg where the proposed interpretation might tend to undermine the policy of the legislation in question), and may in the discretion of the court be permitted to intervene in the proceedings on application of usual principles.
³ See also Practice Direction 19A at paragraphs **6.1–6.6.**
⁴ CPR 19PD 6.4(1).
⁵ *Ghaidan v Godin-Mendoza* [2004] 2 AC 557, is an example of this.

14.51 A declaration of incompatibility does not affect the binding effect of the legislation in question; nor is it binding on the parties to the proceedings in which the declaration is made.[1] If a declaration of incompatibility is made and there is no outstanding right of appeal, the Minister may use the remedial powers specified at s 10 of and Sch 2 to the Human Rights Act. Put shortly, the power to take remedial action permits a Minister to amend legislation to remove the incompatibility. This power to amend includes a power to amend either primary or secondary legislation 'by order'. However, so far as concerns the power to amend primary legislation, this arises only if the Minister considers that there are 'compelling reasons for proceeding' in this way, rather than by addressing the incompatibility by fresh primary legislation.[2] To date, the preference has been not to use the section 10 power, but where necessary to pass amending primary legislation.

1   See the Human Rights Act 1998, s 4(6).
2   The procedure for orders under s 10 is set out in Sch 2 to the Human Rights Act; save in cases of urgency, a positive resolution of each House of Parliament is required. Where urgency exists, there is a modified procedure, under which an order may be made but will cease to have effect if, within 120 days it has not been approved by positive resolution of each House of Parliament.

14.52 Making a declaration of incompatibility is an option of last resort; to be used only after a court has given full consideration to its obligation of interpretation under s 3 of the Human Rights Act.[1]

Whether or not to make a declaration of incompatibility is a matter of discretion for the court. Yet it is realistic to assume that where there is a conclusion of incompatibility, a declaration will be made unless there is good reason to the contrary.[2]

1   See for example, *R v A (No 2)* [2002] 1 AC 45, per Lord Steyn at [44]. See also Chapter 4 for general discussion of the section 3 interpretation obligation.
2   For an example of a situation where there was good reason, see the judgment of the Divisional Court in *R (Conway) v Secretary of State for Justice* [2017] EWHC 640 (Admin). In that case, the court refused to make a declaration directed to s 2(1) of the Suicide Act 1961. In that case it was noted that the same point had already been addressed by the Supreme Court in earlier litigation in which a declaration had been refused on grounds that it was not 'institutionally appropriate' for the court to make a declaration on the issue. The court also noted that since that judgment, the merits of s 2(1) of the 1961 Act had been debated by both Houses of Parliament. That being so, the court concluded that it was institutionally inappropriate for a declaration to be made: see per Burnett LJ at [3] to [27]. See also, the judgment in the earlier Supreme Court case, *R (Nicklinson) v Secretary of State for Justice* [2015] AC 657.

DAMAGES AGAINST THE CROWN

14.53 Until recently, damages have had a very minor role in judicial review proceedings.[1] As a general rule under domestic law, the unlawful exercise of public law powers and duties does not give rise to any liability in damages. However, actions may sometimes lie in relation to the exercise of public law functions, where the exercise has involved the commission of a tort (the main examples are in the fields of negligence[2] and misfeasance in public office[3]): for detailed analysis of these cases, reference should be made to commentaries on the law of tort.

¹ For general discussion of damages and other monetary remedies, see CHAPTER **17**.

² See, for example *X (minors) v Bedfordshire County Council* [1995] 2 AC 633, *Stovin v Wise* [1996] AC 923, *Barrett v Enfield London Borough Council* [2001] 2 AC 550, *Phelps v Hillingdon London Borough Council* [2001] 2 AC 619, *Gorringe v Calderdale Metropolitan Borough Council* [2004] 1 WLR 1057, HL, and *Morrison Sports Ltd v Scottish Power (Scotland)* [2010] 1 WLR 1934, SC.

³ For example, see *Three Rivers District Council v Bank of England (No 3)* [2003] 2 AC 1 and *Watkins v Secretary of State for the Home Department* [2005] 2 WLR 1538, CA.

14.54 Further, developments in EU law have established the existence of a cause of action in respect of damage caused by executive or legislative measures adopted or retained in breach of EU law.¹ The ground was laid by the decision of the Court of Justice in *Francovich and Bonifaci v Italy*: C-6/90 and C-9/90,² but the relevant principles have now been laid down more fully by the ECJ in a series of references from the English courts: *R v Secretary of State for Transport, ex p Factortame Ltd (No 4)*,³ *R v HM Treasury, ex p British Telecommunications plc*: C-392/93⁴ and *R v Ministry of Agriculture, Fisheries and Food, ex p Hedley-Lomas (Ireland) Ltd*: C-5/94.⁵ The House of Lords applied those principles, and awarded damages against the Crown, in *R v Secretary of State for Transport, ex p Factortame Ltd (No 5)*.⁶ In summary, a Member State may be liable in damages for measures that infringe EC law if three conditions are satisfied.⁷ The three conditions are: (a) that the law infringed must be intended to confer rights on individuals; (b) the breach must be 'sufficiently serious'; and (c) there must be a causal link between the breach, and the loss sustained.

¹ General principles of EU law are discussed in CHAPTER **14**.

² [1991] ECR 1–5357.

³ (Joined with a reference from Germany, *Brasserie du Pecheur*) [1996] QB 404. This is the leading authority on the principles to be applied.

⁴ [1996] QB 615.

⁵ [1997] QB 139.

⁶ [2000] AC 524.

⁷ For a recent restatement of these conditions, see Case C-278/05 *Robins v Secretary of State for Work and Pensions* at 69.

14.55 In developing the second condition, the Court of Justice has stated that the decisive test for finding that a breach is sufficiently serious is whether the Member State manifestly and gravely disregarded the limits on its discretion. It has identified a number of factors for the national court to take into consideration when deciding that issue. They include the clarity and precision of the rule breached, the measure of discretion left by the rule to the national authorities, whether the infringement and the damage caused was intentional or involuntary, whether any error of law was excusable or inexcusable, and the position adopted at the material time by the Commission and other Member States.¹

¹ See, eg *Brasserie du Pecheur/ex p Factortame* [1996] QB 404 at 499–500, paragraphs 55–64; see also, *Robins* (above) at paragraphs 70–71 and 76–77.

14.56 A claim for damages under these principles is classified as having the nature of a private law action for breach of statutory duty.¹ It may be commenced either under CPR Part 7 or Part 8. In *R v Secretary of State for*

Employment, ex p Equal Opportunities Commission,[2] the House of Lords declined to grant a declaration in judicial review proceedings as a means of assisting an applicant towards the making of a damages claim (although it granted a declaration on different grounds). Lord Keith stated:[3]

> 'In my opinion it would be quite inappropriate to make any such declaration. If there is any individual who believes that he or she has a good claim to compensation under the *Francovich* principle, it is the Attorney-General who would be a defendant in any proceedings directed to enforcing it, and the issues raised would not necessarily be identical with any of those which arise in the present appeal'.

That reasoning was applied by the House of Lords in *R v Secretary of State for Employment, ex p Seymour-Smith*.[4]

[1]   *R v Secretary of State for Transport, ex p Factortame Ltd (No 7)* [2001] 1 WLR 942; *Phonographic Performance Ltd v Department for Trade and Industry* [2004] 1 WLR 2893.
[2]   [1995] 1 AC 1.
[3]   [1995] 1 AC at 32.
[4]   [1997] 1 WLR 473, 480.

14.57 However, damages claims can also properly be included in proceedings in judicial review under CPR Part 54 (although a Part 54 claim may not seek damages alone: see CPR54.3(2)).

In fact, the relevant principles governing liability have themselves been developed in judicial review proceedings – in all of which there were claims for damages that were the subject of questions referred to the ECJ.[1] Damages will only be awarded in a CPR Part 54 claim if there is a proper cause of action established, eg in tort, under EU law or under the Human Rights Act 1998.

By virtue of CPR54.3(2), the court may award damages on an application for judicial review if: (a) the applicant has joined with his application a claim for damages arising from any matter to which the application relates; and (b) the court is satisfied that, if the claim had been in an action begun by the applicant at the time of making his application, he would have been awarded damages. Thus, if a claim can be brought by way of an ordinary claim against the Attorney-General, as contemplated by Lord Keith in *ex p Equal Opportunities Commission*, it can also be included in an application for judicial review provided that it arises from the matter to which the application relates.

The observations in *ex p Equal Opportunities Commission* are to be seen not as laying down an exclusive procedural route but as emphasising that judicial review is not to be used inappropriately as a step in other proceedings. It is suggested that the real question should be whether proceedings for judicial review are appropriate in themselves, leaving aside the question of damages: if they are, then a consequential claim for damages can properly be included. For example, in *ex p Factortame* the applicants' primary objective was to have certain provisions of national legislation struck down so that they could be registered to fish against British quotas. They included a claim for damages which proceeded (still as part of the judicial review proceedings) when the applicants had succeeded on the substantive issue.[2]

[1]   See, also, *R v Secretary of State for the Home Department, ex p Gallagher* [1996] 2 CMLR 951, where the Court of Appeal, applying the principles laid down by the ECJ, held that a claim for damages was unarguable and for that reason – rather than because of any wider concern about the appropriateness of such a claim being made in judicial review – refused

leave that such a claim to be included by amendment in the judicial review proceedings after the applicant had been successful on one of the substantive issues on a reference to the ECJ.
2   See *R v Secretary of State for Transport, ex p Factortame Ltd (No 5)* [2000] AC 524.

14.58 The decision of the Court of Justice in Case C-224/01 *Kobler v Austria*[1] raises the possibility of damages claims in respect of sufficiently serious breaches of EU law perpetrated by domestic courts. Here, again, the Attorney-General is the appropriate defendant, as representative (in effect) of the State.[2]

1   [2004] QB 848, noted at [2004] CLJ 564.
2   Such a claim was commenced in the domestic courts in relation to a decision of the Appeal Committee of the House of Lords on 9 July 2003 to refuse permission to appeal against the decision of the Court of Appeal in *R (Prokopp) v London Underground Ltd* [2003] EWCA Civ 961, which also entailed a refusal to make a reference to the ECJ under art 234 (the act of the House of Lords which, it is alleged, engages liability in damages under the principle in *Kobler*). The claim was commenced under CPR Pt 54 and naming the Secretary of State for Constitutional Affairs as defendant. The Crown contended that the claim should proceed under CPR Pt 8 and against the Attorney-General as defendant. Richards J, on consideration of the application for permission, indicated his provisional view that the correct procedure would be a claim brought under CPR Pt 8 against the Attorney-General, and invited the claimant to consider adopting that course. The claim did not proceed further.

14.59 Finally, Ministers are liable to damages claims brought under ss 6 to 8 of the Human Rights Act 1998 in the same way as other public authorities. In addition, the Crown has a special role under s 9(4) of the Act as defendant to any claim for damages in respect of a violation of Convention rights by a judicial act. For such a claim, 'the appropriate person' – the Minister responsible for the court concerned or a person or government department nominated by him[1] – must be joined as a party to the proceedings.[2]

1   'Appropriate person' is defined in the Human Rights Act 1998, s 9(5).
2   See, generally, CHAPTER 4.

Chapter 15

EUROPEAN UNION LAW

THE NATURE OF EUROPEAN UNION LAW

15.1 The European Union (EU) is a union of 28 states, established by treaty, on which its Member States have conferred limited competence, authority and legal personality in order to promote the achievement of objectives which they have in common.[1]

The EU acts through institutions in which each Member State participates, in particular the Council, the Commission, the European Parliament, and the European Council.[2] The EU's origins lie in institutions for the promotion of economic and trading freedoms: in particular, rights to trade freely in goods and services and to move freely, reside and establish a business within the territory of other Member States.[3] The achievement of these economic freedoms and progressive development of a single market has also required delegation to the EU of standard-setting competence in various fields.[4] Over time, the EU's obligations and aspirations to protect civil, political, socio-economic, environmental and consumer rights and to promote solidarity and social justice have become increasingly recognised and embedded in its constituent treaties.[5] The competences conferred by Member States on the EU have been extended over time accordingly. Following the entry into force of the Lisbon Treaty[6] on 1 December 2009, the primary source of rights and obligations under EU law are the two main treaties: the Treaty on European Union; (TEU); and the Treaty on the Functioning of the European Union (TFEU) (formerly the EC Treaty).[7]

[1] Articles 1 and 47 TEU; art 335 TFEU; Declaration 24.
[2] Article 13 TEU. The roles of the main EU institutions are defined by arts 14-19 TEU. National parliaments and citizens participate directly in the institutional workings of the European Union in certain significant but limited ways prescribed by arts 9–12 TEU and arts 15, 20 and 24 TFEU. They participate indirectly through their respective national governments: art 12(2) TEU.
[3] Articles 21, 26, 28, 30, 34, 35, 45, 49, 56, 63 TFEU; Charter of Fundamental Rights art 15. These rights are subject to certain preconditions and limitations.
[4] See in particular arts 26 and 114–115 TFEU (formerly arts 14 and 94-95 EC), empowering the Council and the European Parliament to adopt measures for the approximation of laws and administrative practices in Member States where divergence in national rules (on e.g. health, safety or technical specifications) is directly affecting the establishment or functioning of the internal market.
[5] Articles 2, 3, 6 and 21 TEU; arts 8–11, 20–23, 145–169 and 174–178 TFEU; Charter of Fundamental Rights of the European Union.
[6] The eur-lex website has all treaties and all EU legislation searchable under year and number. See: eur-lex.europa.eu/homepage.html. Whilst this website also has all EU caselaw, the Court of Justice of the EU (CJEU) has pdfs of all caselaw most easily accessible by case number from the home page of its curia.eu website. Multilingual versions of both legislation and caselaw are also available on the eur-lex website.
[7] Where the expression 'European Community' and its variants appear in passages quoted in this chapter, such expressions are retained in their original form. It will be noted that they refer to competence and treaty rules derived from the former EC Treaty.

15.2 European Union law is characterised by a system of uniform rules combined with a decentralised system for their administration. It consists of the Treaties, legislation enacted by the EU institutions, international agreements concluded by the Union, general principles of law acknowledged by the CJEU in light of the common constitutional traditions of the EU Member States, and certain principles of international law. The uniform character of European Union law is preserved, in particular, by the principle of uniform interpretation. According to the Court of Justice:

> 'The need for uniform application of Community law and the principle of equality require that the terms of a provision of Community law which makes no express reference to the law of the Member States for the purpose of determining its meaning and scope must normally be given a uniform and autonomous interpretation throughout the Community; that interpretation must take into account the context of the provision and the purpose of the legislation in question'.[1]

[1] Case C-287/98 *Grand Duchy of Luxemburg v Berthe Linster, Aloyse Linster and Yvonne Linster* [2000] ECR I-6917, paragraph 43; see also Case 327/82 *Ekro BV Vee – en Vleeshandel v Produktschap voor Vee en Vlees* [1984] ECR 107 paragraphs 22–23; Case C-58/01 *Océ Van der Grinten NV v Commissioners of Inland Revenue* [2003] ECR I-9809, paragraph 53; Opinion of Advocate-General Stix-Hackl in Case C-320/02 *Forvaltnings AB Stenholmen v Riksskatteverket* [2004] ECR I-3509, paragraph 23; Opinion of Advocate-General Geelhoed in Case C-240/01 *Commission of the European Communities v Federal Republic of Germany* [2004] ECR I-4733, paragraph 54.

15.3 In its seminal judgment in *Van Gend en Loos v Nederlandse Adminis-tratie der Belastingen* the European Court of Justice reasoned that in order to secure the uniform interpretation by national courts of what was then European Community law, it is necessary to acknowledge that articles of the treaties can be invoked before national courts as an independent source of rights and obligations without the need for implementation in national law. The court concluded that the Union (then the Community) constitutes a new legal order of international law for the benefit of which the Member States have limited their sovereign rights, albeit within limited fields, and the subjects of which comprise not only the Member States but also their nationals. It stated that independently of the legislation of Member States, Community law not only imposes obligations on individuals but is also intended to confer on them rights which become part of their legal heritage.[1] This concept has become known as direct effect and is capable of applying not only to Treaty articles but to all binding EU law, including directives, general principles and international agreements.[2]

[1] Case 26/62 *Van Gend en Loos v Nederlandse Administratie der Belastingen* [1963] ECR 1 at 12.

[2] For the preconditions necessary to enable a provision of EU law to have direct effect within national legal orders, see below **15.26–15.28** and **15.41–15.44**.

15.4 The following year, in *Costa v ENEL* the same court added that one of the central features of this new legal order is the supremacy of the Union's rules over national law of the Member States:

'By creating a Community of unlimited duration, having its own institutions, its own personality, its own legal capacity and capacity of representation on the international plane and, more particularly, real powers stemming from a limitation of sovereignty or a transfer of powers from the States to the Community, the Member States have limited their sovereign rights, albeit within limited fields, and have thus created a body of law which binds both their nationals and themselves. The integration into the laws of each Member State of provisions which derive from the Community, and more generally the terms and the spirit of the Treaty, make it impossible for the states, as a corollary, to accord precedence to a unilateral and subsequent measure over a legal system accepted by them on a basis of reciprocity. Such a measure cannot therefore be inconsistent with that legal system. The executive force of Community law cannot vary from one state to another in deference to subsequent domestic laws, without jeopardising the attainment of the objectives of the Treaty . . . '[1]

[1] Case 6/64 *Costa v Ente Nazionale Energia Elettrica* [1964] ECR 585 at 593.

15.5 As a matter of EU law, therefore, any directly effective provision of EU law takes precedence over any inconsistent provision of national law to the extent of any conflict, no matter what the status of the latter within national law.[1] This is so whether the national law provision precedes or post-dates the EU law provision.[2] National courts and administrative institutions must refuse to apply any provision of national law conflicting with directly effective EU law,[3] and must grant such relief (including interim relief) as is necessary to ensure that EU law is given full force and effect.[4] National courts must also interpret national law in such a way as to be applied consistently with EU law, whether that EU law has direct effect within the national legal order or not.[5]

[1]   Case 11/70 *Internationale Handelsgesellschaft mbH v Einfuhr- und Vorratsstelle für Getreide und Futtermittel* [1970] ECR 1125 paragraph 3; Case C-224/97 *Ciola v Land Vorarlberg* [1999] ECR I-2517; Case C-399/11 *Melloni v Ministerio Fiscal* EU:C:2013:107, paragraphs 56–59. See also Declaration 17 Concerning Primacy, adopted together with the Lisbon Treaty.

[2]   Case 6/64 *Costa v Ente Nazionale Energia Elettrica* [1964] ECR 585 at 593; Case 106/77; *Amministrazione delle Finanze dello Stato v Simmenthal SpA* [1978] ECR 629, paragraphs 17–24.

[3]   Case 106/77 *Amministrazione delle Finanze dello Stato v Simmenthal SpA* [1978] ECR 629 paragraph 24; Case C-118/00 *Larsy v INASTI* [2001] ECR I-5063, paragraphs 51–53.

[4]   Case C-213/89 *R v Secretary of State for Transport, ex p Factortame Ltd* [1990] ECR I-2433 [1991] 1 AC 603 paragraphs 19–23;*Factortame Ltd (No 2)* [1991] 1 AC 603. A national court is, however, not obliged to disapply national rules on res judicata in order to review and set aside a final decision which infringes EU law: see Case C-234/04 *Kapferer v Schlanck and Schick* [2006] ECR I-2585; Case C-119/05 *Ministero dell'Industria, del Commercio e dell'Artigianato v Lucchini SpA* [2007] ECR I-6199; Case C-2/08 *Amministrazione dell'Economia e delle Finanze and Agenzia delle entrate v Fallimento Olimpiclub Srl* [2009] ECR I-7501.

[5]   Case 14/83, *Von Colson v Land Nordrhein-Westfalen* [1984] ECR 1891 paragraph 26; Case C-106/89, *Marleasing v La Comercial Internacional de Alimentacion* [1990] ECR 1-4135, paragraph 8; Joined Cases C-397-403/01, *Pfeiffer v Deutsches Rotes Kreuz* [2004] ECR I-8835, paragraphs 110–118; *Autologic Holdings plc and others v Inland Revenue Commissioners* [2005] UKHL 54, AC 118 at paragraphs 16–17 *Vodafone 2 v Revenue and Customs Commissioners* [2010] Ch 77 paragraphs 37–39.

15.6 Whether the principle of supremacy is accepted by the law of the EU Member States, and if so whether that acceptance is subject to qualification or limitation, is a matter for the constitutional law of each Member State. Effect is given to the principle of supremacy in UK law by the European Communities Act 1972, ss 2–3 and the European Union 2011 Act, s 18.[1] These provisions are consistent with the fundamental UK constitutional doctrine of parliamentary sovereignty, because Parliament retains the power to repeal or vary the 1972 Act by express legislation.[2] Thus, while the primacy of EU law as provided for in the UK by the 1972 Act means that (unlike other rules of domestic law) EU law cannot be implicitly displaced by the mere enactment of legislation which is inconsistent with it,[3] the 1972 Act would not prevent Parliament from enacting legislation which expressly alters the domestic constitutional status of EU institutions or of EU law.[4] Acceptance within UK law of the primacy of EU law may be subject to limitations, insofar as the UK courts might refuse to give overriding effect to a provision of EU law that was repugnant to a fundamental or constitutional right guaranteed by UK law.[5] For the UK's right to withdraw from the EU, and the status of EU law within the UK after any such withdrawal, see **15.17–15.22** below.

[1]   *R (Miller) v Secretary of State for Exiting the European Union* [2017] UKSC 5 [2017] 2 W.L.R. 583, paragraphs 60–67.

[2]   *R (Miller) v Secretary of State for Exiting the European Union* [2017] UKSC 5 [2017] 2 W.L.R. 583, paragraph 60.

[3]   *Factortame Ltd (No 2)* [1991] 1 AC 603; *Thoburn v Sunderland City Council* [2003] QB 151 (DC), paragraphs 37–47; *R (Miller) v Secretary of State for Exiting the European Union* [2017] UKSC 5 [2017] 2 W.L.R. 583, paragraphs 66–67.

[4]   *R (Miller) v Secretary of State for Exiting the European Union* [2017] UKSC 5 [2017] 2 W.L.R. 583, paragraph 67.

[5]   *Thoburn v Sunderland City Council* [2003] QB 151 (DC), paragraph 69; *R (Buckingham County Council) v Secretary of State for Transport* [2014] UKSC 3 [2014] 1

WLR 324 at paragraphs 79, 203–207; *Pham v Secretary of State for the Home Department* [2015] 1 WLR 1591, paragraph 90.

15.7 In order to secure the uniformity of the Union's rules, the Union's legislative institutions, with the important exception of the Council, are charged to act independently of the Member States.[1] Indeed, the term 'supranational' originated in the authentic French version of the Treaty establishing the European Coal and Steel Community. It signified the status of the High Authority, now the Commission, which was thus distinguished from an international institution.[2] Even in the case of the Council, which brings together representatives of the Member States, decisions taken by majority vote bind all of them.[3]

[1]   See the references in the Treaties. The European Parliament consists of 'representatives of the Union's citizens': TEU art 14. It appoints an Ombudsman, charged to be completely independent: TFEU, art 228(3). The Commission contains a number of members equal to the number of Member States but 'The Members of the Commission shall refrain from any action incompatible with their duties. Member States shall respect their independence and shall not seek to influence them in the performance of their tasks': TFEU, art 245. Judges and Advocates General of the European Court of Justice are to be 'chosen from persons whose independence is beyond doubt': TFEU, art 253. Members of the Court of Auditors 'shall be completely independent in the performance of their duties, in the Union's general interest': TFEU, art 285(2). Note that amendments have involved renumbering articles of the Treaties: a table of equivalences is annexed to the Treaty of Lisbon pursuant to art 5 thereof and is available on the eur-lex database: eur-lex.europa.eu/collection/eu-law/treaties.html.
[2]   Paris, 18 April 1951, 261 UNTS 140, Cmnd 7641, art 9 (removed by art 19 of the Merger Treaty and replaced by art 10 of that treaty).
[3]   For legislative procedures, see arts 293–299 TFEU. A 'legislative act' is a legal act adopted by legislative procedure (Article 289(3) TFEU).

15.8 The legal competence of the European Union is restricted and defined by the Treaties which enumerates specific fields in which the EU has competence.[1] Since the Lisbon Treaty, the competence of the Union to act in each sphere of action has been categorised as being (i) exclusive, (ii) shared with Member States, or (iii) restricted to carrying out actions to support, coordinate or supplement the actions of Member States.[2] The legal consequences of a competence being exclusive, shared or supporting are defined by Article 2 TFEU. When the Treaties confer on the Union exclusive competence in a specific area, only the Union may legislate and adopt legally binding acts (unless the Member States themselves are empowered to do so by the EU).[3] When the Union has competence in a field shared with Member States, Member States may legislate and adopt legally binding acts in that field, but only to the extent that the Union has not exercised its competence.[4] Where the Union has only supporting competence, the Union may legislate but may not require harmonisation of Member States' laws; and any exercise of competence by the Union does not supersede the Member States' competence in the relevant field.[5] The Union possesses additional competences to act in the spheres of economic and employment policy and the Common Foreign and Security Policy (CFSP), which fall outside the preceding tripartite scheme.[6]

[1]   Article 5(1)–(2) TEU. This principle that the Union must act within the limits of the competences conferred upon it by the Member States in the Treaties (the 'principle of conferral') applies to both the internal action and the international action of the EU: *Opinion 2/94 (Accession to the ECHR)* [1996] ECR I-1759, paragraph 24.
[2]   Article 3 TFEU lists the EU's areas of exclusive competence. Article 6 lists the EU's areas of supporting, coordinating or supplementing competence. Article 4(1) provides that where

neither Art 3 nor Art 6 applies, the EU's competence (if any) shall be shared with Member States. Article 4(2) lists the primary areas of EU shared competence.

3 Article 2(1) TFEU.

4 Article 2(2) TFEU. Protocol 25 to the Lisbon Treaty clarifies that 'With reference to Article 2(2) [TFEU] on shared competence, when the Union has taken action in a certain area, the scope of this exercise of competence only covers those elements governed by the Union act in question and therefore does not cover the whole area.' If the EU decides to cease exercising its competence in the relevant field, the Member States are once again permitted to legislate and adopt legally binding acts.

5 Article 2(5). The fact that the Member States retain competence to act in the field does not mean that any legislation adopted by the EU in that field is any the less binding on Member States.

6 Articles 2(3)–(4) TFEU.

15.9 The competence of the Union to act is limited by the principle of subsidiarity in Article 5(3) TEU.[1] The Union will only act where the proposed action can, by reason of its scale or effects, be better achieved at EU level in view of the objectives of the Union set out in Article 3 TEU and other relevant Treaty articles.[2] Further content to the principle of subsidiarity is provided by Protocols 1 and 2 of the Lisbon Treaty, which require each EU institution to respect the principles of subsidiarity and proportionality, and set out procedural mechanisms (including procedures involving national parliaments) designed to achieve and ensure subsidiarity in practice.[3]

1 Article 5(3) TEU: 'Under the principle of subsidiarity, in areas which do not fall within its exclusive competence, the Union shall act only if and in so far as the objectives of the proposed action cannot be sufficiently achieved by the Member States, either at the central level or at regional and local level, but can rather, by reason of the scale and effects of the proposed action, be better achieved at local level.'

2 C-358/14, *Poland v Parliament and Council (Second Tobacco Directive)* EU:C:2016:323, paragraph 119.

3 Protocol (No 1) on the Role of National Parliaments in the European Union; Protocol (No 2) on the Application of the Principles of Subsidiarity and Proportionality.

15.10 Another expression of the limited scope of European Union law is the principle that EU rules governing freedom of movement will not be applied to 'wholly internal situations', that is to say cases which have no factor linking them with any of the situations governed by EU law and all elements of which are purely internal to a single Member State.[1] A purely hypothetical prospect of exercising such rights or of their being obstructed is not sufficient to establish the necessary connection.[2] As applied to the right to free movement of persons, this means that EU rights to free movement and residence are triggered only where (a) a national of a Member State has crossed a border with another Member State, or (b) there is a real prospect of him / her doing so.[3] The question of whether a situation is 'wholly internal' is in effect the converse of the question of whether the claimant has a fundamental freedom as a matter of EU law in the first place. Under the impetus of recent changes in the founding treaties, including the proclamation of citizenship of the Union and the concomitant right to move freely throughout its territory,[4] the tendency has been to find fewer instances of situations purely internal to a single Member State, as can be seen from the examples in the next paragraph.

1 Case 175/78 *R v Vera Ann Saunders* [1979] ECR 1129; Joined Cases C-64/96 and C-65/96 *Uecker and Jacquet* [1997] ECR I-3171; Case C-60/00 *Mary Carpenter v Secretary of State* [2002] ECR I-6279, paragraph 28; Case C-148/02 *Garcia Avello* [2003] ECR I-11613; Case C-212/06 *Government of the French Community and Walloon Government v Flemish*

Government [2008] ECR I-01683; Joined Cases C-456/12 and C-457/12, *Minister voor Immigratie, Integratie en Asiel*, Opinion of Advocate General Sharpston [2013] ECR.

2   Case C-40/11 Iida [2012] ECR, paragraph 77.

3   Joined Cases C-456/12 and C-457/12, *Minister voor Immigratie, Integratie en Asiel v O*, Opinion of Advocate General Sharpston [2013] ECR, paragraph 38.

4   *Fisher v Revenue and Customs Commissioners* [2014] UKFTT 804 (TC) [2014] SFTD 1341, paragraph 608. Paragraphs 564–603 of this judgment contain a useful summary of the CJEU's case law on 'wholly internal situations', and a summary of relevant legal propositions derived therefrom appears at paragraph 604.

15.11 Where the child born in the UK of Chinese parents, wished to stay in the UK with her mother and had never entered or sought to enter another Member State, the situation was not purely internal since, by birth in Belfast, the child acquired Irish citizenship.[1] Nor was the imposition of dock dues in the French *département* of *Réunion* a 'purely internal' matter, even where the goods arrived after shipment from metropolitan France.[2] In a case referred from an Austrian court, involving the conditions for the acquisition by an Austrian company of land in Austria, the European Court of Justice held that the situation was not wholly internal, since the relevant Austrian legislation applied without distinction to Austrian nationals and to nationals of Member States of the Union.[3] The European Court of Justice applied similar reasoning in a case referred from a French court, before which the accused was a French national charged with an offence, defined by French law,[4] of offering for sale Emmenthal cheese without a rind. The rules of European Union law applied to the case since French law drew no distinction in that respect between cheeses made in France and those made elsewhere.[5]

1   Case C-200/02 *Man Levette Chen v Secretary of State* [2004] ECR I-9925, opinion AG Tizzano and ECJ judgment at paragraph 41.

2   Joined Cases C-363/93 and C-407/93 to C-411/93 *Lancry and Others v Direction Generate des Douanes* [1994] ECR I-3957.

3   Joined Cases C-515/99, C-519/99 to C-524/99 and C-526/99 to C-540/99 *Hans Reisch and Others v Bürgermeister der Landeshauptstadt Salzburg and Grundverkehrsbeauftragter des Landes Salzburg* [2002] ECR I-2157.

4   Decree No 88-1206 of 30 December 1988.

5   Case C-448/98 *Guimont* [2000] ECR I-10663. The judgment is consistent with Joined Cases C-321/94 to C-324/94 *Pistre and Others* [1997] ECR I-2343, paragraph 44: Case 286/81 *Oosthoek's Uitgeversmaatschappij* [1982] ECR 4575, paragraph 9.

15.12 The types of legal acts, including legislation,[1] open to the Union's institutions arc set out in article 288 TFEU. They include directives which, as we shall see,[2] permit Member States a certain flexibility in choice of form and methods providing always that national implementing rules both ensure that the directive is fully effective in accordance with the objective which it pursues[3] and are not liable to nullify the effects of the directive.[4] Such flexibility is absent in the case of measures adopted in the form of regulations and decisions. Regulations in particular would normally require uniform application of detailed criteria throughout the Union. For this reason, Member States may not add supplementary conditions to those provided for in a regulation, as this would put at risk the uniform applicability of the relevant regulation throughout the Union. In so far as national implementation of a regulation is necessary, it must not jeopardise the scope and effectiveness of EU law, including its general principles.[5]

1   The Treaties refer to EU legislation as 'legislative acts', defined by art 289(3) TFEU as 'legal acts adopted by legislative procedure' (whether the 'ordinary legislative procedure' defined by

arts 289(1) and 294 TFEU, or a 'special legislative procedure' as defined by s 289(2) and other treaty articles). Regulations, directives and decisions are all capable of qualifying as 'legislative acts'. The Treaty of Lisbon introduced two further (and subordinate) categories of legal act which do not amount to legislative acts, namely 'delegated acts' and 'implementing acts': arts 290 and 291 TFEU.

2   See **15.37–15.40** below.
3   Case C-268/06 *Impact v Minister for Agriculture and Food* [2008] ECR I-2483, paragraph 40. Variation in implementing legislation between autonomous regions of a Member State is also permissible provided that the allocation of powers within the Member State permits the Community legal measures to be implemented correctly: Case C-429/07 *Horvath v Secretary of State for Environment, Food and Rural Affairs*, [2009] ECR I-4833.
4   Case C-263/08 *Djurgarden-Lilla Värtans Miljöskyddsförening v Stockholms kommun genom dess marknämnd*, [2009] ECR I-9967, paragraph 45. Care must also be taken to ensure that implementation does not rely upon an interpretation of the directive which would be in conflict with fundamental rights or with other general principles of EU law: Case C-275/06 *Promusicae v Telefonica de Espana* [2008] ECR I-271 at paragraph 68.
5   Case C-40/69, *Hauptzollamt Hamburg-Oberelbe v. Firma Paul G. Bollmann* [1970] ECR 69; Joined Cases C-80/99, C-81/99, and C-82/99 *Ernst-Otto Flemmer et al v. Council of the European Union and Commission of the European Communities* [2001] ECR I-7211, paragraph 55.

15.13 The decentralised character of the administration of European Union law arises from the fact that the supervision of its application is entrusted primarily to the authorities of the Member States. Indeed, many of the rules of European Union law are addressed primarily to Member States whose authorities are required thereby to take or abstain from taking certain action. That is the case, for instance, with the Union's rules on taxation,[1] transport,[2] State aid,[3] economic and monetary policy,[4] employment,[5] economic and social cohesion,[6] and government deficits.[7] The Union's rules relating to the free movement of goods apply, in principle, to the removal of obstacles to trade arising from action taken by Member States;[8] and the same is true of the rules relating to the free movement of capital.[9] Where a natural or legal person (other than a Member State or Union institution) maintains that a Member State has failed to take action, or to abstain from taking it, in breach of an obligation owed to that person under European Union law, the function of securing the Member State's compliance with its obligations falls in the first instance on the national courts.

1   Art 110 TFEU: 'No Member State shall impose, directly or indirectly, on the products of other Member States, any internal taxation of any kind in excess of that imposed directly or indirectly on similar domestic products'.
2   Art 90 TFEU: 'The objectives of this Treaty shall, in matters governed by this Title, be pursued by Member States in the framework of a common transport policy'.
3   Art 107(1) TFEU: 'Save as otherwise provided in this Treaty, any aid granted by a Member State or through State resources in any form whatsoever which distorts or threatens to distort competition by favouring certain undertakings or the production of certain goods shall, in so far as it affects trade between Member States, be incompatible with the common market'.
4   Art 120 TFEU: 'Member States shall conduct their economic policies with a view to contributing to the achievement of the objectives of the Community, as defined in Article 3 of the Treaty on European Union, and in the context of the broad guidelines referred to in Article 121(2)'.
5   Art 146 TFEU: 'Member States, through their employment policies, shall contribute to the achievement of the objectives referred to in Article 145 in a way consistent with the broad guidelines of the economic policies of the Member States and of the Union adopted pursuant to Article 121(2)'.
6   Art 175 TFEU: 'Member States shall conduct their economic policies and shall coordinate them in such a way as . . . to attain the objectives set out in Article 174'.
7   Art 126 TFEU: 'Member States shall avoid excessive government deficits'.

[8] According to the famous formula in Case 8/74 *Dassonville* [1974] ECR 837, paragraph 5, all trading rules enacted by Member States which are capable of hindering, directly or indirectly, actually or potentially, intra-Community trade are measures having an effect equivalent to quantitative restrictions within the meaning of art 34 TFEU. In Case 249/81 *Commission v Ireland* [1982] ECR 4005 (the *'Buy Irish'* case) the European Court of Justice held that by adopting a series of measures designed to promote Irish products Ireland had infringed art 30 EEC (now art 34 TFEU). The fact that those measures had been taken by a private company (the Irish Goods Council) was not decisive given that the Council had been set up at the initiative of the Irish Government.

[9] Joined Cases C-163/94, C-165/94 and C-250/94 *Sanz de Lera and Others* [1995] ECR I-4821, paragraphs 40–48.

15.14 However, rules of European Union law may apply 'horizontally' between one natural or legal person and another. In such cases the function of administering the rules falls upon national authorities, including national courts, subject to the possibility of guidance from the European Court of Justice by way of references for preliminary ruling.[1] For instance, the prohibition of obstacles to the free movement of persons or to the freedom to provide services has been construed as extending not only to national authorities but also to groups or organisations that impose on individuals rules of any kind aimed at regulating in a collective manner gainful employment, self-employment and the provision of services which adversely affect the exercise of their fundamental freedoms.[2] In addition, many of the provisions embodying the Union's social policy are designed to apply between one subject and another.[3]

[1] By way of exception art 272 TFEU provides that the CJEU has jurisdiction to give judgment pursuant to an arbitration clause in a contract concluded by or on behalf of the Community, whether that contract be governed by public or private law.

[2] Case 36/74 *Walrave and Koch v Association Union Cycliste Internationale and Others* [1974] ECR 1405; Case C-415/93 *Union Royale Belge des Societes de Football Association and Others v Bosman and Others* [1995] ECR I-4921; Case C-438/05 *International Transport Workers Federation v Viking Line ABP* [2007] ECR I-10779 paragraph 33.

[3] It is settled case law that the prohibition of discrimination between men and women under article 157 TFEU, which is mandatory in nature, applies not only to the action of public authorities, but also extends to all agreements which are intended to regulate paid labour collectively, as well as to contracts between individuals: Case C-91/92 *Faccini Dori* [1994] ECR I-3325, paragraphs 19–26. See also Case C-349/01 *Betriebsrat der Firma ADS Anker GmbH v ADS Anker GmbH* [2004] ECR I-6803.

15.15 EU competition law is the paradigm example of such horizontal application of EU rules. With effect from 1 May 2004, Regulation 1/2003 of 16 December 2002 on the implementation of the rules on competition in arts 101 and 102 of the Treaty[1] provides that art 101(3) TFEU is to be directly applicable both by national competition authorities and national courts. The regulation abolished the former system of notification of agreements. National competition authorities and national courts have the power to assess agreements, for the purpose of determining whether they qualify for exemption under art 101(3). They may, for instance, decide that a particular decision contributes to improving the production of goods or promoting technical progress while allowing consumers a share of the resulting benefit and imposing no restrictions other than those indispensable for achieving this object, thereby permitting an otherwise restrictive agreement to be exempted from the scope of the competition rules.

¹ OJ 2003 L1/1.

15.16 The tension between the Union's system of uniform rules and the decentralised system for their administration gives rise to some special difficulties in the context of judicial review. Rules of national law governing the procedure for judicial review,¹ the remedies available and the conditions for the grant of relief must be modified to the extent necessary to comply with the substantive requirements of the Union's system. The general principles developed by common law courts for the grant of judicial review must be tailored in such a manner as to reflect the principles developed, largely by means of comparative law, in the European Union's system.² Consequences for judicial review in England and Wales are discussed at **15.101–15.105** below.

¹ See by analogy the perceived lack of legal certainty arising from a deadline for public procurement challenges of 'promptly and in any event within three months': Case C-406/08 *Uniplex (UK) Ltd v NHS Business Services Authority* [2010] ECR I-817. However (then) the generous rules on standing in England and Wales were singled out for praise by the Vice President of the Court of Justice, Judge Lenaerts, in a speech to the CCBE in Brussels on 28 April 2014 in the context of challenges to forthcoming national legislation pursuant to obligations on Member States in EU directives and regulations. In this way, national law can help to fill any gap in judicial protection created by the very restrictive EU rules on standing to challenge legislative measures.
² See K Lenaerts, 'In the Union we Trust: Trust Enhancing Principles of Community Law' (2004) 41 CMLRev 317–334.

WITHDRAWAL FROM THE EU AND INCORPORATION OF EU LAW

15.17 Member States are permitted to withdraw from the European Union by Article 50(1) TEU.¹ The terms of a Member State's withdrawal are to be determined by agreement between that Member State and the Union. The Union will act for these purposes through the Commission in the negotiation of the agreement, and through a qualified majority of the remaining members of the Council in the concluding of the agreement. The European Parliament must also give its consent to any withdrawal agreement. If no withdrawal agreement is agreed within two years of notification by the Member State of its intention to withdraw, the Treaties will 'cease to apply' to that Member State, unless the European Council (acting unanimously) and the Member State concerned decide to extend that two-year period.² Any final new agreement(s) between the withdrawing Member State and the European Union is or are highly likely to be (or to include) a 'mixed agreement' under art 218 TFEU to which both the European Union and its remaining Member States are party. This will mean that national and regional parliaments of the Member States are required to ratify the new agreement. A transitional agreement may, however, be capable of being agreed under Article 50 before adoption of such a final agreement.³

¹ Article 50(1) TEU: 'Any Member State may decide to withdraw from the Union in accordance with its constitutional requirements.'
² Article 50(2)–(4) TEU, art 218 TFEU.
³ On the respective scope of art 50 TEU, art 207 TFEU and art 218 TFEU, see House of Commons, Exiting the European Union Committee, 'The process for exiting the European Union and the Government's negotiating objectives' (11 January 2017) paragraphs 53–67,

and House of Commons Foreign Affairs Committee 'Article 50 negotiations: Implications of "no deal"' (7 March 2017), paragraphs 10–15.

15.18 Following the result of a referendum on EU membership in the UK, the UK government gave notification on 29 March 2017 of the UK's intention to withdraw from the EU. The government has stated that its intention is to enact legislation (a 'Great Repeal Bill') to repeal the European Communities Act 1972 and to convert the body of existing directly applicable EU law into domestic law.[1] The government's intended approach is to preserve (in the first instance at least)[2] both the content and the manner of interpretation of that EU law:[3]

'The Government's general approach to preserving EU law is to ensure that all EU laws which are directly applicable in the UK (such as EU regulations) and all laws which have been made in the UK, in order to implement our obligations as a member of the EU, remain part of domestic law on the day we leave the EU.

In general the Government also believes that the preserved law should continue to be interpreted in the same way as it is at the moment. This approach is in order to ensure a coherent approach which provides continuity. It will be open to Parliament in the future to keep or change these laws.'

The Great Repeal Bill is expected to include provision for Ministers by statutory instrument to make necessary logical amendments to transposed EU laws which would not function sensibly if incorporated without amendment. The precise mechanism for doing so, and attendant constitutional safeguards, are not at present clear. There are also significant constitutional questions about the respective roles of the UK and the devolved governments in the repatriation of former EU competencies.[4] The government has acknowledged that UK domestic legislation following withdrawal will need to reflect the content of the UK's withdrawal agreement negotiated with the EU.[5] It is proposed that a dispute resolution mechanism will be instituted to interpret and ensure the enforcement of the EU-UK withdrawal agreement.[6]

[1] HM Government, 'The United Kingdom's exit from and new partnership with the European Union', CM 9417 (February 2017), paragraph 1.1; HM Government, 'Legislating for the United Kingdom's withdrawal from the European Union', CM 9446 (March 2017).
[2] A two-stage process is envisaged for the process of converting EU law into UK law: first, the initial preservation of EU law by converting it into UK law with such amendments as are necessary to make it work sensibly in a UK context; and, second, a longer-term process in which Parliament and the government determine the extent to which (what was) EU law will remain part of UK law. The Great Repeal Bill is intended to facilitate the first stage of this process, with the second stage being achieved through normal parliamentary procedures: see House of Lords Select Committee on the Constitution, HL Paper 123, 'The "Great Repeal Bill" and delegated powers' (7 March 2017), p 3.
[3] HM Government, 'The United Kingdom's exit from and new partnership with the European Union', CM 9417 (February 2017), p 10.
[4] House of Lords Select Committee on the Constitution, HL Paper 123, 'The 'Great Repeal Bill' and delegated powers' (7 March 2017), paragraphs 109–122.
[5] HM Government, 'The United Kingdom's exit from and new partnership with the European Union', CM 9417 (February 2017), paragraph 1.5.
[6] HM Government, 'The United Kingdom's exit from and new partnership with the European Union', CM 9417 (February 2017), paragraphs 2.4–2.10.

15.19 Three overarching questions arise in relation to the operation of the intended Great Reform Bill: the means of incorporation of EU law; the interpretation of such incorporated EU law; and the effect of judgments of the CJEU. As to the first, the government's proposal is: (i) to repeal the European Communities Act 1972; (ii) to re-enact as UK (or devolved) law all directly-applicable EU law as it applied in the UK the moment before the UK's exit from the EU; and (iii) to authorise the government and devolved governments to make secondary legislation so as to make logical amendments to the newly re-enacted 'EU-derived law' and to implement the contents of any withdrawal agreement reached with the EU.[1] The Great Repeal Bill will also preserve (and, where necessary, adapt) the laws that have been made in the UK to implement the UK's EU obligations under s 2(2) of the European Communities Act 1972, or under other primary or secondary domestic legislation. Without such provision, the secondary legislation made under ECA 1972, s 2(2) would cease to have effect when that Act is repealed.[2] The government has estimated that there are over 12,000 EU regulations in force in the UK prior to the 'great repeal', and over 7,900 statutory instruments which have implemented EU legislation.[3]

[1] HM Government, 'Legislating for the United Kingdom's withdrawal from the European Union', CM 9446 (March 2017), Chapter 2.

[2] The general principle is that when an Act is repealed, any rules or regulations made under it cease to have effect: *Surtees v Ellison (1829) 9 B & C 750*; *Watson v Winch* [1916] 1 KB 688. It is thought that ss 16 and 17 of the Interpretation Act 1978 would not be sufficient to preserve the validity of that subordinate legislation. See HM Government, 'Legislating for the United Kingdom's withdrawal from the European Union', CM 9446 (March 2017), paragraph 2.5: 'Once the ECA has been repealed, all of the secondary legislation made under it would fall away'. The government's White Paper acknowledges (at paragraph A.14) that some EU directives have been implemented in the UK by means of primary legislation or by secondary legislation made under statutory powers other than the ECA, s 2(2). These latter UK laws will not require new legislation to preserve them, but may well require amendment in order to function properly post-Brexit.

[3] HM Government, 'Legislating for the United Kingdom's withdrawal from the European Union', CM 9446 (March 2017), paragraph 2.6.

15.20 The Government has indicated that most of the EU law which it is intended to re enact or preserve in this way will not function properly without amendment.[1] This may be for a variety of reasons.[2] First, there will be laws whose existence is predicated on the UK enjoying a benefit of EU membership which will be lost following exit from the EU, unless preserved by transitional arrangements or a new treaty with the EU: an important example is the right to work and reside in other EU countries. Second, there are laws which will become redundant after UK exit from the EU. Third, there are laws which will no longer operate as intended because they require the participation of an EU institution or EU-wide scheme: for example, EU legislation providing rights to benefits (eg the EU basic payment scheme in agriculture) or granting powers to EU institutions to intervene in or consider complaints in relation to a market. Fourth, there are laws which may require more minor textual amendments to reflect the UK's changed constitutional circumstances: for example, references in statutes to 'Member States other than the United Kingdom', to 'EU law' or to the UK's 'EU obligations'. Fifth, there are laws which would work perfectly well as a matter of legal logic without amendment but which, as a matter of policy, the government might not wish to remain in force after exit from the EU: for example, obligations to send information to EU institutions or Member States. The Great Repeal Bill will contain broad delegated powers to enable the government to make the (in many cases) significant and complex amendments to both delegated and primary legislation that will be required as a result. The government has indicated that the implementation of new policies in areas that previously lay within the EU's competence will not be carried out by means of such delegated powers, and that instead new primary legislation will be enacted to deal with such matters (including customs and immigration). Nevertheless, concerns have been expressed as to whether the terms of the delegated powers provided for by the Great Reform Bill will guarantee an appropriate level of parliamentary and judicial scrutiny.[3]

[1] HM Government, 'Legislating for the United Kingdom's withdrawal from the European Union', CM 9446 (March 2017), paragraphs 3.2 and 3.5.
[2] HM Government, 'Legislating for the United Kingdom's withdrawal from the European Union', CM 9446 (March 2017), paragraphs 3.3–3.4.
[3] House of Lords Select Committee on the Constitution, HL Paper 123, 'The 'Great Repeal Bill' and delegated powers' (7 March 2017).

15.21 On the second overarching question, once incorporated into UK law, EU legislation and other directly applicable EU law will need to be interpreted. The standard EU canons of interpretation in accordance with the literal words, the history of the provision, context and purpose differ from the English approach, for example as regards the readiness to look at *travaux préparatoires*. EU rules adopted for application within the UK do not necessarily have the same meaning as the original EU rules.[1] The government has confirmed that it does not intend for Brexit to make any change to the interpretation of EU law as it applied up to the moment of its incorporation into domestic UK law.[2] Judgments of the CJEU delivered before the UK's exit will therefore remain binding, and the government intends that these historic CJEU judgments will be given the same precedential status in UK courts as decisions of the UK Supreme Court.[3] EU-derived law (which ought logically to include the interpretation of that law by the CJEU) will also continue to enjoy supremacy over domestic UK law enacted prior to Brexit.[4] The government's intention is that the Great Repeal Bill will not require UK courts to consider CJEU jurisprudence post-dating Brexit.[5] Whether any statutory guidance is given to UK courts in this regard and what presumptions the UK courts themselves develop with regard to the interpretation of EU-derived law, will be an area of great constitutional and practical significance.

[1] *Cook v Virgin Media* [2015] EWCA Civ 1287, [2017] 1 All ER 929 at paragraph 31.
[2] HM Government, 'Legislating for the United Kingdom's withdrawal from the European Union', CM 9446 (March 2017), paragraph 2.14: 'for as long as EU-derived law remains on the UK statute book, it is essential that there is a common understanding of what that law means. The government believes that this is best achieved by providing for continuity in how that law is interpreted before and after exit day'.
[3] HM Government, 'Legislating for the United Kingdom's withdrawal from the European Union', CM 9446 (March 2017), paragraphs 2.14, 2.16.
[4] HM Government, 'Legislating for the United Kingdom's withdrawal from the European Union', CM 9446 (March 2017), paragraphs 2.19–2.20. It may be argued that the consequence of this is that pre-Brexit CJEU judgments will be superior and not simply equivalent to pre-Brexit Supreme Court judgments.
[5] HM Government, 'Legislating for the United Kingdom's withdrawal from the European Union', CM 9446 (March 2017), paragraph 2.13. Compare paragraphs 24–27 of the House of Lords Select Committee on the Constitution, HL Paper 123, 'The 'Great Repeal Bill' and delegated powers' (7 March 2017), suggesting that the bill provide that UK courts 'may have regard to' the case law of the CJEU (without being bound by them) in relation to judgments made both before and after Brexit in order to assist in the interpretation of UK law.

15.22 Further questions will arise concerning the desirability or otherwise of regulatory equivalence between EU law and UK law in various fields following the UK's withdrawal from the EU, and the legal mechanism for achieving parity between EU law and UK law in particular fields if this is desired. These are political questions yet to be resolved. The government's February 2017 White Paper appears to indicate that it wishes common regulatory frameworks to continue where possible.[1]

[1] HM Government, 'The United Kingdom's exit from and new partnership with the European Union', CM 9417 (February 2017), paragraphs 8.2–8.3, stating that the trade negotiation between the UK and the EU will be 'about finding the best way for the benefit of the common systems and frameworks . . . to continue', and that 'it makes no sense to start again from scratch when the UK and the remaining Member States have adhered to the same rules for so many years'. See too at paragraphs 8.13, 8.25–8.26, 8.32–8.35 and 8.42. The Secretary of State's preface to the White Paper states: 'The focus will not be about removing existing barriers or questioning certain protections but about ensuring new barriers do not arise.'

TREATIES AS SOURCES OF UNION LAW

15.23 In the language of the European Communities Act 1972, s 2(1):

'All such rights powers, liabilities, obligations and restrictions from time to time created or arising by or under the Treaties, and all such remedies and procedures from time to time provided for by or under the Treaties, as in accordance with the Treaties are without further enactment to be given legal effect or used in the United Kingdom shall be recognised and available in law, and be enforced, allowed and followed accordingly; and the expression "enforceable Community right" and similar expressions shall be read as referring to one to which this subsection applies'.

15.24 The treaties to which this section refers include not only those founding the European Union and the European Atomic Energy Community[1] but also a substantial list of associated agreements, among which are the United Kingdom's Treaty and Act of Accession,[2] and the Treaties and acts of accession of other Member States joining the Community after 1973. The founding Treaties have from time to time been amended or supplemented, most notably by the Single European Act,[3] the Treaty on European Union,[4] the Treaty of Nice[5] and, most recently, by the Treaty of Lisbon. The Treaty of Lisbon may be considered to have restored the unity of European law through amendments to the Treaty on European Union and the EC Treaty to create a single legal regime of European Union law. Thus the provisions of EU law are to be found not only in the TFEU (formerly the EC Treaty) but in a combination of both the TEU and the TFEU which are together the founding treaties of the European Union.[6] The Treaties are supplemented by extensive protocols and annexes which 'form an integral part' of the Treaties. Furthermore, Article 6 TEU expressly recognises the Charter of Fundamental Rights[7] as having 'the same legal value as the Treaties'.[8]

[1] Also, in relation to events that occurred prior to its desuetude, the Treaty establishing the European Coal and Steel Community.
[2] Brussels, 22 January 1972, Cmnd 4862. See eur-lex.europa.eu/collection/eu-law/treaties.html for all relevant EU Treaties including Treaties of Accession.
[3] Luxembourg and The Hague 17 and 28 February 1986, OJ 1987 L169/1.
[4] Maastricht, 7 February 1992, OJ 1992, OJ 2002 C325/ 1.
[5] 26 February 2001, OJ 2001 C80/1.

⁶ Art 1(2) TEU and art 1(2) TFEU. Post-Lisbon consolidated versions of the Treaty on European Union and the Treaty on the Functioning of the European Union are also to be found at: eur-lex.europa.eu/legal-content/EN/TXT/?uri=CELEX:12012E/TXT

⁷ A copy of the Charter is also to be found on the eur-lex treaty page: eur-lex.europa.eu/collection/eu-law/treaties.html..

⁸ Protocol No 30 provides that the Charter 'does not extend the ability' of European or Polish/UK courts to find that national provisions are inconsistent with the fundamental rights, freedoms and principles that it reaffirms. Protocol 30 is not an 'opt-out'; instead it appears to be a restatement of the point, already established by art 51(2) of the Charter that the Charter, does not extend the field of application of EU law. See Protocol No 30, preamble 3; Case C-411/10 *NS v Secretary of State for the Home Department* [2006] ECR I-5769, paragraph 120; and see Report of the House of Commons European Scrutiny Committee, HC 979 'The application of the EU Charter of Fundamental Rights in the UK: a state of confusion' (2 April 2014).

15.25 A provision in the EU treaties is 'without further enactment to be given legal effect or used in the United Kingdom' when it gives rise to rights on which individuals may rely or 'produces direct effects'. As noted above,¹ direct effect of certain Treaty articles may be asserted not only against Member States but also against private parties.

¹ Paragraph **15.14**.

15.26 In *Van Gend en Loos v Nederlandse Administratie der Belastingen*, the Court of Justice stated that to ascertain whether a provision in the EC Treaty gives rise to directly effective rights on which individuals may rely in proceedings before national courts, it is necessary to consider the spirit, general scheme and wording of the provision in question.¹ In accordance with the spirit of that Treaty, rights for individuals arise by reason of obligations which the Treaty imposes in a clearly defined way upon individuals as well as the Member States and the institutions. With regard to the general scheme of the Treaty, as it relates to the customs duties and equivalent charges in issue in that case, the court noted that art 12 EC (now art 25 TFEU) 'contains a clear and unconditional prohibition . . . not qualified by any reservation on the part of States which would make its implementation conditional upon a positive legislative measure under national law'.

¹ Case 28/62 *Van Gend en Loos v Nederlandse Administratie der Belastingen* [1963] ECR 1 at 12. See further **15.40–15.48** below.

15.27 The quality of clarity or precision required for the production of direct effects is not to be confused with absence of any ambiguity.¹ The appropriate test is to ask whether the provision in question, properly construed, establishes standards by reference to which an individual's rights can be ascertained. In *Ianelli v Meroni*² the European Court of Justice held that what was then the first paragraph of art 92 EC (now art 107 TFEU) was insufficiently precise to produce direct effects in relation to existing systems of aid. That paragraph prohibited state aid. Article 92(2) provided by way of derogation that certain categories of aid shall be compatible with the common market and art 92(3) provided that other categories may be considered compatible with it. Since the Union institutions enjoyed a discretionary power in determining whether forms of aid are to be considered compatible with the common market, art 92(1) could not be said to be sufficiently clear or precise. Conversely, in *Van Duyn v Home Office*, art 48 EC (now art 45 TFEU) on the free movement of workers was given direct effect, notwithstanding the fact that Member States were permitted by that article to limit a worker's free movement on grounds of public policy, public security, or public health. The Member States' discretion to invoke those limitations was judicially controlled, and was therefore not incompatible with the conferral of enforceable rights on individuals.[3]

¹ Per AG Warner in Case 131/79 *R v Secretary of State for Home Affairs ex p Santillo* [1980] ECR 1585 at 1611.
² Case 74/76, [1977] ECR I-557, paragraphs 11–13.
³ Case 41/74 *Van Duyn v Home Office* [1974] ECR 1337, paragraph 7.

15.28 A provision is sufficiently immediate or unconditional to produce direct effects when it imposes an obligation which is not dependent on the adoption of further measures by the Union or the Member States. In *Schlüter v Hauptzollamt Lörrach*[1] the Court of Justice held that the former arts 5 and 107 EC did not produce direct effects since, in providing for the procedures to be followed in order to co-ordinate the economic policies of the Member States, they allowed Member States 'such freedom of decision that the obligation contained in those Articles 5 and 107 cannot confer on interested parties rights which the national courts would be bound to protect'.[2] The fact that a Treaty article envisages implementing measures at EU or Member State level is not necessarily fatal to the direct effect of that Treaty article. Where the norm can be identified and judicially applied with sufficient precision, the obligation on Member States to enact implementing legislation may be interpreted as being a duty to assist the implementation of the norm, rather than a precondition of the norm having direct effect at all.[3]

¹ Case 9/73 [1973] ECR 1135, at paragraph 39.
² See, further Case 13/68 *Salgoil SpA v Italian Ministry for Foreign Trade* [1968] ECR 453 at 461; art 90(2): Case 10/71 *Ministère Public of Luxembourg v Müller* [1971] ECR 723 at 729; art 97(1): Case 28/67 *Molkerei-Zentrale Westfalen Lippe GmbH v Hauptzollamt Paderborn* [1968] ECR 143 at 156.
³ Case 2/74 *Reyners v Belgium* [1974] ECR 631 (art 52 EC, requiring equal treatment with nationals in the context of freedom of establishment); Case 43/75 *Defrenne v Société Anonyme Belge de Navigation Aérienne (SABENA)* [1976] ECR 455 (art 119 EC: 'Each Member State shall ensure that the principle of equal pay for male and female workers for equal work or work of equal value is applied').

15.29 Even where articles in the Treaties do not confer rights on individuals but give rise to obligations or commitments between Member States at the international level, national courts are under a 'broad and far-reaching' obligation to construe domestic legislation consistently with EU law obligations.[1] This is an aspect of the national courts' duty to do whatever lies within their jurisdiction to ensure that EU law is effective.[2] It is also considered to be justified by s 2(4) of the European Communities Act, which provides in part that:

> 'any enactment passed or to be passed . . . shall be construed and have effect subject to the foregoing provisions of this section'.

The court's duty of consistent interpretation is not constrained by conventional rules of construction; does not require ambiguity in the legislative language; is not an exercise in semantics or linguistics; permits departure from the strict and literal application of the words which the legislature has elected to use; and permits the implication of words necessary to comply with Community law obligations.[3] The only constraints on the obligation are that: (a) the meaning should 'go with the grain of the legislation' and be 'compatible with the underlying thrust of the legislation being construed'; and (b) the exercise of the interpretative obligation cannot require the courts to make decisions for which they are not equipped or give rise to important practical repercussions which the court is not equipped to evaluate. As to the first of these two constraints, an interpretation should not be adopted which is inconsistent with a fundamental or cardinal feature of the legislation, since this would cross the boundary between interpretation and amendment.[4] The same principle applies also to Council Framework Decisions made under the TEU prior to the Lisbon Treaty.[5]

[1] *Vodafone 2 v Revenue and Customs Commissioners* [2010] Ch 77 at paragraph 37, per Morritt C. Paragraphs 37–38 have been cited with approval in numerous subsequent English and Welsh and UK judgments, including *Sub One Limited v Commissioners for Her Majesty's Revenue and Customs* [2014] EWCA Civ 773, [2014] S.T.C. 2508, paragraph 42 and *United States of America v Nolan* [2016] AC 463, paragraph 14.

[2] Case C-378/07 *Angelidaki* [2009] ECR I-3071, paragraph 197.

[3] *Vodafone 2 v Revenue and Customs Commissioners* [2010] Ch 77 at paragraph 37, citing (among other cases) *Pickstone v Freemans plc* [1989] AC 66. *Marleasing SA v La Comercial Internacional de Alimentación SA* [1990] ECR I-4135.

[4] *Vodafone 2 v Revenue and Customs Commissioners* [2010] Ch 77 at paragraph 38, citing *Ghaidan v Godin-Mendoza* [2004] 2 AC 557, *Revenue and Customs Comrs v EB Central Services Ltd* [2008] STC 2209 and *R (IDT Card Services Ireland Ltd) v Customs and Excise Comrs* [2006] STC 1252.

[5] Case C-105/03 *Criminal Proceedings against Maria Pupino* [2005] ECR I-5285.

LEGISLATION AS A SOURCE OF UNION LAW

15.30 In the case of rights, powers, liabilities, obligations and restrictions arising *under* the Treaties, it is necessary, in the first place, to identify the source and hence the limits of the power of the Union institutions to enact legislation.

15.31 The institutions of the Union have no inherent legislative authority:[1] but may enact legislation on the basis of specific authority conferred by the founding treaties and subject to the limits laid down therein. This may give rise to questions as to: (a) whether the Union is empowered to enact a particular legislative act at all; and (b) if so, which Treaty article should be identified as the proper source of the Union's power to do so: in some cases, the legislative act in question may arguably fall within any one of two or more areas of competence. Since the Union's competence and the procedure for the enactment of legislation may be different depending on which Treaty article applies, the question of categorisation may have important legal and practical consequences. The choice of legal basis for a European Union measure must rest on objective factors that are amenable to judicial review; these include the aim and content of that measure.[2] However, as appears below, the Union legislative institutions are afforded a wide degree of discretion in the choice of Treaty basis, and the legality will be affected only if the measure is 'manifestly inappropriate having regard to the objective which the competent institution is seeking to pursue'.[3]

[1] The principle is one of conferral of power by the Treaties: Articles 5(1) and 5(2) TEU. See further **15.8** above.

² Case 491/01 R (*on the application of British American Tobacco (Investments) Ltd v Secretary of State for Health* [2002] ECR I-11453, paragraph 123.

³ Case C-411/06 *Commission v Parliament and Council* EU:C:2009:518, paragraph 45; C-130/10 *Parliament v Council* :EU:C:2012:472, paragraph 42; Case C-43/12 *Commission v Parliament and Council* [2014] ECR, paragraph 29.

15.32 Much of the litigation concerning appropriate choice of legal basis has concerned art 114(1) TFEU, formerly art 100a(1) EC,¹ which provides for the adoption of measures for the approximation of the national law having as their object the establishment and functioning of the internal market.

In proceedings instituted by Germany in 1998, the Court of Justice held that the Council had acted in excess of its authority when enacting a Directive governing tobacco advertising.² It was not open to the Union's legislative institutions to adopt the Directive on the basis of art 100a(l) of the EC Treaty (now art 114 TFEU), for to construe that provision as vesting in the Union legislature a general power to regulate the internal market would be incompatible with the principle embodied in art 3b of the EC Treaty (now in substance art 5 TEU) which provides that the Union shall act within the limits of the powers conferred upon it.

¹ S Weatherill, 'Competence Creep and Competence Control' (2004) 23 YEL 1; S Weatherill 'Better Competence Monitoring' (2005) 30 ELRev 23; L Azoulai (ed) The Question of Competence in the European Union (Oxford University Press, 2014).

² Case C-376/98 *Federal Republic of Germany v European Parliament and Council of the European Union* [2000] ECR I-8419, annulling Directive 98/43/EC of the European Parliament and of the Council of 6 July 1998 on the approximation of the laws, regulations and administrative provisions of the Member States relating to the advertising and sponsorship of tobacco products, OJ 1992 L213, p 9. For a further example, see Case C-43/12 *Commission v Parliament and Council*, 6 May 2014 (exchange of information on traffic offences principally concerned with transport safety with no direct link to police co-operation).

15.33 The principle established by the *Tobacco Directive* case and subsequent cases is that a mere finding of disparities between national rules will not be sufficient to justify having recourse to Article 114 TFEU; however, recourse to Article 114 TFEU will be justified where there are differences between the laws, regulations or administrative provisions of the Member States which are such as to obstruct the free movement of goods, services, persons or capital and thus have a direct effect on the functioning of the internal market.¹ Although recourse to Article 114 TFEU as a legal basis is possible if the aim is to prevent the emergence of future obstacles to trade as a result of divergences in national laws, the emergence of such obstacles must be likely and the measure in question must be designed to prevent them.² Any EU harmonising legislation must also be consistent with the principles of subsidiarity and proportionality.

¹ C-376/98 *Germany v Parliament and Council* EU:C:2000:544, paragraphs 84 and 95; C-491/01 *British American Tobacco (Investments) and Imperial Tobacco* EU:C:2002:741, paragraphs 59 and 60; C 434/02 *Arnold André* EU:C:2004:800, paragraph 30; C 210/03 *Swedish Match* EU:C:2004:802, paragraph 29; C 380/03 *Germany v Parliament and Council* EU:C:2006:772, paragraph 37; C 58/08 *Vodafone* EU:C:2010:321, paragraph 32; C-358/14, *Poland v Parliament and Council (Second Tobacco Directive)* EU:C:2016:323, paragraph 32.

² C-358/14, *Poland v Parliament and Council (Second Tobacco Directive)* EU:C:2016:323, paragraph 33.

15.34 Thus in *R (on the application of British American Tobacco (Investments) Ltd v Secretary of State for Health*,[1] the Court of Justice held that art 95(1) EC (now art 114 TFEU) authorised the adoption of a Directive prohibiting the advertising of tobacco in non-static advertising media, such as periodicals. The court reasoned that by establishing common rules in respect of advertising in such media, the Directive would ensure their free circulation within the Union.[2] The court noted that where national restrictions on the sale and marketing of tobacco products varied, such prohibitions were liable to be circumvented by intra-Union trade. It continued:[3]

'In those circumstances, the ban on manufacture provided for by Article 3(1) of the Directive may be regarded as a measure intended to prevent the circumvention of the prohibitions, also laid down by that provision, of placing cigarettes which do not comply with the requirements of that provision in free circulation or of marketing them in the Member States'.

[1] C-491/01, [2002] ECR I-11453.
[2] Cf art 13 of Council Directive 89/552/EEC of 3 October 1989 on the co-ordination of certain provisions laid down by law, regulation or administrative action in Member States concerning the pursuit of television broadcasting activities, OJ 1989 L 298, p 23 and Case C-222/94 *Commission v United Kingdom* [1996] ECR I-4025.
[3] C-491/01, [2002] ECR I-11453, paragraph 90.

15.35 Although one of the aims pursued by the contested Directive was the protection of human health, this did not make it inappropriate to adopt the measure on the basis of art 95(1) EC:

'If examination of a Community act shows that it has a twofold purpose or twofold component and if one of these is identifiable as main or predominant, whereas the other is merely incidental, the act must be founded on a sole legal basis, that is, the one required by the main or predominant purpose or component. Exceptionally, if it is established that the act simultaneously pursues a number of objectives, indissociably linked, without one being secondary and indirect in relation to the other, such an act may be founded on the various corresponding legal bases.

With regard to judicial review of the conditions referred to in the previous paragraph, the Community legislature must be allowed a broad discretion in an area such as that involved in the present case, which entails political, economic and social choices on its part, and in which it is called upon to undertake complex assessments. Consequently, the legality of a measure adopted in that sphere can be affected only if the measure is manifestly inappropriate having regard to the objective which the competent institution is seeking to pursue'.[1]

[1] Case 491/01 [2002] ECR I-11453, paragraphs 94 and 123.

15.36 Once it is established that the Union's legislature has the power under the treaties to adopt legislation, it is necessary to examine the effects of such legislation.

Measures which may be taken by the Council or the Commission

15.37 Article 288 TFEU envisages five types of measure which may be taken by the Council or the Commission. A Regulation is a measure having general application, binding in its entirety and directly applicable[1] in all Member States. A Directive is binding, as to the result to be achieved, upon each Member State to which it is addressed, but it leaves to national authorities the choice of form and methods. A Decision is binding upon those to whom it is addressed. Recommendations and opinions have no binding force.

¹ In other words, such measures are binding without the necessity of any national legislative or administrative transformation into the domestic legal system. See J Winter, 'Direct Applicability and Direct Effect: Two Distinct and Different Concepts in Community Law' (1972) 9 CMLRev 425.

15.38 Articles contained in regulations made under the TFEU or Euratom Treaty must be regarded, at least prima facie, as measures giving rise to rights, powers, liabilities, obligations or restrictions within the meaning of s 2(1) of the 1972 Act. Decisions made under the TFEU or Euratom Treaty likewise give rise, at least prima facie, to rights or (more commonly) obligations within the meaning of that section. Ultimately, although all provisions of a regulation are directly applicable in the sense that they need no implementing legislation to have legal force, it is a question of interpretation to determine whether a particular provision imposes obligations on an individual or simply on the Member State.¹ In the case of directives made under the EC or Euratom Treaty, the obligation to take the necessary implementing measures is on the Member State. Private individuals or legal persons are not bound directly by provisions of directives.²

¹ *R (on the application of Jaspers (Treburley) Ltd v Food Standards Agency* [2013] EWHC (Admin) 1788, paragraphs 35–36.
² Case 152/84 *Marshall v Southampton and South West Hampshire Area Health Authority (Teaching)* [1986] QB 401, [1986] ECR 723.

15.39 Although Article 288 TFEU provides that Member States may determine the appropriate 'form and methods' to implement directives, it is well established that a Member State fails in its duty to implement a directive when the measures that it takes are insufficiently specific, precise and clear to enable those affected thereby to ascertain the full extent of their rights and obligations. In the words of the Court of Justice:

'the provisions of a Directive must be implemented with unquestionable binding force and with the specificity, precision and clarity required in order to satisfy the requirement of legal certainty, under which, in the case of a Directive intended to confer rights on individuals, persons concerned must be enabled to ascertain the full extent of their rights.'¹

Moreover the fact of implementation does not exhaust the effects of the directive. Member States remain bound to ensure full application of the directive even after adoption of implementing measures. Therefore an individual can rely upon the directly effective provisions of the directive both where the directive has not been implemented correctly and also where, though correctly implemented, the implementing provisions are not being applied in such a way as to achieve the result sought by the directive.² Also, before expiry of the deadline for transposition of a directive, Member States are subject to a form of standstill obligation not to introduce legislation falling below the level of protection of rights afforded by the directive or seriously compromising its goals.³

¹ Case C-354/98 *Commission v France* [1999] ECR I-4927, paragraph 11, quoting Case C-197/96 *Commission v France* [1997] ECR I-1489, paragraph 15. The court has on several other occasions made statements to similar effect. See, eg Case 29/84 *Commission v Germany* [1985] ECR 1661, paragraph 23; Case 247/85 *Commission v Belgium* [1987] ECR 3029, paragraph 9; Case C-96/95 *Commission v Germany* [1997] ECR I-1653, headnote; Case C-217/97 *Commission v Germany* [1999] ECR I-5087, paragraph 31.
² Case C-62/00 *Marks & Spencer v Commissioners of Customs and Excise* [2002] ECR I-6325, paragraph 27.
³ Case C-144/04 *Mangold* [2005] ECR I-9981.

15.40 Directives are by definition addressed to Member States; but the European Court of Justice has concluded that it would be incompatible with their binding effect to exclude, in principle, the possibility that the obligation which it imposes may be invoked by those concerned against a Member State, ie the principle of direct effect.¹ In appropriate cases the binding effect of a directive may be invoked against any body, whatever its legal form, which has been made responsible, pursuant to a measure adopted by the State, for providing a public service under the control of the State and has, for that purpose, special powers beyond those which result from the normal rules applicable in relations between individuals.² On the other hand, the principle whereby directives may be relied upon against State entities is based on the binding nature of those measures, which are binding only with regard to the Member States to which they are addressed. For this reason a directive may not impose obligations directly on an individual: its direct effects are said to be 'vertical', not 'horizontal'³ and the directive cannot therefore be relied on against that individual.⁴

¹ Case 41/74 *Van Duyn v Home Office* [1975] Ch 358, [1974] ECR 1337; Case 148/78 *Pubblico Ministero v Ratti* [1979] ECR 1629, Case 8/81 *Becker v Finanzamt-Münster-Innenstadt* [1982] ECR 53. See **15.26–15.28** above.
² Case C-188/89 *Foster v British Gas plc* [1991] 1 QB 405; Case C-282/10 *Dominguez*, 24 January 2012.
³ Case 152/84 *Marshall v Southampton and South West Hampshire Area Health Authority (Teaching)* [1986] QB 401, [1986] ECR 723, [1986] 1 CMLR 688; Case C-91/92 *Faccini Dori v Recreb* [1994] ECR I-3325, [1995] 1 CMLR 665; Case C-192/94 *El Corte Ingles v Rivero* [1996] ECR I-1281, [1996] 2 CMLR 507.
⁴ Joined Cases C397/01 to C403/01 *Pfeiffer and Ors* [2004] ECR I-8835, paragraph 108 and Joined Cases C-387/02, C-391/02, C-403/02 *Criminal Proceedings against Silvio Berlusconi* [2005] ECR I-3565.

Consequences of insufficiently precise measures

15.41 A measure in the form of a Directive or otherwise will not give rise to rights on which a natural or legal person may rely unless it is sufficiently precise, immediate and unconditional to produce direct effects. Indeed, the propensity to give rise to rights for individuals is so closely allied to the propensity to produce direct effects that in its early judgments the European Court of Justice itself drew no distinction between them. It is now clear, however, that the two propensities are not precisely the same.

15.42 In *Costa v Ente Nazionale Energia Elettrica*¹ the ECJ stated of the final sentence of art 93(3) EC (now art 108 TFEU) that it 'creates individual rights' but subsequently in Case 120/73: *Lorenz v Germany*[2] the court explained its earlier judgment as follows:

'It has already been decided in the judgment of 15 July 1964 . . . that the prohibition on implementation referred to in the last sentence of Article 93(3) has a direct effect *and* gives rise to rights in favour of individuals which national courts are bound to respect'.

[1] [1964] ECR 585 at 596.
[2] [1973] ECR 1471 at 1483, paragraph 8.

15.43 The Advocate-General's Opinion in *Costa v Ente Nazionale Energia Elettrica* explains why a measure which is insufficiently precise, immediate and unconditional is unsuitable for determination by national courts. Such a provision may well entail obligations; but their nature is such as to make them unsuitable for national adjudication:

'As far as the question is concerned whether "any such plan is compatible with the Common Market having regard to Article 92", on which the possible infringement of the Treaty depends, one need only read Article 92, especially paragraph (3), to be convinced that this question of compatibility implies here again a delicate value-judgment, requiring a balancing of the political and economic interests of the State concerned with the requirements of a common market. This judgment cannot possibly be left to the sole appraisal of national courts without any intervention by Community organs or by governments. It is my submission therefore that it is not possible to read the provisions of Article 93 as self-executing'.

15.44 A finding that an article of the treaty or a provision of a directive produces direct effects, is the expression of its suitability for determination by national courts. Precision, immediacy and unconditionality are the indispensable characteristics of a measure which is capable of being enforced before a court. The propensity to give rise to rights for individuals is the normal but not the inevitable consequence of that justiciability.

15.45 Thus in *Bulk Oil (Zug) AG v Sun International and Sun Trading Co*[1] one of the questions arising was whether it was open to a party to national proceedings to rely upon a provision in a Council Decision which required Member States to give prior notice to Union institutions and to consult them before amending their rules governing exports to non-member countries. The Commission contended that the obligation to notify is not a rule of European Union law which has direct effect in the sense of the court's judgment in *Costa v Ente Nazionale Energia Elettrica* since the 1961 decision does not oblige the Member State to obtain or even seek approval for the measures which it envisages.[2] In dealing with this issue, the European Court of Justice was careful to eschew any mention of the phrase 'direct effect'. It stated that the obligation in question:

'concerns only the institutional relationship between a Member State and the Community and the other Member States. In proceedings before national courts between natural or legal persons such persons cannot attack a policy or measure adopted by the Member State on the basis that the Member State has failed to fulfil its obligation to inform the other Member States and the Commission beforehand. Such a failure does not therefore create rights which national courts must protect'.

[1] [1986] ECR 559, [1986] 2 CMLR 732.

15.46 The issue there, on proper analysis, was not a question of direct effect. Indeed, there was no basis for challenging the precision, immediacy or unconditionality of the Decision. The issue was whether the authors intended to create rights for individuals which were enforceable before national courts.¹

¹ This point appears with particular clarity from the Opinion of the Advocate-General in that case. Sir Gordon Slynn. He stated, at p 575:
'If . . . I had come to the view that there was an obligation to notify or consult under Articles 2 and 3 of Regulation No 2603/69 I should not have considered that such a breach invalidated the policy, for the reasons given by Mr Advocate-General Reischl in the final paras of his Opinion in Cases 181 and 229/78 *Van Passen v Staatssecretaris van Financien* . . . Nor do I consider that, if it were possible to read into the Agreement, by virtue of articles 4, 11 and 25, a bar on restrictions on exports, such obligation would be sufficiently clear and precise to be directly applicable between two individuals litigating in national courts'.
Apparently he did not find a lack of clarity or precision in the wording actually included in the instrument in question, which imposed an obligation to consult. The lack of clarity or precision capable of preventing it from producing direct effects was in the imaginary prohibition on exports pending the outcome of the consultation. Unlike the obligation to consult, such a prohibition could arise only by inference.

15.47 The same point emerges from the opinion of Mr Advocate-General Reischl in *Van Passen v Staatssecretaris van Financien*.¹ One of the questions there considered was whether an individual can rely before a national court on a Member State's failure to engage in the consultation envisaged in the Second Council Directive on the harmonisation of turnover tax.² Submissions on the direct effectiveness of the provisions in question were made by the parties to the main action and by the Federal Republic of Germany. The Advocate-General described those submissions and continued:

'In my view these observations on the direct effect of the Second Council Directive need concern us no further. In the present case it is solely a question of interpreting the Directive as to the consequences of failure to comply with the obligation to consult . . . the obligation to consult concerns only the legal relations between the Commission and the Member States and does not affect the interests of individuals'.

¹ [1979] ECR 2063.
² Council Directive 67/228/EEC of 11 April 1967, OJ Sp Ed 1967, p 16.

15.48 Thus, direct effectiveness and the grant of rights to individuals are separate issues, although closely related. A measure itself cannot give rise to rights for individuals before national courts unless it is directly effective; conversely, it is possible to encounter provisions which are sufficiently precise, immediate and unconditional to be directly effective but which only affect the legal relations between the Commission and the Member States and will not affect the interests of individuals.

15.49 The principal consequence of the distinction between direct effectiveness and intention to give rise to rights for individuals is demonstrated in *Francovich and Bonifaci v Italian Republic*.¹ In that case, the ECJ concluded that Council Directive 80/987 on the protection of employees in the event of insolvency² failed to produce direct effects since it did not identify the person liable to provide the guarantee: in that respect, it was insufficiently precise.

Nevertheless, the court indicated that the Directive was intended to confer rights on individuals. Against the submissions of Germany, the Netherlands, Italy and the UK, it held that the Member State should be held liable for failing to implement the Directive within the prescribed period where the result prescribed by the Directive entails the grant of rights to individuals; and it is possible to identify the content of those rights on the basis of the Directive; and there is a causal link between the breach of the Member State's obligation and the loss and damage suffered by the injured parties.[3] The breach of EU law must also be of sufficient seriousness to warrant an action for reparation. Such seriousness[4] can be established by a failure to transpose a directive in time[5] but, when the argument is one of incorrect transposition in circumstances where there is a discretion or policy choice to be exercised, it must be shown that there has been a manifest and grave disregard by the Member State of the limits of its powers.[6] Reduced or a closely circumscribed discretion will give rise to a correspondingly greater risk of a finding of liability.[7]

[1]   [1991] ECR I-5357, [1992] IRLR 84. See further **15.106** below.
[2]   20 October 1980, OJ 1980 L283/24.
[3]   See paragraph **15.100** et seq below.
[4]   Cases C-46/96 and C-48/93 *Brasserie du Pecheur* [1996] ECR I-1029. See also the judgment of Lord Clyde in *R v Secretary of State for Transport ex p Factortame (No 5)* [2000] 1 AC 524 for a discussion of the factors relevant to assessing the seriousness; applied for example in *Delaney v Secretary of State for Transport* [2014] EWHC 1785 (QB) approved in [2015] EWCA Civ 172.
[5]   Case C-178/94 *Dillenkofer v Germany* [1996] ECR I-4845, paragraph 29.
[6]   Joined cases C-283/94, C-291/94, C-292/94 *Denkavit* [1996] ECR I-4845; C-392/93 *R v HM Treasury ex p BT* [1996] ECR I-1631.
[7]   *Delaney v Secretary of State for Transport* [2014] EWHC 1785 (QB) finding liability on the basis of *Francovich*.

15.50 *Francovich* liability does not constitute an exception to, or departure from, the proposition that a provision in the Treaties or their subordinate legislation does not give rise to individual rights enforceable in national courts unless that provision produces direct effects. Any rights conferred by European Union law on the litigants in *Francovich* arose not from the terms of Council Directive 80/987, but from a general principle of European Union law that national courts whose duty it is to apply the provisions of European Union law must ensure the full effectiveness of those rules.[1] Indeed even the decisions of the courts themselves are capable of giving rise to liability under this principle where the legislation or case law was clear.[2]

[1]   Case 106/77 *Amministrazione delle Finanze dello Stato v Simmenthal* [1978] ECR 629, paragraph 16; Case C-213/89 *Factortame* [1990] ECR I-2433. The treaty basis for this principle is found in art 4(3) TEU (formerly EC Treaty, art 10): Case 6/60 *Humblet v Belgium* [1960] ECR 559. See also Article 19 TEU with regard to effective remedies.
[2]   Case C-224/01 *Koebler v Austria* [2003] ECR I-10239, paragraph 29. Case C-160/14 *Ferreira da Silva* EU:C:2015;565.

GENERAL PRINCIPLES OF EUROPEAN UNION LAW

Applicability of general principles

15.51 The sources of law set out above are supplemented by a corpus of general principles of European Union law. These general principles have been drawn primarily from the legal systems and constitutions of the Member States,[1] although references to these principles can also be identified in the founding treaties.[2] General principles are binding both on community institutions[3] and on Member States when implementing Union legislation or acting in the exercise of powers conferred or reserved by Union law.[4] Thus, the general principles may for instance be relied upon to establish the illegality of a Union act under TFEU art 340,[5] or as a ground for annulment of a legislative or administrative measure under Article 263 TFEU,[6] or as a basis for infringement proceedings against a Member State under Article 258 TFEU,[7] or in interpreting provisions of Union law.[8] The list of general principles is not closed, but a number of principles have become particularly well recognised, amongst them: the principles of equality or non-discrimination, proportionality, legal certainty, legitimate expectations, sincere or loyal cooperation, and the protection of fundamental rights.[9]

[1] Tridimas, The General Principles of EC Law (2006) 2nd edn, OUP; Arnull, *The European Union and its Court of Justice* (2006) 2nd edn, OUP.
[2] See, for example, arts 2–6 TEU, arts 2–17 TFEU and arts 1–3 of the Euratom Treaty, and art 340 of the TFEU and art 188 of the Euratom Treaty for express reference to the general principles.
[3] For example, Joined Cases 17, 20/61 *Klöckner-Werke AG and Hoesch AG v High Authority* [1962] ECR 325. First Les Verts case (294/85); [1986] ECR 1365, paragraph 23.
[4] For example, Case C-144/04 *Mangold v Helm* [2005] ECR I-9981 at paragraph 75. See Schermers and Waelbroeck, Judicial Protection in the European Union (2001) 6th edn, Kluwer at paragraph 77.
[5] Schermers and Waelbroeck, Judicial Protection in the European Union (2001) 6th edn, Kluwer at paragraph 59.
[6] For example, *Ireland v Commission* [1987] ECR 5041.
[7] See Case C 257/86 *Commission v Italy* [1988] ECR 3249; Case C-58/90 *Commission v Italy* [1991] ECR-I-4193; Case 104/86 *Commission v Italy* [1988] ECR 1799.
[8] Joined Cases C-90/90 and C-91/90 *Neu and Others* [1991] ECR-I-3617 at paragraph 12.
[9] See K Lenaerts, 'Interlocking Legal Orders in the European Union and Comparative Law' (2003) 52 ICLQ 873.

Equality/Non-Discrimination[1]

[1] For discussion of similar principles in the law of England and Wales and of Scotland, see **8.97** et seq and **22.69** et seq.

15.52 The principle of equality[2] is one of the fundamental principles of European Union law. It requires that similar situations shall not be treated differently and that different situations shall not be treated in the same way, unless such treatment is objectively justified.[3] Numerous provisions of the Treaties contain reference to the principle of equality or to the prohibition of discrimination, both in general terms and in specific contexts;[4] however, the general principle remains useful, both as a safety net to deal with any lacunae in the written texts and as an expression of a fundamental constitutional guarantee.[5] The principle applies to the relationship between the Union institutions and its officials[6] and provides grounds for review of measures adopted by the Union.[7] The principle has also been held to apply to Member States acting within the scope of Union law.[8]

[2] See B Sundberg-Weitman, *Discrimination on Grounds of Nationality: Free Movement of Workers and Freedom of Establishment under the EEC Treaty*, (1977) North Holland; S Kon 'Aspects of Reverse Discrimination in Community Law', 6 EL Rev (1981) 75.

3   Case C 354/95 *R v Minister for Agriculture, Fisheries and Food, ex p National Farmers' Union*
    [1997] ECR- I-4559 at paragraph 61; Case C-152/09 *Grootes* [2010] ECR I-11285,
    paragraph 66; and Case C-236/09*Association belge des Consommateurs Test-Achats and
    Others* [2011] ECR I-773, paragraph 28; Case C 401/11 *Blanka Soukupová v Ministerstvo
    zemědělství* EU:C:2013:223 at paragraph 29.
4   See, eg Articles 20 and 21 of the Charter of Fundamental Rights of the European Union;
    Articles 8, 10, 18, 19, 36, 37, 40, 45 and 95 of the TFEU.
5   Tridimas, *The General Principles of EC Law* (2006) 2nd edn, OUP, Chapter 2.
6   Case 20/71 *Sabbatini v European Parliament* [1972] ECR 345; Case T-60/92 *Noonan
    v Commission* [1996] ECR-II-215.
7   Case 162/82 *Cousin* [1983] ECR 1101; Case C-372/06 *Asda Stores Ltd v Commissioners of
    Her Majesty's Revenue and Customs* [2007] ECR I-11223.
8   Case C-144/04 *Mangold v Rüdiger Helm* [2005] ECR-I-9981.

Proportionality

15.53 The principle of proportionality[1] has now been enshrined in Article 5(4)
TEU, which provides that, 'Under the principle of proportionality, the content
and form of Union action shall not exceed what is necessary to achieve the
objectives of this Treaty', but it had been developed by the Court of Justice as
a fundamental principle well before this. The principle applies to the acts of
Union institutions, and also to Member States when implementing Union law
or when acting within the field of Union law,[2] for instance by imposing limits
on the rights conferred under Union law.[3] The principle of proportionality, as
formulated by the Court of Justice,[4] incorporates a three-stage test: (i) the
measures adopted must not exceed the limits of what is appropriate and
necessary in order to attain the objectives legitimately pursued by the
legislation in question; (ii) when there is a choice between several appropriate
measures, recourse must be had to the least onerous; and (iii) the disadvantages
caused must not be disproportionate to the aims pursued.[5] The existence of the
third limb, sometimes referred to as proportionality stricto sensu, is debatable.[6]

1   For discussion of the scrutiny required to be undertaken by the national court where European
    Union law is involved, see **15.101** et seq below. Further discussion of the principle of
    proportionality as developed by the European Court of Justice, the European Court of Human
    Rights, and national courts in Germany and France, will be found in Chapter 8. For general
    discussion of proportionality in relation to the law of England and Wales and of Scotland, see
    Chapter 9 and **22.74**.
2   Tridimas, *The General Principles of EC Law*, 2nd edn, 2006, OUP, Chapters 3 to 5.
3   Case C-198/01 *Jippes v Minister van Landbouw, Natuurbeheer en Visserij* [2001] ECR
    I-5689; The principle of proportionality also applies to national measures falling within the
    scope of EU law: see the opinion of Advocate General Sharpston in Case C-427/06 *Bartsch v
    Bosch und Siemens Hausgerate (BSH) Altersfursorge GmbH* [2008] ECR I-7245 para 69.
4   Case C-413/99 *Baumbast v Secretary of State for the Home Department* [2002] ECR I-7091;
    Case C-524/06 *Huber v Germany* [2008] ECR I-9705.
5   Case C-343/09 *Afton Chemical v Secretary of State for Transport* [2010] ECR I-7027; Joined
    Cases C-581/10 and 629/10 *Nelson v Deutsche Lufthansa* EU:C:2012:657; Case C-331/88 *R
    v Ministry of Agriculture, Fisheries and Food Ex p. Federation Europeene de la Sante Animale
    (FEDESA)* [1990] ECR I-4023 applied in *R (on the application of) Lumsdon v Legal Services
    Board* [2015] UKSC 41; [2016] AC 697.
6   *R (on the application of) Lumsdon v Legal Services Board* [2015] UKSC 41; [2016] AC 697
    at paragraph 33.

15.54 The proportionality principle is a flexible tool.[1] The court's case law
applying the proportionality principle varies according to context.[2] There are

broadly three types of cases: the review of EU measures, the review of national measures relying on derogations from general EU rights, and the review of national measures implementing EU law. First, proportionality as a ground of review of EU measures is concerned with 'the balancing of private interests adversely affected by such measures against the public interests which the measures are intended to promote'.[3] In that context, proportionality functions as a check on the exercise of public power and cases in which measures adopted by the EU legislator or administration in the public interest are held by the EU judicature to be disproportionate interferences with private interests are likely to be relatively infrequent. Second, proportionality as a ground of review of national measures, has been applied most frequently to measures interfering with the fundamental freedoms guaranteed by the EU Treaties, where the court is concerned, primarily, with 'whether a member state can justify an interference with a freedom guaranteed in the interests of promoting the integration of the internal market and the related social values which lie at the heart of the EU project'.[4] In this context, the principle of proportionality functions as a means of preventing disguised discrimination and unnecessary barriers to market integration and the court applies the principle more strictly. Third, where member states adopt measures implementing EU legislation, the proportionality principle generally functions as a conventional public law principle because member states are seeking to contribute rather than limit the integration of the internal market.[5]

[1] See G de Búrca, '*The Principle of Proportionality and its application in EC Law*' (1993) 13 *YEL 105*.
[2] *R (on the application of) Lumsdon v Legal Services Board* [2015] UKSC 41; [2016] AC 697 at paragraph 34.
[3] *R (on the application of) Lumsdon v Legal Services Board* [2015] UKSC 41; [2016] AC 697 at paragraph 36.
[4] *R (on the application of) Lumsdon v Legal Services Board* [2015] UKSC 41; [2016] AC 697 at paragraph 37.
[5] *R (on the application of) Lumsdon v Legal Services Board* [2015] UKSC 41; [2016] AC 697 at paragraph 38.

15.55 In areas where institutions have a wide legislative discretion or where they are required to undertake complex assessments or to make political, economic or social choices, the legality of a measure can only be affected if it is 'manifestly inappropriate' to the objective pursued.[1] Member States implementing measures in the context of such complex or political areas also benefit from a wide margin of appreciation.[2] In other areas, the Court of Justice may apply more exacting standards, particularly in relation to acts or measures of Union institutions[3] or Member States[4] which restrict or seek to balance the scope of fundamental rights. National measures which derogate from the fundamental freedoms (free movement of goods, the free movement of workers, freedom of establishment, freedom to provide services, and the free movement of capital) come under more scrutiny and the court's approach, in the context of proportionality, is that they must be suitable for securing the attainment of the objective which they pursue and they must not go beyond what is necessary in order to attain it.[5] The position was summarised by Advocate General Sharpston in her opinion in *European Commission v Kingdom of Spain* in which she identified that, where there is a choice of equally effective measures, it is necessary to establish that no other measures could have been equally effective but less restrictive of the freedom in question.[6] The justification for restriction tends to be examined in detail. An economic or social justification must be supported by evidence.[7]

[1]   Case C-331/88 *R v Minister of Agriculture, Fisheries and Food and Secretary of State for Health, ex p FEDESA* [1990] ECR- I-4023; Case C-491/01*R v Secretary of State for Health, Ex parte British American Tobacco (Investments) Ltd and Imperial Tobacco Ltd* [2003] All ER (EC) 604; Case C-343/09 *Afton Chemical v Secretary of State for Transport* [2010] ECR- I-7027; Case C-343/07 *Bavaria NV v Bayerischer Brauerbund e V* [2009] ECR I-05491; *R (on the application of) Lumsdon v Legal Services Board* [2015] UKSC 41; [2016] AC 697 at paragraphs 40–49.

[2]   Case C-4/96 *Northern Ireland Fish Producers' Organisation Ltd v Department of Agriculture for Northern Ireland* [1998] ECR-I-681.

[3]   Case C-293/12 *Digital Rights Ireland Ltd v Minister for Communications, Marine and Natural Resources* ECLI:EU:C:2014:238; Case C-283/11 *Sky Österreich GmbH v Österreichischer Rundfunk* ECLI:EU:C:2013:28.

[4]   Case C-413/99 *Baumbast v Secretary of State for the Home Department* [2002] ECR-I-7091; C-165/14 *Marin v Administración del Estado* EU:C:2016:675.

[5]   Case C-55/94 *Gebard v Consiglio dell'Ordine degli Avvocati e Procuratori di Milano* [1996] 1 CMLR 603 at paragraph 37 *applied in R (on the application of) Lumsdon v Legal Services Board* [2015] UKSC 41; [2016] AC 697 at paragraph 52.

[6]   Case C-400/08*European Commission v Kingdom of Spain* [2011] ECR I-1915 at paragraph 89.

[7]   Case C-319/06*European Commission v Grand Duchy of Luxembourg* [2008] ECR I-4323 at paragraph 51.

Legal certainty[1]

[1]   For discussion of similar principles in the law of England and Wales and of Scotland, see **8.42**, **13.11** and **22.69**.

15.56 The principle of legal certainty, a facet of the rule of law, requires that 'Legal rules be clear and precise, and aim to ensure that situations and legal relationships governed by Community law remain foreseeable'[2] and that an individual must 'be able to ascertain unequivocally what his rights and obligations are and take steps accordingly'.[3] In particular, rules imposing charges on the taxpayer must be clear and precise so that she may know without ambiguity what his rights and obligations are and may take steps accordingly: any ambiguity in such measures should be resolved in favour of the taxpayer.[4] More generally, Union measures should only be enforceable against individuals once the relevant legislative texts have been published[5] and those affected have had the opportunity to acquaint themselves with the measure.[6] Likewise, the principle will usually operate to strike down measures which are retroactive, although retroactive legislation is exceptionally permitted where, 'it clearly follows from their terms or general scheme that such was the intention of the legislature'[7] or 'where the purpose to be achieved so demands and where the legitimate expectations of those concerned are duly respected.'[8] Conversely, in exceptional circumstances, the application of the principle may lead the Court of Justice to limit or to exclude the usual retroactive effect of a ruling.[9] The principle of legal certainty applies to Member States, so for instance rules adopted in accordance with Union law must be clear and certain.[10] However, Member States may also rely upon the principle against the Union institutions, in particular in relation to issues of public finance.[11]

2   Case C-63/93 *Duff v Minister of Agriculture and Food Ireland* [1996] ECR-I-569; Case C-199/03 *Ireland v Commission* [2005] ECR-I-8027.
3   Case C-143/93 *Gebroeders van Es Douane Agenten BV v Inspecteur der Invoerrechten en Accijnzen* [1996] ECR-I-431; Joined Cases C-581/10 and 629/10 *Nelson v Deutsche Lufthansa AG.* ECLI:EU:C:2012:657.
4   Case 169/80 *Administration des Douanes v Gondrand Frères* [1981] ECR 1931.
5   Case C-345/06 *Gottfried Heinrich* [2009] ECR-I-659.
6   Case 98/78 *Racke v Hauptzollamt Mainz* [1979] ECR 69.
7   Case T-357/02 *Freistaat Sachsen v Commission* [2007] ECR II-1261.
8   Case 98/78 *Racke v Hauptzollamt Mainz* [1979] ECR 69.
9   Case 43/75 *Defrenne v SABENA* [1976] 455.
10 Case 102/79 *Commission v Belgium* [1980] ECR I-6267. Case C-144/14 *Cabinet Medical Veterinar Dr. Tomoiagă Andrei v Direcţia Generală Regională a Finanţelor Publice Cluj Napoca prin Administraţia Judeţeană a Finanţelor Publice Maramureş* EU:C:2015:452 at paragraph 35.
11 Case 44/81 *Germany v Commission* [1982] ECR 1855; Case C-84/96 *Kingdom of the Netherlands v Commission* [1999] ECR I-6547 at paragraph 26.

Legitimate expectations

15.57 The principle of legitimate expectations[1] 'is the corollary of the principle of legal certainty'[2] and protects individuals who have relied in good faith upon assurances given by Union institutions. The classic example is found in *Mulder v Minister for Agriculture and Fisheries*,[3] in which a dairy farmer, who had suspended production of dairy products under a non-marketing agreement, was subsequently refused a quota when the non-marketing period came to an end on the grounds that his production in the previous year had been nil. The Court of Justice held that where a producer, ' . . . has been encouraged by a Community measure to suspend marketing for a limited period in the general interest and against the payment of a premium, he may legitimately expect not to be subject, upon the expiry of his undertaking, to restrictions which specifically affect him precisely because he availed himself of the possibilities offered by the Community provisions.' The principle is frequently invoked and, although often unsuccessful, it is capable of leading to significant remedies, for example the annulment of Union law measures,[4] precluding the Commission from relying on a measure until the effects of the measure have been clarified and notified to those affected,[5] and a right to non-contractual damages against the Union institutions.[6] A legitimate expectation will not generally be protected if the institution, in giving the relevant assurance, has acted contrary to Union law. Likewise,[7] the complainant is required to act with 'clean hands' and so will not be entitled to protection if they knew (or ought to have known) that the assurance was illegal or might be withdrawn,[8] or if they themselves have breached applicable Union laws.[9] Furthermore, 'economic operators are not justified in having a legitimate expectation that an existing situation which is capable of being altered by the Community institutions in the exercise of their discretionary power will be maintained, particularly in an area such as that of the common organisation of the markets, the objective of which involves constant adjustment to reflect changes in economic circumstances'.[10]

1   For discussion of similar principles in the law of England and Wales and of Scotland, see **8.80** et seq and **22.79**.
2   Case T-471/11 *Éditions Odile Jacob SAS v Commission* EU:C:2012:555 at para 90.

3   *J Mulder v Minister van Landbouwen Visserij*, Case 120/86 [1988] ECR 2344.
4   Case C-152/88 *Sofrimport v Commission* [1990] ECR I-2477.
5   Case T-81/95 *Interhotel-Sociedade Internacional de Hotéis SARL v Commission* [1997] ECR
    II-1265.
6   Case C-104/89 *Mulder v Council and Commission* [1992] ECR I-3061.
7   Case C-188/92 *Thyssen v Commission* [1983] ECR 3721.
8   Case T-13/99 *Pfizer Animal Health v Council* [2002] ECR II-3305.
9   Case T-234/94 *Industria Pesquera Campos v Commission* [1996] ECR II-247.
10 Case C-310/04 *Kingdom of Spain v Council* [2006] ECR I-07285; Case C-335/09, *Republic
    of Poland v Commission* EU:C:2012:385.

Fundamental rights

15.58 It is well established by the case law of the Court of Justice that both EU institutions and Member States, when acting within the scope of Community law, are bound to respect fundamental rights as general principles of EU law.[1] 'For that purpose, the Court draws inspiration from the constitutional traditions common to the Member States and from the guidelines supplied by international instruments for the protection of human rights on which the Member States have collaborated or to which they are signatories..'[2] Until the entry into force of the Lisbon Treaty amendments, the ECHR was not directly applicable in Union law but rather an important source of fundamental rights. Article 6(3) of the Lisbon Treaty now expressly provides that 'Fundamental rights, as guaranteed by the [ECHR] and as they result from the constitutional traditions common to the Member States, shall constitute general principles of the Union's law.' Article 6 further introduces two potentially significant innovations. First the Union shall accede to the European Convention for the Protection of Human Rights.[3] Secondly, Article 6(1) TEU provides that the Charter of Fundamental Rights of the European Union 'shall have the same legal value as the Treaties'.[4] The provisions of the Charter are, under Article 51(1), addressed to Union institutions and to Member States when implementing Union law. However, in this context, 'implementing' has been given a broad interpretation.[5] The rights, freedoms and principles in the Charter shall be interpreted 'with due regard to' the explanations referred to in the Charter[6] but the Charter shall not extend in any way the competences of the Union as defined in the Treaties.[7] The intent appears to be to avoid the Charter becoming a vehicle through which the Court of Justice would acquire general human rights jurisdiction,[8] albeit that certain rights derived from the ECHR would be more broadly applicable than under the ECHR itself.[9] Protocol No 30 to the TFEU makes special provision for the status of the Charter for the United Kingdom and Poland. This has wrongly been described as an 'opt-out'. The Court of Justice has explained the effect of Protocol 30 in *NS v Secretary of State for the Home Department*[10]: ' . . . Protocol (No 30) does not call into question the applicability of the Charter in the United Kingdom or in Poland, a position which is confirmed by the recitals in the preamble to that protocol. Thus, according to the third recital . . . Article 6 TEU requires the Charter to be applied and interpreted by the courts of Poland and of the United Kingdom strictly in accordance with the explanations referred to in that article. In addition, according to the sixth recital . . . the Charter reaffirms the rights, freedoms and principles recognized in the Union and makes those rights more visible, but does not create new rights or principles. In those circumstances, Article 1(1) of Protocol (No 30) explains Article 51 of the

Charter with regard to the scope thereof and does not intend to exempt the Republic of Poland or the United Kingdom from the obligation to comply with the provisions of the Charter or to prevent a court from one of those Member States from ensuring compliance with those provisions.' In the light of this decision, Mostyn J, in *R (AB) v Secretary of State for the Home Department*[11] has expressed the view that the Charter is now a part of United Kingdom domestic law.

[1] For recent examples, see Case C-300/11 *ZZ v Secretary of State for the Home Department* [2014] I.N.L.R. 368 at paragraph 60 and Joined Cases C-402/05P and C-415/05P *Kadi (Spain, interveners) al Barakaat International Foundation v EU Council* [2008] ECR I-6351 at paragraph 283; Case C-584/10P *Commission v Kadi* (decision of 18 July 2013).

[2] Case C-305/05 *Ordre des Barreaux Francophones et Germanophones v Conseil des Ministres (Conseil des Barreaux de L'Union europeenne, intervening)* [2007] ECR I-5305, paragraph 29 (right to a fair trial, deriving inter alia from Art 6 ECHR, constitutes a fundamental right which the EU respects as a general principle under the former Article 6(2) TEU); *Tariq v Home Office* [2011] UKSC 35 at paragraph 23.

[3] Article 6(2) TEU. A Draft Accession Treaty was concluded on 10 June 2013.

[4] See Hofmann and Mihaescu, 'The Relation between the Charter's fundamental rights and the unwritten general principles of EU law: good administration as the test case', 2013 ECL Review 73.

[5] Case C-617/10 *Åkerberg Fransson; Secretary of State for the Home Department v R. (Davis and Others)* [2015] EWCA Civ 1185 at paragraph 92.

[6] OJ [2007] C 303, p 2. The explanations were originally prepared under the authority of the Praesidium of the Convention which drafted the Charter, albeit that they have since been updated.

[7] Article 6(1) TEU.

[8] Cf. the explanations to Article 51 which refer to the case law on fundamental rights binding Member States when they act 'in the scope of Union law' whereas the text of Article 51(1) of the Charter says 'when they are implementing Union law'.

[9] See eg the guarantee of a fair and public hearing in Article 47 which is not limited to disputes relating to civil law rights and obligations.

[10] Joined Cases C-411/10 and C-493/10 [2011] ECR I-13905, paragraphs 119–120.

[11] [2013] EWHC 3453 (Admin), paragraphs 13–14.

Sincere cooperation

15.59 Article 4(3) TEU provides that 'Pursuant to the principle of sincere cooperation, the Union and Member States shall, in full mutual respect, assist each other in carrying out tasks which flow from the Treaties.' The previous treaty provisions had imposed the duty of sincere cooperation only on Member States, although the Court of Justice had earlier emphasised that the duty also imposed on the Union institutions 'reciprocal duties of sincere cooperation with Member States'.[1] The duty of sincere cooperation, as it relates to Union institutions, in particular requires cooperation with the judicial authorities of Member States, for instance in complying with requests for disclosure of documents or obeying interlocutory orders of national courts.[2] As far as Member States are concerned, the principle of sincere cooperation requires them to take any appropriate measure to fulfill any obligations arising from Union law or the acts of Union institutions and to assist in the achievement of the Union's objectives.[3]

[1] Case C-230/81 *Luxembourg v European Parliament* [1983] ECR 255; Joined Cases C-36/97 and C-37/97 *Kellinghusen (Hilmar) v Amt Für Land und Wasserwirtschaft Kiel; Ketelsen (Ernst Detlef) v Amt Für Land und Wasserwirtschaft Kiel* [1998] ECR I-6337.

² Case C-2/88 *Imm JJ Zwartveld (JJ), Re* [1990] ECR I-3365. *Ibrahimi v Secretary of State for the Home Department* [2016] EWHC 2049 (Admin) at paragraph 81; *R (on the applicaton of Newby Foods Ltd) v FSA (No.7)* [2014] EWHC (Admin) 1340, [2014] 1 WLR 4589.
³ Case 14/83 *Von Colson* [1984] ECR 1891.

Administrative or procedural fairness

15.60 The principles of administrative or procedural fairness acknowledged by the CJEU originate both in the national laws of the Member States and in the ECHR, as an expression of the common legal tradition of the Member States.¹ It has long been recognised as a general principle of EU law.² Among the rules originating in national law and acknowledged by the ECJ is *audi alteram partem*: persons whose interests are affected by a decision-making body must be given an opportunity to make their point of view known.³ Among the rules originating in the ECHR is the requirement of judicial control: Member States are under an obligation to ensure that rights conferred by European Union law can be effectively relied upon before national courts by the persons concerned.⁴ The concept of good administration has now also been recognised as a binding fundamental right under Article 41 of the Charter. Article 41(1) provides that 'Every person has the right to have his or her affairs handled impartially, fairly and within a reasonable time by the institutions, bodies, offices and agencies of the Union.' Article 41(2) elaborates that this right includes (i) the right of every person to be heard before any individual measure which would affect them is taken; (ii) the right of every person to have access to their file; and (iii) the obligation of the administration to give reasons for its decisions. Further, Article 41(3) provides that every person has the right to have the Union make good any damage caused by its institutions or servants in the performance of their duties. However, Article 41 appears to be considerably narrower in scope than the general principle of good administration. In particular, the general principle extends to Member States acting within the scope of Union law⁵ and to general measures as opposed to individual decision-making.

¹ Rome, 4 November 1950, Cmnd 8969.
² Joined Cases 33/79 and 75/79 *Kuhner v EC Commission* [1980] ECR 1677.
³ Case 17/74 *Transocean Marine Paint Association v EC Commission* [1974] ECR 1063 at 1080: Joined Cases 100–103/80 *Musique Diffusion Francaise SA v EC Commission* [1983] ECR 1825 at 1881.
⁴ Case 222/84 *Johnston v Chief Constable of the Royal Ulster Constabulary* [1986] ECR 1651 at 1682.
⁵ Case T-450/93 *Lisrestal – Organizacao Gestao de Restaurantes Colectivos Lda v EC Commission* [1994] ECR II-1177.

INTERNATIONAL LAW AS A SOURCE OF EU LAW

15.61 The EU enjoys legal personality under international law, as an international organisation.¹ It thereby has rights and duties under international law distinct from the rights and duties of its constituent Member States; is entitled to bring a claim in international law for the purpose of maintaining its own rights; and is presumed to be responsible (to the exclusion of Member State responsibility) for the fulfilment of its obligations under international law.² Further, the EU has the power to conclude agreements which are subject to the law of treaties.[3]

[1] Art 47 TEU; Case 22-70 *Commission v Council (AETR/ERTA)* [1971] ECR 263. The capacity of an international organisation to possess international legal personality was established, as a matter of international law, by the International Court of Justice in *Reparation for Injuries Suffered in the Service of the United Nations, Advisory Opinion* (1949) ICJ Reports, 174. Art 335 TFEU provides that, within each of the Member States, 'the Union shall enjoy the most extensive legal capacity accorded to legal persons under their laws'. Declaration 24 concerning the legal personality of the European Union confirms 'that the fact that the European Union has a legal personality will not in any way authorise the Union to legislate or to act beyond the competences conferred upon it by the Member States in the Treaties'.

[2] *JH Rayner (Mincing Lane) Ltd v Department of Trade and Industry* [1989] Ch. 72 (CA), [1990] 2 A.C. 418 (HL).

[3] The EU's power to conclude agreements with third countries and/or international organisations is expressly provided for by art 216 TFEU. See in this context the Vienna Convention on the Law of Treaties between States and International Organizations or between International Organizations (not yet entered into force) (25 ILM 543 (1986)).

15.62 The EU's power to enter into treaties is limited by the principle of conferral of powers: since the EU has conferred powers only, it must tie an international agreement to a Treaty provision which empowers it to approve such a measure. If an incorrect legal basis is specified, this is liable to invalidate the act concluding the agreement and so vitiate the Union's consent to be bound by the agreement it has signed.[1] In such a case, the international agreement will remain binding on the Union as a matter of international law.[2] The EU is in these circumstances required to re-enact its adherence to the agreement, using the correct legal basis;[3] or, if there is no legal basis capable of authorising it, to denounce the agreement.[4]

[1] *Opinion 2/00 on the Cartagena Protocol* [2001] ECR I-9713, paragraph 5; C 370/07 *Commission v Council* [2009] ECR I-8917, paragraph 47; art 218(11) TFEU.

[2] See Article 46 of the 1969 Vienna Convention on the Law of Treaties (1155 UNTS 331); *Opinion 2/15 on the Free Trade Agreement between the European Union and the Republic of Singapore (EUSFTA)*, Opinion of Advocate General Sharpston EU:C:2016:992, paragraph 84, footnote 33.

[3] Case C-327/91 *France v Commission (Re EC-US Anti-Trust Agreement)* [1994] ECR I-3641, paragraphs 22-25; Case C-94/03 *Commission v Council (Rotterdam Convention)* [2006] ECR I-1.

[4] Cases C-317 and 318/04, *European Parliament v Council (PNR)* [2006] ECR I-4721.

15.63 The Union's competence with respect to foreign affairs is divided between the Common Foreign and Security Policy (CFSP) under Title V (arts 21–46) of the TEU, and Part V (arts 205–222) of the TFEU which sets out the Union's remaining external competences. Both are intended to pursue the same objectives, defined by art 21 TEU.[1] The CFSP is a largely intergovernmental regime led by the European Council as well as by the High Representative of the Union for Foreign Affairs and Security Policy.[2] The EU cannot adopt legislation under the CFSP; instead, the products of the CFSP are 'general guidelines', 'decisions', 'positions' and 'arrangements', which (subject to the exceptions in art 40 TEU and art 275 TFEU) are not reviewable by the CJEU.[3] The Union's supranational external competences under Part V of the TFEU include the common commercial policy (CCP),[4] development and humanitarian assistance, and the maintenance of diplomatic relations with foreign countries and international organisations. Article 216(1) TFEU codifies the principle, already established by the Court of Justice's case-law, that the EU has implied competence to conclude international agreements where such agreements are necessary to achieve the objectives specified by the Treaties.[5]

1   Articles 3(5) and 21 TEU; art 205 TFEU.
2   Articles 24, 26, 27 and 31 TEU. The European Council and the Council are comprised
     respectively of Heads of State and Ministers of Member States: arts 15 and 16 TEU.
3   Articles 24, 25 and 31 TEU; art 275 TFEU. The main exception to this principle is that
     the CJEU does have jurisdiction to determine whether action has been properly taken under
     the CFSP or whether it should have been taken using the EU's supranational powers (and vice
     versa): articles 24 and 40 TEU. The CJEU also has jurisdiction to review the legality of EU
     sanctions, the implementation of which falls partly within and partly outside the CFSP: art 24
     TEU; arts 215, 263 and 275 TFEU.
4   Article 206 TEU: 'By establishing a customs union in accordance with Articles 28 to 32
     [TFEU], the Union shall contribute, in the common interest, to the harmonious development
     of world trade, the progressive abolition of restrictions on international trade and on foreign
     direct investment, and the lowering of customs and other barriers.' Article 207(1) TFEU: 'The
     common commercial policy shall be based on uniform principles, particularly with regard to
     changes in tariff rates, the conclusion of tariff and trade agreements relating to trade in goods
     and services, and the commercial aspects of intellectual property, foreign direct investment, the
     achievement of uniformity in measures of liberalisation, export policy and measures to protect
     trade such as those to be taken in the event of dumping or subsidies. The common commercial
     policy shall be conducted in the context of the principles and objectives of the Union's external
     action.'
5   Article 216(1) TFEU: 'The Union may conclude an agreement with one or more third counties
     or international organisations where the Treaties so provide or where the conclusion of an
     agreement is necessary in order to achieve, within the framework of the Union's policies, one
     of the objectives referred to in the Treaties, or is provided for in a legally binding Union act
     or is likely to affect common rules or alter their scope.'

15.64 Where the EU has competence to act externally by the conclusion of an
international agreement, that competence may be exclusive or may be shared
with Member States. Article 3(1) TFEU gives the EU exclusive competence
(internal and external) in five specified fields, including the customs union and
the common commercial policy. Article 3(2) TFEU provides more generally
that the EU 'shall have exclusive competence to conclude an international
agreement' on three grounds, reflecting and codifying earlier case-law: (i)
'when its conclusion is provided for in a legislative act of the Union'; (ii) when
its conclusion 'is necessary to enable the Union to exercise its internal
competence'; or (iii) 'in so far as its conclusion may affect common rules or
alter their scope'.[1] The third of these three limbs refers to the situation where
the scope, nature and content of EU legislative activity in a particular field
means that the conclusion of international agreements by Member States in the
same field is liable to undermine the uniform and consistent application of the
EU rules and the proper functioning of the system which they establish.[2]

1   See *Opinion 2/15 (EUSFTA)*, Opinion of AG Sharpston EU:C:2016:992, paragraphs 64,
     68–70 and 117–131, and cases there cited.
2   Case 22/70 *Commission v Council (AETR / ERTA)* [1971] ECR 263, paragraphs 15–17;
     Opinion 1/03 (Lugano Convention) [2006] ECR I-1145, paragraphs 124–133; Case C-47/07
     Commission v Greece [2009] ECR I-709; Case C-114/12 *Commission v Council (Convention
     on the Rights of Broadcasting Organizations)* EU:C:2014:2151, paragraphs 64–74; *Opinion
     1/13 on the Hague Convention on Child Abduction* EU:C:2014:2292.

15.65 Not infrequently, some parts of an international agreement will fall
within the exclusive competence of the EU, others will fall within shared EU
and Member State competence, and others still will fall within the exclusive
competence of the Member States. Where the Member States enjoy exclusive
competence for part of an international agreement, and the remainder of the

agreement falls within the exclusive or shared competence of the European Union, both the Member States and the European Union must conclude the agreement.[1] This is described as a 'mixed agreement'. Where competence to conclude an international agreement is shared between the European Union and its Member States, the precise extent of both the European Union's exclusive competences and the Member States' shared (or exclusive) competences as regards a specific agreement cannot, as such, have any bearing on the competence of the European Union for concluding that agreement and, more generally, on the substantive or procedural validity of the European Union's decision to conclude it.[2] Where the EU has adopted a decision authorising the Commission to negotiate a multilateral agreement, the Member States are under a duty to cooperate closely with the EU institutions in order to facilitate the achievement of the EU's tasks and to ensure the coherence and consistency of the EU's action and its international representation.[3] This follows from the Member States' duty of cooperation under art 4(3) TEU, and applies whether the EU's competence is exclusive or shared.

[1] Case C-268/94, *Portugal v Council* EU:C:1996:461, paragraph 39; Opinion 2/15 (EUSFTA), Opinion of AG Sharpston EU:C:2016:992, paragraph 78 and CJEU opinion therein, 16 May 2017.
[2] *Opinion 2/00 (Cartagena Protocol)* [2001] ECR I-9713, paragraph 15; *Opinion 2/15 (EUSFTA)*, Opinion of AG Sharpston EU:C:2016:992, paragraph 81.
[3] Case C-266/03 *Commission v Luxembourg (Inland Waterways Agreement)* [2005] ECR I-4805, paragraphs 58-60; Case C-433/03 *Commission v Germany (Inland Waterways Agreement)* [2005] ECR I-701; Case C-45/07 *Commission v Greece* [2009] ECR I-701; Case C-246/07 *Commission v Sweden* [2010] ECR I-3317, paragraph 91.

15.66 If an international agreement is signed by both the European Union and its constituent Member States, both the European Union and the Member States are, as a matter of international law, parties to that agreement. That will have consequences, in particular in terms of liability for a breach of the agreement, the right of action in respect of such a breach, and the Member States' freedom under international law to terminate the agreement.[1] Termination of a mixed agreement would not necessarily prevent an individual Member State from being bound by its obligations, since the effect of art 216(2) TFEU will be that, as a matter of EU law, that Member State continues to be bound by the areas of the agreement concluded under EU competence, unless and until the European Union terminates the agreement. Unilateral termination of the agreement would also be likely to amount to a breach of the Member State's duty of sincere cooperation under art 4(3) TEU.

[1] See *Opinion 2/15 (EUSFTA)*, Opinion of AG Sharpston EU:C:2016:992, paragraphs 76–77.

15.67 Challenges to the legal basis for Union external legal acts have largely concerned the boundaries (i) between the CFSP and other Union competences,[1] and (ii) between Art 207 TFEU (which empowers the European Parliament and the Council to legislate to implement a common commercial policy) and other express and implied external competences.[2] The significance of the latter is that Art 207 is subject to a specific procedural regime which gives the Commission and the European Parliament an enhanced role in the initiation and negotiation of international agreements, and which permits the Council to act (in certain instances) by a qualified majority. By contrast, the general procedure for the negotiation and conclusion of international agreements (Art 218 TFEU) accords a greater role to the Council. Further, the EU

587

has exclusive competence in relation to the common commercial policy.[3] Legal acts need not relate exclusively to commerce in order to fall within the scope of the common commercial policy and Art 207; it is sufficient that the measures have direct and immediate effects on trade with non-member states, and be essentially intended to promote, facilitate or govern trade with such states.[4]

[1] Articles 23–24 and 40 TEU; Case C-91/05 *Commission v Council (ECOWAS)* [2008] ECR I-3651; C-130/10 *Parliament v Council (Al-Qaeda Sanctions)* EU:C:2012:472; C-658/11 *Parliament v Council (EU-Mauritius Agreement)* EU:C:2014:2025.

[2] Opinion 2/00 (Cartagena Protocol) [2001] ECR I-9713; C-281/01 *Commission v Council* EU:C:2002:761; Opinion 1/08 (GATS) [2009] ECR I-11129; C-137/12 *Commission v Council* EU:C:2013:675, paragraph 76.

[3] Art 3(1)(e) TFEU.

[4] Opinion 2/15 (EUSFTA), Opinion of AG Sharpston EU:C:2016:992, paragraphs 101–103, citing Opinion 1/78 of 4 October 1979 [1979] ECR 2871, paragraphs 41 to 46; C 62/88 *Greece v Council* [1990] ECR I-1527, paragraphs 17 to 20; C 70/94 *Werner* [1995] ECR I-3189, paragraph 10; C 83/94 *Leifer* [1995] ECR I-3231, paragraph 11; *Opinion 2/00 (Cartagena Protocol)* [2001] ECR I-9713, paragraph 40; C 414/11 *Daiichi Sankyo* and *Sanofi-Aventis Deutschland* EU:C:2013:520, paragraphs 50–52; C 137/12 *Commission v Council* EU:C:2013:675, paragraphs 56–58; CJEU opinion, paragraph 36.

15.68 The principles governing choice of legal basis mirror those governing the exercise of the EU's internal competences: where an EU agreement pursues more than one purpose or comprises two or more components of which one is identifiable as the main or predominant purpose or component, whereas the other(s) is (or are) merely incidental or extremely limited in scope, the European Union has to conclude that agreement based on a single legal basis, namely that required by the main or predominant purpose or component.[1] Conversely, if the international agreement in question simultaneously pursues a number of objectives, or has several components, which are inextricably linked without one being incidental to the other, such that various provisions of the Treaties are applicable, the European Union's act concluding that agreement would need to be founded on the various legal bases corresponding to those components.[2]

[1] C 281/01 *Commission v Council* EU:C:2002:761, paragraph 43; C 137/12 *Commission v Council* EU:C:2013:675, paragraph 76; *Opinion 2/15 (EUSFTA)*, Opinion of AG Sharpston EU:C:2016:992, paragraph 93.

[2] C-94/03 *Commission v Council* EU:C:2006:2, paragraph 51; C-263/14 *Parliament v Council* EU:C:2016:435, paragraph 44.

15.69 The provisions of an international agreement entered into by the EU become, from its entry into force, an integral part of European Union law, binding the EU institutions and its Member States and prevailing over any inconsistent acts laid down by the EU intitutions.[1] This is true not only of treaties in force exclusively between the Union, on the one hand, and non-Member countries or other legal persons on the other, but also in the case of 'mixed agreements' concluded by both the Union and its Member States.[2] A national court applying EU law must therefore also apply provisions of treaties entered into by the Union, insofar as those provisions have direct effect.[3] The provisions of an international agreement to which the European Union is a party can be relied on in support of an action for annulment of an act of secondary EU legislation or an exception based on the illegality of such an act only where, first, the nature and the broad logic of that agreement do not preclude it and, secondly, those provisions appear, as regards their content, to be unconditional and sufficiently precise.[4] WTO rules do not enjoy direct effect.[5] Even where they do not have direct effect, international commitments binding on the EU will inform the CJEU's interpretation of EU law.[6]

[1] Art 216(2) TFEU, reflecting long-established case-law: Case 181/73 *Haegeman v Belgium* [1974] ECR 449 paragraph 5; *Opinion 1/91 (EEA Agreement)* [1991] ECR I-6079, paragraph 37; Case C-308/06 *The Queen (on the application of Intertanko) v Secretary of State for Transport* [2006] ECR I-4057, paragraph 42. See M *Mendez, The Legal Effect of EU Agreements (OUP, 2013).*

[2] Case C-13/00 *Commission v Ireland* [2002] ECR I-2943, paragraph 14 referring to Case 12/86 *Demirel v Stadt Schwäbish Gmund* [1987] ECR 3719, paragraph 9.

[3] Cases 21-24/72 *International Fruit Company v Prodktschap voor Groenten en Fruit* [1972] ECR 1219; Case 9/73 *Schlüter v Hauptzollamt Lörrach* [1973] ECR 1135; Case 270/80 *Polydor Ltd v Harlequin Record Shops Ltd* [1982] ECR 329; Case 104/81 *Hauptzollamt Mainz v CA Kupferberg & Cie KG* [1982] ECR 3641; Case C-469/92 *Amministrazione delle Finanze dello Stato Chiquita Italia* [1995] ECR I-4533; Case C-377/98 *Netherlands v Council* [2001] ECR I-7079; Case C-2013/03 *Syndicat professional coordination des pêcheurs de l'étang de Berre v EDF* [2004] ECR I-7357, paragraphs 31–47; Case C-351/04 *Ikea Wholesale* [2007] ECR I-7723; Cases C-120 and 121/06 *FIAMM and Fedon v Council and Commission* [2008] ECR I-6513; Case C-308/06 *The Queen (on the application of Intertanko) v Secretary of State for Transport* [2006] ECR I-4057; Case C-366/10 *ATAA v Secretary of State for Energy and Climate Change* EU:C:2011:864; Case C-363/12 *Z v A Government Department* EU:C:2014:159.

[4] Cases C-401 to 403/12 P *Council v Vereniging Milieudefensie* [2015] ECR, paragraph 54.

[5] Case C-149/96, *Portugal v Council* [1999] ECR I-8395, paragraphs 36–47; Case C-307/99 *OGT v Hauptzollamt Hamburg-St Annen* [2001] ECR I-3159; Cases C-27 and 122/00 *The Queen v Secretary of State for the Environment, Transport and the Regions, ex p Omega Air Ltd* [2002] ECR I-2569; Cases C-300 and 392/98, *Dior v Tuk Consultancy* [2000] ECR I-11307; Case C-245/02 *Anheuser-Busch Inc v Budejovicky Budvar* [2003] ECR I-10989; Case C-94/02 P *Etablissements Biret et Cie SA v Council* [2003] ECR I-10565 Cases C-120 and 121/06 *FIAMM and Fedon v Council and Commission* [2008] ECR I-6513.

[6] Case C-61/94 *Commission v Germany (International Dairy Arrangement)* [1996] ECR I-3989; Cases C-300 and 392/98, *Dior v Tuk Consultancy* [2000] ECR I-11307; Case C-245/02 *Anheuser-Busch Inc v Budejovicky Budvar* [2003] ECR I-10989, paragraphs 54–57; Case C-263/08 *Djurgården-Lilla Värtans Miljöskyddsförening* [2009] ECR I-9967, paragraph 51; Case C-240/09 *Lezoochranárske zoskupenie (Brown Bears)* [2011] ECR I-1255; Case C-411/10 *NS v Home Secretary* [2011] ECR I-13905, paragraphs 75–80; Cases C-401 to 403/12 P *Council v Vereniging Milieudefensie* EU:C:2015:4, paragraphs 52–62.

15.70 The EU is bound to respect international law (including customary international law) in the exercise of its powers.[1] This would, for example, require the EU to comply with the rules of customary international law when adopting a regulation suspending the trade concessions granted by, or by virtue of, an agreement which it has concluded with a non-member country.[2] It also means that an EU law provision must be interpreted, and its scope limited, in the light of applicable rules of international law.[3] However, international law may not be relied on in order to oust the Court of Justice's ability to review EU acts for compliance with fundamental rights: even EU legislation implementing resolutions of the UN Security Council adopted under Chapter VII of the United Nations Charter must be subject to review by the Court of Justice for compliance with fundamental rights.[4] Even if an international agreement does not bind the Union but only the Member States, the customary principle of good faith in general international law, in conjunction with the principle of sincere cooperation, mean that it is incumbent on the Court of Justice to interpret EU legislation taking account of the agreement.[5]

[1] Case C-286/90 *Poulsen and Diva Navigation* [1992] ECR I-6019, paragraph 9; Case C-162/96 *Racke* [1998] ECR I-3655, paragraph 45; Joined Cases C-402/05P & C-415/05P *Kadi v Council of the European Union* [2008] ECR I-6351 [2009] 1 A.C. 1225, paragraph 291.

[2] Case C-162/96 *Racke* [1998] ECR I-3655, paragraph 45.

[3] Case C-286/90 *Poulsen and Diva Navigation* [1992] ECR I-6019, paragraph 9; Joined Cases C-402/05P & C-415/05P *Kadi v Council of the European Union* [2008] ECR I-6351 [2009] 1 A.C. 1225, paragraph 291.

[4] Joined Cases C-402/05P & C-415/05P *Kadi v Council of the European Union* [2008] ECR I-6351, [2009] 1 A.C. 1225, paragraphs 280–285 and 326; Case C-584/P *Commission v Kadi* EU:C:2013:518.

[5] Case C-308/06 *The Queen (on the application of Intertanko) v Secretary of State for Transport* [2006] ECR I-4057 at paragraph 52.

ENFORCEMENT OF UNION LAW

15.71 In its judgment dated 1978 in *Amministrazione delle Finanze dello Stato v Simmenthal*[1] the ECJ linked the precedence of European Union law to the duty of national courts to secure the application of that law in the face of national provisions to the contrary. A rule of Italian law, reserving to the Constitutional Court the exclusive authority to determine whether national legislation was unconstitutional, could not be permitted to prevent even a Pretore from setting aside national legislation inconsistent with European Union law. The CJEU held that the provisions of the EC Treaty and directly effective legislation adopted thereunder preclude the valid adoption of new national legislative measures to the extent that they would be incompatible with Union provisions. In the same case, the court stated that:

> 'every national court must, in a case within its jurisdiction, apply Community law in its entirety and protect rights which the latter confers on individuals and must accordingly set aside any provision of national law which may conflict with it, whether prior to or subsequent to the Community rule'.[2]

[1] Case 106/77, [1978] ECR 629, paragraph 17.
[2] Case 106/77, [1978] ECR 629, paragraph 21.

15.72 Whereas in *Simmenthal* the ECJ was careful to qualify its observation to the duties of a national court 'in a case within its jurisdiction', in *Factortame* the same court enlarged its principle, so as to require a national court to grant a remedy that would not otherwise have been available. In that case the House of Lords asked whether an English court must be taken to have the power to grant an interim injunction against the Crown so as to protect the rights that a claimant asserted as a matter of European Union law.[1]

[1] Case C-213/89 *R v Secretary of State for Transport ex p Factortame and Others* [1990] ECR I-2433, paragraphs 14 and 15; see 15.106–15.107 below.

15.73 The ECJ ruled that:

> 'a national court which, in a case before it concerning European Union law, considers that the sole obstacle which precludes it from granting interim relief is a rule of national law must set aside that rule'.

15.74 Even so, the ruling is cautiously expressed. It presupposes that the national court in question has jurisdiction in respect of the dispute and requires only that a national rule precluding the award of a particular remedy must be set aside where its application would impair the full effectiveness of European Union law.

15.75 Accordingly, it is in principle for national law to designate the courts having jurisdiction to protect the rights enjoyed by natural or legal persons in consequence of the operation of European Union law and to prescribe the remedies available in those courts and the applicable procedural conditions, including time limits.[1] This is sometimes referred to as the principle of national procedural autonomy. There are two qualifications to this principle:

(1)   The procedural rules governing actions for safeguarding rights derived from EU law are not to be less favourable than those rules governing similar domestic actions. It must be possible for every type of action provided for by national law to be available for the purpose of ensuring observance of EU provisions having direct effect on the same conditions concerning the admissibility and procedure as would apply if it were a question of ensuring observance of national law. This is the principle of equivalence.[2]

(2)   The remedies created by national law must be effective: that is to say, they must not make it impossible or excessively difficult to exercise the Union rights which national courts have a duty to protect. This is the principle of effectiveness.[3]

---

[1]   Case 68/79 *Hans Just I/S v Danish Ministry for Fiscal Affairs* [1980] ECR 501 at 522; Case 158/80 *Rewe Handelsgesellschaft Nord mbH v Hauptzollamt Kiel* [1981] ECR 1805 at 1838; Case 79/83 *Harz v Deutsche Tradax, GmbH* [1984] ECR 1921 at 1941. For a full account see M Brealey and M Hoskins, *Remedies in EC Law* (1998) Longman.

[2]   Case 158/80 *Rewe Handelsgesellschaft Nord mbH v Hauptzollamt Kiel* [1981] ECR 1805 at 1838. See also *Byrne v Motor Insurers' Bureau* [2008] EWCA Civ 574, [2008] 4 All ER 476 at paragraphs 22–31 (MIB agreement should be subject to a limitation period no less favourable than that which applies to the commencement of court proceedings by a minor under the Limitation Act 1980, ie with suspension of limitation during the period of minority or disability) and Joined Cases C/295-298/04 *Manfredi v Lloyd Adriatico Assicurazioni SpA* [2006] ECR I-6619 (exemplary damages should be available for breach of the law [if available] for similar domestic actions). See *Devenish Nutrition v Sanofi-Aventis* [2008] EWCA Civ 27, [2009] Ch 390 at paragraph 130 for English application of *Manfredi*. In *TA (Iraq) v Home Secretary* [2011] UKSC 22 the Supreme Court considered (i) whether the comparator right needed to be a purely domestic right and also (ii) the degree of similarity which must exist between the compared measures in order for them to be sufficiently similar. It referred various questions to the Court of Justice.

[3]   Case 45/76 *Comet v Produktschap voor Siergewassen* [1976] ECR 2043 at 2053, paragraph 13 reiterated in numerous cases, including Joined Cases C-397 and C-410/98 *Metallgesellschaft Ltd v Commissioners of Inland Revenue; Hoechst v Commissioners of Inland Revenue* [2001] ECR I-1727 paragraph 85. In appropriate cases, the principle of effective protection of Community law rights may authorise the European Commission to require Member States to adopt criminal sanctions: Case C-176/03 *Commission v Council* [2005] ECR I-7879 (in the field of serious environmental offences). In *Comet* the Court used only the formulation 'virtually impossible'. The additional 'or excessively difficult' formulation was added in later cases.

15.76 The principle of effectiveness has now been expressly incorporated into the Treaties as Article 19(1), second paragraph, of the Treaty on European Union:

'Member States shall provide remedies sufficient to ensure effective legal protection in the fields covered by Union law.'

Moreover Article 4(3) TEU not only incorporates the substance of former Article 10 EC but also includes an additional first sentence:

'Pursuant to the principle of sincere cooperation, the Union and the Member States shall, in full mutual respect, assist each other in carrying out tasks which flow from the Treaties.'

These changes appear designed to emphasise Member State obligations with regard to remedies and may encourage the Court of Justice to apply the principles with renewed vigour.

The principle is also stated in Article 47 EU Charter of Fundamental Rights, the first limb of which provides that: 'Everyone whose rights and freedoms guaranteed by the law of the Union are violated has the right to an effective remedy before a tribunal in compliance with the conditions laid down in this Article.'

15.77 Where a question is raised as to whether a national procedural provision renders application of European Union law impossible or excessively difficult, this issue is to be analysed by reference to the role of the provision in national procedure, to the way in which the rule applies and to its special features. Where appropriate, it is also necessary to take into consideration whether the domestic rule can reasonably be justified on grounds of protection of the rights of defence, legal certainty or the proper conduct of proceedings.[1]

[1] Case C-312/93 *Peterbroeck van Campenhout & Cie SCS v Belgium* [1995] ECR I-4599, [1996] 1 CMLR 793; Joined Case C-430–431/93 *Jeroen van Schijndel and Johannes van Veen v Stichting Pensioenfonds voor Fysiotherapeuten* [1995] ECR I-4705, [1996] 1 CMLR 801. Case C-662/13 *Unidades de Saúde SA v Fazenda Pública* EU:C:2015:89, [2015] B.V.C. 12 at paragraph 28.

15.78 As Tridimas[1] points out, the principle of effectiveness confers on Union law a quasi-constitutional status whereby domestic procedural rules are to be reassessed by reference to their impact on the protection of rights derived from EU law. The duty on national courts is therefore to ensure effective protection of EU law rights even if this means applying procedural standards which are more favourable than those applicable to national rights. On the facts of *Peterbroeck*,[2] the relevant Belgian procedural time limit fixed a period of 60 days within which the taxpayer could raise new pleas, such period to run from the date of the lodging by the tax authorities of a certified copy of the contested decision. Under the national procedural rules, the Court of Appeal was the first body in the course of proceedings to have jurisdiction to refer an issue of Community law to the Court of Justice. Before the Court of Appeal, the taxpayer raised a late plea based on EU free movement provisions but the hearing before the Court of Appeal took place after the expiry of the 60-day time limit with the effect that the Court of Appeal had no power to consider the EU argument, whether of its own motion or otherwise. The Court of Justice considered that, whilst a 60-day period was not objectionable *per se*, the effect of the rule was that *no* court could consider the EU argument and that the impossibility for national courts to raise Community law points of their own motion did not appear to be reasonably justified by principles such as legal certainty or proper conduct of procedure. Accordingly the case was treated as being one where it was virtually impossible to rely on EU law in that EU law could not be considered by any court unless invoked by the taxpayer within the 60-day period.

¹   Tridimas, *General Principles of EC law*, 2nd edn, Oxford, 2006, p 423 ff.
²   Case C-312/93, [1995] ECR I-4599, paragraphs 16–21.

15.79 It remains, however, difficult to predict when national procedural rules will be regarded as rendering reliance on Union law to be 'excessively' difficult. By way of example, frequent attempts have been made to circumvent national limitation periods on grounds of the effectiveness of EU law but they have met with little success. In *Emmott*¹ the court held that where a Member State had not properly implemented a directive, where an individual sought to rely upon the provisions of the directive the Member State could not invoke a national time limit for bringing proceedings until the directive was properly implemented. However, this broad exception for non-implementation of directives was not followed in later cases which considered that reasonable time-limits are an application of the principle of legal certainty protecting both individuals and administrations.² In *Tonina Enza Iaia and Others v Ministero dell'Istruzione, dell'Università e della Ricerca* the Court reconciled these two positions by holding that 'EU law does not preclude a national authority from relying on the expiry of a reasonable limitation period unless, by its conduct, it was responsible for the delay in the application, thereby depriving the applicant in the main proceedings of the opportunity to enforce his rights under an EU directive before the national courts.'³ It is clear from *Levez*⁴ that, although a national rule which restricts a claim for arrears of remuneration to a period of two years prior to the date of instituting proceedings is not of itself open to criticism, that rule may not be applied if the delay in making a claim is due to misleading information from the employer because the effect of the rule in such a case would be to 'facilitate the breach of Community law by an employer whose deceit caused the employee's delay'. Application of the principle of effectiveness in those circumstances was not excluded by the fact that there was some prospect of a civil action in deceit for the employer's misleading statement but it was left up to the national court to determine whether such a civil action would be likely to entail procedural rules or other conditions such as delay which are less favourable than those applicable to an action in an Industrial Tribunal.

¹   Case C-208/90 *Emmott v Minister for Social Welfare and the Attorney General* [1991] ECR I-4269 – claim based on Irish failure to implement directive but claimant had been dissuaded by letter from Minister from bringing a claim; Court of Justice held that until such time as directive has been properly transposed, a defaulting Member State may not rely on an individual's delay in instituting proceedings.
²   Case C-338/91 *Steenhorst-Neerings v Bestuur van de Bedrijfsvereniging voor Detailhandel, Ambachten en Huisvrouwen* [1993] ECR I-5475; Case C-410/92 *Johnson v Chief Adjudication Officer* [1997] ECR I-5483; Case C-2/94 *Denkavit International BV v Kamer van Koophandel en Fabrieken voor Midden-gelderland* [1996] ECR I-2827 with Advocate General Jacobs in this last case reviewing *Steenhorst-Nordings* and *Johnson* and rationalising *Emmott* as a case where the Member State was 'in default both in failing to implement a directive and in obstructing the exercise of a judicial remedy in reliance upon it', so that the failure to meet the time limit may be regarded as due to the conduct of the national authorities. Even very short periods of time have, in special circumstances, been held capable of complying with the principle of effectiveness: Case C-349/07 *Sopropé v Fazenda Pública* [2008] ECR I-10369, paragraphs 52–53 (8-day period for importer suspected of having committed customs offence

to submit observations is capable of complying with EU law, given special circumstances of customs system).

3   Case Case C-452/09 *Tonina Enza Iaia and Others v Ministero dell'Istruzione, dell'Università e della Ricerca and Others* [2011] ECR I-4043 at paragraph 21.
4   Case C-329/96 *Levez v Jennings (Harlow Pools)* [1998] ECR I-7835.

15.80 The fundamental requirement of the principle of effectiveness is that limitation periods should be reasonable,[1] but the principle of effectiveness has not only been applied to assess the compatibility of time limits with EU law. It has also been applied to require that a particular remedy be available in respect of a right derived from EU law. In *Metallgesellschaft Ltd v Commissioners of Inland Revenue; Hoechst v Commissioners of Inland Revenue*[2] the Court of Justice considered the position of a company which had been required to pay corporation tax earlier than it should have been required to had Community law been properly applied. The company claimed a sum representing interest for the loss of its money during this period. English law did not permit claims for interest where no principal sum was still due to the claimant. The Court of Justice held that the company was entitled to payment of interest that would have been generated on sums foregone (although it was a matter for national law to decide whether the claim was to be framed as one in restitution or damages). It stated:

> 'The exercise of rights conferred on private persons by directly applicable provisions of European Union law would . . . be rendered impossible or excessively difficult if their claims for restitution or compensation based on European Union law were rejected or reduced solely because the persons concerned had not applied for a tax advantage which national law denied them . . . '.

Other cases have considered the compatibility of national rules allocating the burden of proof and national rules of evidence. These cases date back to *San Giorgio*,[3] in which repayment was sought of a charge levied in breach of EU law. It was held that national provisions preventing recovery of such charges, if it is established that the claimant had in fact passed on the charge, were compatible with Community law. However, presumptions or rules of evidence which placed upon the taxpayer the burden of establishing that the charges had *not* been passed on to other persons or special limitations concerning the form of evidence which could be adduced (such as the exclusion of all evidence save for documentary evidence) would make it virtually impossible or excessively difficult to obtain repayment of sums paid in breach of EC law. Such limitations were not compatible with Community law:

> 'Once it is established that the levying of the charge is incompatible with Community law, the court must be free to decide whether or not the burden of the charge has been passed on, wholly or in part, to other persons.'[4]

It follows that a member state is 'in principle required to repay charges levied in breach of Community law'[5] except where the charge has been passed on by the party who paid it, with the result that he would be unjustly enriched were he to recover it for his own benefit.[6]

If it is clear that one party does not have access to information, at least in the context of litigation between Member States and Community institutions, regard should be had to the party 'best placed to collect and verify' the relevant data when imposing the relevant burden of proof.[7] It would further appear from the *Boiron* case that this approach is to be applied more broadly so that, where a state aid complainant cannot prove the state aid, the national court is required to use all procedural steps available to it under national law including ordering the production of documents.[8] In *Bundeswettbewerbsbehörde v Donau Chemie AG*,[9] the Court of Justice considered the compatibility of Austrian rules regarding third party access to the file of proceedings relating to a cartel.

In *FII Test Claimants v Revenue and Customs Commissioners*, the Supreme Court considered that the principle of effectiveness has a significant impact not just on the procedural law of Members States but also on substantive law, requiring Member States to ensure that domestic law meets minimum standards in order to fully protect EU rights. In so far as the legal system of a member state fails to give adequate effect to directly effective EU law rights, it is incumbent on national courts to give effect to those rights by filling the gap between existing causes of action or if necessary to create a new one. EU law cannot require that national law should create a particular cause of action or remedy but simply requires that the causes of action or remedies that exist in national law be effective.[10]

1 Case 33/76 *Rewe Zentralfinanz eG v Landwirtschaftskammer fur das Saarland* [1976] ECR 1989, para 5; *Comet BV v Produktschap voor Siergewassen (Case 45/76)* [1976] ECR 2043, paras 16–18. Legislation curtailing limitation periods is in principle consistent with the principle of effectiveness provided that a period of grace is allowed, either by giving sufficient advance notice of the change or by including transitional provisions in the legislation: *Aprile Srl v Amministrazione delle Finanze dello Stato (No 2)* (Case C-228/96), [1998] ECR I-07141; *Dilexport Srl v Amministrazione delle Finanze dello Stato* (Case C-343/96), [1999] ECR I-579, *Grundig Italiana SpA v Ministero delle Finanze* (Case C-255/00), [2002] ECR I-8003; *Marks & Spencer plc v Customs and Excise Comrs* (Case C-62/00), [2002] ECR I-6325.

2 [2001] ECR I-1727 at paragraph 106. See, more recently on the question of effective remedy for overpaid tax: *Test Claimants in the FII Group Litigation v Revenue and Customs Commissioners* [2012] UKSC 19, [2012] 2 AC 337.

3 Case 199/82 *Amministrazione delle Finanze dello Stato v San Giorgio* [1983] ECR 3595. These principles were restated in the judgments of the Court of Justice in *Metallgesellschaft* [2001] Ch 620, paras 84–86 and in *FII Test Claimants v Inland Revenue Comrs (Case C-446/04)* ECR I-11753, paras 201–208.

4 Ibid, paragraph 14. The alternative may to be to impose on the claimant the 'probatio diabolica' of which Advocate General Jacobs spoke in Cases C-427/93, C-429/93, and C-436/93 *Bristol-Myers Squibb v Paranova A/S* [1996] ECR I-3457 at paragraph 103.

5 *Société Comateb v Directeur Général des Douanes et Droits Indirects* (Joined Cases C-192 to C-218/95) [1997] ECR I-165, para 20.

6 *Weber's Wine World Handels-GmbH v Abgabenberufungskommission Wien* (Case C-147/01)[2005] All ER (EC) 224, para 94.

7 Case C-28/94 *Netherlands v Commission* [1999] ECR I-1973, paragraph 41.

8 Case C-526/04 *Laboratoires Boiron SA v Union de recouvrement des cotisations de sécurité sociale et d'allocations familiales (Urssaf) de Lyon* [2006] ECR I-7529. See also Case C-147/01 *Weber's Wine World* [2003] ECR I-11365 at paragraph 115 – assumption of burden of proof by public authority may be subject to a requirement of cooperation by the taxpayers.

9 Case C-6/11 [2013] 5 CMLR 19. See also Case 557/12 *Kone* (Austrian rule excluding causation for claim against cartel member for the added cost of products bought from third parties at prices inflated by the existence of the cartel, set aside on grounds of effectiveness).

10 Case C-432/05 *Unibet (London) ltd v Justitiekanslern* [2007] ECR I-2271; paras 40–41; *FII Test Claimants v Revenue and Customs Comrs* [2012] UKSC 19; [2012] 2 AC 337 at paragraphs 147 and 148.

15.81 In short, it is plain that the categories of national procedural rules which may be the subject of modification by the principle of effectiveness is not closed. A full review of this principle is beyond the scope of this chapter but, by way of further examples, it has also been applied to rules specifically introduced to limit Community claims; to the need for effective judicial review;[1] to *locus standi* before national courts;[2] to rules limiting the availability of interim relief in the national courts;[3] to restrictive rules on damages;[4] to a statutory maximum for compensation which precluded the award of interest;[5] to rules limiting recourse to the courts to challenge arbitration awards.[6]

[1] Judicial scrutiny could not therefore be excluded by a certificate to be treated as conclusive evidence that the conditions for derogating from the principle of equal treatment are met: Case 222/84 *Johnston v Chief Constable of the Royal Ulster Constabulary* [1986] ECR 1871.

[2] Case C-263/08 *Djurgarden-Lilla Värtans Miljöskyddsförening v Stockholms kommun genom dess marknämnd*, [2009] ECR I-9967.

[3] Case C-213/89 *R v SoS for Transport ex p Factortame* [1990] ECR I-2433. Particular criteria have been set down where interim relief is sought against the operation of a Union act (or a national implementing measure) which is alleged to be incompatible with the EU legal order. See eg Cases C-143/88 and C-92/89 *Zuckerfabrik Süderdithmarschen and Zuckerfabrik Soest* [1991] ECR I-415.

[4] Case 14/83 *Von Colson and Kamann v Land Nordrhein-Westfalen* [1984] ECR 1891. And see *Sempra Metals Ltd v Inland Revenue* [2005] EWCA Civ 389, [2006] QB 37 where the Court of Appeal held that it was required to grant compound interest on a claim for tax paid too early even though such a claim would not lie under English law (House of Lords did not rely on effectiveness because the right to compound interest arose at common law – [2008] 1 AC 561).

[5] Case C-271/91 *Marshall v Southampton and South-West Hampshire Area Health Authority* [1993] ECR I-4367. Cf the position of the Court of Justice on interest and restitution in Case C-66/95 *R v Secretary of State for Social Security ex p Sutton* [1997] ECR I-2163 unless the payment of interest is not ancillary but is the very objective sought by the action: Joined Cases C-397/98 and C-410/98 *Metallgesellschaft Ltd and Hoechst AG v Commissioners of Inland Revenue* [2001] ECR I-1727.

[6] Case C-126/97 *Eco Swiss China Time Ltd v Benetton International NV* [1999] ECR I-3055. See Tridimas, op cit, Chapter 9 for a comprehensive review of the application by the Court of Justice of the principle of effectiveness.

PRELIMINARY RULINGS

15.82 Where a question arises before a national court or tribunal as to the interpretation of the TEU or the TFEU or the validity or interpretation of acts of Union institutions, bodies, offices or agencies,[1] that court or tribunal may, if it considers that a decision on the question is necessary to enable it to give judgment,[2] request the Court of Justice to give a ruling.[3] In appropriately justified cases, such a request may benefit from an urgent procedure.[4] The fourth paragraph in Article 267 requires the Court of Justice to act with 'the minimum of delay' if a question is raised in a case pending with regard to a person in custody. For the purpose of enabling the High Court and the Civil Division of the Court of Appeal to make such references, explicit provision has been made in CPR 68, and corresponding provision has been made for criminal courts.[5]

[1] The right to make a reference to the Court of Justice for a preliminary ruling must therefore exist in respect of all measures adopted by the Council, whatever their nature or form, which are intended to have legal effects in relation to third parties: Case C-355/04P *Segi v Council* [2007] ECR I-1657 at paragraphs 53–54 (re Council Common Position on application of specific measures to combat terrorism).

[2] The issue to be addressed by the national court is whether a decision on the disputed question of European Union law is necessary in order to enable the national court to give judgment. If such a decision is necessary, the national court has discretion to refer the question. The

reference itself need not be 'necessary'; and any suggestion to that effect in *HP Bulmer Ltd v J Bollinger SA* [1974] Ch 401, [1974] 2 All ER 1226, is per incuriam.

3 Article 267 TFEU; Euratom Treaty, art 106a (which applies art 267 to the European Atomic Energy Community). See D Anderson and M Demitriou *References to the European Court* (2002) Sweet & Maxwell; and R Plender ed, *European Courts Procedure* (2001), Chapter 31.

4 Under art 105 of the Rules of Procedure (2012). See Case C-195/08 PPU *Rinau* [2008] ECR I-5271 at paragraphs 43–46 which considered the urgent procedure previously provided under art 104b of the previous rules of procedure.

5 Criminal Procedure Rules, Part 75.

15.83 Questions may be referred only when they concern the interpretation or validity of measures enumerated in art 267 TFEU or in the corresponding provisions in the other founding treaties. The Court does not have jurisdiction to interpret a provision of a treaty merely because it forms part of an agreement linked to the Union and the functioning of its institutions.[1] On the other hand, treaties concluded between the Union and third countries are, as far as concerns the Union, acts of the institutions, which the European Court has jurisdiction to interpret.[2]

1 Case 44/84 *Hurd v Jones* [1986] ECR 29 at para 20; Case C-132/09 *Commission v Kingdom of Belgium* [2010] ECR I-8695 at para 44.

2 Case 181/73 *R and V Haegeman Sprl v Belgium* [1974] ECR 449; Joined Cases 290–291/81 *Compagnia Singer SpA and Geigy SpA v Amministrazione delle Finanze dello Stato* [1983] ECR 847; Case C-356/12 *Glatzel v Freistaat Bayern* EU:C:2014:350.

15.84 A question should not be referred for preliminary ruling if the answer thereto is so plain that it admits of no difficulty, that is to say, if there is no scope for any reasonable doubt as to the manner in which the question is to be resolved. This is the *acte claire* doctrine. Before it comes to the conclusion that this is the case, the national court or tribunal must be convinced that the matter is equally obvious to the courts of other Member States and to the Court of Justice itself. The national court must bear in mind the special character of EU law and the particular problems which are presented by its interpretation viz: that EU legislation is drafted in several languages (each of which is equally authentic), that EU law uses terminology which is peculiar to it and that every provision of EU law is to be placed in context and interpreted in the light of the provisions of EU law as a whole.[1] The fact that a party contends that a dispute gives rise to a question concerning the interpretation of European Union law does not mean that the court or tribunal is compelled to consider that a question has been raised within the meaning of the relevant treaty provisions.

1 Case 283/81 *CILFIT Srl v Ministry of Health* [1982] ECR 3415: Case 338/85 *Pardini Fratelli SpA v Ministero del Commercio con l'Estero* [1988] ECR 2041; Case C-379/15 *Association France Nature Environnement v Premier ministre and Ministre de l'Écologie, du Développement durable et de l'Énergie* EU:C:2016:603. For some applications in national law, see *Magnavision NV SA v General Optical Council (No 2)* [1987] 2 CMLR 262 (Watkins LJ); *R v International Stock Exchange, ex p Else* [1993] 2 CMLR 677; *Re Societe des Petroles Shell-Berre* [1964] CMLR 462 (French Conseil d'Etat): See H Rasmussen 'The European Court's Acte Clair Strategy in CILFIT' 9 EL Rev (1984) 242; H Schermers. 'The Law as it Stands on Preliminary Rulings', [1974–1] LIEI 93. There has been recent criticism of English courts for failing to make preliminary references, especially in environmental matters: V Heyvaert, J Thornton and R Drabble, 'With reference to the environment: the preliminary reference procedure, environmental decisions and the domestic judiciary' (2014) 130 LQR 413.

15.85 The power to refer cases for preliminary ruling is reserved for courts or tribunals of Member States. That expression denotes not only the central judicial authorities of any Member States but also all tribunals authorised to give binding decisions of a judicial nature.[1] In deciding whether a body is a 'court or tribunal' the European Court takes into account a number of factors, such as whether it is established by law, whether it is permanent, whether its jurisdiction is compulsory, whether its procedure is *inter partes*, whether it applies rules of law and whether it is independent.[2] It does not embrace a body which has before it a request for a declaration relating to a dispute which it is under no legal obligation to resolve.[3] A national competition authority was not considered to be a court or tribunal where it lacked independence from government and having regard to art 11(6) of Regulation 1/2003 which permits the Commission to take over conduct of proceedings.[4] Where, however, the task of implementing provisions of European Union law in a Member State is assigned to a professional body acting under a degree of governmental supervision and that body, in conjunction with the public authorities concerned, creates appeal procedures which may affect the exercise of rights created by European Union law, the appellate body so created is to be regarded as a court or tribunal within the meaning of art 267 TFEU.[5]

1   The relevant tests are set down in the Grand Chamber's decision in Case C-196/09 *Miles v European Schools* [2011] 3 CMLR 25 (holding that the Complaints Board of the European Schools did not qualify).
2   Case C-54/96 *Dorsch Consult Ingenieurgesellschaft v Bundesbaugesellschaft Berlin* [1997] ECR I-4961 para 23; Case C-363/11 *Epitropos tou Elegktikou Synedriou sto Ypourgeio Politismou kai Tourismou v Ypourgeio Politismou kai Tourismou - Ypiresia Dimosionomikou Elenchou* EU:C:2012:825 at paragraph 18.
3   Case 138/80 *Borker* [1980] ECR 1975; Case C-14/08 *Roda Golf & Beach Resort SL* [2009] ECR I-05439 at paragraphs 34–36.
4   Case C-53/03 *Syfait v GlaxoSmithKline plc* [2005] ECR I-4609, where the Greek Competition Commission was held not to be a court or tribunal of a Member State.
5   Case 246/80 *Broekmeulen v Huisarts Registratie Commissie* [1981] ECR 2311 (in respect of a professional disciplinary tribunal for the Dutch medical profession).

15.86 A conventional arbitral tribunal does not fall within the definition of 'court or tribunal', even if the arbitrator also sits in other cases as a judge or the effect of an arbitration agreement precludes recourse to national courts, because the resolution of disputes by means of arbitration is a matter of agreement.[1] However an arbitral tribunal which is established by law (as opposed to by party agreement) and the decisions of which were binding on the parties was held to qualify as a court or tribunal within the meaning of the Article.[2] Conversely, a court or tribunal within the meaning of art 267 does not lose its character as such by reason of the fact that it combines other functions of a non-judicial character. A court of an overseas territory of a Member State, to which Community treaties apply, is to be considered as a court or tribunal of a Member State for the purpose of referring questions for preliminary ruling.[3] In particular, a Manx court and a court of any of the Channel Islands may be considered as competent to refer questions.[4]

1   Case 102/81 *Nordsee Deutsche Hochseefischerei GmbH v Reederei Mond Hochseefischerei Nordstern AG & Co KG* [1982] ECR 1095; Case C-125/04 *Guy Denuit and Betty Cordenier v Transorient – Mosaïque Voyages and Culture SA* [2005] ECR I-00923. See G Bebr, 'Arbitration Tribunals and Article 234 of the EC Treaty' 22 CML Rev (1985) 489.
2   Case C-555/13 *Merck v Accord Healthcare* (Judgment 13 February 2014).
3   Case 14/86 *Pretore di Salo v Persons Unknown* [1987] ECR 2545.

⁴   Joined Cases C-100–101/89 *Kaefer and Procacci v French State* [1990] ECR I-4647.

15.87 Under the third paragraph of art 267 TFEU, a court or tribunal against whose decisions there is no judicial remedy under national law must refer to the Court of Justice a question for preliminary ruling, where any such question is raised in a case pending before it (unless the matter falls within one of the circumstances discussed at **15.84** above where no reference need be made). Plainly, the Supreme Court is a court or tribunal of the kind considered in that paragraph[1] and it has now clarified its duty with regard to references when considering an application for permission to appeal.[2] It is, however, established that even an inferior court seised of a referable question has a duty to refer it where there is no judicial remedy against the decision of that court in the circumstances of the case.[3] Accordingly, Buckley LJ has concluded that the Court of Appeal is obliged to refer when finally determining an issue in respect of which there is no possibility of appeal to the Supreme Court.[4] It is otherwise where the unsuccessful party has the right to apply to the Supreme Court for permission to appeal.[5] A failure to make a preliminary reference in circumstances where Article 267(3) required one to have been made may result in state liability for breach of EU law.[6]

¹   *H P Bulmer Ltd v J Bollinger SA* [1974] Ch 401, [1974] 2 All ER 1226.
²   Supreme Court Rules 2009, Rule 42; UKSC Practice Direction 11.
³   Case 6/64 *Costa v Ente Nazionale Energia Elettrica* [1964] ECR 585.
⁴   *Hagen v Fratelli D and G Moretti SNC* [1980] 3 CMLR 253 at 255 in relation to the House of Lords. See, also, *R v Pharmaceutical Society of Great Britain, ex p the Association of Pharmaceutical Importers* [1987] 3 CMLR 951 at 969.
⁵   *Generics (UK) Ltd v Smith Kline & French Laboratories Ltd* [1990] 1 CMLR 416, per Balcombe LJ; *Chiron v Murex (No 8)* [1995] All ER (EC) 88. For this reason, Rule 42(1) of the Supreme Court Rules requires 'brief reasons' to be given for refusal of the application for permission to appeal where an application for permission raises a question of Community law. See also paragraph 11.1.2 of UKSC Practice Direction 11.
⁶   Case C-224/01 *Köbler v Austria* [2003] ECR I-10239.

15.88 The system of references for preliminary rulings under art 267 TFEU presupposes a distinct separation of functions between the European Court on the one hand and national courts and tribunals on the other. The former has the function of determining authoritatively the abstract question referred for ruling; the latter has the function of determining issues of fact and applying the European Court of Justice's ruling to the case.[1] Article 267 is based on a clear separation of functions between the national courts and the Court of Justice so that, when ruling on the interpretation of validity of Union provisions, the Court of Justice is empowered to do so only on the basis of the facts which the national court put before it and has no power to find the facts. That is the domain of the national court.[2] Article 267 does not give the Court jurisdiction to take cognisance of the facts of the case or to criticise the reasons for the reference.[3] A reference for preliminary ruling is not inadmissible by reason only of the fact that there is a substantial degree of agreement between the parties before the national court as to the answer to be given to the question referred.[4]

¹   Case 35/76 *Simmenthal SpA v Italian Minister for Finance* [1976] ECR 1871; Joined Cases 28–30/62 *Da Costa en Schaake NV v Nederlandse Belastingadministratie* [1963] ECR 31; Joined Cases C-165/09 to C-167/09 *Stichting Natuur en Milieu and Others v College van Gedeputeerde Staten van Groningen* [2011] ECR I-04599.

² HMRC v Aimia Coalition Loyalty UK Ltd [2013] UKSC 42 at 554 and cited there. See to like effect: *De Groot en Slot Allium BV*, Counseil d'Etat, France 10 January 2006 No 234560; *Data Delecta*, Swedish Supreme Court, 13 November 1996, Case Ö 1195/94.

³ Case 117/77 *Bestuur van het Algemeen Ziekenfonds Drenthe-Platteland v Pierik* [1978] ECR 825.

⁴ Case 244/78 *Union Laitiere Normande v French Dairy Farmers Ltd* [1979] ECR 2663; Case C-331/88 *R v Minister of Agriculture, ex p FEDESA* [1990] ECR I-4023.

15.89 In *Kontogeorgas v Kartonpak AE*¹ the Court of Justice reaffirmed that it is for the national court before which the proceedings are pending to determine, having regard to the special features of the case, both the need for a preliminary ruling to enable it to give judgment and the relevance of the questions which it refers to the court and also to decide at which stage in the proceedings to refer such questions.

¹ Case C-105/95 *Kontogeorgas v Kartonpak AE* [1996] ECR I-6643, [1997] 1 CMLR 1093, paragraph 11.

15.90 Nevertheless, it is for the CJEU to examine where necessary the conditions in which a reference has been made in order to confirm its own jurisdiction.¹ If a national court, having referred a question for preliminary ruling, finds that the claims of the appellants have been acceded to and that the national proceedings have been terminated, the CJEU is without jurisdiction.²

¹ Which examination may include providing the national court with all elements for interpreting EU law which may be of assistance in adjudicating on the case pending before it, whether or not the court has specifically referred those questions: Case C-321/03 *Dyson v Registrar of Trade Marks* [2007] ECR I-687 at paragraph 24.

² Joined Cases C-422–424/93 *Zabala and Others v Instituto Nacional de Empleo* [1995] 1 ECR 1567; [1996] 1 CMLR 861; Case C-470/12 *Pohotovost's. r.o.v. Miroslav Vašuta* EU:C:2014:101 at paras 27–34.

15.91 In the context of a reference for preliminary ruling, the Court of Justice has no jurisdiction to decide whether a national provision is compatible with European Union law. Moreover, when referring questions, a national court must give at the very least some explanation of the reasons for its choice of the Community provisions for reference and the link between those provisions and the national legislation applicable to the dispute.¹

¹ Case C-167/94R *Gomis and Others* [1995] 1 ECR 1023; [1996] 2 CMLR 129; [1995] All ER (EC) 668; Case C-116/08 *Christel Meerts v Proost NV* [2009] ECR I-10063 at paras 26–27. On the last point see also Order of Court in Case C-458/93 *Saddick* [1995] ECR I-511; [1995] 3 CMLR 318.

15.92 However, a reference was held inadmissible where the parties before the national court had artificially arranged matters so as to generate a dispute for the purpose of obtaining a ruling to establish the inconsistency of a provision of national law with European Union law.¹ The effect of that ruling was for some time both contentious and uncertain.² It has now been clarified. The Court of Justice has explained that a reference will be inadmissible when it is unnecessary to answer the question for the purpose of resolving the dispute between the parties, even though the referring court may consider it desirable to have the issue determined for the future.³ The Court has stressed that its role under the preliminary reference procedure is to assist in the administration of justice in the member states and not to give advisory opinions on general or hypothetical questions.[4] On the other hand, it will accept a jurisdiction where it is not manifestly apparent from the facts set out in the order for reference that the dispute is fictitious.[5] In one case, the Court of Justice accepted that it had jurisdiction to consider a reference made by a Swedish court in a tax matter even where all of the parties to the proceedings were agreed as to the proper tax treatment of the goods concerned: the purpose of the national proceedings was to review the legality of an opinion which, when it became definitive, would bind the tax authorities and serve as the basis on which the party which had applied for the opinion would be taxed. That was held to make the question referred real and not hypothetical.[6]

[1] Case 104/79 *Foglia v Novello* [1980] ECR 745: Case 244/80 *Foglia v Novello (No 2)* [1981] ECR 3045.

[2] See A Barav, 'Preliminary Censorship' 5 EL Rev (1980) 443; G Bebr, 'The Existence of a Genuine Dispute: An Indispensable Precondition for the Jurisdiction of the Court under Article 234 EEC Treaty?' 17 CML Rev (1980) 525; D Wyatt, 'Following up Foglia: Why the Court is Right to Stick to its Guns', 6 EL Rev (1981) 447; Morten Broberg and Niels Fenger, *Preliminary References to the European Court of Justice* (2010) Oxford University Press at 203–211.

[3] Joined Cases C-422 to 424/93 *Erasun v Instituto Nacional de Empleo* [1995] ECR I-1567, [1996] 1 CMLR 861; *Joined Cases C-261/08 and C-348/08 Garcia and Cabrera v Delegado del Gobierno en la Región de Murcia* [2009] ECR I-10143 at paras 36–41.

[4] Case C-458/06 *Skatteverket v Gourmet Classic Ltd.* [2008] ECR I-4207 para [26], approving Foglia; Case C-440/08 *Gielen v Staatssecretaris van Financiën* [2010] ECR I-2323 at paras 28–29.

[5] Case 267/86 *Van Eycke v ASPA NV* [1988] ECR 4769, [1990] 4 CMLR 330, paragraphs 11 and 12.

[6] Case C-458/06 *Skatteverket v Gourmet Classic Ltd* [2008] ECR I-4207. See Case C-163/09 *Répertoire Culinaire v HMRC* for the issues arising from such an approach.

15.93 A competent national court or tribunal (except one of final instance) enjoys the widest discretion in determining whether to refer questions.[1] It is for the national court or tribunal to determine the stage at which questions shall be referred, although the Court of Justice will often find it convenient to have facts decided first, in order that it may take cognizance of them in framing its ruling.[2] One factor to be taken into account may be the delay of one to two years in obtaining a ruling from the court.[3] Some English courts have refused to make references because of such delay.[4] Given concerns about delay it may be considered appropriate to refer where the judge is convinced that a reference will eventually be necessary, so that an early reference will save time.[5] The decision to refer is that of the national judge, who may consider it appropriate to do so even if both parties object.[6]

[1] Case 166/73 *Rheinmuhlen-Dusseldorf v EVGF* [1974] ECR 33; Case C-689/13 *Puligienica Facility Esco SpA (PFE) v Airgest SpA* EU:C:2016:199 at paragraph 32.

[2] Joined Cases 36, 71/80 *Irish Creamery Milk Suppliers Association v Ireland* [1981] ECR 735; Case C-5/14 *Kernkraftwerke Lippe-Ems GmbH v Hauptzollamt Osnabrück* EU:C:2015:354 at paragraph 31.

[3] *R v Pharmaceutical Society of Great Britain and Secretary of State for Social Services, ex p Association of Pharmaceutical Importers* [1987] 3 CMLR 951; *Customs and Excise Comrs v ApS Samex* [1983] 1 All ER 1042 at 1055.

[4] *B (A Child) (Care Proceedings: Jurisdiction), Re* [2013] EWCA Civ 1434 at paragraph 83

[5] *R v HM Treasury, ex p Daily Mail and General Trust plc* [1987] 2 CMLR 1.

[6] *Direct Cosmetics Ltd v Customs and Excise Comrs* [1983] 3 CMLR 416; *Maxim's Ltd v Dye* [1978] 2 All ER 55, [1977] 1 WLR 1155.

15.94 It is, however, the duty of the national court, when referring questions for preliminary ruling, to define the factual and legislative context of the questions that it is asking, or at least to explain the factual circumstances on which they are based in order to enable the Court of Justice to arrive at an interpretation of European Union law which will be helpful. Where the national court fails to set out the factual circumstances with sufficient particularity to enable the Court of Justice properly to appreciate the context of the request, the questions will be considered manifestly inadmissible.[1] The requirement to set out the facts fully is less pressing, however, where the questions relate to specific technical points and enable the Court of Justice to give a useful reply even in the absence of a full description of the factual and legal context.[2] In the UK, the factual and legislative context will ordinarily be set out, in the form of a judgment of the referring court which explains the issues and the reasons for the reference, by together with an Order, to which questions are scheduled.

[1] Joined Cases C-320 to C-322/90 *Telemarsicabruzzo SpA v Circostel* [1993] ECR I-393 paragraph 6; Case C-157/92 *Pretore di Genova v Banchero* [1993] ECR I-1085 paragraph 4: Case C-378/93 *La Pyramide* [1994] ECR I-3999, paragraph 14; Case C-458/93 *Mostafa Saddik* [1995] 3 CMLR 318, paragraph 15; Case C-234/12 *Sky Italia Srl v Autorità per le Garanzie nelle Comunicazioni* EU:C:2013:496 at paragraphs 30–33.
[2] Case C-316/93 *Vaneetveld v SA Le Foyer and SA Le Foyer v Fédération des Mutualités Socialistes et Syndicales et Syndicales de la Provence de Liege* [1994] ECR I-763, [1994] 2 CMLR 852.

15.95 The questions themselves should be expressed with sufficient clarity to communicate the essential nature of the dispute to a reader who does not have access to the account of the factual and legislative context. This necessity arises from the fact that only the questions are communicated, by publication in the *Official Journal of the European Community*, to the Governments of the other Member States which must decide on that basis whether to intervene in the proceedings;[1] but they should not be unnecessarily prolix.[2] For this reason it is unsatisfactory to refer a series of questions, the product of negotiation between counsel, each designed to encompass phrases considered advantageous to the argument advanced by one party or the other. The English court would tend to give judgment explaining the reasons for making a reference and would append draft questions on which the parties may usually comment before the order for reference is finalised.

[1] Morten Broberg and Niels Fenger, *Preliminary References to the European Court of Justice* (2010) Oxford University Press at 301.
[2] In Joined Cases 115 and 116/81 *Adoui and Cornuaille v Belgium* [1982] ECR 1665, [1982] 3 CMLR 631, the *Tribunal de Liege* asked 29 questions, many of them broken down into subordinate questions. This provoked extra-judicial criticism from Judge Koopmans in 'The Technique of the Preliminary Question – a View from the European Court of Justice' in *Article 234 EEC: Experiences and Problems*, TMC Asser Instituut (1987) The Hague, the Netherlands, 328.

15.96 In the event of a reference for preliminary ruling, the costs incurred at the hearing before the CJEU by the parties to the proceedings before the national court are a matter for that national court.[1] The proceedings before the CJEU are to be regarded for this purpose as a stage in the proceedings before the referring court. By the same token, a grant of legal aid for the purposes of proceedings before an English court automatically encompasses proceedings before the CJEU in the event of a reference.[2] The ECJ has, however, its own resources for the award of legal aid, particularly in the event of a reference for preliminary ruling from a national tribunal before which legal aid is not available.[3]

[1] Case C-472/99 *Clean Car Autoservice GmbH v Stadt Wien* [2001] ECR I-09687.
[2] *R v Marlborough Street Stipendiary Magistrate, ex p Bouchereau* [1977] 3 All ER 365, [1977] 1 CMLR 269.
[3] Rules of Procedure of the Court of Justice, art 115–118.

15.97 Following a substantial revision of its Rules of Procedure in 2012, the Court of Justice has issued Recommendations to national courts and tribunals in relation to the initiation of preliminary rulings proceedings and revised Practice Directions to parties.[1] Also the Council of Bars and Law Societies of Europe (CCBE) has issued Practical Guidance for Advocates before the Court of Justice in Preliminary Reference Proceedings to assist in particular first time advocates before the Court and also guidance for advocates before the General Court.[2]

[1] See http://curia.europa.eu/jcms/jcms/Jo2_7031/en/
[2] See http://www.ccbe.eu/fileadmin/speciality_distribution/public/documents/PD_LUX/PDL_Gu idesrecommendations/ENPDL20150909Practical-Guidance-for-Advocates-before-the-Genera l-Court-in-Direct-Actions.pdf

REMEDIES IN NATIONAL COURTS

Remedies generally

15.98 European Union law requires Member States to provide remedies in national courts to enforce obligations arising under European Union law. The detailed substantive and procedural rules in relation to such remedies are, in general, to be determined as a matter of national law. These domestic rules are, however, subject to the general principles of effectiveness, equivalence and effective judicial protection.[1] Furthermore, Article 47 of the Charter of Fundamental Rights of the European Union provides that '[e]veryone whose rights and freedoms guaranteed by law of the Union has the right to an effective remedy before a tribunal in compliance with the conditions laid down in this article . . . '

[1] Lewis, Judicial Remedies in Public Law (5th edn, 2014) at 17-052 to 17-062.

15.99 The need for a remedy for breach of European Union law may arise in both private and public law cases.[1] As a matter of private law, individuals may, for instance, have a statutory right to enforce obligations arising in European Union law (as is the case in relation to certain obligations imposed in employment law). The right, in Article 47 of the EU Charter of Fundamental Rights, to an effective remedy is in effect accorded 'horizontal direct effect' and can therefore be relied upon by individuals against other individuals because the court is bound by this principle.[2] An individual may alternatively be able to formulate a claim for breach of statutory duty.[3] This is so since there is a duty under s 2 of the European Communities Act 1972 to recognise and enforce rights arising by or under the treaties. Proceedings for breach of statutory duty may, therefore, be brought not only in the event of a breach of a directly effective provision of any of the treaties establishing the European

Union or governing the constitution of the institutions of those Communities,[4] but also in the event of a breach of a directly effective provision of legislation adopted by those institutions,[5] or a breach of directly effective provisions of other Community treaties.[6]

1   Gordon and Moffatt, EU Law in Judicial Review (2ⁿᵈ edn, 2014) at 5.30 ff.
2   In *Benkharbouche v Embassy of Sudan* [2015] EWCA Civ. 33, at [76]–[81], the Court of Appeal held that the right to an effective remedy enshrined in Article 47 of the CFREU could be relied upon horizontally in an employment claim (insofar as the claims fell within the scope of EU law) brought by an employee against an embassy.
3   *Garden Cottage Foods Ltd v Milk Marketing Board* [1984] AC 130 at 141 (Lord Diplock); *Bourgoin SA v Ministry of Agriculture Fisheries and Food* [1986] QB 716, [1985] 3 All ER 585. The previous authorities are reviewed in *R v Secretary of State for Transport ex p Factortame Ltd (No 7)* [2001] 1 WLR 942. There is, however, discussion of whether this classification is correct (P Giliker 'English tort law and the challenge of Francovich liability: 20 years on' (2012) 128 LQR 541) and an action for breach of EU law is sometimes referred to as 'analogous' to one for breach of statutory duty: eg *Sempra Metals Ltd (formerly Metallgesellschaft Ltd) v IRC* [2007] UKHL 34, [2008] 1 AC 561 at para 225.
4   For treaties governing the constitution of the institutions, see **15.3–15.5** above.
5   For reliance on directly effective legislation, see Case 41/74 *Van Duyn v Home Office* [1975] Ch 358, [1974] ECR 1337.
6   For reliance on the EC-Turkey Association Agreement and measures adopted pursuant thereto, see Case 12/86 *Demirel v Stadt Schwäbisch Gmünd* [1987] ECR 3719; *R v Secretary of State for the Home Department ex p Narin* [1990] 1 CMLR 682; Case C-192/89 *Sevince v Staatssecretaris van Justitie* [1990] ECR-I-3461.

15.100 In the public sphere, European Union law may be invoked in judicial review proceedings in a variety of ways. In particular, challenges may be brought in respect of: (i) national legislation which purports to implement European Union law into domestic law or to derogate from European Union obligations; (ii) a failure to implement a European Union obligation; and/or (iii) acts or omissions of public authorities which are justified by reference to European Union law (directly or indirectly). Such challenges may involve an indirect challenge to the validity of European Union law legislation itself. Domestic courts do not, however, have jurisdiction to declare European Union law invalid,[1]. although they may declare the rule to be valid or (if it is considered that the challenge has some merit) make a reference to the CJEU.

1   *Foto-Frost v Hauptzollamt Lubeck-Ost Case 314/85* [1987] ECR 4199.

Judicial review in the context of European Union law

15.101 In situations where European Union law is engaged, the rules of judicial review are different from those that are adopted by the English courts in relation to challenges of administrative decisions based upon English law.[1] As indicated above, the circumstances and context in which the judicial review of a measure based on European Union law arise are many and varied and it is therefore difficult to provide rules of general application. Accordingly, the text below merely considers the broad approach to the modification of the rules of judicial review, subject to the caveat that the rules of judicial review required by European Union law vary according to the particular context.

1   For instance, in *R (oao Lumsdon) v Legal Services Board* [2015] UKSC 41; [2016] AC 697 at [31] the Supreme Court (per Lords Reed or Toulson, with whom the rest of the Court agreed), stated that 'Where the proportionality principle is applied by a national court, it must, as a

principle of EU law, be applied in a manner which is consistent with the jurisprudence of the [CJEU] . . . '

15.102 A distinction can be drawn between the judicial review of measures taken by: (a) the Union institutions, on the one hand; and (b) national authorities, on the other. In both instances, however, and whether the challenge is brought in the Court of Justice of the European Union or in a national court, the grounds of judicial review are similar and are derived from European Union law. Where Union institutions are alleged to have acted inconsistently with European Union law, the right to an effective judicial remedy means that the exercise of the Union institutions' powers may be subject to judicial scrutiny in accordance with the principles of judicial review laid down by European Union law. The grounds of judicial review of the Union institutions' discretion include manifest error of assessment; inadequate reasoning; incorrect reference to the provisions of the treaty under which the measure was adopted; failure to consult and breach of the general principles of European Union law.[1]

[1] See paras **15.51** *et seq.*

15.103 Where decisions of national authorities are subject to judicial review for alleged inconsistency with European Union law, no difficulty of a legal nature arises where the exercise of the discretion is alleged to conflict with a directly effective right emanating from an act of a Union institution whose objective meaning can be determined by judicial process, if necessary accompanied by fact finding. The administrative courts must give effect to the directly effective right and quash as unlawful the purported exercise of administrative power. A measure of a national administrative authority that is allegedly inconsistent with European Union law can also be challenged on the basis that it fails to respect the principles of judicial review laid down by European Union law. As can be seen from the short list provided in the paragraph immediately above, these principles, and therefore the proper approach for English courts to adopt in a judicial review of the exercise of such powers, are in general stricter than the test of *Wednesbury* unreasonableness.[1] The stricter test means that, in such circumstances, in general the exercise of administrative power may be tested and passed only if substantial factual considerations, which are relevant, reasonable and proportionate to the aim in view, are put forward in its justification.[2]

[1] Case C-222/84) *Johnston v Chief Constable of the Royal Ulster Constabulary* [1987] ICR 83 at paragraph 13 et seq. and *R (Mabanaft) Ltd v Secretary of State for Trade and Industry* [2009] EWCA Civ 224 at paragraph 30.
[2] *R v Ministry of Agriculture, Fisheries and Food, ex p First City Trading* [1997] 1 CMLR 250 at 279, paragraph 69. See also *R v Minister of Agriculture, Fisheries and Food, ex p Bell Lines Ltd and An Bord Bainne Co-operative Ltd* [1984] 2 CMLR 502 and *R v Minister of Agriculture, Fisheries and Food, ex p Roberts* [1991] 1 CMLR 555 at paragraph 85 (issue is not *Wednesbury* unreasonableness but whether 'in the court's view the decision was a correct one').

15.104 However, as explained above, the applicable rules for the judicial review of a measure alleged to be inconsistent with European Union law depend upon the context. Where the enactment conferring the relevant power uses elastic terminology such that the Union institution or national authority enjoys a wide power of appraisal in assessing a complex economic or technical situation, the intensity of the review is low. In such situations, the Court of Justice of the European Union has held that the reviewing court may not substitute its assessment of the facts for the assessment made by the relevant authority and must therefore restrict itself to examining the accuracy of the findings of fact and law made by the authority and to verifying that the exercise of administrative power is not vitiated by a manifest error or a misuse of powers and that it did not clearly exceed the bounds of its discretion.[1] However, even the exercise of complex technical evaluations does not exclude the reviewing court from establishing both whether the evidence relied upon is factually accurate, reliable and consistent and also whether the evidence contains all the information which must be taken into account in order to assess a complex situation and whether it is capable of substantiating the conclusions drawn from it.[2]

[1] Case C-120/97 *Upjohn Ltd v Licensing Authority established under the Medicines Act 1968* [1999] ECR I-223. For a comparable case in English law, see the Court of Appeal decision in *R v Radio Authority, ex p Bull* [1997] 2 All ER 561.
[2] Case C-405/07 P *Netherlands v Commission* [2008] ECR I-8301 at paragraph 55 and Case C-525/04 P *P Spain v Lenzing AG* [2007] ECR I-9947 at paragraph 57.

15.105 In order to establish the standard and intensity of review in any given situation it is necessary to consider the grounds of review relied upon and the nature of the decision and to assess the degree of discretion that has been left to the national authorities or Union institution. The starting point where the discretionary power in question is derived from European Union law is that the nature and limits of the discretion and the manner of its exercise must be determined by the national court in accordance with European Union law, assisted if appropriate by the guidance of the Court of Justice of the European Union given by way of preliminary ruling.

Damages

15.106 On the availability of damages for breaches by Member States of directly effective provisions of European Union law, the Court of Justice has rendered a series of seminal rulings.[1] There is, in European Union law, a principle of State liability for loss and damage caused to individuals. That principle is inherent in the Treaty and applies to any case where a Member State acts in breach of its obligations. Two key decisions are *Francovich v Italy*[2] and *Brasserie du Pecheur v Germany*.[3]

[1] For an account of these, see W van Gerven, 'Bridging the Unbridgable: Community and National Tort Laws after *Francovich* and *Brasserie*' 45 ICLQ (1996) 507.
[2] Joined Cases C-6/90 and C-9/90 *Francovich and Bonifaci v Italy* [1991] ECR I-5357.
[3] Joined Cases 46 and 48/93 *Brasserie du Pecheur v Germany and R v Secretary of State for Transport, ex p Factortame Ltd* [1996] ECR I-2553.

15.107 Where there is a breach of European Union law committed by a Member State acting in a field in which it has a wide discretion in taking legislative decisions, the Court of Justice stated in *Brasserie du Pecheur*[1] that European Union law confers a right of reparation where three conditions are met:

(1)   the rule infringed must be one intended to confer rights on individuals;

(2)   the breach must have been sufficiently serious; and
(3)   there must be a direct causal link between the breach and the damage
       sustained by the injured parties.[2]

1   Joined Cases 46 and 48/93 *Brasserie du Pecheur v Germany and R v Secretary of State for
     Transport, ex p Factortame Ltd* [1996] ECR I-2553.
2   In *Barco de Vapor BV v Thanet District Council* [2014] EWHC 490 (Ch) Birss J accepted that
     to show the necessary causal link the claimant needed to satisfy the 'but for' test and prove that
     the damage suffered was as a 'sufficiently direct consequence' of the unlawful act complained
     of: paragraph [70].

15.108 A breach of European Union law is sufficiently serious to give rise to
a liability to make reparation where the Member State has 'manifestly and
gravely disregarded the limits on its discretion'.[1] In *Brasserie du Pecheur*
the Court of Justice gave a non-exhaustive list of the factors which could be
taken into account in deciding whether there had been such a breach:[2]

> 'The factors which the competent court may take into consideration include the
> clarity and precision of the rule breached; the measure of discretion left by that
> rule to the national or Community authorities; whether the infringement and the
> damage caused was intentional or involuntary; whether any error of law was
> excusable or inexcusable; the fact that the position taken by a Community
> institution may have contributed towards the omission, and the adoption or
> retention of national measures or practices contrary to Community law.'

Although national rules relating to compensation for damage may be applied
to such a cause of action, Member States are not permitted to add to the
Francovich conditions so as to make it excessively difficult to obtain damages
or other forms of compensation.[3]

1   Joined Cases 46 and 48/93 *Brasserie du Pecheur v Germany and R v Secretary of State for
     Transport, ex p Factortame Ltd* [1996] ECR I-2553 at paragraph [55]. See *Angus Grow-
     ers Ltd v Scottish Ministers* [2016] CSOH 26; 2016 SLT 529, in which the Court of Session
     (Outer House) held that the breach of EU law by the State (failing to lift the suspension of a
     producer from the fruit and vegetable aid scheme) was sufficiently serious to give rise to a right
     to reparation and the conditions for the imposition of state liability were otherwise fulfilled.
2   Ibid at para [56]. See also the discussion in *R v Secretary of State for Transport, ex p
     Factortame Ltd (No 5)* [2000] 1 AC 524 at 554 et seq (Lord Clyde). There is no requirement
     for exhaustion of domestic remedies before such a claim can be advanced: *Spencer v Secretary
     of State for Work and Pensions* [2008] EWCA Civ 750; [2009] QB 358.
3   Case C-470/03 *AGM-COS.MET SRL v Suomen valtio* [2007] ECR I-2749. Cf. the require-
     ment imposed on a *Francovich* claim in *Poole v Her Majesty's Treasury* [2007] EWCA Civ
     1021, [2008] EuLR 309 at paragraph 36 that an individual right of complaint about failures
     of regulation within the national market be *necessary* to achieve freedom of establishment.

15.109 Where, on the other hand, the Member State when committing the
breach of European Union law was not called upon to make legislative choices
and had considerably reduced discretion, or none at all, the mere infringement
may be sufficient to establish the existence of a sufficiently serious breach. So
where a Member State fails, in breach of the third paragraph of art 288 TFEU,
to take any of the measures necessary to achieve the result prescribed by a
directive within the time there laid down, the State is, *ipso facto*, guilty of a
manifest and grave breach, and is liable to make good in damages any loss
caused directly by that breach to any individual on whom the directive was
intended to confer rights.[1] Indeed, in an exceptional case where a court of a
Member State has manifestly infringed EU law, it is possible for a Mem-

ber State to be liable in damages for the decisions of its courts.[2]

¹ Joined Cases C-6/90 and C-9/90 *Francovich and Bonifaci v Italy* [1991] ECR I-5357; Joined Cases C-178–179 and 188–190/94 *Dillenkofer v Germany* [1996] 3 CMLR 469. Cf the case where it is not possible to establish with precision the minimum of level of protection under the EU provision: Case C-278/05 *Robins v Secretary of State for Work and Pensions* [2007] ECR I-1053 at paragraphs 79–82. In *Delaney v Secretary of State for Transport* [2014] EWHC 1785 (QB) Jay J stated that the test which applies to both the 'little or no discretion' type case and the 'wide discretion' type case is a unitary one, but the conditions for liability are more readily satisfied in cases where the State has little discretion how to comply with its EU obligations: paragraphs [79] and [85]. This was upheld by the Court of Appeal at [2015] EWCA Civ 172.

² Case C-224/01 *Köbler v Austria* [2003] ECR I-10239 at paragraph 53; Case C-173/03 *Traghetti del Mediterraneo SpA v Italy* [2006] ECR I-5177 at paragraphs 32 and 42–46 (Member States may not impose conditions stricter than the *Köbler* conditions to establish liability). See also *Cooper v A-G* [2010] EWCA Civ 464, [2011] QB 976,[2011] 2 WLR 448.

15.110 Different considerations apply where the breach of European Union law is invoked as a basis for an action in damages brought by one private individual against another. It appears from *Garden Cottage Foods Ltd v Milk Marketing Board* that in English proceedings between private individuals or corporations, damages will be available for breaches of those directly effective provisions which are designed to protect private rights.[1] The tort may be characterised as breach of statutory duty, arising from analysis of the Treaty provision in question.[2] This is by no means inconsistent with the conclusion of Neill J in *An Bord Bainne Co-operative Ltd (Irish Dairy Board) v Milk Marketing Board*[3] where he held that the speeches in *Garden Cottage Foods Ltd v Milk Marketing Board* support the proposition that any contravention of a directly effective provision of European Union law creates rights in private law which national courts must protect. The same view was taken by Parker LJ in *Bourgoin SA v Ministry of Agriculture, Fisheries and Food*.[4] Damages claims for losses caused by breach of competition law are an example of a remedy for breach of EU law obtained by one private person against another.[5]

¹ [1984] AC 130, [1983] 2 All ER 770.
² The suggestion that this was a new innominate tort was made by Lord Denning MR in *Application des Gaz SA v Falks Veritas Ltd* [1974] 1 Ch 381 at 395. That view has not however found favour.
³ [1984] 2 CMLR 519 at 528 upheld on appeal [1984] 2 CMLR 584.
⁴ [1986] QB 716 at 787. See also Morritt J in *Plessey Co plc v General Electric Co plc and Siemens* [1990] ECC 384 at 393.
⁵ See, eg, Case C-453/99 *Courage Ltd v Crehan* [2002] QB 507, [2001] ECR I-6297; *Devenish Nutrition Ltd v Sanofi-Aventis SA* [2007] EWHC 2394 (Ch), [2009] Ch 390.

Interim relief

15.111 The obligation imposed by European Union law on the national court to ensure the effective judicial protection of rights directly conferred on the individual by provisions of European Union law includes the obligation, if the need arises and where the factual and legal preconditions are met, to afford interim and urgent protection to rights claimed on the basis of such provisions of European Union law, pending a final determination and any interpretation by way of preliminary ruling given by the Court of Justice.[1] Accordingly, a national court which, in a case before it concerning European Union law, considers that the sole obstacle which precludes it from granting interim relief is a rule of national law, must set aside that rule.[2]

¹   Opinion of Mr Advocate-General Tesauro in Case C-213/89 *R v Secretary of State for Transport, ex p Factortame (No 2)* [1991] 1 AC 603, [1990] 3 CMLR 1.
²   Ruling of the court in Case C-213/89 *R v Secretary of State for Transport, ex p Factortame (No 2)* [1991] 1 AC 603, [1990] 3 CMLR 1.

15.112 In considering whether interim relief should be granted, an English court must consider, first, the availability to either claimant or defendant of an adequate remedy in damages and second, if no such adequate remedy exists, the balance of convenience, taking all the circumstances of the case into consideration; and, in considering the balance of convenience, the court must take into account the interests of the public in general to whom the authority owes duties. There is no rule that the party challenging the validity of the law has to show a strong prima facie case that it is invalid; nevertheless, the court will not restrain the public authority from enforcing the law unless it is satisfied that the challenge to its validity is based sufficiently firmly to warrant that exceptional course of action.[1] Where there has been a breach of a provision of European Union law which does not produce direct effects, and an individual has suffered loss in consequence of that breach, the individual's interest may be protected by means of an action in the European Court by the Commission (or exceptionally by another Member State) against the Member State in default.[2] Where in such proceedings judgment is given against a Member State, the latter is required to take the necessary measures to comply with the judgment of the Court of Justice.[3] In this context, it is thought that the 'necessary measures' could include the payment of an indemnity to compensate individuals for losses occasioned by the breach of the obligation. Where the breach consists in a failure to adopt apt and timeous national legislation, the question arises whether the 'necessary measures' to comply with the judgment may include the making of retrospective legislation to cure the defect *ex post facto*. This possibility cannot be excluded, notwithstanding the fact that such legislation is expressly prohibited by para 1(1)(b) of Sch 2 to the European Communities Act 1972.

¹   *R v Secretary of State for Transport, ex p Factortame (No 2)* [1991] 1 AC 603, [1990] 3 CMLR 1, HL, applying *American Cyanamid Co v Ethicon Ltd* [1975] AC 396, [1975] 1 All ER 504, HL and *Smith v Inner London Education Authority* [1978] 1 All ER 411, CA. For a recent successful application for interim relief against the operation of a decision alleged to be in breach of EU law (so as to permit the shipment of live sheep to France, despite a ban on live animal shipments imposed by the defendant) see *Barco de Vapor v Thanet District Council* [2012] EWHC 3429 (Admin).
²   Arts 258 and 259 TFEU.
³   Art 260 TFEU.

Remedies against Union institutions

15.113 In the case of actions against Union institutions the point of departure is that, save where jurisdiction is conferred on the European Court, disputes to which the Union is a party are not on that ground excluded from the jurisdiction of courts or tribunals of the Member States.[1] The European Court has the sole jurisdiction to annul measures adopted by Union institutions[2] for this jurisdiction is conferred on that court by the Treaties.[3] The European Court also has sole responsibility to determine claims for compensation for damage, pursuant to art 268 and the second paragraph of art 340 TFEU (that is, claims for 'non-contractual liability'). Actions for breach of contract may be brought against Union institutions in national courts, in appropriate cases. In such cases, contractual liability is governed by the law applicable to the contract in question whereas non-contractual liability, including unjust enrichment,[4] is governed 'in accordance with the general principles common to the laws of the Member States'.[5]

[1] Art 274 TFEU. By Protocol (No 7) to the TFEU on Privileges and Immunities of the European Union, the property, funds and assets of the Communities are accorded inviolability and privileges are conferred in respect of customs duties, prohibitions on imports, communications and *laissez-passer*. Officials and servants of the Communities and Members of the European Parliament also enjoy immunities thereunder.

[2] Case 314/85 *Foto-Frost v Hauptzollamt Lübeck-Ost* [1987] ECR 4199.

[3] Art 263 TFEU.

[4] Case C-47/07 P *Masdar (UK) Ltd v European Commission* [2008] ECR I-9761.

[5] Art 340 TFEU.

15.114 Since the administration of European Union law is, in principle, entrusted to the Member States, a practical question arises of determining whether any proceedings in national courts for the damages for non-contractual liability should be brought against the Commission, as representative of the Communities[1] or against national authorities.[2] In relation to claims for sums unduly paid by, or owing to, pursuant to Union law which the national authorities administer, the proceedings must be brought against the national authorities.[3] On the other hand, where a decision adversely affecting the plaintiff was adopted by national authorities acting to ensure the application of Union rules, the attribution of jurisdiction between national courts and the Court of Justice depends upon the division of responsibility between the respective authorities for the adoption of the relevant measure. If the Union institution is entitled to *insist* that the national body take specific action, and does so, the alleged unlawful conduct is to be attributed to the Commission and not to the national authorities; and accordingly the proceedings should be brought against the Commission in the European Court.[4]

[1] In proceedings before national courts, the Commission represents the Union pursuant to art 17 TEU. In proceedings before the European Court, the Community is represented by the institution alleged to be at fault. Joined Cases 63–69/72 *Werhahn Hansamuhle v EC Council* [1973] ECR 1229.

[2] A Durand, 'Restitution or Damages: National Court or the European Court?' (1975–6) 1 EL Rev 431; P Oliver. 'Enforcing Community Rights in the English Courts' (1987) 50 MLR 81.

[3] Case 96/71 *Haegeman (R and V) v EC Commission* [1972] ECR 1005.

[4] Case 175/84 *Krohn & Co Import-Export GmbH & Co KG v EC Commission* [1986] ECR 753.

EUROPEAN COURT ACTIONS AGAINST MEMBER STATES

15.115 The TFEU and the Euratom Treaty provide that the Commission may institute proceedings against a Member State if the former considers that the latter has failed to fulfil an obligation under the Treaties.[1] In such a case, the Commission must first deliver a reasoned opinion on the matter and give the State the opportunity to submit its observations.[2] The Commission's decision must set a time limit for the fulfilment of the obligation. The Member State may institute proceedings before the court within two months of the notification of the decision, with a view to its annulment. In the event that the Court of Justice confirms the Commission's decision, the penalty for continued noncompliance by the Member State with a judgment of the court under art 260(2) TFEU may include both a periodic penalty payment and a lump sum fine.[3]

1   Art 258 TFEU (applied to the Euratom Treaty by Art 106a).
2   The subject matter of the action is determined by the reasoned opinion, accordingly both must be based on the same submissions: Case 211/81 *EC Commission v Denmark* [1982] ECR 4547 at 4558: Case 193/80 *EC Commission v Italy* [1981] ECR 3019 at 3032; Case 85/85 *EC Commission v Belgium* [1986] ECR 1149; Case 508/10 *Commission v Netherlands* EU:C:2012:243 at [34].
3   Case C-304/02 *Commission v France* [2005] ECR I-6263; cf. Case 270/11 *Commission v Sweden* EU:C:2013:339.

15.116 The proceedings may be brought against a Member State irrespective of the identity of the agency of the State whose action or inaction is the cause of the failure to fulfil its obligation, even in the case of a constitutionally independent institution[1] or a fraudulent official.[2] Where, therefore, a Member State delegates powers to regional or local authorities to implement a directive, and those authorities fail to implement it properly, proceedings may be brought against the Member State by the Commission.[3] Moreover, even if a Member State puts an end to its infringement, the Commission remains competent to bring proceedings for a declaration that the Member State failed to fulfil its obligations.[4] The Commission may, if it chooses, discontinue proceedings against the Member State but such discontinuance does not constitute recognition that the contested conduct is lawful.[5] It appears that the decisive date for determining whether the Member State has infringed its obligations is the expiry of the period laid down by the Commission in its reasoned opinion.[6]

1   Case 77/69 EC *Commission v Belgium* [1970] ECR 237.
2   Case 334/08 *Commission v Italy* [2010] ECR I 6865.
3   Case 96/81 EC *Commission v The Netherlands* [1982] ECR 1791.
4   Case 39/72 EC *Commission v Italy* [1973] ECR 101.
5   Joined Cases 15–16/76 *France v EC Commission* [1979] ECR 321.
6   Case 7/61 EC *Commission v Italy* [1961] ECR 317 at 326; Case 26/69 EC *Commission v France* [1970] ECR 565 at 575; Case 69/77 EC *Commission v Italy* [1978] FCR 1749 at 1755.

15.117 Although the Commission's reasoned opinion circumscribes the submissions that may be advanced by the Commission, it does not delimit the grounds which may be advanced before the Court by a Member State.[1] The latter may therefore put forward all possible justifications for its failure to comply with an obligation and, in particular, it may rely on *force majeure* as an excuse for a failure to comply with an obligation by the due date.[2] On the other hand, the court has on many occasions stated that a Member State may not plead provisions, practices or circumstances existing in its internal legal system in order to justify a failure to comply with obligations and time limits imposed by directives.[3]

1   Joined Cases 142, 143/80 *Amministrazione delle Finanze dello Stato v Essevi SpA* [1981] ECR 1413 at 1433; Halsbury's Laws of England, Vol 51, para 2.22.
2   Case 101/84 *EC Commission v Italy* [1985] ECR 2625 (destruction of records by bomb excused delay but did not excuse persistent failure in supplying statistical data).

³   Case 42/80 EC *Commission v Italy* [1980] ECR 3635; Case 43/80 EC Commission v Italy [1980] ECR 3643; Case 46/88 EC *Commission v Belgium* [1989] ECR 1133.

15.118 Where there has been a breach of a provision of European Union law which does not produce direct effects, and an individual has suffered loss in consequence of that breach, the individual's interest may be protected by means of an action in the European Court by the Commission (or exceptionally by another Member State) against the Member State in default.[1] Where in such proceedings judgment is given against a Member State, the latter is required to take the necessary measures to comply with the judgment of the Court of Justice.[2] In this context, it is thought that the 'necessary measures' could include the payment of an indemnity to compensate individuals for losses occasioned by the breach of the obligation. Where the breach consists in a failure to adopt apt and timeous national legislation, the question arises whether the 'necessary measures' to comply with the judgment may include the making of retrospective legislation to cure the defect *ex post facto*. This possibility cannot be excluded, notwithstanding the fact that such legislation is expressly prohibited by para 1(1)(b) of Sch 2 to the European Communities Act 1972.

¹   Articles 258 and 259 TFEU.
²   Article 260 TFEU.

EUROPEAN COURT ACTIONS AGAINST INSTITUTIONS

15.119 The TFEU authorises a form of judicial review proceedings against Union institutions[1] designed to secure the annulment of acts taken by them[2] or to secure redress for their failure to act;[3] and they provide for proceedings for damages[4] as well as special forms of proceedings pursuant to arbitration agreements,[5] and, at the request of a Member State supported by a determination of the Council, to determine the legality of an act adopted by the Council[6] and actions between the Union and its servants.[7]

¹   The institutions, properly so called, are those enumerated in Part Six of the Treaty on the Functioning of the European Union, ie the Parliament, the Council, the Commission and the Court. For the purposes of proceedings by staff, the European Investment Bank is treated as though it were an institution: Case 110/75 *Mills v European Investment Bank* [1976] ECR 955; and art 271 TFEU authorises actions for annulment against the Board of Governors of the Bank.
²   Articles 263–266 TFEU.
³   Article 265 TFEU.
⁴   Articles 268 and 340 TFEU.
⁵   Article 272 TFEU.
⁶   Article 269 TFEU.
⁷   Article 270 TFEU.

15.120 Article 263 TFEU does not define the acts susceptible to annulment. The Court of Justice has rejected the view that its jurisdiction under the Treaties to review 'acts . . . other than recommendations or opinions' was confined to acts (other than recommendations or opinions) of the kind listed in art 288. Rather it has held that any measure is challengeable if its legal effects are binding on and capable of affecting the interests of the applicant. An oral act may therefore be reviewed. Accordingly, the court may annul a Commission notice rejecting a complaint alleging breach of Community competition law[1] or a notice terminating provisional exemption from fines;[2] but it does not have jurisdiction to annul a decision or refusal to give an opinion or advice[3] nor a refusal to initiate action under the Treaties against a Member State.[4]

[1] Case 26/76 *Metro SB-Grossmärkte & Co KG v EC Commission* [1977] ECR 1875; Case 298/83 *CICCE v EC Commission* [1985] ECR 1105 at 1122; Case 210/81 *Demo-Studio Schmidt v EC Commission* [1983] ECR 3045; Case 191/82 *Fediol v EC Commission* [1983] ECR 2913 at 2931.
[2] Joined Cases 8–11/66 *Cimenteries CBR Cementbedrijven NV v EC Commission* [1967] ECR 75.
[3] Case 133/79 *Sucrimex SA v EC Commission* [1980] ECR 1299; Case 15/70 *Chevalley v EC Commission* [1970] ECR 975.
[4] Case 48/65 *Alfons Lütticke GmbH v EC Commission* [1966] ECR 19 at 27.

15.121 The Euratom Treaty incorporates by reference most forms of action available under the TEU/TFEU.[1] In the case of the TFEU, there is express provision for the Court of Justice to have jurisdiction to review the legality of acts adopted jointly by the European Parliament and the Council, of acts of the Council, of the Commission and of the European Central Bank other than recommendations and opinions, and of acts of 'bodies, offices or agencies of the Union' intended to produce legal effects vis-a-vis third parties.[2]

[1] Article 106a of the Euratom Treaty incorporates by reference for example the entire Court of Justice section from the TFEU save for art 271 TFEU and arts 275–276 TFEU.
[2] Article 263 TFEU.

15.122 Article 263 TFEU distinguishes, for the purposes of locus standi, between Member States and Union institutions, on the one hand, and natural or legal persons, or undertakings, on the other. The Member States, the Council and the Commission are privileged applicants in that they may initiate proceedings for annulment under art 263 TFEU without the necessity of proving legal interest. The European Parliament and the European Central Bank may institute proceedings on the same basis for the protection of their prerogatives.[1] Where, however, a natural or legal person[2] institutes proceedings under art 263 TFEU, he must normally show either that the contested measure is a decision addressed to him or that it is a decision in the form of a regulation or in the form of a decision addressed to another person which is of direct and individual concern to him.[3] There is one relaxation to these strict rules of standing in the case of 'regulatory acts' which do not entail implementing measures. For such measures, it is only necessary to show direct and not individual concern.[4]

[1] Case 166/78 *Italy v EC Council* [1979] ECR 2575 at 2596.
[2] For the purposes of intervention the word 'person' includes non-member States: Joined Cases 91, 200/82 *Chris International Foods Ltd v Commission* [1983] ECR 417. It is at least arguable that it has the same meaning for the purposes of actions for annulment. A local authority enjoying legal personality under the law of the State in which it exercises jurisdiction is a 'person' for these purposes: Case 222/83 *Commune de Differdange v EC Commission* [1984] ECR 2889.
[3] Article 263(4) TFEU. The previous wording which required the measure to be a regulation or a decision was removed by the Lisbon Treaty. see J Schwarze. 'The Legal Protection of the Individual against Regulations in European Union Law', 10 Eur Pub L (2004) 285: and K Lenaerts and T Corthout, 'Judicial Review as a Contribution to the Development of European Constitutionalism', 22 Ybk Eur L (2003) 1.

15.123 A person is said to be directly concerned by the disputed act, for the purposes of art 263 TFEU, if it affects his or her interests immediately, independently of the exercise of discretion by another person. Where, therefore, the Commission addresses a decision to two Member States, refusing an import quota, a trader is not directly concerned thereby, for the States would have enjoyed a discretion as to the disposal of any quota that might have been allocated to them for distribution amongst applicants.[1] Conversely, a decision is of direct concern to a legal person when it is addressed to a Member State which has already tied its own hands as to the exercise of any discretion that might otherwise have been retained.[2] A measure is of direct concern to a person if it constitutes a complete set of rules which are sufficient in themselves and which require no implementing provisions, in particular, where their effect on the applicant is automatic.[3] The fourth paragraph of art 263 TFEU requires the Community measure complained of to affect directly the legal situation of the individual and leave no discretion to the addressees of that measure, who are entrusted with the task of implementing it, such implementation being purely automatic and resulting from Community rules without the application of other intermediate rules.[4] In *International Fruit Co NV v EC Commission*,[5] the court noted that under the relevant Regulation the decision on the grant of import licences for dessert apples was a matter for the Commission: the duty of national authorities was merely to collect the data necessary in order for the Commission to take its decision. It concluded that 'The measure whereby the Commission decides on the issues of the import licences thus directly affects the legal position of the parties concerned'. The court has also found a measure to be of direct concern where the Member State enjoyed, nominally, a discretion in the application of the contested decision but the possibility that the Member State might not make use of the authorisation granted to it was entirely theoretical.[6]

1 Case 69/69 *Alcan Aluminium Raeren SA v EC Commission* [1970] ECR 385; Joined Cases 103–109/78 *Sociétés des Usines de Beauport v EC Council* [1979] ECR 17 at 25. See A Barav, 'Direct and Individual Concern: An Almost Unsurmountable Barrier to the Admissibility of Individual Appeal to the European Court', 11 CML Rev (1974) 19; C Harding, 'Decisions Addressed to Member States and Article 230 EEC', 25 ICLQ (1976) 15.
2 Case 62/70 *Book v EC Commission* [1971] ECR 897. In Joined Cases 106, 107/63 *Toepfer v EC Commission* [1965] ECR 405 at 411, the court found the applicants to be directly concerned by a decision validating previous acts since the discretion had already been exercised.
3 Case 294/83 *Parti Écologiste Les Verts v European Parliament* [1986] ECR 1339 at 1367.
4 Case C-404/96 P *Glencore Grain v Commission* [1998] ECR I-2435, paragraph 41; Case C-486/01 P, *Front National v European Parliament* [2004] 2 CMLR 51, paragraph 34.
5 [1971] ECR 411 at 422.
6 Case 11/82 *AE Piraiki-Patraiki v EC Commission* [1985] ECR 207. Similar principles apply where the contested decision is addressed to a person other than a Member State; Case 26/76 *Metro v EC Commission* [1977] ECR 1875.

15.124 The term 'individual concern' in art 263 TFEU denotes the quality, possessed by the contested measure, of affecting the applicant by reason of certain attributes which are peculiar to him or by reason of circumstances differentiating him from all other persons, by virtue of which the applicant is distinguished individually, just as in the case of the person addressed.[1] A measure which affects only one person is not of individual concern to him or it if this fact is fortuitous and if there was a possibility that others might have entered the class of persons affected thereby.[2] The possibility of determining, more or less precisely, the number or even the identity of the persons to whom a measure applies, by no means implies that it must be regarded as being of individual concern to them.[3] On the other hand, a particular factual situation may differentiate the applicant from all other persons;[4] thus, 'individual concern' was established where a regulation named certain undertakings and applied specific measures to them by setting the tonnage of isoglucose that each of them was allowed to produce.[5]

[1]   Case 25/62 *Plaumann & Co v EEC Commission* [1963] ECR 95; Case 40/64 *Sgarlata v EEC Commission* [1965] ECR 288: Case 72/74 *Union Syndicale-Service Public European v Council (No 2)* [1975] ECR 401.
[2]   Case 1/64 *Glucosieries Réunies SA v EEC Commission* [1964] ECR 413; Case 38/64 *Getreide-Import v EEC Commission* [1965] ECR 203.
[3]   Case 123/77 *UNICME v EC Council* [1978] ECR 845.
[4]   Joined Cases 239, 275/82 *Allied Corporation v EC Commission* [1984] ECR 1005.
[5]   Case 138/79 *Roquette Frères SA v EC Council* [1980] ECR 3333. See J Dinnage, '*Locus Standi* and Article 230 EEC', 4 EL Rev (1979) 15; R M Greaves '*Locus Standi* under Article 230 EEC when seeking Annulment of a Regulation', 11 EL Rev (1986) 119.

15.125 Individual concern is not however required to be shown where the act which is the subject of the application is a 'regulatory act' which 'does not entail implementing measures'.[1] The term 'regulatory act' is not defined and is only used in Article 263 TFEU. It had been thought on the basis of the Praesidium Explanations[2] that the objective pursued by the amendment to former Article 230 EC was to relax standing to a certain degree so as to provide access to justice in those cases where there is no implementing measure at national level, thus providing at least access to justice where none existed under the EC Treaty. However the Court of Justice has held that it was not the purpose of the Lisbon amendments to change the system of judicial review as regards legislative acts and that they cannot therefore qualify as regulatory acts.[3] Effective protection of EU law rights is a matter for national courts with the assistance of the preliminary reference procedure. As regards the concept of 'implementing measures', this is to be assessed by reference to the position of the person pleading the right to bring the proceedings and to the subject matter of the action, including whether it attacks only part of an act.[4]

[1]   The background to these changes was the debate between the Court of Justice, the Advocate Generals and the General Court as to the scope of the provisions on standing in: Case C-50/00P *Union de Pequenos Agricultores v Council* [2002] ECR 6677; Case T-177/01 *Jégo-Quéré* [2002] ECR II-2365 and see Case C-263/02P, [2004] ECR I-3425.
[2]   Praesidium Explanations to the European Convention, CONV 734/03, 12 May 2003, p 20.
[3]   Case C-583/11P *Inuit Tapiriit Kanatami v. Parliament and Council*, 3 October 2013, para 61.
[4]   Case C-274/12P *Telefonica v Commission*, 19 December 2013.

15.126 The grounds on which the court may annul acts under art 263 TFEU and under the Euratom Treaty are identical: lack of competence, infringement of an essential procedural requirement, infringement of the Treaty or of any rule of law relating to its application and misuse of powers. 'Lack of competence' means absence of the legal power to adopt the act in question.[1] The court will annul under this heading any act which does not have a legal basis in a relevant Treaty provision.[2] 'Infringement of an essential procedural requirement' denotes an irregularity in the procedure such that, but for the irregularity the decision might have been different.[3] A claim commonly made under this heading is that a measure did not adequately state the reasons on which it is based, contrary to the Treaty.[4] 'Infringement of the Treaty or of any rule of law relating to its application' denotes a breach of the Treaty itself or the implementing legislation or of any general principle of European Union law.[5] Exceptionally, a breach of a rule of international law may amount to an infringement of a rule of law relating to the application of the Treaty.[6] 'Misuse of powers',[7] which is not easily proved, denotes the use of a power for a purpose other than that for which it was conferred.[8] There is a misuse of power when an administrative or legislative act is objectively in accordance with the Treaty but subjectively vitiated by reason of the aim pursued by the respondent authority.[9]

[1] The plea was raised successfully in Case 9/56 *Meroni & Co. Industrie Metallurgiche SpA v High Authority* [1957–58] ECR 133, where the court annulled levies imposed on scrap iron by the High Authority on the basis of decisions taken by a subordinate body. Cf. Case 376/98 *Germany v Parliament and Council (Tobacco Advertising)* [2000] ECR I-8419.

[2] Joined Cases 228, 229/82 *Ford of Europe Inc and Ford-Werke AG v EC Commission* [1984] ECR 1129.

[3] Case 30/78 *Distillers Co Ltd v EC Commission* [1980] ECR 2229 at 2290 (per Mr Advocate-General Warner); Joined Cases 209–288, 218/78 *Heintz Van Landewyck Sarl v EC Commission* [1980] ECR 3125 at 3239.

[4] Article 296 TFEU; Case 25/62 *Germany v EEC Commission* [1963] ECR 63.

[5] Case 4/73 J *Nold KG v EEC Commission* [1974] ECR 491; Case 92/78 *Simmenthal SpA v EEC Commission* [1979] ECR 777.

[6] Breach of international law was alleged in Case 60/81 *International Business Machines Corpn v EC Commission* [1981] ECR 2639.

[7] The term is better rendered in the French *détournement de pouvoir* the Italian *sviamento di potere* or the German *Ermessensmissbrauch*.

[8] Case 8/55 *Fédération Charbonnière de Belgique v High Authority* [1954–56] ECR 245 at 303.

[9] Case 10/55 *Mirossevich v High Authority* [1954–56] ECR 333; Case 5/55 *Assider v High Authority* [1954–56] ECR 135. The expression has no precise parallel in English law but there is an analogy in the House of Lords' wording in *Westminster Corporation v London and North Western Railway Co* [1905] AC 426 at 432 and 439.

15.127 In the case of actions for damages in respect of the non-contractual liability of the EU under Article 340 TFEU, the restrictions as regards locus standi, applied in actions for annulment, are inapplicable.[1] However a claimant may not employ the action for damages so as to circumvent the inadmissibility of an action for annulment.[2]

[1] Joined Cases 9, 12/60 *Societe Commerciale Antoine Vloeberghs SA v High Authority* [1961] ECR 197 at 213; Case 4/69 *Alfons Lutticke GmbH v EC Commission* [1971] ECR 325; Case 153/73 *Holtz and Willemsen GmbH v EC Council and EC Commission* [1974] ECR 675.

[2] Case 59/65 *Schreckenberg v Commission* [1966] ECR 543.

15.128 The treaties impose on the Union the duty to make good any damage caused by their institutions or by their servants in the performance of their duties.[1] The Union is liable only for those acts of its servants which, by virtue of an internal and direct relationship, are the necessary extension of the tasks entrusted to the institutions.[2]

[1] Case 9/69 *Sayag v Leduc* [1969] ECR 329 at 335.

[2] Case 9/69 *Sayag v Leduc* [1969] ECR 329 at 336.

15.129 According to the Court of Justice, the action for damages is an autonomous form of action, the essential feature of which is an unlawful act or omission of a Union institution, causing loss to an applicant.[1] In the *Bergaderm* case,[2] the Court of Justice abandoned the former distinction between administrative and legislative acts and applied the three conditions laid down in *Francovich* for member state liability to the liability of the EU institutions: The rule of law infringed must be intended to confer rights on individuals; the breach must be sufficiently serious; and there must be a direct causal link between the breach and the damage sustained. Mere illegality of an EU act will not therefore suffice to establish liability and account needs to be taken of the degree of discretion enjoyed by the institution when discharging its functions.

[1]   Case 175/84 *Krohn & Co Import-Export GmbH & Co KG v EC Commission* [1986] ECR 753 at 767–768.
[2]   Case C-352/98P *Bergaderm* [2000] ECR I-5291.

15.130 The limitation period for actions for damages is five years from the occurrence of the event giving rise to liability.[1] That period cannot begin before all the requirements governing an obligation to provide compensation for damage are satisfied and, in particular, before the damage to be made good has materialised.[2]

[1]   Statute of the European Court of Justice of the EC, art 43; Statute of the European Court of Justice of Euratom, art 46.
[2]   Joined Cases 256, 257, 265, 267/80 and 5/81 *Birra Würrer SpA v EC Council and EC Commission* [1982] ECR 85 at 106.

15.131 By virtue of the second paragraph of art 340 TFEU, and the general principles to which this provision refers, the liability of the Union presupposes the existence of a set of circumstances comprising actual damage, a causal link between the damage claimed, and the illegality of such conduct.[1] Damage covers not only material loss *(damnum emergens)* but also loss of profit or appreciation *(lucrum cessans).*[2] In quantifying damage the court aspires to restore the applicant to the status quo.[3] A causative connection between the act and the loss is an essential feature of the cause of action.[4] Thus, for example, where an applicant claimed to have suffered damage by reason of the unlawful conduct of Commission officials in connection with the implementation of a public works contract concluded between the Republic of Malagasy and the European Development Fund, the action was dismissed on the ground that the applicant had failed to show that the Commission's action caused it to sustain damage, distinct from the damage in respect of which it ought to have sought compensation from the Malagasy State.[5]

[1]   Case 4/69 *Alfons Lütticke GmbH v Commission* [1971] ECR 325 at 337.
[2]   Joined Cases 5, 7, 13–24/66 *Kampffmeyer v EC Commission* [1967] ECR 245 at 266: Case 74/74 *CNTA v EC Commission* [19751 ECR 533 at 550.
[3]   Case 90/78 *Granaria BV v EC Council and EEC Commission* [1979] ECR 1081 at 1090; Joined Cases, 5, 7, 13–24/66 *Kampffmeyer v EC Commission* [1967] ECR 245.
[4]   Case 169/73 *Compagnie Continentale France v EC Council* [1975] ECR 117 at 135; Joined Cases 64, 113/76, 167, 239/78 and 27, 28, 45/79 *P Dumortier Freres SA v EC Council* [1979] ECR 3091 at 3117.
[5]   Case 33/82 *Murri Frères v EC Commission* [1985] ECR 2759 at 2789.

Chapter 16

QUASHING ORDERS

THE REMEDIES AVAILABLE ON AN APPLICATION FOR JUDICIAL REVIEW

Modernisation of the 'antique remedies'

16.1 In 1976, a Law Commission report[1] critically examined the various 'antique' remedies which then formed the basis of judicial control of enactments and of administrative action by public bodies. This confusion of remedies, considered in detail in CHAPTER 2, was modernised by the introduction of a new Order 53 of the Rules of the Supreme Court in 1977, and by the Supreme Court Act 1981. The present procedure is set out in Part 54 of the Civil Procedure Rules 1998. The available remedies are specified in Part II of the Supreme Court (Senior Courts) Act 1981 and comprise:

- Quashing orders (sections 29(1), 31(1)(a), 31(5) Supreme Court Act 1981);
- Prohibiting orders (sections 29(1), 31(1)(a));
- Mandatory orders (sections 29(1), 31(1)(a));
- A declaration (sections 31(1)(a), 31(2));
- An injunction (sections 30, 37(1));
- Damages (section 31(4)).

[1] Renamed as the Senior Courts Act 1981 by the Constitutional Reform Act 1981.

Combining prerogative orders

16.2 Section 29(2) of the 1981 Act provides that an order granting one or more of these remedies is final, subject to any right of appeal. It is clear from section 31(1) of the Supreme Court Act 1981 and Order 53 rule 2, that these remedies may be claimed as an alternative, or in addition, to each other. It may be difficult in any given case to predict the court's decision as to the respective appropriateness of one or more remedies, and whilst a claim may be amended to add new relief it is advisable to claim all relevant remedies cumulatively or alternatively. It follows that an applicant may seek in a single claim for judicial review all such remedies as might be necessary to review the lawfulness of an enactment, decision, action or failure to act in relation to the exercise of a public function. Accordingly, it is common for a claim for judicial review to seek an order quashing a decision, together with a prohibiting order to prevent implementation of the decision, and/or a mandatory order to compel some further action, such as the taking of a new decision.

Remedies and relevant issues covered in other chapters

16.3 This chapter considers the prerogative orders of certiorari, prohibition and mandamus. Declarations, injunction and damages are considered separately in Chapter 16. Order 53 rule 7(2) provides that any claim for damages is subject to the usual pleading provisions of Order 18 rule 12 and this is further considered in Chapter 16. The restrictions on remedies, including *locus standi*, are considered separately in Chapter 17 and are relevant to this chapter as the court has discretion to refuse to grant a prerogative order even if the defendant public authority is held to have acted unlawfully. Declarations of incompatibility pursuant to section 4 of the Human Rights Act 1988 and damages for the breach of Convention rights pursuant to section 8 are both important remedies and are dealt with in Chapter 16. The prerogative orders are final remedies. Interim relief, including urgent applications for such relief, is dealt with in Chapter 18.

THE PREROGATIVE ORDERS

The development of writs to orders

16.4 Chapter 2 describes the historical background of the complete range of public law remedies in detail, but an understanding of that background informs the present form and use of the prerogative orders. The modern orders derive from three of the old prerogative writs which bore the same names. In their earliest form, they were sealed royal writs by which the Monarch gave orders or notifications. Those writs were converted into judicial orders obtained by application to the Queen's Bench Division by the Administration of Justice (Miscellaneous Provisions) Acts of 1933 and 1938.[1] In 1994 a Law Commission report[2] proposed that these obscurely named prerogative orders should be renamed so as to be more readily understandable, thus certiorari became a 'quashing order', prohibition a 'prohibiting order', and mandamus a 'mandatory order'. The three prerogative orders were formally renamed by s 29 of the Supreme Court Act 1981.[3]

[1] 'Administrative Law: Judicial Review and Statutory Appeals' Law Comm No. 226.
[2] As amended by the Civil Procedure (Modification of Supreme Court Act 1981) Order 2004, SI 2004/1033.
[3] Including the privatisation of hitherto public services, the 'outsourcing of decision-making' to non-governmental bodies, and the development of hybrid public authorities.

16.5 Despite the evolution of modern procedures to adapt to changing constitutional and social circumstances,[1] and the imposition of modern titles, each of the prerogative orders remains substantively unchanged from the predecessor writ. Indeed, in its original form in the 1981 Act it was apparent that section 29 provided a statutory footing for the High Court's power of judicial review by reference to the pre-existing common law powers. The modern approach of the courts is to grant these orders to give effect to the judgement of the court on the substance of the claim: they are applied as practical remedies. However, their origin as prerogative writs means that they are purely public law remedies, available against public bodies alone and obtained exclusively by judicial review.[2]

---

[1] This is the effect of s 31 of the Supreme Court Act 1981 and the procedural requirements of CPR 54.2 and 54.3.

[2] [1985] AC 374.

16.6 Neither the new Order 53 nor the new provisions in the Supreme Court Act 1981 made any express change to the substantive circumstances in which (as opposed to the procedure by which) an order of certiorari, prohibition or mandamus could be obtained.[1] These procedural changes occurred, however, during a period of case law development of the substantive principles of judicial review. With the benefit of the new procedures that development continued apace. While in 1958 it could be said[2] that many of the 'particular ways, manners and caprices' of the prerogative orders had remained 'as unshakeable as those of any other society of noblemen', the attitude of the courts today is that they possess a jurisdiction in which every public body is in principle subject to the supervision of the court as regards every decision it makes. It is not uncommon to find statements of limitations said to apply to particular prerogative writs or orders, but these statements now need to be read subject to what is said about the ambit of judicial review generally in CHAPTER 5 and about the grounds for judicial review as described in CHAPTERS 6–13. Many such statements are likely to have been overtaken by substantive common law developments. In particular, any suggestion that a particular prerogative remedy is available at common law only on particular grounds narrower than those applicable to other such remedies is unlikely to survive the universal analysis by Lord Diplock in *Council of Civil Service Unions v Minister for the Civil Service*.[3]

---

[1] *R v British Broadcasting Corpn, ex p Lavelle* [1983] 1 WLR 23, 30; *Law v National Greyhound Racing Club Ltd* [1983] 1 WLR 1302 at 1308 (Lawton LJ), 1310–1311 (Fox LJ) and 1315 (Slade LJ); *R v East Berkshire Health Authority, ex p Walsh* [1985] QB 152, 179. See, also, Forsyth 'The Scope of Judicial Review: "Public Duty", not "Source of Power" ' [1987] PL 356, 359.

[2] Zamir, 'The Declatory Judgment v The Prerogative Orders' [1958] PL 341.

[3] [1985] AC 374.

Bodies which can be subject to prerogative orders

16.7 The historical rules as to the bodies which might be subjected to mandamus differed from those applicable to certiorari and prohibition. Older cases therefore need to be read with this in mind and interpreted with that context in mind. An important instance is that certiorari and prohibition were said to be limited to persons or bodies whose office was judicial or who had a duty to act judicially. Mandamus was never limited, or indeed primarily concerned with, such persons or bodies: it lay where the thing directed to be done appertained to the respondent or an office held by the respondent, and was in the nature of a public duty.

16.8 All three are final remedial orders which may be granted at the conclusion of the final hearing. Their origin as prerogative writs means that they cannot be granted against superior Courts of Record[1] or against decisions that are in substance, rather than merely form, decisions of the Crown.[2] The Tribunals, Courts and Enforcement Act 2007 designated the Upper Tribunal as a Superior court of Record. This raised constitutional questions as to the relationship between the new tribunal chambers and the ordinary courts and the principles underpinning the supervisory jurisdiction of judicial review. Early challenges met with different conclusions in the lower courts in Engand and Scotland, notwithstanding that the same legislation and tribunal structure applies in both jurisdictions. In *R (Cart) v Upper Tribunal; R (MR (Pakistan)) v Upper Tribunal (Immigration and Asylum Chamber)*[3] and *Eba v Advocate General for Scotland*[4] the Supreme Court held that permission to apply for judicial review should only be granted where the criteria for a second-tier appeal are satisfied, namely where there is an important point of principle or practice or some other compelling reason to review the case.

[1] Such as the Supreme Court, Court of Appeal, High Court, Supreme Court Masters, Employment Appeals Tribunal or Special Immigration Appeal Commission. This is considered in CHAPTER 17.

[2] But see the approach of the Administrative Court in *R (Misick) v Secretary of State for Foreign & Commonwealth Affairs* [2009] EWHC 1039.

[3] [2011] UKSC 28.

[4] [2011] UKSC 29.

16.9 If a remedy against the Crown is sought, general principles discussed in CHAPTER **14** will apply. In the present chapter, reference is made to the Crown's immunity from suit only where a particular point needs to be made in relation to a particular remedy. Thus, while this chapter will touch on some aspects of the bodies which may be subject to prerogative orders, the reader should turn to CHAPTER **5** for a general discussion of amenability to judicial review and to CHAPTER **14** for discussion of the position of the Crown. The traditional view has been that prerogative orders cannot be granted in relation to matters of military discipline or conduct, or against ecclesiastical courts.[1] However, section 6 of the Human Rights Act 1998 requires the High Court to act compatibly with the European Convention on Human Rights, including the Article 6 right to a fair and public hearing to determine civil rights and obligations. Article 13 requires that contracting states must afford an effective remedy before a national authority. This purported immunity from prerogative orders is therefore unlikely to survive.[2] Modern commentaries now commonly state that the decisions of the Church courts are subject to judicial review and that, for the purposes of the Human Rights Act 1998, all courts and tribunals of the Church of England are public authorities and so must act in a way which is compatible with Convention rights.[3]

[1] Save for prohibiting orders which will lie against ecclesiastical courts as the old writ of prohibition was originally typically directed at them.

[2] The modern approach to the courts on such issues can be gleaned from cases such as *Jones v Kaney* [2010] EWHC 61 QB in which a certificate was granted pursuant to s 12(1) of the Administration of Justice Act 1969 to enable the Supreme Court to decide whether to re-visit the issue of witness immunity notwithstanding binding superior court judgements which cannot be distinguished.

[3] M Hill, R Sandberg and N Doe, *Religion and Law in the United* Kingdom, (Kluwer Law International, The Netherlands 2011).

Prerogative origins and the title of proceedings

16.10 The prerogative origins of the modern orders can still be seen in the title of the proceedings, *Regina on the application of [Claimant] v [Defendant]*. Thus it remains the case, at least in name, that the court grants the order at the suit of the Crown.

QUASHING ORDERS

The early form: certiorari

16.11 In its earliest form certiorari was a royal demand for information. By the 13th century it was issuing on the application of a subject. By the 17th century it was established as one of the most common and effective means of supervising local administration which was largely unsupervised by central government.

The modern form: the quashing order

16.12 The modern quashing order is an order granted by the High Court which quashes a decision of an inferior court, tribunal, public authority or any other body or persons who are susceptible to judicial review. It is therefore a declaratory remedy concerned with existing decisions which pronounces upon the lawfulness of that decision. It seeks for the original order or decision to be quashed as, for example, a 'Director of Social Services' decision not to ratify a complaints panel decision that a 17-year-old should be accommodated.[1] Technically it requires the decision to be 'removed' up into the High Court so that its validity can be determined. In modern practice it is an order by which the court rules as to the continuing legal validity of decisions vitiated by illegality. The decision is nullified and is of no continuing effect. It is the most common prerogative order granted in successful judicial review proceedings. The term 'decision' is used in this chapter for ease of reference only, as a quashing order may be granted in respect of not only decisions but also statutory instruments,[2] rules, guidance,[3] circulars, policies, advisory reports, advisory opinions and recommendations. It should be noted that if a quashing order is made, the court may remit the matter to the decision-maker and direct it to reconsider the matter, but if it feels that there is no purpose in remitting, the court retains the discretion to take the decision itself (pursuant to CPR, r 54.19).

[1]   See *Re T (Accommodation By Local Authority)* [1995] 1 FLR 159.
[2]   For a modern use of this order in relation to secondary legislation intended to derogate from Convention rights see *A v Secretary of State for the Home Department* [2004] UKHL 56.
[3]   See *Gillick v West Norfolk & Wisbech Area Health Authority* [1986] AC 112 which related to DHSS guidance on contraception for children, and whether or not a child was able to consent to their own medical treatment without parental knowledge/consent ('Gillick competence').

16.13 The court may grant such an order where a decision is ultra vires, but also where the decision is intra vires but is vitiated by an error of law or fact. If the decision under review is held to be void then the grant of a quashing order has the effect that the decision, measure or instrument is treated as being void ab initio: invalid from the outset. If the decision under review is held to be voidable the grant of a quashing order will have the effect that the decision is deprived of legal effect. The court may not only quash the review decision if it is held to be vitiated by legal misdirection or procedural impropriety or unfairness or bias or irrationality or bad faith, but also if there is no evidence to support factual findings made or they are plainly untenable, or if the decision maker is shown to have misunderstood or been ignorant of an established and relevant fact.[1]

<hr>

1   This modern exposition of the proper exercise of the power to grant a quashing order was given by Lord Bingham in *Runa Begum v Tower Hamlets London Borough Council* [2003] UKHL 5.

16.14 A quashing order is a constitutive remedy[1] in the sense that the grant of such an order by itself destroys the legal validity of the action which is quashed by the order.[2] No further action by the applicant or respondent is required in order to achieve this. This destruction of legal validity may be important, for unless the impugned action is quashed it may be impossible for the body concerned to take a fresh decision.[3] By contrast, it is unclear whether a prohibiting order will of itself invalidate the prohibited act. The order directs the respondent not to proceed with proposed action; but if there is any sign that the respondent does not intend to obey the order, the applicant may be well advised to deploy further remedies in support of the court's order. The discretion to grant a quashing order must be 'exercised judicially and in most cases in which a decision has been found to be flawed it would not be a proper exercise of the discretion to refuse to quash it'.[4] Accordingly, the normal result of a finding of unlawfulness will be a quashing order, subject to any overriding issues of public policy. A partial quashing order, that is an order quashing only part of a decision, may be appropriate where a decision is made up of many elements, but only some of which are unlawful.[5] However, if any unlawful element is central to the decision then a partial quashing order is unlikely to be an appropriate exercise of the court's discretion.[6]

<hr>

1   See Lawson, *Remedies in English Law* (2nd edn, 1980), Ch 17; such remedies differ from coercive orders in not needing execution against an unwilling defendant.
2   The effect will generally be retrospective. It has been held in a particular statutory context that quashing may have effect so as to annul an earlier proceeding only from the time that the quashing order is pronounced: *Hancock v Prison Comrs* [1960] 1 QB 117. Lewis Judicial Remedies in Public Law (3rd edn, 2004) para 6–035 suggests that in a case of non-jurisdictional error of law on the face of the record certiorari would quash only prospectively.
3   An example in the context of a statutory appeal is *Customs and Excise Comrs v Ferrero UK Ltd* [1997] STC 881, CA. The reasoning of the courts has not always been consistent. The need for certiorari was explained by Lord Denning in *Baldwin & Francis Ltd v Patents Appeal Tribunal* [1959] AC 663, 693–694. Subsequently Lord Denning (in company with Danckwerts LJ) considered that certiorari might be postponed: see *R v Paddington Valuation Officer, ex p Peachey Property Corpn Ltd* [1966] 1 QB 380, 401–403, 418, but compare Salmon LJ at pp 418–419. In order for a decision to cease to have effect it is usually necessary for a court to set it aside: *R v Panel on Takeovers and Mergers, ex p Datafin plc* [1987] QB 815, [1987] 1 All ER 564, CA, per Sir John Donaldson MR at 840. Lord Roskill's speech in *Harrington, Re* [1984] AC 473 suggests that where proceedings are a nullity it would not be right to order certiorari as well as mandamus. The Divisional Court in *R v Hendon Justices, ex p DPP* [1994] QB 167 granted an order of mandamus requiring justices to hear informations which they had previously dismissed; no order of certiorari was made, apparently on the footing that the order of mandamus was sufficient to deprive the dismissals (and consequent acquittals) of any ostensible effect. The court added (at 178) that, while the procedure (of quashing a nullity) involved a defiance of logic, 'in practice decisions which are

nullities are quashed as a convenient way of preventing the continuance of any ostensible effect'. For a general discussion of the concept of 'nullity' see CHAPTER 6. See, also, the decision of the Divisional Court in *R (Salubi and Wanogho) v Bow Street Magistrates' Court* [2002] 1 WLR 3073, holding that the Crown Court was entitled, without waiting for judicial review, to ignore a committal made without jurisdiction, where Auld LJ said at para 51, p 3091: 'The fact that this court often loosely uses the word "quash" when marking acts as done without jurisdiction, when it could simply declare them to be so, does not accord them life or effect unless and until they are quashed. Procedural matters designed to simplify and speed the processes of the courts such as this should not turn on arid and philosophical debate as to whether a legal nullity requires recognition by a quashing order to make it so'.

[4] Applied in the contest of pollution & environment in *R (Edwards) v Environment Agency (No 2)* [2008] UKHL 22, and in the context of planning in *R (Corus UK Ltd (t/a Orb Electrical Steels)) v Newport City Council* [2010] EWCA Civ 1626.

[5] See as an example of such an order *R v Inner South London Coroner, ex p Kendall* [1988] 1 WLR 1186.

[6] See as an example *R (Guiney) v Greenwich London Borough Council* [2008] EWHC 2012 (Admin).

Consequential powers: suspension

16.15 One permissible, but perhaps unusual exercise of the court's discretion is to suspend the effect of a quashing order where, for example, it will have a disproportionate effect.[1] However, the general approach of the courts is not to favour suspending on the basis that doing so may defeat or obfuscate the purpose of the judgment.[2]

[1] See *R (Rockware Glass Ltd) v Chester City Council* [2006] EWCA Civ 992 for an example in the context of pollution.

[2] See *R (T) v Chief Constable of Greater Manchester* [2013] EWCA Civ 25 in the context of rehabilitation of offenders and records of spent convictions.

Consequential powers: retrospectivity

16.16 A quashing order ordinarily renders the decision a nullity from the time at which it was made and so will generally have retrospective effect. However, the court has a general inherent power to limit the retrospective effect of such an order to avoid injustice at the time it is granted.[1]

[1] See *Cadder (Peter) v HM Advocate* [2010] UKSC 43 for an example in the context of admissions by an accused obtained in the absence of legal advice.

Consequential powers: remission

16.17 Section 31(5) and (5A) of the Supreme Court Act 1981 and CPR 54.19 provide that where the court quashes a decision it may exercise a consequential power to remit the matter back to the inferior tribunal or decision-maker concerned with a direction to reconsider it and reach a decision in accordance with the findings and judgement of the court. Although the court is exercising a discretionary power to grant relief it may only properly decline to make a quashing order if it is satisfied that a properly directed decision-maker would inevitably reach the same conclusion again if the decision is quashed and the matter remitted back for fresh consideration.[1] CPR 54.19(2)(ii) is sufficiently wide for the court to be able to give practical directions as part of its judgement, such as directing that a differently constituted tribunal should rehear a matter[2], or that the same panel should restrict themselves to deciding one or more issues on which they originally misdirected themselves in law.[3]. It is increasingly common for the court, exercising CPR 54.19, to specify a deadline by which the new decision must be reached. The issue of whether and when the court may itself decide issues of precedent fact is discussed in the 'age assessment' cases. and notably the judgment of the Supreme Court in *R (AA) v Secretary of State for the Home Department.*[4]

[1] See *Barty-King v Ministry of Defence* [1979] 2 All ER 80.
[2] To avoid any appearance of bias or unfairness.
[3] To deliver a not only fair but proportionate remedy.
[4] [2013] UKSC 49.

16.18 By section 31(5) of the Supreme Court Act 1981 if, on an application for judicial review seeking a quashing order, the High Court quashes the decision to which the application relates, then the High Court may remit the matter to the court, tribunal or authority concerned, with a direction to reconsider it and reach a decision in accordance with the findings of the High Court.[1] This provision, by enabling the court to give directions which must be complied with by the body in question, offers an alternative to a mandatory order in the cases to which it applies. It also clarifies that a quashing order may be framed in such a way as to leave on foot earlier parts of the proceedings in question which are not vitiated by any relevant error. An example is *R v Secretary of State for the Home Department, ex p Benwell*[2] where a decision of the Secretary of State to implement the dismissal of the applicant was quashed, and the matter was remitted for reconsideration in accordance with the court's opinion. This left on foot disciplinary proceedings up to the point where they had become tainted with unfairness. It is not uncommon for orders remitting a matter to justices to direct that a new hearing should take place before different justices from those who dealt with the matter earlier. This undoubtedly lies within the court's powers in a case where subsequent proceedings before the same justices would be open to review on grounds of predetermination or bias.[3] Such orders are also made in relation to local government decision-makers whose original decision has been quashed, despite the common judicial deference to the conscientiousness and competence of such decision-makers identified in cases such as *Feld v Barnet London Borough Council.*[4]

[1] This provision was substantially the same as that in RSC Ord 53, r 9(4), now found in CPR 54.19(2).
[2] [1985] QB 554. This case is discussed by Lewis Judicial Remedies in Public Law (3rd edn 2004) para 6–019.
[3] See, eg *R v Hampshire County Council, ex p K* [1990] 2 QB 71. Mann J in *R v Mental Health Review Tribunal, ex p Clatworthy* [1985] 3 All ER 699, 704 did not think that the court had any specific power to direct that a matter should be heard by a differently constituted tribunal; nevertheless, the Divisional Court frequently expresses a desire or gives a direction to that effect, both on judicial review and on appeals by case stated (where such a direction may fall within the Summary Jurisdiction Act 1857, s 6, permitting the court to make 'such other order as it considers fit').
[4] [2004] EWCA Civ 1307.

Consequential powers: substitution

16.19 Judicial review is aptly named. It is a review of legality rather than a fact sensitive determination of any substantive issue. The court will ordinarily follow a finding of illegality with a quashing order and remittal to the appropriate decision-maker. However, where the court is satisfied that remitting the matter would serve no purpose then the consequential power given by CPR 54.19(2)(b) provides that the court may, absent any statutory provision to the contrary, substitute its own decision for the decision to which the claim relates. The statutory foundation for this power was introduced by the Tribunals, Courts and Enforcement Act 2007.[1] This power will be exercised where, on a correct application of the law to the known facts the decision is inevitable. Where a decision is vitiated by a failure to have regard to relevant facts the court may substitute its own decision where there is no real prospect that the decision-maker, acting rationally and with the benefit of further inquiry, might lawfully come to a different decision.[2] In practice the power is exercised sparingly as the court tends to show deference to public authority decision-makers. The text of CPR 54.19.2 cautiously notes that where a statutory power is given to a tribunal, person or other body it may be the case that the court cannot take the decision itself. It will only be in exceptional circumstances that the court will take the decision itself, for ordinarily the decision-maker will be entitled to review the matter having regard not merely to the court's decision, but also to the decision-maker's own assessment of relevant factors as they exist at the time the fresh decision is taken. In a case, however, where, in addition to a quashing order, a mandatory order could properly be made it might be appropriate for the court to exercise the power under CPR 54.19(2)(a).

[1] Section 141 of the 1007 Act amends s 31 of the Supreme Court Act 1981 to add this power.
[2] See *R (A) v Lord Saville of Newdigate (No.2)* [2002] 1 WLR 1249 within the context of judicial decisions relating to Article 6 ECHR and fair hearings by tribunals: see also *Deugi v Tower Hamlets London Borough Council* [2006] EWCA Civ 159 within the context of homelessness decision by local Government officers.

16.20 Where a quashing order is granted to quash a sentence of the Crown Court or of a Magistrates Court on the ground that the first instance court had no power to pass the sentence imposed, the Administrative Court may, instead of remitting the matter back, itself pass any sentence which the first instance court could have passed.[1] By sections 43 and 43ZA of the Supreme Court Act 1981 the High Court may, in certain circumstances, instead of quashing orders of a magistrates' court or Crown Court concerned with conviction, sentence or committal to prison or detention, amend the lower court's order or exercise its powers by way of correction of that order.[2]

[1] Section 43 of the Supreme Court Act 1981.
[2] For examples of the exercise of this power, see *R v Pateley Bridge Justices, ex p Percy* [1994] COD 453 (sentence of one month's imprisonment for contempt quashed for failure to give opportunity to apologise; sentence of one day's imprisonment substituted following apology); *R v Crown Court at Exeter, ex p Chennery* [1996] COD 207 (sentence of 16 months' detention reduced to legal maximum of 12 months).

PROHIBITING ORDERS

The early form: prohibition

16.21 In its original form the writ of prohibition was used primarily to limit the jurisdiction of the ecclesiastical courts. It would issue on the application of a subject. It increasingly came to be used by the common law courts to limit the jurisdiction of the Chancery and Admiralty courts. By the 17th century it too was established as one of the most common and effective means of supervising local administration which remained largely unsupervised by central government.

The modern form: the prohibiting order

16.22 The modern prohibiting order is a coercive remedy granted by the High Court and directed to an inferior court, tribunal, public authority or any other body or persons who are susceptible to judicial review which forbids it to act in excess of its statutory or other public law powers, or forbids it from abusing those powers. It seeks to restrain a body from acting unlawfully, and is therefore a negative order intended to preclude future unlawful action or decisions, or to preclude future actions to implement existing decisions.[1] For that reason a prohibiting order may be granted with a quashing order to avoid the implementation of an unlawful decision.[2] An order will be granted where the public body affected has misdirected itself or is otherwise acting under some misapprehension as to the law or as to its lawful powers. An order will not be granted unless something remains to be done or is intended to be done that the court can prohibit.

[1]   *R v Electricity Commissioners, ex p London Electricity Joint Committee Co Ltd* [1924] 1 KB 171.
[2]   See *R v Horseferry Road Justices, ex p Independent Broadcasting Authority* [1987] QB 54.

The appropriate time for making the application

16.23 Where it is apparent that the court, tribunal or body will be acting in excess of its powers a prohibiting order may be applied for immediately. Where it is arguable but not apparent that the act will be *ultra vires* the application must wait until the body has, or is clearly about to, act in excess of its powers.[1]

[1]   *R v Local Commissioners for Administration for North & East Area of England, ex p. Bradford Metropolitan City Council* [1979] QB 287.

Conditional orders

16.24 The court may make conditional prohibiting orders which are directed at ensuring that a certain steps are taken before the prohibition on the intended act is lifted: for instance the order might require consultation with affected interested parties before the intended act is taken.[1]

[1] Examples of such orders can be found in relation to the closure or radical re-organisation of community based public services, and in relation to changes to local government schemes for licensing and permissions for businesses.

Temporary orders

16.25 At common law the court has power to grant an order which will only restrain the body in question from the impugned action until it has taken steps necessary to render that action lawful. A well-known example is *R v Liverpool Corpn, ex p Liverpool Taxi Fleet Operators Association*.[1] However, in *A-G of Hong Kong v Ng Yuen Shiu*,[2] the Privy Council varied a conditional order of prohibition made by the Court of Appeal of Hong Kong, stating that the appropriate order was an order of certiorari quashing a direction for removal of the applicant, this being without prejudice to the making of a fresh removal order after a fair enquiry had been held.

[1] [1972] 2 QB 299.
[2] [1983] 2 AC 629, 639.

Prohibiting orders and the County Court

16.26 By section 84 of the County Courts Act 1984 (read with s 29(5) of the Supreme Court Act 1981), a County Court Judge is not to be served with notice of an application for a prohibiting order, nor (except by order of a judge of the High Court) is the County Court Judge required to appear or to be heard, or liable for costs. Such an application for a prohibiting order is to proceed and be heard in the same manner as an appeal from a decision of the county court judge. In *R v Leeds County Court, ex p Morris*[1] Watkins LJ said that this section and section 83 of the County Court Act 1984 (which provides that grant of permission to apply for a quashing or prohibiting order directed to a county court shall, if the High Court so directs, operate as a stay of the proceedings) give explicit recognition to the function of the Divisional Court enabling it to review a decision in the county court.[2]

[1] [1990] 1 QB 523, 530.
[2] For an example of certiorari and mandamus to a county court, see *R v Hurst, ex p Smith* [1960] 2 QB 133. See, also, discussion of limitations on review of the county court in CHAPTER 6.

The effect of the order

16.27 By contrast with a quashing order, which is a constitutive remedy in the sense that the grant of such an order by itself destroys the legal validity of the action which is quashed by the order, it is unclear whether a prohibiting order will of itself invalidate the prohibited act. The order directs the respondent not to proceed with proposed action; but if there is any sign that the respondent does not intend to obey the order, the applicant may be well advised to deploy further remedies in support of the court's order.

The modern day decline

16.28 The use of this prerogative remedy has declined in modern times as the court has come to expect that quashing orders together with declarations will be sufficient to ensure that responsible public bodies act lawfully. This is based on the presumption that public bodies will do so due to a variety of factors including respect for the rule of law, democratic accountability, governmental budgetary sanctions and the supervision of the bodies such as the Audit Commission and Ombudsmen.

ISSUE COMMON TO BOTH QUASHING AND PROHIBITING ORDERS

Discretion

16.29 General aspects of the discretionary refusal of relief are dealt with in CHAPTER 18. In deciding whether or not to grant a quashing or prohibiting order, the court will have regard to the effect of doing so.[1] If the remedy is unnecessary[2] or premature,[3] the court may refuse to make an order. Thus, where grounds are made out upon which the court might grant the order, it will not do so when no benefit could arise from granting it. In appropriate cases the court may decline any prerogative order on giving judgment, but nevertheless grant liberty to apply so that either party may bring the matter back before the court (without initiating fresh proceedings) lest there be any need for a coercive order or any doubt about what is required in the light of the court's judgment.[4] A quashing and/or prohibiting order may be refused if there has been undue delay and granting such orders would cause substantial hardship or prejudice to an individual or be detrimental to good administration (see s 31(6) of the Senior Courts Act 1981). The Act intends a wide discretion to enable the court to ensure that the interests of justice are served when considering the consequences of an unlawful decision.

[1] See *R v Hillingdon Health Authority, ex p Goodwin* [1984] ICR 800, and *R v Brent Health Authority, ex p Francis* [1985] QB 869, [1985] 1 All ER 74, DC.
[2] See *R v General Medical Council and the Review Board for Overseas Qualified Practitioners, ex p Popat* [1991] COD 245.
[3] See *R v Greater London Council, ex p Blackburn* [1976] 3 All ER 184, [1976] 1 WLR 550, CA.
[4] Examples are *R v Investors Compensation Scheme, ex p Last* [1994] QB 749, 767 (where a declaration of entitlement to compensation was made); *R v Human Fertilisation and Embryology Authority, ex p Blood* [1999] Fam 161, [1997] 2 All ER 687.

Nullities

16.30 Where proceedings in the inferior tribunal are held to be a nullity, a question might theoretically arise whether there is anything to be quashed. The practical answer is that this does not deprive the court of jurisdiction to quash: the making of a quashing order may well serve a useful purpose by placing the invalidity of the proceedings beyond doubt.

Superior courts

16.31 With one exception, quashing and prohibiting orders cannot be directed by the High Court to any superior court (ie a court which is not inferior to the High Court).[1] Superior courts include the Supreme Court, Court of Appeal, the High Court itself and the Courts-Martial Appeal Court[2](and officers thereof when acting in that capacity). The question whether a tribunal is a superior court of record or is subject to judicial review by the High Court depends in each case on the precise nature and powers of the tribunal. It is necessary to look at all the relevant features of the tribunal including its constitution, jurisdiction and powers and its relationship with the High Court in order to decide whether the tribunal should be properly regarded as inferior to the High Court, so that its activities may appropriately be the subject of judicial review by the High Court.[3] Thus, when judges of the High Court sit as visitors to the Inns of Court to determine appeals against orders by which barristers are to be disciplined by their Inn of Court, they are not sitting as the High Court and there can be judicial review of their decisions.[4]

[1] See *Re Racal Communications Ltd* [1981] AC 374 at 384 (Lord Diplock), 386 (Lord Salmon), 392 (Lord Scarman, pointing out that the High Court has inherited the jurisdiction of the superior common law courts of first instance). The exception is the Crown Court, dealt with below.
[2] Courts-Martial (Appeals) Act 1968, s 1.
[3] See *R v Cripps, ex p Muldoon* [1984] 1 QB 68, DC.
[4] *R v Visitors to the Inns of Court, ex p Calder* [1994] QB 1, CA; the visitors are, however, held in this decision to have the protection afforded in *R v Hull University Visitor, ex p Page* [1993] AC 682 to visitors of charitable foundations (and thus, for example, cannot be reviewed for error of law within their jurisdiction).

The Crown Court

16.32 The Crown Court is a superior court and a branch of the Supreme Court of Judicature. However, when the Crown Court was created by the Courts Act 1971 and took over the jurisdiction formerly exercised at assizes and quarter sessions, it was recognised by Parliament that certain Crown Court decisions should be subject to a supervisory jurisdiction.[1] Accordingly, by ss 28 and 29(3) of the Supreme Court Act 1981 there are conferred on the High Court, subject to certain exceptions, powers to review the Crown Court by way of case stated and by the grant of mandatory, prohibiting and quashing orders. These provisions grant to the High Court a jurisdiction which it would otherwise not have possessed.[2]

[1] Lord Bridge points out in *Re Smalley* [1985] AC 622, 640 that quarter sessions were subject to the prerogative writs and orders, while assizes were not.
[2] See *R v Crown Court at Chelmsford, ex p Chief Constable of Essex* [1994] 1 WLR 359 at 367 and 369. The principal exception, concerning decisions of the Crown Court relating to trial on indictment, is fully discussed by the House of Lords in *Re Ashton* [1994] AC 9 and *R v Crown Court at Manchester, ex p DPP* [1993] 1 WLR 1624; see, also, *R v Crown Court at Southwark, ex p Customs and Excise Comrs* [1993] 1 WLR 764 and *R v Crown Court at Leeds, ex p Hussain* [1995] 1 WLR 1329. For a general examination see Gledhill, 'Judicial Review and the Crown Court' [1996] JR 230. Subsequent cases include *R (Salubi) v Bow Street Magistrates Court* [2002] 1 WLR 3073, expressing no view on the general application of the principle in *R v Maidstone Crown Court, ex p Harrow London Borough Council* [2000] QB 719 that where a judge makes an order that is jurisdictionally flawed the High Court may intervene notwithstanding that it relates to trial on indictment. The effect of s 29(6) of the 1981 Act is that the Crown Court's jurisdiction relating to orders under

s 17 of the Access to Justice Act 1999 (concerning terms of provision of funded legal services) may be supervised by mandatory, prohibiting and quashing orders notwithstanding that the matter relates to trial on indictment. Refusal of bail by the Crown Court may be the subject of judicial review.

Inferior court and tribunals

16.33 Generally speaking, County Courts, justices, coroners,[1] statutory tribunals and other public authorities[2] may be the subject of quashing and prohibiting orders. It has been held that certiorari will not lie to an ecclesiastical court, although prohibition may be granted.[3] Both orders were held to lie to a statutory arbitrator to whom the parties must resort, but not to an ordinary arbitrator to whom the parties resort by consent or to a private tribunal set up by agreement between the parties. The special position of visitors to an educational institution is dealt with in CHAPTER 5. The Tribunals, Courts and Enforcement Act 2007 designated the Upper Tribunal as a Superior Court of Record. This raised constitutional questions as to the relationship between the new tribunal chambers and the ordinary courts and the principles underpinning the supervisory jurisdiction of judicial review. Early challenges met with different conclusions in the lower courts in England and Scotland, notwithstanding that the same legislation and tribunal structure applies in both jurisdictions. In *R (Cart) v Upper Tribunal; R (MR (Pakistan)) v Upper Tribunal (Immigration and Asylum Chamber)*[4] and *Eba v Advocate General for Scotland*[5] the Supreme Court held that permission to apply for judicial review should only be granted where the criteria for a second-tier appeal are satisfied, namely where there is an important point of principle or practice or some other compelling reason to review the case. Post-*Cart* the Court of Appeal has emphasised the high threshold intended by the second tier appeal test,[6] and that the application of that threshold is fact sensitive and must properly take into account all of the circumstances of the individual case.[7] It is becoming increasingly clear that the court will be unforgiving where there are failures to follow the appropriate CPR 54 procedures.[8] It is similarly clear that, once the court has given permission to appeal in a *Cart* case (applying the second tier appeals test), at the substantive hearing that test no longer applies.[9] Nonetheless, judicial restraint and deference in relation to the decisions of statutory tribunals has been re-affirmed in *R (Jones (by Caldwell)) v First-Tier Tribunal & Criminal Injuries Compensation Authority*[10] in which the UKSC overturned the Court of Appeal's decision to quash the decision of the first tier tribunal and remit the matter back to a differently constituted tribunal.

[1] See *R v Greater Manchester Coroner, ex p Tal* [1985] QB 67, [1984] 3 All ER 240 for a discussion of the statutory power to quash.

[2] See *R v Northumberland Compensation Appeal Tribunal, ex p Shaw* [1952] 1 KB 338, [1952] 1 All ER 122, CA. Which holds that this is so irrespective of whether the functions of the public authorities are judicial or administrative.

[3] See *R v St Edmundsbury and Ipswich Diocese Chancellor, ex p White* [1948] 1 KB 195, [1947] 2 All ER 170, CA for an example of the traditional reasoning for excluding certiorari which now seems outdated and ripe for revisiting.

[4] [2011] UKSC 28.

[5] [2011] UKSC 29.

[6] See *PR (Sri Lanka) v Secretary of State for the Home Department* [2011] EWCA Civ 988; and *JD (Congo) v Secretary of State for the Home Department* [2012] EWCA Civ 327 on the threshold for the second tier appeal test.

[7] *JD (Congo)* ibid.

[8] See, for example, *R (Khan) v Secretary of State for the Home Department* [2011] EWHC 2763 (Admin).

[9] See the exposition in *R (HS) v Upper Tribunal (Immigration and Asylum Chamber)* [2012] EWHC 3126 (Admin),[2013] Imm AR 579.

[10] [2013] UKSC 19.

The Crown and Crown servants

16.34 Remedies against the Crown are discussed in CHAPTER **14**, and reference should be made to that chapter for the general principles applicable. Ministers of the Crown have been the subject of certiorari when exercising statutory powers[1] and (by delegation) prerogative powers.[2] In a case where the Queen acted as visitor to a university it was assumed that certiorari would lie.[3] Prohibiting orders, being coercive, are likely to be subject to similar considerations as those which affect mandatory orders insofar as sought against the Crown.[4]

[1] See *R v Secretary of State for the Environment, ex p Brent Londond Borough Council* [1982] QB 593.

[2] A classic example can be found in *Council of Civil Service Unions v Minister for the Civil Service* [1985] AC 374.

[3] See *R v Hull University Visitor, ex p Page* [1993] AC 682; compare *R v HM The Queen in Council* [1990] 2 QB 444, 451.

[4] See, generally, CHAPTER **14**.

Territorial scope

16.35 The territorial scope of certiorari was discussed in *Re Mansergh*, a case where it was sought to quash a decision taken by a Court Martial in India. It was held by two of four judges that the court's supervisory jurisdiction did not extend to tribunals established under the authority of the Crown in its realms and territories overseas, even if the records of any such court should be in England.[1] Blackburn J said that the Court of Queen's Bench in England controlled local tribunals within England and such of its dependencies as were integral parts of England.[2]

[1] (1861) 1 B & S 400. The two judges who rested their decision on territorial jurisdiction were Crompton and Blackburn JJ. Cockburn CJ and Wightman J laid greater emphasis on the fact that the decision of the Court Martial affected the military status only of the applicant: on this point, provision is now made for appeal under the Courts-Martial (Appeals) Act 1968. As to martial law generally, see 8(2) Halsbury's Laws of England (4th edn, Re-issue, 1996) paragraph 821; for judicial review of the Army Board of the Defence Council in relation to its functions under the Race Relations Act 1996, see *R v Army Board of the Defence Council, ex p Anderson* [1992] QB 169.

[2] See, generally, Beloff and Mountfield [1997] JR 131.

16.36 More generally, territorial scope may be determined by the proper construction of a statutory power or duty. In relation to the Human Rights Act 1998, it has been held that although the notion of jurisdiction under the European Convention on Human Rights was essentially territorial, there were exceptional cases in which acts performed or producing effects outside the territories of states which were contracting parties to the Convention could constitute an exercise of jurisdiction by them within the meaning of art 1 of the Convention.[1]

[1] *R (B) v Secretary of State for Foreign and Commonwealth Affairs* [2005] QB 643, CA; *R (Al-Skeini and others) v Secretary of State for Defence* [2005] 2 WLR 1401, DC. In the latter case the Divisional Court held that jurisdiction under art 1 of the Convention did not extend to a broad, worldwide extra-territorial personal jurisdiction arising from the exercise of authority by party states' agents anywhere in the world, but only to an extra-territorial jurisdiction which was exceptional and limited and to be found in specific cases recognised in international law. Accordingly, the doctrine of effective control of an area did not apply in territories outside the regional sphere of the party states of the Convention itself, and it could not be relied upon to make art 1 applicable to deaths of Iraqi civilians caused by British troops in Iraq, which was not within the regional sphere of the Convention. However, the death of an Iraqi civilian in a British military prison, operating in Iraq with the consent of the Iraqi sovereign authorities, and containing arrested suspects, fell within a narrowly limited exception exemplified by embassies, consulates, vessels and aircraft. The 1998 Act had to be construed in conformity with the Convention in the matter of jurisdictional scope. In *R (Quark Fishing Ltd) v Secretary of State for Foreign and Commonwealth Affairs (No 2)* [2005] QB 93, CA, a claim for damages under the First Protocol to the Convention failed because that Protocol had not been extended to South Georgia.

Non-statutory tribunals and public authorities

16.37 Certiorari and prohibition have been held capable of controlling public authorities who act in pursuance of a power derived from a common law, or prerogative,[1] rather than statutory source.[2] The circumstances in which actual or potential proceedings pursuant to non-statutory powers are open to judicial review, and therefore (subject to the court's discretion) may lead today to the grant of quashing or prohibiting orders, are fully discussed in CHAPTER 5. A recent example of the grant of orders prohibiting the continuation of disciplinary proceedings by an NHS Trust can be found in *West London Mental Health NHS Trust v Chhabra*.[3]

[1] On the prerogative generally, see CHAPTER 14.
[2] *Council of Civil Service Unions v Minister for the Civil Service* [1985] AC 374 at 407, [1984] 3 All ER 935 at 948, HL, per Lord Scarman.
[3] [2013] UKSC 80.

Delegated legislation

16.38 At one time declaratory judgments, rather than the prerogative remedies, were regarded as appropriate for challenging delegated legislation.[1] But this ignored the fact that prohibition had been held appropriate to prevent the commencement of a process of delegated legislation in *R v Electricity Comrs, ex p London Electricity Joint Committee Co (1920)*.[2] The ability of the court to quash delegated legislation has been confirmed.[3] Further, it has been held that the court may grant relief on judicial review in respect of a draft Order in Council made under the European Communities Act 1972 to be laid before both Houses of Parliament by the Treasury to implement its undertaking given by Member States of the EEC that the expenditure contemplated by the EEC budget would be met out of funds provided by them.[4] A more recent analysis of the competing merits of the mandatory order and the declaration, and of the relevance of retrospective effect, can be found in the judgment of the Supreme Court in *Raymond Brownlee's application for Judicial Review*

(Northern Ireland).[5]

[1] See, eg *Brownsea Haven Properties Ltd v Poole Corpn* [1958] Ch 574, [1958] 1 All ER 205, CA. The Divisional Court in *R v Legislative Committee of the Church Assembly, ex p Haynes-Smith* [1928] 1 KB 411 held that certiorari and prohibition did not lie against a legislative body because it was not under a duty to act judicially: this reasoning can no longer stand.

[2] [1924] 1 KB 171.

[3] In *R v Secretary of State for Social Services, ex p Association of Metropolitan Authorities* [1986] 1 All ER 164, [1986] 1 WLR 1, certiorari was refused on discretionary grounds by Webster J, who suggested that it would not necessarily be the normal practice, where delegated legislation is held to be ultra vires, to revoke the instrument. Safety regulations laid before Parliament under the Consumer Protection Act 1987, s 11 were quashed by the Divisional Court in *R v Secretary of State for Health, ex p US Tobacco* [1992] QB 353. Lord Keith of Kinkell has said that statutory instruments are capable of being set aside by certiorari: *R v Secretary of State for Employment, ex p Equal Opportunities Commission* [1995] 1 AC 1, 26.

[4] *R v HM Treasury, ex p Smedley* [1985] QB CA.

[5] [2014] UKSC 4.

The requirement of a decision or determination

16.39 This topic is discussed in CHAPTER 5 and reference should be made to that chapter for general considerations. It was at one time said that the remedy of certiorari lay only to bring up to the High Court and quash something which was a determination or a decision. Thus the court in one case, adopting a narrow definition of the word 'decision', held certiorari inapplicable to a report of visitors of a hospital because the report merely advised the board of control as to the need for the continued detention of a mental health patient.[1] But this is inconsistent with the modern recognition that recommendations by ombudsmen,[2] circulars giving legal advice[3] and reports by industrial relations conciliators[4] fall within the scope of judicial review, and that in appropriate circumstances a recommendation in an advisory report may be quashed. Certiorari could issue in respect of decisions as to the gathering of evidence, such as the issue of a search warrant or a witness summons. It also lay in respect of a preliminary decision.[5] Certiorari was also used to quash the inquisition of a coroner's court,[6] which is in modern times a decision only in the sense that the court has decided upon the verdict contained in the inquisition: it determines nothing in terms of rights and obligations.[7] These matters all suggest that 'decisions' in the broadest sense of that word may be quashed on judicial review and it is questionable whether a decision of any kind is essential before a quashing order can be made.

[1] *R v St Lawrence's Hospital, Caterham, Statutory Visitors, ex p Pritchard* [1953] 2 All ER 766, [1953] 1 WLR 1168, DC. There was, of course, a 'decision' to make the recommendation, but this was apparently not such a 'decision' as would be susceptible to certiorari.

[2] See *R v Parliamentary Comr for Administration, ex p Dyer* [1994] 1 WLR 621 and cases there cited.

[3] *Gillick v West Norfolk and Wisbech Area Health Authority* [1986] AC 112.

[4] *Grunwick Processing Laboratories v Advisory, Conciliation and Arbitration Service* [1978] AC 655.

[5] See *R v Boycott, ex p Keasley* [1939] 2 KB 651, [1939] 2 All ER 626, DC. Lord Steyn in *R (Burkett) v Hammersmith and Fulham LBC* [2002] 1 WLR 1693 said at para 38, p 1605: 'for substantive judicial review purposes the decision challenged does not have to be absolutely final. In a context where there is a statutory procedure involving preliminary decisions leading to a final decision affecting legal rights, judicial review may lie against a preliminary decision not affecting legal rights. Town planning provides a classic case of this flexibility. Thus it is in principle possible to apply for judicial review in respect of a resolution to grant outline

permission and for prohibition even in advance of it . . . '. See, also, obiter observations in
R (Davies) v Financial Services Authority [2004] 1 WLR 185, CA, at para 33, p 194.

⁶ See, eg *R v Greater Manchester Coroner, ex p Tal* [1985] QB 67; *R v Southwark Coroner, ex
p Hicks* [1987] 1 WLR 1624.

⁷ See Halsbury's Laws of England (4th edn), para 1143 (dealing with traverse of the inquisition).

16.40 Lord Diplock in *Council of Civil Service Union v Minister for the Civil
Service*¹ said that the subject-matter of every judicial review is a decision or a
refusal to make a decision. Even in the broadest sense of the word 'decision',
and despite the high authority of this obiter dictum, such a proposition cannot
be treated as accurate. First, the House of Lords has now held that an applicant
may seek a declaration by way of judicial review even if there is no decision in
respect of which one of the prerogative orders would be available.² Second, for
reasons discussed below, in relation to prohibiting and mandatory orders there
is no need for any such decision or refusal to make a decision. Third, in
relation to quashing orders, many cases concerned with certiorari examined
the legality of acts, as opposed to decisions. The remedy of certiorari
historically presupposed the existence, or the ability to bring into existence, of
a record which could be certified and removed to the King's court for
quashing.³ It may be thought self-evident that before a quashing order is
granted there must be something which is capable of being quashed, ie
overthrown or annulled.⁴ Given the very substantial developments in the
substantive law of judicial review, the preferable course today is to hold that,
provided the subject matter of a challenge is within the scope of judicial review
as described in CHAPTER 5, a quashing order should, in principle, be available
in all cases where there is a proceeding which can sensibly and usefully be
overthrown to provide a practical remedy.

¹ [1985] AC 374, 408.
² *R v Secretary of State for Employment, ex p Equal Opportunities Commission* [1995] 1 AC
1: and see CHAPTER 18.
³ The 'record' includes oral as well as written reasons given by the body under review: see *R v
Crown Court at Knightsbridge, ex p International Sporting Club (London) Ltd* [1982] QB
304. Prior to CPR, where the relief sought was or included an order of certiorari to remove any
proceedings for the purpose of quashing them, by RSC Ord 53, r 9(2) the applicant might not
question the validity of any order, warrant, commitment, conviction, inquisition or record
unless before the hearing of the motion or summons the applicant had lodged in the Crown
Office a copy thereof verified by affidavit or accounted for the failure to do so to the
satisfaction of the court hearing the motion or summons. RSC Ord 53 r 9(3) stated that in any
case where certiorari is sought to remove any proceedings for the purpose of quashing them,
then if the order were granted it should direct that 'the proceedings shall be quashed forthwith
on their removal into the Queen's Bench Division'. This was subject to RSC, Ord 53, r 9(4).
Production of the actual 'record' was not in practice required.
⁴ See Tanby Cowel's Interpretor (1672): an example of something which cannot sensibly be said
to be 'overthrown' may be a purely internal opinion on a matter of law or fact, such as that
which was held not susceptible to certiorari in *R v Secretary of State for Employment, ex p
Equal Opportunities Commission* [1995] 1 AC 1. Compare *R v London Waste Regulation
Authority, ex p Specialist Waste Management Ltd* [1989] COD 288 where declaratory relief
was sought prior to the Equal Opportunities Commission case, and it was held that advice as
to the respondent's understanding of the law was not amenable to judicial review.

16.41 There is not any a priori reason why a 'decision' should be required
before a prohibiting order may be made. Historically, the writ of prohibition
was available to prevent the conduct of proceedings in a court which lacked
jurisdiction: there was no requirement that the court itself should have decided

to assume jurisdiction.[1]

[1] See per Bayley J in *Byerley v Windus* (1826) 5 B&C 1, 21.

16.42 In *R v Tottenham and District Rent Tribunal, ex p North-field (Highgate) Ltd,* counsel for the tribunal asked the Divisional Court to express an opinion whether it was right for the applicants to have applied to that court for prohibition before there had been any decision on the point by the tribunal. Lord Goddard CJ held that there was no obligation to seek a decision from the tribunal,[1] and added:

'I think it would be impossible and not at all desirable to lay down any definite rule as to when a person is to go to the tribunal or come here for prohibition where the objection is that the tribunal has no jurisdiction. Where one gets a perfectly simple, short and neat question of law as we have in the present case, it seems to me that it is quite convenient, and certainly within the power of the applicants, to come here for prohibition'.

[1] [1957] 1 QB 103, 107–108.

Error of law on the face of the record

16.43 A final aspect of the scope of certiorari should be mentioned. In addition to the historical issue of certiorari where an inferior tribunal had acted 'without jurisdiction', the writ was also available in a case where the tribunal had acted 'within jurisdiction' but an error of law appeared 'on the face of the record'. This aspect of the power to grant certiorari is noteworthy, for it was the rediscovery of the power to quash for error on the face of the record in *R v Northumberland Compensation Appeal Tribunal, ex p Shaw*[1] which led eventually to the recognition that (unless Parliament has granted to the body in question a power to determine issues of law) any error of law by a body which is subject to judicial review will constitute a ground for review.[2] The result of this development is that the historic power of the court to grant certiorari where there has been error of law on the face of the record is unlikely to be of practical importance.[3]

[1] [1952] 1 KB 338.
[2] See Cooke, '*The Struggle for Simplicity in Administrative Law*' in Taggart (ed), Judicial Review of Administrative Action in the 1980s, pp 6–10.
[3] The requirement for error of law to appear on the face of the record was said by the Divisional Court in *R v Greater Manchester Coroner, ex p Tal* [1985] QB 67, 82, to be obsolete. Compare the caution of Cooke, cited in the preceding footnote. For discussion of the limits of the court's power to intervene for error of law on the face of the record, see Lewis Judicial Remedies in Public Law (3rd edn, 2004) paras 6–032 et seq.

MANDATORY ORDERS

The early form: mandamus

16.44 In its original form the writ mandamus emerged to compel the restitution of subjects to offices and liberties which had been unjustly rested from them. By the 18th century its use had extended beyond such restitution to compel the performance of a wide range of public or quasi-public duties which had been unlawfully refused, and require proper election to office. The Kings Bench developed mandamus to compel the proper discharge of duties by judicial and administrative bodies. Reform of local government in the 19ᵗʰ and early 20ᵗʰ centuries provided elected local authorities, regulatory structures, and rights of objection, complaint and appeal. As a result the use of mandamus declined as effective alternative remedies emerged.

The modern form: the mandatory order

16.45 The modern mandatory order is a coercive remedy granted by the High Court and directed to an inferior court, tribunal, public authority or any other body or persons who are susceptible to judicial review which compels it to do some particular thing, specified in the order, which it is under a public law duty to do. It is a discretionary public law remedy distinct from private law mandatory injunctions.[1] It is where a body is ordered to comply with a statutory duty, for example: that the local authority provide some specific support service,[2] or to set up a complaints procedure that complies with certain regulations.[3] Failure to obey a mandatory order is a contempt of court. It is a discretionary remedy and may issue in cases where, although there is an alternative legal remedy, that mode of redress is less convenient, beneficial and effective. It is common practice to apply for quashing and mandatory orders together.[4] A mandatory order may require a public body to take specific steps.[5] However, a mandatory order which requires a particular result will usually only be ordered where the court concludes that it is the sole result that is legally permissible. Even in such circumstances the court repeatedly affirms the principle of deference to public authority decision-making.[6]

[1] *R v Chief Constable of Devon & Cornwall, ex p Central Electricity Generating Board* [1981] 3 All ER 826 CA.

[2] See *R (on the application of Stewart) v Wandsworth, Hammersmith and Fulham, Lambeth London Borough Councils* [2001] EWHC 709, [2002] 1 FLR 469, in which Lambeth and Wandsworth were ordered to make an assessment of whether the children concerned were in 'need' pursuant to Part III of Schedule 2 to the Children Act 1989.

[3] See *R v Barnet London Borough Council, ex p B at 788* [1994] 1 FLR 592 at 598, per Auld J. This case looked in particular at the complaints procedure as set out and prescribed under statute.

[4] For example, to quash a decision of a body and to require that body to go through the decision-making process again (as was sought in *R v Panel on Take-overs and Mergers, ex p Datafin plc* [1987] QB 816, [1987] 1 All ER 564, CA).

[5] See, for example, *R (Kay) v Chief Constable of Northumbria Police* [2010] EWHC 31 (Admin) where the court ordered the chief constable to reinstate a probationary police constable.

[6] See, for example, *R v Ealing London Borough Council, ex p Parkinson* (1995) 29 HLR 179.

Grant is discretionary

16.46 The grant of a mandatory order is, as a general rule, a matter for the discretion of the court.[1] The general principles concerning discretionary refusal of relief (discussed in CHAPTER 18) will apply. In the context of those principles, certain specific cases deserve mention. A mandatory order may be refused where a public authority has done all that it reasonably can to fulfil its duty[2] or where the remedy appears unnecessary. In the latter case, the refusal may be temporary, with liberty to apply. It may also be refused where there are practical problems that would arise from making such an order,[3] for example, if the form of the order may require detailed supervision by the court,[4] or where it appears that it would be futile in its result. Nor will it be issued if it would cause administrative chaos and public inconvenience,[5] nor when the object for which the application was made has already been obtained. In the case of those responsible for the prosecution of offences, to whom a mandatory order may issue if they refuse to perform their duty, the court may prefer to explain their duty to them in general terms and leave them to act on their own responsibility in any particular situation.[6] Similarly, even if there are grounds for interfering with the decision of a body such as the Panel on Take-overs and Mergers, the court may decline to grant the relief claimed.[7] The court may grant permission to apply for a mandatory order even though the right in respect of which it is sought appears to be doubtful. The court will take a liberal view in determining whether or not the order should issue, not scrupulously weighing the degree of public importance attained by the matter which may be in question, but applying the remedy in all cases to which, upon a reasonable construction, it can be shown to be applicable.

[1]   *Chief Constable of the North Wales Police v Evans* [1982] 3 All ER 141, [1982] 1 WLR 1165, HL.
[2]   *R v Bristol Corpn, ex p Hendy* [1974] 1 All ER 1047 at 1051, [1974] 1 WLR 498 at 503, CA, per Scarman LJ.
[3]   *Chief Constable of the North Wales Police v Evans* [1982] 3 All ER 141 at 166, [1982] 1 WLR 1165 at 1176, HL, per Lord Brightman.
[4]   R v Peak Park Joint Planning Board, ex p Jackson (1976) 74 LGR 376 at 380 per Lord Widgery CJ.
[5]   *R v Paddington Valuation Officer, ex p Peachey Property Corpn Ltd* [1964] 3 All ER 200 at 208, [1964] 1 WLR 1186 at 1195, DC: affd [1966] 1 QB 380, [1965] 2 All ER 836, CA. This is a question of degree: see *Secretary of State for Education and Science v Tameside Metropolitan Borough Council* [1977] AC 1014, [1976] 3 All ER 665, HL.
[6]   *R v Metropolitan Police Comr, ex p Blackburn* [1968] 2 QB 118, [1968] 1 All ER 763, CA; *R v Metropolitan Police Comr, ex p Blackburn (No 3)* [1973] QB 241, [1973] 1 All ER 324, CA; *Raymond v A-G* [1982] QB 839; *R v General Council of the Bar, ex p Percival* [1991] 1 QB 212, [1990] 3 All ER 137; and *R v DPP, ex p Langlands-Pearse* [1991] COD 92. In *R v Chief Constable of Kent, ex p L* [1993] 1 All ER 756 it was said that a decision to discontinue proceedings by the Crown Prosecution Service can be equated with a decision by the police not to prosecute and is therefore open to judicial review only upon the restricted basis available to someone seeking to challenge a decision by the police; applications for mandamus to direct the Service to discontinue criminal proceedings were unsuccessful. See, also, *R v IRC, ex p Mead* [1993] 1 All ER 772 and *R v DPP, ex p C* [1995] 1 Cr App Rep 136; *R v Panel on Take-overs and Mergers, ex p Fayed* [1992] BCC 524; *R v Chance, ex p Coopers & Lybrand* (1995) 7 Admin LR 821.
[7]   *R v Panel of Take-overs and Mergers, ex p Datafin plc* [1987] QB 816 at 842, [1987] 1 All ER 564 at 579–580, CA, per Sir John Donaldson MR.

Enforcement of statutory duties

16.47 The coercive and mandatory nature of the order means that it is most appropriate in relation to cases where the public authority has a clear and mandatory statutory duty to do a certain thing such as set a fair rent,[1] secure suitable housing,[2] assess community care needs,[3] or assess appropriate mental health services to be provided to patients discharged in to the community.[4] An order may be granted to compel a public body to perform a specific act that it is under a statutory duty to perform but the court will often prefer to grant a declaration that the body is under a duty to do the act and rely on it to carry out its duty. A mandatory order will be granted ordering to be done that which a statute requires to be done. If a power or discretion only (as distinct from a duty) exists, the order will not be granted by the court except to secure performance of a duty to exercise the discretion when the occasion arises, or a duty to exercise a genuine discretion or a discretion based on proper legal principles.[5] A mandatory order will not be granted to compel anything to be done which is contrary to law. Nor will such an order be granted to compel the performance of a mere moral duty.

1   Pursuant to the Rent Act 1977.
2   For instance section pursuant to the homelessness duty in s 193(2) of the Housing Act 1996.
3   Pursuant to s 47 of the National Health Service & Community Care Act.
4   Pursuant to s 17 of the Mental Health Act 1983.
5   See, eg *R v Port of London Authority, ex p Kynock Ltd* [1919] 1 KB 176, CA; *Padfield v Minister of Agriculture, Fisheries and Food* [1968] AC 997, [1968] 1 All ER 694, HL.

Enforcement of non-statutory duties

16.48 A mandatory order may be sought to enforce a non-statutory duty, such as the duty of the police to prosecute offenders who break the law[1] or the duty of a local authority to produce documents which a councillor reasonably needs for the proper performance of his duties as such[2] or the decision of a regulatory trade body such as the Panel on Take-overs and Mergers.[3] Provided that the duty has a public law element it may arise from statute or otherwise, in accordance with the principles discussed in CHAPTER 5. A mandatory order will not be granted to compel the performance of a mere moral duty.[4]

1   *R v Metropolitan Police Comr, ex p Blackburn* [1968] 2 QB 118 at 138–139, [1968] 1 All ER 763 at 771, CA, per Salmon LJ. On mandamus against those who have the responsibility of prosecuting offenders see note 6, **16.46** above.
2   See *R v Hackney London Borough Council, ex p Gamper* [1985] 3 All ER 275, [1985] 1 WLR 1229.
3   *R v Panel on Take-overs and Mergers, ex p Datafin plc* [1987] QB 816, [1987] 1 All ER 564, CA. See also CHAPTER 5.
4   See by example *Ex p. Napier* (1852) 18 Q.B. 692 where the application related to a military officer's salary.

The requirement of a decision or refusal to make a decision

16.49 Reference has been made earlier in this chapter to an obiter dictum of Lord Diplock asserting that the subject matter of every judicial review was a decision or refusal to make a decision. In relation to mandatory orders, this dictum is inconsistent with a long-standing and important decision of the Divisional Court, and seems wrong in principle. As a matter of practicality there must be some action which remains to be done before an order of mandamus can be made to compel performance of the action. It is difficult to see any reason in principle why there should be any additional formal requirement before mandamus can lie. Suggestions that there is a formal requirement of demand and refusal[1] were discussed by Channell J in *R v Hanley Revising Barrister*,[2] a case where the Divisional Court was confronted with circumstances where a demand to perform would have been pointless, the body under review having become functus officio. Channell J rejected a defence (put forward by an interested party) of absence of demand and refusal:

'The requirement that before the courts will issue a mandamus there must be a demand to perform the act sought to be enforced and a refusal to perform it is a very useful one, but it cannot be applicable to all possible cases'.

1   For example, in *R v Bristol and Exeter Rly Co* (1843) 4 QB 162.
2   [1912] 3 KB 518, 531–532.

16.50 It accords with this statement that mandamus has been held to lie so as to prevent an apprehended breach of duty.[1] At first sight Channell J's statement may seem inconsistent with a holding by Bankes LJ[2] that there must be 'something in the nature of a refusal to exercise jurisdiction'. The case in question concerned an assertion that the Port of London Authority had fettered their discretion and misdirected themselves in law, and Bankes LJ's holding was concerned to demonstrate (at a time when the law was developing in this regard) that grounds for mandamus were not shown where a body had remained willing to depart from its policy in appropriate cases. Channell J's statement was not cited, nor is there any reason to think that Bankes LJ was intending to lay down a proposition which applied to the circumstances contemplated by Channell J, or required, even in a case where grounds for mandamus otherwise existed, a formal demand and refusal. Further, it may be noted that Bankes LJ's proposition focused on the exercise of jurisdiction, a phrase wide enough to include both decisions and other types of proceedings. The preferable view is that, while it will usually be desirable to call for the body in question to fulfil its duty (failing which relief may be refused in discretion),[3] any failure to fulfil a public duty may in principle be the subject of a mandatory order.[4] This analysis must now be read in the context of paragraphs 8–12 of the Pre-Action Protocol for Judicial Review which, whenever appropriate, requires a specific demand or request for the performance in the standard format prescribed in Annex A as a precursor to the issue of an application for judicial review.

1   *R v Kent Police Authority, ex p Godden* [1971] 2 QB 662 (see the form of order proposed at 670–671); Fleming v Lees [1991] COD 50.
2   *R v Port of London Authority, ex p Kynoch Ltd* [1919] 1 KB 176 at 183, CA, where Bankes LJ added that a tribunal will be held to have refused to hear and determine when it has been guilty of such delay as to amount to refusal or when it has, in substance, shut its ears to the application which was made to it and has determined upon an application which was not made to it.
3   Compare in relation to mandatory injunctions *R v Kent County Council, ex p Bruce* (1986) Times, 8 February.
4   Even if (contrary to the propositions in the text) a 'refusal' is required, the courts will intervene where delay amounts to a refusal: *R v Secretary of State for the Home Department, ex p Phansopkar* [1976] QB 606; *R v Tower Hamlets London Borough Council, ex p Kayne-Levenson* [1975] QB 431.

Susceptibility to mandatory orders

16.51 As stated at the outset of this chapter, when dealing with the general nature of the prerogative orders, historical rules as to the bodies which might be subjected to mandamus differed from those applicable to certiorari and prohibition, but it is doubtful whether such differences persist. An example of the issue of mandamus in a case which would today be regarded as a matter of private law rather than public law is the enforcement of the admission of copyholders in manors.[1] It does not seem likely that these historical differences will be of any great importance today: the modern approach is to determine availability of a mandatory order against any particular body by ascertaining whether that body is susceptible to judicial review in accordance with the principles discussed in CHAPTER 5.

[1] See Wade and Forsyth Administrative Law (9th edn, 2004) p 17, referring to *R v Powell* (1841) 1 QB 352 and *R v Garland* (1879) LR 5 QB 269.

Mandatory orders after the expiry of a time limit

16.52 The court may issue mandamus even though the time prescribed by statute for the performance of the duty may have passed. Thus, in *R v Hanley Revising Barrister*,[1] the Divisional Court was concerned with a case where the revising barrister under electoral legislation was required to deliver lists of voters. The lists as delivered had been marked up prior to delivery in a fashion which inaccurately recorded the barrister's decisions and, when the error was noticed, the time for delivery had passed. Channell J applied the decision of the Exchequer Chamber in Rochester Corpn[2] that, in the absence of a successor, even a person who was functus officio may be ordered to act by mandamus. The revising barrister was accordingly directed by mandamus to fulfil his duty of delivering the lists of voters as determined by him, in the place of the original lists which erroneously recorded his determinations.

[1] [1912] 3 KB 518.
[2] (1858) E B & E 1024.

Compelling public official and bodies

16.53 Mandamus, in common with the other prerogative orders, cannot be granted against the Crown directly because there would be an incongruity in the Queen commanding herself to do an act. However, this restriction is of little modern relevance as legislation rarely places duties or confers powers on the Crown as the statutory and prerogative powers are exercised by central government, by Secretaries of State (who are *officers of the* Crown as distinct from the Crown itself) and prerogative order, including mandamus, may be granted against ministers in their official capacity. If public officials (including Ministers of the Crown) or public bodies fail to perform any public duty with which they have been charged, a mandatory order will lie to compel them to carry it out. Thus mandamus has been directed to government officials in their capacity as public officers bound to perform executive duties which affect the rights of private persons.[1] Mandamus was issued to the appropriate authority to hear and determine, in accordance with the provisions of the Education Act 1921, a question arising between the local education authority and the managers of a non-provided school[2] and to pay college lecturers.[3] It was held that in a proper case the order might go to the Board of Trade, for instance, to appoint an inspector to inquire into a company's affairs.[4] It was issued to compel a minister to exercise his discretion according to law, and for the purpose of promoting the objects of the Act in question, in deciding whether to accede to a request to appoint a committee of investigation into a complaint;[5] to direct a minister to hear and determine certain appeals under the Town and Country Planning Act 1971;[6] and to a minister and a prison governor to detain a prisoner according to law.[7] In 1970 the Court of Appeal refused leave to seek mandamus to compel the Parliamentary Commissioner for Administration to investigate a complaint, and the House of Lords refused leave to appeal on the ground that the Commissioner had a discretion whether to investigate or not.[8] However, in subsequent cases, the investigation of complaints by ombudsmen has been treated as falling within the scope of judicial review, the remedy of mandamus being available in principle subject to the court's discretion.[9] A statutory duty must be performed without unreasonable delay and it was on this ground that mandamus was granted against the Home Secretary to determine the application for an entry certificate of a would-be immigrant who was legally entitled to enter the country without let or hindrance.[10] While the court will not compel any authority to do more than consider the exercise of a power which is merely permissive, and which does not impose an obligation to act,[11] it may nevertheless intervene if action is taken inhibiting the exercise of that power.[12] The Supreme Court re-iterated the importance of affording a wide interpretative discretion to local government charged with onerous and far-reaching statutory duties before granting mandatory orders to compel them to comply with such duties in the context of providing accommodation to those in need of care and attention pursuant to the National Assistance Act 1948.[13]

[1] *Income Tax Special Purposes Comrs v Pemsel* [1891] AC 531, HL. In *M v Home Office* [1994] 1 AC 377, 417 Lord Woolf observed that by 1978 prerogative orders were being granted regularly against ministers where an unfulfilled statutory duty was placed on a person in the minister's department.
[2] *Board of Education v Rice* [1911] AC 179, HL.
[3] *R v Liverpool City Council, ex p Coade* (1986) Times, 10 October.
[4] *R v Board of Trade, ex p St Martin's Preserving Co Ltd* [1965] 1 QB 603, [1964] 2 All ER 561, DC.
[5] *Padfield v Minister of Agriculture, Fisheries and Food* [1968] AC 997, [1968] 1 All ER 694, HL.
[6] *R v Secretary of State for the Environment, ex p Percy Bilton Industrial Properties Ltd* (1975) 31 P & CR 164.
[7] *R v Secretary of State for the Home Department, ex p Herbage (No 2)* [1987] QB 1077, [1987] 1 All ER 324, CA.
[8] *Re Fletcher's Application* [1970] 2 All ER 527n.
[9] *R v Broadcasting Complaints Commission, ex p Owen* [1985] QB 1163, [1985] 2 All ER 522, DC; *R v Local Comr for Administration, ex p Eastleigh Borough Council* [1988] QB 855, CA; *R v Parliamentary Comr for Administration, ex p Dyer* [1994] 1 WLR 621. Compare *Padfield v Minister of Agriculture, Fisheries and Food* [1968] AC 997, [1968] 1 All ER 694, HL, which concerned the appointment of a committee of investigation.
[10] *R v Secretary of State for the Home Department, ex p Phansopkar* [1976] QB 606, [1975] 3 All ER 497, CA. As to the requirement that delay be unreasonable, see R v IRC, ex p Opman International UK [1986] 1 WLR 568; *R v Secretary of State for the Home Department, ex p Rofathullah* [1989] QB 219; *Pritchard v Thamesdown Borough Council* (1988) 21 HLR 237, CA.
[11] *Padfield v Minister of Agriculture, Fisheries and Food* [1968] AC 997, [1968] 1 All ER 694, HL.
[12] *R v Secretary of State for the Home Department, ex p Fire Brigades Union* [1995] 2 AC 513.
[13] *R (S) v Westminster City Council* [2013] UKSC 27.

Compelling inferior tribunals

16.54 The principle that an order of mandamus will issue to tribunals exercising an inferior jurisdiction, commanding them to hear and determine according to law is embodied in Lord Mansfield's famous dictum in *R v Barker*:[1]

> 'It [mandamus] was introduced, to prevent disorder from a failure of justice, and defect of police. Therefore it ought to be used upon all occasions where the law has established no specific remedy, and where in justice and good government there ought to be one.'

[1]   (1762) 3 Burr 1265, 1267.

16.55 Both statutory and (in accordance with the principles discussed in CHAPTER 5) non-statutory tribunals may accordingly be subjected to a mandatory order in the absence of any statutory restriction on this remedy. Further, certain tribunals are by statute made subject to mandamus.[1]

[1]   Thus by the Supreme Court Act 1981, s 29(4) the power of the High Court under any enactment to require justices of the peace or a judge or officer of a county court to do any act relating to the duties of their respective offices, or to require a magistrates' court to state a case for the opinion of the High Court, in any case where the High Court formerly had by virtue of any enactment jurisdiction to make a rule absolute, or an order, for any of those purposes, shall be exercisable by mandatory order.
    There appears to be no reason why the modern tribunals (consisting of the first tier and second tier or upper tribunals arranged into chambers) introduced by the Tribunals, Courts and Enforcement Act 2007 may not be subjected to mandatory orders.

The Crown Court

16.56 The statutory jurisdiction to grant prerogative orders in relation to the Crown Court is dealt with earlier in this chapter in the context of quashing and prohibiting orders, and the principles there discussed will be equally applicable to mandatory orders. The statutory power of review reflects the fact that part of the jurisdiction enjoyed by the Crown Court was previously amenable to prerogative writs and orders and, accordingly, cases decided in relation to the issue of mandamus to quarter sessions may be relevant to the position of the Crown Court. For example, the order would lie to courts of quarter sessions to hear and determine an appeal in which they had declined jurisdiction.[1] An order of mandamus has been made to require the Crown Court to grant an applicant leave to appeal out of time against conviction.[2] If a Crown Court refuses to state a case, on the application of a person wishing to question a decision on the grounds of error of law or excess of jurisdiction, for the opinion of the High Court, then a mandatory order may be sought.[3]

[1]   *R v Devon Justices, ex p DPP* [1924] 1 KB 503, DC.
[2]   *R v Crown Court at Croydon, ex p Smith* (1983) 77 Cr App Rep 277, DC.
[3]   Senior Courts Act 1981, ss 28, 29(1).

MAGISTRATES

16.57 A mandatory order may be sought against magistrates who decline to adjudicate on matters within their province.[1] They will be considered to have declined jurisdiction when they have dismissed an information on a point relating to their jurisdiction only, such as that it was necessary to bring all joint owners before them instead of simply the one against whom the information had been laid; or when they have refused to issue summonses in consequence of having acted upon considerations which were extraneous or extra-judicial and which they ought not to have taken into account; or when they have dismissed the information without allowing the prosecution to present its case on the evidence available;[2] or when they have failed to pass sentence, and thus have not disposed of a case;[3] or when they have drawn up a consent order in terms that did not reflect the agreement between the parties.[4] Attempts to obtain a mandatory order against justices were said to be inappropriate, however, when the ground of their decision was that they disbelieved certain evidence,[5] or when the justices had correctly directed themselves on considerations affecting whether or not a matter is to be adjourned.[6] Legislative provisions, now repealed, provided that where justices of the peace refused to do any act relating to the duties of their office the party requiring that act to be done might apply to the High Court for mandamus: these echoed the common law. Where justices refuse to state a case, the High Court may, on the application of the person who applied for the case to be stated, make a mandatory order requiring the justices to state a case.[7] The High Court has, of course, a discretion and may refuse the order. Justices have also been directed to entertain an application for bail.[8]

[1] *R v Newham Justices, ex p Hunt* [1976] 1 All ER 839, [1976] 1 WLR 420, DC.
[2] *Re Harrington* [1984] AC 473, [1984] 2 All ER 474, HL.
[3] See *R v Norfolk Justices, ex p DPP* [1950] 2 KB 558, DC.
[4] *R v Bowman* [1898] 1 QB 663 at 668, DC, per Darling J.
[5] *R v Southampton Justices, ex p Lebern* (1907) 96 LT 697, DC; but on the question of adjournments the court may be entitled to intervene on grounds of procedural propriety (see, eg *R v Panel on Take-overs and Mergers, ex p Guinness plc* [1990] 1 QB 146).
[6] Justices of the Peace Act 1979, s 48.
[7] Magistrates' Courts Act 1980, s 111(6), read in conjunction with the Supreme Court Act 1981, s 29(5).
[8] *R v Blyth Juvenile Court, ex p G* [1991] COD 347.

Licensing justices

16.58 A mandatory order will issue to licensing justices who have failed to hear and determine according to law an application in respect of a licence, commanding them to hear and determine an application for the grant, renewal or transfer of a licence.[1] The licensing jurisdiction of justices was at the turn of the last century an example of an 'administrative' jurisdiction where it was thought that mandamus was the only available prerogative remedy, because certiorari and prohibition were said to be applicable only where there was a 'judicial function'.[2] Although the error was authoritatively corrected,[3] it has been said that, simply as a matter of habit, the standard remedy for judicial control of licensing justices' decisions remains mandamus rather than certiorari.[4]

[1] *Fletcher v London (Metropolitan) Licensing Planning Committee* [1975] AC 160, [1975] 2 All ER 916, HL. But see *R v Kingston Justices, ex p Davey* (1902) 86 LT 589, DC.
[2] *R v Sharman* [1898] 1 QB 578; *R v Bowman* [1898] 1 QB 663.
[3] *Frome United Breweries Co v Bath Justices* [1926] AC 586; see also *R v Woodhouse* [1906] 2 KB 501, reversed (but not on this point) sub nom *Leeds Corpn v Ryder* [1907] AC 420.
[4] Wade and Forsyth Administrative Law (9th edn, 2004) p 25.

County Courts

16.59 Any party requiring any act to be done by a judge or officer of the County Court relating to the duties of his office may apply to the High Court for a mandatory order, and that court may make an order accordingly.[1] A county court judge who mistakenly declined to hear an action for possession by mortgagees on the ground that the court had no jurisdiction was ordered to hear and determine the case.[2] An order of mandamus was issued to direct a county court judge to hear an appeal from a registrar's refusal to grant a certificate under rule 48 of the Matrimonial Causes Rules 1977 that the petitioner was entitled to a decree nisi of divorce.[3] Mandamus has been granted to order the county court to include a penal notice as part of an injunction.[4]

[1] Senior Courts Act 1981, ss 29(4), 31.
[2] *R v Judge Dutton Briant, ex p Abbey National Building Society* [1957] 2 QB 497, [1957] 2 All ER 625, DC.
[3] *R v Nottingham County Court, ex p Byers* [1985] 1 All ER 735, [1985] 1 WLR 403.
[4] *R v Wandsworth County Court, ex p Munn* (1994) 26 HLR 697. See, also, discussion of limitations on review of county court in Chapter 6.

Coroners

16.60 In addition to its powers at common law,[1] the High Court, on application by or under the authority of the Attorney-General, has power to order an inquest to be held touching a death in respect of which a coroner refuses or neglects to hold an inquest, or in respect of which it is necessary or desirable in the interests of justice that another inquest should be held, by reason of fraud, rejection of evidence, irregularity of proceedings, insufficiency of inquiry, the discovery of new facts or evidence or otherwise.[2] Mandamus was granted at common law in *R v Inner London North District Coroner, ex p Linnane*,[3] where the court concluded that the coroner ought to have summoned a jury.

[1] *R v Greater Manchester Coroner, ex p Tal* [1985] QB 67.
[2] Coroners Act 1988, s 13 (which contains supplementary provisions including a power to quash earlier proceedings). See *Re Rapier* [1988] QB 26, DC.
[3] [1989] 1 WLR 395.

The Crown and Crown Servants

16.61 No court can compel the Sovereign to perform any duty, and so no mandatory order will lie to the Sovereign. Lord Denman in *R v Powell*[1] identified two reasons for this:

' . . . both because there would be an incongruity in the Queen commanding herself to do an act, and also because disobedience to a writ of mandamus is to be enforced by attachment.'

[1] *R v Powell* (1841) 1 QB 352 at 361 per Lord Denman CJ.

16.62 But this proposition should not be construed too broadly in relation to those who act in the name of the Crown. The first of the reasons given by Lord

Denman has no logical force where the order is addressed to a person other than the Sovereign, while the force of the second reason is limited to cases where the only method of enforcement is against property of the Sovereign. As long ago as 1850 it was stated:[1]

> 'whenever a person, whether fulfilling an office of the Crown or not has a statutory duty towards another person, a mandamus will lie to compel him to perform it.'

---

[1] *R v Comrs of Woods, Forests, Lands, Works and Buildings, ex p Budge* (1850) 16 QB 761, 768. See, also, *R v Income Tax Special Purposes Comrs* (1888) 21 QBD 313 (where the amenability of the Commissioners to mandamus was upheld despite objection by the Attorney-General): *Income Tax Comrs v Pemsel* [1891] AC 531; Hogg Liability of the Crown (2nd edn, 1989) p 34.

16.63 In 1980 Lord Diplock suggested that mandamus could be awarded against Cabinet Ministers, requiring them to advise the Crown to perform its duty.[1] The modern position concerning the amenability of the Crown to coercive orders is discussed in CHAPTER 14. In the light of Lord Woolf's speech in *M v Home Office*[2] it would seem that all justiciable activities by those who act on behalf of the Crown are subject to mandatory orders, whether those activities are conducted pursuant to statute,[3] or whether they are conducted under the royal prerogative, by delegation pursuant to order in Council[4] or otherwise.[5]

It follows that the historical restriction is of little modern relevance as legislation rarely places duties or confers powers on the Crown as the statutory and prerogative powers are exercised by central government, by Secretaries of State (who are *officers of the* Crown as distinct from the Crown itself) and prerogative orders may be granted against ministers in their official capacity.

---

[1] *Teh Cheng Poh v Public Prosecutor, Malaysia* [1980] AC 458 at 473, [1979] 2 WLR 623 at 633, PC, per Lord Diplock.
[2] [1994] 41 AC 377.
[3] Amenability to mandamus in relation to a statutory discretion was conceded in *Padfield v Minister of Agriculture, Fisheries and Food* [1968] AC 997, 1021.
[4] See *Council of Civil Service Unions v Minister for the Civil Service* [1985] AC 374.
[5] *R v Secretary of State for the Home Department, ex p Bentley* [1994] QB 349.

The Superior Courts

16.64 Subject to any statutory exceptions, a mandatory order will not issue to any of the superior courts. This is an application of the principle discussed earlier, and is subject to the same statutory exception conferring jurisdiction in relation to the Crown Court in particular circumstances. Accordingly, no mandatory order will go to such courts as the Supreme Court, the Court of Appeal, or any of the Divisions which make up the High Court of Justice.

Visitors of charitable foundations

16.65 In 1993 the House of Lords held that charitable foundations which would otherwise be amenable to judicial review have the benefit of certain protections in so far as a complainant may have recourse to a visitor under the rules governing the foundation: with the result that such a complainant must first have recourse to the visitor, who is only subject to judicial review for acting outside jurisdiction (in the narrow sense of entering upon a proceeding when not empowered to do so), abuse of power or breach of natural justice.[1] The main impact of this decision will be on those who seek to challenge action or inaction on the part of colleges and universities, and it is discussed (along with other aspects of review of educational institutions) in CHAPTER 5. It has been said that no mandamus will lie to the benchers of any of the Inns of Court to compel them to admit a certain person as a student of the society or to call a student to the bar, for they have absolute discretion as to the management of their own affairs, and on this basis there would be no legal right that could be enforced against them by mandamus.[2] These statements are of high authority and have stood for many years; but they appear inconsistent with modern notions of judicial review of professional bodies and educational institutions. It is now clear that the visitors to the Inns of Court are subject to judicial review, although it has been held by the Court of Appeal that they have the protection afforded to visitors of charitable foundations (and thus, eg, cannot be reviewed for error of law within their jurisdiction).[3]

[1] *R v Hull University Visitor, ex p Page* [1993] AC 682.
[2] *R v Lincoln's Inn Benchers* (1825) 4 B & C 855 at 860 per Bayley J; *R v Gray's Inn* (1780) 1 Doug KB 353 at 355 per Lord Mansfield. However, the Professional Conduct Committee of the General Council of the Bar has the duty to prefer and prosecute disciplinary charges against members of the Bar before a disciplinary tribunal, and the Bar Council is amenable to judicial review in relation to the performance of that function: *R v General Council of the Bar, ex p Percival* [1991] 1 QB 212, [1990] 3 All ER 137.
[3] *R v Visitors to the Inns of Court, ex p Calder* [1994] QB 1, CA.

The modern day decline

16.66 In common with the other coercive remedy of a prohibiting order, the use of this prerogative order has declined in modern times as the court has come to expect that quashing orders together with declarations will be sufficient to ensure that responsible public bodies act lawfully. This is based on the presumption that public bodies will do so due to a variety of factors including respect for the rule of law, democratic accountability, governmental budgetary sanctions and the supervision of the bodies such as the Ombudsmen, Audit Commission and Homes and Communities Agency. Nonetheless, it is commonly sought in order to compel a public body to consider and determine a case, to discharge a duty or to consider exercising a power. A mandatory order remains the most effective way to compel a public body to act when it is culpable for unreasonable delay. It is similarly effective to compel a decision-maker to give adequate reasons for a decision where there is a statutory duty to do so.

Chapter 17

DECLARATIONS, INJUNCTIONS AND MONEY AND RESTITUTIONARY REMEDIES

INTRODUCTION

Framework of this chapter

17.1 The present chapter gives an account of the principles which govern claims for declarations, injunctions and money and restitutionary remedies in proceedings for judicial review. Before 1977 these remedies were available in private law proceedings only but since then they have been available in judicial review claims. Some account of the position prior to 1977 is necessary in order to understand the current framework but reference is made to the previous editions of this work for a fuller treatment of this topic.

17.2 In this part of the chapter the history of the reforms is discussed briefly, and some general comments are made about declarations, injunctions and money and restitutionary remedies in the context of judicial review. The second part of this chapter deals with the court's jurisdiction to grant declarations and injunctions by way of an application for judicial review (see **17.16** below). The third and fourth parts discuss particular features of declarations (see **17.17** below) and injunctions (at **17.59** below) respectively. The fifth part of this chapter describes the use of declarations and injunctions in cases concerned with public and municipal offices (see **17.80** below), and the final part deals with the award of money and restitutionary remedies on an application for judicial review (see **17.85** below).

The position prior to 1978

17.3 The prerogative orders (discussed in Chapter 16) are not the only remedies open to a person who wishes to challenge administrative action. Rights which would now be described as falling within public law have long been vindicated in England and Wales by actions for damages and for statutory penalties, and such rights have increasingly been the subject of applications for declarations and injunctions. Although the prerogative orders could have effects similar to those of a declaration or an injunction, and might in effect require the payment of money, prior to 1978 none of the remedies of declaration, injunction and damages were granted in their own right as additional or alternative relief consequent upon applications for a prerogative order. Applications for a prerogative Order were processed through the Crown Office, and accordingly fell within the category known as proceedings on the Crown Side of the Queen's Bench Division. They were heard by a Divisional Court of the Queen's Bench Division, using a procedure under which both the ex p motion for leave and (if leave were granted) the substantive motion seeking the prerogative order in question were heard by a panel of three judges.[1] By contrast, applications for other remedies, even though the issues might turn on the legality of administrative action, could normally[2] only be made in ordinary civil proceedings.[3] The result was that a claimant seeking to assert that an administrative act should be the subject of a declaration, an injunction, or an award of damages, was compelled to use a different procedure from that which would have applied had the claimant sought orders of certiorari, prohibition or mandamus – and a claimant who sought remedies falling in both these categories would need to bring two sets of proceedings.

1 See the description by Sir Louis Blom-Cooper in 'The New Face of Judicial Review' [1982] PL 250, 251, and see, generally, at Chapter 3 above.
2 There were (and continue to be) exceptions: eg claims to penalties or other statutory entitlements could involve special procedures and venues, and determinations of qualification for municipal office were dealt with both by the High Court and by courts of summary jurisdiction under the Local Government Act 1933, s 84.
3 This feature assumed great importance in Dicey's exposition of the rule of law, which ignored the prerogative remedies when supporting the assertion that the law of the constitution was the consequence of the rights of individuals as defined and enforced by the courts: see Dicey *Introduction to the Study of the Law of the Constitution*, Ch 4, and the discussion of Dicey's legacy and more general aspects of the history in Chapter 2 above.

The 1977 Reforms and s 31 of the Supreme Court Act 1981

17.4 With effect from January 1978 the new RSC Ord 53 provided that applications for a declaration and an injunction could be made by way of judicial review and that the court had a power to award damages on an application for judicial review in case where damages would have been awarded if the claim had been started by a private action. These rule changes were confirmed in primary legislation in s 31 of the Supreme Court Act 1981 (now Senior Courts Act 1981). By s 31(2):

'A declaration may be made or an injunction granted under this sub-section in any case where an application for judicial review, seeking that relief, has been made and the High Court considers that, having regard to:
(a)   the nature of the matters in respect of which relief may be granted by orders of mandamus, prohibition or certiorari;
(b)   the nature of the persons and bodies against whom relief may be granted by such orders; and
(c)   all the circumstances of the case,

it would be just and convenient for the declaration to be made or the injunction to be granted, as the case may be'.

17.5 Provision continues to be made, by s 30 of the Senior Courts Act 1981, for declarations and injunctions instead of informations or writs of quo warranto.[1] The use of declarations and injunctions for this purpose is discussed at 17.85 below.

Damages and other monetary remedies are dealt with in s 31(4) which now[2] reads:

'(4)   On an application for judicial review the High Court may award to the applicant damages, restitution or the recovery of a sum due if–

    (a)   the application includes a claim for such an award arising from any matter to which the application relates; and

    (b)   the court is satisfied that such an award would have been made if the claim had been made in an action begun by the applicant at the time of making the application.'

[1]   Rules of the Supreme Court (Amendment No 3) Order 1977, now superseded by Section 1 of CPR Pt 54.
[2]   Initially it included damages only but the power to award a restitutionary or other monetary remedy was added by Article 4 of the Civil Procedure (Modification of Supreme Court Act 1981) Order 2004, SI 2004/1033.

CPR Provisions relating to injunctions etc

17.6 CPR Part 54 does not (unlike the former RSC O.53) set out the test for applying for injunctions, declarations or damages by judicial review in the body of the rule but cross-refers to and incorporates the provisions of s 31 of the Senior Courts Act 1981.

By CPR 54.3 a Claimant may use the judicial review procedure where they seek a declaration or an injunction.

However, the judicial review procedure is mandatory if, in addition, the Claimant seeks a remedy listed in CPR 54.2 (mandatory, quashing or prohibiting orders or the injunction formerly known as *quo warranto* – see below).

A claim for judicial review may include a claim for damages, restitution or the recovery of a sum due but cannot include this remedy alone (CPR 54.3). This applies only to the start of the claim rather than to its subsequent progress. Thus if a claim starts by including other remedies but these are later excluded leaving only a claim for a monetary remedy then the court on judicial review still has power to deal with it. Where a claim starts under Part 54 but the public law issue is resolved leaving only a claim for damages requiring live evidence or extensive disclosure, then the proper course will normally be to direct that the case be transferred under CPR 54.20 to continue as if not started under Part 54.[1] However, in this case any grant of legal aid for the earlier judicial review proceedings will not cover the transferred part of the claim.[2]

[1]   See eg *Khalifa v Secretary of State for the Home Department* [2015] EWHC 4017 (Admin) where the only issue remaining was liability for historical unlawful detention.
[2]   Legal Aid Sentencing and Punishment of Offenders Act 2012 Schedule 1, paragraph 19(10).

Claims in the Upper Tribunal

17.7 Where judicial review claims are to be dealt with by the Upper Tribunal the source of the power to make declarations and final injunctions is s 15 of the Tribunals Courts and Enforcement Act 2007. The Upper Tribunal is to apply the same principles as apply in the High Court on an application for judicial review under s 31 of the SCA and where relief is granted then it has the same effect and is enforced in the same way as if the Order had been made by the High Court (s 15(3), (5)). Relief can only be granted where the Tribunal has given permission to apply for it (s 16(2)). In the 4th edition of this work doubts were expressed about whether the Upper Tribunal had power to grant an interim injunction since the powers of the High Court under s 37 of the Senior Courts Act 1981 have not been transferred to it. The Upper Tribunal does not share these doubts and paragraph 11 of the Practice Direction on Judicial Review in the Immigration and Asylum Chamber of the Upper Tribunal Immigration sets out the procedure to be followed where a claimant is seeking an interim injunction.[1]

1 In *R (JW through DW as Litigation Friend) v The Learning Trust* [2009] UKUT 197 (AAC) the Upper Tribunal assumed (para 26) that it had power to grant interim relief but the application was refused on the merits.

Declarations And Injunctions: Questions Of Jurisdiction

17.8 In the early days following the changes to RSC O53 and s 31 there was much debate over the extent of the reforms and how far they had changed the basis on which declarations or injunctions might be granted or whether judicial review was now an exhaustive procedure. In due course each of these questions was answered in favour of a flexible approach that had the practical effect of enlarging access to the new judicial review remedies. The debates are largely now of historical interest only and are simply noted here.[1]

1 The position is more fully discussed in the third edition of this work.

17.9 Initially it was doubted whether a declaration or injunction would be available in respect of decisions where a prerogative order would not have lain. But this was authoritatively resolved in *R v Secretary of State for Employment, ex p Equal Opportunities Commission*[1] where a declaration was made that the threshold conditions for claiming unfair dismissal were incompatible with Community Law despite the fact that there was no decision in respect of which one of the prerogative orders would have been available.

1 [1995] 1 AC 1.

17.10 A further area of debate was over the question whether the reforms had expanded the kinds of bodies against whom relief could be obtained and the circumstances in which relief could be granted against them. This question assumed considerable importance in deciding whether an injunction could be granted against the Crown (declarations had always been available against the Crown in some, but not all cases – see below). At first s 31 was construed restrictively. In *R v Secretary of State for Transport, ex p Factortame Ltd*[1] the applicants had been granted an interlocutory injunction restraining the Secretary of State from enforcing certain legislation against the applicants pending a preliminary ruling on the validity of that legislation by the European Court of Justice. The Court of Appeal had set aside the interlocutory injunction and the House of Lords held that, as a matter of domestic law, they were right to do so. The leading speech was delivered by Lord Bridge, who[2] gave three reasons for holding that s 31 should be given a restricted interpretation. The second and third reasons were that Parliament had eschewed draft legislation[3] expressly conferring a power to grant injunctions against the Crown, and had enacted a provision which was directed to the final, rather than the interlocutory, stage of proceedings. The first reason was as follows:

> 'First, section 31(2) and Order 53, rule 1(2) being in identical terms, the subsection and the sub-rule must have the same meaning and the sub-rule, if it purported to extend jurisdiction, would have been ultra vires'.

[1]   [1990] 2 AC 85.
[2]   At 149–150.
[3]   This had been formulated in the proposed clause 3(2) of the Law Commission's draft Bill.

17.11 Four years later, however, the approach taken by Lord Bridge was rejected by the House of Lords in *M v Home Office*.[1] In this case the House of Lords decided that an order granting an interim injunction against the Secretary of State had been properly made. In the leading speech, Lord Woolf observed that if a statute placed a duty on a specified minister or other official which created a cause of action, an injunction against such an officer of the Crown would not fall within the prohibition in s 21 of the Crown Proceedings Act 1947. It may be commented that there was therefore no difficulty in holding that s 31(2) of the Supreme Court Act 1981 gave jurisdiction to the court on an application for judicial review to grant an injunction against a specified official who was under such a duty: indeed, this involved no extension to the jurisdiction of the High Court in the strict sense of the term prior to 1977, on a proper understanding of s 21 of the Crown Proceedings Act 1947.

[1]   [1994] 1 AC 377. For comment see Gould [1993] PL 568; Harlow (1994) 57 MLR 620. For further discussion of this case and the position of the Crown, see Chapter **14**.

17.12 Nevertheless, Lord Woolf held further that RSC Ord 53 (which was not subject to s 21 of the 1947 Act) extended the circumstances in which remedies could be obtained against the Crown. Lord Woolf[1] explained the position as follows:

> 'Order 53 undoubtedly extended the circumstances in which a declaration could be granted against the appropriate representative of the Crown. Prior to the change no remedy whatsoever in the nature of a declaration could be obtained in prerogative proceedings. Furthermore, there are situations where no declaration could be obtained in private law proceedings against the Crown without the assistance of the Attorney General in circumstances in which it is now available on judicial review. It is not suggested that Order 53 was ultra vires in allowing declarations against Ministers and in my view if it was not ultra vires in relation to declarations there is no reason why it should be regarded as being ultra vires in relation to injunctions, albeit that the effect is that an injunction [can now] be obtained against a Minister of the Crown where previously only an order of mandamus or prohibition could be obtained. However, if Order 53 were to be regarded as being open to challenge on this ground, this would explain why the unusual course was taken, a change having been introduced by an amendment to the Rules of the Supreme Court, of confirming the amendment a substantial period later by the Act of 1981.'

[1]   [1994] 1 AC at 420–421;The authors are indebted to Sir Sydney Kentridge QC for deducing, and to Lord Woolf for confirming, that 'cannot' in the printed text should read 'can now'. For further analysis, see Edwards, 'Interdict and the Crown'(1995) 111 LQR 34.

17.13 Lord Woolf in this passage, regarded s 31 of the Supreme Court Act 1981 as confirming that the entitlement of the court to grant injunctions and declarations under RSC Ord 53, r 1(2) (and now under CPR Part 54.4) is not limited to circumstances where any particular remedies were available in particular proceedings prior to the reform. This may well have involved an alteration to substantive law in the sense that it freed the High Court from restrictions which otherwise would have affected jurisdiction to grant relief: but if so it is an alteration whose practical limits will be for the court itself to determine, by reference to the criteria set out in s 31 of the Supreme Court Act 1981.

17.14 Prior to the 1977 reforms the requirements for standing were more restrictive for an injunction or declaration than they were for the prerogative remedies. The declaration was a private law remedy to establish private law rights or at least or to deal with a case where the plaintiff had suffered special damage through a breach of a public right. An injunction or declaration to vindicate public rights was to be brought by the Attorney General – *Gouriet v Union of Post Office Workers*[1]. In *IRC v National Federation of Self Employed and Small Businesses*[2] the House of Lords held that the restrictive tests for standing to claim declarations and injunctions in private law proceedings did not apply to public law cases. There is now no formal difference in the standing requirement between the various remedies sought on judicial review and older cases in this respect must be treated with considerable caution.[3] Standing generally is dealt with in Chapter **18**.

[1]   [1978] AC 435 HL.
[2]   [1982] AC 617.
[3]   Despite these relaxations in the rules on standing the court will still not grant an injunction (or presumably declaration) in aid of the criminal law at the instance of a private individual with no particular private input or interest to be protected — *R (Islamic Human Rights Commission) v Civil Aviation Authority* [2006] EWHC 2465 (Admin) at paragraphs 38–39.

17.15 Finally, if a claim for a declaration, an injunction or other remedy could be made in a particular case by way of judicial review then the question arose whether judicial review was an exclusive procedure so that the claim could not any longer be made by way of ordinary civil action. The answer initially given to this question in 1982 (by the decision in *O'Reilly v Mackman*)[1] was that, in certain circumstances, the remedies of declaration and injunction must be sought by judicial review alone. However, this restrictive rule has been overtaken by a more liberal approach stressing the broad powers of case management under the CPR and can now be treated as largely obsolete. Following the decision in *Clark v University of Lincolnshire and Humberside*[2] it is rare for a claim to be struck out on procedural exclusivity grounds where there is a private law element to the claim or where the vindication of private law rights requires the examination of the validity of public law action.

Chapter **5** describes the current state of the law in this regard.

[1]   [1983] 2 AC 237.
[2]   [2000] 1 WLR 1988 CA.

Declarations, injunctions and money and restitutionary remedies in the context of judicial review

17.16 As with the discussion of prerogative remedies in CHAPTER 16, certain general points can usefully be made before turning to discuss particular features of the remedies of declaration, injunction, damages, restitution and recovery of a sum due:

(1)   It has now been recognised that the changes initiated by the new RSC Ord 53 extended the circumstances in which declarations and injunctions could be granted (see above).[1]

(2)   The changes have been accompanied by judicial development of the remedies of declarations and injunctions. Citations from earlier cases concerning limitations on the grant of declarations and injunctions should be read with caution.

(3)   Where there is some objection to the grant of any one of the remedies of declaration, injunction, damages, restitution or the recovery of a sum due, the desired result may be achievable by another of those remedies or by the grant of a prerogative order (discussed in CHAPTER 16).

(4)   If a remedy against the Crown is sought, general principles discussed in CHAPTER 14 will apply. In the present chapter, reference is made to the Crown's immunity from suit only where a particular point needs to be made in relation to a particular remedy.

(5)   General principles affecting restrictions on the remedies of declaration and injunction are discussed in CHAPTER 18. In the present chapter, questions of standing, refusal of relief because of the availability of alternative remedies, refusal of relief for delay, and other discretionary bars are discussed only where a special feature of a particular remedy calls for consideration.

(6)   This chapter is concerned with remedies which a court may grant at a final hearing. Interim remedies call for separate discussion and are dealt with in CHAPTER 19.

(7)   The only remedies (other than prerogative orders) which the Civil Procedure Rules currently allow to be sought in judicial review proceedings are those of declaration, injunction, damages, restitution and recovery of a sum due. If other remedies are desired separate proceedings may be needed.[2]

(8)   If one of the remedies sought is the award of a declaration, an injunction, damages, restitution or recovery of a sum due, but the court considers that it should not be granted on an application for judicial review, then by CPR 54.20 the court can order the claim to continue as if it had not been started under Part 54. This means that if the objection to the grant of the remedy is merely that it should not be sought by way of judicial review, all is not necessarily lost.[3]

---

[1]   This is discussed at **17.16** and **17.17**.
[2]   See the discussion at **17.3** et seq.
[3]   The relevant principles are discussed at **5.48** above and at **19.145** and **20.32** below.

DECLARATIONS

Declaratory judgments as a public law remedy[1]

[1] See, generally, Zamir and Woolf *The Declaratory Judgment* (4th edn, 2011) and Lewis *Judicial Remedies in Public Law* (5th edn, 2014), Ch 7. For discussion of whether a declaratory judgment is a constitutive remedy, see Zamir and Woolf at paragraph 1.03, and Cane. 'A Fresh Look at Punton's Case' (1980) 43 MLR 268.

17.17 Following mid-nineteenth century statutory reform,[2] in 1883 the Rules of the Supreme Court expressly provided that the High Court could make a merely declaratory judgment whether or not any consequential relief could be claimed.[3] The rules of 1883 referred to the grant of 'declarations of right'. This was repeated through to the rules of 1965. The words 'of right' were omitted, however, in the Civil Procedure Rules 1998, CPR 40.20 now provides: 'The court may make binding declarations whether or not any other remedy is claimed'. This emphasises the breadth of the remedy of declaration.

[2] Chancery Act 1850; Chancery Procedure Act 1852, s 50.
[3] Order 25, r 5 of the Rules of the Supreme Court 1883. A challenge to the vires of the rule was rejected in *Guaranty Trust Co of New York v Hannay & Co* [1915] 2 KB 536.

17.18 Contentions that declaratory relief could not be obtained against the Crown were rejected, and the real potential for declaratory relief as a remedy for actual or threatened illegal behaviour by the executive was demonstrated, in *Dyson v A-G*[1] where the Court of Appeal granted declarations that a requisition by the Commissioners of Inland Revenue was unlawful and that the claimant was under no obligation to comply with it. Since then the declaration has proved a particularly apt remedy in public law where respondents can generally be expected to comply with the court's decision.[2] The usefulness of the declaration as a flexible remedy, capable of adaptation to new circumstances, was demonstrated in *R v Secretary of State for Employment, ex p Equal Opportunities Commission*,[3] where a declaration was granted to the Equal Opportunities Commission that certain provisions of United Kingdom legislation were incompatible with the Treaty of Rome and the Equal Pay Directive.

[1] [1912] 1 Ch 158; an interlocutory attempt to strike out the claim on the ground that a declaration could not be sought against the Crown was unsuccessful: see *Dyson v A-G* [1911] 1 KB 410, discussed at **17.14** below.
[2] See, eg *R v Liverpool City Corpn, ex p Ferguson* [1985] IRLR 501. A mere declaration may not be appropriate if the respondent cannot be relied upon to act responsibly: see *Webster v Southwark London Borough Council* [1983] QB 698, and the comment on this case in de Smith's *Judicial Review* (7th edn, 2013) 18-037. Consequences of the grant of a declaration are dealt with at **17.32** below.
[3] [1995] 1 AC 1. An attack on the Divisional Court as an appropriate forum for the Commission's claim was rejected (at 27–28): it was the only English forum in which the incompatibility issue could be determined at the instance of the Commission, and (given that the question of objective justification is to be determined by national courts) it was more appropriate than potential proceedings by the European Commission in the European Court of Justice.

17.19 This part of the chapter discusses the nature of the court's power to grant a declaration by way of judicial review, the factors which affect the willingness of the court to grant declarations (including the objection that they are 'advisory'), and the flexibility of declarations (including the use of 'prospective' declarations).

Nature of the declaration by way of judicial review

General principles

17.20 Under s 31 of the Supreme Court Act 1981 the court is required, when considering whether it would be just and convenient for a declaration to be granted on an application for judicial review, to have regard to the nature of the matters in respect of which relief may be granted by way of the prerogative orders, and the nature of the persons and bodies against whom such relief may be granted, as well as to all the circumstances of the case. As noted above, modern developments have largely superseded particular restrictions on particular remedies. Even so, the courts in the application of s 31 can be expected (in accordance with the criteria to which s 31 directs attention) to confine judicial review to cases where it is appropriate for the court to exercise jurisdiction as a matter of public law.[1]

[1] Thus Woolf J in *R v British Broadcasting Corporation, ex p Lavelle* [1983] 1 WLR 23 said at 31 that he regarded the wording of RSC Ord 53 r 1 and the statute as making it clear that the application for judicial review is confined to reviewing activities of a public nature as opposed to those of a purely private or domestic character.

17.21 Accordingly, it remains appropriate to have regard to general principles that the court cannot grant declarations on purely moral, social or political matters in which no legal or equitable rights arise,[1] or concerning the constitutionality of an Act of Parliament,[2] parliamentary privileges,[3] foreign policy or the compliance by other states with international law[4] or concerning the making of treaties.[5] Where a question of criminal law arises, the High Court will be anxious not to usurp the jurisdiction of the criminal courts, and it will not grant a declaration that an accused is innocent after a prosecution has started: *Imperial Tobacco Ltd v A-G.*[6] In *A-G v Able*[7] the Attorney-General contended that distribution of a booklet constituted an offence under the Suicide Act 1961, and sought declarations in various alternative forms; Woolf J held that such a declaration should only be granted if it is clearly established that there is no risk of it treating conduct as criminal which is not clearly in contravention of the criminal law.[8] Similarly, the High Court cannot pronounce on entitlements which are exclusively for adjudication by other tribunals. Thus a special provision for the enforcement of a statutory right to recover in a court of summary jurisdiction the costs of raising a wreck was held to exclude other methods of enforcement in *Barraclough v Brown, The J M Lennard.*[9] Two points should be noted here. First, this was a restriction on the court's original jurisdiction:[10] there was no restriction of the court's power to supervise the statutory enforcement procedure.[11] Second, it is to be noted that the mere provision of a particular method for determining rights in particular cases will not of itself compel the conclusion that the court's jurisdiction to grant a declaration has been excluded.[12]

[1] *Malone v Metropolitan Police Comr* [1979] Ch 344, per Sir Robert Megarry V-C at 353. Note also Lord Bridge in *Gillick v West Norfolk and Wisbech Health Authority* [1986] AC 112, 193–194: the jurisdiction to correct error of law in a government circular should be exercised by the court with the utmost restraint, avoiding 'expressing ex cathedra opinions in areas of social and ethical controversy in which it has no claim to speak . . . '.
[2] *Shindler & anor v Chancellor of the Duchy of Lancaster & anor* [2017] Q.B. 226 discussed at 17.38 below.

³ *Bradlaugh v Gossett* (1884) 12 QBD 271; but this does not prevent the court from considering whether delegated legislation about to be laid before parliament is lawful: *R v HM Treasury, ex p Smedley* [1985] QB 657.

⁴ See eg *R (Gentle) v Prime Minister* [2007] QB 689 at 33-4 CA; *R (Khan) v Secretary of State for Foreign and Commonwealth Affairs* [2014] 1 WLR 872 CA. This is subject to exceptions and will, for example 'not apply to foreign acts of state which are in breach of clearly established rules of international law or are contrary to English principles of public policy, as well as where there is a grave infringement of human rights' *Khan* at para 28 per Lord Dyson MR.

⁵ See *ex p Molyneux* [1986] 1 WLR 331. But a declaration whether legislation is compatible with the Treaty of Rome is permissible, reflecting the primacy of European Community law enshrined in s 2 of the European Communities Act 1972: *R v Secretary of State for Employment, ex p Equal Opportunities Commission* [1995] 1 AC 1, 27. See, also, *R v Secretary of State for Foreign & Commonwealth Affairs, ex p Rees-Mogg* [1994] QB 552.

⁶ [1981] AC 718, [1980] 1 All ER 866, HL. See further **17.46** below.

⁷ [1984] QB 795, [1984] 1 All ER 277.

⁸ None of the various alternatives proposed by the Attorney-General met this test, and his application was refused. A declaration of non-criminality sought by the respondents was also refused, because supply of the booklet could constitute an offence. Where criminality depends on the lawfulness of executive action, it may be highly convenient and appropriate to grant a declaration: *Dyson v A-G* [1911] 1 KB 410, CA, [1912] 1 Ch 158, CA. For declarations as to the accuracy of government advice on the criminal law, and as to the criminality of proposed conduct by medical practitioners, see the discussion of *Gillick v West Norfolk and Wisbech Area Health Authority* [1986] AC 113, and *Airedale NHS Trust v Bland* [1993] AC 789 below.

⁹ [1897] AC 615. See, also, Argosam Finance Co Ltd v Oxby [1965] Ch 390; Jensen v Corpn of the Trinity House of Deptford, The Dana Anglia, Dana Regina and Dana Futura [1982] 2 Lloyd's Rep 14, CA.

¹⁰ For the distinction between the court's original and supervisory jurisdiction, see **17.24**. Exclusion of the court's supervisory jurisdiction is discussed in CHAPTERS 5 and 6.

¹¹ Although even where the court is exercising its supervisory jurisdiction it will not grant a declaration framed in terms that trespass on the decision-making functions of another body. In *R (Licensed Taxi Driver's Association) v TFL* [2016], R.T.R Patterson J refused to grant a declaration that works carried out by the defendant were a breach of planning control because that could pre-empt a decision by the relevant planning authorities.

¹² See *Pyx Granite Estates Ltd v Ministry of Housing and Local Government* [1960] AC 260; *Ealing London Borough Council v Race Relations Board* [1972] AC 343. Although a declaratory action is not admissible to circumvent appeal procedures under the Income Tax Acts (*Soul v Marchant* (1962) 40 TC 508) it was held in *Beecham Group plc v IRC* [1992] STC 935 that a declaration may be obtained as to the lawfulness of procedures proposed by the Inland Revenue Commissioners.

17.22 By contrast, s 31 may well be prayed in aid to overcome certain technical restrictions, discussed below. Also discussed below are the supervisory and original aspects of the court's jurisdiction, the relevance of reliance on public law grounds of review, the relevance of the relationship between the High Court and other courts, the inability to grant interim declarations, questions concerning declarations against the Crown, the consequences of grant of a declaration, and cases that are unsuitable for judicial review.

Technical restrictions

17.23 Restrictions on the grant of declarations are unlikely to have survived the new RSC Ord 53 and its statutory confirmation if they are founded on technical points unrelated to the question of whether it is appropriate for the court to exercise its jurisdiction as a matter of public law. Lord Woolf in *M v Home Office*¹ observed that there are situations where no declaration could be obtained in private law without the assistance of the Attorney-General in circumstances in which a declaration is now available on judicial review. This observation reflects the fact that it was undoubtedly the intention of the new RSC Ord 53 in the 1981 Act to do away with technical restrictions on standing.[2] Similarly, in so far as there may be any technical restrictions on the court's ability to grant 'advisory' declarations otherwise than on judicial review, such restrictions should not prevent the court on judicial review from granting a declaration where it is appropriate to do so as a matter of public law.[3] A further possible example of a technical restriction is *Punton's case*,[4] which has been thought to preclude a grant of a declaration that a voidable decision was invalid.[5] In such rare cases as may involve a truly voidable decision, it seems desirable in principle that the court should be able to declare by way of judicial review (in a case where this will serve a useful purpose) that the decision while valid in the meantime, now that it has come before the court, can – prospectively – be treated as no longer valid.[6] As a matter of discretion the court would only make such a declaration in a case where it was right to treat the decision as having been avoided.[7]

[1]   [1994] 1 AC 377, 420–421.
[2]   The new principles governing standing were the subject of express provision, and are discussed in Chapter 18.
[3]   See the discussion of advisory declarations at 17.37–17.55.
[4]   *Punton v Ministry of Pensions* [1963] 1 WLR 186, *Punton v Ministry of Pensions (No 2)* [1963] 1 WLR 1176 (Phillimore J); affd, [1964] 1 WLR 226, CA. For criticism, see Cane, 'A Fresh Look at Punton's Case' [1980] 43 MLR 266. The actual decision is of limited practical effect now that errors of law are generally treated as going to jurisdiction.
[5]   The reasoning is that mere declaration of intra vires error leaves a voidable decision intact.
[6]   A similar outcome is achieved when the court grants a prospective declaration: see 17.55.
[7]   Lewis *Judicial Remedies in Public Law* (4th edn, 2008) paragraph 5–031 objects that such a declaration would be constitutive; but compare Cane, 'A Fresh Look at *Punton's Case*' [1980] 43 MLR 266.

Original and supervisory jurisdiction

17.24 It has been said that the court's jurisdiction to grant a declaration is both original and supervisory.[1] Original jurisdiction is invoked by declaration or otherwise where one person asserts an actual or threatened infringement of private rights, or special damage suffered, as a consequence of some breach of public duty by another person. Supervisory jurisdiction involves control (by declaration or otherwise) of bodies whose acts or decisions themselves may affect the rights of the parties. Thus in *R v Port Talbot Borough Council, ex p Jones*[2] the court exercised its supervisory role by quashing a determination to grant a tenancy and made a declaration that the tenancy granted pursuant to the decision was void: this declaration was an exercise of the court's original jurisdiction. As pointed out by Craig,[3] the duality of role is one of the strengths of the declaration, for it allows a court to declare invalid certain action by a public body (the supervisory role) and then, if appropriate, to pronounce on the rights which the parties actually have (the original role). So, where the court has declared that an office holder has been unlawfully dismissed then it may go on to explain the impact that it has on their right to arrears of salary.[4]

Conversely, a supervisory declaration may have no direct impact on a private claim because it relates solely to public law issues. In *Tchenguiz v Director of the Serious Fraud Office*[5] T brought judicial review proceedings to quash a search warrant. The court quashed the warrants and 'consequently . . .

declare[d] the entries, searches and seizures conducted pursuant to the warrants to be unlawful on the grounds set out in the judgment'. On a subsequent claim for damages (which had been remitted to the QBD under CPR 54.20) T argued that it necessarily followed from the declaration that the SFO had been guilty of trespass. The Court of Appeal disagreed. The declaration related only to public law unlawfulness entitling the claimant to challenge the order made (para 14, 19). In other words, it was an expression of the court's supervisory jurisdiction. It did not deal with the consequences in private law and whether officers who executed the warrants would be liable in trespass.

1   Zamir and Woolf *The Declaratory Judgment* (44th edn 2011) paragraph 3–004.
2   [1988] 2 All ER 207.
3   *Administrative Law* (7th edn, 2012) 26-017.
4   See paragraph 17.39.2 below. In *McLaughlin v Governor of the Cayman Islands* [2007] UKPC 50, [2007] 1 WLR 2839, PC the court granted a declaration that 'the purported dismissal . . . was ineffective in law to determine [Dr McLaughlin's] tenure of office, and . . . that [he] is entitled to recover arrears of salary . . . and to the payment of pension contributions . . . until he resigns or his tenure of office lawfully comes to an end'.
5   [2014] EWCA Civ 472.

17.25 The Court may also make a declaration exercising its original jurisdiction as to the status of an individual so as to regulate the legal relationship between the parties in future. So in *R (on the application of D) v Southwark LBC*[1] a declaration was granted as to the status of a formerly looked after child even though they were no longer being looked after because it would form the basis on which the authority should assess what services to provide. However, this technique cannot be used improperly to circumvent the ordinary time limits for judicial review.[2]

1   [2006] EWHC 2280 (Admin); *R (TG) v Lambeth London Borough Council* [2012] PTSR 364, CA
2   *Stancliffe Stone Co Ltd v Peak District National Park Authority* [2005] EWCA Civ 747 – Planning status and *Rusby v Harr* [2006] EWCA Civ 865, [2007] JPL 262 – whether a highway had been validly adopted so as to afford a defence to an action for trespass. In both cases the court held that the statutory framework did not permit any challenge other than a timely claim for judicial review.

17.26 The court must take care not to infringe any statutory exclusion of jurisdiction, and cannot use its original role to interfere with the functions of a public authority that are only subject to control in its supervisory role. Thus in *A (A Patient) v A Health Authority; Re J; The Queen on the Application of S v Secretary of State for the Home Department*[1] a dispute arose between the authority and the father of A, an adult with severe learning difficulties, as to where he should live. The applicant brought proceedings for a declaration as to best interests under the inherent jurisdiction of the High Court[2]. Having extensively reviewed the authorities, Munby J held at paragraph 97: 'if the task facing the judge is to come to a decision for and on behalf of a child or incompetent adult then the welfare of that person must be the paramount consideration. If the task for the judge is to review the decision of a public authority taken in the exercise of some statutory power then the governing principles are those of public law'. To the extent that the claim involved a challenge to the community care assessment carried out by the authority it was a public law matter to which the supervisory standards of judicial review applied.[3]

This approach was confirmed in *N v A Clinical Commissioning Group and others* [2017] UKSC 22 where the Supreme Court held that the powers to make a declaration as to best interests and to make a decision on behalf of an incapacitated adult under the Mental Capacity Act 2015 did not enable the court to require care providers to do that which they were unwilling or unable to do.

1. [2002] 1 FLR 845.
2. Now the application would be to the Court of Protection under the Mental Capacity Act 2005.
3. See the discussion at **17.21** above of *Barraclough v Brown* [1897] AC 615. Where there is only one conclusion open to the Defendant or only one course of action they can take then the court can, even in the exercise of its supervisory jurisdiction, declare that to be the case. So, in *R (MM) v Lewisham London Borough Council* [2009] EWHC 416 (Admin) the court granted a declaration that the authority owed a duty to house the claimant, that being the only decision it could properly have reached had it acted lawfully.

Reliance on public law grounds of review

17.27 An application for a declaration by way of judicial review will normally invoke the court's supervisory jurisdiction discussed above. In this regard, before proceeding to consider whether public law grounds of challenge are made out so as to warrant the grant of a declaration, the court will need to satisfy itself that the matter is of a public law nature, in which public law grounds of challenge are properly brought into play. This is a matter of substantive law. A useful analogy here is *R v British Broadcasting Corporation, ex p Lavelle*[1] where the applicant's claim was held to be a matter of private law, and so could not proceed by judicial review.[2] Provided that the case raises public law issues, it may well be appropriate for the court on judicial review, having determined those issues, to make a declaration of the consequential private law rights of the parties. But if the case raises no public law issue, it will not be appropriate to grant a declaration of private law rights on an application for judicial review. In such a case it may be appropriate under CPR 54.20 to order the claim to continue as if it had not been started under Part 54.[3]

In a private law claim for a declaration the court may refuse relief where it considers that the claim really raises matters of public law that ought to be dealt with on an application for judicial review. In *Milebush Properties Ltd v Tameside Metropolittan Borough Council*,[4] M sought a declaration as to the meaning of an obligation to grant a right of way contained in a section 106 agreement between the authority and T who had acquired the property from the developers. M was not a party to the agreement. The Court of Appeal (Moore Bick LJ dissenting) held that while there was power to grant a declaration as to the meaning of an agreement to which M was not a party the real issue was one of planning policy and its enforcement by H which ought to be determined, if at all, on an application for judicial review.

1. [1983] 1 WLR 23.
2. The remedy sought in that case was an injunction, but similar considerations would have applied had a declaration been sought.
3. The court in the *Lavelle* case was willing to treat the matter as if an order had been made under RSC Ord 53 r 9(5) for the case to proceed as if begun by writ. This has been replaced by CPR 54.20, discussed at **5.48** above and **19.145** and **20.32** below.
4. [2011] PTSR 1654.

Relationship between the High Court and other courts

17.28 The determination of the limits of the court's supervisory jurisdiction may require analysis of the relationship between the High Court and other courts.[1] Thus in *R v Crown Court at Chelmsford, ex p Chief Constable of Essex*[2] the High Court was asked to make a declaration concerning the extent of public interest immunity in relation to certain proceedings in the Crown Court. After examining the statutory provisions governing the creation of the Crown Court, and the historical role of the assizes which the Crown Court had replaced, the High Court held that it had no general supervisory jurisdiction over proceedings in the Crown Court. Section 29 of the Senior Courts Act 1981 allows orders of mandamus, prohibition or certiorari to be made in respect of proceedings in the Crown Court other than in matters relating to trials on indictment but since the claim did not fall within that statutory exception it was dismissed. In *R (on the application of B) v Stafford Combined Court*[3] the court granted a declaration that a witness was entitled to service of a witness summons requiring production of her medical notes and to make representations. This was not a breach of s 29(3) of the Senior Courts Act 1981. The reasoning behind that rule was to prevent trials being delayed in respect of matters that could be appealed in the event of a conviction. The claimant was a witness and could not appeal and her application would have no impact on any trial.

[1] Such an analysis may also be required in relation to the original jurisdiction of the High Court: see the discussion at **17.20** of *Barraclough v Brown* [1897] AC 615.

[2] [1994] 1 WLR 359.

[3] [2007] 1 WLR 1524.

Interim declarations

17.29 An interim declaration may now be granted under CPR 25.1, whether or not a final declaration is sought.[1]

[1] For the position prior to CPR, see p 14.14 of the second edition of this work. For comment on the current position, see **19.104** below.

Declarations affecting the Crown

17.30 The position of the Crown is discussed in CHAPTER **14**, to which reference should be made for general principles. Contentions that a declaration could not be granted against a representative of the Crown were rejected by the Court of Appeal in *Dyson v A-G*.[1] The court referred to the principle that the Crown could not be ordered to convey its estate without the permission of the Crown, but held that a declaratory order would not infringe this principle because it affected the interests of the Crown only indirectly.[2] Identification of the appropriate respondent is not governed by the Crown Proceedings Act 1947, because claims for judicial review are not civil proceedings for the purposes of Part II of that Act.[3] The Crown has been permitted to intervene in cases where it desires to be heard on questions which may affect government.[4] The Crown is entitled to be made a defendant whenever a declaration sought may directly or indirectly affect the rights of the Crown.[5] and by analogy if such a declaration is sought by way of judicial review the Crown should be entitled to be joined.[6] The Crown could also be heard in any appropriate case (but not as a party) under CPR 54.17. It should also be noted that proceedings against one minister of the Crown may not be apt to decide aspects of the case which affect other ministers or the Crown itself. Thus in *R v Secretary of State for Employment, ex p Equal Opportunities Commission*[7] the applicant, who was granted a declaration that threshold provisions for compensation for unfair dismissal in the Employment Protection (Consolidation) Act 1978 were incompatible with the Equal Treatment Directive, also sought a declaration that the Secretary of State was in breach of those provisions of that directive which required member states to abolish any laws contrary to the principle of equal treatment. This declaration was sought in order to enable certain classes of employee to take proceedings against the UK for compensation under the principles in *Francovich v Italian Republic*.[8] Lord Keith said of this:[9]

> 'In my opinion it would be quite inappropriate to make any such declaration. If there is any individual who believes that he or she has a good claim to compensation under the *Francovich* principle, it is the Attorney-General who would be defendant in any proceedings directed to enforcing it, and the issues raised would not necessarily be identical with any of those which arise in the present appeal'.

[1]   [1911] 1 KB 410; [1912] 1 Ch 158.
[2]   See [1911] 1 KB 410 per Cozens-Hardy MR at 417 and per Farwell LJ at 421: in the subsequent proceedings Fletcher Moulton LJ agreed with both these judgments: [1912] 1 Ch 158, 168.
[3]   *M v Home Office* [1994] 1 AC 377, per Lord Woolf at 412. It seems that in a case where the Crown was a university visitor, the Lord President of the Council was the appropriate Crown agent: see Wade & Forsyth *Administrative Law* (9th edn, 2004) p 73.
[4]   *Rio Tinto Zinc v Westinghouse Electric Corporation* [1978] AC 547; *Western Fish Products v Penwith District Council* [1981] 2 All ER 204.
[5]   Zamir & Woolf *The Declaratory Judgment* (4th edn, 2011) paragraph 6.23.
[6]   This point does not appear to have arisen in *R v Rent Officer Service, ex p Muldoon* [1996] 1 WLR 1103, where an unsuccessful attempt was made by the Secretary of State for Social Services to rely on RSC Ord 53, r 5(3) (now CPR 54.7) to be joined as an interested party. The House of Lords held that his obligation to reimburse housing benefit payable by the Respondent in the event that the claim succeeded did not make him 'directly affected' so as to come within the definition of interested person.
[7]   [1995] 1 AC 1.
[8]   Cases C-6/90, C-9/90 [1991] ECR 1–5357.
[9]   [1995] 1 AC 1, 32.

17.31 This approach was also adopted by the House of Lords in R v Secretary of State for Employment, ex p Seymour-Smith.[1]

[1]   [1997] 1 WLR 473: see per Lord Hoffmann at 480.

Consequences of grant of a declaration

17.32 Acting incompatibly with a declaration cannot be punished as a contempt of court, nor can a declaration be enforced by any normal form of execution.[1] In a private law case it creates an estoppel *per rem judicatam* between the parties and their privies,[2] but the position in public law is less rigid[3] at least where the declaration is not *in rem*. This does not mean that a declaration is pointless: public law defendants can generally be expected to proceed on the footing that the law is as the court has declared it to be. If there is good reason to doubt that the defendant will do so, then a mandatory order or an injunction may be sought. When granting a declaration the court may also grant liberty to apply so that either party may bring the matter back before the court (without initiating fresh proceedings) lest there be any need for a coercive order or any doubt about what is required in the light of the court's judgment.[4]

1 *St George's Healthcare NHS Trust v S* [1999] Fam 26, 60, where it is added that exceptionally a writ of sequestration might be appropriate: see *Webster v Southwark London Borough Council* [1983] QB 698. It may also be a contempt of court deliberately to interfere with a legal situation as declared by the courts, and a minister or other officer who acted in disregard of a declaration would expose himself to a personal liability — *M v Home Office* [1994] 1 AC 377 at 397A. As to whether a declaration is constitutive, see the note to the heading at **17.17** above.

2 Re F (Mental Patient: Sterilisation) [1990] 2 AC 1, 64.

3 See **18.65** below. Although CPR 40.20 refers to 'binding declarations', it is unlikely that this was intended to indicate that private law principles of issue estoppel were to apply with full effect in public law. In *Glenharrow Holdings Ltd v Attorney-General* [2005] 2 NZLR 289, PC, declarations had been granted against the New Zealand government in earlier proceedings. Although the government did not appeal, it did not act in accordance with the declarations. On a fresh judicial review claim by the same plaintiff, the High Court permitted an interested party which had been aware of, but had not been served with, the earlier proceedings to be joined as second defendant. In the High Court it was accepted that the second defendant was not bound by the declarations, and in the Court of Appeal and Privy Council, without objection by the plaintiff, the government advanced arguments inconsistent with the declarations. The advice of the Board, paragraph 11, described as 'prima facie . . . surprising' the government's delay in proceeding in accordance with the declarations, but in the light of the plaintiff's stance made no further comment. In argument counsel for the government said that estoppel ought not to apply in a public law context, and that the Attorney-General had a legitimate interest in the interpretive process regarding the proper limits of a Minister's power: [2005] 2 NZLR at p 293.

4 Examples are *R v Investors Compensation Scheme, ex p Last* [1994] QB 749, 767 (where a declaration of entitlement to compensation was made); *R v Human Fertilisation and Embryology Authority, ex p Blood* [1999] Fam 151, [1997] 2 All ER 687; *R (Khan) v Secretary of State for Health* [2004] 1 WLR 971 – where the appeal was adjourned to give the Secretary of State an opportunity to decide what action to take in the light of the legal position declared by the court; *R (Shoesmith) v Ofsted* [2011] PTSR. 1459 where the court declared that S's dismissal was unlawful and that she was entitled to some compensation. Quantum was remitted to the Administrative Court.

17.33 In some circumstances a declaration may take effect as a declaration *in rem* so that it binds even those who are not parties to the proceedings. This does not depend on any rule or principle specifically applicable to judicial review claims. The power to grant such a declaration will ordinarily only arise where either the court or tribunal is expressly empowered to make such a declaration or where the relevant statutory provisions, properly construed, confer such a power.[1] In *PM* Hickinbottom J observed that the court may well have had jurisdiction to make a declaration as to age, even against the world, if it was appropriate to do so [para 54]. However, in that case he also explained that the power to make judgments *in rem* is a severe and exceptional one that would normally bear the hallmark of injustice. It follows that the power to make such a declaration, if it exists at all, will only be exercised rarely. In practice the issue will not normally arise. Where a declaration is as to matters of law then it will apply to third parties through the doctrine of *stare decisis*.

1 *R (PM) V Hertfordshire County Council* [2011] PTSR 269 at 34-67, cited with approval in *MWA (Afghanistan) v Secretary of State for the Home Department* [2014] EWCA Civ 706. An example of an express statutory power is a declaration as to marital status (Family Law Act

1986). Two cases concerning age assessments at first instance have suggested that decisions of the High Court (or Upper Tribunal) declaring somebody to be a child for the purposes of the Children Act 1989 are binding on other parties including other authorities and the Border Agency as judgments in rem (*AS v Croydon London Borough Council* [2011] EWHC 2091 (Admin) and *R (TS) v Croydon London Borough Council* [2012] EWHC 2389 (Admin)). However, neither case was relied on in the Court of Appeal in *MWA* where a declaration by the High Court as to a Claimant's status under the Children Act 1989 did not prevent the Secretary of state from challenging his age for immigration purposes (see para 26).

Cases unsuitable for declaration by way of judicial review

17.34 The factors which are by s 31 of the Supreme Court Act 1981 to be taken into account by the court when considering whether it would be just and convenient for a declaration to be granted on an application for judicial review, include 'all the circumstances of the case'. Whether or not there is an objection to declaratory relief as such, the circumstances could make the case unsuitable for judicial review. This may be so where resolution of the issues requires oral evidence, and is better suited to determination in ordinary proceedings rather than by the exceptional course of cross-examination on written evidence lodged for the purpose of judicial review.[1]

[1] *R v Gloucestershire County Council, ex p P* [1994] ELR 334, 340; in this case a declaration was sought so that there would be an issue estoppel in subsequent proceedings for damages (p 337 of the report), but as to this, see **18.65** below. The question whether remedies by way of judicial review can be sought in order to found a claim for damages is considered in the final part of this chapter.

17.35 It may also be that a different tribunal is the appropriate forum. Thus in *R v Secretary of State for Employment, ex p Equal Opportunities Commission*,[1] the second applicant, Mrs Day, was an employee of Hertfordshire County Council. While holding that the Equal Opportunity Commission's claim against the Secretary of State for Employment was appropriate for the grant of a declaration by way of judicial review, Lord Keith held that Mrs Day's claim, unlike that of the Equal Opportunities Commission, was unsuitable for the Divisional Court.[2] His reasoning was that Mrs Day had a good claim against her employers in the industrial tribunal: this was a claim in private law to which the Secretary of State was not a party. A suggested danger that different industrial tribunals might reach different conclusions on the same issue of statutory validity under European Community law was rejected: this danger could be avoided by a test case on the question. Lord Keith's reasoning was adopted by Lord Hoffmann in a later case, *R v Secretary of State for Employment, ex p Seymour-Smith*,[3] holding that a person claiming to be entitled as a matter of private law to compensation for unfair dismissal should ordinarily bring her proceedings in the industrial tribunal, even if they will raise an issue of incompatibility between domestic and Community law. However, for exceptional reasons in that case it was decided that, the Court of Appeal having permitted the matter to proceed by way of judicial review, the House should deal with the appeal.[4]

[1] [1995] 1 AC 1. See, also, *R v British Broadcasting Corporation, ex p Rossi* [1997] EMLR 71, and contrast *R v Hertfordshire County Council, ex p NUPE* [1985] IRLR 258, applied in *R v Liverpool City Corpn, ex p Ferguson* [1985] IRLR 501, for the position where an applicant argues that a public authority has behaved unreasonably.

[2] [1995] 1 AC 1, 25. Lord Lowry, Lord Browne-Wilkinson and Lord Slynn agreed: see pp 34 and 37.

3   [1997] 1 WLR 473, 481.

4   The issue to be determined on appeal was whether the period of employment required in order for an employee to be able to claim for unfair dismissal was incompatible with art 119 of the Treaty of Rome: in order to determine this issue the House referred various questions to the European Court of Justice.

17.36 Of course, even when it is appropriate for the court to intervene it will not do so in a way which will usurp the authority of the public body in question. The court may grant a mandatory order to require reconsideration by the decision-maker, but not a declaration as to what the result of reconsideration should be, unless all the facts and circumstances were established and fixed and only one decision could be reasonable.[1]

1   *Shah v Barnet London Borough Council* [1983] 2 AC 309, [1983] 1 All ER 226, HL; *Barty-King v Ministry of Defence* [1979] 2 All ER 80; *R v Westminster City Council, ex p Tansey* [1988] COD 114; *West Glamorgan County Council v Rafferty* [1987] 1 WLR 457, 478. If a quashing order is made in such a case consideration could be given to the exercise of the ancillary powers in CPR 54.19 – see CHAPTER 16.

Factors affecting the grant of declarations

17.37 Certain restrictions on remedies (namely, standing, availability of alternative remedies, delay and other discretionary bars) raise issues in common with other remedies on judicial review, and are dealt with in CHAPTER 18. In this part of the present chapter certain factors which have caused concern specifically in relation to declarations are discussed. These factors must be considered in the context of the court's general approach to declaratory relief, which (as with other discretionary remedies) will be to look at the substance of the matter rather than the form,[1] and to grant declaratory relief where this will be of practical utility.[2] Thus in *R v Secretary of State for the Home Department, ex p Abdi*[3] the outcome of the appeal would not directly affect the applicants, but the appeals raised a question of fundamental importance which the House of Lords proceeded to decide. By contrast in *R v Secretary of State for Education, ex p Birmingham City Council*[4] leave to move for judicial review was set aside because in the circumstances of the case the declaration sought was not connected with any relevant decision; while in *R v Ministry of Agriculture Fisheries and Food, ex p Live Sheep Traders Ltd*[5] the case was not suitable for declaratory relief because the declaration sought looked only to the past and had no prospective relevance. Similarly a declaration in order that the Defendant might 'learn the error of its ways' was refused in circumstances where it had already accepted that it had erred and so a declaration would serve no purpose.[6] In many cases a declaration can only meaningfully be made on the basis of specific fact findings and this may make it unsuitable for decision on an application for judicial review – particularly where an appeal or review on the facts lies to some other body or tribunal.[7] Other examples of the approach of the courts can be found at **17.46** below.

The modern cases repeatedly emphasise that the discretion to grant a declaration is a broad one and 'uniquely flexible, in that the courts may in their own words identify and particularise what is objectionable in legal terms'.[8] This reflects developments in private law claims where the grant or refusal of declaratory relief is not now constrained by artificial limits but is kept in proper bounds by the exercise of the court's discretion.[9] In *Financial Services*

Authority v Rourke[10] Neuberger J suggested that the court should 'take into account justice to the claimant, justice to the defendant, whether the declaration would serve a useful purpose whether there are any other special reasons why or why not the court should grant the declaration.' Where in a public law claim the claimant has succeeded in showing that a public body has acted unlawfully, but it is not appropriate to make a mandatory, prohibitory, or quashing order[11], then it will usually be appropriate to make some form of declaratory order to reflect the court's finding.[12] This does not mean that the court is obliged to act of its own motion where a declaration is not asked for (*Hunt* – see below) and normally a claim for a declaration must be pleaded. If it is not then the court may refuse to entertain it.[13]

[1] See, eg *R v Monopolies and Mergers Commission, ex p Argyll Group plc* [1986] 1 WLR 763 per Sir John Donaldson MR at 774.
[2] Thus where it was not possible to formulate a declaration which would be both helpful and correct, this was a sufficient reason for not granting any declaration at all: *R v Legal Aid Board, ex p R M Broudie & Co* [1994] COD 435. See, also, Lord Templeman's observation in *R v Northavon District Council, ex p Smith* [1994] 1 WLR 403, 409 to the effect that where two authorities were required to co-operate, but the court cannot decide what form co-operation should take, judicial review was not the way to obtain co-operation.
[3] [1996] 1 WLR 298.
[4] Brooke J, 14 May 1991; see *R v Birmingham City Council, ex p Equal Opportunities Commission* [1994] ELR 282, 292.
[5] [1995] COD 297.
[6] *UK Uncut Legal Action Ltd v Revenue and Customs Comrs, Goldman Sachs International and Goldman Sachs Services Ltd* [2013] EWHC 1283 (Admin) at para 58.
[7] *R (Anti-Waste Ltd) v Environment Agency* [2008] 1 WLR 923 disapproved declarations that did not address the 'technical facts', warning that they were of 'delphic generality' and said little of any utility. The correct procedure in that case was to exercise a statutory right of appeal to the Secretary of State.
[8] *R (Robert Hitchins Ltd v Worcestershire CC* [2014] EWHC 3809 (Admin) §§72-3, *R (Joanne Dennehy) v SSJ, Sodexo Ltd* [2016] EWHC 1219 (Admin) §74 approving the passage cited from Lewis: *Judicial Remedies in Public Law* 5th edn, 7-009-7-010.
[9] *Fujifilm Kyowa Kirin Biologics Co Ltd v Abbvie Biotechnology Ltd* [2017] EWCA iv 1 §58–9.
[10] 10 [2002] CP Rep 14.
[11] For example, because of the passage of time or because a mandatory order for the future cannot be drafted with sufficient precision (as in *R. (on the application of Walker) v Secretary of State for Justice* [2009] UKHL 22; [2010] 1 A.C. 553 §37 with the result that a declaration was granted as regards past unlawfulness).
[12] *R (Hunt) v North Somerset Council* [2015] 1 W.L.R. 3575 §11 per Lord Toulson, *R (Bibi) v Secretary of State for the Home Department* [2015] 1 WLR 5055. In *R (O by her litigation friend H) v Peterborough City Council & anor* [2016] EWHC 2717 (Admin) Singh J quashed a child protection plan, but also granted a declaration in order to assuage the parents' concerns about future impact. They would then have the declaration 'if ever necessary in the future to demonstrate to anyone concerned that, if they come across a record of a child protection plan in this case, it was as a matter of law null and void and of no effect' [55].
[13] *R (Waters) v Breckland DC* [2016] EWHC 951 (Admin) Lang J.

Primary legislation

17.38 The conventional rule is that the Courts will not pronounce on the validity of primary legislation (see *Pickin v BRB*)[1] but in *R (on the application of Jackson) v Attorney General*[2] the court entertained an argument (which proved to be unsuccessful) that the Parliament Act 1949 had not been validly made under the Parliament Act 1911 and that consequently the Hunting Act 2004 had not been validly made. This was despite the misgivings of Lord Bingham [paragraph 27] that even to embark on the enquiry was to invite the court to enquire into matters outside its competence. However, the enquiry was in reality to determine whether or not the Act was 'enacted law' and so outside the rule preventing enquiry into its validity. *Shindler & anor v Chancellor of the Duchy of Lancaster & anor*[3] rejected a claim for a declaration that the European Union Referendum Act 2015 was unconstitutional because it conflicted with a fundamental right to vote by excluding certain expatriates. However, the court noted the possibility, canvassed in *Moohan v Lord Advocate*[4] that 'in the very unlikely event that a parliamentary majority abusively sought to entrench its power by a curtailment of the franchise or similar device, the common law, informed by the principles of democracy and the rule of law and international norms, would be able to declare such legislation unlawful.'

[1]   [1974] AC 765.
[2]   [2006] 1 AC 262.
[3]   [2017] Q.B. 226 .
[4]   [2015] AC 901 per Lord Hodge §35.

Advisory declarations

17.39 A declaration is usually advisory in the sense that it merely informs and does not of itself compel any particular course of action. Suggestions that the court cannot or should not grant advisory declarations are usually directed at some feature other than the lack of any coercive element in the order sought. Among such features are the undesirability of giving advice at the request of the executive, the absence or unwillingness of a proper contradictor (including the misuse of negative declarations), prematurity (including the lack of a defined issue and the hypothetical nature of the dispute), and the lack of any practical significance (including cases where the point is moot). Each of these factors is briefly discussed below. As will be seen, their importance may depend on the circumstances of the case, and may sometimes be outweighed by the public interest in the grant of a declaration. It has been said that the High Court has inherent jurisdiction to make advisory declarations as a matter of discretion[1]. In *R (Campaign for Nuclear Disarmament) v Prime Minister*[2] Simon Brown LJ expressly accepted that the court's jurisdiction to grant such relief 'rarely though it is exercised, cannot be doubted', and it is suggested that the cases discussed below are, in the result if not always in the reasoning, consistent with this. Further, even if the court's power to grant declarations otherwise than on judicial review were limited in respect of advisory declarations, it is arguable that s 31 of the Supreme Court Act 1981 has removed any such limitation in a case where it is appropriate to grant a declaration as a matter of public law.[3] Recommendations that there should be express provision for the grant of advisory declarations, but subject to certain qualifications, have been made by both the Law Commission[4] and Lord Woolf's inquiry into civil justice.[5] However, the courts remain extremely hesitant about granting declarations in circumstances where there is no defined set of facts and where the court may not fully appreciate the impact that its decision may have on other cases.[6]

[1]   *R v Secretary of State for the Home Department, ex p Mehari* [1994] QB 474 per Laws J at page 491; Sir John Laws. 'Judicial Remedies and the Constitution' [1994] 57 MLR 213; *R v Ministry of Agriculture, ex p Live Sheep Traders* [1995] COD 297; *Re S* [1996] Fam 1, per Sir Thomas Bingham MR at 18 and per Millet LJ at 21–22. As to the approach of the

European Court of Justice in cases where there is a substantial degree of agreement between the parties, and in cases where the parties have arranged their mutual affairs so as to provoke litigation, see **15.88** et seq above.

2 [2002] EWHC 2777 (Admin) at para 15. The declaration, which was as to whether UN Resolution 1441 permitted military action in Iraq, was not granted for reasons summarised at paras 46 and 47. Richards J also considered that there was power to make an advisory declaration in 'exceptional circumstances' [para 52].

3 See **17.23** above.

4 Report No 226, from paragraph 8.9: 'We recommend that where the judge is satisfied that the application is for an advisory declaration, he should also be satisfied that the point concerned is one of general public importance, before he makes the advisory declaration . . . '.

5 *Access to Justice. Final Report* (June 1996) p 251: 'The court should have an express power to grant advisory declarations when it is in the public interest to do so. However, this should be limited to cases where the issue was of public importance and was defined in sufficiently precise terms, and where the appropriate parties were before the court'.

6 *R (Burke v General Medical Council* [2006] QB 273 at 21. See *Birmingham CC v Clue* [2010] EWCA Civ 460 where the court refused to rule on 6 hypothetical scenarios put forward by the Claimants. In *R (Customs and Excise Comrs) v Crown Court at Canterbury* [2002] EWHC 2584 (Admin) Admin the court granted what Laws LJ accepted was an advisory declaration but limited to the specific terms of the judgment under challenge. No wider declaration was granted because other different sets of circumstances might arise. See also generally Davin Elvin: Hypothetical, academic and premature challenges J.R. 2006 11(4) 307–324.

Giving advice at the request of the executive

17.40 The Stuart kings found it a useful precaution to seek advice from the judges as to their views of proposed courses of action. When Sir Ranulph Crewe advised that forced loans would, in his view, be illegal, he was dismissed as Chief Justice of the King's Bench and replaced by the more amenable Sir Nicholas Hyde.[1] It would be no surprise to find that since the seventeenth century the judges have expressed themselves as antagonistic to the giving of advice to government; but the Act of Settlement removed the risk of arbitrary dismissal, and the judges advised Parliament and (as Privy Councillors) took part in legislative and executive functions until late in the nineteenth century.[2] The Judicial Committee Act 1833 (s 4) rendered it lawful for the Crown to refer to the Privy Council a question for advice; however, the advice is not binding and the power is little used. In *Chief Justice of the Cayman Islands v Governor of the Cayman Islands*[3] the Privy Council advised that it was not appropriate to give substantive advice on a petition that had been submitted to it. It considered that the s 4 procedure was not intended to deal with matters that could be raised through the ordinary judicial process. Provision for binding decisions of the Judicial Committee of the Privy Council is made in the Northern Ireland Act 1998, the Scotland Act 1998 and the Government of Wales Act 1998.

1 When Sir Thomas Darnel and others were imprisoned for refusing to pay forced loans. Hyde CJ refused habeas corpus: *The Five Knights Case* (1627) 3 State Trials 1.

2 Robert Stevens, 'The Independence of the Judiciary: The View from the Lord Chancellor's Office' (1993).

3 [2012] UKPC 39, [2014] AC 198, [2013] 3 WLR 457.

17.41 There can be no doubt that it is undesirable for the court to be asked to form an opinion without the benefit of adversary argument. But if there is a question of public importance to be determined, and it is not possible to identify an appropriate respondent willing to argue against the proposed declaration, the court may consider requesting the Attorney-General to appoint a friend of the court.[1]

[1] The need for a proper contradictor, and the court's reluctance to compel a respondent to take a stand, is discussed below. In *Re Parliamentary Privilege Act 1770* [1958] AC 331 (a case under the Act of 1833) the Attorney-General, with the support of an interested party, sought an affirmative answer to the question posed, while separate counsel instructed by the Treasury Solicitor argued (successfully) for a negative answer.

17.42 It may well be appropriate for government to invoke the supervisory jurisdiction of the court. A declaration has been held to have been properly sought by a local authority which desired to establish that structures erected by the defendants could lawfully be removed by the authority.[1] Similarly, in *R v London Transport Executive, ex p Greater London Council*,[2] the Greater London Council was granted a declaration that new proposals for the making of grants to London Transport were within their statutory powers. In *Islington London Borough Council v Camp*[3] Richards J entertained an application for a declaration as to whether a councillor was disqualified by reason of her employment. Further, as against a respondent which exercised public law powers, the Secretary of State for the Environment has been held entitled to orders by way of judicial review.[4] Judicial testing of prospective changes to regulations may be particularly advantageous in the fields of social security and immigration, and there are other circumstances where decisions on proposed changes of policy may, in suitable cases, be useful.[5] Given that the legality of proposed executive action can be tested by claimants bringing an application for prohibition, there seems no good reason in principle why the executive should not test that legality in proceedings against a party who is willing to contest that legality. There may, of course, be other reasons why a declaration should be refused: for example in *Re Carnarvon Harbour Acts, 1793–1903*[6] there was no actual dispute which could be settled by the declaration claimed,[7] the issues which would have arisen in the event of an actual dispute do not seem to have been defined,[8] and there was not an appropriate respondent before the court in order to ensure, as discussed below, that the court has full argument on both sides.

[1] *Ruislip-Northwood Urban District Council v Lee* (1935) 145 LT 208.
[2] [1983] QB 484.
[3] [2004] LGR58.
[4] *R v Haringey London Borough Council, ex p Secretary of State for the Environment* [1990] RVR 261.
[5] Sir John Laws, 'Judicial Remedies and the Constitution' [1994] 57 MLR 213, 218, 219.
[6] [1937] Ch 72.
[7] See Zamir and Woolf *Declaratory Judgment* (4th edn, 2010) paragraphs 4.063–4.
[8] See the discussion of prematurity below.

Need for a proper contradictor, and negative declarations

17.43 It has been held that if the court is to grant a declaration the person raising the question must not only have a real interest to raise but also be able to secure a 'proper contradictor', that is to say someone presently existing who has a true interest to oppose the declaration sought.[1] The court should not be put in a position where it has to make a decision without hearing full argument from both sides.[2] In this context, the court must be alert to the possibility that a declaration which seems apt in the circumstances may be sought to be deployed in different circumstances where different issues would arise: if the appropriate person to argue those issues is not before the court, the declaration may need modification or may be inappropriate.[3] While a negative declaration may be a perfectly appropriate way of determining a real dispute, the courts were formerly reluctant to permit an application for a negative declaration to be used to force an unwilling respondent to take a stand. Thus, in *Re Clay*,[4] a defendant had reserved his rights under a deed of indemnity to claim certain costs from the claimants, but had made no actual claim upon them. The Court of Appeal held that the claimants, who wished to know where they stood, were not entitled to cut the matter short by bringing an action at their option. Similarly, in *Re Barnato*[5] trustees wished to advance monies to a child, but had been informed by the Inland Revenue that if the child's mother died within five years from the date of the advance the Crown would claim estate duty from the trustees. When the trustees sought a declaration as to the position if the mother should die, the Crown's objection was upheld: the Inland Revenue had not made a claim, and there was no certainty that they would (because it was uncertain when the mother would die).

[1]   *Russian Commercial and Industrial Bank v British Bank for Foreign Trade Ltd* [1921] 2 AC 438 at 448 per Lord Dunedin. See, also, *Gouriet v Union of Post Office Workers* [1978] AC 435 per Lord Diplock at 501.

[2]   *Maerkle v British Continental Fur Co Ltd* [1954] 1 WLR 1242, 1248.

[3]   For this reason one of the declarations sought in *R v Secretary of State for Employment, ex p Equal Opportunities Commission* [1995] 1 AC 1 was refused (see p 32);see, also, *R v Secretary of State for Employment, ex p Seymour Smith* [1997] 1 WLR 473. In *Human Fertilisation and Embryology Authority v Amicus Healthcare Ltd* [2005] EWHC 1092 all relevant parties were represented at the hearing, and sought the grant of three declarations by consent. The court noted that it was highly desirable before making a declaration to hear argument both for and against what was proposed. Having concluded that the first two declarations sought were sound, the court exercised its discretion in favour of granting the declarations: this was appropriate because there was concern whether actual or proposed decisions of regulatory and prosecuting authorities would be lawful. The third declaration was addressed to whether a 'substantive legitimate expectation' had arisen. This was refused as a matter of discretion: one of the reasons was that it involved too many assumptions for a case where the proposed declaration had not been in contest. In *S, C (by her litigation friend S), D (by his litigation friend S) v The Secretary of State for the Home Department* [2007] EWHC 1654 (Admin) a declaration that the Children Act 1989 applied to children in immigration detention was refused as unnecessary because the Defendant had not disputed the point in the course of the proceedings.

[4]   [1919] 1 Ch 66 but see **17.45** fn 1 below.

[5]   [1949] Ch 21; affd [1949] Ch 258, CA.

17.44 By contrast, a declaration was granted when a local housing authority took issue with the Race Relations Board who had formed the opinion that the authority's waiting list and points scheme was unlawful discrimination contrary to the Race Relations Act 1976: *Ealing London Borough v Race Relations Board*.[1] Swanwick J at first instance[2] distinguished *Re Clay* and *Re Barnato* because the Board had 'formed and communicated a formal opinion that the council have been guilty of unlawful conduct and have sought an assurance against repetition' and because the council were 'a public body who are entitled in those circumstances to seek a ruling as to the legality of their rule, provided of course that there is a defendant with sufficient interest in the matter'. His conclusion that there was jurisdiction to grant a declaration was affirmed by the House of Lords on appeal.[3]

[1]   [1972] AC 342, [1972] 1 All ER 105, HL.

[2]   [1971] 1 QB 309 at 319.

³   [1972] AC 342, 353. The House of Lords reversed Swanwick J, however, on the substantive issue.

17.45 The modern private law cases have also tended to take a more liberal approach and in *Messier-Dowty Limited v Sabena SA*[1] Lord Woolf MR held that while the unusual nature of a negative declaration justified caution 'subject to the exercise of appropriate circumspection, there should be no reluctance to their being granted when it is useful to do so' (paragraph 42). The fact that a defendant is unwilling to have matters tested in this way justifies caution but is no longer a bar.[2] In private cases the rule that a declaration will not be made by consent has also been relaxed since it has only ever been a rule of practice. The position now is that a declaration will not be refused on this basis if that would deny the party seeking it the 'fullest justice to which he is entitled'. However, the court will still only grant a declaration without a trial where satisfied that the claim was seriously arguable and that if fought to trial the court would have been likely to have been satisfied that the order was necessary. It must also be satisfied that there will be no adverse consequences for third parties.[3]

¹   [2000] 1 WLR 2040. In *Actavis UK Ltd v Eli Lilly & Co* [2014] EWHC 1511 (Pat) Arnold J said that the effect was that the old restrictive approach in *re Clay* (ie that no declaration would be made where no claim of right had been asserted against the person seeking the declaration) had been 'abandoned' (para 304).
²   [2010] Lloyds Rep IR 358.
³   *Hayim v Couch* [2009] EWHC 1040 (Ch) per Stephen Smith QC, In *Pavilion Property Trustees Ltd. And another v Permira Advisers LLP and another* [2014] EWHC 1451 (Ch) Morgan J said that the court would have to be satisfied that the declaration was right.

Prematurity: lack of a defined issue and hypothetical disputes

17.46 Applications for declarations are prone to raise hypothetical questions. The court will not give advisory opinions to those who wish guidance as to the ordering of their affairs by way of a general exegesis on a topic.[1] It is wary about decisions that either (for example, through lack of a defined issue) will not bind potentially affected parties, and so will not prevent litigation in the future, or are sought to bind everyone, with the danger that they may be a cause of grievance to a party not present before the court.[2] There is a legitimate concern that the court's resources may be wasted by asking it to pronounce on circumstances which may never occur.[3]

¹   See, eg *R v Department of Social Security, ex p Overdrive Credit Card Ltd* [1991] 1 WLR 635, 641. In *Human Fertilisation and Embryology Authority v Amicus Healthcare Ltd* [2005] EWHC 1092 (see the note to **17.43**) the court refused to grant a declaration that a 'substantive legitimate expectation' had arisen in favour of a clinic. One of the reasons was that whether, and in what circumstances, regulatory and prosecuting authorities were fettered by what they said or did might give rise to a variety of issues. The court considered that the clinic could and should rely on its own legal advice as to the consequences of anything said or done by the regulatory and prosecuting authorities. This may be contrasted with a ruling on the true meaning of a licence condition, which is a key question for the purposes of negotiations which the parties are required to conduct: see *Mercury Communications Ltd v Director General of Telecommunications* [1996] 1 WLR 48 and *R (Burke) v General Medical Council* [2006] QB 273; 'In judicial review proceedings, it is not the role of this court to give general advice or make general pronouncements about what might hypothetically be lawful and what not. This court's role is primarily to determine the legality of the challenged decision, and to quash it if it is unlawful' – *R (Great Yarmouth Port Company Ltd) v Marine Management Organisation* [2013] EWHC 3052 (Admin), 59.

2   See *Re Carnarvon Harbour Acts 1793 to 1903* [1937] Ch 72 and *Lever Bros v Manchester Ship Canal* (1945) 78 Ll L Rep 507.

3   As in *Re Barnato* [1949] Ch 21; affd [1949] Ch 258, CA and in *Rusbridger* (below) where the litigation was unnecessary. In *R (Raw) v LB Lambeth* (below) Stadlen J considered it a relevant factor to consider whether the grant or refusal of application would encourage or discourage litigation in the future.

17.47 While the court is reluctant to grapple with matters that are contingent or premature (see **5.5** above), it is concerned with genuine and immediate disputes based upon existing facts. Accordingly, it may be willing to resolve threatened or apprehended disputes, where a proposed course of action is put in jeopardy by a concern that it may be unlawful.

17.48 Thus in *Dyson v A-G*[1] Dyson was entitled to seek a declaration (against the Crown) that a demand made upon him by the Inland Revenue to furnish particulars was ultra vires. He did not have to wait to be sued for a penalty, a penalty having been threatened. In *Ruislip-Northwood UDC v Lee*[2] the Council was entitled to seek a declaration that the defendant's caravans were liable to be removed and thereby clarify the legal position. It did not have to take precipitate physical action that may have occasioned a breach of the peace. Greer LJ said, at 214:

> 'In a case where it is important to have a decision between the parties, then that decision may be given in the form of a declaration even though there is no other cause of action than the right of relief in the form of a declaration . . . The present case is a case where the wrong had in fact been done, and was continuing in existence at the date the writ was issued, and if ever there was a case in which it is convenient and right that there should be on the part of a claimant a right to a declaration which will make it safe if he acts in accordance with his rights, that is the present case'.[3]

1   [1911] 1 KB 410 at 417 and 421, [1912] 1 Ch 158 at 166–168 and 172.

2   (1931) 145 LT 208.

3   Contrast *Re Clay* [1919] 1 Ch 66; *Draper v British Optical Association* [1938] 1 All ER 115 at 119–120; *Re Barnato* [1949] Ch 258; and *British Oxygen Co Ltd v Board of Trade* [1969] 2 Ch 174, [1969] 2 All ER 18, CA.

17.49 In order for there to be a present dispute between parties it is not necessary for there to have been a decision. This was established in relation to prohibition by *R v Electricity Comrs, ex p London Electricity Joint Committee Co (1920) Ltd*,[1] discussed in CHAPTER **16**. In *R v HM Treasury, ex p Smedley*,[2] the decision in *R v Electricity Comrs* was applied in relation to a draft Order in Council laid before Parliament. The court's intervention at an early stage would be of assistance to, rather than a challenge to the supremacy of, Parliament. Slade LJ said:[3] 'I conceive that in at least most such cases the only appropriate form of relief (if any) could be by way of declaration'.

1   [1924] 1 KB 171.

2   [1985] QB 657, [1985] 1 All ER 589.

3   At 672 (see also per Sir John Donaldson MR at 666–667). Similar reasoning was applied in *R (Buckinghamshire County Council) v Secretary of State for Transport* [2014] 1 WLR 324 where the Supreme Court addressed the question whether EU law required a strategic environmental assessment in advance of the relevant Hybrid Bill being considered by Parliament [93-7 per Lord Carnwath].

17.50 Similarly, in *Pharmaceutical Society of Great Britain v Dickson*[1] it was held that a member of the society was entitled to test in the courts the validity of a proposed rule of professional conduct, while in *Mercury Communications Ltd v Director General of Telecommunications*[2] a declaratory judgment was held appropriate to determine validity of the Director General's interpretation of a clause in a licence, the meaning of which was a key question in negotiations required to be conducted between two utility companies and in a decision to be made by the Director General. In *Office of Fair Trading v Foxtons Ltd*[3] a regulator was entitled to a declaration to the effect that a term in a contract between an estate agent and its customers was a breach of the Unfair Terms in Consumer Contracts Regulations 1999. The subject matter of the declaration did not have to be a right claimed by one of the parties to the action as long as it was contested by them (applying *Re S (Hospital Patient: Court's Jurisdiction)*)[4]. Otherwise the ability of the Regulator to make general challenges would be frustrated.

The pragmatic approach in the cases cited above has also been mirrored in the recent case law with regard to private law claims under CPR Part 8. In *Rolls Royce plc v Unite the Union*[5] the employer sought a declaration as to whether a length of service redundancy criterion was unlawfully discriminatory on the ground of age. No redundancies had been made and as and when they were, the affected employees could bring a claim in the employment tribunal. Aikens LJ noted that the circumstances in which the courts will grant declaratory relief have widened in recent times and that nothing in the modern cases required that there should be an actual or imminent threat to a legal right.[6] The courts may make declarations as to rights that may arise in the future or that are academic.[7]

[1]   [1970] AC 403, [1968] 2 All ER 686, HL.
[2]   [1996] 1 WLR 48.
[3]   [2010] 1 WLR 663.
[4]   [1996] Fam 1.
[5]   [2010] 1 WLR 318.
[6]   At 188-120.
[7]   *Milebush Properties Ltd v Tameside Metropolitan Borough Council* [2011] PTSR 1654; *Pavledes v Hadjisavva* [2013] EWHC 124 (Ch) at paras 24–25.

17.51 Perhaps the most striking examples of declarations addressed to an anticipated future event are those concerning the criminality of medical matters. In *Royal College of Nursing of the United Kingdom v Department of Health and Social Security*[1] the House of Lords resolved a dispute when the Department of Health and Social Security gave advice on abortion. This precedent was successfully invoked when the DHSS gave non-statutory advice on contraception: *Gillick v West Norfolk and Wisbech Area Health Authority*.[2] A case which solely concerned future choices was *Airedale NHS Trust v Bland*,[3] where the House of Lords granted to a health authority a declaration that it would be lawful to stop feeding an accident victim who was in a persistent vegetative state. It has been said that these cases are examples of a principle that the court may give an advisory opinion so that persons with onerous duties towards another might know how the law permitted them to act.[4]

[1]   [1981] AC 800, [1981] 1 All ER 545, CA.
[2]   [1986] AC 112, [1985] 3 All ER 402, HL.

[3] [1993] AC 789.

[4] See the discussion of the court's role where a claimant needs to know the answer to a question of law in order to know how to perform duties owed, or which will be owed, to third parties by Sir John Laws, 'Judicial Remedies and the Constitution' [1994] 57 MLR 213–217. The two declarations granted in *Human Fertilisation and Embryology Authority v Amicus Health-care Ltd* [2005] EWHC 1092 (see the footnote to paragraph **17.43**) may be said to fall into this category.

17.52 However, a declaration will not be granted as to the meaning of a criminal provision unless the circumstances are exceptional. In *R (Rusbridger) v Attorney General*[1] the claimant sought a declaration that s 3 of the Treason Felony Act 1848 had to be interpreted compatibly with art 10 of the ECHR in order to allow articles to advocate the non-violent abolition of the monarchy. No prosecution had been initiated and there was no realistic possibility of this. The House of Lords held that no useful purpose would be served by entertaining the claim since the outcome was obvious and s 3 of the Human Rights Act 1998 meant that no prosecution could succeed. It was not the function of the courts to keep the statute book up to date. Lord Steyn, with whom the majority agreed, accepted that the courts should adopt a structured approach when dealing with applications for declarations against the Crown about the lawfulness of proposed future conduct. There were three factors to be considered (assuming in the first place that the Claimant had standing): firstly whether or not there was a genuine dispute, secondly whether the matter was fact sensitive (described as a factor of great importance such that most claims will founder on this ground) and thirdly whether there was a cogent public or individual interest to be advanced by the declaration. The opposite result was reached in *Transport for London v Uber London Ltd*[2] where Ouseley J granted a declaration that the 'Uber App' was not a taximeter and so minicabs using it did not commit an offence under the Private Hire Vehicles (London) Act 1998. The judge affirmed as 'correct' the propositions set out by Walker J in Haynes (below) and took into account the following: extant criminal proceedings had been withdrawn to enable the civil claim to proceed; there was a clear dispute of statutory construction on specific facts; the system was in use and the dispute was not hypothetical; the claim was brought by the statutory regulator.

[1] [2004] 1 AC 35, 7.

[2] [2016] R.T.R. 12.

17.53 The courts will not grant a declaration about the meaning or applicability of a criminal provision once criminal proceedings have begun. The court will be more reluctant to grant a declaration that conduct *is* criminal than a declaration that it is not. It should be particularly cautious about granting such a declaration in relation to existing conduct rather than prospective conduct and should be wary about embarking on a claim than that conduct is criminal other than at the suit of the Attorney General.[1] In *R (Freedom and Justice Party) v FCO*[2] the court granted a declaration about whether or not members of a special mission were immune from arrest. This raised a defined issue of law untrammelled by political or social questions and that was likely to arise so was not academic even if it was hypothetical. The court was influenced by the fact that the DPP supported the application.

[1] *R (Haynes) v Stafford BC* [2007] 1 WLR 1365, in which Walker J granted a declaration as to the meaning of the term market after satisfying himself that he would not be declaring that any

particular person had committed an offence and so would not be usurping the function of the criminal court. He set out eight propositions derived from the authorities that have since been approved in *TfL v Uber* – see above. In contrast in *Regina (Robinson) v Torridge District Council* [2007] 1 WLR 871 a declaration as to whether a river intermittently choked by a bridge could be a statutory nuisance was refused as hypothetical where the issues were highly factually dependent and where the underlying claim for a mandatory order had become academic.

²   [2016] EWHC 2010 (Admin).

Lack of practical significance

17.54 While final declarations may be made if they have some current or future value, they will not be made just as a comment on past events,[1] whether or not the applicant had a legal right at the time when the proceedings were begun.[2] It does not follow from this that a moot point is necessarily inappropriate for relief by way of a declaration. Mootness will often render litigation inappropriate. Thus in *Ainsbury v Millington*[3] the House of Lords protested against the continuation of an appeal when the dispute between the parties had been resolved. Similarly, in *R v Registered Designs Appeal Tribunal, ex p Ford Motor Co Ltd*[4] the court refused to discuss the meaning of statutory provisions which did not need to be determined in the circumstances of the case and should be resolved with reference to specific issues illuminated by concrete evidence. On the other hand, where a point is one of real public importance the court has been willing to give guidance even though it does not actually arise on the facts of the case,[5] the court has resolved procedural questions which were immaterial to the outcome of the case but nevertheless had far reaching implications[6] and the court has answered questions of general public interest even though they no longer had any potential impact on the applicant.[7] The authorities suggest that the court is more likely to entertain an academic issue in a case involving public law issues than it will in a purely private law case.[8] Nonetheless, the power to proceed is to be exercised with caution and the case will not proceed unless there is good reason to do so in the public interest. Factors to be considered will include (but not be limited to) whether there are a large number of cases raising the same issue, whether the issue is fact sensitive or can be dealt with as a discrete point of principle (for example a point of statutory construction),[9] whether the case involves an arguably unlawful policy that will otherwise never be able to be challenged (for example because the impact is transient so that cases will always become academic),[10] and whether the Court can give meaningful guidance.[11] Further, as discussed below, the courts have been willing to contemplate prospective declarations. The result is that while mootness may mean that as between the parties the question has no potential to arise, nevertheless (as with hypothetical questions) the court may deal with the matter if it is of sufficient public importance.[12]

¹   See, eg *A-G v Colchester Corpn* [1955] 2 QB 207, [1955] 2 All ER 124; Williams v Home Office (No 2) [1981] 1 All ER 1211; *R v Bromley Licensing Justices, ex p Bromley Licensed Victuallers Association* [1984] 1 All ER 794, [1984] 1 WLR 585; *R v Secretary of State for the Home Department, ex p Anderson* [1984] QB 778, [1984] 1 All ER 920 and *R v Panel on Take-overs and Mergers, ex p Datafin plc* [1987] QB 815, [1987] 1 All ER 564, CA (prospective declaration); *R v Gloucestershire County Council, ex p P* [1994] ELR 334, 340. See also *R v Secretary of State for the Home Department, ex p Abdi* [1996] 1 WLR 298 and other cases discussed above in the context of general factors affecting the grant of declarations.

2   *R v Secretary of State for the Environment, ex p Nottinghamshire County Council* [1987] LG
    Rev 551 (retrospective legislation had been passed after the commencement of the proceedings
    which had the effect of validating the Rate Support Grant Report in question). The
    observations in the text must also be considered in the light of the cases cited at **17.17** above
    and which show that where the court finds unlawful conduct then it should normally reflect
    that in a declaration.
3   [1987] 1 WLR 379n. See, also, *Sun Life Assurance v Jervis* [1944] AC 111, and Sir John Laws.
    'Judicial Remedies and the Constitution' [1994] 57 MLR 213, 214–215.
4   [1995] 1 WLR 18.
5   *Gaming Board for Great Britain v Rogers* [1973] AC 388, 411.
6   *Chief Adjudication Officer v Foster* [1993] AC 754.
7   Examples are *R v Board of Visitors of Dartmoor Prison, ex p Smith* [1987] QB 106 and *R (H)
    v Ashworth Hospital Authority* [2003] 1 WLR 127.
8   *R (Salem) v Secretary of State for the Home Department* [1999] 1 AC 450.
9   Salem ibid at p 457; *R (Zoolife International Ltd) v Secretary of State for Environment* [2007]
    EWHC 2995 (Admin).
10 *R (Raw) v Lambeth LBC* [2010] EWHC 507 (Admin) at paragraph 60.
11 *R (Limbuela) v Secretary of State for the Home Department* [2006] 1 AC 396 at paragraph 81.
12 For further discussion of mootness and hypothetical questions, see **20.13**.

Flexibility of declarations and prospective declarations

17.55 The flexibility of the declaratory judgment is demonstrated by the circumstances in which a final declaration has been available, which have included:

(1)   when a Minister gave 'guidance' (approved by Parliament) requiring the Civil Aviation Authority to revoke a commercial airline's licence: *Laker Airways Ltd v Department of Trade*;[1]

(2)   To establish that a policy practice or act of a public body is unlawful — *R (on the application of European Roma Rights Centre) v Immigration Officer, Prague Airport.*[2]

(3)   when ACAS recommended the recognition of a trade union: *Grunwick Processing Laboratories Ltd v Advisory Conciliation and Arbitration Service*,[3] and when ACAS reported on a recognition issue: *United Kingdom Association of Professional Engineers v Advisory Conciliation and Arbitration Service*;[4] and

(4)   when the Department of Health and Society Security gave advice on abortion – *Royal College of Nursing of the United Kingdom v Department of Health and Social Security*[5] – and when the DHSS gave non-statutory advice on contraception: *Gillick v West Norfolk and Wisbech Area Health Authority.*[6] in which Lord Bridge of said, at 193:

> 'We must now say that if a government department, in a field of adminis-
> tration in which it exercises responsibility, promulgates in a public docu-
> ment, albeit non-statutory in form, advice which is erroneous in law, then
> the court, in proceedings in appropriate form commenced by an applicant or
> claimant who possesses the necessary locus standi, has jurisdiction to correct
> the error of law by an appropriate declaration. Such an extended juris-
> diction is no doubt a salutary and indeed a necessary one in certain
> circumstances, as the Royal College of Nursing case itself well illustrates.
> But the occasions of a departmental non-statutory publication raising, as in
> that case, a clearly defined issue of law, unclouded by political, social or
> moral overtones, will be rare. In cases where any proposition of law implicit
> in a departmental advisory document is interwoven with questions of social

and ethical controversy, the court should, in my opinion, exercise its jurisdiction with the utmost restraint, confine itself to deciding whether the proposition of law is erroneous and avoid either expressing ex cathedra opinions in areas of social and ethical controversy in which it has no claim to speak with authority or proffering answers to hypothetical questions of law which do not strictly arise for decision'.

(5) on the question whether a care home was operating as a public body for the purposes of the Human Rights Act 1998 *YL v Birmingham CC*.[7]

(6) To establish that the DWP could only recover overpaid benefits through the statutory procedure and not using common law powers.[8]

(7) Where a defendant had succeeded overall but wished to test the question whether or not the claimant was amenable to judicial review, a declaration was granted that they were not reviewable so that the defendant could appeal.[9]

[1] [1977] QB 643, [1976] 3 WLR 537.
[2] [2005] 2 AC 1.
[3] [1978] AC 655, [1978] 1 All ER 338.
[4] [1981] AC 424, [1980] 1 All ER 612, HL.
[5] [1981] AC 800, [1981] 1 All ER 545, CA.
[6] [1986] AC 112, 193, [1985] 2 All ER 402, HL.
[7] [2008] 1 AC 95.
[8] *R (Child Poverty Action Group) v Secretary of State for Work and Pensions* [2010] UKSC 54, [2011] 2 AC 15.
[9] *R (Weaver) v London and Quadrant Housing Trust (Equality and Human Rights Commission intervening)* [2010] 1 WLR 363 at 5-6. See also *R TN (Vietnam) v SSHD* [2017] EWHC 59 (Admin) §47. In *Re: W (A child)* [2016] EWCA Civ 1140 the Court of Appeal held that it could deal with a case where adverse findings had been made against witnesses that had had a serious impact on their private lives when they had not had a proper opportunity to respond. This was a free-standing breach of Art 8 and it did not require a declaration or recourse to the 'contrived vehicle' [118] of appealing against a failure to make a declaration on the relevant point.

17.56 A declaration will be especially appropriate in circumstances where it is undesirable for a decision to be rendered a nullity for all purposes or none.[1] Thus it may be appropriate for a declaration of invalidity to be made without quashing a decision which needs to remain in place if the parties are not to be placed in an impractical position,[2] or where the decision under challenge would not have been different and so should not be quashed, but nonetheless raises a question of general importance.[3] Equally a prospective declaration,[4] designed to give guidance for the future, may be the solution where it is inappropriate to quash regulations because of the administrative inconvenience which would result,[5] where a court considers that delay precludes the quashing of a decision,[6] and where a contemporaneous or retrospective ruling would interfere with the orderly operation of financial markets.[7] In *R (Tigere) v SSBIS*[8] a quashing order was inappropriate because there were many cases unaffected by the unlawfulness, but simply to read down the provision so that it was compatible with Convention rights would give insufficient guidance to decision makers. The Supreme Court therefore made a declaration leaving it to the Secretary of State to devise a more carefully tailored criterion. However, there may be cases where a claimant's arguments on a judicial review application have been successful in whole or in part, but the preferable course is that the court's judgment should simply speak for itself without the grant of declaratory relief.[9]

1   See *Ridge v Baldwin* [1964] AC 40, [1963] 2 All ER 66, HL and *Chief Constable of the North Wales Police v Evans* [1982] 3 All ER 141, [1982] 1 WLR 1155, HL and the Supreme Court Act 1981, s 31(6). However, in *R (TN Vietnam) v SSHD* [2017] EWHC 59 (Admin) Ouseley J pointed out the Regulations in question were ultra vires: the difference between granting a declaration to that effect and not doing so was merely formal since the effect on the estimated 10,000 cases decided under them would be the same. In fact he went on to hold that the individual appeals were not nullified.

2   See, eg *R v Secretary of State for the Environment, ex p Birmingham City Council* (Mann J, unreported, 15 April 1986) where a declaration was made that determinations in a Rate Support Grant Report were invalid; had the Report been quashed it would have been impossible to maintain the payments of subventions to local authorities without emergency legislation.

3   For example in *R (Brooke) v Parole Board* [2007] EWHC 2036 (upheld on appeal at [2008] 1 WLR 1950) where a declaration was granted that the Parole Board lacked sufficient independence even though the actual decisions would have been no different. See now the Senior Courts Act 1981 – below.

4   *R v Secretary of State for Social Services, ex p Association of Metropolitan Authorities* [1986] 1 WLR 1. *R v Governor of Brockhill Prison ex p Evans (No2)* [1999] QB 1043 1058F-G and [2001] 2 AC 19 at 26H.

5   See Clive Lewis, 'Retrospective and Prospective Rulings in Administrative Law' [1988] PL 78.

6   *Caswell v Dairy Produce Quota Tribunal* [1990] 2 AC 738; *R (on the application of Friends of Hethel Ltd) v South Norfolk DC* [2009] EWHC 2856 (Admin).

7   *R v Panel on Take-overs, ex p Datafin plc* [1987] QB 815; for comment, see Cane, 'Self-Regulation and Judicial Review' (1987) 6 Civil Justice Quarterly 324. A more general power of prospective over-ruling was discussed in *R v Governor of Brockhill Prison, ex p Evans (No 2)* [2001] 2 AC 19, where the House of Lords concluded that even if there were power to limit the declaratory effect of a judgment this was not a case calling for such a course. See, also, *R (Richards) v Secretary of State for the Home Department* [2004] ACD 69.

8   [2015] 1 WLR 3820 §49.

9   An example is *(Kent Pharmaceuticals) v Director of the Serious Fraud Office* [2004] ACD 23. In *Regina (Equal Opportunities Commission) v Secretary of State for Trade and Industry* [2007] ICR 1234 Burton J gave judgment on a number of respects in which new sex discrimination regulations failed to comply with Council Directive 76/207/EEC. The object was 'to give the defendant the opportunity to consider the effect of my conclusions without any formal order'. However, in *Office of Fair Trading v Foxtons Ltd* [2010] 1 WLR 663 the Court of Appeal held that it ought specifically to identify the term in question and what aspect of it was unfair rather than 'forcing persons to analyse the judgment in order to assess precisely what it decides'. See also the general approach now commended in *Hunt v North Somerset Council* [2015] 1 WLR 3575.

17.57 A declaration will also be appropriate where the decision under challenge is not something that has direct legal effect and so is not the appropriate target for a quashing order. So in *R (on the application of Greenpeace Ltd) v Secretary of State for Trade and Industry*[1] a declaration was granted 'in the case of a document of this kind' where a white paper was inadequate as a consultation paper as to whether or not nuclear new build had a role to play. In *Shrewsbury and Atcham BC v Secretary of State for Communities and Local Government*[2] Carnwath LJ said: 'To avoid confusion, in my view, the word 'quashing' order as used in the Supreme Court Act 1981 s 31(1) (like the term 'certiorari' which it replaced) is best confined to its historical role as directed to orders or decisions which otherwise would have substantive legal effect: see eg *R v Electricity Commissioners*,[3] per Atkin LJ. In other contexts, a declaration or injunction is likely to be the more appropriate remedy.' If this is correct then for many types of decision a declaration or injunction would be the only appropriate remedy in respect of invalidity.

The Court may suspend the making or effect of any declaration. However, when the Supreme Court had ruled that Orders freezing the assets of suspected terrorists were unlawful it refused an application by the Secretary of State to suspend making of any declaration pending the making of new Regulations. Since the provisions had been found to be ultra vires suspension of the court's order declaring them to be so and quashing them did not alter the position in law that they were of no effect and a suspension might obfuscate and give a misleading impression about their validity.[4] If such a suspension had been granted then it is unclear what effect it would have in law since on ordinary ultra vires reasoning the order subject to challenge was void and could not be given temporary validity by withholding the declaration.[5]

There is limited authority that a declaration (and a quashing order) may be made with prospective effect only. In *Sabha v Attorney General* [2009] UKPC 17, para 42 the Privy Council limited the retrospective effect of an order that the grant of an honour breached the Constitution of Trinidad and in *R (British Academy of Songwriters Composers and Authors) v SSBIS* [2015] Bus LR 1435 Green J quashed Regulations that had permitted the private copying of musical and other copyright works and in reliance on which millions of copies had been made. However, given the potential impact on private rights, he made the order prospective only and expressly declined to make a declaration that Regulations were retrospectively unlawful [supplementary judgment 19].

1   [2007] Env. LR 29.
2   [2008] EWCA Civ 148.
3   [1924] 1 KB 171, 204–5.
4   *Ahmed and others v HM Treasury (Justice intervening) (Nos 1 and 2)* [2010] 2 AC 534 in *R (T) v Chief Constable of Greater Manchester* [2013] 1WLR 2515, CA where the court held further that its declaration must 'reflect the true effect of our reasoning' [para 83].
5   See [2010] 2 AC 534 @ 7, 8 and 20 per Lord Hope dissenting. See also in a different context *R (TN Vietnam)* above. Nadhamuni argues that the suspension does have a substantive legal effect but that since the nullity *ab-initio* doctrine is founded on the rule of law it can be departed from where fundamental rule of law principles are at stake and require it – 'Suspending invalidity while keeping faith with nullity: an analysis of the suspension order cases and their impact on our understanding of the doctrine of nullity' [2015] PL 596.

Where the outcome would have been no different

17.58 Important changes to the Senior Courts Act 1981 have been made by the Criminal Justice and Courts Act 2015. This inserts a new s 31(2A) for cases started on or after 13 April 2015, under which the court must refuse relief if 'if it appears to the court to be highly likely that the outcome for the applicant would not have been substantially different if the conduct complained of had not occurred'. The court can still grant relief if 'it is appropriate to do so for reasons of exceptional public interest' [s 31(2B)]. The court may also address this issue at the permission stage and must consider it if the defendant asks it to do so [s 32(2B)]. This restriction on relief applies to orders for a declaration but it was accepted by counsel for all parties in R (Logan) v Havering BC[1] that the section does not prevent the court from giving a judgment having the same effect but without an order for a declaration.

1   [2015] PTSR 603.

INJUNCTIONS

The injunction as a public law remedy

17.59 This section deals with final injunctions, being injunctions granted by the court after full argument of the substantive issues of law.[1] Interim injunctions raise separate considerations and are dealt with in CHAPTER **19**. Injunctions may be mandatory (requiring that certain action be taken) or prohibitory (ordering that specified things should not be done). The statutory provisions creating the Supreme Court of Judicature empowered all divisions of the High Court to grant an injunction where that remedy appeared to be just and convenient:[2] this was held to mean that the court could grant an injunction where it would previously have granted a remedy either at common law or in equity.[3]

[1] On injunctions generally, see Bean *Injunctions* (12th edn, 2015); McGhee *Snell's Equity* (3rd edn, 2016).
[2] See now the Senior Courts Act 1981, s 37.
[3] *North London Rly Co v Great Northern Rly Co* (1883) 11 QBD 30.

17.60 It was argued on behalf of the respondent in *R v Kensington and Chelsea Royal London Borough Council, ex p Hammell*[1] that because an injunction could only be granted to protect a legal or equitable right[2] it followed that a homeless person could not seek injunctive relief against a housing authority. This argument was rejected by the Court of Appeal: the injunction lies to protect a public law right.[3] The leading speech of Parker LJ[4] relied on passages in *O'Reilly v Mackman*[5] where Lord Diplock explained that previous disadvantages under the old RSC Ord 53 had justified the courts in permitting resort to an alternative procedure by way of action for an injunction (not then available on an application under RSC Ord 53). An example of such a case is *Legg v Inner London Education Authority*[6] where the ILEA had failed to follow the statutory procedure for ceasing to maintain a school: Megarry J held that parents of children at the school were entitled to an injunction against the ILEA.[7]

[1] [1989] QB 518.
[2] *South Carolina Insurance Co v Assurantie Muatschappij 'De Zeven Provincien' NV* [1987] AC 24.
[3] In *Pickering v Liverpool Daily Post and Echo Newspapers plc* [1991] 2 AC 370, a case where the defendant was not a public authority, Lord Bridge (at 420) said obiter that an injunction could only be granted to a private individual (to compel performance of a statutory obligation) if that person fell within a class on whom the legislation conferred a cause of action in damages;but compare the reasoning in the Court of Appeal [1990] 2 WLR 494.
[4] See pp 530–531; see also Croom-Johnson LJ at 539–540; Fox LJ agreed with Parker LJ.
[5] [1983] 2 AC 237, 283–284 and 285.
[6] [1972] 1 WLR 1245.
[7] In the event, the court refrained from granting an injunction because suitable undertakings were given: see **17.77**.

17.61 In the *Legg* case the remedy of injunction was available to ensure that a public authority did not infringe the requirements of public law. This is not the only type of injunction in ordinary civil proceedings which may be seen as falling within public law. For example, those charged with enforcement of the criminal law, or concerned to prevent a public nuisance may seek the aid of the civil courts. The criteria for the grant of an injunction in a law enforcement case were summarised as follows by Bingham LJ in *City of London Corpn v Bovis Construction Ltd*:[1]

'(1)   The jurisdiction is to be invoked and exercised exceptionally and with great caution . . .

(2)   that there must certainly be something more than mere infringement of the criminal law before the assistance of civil proceedings can be invoked and accorded for the protection or promotion of the interests of the inhabitants of the area . . .

(3)   that the essential foundation for the exercise of the court's discretion to grant an injunction is not that the offender is deliberately and flagrantly flouting the law but the need to draw the inference that the defendant's unlawful operations will continue unless and until effectively restrained by the law and that nothing short of an injunction will be effective to restrain them'.

It is also a requirement that the criminal provision sought to be enforced is clear.[2]

[1]   (1988) 86 LGR 660 at 682; *Nottingham City Council v Zain* [2001] EWCA Civ 1248, [2002] 1 WLR 607. Express statutory provisions (for example anti-social behaviour orders) now apply in many cases where authorities used to seek injunctions under the principles discussed in this case. This does not exclude the power of a local authority to seek an injunction under s 222 of the Local Government Act 1972 but ordinarily the authority should be required to use the statutory route designed for the purpose *Birmingham CC v Shafi* – [2009] 1 WLR 1961. In an appropriate case an injunction can be granted to enforce a byelaw – *Hall v Mayor of London* [2010] EWCA Civ 817 at paras 52-7. See Encyclopedia of Local Government Law para 2.526.1 for a fuller discussion of the case law under s 222.

[2]   This was an additional reason for refusing the Order in *The Queen on the Application of Islamic Human Rights Commission v Civil Aviation Authority, The Foreign and Commonwealth Office, The Ministry of Defence* [2006] EWHC 2465 (Admin).

17.62 Other types of injunction which may fall within public law are applications by the Attorney-General in the public interest (on behalf of the Government or at the relation of a private individual) to restrain unlawful conduct,[1] and applications by private individuals who claim that a public authority threatens to act in breach of a duty owed to them in tort or contract.[2] Such injunctions will not generally be sought by way of judicial review and are not discussed further here.

[1]   See de Smith Woolf and Jowell *Judicial Review of Administrative Action* (7th edn, 2013) paragraphs 2-014.

[2]   See *Clerk & Lindsell on Torts* (21st edn, 2016), Ch 29: *Chitty on Contract* (32nd edn, 2016), Ch 27.

Nature of an injunction by way of judicial review

17.63 In relation to injunctions, in the same way as in relation to declarations, the court is required[1] when considering whether it would be just and convenient for an injunction to be granted on an application for judicial review, to have regard to the nature of the matters in respect of which relief may be granted by way of the prerogative orders, and the nature of the persons and bodies against whom such relief may be granted, as well as to all the circumstances of the case. Full recognition of the effect of these provisions in relation to injunctions was achieved only with the decision of the House of

Lords in 1993 in *M v Home Office*,[2] discussed above. Their essential nature, however, had been explained ten years earlier by Woolf J in *R v British Broadcasting Corporation, ex p Lavelle*.[3] In that case an employee of the BBC had been dismissed when tapes belonging to the BBC were found at her home, and she sought (among other things) an order staying the hearing of an appeal under the BBC's disciplinary procedure pending her criminal trial. In seeking a stay the applicant was seeking, in effect, an injunction, and the matter was argued on the basis that relief by way of an injunction was being sought on the application for judicial review. Woolf J, having observed that the new RSC Ord 53 did not strictly confine applications for judicial review to cases where an order for mandamus, prohibition or certiorari could be granted,[4] held that having regard to the nature of the matters in respect of which relief by prerogative order could be granted it was clear that the application for judicial review was confined to reviewing activities of a public nature as opposed to those of a purely private or domestic character.

[1] By the Senior Courts Act 1981, s 31, as noted in CPR 54.3(1)(b).
[2] [1994] 1 AC 377.
[3] [1983] 1 WLR 23.
[4] See **17.7** above.

17.64 Applying these principles, as described in relation to declarations above,[1] the court may be expected not to trespass by way of injunction upon purely moral, social or political matters, parliamentary privileges,[2] or upon the royal prerogative in relation to the making of treaties. Nor is it to be anticipated that the court would grant an injunction which usurped the jurisdiction of the criminal courts[3] or pronounced on entitlements which are exclusively for adjudication by other tribunals.[4]

[1] See **17.20fn 1** above.
[2] See **17.75** below.
[3] See **17.69** below.
[4] *Stannard v St Giles's, Camberwell, Vestry* (1882) 20 Ch D 190. The position is otherwise where the other tribunal has no jurisdiction: *Auckland (Lord) v Westminster Local Board of Works* (1872) 7 Ch App 597; compare, however, *North London Rly Co v Great Northern Rly Co* (1883) 11 QBD 30 and *Johns v Chatalos* [1973] 1 WLR 1437. See the discussion of declaratory relief at **17.20** above.

17.65 The removal of technical restrictions on the grant of an injunction is discussed below, along with the supervisory and original aspects of the court's jurisdiction, the need for reliance on public law grounds of review, the relationship between the High Court and other courts, questions concerning injunctions against the Crown, the effect of European Union law, and the impact of injunctions on parliamentary proceedings.

Technical restrictions

17.66 As noted earlier, the House of Lords in *M v Home Office*[1] held that the new RSC Ord 53 (with the benefit of statutory confirmation in the Senior Courts Act 1981, s 31) extended the circumstances in which injunctions could be granted against the Crown. Applying this reasoning, the broad language of the relevant provisions and the considerations to which they direct attention suggest that technical restrictions should no longer stand in the way of the grant of an injunction where such a remedy is appropriate as a matter of public law.[2] Thus, if in *R v Kensington and Chelsea Royal London Borough Council, ex p Hammell*[3] there had been any doubt as to the ability of the court to grant an injunction to protect a public law right, such doubts could have been assuaged by reasoning similar to that in the *M* case. Further, as discussed below, any restrictions imposed by domestic law on the grant of an injunction may be trumped by European Union law in accordance with the European Communities Act 1972.

[1] [1994] 1 AC 377; see **17.16** above.
[2] As to the effect of these provisions on the requirements of standing, see CHAPTER **18**.
[3] [1989] QB 518; see **17.59** above.

Supervisory jurisdiction

17.67 As with declarations, it is possible to classify injunctions as either original or supervisory: original where they give effect to rights as between the parties, and supervisory when they are directed to a body with power to affect the rights of the parties. Cases in which a final injunction is needed in order to give effect to the court's supervisory jurisdiction are likely to be rare: in ordinary circumstances, the desired outcome will be achievable by orders of prohibition or mandamus.[1] Nevertheless, in a case where an interlocutory injunction has been granted it may be convenient to order at the final hearing that the interlocutory injunction should continue.[2]

[1] See per Lord Woolf in *M v Home Office* [1994] 1 AC 377, discussing the availability of injunctions against ministers at 418. In *Speciality Produce Ltd v Secretary of State for the Environment, Food and Rural Affairs* [2009] EWHC 1245 (Admin) an injunction requiring the defendant to give effect to the decision was refused because the court would not step into the shoes of the decision maker and it was for the authority to apply the judgment.
[2] See, eg *R v North Yorkshire County Council, ex p M* [1989] QB 411. The Court may also grant an injunction even after the claimant has failed at the final hearing as a means of achieving the same result as a stay pending appeal. Normally an injunction in such terms will be granted for a short period only – *The Queen on the Application of Rutter v Stockton on Tees Borough Council* [2008] EWHC 2651 (Admin) where the issue was the removal of a long-term resident from a care home.

Reliance on public law grounds of review

17.68 The court will not deal with a claim for injunction by way of judicial review unless the matter raises issues of public law.[1] Where public law issues are raised, it may well be appropriate for the court to grant an injunction by way of judicial review to protect the applicant's private law rights in consequence of the determination of the issues of public law.[2] If it is established that no issue of public law arises, or if the public law issues have been dealt with but other issues remain before the claim to an injunction can be determined, the court may direct under CPR 54.20 that the matter proceed as if not begun under Section 1 of CPR Pt 54.[3]

[1] *R v British Broadcasting Corporation, ex p Lavelle* [1983] 1 WLR 23; see the discussion at **17.16** et seq and **17.27** above. In *R (on the application of Supportways Community Services Ltd) v Hampshire CC* [2006] EWCA Civ 1035; [2006] BLGR 836 the claimant complained about the way in which their contract to provide housing related services had been terminated. An order for specific performance was granted but overturned on appeal because the contract had come to an end and with it any contractual procedural duty. Like relief in

public law was rejected because the dispute was essentially about the terms of the contract rather than the unlawful exercise of public power [see paras 34–48 and 51–62].

2   For an example of a case which might be dealt with in this way today, see *Repton School Governors v Repton Urban District Council* [1918] 2 KB 133 (injunction to prevent tortious conduct).

3   Prior to CPR there was power to direct that the matter proceed as if begun by writ under RSC Ord 53, r 9(5), a course deemed to have been taken in the *Lavelle* case. See **5.48, 19.145,** and **20.32** for discussion of the current powers of the court under CPR 54.20.

Relationship between the High Court and other courts

17.69 In *Saull v Browne*[1] it was envisaged that there may be cases in which criminal proceedings instituted by a party to civil litigation were so identical with the civil proceedings as to induce the court to restrain the prosecution of the criminal proceedings by injunction. Such an injunction was granted against a defendant in civil proceedings by Buckley J in *Thames Launches Ltd v Trinity House Corpn (Deptford Strond)*.[2] An injunction of this kind is directed to the litigant, not to the criminal court, and is granted so as to enable the High Court to exercise its original jurisdiction without hindrance. It is unlikely that an injunction, rather than an order of prohibition or mandamus, would be an appropriate exercise of the High Court's supervisory jurisdiction over other courts. In principle an injunction can lie in judicial review against a decision to prosecute but this is an exceptional remedy and it would be necessary to show that the issue could not adequately be resolved in the criminal proceedings – for example by an argument based on abuse of process.[3] The extreme reluctance of the High Court to interfere with the decision-making processes of the criminal courts is noted above (see **17.21** and **17.60**) in connection with declarations as to the meaning of the criminal law, and similar principles apply here.

1   (1874) 10 App Ch 64.

2   [1961] Ch 197; this decision was described as a 'high water-mark' by Lord Lane in *Imperial Tobacco Ltd v A-G* [1981] AC 718, 750.

3   Sharma v Browne-Antoine [2007] 1 WLR 780 PC, R *(SOMA Oil & Gas Ltd) v Director of the Serious Fraud Office* [2016] EWHC 2471 (Admin) DC.

17.70 In certain circumstances it may be necessary for the Administrative Court to grant an injunction to restrain the local authority from acting on an unlawful care plan pending care proceedings. For this purpose the judge hearing an appeal in the Family Division ought also to be an administrative court judge.[1] Where an inferior tribunal has no power to grant interim relief then an injunction may be granted in judicial review proceedings to achieve the same substantive result. In *R (JW through DW as Litigation Friend) v The Learning Trust*[2] a child's parents appealed against a statement of special educational needs (which did not provide for a placement at Z College) to the First Tier Tribunal (FTT). The Upper Tribunal held that it could grant an injunction requiring the Respondent to provide schooling at Z despite the fact that the FTT could not grant interim relief. However the power was exceptional and had to be exercised with restraint given the statutory context and relief was refused on the facts.

Where separate proceedings are brought, by a local authority for an injunction to restrain a breach of statute (eg, the Shops Act 1950), and against the authority for judicial review of its decision to pursue the injunction (and bring criminal proceedings in the magistrates' court), it is not necessary for the injunction case to be delayed until the outcome of the judicial review proceedings. The same judge (who may be a Chancery judge, sitting as an additional judge of the Queen's Bench Division) can hear both applications. Indeed, it will generally be possible for the affected individual to raise a public law challenge to the decision to bring proceedings against them by way of defence, without the need to start separate proceedings.

1 *Re S (Children)* [2007] EWCA Civ 232, [2007] 2 FLR 275 paragraph 50-1 and 89.
2 [2009] UKUT 197 (AAC).

Injunctions against the Crown

17.71 No injunction can issue against the Crown as sovereign. General principles in this regard are discussed in CHAPTER **14**. In civil proceedings against the Crown other than an application for judicial review, the Crown Proceedings Act 1947, s 21(1), provides that the court:

(1) shall not grant an injunction, make an order for specific performance, or make an order for recovery of land or delivery of property, but

(2) may in lieu thereof make an order declaratory of the rights of the parties.

17.72 Section 21(2) provides that the court shall not in any civil proceedings grant any injunction or make any order against an officer of the Crown if the effect of granting the injunction or making the order would be to give any relief against the Crown which could not have been obtained in proceedings against the Crown. The interpretation to be given to this section is dealt with by the House of Lords in *M v Home Office*;[1] where, prior to 1947, an injunction could be obtained against an officer of the Crown, because that officer had personally committed or authorised a tort, an injunction in civil proceedings can still be granted on precisely the same basis as previously, since the grant of an injunction could not affect the Crown (given the assumption that the Crown can do no wrong). Such proceedings would have to be brought against the tortfeasor personally; if, on the other hand, the officer was being sued in civil proceedings in a representative capacity (eg as Attorney-General), no injunction could be granted because in such a situation the effect would be to give relief against the Crown.

1 [1994] 1 AC 377.

17.73 However, s 21 does not apply to judicial review proceedings. Accordingly, in such proceedings an injunction under s 31 of the Supreme Court Act 1981 can be obtained against an officer of the Crown sued in a representative capacity, there being no justification for limiting the remedy in the absence of clear language such as that in s 21(2) of the 1947 Act.[1]

1 See [1994] 1 AC at 422; see also **17.16** above which deals with the jurisdiction of the court to grant declarations and injunctions on judicial review, and the discussion of remedies against the Crown generally in CHAPTER **13**. As discussed below, immunities of the Crown may be overridden by European Union law. At first the position was held to be different in Scotland on the ground that there was no precise counterpart to proceedings on the Crown Side of the Queen's Bench Division. But this anomaly was dealt with by the HOL in *Davidson v Scottish Ministers No 2* [2005] UKHL 74 2006 SC (HL) 41. It is now clear that the Court of Session

may grant an injunction against the Crown when exercising its supervisory jurisdiction in cases involving other than private law rights.

European Union law

17.74 Such immunities as the Crown continues to possess, and any other domestic law restrictions on the grant of an injunction, will be overridden in a case where European Union law so requires. This was established in the *Factortame* litigation, where the House of Lords had regarded itself as unable to grant interlocutory relief because of a rule rendering the Crown immune from an injunction.[1] The European Court of Justice held, in answer to questions posed by the House of Lords,[2] that if a rule of national law is the sole obstacle to the granting of interim relief, the national court must set aside that rule. This ruling of the European Court was then duly applied by the House of Lords.[3] These principles will be equally applicable to the case of a final (rather than an interim) injunction.

[1] *R v Secretary of State for Transport Ltd, ex p Factortame Ltd* [1990] 2 AC 85 ('Factortame I'); the reasoning, and its subsequent disapproval, is discussed at **17.16** above.
[2] *Factortame II* [1991] 1 AC 603, [1991] 1 All ER 70.
[3] *Factortame II* [1991] 1 AC 603 at 658ff, [1991] 1 All ER 70.

Injunctions and Parliament

17.75 While an injunction will not be granted which will infringe parliamentary privilege, the court will determine the extent of the privilege. Thus a mandatory injunction to seek leave to withdraw a private Bill was held by Millett J not to affect parliamentary privilege in *Fairfold Properties v Exmouth Docks Co*.[1] The court may be confronted with difficult questions where injunctions are sought which will affect statutory instruments laid, or to be laid, before Parliament.[2] It will usually be possible to avoid conflict, even when the court is dealing with potential but uncertain privileges. Thus in *R v Secretary of State for the Environment, ex p Doncaster Metropolitan Borough Council*,[3] the court discussed the principles which underlay the decision of the Court of Appeal in *R v Electricity Comrs, ex p London Electricity Joint Committee Co*,[4] where it was held that the court had power by way of prohibition to prevent a scheme going forward for approval by the Minister, even though the scheme could only take effect should it be approved by the House of Commons. The court in the *Doncaster* case declined to take any action that would inhibit the freedom of the Secretary of State to lay a draft order before a House of Parliament for its approval by affirmative resolution: the parliamentary timetable was such that the laying of the draft order would not interfere with the resolution of legal questions by the court. The court has a statutory jurisdiction in relation to elections to the House of Commons; this is discussed below.[5]

[1] (1990) Times, 15 October; see also Sir John Laws, 'Judicial Remedies and the Constitution' (1994) 57 MLR 213, 219–221.
[2] See *R v HM Treasury, ex p Smedley* [1985] QB 657, and *R v HM Treasury, ex p British Telecommunications plc* [1995] COD 56.
[3] (15 May 1990, unreported) CA.
[4] [1924] 1 KB 171, CA.

Factors affecting the grant of injunctions

17.76 Questions of standing, availability of alternative remedies, delay and other discretionary bars raise issues in common with other remedies on judicial review, and are dealt with in CHAPTER **18**. A primary consideration affecting the grant of an injunction will be its practical consequences. An order will not be made which requires the person injuncted to do something which is impossible.¹ On the other hand, the court will not be unduly tender to a public authority which complains of the difficulty of complying with the law.² But this does not mean that an individual who has shown that proposed conduct would be unlawful will be entitled to an injunction as of right: the remedy of injunction will not be granted if it is disproportionate in the circumstances. Thus in *Coney v Choyce*³ Templeman J, having held that the action in question would not be unlawful, nevertheless went on to add that if he had found unlawfulness:

'I should be very slow to introduce the swingeing weapon of an injunction, interfering in administrative and educational matters of great moment by the sledge hammer of an injunction which would bring to a grinding halt all the co-operation . . . in the course of the past few years.'

¹   *A-G v Colchester Corpn* [1955] 2 QB 207.
²   *Bradbury v Enfield London Borough Council* [1967] 1 WLR 1311.
³   [1975] 1 WLR 422, 437.

Practice and procedure

17.77 An injunction operates in personam. Accordingly, if the respondent is an administrative tribunal which has no legal personality,¹ it seems likely that in order to secure an effective injunction the relevant natural persons would need to be made parties. It seems that in the exercise of its original jurisdiction the court can grant an injunction that is binding on non-parties.² However, this may not be the case in respect of the court's supervisory powers. In *R (Health and Safety Executive) v Wolverhampton City Council*³ Collins J held that there was no power to make a final injunction against an interested party restraining them from completing a development on an application to quash the associated planning permission. In a case where the court has concluded that an injunction is appropriate, the court will nevertheless not grant an injunction if the respondent offers a suitable undertaking.⁴

¹   Lord Denning's discussion of the grant of injunctions in *Barnard v National Dock Labour Board* [1953] 2 QB 18, 41–42, did not deal with the question of legal personality.
²   For example *R v Tower Bridge Magistrates' Court, ex p Osborne* (1987) 88 Cr App Rep 28 where the Divisional Court granted an injunction restraining publication of proceedings in the magistrates' court.
³   [2010] PTSR (CS) 1 at para 43. This issue was not addressed on appeal to the Court of Appeal and Supreme Court [2012] 1 WLR 2264.
⁴   See, eg *Legg v Inner London Education Authority* [1972] 1 WLR 1245.

17.78 Where a minister gives an undertaking then the responsibility for acting in accordance with it cannot be delegated to civil servants. They are not in the same position as employees because they are not agents of the minister but servants of the Crown. The minister is responsible for the acts or omissions of civil servants because they are under his or her control but it is the minister in person who is responsible for any breach of an undertaking. It follows that it is wrong in principle to require a civil servant whose conduct is criticised as a breach of the undertaking to attend court under pain of punishment if they do not do so.[1] However, civil servants may be liable if they are aware of an order or undertaking but wilfully breach it.[2]

[1] *Beggs v Scottish Ministers* [2007] 1 WLR 455 at paragraphs 8–9.
[2] Ibid paragraphs 10–11. They are liable in this case in the same way as a director of a company who is aware of an order against the company but acts in breach of it – See *AG for Tuvalu v Philatelic Distribution Corpn Ltd* [1990] 1 WLR 926.

17.79 It is not the normal practice of the Administrative Court to attach a penal notice to an injunction since it is to be expected that a public body will not deliberately flout an order of the court and the risk of adverse findings and liability to pay indemnity costs in the event of breach will normally be sufficient. In the case of a persistent failure to comply a further order can be made with a penal notice. If a Claimant has reason to think that a penal notice is required then a specific request should be made to the judge to that effect.[1]

[1] *R (JM) v Croydon LBC* [2010] PTSR 866, Collins J. In *R (Lamari) v Secretary of State for the Home Department* [2012] EWHC 1895 (Admin) an undertaking to release a detainee was not complied with. HHJ Cotter QC made a formal finding of contempt and observed that such failures might force the court to consider whether it could accept undertakings or whether orders with a penal notice would become necessary.

PROCEEDINGS CONCERNING PUBLIC AND MUNICIPAL OFFICES

17.80 Section 30 of the Senior Courts Act 1981 provides for declarations and injunctions in relation to the holder of certain public offices:

'30
(1) Where a person not entitled to do so acts in an office to which this section applies, the High Court may:
    (a) grant an injunction restraining him from so acting; and
    (b) if the case so requires, declare the office to be vacant.
(2) This section applies to any substantive office of a public nature and permanent character which is held under the Crown or which has been created by any statutory provision or royal charter.'

17.81 This provision re-enacts with modifications the Administration of Justice (Miscellaneous Provisions) Act 1938, s 9, which introduced these measures as a replacement for the information in the nature of *quo warranto*.[1]

[1] The writ of *quo warranto*, which was a procedure to challenge the usurpation of an office fell into disuse. Whereas the 1938 Act defined the circumstances in which the injunction and declaration could be sought by reference to those in which an information in the nature of *quo warranto* could be obtained, s 30 of the Supreme Court Act 1981 has identified the offices to which the section applies and has abandoned the requirement that an applicant for the statutory remedies must have sufficient standing for an information in the nature of *quo warranto*. The defendant must have acted in the office and the procedure does not extend to contracts of employment.

17.82 By the Supreme Court Act 1981, s 31(1)(c), an application for an injunction under s 30 must be made by application for judicial review;[1] presumably a declaration under s 30 may be sought by application for judicial review pursuant to s 31(2) of the 1981 Act. In practice an application for a declaration will have to be brought by judicial review because it will always be linked to a claim for an injunction (which falls within CPR 54.2). CPR 54.3 therefore makes the use of judicial review mandatory.

[1] This requirement is reflected in CPR Part 54.2(d) under which an application for an injunction must be by judicial review.

17.83 Special provision has long been made for proceedings in relation to municipal offices. The Mandamus Act of 1710[1] gave authority to file informations in the nature of *quo warranto* in the case of municipal corporations on the relation of private persons. This provision was abolished by the Local Government Act 1933, s 84 of which established a procedure for declarations and injunctions (and forfeiture) in the High Court, as well as for fines in the magistrates' court. Now by the Local Government Act 1972, s 92(5), the exclusive method of proceeding against a person on the ground of acting or claiming to be entitled to act as a member of a local authority[2] while disqualified is by proceedings under that section, pursuant to which the High Court may make a declaration of the disqualification and that the office in which the defendant has acted is vacant, and may grant an injunction restraining the defendant so acting.[3] If proceedings under s 92 of the 1972 Act are begun in the High Court a Part 8 claim form must be used.[4]

[1] 9 Anne c 20 (sometimes described as 9 Anne c 25).
[2] Section 92 is also applicable to membership of other bodies: eg Committees (and joint Committees of local authorities (s 104(3)) of the Local Government Act 1972), joint authorities (s 92(7)), joint waste authorities (s 97(2A), the Broads Authority (s 92(8)) and National Park Authorities (Environment Act 1985, s 63(5) and Sch 7, paragraph 7(3)).
[3] The High Court may also order that the defendant shall forfeit a sum (subject to a specified maximum) for each occasion on which the defendant acted while disqualified; under an alternative procedure in the Magistrates' Court the defendant may be convicted and fined.
[4] Section B of the Practice Direction supplementing CPR Pt 8. This Practice Direction contains further procedural provisions.

17.84 A special jurisdiction also exists in relation to certain local, national and European elections. Section 11 of the European Parliamentary Elections Act 2002 empowers the High Court to make a declaration that a person purporting to hold office as a representative to the European Parliament is or was disqualified at the time of, or at any time since, election. Under the Representation of the People Act 1983, Pt III, there is provision for a petition to the court for determination of the validity of parliamentary and local government elections. Similar provisions apply to election of representatives to the European Parliament.[1] The House of Commons Disqualification Act 1975 provides for an application to the Judicial Committee of the Privy Council for a declaration that a person is disqualified from membership; and it is possible for there to be a special reference by the Crown to the Judicial Committee of the Privy Council under the Judicial Committee Act 1833, s 4.[2]

[1] Part 4 of the European Parliamentary Elections Regulations 2004 (SI 2004/293).
[2] See *Re Sir Stuart Samuel* [1913] AC 514, PC and *Re Macmanaway* [1951] AC 161. See, also, 17.40 above.

MONEY AND RESTITUTIONARY REMEDIES

General

17.85 Three additional types of remedy are obtainable on an application for judicial review. As explained below, they are described as 'damages, restitution, or the recovery of a sum due'. Proceedings seeking the first and third of these will invariably be money claims. Proceedings for the second (described below as 'restitutionary claims') will often be money claims, but need not be – for example, the law of restitution enables a party to recover all types of property.[1] This part of the chapter discusses briefly the relationship between money and restitutionary claims and the public law obligations which underlie judicial review, it then turns to examine the circumstances in which such claims can be made on an application for judicial review.

[1] See Goff and Jones *Law of Unjust Enrichment* (9th edn, 2016).

Money and restitutionary claims and public law

17.86 The mere fact that there has been a breach of a public law duty does not normally give rise to a cause of action for a money or restitutionary claim. As was said by Laws J in *R v Ealing London Borough Council, ex p Parkinson*:[1]

'the starting point . . . consists in a general principle of administrative law, namely that the law recognises no right of compensation for administrative tort; by "administrative tort" I mean breach of a duty owed by a public body arising only in public law. This principle is clearly established. A public body condemned by the court as having acted irrationally, unfairly or illegally is not thereby rendered liable to damages. There are exceptions. If the public body is convicted of misfeasance in public office, damages may be recovered; strictly, however, this is no exception since misfeasance is recognised as a tort sounding in private law . . . There is a further, and true, exception where the public law breach consists in a failure to fulfil an obligation arising under EC law and is of a kind such that compensation may be payable according to the jurisprudence of the Court of Justice . . . There may also be cases where in the purported performance of a public duty, a body commits what is plainly a private wrong: it may be false imprisonment, or in some cases negligence . . . but again, these are not exceptions to the principle which I have stated.'

[1] (1995) 8 Admin LR 281, 285. See also *R (Quark Fishing Ltd) v Secretary of State for Foreign and Commonwealth Affairs* [2006] 1 AC 529 [96]; *Tchenguiz v Director of the Serious Fraud Office* [2014] EWCA Civ 472 at 8 and 14, approving the statement from De Smith Judicial review (7th edn), 19–25: 'while in some cases it may be a necessary condition, it is never a sufficient one for the award of damages that the act or omission complained of be "unlawful" in a public law sense'.

17.87 In conformity with these observations, it is no exception to this general principle that damages have long been awarded in England and Wales as a vindication of rights which today would be regarded as falling within public law.[1] Two of many examples may be given from the law of tort. The tort of misfeasance in a public office will entail liability in damages where certain public officers have acted unlawfully and in bad faith.[2] Certain public bodies which act in breach of statutory duty will be held liable in damages if the duty under the statute was owed to individuals.[3] In such cases the courts have, in effect, held that their supervisory jurisdiction is not enough to vindicate the claimant's rights, and that the claimant in vindication of his rights may in certain circumstances invoke the court's ordinary jurisdiction to award damages. However, in such cases the claimant will have to establish loss in the ordinary way. Where, in a claim for false imprisonment, the claimant would inevitably have been imprisoned in the same way if the public authority had not acted unlawfully then there will be no award of compensatory damages and the common law does not recognise a separate head of vindicatory damages.[4] Where exemplary damages are available then a sufficiently serious breach of public law duty may support a claim to them even though it could not give rise to a claim for damages in its own right.[5]

[1] A celebrated example is *Ashby v White* (1703) 2 Ld Raym 938: the House of Lords, upholding the dissent of Holt CJ in the Court of King's Bench, permitted an action on the case for wrongful refusal of a returning officer to accept the claimant's vote. For discussion of the consequent conflict between the House of Lords and the House of Commons, and the question whether malice was a necessary averment, see *Smith's Leading Cases* (13th edn, 1929) pp 281–283.

[2] See *Clerk & Lindsell on Torts* (21st edn, 2016), Ch 14 section 4.

[3] See *Clerk & Lindsell on Torts* (21st edn, 2016) Ch 9.

[4] *R (Lumba) v Secretary of State for the Home Department* [2012] 1 AC 245. Subsequent cases have held that the correct test is whether, on a balance of probabilities, the claimant would have been detained in any event but for the error – *R (Ageyikum) v Secretary of State for the Home Department* [2013] EWHC 1828 (Admin) at para 84. Where exemplary damages are available then a sufficiently serious breach of public law duty may support a claim to them even though it could not give rise to a claim for damages in its own right. *R (Santos) v SSHD* [2016] EWHC 609 (Admin).

[5] *R (Santos) v SSHD* [2016] EWHC 609 (Admin).

17.88 Dicey described the third aspect of the rule of law as being that the general principles of the constitution (as for example the right to personal liberty, or the right of public meeting) are the result of judicial decisions determining the rights of private persons in particular cases brought before the courts.[1] This proposition required considerable qualification if it were to be regarded as correct even in Dicey's time, but it reflects the importance of the law of tort in the vindication of rights which today can be described as falling within the field of public law. At the same time it hindered the development of the concept that there could be public law rights which differed from those in private law. As late as 1984 Lord Wilberforce[2] expressed reserve about the use of the terms 'public law' and 'private law', but in the words of Sir John Laws, that reserve 'has been washed away by the tide of judicial review'.[3] With the recognition that public law rights may differ from those in private law there has come a perception that pecuniary remedies against public authorities might be available in circumstances where they would not necessarily be available against private persons. Three features may be mentioned. The first concerns the European Convention on Human Rights. The grant of the right of individual petition meant that where the UK infringed the Convention, monetary awards might be made against the UK in favour of the victim of that infringement. Now, under s 8 of the Human Rights Act 1998, domestic courts are empowered to award damages against public authorities as 'just satisfaction' to those who are victims of the breach of certain provisions of the European Convention on Human Rights.[4] Second, the role of the domestic courts in giving effect to the supremacy of European Union law is now established to include the award of damages against the UK Government where it is in breach of a rule of community law intended to confer rights on individuals, the breach is sufficiently serious and there is a direct causal link between the breach and the damage sustained by those individuals.[5] Third, the House of Lords has held that in the case of a tax or similar impost on the claimant by the state there is a prima facie right of recovery based solely on payment of money pursuant to an ultra vires demand by a public authority.[6] Factors which in that case were held to warrant a reformulation of the law of restitution may well have a similar effect in cases where recovery of something other than money is sought.

[1] A V Dicey, An Introduction to the Study of the Law of the Constitution (10th edn, 1959) p 195.

[2] *Davy v Spelthorne Borough Council* [1984] AC 262, 276.

[3] Sir John Laws, 'Judicial Remedies and the Constitution' (1994) 57 MLR 213.

[4] See, generally, CHAPTERS 4 and 14. In other jurisdictions the enactment of constitutional rights has been held to carry with it an entitlement to public law compensation: see *Maharaj v A-G of Trinidad and Tobago (No 2)* [1979] AC 385 and two New Zealand cases, *Simpson v A-G, Baigent's case* [1994] 3 NZLR 667 and *Auckland Unemployed Workers Rights Centre Inc v A-G* [1994] 3 NZLR 720, discussed by Dr Rodney Harrison QC in Huscroft and Rishworth (eds) *Rights and Freedoms: The New Zealand Bill of Rights Act 1990 and the Human Rights Act 1993* (1995).

[5] See Joined Cases C-6, 9/90 *Francovich and Bonifaci v Italy* [1991] ECR 1–5357, [1992] IRLR 84 and ECJ III [1996] QB 404, Joined Cases C46/93 and C48/93 *(Factortame III)*, and W van Gerven, 'Bridging the Unbridgable: Community and National Tort Laws after *Factortame* and *Brasserie*' (1996) 45 ICLQ 507. In CHAPTER 15 there is discussion of the EC law principle of state liability for loss and damage caused to individuals (see **15.98**), and this is contrasted with the different considerations which apply where the breach of Community law is invoked as a basis for an action in damages brought by one individual against another. Claims against Community institutions are also discussed in CHAPTER 15.

[6] *Woolwich Equitable Building Society v IRC* [1993] AC 70. See Goff and Jones, *Unjust Enrichment* (9th edn) at 22.17–22.47 for a discussion of this principle. In *Hemming (t/a Simply Pleasure Ltd) v Westminster City Council* [2013] PTSR 1377(see also [2015] UKSC 25 and [2017] P.T.S.R. 325 (C.J.E.U.)) it was held that money paid to a person in a public or quasi-public position to obtain the performance by him of a duty which he is bound to perform for nothing, or for less than the sum demanded by him, is recoverable to the extent that he is not entitled to it.

17.89 In the examples just given the link between the claim to a money or restitutionary remedy and the public law duties of the defendant is very strong – the former will be determined by the latter, albeit on occasion with qualifications. In other cases, however, the strength of the link will depend upon the facts of the case and the principles of substantive law involved in the money or restitutionary claim, such principles often being different from those governing the public law duty. The result of the absence of a general right to damages for maladministration is that money claims and restitutionary claims against public authorities are generally dependant upon an array of differing principles of substantive private law. This is a feature of the law of England and Wales which has not received universal approval,[1] and is only partially ameliorated by the entitlement to damages under the Human Rights Act 1998 (discussed in CHAPTERS 4 and 14) and the possibility of resorting to the Parliamentary Commissioner for Administration and other ombudsmen who have varying powers to recommend (or occasionally enforce) compensation.[2]

[1] See, eg, Schiemann LJ in *R v Knowsley Borough Council, ex p Maguire* (1992) 90 LGR 653, 'our law in relation to claims for damages for administrative wrongdoings is notoriously unsatisfactory from the claimant's point of view'. See, also, JUSTICE – All Souls, *Administrative Justice: Some Necessary Reforms*, (1988), Ch 11.

² As to the inter relationship of the role of ombudsmen and the court, see Woolf *Protection of the Public – A New Challenge,* and JUSTICE – All Souls, *Administrative Justice: Some Necessary Reforms* (1988), Ch 5.

17.90 Between October 2004 and May 2010 the Law Commission conducted a detailed review of this issue.¹ In its consultation paper it recognised that the current position was untenable. Compensation was rarely available in domestic judicial review cases and lacked a coherent foundation whereas the boundaries of liability in private law were unprincipled and unpredictable. It recommended reform in both private and public law so that financial redress would be available in cases involving the discharge of certain public functions² but where the core requirement, (inspired by the example of EU law) would be to show serious fault rather than merely illegality or negligence. These proposals were subject to considerable criticism for themselves being unprincipled.³

¹ The initial discussion paper was Monetary Remedies in Public Law – 11 October 2004. This was followed by Consultation Paper no 187 Administrative Redress: Public Bodies and the Citizen in June 2008. The Final Report; Law Com No 322 was published in May 2010.
² In judicial review the proposal was that the common law or statutory regime in issue must be one conferring some form of benefit corresponding to the harm suffered by the claimant.
³ See eg Cornford 2009 Public Law 70–88. And see the summary of consultation responses at paragraph 2 of the final report.

17.91 In its final report the Law Commission accepted it had not persuaded consultees of the need for change from the current incremental approach to liability in private law cases.¹ As far as monetary remedies in public law were concerned it maintained its position that there were significant gaps in the current regime and that there were important situations where the award of damages would be considered appropriate in a public law case in the interests of justice.² It considered that the basic structure of the consultation proposals remained sound and that there was a good argument for reforming the law on those lines. Despite this the Commission did not recommend any changes because it had been unable to assess how the proposals would work in practice. It had been unable to show how many new cases would be launched and could not show that the proposals would not impose an unacceptable burden on public bodies. As the Commission put it at paragraph 2.95:

'It has always been fundamental to our approach that the liability of public bodies raises different issues to the law governing compensation between private individuals. The imposition of liability on public bodies can divert resources allocated for the public good to individual compensatory awards and legal costs. We do not see this as the end of any argument. There are good reasons why liability should be imposed on public bodies in certain circumstances, for instance in the interests of justice and to prevent recurrent failures in service delivery. What this does mean though, is that assessing the financial implications of any reforms is particularly important. Our inability to create an assessment of the financial effects of our proposals made it impossible to address certain concerns expressed by Government'.³

And at paragraph 6.7:

'However, given the substantial opposition to our proposals – in particular from Government but also from others – coupled with the lack of a dataset that would have assisted in addressing some of these concerns, we accept that we cannot take this part of the project any further.'

This was a remarkable conclusion for the Commission to have to reach. It devoted a section of its report to the difficulties it had encountered in obtaining the relevant data and made specific recommendations for reform 'to fulfil the requirements of accountability and transparency that are key to our system of governance'.[4] The proposals were controversial and may have proved impossible in any event, but what defeated them on this occasion was the lack of proper record keeping by the very bodies against whom claims would have been made.[5]

[1] See paragraphs **6.56–6.64**.
[2] The classic example, used in both the consultation and final papers was the unlawful removal of a licence to carry out an economic activity – Final Report paragraph 2.51.
[3] The Commission experienced a similar difficulty in assessing the impact of its proposals in private law – paragraph 3.78.
[4] Paragraph 6.12.
[5] See further the observations of Sedley LJ in *Mohammed v Home Office* [2011] 1 WLR 2862 [23] describing the fate of the proposals as a 'debacle' and as 'a troubling comment on the functioning of the separation of powers'.

17.92 This part of the chapter discusses types of money and restitutionary claims that can be included on an application of judicial review,[1] but it is not proposed here to give an account of the substantive principles of law giving rise to money and restitutionary remedies. The substantive merits of such claims will depend on the application of principles of substantive law in particular fields. Those principles are discussed in texts dealing with the subject matter in question, and will call for careful scrutiny before any damages claim is pleaded on an application for judicial review. Here it may be noted that among such fields are European Union law,[2] as well as the law of tort (especially misfeasance in a public office, breach of statutory duty, and negligent mis-statement and negligence generally, also false imprisonment, malicious prosecution and the torts protecting rights in real and personal property, protecting economic interests and protecting reputation),[3] equitable obligations (especially obligations of confidence),[4] contract (especially public procurement contracts)[5] and restitution.[6] Further, vicarious liability[7] may arise, principles of quantification of damages (including exemplary damages)[8] may be relevant, and specific immunities may attach to specific defendants (for example the Crown[9] and judicial officers).[10]

[1] In CHAPTER 5 there is discussion of the separate question whether a claim to damages which can be made on an application for judicial review will be barred from proceeding in any other way (see *Guevara v Hounslow London Borough Council* (1987) Times, 17 April. Contrast *An Bord Bainne Co-operative Ltd (Irish Dairy Board) v Milk Marketing Board* [1984] 2 CMLR 584).
[2] See CHAPTER 15 above; also Vaughan and Robertson, *Law of the European Union.*
[3] See Clerk and Lindsell on Torts (21st edn, 2016).
[4] See *Snell's Equity* (33rd edn, 2016); Gurry *Breach of Confidence* 2nd edn, 2012.
[5] See *Chitty on Contracts* (32nd edn, 2016); Treitel, *Law of Contract* (14th edn, 2015); Arrowsmith Law of Public and Utilities Procurement (3rd edn, July 2014).
[6] See Goff & Jones *Law of Unjust Enrichment* (9th edn, 2016). Virgo, Restitution from Public Authorities: Past Present and Future; Judicial Review 2006 11(4) 370–383.
[7] *Clerk and Lindsell on Torts* (21st edn, 2016), Ch 6.
[8] See, generally, *McGregor on Damages* (19th edn, July 2014) and Law Commission *Aggravated, Exemplary and Restitutionary Damages* (1993).
[9] See CHAPTER 14 above.
[10] See Olowofoyeku, 'Suing Judges: A Study of Judicial Immunity' (1993).

Claims for money and restitution on an application for judicial review

17.93 Section 31(4) of the Senior Courts Act 1981[1] provides for money and restitutionary remedies in this way:

'On an application for judicial review the High Court may award to the applicant damages, restitution or the recovery of a sum due if:

(a)   he has joined with his application a claim for such an award arising from any matter to which the application relates; and

(b)   the court is satisfied that such an award would have been made if the claim had been made in an action begun by the applicant at the time of making his application.'

---

[1]   This section as originally enacted confirmed (with slight differences in wording) the earlier provision in RSC Ord 53, r 7(1); it is set out in the text as amended by art 4 of the Civil Procedure (Modification of Supreme Court Act 1981) Order 2004 which extends the section beyond award of damages so as to permit the award of restitution and recovery of a sum due. Corresponding provision is made in respect of the Upper Tribunal by s 16(6) of the Tribunals Courts and Enforcement Act 2007. A monetary award made by the Upper Tribunal is enforceable as if it were an award of the High Court (s 16(7)).

17.94 It follows from this provision that, as was observed at the outset of this chapter, an award of a money or restitutionary remedy (by contrast with an injunction or declaration) is not a form of relief by way of judicial review. What s 31(4) (and s 16(6)) achieve is that if a matter gives rise, not only to grounds for judicial review, but also to a claim for a money or restitutionary remedy, then in certain circumstances the application for judicial review and the claim for a money or restitutionary remedy may be joined.[1] The following paragraphs examine those circumstances. It should be borne in mind that if the court concludes that a money or restitutionary claim cannot or should not be considered on an application for judicial review, the proceedings can be directed to continue as if begun in some other way.[2]

---

[1]   See **17.4** above. If the claim has not included a claim for a monetary remedy then there is no power to award it *R (Bamber) v Revenue & Customs Commissioners* [2008] STC 1864. In that case there was in any event no valid restitutionary claim.

[2]   This can be done under CPR 54.20, as to which see **5.48**, and **21.35**.

No new cause of action

17.95 The reform begun by the new RSC Ord 53 was concerned with remedies and with public law, not extending, or diminishing, substantive rights in private law. It created no new cause of action.[1] It enabled a claim for damages resulting from unlawful conduct by a public authority to be joined with a public law application to establish the unlawfulness rather than being claimable only in an action begun by writ.[2] This was of value because it avoids the instigation of duplicate proceedings.

---

[1]   *Calveley v Chief Constable of the Merseyside Police* per Lord Donaldson MR and Glidewell LJ in the Court of Appeal [1989] QB 136, 151–152, 154; Staughton LJ agreed with both judgments. The point is not dealt with in the speeches in the House of Lords [1989] AC 1228, [1989] 1 All ER 1025.

[2]   For detailed consideration of the position prior to the extension of s 31 (4) of the Supreme Court Act 1981, see CHAPTER 16 of the second edition of this work.

17.96 In *Chief Constable of the North Wales Police v Evans*,[1] the House of Lords held that the Chief Constable, when dismissing the applicant, had failed to deal fairly with him in relation to the adverse factors relied upon, but would not grant an order of mandamus for his reinstatement because such an order might border on usurpation of the powers of the Chief Constable. A declaration that the decision of the Chief Constable was void would be unsatisfactory because it was not clear what consequences would flow from it, and instead a carefully formulated declaration was granted stating that, by reason of his unlawfully induced resignation, the applicant had thereby become entitled to the same rights and remedies, not including reinstatement, as he would have had if the Chief Constable had unlawfully dispensed with his services. The effect of such a declaration was considered in *R v Chief Constable of the Thames Valley Police, ex p Cotton*,[2] Simon Brown J said at 320:

'The mere fact of succeeding in judicial review proceedings does not supply [an applicant with a cause of action]. Successful natural justice challenges do not carry in their wake damages claims. They entitle the applicant to a fresh decision but it is generally well recognised that the mere quashing of a decision and the recognition that the state of affairs which it brought about was unlawfully occasioned does not carry with it an entitlement to damages . . . [Chief Constable of the North Wales Police v Evans] is to be regarded as a case where it was recognised, in the light of the court's conclusions as to the "outrageous" nature of the process that had been followed against the officer, that the only reasonable conduct by the Chief Constable thereafter would be to pay compensation as if there was in law a right to damages. Strictly, however, that compensation would fall to be paid on an ex gratia basis, there being no private law entitlement to it. I do not read Evans as authority for the proposition that a private law right to damages for breach of statutory duty arises when a decision to dispense with a police officer's services is held to have been unlawfully taken by reason of procedural improprieties . . . '.

Other cases where office holders have been unlawfully dismissed have attracted a range of responses from the courts. If the dismissal is void then the consequence of a declaration to that effect ought to be that they remain entitled to the salary and other benefits of their office even if they are not re-instated. This was ordered in *McLaughlin*.[3] But other cases have not gone so far since the claimant might have been lawfully dismissed. In *R (Shoesmith) v OFSTED*[4] the court declared the dismissal to be unlawful and then directed a further hearing on the issue of damages. The options were said to be 'at the outer limits' that the claimant would recover her notice pay or her ongoing losses.

[1] [1982] 3 All ER 141, [1982] 1 WLR 1155, HL.
[2] [1989] COD 318, [1990] I.R.L.R. 344.
[3] [2007] 1 WLR 2839.
[4] [2011] PTSR 1459 at 128–132.

17.97 By parity of reasoning s 31(4) does not give rise to a right to claim interest on judicial review where none could have been claimed in other proceedings. It remains the case that the mere fact that a delay in the award of a grant was caused by breach of a public law duty will not give rise to a claim to interest.[1] However, where a sum is outstanding at the time that a claim for it is made in judicial review proceedings then the Court has power to award interest under s 35A of the Senior Courts Act 1981 even where the amounts are paid prior to judgment on the remainder of the claim – *R (Kemp) v Denbighshire Local Health Board* (a restitutionary claim for overpaid care home fees).[2]

[1] *R v Secretary of State for Transport, ex p Sherriff & Sons* (1988) Independent, 12 January. For comment see Bradley [1989] PL 197. The Law Commission in Report 226, paragraph 8.8 recommend that there should be express power to award interest on claims to damages, liquidated sums and restitution; this would not, however, meet the problems of the Sherriffs, which raise wider questions of compensation for unlawful administrative action (or inaction).

[2] [2007] 1 WLR 639.

Need for a genuine primary claim to judicial review

17.98 An attempt to claim a money or restitutionary remedy under CPR Pt 54 will not be possible if the matter raises no issue of public law. This is because, under s 31(4) of the Supreme Court Act 1981 the claim to a money or restitutionary remedy must arise from any matter to which the application for judicial review relates. Accordingly, principles governing the ambit of judicial review, discussed in Chapter 5, will come into play. Taking, by way of example, the facts in *R v Lord Chancellor, ex p Hibbit and Saunders*,[1] a decision by a government department to reject a tender may lack the public law element necessary to render it amenable to judicial review. Similarly, in *R v East Berkshire Health Authority, ex p Walsh*,[2] a claim by a health authority employee was in truth founded on the contract of employment and unsuitable for judicial review. It would follow that in such cases, from the time that the matter was held unsuitable to proceed by way of judicial review,[3] any claim to a money or restitutionary remedy could no longer proceed under Section I of CPR Pt 54, but might be directed to continue as if it had not been started under that Section.[4] However, where there is a public law element then the claim may also remain in the Administrative Court for determination of any issues relating to damages. When this happens then the approach of the court to evidence is no different to that which applies in an ordinary action and Part 54 does not operate to provide "'a passport to avoid the usual procedures which the courts employ to resolve substantial disputes of fact'.[5] The court will order the attendance of witnesses and cross examination where that is necessary.

[1] [1993] COD 326.

[2] [1984] ICR 743; see also the discussion of when an employee of a public authority can seek judicial review in *R v Derbyshire County Council, ex p Noble* [1990] ICR 808 and *McClaren v Home Office* [1990] ICR 824. Contrast *Shoesmith v OFSTED* where the dismissal of a director of children's services and education was held to have a sufficient public law element despite the possibility of a claim for unfair dismissal.

[3] Compare the position where a claim to an injunction was held unsuitable for judicial review: *R v British Broadcasting Corpn, ex p Lavelle* [1983] 1 WLR 23.

[4] See CPR 54.20, discussed at **5.48, 19.145** and **20.32**. In *Anufrijeva v Southwark LBC* [2004] 2 WLR 603, the Court of Appeal suggested at paragraph 81(ii) that while a claim for damages alone could not be brought by way of judicial review, where damages under the Human Rights Act 1998 are sought the proceedings should still be brought in the Administrative Court by an ordinary claim. In *Andrews v Reading Borough Council* [2005] Env LR 2, [2005] ACD 11 Collins J noted the problems that strict adherence to such a procedure could cause including excessive cost and conflict with the jurisdictional limits on bringing low value claims in the High Court (at the time the limit was £25,000 but since April 2014 CPR 7.1 and paragraph 2.1 of PD 7A require that 'proceedings (whether for damages or for a specified sum) may not be started in the High Court unless the value of the claim is more than £100,000'). Collins J explained the procedure advocated in *Anufrijeva* as applying only where

A the claimant still needed to establish maladministration in a judicial review claim. In practice, many claims for damages under the HRA are started in the county court.

5   *The Queen on the Application of Mowleed Mohammed Hussein v The Secretary of State for the Home Department* [2009] EWHC 2506 (Admin). In that case the defendant made an application to cross-examine but it was rejected as being too late. Sales J therefore applied a 'measure of generosity' to the claimant's evidence since he had not been challenged on it [paragraph 10].

17.99 Sometimes the grant of a public law remedy will itself enable the pursuit of consequent private law proceedings. Examples are: *R v Governor of Brockhill Prison ex p Evans (No 2)*[1] where declarations that the claimants had been unlawfully held in prison after their release date enabled proceedings for damages for false imprisonment;[2] *R v IRC ex p Woolwich Equitable BS*[3] where a declaration that Regulations under which tax had been claimed were invalid produced the restitution claims in *Woolwich v IRC*[4] and *McLaughlin v Governor of the Cayman Islands*[5] where a declaration was granted that the dismissal of a public servant was unlawful with the result that he was entitled to recover arrears of salary and the payment of pension contributions on his behalf until either he resigned or his tenure of office lawfully came to an end.

In these cases the earlier public law action is not a necessary pre-condition for bringing the damages claim because the public law fault giving rise to the claim for damages was present whether or not there has been a separate public law remedy to that effect. Now that the rules on procedural exclusivity have been relaxed the decision whether the public law issue should be addressed in judicial review proceedings or in a separate civil claim will depend on the nature of the issues. If the case is one where there are significant factual disputes then a separate civil claim may be appropriate.[6] The opposite applies where the real challenge is to a public law decision.[7]

1   [2001] 2 AC 19.
2   In fact the initial claims had included claims for damages but the result would have been no different if the actions had been sequential.
3   [1990] 1 WLR 1400.
4   [1993] AC 70.
5   [2007] 1 WLR 2839.
6   *R v London Commodity Exchange, (1986), ex p Brearly* [1994] COD 145.
7   See eg *Jones v Powys Local Health Board* [2009] C.C.L. Rep 68 where a claim for reimbursement of nursing fees was in reality a challenge to the decision of a review panel and the claim was struck out as an abuse of process. The opposite result was reached in *Richards v Worcestershire CC* [2016] EWHC 1954 (Ch) where the claimant sought restitution of sums he claimed were wrongly charged for mental health after-care services. His concern was to obtain financial redress rather than other relief and there was no reason why his claim should be subject to judicial review time limits [50].

17.100 The modern approach to exclusivity renders many of the earlier cases on this topic obsolete. It was formerly suggested that where the claim was for damages which were non-discretionary then judicial review was wholly inappropriate.[1] That may be so where no public law remedy is sought (as it was not in that case) but where the claimant has a sound claim for a public law remedy. Then even though the entitlement to damages may be non-discretionary should the public law claim succeed, it will be contrary to the purpose of the 1977 reform to require that separate proceedings be issued in respect of the damages claim. The same is true of claims to restitution and recovery of a sum due following the 2004 reform. It follows from this that so long as the claim for judicial review is genuine and subsisting, and the claim to a money or restitutionary remedy is otherwise within Section 1 of Part 54, then a money or restitutionary claim should not be struck out merely because it might alternatively have been made in proceedings other than judicial review.

[1] *An Bord Bainne Co-operative Ltd (Irish Dairy Board) v Milk Marketing Board* [1984] 2 CMLR 584; see, also, R v Ministry of Agriculture, ex p Live Sheep Traders [1995] COD 297.

17.101 An extreme case was *R v Northavon District Council, ex p Palmer*,[1] where Sedley J was willing to grant leave to bring a claim for a declaration by way of judicial review, even though the point in question had become moot, because of a concern that if a claim to a money remedy were not able to be tacked on to the application for judicial review, the applicant might have no way of securing compensation, given the risk that a writ action might be struck out as an abuse of process. Where there is no element in the claim which calls for judicial review and the claim turns on disputes between the parties as to matters of fact, proceedings for judicial review may be stayed while the matter proceeds otherwise than under Pt 54[2] In particular, if in a criminal case an application for judicial review is academic in the sense that its sole purpose is to prime the pump for a money or restitutionary claim, the preferable course is for the court to decline as a matter of discretion to deal with the application for judicial review and to allow the money or restitutionary claim to proceed as if not begun under s 1 of CPR Pt 54.[3]

[1] (1993) 25 HLR 674. The claim for damages in that case would be unsustainable following *O'Rourke v Camden London Borough Council* [1998] AC 188 which established that there was no private law right to damages arising from a homelessness decision.
[2] Compare, prior to CPR, *R v London Commodity Exchange, ex p Brealey* [1994] COD 145.
[3] Compare, prior to CPR, *R v Blandford Justices, ex p Pamment* [1990] 1 WLR 1490; the court was particularly concerned with the problem of whether an appeal from the divisional court in such a case could be dealt with by the Court of Appeal (Civil Division) rather than the House of Lords, as to which see the discussion in relation to practice and procedure below.

17.102 It may also be argued that in some cases it will be an abuse *not* to bring a private law claim and a judicial review claim together and that a later claim for damages should be struck out. In the cases discussed above it seems not to have mattered when the money claim was raised. The point was not taken that since it could have been included in the judicial review proceedings then it is an abuse of process under the rule in *Henderson v Henderson*[1] to seek to introduce it later as a separate claim. Estoppel and this type of abuse of process is normally said not to be strictly applicable in public law but the point about money claims in judicial review is that they are private law cases included to avoid multiplicity of actions. There ought therefore to be no reason why the rule should not apply in principle because if a party can bring forward their whole claim at once then they should do so. In many cases there will be a factual dispute, or the damages claim will otherwise be unsuitable for determination in judicial review and this will be a reason why the subsequent action is not abusive. But this will not always be the case and *BA v Secretary of State for the Home Department (Bail for Immigration Detainees intervening)*[2] confirms that the approach to abuse of process outlined in *Johnson v Gore Wood & Co (a firm)*[3] applies in this context. In that case a claim for damages for unlawful detention was made after a claim for judicial review had been refused permission. The sequential claims were the result of the way that legal aid contracts were arranged and in the special circumstances of that case this was not held to be an abuse. However, the court also indicated that ordinarily the claims ought to be brought together in view of the overlap between the issues and the fact that the lawfulness of detention was apt for determination by the Administrative Court. If the legal aid position changed then it might well be an abuse not to seek to include a damages claim in the judicial review claim and to bring it later.[4]

1   67 ER 313.
2   [2012] EWCA Civ 944.
3   [2002] 2 AC 1 'a broad, merits-based judgment which takes account of the public and private interests involved and also takes account of all the facts of the case, focusing attention on the crucial question whether, in all the circumstances, a party is misusing or abusing the process of the court by seeking to raise before it the issue which could have been raised before'.
4   [2002] 2 AC 1 at paras 27 and 36.

Claims for costs of legal proceedings

17.103 Where claims to a money remedy arise in relation to the costs of legal proceedings, it may be possible to seek from the court having jurisdiction over those proceedings an order for payment against a party or, exceptionally, a non-party. Circumstances where this may be the case in relation to judicial review proceedings are discussed in CHAPTER 20.

Practice and procedure

17.104 The court has a discretion whether to permit a claim for a money or restitutionary remedy on a claim for judicial review. Practice and procedure (generally) are discussed in later chapters, and reference should be made to them for detailed analysis.[1] Because the judicial review procedure is not well suited to determining factual disputes, it will often be desirable for the court first to determine the public law issues. In *Anufrijeva v Southwark LBC* the Court of Appeal[2] suggested that in claims for damages under the Human Rights Act, permission to apply for judicial review should if appropriate be limited to relief other than damages and consideration given to deferring permission for the damages claim, adjourning or staying that claim until use has been made of alternative dispute resolution,[3] or remitting that claim to a district judge or master.[4] Alternatively, the court may make an award of a money remedy to be assessed, giving case management directions for quantum to be determined by a Master. If the application for judicial review concerns a criminal cause or matter, there may be difficulty in taking a money or restitutionary claim (forming part of the application) on appeal: in *R v Blandford Justices, ex p Pamment*[5] the Court of Appeal (Civil Division) held that it had no jurisdiction to hear an appeal from the Divisional Court in a case where damages were sought for alleged unlawful conduct of magistrates when remanding the applicant. Claims for a money or restitutionary remedy may require further evidence or argument: in *R v Lambeth London Borough Council, ex p Campbell*[6] Laws J granted an order of certiorari, but directed that the application for damages stand adjourned and (subject to further submissions) that if the applicant sought to pursue the damages claim she should issue a summons before the Master of the Crown Office for directions as to the further conduct of the damages claim. In *R v Tower Hamlets London Borough Council, ex p Khalique*,[7] Sedley J made an order for damages to be assessed, and contemplated that discovery would be ordered for that purpose.

[1] See CHAPTERS **19** and **20**.

[2] [2004] 2 WLR 603, CA. This approach may be suitable in many non-HRA claims as well.

[3] Whether by a reference to a mediator or an ombudsman or otherwise.

[4] If it cannot be dismissed summarily on grounds that in any event an award of damages is not required to achieve just satisfaction. Where a claim for HRA damages proceeds, it should generally remain in the Administrative Court even if it is not, or is no longer, brought on an application for judicial review: *Anufrijeva v Southwark LBC* [2004] 2 WLR 603, CA. Conversely, where the damages claim is straightforward and does not involve further investigation of the facts, then the judge dealing with the public law issues should decide it rather than directing a 'laborious assessment' – in *R (Sino) v SSHD* [2016] 4 WLR 80 [12–13].

[5] [1990] 1 WLR 1490.

[6] (1994) 26 HLR 618.

[7] (1994) 26 HLR 517.

Chapter 18

RESTRICTIONS ON THE AVAILABILITY OF JUDICIAL REVIEW

INTRODUCTION

18.1 The court's permission to proceed is required in a claim for judicial review.[1] Permission will not be granted unless the court is satisfied that there is an arguable case that a ground for seeking judicial review exists.[2] If permission is granted then the claim will be determined at a full hearing,[3] otherwise the claim will go no further. Much of this book is taken up with explaining the various grounds upon which judicial review can be sought.

[1] CPR 54.4.
[2] See Civil Procedure 2017, Vol 1 at 54.4.2; *R v Legal Aid Board, ex p Hughes* (1992) 5 Admin L Rep 623; *R v Secretary of State for the Home Department, ex p Rukshanda Begum and Angur Begum* [1990] COD 107; *Sharma v Brown-Antoine* [2007] 1 WLR 780.
[3] Subject to the court's power to decide a claim for judicial review without a hearing, if all the parties agree: CPR 54.18.

18.2 However, even where the claim falls within the ambit of judicial review,[1] a claimant who can show an arguable case that a ground for seeking judicial review exists may nevertheless be refused permission to proceed. Likewise, a claimant who succeeds at the full hearing in establishing that the defendant has acted unlawfully may be refused a remedy. This may be because the court concludes that the claimant lacks standing to bring the claim; or it may be because the court refuses to grant permission, or to grant a remedy, for some other reason. Standing is discussed in the first part of this chapter, and the various other restrictions on the availability of judicial review are considered in the second part of the chapter.[2]

[1] The ambit of judicial review is discussed in CHAPTER 5.
[2] For general discussion in other works, see Lewis *Judicial Remedies in Public Law* (5th edn, 2014) Chapters 11 and 12; Cane *Administrative Law* (5th edn, 2011) Chapters 12 and 13.

STANDING

18.3 CPR Pt 54 does not specifically deal with the question of standing.[1] However, s 31(3) of the Senior Courts Act 1981 (SCA 1981) provides that a court may not grant permission to make an application for judicial review unless the claimant has sufficient interest in the matter to which the claim relates. Section 31(3) predates CPR Pt 54, and reflects the language of the former Order 53 of the Rules of the Supreme Court. Hence a brief explanation of the development of judicial review procedure prior to CPR Pt 54 is of assistance in understanding how the sufficient interest test emerged, and how it should be applied.

[1] For Scots law, see CHAPTER 22 below.

History prior to CPR Pt 54

18.4 Before the important procedural reforms made in 1977,[1] administrative law operated with two quite different sets of remedies. In the first place there were the 'prerogative orders' of certiorari, mandamus and prohibition. These were available only against public bodies. Second, there were the remedies of declaration and injunction, available against both public bodies and other sorts of defendant. The two groups of remedies were governed by different rules as to standing. There were also differences between the three prerogative orders, though the significance of these differences was decreasing: in general, the standing rules for mandamus were thought to be stricter than for the other two prerogative orders. There is a more detailed account of the pre-1977 rules as to standing in the second edition of this book.[2]

[1] For discussion of aspects of the history, see CHAPTER 2 and CHAPTER 3.
[2] At pp 15.2–15.5.

18.5 The 1977 procedural reforms introduced the application for judicial review, governed by a new Order 53 of the Rules of the Supreme Court (RSC Ord 53).[1] Any application for mandamus, prohibition or certiorari was to be made by way of an application for judicial review under RSC Ord 53; and an applicant proceeding under RSC Ord 53 could also seek a declaration, an injunction, or an award of damages. Whichever form of relief was sought, the applicant required the leave of the court in order to proceed. RSC Ord 53(7) provided that the court should not grant leave unless it considered that the applicant had a sufficient interest in the matter to which the application related. This formula was subsequently repeated in SCA 1981, s 31(3).

¹ The new RSC Ord 53 was substituted by the Rules of the Supreme Court (Amendment No 3) 1977, SI 1977/1955. It came into effect on 11 January 1978.

18.6 RSC Ord 53 has subsequently been revoked as a result of the introduction of the Civil Procedure Rules. Claims for judicial review are now governed by CPR Pt 8 and CPR Pt 54, read together with SCA 1981 s 31.¹ The new rules use the terms 'claim', 'claimant' and 'defendant' in place of 'application', 'applicant' and 'respondent', and they refer to 'quashing orders, prohibiting orders and mandatory orders' rather than to orders for certiorari, prohibition and mandamus: for ease of understanding, the remainder of this chapter uses the new terminology even when referring to pre-CPR case law. As already indicated, CPR Pt 54 (and, indeed, CPR Pt 8) do not deal with standing to bring a claim for judicial review, but SCA 1981, s 31(3) remains in force. In other words, the revocation of RSC Ord 53 and the introduction of CPR Pt 54 has not in itself led to any change in the way in which the test for standing is formulated.

¹ The change was effected by the Civil Procedure (Amendment No 4) Rules 2000, SI 2000/2092, which came into force on 2 October 2000. Rule 22 and Sch 1 to the rules inserted CPR Pt 54 into the CPR. Rule 23 revoked RSC Ord 53.

General principles

18.7 *IRC v National Federation of Self Employed and Small Businesses*¹ remains the leading case, notwithstanding that the decision predates SCA 1981 and considers only RSC Ord 53. The federation was a body 'whose name sufficiently describes its nature', in the words of Lord Wilberforce.² It sought judicial review in respect of arrangements made by the Inland Revenue for taxing the earnings of a group of workers in the printing industry referred to collectively as 'Fleet Street casuals'. The complaint was that the Inland Revenue had chosen not to investigate or seek to collect taxes unpaid in certain previous years.³ The claimant contrasted this approach with the Inland Revenue's treatment of the claimant's own members in cases where non-payment was suspected;⁴ it contended that the 'amnesty' (as the claimant described it) given to Fleet Street casuals was unlawful because, inter alia, it was a breach of the duty to act fairly as between different taxpayers.

¹ [1982] AC 617.
² See at 629B.
³ It appeared that there had previously been a practice by Fleet Street casuals of filling in pay slips with fictitious names and addresses so as to hide their true identity from the Inland Revenue. One favourite was 'Mickey Mouse of Sunset Boulevard': see the decision of the Court of Appeal, [1980] 1 QB 407 at 418A–418B, per Lord Denning MR. Hence the case is sometimes referred to as 'the Mickey Mouse case'.
⁴ See at 647E, per Lord Scarman.

18.8 The claimant sought a declaration that the Inland Revenue had acted unlawfully, together with a mandatory order that the Revenue assess and collect income tax from the Fleet Street casuals according to law. The Divisional Court granted permission, but at the full hearing it considered the question of standing as a preliminary point and dismissed the claim for want of standing. The Court of Appeal reversed this decision. The House of Lords in turn reversed the decision of the Court of Appeal and dismissed the claim, on the basis both that the claimants lacked standing and that the claim was without merit.[1]

[1] Lord Wilberforce considered that the claimants had not shown a sufficient interest, and also that the case against the Inland Revenue 'did not leave the ground': 635F–636A. Lord Diplock would have preferred to decide the case on the basis that it had not been shown that the Inland Revenue had acted unlawfully: 637D–637F. Lord Fraser considered that the claim should be dismissed for want of sufficient interest, but that it would also fail on its merits: 645E–645G. Lord Scarman considered that the claimant had failed to show sufficient interest precisely *because* it had failed to show any grounds for believing the Inland Revenue had failed to perform its statutory duty: 654H–655B. Lord Roskill considered that the claim should be dismissed both for want of sufficient interest and for lack of merit: 664A–664C.

18.9 The decision of the House of Lords considered the procedure to be adopted in determining questions of standing, and how the test of sufficient interest is to be applied. Both questions are discussed below: the discussion starts with the decision in the *IRC* case and then considers some of the later authorities.

Procedure

18.10 The House of Lords disapproved of the way in which the question of standing had been approached. In the Divisional Court it had been taken as a preliminary point, before consideration of the merits; in the Court of Appeal argument had again concentrated on the preliminary point; and before the House of Lords both sides had approached the case on the basis that the only issue to be decided at that stage in the proceedings was whether the claimant had a sufficient interest. Their Lordships considered that this was inappropriate. Except in simple cases, the question of standing should be considered in its full factual and legal context, and hence the question of standing had to be considered in conjunction with the merits of the case as a whole.[1]

[1] See at 630C–630E, per Lord Wilberforce; at 636B–636F, per Lord Diplock; at 645A–645F, per Lord Fraser; at 649B–649C, per Lord Scarman; at 656B–656E, per Lord Roskill.

18.11 SCA 1981, s 31(3) states that the requirement of 'a sufficient interest' is a precondition for the grant of *permission* to apply for judicial review. RSC Ord 53, r 3(7) was to the same effect. This might suggest that the question of standing is to be considered at the permission stage only, and that a grant of permission conclusively determines the question of standing in the applicant's favour.[1] The *IRC* case and the subsequent authorities have firmly rejected that approach: indeed, such an approach would be entirely inconsistent with what is said in *IRC* about the difficulty of considering standing in isolation from all of the facts and circumstances of the case. Instead, the question of standing is dealt with in two stages. At the permission stage the court should take a preliminary view as to whether or not the claimant has standing. If its preliminary view is in the claimant's favour then permission to bring the claim should be granted. The purpose of the permission requirement is to identify hopeless cases: permission should be refused for want of standing only in circumstances where the lack of sufficient interest is very clear.[2] Once permission has been granted, the question of standing can then be reconsidered at the full hearing in the light of all the evidence.[3] There are very many examples of cases where the question of standing has been considered at the full hearing only after an extensive discussion of the merits of case.[4]

[1] Compare the discussion in *R v Secretary of State for the Environment, ex p Rose Theatre Trust Co Ltd* [1990] 1 QB 504 at 519F–519G.

[2] As in *R v Dean and Chapter of St Paul's Cathedral and The Church in Wales* [1996] COD 130: priest in Church of England seeking judicial review of decision of Church in Wales to ordain women to the priesthood.

[3] See the IRC case at 645C–645G, per Lord Fraser; at 654A–654D, per Lord Scarman. For a similar two-stage approach, see eg *R v Inspectorate of Pollution, ex p Greenpeace Ltd (No 2)* [1994] 4 All ER 329 at 346G–352A.

[4] See, for instance, *R v Boundary Commission for England, ex p Foot* [1983] QB 600 at 627D–627F; *R v Secretary of State for the Environment, ex p Rose Theatre Trust Co* [1990] 1 QB 504.

Application of the 'sufficient interest' test

18.12 In the *IRC* case, the question of standing was described as being a mixed question of fact and law, to be decided on legal principles, and as being a question of fact and degree.[1] The question of what constitutes a sufficient interest is not, therefore, one that exists in the realm of pure discretion.

[1] See at 631C, per Lord Wilberforce; at 646A, per Lord Fraser; and at 648C–648D, per Lord Scarman and at 659A–659B, per Lord Roskill.

18.13 It was, however, also accepted in the *IRC* case that there are a wide range of factors to be taken into account in answering that question. The case refers to the need to consider such matters as the duties (if any) which the claimant contends the defendant was under; the respects (if any) in which any such duties have been breached; and the proper construction of any relevant statutory material.[1] Inevitably this approach makes it impossible in most cases to consider the question of standing prior to, or in isolation from, the merits; hence the procedural approach explained above. The practical effect is to reduce the importance of the standing requirement as an independent constraint on the availability of judicial review. If after considering the merits, the court forms the view that the defendant has acted unlawfully, then the court may well be reluctant to refuse relief for want of standing.

[1] See at 630D–630E, per Lord Wilberforce; at 636C–636F, per Lord Diplock; at 662E–663B, per Lord Roskill.

18.14 One question addressed in the *IRC* case was whether the new RSC Ord 53 was intended to sweep away any differences between the standing rules governing the different prerogative orders, and also between the prerogative orders and the remedies of declaration and injunction. Different views were expressed on this issue. For instance, Lord Diplock considered RSC Ord 53 was intended to remove any differences in standing rules between the different remedies.[1] By contrast, Lord Wilberforce took the view that it would, in general, be harder to demonstrate a sufficient interest in a case where a mandatory order was sought than in a case where other forms of relief were sought: this was a matter of common sense rather than a technical rule.[2]

[1] See at 638C–638G and 639B–639E.

2   See at 631D–631E.

18.15 The subsequent authorities do not suggest that what constitutes a sufficient interest will vary depending on whether the claimant is seeking a mandatory order, a prohibiting order, a quashing order, a declaration or an injunction. What will always be of importance, however, is to pay close attention to the factual context and to the precise content of the remedy sought. What is it exactly that the claimant is asking the court to order the defendant to do? What is it that the claimant is asking the court to declare? Questions like this require one to focus on the specific circumstances of the individual case, rather than on the more abstract question of whether the remedy sought is (say) a mandatory order or a declaration.

18.16 A good example of this approach is *R v Felixstowe Justices, ex p Leigh*.[1] Justices who tried a case against six defendants in 1985 ('the *Sangster* case') made a restricted reporting order to restrict the publication of details which might identify a particular child. It was clear from the newspaper coverage of the case that different newspapers had received different legal advice about the effect of the order. A journalist working for the *Observer* newspaper wished to write an article about the case and the way in which it had been covered in the press. He asked the deputy clerk to the justices for the names of the chairman and the other justices who heard the *Sangster* case. His request was refused, and he was told that it was the policy of these justices and their clerk to withhold from the press and public the names of the justices who heard particular cases. The journalist, and the *Observer*, sought a mandatory order directing the clerk to reveal to the journalist the names of the justices who tried the *Sangster* case, and a declaration that the policy of withholding justices' names was unlawful.

1   [1987] QB 582: discussed in Cane *Administrative Law* (5th edn, 2011) at section 12.3.2.

18.17 The Divisional Court held that the journalist[1] had standing in relation to the proposed declaration but not in relation to the proposed mandatory order. This was not because there were different standing requirements for mandatory orders and for declarations: Watkins LJ (with whom the other two judges agreed)[2] was inclined to think that there were not, but did not consider it necessary to decide the question. Rather what was important was the factual context in relation to both remedies. The journalist had not been present in court during the *Sangster* trial. His aim was to write an article about the way in which the case had been covered by the press, not about the case itself. The identity of the justices who heard the case was not essential or even material for that purpose. Hence the journalist did not have sufficient interest to obtain an order that their names be disclosed. On the other hand, the general policy of non-disclosure raised issues of public importance; the applicant had sufficient interest to challenge that policy and hence was entitled to the declaration sought.

1   The court clearly did not consider that there was any difference in terms of standing between the journalist and the newspaper. Indeed, the discussion of standing appears to proceed as if the journalist was the only applicant.
2   See at 595F–598E for the discussion of standing.

18.18 A subsequent example of the need to pay close attention to the factual context of the individual case in determining issues of standing is *R (Bulger) v Secretary of State for Home Department*.[1] When taking a decision on the appropriate tariff of a juvenile detained for murder, the Lord Chief Justice invited written representations from members of the victim's family. They were held to have no standing to bring judicial review proceedings challenging the decision as to what should be the appropriate tariff. Lord Justice Rose said that the threshold for standing in judicial review had generally been set at a low level because of the importance in public law that someone should be able to call decision-makers to account, lest the rule of law break down and private rights be denied by public bodies. In criminal proceedings, however, the Crown and the defendant were both able to challenge those judicial decisions which were susceptible to judicial review and there was no need for a third party to be able to do so. A proper discharge of judicial functions in relation to sentencing required the judge to take into account the impact of the offence and the sentence on the public generally, and on individuals including the victim, the defendant, and their respective families, and this was properly channelled through the Crown and the defendant. The family had not been invited to indicate views on the appropriate tariff. At best, therefore, they had only limited standing to enable them to challenge any failure to have regard to the impact of the offence on them personally.

[1] [2001] 3 All ER 449.

Different bases upon which claimant may assert that he has standing

18.19 A useful general distinction is between cases where the claimant relies on his own personal interests as constituting a sufficient interest to bring a claim, and cases where the claimant alleges that he acts on behalf of some particular section of society or on behalf of the public interest. The first situation may be described as a case of 'personal standing', and the second as 'representative standing'. This terminology is useful and helpful, although it has not yet been deployed in the case law.[1]

[1] It has been adopted from the writing of Peter Cane. See, in particular, 'Standing up for the Public' [1995] PL 276; Cane *Administrative Law* (5th edn, 2011) at section 12.3.2–12.3.3.

18.20 Cases of personal standing include cases where the decision is taken specifically in relation to the claimant, and is based on facts personal to the claimant. They also include cases where the decision affects the financial interests of the claimant. A good example is the decision taken by a medical referee under the Police Pensions Regulations 1987 as to whether an officer is permanently disabled by an injury received in the execution of duty, and therefore entitled to an injury award.[1] Clearly, both the individual officer and his police authority (upon which the financial burden of paying the award would fall) would have standing to challenge the referee's decision.

[1] As in, eg *R (Stunt) v Mallett* [2001] ICR 989.

18.21 Cases of representative standing fall in turn into two main types. There are cases of *associational* standing, where the claimant is a body acting on behalf of the interests of its own members. There are also cases of *public* *interest* standing, where the claimant alleges that it acts on behalf of the public or a sector of the public. This distinction is a useful one so long as it is not applied over-rigidly: there are, of course, borderline cases.

Personal standing

18.22 A wide range of different types of personal interest have been held to constitute sufficient interest for the purposes of standing. The claimant may have a direct financial or legal interest; his financial position may be indirectly affected: he may be factually affected in some other way; or his interest may derive from a family relationship. It is, of course, impossible to give an exhaustive list of the circumstances that are capable of giving rise to a sufficient interest. The approach taken here is to illustrate the range of potentially relevant circumstances, by considering four categories of case:

(1)   planning cases;
(2)   education cases;
(3)   cases about public sector contracts; and
(4)   tax cases.

18.23 Most judicial review cases relating to planning are about decisions to grant planning permission.[1] Note that judicial reviews or statutory challenges involving planning permission (or any of the other matters listed in CPR 54.21(2)(a)) are now dealt with in the Planning Court; this is a specialist list in relation to judicial reviews and statutory challenges in planning-related matters, established under CPR 54.21 and 54.22. The following are examples of cases where a claimant has had standing to challenge a decision to grant planning permission.

---

[1]   Judicial review cases about refusal of planning permission are rare, because of the existence of an alternative remedy by way of appeal.

18.24 A local authority granted planning permission for a supermarket. At the same meeting it rejected six other applications for the development of supermarkets on other sites. One of the unsuccessful applicants sought judicial review of the decision to grant planning permission. The claim failed on the merits, but the court accepted (without specific discussion) that the claimant had standing.[1]

---

[1]   *R v St Edmundsbury BC, ex p Investors in Industry Commercial Properties Ltd* [1985] 1 WLR 1168.

18.25 Outline planning permission was granted for a food store and associated development on a particular site. The claimant had an option to purchase certain other land, and wished to obtain planning permission for retail development on that land, but had not yet made an application. The court held that the claimant had standing to challenge the grant of planning permission, on the basis that it could well prejudice the chances of success of the claimant's own proposed planning application.[1]

---

[1]   *R v Canterbury City Council and Robert Brett & Sons Ltd, ex p Springimage Ltd* (1993) 68 P & CR 171, especially at 173–176.

18.26 Judicial review cases about education can cover a wide range of subject matter, including decisions about the admission or exclusion of individual pupils, or the closure and reorganisation of schools. Where decisions relate to specific individual pupils, then in general those individuals will have standing to challenge them by way of judicial review.[1] Where decisions relate to an entire school then there is likely to be a wider range of persons having a sufficient interest to bring a judicial review claim. For instance, decisions to reorganise schools may be challenged by parents of children at the schools in question, or by governors of the schools.[2]

[1] There may, of course, be other reasons why judicial review is not available: in particular, there may be alternative remedies by way of statutory appeal.

[2] See *R v Kirklees Metropolitan Borough Council, ex p Molloy* (1987) 86 LGR 115; *R v Secretary of State for Education and Science and another, ex p Threapleton* [1988] COD 102. Also see *R (WB) v Leeds School Organisation Committee* [2002] EWHC 1927 (Admin) where parents and children had standing in relation to decisions of the Committee.

18.27 As far as the award of public sector contracts is concerned, there was at one point a trend in the case law towards a more liberal approach to standing. In *R v Hereford Corporation, ex p Harrower*,[1] it was held that contractors did not have standing to seek a mandatory order to enforce local authority standing orders relating the grant of contracts; but in a later case, companies seeking to enter into contracts with a local authority were permitted to bring a claim in order to ensure that the proposed contractual terms did not breach statutory requirements.[2]

[1] [1970] 1 WLR 1424.

[2] See *R v Islington Borough Council, ex p Building Employers Confederation* [1989] COD 432.

18.28 Note, however, that the courts have subsequently taken a more restrictive approach in cases under the procurement legislation. A recent example is *Wylde v Waverley Borough Council* [2017] EWHC 466 (Admin). This was a challenge to a decision to amend a redevelopment agreement, based on alleged failure to comply with the requirements of the 2006 Public Contracts Regulations. The court held that the claimants lacked standing. It was not sufficient that they were council taxpayers, members of relevant local authorities, or persons concerned with the impact of the development. The question of standing had to be considered in the specific legislative context of the procurement regime. The approach to standing in that context was more restrictive than for judicial review generally, and the right approach was to ask whether the claimants could establish that compliance with the procurement regime might have led to a different outcome with a direct impact upon them: see the decision of the Court of Appeal in *R (ota Chandler) v Secretary of State* [2009] EWCA Civ 1011.

18.29 In tax cases it has generally been held that one taxpayer does not have standing to challenge the assessment of another taxpayer (the *IRC* case is itself an example of this approach). However, in *R v Attorney General, ex p ICI plc*,[1] the claimant was permitted to challenge the way in which another company's profits had been valued. The claimant contended that the company was one of its competitors and that the proposed valuation gave it a commercial advantage over the claimant itself.

¹ [1987] 1 CMLR 72.

Representative standing

18.30 There are many examples of cases where organisations have been permitted to bring claims on behalf of their members. This is the situation that was described above as involving issues of 'associational standing'. For instance, a community association formed to represent and safeguard the interests of Covent Garden residents had standing to challenge a grant of planning permission for a change to office use of certain premises in the Covent Garden area;¹ the Royal College of Nursing had standing to challenge a circular giving advice to nurses in relation to their participation in abortions;² and trade unions have been given standing to challenge decisions affecting their members.³ A company formed by local residents opposed to an application for planning permission had standing to challenge the decision to grant permission, despite the fact that the company was not formed until after that decision had been taken.⁴

¹ *Covent Garden Community Association Limited v Greater London Council* [1981] JPL 183.
² *Royal College of Nursing of the United Kingdom v Department of Health and Social Security* [1981] AC 800.
³ See, eg *R v Chief Adjudication Officer, ex p Bland* (1985) Times, 6 February.
⁴ See *R (Residents against Waste Site Ltd) v Lancashire County Council* [2007] EWHC 2558 (Admin), at paragraphs 14–22.

18.31 There have also been a number of cases in recent years in which individuals or organisations have claimed standing on the basis that they are acting in the public interest, rather than on the interest of their own members. Typically, the claimants in these cases are campaigning groups or pressure groups active in areas such as environmental policy or overseas aid, as distinct from groups (for example, residents' associations, trade unions or professional bodies) that exist primarily to defend the interests of their own members.

18.32 At one point it appeared that the courts were adopting a restrictive approach on the issue of public interest standing. In *R v Secretary of State for the Environment, ex p Rose Theatre Trust Co*,¹ Schiemann J held that the claimant (which had been set up with the object of preserving the remains of the Rose Theatre and making them accessible to the public) did not have sufficient interest to challenge by way of judicial review the Secretary of State's decision not to list the remains in the Schedule of Monuments made under the Ancient Monuments and Archaeological Areas Act 1979. The decision recognises that the effect may be that there is nobody at all with standing to challenge the decision. In a more recent case, however, the court has been reluctant to accept such an outcome. The Court of Appeal in Northern Ireland held that a mother had standing to seek judicial review of a decision to retain in the armed forces two soldiers despite conviction for the murder of her son. Carswell LCJ said that he was not attracted to the idea that there is a category of unchallengeable decisions in the public sector.²

¹ [1990] 1 QB 504.

² *Re McBride's Application for judicial review* [2003] NICA 23 at paragraph 27. Note, however, paragraph 49 of the judgment of McCollum LJ, holding that the mother's interest was sufficiently met by a declaration.

18.33 Most of the authorities have taken a more expansive approach than the *Rose Theatre* case to the question of representative standing for groups or organisations acting in the public interest. Some examples are set out below.

(1)   *R v Inspector of Pollution, ex p Greenpeace Ltd (No 2)*¹ — Otton J held that Greenpeace had standing to challenge the decision of the respondents (who were the regulatory authorities for the purposes of the Radioactive Substances Act 1960) to allow British Nuclear Fuels Limited (BNFL) to discharge radioactive waste in testing a new reprocessing plan at Sellafield. The decision is based both on public interest standing and on associational standing: Greenpeace was permitted to bring the claim both because of its general interest in environmental issues and because it had a number of members in the Sellafield area. Otton J considered that if Greenpeace were not permitted to bring the challenge then any challenge would need to be brought instead by an individual who was a near neighbour or employee of BNFL. Such a challenge might well be less well-informed and more time consuming to resolve.

(2)   *R v Secretary of State for Foreign Affairs, ex p World Development Movement*² — the Secretary of State approved a proposal for aid and trade provision to assist in funding the Pergau Dam scheme, which involved the construction of a dam and hydro-electric power station in Malaysia. The claimant was a pressure group that campaigned to increase the amount and quality of British overseas aid. It was granted standing to apply for a declaration that the decision was unlawful. Rose LJ, who gave the main judgment, identified four main factors in favour of this outcome. He referred to the importance of vindicating the rule of law, the likely absence of any responsible challenger, the nature of the alleged breach of duty by the Secretary of State, and the prominent role of the claimant in relation to aid issues.

(3)   *R v Secretary of State for Employment, ex p Equal Opportunities Commission*³ — the claimant (the EOC) brought judicial review proceedings raising the question whether certain provisions of UK statute law were contrary to EU law as involving impermissible indirect sex discrimination. By a majority of four to one (Lord Jauncey dissenting) the House of Lords considered that the EOC had standing on the basis of its statutory duty under s 53(1) of the Sex Discrimination Act 1975 to work towards the elimination of sex discrimination. There is a difference between this case and the two previous cases, in that the EOC is a statutory body rather than a campaigning group.

(4)   *R (Quintavalle) v HFEA*⁴ — judicial proceedings were brought on behalf of a group concerned with ethical issues in relation to embryology. The group had standing to challenge the defendant's decision to licence IVF treatment that included pre-implantation testing to ascertain whether the embryo had a particular genetic condition.

(5)   *R (Plantagenet Alliance Ltd) v Secretary of State for Justice*[5] — a campaigning organisation representing a group of Richard III's collateral descendants had standing to challenge decisions about the deceased king's re-interment, both on conventional principles and in the unusual circumstances of the case, which involved the discovery of the proven remains of a former monarch.

[1]   [1994] 4 All ER 329.
[2]   [1995] 1 All ER 611.
[3]   [1995] AC 1.
[4]   [2004] QB 168; [2005] UKHL 28, [2005] AC 561.
[5]   [2013] EWHC B13 (Admin).

18.34 It is suggested that at present the courts are likely to grant standing to groups that bring judicial review claims acting in the public interest, provided that:

(1)   the group in question is regarded as reputable and responsible and as having significant expertise in the area with which the claim is concerned;
(2)   the issue raised is accepted as being of real importance; and
(3)   there is no potential claimant that is better placed to bring the matter to court.

On the other hand, if a decision relates specifically to the position of a particular individual then the courts may well consider that the only person with standing to bring a claim for judicial review is the individual himself.

18.35 Where the claimant is an individual purporting to act in the public interest, the courts may take a more cautious approach. Thus, in *R (Feakins) v Secretary of State for Environment Food and Rural Affairs*,[1] the court considered that, where an individual claimed to be acting in the public interest, it was relevant to take account of whether that was his true reason for acting, or whether he had some ulterior motive. On the particular facts of that case, the court accepted that the claimant had standing. In *R (Edwards) v Environment Agency* [2004] 3 All ER 21 an individual sought judicial review of the decision by the Environment Agency to grant a permit to a company under the Pollution Prevention and Control (England and Wales) Regulations 2000,[2] enabling the company to carry out certain operations at its cement plant near Rugby town centre. The claimant asserted that he had standing as a local resident affected by the operation of the company's works. There had been considerable opposition to the company's plans from a range of local groups, and it was suggested that the claimant was, in effect, acting on behalf of those groups, and that he had been put forward as claimant in order to secure funding for the challenge from the Legal Services Commission. The court held that the claimant had standing as an inhabitant of Rugby affected by the decision. The fact that the claimant had not personally taken part in the consultation exercise that preceded the grant of the permit did not deprive him of standing. There was evidence that the Legal Services Commission had been aware of all the relevant facts before deciding to fund the claim; the court held that it must be taken that the Commission had considered whether the claim involved an abuse of the system for public funding of litigation.

[1]   [2004] 1 WLR 1761, CA.

18.36 Some cases of representative standing have given rise to difficulty because the claimant is an unincorporated association. These difficulties are discussed below (although strictly speaking they are not difficulties about standing at all).¹

¹   See **18.42**.

Standing under the Human Rights Act 1998

18.37 There is a special test for standing in judicial review claims that are based on the Human Rights Act 1998 (HRA 1998). As explained in Chapter 4, under s 6(1) of the Act, public authorities are under a duty not to act in a way which is incompatible with a Convention right. A person who claims that a public authority has acted or proposes to act in a way which is made unlawful by s 6(1) may either bring proceedings against the authority under the Act in the appropriate court or tribunal, or rely on the Convention right or rights concerned in any legal proceedings, but only if he or she is, or would be, a victim of the unlawful act.¹ If the proceedings are brought on an application for judicial review, the applicant is to be taken to have a sufficient interest in relation to the unlawful act only if he or she is, or would be, a victim of that act.² The effect of this is that only a 'victim' has standing to complain in judicial review proceedings that a public authority has breached s 6(1) of the HRA 1998.

¹   HRA 1998, s 7(1).
²   HRA 1998, s 7(3).

18.38 HRA 1998, s 7(7) explains what is meant by 'victim' in the context. A person is a victim of an unlawful act only if he or she would be a victim for the purposes of art 34 of the European Convention on Human Rights if proceedings were brought in the European Court of Human Rights in respect of that Act. In other words, the test as to whether a person is a victim is the same test as applied by the Strasbourg Court.¹ The general approach taken by the Strasbourg Court is that a victim of a violation is a person directly affected by the impugned measure.²

¹   See *R (Hooper) v Secretary of State for Work and Pensions* [2005] 1 WLR 1681 at 1697C–F (paragraphs 54–56).
²   See, eg *Buckley v United Kingdom* (1996) 23 EHRR 101 at paragraphs 56–59.

18.39 In the *Hooper* case, the claimants were widowers who were refused benefits under the Social Security Contributions and Benefits Act 1992 which would at the relevant time and in equivalent circumstances have been available to widows. They sought judicial review of the refusal, contending that it was a breach of their Convention rights. The conclusions reached by the House of Lords on the merits of the claims made it strictly unnecessary to decide whether the claimants were victims for the purposes of bringing an action under s 7(1)(a).¹ However, Lord Hoffmann expressed the view that an individual would be a 'victim' in relation to survivors' benefits if he had done something which identified him as having wished to make a claim. It was not necessary for that intention to have been expressed in writing. Claims made before 2 October 2000 (when the Human Rights Act 1998 came into force) did not count; but a post-2 October 2000 reaffirmation of an earlier claim (expressly or by implication) would suffice.[2]

[1] See *R (Hooper) v Secretary of State for Work and Pensions* [2005] 1 WLR 1681 at 1697B (paragraph 53).
[2] See *R (Hooper) v Secretary of State for Work and Pensions* [2005] 1 WLR 1681 at 1697E–1698D, paragraphs 56–59. The other members of the House of Lords expressed general agreement with Lord Hoffmann's speech but did not specifically discuss the 'victim' test.

18.40 The effect of s 7(3) is that pressure groups or campaigning organisations acting in the public interest will not be entitled to bring a claim for judicial review in their own name alleging a breach of the duty under s 6(1) of the Act. If such a breach of duty is to be asserted, then the claim must be brought by a victim.[1] It should be noted that the restriction in s 7(3) of the Human Rights Act 1998 applies only in so far as a claim asserts breach of s 6(1). A claimant with standing at common law can rely on other aspects of the Human Rights Act 1998 whether or not the 'victim' test is satisfied.[2]

[1] Others — including pressure or campaigning groups — may wish to fund such a victim. They will need to ensure that there is no abuse of process (see **18.61** et seq), and to consider consequences as to costs (see **20.126**).
[2] See note 1, **4.63**.

18.41 Note, however, that in *Lancashire CC v Taylor*[1] the claimant sought possession of a farm from the defendant tenant, the termination of the tenancy being governed by the Agricultural Holdings Act 1986. The defendant asserted that the 1986 Act was incompatible with the Convention, and sought a declaration of incompatibility under HRA 1998, s 4. The court held that he did not have standing to seek such a declaration: the question of standing was governed by HRA 1998, s 7, and the defendant was not a 'victim' as he was not personally affected by any of the features of the 1986 Act which he alleged were contrary to the Convention.

[1] [2005] 1 WLR 2668.

Standing and capacity to bring a claim

18.42 Questions of standing and of capacity to claim need to be distinguished. The capacity of unincorporated associations to bring claims for judicial review has been doubted. This is nothing to do with the question of whether the association has sufficient interest in the subject matter of the claim. The difficulty is more fundamental: unincorporated associations have no legal personality and so the question is whether they can ever bring claims for judicial review, whatever the subject matter.

18.43 Auld J in *R v Darlington Borough Council, ex p Association of Darlington Tax Owners and Darlington Owner Drivers Association*[1] held that an unincorporated association could not generally bring proceedings for judicial review in its own name. Other authorities have taken a different view.[2] The Law Commission has proposed that unincorporated associations should be permitted to bring proceedings for judicial review in their own name.[3]

1   [1994] COD 424.
2   See *R v London Borough of Tower Hamlets, ex p Tower Hamlets Combined Traders Association* [1994] COD 325; *R v Traffic Commissioner for North Western Traffic Area, ex p Brake* [1996] COD 248; *R v Leeds City Council, ex p Allwoody* [1995] New Property Cases 149.
3   See Administrative Law: Judicial Review and Statutory Appeals Law Com no 226, (1994) HC 669.

18.44 There may be practical difficulties in relation to costs: for instance, an unincorporated association may have no assets against which a costs order can be enforced. It is suggested that these can be dealt with by imposing conditions on the grant of permission, for instance, by requiring security for costs to be provided, or by requiring an individual member of the association to be joined as a party so that if necessary a costs order can be made against him.[1]

1   In *R v Minister of Agriculture Fisheries and Foods, ex p British Pig Industry Support Group* [2000] EULR 724 at paragraph 108, Richards J said, 'I do not think that there is any over-riding requirement for [a claimant] for judicial review to have legal personality, but it is important in such a case that adequate provision should be made for the protection of the defendant in costs'.

OTHER RESTRICTIONS ON REMEDIES

18.45 Judicial review remedies are discretionary.[1] There are several bases upon which the court in the exercise of its discretion may refuse to grant a remedy — and in an appropriate case, for that reason refuse permission to bring a claim. The various discretionary bars overlap to some extent. In addition, proposed legislation currently before Parliament (the Criminal Justice and Courts Bill) would introduce new restrictions on the circumstances in which the court can grant permission, or remedies, in judicial review cases. This chapter considers the following bars to relief:

(1)   delay by the claimant;
(2)   other conduct of the claimant;
(3)   the existence of an alternative remedy;
(4)   the absence of any practical purpose in granting a remedy; and
(5)   the effect of a remedy on the defendant or on third parties.
(6)   the additional restrictions imposed by the Criminal Justice and Courts Act 2015.

1   For Scots law, see **22.82** et seq.

18.46 As was the case in relation to standing, these issues may be considered at the permission stage (and may be a basis for refusing permission). Alternatively, they may be considered at the substantive hearing as a basis for refusing to grant the claimant a particular remedy, or any remedy at all.

18.47 There are a number of other possible bases upon which the court may be required to hold that a claim may not be brought by way of judicial review. For instance, there may be a specific statutory exclusion of judicial review, by way of an ouster clause.[1] Other matters which will cause a claim to be outside the ambit of judicial review are discussed elsewhere in this book.[2]

[1]   See CHAPTER 6.
[2]   See, in particular, CHAPTER 5.

Delay by the claimant

18.48 The relevant provisions are in CPR Pt 54 and in s 31 (6) of the Senior Courts Act 1981. These impose a tight time limit for bringing judicial review claims, and deal with the consequences of delay by the claimant.

18.49 CPR 54.5 provides that the claim form must be filed promptly, and in any event not later than three months after the grounds to make the claim first arose.[1] This time limit may not be extended by agreement between the parties.[2] It does not apply when any other enactment specifies a shorter time limit for making the claim for judicial review.[3] However, the court does have power to extend time for bringing a claim under CPR 3.1(2)(a). Note that there is no specific provision about extension of time in CPR Pt 54 itself.

[1]   As to the precise calculation of the three-month time limit, in *Crichton v Wellinborough Borough Council* [2002] EWHC 2988 (Admin), [2004] Env LR 11 Gibbs J was inclined to the view that time runs so as to include the date on which the decision challenged was taken. For detailed argument to the contrary, see Taylor [2005] JR 249.
[2]   CPR 54.5(2).
[3]   CPR 54.5(3).

18.50 Section 31(6) of the 1981 Act provides:

> 'Where the High Court considers that there has been undue delay in making an application for judicial review, the court may refuse to grant (a) leave for the making of an application, or (b) any relief sought on the application, if it considers that the granting of the relief sought would be likely to cause substantial hardship to, or substantially prejudice the rights of, any person or would be detrimental to good administration'.

18.51 The first and most important practical point for an adviser arising from these provisions is that a claim may be out of time because it was not made promptly, even if it was made within the three-month period. Thus, in *Re Friends of the Earth Ltd*[1] a challenge to the grant of planning permission for the Sizewell power station was held not to have been made promptly even though it was made (by one day) within the three-month period. It is inadvisable to wait until the end of the three-month period to bring a claim: in general, the safest course is to lodge the claim as soon as possible.[2] The requirement to act promptly is particularly important in cases where third parties are likely to have committed themselves to expenditure on the basis of the decision under challenge.[3] In *R (Burkett) v Hammersmith LBC*[4] (discussed further below) two members of the House of Lords expressed doubt as to whether the requirement to act 'promptly' was sufficiently certain to comply with European Community law and the European Convention.[5] However, subsequent cases have emphasised that notwithstanding these remarks the obligation to act promptly remains a feature of English law.[6]

[1]   [1988] JPL 93.
[2]   See, also, *R v Cotswold District Council, ex p Barrington Parish Council* (1997) 75 P & CR 515 at 523.

3 See, eg *R v Independent Television Commission, ex p TV NI Ltd* (1991) Times, 30 December. See, also, *R v Rochdale MBC, ex p B* [2000] Ed CR 117, 120 (allocation of places at secondary school for children; essential, absent exceptional circumstances, for matter to be determined before term started).

4 [2002] 1 WLR 1593.

5 See at [2002] 1 WLR 1611A–1611D (Lord Steyn) and at [2002] 1 WLR 1612C–1614E (Lord Hope).

6 See, eg *R (Young) v Oxford City Council* [2002] 3 PL 86 at paragraph 38. See, also. Taylor [2005] Judicial Review 249, suggesting that the comments made in *Burkett* did not address the decision of the European Court of Human Rights in *Lamm v United Kingdom* (Application No 41671/98: 5 July 2001), a case which supports the compatibility with art 6 of a requirement for an application to be made promptly.

18.52 A second practical point is that the need to comply with the pre-action protocol[1] does not affect the obligation to comply with the time limit in CPR 54.5. If time is short, it is suggested that the better course is to file the claim form within the three-month time limit, and to explain in the form itself why it has not been possible to comply fully with the pre-action protocol. In these circumstances the claimant should still, if all possible, write a letter before claim in accordance with the protocol, but it may not be possible to give the defendant 14 days to reply before issuing proceedings: the letter itself should explain this. One possible approach is to state in the letter that although the claimant will need to lodge the claim shortly in order to comply with time limits, if the defendant answers the pre-action letter within 14 days then the claimant will take account of that answer in deciding whether to continue with the claim. It goes without saying that a much better course is to ensure from the outset, where possible, that there is time both to comply with the protocol and to lodge the claim well within the three-month period.

1 See CHAPTER 19.

18.53 Although the court has power to extend time and hence to grant permission even though the claim has been filed late, it likely to require a good explanation for the delay and it may also consider whether an extension of time will not cause hardship or prejudice or be detrimental to good administration. However, the fact that the claim is of substantial public importance may in itself be a factor in favour of extending time.[1]

1 See, eg *R v Secretary of State for Foreign and Commonwealth Affairs, ex p World Development Movement* [1995] 1 WLR 386 at 402.

18.54 There is, however, an issue as to whether these requirements are compatible with the obligation to provide an effective remedy for the enforcement of rights based on EU law. There are potentially two difficulties: the uncertainty inherent in the requirement to act 'promptly'; and the fact that the three month time limit runs from the date when the grounds for the claim first arose, not from the date when the claimant knew or ought to have known of those grounds.

18.55 A similar issue has arisen in cases about UK regulations implementing an EU Procurement Directive, and including a time limit in similar terms to the judicial review time limit. In *Uniplex (UK) Ltd v NHS Business Services Authority*[1] the Court of Justice of the European Union held that a requirement for the claimant to act 'promptly' was incompatible with the relevant Directive, as it failed to comply with the requirement of legal certainty. The court held that domestic legislation giving effect to a Directive should be interpreted by the domestic court in the light of the wording and purpose of the Directive. That interpretation should if possible ensure that any limitation period ran from the date when the claimant knew or ought to have known of the breach. If such an interpretation was not possible, then any discretion available to the national court should be exercised so as to reach an equivalent result, or else the national time limit provisions should be disregarded. Subsequently in *Sita UK Ltd v Greater Manchester Waste Disposal Authority*[2] the Court of Appeal held that the proper approach in the light of *Uniplex* was for the UK court to exercise its discretion in relation to time limits, so as to provide for a three month period starting on the date when the claimant knew or ought to have known of the alleged breach of EU law. *Uniplex* and *SITA* are both procurement cases, but a similar approach is likely to be applicable in other cases where judicial review proceedings are brought in order to enforce rights derived from EU law.

[1]   [2010] 2 CMLR 1255.
[2]   [2011] EWCA Civ 156.

18.56 The requirement to act promptly and in any event within three months remains applicable in cases not involving EU law: see *R (Berky) v Newport City Council*.[1]

[1]   [2012] Env LR 35.

18.57 The House of Lords considered the relationship between s 31(6) of the Senior Courts Act 1981 and RSC Ord 53, r 4 in *Caswell v Dairy Produce Quota Tribunal for England and Wales*[1] and again in *R v Criminal Injuries Board, ex p A*.[2] It is suggested that in cases not involving EU law the following propositions, derived from these two authorities, remain good law. They are not displaced either by the substitution of CPR Pt 54 for RSC Ord 53, or by the subsequent decision of the House of Lords in *R (Burkett) v Hammersmith and Fulham London Borough Council*.[3]

(1)   The reference to 'an application for judicial review' in s 31(6) is a reference to the application for permission.[4]

(2)   If a claim is not made promptly or within three months then there will be undue delay for the purposes of s 31(6).[5]

(3)   The court has power to grant permission to apply despite the fact that the application is late. It does this by extending the time for bringing the application.[6] The claimant must show good reason for extending time. Even if the claimant does so, the court may refuse permission on the grounds of hardship, prejudice and detriment to good administration.[7]

(4)   At the substantive hearing, the question whether permission ought to have been refused on grounds of delay ought not to be re-opened.[8] However, what the court can do at the substantive hearing is to refuse to grant relief because of the matters referred to in s 31(6).[9]

[1]   [1990] 2 AC 738.
[2]   [1999] 2 AC 330.
[3]   [2002] 1 WLR 1593, discussed further below.
[4]   See per Lord Goff at 1326B.
[5]   *Caswell v Dairy Produce Quota Tribunal for England and Wales* [1990] 2 AC 738 at 746H–747B.

⁶ At 1326C.

⁷ *R v Criminal Injuries Board, ex p A* [1999] 2 AC 330 at 341B–C.

⁸ *Ex p A*, above, at 341D–E. Hence the defendant's acknowledgment of service ought to deal fully with any submission that permission ought to be refused on grounds of delay: see **19.44**.

⁹ *Ex p A*, above, at 341E–F. The Court of Appeal has suggested that the defendant ought only to be able to raise the issue of delay at the substantive hearing, as a basis for refusing relief, in limited circumstances: see *R (Lichfield Securities Ltd) v Lichfield District Council* [2001] EWCA Civ 304. For a recent case where permission was granted despite a failure to act promply, but relief was refused partly on the basis of section 31(6), see *R (Corus UK Ltd (t/a Orb Electrical Steels)) v Newport City Council* [2010] EWHC 1279 (Admin), at paragraphs 104–130.

18.58 Hence there may be cases where the court is persuaded to extend time and grant permission, but where the issues of hardship, prejudice and detriment to good administration are nevertheless considered at the substantive hearing and where consideration of those issues leads the court to deny a remedy. *Caswell* itself was such a case. The claimant sought to quash a decision fixing his dairy quota. The court considered that if the claim succeeded then it might prompt a considerable number of similar claims. This could lead to the allocation quota being re-opened going back over a period of some years. The prejudice to good administration that this would cause outweighed the financial effect of the decision on the claimant.

18.59 In applying the three-month rule, it is, of course, important to ascertain when time will start to run against the claimant. In *Burkett* the House of Lords considered that where a decision-maker indicates that he is provisionally minded to make a particular decision, subject to hearing further representations, then time should not start to run until a final decision is made.¹ Applying this general approach the court held that time for challenging a decision to grant planning permission ran from the date when permission was granted, not from the date when a resolution was passed in favour of granting planning permission.

¹ See at [2002] 1 WLR 1607F–1607H.

18.60 In two classes of case, CPR 54.5 prescribes a shorter time limit. First, where the application relates to a decision of the Secretary of State or local planning authority under the planning acts (as defined in CPR 54.5(Λ1)) then the claim form must be filed not later than six weeks after the grounds to make the claim first arose: CPR 54.5(5). Secondly, where the application relates to a decision governed by the Public Contracts Regulations 2015, the claim form must be filed within 30 days beginning with the date when the claimant first knew or ought to have known that grounds of challenge had arisen: CPR 54.5(6).¹ Note also that CPR 54.7A makes special provision where an application is made, following refusal by the Upper Tribunal of permission to appeal against a decision of the First-tier Tribunal, for judicial review: of the decision of the Upper Tribunal refusing permission to appeal; or in relation to the decision of the First-tier Tribunal which was the subject of the application for permission to appeal. In such a case, the claim form (with the various supporting documents required by CPR 54.7A(4)) must be filed no later than 16 days after the date on which notice of the Upper Tribunal's decision was sent to the applicant. There are limitations on the circumstances in which permission to proceed will be given in these cases: see CPR 54.7A(7), discussed further below.

1   This result is achieved by cross-referring to reg 92(2) of the 2015 Regulations. For an explanation of the practical effect see the commentary in Civil Procedure 2017 Volume 1 at 54.5.1.

Abuse of process and other conduct of the claimant

18.61 Delay by the claimant is the most significant respect in which the claimant's conduct may lead the court to deny a remedy. Other examples of conduct which may lead to the refusal of relief can generally be seen to involve some abuse of process.

18.62 *Non-disclosure*: The obligation to give full and frank disclosure generally arises where a court makes an order without notice to the other party. The extent to which it applies to judicial review following the introduction of CPR Pt 54 is discussed in Chapter 19. Non-compliance gives rise to a discretion to refuse relief.[1]

1   It has been said that an inadvertent mis-statement of fact will ground refusal of relief: see *R v North East Thames Regional Health Authority, ex p De Groot* [1988] COD 25. This ground of refusing relief has not often arisen in judicial review. Principles developed in the analogous field of emergency injunctions are discussed in *Civil Procedure 2014* Vol 1 at paragraph 25.3.5.

18.63 *Turpitude or lack of merit*: In an exceptional case turpitude or lack of merit in the claimant may lead to discretionary refusal of relief. An example is *Dorot Properties v Brent London Borough Council*[1] (ratepayer challenged a refusal to refund rates: remedy refused because he had previously withheld payment of rates without justification).

1   [1990] RA 137.

18.64 *Abusive motive*: Relief may be refused where there is an ulterior or improper motive for seeking judicial review.[1]

1   See, eg *R v Customs and Excise Commissioners, ex p Cooke and Stevenson* [1970] 1 All ER 1068.

18.65 *Estoppel, waiver or omission to act*: It has now been established that a decision in earlier judicial review proceedings does not give rise to an issue of estoppel. However, it remains possible that it may be an abuse of process for a party to seek to reopen debate on an issue decided in earlier proceedings.[1] Similarly, waiver and acquiescence may lead to discretionary refusal of relief.[2] Relief may also be refused where there has been a failure to raise a point at a time when it was reasonably open to the claimant to do so.[3]

1   See *R (Munjaz) v Mersey Care NHS Trust* [2004] QB 395, CA, at paragraph 79, and *R v Crown Court at Knightsbridge, ex p Quinlan* [1989] COD 287. As to seeking to reopen a decision limiting issues on which permission to apply for judicial review is given, see **19.67**.
2   *R v Port Talbot Borough Council, ex p Jones* [1988] 2 All ER 207.
3   See *R v Governors of Small Heath School, ex p Birmingham City Council* [1990] COD 23.

The existence of alternative remedies

18.66 The question considered here is whether the courts will refuse to grant relief when there are alternative remedies available to the claimant and those remedies have not been exhausted.[1] The question arises in cases where the claimant has a right of appeal against the decision that is under challenge, but chooses not to exercise that right. If, in such a case, the claimant is required to exhaust his or her right of appeal then he or she may in practice lose the right to challenge the original decision in a claim for judicial review. By the time any appeal has been concluded, a challenge to the original decision in judicial review proceedings may be out of time. However, it may be that the appeal decision is itself susceptible of challenge (by way of further appeal or of judicial review). Issues as to the availability of an alternative procedure will normally be considered on the application for permission to apply for judicial review, rather than at the substantive hearing.[2]

---

[1] In *R (M) v Bromley LBC* [2002] EWCA Civ 1113 Buxton LJ said, 'It is . . . important to bear in mind that the jurisprudence relating to alternative remedies and their relevance to relief in judicial review do not form a separate chapter in the law of judicial review, but are only one aspect of a more general discretionary power of the court to refuse relief in an appropriate case."

[2] *R v Chief Constable of West Yorkshire, ex p Wilkinson* [2002] EWHC 2353 (Admin).

18.67 There has been a considerable amount of discussion in the case law as to whether the courts should refuse relief on the grounds of a failure to exhaust alternative remedies. There are competing considerations at work here. On the one hand there are arguments of principle in favour of permitting an application for judicial review. In theory, review and appeal fulfil different functions: review is concerned with the legality of a decision, and appeal with its merits. This suggests that a claimant who has a good case for judicial review should be permitted to proceed with it even if he or she could also proceed by way of appeal. An argument of principle on the other side of the equation, however, is that where there is a statutory appeal then the courts should not undermine the choice of Parliament to provide an appeal route, by allowing the claimant instead to proceed by way of judicial review. There are also pragmatic factors to take into account: the court may be concerned to avoid excessive numbers of applications for judicial review, in order to avoid delay in dealing with those applications. And, finally, there may be considerations about comparative expertise. The court may be reluctant to usurp the role of a specialist appellate body with expert knowledge of the subject matter. On the other hand, if a challenge raises an issue of general legal principle, then the court may consider that it is better placed than the specialist appellate body to resolve that challenge. Given these competing considerations it is not surprising that the case law is not wholly consistent.

18.68 There are a number of strong statements of principle that judicial review will generally not be available when an alternative remedy by way of appeal has not been exhausted. Thus, in *R v Epping and Harlow General Commissioners, ex p Goldstraw*,[1] Sir John Donaldson MR (with whom Purchase LJ agreed) described it as a 'cardinal principle' that, 'save in the most exceptional circumstances', the judicial review jurisdiction would not be exercised where other remedies were available and had not been used.[2] In *Re Preston*[3] Lord Scarman described it as a proposition of great importance that a remedy by way of judicial review should not be made available where an alternative remedy existed.[4] Sir John Donaldson MR reaffirmed what he had said in *Goldstraw* in the later case of *R v Chief Constable of Merseyside Police, ex p Calveley*[5] while emphasizing that he did not mean that judicial review was *never* available in cases where there was an alternative remedy. In the *Burkett* case Lord Steyn emphasised that judicial review is a remedy of last resort.[6] In *R (Pepushi) v CPS*[7] it was stated that the LSC and those advising prospective applicants should always realise that judicial review is very rarely appropriate where an alternative remedy is available.

[1]   [1983] 3 All ER 257.
[2]   See at 262J.
[3]   [1985] AC 835.
[4]   See at 852D. See, also, per Lord Templeman at 862C–862D.
[5]   [1986] QB 424 at 433A–433D.
[6]   [2002] 1 WLR 1592 at paragraph 42.
[7]   [2004] EWHC 798 (Admin), [2004] INLR 638.

18.69 Notwithstanding the above, in numerous cases the courts have granted judicial review even where alternative remedies have not been exhausted. *Calveley* is itself an example, and is not easy to discern what it was about the facts of the case that the court regarded as being exceptional and as justifying departure from the usual principle. In other cases the courts have attempted to set out in general terms the circumstances in which a departure from the usual principle will be permitted. For instance, in *ex p Waldron*,[1] Glidewell LJ suggested that the relevant factors included whether the alternative statutory remedy would resolve the question at issue fully and directly; whether the statutory procedure would be quicker, or slower, than procedure by way of judicial review; and whether the matter depended on some particular or technical knowledge which was more readily available to the alternative appellate body. Some examples of the factors that may influence the courts in deciding whether a claimant who has failed to exercise a statutory right of appeal should nevertheless be permitted to proceed with a judicial review claim are set out below, although there is as yet no generally accepted statement of principle in this area.[2]

(1)   *Nature of the issues* — where the claimant contends that there has been an error in applying the particular statutory regime that an appellate tribunal is specifically set up to deal with, then in general the claimant should proceed by way of appeal not judicial review.[3] On the other hand, where the claim raises general issues of public law, the courts may well consider that it is appropriate to permit a judicial review claim.[4]

(2)   *Adequacy of remedies* — if the court considers that the alternative remedy is inadequate then it is unlikely to require that the claimant pursue it.[5] A statutory appeal may offer an inadequate remedy because, for instance, there is no power to quash the disputed decision (but merely to alleviate its consequences).[6]

(3)   *Interim remedies* — the case may be one in which urgent interim relief is required. It is unlikely that a statutory appeal will meet this need.

[1]   [1986] 1 QB 824 at 852G–852H.
[2]   For further discussion, see Beloff and Mountfield [1999] JR 143, cited with approval in *Re: Director of Public Prosecutions for Northern Ireland's application* [2000] NI 174.
[3]   See, eg *R v Secretary of State for the Home Department, ex p Swati* [1986] 1 WLR 477.
[4]   See, eg *R v Devon County Council, ex p Baker* [1995] 1 All ER 73.

⁵   See, eg *R (Sivasubramaniam) v Wandsworth County Court* [2003] 1 WLR 475, especially at paragraphs 47–48.
⁶   See *R v Deputy Governor of Parkhurst Prison, ex p Leech* [1988] AC 533.

18.70 There is now an increasing emphasis in the courts on the desirability of avoiding litigation where possible, and on the need to encourage alternative dispute resolution. This is likely to lead to an increasingly willingness on the part of the courts to encourage the use of methods such as complaints procedures, or mediation, to resolve disputes between public authorities and members of the public: see the strongly worded comments of the Court of Appeal in *R (Cowl) v Plymouth City Council*.[1]

¹   [2002] 1 WLR 803.

18.71 The following are some specific situations in which the courts have considered the relationship between judicial review and alternative remedies.

Decisions of the Financial Services Authority

18.72 The Financial Services Authority is established under the Financial Services and Markets Act 2000. That Act provides for an appeal to the Financial Services and Markets Tribunal against various decisions of the Authority, with a further right of appeal (with permission) to the Court of Appeal on a point of law. In *R (Davies) v Financial Services Authority*[1] the Court of Appeal held that it was only in the most exceptional circumstances that the Administrative Court should permit a claimant to proceed by way of judicial review rather than by using the statutory appeal procedure.[2]

¹   [2004] 1 WLR 185.
²   [2004] 1 WLR 185 at 193A–193G, paragraphs 29–32.

Decisions of the county court

18.73 The county court is an inferior court created by statute and is in principle subject to control by judicial review.[1] There is a complex statutory scheme providing for the right to appeal against county court decisions; the effect of s 54 of the Access to Justice Act 1999 (together with CPR 52.3 and the Practice Direction supplementing CPR Pt 52) is that, in most cases, an appeal requires permission. In *Sivasubramanian* the Court of Appeal held that s 54 of the 1999 Act did not oust the jurisdiction of the High Court to subject decisions of the county court to judicial review.[2] However, where there had been a failure to seek permission to bring a statutory appeal, permission to proceed by way of judicial review should be refused save in exceptional circumstances, and the Court of Appeal found it hard to envisage what these could be.[3] Where permission to appeal had been sought and refused then applications for judicial review of the refusal of permission should usually be summarily dismissed. Such applications should only be entertained in very rare cases, where there was an allegation of jurisdictional error in the narrow, pre-*Anisminic* sense, or procedural irregularity such as to constitute a denial of the right to a fair hearing.[4]

¹   See *R v Worthington-Evans, ex p Madan* [1959] 2 QB 145; *R (Sivasubramaniam) v Wandsworth County Court* [2003] 1 WLR 475 at 486, paragraph 33.

² See *R (Sivasubramaniam) v Wandsworth County Court* [2003] 1 WLR at 489F–489H, paragraph 44.
³ [2003] 1 WLR at 490E–490G, paragraph 48.
⁴ [2003] 1 WLR at 492A–492H, paragraphs 54–56; see, also, *Gregory v Turner* [2003] 1 WLR 1149.

Absence of any practical purpose in granting a remedy

18.74 The court does not beat the air in vain.¹ It may have become otiose or pointless to grant a remedy because the relevant detriment to the claimant has been removed² or because nothing in practice will change if the remedy is granted.³ However, the court will not readily assume that a declaration will be ineffective.⁴ Nor should it be deterred from granting relief merely because it considers it likely that the same decision would be reached a second time if the first decision were to be quashed.⁵

¹ The principles which follow in the text, as set out in the first edition of this work, were cited with approval by Turner J in *R v Neale, ex p S* [1995] ELR 198 at 210.
² See, eg *R v Secretary of State for Foreign and Commonwealth Affairs, ex p Everett* [1989] QB 811.
³ See *Cinnamond v British Airports Authority* [1980] 2 All ER 368; *R v Secretary of State for the Environment, ex p Brent London Borough Council* [1982] QB 593; *R v Monopolies and Mergers Commission, ex p Argyll Group plc* [1986] 1 WLR 763. However, the court should be slow to conclude that the error made no difference to what would have happened: see *R v Chief Constable of the Thames Valley Police Force, ex p Cotton* [1990] IRLR 344 at 352; Bingham [1991] PL 64; and *R v Camden LBC ex p Paddock* [1995] COD 130.
⁴ See *Eastham v Newcastle United Football Club Ltd* [1964] Ch 413 at 449–451.
⁵ *R v Secretary of State for Education and Science, ex p Inner London Educational Authority* (1990) Times, 3 March.

18.75 For a recent example of a case where relief was refused on the ground that there was no need for any remedy, see *R (Rusbridger) v Attorney General*¹ (no need for a declaration that a newspaper publishing a series of articles advocating the abolition of the monarchy would not thereby commit an offence under s 3 of the Treason Felony Act 1848).

¹ [2003] 3 WLR 232.

Effect of remedies on the defendant or on third parties

18.76 A remedy may be denied in order to avoid wide implications or unacceptable adverse impact on third parties. This is the converse of the situation discussed in the previous section: the difficulty here is that a grant of a remedy would have too great a practical effect, rather than that it would have no practical effect. For examples of cases where relief has been refused on this basis, see *R v Brentwood Superintendent Registrar of Marriages, ex p Arias*,¹ *R v Secretary of State for Social Services, ex p Association of Metropolitan Authorities*,² and *R v Monopolies and Mergers Commission, ex p Argyll Group plc*.³

¹ [1968] 2 QB 956.
² [1986] 1 All ER 164.
³ [1986] 2 All ER 257.

Criminal Justice and Courts Act 2015

18.77 The Criminal Justice and Courts Act 2015 amended s 31 of the Senior Courts Act 1981, by inserting subsections (2A)–(2C), (3C)–(3F), and (8). These came into force with effect from 13 April 2015: see SI 2015/778. The effect of these new provisions is to require the court to refuse to grant relief, or to grant permission to apply for judicial review, in specified circumstances. The court must refuse to grant relief on an application for judicial review, and may not make an award under s 31(4) (which deals with damages and other money awards), if it appears to the court to be highly likely that the outcome for the applicant would not have been substantially different if the conduct complained of had not occurred. When considering whether to grant permission, the court may consider this question of its own motion, and must do so if asked by the defendant. If on such consideration it appears to the court to be highly likely that the outcome for the applicant would not have been substantially different, then the court must refuse to grant permission. The court may disregard these requirements to refuse relief (or money awards), or to refuse leave, if it considers that it is appropriate to do so for reasons of exceptional public interest. CPR 54.11A allows the court to direct a hearing at the permission stage, where it wishes to hear submissions on: whether it is highly likely that the outcome would not have been substantially different; or whether there are reasons of exceptional public interest that would nevertheless make it appropriate to grant permission.

18.78 The Criminal Justice and Courts Act 2015 also includes provisions that will require applicants for permission to provide the court with information (to be specified in rules of court) as to the financing of their application, as a condition of obtaining permission to apply for judicial review: see s 85(1) and (2) of the 2015 Act, amending s 31(3) of the Senior Courts Act 1981, and inserting new sub-ss (3A) and (3B) into s 31. These provisions are not yet in force.

Chapter 19

PROCEDURE: THE EARLY STAGES

INTRODUCTION

19.1 Judicial review claims are governed by Part 54 of the Civil Procedure Rules,[1] which modifies Part 8 of the CPR and must be read with s 31 of the Senior Courts Act 1981. Part 54 came into force on 2 October 2000 and replaced the old RSC Order 53. Part 54 is now supplemented by Practice Direction 54A – Judicial Review ('CPR Pt 54A PD'), Practice Direction 54D – Administrative Court (Venue) ('CPR Pt 54D PD'), Practice Direction 54E – Planning Court Claims ('CPR Pt 54E PD') and by the Pre-action Protocol for Judicial Review.

> [1] Introduced on the recommendation of the Bowman Report submitted to the Lord Chancellor in March 2000.

19.2 The main features of the present regime, as distinguished from the previous Order 53 procedure, are:

(1) a pre-action protocol for judicial review formalising and extending a number of 'best practice' considerations which had previously been developed by the court on an *ad hoc* basis;[1]

(2) the defendant will now routinely be notified of, and involved in, the claim *before* consideration by the court of whether to grant permission. Under Order 53 the application for leave to apply for judicial review was made on an *ex p* basis;

(3) the integration of Part 54 into the CPR as a whole, so that issues such as disclosure and interim relief are dealt with by the relevant parts of the CPR as opposed to special rules applicable only to judicial review.

> [1] See, for example, *R v Borough of Milton Keynes, ex p Macklen* [1996] CLY 5445.

19.3 This chapter describes the procedure involved in a judicial review claim up to the period shortly before the hearing. Procedure from that time onwards is discussed in Chapter 20.

THE PRE-ACTION PROTOCOL FOR JUDICIAL REVIEW

19.4 Before commencing a claim for judicial review, it is necessary to have regard to the judicial review pre-action protocol.[1] As with any pre-action protocol, the intention behind the judicial review protocol is, in the words of Lord Woolf:[2]

> 'to build on and increase the benefits of early but well informed settlements which genuinely satisfy both parties to disputes'.

> [1] The protocol is set out at paragraph C8-001 of *Civil Procedure 2014* and is available online at www.justice.gov.uk/civil/procrules_fin/contents/protocols/prot_jrv.htm
> [2] Access to Justice 1996, Chapter 11.

19.5 The essence of the protocol is the requirement that the parties enter into correspondence, in the form of a formal letter before claim and response, before starting proceedings. If carried through properly, this is intended to foster non-judicial resolution of the problem, and even if such resolution is not possible will help to clarify issues. In judicial review the protocol brings the particular benefits of identification and notification of interested parties[1] in advance of the claim and the opportunity thereby given to them to take an active part in the proceedings from an early stage.

[1] An 'interested party' is defined in CPR 54.1 as 'any person (other than the claimant and defendant) who is directly affected by the claim'. The meaning of this expression is discussed at **20.17**.

The need to follow the protocol

19.6 The protocol describes itself as 'a code of good practice' containing 'the steps which the parties should generally follow' before bringing proceedings for judicial review. Thus a failure to follow the protocol will not as such be a bar to a claimant bringing a claim for judicial review or obtaining relief therein, nor to a defendant in successfully resisting such a claim. Nevertheless, in a case where there is no good reason for a failure to comply with the protocol, the court is unlikely to view that failure favourably. The protocol warns in a number of places of possible sanctions for failure to comply with its provisions.[1]

[1] Protocol, paragraphs 3, 6, 7, 13 and 14.

19.7 In considering whether or not to follow the protocol, it should always be borne in mind that all remedies in judicial review proceedings are discretionary and may be withheld by the court notwithstanding that illegal conduct on the part of a public body has been established.[1] The most likely consequence may, however, be in terms of costs.[2]

[1] It may be noted that the *Practice Direction – Protocols*, which is of general application to all protocols, indicates that a party who fails to comply with a protocol may be penalised in certain ways (paragraphs 13–16), but does not envisage that a remedy would be denied on that account alone. The discretionary nature of remedies is discussed in Chapter **18**, but we think it would be highly exceptional for a remedy to be refused solely on account of non-compliance with the protocol.

[2] Paragraph 9 of the Protocol warns parties that if the protocol is not followed then the Court must have regard to such conduct when determining costs.

19.8 The protocol states that following the protocol will not be appropriate:

– in urgent cases, such as where a person may be about to be removed from the United Kingdom or where there is an urgent need for an interim order to compel a body to act where it has unlawfully refused to do so, such as a failure to provide interim accommodation for a homeless claimant.[1]

In such cases a claim should be made immediately because, as the protocol points out, the sending of a letter before claim will not in itself prevent the implementation of a disputed decision. In such cases the protocol recommends that it is good practice to send the draft Claim Form by email or fax to the defendant before issuing, and states that the claimant will normally be required to notify a defendant where an interim mandatory order is made against it is sought.[2]

[1] Protocol, paragraph 6.

2   Protocol, paragraph 6. As to urgent applications and interim relief generally, see **19.96** and **19.106**.

19.9 In practical terms, however, it will usually be best to follow the protocol where this is at all possible. In cases where it is not possible to follow the strict letter of the protocol, parties should still endeavour to observe its spirit so far as they are able. In cases where there has been a failure to observe the provisions of the protocol prior to the commencement of a claim, whether justified or not, there is nothing to prevent the parties from corresponding with a view to resolving, or narrowing, the issues prior to any consideration of the claim by the court – something which the court would encourage.

The time limit for bringing judicial review in claims under the Planning Acts and in relation to public procurement has been shortened to six weeks and 28 days respectively. In many planning cases, and likely also in many procurement cases, the defendant will not have the legal power to withdraw the decision under challenge. This is the case, for example, in the most common case of a planning judicial review, involving a challenge to a grant of planning permission. Although claimants have in general seen themselves as obliged to follow the protocol in such cases, there is a strong argument that they are not in fact required to do so. Nevertheless, we suggest that it would be wise to seek to comply in so far as practicable, and there may also be advantages to doing so for tactical reasons or to secure agreement on issues relating to costs or disclosure.

Alternative dispute resolution

19.10 The Protocol states that parties should consider whether some form of alternative dispute resolution procedure would be more suitable than litigation, and if so, endeavour to agree which form to adopt. The Protocol warns that both the claimant and defendant may be required by the Court to provide evidence that alternative means of resolving the dispute was considered.[1] In *Cowl v Plymouth City Council*,[2] Lord Woolf considered that the failure to attempt ADR was 'indefensible'. Whilst a party's refusal to participate in ADR, or silence in response to an invitation to participate in ADR, could be considered unreasonable by the court in some circumstances, and could lead to the court ordering that party to pay additional costs, ADR remains the exception rather than the rule in judicial review. Parties are not routinely denied their costs, let alone refused a remedy, for failure to participate in ADR. The court cannot compel a party to mediate or enter any form of ADR.[3] Further, unless there is a form of ADR which amounts to an 'alternative remedy', properly understood, the court is unlikely to refuse to grant relief in the absence of evidence of attempts to resolve the dispute by ADR, and, since it requires participation by both sides, it is difficult to see how it could provide a remedy where a defendant does not offer it.[4] *Cowl* has been cited in later cases but not applied in a way which creates a routine expectation of mediation. There will be cases where the history of the case makes clear why ADR is unrealistic or inappropriate or shows that something akin to ADR has been attempted before the claim was lodged (see, for example, *R (Crawford) v Newcastle upon Tyne University)* [2014] EWHC 1197 (Admin).

1   Protocol, paragraph 9.

²   [2002] 1 WLR 803.

³   In *Halsey v Milton Keynes General NHS Trust* and *Steel v Joy and Halliday* [2004] EWCA Civ 576; [2004] 4 All ER 920, mandatory mediation was considered to be a breach of art 6 ECHR.

⁴   However, see *Anufrijeva v Southwark London Borough Council* [2003] EWCA Civ 1406, where the Court of Appeal set out guidance for dealing with damages claims under the Human Rights Act 1998 for maladministration. In that case, the court suggested that a claim to the Parliamentary Commissioner for Administration or the Local Government Ombudsman might be required before the Administrative Court would entertain the claim. For more on alternative remedies as a discretionary bar to relief, see CHAPTER 18.

Letter before claim

19.11 The protocol states that the purpose of the letter before claim is 'to identify the issues in dispute and establish whether they can be narrowed or litigation can be avoided'. Any interested parties identified by the claimant should be sent a copy of the letter before claim for information.[1] Where the claimant considers a claim to fall within the Aarhus Convention, the letter before claim should clearly state this and explain the reason.[2]

¹   Protocol, paragraph 17. See also *R (Candlish) v Hastings Borough Council* [2005] EWHC 1539 (Admin) where it was emphasised that claimants should copy in third parties to pre-action correspondence.

²   Protocol, paragraph 10.

19.12 Annex A of the Protocol provides a standard form letter before claim, which should 'normally' be used,[1] although the real question will be whether the letter, whatever its precise format, contains the information that it ought to contain. Slavish adherence to the standard form letter is not necessary, but there will generally be little to be gained by departing from it. The letter must contain the details of the claimant and defendant and their legal advisers (if any), any interested parties known to the claimant, ADR proposals and any reference details. It must also contain a summary of the facts which give rise to the claim, the details of the decision under challenge and a brief statement of why it is said to be wrong. It should also state the detail of any information or disclosure that is sought. Finally, it should set out a proposed date by which a reply is expected.[2] The standard period for reply is said to be 14 days but a longer or shorter period may be appropriate depending on the nature of the claim. If a claim is considered appropriate for allocation to the Planning Court and/or for classification as 'significant' within that court for the purposes of CPR 54.22(3) and Practice Direction 54E, the letter before claim should state this clearly and explain the reasons.[3] If a claimant intends to ask for a capping order (an order that the claimant will not be liable for costs of the defendant or any other party, or to limit such liability), or contends that the claim is an Aarhus Convention claim, then this should be stated in the letter before the claim, which should give the reasons, including an explanation — in the context of a costs capping order — of the limit of the financial resources available to the claimant.[4] The claim should not normally be made until the proposed reply date has passed,[5] unless a reply has been received. For the precise format of the letter, reference should be made to Annex A of the Protocol.

¹   Protocol, paragraph 15.

²   Protocol, Annex A.

³   Protocol, paragraph 16.

Letter of response

19.13 The defendant should normally reply within the proposed time limit, although neither the defendant nor the claimant will be bound by time limits unilaterally imposed by the other side. If unable to reply within the time proposed, it would be good practice to send an interim reply, giving a date by which the defendant expects to respond substantively. Where an extension of time is sought, reasons should be given. The defendant in its response should identify any additional interested parties and provide relevant details not provided in the letter before claim.[1] The response should also set out the defendant's position to any ADR proposals made in the letter before the claim, as well as any ADR proposals by the defendant. Where the claimant is a litigant in person, the defendant should enclose a copy of the Protocol with its letter.[2] Where the letter before claim asserts that the claim is an Aarhus Convention claim, but the Defendant disputes this, then the reply should state this clearly, giving reasons.[3] Where the letter before claim asserts that the claim is suitable for the Planning Court or categorisation as 'significant' within the court, but the defendant does not accept this, then the reply should state this clearly, giving reasons.[4] Where the claimant has stated an intention to ask for a costs capping order, the defendant's response to this should be explained.[5]

[1] Annex B to the Protocol sets out the information required in a response to a letter before claim.
[2] Protocol, paragraph 20.
[3] Protocol, paragraph 23.
[4] Protocol, paragraph 23.
[5] Protocol, paragraph 23.

19.14 If the claim is being conceded in full, the response should say so in clear and unambiguous terms. If it is being contested, either in full or in part, that should also be stated in clear terms and reasons given. A fuller explanation of the decision may be provided if it is considered appropriate to do so. Where it is not possible to address a particular point, an explanation should be given for this.

19.15 Where a request has been made for information or disclosure, an explanation should be given for any failure or refusal to comply with that request. Where documents cannot be provided within the timescales required, a clear timescale for provision should be given.

19.16 As with the letter before claim, copies should be sent to any interested party identified by either side.

The relevance of the protocol to delay

19.17 The protocol states in clear terms that it does not affect the time limit for judicial review specified by CPR 54.5(1), or the shorter time limits specified by CPR 54.5(5) and (6).[1] The protocol also emphasises the fact that a defendant's request for an extension of time for responding to a letter before claim will not affect those time limits.[2]

---

[1]   Protocol, paragraph 1. Compliance with the protocol should normally be seen as relevant to whether time should be extended, and may be of some importance where delay is slight and a claimant can show that the defendant was made aware of the claim, via a letter before claim, prior to the expiry of the three months. For discussion of the time limit for judicial review, see CHAPTER 18.

[2]   Protocol, paragraph 21. CPR 54.5(2) provides that the time limit for filing the claim form cannot be extended by agreement between the parties.

19.18   That can leave claimants and their advisers in a difficult position in that they may have to choose between bringing a claim within the time limit and compliance with the protocol. It is suggested that in such cases the cardinal rule should be that the claim should be brought within the three-month or six-week time limit in order to protect the claimant's position.[1] Failure to bring a claim within that time limit, where no extension of time is granted, will prevent the claim from continuing at all, whereas a failure to comply with the protocol should not generally debar the claim as a whole. Once a claim has been brought, the claimant who has so far failed to comply with the protocol should do everything possible to comply with its spirit, by attempting so far as possible to reach agreement, or clarify the disagreement, with the defendant and other parties. If necessary, a stay may be applied for.[2] If the three-month period has yet to expire but will do so before the expiration of the normal time for the defendant to respond, a letter before claim can be sent giving an abridged time for response that will expire just before the end of the three months.

---

[1]   As Keith J observed in *Domi v Secretary of State for the Home Department* [2006] EWHC 1314 (Admin), 'if you are up against a time limit, you do not delay the filing of the claim to comply with a pre-action protocol'.

[2]   *Practice Direction – Protocols*, paragraph 17. In practice, this may be unnecessary in that the major steps required by the Protocol can probably in most cases be conducted before the court is likely to consider the matter on the papers. An alternative may be a joint application to extend the defendant's time for acknowledgement of service.

19.19   In a case where the three-month period has yet to expire, but there is thought to be a potential issue about acting 'promptly' within that period, it is suggested that it will almost always be preferable to comply with the protocol. A defendant will be on notice of the potential application from the time that he receives the letter before claim, and the claimant's compliance with the protocol is potentially to his or her advantage in that it may avoid any need for litigation at all. In circumstances where a defendant has been notified of the claim and the proposed grounds in accordance with the protocol, it would be difficult to argue that a failure to actually bring the claim caused any prejudice. However, in a case where there may be an issue as to promptness even within the three-month time limit, it will be particularly important to identify any potential interested parties or alternative defendants and ensure that they are also informed of the potential claim.[1]

---

[1]   That is well illustrated by *R (Camacho) v RB Kensington and Chelsea* [2003] EWHC 1497 (Admin), a case about student loans. The claimants had entered into correspondence with the relevant local authorities and it had been agreed that no claim would be brought until judgment was given on another case being referred to the ECJ, but that no point would be taken on delay by the local authorities in the event that a claim was later brought. However, no similar discussion had taken place with the Secretary of State for Education and Skills, who was ultimately liable to pay for any loan out of central government funds, the local authorities'

role being essentially administrative. The failure to notify the Secretary of State led to the claims being struck out for delay.

BEGINNING THE CLAIM

Venue

19.20 Claims for judicial review in England and Wales must be issued either in the Administrative Court or in the Upper Tribunal. The decision will depend on whether the claim falls within the jurisdiction of the Upper Tribunal. Claims considered by the Upper Tribunal are subject to statutory rules rather than the CPR. Accordingly, while some of what follows is applicable to both Administrative Court and Upper Tribunal claims, readers should additionally refer to paragraph **19.152** et seq in respect of Upper Tribunal claims.

19.21 In respect of Administrative Court claims, the Administrative Court operates from a number of regional centres in addition to the Royal Courts of Justice in London, including Birmingham, Cardiff, Leeds and Manchester. The five centres are located at:

- Cardiff Civil Justice Centre, 2 Park Street, Cardiff, CF10 1ET;
- Birmingham Civil Justice Centre, Priory Courts, 5th Floor, 33 Bull Street, Birmingham B4 6DS;
- Bristol Civil and Family Justice Centre, 2 Redcliff Street, Bristol BS1 6GR;
- Leeds Combined Court, 1 Oxford Row, Leeds, West Yorkshire. LS1 3BG;
- Manchester Civil Justice Centre, 12th Floor, 1 Bridge Street West, Manchester. M3 3FX.

However, as at January 2017, the Administrative Court in Bristol does not have facilities for the lodging of papers.

Choice of Venue

19.22 Practice Direction 54D – Administrative Court (Venue) ('CPR Pt 54D PD') provides guidance on where to issue a claim in the Administrative Court. It provides that, subject to certain exceptions, a claim form may be issued at the Administrative Court Office of the High Court at the Royal Courts of Justice in London, or at the District Registry of the High Court at Birmingham, Cardiff, Leeds, or Manchester.[1]

[1] CPR Pt 54D PD2.

19.23 The exceptions to the ordinary rule include proceedings under the Prevention of Terrorism Act 2005, and the Counter Terrorism Act 2008, and Part 1 of the Terrorist Asset-Freezing etc. Act 2010, proceedings to which RSC Order 115 applies, proceedings under the Proceeds of Crime Act 2002, appeals to the Administrative Court under the Extradition Act 2003, proceedings which must be heard by a Divisional Court, and proceedings relating to the discipline of solicitors. These categories of claim must be issued at the

Royal Courts of Justice in London.[1]

¹   CPR Pt 54D PD3.1.

19.24 The general expectation is that proceedings will be administered and determined in the region with which the claimant has the closest connection, but CPR Pt 54D PD5.2 provides a list of considerations relevant to deciding the appropriate venue, including:

(1)   Any reason expressed by any party for preferring a particular venue;
(2)   The region in which the defendant, or any relevant office or department of the defendant, is based;
(3)   The region in which the claimant's legal representatives are based;
(4)   The ease and cost of travel to a hearing;
(5)   The availability and suitability of alternative means of attending a hearing (for example, by videolink);
(6)   The extent and nature of media interest in the proceedings in any particular locality;
(7)   The time within which it is appropriate for the proceedings to be determined;
(8)   Whether it is desirable to administer or determine the claim in another region in the light of the volume of claims issued at, and the capacity, resources and workload or, the court at which it is issued;
(9)   Whether the claim raises issues sufficiently similar to those in another outstanding claim to make it desirable that it should be determined together with, or immediately following, that other claim; and
(10)   Whether the claim raises devolution issues and for that reason whether it should more appropriately be heard in London or Cardiff.

19.25 It is notable that the list of relevant considerations includes the time within which it is appropriate for the proceedings to be determined and the workload of the court at which the claim is issued. Experience suggests that the delay of the Administrative Court in London may be an increasingly important factor in the growth of the regional Administrative Courts. Claimants who want their claims to be dealt with quickly, but who are unable to expedite the claims, may well be advised to issue in a regional Administrative Court.

19.26 The court may transfer proceedings to another region for hearing when giving directions under rule 54.10, taking into account the considerations set out in CPR Pt 54D PD5.4.

19.27 Proceedings commenced elsewhere in the High Court may be transferred to the Administrative Court. The application should be lodged at the Administrative Court Office and will be dealt with by a judge nominated to hear cases in the Administrative Court.[1] A case transferred in this way will require permission in the ordinary way.[2] There is also power under CPR 30.2 to transfer an application for judicial review to a district registry, or (without transferring the case) under CPR 30.6 to specify a place where a trial or other hearing is to be held.[3]

¹   CPR 30.5.
²   CPR 54.4.
³   The ability to exercise powers under CPR Pt 30 in an application for judicial review is confirmed at CPR 54.20. Practice Direction 54A draws attention, at paragraph **14.1** to CPR 30.5 (the power to transfer to or from a specialist list) and adds that in deciding whether a

claim is suitable for transfer to the Administrative Court, the court will consider whether it raises issues of public law to which Pt 54 should apply.

The Claim Form

19.28 A claim for judicial review commences by completing, and filing at the appropriate venue, High Court form N461.[1] N461 is a standard form and can be found in the Civil Procedure loose-leaf binder, 'Forms'. It is also available on the Court Service Website.[2] Requirements as to the time within which the form must be issued, and consequences where those requirements are not met, are discussed in CHAPTER **18**. The claim form must be served on the defendant and, unless the court otherwise directs, any interested party within seven days of filing at the court.[3]

[1] Since the previous edition, the fee on lodging the claim has increased from £140 to £154 (the Civil Proceedings Fees (Amendment) Order 2014,SI 2014/874) as amended by the Civil Proceedings, First-tier Tribunal, Upper Tribunal and Employment Tribunals Fees (Amendment) Order 2016/807. Claimants in receipt of certain types of benefit may be entitled to exemption or remission of fees. In such a case application should be made by form EX160A to the office of the relevant court.

[2] At www.justice.gov.uk/civil/procrules_fin/menus/forms.htm

[3] CPR 54.7. An application for a direction excusing service on an interested party should be included in Section 7 of the claim form. CPR 6.14 and 7.5 identifies the deemed day of service where particular methods of delivery are used.

19.29 The Claim Form should be headed 'The Queen (on the application of) [Claimant] –v– [Defendant]. It requires details of the name of the claimant and his or her solicitor's name and address and the name and address of the defendant and any interested parties known to the claimant. The Claim Form requires the claimant to identify the decision, act or omission that is being challenged and to specify the remedies sought, including any interim remedy.[1] It should state that the claimant is seeking permission to apply for judicial review.[2] It should either confirm that the pre-action protocol has been complied with or give the reasons for non-compliance.[3] Where the claim is brought outside of the three months for bringing a claim for judicial review, it must contain an application to extend the time limit.[4] When s 85(1) of the Criminal Justice and Courts Act 2015 is brought into force, a claimant will be required to provide information about the financing of the claim before an application for judicial review can be made.[5]

[1] CPR 54.6(1)(c). Interim remedies are discussed below at **19.96** et seq.

[2] And may state that the claimant believes that an oral permission hearing is appropriate although the court will certainly not see itself as bound by this. In practice, with the exception of cases where urgent interim relief is sought, it is difficult to see why a claimant would seek an oral permission hearing at this stage given the right to renew any application orally if permission is refused.

[3] See N461, section 4.

[4] CPR Pt 54A PD 5.6(3).

[5] Section 85(1) would modify s 31(3) of the Senior Courts Act. The provision had not been brought into force at the time of writing.

19.30 Claimants should also be aware, where their case involves any issue under the Human Rights Act 1998, of the need to state that fact and to comply with a number of provisions under CPR Pt 16 PD, and, where the case raises a 'devolution issue',[1] to state that fact, identify the relevant provisions of the devolution legislation and contain a summary of the facts, circumstances and points of law on which the issue is based.[2] Where relevant, the Claim Form should include the grounds on which it is contended that the claim falls under the Aarhus Convention.[3]

[1]   As defined in Northern Ireland Act 1998, Sch 10, paragraph 1; and the Scotland Act 1998, Sch 6, paragraph 1 (see CPR Pt 54 PD 5.5). Devolution issues are discussed in Chapter 21.

[2]   CPR Pt 54A PD 5.4.

[3]   CPR 54.6(1)(d).

19.31 The Claim Form requires the claimant to set out a detailed statement of grounds and the facts relied upon,[1] and this will generally be the most involved aspect of the Claim Form. It is common practice, and generally sensible, to combine those two sections of the Form in a separate document which may be drafted by Counsel. It is this document that will summarise the claimant's arguments when the judge considers, initially on the papers alone, whether to grant permission, and which therefore provides the claimant with the opportunity to persuade the judge that permission should be granted. It is, therefore, important that it provides a succinct, and above all clear, summary of the claimant's arguments,[2] and careful 'sign-posting' to the documentation that is likely to be of value to the judge. A short summary of the legislative framework may also assist. A further benefit of a well-drafted statement of facts and grounds is that it may, in a clear case, persuade the defendant to concede the claim.

[1]   CPR Pt 54A PD 5.6(1)–(2)

[2]   It is important that the statement of facts and grounds is not overloaded with arguments, but is well focused: see *R (Naing) v Immigration Appeal Tribunal* [2003] EWHC 771 (Admin) at [59].

19.32 The claimant must file a certificate of service (form N215) within 21 days of service of the Claim Form.[1]

[1]   CPR 6.17. See paragraph 6.8.3 of the Judicial Review Guide 2016 published by the Administrative Court Office and available at https://www.gov.uk/government/uploads/system/uploads/attachment_data/file/540607/administrative-court-judicial-review-guide.pdf

The claimant's duty of candour

19.33 Under the old Order 53 procedure, the application for leave was made without formal notice to the defendant, which gave rise to a duty on the claimant to provide full and frank disclosure of all relevant matters,[1] including in particular those unfavourable to the claimant's case. The Part 54 procedure requires the claim form be served on the defendant and interested parties and an opportunity be given to them to respond prior to the determination of the application for permission. It might be argued that this change removed, to some extent, the rationale for this duty. However, the duty remains essentially the same post-CPR. A claimant is expected to provide the court with a full account of all relevant matters and to draw the court's attention to documents that both support and undermine the claim. In R *(Mohammad Khan) v Secretary of State for the Home Department,*[2] the Court of Appeal held that whilst the duty on claimants does not equate exactly with that on respondents, the duty of candour requires more from claimants than merely furnishing material documents (without drawing its significance to the attention of the court). Beatson LJ said: 'If, as Collins stated in *R (I) v Secretary of State for the Home Department*,claimants in judicial review proceedings must ensure that the judge dealing with the application has the full picture: in some circumstances to ensure this they will have to do more than just furnish the document [. . .] providing a partial explanation in the statements of grounds and facts which is misleading will be a breach of the duty of candour in an application for judicial review even where it is not linked with a without notice application for an injunction. Beyond that, in particular, I do not consider that it suffices to provide a pile of undigested documents, particularly in a document heavy case, or where the claimant has knowledge which enables him or her to explain the full significance of a document. I also consider that in considering the effect of a failure to explain material in a disclosed document hat is adverse to the claim, it is relevant to consider whether the failure to explain the material was innocent in the sense that the relevance of the material was not perceived.' (emphasis added). Further, in urgent cases, where permission or interim relief may fall to be considered before the defendant has an opportunity to respond, the duty applies with full rigour.[3]

1   For a general summary of the duty see *R v Jockey Club Licensing Committee, ex p Wright* [1991] COD 306. Consequences where the duty is not fulfilled are discussed in CHAPTER 18.
2   R *(Mohammad Khan) v Secretary of State for the Home Department* [2016] EWCA Civ 416 at paragraphs 45–46. The judgment of Beatson LJ provides an overview of the applicable principles in the context of the claimant's duty of candour.
3   And see, also, CPR Pt 25A PD 3.3, on the duty to disclose all material facts when applying for an interim injunction.

19.34 The claimant's duty of candour requires the claimant to provide full information about the following, at least:

(1)   any legislative material, or any body of authority, that is against the claimant's case[1] (and state why that is distinguishable);

(2)   the existence of any alternative remedy, ouster clause,[2] or question of delay,[3] and why that should not bar the claimant's case;

(3)   all material facts, not being limited to those perceived to be material by the claimant and including such as may have been available to the claimant following proper inquiry.

1   *R v CPS, ex p Hogg* [1994] COD 237; *R v Secretary of State for the Home Department, ex p Li Bin Shi* [1995] COD 135.
2   *R v Cornwall County Council, ex p Huntington* [1992] 3 All ER 566.
3   *R v Bromley London Borough Council, ex p Barker* [2001] Env LR 1.

19.35 In an application for interim relief without notice in the Administrative Court, it has been held that the obligation to make full and candid disclosure includes a duty to make proper inquiries before making the application, so that there is a breach of the duty if the claimant fails to disclose any additional material facts which he would have known if he had made proper inquiries before making the application. Proper disclosure for this purpose means specifically identifying all relevant documents for the judge, taking him to the particular passages in the documents which are material and taking appropriate steps to ensure that the judge correctly appreciates the significance of what he is being asked to read. That burden of full and frank disclosure is more onerous where a telephone application is being made to a judge who has none of the papers before him.[1] It has also been held, in the context of an application for an injunction in a non-judicial review case, that the duty encompasses a duty to disclose any defence that the claimant has reason to anticipate may be advanced,[2] although that does not extend to a duty to second-guess the defendant's position.

[1] *R (Lawer) v Restormel Borough Council* [2007] EWHC 2299 (Admin)
[2] *Lloyds Bowmaker Ltd v Britannia Arrow Holdings* [1988] 1 WLR 1337. In *Brink's Mat Ltd v Elcombe* [1988] 1 WLR 1350 it was recognised that 'the borderline between material facts and non-material facts may be a somewhat uncertain one' and the duty should not be 'carried to extreme lengths'.

19.36 It is important to bear in mind that the duty must be balanced against the need to avoid overloading the court with documentation. In preparing the documentation care should be taken only to exhibit documentation that is truly relevant. Cases turning on statutory construction, for example, require relatively little background information. The courts do not welcome large amounts of extraneous material that do not advance consideration of the legal issues involved.[1]

[1] For an example among many of strong judicial dicta on this point, see *R (Prokopp) v London Underground Ltd* [2004] Env LR 170, per Schiemann LJ at paragraph 52 and Buxton LJ at paragraph 90. Regarding the citation of Strasbourg case law, regard should be had to the guidance in *R (Sturnum); R (Faulkner) v Parole Board* [2013] 2 AC 254 per Lord Reed JSC at paragraph 103 and Lord Carnwath JSC at paragraph 114.

19.37 The claim form must be verified by a statement of truth.[1] Where the statement of facts and/or grounds are drafted as separate documents, they are nevertheless incorporated into the claim form as sections 8 and 5 respectively. It is therefore unnecessary that they include any additional statement of truth.

[1] CPR 8.2 and 22.1.

Documents filed with the claim form

19.38 The claimant should lodge in the Administrative Court Office two copies of an indexed paginated bundle containing the claim form and all documents by which it must be accompanied.[1] Those documents are:[2]

(1) any written evidence in support of the claim or application to extend time;
(2) a copy of any order that the claimant seeks to have quashed;
(3) where the claim for judicial review relates to a decision of a court or tribunal, an approved copy of the reasons for reaching the decision;
(4) copies of any documents on which the claimant proposes to rely;
(5) copies of any relevant statutory material; and
(6) a list of essential documents for advance reading by the court (with page references to the passages relied on).

[1] CPR Pt 54A PD 5.9.
[2] CPR Pt 54A PD 5.7.

19.39 Where it is not possible to file all of the above documents, the claimant must indicate which documents have not been filed and the reasons why they are not currently available.[1]

[1] CPR Pt 54A PD 5.8. Section 10 of the claim form provides a checklist for the above documents. Unlike the Practice Direction it requires not only the reasons why they are not available but also the date when it is expected to be available.

19.40 The claim form must include a statement of the facts relied upon and must be verified by a statement of truth.[1]

[1] CPR 22.1(1)(a). The claimant may rely on the contents of the claim form as evidence, provided it has been verified by a statement of truth: CPR 8.5(7).

19.41 If written evidence is to be relied upon, it should be filed with the claim form.[1] It is generally advisable that some written evidence is provided, if only in order to exhibit documents on which reliance is placed. In such cases, especially where the case turns on points of pure statutory construction or the adequacy of reasoning in a decision letter, a relatively short formal statement by the claimant's solicitor may suffice. In other cases, however, even where the court has no primary fact-finding role, the value of a witness statement from the claimant in person should not be underestimated, by providing the court with information as to the relevant background and the claimant's interest in the case.

[1] CPR Pt 54A PD 5.7(1). The court has power to grant permission for a statement to be relied upon by the claimant notwithstanding that it was not filed with the claim form. In practice it is very unusual for a court to exclude such evidence in the absence of real prejudice to the other side, such as where a party is unfairly taken by surprise.

19.42 In 'Cart' judicial reviews,[1] that is, applications for judicial review of a decision of the Upper Tribunal to refuse permission to appeal from the First-tier Tribunal, supporting documents which must be sent with the claim form are set out in CPR 54.7A(4). These are:

(a) the decision of the Upper Tribunal to which the application relates, and any document giving reasons for the decision;

(b) the grounds of appeal to the Upper Tribunal and any documents which were set with them;

(c) the decision of the First-tier Tribunal, the application to that Tribunal for permission to appeal and the reasons for refusing permission; and

(d) any other documents essential to the claim.

[1] See **19.57**.

ACKNOWLEDGEMENT OF SERVICE

19.43 A person served with a claim form, who wishes to take part in the proceedings, must file and serve an acknowledgement of service on the appropriate form, namely N462.[1] This obligation is not limited to the defendant, but applies to any interested party on whom the claim form was served. Subject to any direction from the court to the contrary, the acknowledgement must be filed not more than 21 days after service of the claim form,[2] and must be served on the claimant and any other person named in the claim form as soon as practicable and, in any event, not more than seven days after filing.[3] Applications for extension of time to file Acknowledgements of Service in twenty cases were considered by Hickinbottom J in *R (Singh) v Secretary of State for the Home Department*.[4] It was held that, even despite the considerable pressures upon the Secretary of State, acknowledgements of service should generally be filed within the 21 day time limit. A first application for extension of time will not need full grounds, and should be 'treated generously by the court'. However, subsequent applications for extension of time should be supported by full reasons and a firm promise as to when the acknowledgement of service would be filed. If good reasons are not provided, the court should not hesitate to impose sanctions, including costs sanctions.[5]

[1] Available, as with the claim form, on the Ministry of Justice Website: see **19.28**.
[2] CPR 54.8(2)(a). A claimant may, however, seek an abridgement of time for filing of the acknowledgement when the claim is made, so it should not be assumed that the court has not directed a shorter timescale. It is also not unknown for the court to proceed to consider the application for permission on paper prior to the expiry of the 21 days, so it is always preferable that the acknowledgement be filed as soon as possible. Where this is not possible, it may be advisable to inform the Administrative Court office that a full response will be filed within the time limit. Where it is not possible to file within the time limit but the defendant intends to defend the claim, it is advisable to keep the Administrative Court Office informed and/or apply for an extension of time within the time limit.
[3] CPR 54.8(2)(b).
[4] [2013] EWHC 2873 (Admin).
[5] For equivalent rules in the Upper Tribunal see below at **19.166**.

19.44 In *R (Mount Cook Land Ltd) v Westminster City Council*,[1] Auld LJ said that the object of the acknowledgment of service was twofold:

i) to assist claimants with a speedy and relatively inexpensive determination by the court of the arguability of their claims; and
ii) to prompt defendants – public authorities – to give early consideration to and, where appropriate, to fulfil their public duties'.

It may well be the case that the acknowledgment of service achieves both ends. However, the introduction of the acknowledgment of service appears to have benefited defendants more than claimants. It has the effect of giving defendants the final word on the arguability of permission applications and it has been argued that the ability of the judge to hear arguments from both sides may well have raised the threshold of 'arguability'.[2]

[1] [2003] EWCA Civ 1346.
[2] See Bondy V and Sunkin M, 'The Dynamics of Judicial Review Litigation', available online at the time of writing at http://www.publiclawproject.org.uk/data/resources/9/TheDynamicsofJudicialReviewLitigation.pdf

19.45 The acknowledgement of service form contains four main parts:

(1) *Acknowledgement of claim (sections A, B and F)* – Section A of form N462 requires the defendant[1] to indicate whether he or she intends to contest the whole or part of the claim, or does not intend to contest the claim, and where the defendant is a court or tribunal, it should indicate whether or not it intends to make a submission.[2] Section B allows the defendant to give details of any further interested party not named in the claim form. Section F allows the defendant to indicate the address to which any notices should be sent and give details of counsel (if any).

(2) *Summary of grounds for contesting the claim (section C)* – A defendant may plead a defence to the claim prior to the consideration of permission. Points to bear in mind are:

(i) The summary grounds for contesting the claim serve a similar purpose to the claimant's grounds and, as with sections 5 and 8 of the claim form, it is common for the summary grounds to be attached to the acknowledgement of service as a separate document. This is the defendant's opportunity to influence the judge prior to the determination of permission on the papers.

(ii) The defendant is required to do no more than summarise the grounds by indicating the main points of resistance, and will not be prevented from making different arguments at a later stage. There are, however, two exceptions. The first is the issue of delay, which should normally not be re-opened at the substantive hearing[3] and which should therefore be fully argued in the acknowledgement of service. The second is where the defendant intends to contest the application on the basis that it is highly likely that the outcome for the claimant would not have been substantially different if the conduct complained of had not occurred, in which case the defendant must set out the grounds for doing so.[4] It may also be advisable to raise other points – such as the existence of an alternative remedy, issues of standing, or whether the defendant is a public body amenable to judicial review – at this stage,[5] but it does not appear a failure to do so will not prevent them being raised at a later stage.[6]

(iii) The purpose of summary grounds is to assist the judge in determining whether to grant permission. It is not to be the basis for resisting the substantive claim: this is the role of detailed grounds.[7] The courts have been very critical of lengthy summary grounds, and the costs of preparing them may not be recoverable.[8]

(iv) An interested party will not be limited to contesting the claim and may, in practice, wish to support the claim, in which case it may take the opportunity provided by Part C to set out its reasons for doing so and why it believes the claim should succeed (it is not limited to the reasons put forward by the claimant and it may, for example in the case of an interested NGO, wish to support the claim on more wide-ranging grounds than those relied upon by the claimant). Whether an interested party wishes to support or contest the claim, it is advisable to set out the basis of its interest in the claim.

(3) *Application for directions (section D)* – This section enables the defendant to apply for any directions. This is not limited to cases where permission is granted; for example, the defendant may wish to apply for a stay of the proceedings prior to the determination of permission, and any application for the costs of filing an acknowledgement of service should be included in section D.[9] In practice, however, the defendant is most likely to require directions where permission is granted. Applications for interim relief should be supported by evidence in the normal way. In immigration cases, a common direction sought is that oral renewal of the application should not be a bar to the claimant's removal, see for instance *R (MD (Afghanistan) v Secretary of State for the Home Department.*[10]

(4)   *Response to the claimant's contention that the claim is an Aarhus claim (section E)* — Where a claimant contends the claim is an Aarhus Convention claim, the defendant must indicate whether they deny that the claim is an Aarhus Convention claim and, if so the grounds for the denial.[11]

[1]   In this section a reference to the defendant should be taken to include any other person filing an acknowledgement of service.

[2]   Defendants who consider their factual case to be so strong that permission should be refused often file witness evidence with the acknowledgement of service. Form N462 states that a defendant court or tribunal need only provide the Administrative Court with such evidence as it can about the decision in order to help the Administrative Court perform its judicial function.

[3]   *R v Criminal Injuries Compensation Board, ex p A* [1999] 2 AC 330, and see also *R (Lichfield Securities Ltd) v Lichfield District Council* [2001] 3 PLR 33 (per Sedley LJ at 34), and *R v Chief Constable of West Yorkshire, ex p Wilkinson* [2002] EWHC 2353 (Admin), per Davis J.

[4]   CPR 54.8(4)(ia). Criminal Justice and Courts Act 2015, s 84(2) inserted subsections 31(3C)–(3F) into the Senior Courts Act 1981. By virtue of the new provisions, if the court considers it highly likely that the outcome for the applicant would not have been substantially different if the conduct complained of had not occurred, it must refuse to grant leave: s 31(3D). The court may consider that question of its own motion, but must consider it if the defendant asks it to: s 31(3C).

[5]   Especially where they are likely to be dispositive of the claim. In such a case (or in cases of delay) consideration should be given to requesting an oral hearing of the permission application.

[6]   See *R (McIntyre) v Gentoo Group Ltd* [2010] EWHC 5 (Admin); *IRC v National Federation of Self Employed and Small Businesses Ltd* [1982] AC 617 (standing).

[7]   See *R (Singh) v Secretary of State for the Home Department* [2013] EWHC 2873 (Admin), paragraph **4**. See *Ewing v Office of the Deputy Prime Minister (Practice Note)* ([2006] 1 WLR 1260), where the court indicated that Defendants would generally be entitled to the costs of 'summary' grounds only, and would not be able to recover the costs of lengthy, detailed grounds at the permission stage. Confirmed in *Davey v Aylesbury District Council* [2007] EWCA Civ 1166; See **19.82**.

[8]   R (Ewing) v Office of the Deputy Prime Minister [2005] EWCA Civ 1583, paragraph 53.

[9]   See **19.80**.

[10]   [2012] 1 WLR 2422, paragraph 6.

[11]   See **19.93**.

19.46   It has been suggested that a defendant may effectively secure a right of appeal against a grant of permission by including, within or alongside, the defendant's acknowledgement of service an application for summary judgment under CPR Pt 24, because appeal does lie against a refusal of summary judgment. Without finding it necessary to decide whether this could be done, this was, however, described by Richards J as a 'somewhat bold submission' in *R (Kurdistan Workers Party) v Secretary of State for the Home Department.*[1] To allow this would undermine the provisions of CPR 54, by allowing an appeal where none is envisaged by the CPR itself, and a defendant who considers itself to be prejudiced by the grant of permission can be adequately protected in an appropriate case by the court ordering expedition of the substantive hearing, or in limited circumstances by applying to have permission set aside.[2] Similar considerations would apply to an application to strike out the claim form under CPR 3.4.

[1]   [2002] ACD 560.

[2]   For the general prohibition on seeking to set aside grant of permission, see **19.71**.

Duty of Candour[1]

[1] Also see discussion in relation to disclosure at 19.116. In April 2016, the Lord Chief Justice issued a consultation in relation to proposed reforms to CPR PD 54A to: (i) clarify the general position governing the defendant's duty of candour and ensure it more closely reflected the case law; (ii) make provision for a specific disclosure procedure; and (iii) provide guidance in respect of the content of any acknowledgment of service filed by a defendant. At the time of writing, the responses were still under consideration by the Lord Chief Justice.

19.47 Although the standard civil rules of disclosure do not apply to judicial review proceedings, (unless the court orders otherwise)[2] both claimants and public authorities who are defendants to applications for judicial review are subject to a duty of candour.[3] Once a claim is issued, the duty requires the parties to assist the court by disclosure of materials that are reasonably required for the court to reach an accurate decision.[4] The duty is a wide one.[5] The objective of the duty is to ensure that public law litigation is a process 'which falls to be conducted with all the cards face upwards on the table'; however 'the vast majority of the cards will start in the authority's hands'.[6] As a result, consideration of the duty of candour has tended to focus on the defendant's duty.[7] The duty requires defendants to provide the court and the claimant with all documents and information that may help the claimant's case or give rise to additional grounds of challenge.[8] The duty requires defendants to give a true and comprehensive account of the way that the relevant decisions were arrived at and, if the court, at a later stage, discovers that this has not occurred, it may draw inferences against the Secretary of State upon points which remain obscure.[9]

[2] See *R (Plantagenet Alliance Ltd) v Secretary of State for Justice* [2013] EWHC 3164 (Admin), paragraph 70, citing Fordham Judicial Review Handbook at 10.4.

[3] *R (Bilal Mahmood) v Secretary of State for the Home Department* [2014] UKUT 00439.

[4] *R (Al Sweady) v Secretary of State for Defence* [2009] EWHC 2387 (Admin); *R (Quark Fishing Ltd) v Secretary of State for Foreign and Commonwealth Affairs* [2002] EWCA Civ 1409; *R v Secretary of State for the Home Department ex p Al-Fayed (No1)* [1998] 1 WLR 763.

[5] *R (Mohammad Khan) v Secretary of State for the Home Department* [2016] EWCA Civ 416 at paragraphs 45–46. The judgment of Beatson LJ provides an overview of the applicable principles in the context of the claimant's duty of candour.

[6] *R v Lancashire County Council, ex p Huddleston* [1986] 2 All ER 941.

[7] See comments of Beatson LJ in *Mohammad Khan* [2016] EWCA Civ 416 at paragraph 39.

[8] *R v Barnsley Metropolitan Borough Council, ex p Hook* [1976] 1 WLR 1052.

[9] *Padfield v Minister of Agriculture* [1968] AC 997, per Lord Upjohn at 1061G–1062A; approved of in R (Quark Fishing Ltd) v Secretary of State for Foreign and Commonwealth Affairs [2002] EWCA Civ 1409, itself applied by the Court of Appeal in R (I) v Secretary of State for the Home Department [2010] EWCA Civ 727.

19.48 In *R (Al Sweady) v Secretary of State for Defence*,[1] the Divisional Court identified serious failings in the defendant's compliance with its duty of candour, and emphasised the heightened duty of candour where a claimant alleged a breach of arts 2, 3 or 5 of the ECHR. In response, the Treasury Solicitor's Department published, in January 2010, a document entitled *'Guidance on Discharging the Duty of Candour and Disclosure in Judicial Review Proceedings'* which now sets out the standard procedure for Government Departments and Agencies when discharging the duty of candour.[2] In *R (Shoesmith) v Ofsted*,[3] Foskett J quoted from and approved the following paragraphs from that document:

'[Observance of the duty of candour] is particularly important when evidence is being prepared. When evidence is served in response to an application for judicial review, what is required is that that evidence read as a whole (i.e. the witness statement and the documents served in support of it) must be such as to meet the obligation of candour . . .

When preparing evidence in response to a claim for judicial review, one issue that frequently arises concerns the extent to which the duty of candour can be satisfied by providing a full and fair explanation of all relevant matters in a witness statement, and the extent to which such evidence must be supported by exhibiting relevant documents. Usually a mix of explanation by way of witness statement, and exhibiting key documents will be appropriate . . .

The duty of candour continues to apply throughout the proceedings. For example, if after the service of evidence, further relevant information comes to light, that information must be disclosed to the other parties to the proceedings and put before the Court at the earliest possible opportunity.'

[1]   [2009] EWHC 2387 (Admin).
[2]   Available online at the time of writing at: https://www.gov.uk/government/uploads/system/upl oads/attachment_data/file/285368/Tsol_discharging_1_.pdf
[3]   [2010] EWHC 852 (Admin). This aspect was undisturbed on appeal: [2011] PTSR 1459.

19.49 Accordingly, before filing the acknowledgment of service, it is important that defendants address their mind to what documents and information ought to be provided to the court to discharge the duty of candour. However, some proportionality is required in doing so; while it is not possible to prescribe the appropriate volume of material that ought to be disclosed at the permission stage, the nature of the claim and the stage of proceedings should be borne in mind to ensure that all pertinent and relevant documents are provided, without overloading the court. As the duty of candour is an ongoing duty, it may be appropriate to file further documents after the grant of permission.

Consequences of failure to file an acknowledgement of service

19.50 The consequences of failure to file an acknowledgement in time are less draconian for the defendant than in ordinary civil action under Part 8,[1] and are limited to preventing the defendant from taking part in any hearing to decide whether permission should be granted without the consent of the court.[2] The defendant or any other person served with the claim form can participate in any substantive hearing of the claim notwithstanding a failure to file an acknowledgement provided that they comply with the rules for filing and service of detailed grounds and written evidence.[3] A failure to file an acknowledgement by a person who subsequently takes part in the substantive hearing may also be taken into account by the court in considering what order to make about costs.[4] Failure to file an acknowledgement of service on time has the result that the general rule that the claimant should pay the defendant's costs of the acknowledgement if permission is refused, does not apply.[5]

[1]   CPR 8.4, disapplied by CPR 54.9(3).
[2]   CPR 54.9(1)(a).

³ CPR 54.9(1)(b). For the rules regarding filing/service of detailed grounds etc, see CPR 54.14, which requires that such documents be served within 35 days of the service of the order granting permission.
⁴ CPR 54.9(2); and see discussion of this rule in *R (Leach) v Local Administration Comr* [2001] EWHC 455 (Admin) and *R (Mount Cook Land Ltd) v Westminster City Council* [2003] EWCA Civ 1346.
⁵ *R (Riniker) v Employment Tribunals and Regional Chairmen* [2009] EWCA Civ 1450.

Reply to acknowledgement of service

19.51 There are currently no prescribed rules in the CPR in relation to a claimant's reply to the acknowledgement of service. There is nothing in principle to prevent a claimant from seeking to reply, by way of additional evidence or even written submissions, to the matters put forward by the defendant in its acknowledgement of service. While it is impossible to be prescriptive about the circumstances which might justify a reply, it may be appropriate where the acknowledgment of service is misleading in some way, or where the claimant is able to point to an authority or factual evidence which makes a definitive response to an argument raised by the defendant. However, it would not be justified to make a reply as a matter of course, and the court will not generally wish to be bombarded with additional material or argument prior to consideration of the paper application. The costs of producing an unnecessary reply may not be recoverable even by a successful party.

GRANT OF PERMISSION

19.52 CPR 54.4 provides that no claim for judicial review may proceed without the permission of the court, whether or not the claim is started under Part 54 or begun by ordinary action and transferred to the Administrative Court.

19.53 The purpose of the permission stage is to 'protect public bodies against weak and vexatious claims'.[1] The general test for the grant of permission in judicial review is that a case is arguable. It is not enough that a case is potentially arguable; there must be a realistic prospect of success.[2] However, the grant of permission remains a matter of discretion for the court.

¹ Per Lord Bingham in *R v Secretary of State for the Environment, ex p Eastway* [2000] 1 WLR 2222, at 2227. To similar effect, see Lord Diplock in *IRC v National Federation of Self Employed and Small Businesses Ltd* [1982] AC 617.
² Per Lord Bingham in *Sharma v Brown-Antoine* [2007] 1 WLR 780.

19.54 In addition to the arguability of the substantive case, consideration should also be given to whether any of the discretionary restrictions on remedies in judicial review[1] are applicable, whether the defendant is indeed a public body[2] and whether judicial review provides the appropriate forum for the claim.[3] The question of delay should normally be dealt with at the permission hearing and, in the ordinary case, should not be re-opened at the substantive hearing.[4] Other such issues may prove dispositive and may also affect the future course of the litigation so that, as a matter of good case management, they should be raised at this stage.

¹ Considered in CHAPTER **18** above.

2   See CHAPTER 5.
3   The public/private law divide, considered in CHAPTERS 5 and 6.
4   See **19.45**(2)(ii) above.

The public interest

19.55 The public interest may be a relevant factor in deciding whether to grant permission, though in most cases, arguments over the public interest will not arise. In *R (Gentle) v Prime Minister*, the Court of Appeal granted permission to apply for judicial review of the government's decision to refuse to hold an inquiry into the Iraq war. In so doing, the Court noted that permission was granted not on the basis that the application for judicial review had a real prospect of success, but because of the importance of the issues involved.[1] The public interest may also weigh against the grant of permission. In *Mass Energy v Birmingham City Council*,[2] Glidewell LJ adopted a higher threshold of whether the claim was 'strong', on the basis that the court had heard detailed argument and considered most, if not all, of the relevant documentation in detail, and that this was a case where there was considerable public disadvantage in delay. Accordingly, it was considered appropriate to apply a higher test at the permission stage. The *Mass Energy* approach has been said not to be limited to permission applications before the Court of Appeal and could apply:

> 'where the court was satisfied that it had heard as much argument and dealt with the matter in as much depth as was normally likely at a substantive hearing'.[3]

1   [2006] EWCA Civ 1078 at paragraph 1; cf CPR Pt 52.3(6)(b).
2   [1994] Env LR 298; see also *R (Federation of Technological Industries) v Customs and Excise Comrs* [2004] EWHC 254 (Admin).
3   *R v London Docklands Development Corpn, ex p S Frost* (1997) 73 P & CR 199. In such a case, the Defendant may get their costs of attending the oral renewal hearing if permission is refused: *R (Salt Union Ltd) v The Health and Safety Executive* [2012] EWHC 2611 (Admin), [73].

19.56 A similar, if generally less onerous, approach has been taken in other cases where fuller argument than usual has been addressed to the court and the public interest was not advanced by continuing uncertainty brought about by ongoing litigation.[1] In *R (Johnson) v Professional Conduct Committee of Nursing and Midwifery Council*,[2] Beatson J considered that, after a three-day permission hearing, it was 'a classic case for the application of the modified test for permission'. The general purpose of the permission stage is, however, to act as a filter against unmeritorious applications, so that it should not become common practice for defendants to seek an extended hearing at the permission stage in order to secure a heightened test for permission.

1   See eg *R v Cotswold District Council, ex p Barrington Parish Council* (1997) 75 P & CR 515 (Keene J required the applicant to show 'a reasonably good chance of success' after hearing full argument from leading Counsel); *R v Derbyshire CC, ex p Woods* [1998] Env LR 277 (a less onerous test than the *Mass Energy* case, but more so than 'a reasonable prospect of success', adopted by CA as a discretionary matter); *R and Northampton Borough Council, ex p Northampton Rapid Transit System* [2000] EWHC 367 (Admin) (10 July 2000) (permission granted applying the *Woods* test); *R (Federation of Technological Industries) v Customs and Excise Comrs* [2004] EWHC 254 (Admin), [2004] STC 1008.

19.57 A different test applies for permission to bring judicial review in so-called 'Cart' judicial reviews.[1] These cases concern situations where a decision in the First Tier Tribunal has been appealed to the Upper Tribunal, but permission to appeal has been refused. Where the decision of the Upper Tribunal in refusing permission is challenged by way of judicial review, then a higher threshold applies,[2] mirroring the so-called 'second appeals' test applicable where the Court of Appeal is called upon to consider permission to appeal to itself from a decision of the Upper Tribunal. The two limbs to the test are now embodied in CPR 54.7A. The claimant must show that there is an arguable case, which has a reasonable prospect of success, that both the decision of the First-tier Tribunal and that of the Upper Tribunal refusing permission were wrong in law, and that *either* the claim raises an important point of principle or practice, or there is some other compelling reason to hear it.

[1] *R (Cart) v Upper Tribunal* [2012] 1 AC 663.
[2] CPR 54.7A(7).

19.58 The first limb, requiring an 'important point of principle or practice', requires little by way of elucidation.[1] The second limb, requiring 'some other compelling reason', has proved more controversial. It was considered by the Court of Appeal in considering permission to appeal in *PR (Sri Lanka) v Secretary of State for the Home Department*,[2] but the guidance in that case is now largely overtaken by the subsequent decision of the Court of Appeal in *JD (Congo) v Secretary of State for the Home Department*.[3]

[1] Unsurprisingly, it was held in *Uphill v BRB (Residuary) Ltd* [2005] 1 WLR 2070 that it must be a controversial point of principle, so that the court's guidance on the issue was required. A claimant who is able to point to a clear error in relation to a settled point of principle may still be able to rely on the second limb however.
[2] [2012] 1 WLR 73.
[3] [2012] 1 WLR 3273.

19.59 It is important to note that some of the guidance in *JD (Congo)*[1] is not directly relevant to *Cart* judicial reviews,[2] because that case does not relate directly to an application to set aside a decision of the Upper Tribunal refusing permission to appeal from the First-tier. However, the key observation of the court is that the 'compelling reason' test is flexible.[3] It may be satisfied by demonstrating a more than merely arguable case, but the court will be flexible as to how much higher than merely arguable the case would need to be. Serious consequences for the claimant, such as might often arise in the asylum context among others, would be one of a number of factors which would be relevant:[4]

'We have deliberately used the phrase "sufficiently serious legal basis for challenging the UT's decision" because the threshold for a second appeal must be higher than that for an ordinary appeal—real prospect of success. How much higher, how strongly arguable the legal grounds for the challenge must be, will depend upon the particular circumstances of the individual case and, for the reasons set out above, those will include the extremity of the consequences of the UT's allegedly erroneous decision for the individual seeking permission to appeal from that decision. It may well be the case that many applicants in immigration and asylum cases will be able to point to the "truly dire consequences" of an erroneous decision. As Mr Husain pointed out, a decision to remove an asylum applicant from the United Kingdom's jurisdiction to the place where he claims to fear persecution will be irreversible. Just as there is no case for applying a different test to applications for permission to appeal from the Immigration and Asylum Chamber of the UT (see Lord Dyson JSC at para 125 of the *Cart case* [2012] 1 AC 663), so also there is no reason to minimise the significance of the consequences of a decision in the immigration and asylum field merely because legal errors in that field are often capable of having dire consequences for appellants.

1   [2012] 1 WLR 3273.
2   [2012] 1 AC 663.
3   Paragraph 23.
4   Paragraph 27.

Consideration on the papers

19.60 The court has power to determine the application for permission without a hearing,[1] and in the ordinary case, permission will first be considered on the papers only, following receipt of the defendant's (and any interested party's) acknowledgement of service.[2] Where permission is granted it may be on all grounds relied upon in the claim form, or on limited grounds only, and when granting permission the court may proceed to make any directions it considers necessary for the future conduct of the claim. Any order must be served on the claimant, the defendant and any other party who has filed an acknowledgement of service.[3]

1   CPR 54.12.
2   CPR Pt 54A PD 8.4.
3   CPR 54.11.

19.61 As an alternative to granting permission, the court may adjourn the permission application into open court, and may consider it appropriate to do so in cases it considers to be at the borderline of arguability, where the defendant raises issues about delay or other bars to relief, where interim relief is sought or for case management reasons.

Renewal of the permission application

19.62 Where permission is refused, or permission is granted on certain grounds only or subject to conditions, the court will serve its reasons for the decision with the order giving or refusing permission.[1] There is no right of appeal,[2] but the claimant may renew the application by filing a request for a renewal within seven days of service of the reasons for the decision.[3] The claimant is entitled as of right to renew the application,[4] but must specify the reasons why renewal is sought in the light of the reasons given by the judge for refusing permission.[5] A fee of £385 is payable on renewal of the application, but this is subtracted from the sum payable for continuing with the claim if permission is granted.[6]

1   CPR 54.12(2).
2   CPR 54.12(3). The Court of Appeal considered, but did not determine, an argument in *R (MD (Afghanistan) v Secretary of State for the Home Department* [2012] 1 WLR 2422 to the effect that, in this regard, CPR 54.12(3) is ultra vires the Senior Courts Act 1981, s 16(1).

3 CPR 54.12(3) and (4).
4 Subject to the exceptions at **19.65** below.
5 Practice Statement (Administrative Court: Listing and Urgent Cases) [2002] 1 WLR 810.
6 This fee being £700: see the Civil Proceedings Fees (Amendment) Order 2014, SI 2014/874.

19.63 Renewed applications are by way of rehearing and are usually heard in open court,[1] to be listed for half an hour unless the parties indicate that a longer period will be required.[2] In a criminal cause or matter, the renewed application is generally made to a Divisional Court comprising two judges; in a civil cause or matter, it will generally go before a single judge. The court can make any directions it considers appropriate if it grants permission. Where permission is refused following an oral hearing, the claimant may appeal to the Court of Appeal. Appeals, including appeals against the refusal of permission, are dealt with in CHAPTER 20. Subject to any appeal, refusal of permission following a renewed application will normally be the end of the matter.[3]

1 Subject to the exceptions listed at CPR 39.2.
2 See paragraph **8.5** of the Judicial Review Guide 2016 published by the Administrative Court Office and available at https://www.gov.uk/government/uploads/system/uploads/attachment_d ata/file/540607/administrative-court-judicial-review-guide.pdf
3 For appeals at the permission stage, see **20.76**. As to whether a fresh application based on arguments rejected at the permission stage would be an abuse of process, see CHAPTER **18**, and the discussion of limited permission below.

19.64 If permission is refused on the papers, or after a hearing, the court may follow procedures designed to identify litigants who make claims that are totally without merit[1]. These procedures are explained at **20.89** below.

1 For an analysis of what 'totally without merit' means see *Samia Wasif v SSHD* [2016] EWCA Civ 82.

19.65 Where permission is considered on the papers, and the judge records the fact that the application is totally without merit, then the Claimant's right to request that the decision be reconsidered at a hearing does not apply.[1] The right to oral renewal also does not apply in the case of 'Cart' judicial reviews.[2] The absence of a right to oral renewal (whether because of CPR 54.7A, or a 'totally without merit' finding) is relevant to onward appeal rights. (See CHAPTER 20.)

1 CPR 54.12(7).
2 CPR 54.7A(8). For the meaning of 'Cart' judicial review, see **19.57** above.

Limited grant of permission

19.66 CPR 54.12(1)(b) makes clear that any grant of permission may be made (i) subject to conditions or (ii) on limited grounds only. In exercising that power the court must have regard to the overriding objective[1] and to its duties of active case management.[2] Where permission has been granted on limited issues following consideration on the papers, the claimant has a right to renew the application for permission orally.[3]

1 CPR 1.1.
2 CPR 1.4. This duty includes early identification of the issues and the summary disposal of those issues not requiring full investigation (CPR 1.4(2)(b) and (c) respectively).

³ Where permission has been granted on some issues on the papers, but refused on others, it should not be open to a defendant, at an oral renewal hearing, to question permission on the issues where permission has already been granted, except in the very limited circumstances where it would be open to the defendant to apply to set aside permission.

19.67 The effect of a grant of permission being limited to certain grounds only is not to wholly exclude reliance on the grounds on which permission was refused at the substantive hearing. CPR 54.15 expressly contemplates that a claimant may obtain the court's permission to rely on grounds other than those for which permission is originally granted. Whether or not such permission should be granted is a matter for the discretion of the judge hearing the substantive application, and guidance as to the exercise of that discretion was given by Lord Woolf CJ in *R (Smith) v Parole Board*.¹ There is no requirement for a 'new situation', in the sense of new material or a change in the law; rather, the judge has a broad discretion to consider whether there is 'good reason' to take a different view from the single judge at the permission stage, albeit that where the judge who granted permission heard detailed argument 'significant justification' would be required before a trial judge took a different view (in *Smith*, argument at the permission stage before Silber J had lasted some three hours). The discretion must be exercised having regard to the interests of the defendant not to be presented with an argument for which they are unprepared, and a claimant would be expected to notify the defendant of the intention to rely on the ground on which permission had been refused.² It appears that the above approach is correct even where the limited permission has been granted by the Court of Appeal.³

¹ [2003] 1 WLR 2548.
² Smith, and see, also, *R (Hunt) v Criminal Cases Review Commission* [2001] QB 1108, and *R v Bow Street Stipendiary Magistrate, ex p Roberts* [1990] 1 WLR 1317.
³ *R v Radio Authority, ex p Wildman* [1999] COD 255, *R (Pelling) v Bow County Court* [2001] ACD 1, albeit that (per Lord Woolf MR in *Wildman*) a first instance judge would 'naturally pay the greatest of attention to the views expressed by the Court of Appeal' and 'would be expected, in normal circumstances, not to take a different view' absent developments of which the Court of Appeal was unaware.

19.68 *Smith* was a case where permission was only granted following an oral hearing. Where limited permission is granted on the papers, the fact that a claimant may renew the application may suggest that this route should be used where the claimant wishes to pursue a ground for which permission has been refused on the papers. However, there may be cases where this would add unnecessarily to the costs. Early communication with the defendant may be the key, so that the parties can agree the approach to procedure.

Procedure from grant of permission onwards

19.69 *Service of the order granting permission* – The order granting permission will be served by the Administrative Court Office on each claimant and defendant along with any other person who has filed an acknowledgement of service.¹ The order will be served along with the Court's reasons for making the decision.²

¹ CPR 54.11, which also provides for any directions by the court to be similarly served. Such directions are likely to be concerned with one or more of the topics discussed in the remainder of this chapter.

² CPR 54.12(2).

19.70 *Payment of fee to continue* – Within seven days of the service of the order granting permission, the claimant must pay a further fee, or lodge a fees exemption certificate,¹ to continue the proceedings. Since 22 April 2014, the fees are £770, unless £385 has already been paid for oral renewal, in which case the fee on the grant of permission is £385. Failure to pay the fee or lodge a certificate within the specified period may result in the claim being struck out.²

¹   See the note to **19.28** above.
²   See the Civil Proceedings Fees (Amendment) Order 2014, SI 2014/874 as amended by the Civil Proceedings, First-tier Tribunal, Upper Tribunal and Employment Tribunals Fees (Amendment) Order 2016/807. Sanctions for non-payment are dealt with at CPR 3.7; in addition to the claim being struck out, the claimant becomes liable for costs which the defendant has incurred unless the court orders otherwise.

19.71 *Setting aside and revoking permission* – CPR 54.13 now provides that neither 'the defendant nor any other person served with the claim form' may apply to set aside an order giving permission to proceed. However it is clear that the court can revoke permission on its own motion where permission has been granted, through oversight, without sight of the acknowledgment of service¹ and defendants may wish to invite the court to revoke permission where they have not been notified of the application for permission, although this is not likely to arise often.² In *(Mohammad Khan) v Secretary of State for the Home Department*, the Court of Appeal set aside a grant of permission due to a serious breach of the duty of candour; the claimant had failed to bring to the court's attention a significant discrepancy which was both within the claimant's knowledge and fatally undermined the main plank in their application.³

¹   See *R (Candlish) v Hastings Borough Council* [2005] EWHC 1539 (Admin).
²   For discussion of whether a defendant can secure a right of appeal by applying for summary judgment, see 19.46.
³   [2016] EWCA Civ 416, paragraph 46. See also *R (Sabir) v Secretary of State for the Home Department* [2015] EWCA Civ 1173.

19.72 *Applications by a third party to set aside permission* – The wording of CPR 54.13 is limited to a defendant or other person served with the claim form, so a person not served is not prevented by this rule from making an application to set aside permission. It may nevertheless be unusual for such an application to succeed where the interested party is unable to raise points that were, or could have been, raised by a defendant who was properly served. However, the position may be different where, for example, the interested party can show a prejudice to itself occasioned by delay that would not have affected the defendant. In a case where there is a clear answer to the claim that had not been taken by the defendant at the permission stage, such as where the claim is prevented by ouster or the defendant is not a public body, it may as an alternative be possible to treat that as a preliminary issue at an early hearing.¹

¹   See *R v Association of British Travel Agents, ex p Sunspell Ltd* [2001] ACD 16.

19.73 *Grounds of opposition* – A defendant and any other person served with the claim form who wishes to contest the claim or support it on additional grounds must file and serve detailed grounds for contesting the claim or supporting it on additional grounds, and any evidence, within 35 days after service of the order giving permission.[1] In this regard, public bodies are expected to assist the court by producing documents and giving such reasons as are needed to enable the court to fulfil its judicial function.[2]

[1] CPR 54.14(1). See **19.45**(2)(iii) above distinguishing the purpose of summary and detailed grounds.
[2] As to disclosure of documents generally, see **19.116** et seq. As to reasons. Sir John Donaldson MR said in *R v Lancashire County Council, ex p Huddleston* [1986] 2 All ER 941 that a local authority whose decision is challenged in judicial review proceedings should, like the judge of an inferior court, not be partisan in those proceedings and should, in the interests of high standards of public administration, assist the court by disclosing, so far as necessary, such reasons as are adequate to enable the court to ascertain whether the local authority was in error in reaching its decision by taking into account irrelevant considerations or not taking into account relevant considerations.

19.74 *Further interested parties and interveners* – Persons who are interested parties but were not identified earlier as such, or persons who are not interested parties but wish to be heard, may apply to the court in that regard.[1]

[1] See **20.17** and **20.18**.

19.75 *Reconsideration of merits* – When the Administrative Court serves the order granting permission it is accompanied by notes reminding claimants and their legal advisers of their obligation to reconsider the merits of their application in the light of the defendant's evidence.[1]

[1] See Hodgson J in *R v Secretary of State for the Home Department, ex p Brown* (1984) Times, 6 February.

ROLLED UP HEARINGS

19.76 In certain cases, the permission and substantive stages may be considered together at a 'rolled up' hearing. This can be called for by the parties, or ordered by the judge on review of the papers. In *R (WJ (China)) v Secretary of State for the Home Department*,[1] Beatson J referred to rolled up hearings as 'a relatively recent development' and acknowledged that they involve procedural uncertainties, as they are not specifically catered for by the CPR. However, he noted that it might be appropriate to order a rolled up hearing when

'there is an issue of delay which, if permission is granted, cannot be raised at the substantive hearing. They may also be justified where there is an issue that has to be determined urgently, its arguability is not clear on the material before the court, but the relevant evidence has either been adduced by the time the papers are considered by the court or it can be adduced within a shortened timescale'.

In the view of the authors, the rolled up hearing procedure does provide the court with a very useful flexibility, especially in dealing with factually complex cases which need to be determined urgently. When a rolled-up hearing is ordered, it is desirable to have directions given to ensure a pre-hearing timetable is set down, as the ordinary rules of CPR Pt 54.14(1) and CPR Pt 54A PD 15.1 do not apply. Claimants should be aware that rolled up hearings carry a significant costs risk, as the ordinary rules applicable to the costs of permission hearings do not apply.[2] In a rolled up hearing, if the court grants permission, it will do so on the condition of the claimant's representatives giving an undertaking that the fee to proceed to substantive challenge is paid.

[1]   [2010] EWHC 776 (Admin).
[2]   See below at **19.80–19.86**.

19.77 The introduction of legal aid rules which mean that providers will only be paid if permission is granted[1] is leading to a reluctance by claimants to seek, and the courts to order, rolled up hearings, at least in legally aided claims.

[1]   See reg 5A of the Civil Legal Aid (Remuneration) Regulations 2013, SI 2013/422. See also the challenge to reg 5A in *R (on the application of Ben Hoare Bell Solicitors) v Lord Chancellor* [2015] EWHC 523 (Admin).

COSTS IN THE EARLY STAGES

19.78 Costs are awarded in judicial review proceedings under the broad discretionary powers given to the High Court and Court of Appeal by s 51 of the Senior Courts Act 1981,[1] but the costs provisions of the CPR apply.[2]

[1]   See *R v Camden London Borough Council, ex p Martin* [1997] 1 WLR 359 per Sedley J at 365A.
[2]   CPR Parts 43, 44, 47 and 48.

Costs where permission, or other application, granted

19.79 CPR 44.13(1A) provides that, where the court makes an order granting permission to apply for judicial review, and the order does not mention costs, it will be deemed to include an order for costs to be in the case.[1] It may be that the court should take that default position as its starting point in considering whether to make any different order. This rule would also apply where the court makes an order for interim relief following an application without notice to the defendant.

[1]   CPR 44.13(1B) enables any party affected by such a deemed order to apply at any time to vary the order.

Costs where permission refused

19.80 Where permission is refused, the general rule is that (i) the defendant is entitled to its costs of preparing an acknowledgement of service but (ii) it is not entitled to the costs of attending an oral hearing to resist permission.[1] That general presumption reflects the fact that preparation of an acknowledgement of service is mandatory and a failure to produce one can disentitle the defendant to costs subsequently, whereas attendance at an oral permission hearing is not required unless the court directs otherwise.[2] In *R (Mount Cook Land Ltd) v Westminster City Council*, Auld LJ stated that the general rule should only be departed from where the court considers that there are 'exceptional circumstances for doing so'. As an example of exceptional circumstances that may justify an award of the defendant's costs of attending the permission hearing, the following non-exhaustive list was provided:

(a)   the hopelessness of the claim;

(b)   the persistence in it by the claimant after having been alerted to facts and/or of the law demonstrating its hopelessness;

(c)   the extent to which the court considers that the claimant, in the pursuit of his application, has sought to abuse the process of judicial review for collateral ends – a relevant consideration as to costs at the permission stage, as well as when considering discretionary refusal of relief at the stage of substantive hearing, if there is one; and

(d)   whether, as a result of the deployment of full argument and documentary evidence by both sides at the hearing of a contested application, the unsuccessful claimant has had, in effect, the advantage of an early substantive hearing of the claim'[3]

[1]   See, generally, *R (Mount Cook Land Ltd) v Westminster City Council* [2004] 1 PLR 29, giving judicial recognition to the presumption contained in CPR Pt 54 PD 8.6.

[2]   CPR Pt 54 PD 8.5.

[3]   Costs awarded at the permission stage can include wasted costs: *R (F) v Head Teacher of Addington High School* [2003] EWHC 228 (Admin). For further discussion of wasted costs orders see **20.31**.

19.81 In *Mount Cook*, it was also said that the availability or otherwise to the claimant of 'substantial resources . . . used to pursue the unfounded claim and which are available to meet an order for costs' was a relevant factor for the court in the exercise of its discretion to award costs on the grounds of exceptional circumstances, although it is not (it is submitted) itself an exceptional circumstance justifying the award of costs.[1] In all but the most exceptional case the costs of a permission hearing would be dealt with by summary assessment.[2]

[1]   For a discussion of the court's practice in awarding costs at the permission stage, see Kate Markus, 'Urgent Applications, Interim Relief and Costs' [2004] JR 256. In particular, the author makes the point that a distinction needs to be drawn between a case that is unarguable, in the sense that leads to the refusal of permission, and true 'hopelessness' in the sense envisaged by Auld LJ in *Mount Cook*, lest the presumption that a defendant's costs should not be awarded merge into a practice that they will ordinarily be awarded.

[2]   CPR Pt 44 PD 9.2(b) provides that the court should normally make a summary assessment at the conclusion of any hearing which lasted not more than one day. Also see *R (Ewing) v Office of the Deputy Prime Minister* [2005] EWCA Civ 1583, discussed below.

19.82 The general rule must be read in light of the Court of Appeal's judgment in *R (Ewing) v Office of the Deputy Prime Minister*,[1] in which Carnwath LJ (as he then was) warned defendants that they would not be entitled to substantial costs of preparing the acknowledgment of service. He said:

'The purpose of the "summary of grounds" is not to provide the basis for full argument of the substantive merits, but rather . . . to assist the judge in deciding whether to grant permission, and if so on what terms . . . it should be possible to do what is required without incurring substantial expense at this stage'.

He referred to the 2½ page grounds of the interested party as a 'model', in contrast to the defendant's 50-page submission. In light of this judgment, defendants who choose to put in lengthy grounds at the permission stage should not expect to recover all the costs involved in doing so.[2]

1   [2005] EWCA Civ 1583.
2   Confirmed in *Davey v Aylesbury District Council* [2007] EWCA Civ 1166 (discussed in more detail at **19.45** above).

19.83 In *Ewing*, Carnwath LJ set out the following procedures to be adopted by the parties to judicial review litigation in relation to costs at the permission stage:[1]

(a)   Where a proposed defendant or interested party wishes to seek costs at the permission stage, the Acknowledgment of Service should include an application for costs and should be accompanied by a Schedule setting out the amount claimed.

(b)   The judge refusing permission should include in the refusal a decision as to whether to award costs in principle and if so, an indication of the amount which he proposes to assess summarily.

(c)   The claimant should be given 14 days to respond in writing and should serve a copy on the defendant.

(d)   The defendant should reply in writing within seven days.

(e)   The judge will then decide and make an award on the papers.

1   At paragraph **47**.

19.84 Parties should be aware that the guidance provided in *Mount Cook* and in *Ewing* assume compliance with the CPR and with the pre-action protocol. Where either party has failed to comply with a procedural rule, the court may take a different approach on costs. In *Ewing*, Brooke LJ said that a claimant who chooses to skip the pre-action protocol stage 'must expect to put his opponents to greater expense in preparing the summary of their grounds for contesting the claim, and this may be reflected in the greater order for costs' made against him.[1] Similarly, where the defendant has filed his acknowledgment of service after the deadline for submission, he will not be entitled to his costs of producing the same.[2]

1   At paragraph **54**.
2   *R (Riniker) v Employment Tribunals and Regional Chairmen* [2009] EWCA Civ 1450.

19.85 The well-established general rule is that the court will only award one set of costs against a claimant in judicial review (see generally Chapter 20 at **20.117**).[1] A literal reading of para 76(1) of *Mount Cook* suggests that this general rule does not apply in relation to Acknowledgement of Service Costs, so that a second defendant or interested party who files an Acknowledgement of Service will generally be entitled to their costs of doing so where permission is refused, even where that leads to a claimant having to pay more than one set of costs. Previous editions of this chapter have doubted whether the Court of Appeal intended that result. It is unclear whether the Court of Appeal had its attention drawn to the general rule on second sets of costs, or whether it intended what is said about acknowledgement of service costs to be subject to that more general rule. Further, given the significant barrier to access to justice that high costs exposure can give rise to, there would appear to be strong policy arguments in favour of enforcing the general rule in this context. Of course, as HHJ Richardson QC recognised in *R (Salford Estates Ltd) v*

Durham CC (Costs), the general rule that a second set of costs is not payable can always be departed from if exceptional circumstances are made out to justify that.[2] However, some recent authority does appear to indicate that a second defendant or interested party who files an Acknowledgement of Service should be entitled to their costs of doing so as of right where permission is refused. That was accepted by Walker J in R *(Kenyon) v Wakefield Council* [2013] EWHC 1269 (Admin),[3] albeit only in a post-judgment ruling, and that was in turn followed by Holgate J *in R (Luton BC) v Central Bedfordshire Council*.[4] The extent to which the point was fully argued in either case is unclear. Holgate J was upheld on appeal,[5] but again it does not appear that the question of whether a second set of costs should be made as of right was put in issue. The position is therefore not completely clear but we suggest that the Kenyon and Luton cases should not necessarily be seen as determinative.

[1]   Also see *Bolton Metropolitan District Council v Secretary of State for the Environment* [1995] 1 WLR 1176; *R (Smeaton) v Secretary of State for Health* [2002] EWHC 610 (Admin).
[2]   [2013] EWHC 776 (Admin) at paragraph 13.
[3]   [2012] EWHC 1785 (Admin). Kensington and Chelsea RLBC was a section 288 challenge, where the interested party was in substance treated as a second defendant throughout the proceedings.
[4]   [2014] EWHC 4325 (Admin), at paragraph 221.
[5]   [2015] EWHC Civ 537, per Sales LJ at paragraph 81.

19.86 The general principles in *R (Mount Cook Land Ltd) v Westminster City Council*,[1] are not displaced by CPR 38.6 where the claimant issues a notice of discontinuance shortly before an oral renewal application: *R (Smoke Club Ltd) v Network Rail Infrastructure Ltd*.[2] However, in *Smoke Club*, the defendant was nevertheless awarded one-third of its costs subsequent to acknowledgement of service.

[1]   [2004] 1 PLR 29. See **19.80** below.
[2]   [2013] EWHC 3830 (Admin).

19.87 In relation to the award of any costs to interveners in judicial review claims, the court must now take into account s 87 of the Criminal Justice and Courts Act 2015. This provision provides that:

(i)   a party may not be ordered to pay an intervener's costs unless there are exceptional circumstances making it appropriate to do so;[1] and

(ii) on an application for costs by a party to the claim, the court must order an intervener to pay costs specified in the application that the court considers have been incurred by the relevant party as a result of the intervener's involvement in that stage of the proceedings: where the intervener has acted, in substance, as the sole or principal applicant, defendant, appellant or respondent; where the intervener's evidence and representations, take as a whole, have not been of significant assistance to the court; where a significant part of the intervener's evidence and representations relates to matters that were not necessary for the court to consider in order to resolve the issues; or where the intervener as behaved unreasonably.[2]

[1]   Section 87(3)–(4).
[2]   Section 87(5)–(6).

Costs following settlement concession by defendant

19.88 There has recently been a significant change in the approach of the court to costs in cases where a claim is compromised before a final hearing, in circumstances where this leads to the claimant achieving a favourable outcome. If that is because the claim becomes academic for reasons outside of the control of the parties, the appropriate order, at least by way of starting point or default position, is likely to be that each side will bear its own costs: see *R (Naureen) v Salford City Council*.[1] The court will however retain a discretion to make a different order. By contrast, where a claim is compromised in the claimant's favour as a result of the litigation, the ordinary rule is that the defendant should pay the claimant's costs. The principles applicable to the latter situation were set out in a number of recent decisions of the Court of Appeal, including most notably *R (Bahta) v Secretary of State for the Home Department*,[2] *M v Croydon London Borough Council*,[3] and *R (Tesfay) v Secretary of State for the Home Department*.[4]

These cases make clear that the general rule, that costs follow the event, applies with equal rigour in judicial review (and other public law proceedings: see *AL (Albania) v Secretary of State for the Home Department*[5]), even in cases which settle at an early stage of the proceedings. They also give effect to the obligations on parties to proceedings to comply with the pre-action protocol.

The ratio of *Bahta* (as identified in the subsequent case of *AL (Albania)*, is as follows:[6]

> When relief is granted,[7] the defendant bears the burden of justifying a departure from the general rule that the unsuccessful party will be ordered to pay the costs of the successful party and that the burden is likely to be a heavy one if the claimant has, and the defendant has not, complied with the Pre-Action Protocol. I regard that approach as consistent with the recommendation in para 4.13 of the Jackson Report.

In *M v Croydon* Lord Neuberger MR (as he then was) distinguished between three types of case:[8]

(i)   a case where a claimant has been wholly successful whether following a contested hearing or pursuant to a settlement, where costs would generally follow;

(ii)   a case where he has only succeeded in part following a contested hearing, or pursuant to a settlement, where costs may also follow but no order for costs may also be appropriate;

(iii)   a case where there has been some compromise which does not actually reflect the claimant's claims, where there is a default position of no order but a claimant may nevertheless seek a different order.

The question of what is meant by a claimant being 'wholly' or 'partly' successful in the context of a judicial review claim was considered by the Court of Appeal in *R (Tesfay) v Secretary of State for the Home Department*, where Lloyd Jones LJ noted that:[9] 'Whereas in a settlement of private law litigation it is usually possible to identify with some precision the extent to which a party has been vindicated, the position following compromise of public law litigation is often not so clear cut. Proceedings for judicial review are brought by persons dissatisfied with decisions of public bodies. However, the courts are not the decision-makers and often in public law the most that can be achieved is an order that the decision-maker reconsider on a correct legal basis. That may not lead to ultimate victory for the applicant because the new decision may be a lawful decision against the interests of the applicant. Nevertheless, to achieve an order for reconsideration will often be a substantial achievement. Success in public law proceedings must be assessed not only by reference to what was sought and the basis on which it was sought and on which it was opposed, but also by reference to what was achievable.' The judge went on to note that, in public law challenges, securing reconsideration of a decision would usually be considered a success.[10] An example of a partial success can be found in Lloyd Jones LJ's consideration of one group of claimants, identified as 'the Malta claimants'. The judge found that the Malta claimants could not recover their costs because, despite having in substance achieved the outcome that they sought, this outcome was not as a result of their arguments succeeding — their arguments had been rejected, but they benefitted from the defendant's withdrawal of the decisions relating to them on the basis of a decision of the Supreme Court. Thus, the fact that they had achieved the outcome they sought 'represented only a very limited success'.[11] Obversely, a claimant who has achieved a quashing order in relation to an impugned decision will not be denied his full costs just because the pleaded relief referred to a mandatory order or declaration (and vice versa) and he will only be denied his full costs for pursuing unsuccessful arguments as well as successful ones if there is reason to think that that has had a significant effect on the overall costs of the parties (as it may *sometimes* do after a contested hearing, but is very unlikely to have done if a claim is settled early on). The later observations of Sullivan LJ in *AN (Afghanistan) v Secretary of State for the Home Department*[12] are instructive:

'While I accept that there might be exceptional cases where it is plain that considerable expense has been incurred on grounds on which permission to appeal has not been given, there is no suggestion in this case that significant additional costs were incurred in respect of those grounds where permission to appeal was not granted. This is another example of what would be a wholly disproportionate use of the court's time: seeking to distinguish the costs that have been incurred in respect of rejected grounds from those which have been incurred in respect of grounds of appeal in respect of which permission to appeal was granted. Save in exceptional cases, a successful appellant is entitled to his costs. I would order accordingly.'

It is clear from *R (KR) v Secretary of State for the Home Department*[13] that non-compliance with the Pre-action Protocol by a claimant is not in itself a sufficient reason to disapply the general rule that costs follow the event, and will not be so where defence of the claim post-issue makes it clear that non-compliance had no causal relevance (because compliance with the pre-action letter would not have led to pre-action settlement). It may, however, be a good reason not to award costs where a defendant concedes immediately after lodging the claim.

1   [2013] 2 Costs LR 257.
2   [2011] CP Rep 4.
3   [2012] 1 WLR 2607.
4   [2016] EWCA Civ 415.
5   [2012] 1 WLR 2898.
6   [2011] CP Rep 4, paragraph 65.
7   The context of *Bahta* itself makes clear that 'granted' here includes granted or conceded, or otherwise provided, by the defendant, as well as granted by the court. *Bahta* itself was a case where the defendant in fact provided different (albeit more extensive) relief than that sought in the claim, outside of the proceedings, but the above approach was found to be applicable.

8 [2012] 1 WLR 2607, paragraphs 60–63.
9 [2016] EWCA Civ 415, paragraph 57.
10 [2016] EWCA Civ 415, paragraph 67.
11 [2016] EWCA Civ 415, paragraph 114. The judge also found that there were other reasons why costs should be denied, such as the fact that the Malta claimants had given false accounts to the defendants and the Administrative Court.
12 [2012] EWCA Civ 1333, *paragraph 23.*
13 [2012] EWCA Civ 1555.

19.89 Parties to judicial review claims need to be aware that the Administrative Court has issued guidance as to the procedure to be followed where cases settle on all issues but costs[1].

The essential procedural requirements of the guidance are as follows:

— The parties should seek to resolve the issue of costs before asking the court to resolve it: the parties shall not make submissions to the court after compromise of the proceedings without attempting to resolve the issue of costs through negotiated agreement. This negotiation should reveal the points of dispute to be addressed in the costs submissions;

— The Guidance provides that the following procedure for submissions on costs should be set out within any consent order: Within 28 days of the consent order, the defendant may file and serve submissions as to what the appropriate costs order should be. If the defendant does not file such submissions, the order will be that the defendant pays the claimant's costs on the standard basis, to be the subject of detailed assessment if not agreed; where the defendant does file, the claimant or any other party may file and serve submissions with 14 days of service; otherwise, the costs order will be in the terms sought by the defendant; where the claimant/any other party files submissions, the defendant shall have 7 days to file and serve a reply; the matter is then put before the judge for a decision on costs or further order;

— The submissions should confirm that the parties have used reasonable endeavours to reach a costs settlement, identify what issues prevented agreement, state the amount of costs likely to be involved in the case, clearly identify the level of compliance with the pre-action protocol, state what relief was sought in the claim form, and what relief was obtained, and specifically address how the claim and basis of settlement fits the principles in *M v Croydon* (including the significance/effect of any action or offer by the defendant) and *R (Tesfay) v SSHD*;

— Documents normally not to exceed two, A4 pages in normal print size, unless there is a good reason for this, properly explained in the submissions;

— Documents should be accompanied by the pre-action correspondence (where this has not already been included in the documents supporting the claim), the correspondence in which the costs claim is made and defended, correspondence necessary to show why the claim was brought (in the light of the pre-action correspondence), or why the step leading to settlement was not taken before the claim was issued;

— Unless otherwise advised, the parties should assume that the court has the claim form and grounds, the acknowledgement of service and evidence in support, and should not provide further copies unless requested by the court.

1   Section 23.5 of the Administrative Court Judicial Review Guide 2006, available online at the
     time of writing at https://www.gov.uk/government/uploads/system/uploads/attachment_data/f
     ile/540607/administrative-court-judicial-review-guide.pdf

Protective costs orders / cost capping orders

19.90 The court may, at or in advance of a hearing, make an order protecting
a claimant from liability to pay some or all of the costs of other parties. The
circumstances when this will be done are discussed in CHAPTER **20**.[1] A new
statutory regime has recently been introduced in ss 88–90 of the Criminal
Justice and Courts Act 2015 setting out a comprehensive statutory code
governing when a protective costs order (now termed a 'cost capping order' or
CCO) can be made. The provisions make a number of important changes to
the previous position with respect to protective costs orders. These include the
fact that a CCO can only be made if permission has been granted,[2] and can
only be made on the application of a party and not on the court's own motion.[3]
Section 89(1) sets out the factors that a court is required to take into account
when considering an application for a CCO. The new regime is limited to
judicial reviews; therefore statutory challenges, such as under s 288 of the
Town and Country Planning Act 1990, would appear to be excluded.[4]

1   See **20.103** below.
2   Section 88(3), Criminal Justice and Courts Act 2015.
3   Section 88(4), Criminal Justice and Courts Act 2015.
4   See **19.91** below and *Venn v Secretary of State for Communities and Local Government*
     [2014] EWCA Civ 1539 for discussion of this distinction in the context of an Aarhus Con-
     vention claim. The changes do not apply to costs protection for Aarhus Convention claims; see
     the note to 19.91 below.

19.91 The CPR provides for favourable protective costs protection in
Aarhus Convention claims[1]. An Aarhus Convention claim is defined as:[2]

> 'A claim for judicial review of a decision, act or omission all or part of which is
> subject to the provisions of the UNECE Convention on Access to Information,
> Public Participation in Decision-Making and Access to Justice in Environmental
> Matters done at Aarhus, Denmark on 25 June 1998, including a claim which
> proceeds on the basis that the decision, act or omission, or part of it, is so subject.'[3]

1   The costs protection under the CPR is not a protective costs order, but an instance of a fixed
     costs regime: see *Howard v Wigan Council* [2015] EWHC 3643 (Admin) at paragraph 30.
2   CPR Pt 45.41(2). Following a consultation on cost capping in environmental claims, the
     government stated in its response in November 2016 that it would extend the definition of an
     Aarhus Convention claim in the CPR to include environmental reviews under statute which
     engage Article 9(2) of the Aarhus Convention. The restriction of the definition of an
     Aarhus Convention claim to claims for judicial review and the exclusion of statutory
     challenges was considered to not be compliant with the UK's obligations under the
     Aarhus Convention in the case of *Secretary of State for Communities and Local Government
     v Venn* [2014] EWCA Civ 1539. The proposed changes have yet to be introduced at the time
     of writing.
3   The Aarhus Convention does not define 'environmental matters'. However, there is a detailed
     definition of 'environmental information' in Article 2(3) of the Convention. The *Aarhus Con-
     vention: An Implementation Guide* applies the definition of 'environmental information' to the
     meaning of 'environmental matters' more broadly, and provides guidance on interpretation of
     it. In *Venn v Secretary of State for Communities and Local Government* [2013] EWHC 3546
     (Admin), Lang J held that 'there is a distinction between pure planning issues and environ-

mental issues'. Despite the broad meaning of environmental matters in the Convention, not every planning matter would be an environmental matter. However, a challenge based on the failure to properly apply a planning policy relating to maintaining a garden in the borough was found to be an environmental matter.

19.92 The Claim Form allows a claimant to indicate whether the claim is an Aarhus Convention claim or not.[1] While the claimant may opt out of the protective costs scheme applicable to Aarhus Convention claims, the following provisions will ordinarily apply:[2]

'Where a claimant is ordered to pay costs, the amount specified for the purpose of rule 45.43(1) is—
(a) £5,000 where the claimant is claiming only as an individual and not as, or on behalf of, a business or other legal person;
(b) In all other cases, £10,000.

Where a defendant is ordered to pay costs, the amount specified for the purpose of rule 45.43(1) is £35,000.'

---

[1] CPR Pt 45.42.
[2] CPR Pt 45 PD 5.1-5.2. In its response to the consultation on cost capping in environmental claims (see note above at **19.91**), the government indicated its intention to replace the cost-capping regime in CPR 45 with a system of variable caps, with caps to be set by the court in line with the principle that the costs of the proceedings must not exceed the financial resources of the claimant and must not appear to be objectively unreasonable. The current levels would represent the default starting points for cost caps, which the court could then vary upward or downward. Claimants would have to file and serve a schedule of their financial resources with the claim form to enable the court to make a decision about the appropriate level for the cost cap. These changes have yet to be introduced at the time of writing.

19.93 There is a strong incentive in the rules for a defendant not to dispute that the claim is an environmental claim. The Court will determine this issue at the earliest opportunity.[1] CPR 45.44(3) provides:

'In any proceedings to determine whether the claim is an Aarhus Convention claim-
(a) if the court holds that the claim is not an Aarhus Convention claim, it will normally make no order for costs in relation to those proceedings;
(b) if the court holds that the claim is an Aarhus Convention claim, it will normally order the defendant to pay the claimant's costs of those proceedings on the indemnity basis, and that order may be enforced notwithstanding that this would increase the costs payable by the defendant beyond the amount prescribed in Practice Direction 45.'

The regime therefore provides that there is limited risk to a claimant in contending that a matter is environmental in nature, as there will be no order for costs. A substantial costs order may however be made against a defendant who fails to persuade the court that the matter does not fall within the Aarhus Convention.

---

[1] CPR 45.44(2). In its response to the consultation on cost capping in environmental claims (see notes above at **19.91** and **19.92**) the government described CPR 44.3(b) as creating 'an uneven playing field', and indicated its intention to replace the provision such that unsuccessful defendants could still expect to be ordered to pay costs, but on the standard rather than indemnity basis.

Security for costs

19.94 An application for security for costs may be made by a defendant in accordance with CPR 25.12. Such an application must be supported by written evidence,[1] and the court must determine the amount of any security and direct the manner and time in which it is to be paid.[2] The conditions, which must be satisfied for an order for security for costs to be made, are set out in CPR 25.13(2), and the court may only make an order where it considers that in all the circumstances it is just to do so.[3] The public nature of the jurisdiction should point against a requirement for giving security where the effect would be to rule out a claim that should be ventilated in the public interest.[4] As a consequence, the use of security for costs applications in public law cases have fallen into abeyance in recent years. Outside of the context of commercially motivated cases, applications for security for costs orders are unlikely to succeed and will be closely scrutinised. This is particularly the case where a claimant is challenging a decision which affects his human rights or some basic welfare entitlement. It is also likely to be the case in environmental cases, where the application of the Aarhus Convention[5] may weigh heavily against such orders.[6]

1   CPR 25.12(2).
2   CPR 25.12(3).
3   CPR 25.13(1)(a).
4   A consideration that is supported by the fact that the court now has power to make a pre-emptive costs order.
5   UNECE Convention on Access to Information, Public Participation in Decision-making and Access to Justice in Environmental Matters.
6   See, in particular, the 'Report of the Working Group on Access to Environmental Justice', May 2008, chaired by Sullivan J; see also the update report: *'Ensuring access to justice in England and Wales: Update report, August 2010'*. See generally *R (Garner) v Elmbridge Borough Council* [2010] EWCA Civ 1006; *Coedbach Action Team Ltd v Secretary of State for Energy and Climate Change* [2011] 1 Costs LR 70.

19.95 While it is possible that some guidance can be obtained from past cases in which security for costs has been granted,[1] such cases must be treated with care in that they were all decided under the provisions of old RSC Ord 53, r 3(9), which provided a more general power to the court, in granting leave to apply for judicial review, to 'impose such terms as to costs and as to giving security as it thinks fit'. Security for costs in judicial review has now been brought into line with the rules governing security for costs in ordinary civil actions.[2]

1   See *R v Westminster City Council, ex p Residents' Association of Mayfair* [1991] COD 182, *R v Leicestershire County Council, ex p Blackfordby & Boothorpe Action Group Ltd* [2001] Env LR 35, *R v Common Professional Examination Board, ex p Meadling-McCleod* (2000) Times, 2 May.
2   Examples in case law of the operation of the new rule are *Olatawura v Abiloye* [2002] 4 All ER 903; and *R v Leicester City Council, ex p Blackfordby and Boothorpe Action Group Ltd* [2001] Env LR 35 at 37. In *R (Residents Against Waste Site Ltd) v Lancashire County Council* [2008] Env LR 27, Irwin J held that, in the context of a challenge by a local interest group to the grant of planning permission for a major waste recycling and processing plant, 'it is perfectly open to a defendant in this situation to make energetic attempts for adequate security before costs'. In *R (Plantagenet Alliance Ltd) v Secretary of State for Justice* [2013] EWHC 3164 (Admin), Haddon-Cave J refused an application for security for costs made by the Secretary of State for Justice. He held that such an order would be inappropriate: it could not be concluded from the formation of a limited liability company that there was any improper motive given that reasons had been given for the incorporation;

an order for security for costs would stifle the claim; and the maintenance of a Protective Costs Order meant that the application for security for costs fell away.

INTERIM RELIEF[1]

[1] CPR 25 1(1)(a).

19.96 Interim relief is governed by CPR Pt 25, and the court may, at any time during proceedings for judicial review, grant such interim relief as is provided for in that Part, including interim injunctions and interim declarations.[2] The power to grant a stay is given by CPR 54.10(2).

[2] CPR 25 1(1)(b).

19.97 Unless the urgency of the case justifies or requires earlier consideration, the court will generally consider any issue of interim relief at the same time as it makes a decision on permission (and where appropriate, consideration of permission can itself be expedited). The court does, however, undoubtedly have jurisdiction to grant relief prior to consideration of permission,[1] albeit that it is not possible for interim relief to continue or be granted once permission has been refused. The procedure to be adopted is described in the next section of this chapter.

[1] *M v Home Office* [1994] 1 AC 377 at 423B–F, approving a note from the Supreme Court Practice 1993. For further discussion of this case, see CHAPTERS 14 and 17.

19.98 The long-standing dispute as to whether injunctions are available against Ministers of the Crown was finally settled in *M v Home Office*, following the earlier case of *R v Secretary of State for Transport, ex p Factortame*,[1] albeit that it was a jurisdiction to be exercised in limited circumstances. In the second *Factortame*[2] case, the House of Lords observed that, where an interim injunction was sought to prevent a minister from applying national legislation that was said to contravene Community law, the challenge had to, prima facie, be so firmly based as to justify such an exceptional course being taken.[3] Over time, however, the courts have become far more disposed to ordering interim relief against public bodies, including the Crown.

[1] [1990] 2 AC 85. See, also, CHAPTERS 14 and 17.
[2] [1999] Q.B. 1161.
[3] See, for example, Lord Goff at 674B–674D.

19.99 The test for the grant of an interim injunction in judicial review proceedings is somewhat modified from the *American Cyanimid*[1] principles governing such interim injunctions in private law, although that case still provides the starting point.[2] In private law, if a claimant can show that there is a serious question to be tried, the court considers whether the claimant would be adequately compensated in damages if ultimately successful at trial. The court also considers whether a cross-undertaking in damages by the claimant would adequately compensate the defendant if an injunction is granted but the claimant is ultimately unsuccessful at trial. If there is doubt as to the adequacy of these remedies in damages, then the court applies a balance of convenience test. In *Factortame*[3] Lord Bridge spoke of the court, in private law claims, making a 'pragmatic decision as to who is likely to suffer the greater injustice' as between an ultimately successful claimant denied relief, and an ultimately successful defendant wrongly restrained, each being left to a remedy in damages. The approach in public law cases was described in the following terms by the Privy Council in *Belize Alliance of Conservative Non-Governmental Organisation v Department of the Environment (Practice Note):*[4]

> 'Counsel were agreed (in the most general terms) that when the court is asked to grant an interim injunction in a public law case, it should approach the matter on the lines indicated by the House of Lords in *American Cyanimid Co v Ethicon Ltd* [1975] AC 396, but with the modifications appropriate to the public law element of the case. The public law element is one of the possible "special factors" referred to by Lord Diplock in that case, at p 409. Another special factor might be if the grant of interim relief were likely to be, in practical terms, decisive of the whole case'.

[1] *American Cyanimid Co v Ethicon Ltd* [1975] AC 396.
[2] *R v MAAF*, ex p. Monsanto [1999] Q.B. 1161.
[3] At 439G.
[4] [2003] 1 WLR 2839.

19.100 A further difference in public law cases is that a broader consideration of the 'public interest' which the public body exists to protect will be required rather than merely the narrow interests of the parties.[1] As such, there is authority to suggest that there may be a requirement that a claimant seeking interim relief in a public law case may be required to show more than merely a serious issue to be tried, but must show rather a strong *prima facie* case before the court will be prepared to grant relief.[2]

[1] *Smith v Inner London Education Authority* [1978] 1 All ER 411.
[2] Notably *Smith v Inner London Education Authority* [1978] 1 All ER 411, per Lord Denning MR and Geoffrey Lane LJ (but compare Browne LJ in the same case); *R v Secretary of State for Transport, ex parte Factortame Ltd* (No 2) [1991] 1 A.C. 603, per Lord Goff at 674B–674D. In *Spl (2004) Ltd v Secretary of State for Health* [2013] EWHC 4520 (Admin), Singh J held that the public interest, considered as part of the balance of convenience, tipped the balance against granting interim relief (paragraph 22).

19.101 However, that is clearly not a rule of universal application, as is shown by *R v Cardiff City Council, ex p Barry*,[1] where it was said that in homeless persons' cases, where a court has granted permission it would normally be right to 'hold the ring' by granting interim relief until the substantive hearing.[2] Similarly, in immigration cases, where the effect of refusal to grant relief would undermine or render nugatory any subsequent order of the court, the court should normally prevent the claimant from being removed from the jurisdiction.[3] It is suggested, therefore, that there is no absolute requirement to show a strong *prima facie* case, but that, in cases where a claimant will not suffer 'serious and irreparable harm',[4] the court will 'have to form some view of the strength' of the claim.[5] In *Practice Statement (Judicial Review: Asylum Support)*[6] it was said that 'an interim order should not be granted unless the judge is persuaded that there seems to be an arguable case'. This appears to be a lower threshold than that applied at the permission stage.

[1] (1990) 22 HLR 261.
[2] See also, *R (Casey) v Restormel BC* [2007] EWHC 2554 (Admin).

³   *R v Secretary of State for the Home Department, ex p Muboyayi* [1992] QB 244. In *R (Pharis) v Secretary of State for the Home Department* [2004] 3 All ER 310, the Court of Appeal had to consider the undertaking given by the Government that if specified procedural requirements were followed then removal directions would not be implemented after issue of proceedings, and made clear that this does not automatically prevent removal where a claimant seeks to appeal to the Court of Appeal following refusal of permission at an oral hearing. In such a case a claimant will need to make express application for a stay.

⁴   Per Lord Goff in *R v Secretary of State for the Transport, ex p Factortame Ltd (No 2)* [1991] 1 AC 603.

⁵   Per Lord Walker in *Belize Alliance of Conservative Non-Governmental Organisation v Department of the Environment (Practice Note)* [2003] 1 WLR 2389, at paragraph 40.

⁶   [2004] 1 WLR 644.

19.102 A further consideration in judicial review is that questions as to the adequacy of damages will rarely be determinative of whether it is appropriate to grant relief.¹ The claimant will not in the vast majority of cases have any entitlement to damages arising directly out of success in the judicial review claim, and his potential loss will be difficult or impossible to quantify. From the point of view of the defendant, the prejudice it suffers by being prevented from enforcing a decision pursuant to its view of the public interest will rarely have direct financial consequences and it will be difficult to identify affected third parties or quantify the loss they may suffer. Where a claimant is able to give a cross-undertaking in damages, that may be taken into account in assessing the wider balance of convenience² but an inability to provide such an undertaking will not be fatal to the claim.³ Much will depend on the nature of the case.⁴ The court should not deprive a person of liberty by injunction, or compel a person to submit to treatment, save in the most exceptional cases.⁵ There is a separate rule concerning cross-undertakings in damages in the environmental context:⁶

> 'If in an Aarhus Convention claim the court is satisfied that and injunction is necessary to prevent significant environmental damage and to preserve the factual basis of the proceedings, the court will, in considering whether to require an undertaking by the applicant to pay any damages which the respondent or any other person may sustain as a result and the terms of any such undertaking–
> (a)   have particular regard to the need for the terms of the order overall not to be such as would make continuing with the claim prohibitively expensive for the applicant; and
> (b)   make such directions as are necessary to ensure that the case is heard promptly.'

¹   See, generally, *R v Secretary of State for the Transport, ex p Factortame Ltd (No 2)* [1991] 1 AC 603.

²   *R v Secretary of State for the Environment, ex p RSPB* (1995) 7 Admin LR 434 and see *Belize Alliance of Conservative Non-Governmental Organisation v Department of the Environment (Practice Note)* [2003] 1 WLR 2389.

³   *R v Durham City Council, ex p Huddleston* [2000] Env LR D21; *R v Servite Houses and Wandsworth London Borough Council, ex p Goldsmith* (2000) 3 CCLR 354.

⁴   Interim relief in order to avoid irrecoverable damage pending a decision of the European Court of Human Rights is discussed in *Human Fertilisation and Embryology Authority v Amicus Healthcare Ltd* [2005] EWHC 1092 (QB).

⁵   *R (Ashworth Hospital Authority) v Mental Health Review Tribunal for West Midlands and North West Region* [2003] 1 WLR 127 (CA).

⁶   CPR Pt 25A PD 5.1B(1). 'Aarhus Convention claim' has the same meaning as in rule 45.41(2): CPR Pt 25A PD 5.1B(2), see **19.91**. When assessing UK law before the implementation of this provision, the CJEU found that the UK was in breach of the requirement of Article 10a of the EIA Directive that proceedings shall not be prohibitively expensive: *European Commission v*

United Kingdom C-530/11. [2014] All ER (D) 121 (Feb). In its response to the consultation on cost capping in environmental claims (see notes above at **19.91–19.93**), the government set out its intention to introduce an amendment so as to define 'prohibitively expensive' with reference to the principles set out by the CJEU in Case C-260/11 *Edwards v Environment Agency* [2013] 1 W.L.R. 2914.

19.103 Particular considerations apply where the grant of interim relief would restrict the right to freedom of expression. There is Practice Guidance with recommended practice for an interim non-disclosure order.[1] Detailed principles are set out by the Court of Appeal in cases where a claimant seeks an anonymity order or restraint on publication of matters normally in the public domain.[2] The Human Rights Act 1998 provides that,[3] when deciding whether to grant relief which may affect the exercise of the right to freedom of expression protected by the European Convention on Human Rights, the court must 'have particular regard to the importance of that right'. When considering interim relief, s 12(3) applies, to the effect that 'No such relief is to be granted so as to restrain publication before trial unless the court is satisfied that the applicant is likely to establish that publication should not be allowed'. This sets a higher threshold than the usual *American Cyanamid* test, in order to protect freedom of expression in the face of privacy arguments arising under the Human Rights Act.[4] No such relief is to be granted so as to restrain publication before trial unless the court is satisfied that the applicant is likely to establish that publication should not be allowed.

[1] *Practice Guidance: Interim Non-Disclosure Orders* [2012] 1 WLR 1003.
[2] *J I H v News Group Newspapers Ltd* [2011] 1 WLR 1645.
[3] Section 12.
[4] The effectiveness of s.12 HRA 1998, s 12 is the subject of significant debate. It is not clear to what extent s 12 can affect the balancing of Article 8 and Article 10 rights that is required by the ECHR. See Civil Practice (2014), 15–42 and discussion in *PJS v News Group Newspapers* [2016] UKSC 26.

19.104 As noted,[1] the court has power to grant a stay on proceedings, the effect of which is generally to preserve the status quo by suspending the proceedings under challenge and preventing the implementation of the decision reached.[2] Although the effect may, in practice, be similar to an interim injunction, the court will generally prefer to order a stay where that is likely to provide effective relief.[3]

[1] At **19.96**, which explains the court's power to grant a stay under CPR Pt 54.
[2] *R (Ashworth Hospital Authority) v Mental Health Review Tribunal for West Midlands and North West Region* [2003] 1 WLR 127, per Dyson LJ.
[3] *R v Secretary of State for Education and Science, ex p Avon County Council* [1991] 1 QB 558.

19.105 The court has power to grant interim declarations.[1] The power has been exercised infrequently and it is hard to draw any clear principles from the caselaw.[2] As Tomlinson J observed in *Amalgamated Metal Trading Ltd v City of London Police Investigation Unit*: 'it remains to be worked out what are the circumstances in which it might be appropriate to resort to this new jurisdiction'.[3] It seems likely that principles similar to those for interim injunctions apply.[4] An interim declaration was granted in *R (AM) v DPP*.[5] The Claimant was terminally ill and wished to end his life. He sought judicial review of the DPP's policy regarding assisted suicide which was introduced after the House of Lords' decision in *R (Purdy) v DPP*.[6] His solicitors sought an interim declaration that they could act for him without risking prosecution or disciplinary sanction, for assisting suicide contrary to section 2 of the Suicide Act 1961. This declaration was granted. In *R (H) v Secretary of State for the Home Department*,[7] Karon Monaghan QC, sitting as a Deputy High Court Judge, considered a challenge to decisions of the Home Secretary and local authority arising from the claimant's assertion that he was in fact a child. The Deputy Judge ordered that the claimant not be removed, and that the local authority provide support under sections 20-23 of the Children's Act 1989. She also indicated her willingness to grant an interim declaration that the claimant was a child. Interim declarations have also been granted to give parties certainty as to how to regulate their conduct pending the outcome of a reference to the CJEU.[8]

[1]   CPR 25.1(b).
[2]   But see, for example, *R v Environment Agency, ex p Mayer Parry Recycling Ltd (No 2)* [2001] Env LR 630; and *B Borough Council v S (by the Official Solicitor)* [2006] EWHC 2584 (Fam).
[3]   [2003] 1 WLR 2711 at paragraph 10.
[4]   See **19.102**.
[5]   [2012] EWHC 470 (Admin).
[6]   [2010] 1 AC 345.
[7]   [2010] EWHC 2414 (Admin).
[8]   See, for example, R v Secretary of State for Trade and Industry, ex p. Trades Union Congress [2001] C.M.L.R. 8.

PROCEDURE: URGENT APPLICATIONS FOR PERMISSION OR INTERIM RELIEF[1]

[1]   See, generally, Marcus, (2004) 9 JR 256.

19.106 In the light of differences which arose as to how claimants should go about applying for interim relief, the Administrative Court issued a Practice Statement *Practice Statement (Administrative Court: Listing and Urgent Cases)*.[2] The Practice Statement recognises that applications for interim relief are likely to have, by their very nature, a degree of urgency, and the procedure is accordingly the same for both kinds of application. The Divisional Court has pointed out that such applications are extremely costly in terms of the court's resources, and now takes a strict approach to representatives in circumstances where such applications are made not in the correct form, or are made without merit. The Divisional Court has threatened to report representatives who do not comply with the requirements to their regulators: *R (Hamid) v Secretary of State for the Home Department*;[3] *Awuku v Secretary of State for the Home Department (No 2)*;[4] *B&J v Secretary of State for the Home Department*;[5] *R (B) v Secretary of State for the Home Department*;[6] *R (Akram) v Secretary of State for the Home Department*.[7]

[2]   [2002] 1 WLR 810.
[3]   [2013] CP Rep 6.
[4]   [2012] EWHC 3690 (Admin).
[5]   [2012] EWHC 3770 (Admin).
[6]   [2014] EWHC 264 (Admin).
[7]   [2015] EWHC 1359 (Admin).

19.107 The basic procedural requirement is that the claimant should, in any case where either (i) there is an application that permission be considered as a matter of urgency, or (ii) an application for interim relief, complete form N463. Representatives must be sure to use the most up-to-date form. That requires that the claimant:

(1) specify the reasons for urgency;

(2) give the proposed timetable for consideration of permission and/or the substantive hearing, and any abridgement of time for acknowledgement of service;

(3) state the nature of any interim relief sought and why (a draft order should be attached);

(4) state what steps have been taken to put the Defendant or interested party on notice of the application

(5) confirm that all relevant facts have been disclosed in the application

(6) if interim relief is sought an application must also be included on the claim form.[1]

---

[1]   CPR 54.6 (1)(C).

19.108 A copy of Form N463 and any draft order should be served, by fax or post, on the defendant and any interested party before proceedings are issued. The Form allows the claimant to specify how it was delivered to the Defendant/Interested Party, whether by fax, handing it or leaving it with someone, or by email, as well as the date served.

19.109 Urgent applications should, of course, be lodged as early as possible. In cases where urgency is measured in hours rather than days, it would be sensible to telephone the Administrative Court Office and warn them of the application. In certain cases the Administrative Court is willing to accept documents sent by fax[1] and may be prepared to issue the claim upon an undertaking to provide the issue fee within a certain time, usually the following day. Although the Administrative Court accepts some documents by email, a claim form cannot be lodged electronically.[2]

---

[1]   See CPR Pt 5A PD 5.3(9) 'Filing by Facsimile', which indicates, inter alia, that in the case of a document attracting a fee (which of course includes a claim form) a fax should not be used except in 'an unavoidable emergency', and should include an undertaking to pay by the end of the following day. The Administrative Court has a standard form of undertaking to be completed in cases where the documents supplied with the claim form do not comply with those required by CPR Pt 54 PD, which makes specific reference to supplying the court fee.

[2]   See CPR Pt 5B PD 2.2, which states that a party must not send by email any application or other document where a fee is payable for that document to be filed with the court.

19.110 *Urgent applications for interim orders*: If satisfied that the claim has sufficient merit and urgency and that an appropriate interim order can be formulated, the judge may make an order without a hearing and without receipt of an acknowledgment of service. If the judge is not so satisfied, the application may be refused on the papers (in which event it may be renewed orally) or directions may be given for an urgent oral hearing.

19.111 *Urgent applications for permission*: Only in exceptional cases will permission for judicial review be granted without giving a defendant an opportunity to make representations by way of an acknowledgment of service. In a case of urgency, the time for filing an acknowledgement of service can be abridged and the greater the degree of urgency, the more significantly the time can be abridged.[1]

[1]   *R (BG) v Medway Council* [2006] 1FLR 663 at [40].

Out of hours applications

19.112 In the most urgent cases the above procedure may break down. It may not be possible for a claim to be issued by 4.30 pm (or 4:00 pm by fax)[1] or it may in any event prove impossible for the application to be considered by the duty judge. Where the application cannot wait until the next day, an application can be made to the out-of-hours judge by telephone.[2]

[1]   CPR Pt 5A PD5.3(6).
[2]   The out-of-hours judge can be reached by telephoning the Royal Courts of Justice on 020 7947 6000. There is no out-of-hours judge for the regional Administrative Courts so all out-of-hours applications must be made to the Royal Courts of Justice (CPR 54D PD4.2). Once the out-of-hours duty clerk has been spoken to, an Out of Hours Application Form (available, at the time of writing, online at http://hmctsformfinder.justice.gov.uk/HMCTS/GetForm.do?cou rt_forms_id=3007) will need to be completed and sent by email to the clerk, together with any relevant supporting documents (see **19.114** below).

19.113 It is necessary to exercise caution in judging whether the nature of the application is so urgent as to justify this course, having regard to the guidance given by Maurice Kay J (as he then was) in *R (Q) v Secretary of State for the Home Department*:[1]

'It is axiomatic that anyone who is deserving of interim relief is suffering or is about to suffer real hardship. If they are so deserving, they are entitled to expect that the court will act quickly. However, in most cases, the circumstances do not justify an application to the out-of-hours judge. In most cases, the hardship which has been endured for days or hours can be endured until the following day without serious further risk. No doubt there are some truly exceptional cases which merit the most urgent and immediate attention. However, I repeat, out-of-hours applications should only be made in such truly exceptional cases. I well understand that committed legal advisers are anxious to get a result for their clients at the earliest opportunity, but I remain of the view that, notwithstanding the impassioned submissions, there are many cases presented late in the day which could reasonably wait until the next morning'.[2]

[1]   [2003] EWHC 2507 (Admin) paragraph 13.
[2]   These remarks were made in the context of the large number of applications for interim relief received by the court in respect of asylum seekers denied support under s 55 of the Nationality Immigration and Asylum Act 2002, but would appear to have potentially wider effect.

19.114 While there is no absolute requirement to do so, a judge is likely to be assisted if certain documents can be sent to him by fax or email, including, if possible, a summary of the case, documents relating to the decision under challenge, and a draft order. Such an order should ordinarily include, in addition to the substantive relief sought:

'(1)   (where this has not been done) an undertaking to issue the claim by a certain time, normally by 4.00 pm on the next working day, and provision that this may be extended by agreement between the parties;[1]

(2)   an order that the defendant have liberty to apply to vary or revoke the order for interim relief upon giving not less than 48 hours'[2] written notice to the claimant'.

[1]   This latter element may avoid the need to issue a redundant claim where the defendant concedes the substantive claim before proceedings have been issued.
[2]   Or such other time as may be appropriate.

19.115 In urgent cases without notice, it should be remembered that the duty of full and frank disclosure is heightened.[1] If at all possible, the defendant should be notified of the application and given the opportunity to take part. It is also vital in urgent cases that the claimant's solicitor has some way of serving the order so that it can be implemented. Additions to the required form now oblige lawyers to certify that an out of hours application is in accordance with professional obligations. This was intended to make it abundantly clear that without notice applications should not be made in a case which is not properly arguable.[2] A without notice application must be fully scrutinised by a properly qualified lawyer.[3]

[1]   See discussion at **19.35** above.
[2]   *Awuku v Secretary of State for the Home Department (No 2)* [2012] EWHC 3690 (Admin), paragraph 4. For submissions which are not properly arguable and will give rise to action by the court, see *R (B) v Secretary of State for the Home Department* [2012] EWHC 3770 (Admin). In *R (Butt) v Secretary of State for the Home Department* [2014] EWHC 264 (Admin), the Divisional Court required an undertaking by a solicitor's firm where an application for judicial review was made almost 3 years after the decision under challenge.
[3]   *Awuku (No 2)*, paragraphs 16–17.

DISCLOSURE[1]

[1]   Also see discussion on duty of candour at **19.47**.

19.116 The ordinary rule is that there is no disclosure in judicial review proceedings unless the court orders otherwise,[2] and traditionally the courts have been extremely reluctant to make such orders. In *R v Secretary of State for the Home Department, ex p Fayed*,[3] Lord Woolf MR attributed that reluctance to the continuing duty of candour owed to the court by public bodies. He said: 'On an application for judicial review there is usually no [disclosure] because [it] should be unnecessary because it is the obligation of the . . . public body in its evidence to make frank disclosure to the court of the decision making process'.[4] Nonetheless, the courts have historically ordered disclosure in judicial review proceedings, albeit rarely.[5]

[2]   CPR Pt 54A PD12.1.
[3]   [1998] 1 WLR 763.
[4]   At 775C. See also *R v IRC ex p Federation of Self Employed and Small Businesses* [1982] AC 617, per Lord Scarman at p 654E; *R v Arts Council of England and Wales, ex p Women's Playhouse Trust* [1998] COD 175, per Laws J; *R (Quark Fishing Ltd) v Secretary of State for Foreign and Commonwealth Affairs (No 1)* [2002] EWCA Civ 1409. In *R v Secretary of State for the Home Department, ex p Harrison (No 1)* (10 December 1987, unreported), CA) Glidewell LJ considered that the reluctance to order disclosure was due to the limited fact-finding role of the court in judicial review.
[5]   See, for example: *Anisminic Ltd v Foreign Compensation Commission* [1969] 2 AC 147; *R v IRC, ex p J Rothschild Holdings plc* [1986] STC 410 It was confirmed in British Union for the Abolition of Vivisection (BUAV) v Secretary of State for the Home Department [2014] EWHC

43 (Admin) that the CPR did not exclude pre-action disclosure in judicial review proceedings, although it was indicated that such applications would rarely be successful.

19.117 The traditional rule was that disclosure which seeks to go behind the defendant's evidence to check its accuracy will, in general, only be ordered if the defendant's evidence is, on its face, inaccurate, misleading or incomplete.[1]

[1] See *R v Arts Council of England, ex p Women's Playhouse Trust* [1998] COD 175 and *R v Secretary of State for Foreign and Commonwealth Affairs, ex p World Development Movement Ltd* [1995] 1 WLR 386 at 396B–C, 397F–H.

19.118 However, the traditional approach has changed in light of two recent cases. In *Tweed v Parades Commission for Northern Ireland*[1] the House of Lords ruled that a 'more flexible and less prescriptive' approach to disclosure was necessary in judicial review proceedings, especially in light of the introduction of the Human Rights Act 1998. In summary, the following principles can be derived from the judgment:

(i)   The test for whether to order disclosure is whether it is necessary in order to resolve the issues in the proceedings fairly and justly;[2]

(ii)   Where there is no substantial issue of fact between the parties, disclosure is unlikely to be appropriate, but where substantial disputes of fact are involved, there may be a case for disclosure;[3]

(iii)   Where the claim involves an allegation of a breach of human rights, and a judgment on proportionality is required, disclosure is more likely to be appropriate;[4]

(iv)   There is no presumption that documents referred to in a witness statement are required to be disclosed as a matter of course.[5] However, where a public authority relies on a document as significant to its decision, it is ordinarily good practice to exhibit it as the primary evidence. Any summary, however conscientiously and skilfully made, may distort. But where the authority's deponent chooses to summarise the effect of a document it should not be necessary for the applicant, seeking sight of the document, to suggest some inaccuracy or incompleteness in the summary, usually an impossible task without sight of the document. It is enough that the document itself is the best evidence of what it says. There may be reasons (arising, for example, from confidentiality, or the volume of the material in question) why the document should or need not be exhibited but it is for the judge to whom application for disclosure is made to decide whether, and to what extent, disclosure should be made.

(v)   Nonetheless, disclosure orders will remain exceptional, even in cases that raise questions of proportionality, and disclosure will not be ordered to facilitate a 'fishing expedition'.

[1] [2006] UKHL 53.
[2] Per Lord Bingham, paragraph 3; Lord Brown, paragraph 52.
[3] Per Lord Bingham, paragraph 2; Lord Carswell, paragraph 32.
[4] Per Lord Bingham, paragraph 3; Lord Carswell, paragraph 39; Lord Brown, paragraph 57.
[5] Query, however, how this relates to CPR Rule 31.14, which gives a party the right to inspect any document contained in a statement of case or witness statement. *Tweed* was a case addressing the duty of candour in Northern Ireland where there was no equivalent rule. It is at least arguable that the right to inspect does apply to judicial review proceedings, although the court retains an inherent jurisdiction to restrict inspection under CPR Rule 31.14 to those

documents that are 'necessary for the fair disposal of the claim' (*Danisco v Novzymes* [2012] EWHC 389 (Pat)) which may align with the principles governing the duty of candour.

19.119 In *R (Al Sweady) v Secretary of State for Defence*,[1] the Divisional Court went further than the House of Lords in *Tweed*. In that case, the Court made an order for disclosure where it had identified serious failings in the defendant's compliance with its duty of candour. In so doing, the Court gave further guidance on when it would be appropriate to make orders for disclosure in judicial review proceedings. Scott Baker LJ said:

'We concluded that it is vital that when it becomes clear that the outcome of a judicial review application might depend on the determination of a factual dispute, urgent consideration should be given to ordering disclosure and cross-examination. Rule 12.1 of the Practice Direction to CPR Pt 54 provides that "disclosure is not required unless the court orders otherwise".

'In our view, the parties and the court should always scrutinise with care the stance of parties to judicial review applications (and in particular those concerning human rights claims) to ascertain if there is any critical factual issue which requires orders for cross-examination of the makers of witness statements or disclosure as being (in the words of Lord Bingham in the Tweed case which we have quoted in [23] above) "necessary in order to resolve the matter fairly and accurately". Courts should not be reluctant to make such orders in suitable cases, which are especially likely to arise in claims based on the ECHR.'

[1]   [2009] EWHC 2387 (Admin).

19.120 An interesting feature of *Al Sweady* was that a disclosure order followed on from an order for cross examination of witnesses. It seems likely that whenever cross examination is ordered, some form of disclosure order is inevitable in order to allow effective cross-examination.[1] However, even in the absence of an order for cross examination, it now appears that where a judicial review claim involves a substantial dispute of fact, and where that dispute involves an allegation of a breach of human rights (especially a breach of arts 2, 3 and 5 ECHR) then a disclosure order will be appropriate. In cases not involving a human rights challenge, it will still be open to a party to seek disclosure on the grounds that it is necessary in order for the court to resolve the proceedings justly and fairly.

[1]   See discussion on cross-examination at **19.129**.

19.121 The Treasury Solicitor's Department has published guidance in light of *Tweed* and *Al Sweady* to facilitate Government Departments and Agencies in discharging their duty of candour and dealing with applications for disclosure in judicial review litigation.[1] The Guidance suggests that best practice is to follow the principles set out in CPR Part 31, including:

(a)   the parties are required to help the court further the overriding objective which is to deal with cases justly. Dealing with a case justly includes dealing with the case in ways which are proportionate. CPR 31(2)(c);

(b)   parties are required to disclose only the documents which:
 (i)   they rely upon;
 (ii)   adversely affect their own, or another party's, case;
 (iii)   support another party's case;

(c)   document means anything in which information of any description is recorded. It will include, for example, not only letters and emails, but drafts, calendars, manuscript and post-it notes, voicemails, computer disks, documents stored on servers and back-up systems and documents that have been deleted and blogs;

(d)   disclosure is required if a party has or at any time has had a document so that the existence of destroyed or lost documents or documents which have been passed on must be disclosed;

(e)   parties are required to undertake a reasonable search for disclosable documents.

---

[1]   'Guidance on Discharging the Duty of Candour and Disclosure in Judicial Review' January 2010; available at the time of writing at: www.gov.uk/government/uploads/system/uploads/att achment_data/file/285368/Tsol_discharging_1_.pdf

19.122 There may be a number of grounds on which defendants may resist disclosure, including, *inter alia*, that:

(i)   the information is not relevant,

(ii)   the volume of material is too great;[1]

(iii)   the information is confidential or privileged;[2] or

(iv)   the information is protected by public interest immunity.[3]

---

[1]   See paragraphs 4 and 37 of the speeches in *Tweed*.
[2]   See paragraphs 33, 37 and 57 of the speeches in *Tweed*.
[3]   See *Al Sweady*.

Statutory rights to access government information[1]

[1]   See P Coppel, *Information Rights*, 4th edn (2014: Hart Publishing).

19.123 The rules on disclosure must be seen in addition to the statutory rights to access government information under the Data Protection Act 1999, and the Freedom of Information Act 2000. Neither statute has radically altered the extent to which a claimant in judicial review proceedings may be able to access information of potential relevance to his or her claim, but there are a number of examples of where the statutory rights have been deployed effectively to access information that is pertinent to a judicial review.[2] It is also important to be aware of more extensive rights of access that may exist under legislation concerned with particular subject areas, such as the Access to Environmental Information Regulations 2004.[3] In *Kennedy v Charity Commission*, the Supreme Court rejected a submission that there was a general right to information under Article 10 of the European Convention on Human Rights.[4]

---

[2]   See *R (Lord) v Secretary of State for the Home Department* [2003] EWHC 2073 (Admin), a case concerning access to personal information under the Data Protection Act 1999 (DPA 1999) for the purposes of a hearing to review a prisoner's categorisation. Access to the information was thus the subject matter of the judicial review claim rather than something sought to be relied on for the purposes of bringing the claim, but it is nevertheless an example of use of the DPA 1999 to obtain information for the purposes of litigation. See, however, the remarks of Auld LJ in *Durant v Financial Services Authority* [2003] EWCA Civ 1746, [2004] FSR 573, that s 7 of the DPA 1999 is not to 'assist him for example, to obtain discovery of documents that may assist him in litigation or complaints against third parties'.

[3] SI 2004/3391. See *R (Bard Campaign) v Secretary of State for Communities and Local Government* [2009] EWHC 308 (Admin), for an example of the use of these regulations to obtain information relevant to a judicial review claim.

[4] [2014] 2 WLR 808. However, see paragraph 135 for a suggestion of common law routes to obtaining information.

19.124 A detailed consideration of this legislation is outside the scope of this chapter but the basic mechanism for seeking to obtain information under the Freedom of Information Act 2000 or the Data Protection Act 1999 is not complex. The Freedom of Information Act contains two separate rights, namely a right to be informed whether a public body holds information, and a right to have the information communicated to him or her.[1] Any request for information must be made in writing,[2] and the applicant must state his or her name, an address for correspondence and the information requested,[3] and a response must be made promptly and, ordinarily,[4] within 20 days of receipt of the request.

[1] Freedom of Information Act 2000, s 1(1).
[2] Freedom of Information Act 2000, s 8(1)(a).
[3] Freedom of Information Act 2000, s 8(1)(b) and (c).
[4] Subject to exceptions where further information is required from the applicant in order to comply (s 1(3)), where the public body has sent a fees notice to the applicant (s 10(2)).

19.125 The two information rights contained in s 1 are not unfettered. Information *may* be immune from an obligation (but not a power) to disclose if it is 'exempt information'.[1] Exempt information falls into two categories: 'absolute' exemptions,[2] which need not be disclosed by reason simply of being with that category,[3] and qualified exemptions. In respect of the latter the duty to confirm or deny[4] or communicate[5] the information does not arise where 'the public interest' in not complying with the duty outweighs the public interest in its disclosure. Where a public body does intend to rely on an exemption it must notify the applicant within the time limit for complying with the duty.[6]

[1] As defined in Freedom of Information Act 2000, s 84 and given effect by s 2.
[2] All categories of information classified as conferring absolute exemption are specified as such in Freedom of Information Act 2000, s 2(3).
[3] Freedom of Information Act 2000, s 2(1)(a) and 2(2)(a).
[4] Freedom of Information Act 2000, s 2(1)(b).
[5] Freedom of Information Act 2000, s 2(2)(b).
[6] Freedom of Information Act 2000, s 17(1).

19.126 Thus, provided that a potential claimant is able sufficiently to identify information that may assist him in his claim, and that information is not somehow excluded from any duty to disclose, he may be able to secure, in advance of bringing any claim it seems, any information that was taken into account in reaching a particular decision. Where a public body does not rely on an exemption, the time limits for compliance with a request are sufficiently short to be compatible with the time for bringing a claim for judicial review provided that a claimant acts quickly. A request for information may be made in parallel with, or even as part of, a letter before claim.

19.127 Problems may arise where a public body relies on an exemption. That may be challenged, by internal review[1] or by recourse to the Information Commissioner,[2] the Information Tribunal[3] or the courts.[4] The likely timescale for any such challenge may cause problems in terms of delay in judicial review, although it is to be hoped that in an appropriate case the court will see a refusal by a public authority to disclose information that was later successfully challenged as at least potentially giving grounds for extending time.

¹ See the Lord Chancellor's Code of Practice on the Discharge of Public Authority Functions under Part I of the Freedom of Information Act 2000.
² By application under Freedom of Information Act 2000, s 50(1).
³ On appeal from the Information Commissioner under Freedom of Information Act 2000, s 57(1).
⁴ Under Freedom of Information Act 2000, s 59 there is an appeal on a point of law from the decision of the Information Tribunal to the appropriate court.

19.128 Section 7 of the Data Protection Act 1998 gives rights to 'data subjects' to access data held by 'data controllers'. It applies to public authorities. Access rights apply only to 'personal data' (data by which the data subject may be identified, either on the face of the data alone, or in combination with data and other information held by the data handler).[1] A data controller is one "who (either alone or jointly or in common with other persons) determines the purposes for which and the manner in which any personal data are, or are to be, processed".[2] There are four rights set out in s 7:

(i)   The right to be informed whether the data controller is processing data relating to that data subject;

(ii)   If so, to be given a description of the personal data, the purposes for which they are or will be processed, and the recipients or classes of recipients to whom they are or may be disclosed;

(iii)   To have communicated in an intelligible form the information constituting the data subject's personal data, and the information available to the data controller as to the source of the data;

(iv)   Where a decision significantly affecting the data controller will be solely based on the processing by automatic means of the data subject's personal data, to be informed of the logic of the decision.

To have the benefit of the rights in s 7, the request must be made in writing, and the relevant fee must be paid. The maximum fee is generally £10, except for educational and health records.[3] Where a request is for 'unstructured' data held by a public authority, the public authority need not provide the data unless the request contains a description of the data. The public authority is also exempt from providing the data where it estimates that the cost of supplying the data would exceed a limit prescribed by regulations by the Secretary of State.[4]

¹ Data Protection Act 1998, s 1(1).
² Data Protection Act 1998, s 1(1).
³ See Coppel, 'Information Rights', 4th edn, 5-046.
⁴ £450 or £600, depending on the public authority: Freedom of Information and Data Protection (Appropriate Limit and Fees) Regulations 2004/3244, Regulation 3.

CROSS-EXAMINATION

19.129 Cross-examination in proceedings for judicial review remains rare, but is increasingly ordered. That there is jurisdiction to order cross-examination was, however, stressed by Lord Diplock in *O'Reilly v Mackman*,[1] in a passage in which he explained that it would only rarely be appropriate to exercise that jurisdiction because the public body's findings of fact are essentially matters for it to determine for itself, and are open to review only on limited grounds, so that:

' . . . to allow cross-examination presents the court with a temptation, not always easily resisted, to substitute its own view of the facts for that of the decision-making body upon whom the exclusive jurisdiction to determine facts has been conferred by Parliament'.

¹　[1983] 2 AC 237.

19.130 CPR 54.16 as originally enacted appeared to indicate, by its disapplication of CPR 8.6, that the court's power to order cross-examination had been removed, but an argument to that effect was rejected by the High Court in *R (PG) v Ealing London Borough Council (No 2)*.¹ Any lingering doubts as to whether the power to order oral evidence and cross-examination has been removed by the subsequent amendment of CPR 54.16 so that it disapplies CPR 8.6(1)² only, thereby leaving the express power to order oral evidence and cross-examination under CPR 8.6(2) and 8.6(3) intact. If it is proposed to cross-examine witnesses then the terms of an appropriate order should be canvassed with other parties. Application can then be made to the court, setting out the views of the parties and the applicant's comments along with a draft order.

¹　[2002] EWHC 250 (Admin), [2004] INLR 638.
²　CPR 8.6(1) is concerned with written evidence.

19.131 Rare cases in which cross-examination may be appropriate will most often fall into one of three categories, all cases where there may be a dispute as to some factual matter that falls within the jurisdiction of the court, rather than the decision-maker, to determine:

(1)　*Cases involving questions of jurisdictional fact* – This exception was recognised by Lord Diplock in *O'Reilly*. Two established examples are that of whether someone is an illegal entrant under the Immigration Act 1971¹, and the question of whether someone is a minor child for the purposes of the Children Act 1981.² In both cases the issue must be determined as a question of primary fact by the court, which may necessitate cross-examination. However, whether this is necessary is a matter for the discretion of the court.³

(2)　*Cases involving disputes as to procedure or bias* – Once again, this potential exception was recognised by Lord Diplock in *O'Reilly*.⁴ The question of whether in fact a particular procedure was followed, or whether there was bias, is not a matter for the exclusive determination of the decision-maker; that would indeed make him a judge in his own case. Once again, the fact that there is a disputed allegation as to whether some procedure was or was not followed will not, without more, be sufficient for cross-examination, and the court will often be reluctant to order cross-examination of a decision-maker (see eg Lord Denning MR in *George v Secretary of State for the Environment*).⁵ *George* was distinguished in *Jones v Secretary of State for Wales*,⁶ where a majority of the Court of Appeal, whilst recognising the general undesirability of exposing those holding quasi-judicial office to cross-examination, nevertheless considered that cross-examination was appropriate. Balcombe LJ set out the guiding principle as follows:

> ' . . . if there is evidence before the court which, unless satisfactorily explained, could lead to an inference of improper behaviour on the part of the inspector, then, in my judgment, the court should allow cross-examination on the affidavits. If the appellant's allegations should turn out to be unjustified then the court has sufficient power to mark its disapproval of their conduct by an award of costs, even if they were to establish their challenge to the validity of the decision letter on other, less contentious, grounds.

> This exception will also extend, in rare cases, to questions as to what was actually in the mind of the decision maker,[7] a question not of procedure but of what considerations actually motivated a decision. The fact that only the decision maker himself can give evidence on such a matter will make it particularly rare for such a course to be appropriate'.[8]

(3) *Cases involving fundamental rights* – That a different approach may be required in cases involving fundamental rights was recognised by the Court of Appeal in *R (Wilkinson) v Responsible Medical Officer Broadmoor Hospital*,[9] because the court in such cases may be in a position where it must 'reach its own view' on disputed questions of fact. The precise nature and extent of this exception remains unclear; later decisions such as *Runa Begum v Tower Hamlets LBC*,[10] indicate that art 6 does not, without more, require or permit the court to substitute its own view on the facts for those of the decision-making body. However, the true basis for this exception is not so much what is required by Article 6 ECHR, but again the court's role as primary decision maker in cases under the Convention: see *R (SB) v Denbigh High School* [2007] 1 AC 100, *R (Begum, Miss Behavin' Ltd) v Belfast CC* [2007] 1 WLR 1420. It will by no means follow that cross-examination will be required in most, or even many, cases, but it may well be needed where the court's expanded role requires it to determine some question of primary fact. An example of this in action can be found in *R (Mousa) v Secretary of State for Defence*,[11] a challenge to the UK Government's investigation into allegations of ill-treatment by British armed forces in Iraq. The Divisional Court held that 'it became obvious that we had to hear oral evidence' in relation to whether the investigation set up by the government was sufficiently independent. This was a case which involved both fundamental rights, and a dispute as to procedure. In *R (N) v M*,[12] another case concerning administration of treatment of a mental health patient without consent, Dyson LJ, giving the judgment of the court, approved Hale LJ's qualification, in *Wilkinson*, that cross-examination would be ordered 'if necessary' to the resolution of the issues, because it may be possible for the court to resolve the issue or disputed fact simply by reference to the written evidence. The court went on to say:

> '39. We suggest that it should not often be necessary to adduce oral evidence with cross-examination where there are disputed issues of fact and opinion in cases where the need for forcible medical treatment of a patient is being challenged on human rights grounds. Nor do we consider that the decision

in Wilkinson should be regarded as a charter for routing applications to the court for oral evidence in human rights cases generally. Much will depend on the nature of the right that has allegedly been breached, and the nature of the alleged breach. Furthermore, although in some cases (such as the present) the nature of the challenge may be such that the court cannot decide the ultimate question without determining for itself the disputed facts, it should not be overlooked that the court's role is essentially one of review:[13] see per Lord Steyn in *R (Daly) v Secretary of State for the Home Department* [2001] UKHL 26, [2001] 2 AC 532, paragraph 27'.

[1] *R v Secretary of State for the Home Department, ex p Khawaja* [1984] AC 74.
[2] *R (A) v Croydon London Borough Council* [2009] UKSC 8.
[3] In *Khawaja*, Lord Bridge recognised that in 'the vast majority of cases' the relevant jurisdictional fact could be proved by written evidence (at 124F–124G), but also commented that 'it may be that the express discretion . . . to permit cross-examination . . . has been too sparingly exercised when deponents could readily attend court' (124H–125A). For other examples of precedent facts, see CHAPTERS 7 and 8.
[4] At [1983] 2 AC 282E.
[5] (1979) 77 LGR 689, at 693–694.
[6] [1995] 2 PLR 26.
[7] Examples include *R v Waltham Forest LBC, ex p Baxter* [1988] QB 419 at 422B (cross-examination of councillors as to whether their discretion was fettered by Labour group decision; *R v Derbyshire CC, ex p Times Supplements Ltd* [1991] 3 Admin LR 241 (cross-examination as to whether Labour councillors were truly influenced by educational considerations in banning council advertisements in the Times Educational Supplement; *R v IRC, ex p J Rothschild Holdings plc* [1986] STC 410 (cross-examination of Inland Revenue officials as to Departmental practice; case described by Simon Brown J as 'a case where inevitably the court is, in any event, going to exercise a first instance fact finding jurisdiction' – p 413d); *R (Bancoult) v Secretary of State for Foreign and Commonwealth Affairs* [2012] EWHC 2115 (Admin) (questions regarding the motivation for creating a Marine Protected Area arose from leaked documents released by Wikileaks); *Jedwell v Denbighshire County Council* [2015] EWCA Civ 1232, where the Court of Appeal held that the judge had erred in failing to accede to an application to cross-examine a planning officer where there had been inconsistencies between the stated basis for a decision and the subsequent explanation of the basis for that decision in a witness statement by the planning officer.
[8] It is unlikely that this approach extends to the situation where the decision maker is a judge: see *Locobail (UK) Ltd v Bayfield Properties Ltd* [2000] QB 451 at [19], where Lord Bingham said that there can be no question of cross-examining or seeking disclosure from the judge in cases of alleged bias.
[9] [2002] 1 WLR 419.
[10] [2003] 2 AC 430.
[11] [2013] HRLR 32. The conclusions on the analysis of witness evidence is at paragraphs 105–109.
[12] [2003] 1 WLR 562; see, also, *S v Airedale NHS Trust* [2002] EWHC 1780 (Admin),; *R (Munjaz) v Mersey Care NHS Trust* [2004] QB 395, where cross-examination was limited to expert witnesses; and *R (B) v Haddock* [2006] EWCA Civ 961.
[13] Although see now *R (SB) v Governors of Denbigh High School* [2007] 1 AC 100; *Miss Behavin' Ltd v Belfast City Council* [2007] 1 WLR 1420.

19.132 In *R (Al-Sweady) v Secretary of State for Defence*, Scott Baker LJ confirmed the approach set out in *Wilkinson* and in *R (N) v M* he addressed the court's difficulty when faced with factual disputes in human rights cases and confirmed that where the court was faced with 'hard edged' questions of fact,[1] it might be appropriate to order cross-examination of witnesses. He said:

'The difficulty confronting us was that, as is well known, the usual procedure in judicial review cases is first for there to be no oral evidence and secondly, insofar as there are factual disputes between the parties, the court is ordinarily obliged to resolve them in favour of the defendant (see, for example, *R. v Board of Visitors of Hull Prison ex p St Germain (No 2)* [1979] 1 WLR 1401 at 1410H, per Geoffrey Lane LJ (as he then was)).

If that approach had been adopted in this case, the Secretary of State would have succeeded and it would also have had the more far-reaching consequence that a defendant would always succeed if sued for an infringement of human rights which was disputed. So a different approach was needed because these "hard-edged" questions of fact represented an important exception to the rule precluding the court substituting its own view in judicial review cases. It is noteworthy that Lord Mustill has distinguished between "a broad judgment whose outcome could be overruled only on grounds of irrationality" and "a hard-edged question [where t]here is no room for legitimate disagreement" (*R. v Monopolies & Mergers Commission ex p South Yorkshire Transport Ltd* [1993] 1 WLR 23 at 32D–32F).

In our view, it was necessary to allow cross-examination of makers of witness statements on those "hard-edged" questions of fact. We envisage that such cross-examination might occur with increasing regularity in cases where there are crucial factual disputes between the parties relating to jurisdiction of the ECHR and the engagement of its articles.'

> [1] For a discussion of 'hard edged' questions, see Fordham, '*Judicial Review Handbook*', 6th edn, paragraph 16.1.

19.133 In *R (Bancoult) v Secretary of State for Foreign and Commonwealth Affairs*,[1] Stanley Burnton LJ allowed an application for cross examination regarding the purposes behind designating the British Indian Ocean Territory as a Marine Protected Area. The Claimant relied upon leaked information released by the internet organisation Wikileaks, which suggested that the purpose behind the designation of the British Indian Ocean Territory as a Marine Protected Area was to prevent the former inhabitants of the Chagos Islanders from resettling there.

Stanley Burnton LJ held:

> 'I acknowledge that cross examination is exceptional in judicial review proceedings. This is largely because the primary facts are often not in dispute, or at least those asserted by the defendant public authority are undisputed. In addition, the defendant public authority may normally (but not invariably) be relied upon to disclose its relevant documents, thus fulfilling its duty of candour in relation to its documents. However, the Court retains a discretion to order or to permit cross examination, and it should do so if cross examination is necessary if the claim is to be determined, and is seen to be determined, fairly and justly.'

Stanley Burnton LJ held that this test was satisfied.

> [1] [2012] EWHC 2115 (Admin).

19.134 No doubt the above categories should not be seen as exhaustive. It is submitted that the essential question is whether there is some disputed question of primary fact that the court must determine for itself, and if so, whether 'the justice of the particular case'[1] requires that there be cross-examination. Even in such a case, it is considered unlikely that the court is obliged to order the cross-examination of witnesses in the absence of any application from the parties.[2]

[1] Per Lord Diplock in *O'Reilly*. The case of *R v Mental Health Act Commission, ex p Mark Witham*, (26 May 1988, unreported) provides a striking example of a case where cross-examination was ordered which cannot readily be fitted into any of the above categories. The issue was whether or not a particular form of treatment fell within a statutory definition as being 'the surgical implementation of hormones for the purposes of reducing the male sexual drive'.

[2] See *R (B) v Haddock* [2006] EWCA Civ 961 at [65] paragraph 65 and *Jedwell v Denbighshire County Council* [2015] EWCA Civ 1232 at paragraphs 53–54, where Lewison LJ confined the comments of Stanley Burnton J in *S v Airedale NHS Trust* [2002] EWHC 1780 (Admin) to situations where there had been no application made for cross-examination of a witness.

OTHER DIRECTIONS AND ORDERS

19.135 The court has power to give directions when granting permission,[1] and the grant of permission provides both a useful opportunity for case management and also an occasion for dealing with certain other consequential matters. In addition to questions of interim remedies and costs, matters which may be dealt with at the permission stage – if not earlier or later – include those set out below.

[1] CPR 54.10(1).

Amendment

19.136 The court has power to allow a claimant to amend the claim form[1] and may consider it appropriate to do so at the permission stage. Amendment of statements of case generally is discussed in CHAPTER 20.[2]

[1] CPR 17.1(2).
[2] See **20.5** et seq.

Expedition

19.137 Many of the cases dealt with by the Administrative Court will have some, perhaps a high degree of, urgency, and it is in that context that a party, or both parties, will need to show that there is some good reason why a case merits earlier consideration than other cases in what is generally a long queue. In appropriate cases an order for expedition may be accompanied by orders for abridgement of time for service of grounds of opposition, evidence and skeleton arguments.[1] In the new Planning Court, the Planning Liaison Judge may categorise claims as 'significant'.[2] The consequences of this are that target timescales (subject to the overriding objective of the interests of justice) apply for determination of written applications for permission, hearing of oral renewal applications and, in the case of challenges under s 288 of the Town and Country Planning Act 1990, substantive applications.[3] However, this does not prevent the Planning Liaison Judge granting expedition regardless of the designation of the claim, if this is necessary to deal with the case justly.[4]

[1] See paragraph **19.106** above in respect of potential amendments to the CPR affecting the expedition of claims.

Hearing of a preliminary issue

19.138 The court may decide to order a hearing on a preliminary issue[1] in pursuance of its powers of case management. This course is most likely where there is some issue as to the whether the case is suitable for judicial review due to the existence of an alternative remedy,[2] doubts about the amenability of the defendant to judicial review[3], whether the subject matter of the claim is justiciable,[4] whether the court has jurisdiction,[5] or what the appropriate standard of review might be.[6]

1   See, especially, CPR 1.4(1) and (2)(d) and (f).
2   For example, *R v Chief Adjudication Officer, ex p Bland* (1985) Times, 6 February.
3   Examples are *R v Disciplinary Committee of the Jockey Club, ex p Aga Khan* [1993] 1 WLR 909; *R v Association of British Travel Agents, ex p Sunspell Ltd* [2001] ACD 88; *R (A) v Partnerships in Care Ltd* [2002] 1 WLR 2610
4   For example, *R (Campaign for Nuclear Disarmament) v Prime Minister* [2002] EWHC 2777 (Admin), (2002) Times, 27 December, [2003] 3 LRC 335; *A v B* [2008] EWHC 1512 (Admin).
5   *R (Bredenkamp) v Secretary of State for Foreign and Commonwealth Affairs* [2013] 2 CMLR 238, paragraphs 7–8.
6   *R (A) v Croydon London Borough Council* [2009] UKSC 8.

Bail

19.139 There is jurisdiction to grant bail in judicial review proceedings, as established by the Court of Appeal in *Vilvarajah v Secretary of State for the Home Department*[1] and *R (Sezek) v Secretary of State for the Home Department*.[2] However, a recent decision of the Supreme Court, *Corey for Judicial Review (Northern Ireland), Re*,[3] distinguished *Vilvarajah* and *Sezek*, on two grounds. The first ground (that the exercise of the inherent jurisdiction of the High Court of Northern Ireland was contrary to the legislative framework) is not of great direct significance for English and Welsh cases. However, the Supreme Court also distinguished *Vivarajah* and *Sezek* on the grounds that, in those cases, the release of the claimant was being sought as relief in the claim. By contrast, in *In re Corey*, the relief sought was that the applicant's detention had not been reviewed as required by article 5.4 of the ECHR. Lord Kerr JSC held:[4]

> ' . . . in both *Tukoglu* and *Sezek* it was accepted by the Secretary of State that the relevant courts had power to grant bail. It should also be remembered that in *Sezek* the Court of Appeal considered that it was by recourse to an original, as opposed to inherent, jurisdiction, that the grant of bail might be made. All that aside, the principle difficulty with [the claimant's] argument is that in both cases the applicants were asserting their right to liberty. If their claims were upheld, they were entitled not to be detained, whereas what Mr Corey claims is the right to have his valid recall to prison reviewed in a way that is compliant with article 5.4 of the Convention. A power to grant bail ancillary to the declaration that the appellant was entitled to that particular form of relief was not only unnecessary in order to make the grant of relief practical and effective, it was unrelated to it.

Quite apart from the inaptness of recourse to an inherent jurisdiction for the purpose of making the judge's order practically and meaningfully effective, to recognise an inherent jurisdiction to order release in the circumstances of this case would run directly counter to the operation of the [Life Sentences (Northern Ireland) Order 2001]'

¹   [1988] QB 398.
²   [2002] 1 WLR 348.
³   [2014] AC 516.
⁴   Paragraphs 30–31. See also discussion of Corey in *Mullan v Secretary of State for Northern Ireland* [2016] NIQB 42.

19.140 Challenges to immigration detention will give rise to a jurisdiction to grant bail. It remains to be seen, in the aftermath of *In re Corey*, whether bail is available in circumstances other than where the primary relief sought is the release from detention of the claimant. It is considered that this jurisdiction should be available, at least in circumstances where, if the primary relief sought is granted, then the claimant will be released from detention. An example would be a judicial review of a decision to remove an individual and to refuse to grant them leave to remain. If the detained claimant is successful and it is found that the refusal to grant leave to remain would be in breach of his human rights, then he will inevitably be released from detention if the claim is successful. Therefore, whilst release from detention is not primary relief sought in the claim, it is a necessary corollary of the success of the claim. In those circumstances, a jurisdiction to grant bail would appear suitable.¹

¹   See discussion of Corey for Judicial Review (Northern Ireland), Re in *Mullan v Secretary of State for Northern Ireland* [2016] NIQB 42.

19.141 Less clear are those cases where it is not certain that an individual would be released even if the primary relief is granted. For example, if a detained claimant seeks judicial review of a decision by the Home Secretary to refuse to treat further asylum representations as a fresh claim for asylum, then a challenge to detention is not primary relief in the claim. It is however fairly likely that, if the decision to refuse to treat the representations as a fresh claim is quashed, then the claimant would be granted temporary admission whilst his asylum claim (and any subsequent appeal) is resolved.

19.142 In *Sezek*, the Court of Appeal's suggestion that 'great weight' should be given to the decision of the Secretary of State to detain may be contrasted with the guidance on bail prepared for First-tier Tribunal Judges,¹ which emphasises the presumption in favour of liberty and states that the burden of showing that detention is justified falls on the Secretary of State.² In any event, as the Court of Appeal held in *R (A) v Secretary of State for the Home Department*,³ the court is the primary fact finder in relation to the legality of administrative detention, which will require it to make findings about matters such as the risk of absconding. It is suggested therefore that *Sezek* should be read as saying no more than that a judge will always listen carefully to the reasons for detention given by the Secretary of State. In both *Sezek* and *Vilvarajah* it was recognised that the absence of any power in the Secretary of State to make release subject to sureties meant that he may on occasion welcome such applications for bail.

¹   See, generally, the '*Bail Guidance for Judges Presiding Over Immigration and Asylum Hearings* Presidential Guidance Note 1 of 2012, implemented on 11 June 2012, and in particular paragraphs 1, 2 and 27.
²   Note however, that this presumption may not apply to foreign nationals pending deportation: see *R (WL (Congo)) v Secretary of State for the Home Department* [2010] EWCA Civ 111. This was approved by Lord Dyson JSC in the Supreme Court [2012] 1 AC 245, paragraph 54, so long as the reference to a presumption is to normal practice, and the principles in *R v Governor of Durham Prison, ex p Singh (Hardial)* [1984] 1 WLR 704 are applied, and each case is considered individually.
³   [2007] EWCA Civ 804.

19.143 In cases where an application may be made to the First-tier Tribunal for bail, the application of ordinary principles governing the use of alternative remedies where available requires that the bail application should be made to the First-tier Tribunal in the first instance. In *R v Secretary of State for the Home Department, ex p Kelso*,¹ Collins J was willing to take a pragmatic approach; having first reached the view that the objections to bail were 'insubstantial' on the facts of the case, it was not sensible to require the matter to go back to an adjudicator for consideration of bail only to face the possibility of it then coming back to the High Court if the decision went against the applicant. It is also suggested that there may be circumstances where it may be appropriate for the court to give consideration to bail if some other aspect of the substantive case is before it and its decision on that has implications for bail, notwithstanding that the application could be made to an adjudicator. The clearest example would be where an adjudicator had thought it appropriate to refuse bail pending a decision from the High Court on whether permission was to be granted, and the High Court subsequently grants permission.

¹   [1998] INLR 603.

19.144 The Administrative Court has also dealt with a number of applications for bail in criminal cases. Following abolition of the general right to apply to a judge of the High Court for bail,¹ it has been held that bail may be sought on an application for judicial review of the decision of the court which refused it.² This appears to be consistent with the approach to *In re Corey*, since if a defendant in a criminal prosecution is acquitted then (unless he is already serving a sentence for another offence), he will be released: the defendant's liberty is clearly at issue in the case. The approach is one of review rather than appeal. Guidance as to the procedure to be adopted was given in *R (Allwin) v Snaresbrook Crown Court*.³ Stressing that the jurisdiction would only be exceptionally exercised, Collins J said that the prosecutor should be notified and the matter dealt with under the court's procedures for urgent applications – but not as an out-of-hours application.⁴ In general, it would not be appropriate that bail be granted on an interim application on the papers, and the claimant should request an oral hearing on notice within as short a time as reasonably possible. Following this decision, the general practice of judges in the Administrative Court has been, unless the claim is unarguable, to direct an oral hearing on two days' notice to the prosecutor. At the oral hearing – normally before a single judge – the court will effectively determine the issue. If it decides that it is an appropriate case to grant bail, it will grant permission, it will abridge all the other procedural requirements and it will make that

Listing **19.148**

decision then and there. Otherwise, it will decide either to grant permission and dismiss the application or to regard the application as unarguable and so refuse permission.

¹ See s 17(6)(b) of the Criminal Justice Act 2003.
² *R (M) v Isleworth Crown Court* [2005] EWHC 363 (Admin), where there is a discussion of the principles upon which the reviewing court will act. However, this jurisdiction is precluded in relation to refusals of bail made in the middle of a trial by virtue of s 29(3) of the Senior Courts Act 1981; see *R (on the application of Uddin) v Leeds Crown Court* [2013] EWHC 2752 (Admin).
³ [2005] EWHC 742 (Admin); confirmed in *R (Mongan) v Isleworth Crown Court* [2007] EWHC 1087 (Admin).
⁴ See **19.106** above.

Transfer

19.145 CPR 54.20 provides that the court may order a claim to continue as if not begun under Part 54, and where it does so, the court may give directions about the future management of the claim. The court also has power to transfer an application for judicial review to be transferred to a district registry, or (without transferring the case) to specify a place where a trial or other hearing is to be held: this is discussed at **19.20** above. In *R (West) v Lloyd's of London*¹ the Court of Appeal concluded that proceedings, if they were to be brought at all, should have been issued in the Chancery Division. Brooke LJ, having considered the possibility of retaining the matter in the Administrative Court or transferring it to another division, said that he would usually be keen to take one or other of these courses, but that the case required such entire reshaping that the claimant would have to begin again.

¹ [2004] 3 All ER 251, at paragraph 41 (p 264). For consideration of transfer by the court at the hearing of a claim for judicial review, see **20.32**.

19.146 The procedure where proceedings issued elsewhere are proposed to be transferred to the Administrative Court is discussed earlier in this chapter.¹

¹ See **19.27**.

LISTING¹

¹ See Judicial Review Guide 2016 published by the Administrative Court section 13, available at the time of writing at https://www.gov.uk/government/uploads/system/uploads/attachment_data/file/540607/administrative-court-judicial-review-guide.pdf

19.147 The *Practice Statement (Administrative Court: Listing and Urgent Cases)*² deals with the fixing of substantive hearings, the short-warned list, and what happens when fixtures have to be vacated.

² [2002] 1 WLR 810. The context in which listing decisions are taken, and the current state of the list, is described in annual statements published by the Administrative Court and available on the HM Courts Service website.

19.148 *Fixing substantive hearings* – Where a case is ready to be heard substantively, it enters a warned list and all parties are informed of this by letter. Some cases require an early hearing date and take priority over other cases waiting to be fixed – these enter the expedited warned list. Where counsel have been identified, their chambers are contacted by the Administrative Court list office in order to agree a convenient date for the hearing. Counsel's clerks are offered a range of dates and have 48 hours to take up one of the dates offered. If counsel's clerk fails to contact the list office within 48 hours, the list office will fix the hearing on one of the dates that was offered, without further notice and the parties will be notified of that fixture by letter. Where a hearing is listed in this way the hearing will only be vacated by the Administrative Court Office if both parties consent. Failing that, a formal application for adjournment must be made (on notice to all parties) to the court. The same procedure is followed where a claimant is in person.

19.149 *Short warned list* – Whilst the Administrative Court usually gives fixed dates for hearings, there is also a need to short warn a number of cases to cover the large number of settlements that occur in the list. Parties in cases that are selected to be short warned will be notified that their case is likely to be listed from a specified date, and that they may be called into the list at less than a day's notice from that date. Approximately six cases are short warned for any specified week. If the case does not get on during that period, a date as soon as possible after that period will be fixed in consultation with the parties.

19.150 *Vacating fixtures* – There are occasions when circumstances, outside the control of the list office, may necessitate them having to vacate a hearing at very short notice. Sometimes this can be as late as 4.30 pm the day before the case is listed. This could be as a result of a case unexpectedly overrunning, a judge becoming unavailable, or other reasons. In deciding which hearing has to be vacated, the list office will assess the cases listed for the following day and take the following factors into consideration:

(1)   which case(s), if removed, will cause the least disruption to the list (the aim is to adjourn as few cases as possible, ideally one);

(2)   how many cases need to be adjourned given the reduced listing time available;

(3)   have any matters previously been adjourned by the court;

(4)   the urgency and age(s) of the matter(s) listed;

(5)   where the parties and/or their representatives are based (this is relevant as in some cases the parties travel to London the day before the hearing);

(6)   whether it is appropriate to 'float' the case in the event of another listed matter going short (cases will not be floated without the consent of the parties);

(7)   the likelihood of a judge becoming available to hear a floated case.

19.151 After taking these factors into account, the list office decides upon the case(s) which will have to be refixed and will inform the parties concerned that their hearing has been vacated. The case record will note that the matter is not to be adjourned by the court again. The court will also endeavour to refix the case on the next available date convenient to the parties.

JUDICIAL REVIEW PROCEDURE IN THE UPPER TRIBUNAL

19.152 Under the Tribunals, Courts and Enforcement Act 2007, the Upper Tribunal has power to hear judicial review claims in two circumstances. Firstly, the Upper Tribunal has a general jurisdiction to accept judicial review cases transferred to it by the High Court. The High Court may, subject to certain limitations,[1] transfer any case where it considers that it is just and convenient to do so. Secondly, the Upper Tribunal has jurisdiction to accept applications for judicial review in any case which falls within a class specified in a Direction by the Lord Chief Justice in agreement with the Lord Chancellor.[2] By Directions dated 29 October 2008 and 21 August 2013,[3] the Lord Chief Justice transferred to the jurisdiction of the Upper Tribunal:

(i)   appeals against reviews of decisions under the Criminal Injuries Compensation Scheme, and

(ii)   reviews of a decisions of the First-tier Tribunal made under the new Tribunal Procedure Rules where there is no appeal to the Upper Tribunal against the decision.

(iii) any application calling into question a decision (or failure to make a decision) made under the Immigration Acts (or under an instrument under the Immigration Acts), or otherwise relating to leave to enter or remain in the United Kingdom outside the immigration rules, or a decision of the Immigration and Asylum Chamber of the First-tier Tribunal, from which no appeal lies to the Upper Tribunal except for:

–   Challenges to the validity of primary or subordinate legislation, or the immigration rules;

–   Challenges to the lawfulness of detention (beyond a challenge to a decision in relation to bail);

–   Challenges to a decision concerning licensing of Sponsors by the UK Border Agency;

–   Challenges to citizenship decisions;

–   Challenges relating to support under s 4 or Part VI of the Immigration and Asylum Act 1999;

–   Challenges to decisions under Part II or Part II of the Nationality, Immigration and Asylum Act 2002;

–   Challenges to decision of the Upper Tribunal;

–   Challenges to decisions under Part II or Part III of the Nationality, Immigration and Asylum Act 2002;

–   Applications for a declaration of incompatibility under s 4 of the Human Rights Act 1998.

A further Direction was made on 24 October 2013, dealing with transitional matters.[4]

[1] Section 19 of the 2007 Act inserted the conditions for transfer into s 31A of the Senior Courts Act 1981. The main limitations on the power to transfer are: (i) where the claim seeks to call into question anything done in a Crown Court and (ii) where the claimant seeks a declaration of incompatibility under section 4 of the Human Rights Act 1998.

[2] Section 18(6) of the 2007 Act.

[3] Available at time of writing at www.judiciary.gov.uk/wp-content/uploads/JCO/Documents/Practice+Directions/Tribunals/lcj-direction-jr-iac-21-08-2013.pdf — Also see a further Direction made on 24 October 2013, dealing with transitional matters: https://www.judiciary.gov.uk/wp-content/uploads/2014/05/Lord-Chief-Justice%E2%80%99s-further-Direction-regarding-the-transfer-of-immigration-and-asylum-Judicial-Review-case.pdf

[4] Available at time of writing at www.judiciary.gov.uk/wp-content/uploads/2014/05/Lord-Chief-Justice's-further-Direction-regarding-the-transfer-of-immigration-and-asylum-Judicial-Review-case.pdf.

19.153 The upshot of s 31A of the SCA 1981, the 2007 Act and the 2013 Transfer Directions is as follows:

(1)   All judicial reviews specified in the Transfer Directions must be submitted to and determined by the UT, unless they fall within a specified exception;

(2)   All other JRs, including those which fall within the specified exceptions must be submitted to the High Court, which may, in its discretion, transfer the case to the UT if it considers it "just and convenient" to do so, unless: (i) The relief sought goes beyond that specified in s.15(1) of the 2007 Act; or (ii) the claim challenges a decision of the Crown Court.

19.154 In practice, at the time of writing the only class of case that is routinely transferred to the UT from the High Court as a matter of discretion is Age Dispute judicial reviews, in which the court is asked to determine a claimant's age as a primary fact. Age Dispute claims *may* be transferred to the UT, but need not be, as they are not specified in an order under s 18(6) of the 2007 Act or in accordance with Part 1 of Schedule 2 to the Constitutional Reform Act 2005. Nonetheless, in *R (FZ Acting by his Litigation Friend Parivash Ghanipour) v Croydon London Borough Council*,[1] the Court of Appeal gave a strong indication that transfer would ordinarily be appropriate in such a case:

> 'The Administrative Court does not habitually decide questions of fact on contested evidence and is not generally equipped to do so. Oral evidence is not normally a feature of judicial review proceedings or statutory appeals. We would therefore draw attention to the power which there now is to transfer age assessment cases where permission is given for the factual determination of the claimant's age to the Upper Tribunal under section 31A(3) of the Senior Courts Act 1981, as inserted by section 19 of the Tribunals, Courts and Enforcement Act 2007 . . . Transfer to the Upper Tribunal is appropriate because the judges there have experience of assessing the ages of children from abroad in the context of disputed asylum claims . . . '.

[1]   [2011] EWCA Civ 59.

Applications to the Upper Tribunal

19.155 Where a judicial review claim relates to proceedings that fall within a class specified in a Direction by the Lord Chief Justice, those proceedings should be issued in the Upper Tribunal. Although the High Court may transfer any claim wrongly issued in the Administrative Court, it will save time and costs by issuing in the right place. With this in mind, claimants are advised to keep informed of any future directions transferring further classes of case to the jurisdiction of the Upper Tribunal. When a claim is transferred to the Upper Tribunal, the Upper Tribunal must inform the parties and give directions.[1]

[1]   Rule 27(1), Tribunal Procedure (Upper Tribunal) Rules 2008.

19.156 In England, the address for any correspondence relating to a judicial review, and the relevant addresses at which to issue a claim are:

For immigration and asylum judicial reviews: Upper Tribunal Immigration and Asylum Chamber, Field House, 15–25 Breams Buildings, London, EC4A 1DZ.

For other judicial reviews in London: The Upper Tribunal Office (Administrative Appeals Chamber), 5th Floor, Chichester Rents, 81 Chancery Lane, London WC2A 1DD. In Wales, the relevant address is The Upper Tribunal Office (Administrative Appeals Chamber), Civil Justice Centre, 2 Park Street, Cardiff CF10 1ET. For the Birmingham Regional Centre, the address is Birmingham Civil Justice Centre, Priory Courts, 5th Floor, 33 Bull Street, Birmingham, B4 6DS. For the Leeds Regional Centre, the address is Leeds Combined Court, 1 Oxford Row, Leeds, LS1 3BG. For the Manchester Regional Centre, the address is Manchester Civil Justice Centre, 1 Bridge Street West, Manchester, M60 9DJ. For the Welsh Centre, the address is Cardiff Civil Justice Centre, 2 Park Street, Cardiff, CF10 1ET.

19.157 Urgent applications made out of hours should be made to the Royal Courts of Justice Queen's Bench Division.[1]

---

[1] For guidance on out of hours applications, see **19.112** above.

19.158 The procedural rules relating to judicial review proceedings in the Upper Tribunal are set out at sections 27–33 of The Tribunal Procedure (Upper Tribunal) Rules 2008 (SI/2008/2698) ('the Rules'). The Rules are not extensive, and it may be that they do not cover all situations that could arise. In the event that the Rules do not prescribe the appropriate procedure to be followed, it may well be appropriate to have regard to the CPR, and the relevant case law relevant to the CPR, even though it is not binding on the Upper Tribunal.[1]

---

[1] The Rules mirror many of the provisions in the CPR. See, for example, the overriding objective at rule 2, and the Tribunal's general case management powers at rule 5.

19.159 Rule 2 of the Upper Tribunal Rules contains the Overriding Objective. Although this is the functional equivalent of the Overriding Objective in Part 1 of the CPR, there are some important differences between them:

(i)   The overriding objective in the CPR is dealing with cases 'justly and at proportionate cost'. The overriding objective in the Upper Tribunal Rules is dealing with cases 'fairly and justly'.

(ii)   The CPR puts more weight on costs. The overriding objective of the CPR includes saving expense, dealing with a case in ways proportionate to the amount of money involved and the financial position of each party, and allocating to it an appropriate share of the court's resources. The overriding objective in the Upper Tribunal Rules considers costs much more briefly, although consideration of proportionality is to include 'the anticipated costs and the resources of the parties'.

(iii) The overriding objective in the Upper Tribunal Rules involves avoiding unnecessary formality, and seeking flexibility in the proceedings. There is no equivalent to this in the overriding objective to the CPR.

(iv)   The overriding objective in the Upper Tribunal Rules includes 'ensuring, so far as practicable, that the parties are able to participate fully in the proceedings'. There is no direct equivalent in the CPR, although the requirement that the court ensure that the parties are on an equal footing may achieve a similar result, as may the requirement that the court ensures the case is dealt with expeditiously and fairly.

(v)   The overriding objective in the Upper Tribunal Rules includes 'using any special expertise of the Upper Tribunal effectively'. There is no analogue in the CPR.

19.160 *The Claim*: A person seeking permission to bring judicial review proceedings before the Upper Tribunal must make a written application to the Upper Tribunal for permission.[1] Section 28(4) of the Rules states that the application must contain:

'(a)   the name and address of the applicant, the respondent and any other person whom the applicant considers to be an interested party;
(b)   the name and address of the applicant's representative (if any);
(c)   an address where documents for the applicant may be sent or delivered;
(d)   details of the decision challenged (including the date, the full reference and the identity of the decision maker);
(e)   that the application is for permission to bring judicial review proceedings;
(f)   the outcome that the applicant is seeking; and
(g)   the facts and grounds on which the applicant relies.'

In addition, section 28(5) of the Rules states that if the application relates to proceedings in a court or tribunal, the application must name as an interested party each party to those proceedings who is not the applicant or a respondent. Where a claim is brought for immigration judicial review, special rules apply,[2] including that a claim must not proceed without the relevant fee being paid, or the Upper Tribunal accepting an undertaking that it will be paid.

[1]   Rule 28(1).
[2]   Rule 28A.

19.161 An application for permission to apply for judicial review falling within the Lord Chief Justice's direction of 21 August 2013 should be made on form T480.[1] A judicial review in the Upper Tribunal Administrative Appeals Chamber will be on form JR1, or in the case of criminal injuries compensation cases, on form JRC1.[2] An application for urgent consideration is to be made on form T483. When the Upper Tribunal receives an application for judicial review it must send a copy of the application and any accompanying documents to each person named in the application as a respondent or interested party.[3]

[1]   Available online at: https://formfinder.hmctsformfinder.justice.gov.uk/t480-eng.pdf
[2]   Available online at: https://hmctsformfinder.justice.gov.uk/HMCTS/GetForms.do?court_form s_category=Administrative%20Appeals%20Chamber%20(Upper%20Tribunal.
[3]   Rule 28(8).

19.162 To comply with the requirements of rule 28A of the Upper Tribunal Rules, the applicant for permission to bring judicial review must provide a written statement of when and how the application and supporting documents were made; this is done on form T485.

19.163 *Method of delivery*: Litigants should ensure that, unless directed otherwise, claim forms and other documents are sent by pre-paid post, DX, hand delivery, or fax. By contrast to the Administrative Court, it appears that the Upper Tribunal will accept a claim form by fax as a matter of course.[1] While the submission of a document by email may be permitted by the Upper Tribunal,[2] it is not, in the ordinary course of events, a prescribed method of delivery

¹   Rule 13(1)(b).
²   Rule 13(1)(c).

19.164 *Time Limits*: The same time limits applicable to a judicial review claim in the Administrative Court apply to the Upper Tribunal, save that applications for permission to bring a judicial review of a decision of the First-tier Tribunal may be made later than three months after the date of the decision if it is made within one month after the date on which the First-tier Tribunal sent written reasons for the decision¹. The Upper Tribunal has the power to extend time for complying with any rule².

¹   Rule 28(3).
²   Rule 5(3)(a).

19.165 *Acknowledgment of Service*: A person who is named as a defendant or interested party in an application for judicial review, and is sent a copy of the application by the Upper Tribunal, must send an acknowledgment of service to the Upper Tribunal within 21 days of the date the Upper Tribunal sent him the application.¹ If an acknowledgment of service is not returned within that time, the person will not be entitled to take part in the application for permission, but may take part in the subsequent proceedings if permission is granted.² The acknowledgment of service is made on form T482 in the Immigration and Asylum Chamber, or on form JR2 in the Administrative Appeals Chamber. It must state:

(i)   Whether the person intends to support or oppose the application for permission;
(ii)   Their grounds for any support or opposition, or any other information which it considers might assist the Upper Tribunal;
(iii)   The name and address of any other person who might be a respondent or interested party in the claim.³

¹   Rule 29(1).
²   Rule 29(3); but note that the Tribunal has the power to extend any time limit provided in the Rules under r.5(3)(a).
³   Rule 29(2).

19.166 In *R (Kumar) v Secretary of State for the Home Department (acknowledgement of service; Tribunal arrangements) IJR*,¹ the Upper Tribunal considered the Home Secretary's difficulties in filing acknowledgements of service within the required time limits, in immigration judicial reviews. This case is the equivalent of *R (Singh) v Secretary of State for the Home Department* [2013] EWHC 2873 (Admin) in the High Court, considered above at **19.43**.

The Upper Tribunal held that the Tribunal would generally not consider applications for permission within six weeks of being lodged; unless there was an application for urgent consideration by the applicant, it was therefore not necessary for the Secretary of State to request a first extension of time from 21 days to six weeks. Nevertheless, this does not absolve the Secretary of State of responsibility for filing an acknowledgement of service within 21 days. The Tribunal held:

'Any application for further time to file the acknowledgement of service after the six-week period would have to comply with the requirements in *Singh* for second extensions of time, ie giving "compelling reasons specific to the case as to why further time is needed", together with "a firm promise . . . as to when the Acknowledgement of Service and summary grounds will be filed". Any such application should be made on 72 hours' notice to the applicant. Where there is no application within the six-week period, and the acknowledgement of service and summary grounds have not been filed, the Upper Tribunal will consider permission without those documents. The Secretary of State should however provide the Tribunal with its response to the applicant's pre-action protocol letter (or state that none was sent), and the Tribunal will consider that response. The Tribunal should give a specific direction that the Secretary of State file summary grounds by a certain date only "where the judicial review application is based on an asserted factual position, which it appears the Secretary of State is in a position to confirm or deny"'.

Where the acknowledgment of service and summary grounds is filed after the expiry of the six-week time limit but before the judge considers the application for permission, the judge should consider those documents when making a decision regarding permission.

The Upper Tribunal also considered costs. First, it held that, where an application would have been dismissed as totally without merit on the papers had a judge seen an acknowledgement of service and summary grounds, and the applicant renews the application orally, the Secretary of State would generally have to pay the applicant's costs in connection with the oral renewal hearing. Secondly, it held that where permission is granted but, after seeing the Secretary of State's detailed grounds of defence, it is clear that permission would be refused had the grounds been expressed in summary grounds of defence, then the applicant's costs, up to the point where the detailed grounds were filed, would ordinarily be payable by the Secretary of State. Finally, if the acknowledgement of service and summary grounds are served outside the six-week period, this is not itself a reason for the Tribunal to refuse to make an order that the Secretary of State's reasonable costs of preparing the acknowledgement of service be paid by the applicant.

[1]   [2014] UKUT 00104 (IAC).

19.167 *Costs*: The Upper Tribunal has power to make orders for costs in judicial review proceedings whether the claim was initiated in the Upper Tribunal or in the High Court[1]. The principles discussed above at **19.78** apply. An award of costs will not be made without giving the paying party the opportunity to make representations.[2]

[1]   Rule 10(3)(a).
[2]   Rule 10(7).

19.168 In an immigration judicial review, where permission is refused on the papers, or where a late application for permission to bring immigration judicial review proceedings is refused, and the Upper Tribunal considers the application to be entirely without merit, it shall record this fact, and the applicant may not request the claim to be reconsidered at an oral hearing.[1]

¹ Rule 30(4A).

19.169 After the grant of permission, a defendant or interested party has 35 days from the Upper Tribunal sending notice of the grant of permission in which to file detailed grounds of resistance.

Transfers to and from the High Court

19.170 Applications for judicial review may be transferred from the High Court to the Upper Tribunal pre or post permission. Such transfers will occur where the application falls into a class of case that has been made subject to the jurisdiction of the Upper Tribunal by Direction of the Lord Chief Justice, or where the High Court considers it is just and convenient to transfer the case. The factors that will be relevant to the Administrative Court's decision on whether it is just and convenient to transfer a case are uncertain. When the Administrative Court transfers a claim to this Upper Tribunal, the Tribunal must give directions as to the future conduct of the proceedings.[1]

¹ Rule 27(1)(b).

19.171 Where an application is made to the Upper Tribunal, but the Tribunal is not empowered to grant the remedy sought, or where it is prevented by statute from hearing a particular class of case, it must transfer that case to the High Court. Where the application is transferred, the application is to be treated for all purposes as if it had been made to the High Court, and any steps taken by the Upper Tribunal, including the grant of permission, are to be treated as having been taken by the High Court.[1]

¹ Tribunals, Courts and Enforcement Act 2007, s 18(9).

19.172 Rule 33A sets out particular rules for judicial review in England and Wales, relating to amendment of claims. This rule gives the Upper Tribunal the power to allow amendments which would require a transfer of a claim back to the High Court.[1] Additional grounds which would require the transfer to the High Court are not to be advanced without the permission of the Upper Tribunal.[2]

¹ Rule 33A(2)(a).
² Rule 33A(2)(b).

JUDICIAL REVIEW PROCEDURE IN THE PLANNING COURT
19.173

In 2014, a specialist Planning Court was established. The government considered having the Planning Court as part of the Upper Tribunal, but it is instead part of the High Court. The Planning Court has its own Practice Direction (54E), but the Civil Procedure Rules will apply as normal unless specifically provided in CPR 54.21-24, or on Practice Direction 54E.[1] A Planning Court claim is one which involves any of the following:[2]

(i)   planning permission, other development consents, the enforcement of planning control and the enforcement of other statutory schemes;

(ii)   applications under the Transport and Works Act 1992;

(iii)   wayleaves;

(iv)   highways and other rights of way;

(v)   compulsory purchase orders;

(vi)   village greens;

(vii)   European Union environmental legislation and domestic transpositions, including assessments for development consents, habitats, waste and pollution control;

(viii)   national, regional or other planning policy documents, statutory or otherwise; or

(ix)   any other matter the judge appointed under rule 54.22(2) considers appropriate;

and which has been issued in or transferred to the Planning Court.

¹   CPR 54.23.
²   CPR 54.21(2).

19.174 Planning Court claims form a specialist list.¹ A judge of the Queen's Bench Division will be designated the Planning Liaison Judge.² CPR 30.5 provides for transfer in the High Court between specialist divisions. A Planning Court judge may order that a case is transferred to or from the Planning Court.³

¹   CPR 54.22(1).
²   CPR 54.22(2). At the time of writing, the Planning Liaison Judge is Lindblom J.
³   CPR 30.5.

19.175 The purpose of the creation of the Planning Court is to ensure that major planning cases are dealt with swiftly. On designation of a Planning Court claim as 'significant' by the Planning Liaison Judge, tight timescales apply. A significant planning case will be one which:¹

(a)   relate to commercial, residential, or other developments which have significant economic impact either at a local level or beyond their immediate locality;

(b)   raise important points of law;

(c)   generate significant public interest; or

(d)   by virtue of the volume or nature of technical material, are best dealt with by judges with significant experience of handling such matters.

The parties wishing to make representations regarding the characterisation of a Planning Court claim must do so in writing, on filing the claim form or the acknowledgement of service.²

¹   CPR Pt 54E PD 3.2.
²   CPR Pt 54E PD 3.3.

19.176 The target timescales are set out in paragraph 3.4 of Practice Direction 54E. They are to apply subject to the overriding objective of the interests of justice. The time limits are:

(a)   applications for permission to apply for judicial review are to be determined within three weeks of the expiry of the time limit for filing of the acknowledgment of service;

(b)   oral renewals of applications for permission to apply for judicial review are to be heard within one month of receipt of request for renewal;

(c)   applications for permission under section 289 of the Town and Country Planning Act 1990 are to be determined within one month of issue;

(d)   substantive statutory applications, including applications under section 288 of the Town and Country Planning Act 1990, are to be heard within six months of issue; and

(e)   judicial reviews are to be heard within ten weeks of the expiry of the period for the submission of detailed grounds by the defendant or any other party as provided in Rule 54.14.

19.177 Regardless of the designation of a Planning Court claim, the Planning Liaison Judge may direct its expedition if he considers it necessary to deal with the case justly.[1]

1   CPR Pt 54E PD 3.6.

Chapter 20

PROCEDURE: HEARINGS AND APPEALS

INTRODUCTION

20.1 Procedure is the ugly duckling of administrative law. In many respects – and despite the existence of CPR Pt 54 and the various Practice Directions that exist – the Administrative Court is the High Court jurisdiction that is least enslaved to the speed bumps of procedural rules. Many hearings appear to pass by without any thought to any point of procedure, or should any such point arise it is dealt with wholly pragmatically depending on the specific circumstances in hand. Yet in many respects this appearance is deceptive. The impact of CPR Pt 54 was to underline and increase the already front-loaded nature of applications for judicial review, at least in procedural terms. The bulk of the claimant's case and evidence is presented with the Claim Form at the outset of the claim; the compulsory permission stage also allows an early opportunity for obvious procedural issues to be addressed and resolved; the rules also require the defendant's evidence to be served shortly after the grant of permission. In some instances directions given at the permission stage will set a date for the service by the claimant of any evidence in reply. This is a sensible step since it can avoid problems at the hearing associated with the late service of evidence. All these matters combine – in the vast majority of claims – to ensure that by the time of the final hearing of the application the court's focus is on substantive issues rather than procedural ones. Thus in most instances the procedural hard graft has already been applied and completed well in advance of the final hearing.

20.2 This chapter will focus on specific issues that can arise immediately before or in the course of a final hearing, at the conclusion of the hearing, in relation to orders on costs (both in advance of and at the end of hearings), and in relation to any appeals (including appeals that arise after permission applications).[1] In most instances the approach that will, or should, be taken on these issues on an application for judicial review should be no different to those that would be taken in the course of any other claim under the CPR. If there are divergences most are explained by the fact that they arise in the context of a public law claim. In procedure, as in law, context is everything.

---

[1]   Procedure at earlier stages is described in CHAPTER 19. See the start of that chapter for cross-reference to Supperstone and Knapman *Administrative Court Practice – Judicial Review* (2008 edition) and to material produced by the Administrative Court and available on the internet.

IMMEDIATELY BEFORE THE HEARING

20.3 What happens immediately prior to a hearing[1] falls into one of two categories: the expected and the unexpected. What is expected is the service of skeleton arguments in accordance with the timetable in the first Practice Direction accompanying CPR Pt 54, Practice Direction 54A. First, the skeleton argument from the claimant should be lodged 21 working days prior to the hearing. Next, skeleton arguments from the defendant and other participants should be lodged 14 working days prior to the hearing.[2]

The skeletons must identify the issues and points of law in the case, set out a chronology of events, identify and list the persons referred to in the claim, and identify and list the documents in the bundle that should be read by the court in advance of the hearing. The papers in the case should be assembled in paginated bundles and filed by the claimant 21 days before the hearing.[3] All this is well known and predictable.

The unexpected is more difficult to predict; the possibilities can appear limitless. That said, there are 'usual suspects'. For example:

(1)   the production of late evidence;

(2)   attempts to amend cases or even to attach challenges to decisions taken since the grant of permission;

(3)   attempts to re-open points which failed at the permission stage:

(4)   late attempts to intervene in proceedings.[4]

[1]   As to the listing of final hearings see **19.147**.
[2]   See CPR Pt 54A PD.15.
[3]   These requirements are all set out in Practice Direction 54A, where reference is made to more general directions about citation of authorities and similar matters.
[4]   On this latter point, see **20.15**.

20.4 *Late evidence* – In some instances, the nature of the claim before the court means that the service of late evidence is almost inevitable. This will be the case if the dispute concerns on-going or developing issues such as challenges to assessments made by social services authorities. Such evidence may be relied on with the permission of the court.[1] However, whether such evidence should be admissible (and therefore whether the court should grant permission to deploy it) requires careful attention to the true purpose of the evidence presented and the nature of the challenge that is in fact before the court. Although the court has a general discretion to admit evidence that comes into existence outside the timetable set either by CPR Pt 54 or by the court itself,[2] this begs, rather than answers, any relevant question. The starting point must be the actual challenge before the court. In most, if not all, instances the issue is to determine the legality of the decision taken as at the time that it was taken. This is likely to count against most late evidence that relates only to events that have taken place after the decision under challenge. In reality such evidence may well not be evidence in support of the original challenge, but rather evidence in support of a challenge to a different decision taken after the grant of permission in response to changing circumstances. Clearly, however, these concerns will not apply if the evidence is material to any issue as to remedies that might arise if the claim succeeds. The discretion as to remedies is one which the court ought to consider on the basis of all material evidence – even (or perhaps, in particular) evidence coming into existence after the date of the decision that is under challenge. In an extreme case the change of circumstances could be such either as to render the grant of any remedy pointless, or so as to render the claim itself academic.

In all instances the exercise of the discretion to admit late evidence is premised on the principles set out in the CPR 'overriding objective'. Following the Jackson reforms, the amendments to the overriding objective include the need to deal with cases at a proportionate cost. Changes were also made to rule 3.9, making it more difficult to obtain relief from sanctions imposed for a failure to comply with any rule, practice direction or court order, which includes any timetable for filing evidence. The court will consider all the circumstances of the case, so as to enable it to deal justly with the application, including the need (a) for litigation to be conducted efficiently and at proportionate cost; and (b) to enforce compliance with rules, practice directions and orders. In *Denton v TH White Ltd*,[3] the Court of Appeal has recently given guidance on the approach to be taken to an application for relief from sanctions. The first stage is to identify and assess the seriousness and significance of the individual failure to comply. The second stage is to consider why the default occurred. The third stage is to consider all the circumstances of the case, accordingly particular, but not paramount, importance or weight to be given to the two factors set out in CPR 3.9. The Court emphasised that there is to be a new 'culture of compliance', but that parties who fail to cooperate in agreeing extensions of time or who 'opportunistically and unreasonably oppose applications for relief from sanctions' will be heavily penalised in costs.[4]

It is important to distinguish between the production of evidence that is late because it is produced after the procedural deadline and evidence that is late because it 'supplements' that provided at the time of the defendant's decision; the latter is discussed at **20.36** and **20.47** below.

[1] See CPR 54.16.
[2] See CPR 54.16.
[3] [2014] EWCA Civ 906.
[4] This decision 'modified' the approach laid down by the Court of Appeal in *Mitchell v News Group Newspapers Ltd* [2013] EWCA Civ 1537; [2014] 1 WLR 795, which, it was said, had elevated the two factors in CPR 3.9 too far, and had led to the imposition of disproportionate penalties for breaches that had little practical effect on the course of litigation.

20.5 *Applications to amend* – Generally, amendments to statements of case will be governed by CPR Pt 17. However, an application to add further grounds to the claim form will fall to be considered under CPR 54.15. The permission of the court is required, and, in the most general terms, the discretion to permit an amendment in a claim for judicial review should be exercised on the basis of precisely the same principles that would apply in any other action (ie can the 'injustice' of an amendment be adequately relieved by an appropriate adjournment or orders for costs?).

In *San Vicente v Secretary of State for Communities and Local Government*,[1] the Court of Appeal held that CPR Part 17.4 (which restricts amendments to statements of case after the end of a relevant limitation period) did not apply to public law proceedings. To allow an amendment to an in-time public law challenge only if the application to amend is made within the relevant statutory period, where the amended grounds relied on the same or substantially the same facts as the original grounds, would be inflexible. It would inhibit the ability of the court to vindicate the principle of legality or to consider the real issues of public interest and policy. Applications to amend in public law claims will therefore continue to be considered under the general discretion in rule 17.1(2)(b), regardless of whether they are made before or after the expiry of the time limit for bringing a claim for judicial review.

There are, however, two possible situations that require special consideration in the context of a claim for judicial review – in most, if not all, instances these will be situations that arise at the instigation of the claimant.

[1] [2014] 1 WLR 966.

20.6 First, the amendment may in substance be a means of seeking to challenge a decision that has occurred since the grant of permission. In some instances the amendment may give the appearance of a fresh challenge, but in substance is only aimed at identifying the decision that should have been the target of the challenge in the first place.[1] If the proposed amendment is in substance a challenge to a later decision, what should be considered is its effect on the original challenge, and whether or not it is appropriate to deal with the new challenge by way of amendment, or whether it should be the subject of a fresh claim. Consideration of these issues is an exercise in pragmatism. In some instances it will be clear that, in substance, the amendment supersedes the original claim. If this is the position, the first point is to consider how the original claim should be disposed of: does any point of principle remain which ought to be considered by the court, or has the original claim become purely academic; what should happen in relation to the costs incurred in relation to the original claim that, in light of the proposed amendment, were unnecessary? In any event, and regardless of whether the proposed amendment overtakes the original claim, issues relating to permission (in the judicial review sense of the term) are also paramount. One purpose of the permission stage is to protect defendants from devoting unnecessary time and expense to claims if there is a short point that may dispose of claim. The importance of this protection is not to be overlooked, and it is important that applications to amend should not form the means by which defendants are bounced into unnecessary preparation to deal with issues that would not withstand consideration at the summary permission stage. In some instances these considerations will point in favour of a decision to refuse an application to amend and leave the claimant to issue new proceedings in relation to the later decision;[2] in others a permission-type exercise could be built into the existing proceedings. The actual resolution ought in all instances to pay close regard to the balance of inconvenience as between the parties.

[1] See, for example, the situation considered in *R (Burkett) v Hammersmith and Fulham London Borough Council* [2002] 1 WLR 1593. Compare *R (Nash) v Barnet LBC* [2013] EWCA Civ 1004 and [2013] EWHC 1067 (Admin) where, although the claimant purported to challenge the local authority's decision to award a contract to a particular provider, in substance the challenge was to the local authority's earlier decision to outsource that function. Therefore, the challenge was out of time.

[2] See, for example, *R (Bhatti) v Bury Metropolitan Borough Council* [2013] EHWC 3093 (Admin), where the court refused to allow judicial review proceedings that had been stayed by consent to be reinstated and amended to challenge a subsequent decision where that challenge did not involve even an incidental consideration of the decision originally challenged, and there was an adequate alternative remedy in the form of a statutory complaints procedure in respect of all the new grounds of challenge.

20.7 *Re-opening points which failed at the permission stage* – The second situation is that where, having failed on one of several grounds at the permission stage, the claimant seeks to revive the ground at the full hearing. This topic is discussed in CHAPTER 19.[1]

[1] See 19.67 et seq.

20.8 *Late applications by interested parties or interveners* – General principles concerning interested parties and interveners are discussed below.[1] If an application is made late and would delay the hearing, the court may be expected to require a strong case before allowing such an application.

[1] See 20.17 et seq.

NO HEARING

20.9 CPR 54.18 permits a court to determine an application for judicial review without a hearing where all parties agree. This includes both situations where the application is uncontested and those where, although a live dispute remains between the parties, all are content for it to be resolved on paper.

20.10 There are, however, other situations in which a hearing will not occur: some friendly, others not so friendly.[1] Squarely in the first category are situations in which at a late stage a claim is settled or withdrawn.[2] Practice Direction 54A indicates that if the parties have agreed the terms of an order it is sufficient to lodge this together with a short statement of the matters relied on as justifying the order and copies of any material authorities.[3] If the court is satisfied that the order should be made, it will make the order without any requirement for attendance. Things may not, however, always be so simple – at least in situations where the agreed order takes the form of a proposed declaration. In private law actions there is a long-standing practice that declarations will not be made in the absence of a full hearing.[4] This is a rule of practice, not a rule of law and as such can be departed from in appropriate cases, for example, if the declaration will not affect the rights of anyone other than the parties to the action.[5] Yet in public law actions this is less likely to be the case, certainly in any instance in which the declaration proposed is premised on any point of statutory construction, and possibly also in other circumstances. This possibility underlines the importance of the explanatory statement that (under the Practice Direction) must accompany any proposed agreed order. There may well be occasions where some form of hearing – even if not a full hearing – is required before the court can properly be satisfied that the agreed order is the order that should be made.[6]

[1] One short point worth mentioning is the position when it is contended that a court should stay its proceedings pending the decision of a different court. If such a step might avoid the need to litigate at all, it is plainly a weighty consideration. However, this is a discretion exercised carefully: see, for example, *R (Anderson) v Secretary of State for the Home Department* [2002] ACD 91 (no stay granted pending consideration of similar issue by the European Court of Human Rights).

[2] In this context, note the important comments made by Hodgson J in *R v Secretary of State for the Home Department, ex p Brown* (1984) Times, 6 February, as to the obligation of a claimant to reconsider the substantive merits of his claim in light of the defendant's evidence. In practice the same should apply to a defendant if following the preparation of his own evidence, or receipt of evidence in reply it becomes apparent that the claim will succeed.

[3] See Practice Direction 54A at §17. Where the agreement relates to an order for costs only, the parties need only file a document signed by all the parties setting out the terms of the proposed order.

[4] See *Wallersteiner v Moir* [1974] 1 WLR 991 per Buckley LJ at 1029A–D.

[5] See also *FSA v Rourke* [2002] CP Rep 14. Here Neuberger J gave consideration to this rule of practice but decided to grant a declaration following summary judgment in circumstances where he was satisfied that there was no realistic possibility that the facts on which the declaration were based would be shown to be wrong at any trial of the action. In considering whether or not to grant declaratory relief the court should take into account justice to the claimant, justice to the defendant, whether the declaration would serve a useful purpose and whether there are any special reasons tending towards the grant or refusal of declaratory relief; see also *FSA v Watkins (Stephen Ronald) (t/a Consolidated Land UK)* [2011] EWHC 1976 (Ch).

[6] Quite apart from any issue of this sort, an agreement between the parties, or a late withdrawal may well leave open the issue as to what order should be made as to costs. On this, see **20.90** below.

20.11 A further situation in which a hearing could be rendered unnecessary will be where the parties have resorted to mediation in order to resolve the issues arising. Clearly, there will be some judicial review actions which by their nature are not suited to mediation or any other form of alternative dispute resolution. That said, it is clear that the courts are positively in favour of the use of mediation and other administrative dispute resolution (ADR) routes where the opportunity presents itself. In a judicial review context this first achieved prominence in *R (Cowl) v Plymouth City Council*.[1] Lord Woolf's judgment in that case made it clear that it was little less than an obligation on the parties to proceedings to consider whether ADR could provide a more effective and cost-effective resolution of any dispute. Moreover it is open to the court to promote ADR wherever possible, and if necessary require the parties to explain why ADR should not be tried. So far, so sensible, but then came *Shirayama Shokusan v Danovo*.[2] Blackburne J concluded that the courts' powers under CPR 1.4(2)(e) to 'encourage' parties to use ADR as an alternative to litigation in fact enabled it to order parties to submit a dispute to ADR even if one of the parties was unwilling to do so.[3] This form of sub-contracting by the court has potentially remarkable consequences. While it is quite obvious why judges – who see nothing but litigation – are highly sympathetic to the notion that there 'must be a better way', it should not be overlooked that, for all its perceived faults, litigation is an attempt to obtain the right answer to a dispute, while for all its perceived merits, ADR is merely an attempt to reach a position that all parties will live with. In some instances the latter may well be as good as the former. But for public authorities there will be many instances in which a court decision in one case will itself prevent other claims arising or surviving the permission stage. Similarly for claimants the importance of a court judgment should not be underestimated, particularly if the claimant relies on a public authority for the day-to-day provision of an essential service. In *Halsey v Milton Keynes General NHS Trust*[4] the Court of Appeal noted that the hallmark of ADR procedures, and perhaps the key to their effectiveness in individual cases, is that they are processes voluntarily entered into by the parties in dispute. The Court observed (obiter) that CPR 1.4(2)(e) does not expressly permit the court to direct that such ADR procedures be used, but may merely encourage and facilitate. The court held that it was likely that compulsion of ADR would be regarded as an unacceptable constraint on the right of access to the court and therefore a violation of Article 6 of the European Convention on Human Rights. Even if the court did have jurisdiction to order unwilling parties to refer their disputes to mediation, the court found it difficult to conceive of circumstances in which it would be appropriate to exercise it. There may, however, be costs consequences if the unsuccessful party can show that the successful party acted unreasonably in refusing to agree to ADR.[5]

[1]   [2002] 1 WLR 803.
[2]   [2004] 1 WLR 2985.
[3]   Compare on this point *Hurst v Leeming* [2003] 1 Lloyd's Rep 379, where Lightman J concluded that an order could only be made with the consent of the parties.
[4]   [2004] EWCA Civ 576; [2004] 1 WLR 3002, CA; see also *Mann v Mann* [2014] EWHC 537 (Fam).
[5]   See **20.97** below and in particular, *R (Crawford) v University of Newcastle upon Tyne* [2014] EWHC 1197 (Admin) where a university student had issued judicial review proceedings against his university while simultaneously pursuing a complaint to the Office of the Independent Adjudicator for Higher Education. The university had not been unreasonable in failing to accept the student's invitation to attempt mediation. The adjudication process was effectively a form of ADR, so the court would not characterise a failure to engage in a different and further form of mediation as unreasonable.

20.12 If it is contended that a particular claim has been rendered academic, whether or not a hearing should take place may well be a more contentious issue. If a claim that has been overtaken by events raises no issue that can be termed an issue of principle, it is unlikely that it will be in the interests of either party to pursue it to a full hearing.[1] More difficult is the situation where one party contends not only that a point of principle is in issue, but also that despite the absence of a real dispute between the parties, that point of principle should still be resolved.

[1] In many instances the choice to be made will be between withdrawal of the claim, or a stay of the action (if that could serve any purpose): see for one consideration of the merits of each option *R v Commissioner for Local Administration, ex p Abernethy* [2000] COD 56. The only exception to this will be if it is not possible for the parties to agree what the position should be in relation to costs. On these sorts of costs issues, see *Brawley v Marczynski* [2003] 1 WLR 813.

20.13 It is clear that the court does have jurisdiction to entertain academic issues. In *R v Secretary of State for the Home Department, ex p Salem*,[1] Lord Slynn indicated that even in public law cases, and if the decision would no longer affect the rights and obligations of the parties themselves, it was open to the court to decide a point, if there was good reason to do so in the public interest. By way of example of such good reason, Lord Slynn suggested that a point could still be resolved if the point in issue did not require detailed factual consideration and its determination could affect a large number of pending or anticipated cases.[2] It is important to consider this reasoning in its context. *Salem* was a situation in which the issue was whether or not the House of Lords should proceed to resolve a point of law where events had overtaken the practical dispute between the parties. While the example provided by Lord Slynn was wholly appropriate in relation to the question whether an appeal should go ahead, it is less relevant in relation to first instance proceedings. In such proceedings, even if there is a point of law of some importance, there will often be much to recommend the view that any important legal issue is likely to be best considered in the context of a real dispute, rather than on assumed facts.[3] This may well be preferable even if the point is not self-evidently fact-sensitive. From the point of view of a first instance court, even if there may be other cases waiting, this is a less pressing reason for going ahead with the case in hand since the point can be considered fully in the next contested claim. In short, the notion of 'good reason in the public interest' must be carefully considered: deciding the point 'right now' is not necessarily in the public interest if there are cogent reasons to conclude that awaiting a case where the point is live will improve the quality of the decision-making process. This may well be a difficult point to pin down. For this reason discretion ought often to triumph over valour. One instance that fell the other side of the line was that considered in *Islington LBC v Camp*.[4] The issue before the court on this occasion was academic in the sense that the court was being asked to resolve a matter because the local authority felt unable to do so. In effect, a form of advisory opinion was being sought.[5] On its facts the case raised highly delicate issues for the local authority, and the strong likelihood was that whatever decision it took would prompt a 'live' challenge. These practical considerations swung the balance in this case. Nevertheless, the court was cautious to entertain only those points that were strictly necessary on the information before it.

An advisory opinion of a different class was considered in *R (Rusbridger) v Attorney General*,[6] a case in which a declaration was sought on a point of criminal law. In truth, these proceedings were little more than vanity litigation.[7] Lords Hutton, Rodger and Walker were emphatic that it was not the function of the courts to 'keep the statute book up to date'. As such it was not appropriate to resolve hypothetical issues which did not impact on the parties before them. Perhaps out of kindness, and giving the claim more dignity than it deserved, Lord Steyn adopted and applied three criteria:

(1) was there an absence of any genuine dispute about the subject matter;
(2) was the case fact-sensitive; and
(3) was there a cogent public or individual interest which could be advanced by the grant of the declaration sought?

The Court of Appeal cautioned against litigating academic issues where there was no real dispute between the parties in *Re X (Deprivation of Liberty)*.[8] The President of the Court of Protection had listed together a number of similar applications in order to determine various issues of principle or practice. The aim was to devise a 'streamlined' process for dealing with those sorts of applications because the number was expected to increase dramatically in light of a Supreme Court decision.[9] The parties sought to appeal to the Court of Appeal. The parties had agreed that there was a 'decision' to appeal; however the Court of Appeal disagreed and found that it did not have jurisdiction. The points concerned were hypothetical and were not live issues in the cases concerned. In the context of Mental Capacity Act 2005, s 53(1), the word 'decision' could not mean any decision made by the Court of Protection; it had to mean a decision taken about or in some way involving the individual concerned. The parties had also argued that modern courts had shown a greater willingness to entertain cases that raised academic or hypothetical points of law of public interest, or alternatively sought to apply the provisions of CPR 19 regarding group litigation. However, these arguments were also rejected. In each of the cases where the Court of Appeal had entertained cases raising academic or hypothetical issues, the matter had begun as a real dispute between parties to conventional litigation, but the issue had been resolved before it reached the appeal court. The Court of Appeal found that the President had exceeded his jurisdiction in acting as he did and could instead have used a practice direction.

---

1   [1999] 1 AC 450.
2   In the circumstances before them, the House of Lords dismissed the appeal without deciding the substantive issue. For instances where an appellate court has gone on (in a private law context) to determine an 'academic' point, see *Fawdry v Murfitt* [2003] QB 104 (judgment on a point of jurisdictional importance after full argument); *Williams v Devon Council* [2003] CP Rep 47 (again, point of general importance as to the application of CPR Pt 36 where social security benefits were recoverable, and again full argument heard including the Secretary of State, who had intervened); *A v B Plc* [2002] 2 All ER 545 (point determined, both parties agreed and the matter was relevant to the issue of costs).
3   This was the view ultimately taken by Silber J in *R (DB) v Dr. SS and others* [2005] EWHC 86 (Admin) at paragraphs 39–71. In reaching this conclusion he also stated that as a matter of principle the court's approach should be the same even if the claimant was seeking a declaration of incompatibility – ie such a claim was not of itself a reason for reaching a substantive conclusion on an issue that was academic. Yet in public law cases a declaration may still serve an important public interest function even though the dispute between the parties has disappeared: see *R v Oxfordshire County Council, ex p Pittick* [1996] ELR 153, per Laws J at 157; and *Levy v Environment Agency* [2002] EWHC 1663 (Admin) per Silber J at paragraph 127.
4   [2004] BLGR 58.
5   See per Richards J at 63D–68A.
6   [2004] 1 AC 356.

[7] Lord Scott at paragraph 44 expressed sympathy with the view of the Administrative Court that the claimant's application was not one to be taken seriously: Lord Steyn, at paragraph 28, described the litigation as 'unnecessary'.

[8] [2015] EWCA Civ 599.

[9] *Cheshire West and Chester Council v P* [2014] UKSC 19.

20.14 In many instances, the third criterion may turn out to provide the most compelling reason for entertaining an apparently academic claim.[1] However, in all cases restraint is appropriate: if proper regard is to be had to the views of Lords Hutton, Rodger and Walker, the public interest element should derive from something more than lawyer's curiosity as to what the law ought to be. There should be some form of practical imperative.

In *R (Zoolife International Limited) v Secretary of State for Environment, Food and Rural Affairs*[2] the court conducted a detailed review of the authorities and concluded that the factors identified in *Salem* applied to first instance decisions. The court declined to decide what had become an academic issue on the grounds that the exceptional circumstances identified in *Salem* had not been met – ie that other similar cases existed or were anticipated and that the decision was not fact-sensitive. The court identified a number of factors which indicated that the claim should not be heard as it was academic: (1) that any decision on the facts of that case would be fact-sensitive; (2) that since the duties of the claimants were not the same in the instant case and in all other potential cases, the result in the instant case would not necessarily be the same in any other cases; (3) there was no certainty or even probability that other claims would be brought; (4) even if there were subsequent claims, other parties might wish to adduce evidence so that the court on a subsequent occasion would have to consider different material; (5) that because any decision in the instant case would depend on assumed facts it would be unlikely to be determinative or of any value in subsequent cases; (6) that because the factual situation in a subsequent case might be different a decision in the instant case would not constitute a precedent for future applications; (7) that not all interested parties had been served with details of the claim; and (8) finally, that there was no good reason in the public interest for the claim to be determined at the present time by the court. If the courts were to entertain academic disputes in judicial review cases in these circumstances, the consequence would be a regrettable waste of valuable court time and the incurring by one or more parties of unnecessary costs. There was accordingly no reason in the public interest for hearing the claim.[3]

The policy reasons for the rule were examined again in *R (Colin Raw) v Lambeth London Borough Council*.[4] The court recognised that in principle, in a hypothetical case in which a claimant was able to identify an unlawful policy implemented by a public body which could never be challenged by a person adversely affected by it, either because the illegality was so transient that it would always cease before it could be brought to court or where the public body deliberately disapplied it so as to render all claims academic, there might be a good reason in the public interest for the court to entertain an academic claim for a declaration that the policy was unlawful.[5]

Hamnett v Essex CC[6] re-iterated the principle that, in a case involving a public authority and raising a question of public law, the court has a discretion to hear an appeal even if it is academic as between the parties. However, the discretion should not be exercised without good reason in the public interest. Save in exceptional circumstances, there had to be a point of general importance; the respondent had to have agreed to the appeal being heard, or had to have at least been completely indemnified on costs; and there had to be the prospect of the competing arguments being properly ventilated.[7] The fact that the outcome of the appeal might affect the costs position as between the parties could be a relevant factor, but the court must be cautious about exercising its discretion on that basis.

In certain cases, the parties may reach agreement as to a particular point of statutory construction, and the court has to consider whether to give a judgment where one party is prepared to consent to dismissing or allowing an appeal so that the issue has become academic. In *QI (Pakistan) v Secretary of State for the Home Department*,[8] the Court of Appeal held that where a case involves a point of statutory construction of very general application, it was appropriate for the court to give a reasoned judgment. It would be wrong to allow the case to be decided by way of a consent order and supporting reasons. It is for the judiciary to construe the effects of statutes, and judicial decisions should be declared in judgments and not inferred without argument from statements of reasons supporting a consent order agreed by the Secretary of State.

1   One example of a plainly exceptional set of circumstances that certainly met Lord Steyn's first and third criteria is that considered in *Airedale NHS Trust v Bland* [1993] AC 789.
2   [2007] EWHC 2995 (Admin); [2008] ACD 44.
3   Despite this, Silber J still went on to consider the merits of the application, as he considered that it was necessary for him to resolve the outstanding issues in case he was wrong on the academic point. This seems to undermine the policy reasons for not entertaining academic claims, particularly the policy objective of discouraging the proliferation of such claims. As Stadlen J recognised in *R (Raw) v Lambeth London Borough Council* [2010] EWHC 507 (Admin) at [68]–[71], there is a risk of defeating that objective, if, having declined to adjudicate upon a claim on the ground that it is academic, the court proceeds to set out what its views would have been if it had adjudicated upon it. While such views would be strictly obiter and would have no binding effect, the fact that the court might be prepared to express them might nonetheless encourage future claims; see for recent examples of this approach, *E v Secretary of State for the Home Department* [2014] EWHC 1030 (Admin); and *R (LM) v Secretary of State for the Home Department* [2014] EWHC 2015 (Admin).
4   [2010] EWHC 507 (Admin). See also *R (McKenzie) v Waltham Forest London Borough Council.* [2009] EWHC 1097 (Admin).
5   [2010] EWHC 507 (Admin). There was no evidence to suggest that this was the case in *Raw* itself.
6   [2017] EWCA Civ 6.
7   See also *Hutcheson (formerly WER) v Popdog Ltd (formerly REW)* [2011] EWCA Civ 1580).
8   [2011] EWCA Civ 614.

ASPECTS OF A HEARING: GENERAL

20.15 The basic structure of a judicial review hearing is well known. In the vast majority of instances the hearing is based on consideration of documentary evidence and witness statements,[1] and legal submissions (either oral or written – usually a combination of both). The parties appear either in person or through legal representation. The claimant opens the case; the defendant responds; and the claimant is entitled to reply. A civil standard of proof is applied, and the burden of proof rests on the claimant.[2] The court delivers judgment. Yet some points are worth considering.

[1]   As explained in Chapter 19, the court may permit cross-examination of witnesses on their statements when a factual dispute arises which the court must resolve in order to determine the claim. Such applications are usually made in advance of the hearing (at the latest shortly after service of the defendant's evidence). For a time after the introduction of the CPR there was doubt as to whether the court retained the power to order cross-examination. This point was considered by Munby J in *R (PG) v London Borough of Ealing* [2002] EWHC 250 (Admin), [2002] ACD 48: he considered that the power remained. The point was confirmed by a subsequent amendment to CPR 54.16.

[2]   See *R v Secretary of State for the Home Department, ex p Khawaja* [1984] AC 74 per Lord Fraser at 97G. However, where a claimant demonstrates that there has been an interference with his or her Convention rights, or constitutional rights, it is for the defendant to show that the relevant interference was justified.

20.16 First, who is entitled to appear at a hearing? Self-evidently, the claimant and the defendant. But where the defendant is an inferior court, the defendant is not usually expected to appear at the judicial review hearing.[1] An exception to this presumption is where on the judicial review claim the bona fides of the court is challenged, or there is some other exceptional reason. Yet this does not mean that the inferior court should play no part in the litigation at all. It is expected that once a claim has been made, the inferior court will make clear what its position on the claim is, usually in writing.[2] In some instances a fuller written explanation of what happened may also be of assistance to the court at the judicial review hearing.[3]

[1]   See *R v Newcastle-under-Lyme Justices, ex p Massey* [1994] 1 WLR 1684.

[2]   See *R v Gloucester Crown Court, ex p Chester* [1998] COD 365. As to the approach the court will not take where there is a challenge to the decision of an inferior court see *R v Reigate Justices, ex p Curl* [1991] COD 66. There the Divisional Court stated that it could envisage 'virtually no circumstances' in which it would be appropriate to require Justices to attend for cross-examination as to what had occurred in the course of a hearing before them.

[3]   For example, *R v Feltham Justices, ex p Haid* [1998] COD 440. In relation to any issue as whether costs ought to be awarded against the inferior court, see **20.90** below.

20.17 Interested parties are also permitted, but not required to attend. Under CPR 54.1(2)(f) an 'interested party' is any person other than the claimant or defendant who is directly affected by the claim. Interested parties ought to be served with the claim and defence,[1] and on this basis should be in a position at an early stage to determine what sort of role they intend to play in a claim. However, this means of identifying interested parties is an imprecise one since it depends wholly on the views and possibly also the diligence of the claimant. In general terms, a person is directly affected if he is affected simply (ie directly) by reason of the grant of a remedy.[2] This standard has been rigorously applied. In *R v Rent Officer Service, ex p Muldoon*[3] the court concluded that the Secretary of State for Social Security would not be directly affected by an order requiring a local authority to pay housing benefit to specific applicants. Even though if the benefit was payable by the local authority the Secretary of State would be required to increase the housing benefit subsidy to the local authority, this was merely a collateral matter, not a direct effect of any relief granted by the court. A similar approach was taken in *R v Monopolies and Mergers Commission, ex p Milk Marque*,[4] albeit that in that case, having failed to convince the court that it was an interested party, the Dairy Federation (which had applied to be heard as an interested party) was heard as an intervener under the power now contained in CPR 54.17.

In *R (McVey and Others) v Secretary of State for Health*[5] Silber J gave useful guidance on the limits of the role of an Interested Party. The interested parties had sought different relief from that being claimed by the claimants at the main hearing. The court concluded that the role of an Interested Party is limited to making submissions in relation to the main claim, and only to the extent that he or she is 'directly affected' by it. If the main claim is altered so that the Interested Party is not 'directly affected' by it, the court ceases to have jurisdiction to hear the Interested Party's claim. There is nothing in the CPR which enables an Interested Party to make an independent discrete claim against a defendant. Any independent and discrete claim by any party in a judicial review application requires permission to proceed – and without it, the court has no power to deal with the claim.

[1] See CPR 54.7 and 54.8.
[2] This would include, for example, the owner or developer of the land that benefits from planning permission if a decision by a planning authority to grant the planning permission is challenged. It would also include a situation where a decision of an inferior court or tribunal is challenged. The court or tribunal will be the defendant, while the other parties to the proceedings before that court or tribunal will be Interested Parties. In all *Cart* judicial reviews, the Upper Tribunal is the defendant and the other party to the appeal is an Interested Party.
[3] [1996] 1 WLR 1103.
[4] [2000] COD 329.
[5] [2010] EWHC 1225 (Admin).

20.18 Under CPR 54.17, the court has a discretion to permit 'any person' either to file evidence or to make representations at the hearing.[1] When exercising this discretion it is clearly open to the court to grant permission to intervene on terms. Any such intervener is inevitably subject to the full range of case management powers available to the court under the CPR. For example, in relation to the intervener's costs (that he should bear his own in any event),[2] or in relation to whether any representations at the hearing should be written or oral, or if oral that they should be time-limited. When considering whether to grant an application for permission to intervene, the court will consider the practical value of the applicant's involvement.[3] A final point to note on the subject of parties is the effect of s 5 of the Human Rights Act 1998. Under this provision, the relevant Minister of the Crown (or devolution equivalent) is entitled to be joined as a party to proceedings in which a court is considering granting a declaration of incompatibility under s 4 of the Act.

[1] The existence of this power does of course go a long way to rendering pointless the sort of debate that took place in the ex p Milk Marque case. Note, where the intervener is a statutory body, issues may arise as to the vires of the body to intervene in proceedings at all. See, for example, *R (Northern Ireland Human Rights Commission) v Greater Belfast Coroner* [2002] ACD 95. As to late interventions by interested parties and others, see **20.8**.
[2] Section 87 of the Criminal Justice and Courts Act 2015 provides that, in the absence of exceptional circumstances, parties who have been granted permission to intervene in judicial review proceedings will have to pay their own costs and, on an application by another party, any costs they have caused to that party as a result of their intervention.
[3] *R (British American Tobacco UK Ltd) v Secretary of State for Health* [2014] EWHC 3535 (Admin).

20.19 Parties at a hearing may also be assisted by *McKenzie* friends[1] – ie lay assistance. The true role of a *McKenzie* friend is set out in *R v Bow County Court, ex p Pelling (No 1)*:[2] he has no right to act as such; the only right is that of the litigant to have reasonable assistance; he is not entitled to address the court. Generally, a litigant in person who wishes to have a *McKenzie* friend will be permitted to do so. In fact, there is a strong presumption that such assistance will be permitted.[3] However, this is within the discretion of the court and will turn on whether such assistance is consistent with the requirements of fairness and the interests of justice. It is well within this discretion for the court to refuse to permit such assistance on the grounds that the proposed 'friend' is unsuitable.[4]

[1] See *McKenzie v McKenzie* [1971] P 33; Practice Note (Sen Cts: McKenzie Friends: Civil and Family Courts) [2010] 1 WLR 1881.
[2] [1999] 1 WLR 1807, in the judgment of Otton LJ.
[3] See *Re O (children)* [2005] EWCA 759.
[4] See, eg *Paragon Finance v Noueiri* [2001] 1 WLR 2357, where the court concluded that the discretion should only exceptionally be exercised in favour of a *McKenzie* friend who made a practice of seeking to represent or assist litigants in person.

ASPECTS OF A HEARING: OPEN JUSTICE

20.20 The starting point and default position is that hearings should take place in public. This is the position both at common law and under art 6 of the European Convention on Human Rights (ECHR). The idea of a court hearing evidence or argument in private is contrary to the principle of open justice, which is fundamental to the dispensation of justice in a modern, democratic society.[1] However, neither establishes an absolute standard.[2] In any situation where a departure from this position is proposed, competing interests collide: the specific personal or public interests that have prompted the proposal; the general public interest that court proceedings should be in public and be capable of being fully reported; in some cases the interests of one or more parties to the proceedings not to be excluded from any part of them; and third party interests, most often those of the press and other media, to hear, see and report what goes on. Two aspects of open justice can be identified:

(1) in what circumstances will a court protect the anonymity of a party to proceedings; and

(2) in what circumstances and to what extent will a court depart from the open justice principle and permit hearings or parts of them to take place in private or in some instances in the absence of one or more of the parties?

[1] See *Bank Mellat v Her Majesty's Treasury (No 1)* [2013] UKSC 38, at paragraph 2.
[2] See *R v Bow County Court, ex p Pelling (No 2)* [2001] ACD 1.

20.21 It has, however, long been accepted that, in rare cases, a court has inherent power to receive evidence and argument in a hearing from which the public and the press are excluded, and that it can even give a judgment which is only available to the parties. Such a course may only be taken: (i) if it is strictly necessary to have a private hearing in order to achieve justice between the parties; and (ii) if the degree of privacy is kept to an absolute minimum.[1]

Other aspects of this issue are premised on the same basic question: what interests (and in what circumstances) are such so as to justify a court modifying its procedures and permit it to move away from the default position – namely that hearings should take place in open court, and be capable of being reported in full?[2] As a general proposition, if the possibility of modification is canvassed, the court should seek first to identify whether a sufficiently important interest (either personal or public) does exist and, second, then seek to identify the measures that are the minimum necessary in order to protect that interest while at the same time affording proper weight to the general public interest that justice should be done in public.

[1]   See *Bank Mellat v Her Majesty's Treasury (No 1)* [2013] UKSC 38 at paragraph 2; *Independent News & Media Ltd v A (by his litigation friend the Official Solicitor)* [2010] 1 WLR 2262; and *JIH v News Group Newspapers Ltd* [2011] 1 WLR 1645.
[2]   This default position is clearly demonstrated by the provisions of CPR 39.2. See also *Attorney General v Leveller Magazine* [1979] AC 440 per Lord Diplock at 449–450. In *Re S (a child)* [2005] 1 AC 593, the House of Lords concluded that in most cases the discretion would now emerge not from the inherent jurisdiction of the court, but rather from the application of ECHR rights (per Lord Steyn at paragraph 23). From the standpoint of the ECHR, the relevant considerations are those arising under art 6 (the hearing), art 8 (the right to respect for private and family life) and art 10 (the right to receive/impart information). The importance that is to be attached to the art 10 rights should not be underestimated, see, for example, *Reynolds v Times Newspapers Limited* [2001] 2 AC 127 per Lord Nicholls at 200.

20.22 It is unwise to seek to identify any closed list of interests that are capable of justifying alterations to this default position. Examples include litigation where children are involved, where threatened breaches of privacy are being alleged, and where commercially valuable secret information is in issue. Some have been specifically identified in legislation;[1] others arise from legislative provisions of general application (for example, the interests protected by ECHR, arts 2, 3 and/or 8[2]) which are brought into play by the specific circumstances of the case. General state interests, for example, the protection of national security,[3] or the prevention of crime[4] and other legitimate interests that qualify rights arising under the ECHR, are also capable of justifying alterations to court procedures.

[1]   For example, s 39 of the Children and Young Persons Act 1933: the power to prohibit the publication of information arising in court proceedings so as not to reveal the identity of any child or young person concerned in the proceedings.
[2]   On such issues, see, for example, *Re S (a child)* [2005] 1 AC 593 (Article 8); *Re C* [2016] EWCOP 21 (Articles 8 and 10); In *Re Officer L* [2007] 1 WLR 2135 (Article 2) and *Secretary of State for the Home Department v AP* [2010] UKSC 24; [2011] 2 AC 1 (Article 3).
[3]   See, eg *R v Home Secretary ex p Ruddock* [1987] 1 WLR 1482 per Taylor J at 1491–2; and *R v Shayler* [2003] 1 AC 247 per Lord Bingham at paragraph 34.
[4]   See, eg the modifications adopted by the court in *R (Lord) v Secretary of State for the Home Department* [2003] EWHC 2073 (Admin) per Munby J at paragraphs 25–27.

20.23 Yet this cacophony of interests must be resolved. Some form of accord must be achieved, and this is likely to be highly case-sensitive. In principle there ought to be little difference in the nature of the balancing exercise regardless of whether it occurs in the context of a specific legislative provision, or in the application of generally applicable legal principles. For example, *R v Leicester Crown Court, ex p S*,[1] a case under s 39 of the Children and Young Persons Act 1933, clearly indicated that the correct approach for determining whether or not reporting of court proceedings should be restricted required a balance to be struck between the interests of the child, the public interest that criminal proceedings should take place in public, and the additional public interest that those living in the community should be aware of present threats or dangers. Although the precise competing interests, and the weight to be attached to them may vary from case to case, it is clear that the same type of exercise is required in the context of competing ECHR rights. Later decisions, both where the provisions of s 39 have been seen through the lens of the ECHR (or other international conventions) and where s 39 has had no role to play at all, have adopted the same basic approach.[2] No single interest or consideration will of necessity trump all others in all situations; but as a matter of principle, if the interests under ECHR, arts 6 and 10 are to give way, some form of compelling reason is required, eg the protection of other interests under the ECHR (Article 2, Article 3 and Article 8). How this threshold is characterised will depend on the importance of the interest relied on to defeat the application of the default provision, and the particular circumstances of any given case.[3]

[1]   [1993] 1 WLR 111.
[2]   See, eg *McKerry v Teesdale and Wear Valley Justices* [2000] COD 199; *R v Central Criminal Court, ex p W, B, and C* [2001] 1 Cr App R 2; and *Re S (a child)* [2005] 1 AC 593. In the latter case, s 39 did not strictly apply since the proceedings concerned the child's mother and brother.
[3]   See, eg *In Re Officer L* [2007] 1 WLR 2135 where in the context of ECHR, art 2 the House of Lords held that an anonymity order may be required if it was necessary to avoid a breach of Article 2. The positive obligation to take steps to prevent the loss of life at the hands of third parties arises only where the risk was 'real and immediate'. The threshold is high, the standard is constant and it is not variable with the type of act in contemplation (see also *Van Colle v Chief Constable of Hertfordshire Police* [2009] 1 AC 225, confirming that there is no lower threshold for art 2 cases when an individual is called by the state as a witness in court proceedings). If the art 2 test is not met, the court or tribunal will need to consider the 'common law duty of fairness' to a witness. This may require anonymity for a witness based on an increased risk to life as a result of giving evidence, and the subjective fears which an individual may express. A balancing exercise will need to be carried out between protecting the applicants and easing their fears, and the need for public confidence in the judicial system. In relation to art 3, see *Secretary of State for the Home Department v AP* [2010] UKSC 24. This was a control order case, where after giving judgment on the substantive claim, the Supreme Court considered whether to continue an anonymity order. The test applied by the Supreme Court was whether the public interest in publishing a full report of the proceedings and a judgment which identifies AP, has to give way to the need to protect AP from the risk of racist or other extremist abuse or the risk of physical violence so as to breach Article 3. In control order cases, the Supreme Court accepted that an interim anonymity order would be appropriate at the initial stages, but such an order should not be continued automatically and the need for it in the particular circumstances of the case should be reviewed at the earliest suitable opportunity. In relation to art 8, see *Z v Finland* (1998) 25 EHRR 371 where the art 8 interest was particularly strong. There the Strasbourg Court concluded that the protection that had been afforded to the art 8 considerations (a ten-year prohibition on publication of medical records used in court) was insufficient; see also *Michael Stone v South East Coast Strategic Health Authority and others* [2006] EWHC 1668 (Admin), where the claim to a right of privacy in respect of medical information was outweighed by a number of other considerations, including the public interest in knowing the actual care and treatment supplied to the claimant, and the failures identified and steps that might be recommended to address inadequacies to prevent repetition. The Supreme Court recently set out the correct approach to the balancing exercise between art 8 and art 10 interests in the case of *In re Guardian News and Media Ltd* [2010] 2 WLR 325, where an application was successfully made by various media to set aside anonymity orders in proceedings relating to orders freezing the assets of suspected terrorists. The Supreme Court applied Lord Hoffmann's guidance in *Campbell v MGN Ltd* [2004] 2 AC 457, and held that the court must ask itself, 'whether there is sufficient general, public interest in publishing a report of the proceedings which identifies [the individual] to justify any resulting curtailment of his right and his family's right to respect for their private and family life.' See also *R (Fagan) v Secretary of State for Justice and Times Newspapers* [2013] EWCA Civ 1275, considering Article 8 and the disclosure of an offender's identity.

20.24 If a balance is struck in favour of some form of restriction, the court must ensure that the measures adopted for this purpose are necessary and proportionate. To this end, the court may either adopt well-known and often used devices (such as reporting restrictions, or true anonymity orders), or solutions that are bespoke for the occasion.[1]

[1] See Practice Guidance (Interim Non-disclosure Orders) [2012] 1 WLR 1003 issued by the Master of the Rolls setting out recommended practice regarding any application for interim injunctive relief in civil proceedings to restrain the publication of information.

20.25 In recent years, there has been an increased use of 'closed material procedures'. A closed material procedure involves the production of material which is so confidential and sensitive that disclosure would be contrary to the public interest. A closed material procedure requires the court not only to sit in private, but to sit in a closed hearing (ie a hearing at which the court considers the material and hears submissions about it without one of the parties to the case/appeal ever having seen the material or being present to hear submissions). Special advocates will generally be appointed to act on a party's behalf in relation to the evidence or material which is disclosed neither to the party nor his instructed lawyers. The court has to contemplate giving a partly closed judgment (a judgment part of which will not be seen by one of the parties).

The precise format of closed material procedures will vary depending on the forum. Parliament made express provision for closed material procedures to be adopted by courts and tribunals in several areas, including the Special Immigration Appeals Commission Act 1997,[1] the Counter-Terrorism Act 2008[2], the Terrorism Prevention and Investigation Measures Act 2011.[3] It is crucial that a proper summary, or gist, of the closed material is provided to the party excluded from the closed material procedure.[4]

[1] See the Special Immigration Appeals Commission Act 1997, s 5 and the Special Immigration Appeals Commission (Procedure) Rules 2003, SI 2003/1034.
[2] See Parts 5 and 6 of the Counter-Terrorism Act 2008 which enables steps to be taken to prevent terrorist financing and the proliferation of nuclear weapons and provides for 'financial restrictions proceedings' which includes a closed material procedure. The procedure is governed by Part 79 of the Civil Procedure Rules.
[3] See Part 80 of the Civil Procedure Rules which govern proceedings under the Terrorism Prevention and Investigation Measures Act 2011.
[4] See *Secretary of State for the Home Department v AF (No 3)* [2010] 2 AC 269, para 59 and *Bank Mellat v HM Treasury* [2015] EWCA Civ 1052.

20.26 Prior to the decision in *Al-Rawi v The Security Services and Others*[1] it was thought that the inherent jurisdiction of the Administrative Court permitted similar schemes to be adopted ad hoc where national security issues arose. However, in *Al-Rawi*, the Supreme Court held that as closed material procedures are contrary to the common law principles of fairness applicable to civil trials, a court can only adopt a closed material procedure where this is provided for by statute.

It was previously suggested that different considerations might apply where the proceedings did not only concern the interests of the parties, but also had a significant effect on a vulnerable third party or the wider public interest. For example, where a case directly impinges on the interests of a child, it may be justifiable for the court to see a document which is not seen by the parties to the proceedings, or where a tribunal has a 'triangulation' of interests.[2] It is likely that these suggestions would need to be revisited in light of the Supreme Court's decision in *Al-Rawi*.

In *Bank Mellatt v HM Treasury (No 1)*,[3] the Supreme Court emphasised the importance of open justice. The issue was whether the Supreme Court had the power to hold closed hearings to consider a closed judgment given in financial restriction proceedings. A majority of the Supreme Court considered that the Constitutional Reform Act 2005 and the Supreme Court Rules gave it the power to conduct a closed material procedure where it was satisfied that it might be necessary to do so in order to dispose of an appeal. While judges would regard the prospect of a closed material procedure with distaste and concern, on any appeal where the judgment was wholly or partially closed, there would be a very serious risk of not doing justice if the court could not consider the closed material, and it could only do so if it adopted a closed material procedure. The court gave useful guidance in respect of applications for closed material hearings on appeal:

(1) First, where a judge gives an open judgment and a closed judgment, it is highly desirable that in the open judgment, the judge (i) identifies every conclusion in that judgment which has been reached in whole or in part in light of points made or evidence referred to in the closed judgment; and (ii) that the judge says that this is what he or she has done.

(2) Second, a judge who has relied on closed material in a closed judgment, should say in the open judgment as much as can properly be said about the material.

(3) Third, on an appeal against an open and closed judgment, an appellate court should only be asked to conduct a closed hearing if it is strictly necessary for fairly determining the appeal.

(4) Fourth, if the appellate court decides that it should look at closed material, careful consideration should be given by the advocates and by the court to the question whether it would nonetheless be possible to avoid a closed substantive hearing. It is quite feasible for a court to consider, and be addressed on, confidential material in open court.

(5) Fifth, if the court decides that a closed material procedure appears to be necessary, the parties should try and agree a way of avoiding, or minimising the extent of, a closed hearing. If a closed hearing is needed, the legal representatives should do their best to agree a gist of any relevant closed document, including any closed judgment below.

(6) Sixth, if there is a closed hearing, the lawyers representing the party who is relying on the closed material should ensure that, well in advance of the hearing of the appeal, (i) the excluded party is given as much information as possible about any closed documents (including any closed judgment) relied on; and (ii) the special advocates are given as full information as possible as to the nature of the passages relied on in such closed documents and the arguments which will be advanced in relation thereto.

(7) Finally, appellate courts should be robust about acceding to applications to go into closed session or even to look at closed material. There must be very few appeals where any sort of closed material procedure

is likely to be necessary. The onus is on the requesting party to show why it is necessary. In the instant case, the Treasury's approach fell far short of what was needed to show that it was necessary for the closed material procedure to be resorted to.[4]

¹   [2012] 1 AC 531.

²   See *Official Solicitor to the Supreme Court v K* [1965] AC 201 at paragraphs 240–241 and *R (Roberts) v Parole Board* [2005] 2 AC 738, where the Parole Board had obligations to the prisoner, to protect society as a whole, and to protect third parties. Even without statutory rules which permitted a closed material procedure, a special advocate procedure was permissible, to enable the board to perform its statutory duty to protect the public.

³   [2013] UKSC 38.

⁴   This ruling does not cast doubt on the availability of a closed hearing to determine whether public interest immunity ("PII") can be claimed in respect of documents. The Court of Appeal in *Al-Rawi* considered that the issue at a PII hearing is whether the material in question is immune from inspection on the ground that the public interest would be harmed by its release into the public sphere. The PII hearing is not the trial of the action: it is merely concerned with an interlocutory matter ahead of the trial, and is bound to result in the material either being available for use in the litigation by both parties, or by neither party. A PII hearing simply could not occur other than on a closed basis. See also *R (Mohammed) v Secretary of State for Defence* [2012] EWHC 3454 (Admin), [2014] 1 WLR 1071, which confirms that principles applicable to public interest immunity apply in judicial review proceedings as in ordinary litigation. See Chapter 14.

20.27 The highly controversial Justice and Security Act 2013 was enacted partly in response to *Al-Rawi*. Part 2 of this Act provides for closed material procedures in relevant civil proceedings. Section 6(11) defines 'relevant civil proceedings' as meaning 'any proceedings (other than proceedings in a criminal cause or matter) before (a) the High Court, (b) the Court of Appeal; (c) the Court of Session or (d) the Supreme Court'.

Section 6(1) states that such a court, when seized of relevant civil proceedings, may declare that a closed material application may be made to the court. The application is for permission not to disclose material otherwise than to the court or a special advocate: s 8(1)(a). The court may make a declaration if two conditions are met.

(1)   The first condition is that (a) a party to the proceedings would be required to disclose sensitive material, being material the disclosure of which would be damaging to the interests of national security, in the course of proceedings to another person; or (b) a party to the proceedings would be required to make such a disclosure were it not for (i) the possibility of a claim for public interest immunity in relation to the material; (ii) the fact that there would be no requirement to disclose if the party chose not to rely on the material; (iii) section 17 of the Regulation of Investigatory Powers Act 2000 (exclusion for intercept material); or (iv) any other enactment that would prevent the party from disclosing the material but would not do so if the proceedings were proceedings in relation to which there was a declaration under this section of the Act.

(2)   The second condition is that it is in the interests of the fair and effective administration of justice in the proceedings to make a declaration.

Section 7 of the Act provides for the review and revocation of a declaration made under s 6, and the court is required to keep such a declaration under review. It can be revoked at any time if the court considers that the declaration is no longer in the interest of the fair and effective administration of justice in the proceedings. Section 8 sets out how courts are to determine applications in section 6 proceedings. If permission is given not to disclose material, the court must consider requiring the relevant person to provide a summary of the material to every other party to the proceedings, so long as that summary does not itself contain material the disclosure of which would be damaging to the interests of national security. Section 8(3) gives the court the power to make directions that certain points may not be relied on in the relevant person's case, or that concessions must be made.

Closed material procedures are governed by Part 82 of the Civil Procedure Rules in England and Wales. Part 82 modifies the other rules in the CPR so that all rules are read and given effect in a way which is compatible with the duty on the court to ensure that information is not disclosed in a way which would be damaging to the interests of national security. Subject to this duty, the court must satisfy itself that the material available to it enables it properly to determine proceedings. The rules contain express powers to hold hearings in private, and make provision for the appointment of special advocates and sets out their functions.

Part 2 of the Act and the role of the rules in Part 82 were considered in *R (Sarkandi) v Secretary of State for Foreign and Commonwealth Affairs*.[1] The court recognised that the closed material procedure was a serious, exceptional departure from the fundamental principles of open justice and natural justice; however, it was a departure authorised by Parliament in defined circumstances for the protection of national security. It was held that appropriate safeguards were built in, eg conditions for a section 6 declaration, provisions for review and revocation of a declaration, and for applications for permission not to disclose material in proceedings in relation to which a declaration was in place. There was no reason to give the Act a narrow or restrictive construction; the statutory conditions should be given their natural meaning. In *McGartland v Attorney General*[2] it was stated that the court can be expected to carefully scrutinise the asserted justification for withholding material. Courts can consider whether material could be disclosed to the claimants and their open representatives without damage to the interests of national security. If this could be done with terms as to confidentiality and/or hearings in private without damage to the interests of national security, then the court can be expected to refuse permission for the material to be withheld to that extent, whilst still giving permission for it not to be disclosed on any wider basis. In addition, if permission is given for material to be withheld from the claimants and their open representatives, the court must go on to consider whether to direct service of a summary. Throughout the process, the court must ensure compliance with the claimants' rights under article 6. If the court considers at any time that the section 6 declaration is no longer in the interests of the fair and effective administration of justice in the proceedings, it must revoke the declaration pursuant to s 7.

[1]   [2015] EWCA Civ 687; applying *CF v Security Service* [2013] EWHC 3402 (QB); [2014] 1 WLR 1699. For another recent example of a section 6 determination, see *XH v Secretary of State for the Home Department* [2015] EWHC 2932 (Admin) which examined the pre-condition for the Secretary of State to consider a claim for public interest immunity before inviting the court to make an application under s 6 of the 2013 Act (see s 6(7)).
[2]   [2015] EWCA Civ 686.

ASPECTS OF A HEARING: JUDGMENTS

20.28 Under the practice statements of 22 April and 25 November 1998,[1] a draft of a reserved judgment is normally provided to lawyers in advance of the time it is formally handed down. Spell-checking and sense-checking draft judgments are the bane of many an advocate's life.[2] But there is the possibility that a judgment can contain more than mere grammatical or linguistic errors. In *Perotti v Collyer-Bristow (No 2)*,[3] when considering the comments of a litigant in person on a draft judgment, the Court of Appeal was reluctant to consider anything beyond suggestions as to 'typing errors, wrong references and other errors of that kind'.

[1]   [1998] 1 WLR 825, [1999] 1 WLR 1. Drafts are usually provided by 4pm two working days before the date on which the judgment is to be handed down, or at such other time as the court may direct: see CPR Practice Direction 40E.

[2]   Although this can be a matter of vital importance. One decision of an Australian court was spared notoriety when it was recognised – when the judgment was in draft – that the persistent references by the court to the 'headless whore' were in fact references to the 'head lessor': see (2003) 77 Australian Law Journal 410.

[3]   [2004] 4 All ER 72.

20.29 In *Noga v Abacha*[1] a more concerted attempt was made. In that case judgment had been given in draft, but had not been handed down. One of the parties applied to the trial judge[2] to the effect that he should reconsider part of the reasoning in his judgment on the basis that he had made an error of law. The application was ultimately refused, but the following points emerge from the decision. First, until an order is perfected (ie sealed by the court under CPR 40.2(b)), the judgment remains in the control of the court. As such, the court can permit argument to be reopened, and it is open to the court either to modify or reverse a conclusion reached by it.[3] However, this is a jurisdiction that is to be exercised 'very sparingly', and only for good reason since the court must also give due regard to the principle of finality in litigation.[4] Also, there is a need to preserve the line between a first instance judgment and an appeal. In most instances, if the first instance judge has made an error, that is why the appeal courts exist: a process by which at first instance a draft judgment became a document for renewed lengthy debate would either subvert the appeal process, or create a situation in which an appeal was inevitable regardless of the outcome of the first instance reconsideration. The exceptional cases will be rare, but might include situations where the first instance decision is overtaken by an appellate decision in another case;[5] where the error, either of fact or of law is too clear for argument. Neither the discovery of fresh evidence nor the formulation of a new point of law previously overlooked is likely to fall into this category.[6]

[1]   [2001] 3 All ER 513.

[2]   Who was Rix J: by the time the application came on for hearing, he was Rix LJ.

[3]   This rule of practice was established in the case of *Re Barrell Enterprises* [1973] 1 WLR 19 and survived the introduction of the CPR: see *Stewart v Engel* [2000] 1 WLR 2268. This case concerned a (very) late application to amend pleadings. The Court of Appeal (by a majority) confirmed that the threshold test was one of exceptional circumstances, not merely the interests of justice. See also on this point (in relation to re-opening hearings), *Taylor v Lawrence* [2002] 2 All ER 353; and *Seray-Wurie v London Borough of Hackney* [2002] 3 All ER 448. On the re-opening of appeals, see CPR 52.17.

[4]   See *Noga v Abacha* [2001] 3 All ER 513 per Rix LJ at paragraphs 42 and 43.

[5]   See *Re Harrison's Share Under a Settlement* [1955] 1 All ER 185.

20.30 The decision in *Noga* was considered by the Court of Appeal in *Robinson v Fernsby*.[1] The Court of Appeal characterised *Noga* as a situation where a reserved judgment had been handed down, and contrasted that position with the one before it where the judgment had been handed down in draft pursuant to the provisions of the relevant Practice Statements.[2] Based on the account of the facts in *Noga*, it is far from clear that there was any such distinction between the two situations at all;[3] nevertheless, the Court of Appeal regarded *Noga* as a situation where a judgment had been handed down, but the order not yet perfected. In true 'draft judgment' situations, the Court of Appeal was not convinced that 'exceptional circumstances' was the correct threshold.[4] The court preferred the phrase 'strong reasons' for re-opening the judgment. The court concluded that in such cases if, after a draft judgment had been handed down, the judge reached the conclusion that it contained an error, it was his duty to correct the error,[5] although bets were hedged by the further conclusion that, just in case they were required, exceptional circumstances did exist for the course taken by the first instance judge.

1   [2003] EWCA Civ 1820.
2   There are two: [1998] 1 WLR 825 and [1999] 1 WLR 1.
3   Compare on this point, *Noga v Abacha* [2001] 3 All ER 513 per Rix LJ at paragraph 8.
4   See also *Re L-B* [2013] 1 WLR 634, below.
5   See *Robinson v Fernsby* [2003] EWCA Civ 1820 per May LJ at paragraphs 69–99, in particular at paragraphs 76, 94–96 and 98. Under CPR 40, Practice Direction E, paragraph 4.4 where a party wishes to apply for an order consequential to the judgment (eg permission to appeal) the application must be made by filing written submission with the judge's clerk. It may be that the existence of an error in the draft judgment is only drawn to the judge's attention after he receives such written submissions. In those circumstances, it would appear that it is legitimate for a judge to correct any error in the judgment, the policy rationale being that this will save the parties the expense of an appeal. However, this gives the judge a 'second bite' of the cherry, and the party drawing the error to the judge's attention may find that his grounds of appeal disappear in the re-drafted judgment.

20.31 The outcome in *Robinson* may well have been influenced that in that instance it was the judge who invited further submissions on the case after handing down the judgment in draft (in *Noga*, what happened took place at the instigation of one of the parties). Yet the reasoning in *Robinson* is not framed in this way, and as a matter of logic it could not be so. The only logical dividing line between the two would appear to be based on just how 'draft' the draft judgment is: if the judgment has been handed down but the order is not perfected, 'exceptional circumstances' is the test; if it is draft in the sense of awaiting suggested corrections from the parties, a different approach prevails. There is logic to this, but this does not appear to be the actual distinction between the circumstances considered in *Noga* and those in *Robinson*. What remains is a position that is far from satisfactory.

In *Paulin v Paulin (Note)*,[1] the Court of Appeal attempted to resolve the confusion. It set out the principles as follows:[2]

(1)   A judge's reversal of his decision is distinguished from his amplification of the reasons which he has given for it. If a party contends that the reasons for his decision are inadequate, he should invite the judge to

amplify them before complaining of inadequacy in the Court of Appeal. A judge has an untrammelled jurisdiction to amplify his reasons at any time prior to the sealing of his order;

(2)   A judge has jurisdiction to reverse his decision at any time until his order is perfected (by being sealed under CPR 40.2(2)(b)) but not afterwards;

(3)   A written reserved judgment is less open to reversal by the judge than an ex tempore judgment. If a written judgment has been disseminated only as a draft, it may be more open to reversal by the judge than if it has been handed down and thus finally delivered;

(4)   The formula in *Barrell* governs the circumstances in which it is proper for a court to reverse its decision prior to sealing the order: ie that the circumstances must be 'exceptional'. This phrase is not a statutory definition, and a formula of 'strong reasons' is an acceptable alternative to that of 'exceptional circumstances'.

(5)   It is instructive to note examples of situations where the jurisdiction to reverse a decision prior to the sealing of the order has been exercised.

In the case of *Re L-B (children) (care proceedings: power to revise judgment)*,[3] the Supreme Court gave detailed consideration to the circumstances in which a judge can amend a judgment. The Supreme Court concluded that, in giving judgment, a judge has jurisdiction to change his or her mind up until the order carrying the judgment into effect is drawn up and perfected. That power is not limited to exceptional circumstances. The overriding objective in the exercise of the power is to deal with the case justly. Whether a judge should exercise the discretion to reverse his decision should include factors such as: (i) whether a party has already acted on the decision to his detriment; (ii) existence of a mistake by the court; (iii) a failure to draw the court's attention to a relevant fact or point of law; or (iv) the discovery of new facts after judgment had been given. Justice might require the revisiting of a decision for no more reason than the judge having had a carefully considered change of mind. Each case would depend on its own circumstances, but the need for the power to be exercised judicially and not capriciously requires that consideration be given to offering the parties the opportunity of addressing the judge on whether he should change his decision.

The Court of Appeal in *R (Binyam Mohamed) v Secretary of State for Foreign and Commonwealth Affairs*, emphasised that 'on rare occasions' and 'in exceptional circumstances' the court may properly be invited to reconsider part of the terms of its draft. The example given in that case was where a judgment contains detrimental observations about an individual or his lawyers, which on the face of it are not necessary to the judgment of the court and appear to be based on a misunderstanding of the evidence, or a concession, or a submission. When an invitation to go beyond the correction of typographical errors is proposed, the court held that it is a 'fundamental requirement' that the other parties should immediately be informed, so as to enable them to make objections to the proposal if there are any.[4]

In *Egan v Motor Services (Bath) Ltd*,[5] the Court of Appeal noted and deprecated the growing practice of counsel writing to the judge upon receipt of draft judgment, asking him to reconsider his conclusions. The court stated that (a) circulation of a draft is not intended to provide counsel with an opportunity to re-argue the issues in the case, and (b) only in the most exceptional circumstances is it appropriate to ask the judge to reconsider a point of substance; for example, where counsel feels that the judge (i) had not given adequate reasons for some aspects of his decision; or (ii) had decided the case on a point which was not properly argued or has relied on an authority which was not considered.[6]

Two further points may be noted. First, in *Taylor v Lawrence*,[7] the Court of Appeal (which has a statutory jurisdiction) held that it has power to re-open its own decisions in very exceptional cases where the interests of justice require it. The reasoning of the court was based in large part on the fact that, for practical purposes, that court is a court of last resort, because of the limited circumstances in which the House of Lords will grant leave to appeal.[8] Second, considerations of finality are to be weighed in public law cases against the public interest.[9]

1   [2009] EWCA Civ 221; [2010] 1 WLR 1057.
2   At [30].
3   [2013] 1 WLR 634.
4   [2010] EWCA Civ 158, [2011] QB 218 at [3]–[4]. The court held that, as draft judgments are necessarily circulated in confidence, it followed that all communications in response are covered by the same principle. In *Binyam Mohamed*, that confidentiality was broken when the letter from the Secretary of State's counsel was circulated to the media and published. The court held that CPR 31.22 did not apply to submissions and discussions about draft judgments which took place in open court. The minimum requirement before circulation other than to the parties is permissible must be an application to the court for the confidentiality principle to be reviewed in the context of the individual case: at [11]–[12]. In that case, as the letter had been published which referred to the substance of the earlier draft judgments, the court ordered the publication of the first draft of the disputed paragraph. See also *All Party Parliamentary Group on Extraordinary Rendition v Foreign and Commonwealth Office* [2013] UKUT 0560 (AAC), where the Upper Tribunal allowed an appeal on the basis that the First tier Tribunal erred in law in failing to reopen the hearing or permit further submissions. The First-tier Tribunal had heard evidence in closed session, from which the Appellant and its legal representatives were excluded. The draft judgment, for the first time, revealed the nature of the respondent's case, and the Appellant made an application to re-open the hearing so as to address those points.
5   [2007] EWCA Civ 1002, [2008] 1 All ER 1156, CA.
6   See also *R (Edwards) v Environment Agency* [2008] 1 WLR 1587, HL. In the House of Lords, drafts of speeches to be delivered are provided to counsel in confidence with a request that counsel should identify any misprints, inadvertent errors of fact or ambiguities of expression. The solicitors for the appellant then submitted a memorandum containing reference to three Directives which had not been mentioned in the appellant's submissions, and repeating other arguments that had already been considered. The Law Lords said that this was an abuse of the procedure of the House. See now paragraph 6.8.4 of Supreme Court Practice Direction 6 ('the purpose of disclosing the judgment is not to allow counsel to re-argue the case and attention is drawn to the opinions of Lord Hoffmann and Lord Hope in *R (Edwards) v Environment Agency*').
7   [2003] QB 528.
8   For further discussion see **5.65**.
9   On similar principles, in *Steward v DPP* [2004] 1 WLR 592, the Divisional Court held that it was open to justices to revisit an announced conclusion that there was no case to answer, where in subsequent discussion an error was identified, was agreed by the defendant's solicitor and was admitted to by the justices.

TRANSFER OF PROCEEDINGS

20.32 CPR 54.20 provides a power for the court to order that a claim commenced under CPR Pt 54 be continued as if it had not been so started.[1] This provides the procedural tool not only to remove from the Administrative Court claims that turn out not to have a sufficient public law element at all,[2] but also to ensure that even those claims which are true public law claims can be dealt with appropriately if they also raise issues that are better considered under the usual Part 7 procedures.[3] Consequential claims for damages are obvious candidates for such treatment, and it is common practice for damages claims to be considered separately and only after the strictly public law issues have been determined.[4]

[1] For use of this power prior to the hearing, see **19.145**.
[2] For example, *R (West) v Lloyd's* [2004] 3 All ER 251.
[3] Thus the CPR power is significantly broader and more flexible than its RSC predecessor, compare, for example, *R v Home Secretary, ex p Dew* [1987] 1 WLR 881 per McNeill LJ at 901 (under the RSC) and *R (Heather) v Leonard Cheshire Foundation* [2002] 2 All ER 936 (under the CPR).
[4] See, for such an approach. *R v Chief Constable of Lancashire, ex p Parker* [1993] QB 577 at 588G; *R v Coventry City Council, ex p Phoenix* [1995] 3 All ER 37; and *R v Governor of Brockhill Prison, ex p Evans (No 2)* [2000] 3 WLR 843. In each of these cases the damages issues were stood over for separate consideration.

EVIDENCE

General

20.33 At the time the claimant files his skeleton argument, he must also file a paginated and indexed bundle of all the documents that are required. This must be done at least 21 working days before the hearing. The bundle will contain the claim form, the claimant's written evidence (normally in the form of witness statements) and the documents upon which he proposes to rely.[1] It must also include all those documents required by the defendant and by any other party who is to make representations at the hearing.[2]

[1] In relation to bundles for hearings before the Court of Appeal see the comments in *Harvey Shopfitters Limited v ADI Limited* [2004] 2 All ER 982 as to the importance of compliance with the requirements of the Practice Direction under CPR Pt 52 (per Brooke LJ at paragraphs 14–18.
[2] See CPR Pt 54, Practice Direction A at § 16.

20.34 It is wise to pay some careful thought to whether or not evidence and documents are relevant to the matters at stake in the proceedings. Judges are expressing increasing impatience with the inclusion of large quantities of superfluous material, and are unlikely to be well disposed towards those who file unnecessary documents.[1]

[1] For a strongly stated example, see *R (Prokopp) v London Underground Ltd* [2003] EWCA Civ 961, [2004] Env LR 170 at paragraph 52; in more measured terms, per Booke LJ in *R (Goldsmith) v London Borough of Wandsworth* [2004] EWCA Civ 1170, (2004) 7 CCL Rep 472 at paragraph 101.

20.35 In a judicial review claim, all parties will have filed their written evidence long before the matter comes to a hearing: the claimant at the time of filing the claim form, other parties at the time of filing their detailed grounds. Indeed, no further written evidence may be relied upon unless the court directs or gives permission.[1] Common reasons to wish to seek to serve new evidence are that the claimant wishes to reply to the evidence of the defendant or interested party. The factual situation may have changed. Relevant events may have taken place between the time for filing evidence and the substantive hearing. In these circumstances, a court may allow a party to file new evidence before the hearing – but issues of relevance and fairness are important considerations.[2]

1   CPR 54.16.
2   See **20.3** above.

Relevance and admissibility

20.36 The usual rules with regard to the admissibility of evidence apply to judicial review claims as to other types of civil claims. The only general (if a little unhelpful) rule is that all relevant evidence is admissible, except where it is inadmissible.

20.37 However, the context and proper scope of the judicial review procedure mean that the evidence is usually restricted to that which was before the public body at the time of the challenged act or decision. If 'fresh' evidence were admissible, the court would be likely to find itself in the position of being asked to decide the merits of the case rather than acting as a court of review.[1]

1   See *Dŵr Cymru Cyfyngedig v Environment Agency of Wales* [2003] EWHC 336 (Admin) at paragraph 58 where the court refused to consider fresh evidence on this basis; and to similar effect *R (Goldsmith) v London Borough of Wandsworth* [2004] EWCA Civ 1170, (2004) 7 CCL Rep 472 per Wall LJ at paragraphs 6–9. The fact that the defendant is under a continuing obligation to revisit the issue in dispute if there is a material change of circumstances is often an argument for not admitting late evidence, since it will inevitably need to be considered by the decision-maker when he revisits the decision: see, for one example, *Machado v Secretary of State for the Home Department* [2005] EWCA Civ 597 per Sedley LJ at paragraphs 22, and 23.

20.38 For this reason it has been held that later evidence, even if it clearly shows that an earlier decision was in fact erroneous, is unlikely to be admissible. This has been stated to be because a decision-making body cannot be criticised for failing to consider evidence which was not before them at the time the decision was taken.[1]

However, if a claim alleges a breach of a Convention right, any evidence relating to any justification for an interference with the right may be relevant and admissible. The court is not restricted to matters before the decision maker: see *R (Middlebrook Mushrooms Ltd) v Agricultural Wages Board of England and Wales* and *R (L) v Chief Constable of Cumbria Constabulary*[2].

1   See *R v Immigration Appeal Tribunal, ex p Jaifor Ali* [1991] COD 37. For a contrary view, see Denning MR in the minority in the Court of Appeal in *R v West Sussex Quarter Sessions, ex p Johnson Trust Ltd* [1974] 1 QB 24 at 36G–H.
2   [2004] EWHC 1447 (Admin), at [84] and [2013] EWHC 869 (Admin); [2014] 1 WLR 601.

20.39 There are some long accepted and uncontroversial exceptions to the exclusion of evidence that was not before the defendant public authority. The court will generally allow fresh evidence in at least the following four circumstances:[1]

(1)   the court will receive evidence to show the nature and details of the material that was before the defendant public body at the relevant time;

(2)   a court will consider evidence to determine a question of fact where the jurisdiction of a public body depends on that fact. In that situation, the court is entitled to look at new evidence as its role goes beyond that of reviewing the decision. It must instead make up its own mind as to the 'jurisdictional fact';[2]

(3)   similarly to (2) above, a court can consider additional evidence to determine whether procedural requirements were observed. Where the challenge is on the basis of failure to consider a relevant consideration, this might include evidence to assess the significance of the alleged failure;

(4)   the court can consider evidence where the challenged act or decision is alleged to have been tainted by misconduct. Examples of such misconduct include bias or fraud. Fresh evidence is admissible to prove the particular misconduct alleged.

[1] This is a restatement of the dicta in *R v Secretary of State for the Environment, ex p Powis* [1981] 1 WLR 584 at 595G ff.

[2] See *R v Secretary of State for the Environment, ex p Davies* (1991) 61 P & CR 487 at 492.

20.40 On analysis, these exceptions relate to the situations in which evidence not before the defendant public authority will be *relevant* to the questions that are to be decided in the challenge. Different evidence will be relevant depending on whether the decision is challenged for lack of jurisdiction, unreasonableness or failure to consider a relevant consideration. All that is required is a consideration of whether a specific piece of evidence would tend to prove or disprove the facts that are in issue in a judicial review. A classic illustration is *R v Boycott, ex p Keasley*.[1] In that case, the court was asked to review a decision taken by a doctor that a boy was an 'ineducable imbecile'. Under the provisions of the Mental Deficiency Act 1913 and the Education Act 1921, a doctor had the power to issue a certificate to this effect only if there was no doubt about the child's mental capacity. If the matter was open to doubt, a decision could only be made by the Board of Education. Thus, whether or not the case under consideration was a case of a doubt was a matter of jurisdictional fact. In these circumstances, the court admitted evidence from other doctors contradicting the original opinion that the child was not imbecile. This evidence was admitted not with a view to proving that he was not an imbecile, but in order to address the jurisdictional issue as to whether there was any doubt about the matter.

[1] [1939] 2 KB 651.

20.41 The question of relevance will not always be determinative of the question of admissibility, however. The courts have not always been careful to make the distinction between relevance and admissibility explicit. It is, however, an important distinction, which has become more important in the context of the newly recognised ground of review on the basis of material error of fact. The ordinary requirements for such a finding are that there must be a mistake as to an existing established and material fact, and that the party seeking to rely on the fresh evidence must not have been responsible for the mistake.[1] In these cases, fresh evidence as to the fact alleged to be erroneous will almost invariably be relevant to the questions that are to be decided. But it seems there is a further question as to whether or not such fresh evidence is *admissible,* even if it is relevant.

¹ See *E v Secretary of State for the Home Department* [2004] EWCA Civ 49, [2004] QB 1044 at paragraph 66.

20.42 In *E v Secretary of State for the Home Department,*¹ the Court of Appeal considered the key authorities and addressed this issue in some detail. The court appears to have put considerable weight on the distinction between two categories of decision-making bodies who might be subject to review.² The first category of subjects are those who have a 'continual responsibility' over a matter. The second category of bodies are those with a finite jurisdiction at a particular time.

¹ [2004] EWCA Civ 49.
² See *E v Secretary of State for the Home Department* [2004] EWCA Civ 49, [2004] QB 1044 at paragraphs 74, 75 and 77.

20.43 An example of the first type of case is where the Secretary of State has decided to extradite the applicant or not to grant her exceptional leave to remain. In *E*, the Court of Appeal described these as situations where the decision-maker has a 'continuing public responsibility in the matter'.¹ In these cases, fresh relevant evidence is likely to be admissible, and not strictly limited to that which was or should have been before the decision-maker at the time of the decision.² Further examples of this sort of case are *R v Secretary of State for the Home Department, ex p Turgut*³ and *R (Hussain) v Secretary of State for Justice.*⁴ In Hussain, the respondent assessed the claimant prisoner's escape risk every six months. Therefore, any subsequent decision rendered the previous decision academic.

¹ See *E v Secretary of State for the Home Department* [2004] EWCA Civ 49, [2004] QB 1044, particularly at paragraph 77.
² See *R v Secretary of State for the Home Department Launder* [1997] 1 WLR 839, especially at 860–861 per Lord Hope and *R v Secretary of State for the Home Department, ex p Turgut* [2001] 1 All ER 729 at 735g.
³ [2001] 1 All ER 729 at 735g.
⁴ [2016] EWCA Civ 1111.

20.44 A challenge to a decision of what was the Immigration Appeal Tribunal provides an example of the second type of case.¹ In these cases, it cannot be said that the decision-making body has a continuing responsibility to keep the decision under review. The Court of Appeal in *E* decided that in a review of the decision of this latter type of body, fresh evidence is only *admissible* in asylum cases when the '*Ladd v Marshall*'² principles apply, but these may be departed from in 'exceptional circumstances where the interests of justice require'. The '*Ladd v Marshall*' principles can be summarised as follows. Fresh evidence can be adduced where it could not have been obtained with reasonable diligence for use at the first hearing, it would have an important bearing on the case and it is apparently credible, although not necessarily incontrovertible. Unfortunately, no guidance was given in *E* as to what might and what might not be considered 'exceptional circumstances'.

¹ This was the situation under consideration in *E v Secretary of State for the Home Department* [2004] EWCA Civ 49, [2004] QB 1044.
² [1954] 1 WLR 1489.

20.45 It might be thought that such procedural rules should be relaxed where the subject matter of the decision being challenged requires the 'anxious scrutiny' of the court, such as with regard to immigration issues. However, it has been held that the requirement of anxious scrutiny cannot alter the statutory limits of the procedure, even though it will be very relevant to the consideration of the facts.[1] For this reason, the '*Ladd v Marshall* Plus Exceptional Circumstances' Rule will apply to 'anxious scrutiny' cases as much as to all other cases.

[1] See *E v Secretary of State for the Home Department* [2004] EWCA Civ 49, [2004] QB 1044 at paragraph 85.

Disclosure and cross-examination

20.46 Applications for the disclosure of documents and for cross examination of witnesses are dealt with elsewhere in this book.[1]

[1] Disclosure and cross-examination are dealt with generally in CHAPTER 19; as to failure to give reasons for a decision where there is a challenge to the reasonableness of a decision, see CHAPTER 8.

'Supplementing' the reasons for a decision

20.47 There can be a fine line between explaining and rationalising a decision. The court has the power to order a party to clarify any matter which is in dispute in the proceedings or give additional information in relation to any such matter.[1] The court may do this on its own initiative or upon the application of a party. When considering whether or not to make such an order, the court must have regard to the overriding objective and, in particular, to the costs and benefits of making the order. The court can use this power to require a defendant to give further details as to how and why it arrived at a particular decision or course of action.

[1] Under CPR Pt 18.

20.48 However, the courts have treated the provisions of late reasons by defendants to judicial review with some care. They are astute to the possibility that a public body will embark on a process of after-the-event rationalisation when faced with a potential challenge.

20.49 Evidence is therefore not admissible to show that the appeal committee meant something different from what was unambiguously stated in a reasoned decision.[1] A public body cannot retrospectively change and improve upon its earlier decision when that decision comes under challenge. If, for example, a later witness statement discloses reasons that would have been proper but are inconsistent with the reasons adopted at the relevant time, the court would not allow the later reasoning to 'cure' the earlier defects.[2]

[1] *Re C and P* [1992] COD 29.
[2] *R (Li) v Mental Health Review Tribunal* [2004] EWHC 51 (Admin), [2004] ACD 74.

20.50 Where there is a statutory duty to give reasons for a decision, the courts have been particularly wary of allowing late reasons. In *R v Westminster*

City Council, ex p Ermakov,[1] Hutchinson LJ set out the criteria for the admissibility of late reasons. He stated that the court should admit evidence 'to elucidate or exceptionally correct or add to reasons' but it should 'be very cautious about doing so'. The examples he gave are of errors in transcription or expression, or the inadvertent omission of words, or where language is lacking clarity.[2]

[1] [1996] 2 All ER 302.
[2] In some instances, the line between admissibility and inadmissibility will depend on whether the duty to give reasons bites at a specific point in time. Usually it will bite at the time the decision is made, but this will not always be so. For an instance where the duty to give reasons did not arise as at the point of decision-making, see *Machado v Secretary of State for the Home Department* [2005] EWCA Civ 597 per Sedley LJ at paragraphs 17–21, under the provisions of the Immigration (EEA) Regulations.

20.51 The appropriate response of public bodies, which are required to give reasons of decisions to an appeal should not be to purport to amplify the decision. The better approach is to supply evidence as to the relevant notes and materials.[1] Fresh reasons would also be likely to be allowed where they merely explain the effect of a certain piece of information on an earlier decision where this is otherwise unclear.[2] However, save in exceptional circumstances, a public body should not be permitted to adduce evidence directly contradicting its own official records of decisions.[3] Of course, where there is a statutory duty to give reasons, reasons supplied after the event cannot make up for breach of a statutory duty to provide reasons in the first place, even if they are admissible for the review.[4]

[1] Oxfordshire County Council v GB [2002] ELR 8, *A v Birmingham City Council* [2004] EWHC 156 (Admin), [2005] ACD 7, and *R (Nash) v Chelsea College of Art and Design* [2001] EWHC 538 (Admin).
[2] See *Ali v Kirklees Metropolitan Borough Council* [2001] LGR 448.
[3] See *R (Lanner Parish Council) v Cornwall Council* [2013] EWCA Civ 1290, where the Court of Appeal held that evidence indicating that the 'real' reasons for the decision were different from the stated reasons was not to be admitted.
[4] *R v Legal Aid Area No 8 (Northern) Appeal Committee, ex p Angell* [1990] COD 355; see also *Caroopen v Secretary of State for the Home Department* [2016] EWCA Civ 1307.

20.52 The courts have been a little more flexible in circumstances where there is no statutory duty to give reasons. Some authorities even appear to suggest that, where there is no statutory duty to give reasons, a defendant will be able to give late reasons and this might even be encouraged.[1]

[1] *R v Legal Aid Area No 8 (Northern) Appeal Committee, ex p Angell* [1990] COD 355.

20.53 However, even in these situations, the court has been (increasingly) cautious about accepting late reasons. In the case of *R (Richards) v Pembrokeshire County Council,*[1] the Court of Appeal stressed that the primary source for identifying the reasons for an impugned measure will always be the contemporaneous documented reasoning. It held that where it is credible and authoritative, fresh evidence may be relied upon to resolve or explain any ambiguity. However, without an ambiguity, fresh evidence as to reasoning will only be appropriate in 'exceptional circumstances'.

[1] [2004] EWCA Civ 1000; [2005] LGR 105. A cautious approach was approved in *Caroopen v Secretary of State for the Home Department* [2016] EWCA Civ 1307.

20.54 It should also be noted that the Court of Appeal in *Richards* expressly warned that whether late reasons are admissible will be dependent on the precise statutory provisions at issue. The admissibility of late reasons where there is no statutory duty to supply reasons is also highly situation sensitive. Relevant considerations to include:

(1)   whether the new reasons were consistent with the original reasons:

(2)   whether it was clear that the new reasons were the original reasons;

(3)   whether there is a real risk that the later reasons had been composed subsequently in order to support the decision, or were a retrospective justification of the original decision;

(4)   the delay before the later reasons were put forward;

(5)   the circumstances in which the later reasons were put forward;

(6)   the subject matter of the administrative decision;

(7)   the qualifications and experience of the persons involved;

(8)   whether the decision-maker would have been expected to state the reasons in the contemporaneous decision; and

(9)   whether it would be just in all the circumstances to refuse to admit the subsequent reasons.[1]

Where the decision-maker originally gave no reasons at all for the decision, it has been held that the public body should not be prevented from articulating the reasons for the first time at the time when the decision is challenged, and the principles set out above do not apply.[2]

[1]   *R (Leung) v Imperial College of Science, Technology and Medicine* [2002] ELR 653 at paragraphs 28–30, approving and adding to the list set out in *R (Nash) v Chelsea College of Art* [2001] EWHC Admin 538.

[2]   See *R v Secretary of State for the Home Department, ex p Peries* [1998] COD 110.

20.55 Once the defendant has filed its evidence, the claimant should have a far better understanding of the way in which the act or decision under challenge was reached. The claimant's advisers now come under a duty to reassess the merits of the review, and reconsider whether or not the matter has sufficient merit to proceed to a hearing.[1] If, on receiving the evidence, it becomes clear that the decision was properly taken, the matter should not be allowed to proceed to trial.

[1]   *R v Liverpool City Justices, ex p Price* [1998] COD 453, *R v Commissioners of Inland Revenue, ex p Continental Shipping Ltd* [1996] COD 335; see also *R (Gul) v Secretary of State for Justice* [2014] EWHC 373 (Admin).

Use of Parliamentary materials: the rule in *Pepper v Hart*

20.56 In *Pepper v Hart*,[1] the House of Lords allowed reference to *Hansard* as an aid to construction in certain well-defined situations. The criteria are, first, that the court is faced with an unclear or ambiguous legislative provision,[2] and second, that *Hansard* reveals a clear statement by the Minister or promoter of the relevant Bill as to what the provision was intended to mean. If the criteria are met, *Pepper v Hart* allows the court to rely on that statement as an indication of the true meaning of the provision.

[1]   [1993] AC 593. The use of other categories of Parliamentary material has been considered in *Black-Clawson International Limited v Papierwerke Waldhof-Aschaffenberg AG* [1975] AC

591 (at 613–615, white papers admissible for the purpose of ascertaining the mischief at which legislation is aimed); *R v Secretary of State for Environment Transport and the Regions ex p Spath Holme Limited* [2001] 2 AC 349 (at 379, use of other background material including Royal Commission reports and Law Commission reports admissible to establish the context and purposes of legislation); *Westminster City Council v NASS* [2002] 1 WLR 2956 (at paragraphs 1–6, explanatory notes admissible 'for what logical value they have' with the caution that these will reflect the views of the executive which may not be the same as those of Parliament); and *R v Montilla* [2004] 1 WLR 3141 (side notes and headings could be considered).

2   As to ambiguity, see *Re OT Computers Limited* [2004] Ch 317 per Longmore LJ at paragraphs 39–41.

20.57 The decision in *Pepper v Hart* has drawn considerable criticism. Many have considered that a liberal approach to admitting *Hansard* offends against fundamental constitutional principles. Wherever a statute is ambiguous, the principle in *Pepper v Hart* appears to allow clear statements from the promoter of a Bill to determine statutory meaning. This runs contrary to the separation of powers in two ways. First, it allows the executive to acquire legislative power. This is because the promoter of the Bill will be expressing the executive's intention with regard to the meaning of its provisions, which may bear scant resemblance to the intention of the legislature as a whole. Second, it allows the executive to interpret legislation, thus allowing it to encroach upon judicial power.[1]

1   For a detailed consideration of this point and the rule in general, see Aileen Kavanagh '*Pepper v Hart* and Matters of Constitutional Principle' (2005) 121 LQR 98. See, also, the speech of Lord Steyn in *McDonnell v Christian Brothers Trustees* [2004] 1 AC 1101 (referring to his own extra-judicial statements at (2001) 21 OJLS 59) to the effect that a better approach would be to regard (and recast) the rule in *Pepper v Hart* as applicable only to prevent a government retreating from specific assurances given as to the meaning of legislation in the course of Parliamentary debate – effectively a form of estoppel that could only be raised against the government itself. See, also Stefan Vogenauer, 'A Retreat from *Pepper v Hart*? A Reply to Lord Steyn' (2005) 25 OJLS 629 and Philip Sales, '*Pepper v Hart*: A Footnote to Professor Vogenauer's reply to Lord Steyn' (2006) 26 OJLS 585.

20.58 There have also been more pragmatic fears that conscientious lawyers have been spurred to spent considerable time, and incurred significant costs, researching *Hansard* references. Indeed, one of Lord Mackay's major concerns in his minority speech in *Pepper v Hart* itself was that the decision would increase the expense of litigation without contributing very much of value to the quality of decision-making. This practical concern as to cost soon became reality. There is also much to be said in support of Lord Mackay's concern that little value is added to the decision-making process. In most situations the search for 'Parliamentary intent' bears many of the hallmarks of a wild goose chase since it requires many (unwarranted) assumptions as to why individual legislators have voted for a particular provision or Bill. In most instances, the Hansard search is not in truth a search for the intention of Parliament, but merely an exercise in attempting to perceive the intentions of the promoter of the Bill in issue.[1]

1   As to this, see *Black-Clawson International Limited v Papierwerke Waldhof-Aschaffenberg AG* [1975] AC 591 at 613–615; and *Davis v Johnson* [1979] AC 264 per Lord Scarman at 350.

20.59 There have been a number of judicial dicta responding to these perceived problems, and expressing doubts about the proper scope of *Pepper* *v Hart*. In *R v Secretary of State for the Environment, Transport and the Regions, ex p Spath Holme Ltd*,[1] four of the five members of the House of Lords expressly stated that the principles laid down in *Pepper v Hart* should be strictly insisted upon.[2] This emphasis on strict insistence has been cited with approval in subsequent cases.[3] 'Ambiguity' has also been narrowly interpreted. It has been held that the fact that two judges differ as to the correct construction of a statute does not necessarily demonstrate ambiguity.[4] Judicial dicta regarding the use of *Hansard* have made reference to matters of constitutional principle. Lord Bingham stated that the overriding aim of statutory interpretation by the courts must always be to give effect to the intention of Parliament as expressed in the words used.[5] Lord Nicholls expressed the view that:

> 'it is not the Minister's words, uttered as they were on behalf of the executive, that must be referred to in order to understand what Parliament intended'.[6]

---

[1] [2001] AC 349.

[2] Lord Bingham at 393, Lord Nicholls at 399, Lord Hope at 409, Lord Hutton at 414.

[3] See *Robinson v Secretary of State for Northern Ireland* [2002] UKHL 32, the House of Lords declined to admit ministerial statements as an aid to statutory construction because they were unclear and inconclusive. In his speech, Lord Hoffmann emphasised (at paragraphs 36–40) that it would be a rare occasion for an Act of Parliament to be construed as meaning something 'different from what it would be understood to mean by a member of the public who was aware of the material forming the background to its enactment but who was not privy to what had been said by the individual members during the debates in one or other House of Parliament'. See also, per Lord Hobhouse at paragraph 65; and *R v A (No 2)* [2002] 1 AC 45 at 79.

[4] See *Re OT Computers* [2004] Ch 317 at paragraph 39.

[5] *R v Secretary of State for the Environment, Transport and the Regions, ex p Spath Holme Ltd* [2001] AC 349 at 388.

[6] *Parochial Church Council of the Parish of Aston Cantlow, Wilmcote in Bellesley, Warwickshire v Wallbank* [2003] UKHL 37, [2003] 3 WLR 283.

20.60 Against this background, an opportunity for the House of Lords to reconsider the principle in *Pepper v Hart* arose in *Wilson v First County Trust*.[1] There was a question in that case as to whether provisions of the Consumer Credit Act 1974 were compatible with art 6 (Right to a Fair Trial) of the ECHR, incorporated into domestic law by the Human Rights Act 1998 (HRA 1998). A key issue was whether the interference with art 6 rights was justified, that is, whether the provisions pursued a legitimate policy aim and whether the measures taken were proportionate to that aim. In the Court of Appeal, Sir Andrew Morritt V-C, examined the preparatory materials including the Parliamentary debates in order to determine what reason of policy led to the enactment of the legislation. Upon finding that these materials tended to 'confuse rather than illuminate', he found that the encroachment on art 6 rights was not justified.

---

[1] [2004] 1 AC 816.

20.61 On appeal to the House of Lords, three key points were made. First, their Lordships emphasised that in seeking to give effect to the will of Parliament, the primary task was to enforce Parliament's enacted intention.[1] Second, the House held that ministerial statements of intent should not be treated as sources of law. Lord Hobhouse stated that:

'the source of the new law is the document itself not what anyone may have said about it or some early form of it . . . it is a fundamental error of principle to confuse what a Minister or a Parliamentarian may have said (or said he intended) with the will and intention of Parliament itself.'[2]

[1]   At paragraph 67.
[2]   At paragraph 139.

20.62 Finally, the House of Lords held that ministerial statements, however clear and explicit they may be, cannot control the meaning of an Act of Parliament. They should instead be treated as no more than part of the background.[1]

Wilson also provided important and necessary guidance as to the relationship between the principles of statutory interpretation and the obligations under the HRA 1998. When considering proportionality, the court should focus on the legislation, rather than the adequacy of the reasons put forward by the promoter of the Bill. The absence of expressed reasons in a Parliamentary debate should not be relevant to whether or not a measure is justified in the context of the ECHR.[2]

[1]   At paragraph 58 per Lord Nicholls.
[2]   At paragraph 67.

20.63 But *Pepper v Hart* has not been overruled. Following *Wilson*, the court retains a discretion to consult Parliamentary debates as background material which may shed light on the intention of the legislature. Yet there must be real doubt that the views of an individual minister can properly be regarded as indicative of the intention of Parliament as a whole. Ministerial statements should never be given the status of law, no matter how clear and unambiguous they are. The admissibility criteria set out in *Pepper v Hart* must be very strictly applied.[1]

If a party wishes to rely on material from *Hansard*, notice must be served in accordance with the relevant Practice Direction (*Hansard Citation*).[2]

In *Agricultural Sector (Wales) Bill, Re, A-G v Counsel General for Wales (A-G for Northern Ireland intervening)*,[3] the Supreme Court held that correspondence between the Government in Westminster and the Welsh Government setting out the joint intention of both parties as to the meaning of clauses in the Government of Wales Bill 2006 was not admissible in a devolution reference to interpret the Government of Wales Act 2006.

[1]   For a recent example where Parliamentary debates have been admissible under *Pepper v Hart*, see *R v JTB* [2009] UKHL 20,[2009] 1 AC 1310.
[2]   [1995] 1 WLR 192.
[3]   [2014] UKSC 43.

Expert evidence

20.64 The general rules on expert evidence are set out in CPR Pt 35 and its accompanying Practice Direction. Expert evidence must be restricted to that which is reasonably required to resolve the proceedings.[1] If a party wishes to call an expert or put in expert evidence, it must apply to the court for permission.[2]

1 CPR 35.1.
2 CPR 35.4(1).

20.65 As with other evidence in judicial review, it is necessary to distinguish between that evidence which was before the decision-maker when it made the decision and fresh evidence. Expert evidence that was before the decision-maker may be relevant in a subsequent judicial review and its admissibility is unlikely to be controversial.

20.66 Expert evidence which was not before the decision-maker may cause more problems. In *R (Lynch) v General Dental Council*.[1] Collins J explained that fresh expert evidence should, in general, only be admitted in the same situations as fresh non-expert evidence. However, he held that fresh expert evidence will be admitted in a truly technical field, where the court needs assistance to explain a process and its significance. Although this went beyond the *Powis* guidelines, such evidence would be required where the court needs to understand matters in order to reach a just conclusion.

1 [2003] EWHC 2987 (Admin), [2004] 1 All ER 1159.

20.67 The courts have been more willing to entertain fresh expert evidence where there are issues relating to proportionality under the ECHR and European Community Law. With regard to the question of whether a provision was made in pursuit of a legitimate aim, the courts may require expert evidence to assess what the needs are from a sociological perspective.[1] At the stage of whether the precise provision is proportionate to a given aim, the court may desire expert evidence to assess the practicability of suggested alternative measures.[2] However, even though such evidence is admissible, restraint should be exercised to ensure that thought is given to the precise point the evidence is intended to address.[3]

1 *Sec Wilson v First County Trust Ltd* [2003] UKHL 40, [2004] 1 AC 816 at paragraphs 141 and 142.
2 See *R (Seahawk Marine Foods Ltd) v Southampton Port Health Authority* [2002] EWCA Civ 54, [2002] EHLR 15 at paragraph 34.
3 *CF v Secretary of State for the Home Department* [2004] EWHC 111 (Fam), [2004] 1 FCR 577 at paragraphs 217–219. Any expert evidence must be careful not to stray beyond the expert's area of expertise: see, for example, *R (AB) v Secretary of State for the Home Department* [2013] EWHC 3453 (Admin), [67] and *MF (Albania) v Secretary of State for the Home Department* [2014] EWCA Civ 902.

PRECEDENT

20.68 The same rules of precedent apply in judicial review as in other proceedings. The general rule is that the court is bound by the result and decisive reasoning in any substantive decision of a higher court. It will follow a court of the same level as a matter of 'judicial comity' unless it is satisfied that that decision is plainly wrong.[1] The Court of Appeal is bound to follow a previous decision unless (i) there are two conflicting decisions of the Court of Appeal (in which case it is free to choose between them); (ii) the decision cannot stand with a decision of the House of Lords; or (iii) the decision was given *per incuriam*.[2]

1   *R v Greater Manchester Coroner, ex p Tal* [1985] QB 67 at 81A–B.
2   *Young v Bristol Aeroplane Co Ltd* [1944] KB 718, 729-730; re-affirmed in *Davis v Johnson* [1979] AC 264.

20.69 There are some limited exceptions to this rule. First, a decision which was clearly taken in the absence of relevant information such as a binding previous authority or a statutory provision, will not bind a future court.[1] Second, there is a principle that a subsequent court will not be bound by a proposition of law which was not the subject of any argument or consideration by the earlier court. This principle is applied only in the most obvious of cases and with great care.[2]

1   See, for example, *R v Simpson* [2004] QB 118.
2   *R (Kadhim) v Brent London Borough Council Housing Benefit Review Board* [2001] QB 955 at paragraphs 33–39.

20.70 There are some special considerations with regard to cases involving the HRA 1998. Where the interpretative obligation under s 3(1) of the HRA 1998 is at issue, previous authority as to the proper construction of the legislative provision under consideration is not binding.[1] However, the court is bound by a decision within the normal domestic hierarchy as to the meaning of an ECHR provision in the same way as it is bound by a decision as to the meaning of purely domestic law.[2]

1   See, for example, *R v Lambert* [2001] UKHL 37, [2002] 2 AC 545 at paragraph 81.
2   *R (Williamson) v Secretary of State for Education and Employment* [2002] EWCA Civ 1926, [2003] QB 1300 at paragraph 41; and *Kay v Lambeth London Borough Council* [2006] UKHL 10; [2006] 2 AC 465. While UK courts are under a duty under s 2 of the HRA to take ECHR judgments and opinions into account, and a duty under s 6 of the HRA not to act incompatibility with Convention rights, domestic rules of precedent should not be modified. The ECtHR was responsible for interpreting Convention rights, but it is for domestic courts to determine initially how the principles laid down by the ECtHR are to be applied in the domestic context. Adherence to precedent is a cornerstone of the domestic legal system. Courts should follow the ordinary rules of precedent, save in an extreme case where the decision of the superior court could not survive the introduction of the HRA. Judges could give leave to appeal where they considered that a binding precedent was inconsistent with ECtHR authority. See also *R (M) v Secretary of State for Work and Pensions* [2009] 1 AC 311, para 60-66 per Lord Neuberger. Where the Court of Appeal is faced with a conflict between one of its own previous decisions and a subsequent decision of the European Court of Human Rights, the Court of Appeal is free, but not obliged, to depart from that previous decision.

20.71 Where a Court of Appeal decision is inconsistent with an earlier House of Lords decision, or inconsistent with a wrongly distinguished earlier Court of Appeal authority, a later Court of Appeal is free to disregard its earlier decision and follow the first decision.[1] However, disapproval of a previous Court of Appeal decision by the Privy Council does not entitle the Court of Appeal to depart from that previous decision. The Court of Appeal remains bound by its previous authority.[2]

1   See *Great Peace Shipping Ltd v Tsavliris Salvage (International) Ltd* [2003] QB 679, *Starmark Enterprises Ltd v CPL Distribution Ltd* [2002] Ch 306 at paragraphs 65, 67, 97.
2   *Re Spectrum Plus Ltd (in liquidation)* [2004] Ch 337 at paragraph 58.

20.72 It should also be noted that permission decisions are not technically binding, although they may be persuasive.[1]

[1] *R (Burkett) v Hammersmith and Fulham LBC* [2002] UKHL 23, [2002] 1 WLR 1593 at paragraph 41. Judgments on applications for permission to apply for judicial review are generally not regarded as authoritative: see *Clark v University of Lincolnshire and Humberside* [2000] 1 WLR 1988, 1998–1999, paragraphs 40–43, per Lord Woolf MR.

20.73 Questions of precedent should be distinguished from questions of issue estoppel. Such questions, and other aspects of abuse of process, are discussed in CHAPTER **18**.[1]

[1] See **18.61**.

20.74 Practitioners should have well in mind the Practice Direction which sets out restrictions on the citation of excessive authority.[1]

[1] *Practice Direction (Citation of Authorities)* [2001] 1 WLR 1001.

APPEALS

Introduction: civil matters and criminal matters

20.75 Rights of appeal arise both at the permission stage and following a full hearing.[1] In relation to each appeal stage, an important distinction exists between criminal matters and civil matters: generally the options for appeal are more limited where the matter is a criminal one. Whether a matter is categorised as a criminal matter or a civil one depends entirely on the nature of the underlying decision.[2] If the decision is taken in the context of criminal proceedings (ie proceedings that might result in conviction and punishment), the matter is, in all probability, a criminal one.[3] This includes matters occurring in the course of a criminal trial, and also occurring in the course of a criminal investigation, even if criminal proceedings have not actually been commenced.[4] A matter may remain a criminal matter even if the judicial review proceedings are commenced only after the conclusion of the criminal proceedings.[5] However, the fact that the underlying proceedings are criminal does not always require the conclusion that the decision under challenge will be categorised as a criminal matter. If the decision under challenge is, in fact, collateral to the criminal proceedings, it will not be a criminal matter.[6]

[1] In relation to the logistics for any hearing before the Court of Appeal anxious regard must be had to the provisions of the Practice Direction under CPR Pt 52. On this, see the comments of Brooke LJ in *Harvey Shopfitters Limited v ADI Limited* [2004] 2 All ER 982.

[2] See *Carr v Atkins* [1987] QB 963 and *R v Secretary of State for the Home Department, ex p Garner* [1990] COD 457. In relation to matters 'relating to trial on indictment' there is no judicial review jurisdiction at all: see s 29(3) of the Supreme Court Act 1981, and *R (Salubi) v Bow Street Magistrates Court* [2002] 1 WLR 3073.

[3] See *Armand v Home Secretary* [1943] AC 147.

[4] See *Carr v Atkins* [1987] 1 QB 963 and *Re Smalley* [1985] AC 622.

[5] *R v Blandford Justices, ex p Pamment* [1990] 1 WLR 1490 (challenge to a decision to refuse unconditional grant of bail).

[6] *Government of the United States v Montgomery* [2001] 1 WLR 196 at paragraph 19; *Re O* [1991] 2 QB 520 (order restraining disposal of assets in anticipation of a confiscation order); *M v Isleworth Crown Court* [2005] EWHC 363 (Admin).

Appeals at the permission stage

20.76 Since 1 July 2013, CPR 54.12(7) has provided that where a court refuses permission to apply for judicial review on the papers and records that the application is 'totally without merit', the claimant may not apply to have that decision reconsidered at an oral hearing. In *R (Grace) v Secretary of State for the Home Department*[1] the Court of Appeal held that the phrase 'totally without merit' meant simply that the claim was 'bound to fail'. (see Chapter CHAPTER 19); however in *R (W) v Secretary of State for the Home Department*,[2] it was found that phrases such as 'bound to fail', 'hopeless' and 'no rational basis' were helpful but imprecise. It was a matter for the judge's assessment in each case and the scope for general guidance was limited. Where an application was certified as being totally without merit, all of the claimant's arguments raised in the grounds should be properly addressed in the judge's reasons (which need not be lengthy). Reasons for a totally without merit certification should be separated from the reasons for refusing permission. Crucially, the court found that neither s 16(1) of the Senior Courts Act 1981 nor s 13 of the Tribunals, Courts and Enforcement Act 2007 conferred any right to appeal against a totally without merit certification as such. A claimant whose application for permission had been refused and so certified could only seek permission to appeal against the refusal.

If, in a civil matter, permission is refused after an oral hearing, the claimant may make an application to the Court of Appeal for permission to appeal to the Court of Appeal.[3] There is a time limit of seven days from the date of the decision of the High Court refusing permission to apply for judicial review.[4] On such an application the Court of Appeal may refuse permission to appeal, grant permission to appeal, or (instead of giving permission to appeal) give permission to apply for judicial review.[5] CPR 52.15(4) provides that in the latter event the case will proceed in the High Court unless the Court of Appeal orders otherwise. Retention of the case in the Court of Appeal will be appropriate where, for example:

(1) the fact that the point in issue is unlikely to be resolved without consideration at an appellate stage;[6] or
(2) that the issues raised in the claim are matters of acute importance;[7] or
(3) that they are time-sensitive such that remitting the case to the Administrative Court would render any relief sought pointless.[8] Where a claim has been certified as totally without merit at the paper stage, the applicant may apply to the Court of Appeal for permission to appeal, but the application will be determined on paper without an oral hearing: see CPR 52.15(1A).

Where permission to apply for judicial review of a decision of the Upper Tribunal (in a *Cart* judicial review claim – see CHAPTER 16 and CHAPTER 19) has been refused by the High Court, then once again, any application for permission to appeal to the Court of Appeal will be determined on paper without an oral hearing.[9]

---

1   [2014] EWCA Civ 1091; [2014] 1 WLR 3432.
2   [2016] EWCA Civ 82. The judgment also offers further guidance as to when claims should be certified as 'totally without merit'.
3   See CPR 52.8.
4   CPR 52.8(5). The High Court judge cannot give permission to appeal.

5   CPR 52.8(5). The latter procedure will, in many cases, be the most efficient, for if the judge considering the application for permission to appeal concludes that there is an arguable point, then there is likely to be little point in further examination of whether the case passes a filter whose purpose is to exclude unarguable cases.

6   As in *R (Smith) v Parole Board* [2003] 1 WLR 2548 at paragraph 20. *R (West) v Lloyd's* [2004] 3 All ER 251.

7   As in *R (Abassi) v Secretary of State for Foreign and Commonwealth Affairs* [2003] UKHRR 76 at paragraph 2.

8   As in *R v Take-over Panel, ex p Datafin* [1987] 1 QB 815 at 834F.

9   See CPR 52.9 and *R (Parekh) v Upper Tribunal (Immigration and Asylum Chamber)* [2013] EWCA Civ 679.

20.77 In civil cases the ability to appeal, at the stage of permission to apply for judicial review, from the Court of Appeal to the House of Lords was held in *R (Burkett) v Hammersmith and Fulham LBC* to depend on whether the Court of Appeal gave permission to appeal from the decision of the High Court. In civil cases when the Court of Appeal has refused permission to appeal in the face of a first instance refusal of permission to seek judicial review, the House of Lords had no jurisdiction to give leave to appeal.[1] If, by contrast, the Court of Appeal grants permission to appeal, then a decision to dismiss the appeal, or even a decision to refuse permission to apply for judicial review in the event that that was determined by the Court of Appeal, could be the subject of an application for leave to appeal to the House of Lords.[2] This would be the appropriate course to follow if a matter is considered potentially suitable for consideration by the House of Lords. It is submitted that the position is the same with respect to an appeal to the Supreme Court, where s 40(2) of the Constitutional Reform Act 2005 provides that an appeal lies to the Supreme Court from "'any order or judgment of the Court of Appeal in England and Wales in civil proceedings'.[3]

1   See the analysis of *R v Secretary of State for Trade and Industry, ex p Eastaway* [2000] 1 WLR 2222 by Lord Steyn in *R (Burkett) v Hammersmith and Fulham LBC* [2002] 1 WLR 1593 at paragraph 13, p 1598. This relied on the approach set out in *Lane v Esdaile* [1891] AC 210, to the effect that whenever a power is given to a court or tribunal by legislation to grant or refuse leave to appeal, the decision of that authority is, from the very nature of the thing, final and conclusive.

2   *R (Burkett) v Hammersmith and Fulham LBC* [2002] 1 WLR 1593.

3   See paragraph 1.2.20 of Practice Direction 1 of the Supreme Court. If it is plainly a matter that should go to the Supreme Court, the Court of Appeal could grant leave; if not, the Court of Appeal would refuse leave so that the Supreme Court could determine whether it would hear an appeal.

20.78 In criminal matters there is no appeal to the Court of Appeal.[1] The analysis in *Burkett* suggests that in a criminal case a refusal to grant permission to apply for judicial review could not be the subject of an application for leave to appeal to the Supreme Court. For these purposes, whether or not any right of appeal at all is preserved is a matter for the Administrative Court.[2] This can be achieved if the Administrative Court grants permission to apply but refuses the substantive application for judicial review and certifies that a question of general public importance arises. If this occurs the claimant can petition the Supreme Court for permission to appeal against the decision to dismiss the claim.[3]

1   Section 18(1) of the Senior Courts Act 1981; *R (Aru) v Chief Constable of Merseyside Police* [2004] 1 WLR 1697; *Hull and Holderness Magistrates' Court v Darroch* [2016] EWCA Civ 1220.

2   And, even in a criminal matter, this can be a single judge rather than a Divisional Court.
3   See, for example. *R v DPP, ex p Camelot plc* (1998) 10 Admin LR 93 at 105E–G.

20.79 The position of a defendant or other party who objects to the grant of permission is considered in CHAPTER **19.**[1]

1   See **19.45.**

Appeals against interim remedies

20.80 Appeals may be made against interim orders.[1] Permission to appeal is required either from the Administrative Court, or from the Court of Appeal itself.[2] It is important to note that where the Administrative Court refuses an application for an interim remedy without a hearing, if the claimant wishes to pursue the application, it should first be renewed at a hearing before the Administrative Court. It is only if an interim remedy is refused at an oral hearing that the claimant should seek to appeal to the Court of Appeal.[3]

1   An example of such an appeal is *R (Wilkinson) v Broadmoor Special Hospital Authority* [2002] 1 WLR 419, an appeal against an order refusing permission to cross-examine the makers of witness statements.
2   See CPR PD 52A paragraphs 3.5, 4.1 and 4.6.
3   See *R (MD (Afghanistan)) v Secretary of State for the Home Department* [2012] EWCA Civ 194; [2012] 1 WLR 2422, para 21.

Parties to an appeal

20.81 In most instances the parties to an appeal will be the same as those party to the decision at first instance. CPR 51.2 defines the 'appellant' as the person who brings or seek to bring the appeal; and the 'respondent' as a person other than the appellant who was a party to the proceedings in the lower court. These definitions might appear to beg some questions. First, who is capable of being the appellant – does it include a person who was an interested party in the proceedings below, or a person who intervened in those proceedings? Section 151 of the Senior Courts Act 1981 defines a party as any person served with the proceedings in accordance with the rules and any person who has intervened. Thus, as a matter of principle, either an interested party or an intervener can seek to appeal a decision of a lower court. However, it is important to realise that all appeals are discretionary in the sense that permission to appeal is required. Thus, although an intervener could apply for permission to appeal, that permission will not be granted unless there is a substantial and proper issue to be determined, and the intervener is an appropriate appellant for that purpose. This point is also material generally as to the role of interveners at the appeal stage. Even though an intervener is a 'party' to the proceedings under the provisions of the Senior Courts Act 1981 (by reason of his participation at first instance) it does not follow that he may continue to intervene as of right in an appeal.[1] The discretion to permit the intervention is within the control of the appeal court.[2] In addition, the Court of Appeal can itself join additional persons as parties to the appeal even if they were not parties at first instance.[3]

1 This explains the wording of CPR 52.1(3)(e) to the effect that the 'respondent' is a person who
   was a party below who is also a person affected by the appeal.
2 For examples of the exercise of this discretion, see *R v Licensing Authority, ex p Smith Kline
   & French Laboratories Limited* [1988] COD 62; and R v Department of Health, ex p Source
   Informatics Limited [2000] COD 114.
3 See, for example *DK v Bryn Aleyn Community (Holdings) Limited (in liquidation)* [2003]
   EWCA Civ 783; *MA Holdings Ltd v George Wimpey UK Ltd and Tewkesbury BC* [2008] 1
   WLR 1649; *Re W (a child)* [2016] EWCA Civ 1140.

Appeals following a final determination

20.82 Appeals are made against orders,[1] not against reasons given in a
judgment.'[2] Thus a party who has been wholly successful cannot appeal merely
as to the correctness of an aspect of the reasoning of the court.[3]

By way of an exception to these principles, in *Morina v Secretary of State for
Work and Pensions*,[4] the Court of Appeal held that it was not precluded from
hearing appeals by the Secretary of State on jurisdictional points from a social
security commissioner, even though the Secretary of State had 'won' before the
commissioner. In each of the cases, the Secretary of State had lost on
jurisdictional points, but won on the merits, so the Secretary of State was the
overall winner below. However, the appeal was governed by s 15 of the Social
Security Act 1998 and not s 16 of the Senior Courts Act 1981. This provided
for an appeal on a question of law relating to 'any decision of a commissioner'
as opposed to an appeal which lies against 'any judgment or order of the
High Court.' In *Morina*, the Court of Appeal considered that the commissioner had made two 'decisions': first, that he had jurisdiction to hear the
appeal and secondly, that the appeal should be dismissed on the merits.[5]

1 This includes orders as to costs, see *R v Holderness Borough Council, ex p James Robert
   Developments Limited* (1993) 66 P&CR 46; and also an order as to the grant of relief *R v
   IRC, ex p National Association of Self-Employed etc* [1982] AC 617. If the appeal concerns
   other matters in addition to costs, but the appeal on those other matters fails, see *Wheeler v
   Somerfield* [1966] 2 QB 94.
2 See Senior Courts Act 1981, s 16.
3 *Lake v Lake* [1955] P 336; and *Noga v Abacha (No.3)* [2003] 1 WLR 307 per Waller LJ at
   paragraphs 26–28. The position would be different if the specific factual finding/point of
   reasoning has been made by way of declaration.
4 [2007] EWCA Civ 749; [2007] 1 WLR 3033.
5 The court was anxious not to encourage a raft of 'winner's appeals'. The judge stated that he
   would expect the Court of Appeal to refuse the successful party below permission to appeal
   'against an immaterial finding of no general significance': see paragraph [10].

20.83 As to whether or not the opportunity to appeal exists (and, if so, to
where) the civil/criminal distinction is important. In criminal cases, the only
possible appeal is to the Supreme Court on a point of law of general public
importance. In civil matters, there is the possibility of appeal first to the Court
of Appeal (with either the permission of the Administrative Court, or of
the Court of Appeal), and thereafter to the Supreme Court (again, either with
the permission of the Court of Appeal or of the Supreme Court itself).

20.84 An appeal does not usually of itself operate as a stay of the judgment
below.[1] The normal rule is that there should be no stay.[2] If an application for
a stay is made, a balance must be struck between the risks of refusal and the

risks of making such an order.[3]

[1] See CPR 52.16. *R (Pharis) v Secretary of State for the Home Department (Practice Note)* [2004] 1 WLR 2590 and *WK (Eritrea) v Secretary of State for the Home Department* [2016] EWCA Civ 502 are to the same effect, and also deal with the position in immigration claims if removal directions have been set (per Brooke LJ at paragraphs 12–20). If the appeal is from the Immigration and Asylum Chambers of the Upper Tribunal, such an appeal operates as an automatic stay of proceedings: CPR 52.16(b).

[2] *Leicester Circuits Limited v Coates Brothers plc* [2002] EWCA Civ 474. In *DEFRA v Downs* [2009] EWCA Civ 257 at [8]–[9], Sullivan LJ stated that a stay is the exception rather than the rule, and that the solid grounds which an applicant must put forward are normally 'some form of irremediable harm' if no stay is granted.

[3] See *R (van Hoogstraten) v Governor of Belmarsh Prison* [2002] EWHC 2015 (Admin); *Gater Assets Ltd v Nak Naftogaz Ukrainiy* [2008] EWCA Civ 51; *Hammond Suddard Solicitors v Agrichem International Holdings Ltd* [2001] EWCA Civ 2065 per Clarke LJ at paragraph 22; *Wittman (UK) Ltd v Walldav Engineering SA* [2007] EWCA Civ 521. A stay may be granted on terms: *Contract Facilities Limited v Estate of Rees (deceased)* [2003] EWCA Civ 465.

20.85 The hearing and determination of appeals is governed by CPR 52.21(3): an appeal is to be allowed if the decision was 'wrong',[1] or 'unjust because of a serious procedural or other irregularity in the proceedings in the lower court'.[2] On appeal, the court has a discretion to permit argument on both points not raised below, but this discretion is usually exercised sparingly.[3] The nature of the court's function on an application for judicial review means that it will be rare for new evidence to be admissible at the appeal stage.[4] If evidence that is genuinely relevant to the judicial review claim emerges only at the appeal stage, the court will apply a *Ladd v Marshall* type approach.[5] Although, in principle, the discretion to admit new evidence on an appeal in a public law claim might be wider than in a private law action, in practice, the discretion is one that is only exercised in exceptional circumstances.

[1] In relation to whether the exercise of a judicial discretion was 'wrong' see the decisions in *Tanfern Limited v Cameron MacDonald* [2000] 1 WLR 1311; *AEI Rediffusion Music v Phonographic Performance Limited* [1999] 1 WLR 1507 per Lord Woolf MR at 1523; and *Price v Price* [2003] 3 All ER 911; *Aldi Stores Ltd v WSP Group Ltd* [2007] EWCA Civ 1260; [2008] 1 WLR 748; *Stuart v Goldberg* [2008] EWCA Civ 2 at [76]. In principle, it must be shown that the exercise of the direction below was based on some error of principle, or on the basis of some immaterial (and important) consideration. The latter does not provide licence to interfere merely because the appellate court would have exercised the discretion differently: there is a 'generous ambit' within which reasonable disagreement should be tolerated.

[2] This ground can bite even if the decision itself was correct: see *Storer v British Gas* [2000] 1 WLR 1237. However, in most instances the procedural irregularity must have had a significant impact on the proceedings at first instance: for example, *Hayes v Transco plc* [2003] EWCA Civ 1261 (exclusion of evidence/cross-examination on a point central to the claim.

[3] For an example, see *R (H) v Secretary of State for the Home Department* [2002] 3 WLR 967 at paragraphs 3 and 47. On the facts of that case, entertaining the new ground would have required the attendance of new parties, both as 'wrongdoers' and possibly also as interveners. As to the general importance of finality in litigation as a factor against new points etc, see *Jones v MBNA International Bank* (CA) 30 June 2000, per May LJ at paragraph 52.

[4] See *R (Goldsmith) v London Borough of Wandsworth* [2004] EWCA Civ 1170, (2004) 7 CCL Rep 472 per Wall LJ at paragraphs 4–9.

[5] *Ladd v Marshall* [1954] 1 WLR 1489. See **20.33** above. For examples of the approach generally, see *Hertfordshire Investments Ltd v Bubb* [2000] 1 WLR 2318; and in the judicial review context, see *R v Home Secretary, ex p Momin Ali* [1984] 1 WLR 663 per Sir John Donaldson MR at 669E–670E, per Fox LJ at 673H, per Sir Stephen Brown LJ at 673–4; and *R v Secretary of State for Education, ex p Amraf Training plc* (2001) Times, 28 June. In *R v Chief Constable of Sussex, ex p International Trader's Ferry Limited* [1998] 3 WLR 1260, the interests of justice required a departure from this strict approach.

Permission to appeal

20.86 The test for granting permission to appeal is whether the appeal either has a real prospect of success, or there is some other compelling reason why the appeal should be heard.[1] If the appeal is a second appeal, permission will only be granted either on the 'compelling reason' basis, or if the appeal raises an important point of principle or practice.[2] A real prospect of success is a prospect that is realistic as opposed to fanciful.[3] What is a 'compelling reason' is more difficult to pin down, particularly since it is an alternative criterion, applicable even if the appeal has no realistic prospect of success. The best statement of what the 'compelling reason' rubric might mean is that given by the Court of Appeal in *Uphill v BRB (Residuary) Ltd* and *Smith v Cosworth Casting Processes Limited*.[4] First, it is unlikely that the court will find that there is a compelling reason to give permission for a second appeal unless it forms the view that the prospects of success are very high. Secondly, the fact that the prospects of success are very high will not necessarily be sufficient. An examination of all the circumstances of the case may lead the court to conclude that, despite the existence of very good prospects of success, there is no compelling reason for giving permission. Thirdly, there may be circumstances where there is a compelling reason to grant permission even where the prospects of success are not very high. This may occur where the court is satisfied that there are good grounds for believing that the hearing was tainted by some procedural irregularity so as to render the first appeal unfair.

However, the *Uphill* guidelines should not be permitted to ossify into a rule. In *Esure Insurance Ltd v Direct Line Insurance plc*[5] the court held that the complexity of the case and the real prospect of showing that the judge had incorrectly exercised his appellate function were sufficient to amount to 'compelling reasons' for allowing a second appeal.

It is submitted that the 'compelling reasons' test should also include cases which should be considered at appellate level as a matter of public interest, or in order to clarify the law. The latter might be thought to be already well-covered by the real prospect of success criterion, and in many instances it will be – if the law is unclear there will in all likelihood be a realistic prospect that the appeal could succeed. However, this might not be the position if the existence of Court of Appeal authority renders it inevitable that the appeal to the Court of Appeal will fail, but the point is one that could properly be considered by the Supreme Court. In such a case the Court of Appeal can grant permission to appeal but then dismiss the substantive appeal leaving the way open to the appellant to seek permission to be heard in the Supreme Court.[6] Thus, in practice, the 'compelling reason' rubric is a useful and adaptable tool.

---

[1]   CPR 52.6(1). In relation to the exercise of the discretion to permit applications for permission to appeal made late, see *Sayers v Clarke Walker* [2002] 1 WLR 3095 and *R (Hysaj) v Secretary of State for the Home Department* [2014] EWCA Civ 1633; [2015] 1 W.L.R. 2472, exercising the discretion by reference to the checklist at CPR 3.9.

[2]   CPR 52.7(2). If the appeal is from a specialist tribunal a more cautious approach is appropriate to whether or not permission should be granted: see *Cooke v Secretary of State for Social Security* [2002] 3 All ER 279 per Hale LJ at paragraph 15; and *Napp Pharmaceutical Holdings Limited v Director General of Fair Trading* [2002] 4 All ER 376.

[3]   See *Swain v Hillman* [2001] 1 All ER 91; and *Tanfern v Cameron-MacDonald (Practice Note)* [2000] 1 WLR 1311 per Brooke LJ at paragraph 21.

[4]   [2005] EWCA Civ 60; [2005] 1 WLR 2070 and [1997] 1 WLR 1538.

[5]   [2008] EWCA Civ 842.

⁶   This was the course adopted in *Beedell v West Ferry Printers Limited* [2001] ICR 962 per
    Mummery LJ at paragraphs 9–16. In *PR (Sri Lanka) v Secretary of State for the Home
    Department* [2011] EWCA Civ 988, the Court of Appeal rejected argument that there was
    some other compelling reason because removal would expose the applicants to the risk of
    serious harm in violation of international obligations. In this context, compelling meant legally
    compelling, rather than compelling from a political or emotional point of view. The question
    is not whether there could be drastic consequences, but whether there was a compelling reason
    why the issue on which the appellants had twice failed should be subject to a third judicial
    process.

20.87   Under CPR 52.18(1)(b), the Court of Appeal may set aside the grant of
permission to appeal, but only where there is a compelling reason to do so.¹
Similarly, it is open to the court to attach conditions to the grant of permission
where such conditions had not previously been imposed, but if any such
application is to be made, it should be made promptly.²

¹   See *Nathan v Smilovitch* [2002] EWCA Civ 759. Compelling reasons may exist where the
    materials before the judge granting permission were so inaccurate that it is clear that, on full
    information, permission would not have been granted – *Hertsmere Borough Council v Harty*
    [2001] EWCA Civ 1238; or where some decisive authority has been overlooked, *Smilovitch*
    (above); or where there is a want of jurisdiction, *Athletic Union of Constantinople v NBA (No
    2)* [2002] 1 WLR 2863; *Angel Airlines SA v Dean & Dean* [2006] EWCA Civ 1505. The fact
    that changing circumstances mean that the appeal has become, in substance an appeal about
    the costs order made below is not necessarily a compelling reason, *Barings Bank plc (in
    liquidation) v Coopers & Lybrand* [2002] EWCA Civ 1155. See also *Obsession Hair and Day
    Spa Ltd v Hi-Lite Electrical Ltd* [2011] EWCA Civ 1148.
²   *Okta Crude Oil Refinery v Moil-Coal Trading Co* [2003] 2 Lloyds Rep. 645. In rare cases, an
    application can be made on the basis of the conditions imposed at the time permission was
    granted.

20.88   In relation to appeals to the Supreme Court, the standard to apply on
civil matters is whether, in the opinion of the Appeal Panel, the appeal raises
an arguable point of law of general public importance which ought to be
considered by the Supreme Court at that time, bearing in mind that the matter
will already have been the subject of judicial decision and may already have
been reviewed on appeal.¹

On criminal matters the appeal must have been certified by the High Court as
involving a point of law of general public importance. In such cases it is then
for the Supreme Court to determine whether the point is one that ought to be
considered by the House.²

Section 12 of the Administration of Justice Act 1969 provides the mechanism
for so-called 'leap-frog' appeals from the High Court to the Supreme Court.
The restrictions were loosened by the Criminal Justice and Courts Act 2015
and this option is now available where there is a point of law of general public
importance and either:

(a)   it relates to either the meaning of a legislative provision that has been
      fully considered by the High Court, or to a point of law on which there
      is already binding Court of Appeal or Supreme Court authority;
      or

(b)   (i) the proceedings entail a decision relating to a matter of national
      importance; (ii) the result of the proceedings is so significant that a
      hearing by the Supreme Court is justified; or (iii) the judge is satisfied
      that the benefits of earlier consideration by the Supreme Court out-
      weigh the benefits of consideration by the Court of Appeal.

Even if these conditions are met, the judge is not required to make the certificate.[3] Second, if the first set of conditions are met, the Supreme Court itself must grant permission to pursue the appeal.[4] If the Supreme Court grants leave, no appeal from the decision of the judge to which the certificate relates shall lie to the Court of Appeal. If, however, the Supreme Court grants permission to appeal subject to conditions, and the appellant does not wish to appeal subject to those conditions, then his right of appeal to the Court of Appeal revives.[5]

[1]   Supreme Court Practice Direction 3, paragraph 3.3.3.
[2]   Administration of Justice Act 1960, s 1(1)–(2).
[3]   See *IRC v Church Commissioners for England* [1975] 1 WLR 251. For an example of a case in which a certificate was granted, see *Ealing Borough Council v Race Relations Board* [1972] A.C. 342 and *R (Miller) v Secretary of State for Exiting the European Union* [2017] UKSC 5..
[4]   See Administration of Justice Act 1969, s 13.
[5]   See *R (Jones) v Ceridigion County Council* [2007] UKHL 24; [2007] 1 WLR 1400.

20.89 Under CPR 3.11 and *Practice Direction 3C – Civil Restraint Orders*, litigants who make hopeless claims may find that their ability to commence or continue litigation is subject to restrictions under a civil restraint order. Provision is made for various types of civil restraint orders. They can be made where the court has dismissed an application or on its own initiative has struck out a statement of case, and considers that the application or claim was totally without merit. An 'application' for these purposes includes applications for permission to apply for judicial review and those for permission to appeal. Where a court dealing with such an application considers it to be totally without merit, CPR 3.3(7) and CPR 23.12 provide that the court's order must record that fact, and the court must, at the same time, consider whether it is appropriate to make a civil restraint order. Where a judge refuses permission to appeal without a hearing and considers that the application is totally without merit, the judge may make an order that the person seeking permission may not request the decision to be reconsidered at a hearing: CPR 52.4(3).

COSTS

20.90 The court has a very broad jurisdiction to consider questions relating to costs in all civil matters. This applies equally to first instance and appellate courts. The jurisdiction is derived from s 51(1) of the Senior Courts Act 1981. This provides that the costs of, and incidental to, any proceedings are in the discretion of the court and the court has full powers to determine by whom and to what extent such costs are to be paid. The general principle is that the unsuccessful party will normally be ordered to pay the costs of the successful party. However, other orders are frequently made.[1] In exercising the general discretion, the court will have regard to all the circumstances of the case including the conduct of all the parties, whether a party has succeeded on all or part of his case and any payment into court or admissible offer to settle.[2] Significant amendments were made to costs rules as a result of the Jackson Reforms. These took effect from 1 April 2013. However, the cost management and cost budgeting provisions in Part II of CPR rule 3 do not automatically apply to judicial review claims. The rules apply only to Part 7 multi-track cases, although courts have a discretion to apply the rules to any other proceedings where the court so orders.[3]

[1] CPR 44.2(2).
[2] CPR 44.2(4).
[3] CPR 3.12.

Costs at the permission stage

20.91 The award of costs at the permission stage is discussed in CHAPTER **19.**[1]

[1] See 19.80.

The exercise of the discretion generally

20.92 Under the pre-CPR rules,[1] there was a presumption that costs should 'follow the event'. This is no longer the case. Although the 'general rule' is that the unsuccessful party pays the costs of the successful party, the court is entirely free to make a different order[2] The CPR encourages the courts to make precise orders to reflect the outcome of different issues.[3] CPR 44.2 sets out a non-exhaustive list of possible orders which the court might make. The decision in each case will, of necessity turn on its facts. It is impossible to list any firm rules that yield predictable results. However, there are some themes, which have emerged from the cases.

[1] RSC Ord 62, r 3(3).
[2] CPR 44.2(2).
[3] See *AEI Rediffusion Music Ltd v Phonographic Performance Ltd* [1999] 1 WLR 1507 at 1522H–1523B, where Lord Woolf MR hoped that this would encourage parties to be selective in their choice of arguments.

20.93 The starting point is that the approach to costs is the same in judicial review as in other civil proceedings.[1] However, as each decision is tied to the facts of the individual case, there are some considerations that are specific to the judicial review context.

[1] *R (Smeaton) v Secretary of State for Health* [2002] EWHC 886 (Admin) at paragraph 8.

20.94 The court will generally look at the substance of the matter rather than who was technically 'successful' in the proceedings. For example, where a claimant wins on a key issue but failed on the facts, a defendant might expect to pay a substantial proportion of the claimant's costs.[1] If a claimant establishes that a defendant has acted unlawfully, but the court declines to grant a remedy, whether the claimant or defendant is to be treated as the successful party will depend on the particular circumstances of the case.[2]

[1] For example, a defendant was required to pay 35% of the claimant's costs in *R (Watts) v Bedford Primary Care Trust* [2003] EWHC 2401 (Admin).
[2] *R v Trafford Borough Council, ex p Colonel Foods Ltd* [1990] COD 351 and compare *R v Swale Borough Council and Medway Ports Authority, ex p Royal Society for the Protection of Birds* (1990) 2 Admin LR 760 where the claimant was successful, no remedy was awarded and no order was made as to costs. See also *R (Hunt) v North Somerset Council* [2013] EWCA Civ 1483, where the appellant succeeded on the legal issues but had failed to achieve any relief because the court considered the claim had been brought too late. The Court of Appeal held that it would be wrong in principle to award any costs to the appellant, as the appeal had been of no practical value to him and had always been destined to fail. The local authority, having

been successful, was in principle entitled to its costs. However, it had resisted the appeal not only on the basis that relief should be refused as a matter of discretion, but also on the two substantive grounds, upon which it had lost. In the circumstances, the local authority was entitled to recover 50% of its costs from the appellant.

20.95 The court may also look to the purpose of bringing the judicial review. For example, where a claimant brings a test case which will have far-reaching implications, a court might consider it wrong for a person of insubstantial means to bear his own costs.[1] In some proceedings, even where a claimant wins, he or she may be ordered to bear the costs of the proceedings where litigation is commenced in order to obtain an unnecessary result.[2] However, if the claimant in judicial review proceedings succeeded in establishing that the defendant had acted unlawfully, the Supreme Court has held that some good reason would have to be shown why he should not recover his reasonable costs, even if the judgment had not resulted in any practical benefit to him.[3]

[1]   *Minister for the Civil Service v Oakes (No 2)* [2003] EWHC 3314 (Ch) Lindsay J.
[2]   *Rusbridger v HM Attorney General* [2003] UKHL 38, [2004] 1 AC 357.
[3]   *R (Hunt) v North Somerset Council* [2015] UKSC 51; [2015] 1 WLR 3575.

20.96 Under the CPR, the courts attempt to apportion the costs, to take into account the proportion of points upon which the claimant succeeded, even where the defendant was successful overall. A court will be likely to consider the reasonableness of taking the unsuccessful points, the manner in which such points were taken, the extra costs and time taken up by the particular issue, the extent to which the point was interrelated with the points upon which the party was successful and, more globally, the extent to which it is just to deprive the successful party of all or any of its costs on this basis.[1] An example of this is *R (Turpin) v Commissioner for Local Administration*,[2] where the defendants were required to pay 80% of the claimant's costs to take account of the fact that one of three grounds of judicial review had failed. Where a claimant takes futile or hopeless points, the court will take particular care to reduce any award for costs in approximate proportion to the fraction of such points to encourage litigants to be selective.[3] However, a court may refrain from reducing a claimant's costs where pursuing an unsuccessful issue has not lengthened the preparation, evidence or hearing in any way.[4]

[1]   See the guidance from Neuberger J in *Antonelli v Allen (No 2)* (2000) *Times*, 8 December.
[2]   [2001] EWHC Admin 503, [2003] LGR 133. For recent examples, see *R (Essex County Council) v Secretary of State for Education* [2012] EWHC 1460 (Admin) and *R (Luton Borough Council) v Secretary of State for Education* [2011] EWHC 556 (Admin).
[3]   *R (Bateman and Bateman) v Legal Services Commission* [2001] EWHC Admin 797, [2002] ACD 29.
[4]   See, for example, *R v Kirklees Metropolitan Borough Council, ex p Beaumont* [2001] ELR 204.

20.97 The court (so far) has refrained from ordering the payment of costs to a successful defendant for refusing to explore the possibility of seeking recourse to alternative dispute resolution (ADR). This was so even where the reason for the refusal was that the defendant was confident of winning and did not wish to incur the associated costs.[1] However, the court will only deprive a party of costs on this basis where it considers that the successful party acted unreasonably in refusing to agree to ADR.[2] Relevant factors in this regard would include the nature of the dispute, the merits of the case, the extent to which other settlement methods have been attempted, the costs of the ADR, whether any delay caused by the ADR would be prejudicial and whether the ADR would have a reasonable prospect of success.[3] It should also be borne in mind that a mediator may be able to provide solutions which are beyond the power of the court to provide.[4] In *R (Crawford) v University of Newcastle upon Tyne*,[5] the unsuccessful claimant argued that the university should be deprived of its costs because it had unreasonably refused to engage in mediation. Grubb J held that in a public law context, ADR could include proceedings before an ombudsman, and included proceedings before the Office of the Independent Adjudicator for Higher Education. An unreasonable refusal to engage in ADR before such bodies could have cost consequences for a public body. Conversely, refusing more traditional ADR, or even maintaining silence in the face of an invitation to participate in traditional ADR, might be excused where proceedings that amount to ADR are in hand before an ombudsman or the Office of the Independent Adjudicator for Higher Education.

[1] *Dunnett v Railtrack plc* [2002] EWCA Civ 303, [2002] 1 WLR 2434 and see *R (Nurse Prescribers Ltd) v Secretary of State for Health* [2004] EWHC 403 (Admin).
[2] *Halsey v Milton Keynes General NHS Trust* [2004] 1 WLR 3002. See also *R (Crawford) v University of Newcastle upon Tyne* [2014] EWHC 1197 (Admin)
[3] *Halsey v Milton Keynes General NHS Trust* [2004] 1 WLR 3002 at paragraph 16, and see *Hurst v Leeming* [2003] 1 Lloyd's Rep 379.
[4] *Dunnett v Railtrack* [2002] EWCA Civ 303 at paragraph 14, quoted with approval in *Halsey v Milton Keynes General NHS Trust* [2004] 1 WLR 3002 at paragraph 16 and see *R (Johnson) v Reading Borough Council* [2004] EWHC 765 (Admin), [2004] ACD 72, QBD where the defendant was awarded its costs in an unsuccessful judicial review, notwithstanding that the claimants had requested ADR in a letter before claim.
[5] [2014] EWHC 1197 (Admin).

20.98 The court will also consider any admissible offers to settle that have been made, which is not an offer to which costs consequences under Part 36 apply.[1] If the successful party fails to better an offer made without prejudice save as to costs, the court may decline to award the successful party its costs after the date of the offer and may permit the unsuccessful party to recover its costs after the date of the offer.

The principles governing Part 36 offers also apply in judicial review claims. In *Hemming (t/a Simply Pleasure Ltd) v Westminster City Council*,[2] the defendant local authority had refused the claimant's Part 36 offer early in proceedings and the claimant obtained a more advantageous award at trial. Keith J subsequently ordered the defendant to pay the claimant's costs on an indemnity basis, notwithstanding that the claim concerned the 'as yet untested new legal regime' under the Provision of Services Regulations 2009.[3] The Court of Appeal, while expressing some sympathy for the defendant and hinting that the order was a harsh one, found that it was nonetheless within the discretion of the trial judge. However, the Court of Appeal suggested that in a test case about a new legal regime, an unsuccessful public law defendant who has rejected a Part 36 offer has a good argument for saying that it should not be subject to the CPR 36.17(3) consequences.

[1] CPR 44.2(4)(c).
[2] [2013] EWCA Civ 591.
[3] [2012] EWHC 1260 (Admin).

20.99 The court will also consider procedural compliance when making orders as to costs. In particular, regard will be had to compliance or noncompliance with the Judicial Review Pre-Action Protocol where it applies.[1] The court may also take into account a failure to file an acknowledgment of service.[2]

[1] See paragraph 7 of the Protocol.
[2] CPR 54.9(2), but see *R (Kelly) v Hammersmith and Fulham London Borough Council* [2004] EWHC 435 (Admin), (2004) 7 CCL Rep 542, QBD where the defendant was awarded costs despite the fact that the acknowledgment of service was deficient where the claim was misconceived.

20.100 When the court comes to assess the costs, the court will consider whether or not the costs incurred were 'proportionate' to the outcome in any individual case. Proportionality is considered, both globally and on an item-by-item basis. No greater sum can be recovered than that which was necessary had the litigation been conducted in a proportionate manner.[1] Where the amount of costs is to be assessed on the standard basis, the court will only allow costs which are proportionate to the matters in issue. Costs which are disproportionate in amount may be disallowed or reduced even if they were reasonably or necessarily incurred.[2] Any doubt as to whether costs were reasonably or proportionately incurred or are reasonable and proportionate in amount will be resolved in favour of the paying party.

Costs incurred will be proportionate if they bear a reasonable relationship to the sums in issue in the proceedings, the value of any non-monetary relief in issue in the proceedings, the complexity of the litigation, any additional work generated by the conduct of the paying party, and any wider factors involved in the proceedings, such as reputation or public importance.[3]

[1] For a discussion of this, see *Lownds v Home Office* [2002] EWCA Civ 365, [2002] 1 WLR 2450.
[2] CPR 44.3(2).
[3] CPR 44.3(5).

20.101 Costs in judicial review can be awarded on an indemnity basis.[1] The courts have a wide discretion in this area. However, the general approach is that the conduct of a party would need to be 'unreasonable to a high degree' before costs are awarded on this basis.[2] In the judicial review context, the matters which have been considered to be important have been whether the conduct of a party has been generally unreasonable throughout the proceedings, such that it falls far short of the standard to be expected of a public authority conducting judicial review proceedings, and whether a party has failed to comply with its duty to give full and frank disclosure.[3]

[1] CPR 44.3(1)(b). *Kiam v MGN Ltd (No 2)* [2002] EWCA Civ 66, [2002] 1 WLR 2810.
[2] *R (Banks) v Secretary of State for the Environment, Food and Rural Affairs* [2004] EWHC 1031 (Admin) where Sullivan J commented that obtaining information from DEFRA was like 'drawing teeth without an anaesthetic'. For recent examples of awards of indemnity costs against public bodies, see *R (O) v Secretary of State for the Home Department* [2010] EWHC 709 (Admin) and *R (CPW) v Harrow Crown Court* [2014] EWHC 2061 (Admin).
[3] *R (Al-Sweady) v Secretary of State for Defence* [2009] EWHC 2387 (Admin), where the court described the Secretary of State's approach to disclosure as 'lamentable'.

20.102 Under CPR 44.2(8), where the court has ordered a party to pay costs subject to detailed assessment, it will order that party to pay a reasonable sum on account of costs, unless there is a good reason not to do so. An interim payment on account of costs should generally be ordered in favour of a successful party where there has been a full trial.[1]

[1] *Mars UK LTd v Teknowledge Ltd (Costs)* [1999] 2 Costs LR 44. The general principle is that the claimant is entitled to something by way of costs and he should be paid it without delay. However, the court has to take into account all the circumstances in a particular case, including the unsuccessful party's wish to appeal, the relative financial position of each party, and the court's overriding objective to deal with cases justly.

Costs protection: public interest litigation

20.103 The tension between the costs rules of adversarial civil litigation and the judicial review context is most apparent where litigation is conducted in the public interest. In these cases, it becomes more difficult to see why an unsuccessful claimant should pay costs as a matter of course.

20.104 Where a matter raises a legal question of genuine public concern, the courts have sometimes held that it is inappropriate to make a costs order against a claimant, even where the judicial review is wholly unsuccessful.[1] This approach was adopted where issues of public health and well-being were at stake and so it was important that the issues were properly examined.[2] The court has also declined to deprive a claimant of its costs with regard to unsuccessful issues where 'fundamental human rights and the liberty of the subject' were involved such that there was a public interest in the issues beyond that of the individual parties. In those circumstances it would be wrong to discourage any party from raising any proper and reasonable argument even if it ultimately proved unsuccessful.[3]

[1] See the pre-CPR case of *R v Secretary of State for the Environment, ex p Shelter* [1997] COD 49.
[2] *R (Friends of the Earth and Greenpeace) v Secretary of State for Environment Food and Rural Affairs* [2001] EWCA Civ 1950; *R (Greenpeace Ltd) v Secretary of State for Environment, Food and Rural Affairs* [2005] EWCA Civ 1656.
[3] *R (Munjaz) v Mersey Care NHS Trust* [2003] EWCA Civ 1036, [2003] 3 WLR 1505 at paragraph 89.

20.105 It should be noted that matters involving children are a special case. The general practice is that no orders are made as to costs in cases involving the welfare of children, unless a party is guilty of unreasonable conduct. This is in view of the importance of the child's welfare and the best interest of the child.[1]

[1] *C v FC (Children Proceedings: Costs)* [2004] 1 FLR 362.

20.106 Despite some regret expressed in judicial dicta, there is no power to award costs to claimants from central funds, however meritorious the individual case.[1]

[1] Brooke LJ lamented this in *R (Davies) v Birmingham Deputy Coroner* [2004] EWCA Civ 207, [2004] 3 All ER 543 at paragraph 44.

20.107 Another possible response to public interest litigation is the costs order, protecting a party to judicial review proceedings against the risk of a substantial costs order should he be unsuccessful or limiting the amount of costs which might be ordered. The circumstances in which such orders can be made are now set out in the Criminal Justice and Courts Act 2015 (see 20.117 below); however, the following provides background, which has largely been reflected in the 2015 Act.

In *R v Lord Chancellor, ex p Child Poverty Action Group*,[1] Dyson J stated that such an order could be made in exceptional circumstances in litigation that amounted to a public interest challenge. He stated:

(1)   the court must be satisfied that the issues raised are truly of general public importance:

(2)   it must also be satisfied that it has a sufficient appreciation of the merits of the claim that it can conclude that it is in the public interest to make the order;

(3)   it must have regard to the financial resources of the parties, and the amount of costs likely to be in issue; and

(4)   it will be more likely to make an order where the defendant has a superior capacity to bear the costs of the proceedings than the claimant, and where it is satisfied that the claimant would be likely to discontinue the proceedings if an order were not made.

An order may be made even before permission has been granted.[2]

[1]   [1999] 1 WLR 347 at 358C–E.
[2]   *R (Campaign for Nuclear Disarmament) v Prime Minister* [2002] EWHC 2712 (Admin), [2003] ACD 83. This case also emphasised that an order should only be made in exceptional cases.

20.108 In *R (Refugee Legal Centre) v Secretary of State for the Home Department*[1] (a post-CPR case) Brooke LJ doubted the continuing relevance of the *Child Poverty Action Group*, and stated that this matter should be given careful scrutiny. He made a preliminary protective costs order. The matter was never given full consideration, however, as the full protective costs order was later made with the defendant's consent.

[1]   [2004] EWCA Civ 1239.

20.109 In *R (Corner House) v Trade and Industry Secretary*, Brooke LJ took the opportunity to carry out the 'careful scrutiny' he had suggested was necessary.[1] The court endorsed Dyson J's first, third and fourth points, but in relation, to the second criterion stated[2] that this should be recast so as to require only a conclusion that the party's case had a real (as opposed to merely fanciful) prospect of success and that it is in the public interests to make the order.

[1]   [2005] 1 WLR 2600: the judgment of the court, handed down by Lord Phillips MR was credited as being the work of Brooke LJ.
[2]   Judgment at paragraph 73.

20.110 As a result, the applicable principles were restated as follows.[1] A protective costs order may be made at any stage of the proceedings, on such conditions as the court thinks fit, provided that the court is satisfied that:

(1)   the issues raised are of general public importance;[2]

(2)   the public interest requires that those issues should be resolved;

(3)   the applicant has no private interest in the outcome of the case;[3]

(4)   having regard to the financial resources of the applicant and the respondent(s) and to the amount of costs that are likely to be involved it is fair and just to make the order;

(5)   if the order is not made the applicant will probably discontinue the proceedings and will be acting reasonably in so doing.[4]

---

[1]   See judgment at paragraph 74. Subsequent judgments have emphasised that the guidance given in *Corner House* is not be treated as laying down hard and fast rules: see *R (Compton) v Wiltshire Primary Care Trust* [2009] 1 WLR 1436; *Morgan v Hinton Organics* [2009] EWCA Civ 107 and *R (Buglife) v Thurrock Thames Gateway Development Corporation* [2008] EWCA Civ 1209. There is no additional requirement that the applicant must show that his is an exceptional case: *R (British Union for the Abolition of Vivisection) v Secretary of State for the Home Department* [2006] EWHC 250 (Admin). This is not an additional hurdle to be overcome, but merely a reflection of the fact that PCOs will not be made routinely.

[2]   On the question of what constitutes an issue of general public importance, see *R (Compton) v Wiltshire PCT* [2009] 1 WLR 1436 and *R (Plantagenet Alliance Ltd) v Secretary of State for Justice* [2013] EWHC 3164 (Admin).

[3]   See **20.113** below.

[4]   See *R (Litvinenko) v Secretary of State for the Home Department* [2013] EWHC 3135 (Admin), where the court held that the claimant's assets outweighed the value of the Secretary of State's estimated costs and she had the financial means to bring the proceedings if she chose to and it would not be reasonable for her to withdraw proceedings on the basis that she did not have a PCO.

20.111 The court went on to state that if those acting for the applicant are doing so pro bono, this would be likely to enhance the merits of the application for a protective costs order, and that it is for the court, in its discretion, to decide whether it is fair and just to make the order in the light of the considerations set out above. Any such order can take a number of different forms and the choice of the form of the order is also an important aspect of the discretion exercised by the court.

20.112 The court also provided[1] guidance as to the practice to be followed in any application for a pre-emptive costs order:

(1)   that in any situation where the claimant was still seeking an order for costs in *its* favour (ie where the claimant's lawyers are not acting pro bono), the court should make a reciprocal cost-capping order, to restrict the possible costs liability of the defendant to a 'reasonably modest amount'. The claimant should expect the capping order to restrict it to solicitors' fees and a fee for a single advocate of junior counsel status that are no more than modest;[2]

(2)   any order should be sought on the face of the claim form, and be supported by a schedule of the claimant's costs. The court recognised that by making the application, the claimant was at risk of liability for the defendant's costs of resisting it; but observed that it would not normally expect a defendant to be able to demonstrate costs of such a point at the paper stage exceeding £ 1,000;

(3)   if the judge refused to make an order on the papers, that decision could be reconsidered at an oral hearing;[3]

(4)   that if an order is made on the papers, an application to vary it or set it aside should only succeed if there was a compelling reason for so doing.[4] An unmeritorious application to set aside an order made on the

papers could result in an order for costs on an indemnity basis (to which any cost cap otherwise applicable by reason of the pre-emptive order would not apply).

There is no assumption that it is appropriate where the claimant's liability for costs is capped, that the defendant's liability for costs should be capped in the same amount. Where a defendant wishes to seek an order capping its liability for costs, it should do so in the acknowledgment of service.[5]

In *Drummond v Revenue and Customs Commissioners*,[6] the Upper Tribunal held that it had the same jurisdiction as the High Court to make protective costs orders, costs capping orders and orders limiting costs in appeals. It then provided guidance that applications for such orders should include: (a) a description of the circumstances of the case, including the amount involved, the financial resources of the applicant, the level of costs already incurred and the further costs likely to be incurred in the appeal (including whether the applicant's representative was acting pro bono); (b) the order sought and why the order should be made; (c) what consequences were likely to follow if the application was not granted. Any statements about the applicant's financial resources, the costs already incurred and likely to be incurred in the appeal should be supported by evidence. In addition, an application for a protective costs order should state why the issues raised were of general public importance and the public interest required that they should be resolved, and the interest the applicant had in the outcome of the case. In the case of a costs capping order, the application should also state why the applicant considered that there was a substantial risk that, without the order, costs would be disproportionately incurred and why that risk could not be adequately controlled by effective case management or detailed assessment of costs. Any response should state whether the application was opposed and, if so, on what grounds. It should also include an estimate of the costs likely to be incurred by the respondent in the appeal that were potentially recoverable from the applicant.

[1] Paragraphs 75–81.

[2] Subsequent cases have recognised that a protective costs order may cover the fees of leading counsel in appropriate cases: see, for example, *R (Buglife) v Thurrock Thames Gateway Development Corporation* [2008] EWCA Civ 1209 at [25]-[27]. The amount of any cap on the defendant's liability for costs will depend on all the circumstances of the case. Under the previous CFA regime, the agreed success fee is relevant to the likely amount of the liability of the defendant to the claimant if the claimant won, and the court should know the level of the success fee when deciding on what the cap should be. At least in cases against central government, the rates payable by the Secretary of State may provide a 'suitable benchmark' of modesty: *R (Medical Justice) v Secretary of State for the Home Department* [2010] EWHC 1425 (Admin).

[3] On this, the court made further observations as to the extent of the costs risk to a claimant, stating that it would not expect a defendant to be able to demonstrate recoverable costs of more than £2,500.

[4] This, of course, assumes that at the paper stage, the defendant had already had a fair opportunity to respond to the application for the pre-emptive costs order. See also *Lumsdon v Legal Services Board* [2013] EWHC 3289 (Admin), where the claimants in the QASA judicial review applied to reduce a cost cap of £150,000 made on the papers to £75,000. The Court confirmed that the same approach applied whether the application to vary the order made on paper was made by a claimant or defendant.

[5] *R (Buglife) v Thurrock Thames Gateway Development Corporation* [2008] EWCA Civ 1209.

[6] [2016] UKUT 221 (TCC); [2016] 4 All ER 884, see paragraphs 43–45.

20.113 Although the court endorsed the requirement, stated in the *CPAG* case, that the litigation be litigation in which the claimant had no private interest, it should be noted that this point was not directly in issue either in *Corner House* itself or in the *CPAG* case. There may well be instances where this should not be regarded as an absolute requirement, if the claimant does have a private interest but where the *public* interest in the point justifies freeing him from the normal costs consequences of litigation. Social security test cases are one possible context in which this convergence of private and public interest may exist – the claimant may have a small financial stake in an issue which has wide-ranging implications for others. The point could be taken by a representative body such as CPAG, which could take advantage of the *Corner House* principles. However (absent the availability of public funding for such cases), it is difficult to see why different principles should apply to an action brought by an individual claimant, with a small financial stake in the matter, than would apply if the same claim was pursued by a representative body with no such stake.

Cases following *Corner House* had emphasised the need for flexibility when considering the requirement that an applicant should have no private interest in the case.[1] A private interest in a judicial review claim is not fatal to the application for a PCO. An applicant's private interest was a factor to be considered when balancing against the other elements of the *Corner House* guidance. In *R (Litvinenko) v Secretary of State for the Home Department*,[2] the court held that Mrs Litvinenko's private interest would not of itself have prevented the making of a PCO.

[1]   However, the point was directly in issue in *Weir v Secretary of State for Transport* [2005] EWHC 812 (Ch). In that case, Lindsay J – albeit in the context of a private law claim – considered the judgment in Corner House and concluded that the existence of the private interest precluded the making of a pre-emptive costs order (see judgment at paragraph 12); see also *Goodson v HM Coroner for Bedfordshire* [2005] EWCA Civ 1172 and *R (A and others) (Disputed Children) v Secretary of State for the Home Department* [2007] EWHC 2494 (Admin). However, serious doubts were expressed about the correctness of this guidance in *Morgan v Hinton Organics (Wessex) Ltd* [2009] EWCA Civ 107 (impossible to ignore the criticisms of a narrow approach); in *R (Eley) v Secretary of State for Communities and Local Government R (England) v London Borough of Tower Hamlets* [2006] EWCA Civ 1742 and *R (Young) v Oxford City Council* [2012] EWCA Civ 46.

[2]   [2013] EWHC 3135 (Admin).

20.114 Article 9(4) of the UNECE Convention on Access to Information, Public Participation in Decision-Making and Access to Justice in Environmental Matters ('the Aarhus Convention') provides that procedures for access to justice in environmental litigation must be 'fair, equitable, timely and not prohibitively expensive'.

From 1 April 2013, the CPR was amended to provide new costs rules for judicial reviews which fall within the Aarhus Convention.[1] An Aarhus Convention claim is a claim for judicial review of a decision, act or omission all or part of which is subject to the provisions of the Convention.[2] Rule 45.43 provides that, subject to rule 45.44, a party to an Aarhus Convention claim may not be ordered to pay costs exceeding the amount prescribed in Practice Direction 45. The standard cost caps are found at paragraph 5 of the Practice Direction to CPR Part 45 and limit the claimant's costs to £5,000 (for an individual) or £10,000 (for any other claimant) and limit the defendant's costs to £35,000.

The cost limit does not apply where the claimant: (a) has not stated in the claim form that the claim is an Aarhus Convention claim, or (b) has stated in the claim form that the claim is not an Aarhus Convention claim or, although it is such a claim, the claimant does not wish those rules to apply.

A defendant may challenge the claimant's contention that the claim is an Aarhus Convention claim. Any question of whether the claim is an Aarhus Convention claim must be determined at the earliest opportunity. If the court decides that the claim is an Aarhus Convention claim, it will normally make a costs order against the defendant on the indemnity basis, even if that would increase the costs payable by the defendant beyond the amount set out in Practice Direction 45. If the court holds that the claim is not an Aarhus Convention claim, it will normally make no order for costs in relation to those proceedings.[3]

[1] CPR Part 45, Chapter 7.
[2] For guidance on cases that fall within this definition, see *Venn v Secretary of State for Communities and Local Government* [2014] EWCA Civ 1539; *R (Dowley) v Secretary of State for Communities and Local Government* [2016] EWHC 2618 (Admin); and *R. (on the application of HS2 Action Alliance Ltd) v Secretary of State for Transport* [2015] EWCA Civ 203.
[3] CPR 45.44(3).

20.115 Prior to 1 April 2013, attempts had been made to develop separate principles for costs in environmental cases, building on the principles of the Aarhus Convention to the effect that judicial procedures allowing members of the public to challenge acts of public authorities which contravene laws relating to the environment should not be 'prohibitively expensive'. The courts had originally rejected such attempts, holding that the principles governing the grant of protective costs orders apply alike to environmental and other public interest cases. The principles of the Aarhus Convention were said to be at most a matter to which the court may have regard in exercising its discretion (save, possibly, in cases concerning directly effective EU Directives which have incorporated principles of the Aarhus Convention): *Morgan v Hinton Organics (Wessex) Ltd, Coalition for Access to Justice for the Environment (CAJE) intervening.*[1]

While the Aarhus Convention is not part of UK domestic law (except where incorporated through European directives),[2]), UK law should be interpreted and applied in harmony with its provisions where possible. However, the Court of Justice of the European Union held that the UK costs regime did not properly implement the requirement in the Aarhus Convention that access to environmental justice must not be prohibitively expensive: *European Commission v United Kingdom.*[3] The Court of Appeal also found that CPR 45.41 does not comply with the obligations of the Convention; it is confined to applications for judicial review and does not extend to statutory appeals or applications: *Venn v Secretary of State for Communities & Local Government.*[4] Therefore, the court cannot make an order in a private nuisance claim even if it raised issues to which the Convention applies[5] and a defendant to a claim for private nuisance cannot rely on the Convention to limit its liability for costs.[6] However, the costs protection extends to a local authority claimant: *R (HS2 Action Alliance Ltd) v Secretary of State for Transport.*[7]

The courts have considered whether, in determining whether costs render proceedings 'prohibitively expensive', the court should adopt an objective approach (by considering the ability of an ordinary member of the public to meet the potential liability for costs), a subjective approach (by considering the means of the particular claimant) or some combination of these two approaches. This question was referred to the CJEU in *R (Edwards) v Environment Agency*[8]. The Court of Justice held that the test is not purely subjective. The cost of proceedings must not exceed the financial resources of the person concerned nor 'appear to be objectively unreasonable'. The justification is related to the objective of the relevant European legislation, which is to ensure that the public 'plays an active role' in protecting and improving the quality of the environment. The CJEU did not give definitive guidance as to how to assess what is 'objectively unreasonable'. In particular it did not in terms adopt the suggested alternative of an 'objective' assessment based on the ability of an 'ordinary' member of the public to meet the potential liability for costs. While the court did not apparently reject that as a possible factor in the overall assessment, 'exclusive' reliance on the resources of an 'average applicant' was not appropriate, because it might have 'little connection with the situation of the person concerned'. The court could also take into account what might be called the 'merits' of the case, ie 'whether the claimant has a reasonable prospect of success, the importance of what is at stake for the claimant and for the protection of the environment, the complexity of the relevant law and procedure, the potentially frivolous nature of the claim at its various stages'. That the claimant has not in fact been deterred for carrying on the proceedings is not 'in itself' determinative.

The case returned to the Supreme Court in *R (Edwards) v Environment Agency (No 2)*.[9] The claimant had already paid £25,000 into court and as there was no evidence that an order for payment of that sum would be beyond her means or cause her hardship, it was impossible to say that the award of such a figure would be subjectively unreasonable or objectively unreasonable.

[1] [2009] EWCA Civ 107; [2009] Env LR 30. See also *R (Dullingham Parish Council) v East Cambridgeshire District Council* [2010] EWHC 1307 (Admin).

[2] When the Arhus Convention has been incorporated into European Union Directives (the Environmental Impact Assessment Directive and the Integrated Pollution Prevention and Control Directive) it has direct effect, and in cases where these two directives apply, the court will have to exercise its discretion as to costs so as to ensure that the proceedings are not prohibitively expensive. At the time of writing, the Government have published a White Paper on leaving the EU. It is unclear to what extent this will change the law, and the consequences of 'Brexit' are outside the scope of this publication. However, it is notable that the white paper states: '*The Government's general approach to preserving EU law is to ensure that all EU laws which are directly applicable in the UK (such as EU regulations) and all laws which have been made in the UK, in order to implement our obligations as a member of the EU, remain part of domestic law on the day we leave the EU. In general the Government also believes that the preserved law should continue to be interpreted in the same way as it is at the moment.*'

[3] [2014] EUECJ C/530/11.

[4] [2014] EWCA Civ 1539.

[5] *Austin v Miller Argent (South Wales) Limited* [2014] EWCA Civ 1012.

[6] *Coventry v Lawrence* [2014] UKSC 46.

[7] [2015] EWCA Civ 203.

[8] [2013] 1 WLR 2914, ECJ.

[9] [2014] 1 WLR 55.

20.116 The *Corner House* principles have been taken to apply in relation to an application for a protective costs order on appeal, although the fact that the issue arises at the appellate stage may affect the exercise of the court's discretion: see *R (Goodson) v Bedfordshire and Luton Coroner*,[1] *and Revenue and Customs Commissioners v TGH (Commercial) Ltd*.[2] In *Weaver v London and Quadrant Housing Trust*,[3], the Court of Appeal gave guidance on the approach to be adopted when making a protective costs order by the respondent to an appeal. The key question was whether the effect of refusing the order would be that the applicant would no longer take part in the appeal and whether she would be acting reasonably in so doing.

The position on appeal is now governed by CPR 52.19. This states that in any proceedings in which costs recovery is normally limited or excluded at first instance, an appeal court may make an order that the recoverable costs of an appeal will be limited to the extent which the court specifies. In making such an order, the court will have regard to (a) the means of both parties; (b) all the circumstances of the case; and (c) the need to facilitate access to justice. If the appeal raises an issue of principle or practice upon which substantial sums may turn, it may not be appropriate to make such an order. An application for an order under this rule must be made as soon as practicable and will be determined without a hearing unless the court orders otherwise.[4]

[1]   [2005] EWCA Civ 1172.
[2]   [2016] UKUT 519 (TCC).
[3]   [2009] EWCA Civ 235.
[4]   For guidance on the application of CPR 52.19, see *R (Manchester College) v Hazel* [2013] EWCA Civ 281; *R (Edwards) v Environment Agency (No 2)* [2014] 1 WLR 55, paragraph 24; *Akhtar v Boland* [2014] EWCA Civ 943; and *JE (Jamaica) v Secretary of State for the Home Department* [2014] EWCA Civ 192.

Costs Capping Orders under the Criminal Justice and Courts Act 2015

20.117 Sections 88–90 of the Criminal Justice and Courts Act 2015 provide new rules governing the circumstances in which Costs Capping Orders (CCOs) can be made. As per *Venn v Secretary of State for Communities and Local Government*,[1] they apply only to judicial review claims and not to statutory reviews (such as those under s 288 of the Town and Country Planning Act 1990). Under s 88(4), an application must be made in accordance with the CPR (see CPR 46.16–19).

Section 88 limits CCOs to cases where: (a) permission has been granted[2] ; and (b) the proceedings are public interest proceedings, defined as cases concerning an issue of general public importance, the public interest requires the issue to be resolved and the proceedings are likely to provide an appropriate means of resolving it;[3] and (c) in the absence of a PCO, the claimant would reasonably withdraw the application for judicial review or cease to participate in the proceedings.[4] As a result, it seems likely that claimants will be dissuaded from seeking a 'rolled up' hearing, given that a CCO cannot be made until permission is granted. It may also mean that CCOs cannot in practice be made in urgent matters that require a 'rolled up' hearing. Claimants are also likely to have to incur significant costs prior to obtaining permission without the protection of a CCO. If proceedings are discontinued as a result of a CCO not being granted, CPR 38.6 provides a presumption that the claimant will pay the costs of the defendant. Therefore, claimants applying for a CCO may also wish to seek an order from the court that they will not be liable for the defendant's costs if the CCO application is not successful.

Section 88(6) further provides that in determining whether proceedings are 'public interest proceedings', the court must consider the number of people likely to be directly affected if relief is granted to the applicant for judicial review; how significant the effect on those people is likely to be; and whether the proceedings involve consideration of a point of law of general public importance. Section 89 sets out further matters that should be considered before granting a CCO, including the applicant's financial standing. If a claimant has the benefit of a CCO but does not have relief granted in the proceedings, section 89(2) provides that the court must also limit or remove the liability of the other party to pay their costs.

Section 90 provides that regulations may be made providing that ss 88 and 89 do not apply to cases which relate entirely or partly to the environment. However, it will not usually be necessary to apply for a CCO in these circumstances because the CPR prevents adverse costs orders being made even if the claim is unsuccessful (see **20.114** above).

[1]   [2014] EWCA Civ 1539; [2015] 1 WLR 2328.
[2]   Section 88(3).
[3]   Section 88(6)(a) and (7).
[4]   Section 88(6)(b) and (c).

Costs: interested parties

20.118   The general rule is that an unsuccessful claimant is not required to pay for more than one set of costs.[1] Where several parties appear to defend a judicial review, they will usually only be allowed one set of costs between them. However, the court may order the payment of further costs in certain circumstances. It is only where an interested party can show that there was likely to be a separate issue on which he was entitled to be heard, or if he has a particular interest which requires separate representation, that the court will order a 'second set of costs'.[2] However, even a separate interest and an entitlement to separate representation may not be sufficient to warrant the grant of a second set of costs in the absence of a conflicting interest which must be promoted. Accordingly, an interested party with a separate, but not conflicting, interest was not awarded its costs in the case of *R (Bedford) v Islington London Borough Council*.[3] The courts have tended to allow two sets of costs more frequently where the claimant to the judicial review is a company rather than an individual of limited means.[4] The court may also consider whether an interested party could have filed evidence but left it to the first defendant to make submissions.[5]

[1]   See, among many examples, *R (Smeaton) v Secretary of State for Health* [2002] EWHC 610 (Admin), [2002] 2 FLR 146 at paragraph 431; *Re G (An Adult) (Costs)* [2015] EWCA Civ 446.
[2]   *Bolton Metropolitan District Council v Secretary of State for the Environment* [1995] 1 WLR 1176 at 1178F–1179A.
[3]   [2002] EWHC 2044 (Admin), [2003] Env LR 463 at paragraph 296. For recent examples of the award of two sets of costs, see *Austin v Secretary of State for Communities and Local Government* [2008] EWHC 3200 (Admin) (separate representation justified on the facts of the case); *R (Bennett) v Secretary of State for Communities and Local Government* [2007] EWHC 737 (Admin); *R (A, B, X and Y) (A and B by their litigation friend the Official Solicitor to the*

Supreme Court) v East Sussex County Council [2005] EWHC 585 (Admin) (fair, just and appropriate to depart from the ordinary rule); *R (London & South East Railway Ltd) v British Transport Police Authority* [2009] EWHC 1255 (Admin); see also *Ong v Ping* [2015] EWHC 3258, where the court found that co-claimants had not required separate representation and so recoverable costs were limited to those for one firm of solicitors.

4   Compare, for example, *R v Director General of Telecommunications, ex p Cellcom Ltd* [1999] COD 105 with *R (Bedford) v London Borough of Islington* [2002] EWHC 2044 (Admin), [2003] Env LR 463.

5   For example, see *R v Secretary of State for the Environment, ex p Kirkstall Valley Campaign Ltd* [1996] 3 All ER 304 at 342–343. However, see also *R (William Hill Organisation Ltd) v Horserace Betting Levy Board* [2013] EWCA Civ 487; [2013] 1 WLR 3656, where an interested party was awarded part of its costs of the claim where the claim was in reality a commercial dispute between the claimant and the interested party.

20.119 Where an interested party has a special interest in a matter, such as that his liberty is at stake, the courts will make him an award of costs.[1] The court may also consider that a second set should be ordered where the interests of the parties are complex such as to justify the need for them both to appear.[2]

1   R (Secretary of State for the Home Department) v Mental Health Review Tribunal [2002] EWCA Civ 1868, (2003) 6 CCLR 319 at paragraphs 32–33.

2   See *R v Registrar of Companies, ex p Central Bank of India* [1986] QB 1114 at 1162 F-H.

20.120 In *Bolton*, it was also held that a second set of costs is more likely to be awarded at first instance than in the Court of Appeal or the House of Lords and that a third set of costs is rarely justified, even if there are in theory three or more separate interests.[1]

1   *Bolton Metropolitan District Council v Secretary of State for the Environment* [1995] 1 WLR 1176 at 1178F–1179A. see *R (Lewisham London Borough Council) v Assessment and Qualifications Alliance* [2013] EWHC 962 (Admin) (costs awarded to three defendants in a claim for judicial review).

20.121 Costs can also be awarded in favour of interested parties who support the application for judicial review. For example, a defendant might be ordered to pay the costs of an interested party where that party would have been entitled to bring their own proceedings.[1]

1   *R v Secretary of State for Health, ex p Eastside Cheese Co* (1999) 11 Admin LR 254; see also *R (London & South Eastern Railway Ltd) v British Transport Police Authority* [2009] EWHC 1255 (Admin).

Costs: defendants who do not appear

20.122 Costs orders are not usually made against those tribunals who do not normally appear to defend their decisions. Brooke LJ summarised the position in *R (Davies) v Birmingham Deputy Coroner*[1] as follows:

'(i)   The established practice of the courts was to make no order for costs against an inferior court or tribunal which did not appear before it except when there was a flagrant instance of improper behaviour or where the inferior court or tribunal unreasonably declined or neglected to sign a consent order disposing of the proceedings.

(ii)   The established practice of the courts was to treat an inferior court or tribunal which resisted an application actively by way of argument in such a way that it made itself an active party to the litigation, as if it was such a party, so that in the normal course of things costs would follow the event.

(iii)　If, however, an inferior court or tribunal appeared in the proceedings in order to assist the court neutrally on questions of jurisdiction, procedure, specialist case-law and such like, the established practice of the courts was to treat it as a neutral party, so that it would not make an order for costs in its favour or an order for costs against it whatever the outcome of the application.

(iv)　There are, however, a number of important considerations which might tend to make the courts exercise their discretion in a different way today in cases in category (iii) above, so that a successful [claimant] . . . who has to finance his own litigation without external funding, may be fairly compensated out of a source of public funds and not be put to irrecoverable expense in asserting his rights after a coroner (or other inferior tribunal) has gone wrong in law, and there is no other very obvious candidate available to pay his costs.'

[1]　[2004] EWCA Civ 207, [2004] 3 All ER 543 at paragraph 47. See, also, *R v Newcastle-under-Lyme Justices, ex p Massey* [1994] 1 WLR 1684; *R v Gloucester Crown Court, ex p Chester* [1998] COD 365; and *R v Feltham Justices, ex p Haid* [1998] COD 440. See subsequently *R (Varma) v Redbridge Magistrates' Court* [2009] EWHC 836 (Admin) (costs shared equally between the CPS and the Magistrates' Court where the CPS should not have contested the appeal and the Magistrates' Court unreasonably failed to sign a consent order); *LT and DT v Cardiff City and County Council and Gwyn Eirug Davies (Chair of Special Educational Needs Tribunal for Wales)* [2007] EWHC 2568 (Admin); and *R (Tull) v Camberwell Green Magistrates' Court and Lambeth Borough Council* [2004] EWHC 2780 (Admin).

20.123 Where the real dispute is between the claimant and an interested party, and the defendant has not participated in the judicial review, it is only in very limited circumstances that it will be held liable for costs. It has been held that a mistake of law will not suffice and it is only when the body has shown a flagrant disregard to principle that an award will be made.[1] If a costs order is made against a person who has not appeared, the proper practice is to make an 'unless' order, ie that the order is not to take effect for a specified period so as to allow an application to set aside the order.[2]

[1]　*R (Towry Law Financial Services plc) v Financial Ombudsman Service Ltd* [2002] EWHC 1603 (Admin) at paragraph 20.
[2]　*R v Doncaster Justices, ex p Christison* [2000] COD 5 (magistrates successfully applied to set aside order as unjustified by explaining evidence).

20.124 The costs practice will depend on the nature of an individual challenge. Even where the real dispute is between the claimant and an interested party, the presence of the defendant may well be of assistance to the court. This is particularly so where difficult questions of fact or law arise in a judicial review. Accordingly, the courts have been reluctant to adopt a practice on costs which might discourage their attendance. They have, for example, ordered that the Pension Ombudsman should only be held liable for costs to the extent that they had been increased by his attendance.[1]

[1]　*University of Nottingham v Eyett* [1999] 1 WLR 594; but see also *Moore's (Wallisdown) Ltd v Pensions Ombudsman (Costs)* [2002] 1 W.L.R. 1649.

Costs orders against third parties

20.125 A third party's involvement in a judicial review may make it liable to pay the costs of the claimant and the defendant. In *R (Holmes) v General Medical Council*,[1] the third party had alone and unsuccessfully sought to uphold the decision of the defendant when both the claimant and the defendant had agreed that judicial review should be granted. Consequently, it was ordered to pay the costs of both the claimant and the defendant.[2] If a third party introduces new points that were not otherwise in issue between the parties, the court may order that the third party pay the costs of the parties to the extent that they were incurred as a result of the issues the third party introduced.[3] However, if a third party is merely performing a public function in supplying the court with information, it is unlikely to become liable for costs.[4]

Section 87 of the Criminal Justice and Courts Act 2015 provides that, in the absence of exceptional circumstances, parties who have been granted permission to intervene in judicial review proceedings will have to pay their own costs and, on an application by another party, any costs they have caused to that party as a result of their intervention.

1   [2001] EWHC 321 (Admin), [2001] Lloyd's Rep Med 366.
2   See, also, *R (Sussex Police Authority) v Cooling* [2004] EWHC 1920 (Admin) where costs were awarded against a third-party beneficiary of decision who with legal representation unsuccessfully defended the impugned decision.
3   *R (Munjaz) v Mersey Care NHS Trust* [2003] EWCA Civ 1036, [2003] 3 WLR 1505 at paragraph 90.
4   For example, this is the role of the police with regard to licensing appeals from magistrates, see *R v Crown Court at Merthyr Tydfil , ex p Chief Constable of Dyfed Powys* (1998) Times, 17 December.

Costs against non-parties

20.126 The power under s 51 of the Supreme Court Act 1981 includes the power to make an award against a non-party. In considering whether to make such an award, the non-party must be added as a party for the purposes of costs only and they must be given a reasonable opportunity to attend a hearing at which the court will consider the matter further.[1] Such an order will only be made in exceptional circumstances.[2]

1   CPR 48.2.
2   *Byrne v South Sefton (Merseyside) Health Authority* [2001] EWCA Civ 1904, [2002] 1 WLR 775 and, for an example in a judicial review, see *R (Davies) v Secretary of State for the Environment, Food and Rural Affairs* [2002] EWHC 2762 (Admin).

20.127 A possible application of this power is where it appears that an unincorporated association is not likely to meet a costs order. In that case, costs can exceptionally be sought against the individual members of the society who are non-parties to the proceedings.[1] However, the more appropriate course may be to seek an order for security for costs against the named claimant.

¹   *R v Secretary of State for Foreign and Commonwealth Affairs, ex p British Council of Turkish Cypriot Associations* [1998] COD 336. See also *Metalloy Supplies Ltd (in liq) v MA (UK) Ltd* [1997] 1 WLR 1613.

Costs against publicly-funded parties

20.128 The same general principles apply as for non-publicly funded litigants, ie that costs normally follow the event. However, where the claimant is funded by the Legal Aid Agency, a successful defendant may apply for an order for costs against the Lord Chancellor.¹ In this context a distinction must be made between being able to obtain an order from the trial court (as against the funded party), and being able in practice to realise any value on such an order (by means of obtaining a further order as against the Lord Chancellor).² The former is straightforward; the latter is very difficult, at least in relation to first instance proceedings.

¹   The Lord Chancellor is responsible for ensuring that legal aid is made available in accordance with Part 1 of the Legal Aid, Sentencing and Punishment of Offenders Act 2012 ('the 2012 Act'). Costs orders against a legally aided party and the Lord Chancellor are governed by s 26 of the 2012 Act and regulations made thereunder, being the Civil Legal Aid (Costs) Regulations 2013, SI 2013/611.
²   See also the Guidance Notes on the Application of s 26(1) of the Legal Aid, Sentencing and Punishment of Offenders Act 2012 issued by the Senior Costs Judge (paragraph 48GP.01 onwards of the White Book).

20.129 In deciding whether and, if so, what costs order to make between the parties, the trial court will not normally take into account whether or not a party is publicly funded.¹ The trial court will exercise this discretion as it would in any other case. However, the power to make an order against the Lord Chancellor is governed by Part 3 of the Civil Legal Aid (Costs) Regulations 2013. Where the relevant proceedings are finally decided in favour of a non-legally aided party, the court may make an order for the payment by the Lord Chancellor to the non-legally aided party of the whole or any part of the costs incurred by that party in the proceedings (other than the costs that the legally aided party is required to pay himself under a costs order made under s 26(1) of the 2012 Act). The non legally aided party must make a request under reg 16(2) within three months of the date on which the s 26(1) costs order is made. At this stage the position of the party seeking the costs becomes significantly more difficult. In relation to first instance decisions, an order will only be made if, (i) the proceedings were instituted by the legally aided party; (ii) the non-legally aided party is an individual; and (iii) the court is satisfied that the non-legally aided party will suffer financial hardship unless the order is made. In all cases, the court must also be satisfied that it is just and equitable in the circumstances that provision for the costs should be made out of public funds.²

¹   See s 26 of the 2012 Act and reg 15 of the Civil Legal Aid (Costs) Regulations 2013, SI 2013/611. However, the legally aided party has cost protection in respect of costs incurred by the receiving party in relation to relevant proceedings under reg 5. The court must consider whether, but for costs protection, it would have made a costs order against the legally aided party and, if so, whether it would have specified the amount to be paid under that order.
²   See reg 10 of the Civil Legal Aid (Costs) Regulations 2013, SI 2013/611.

20.130 As regards the costs of an appeal, the only condition is that the court is satisfied that it is just and equitable in the circumstances that provision for the costs should be made out of public funds. Under the previous costs regime, in *R (Gunn) v Secretary of State for the Home Department*[1] the Court of Appeal concluded that, in relation to the costs of an appeal, it will normally be just and equitable for a Costs Judge to order that the costs of an unsuccessful funded party be paid by the Legal Services Commission. In *Gunn* the court further concluded that the jurisdiction of the Costs Judge to make an order as against the Commission (whether after a first instance hearing or an appeal) was not ousted by the fact that the party seeking the order was a public authority (and as such in receipt of public funding of a different sort).[2] Costs judges and District Judges proceeded on the basis that it is just and equitable that the Commission should stand behind the Commission-funded client unless there are circumstances which render that result unjust or inequitable.[3] The same approach is being taken under the 2012 Act and the Civil Legal Aid (Costs) Regulations 2013.

[1] [2001] EWCA Civ 891, [2001] 1 WLR 1624 at paragraph 50.
[2] [2001] EWCA Civ 891, [2001] 1 WLR 1624, at paragraph 51 (although note the pragmatic caveat from the court).
[3] See paragraph 48GP.06 and following, of the White Book.

Costs in discontinued or compromised claims

20.131 A claim for judicial review might not proceed to a substantive hearing because it is discontinued, withdrawn or settled, whether before or after permission to apply for judicial review has been granted. The court retains a power to make an order for costs. The question of what order should be made depends on all the circumstances of the case.

20.132 A claimant who chooses to discontinue when the defendant has not agreed to reconsider the decision and there has been no change of position by the defendant can expect to pay the costs incurred up to the date of discontinuance.[1]

[1] See CPR Part 38.6 (liability for costs on discontinuance) and the *Practice Statement (Administrative Court: Uncontested Proceedings)* [2008] 1 WLR 1377.

20.133 The court's previous practice on costs awards when claims were settled was set out in the decision in *R (Boxall) v Waltham Forest London Borough Council*.[1]

However, the Court of Appeal has recently overturned this approach in a series of cases, including *R (Bahta) v Secretary of State for the Home Department*;[2] *M v Croydon London Borough Council*;[3] and *Emezie v Secretary of State for the Home Department*;[4] and *R (Tesfay) v Secretary of State for the Home Department*.[5]

The starting point is to ask whether the claimant has been wholly successful in obtaining the remedy that he or she sought, or something substantially similar. If so, the unsuccessful defendant will usually be ordered to pay the claimant's costs, unless there is a good reason to the contrary. While a defendant might argue that they were realistic in settling, and should not be penalised in costs, the time for settlement was in response to the Pre-Action Protocol letter. Concessions made subsequently are unlikely to justify a departure from the general rule that a party who succeeds in obtaining that which was sought should recover his or her costs from the unsuccessful party.[6]

If the claimant has only succeeded in part, the court will consider whether it can form a view on the appropriate costs order. It will consider factors such as how reasonable the claimant was in pursuing the unsuccessful parts of the claim, how important it was compared with the successful claim, and how much the costs were increased as a result of the claimant pursuing the unsuccessful claim. A court may feel that the appropriate order is that there be no order for costs. However, if it is tolerably clear who would have won if the matter had proceeded to trial, the court may make an order in favour of the party that would have won.[7]

If, however, there has been some compromise that did not actually reflect the claimant's claims, the court will often be unable to gauge whether there is a successful party in any respect and, if so, who it is. There is then an even more powerful argument that the default position should be no order for costs. Again, however, the court may look at the underlying claims and inquire whether it was tolerably clear who would have won if the matter had not settled. If it is, then that may well strongly support the contention that the party who would have won did better out of the settlement, and should recover his costs.[8]

The court will not spend a disproportionate amount of time in considering the merits of the case for the purposes of making a costs order. No order for costs will be the default order when the judge cannot without disproportionate expenditure of judicial time, if at all, fairly and sensibly make an order in favour of either party.[9]

1   (2001) 4 CCL Rep 258.
2   [2011] EWCA Civ 895.
3   [2012] EWCA Civ 595; [2012] 1 WLR 2607.
4   [2013] EWCA Civ 733; [2013] 5 Costs LR 685.
5   [2016] EWCA Civ 415.
6   *M v Croydon*, para 61–64.
7   *M v Croydon*, para 61–64.
8   *M v Croydon*, para 61–64.
9   *M v Croydon*, para 64, 73, 77.

20.134 Part 23 of The Administrative Court Judicial Review Guide 2016 provides guidance on the approach that parties should take to applications for costs made following the settlement of claims for judicial review.[1]

The guidance was issued in response to 'a significant number of cases, poorly considered and prepared by the parties, which can consume judicial time far beyond what is proportionate to deciding a costs issue after the parties have settled the case'. The guidance re-iterates the authority of *M v Croydon* and *Tesfay* and emphasises that the onus is on the parties to reach agreement on costs wherever possible in advance of asking the court to resolve the issues. It lays down strict procedural requirements for costs submissions to the court:

(a)   **Timetable**: submissions seeking costs must be filed and served within 28 days of approval of the consent order; submissions in reply within 14 days thereafter; any further submissions in response within 7 days of the response.

(b) **Content:** submissions must:
  (i)   confirm that the parties have used reasonable endeavours to negotiate a costs settlement;
  (ii) identify what issues or reasons prevented the parties agreeing costs liability;
  (iii) state the approximate amount of costs likely to be involved in the case;
  (iv) identify the extent to which the parties complied with the pre-action protocol;
  (v)   state the relief the claimant (i) sought in the claim form and (ii) obtained;
  (vi) address specifically how the claim and the basis of its settlement fit the principles in *M v Croydon* and *Tesfay*, including the relationship of any step taken by the defendant to the claim.

(c) **Format:** Submissions should not without good reason (explained in the submissions) exceed two A4 pages in length and should be accompanied by the pre-action protocol correspondence, along with any other correspondence necessary to demonstrate why the claim was brought in the light of the pre-action protocol correspondence or why the step which led to settlement was not taken until after the claim was issued. Parties should assume that the court has the claim papers originally lodged by the parties.

[1]   See website at: https://www.gov.uk/government/uploads/system/uploads/attachment_data/file/540607/administrative-court/judicial-review-guide.pdf

20.135 Proceedings on judicial review may, on occasion, prove ineffective or may become academic through no fault of the parties. The general costs order in such circumstances is that there be no order as to costs. The Lord Chancellor, on occasion, has made ex gratia payments out of the funds allocated to his department by Parliament when litigants complained that they had been put to unnecessary expense by reason of some form of maladministration in the operation of the courts.[1] The House of Lords held in *Steel Ford & Newton v Crown Prosecution Service (No 2)*[2] that s 51 of the Supreme Court Act 1981 gave a court no implied power to make an order out of central funds in civil litigation to compensate a litigant for wasted costs. There may be, however, power to make an order against the Lord Chancellor in a case where costs are wasted by a breach of the European Convention on Human Rights.

[1]   See *Re Medicaments and Related Classes of Goods (No 4)* [2002] 1 WLR 269 at paragraph 4, p 273.
[2]   [1994] 1 AC 22.

Wasted costs

20.136 A wasted costs order is an order that a legal representative pay the costs of a party. The statutory basis for the jurisdiction to make such an order is s 51(6) and (7) of the Senior Courts Act 1981. Where the court is considering whether to make such an order, it must give the legal representative a reasonable opportunity to make written submissions or, if the legal representative prefers, to attend a hearing to give reasons why it should not make such an order.[1] A wasted costs order can be made at any stage in the proceedings, although in general, applications for wasted costs are best left until after the end of the trial. It may be made on the court's own initiative or on the application of a party, by filing an application notice in accordance with Part 23 or by making an application orally in the course of any hearing.

[1] CPR 46.8. and Practice Direction 46 – Costs Special Cases, paragraph 5.

20.137 A wasted costs order should only be made if the legal representative has acted improperly, unreasonably or negligently, his conduct has caused another party to incur unnecessary costs or has meant that costs incurred by a party prior to the improper, unreasonable or negligent act or omission have been wasted and it is just in all the circumstances to order him to compensate that party for the whole or part of those costs.[1] The court will usually consider the matter in two stages. The first stage is to ask whether the court satisfied that it had before it evidence which would, if unanswered, be likely to lead to a wasted costs order being made; and the wasted costs proceedings are justified notwithstanding the likely costs involved. The second stage is whether, having given the legal representative an opportunity to make representations in writing or at an oral hearing, it is nevertheless appropriate to make the order. The court may proceed to the second stage without first adjourning the hearing if it is satisfied that the legal representative has already had a reasonable opportunity to make representations.[2]

In judicial review claims, the court identified a very important public interest in ensuring the prompt and proper withdrawal of claims where they are manifestly hopeless. A public body is justified in seeking a wasted costs order where despite the clearest warnings that costs were likely to be sought, the claim was not withdrawn.[3]

In *R (Hide (Eugene)) v Staffordshire County Council*[4] the court declined to make a wasted costs order against a solicitor advocate, even though her behaviour had been unreasonable and negligent during judicial review proceedings. In considering whether it is just in all the circumstances to order the representative to pay wasted costs, the court should consider the effect of the order upon the person against whom it was sought.

[1] CPR PD 46, paragraph 5.5.
[2] CPR PD 46, paragraph 5.6 to 5.8.
[3] *R (Tezel) v Secretary of State for the Home Department* [2008] EWHC 3609 (Admin), See also *R (Gransian Ltd) v Secretary of State for the Home Department* [2008] EWHC 3431 (Admin).
[4] [2007] EWHC 2441 (Admin). In the present case, it was not just to order wasted costs as such an order carried a significant risk of causing the solicitor advocate to become bankrupt, which would be a disproportionate consequence of her unreasonable and negligent conduct in the litigation.

20.138 There is some debate as to whether or not a non-party can apply for a wasted costs order. In *R v Camden London Borough Council, ex p Martin*,[1] an application for a wasted costs order could not be made by a party who volunteered to attend as respondent to the hearing of an application for leave to appeal for judicial review. This was because such a party is not a 'party' within the meaning of ss 51(6) and (7) and 151 of the Senior Courts Act 1981. However, in *R v Immigration Appeal Tribunal, ex p Gulson*[2] the court held that it has a residual common law jurisdiction to make wasted costs orders even in these circumstances.

¹ [1997] 1 WLR 359.
² [1997] COD 430.

20.139 Where a wasted costs order is sought against a legal representative who is unable to defend his or her conduct due to legal professional privilege, the court will not make a wasted costs order unless, proceeding with extreme care, it is satisfied that there was nothing that the representative could have said, if unconstrained by the requirements of professional obligation, to resist the order.¹

¹ *Medcalf v Mardell* [2002] UKHL 27, [2003] 1 AC 120.

Chapter 21

DEVOLUTION

AIM OF THIS CHAPTER

21.1 Arrangements for devolution in each of Northern Ireland, Scotland and Wales have taken different forms. They raise constitutional issues which are not discussed in detail here. The aim of this chapter is to give a brief account of the impact of those arrangements so far as proceedings for judicial review are concerned.[1]

---

[1]   The law of judicial review in Scotland, other than as regards devolution issues, is described in CHAPTER 22.

NORTHERN IRELAND

Introduction

21.2 The Northern Ireland Act 1998 (hereafter 'the 1998 Act') is more than a scheme of devolution. While it makes provision for the government of Northern Ireland (as other Northern Ireland schemes of devolution had[1]) it is said to be 'for the purpose of implementing the agreement reached at multi-party talks on Northern Ireland', otherwise known as the Belfast Agreement.[2] That Agreement, which brought forward related legislation to complement the 1998 Act,[3] has since had a contested political existence and several of its key provisions have been revised in later accords intended to sustain the Northern Ireland peace process.[4] The amended 1998 Act,[5] in addition to prescribing how the devolved institutions are to operate,[6] thus deals with a wide range of matters that include the constitutional status of Northern Ireland,[7] arrangements for the workings of a North/South Ministerial Council and a British-Irish Council,[8] the establishment of cross-border implementation bodies,[9] and special provision for human rights and equal opportunities.[10] The 1998 Act has also been amended to provide for a Department with policing and justice functions[11] and to reduce the number of Members of the Legislative Assembly from 108 to 90.[12] In addition, it is now possible for political parties who are eligible for, but who do not wish to take, Ministerial positions in the Executive Committee, to enter into a formal opposition within the Northern Ireland Assembly.[13]

[1] Such as the Government of Ireland Act 1920 and the Northern Ireland Constitution Act 1973. See further B Hadfield, *The Constitution of Northern Ireland* (SLS Legal Publications, Belfast, 1989).

[2] The words are taken from the long title of the 1998 Act. The Belfast Agreement is published as Command Paper 3883 of 1998.

[3] For instance, the Northern Ireland (Sentences) Act 1998; the Police (Northern Ireland) Act 2000; and the Justice (Northern Ireland) Act 2002.

[4] See **21.4**.

[5] See the Northern Ireland Act 2009; the Northern Ireland (St Andrews Agreement) Act 2007; the Northern Ireland (St Andrews Agreement) Act 2006; and the Northern Ireland (Miscellaneous Provisions) Act 2006.

[6] See Part II on the Assembly's legislative power and Part III on executive authorities, the First Minister and Deputy First Minister and the Northern Ireland Ministers.

[7] Section 1.

[8] Sections 52A–54. The Councils were formally created by the British-Irish Agreement 1999, as read with the North/South Co-operation (Implementation Bodies) (Northern Ireland) Order 1999 and, in the Republic of Ireland, the British-Irish Agreement Act 1999.

[9] Section 55.

[10] Part VII which deals, inter alia, with the establishment of the Northern Ireland Human Rights Commission and the Equality Commission for Northern Ireland and discrimination on grounds of religious belief or political opinion by public authorities carrying out functions in respect of Northern Ireland. See, too, Schs 7–9 to the 1998 Act. Note that the powers of the Human Rights Commission were added to significantly by the Justice and Security (Northern Ireland) Act 2007, ss 14–20.

[11] Section 21(A). See, too, the Department of Justice Act (Northern Ireland) 2010; and Northern Ireland Act 1998 (Devolution of Policing and Criminal Justice) Order 2010, SI 2010/976 and Northern Ireland Act 1998 (Amendment of Schedule 3) Order 2010, SI 2010/977.

[12] Assembly Members (Reduction of Numbers) Act (Northern Ireland) 2016.

[13] The Assembly and Executive Reform (Assembly Opposition) Act (Northern Ireland) 2016.

21.3 The corresponding arrangements for the internal operation of the institutions of devolved government may reasonably be described as complex.

While the competence of the institutions – is defined in a conventional manner,[1] there are novel provisions prescribing how both the Assembly and the Executive Committee are to function. These provisions are the result of lengthy political negotiation and they require, among other things, that certain matters be dealt with only by or with 'cross-community' support;[2] that the First Minister and Deputy First Minister be appointed on the basis of party political strength;[3] and that Ministerial decisions can be subject to fuller control within the framework of the Executive Committee.[4] These, and other provisions, have had to operate in a highly party political context and they have given rise to litigation that has revealed much about the 'constitutional' nature of the 1998 Act and its mechanisms for allocating and controlling political power. The case law has also given insights into the interface between law and politics and, indeed, the weakness of institutional structures at times of political distrust.

[1] By reference to a division of powers between excepted and reserved matters (retained at the centre) and others (which are transferred to the devolved institutions): 1998 Act, ss 4–8 & Schs 2, 3. For the leading case law on the powers of the devolved institutions see, by analogy, *AXA General Insurance Ltd v Lord Advocate (Scotland)* [2011] UKSC 46, [2012] 1 AC 868; *A-G v National Assembly for Wales Commission* [2012] UKSC 53, [2013] 1 AC 792; *Imperial Tobacco Ltd v The Lord Advocate (Scotland)* [2012] UKSC 61, 2013 SC (UKSC) 153; *Recovery of Medical Costs for Asbestos Diseases (Wales) Bill* [2015] UKSC 3, [2015] AC 1016; and *R (Miller) v Secretary of State for Exiting the European Union* [2017] UKSC 5, [2017] 2 WLR 583.

[2] For example, s 39(7) dealing with the election of the presiding officer; s 41(2) on the making and amendment of standing orders; and s 42 on 'petitions of concern'. The meaning of 'cross-community support' is dealt with by s 4(5): "cross-community" support, in relation to a vote of any matter, means (a) the support of a majority of members voting, a majority of the designated Nationalists voting and a majority of the designated Unionists voting; or (b) the support of 60 per cent of the members voting, 40 per cent of the designated Nationalists voting and 40 per cent of the designated Unionists voting'.

[3] Section 16A–C.

[4] Sections 28(A) and 28(B).

21.4 This chapter provides an overview of some of that case law and of related proceedings that have considered the out-workings of the Belfast Agreement. It begins with a section that considers the operation and amendment of the 1998 Act, and it next examines some of the leading judicial review case law that has arisen within the framework of that Act. There then follows a section on the 1998 Act's provisions for the resolution of devolution issues, as defined by Sch 10 to the 1998 Act. The conclusion provides some evaluative comments.

The operation of the Northern Ireland Act 1998

21.5 The first point to be made about devolution within the framework of the 1998 Act is that it had only a 'staccato' existence until 8 May 2007.[1] Prior to that date – the day that marked the restoration of devolved government on the basis of the St Andrews Agreement of 2006[2] – the local institutions had been suspended for evermore lengthy periods of time under the Northern Ireland Act 2000[3] (indeed, at the time of writing there is an ongoing political disagreement that means that the institutions presently are not functioning). That Act, which provided for Northern Ireland legislation to be made by way of Order in Council, had been enacted given ongoing political difficulties and distrust as the Belfast Agreement was being implemented. Initially, much of the distrust was caused by an absence of decommissioning of paramilitary weapons and unilateral Unionist decisions to collapse the power-sharing institutions in the absence of movement on the arms issue. However, with the passage of time the difficulties became more widely drawn due to changing electoral patterns within Northern Ireland's two ethno-national communities. Not only did Sinn Féin emerge as the largest party within the nationalist/republican community, the Democratic Unionist Party (DUP) – which had been opposed to the original Agreement of 1998 – achieved electoral dominance within unionism/loyalism. The result was increased political polarisation within constitutional structures that could function only where all of the main parties were willing to work together in a spirit of common endeavour.

[1] The term was used by Lord Bingham in *Robinson v Secretary of State for Northern Ireland* [2002] NI 390, 395. The case is discussed below.
[2] The Northern Ireland Act 2000 (Restoration of Devolved Government) Order 2007, SI 2007/1397. For the St Andrews Agreement 2006 see www.gov.uk/government/uploads/syste m/uploads/attachment_data/file/136651/st_andrews_agreement-2.pdf.
[3] Now repealed: Northern Ireland (St Andrews Agreement) Act 2006, Sch 4 and Northern Ireland (St Andrews Agreement) Act 2007.

21.6 The agreement reached at St Andrews in 2006 (hereafter 'St Andrews') was almost as significant as the original Belfast Agreement. In general terms, St Andrews was the culmination of extensive Irish and UK government efforts to engage all of the main parties in the institutions whether through negotiations with them or through the use of 'confidence building' measures intended to engender (primarily) unionist support for devolution. Of course, the very fact of a further agreement did not remove discord entirely from the political process – further agreements were needed in 2010 and 2014/5[1] – but it did allow for a redrawing of some of the institutional features of the 1998 Act. Principal among these was a somewhat controversial change to the manner of choosing the First and Deputy First Ministers as, rather than being elected with cross-community support, the 1998 Act was amended to provide for appointment through a process of nomination in the light of party strength in the Assembly.[2] Also important were changes to pursue heightened levels of Ministerial accountability. At the centre of these was a commitment to adopt a statutory Ministerial Code which would tie the holders of Ministerial positions to a range of duties, including duties to pass certain Ministerial decisions over to the collective decision-making forum of the Executive Committee[3] (this aspect is discussed more fully below[4]). This emphasis on collective decision-making was likewise to be complemented by a provision that would allow a minimum of 30 Members of the Assembly to ask for a Ministerial decision to be referred to the Executive Committee where the Members consider that the decision may have been taken in contravention of the Ministerial Code or where it relates to a matter of 'public importance'.[5]

[1] Viz, the Hillsborough Agreement 2010 (www.parliament.uk/briefing-papers/SN05350/the-hi llsborough-agreement) and the Stormont House and Fresh Start Agreements of 2014 and 2015, respectively (https://www.gov.uk/government/publications/the-stormont-house-agreeme nt AND https://www.gov.uk/government/news/a-fresh-start-for-northern-ireland).
[2] Section 16A-C.
[3] Section 28A(5). The text of the Code is available at https://www.northernireland.gov.uk/sites/ default/files/publications/nigov/Northern%20Ireland%20Ministerial%20Code.pdf
[4] Paragraphs **21.18–21.22**.

Section 28B. Note that such referrals can be made only once and within a seven-day time-frame and that the question whether a decision touches upon matters of 'public importance' is one for the Presiding Officer.

21.7 In terms of judicial review, this experience with devolution as an initially 'stop-start' enterprise revealed much about the role of law at a time of profound political change. For instance, in the immediate post-Belfast Agreement years, when the workings of the institutions were at their most unpredictable, the courts stated that the 1998 Act is a 'constitution' for Northern Ireland and that its institutions should be given every legal chance to function.[1] On the other hand, the courts also held that some 'confidence building' measures were unlawful notwithstanding the political context within which the measures were adopted.[2] While this did not mean that confidence building measures *per se* were deemed unlawful – some applications for judicial review of governmental choices were dismissed[3] – it did mean that political convenience was not allowed to trump core requirements of the rule of law. The same was true in a case arising under the statutory Ministerial Code that was adopted after the St Andrews Agreement, where the High Court held that a Minister had acted unlawfully by failing to observe procedural limitations on her powers.[4]

[1] *Robinson v Secretary of State for Northern Ireland* [2002] NI 390, discussed at **21.8–21.11**. And see, by analogy, *Re Toner's Application* [2007] NIQB 18, paragraph 9(x)(a), Gillen J; and *Re Williamson's Application* [2009] NIQB 63, paragraph 66, Gillen J.
[2] *Re Duffy* [2008] UKHL 4, [2008] NI 152; and *Re Downes' Application* [2006] NIQB 77, [2007] NIQB 1, [2009] NICA 26 discussed below at **21.14.–21.15**.
[3] *Re Murphy's Application* [2001] NI 425, discussed below at **21.13**.
[4] *Re Solinas' Application* [2009] NIQB 43, discussed below at **21.19–21.21**.

Judicial Review

The 1998 Act as 'a constitution'

21.8 The case in which the courts first described the 1998 Act as a 'constitution' was *Robinson v Secretary of State for Northern Ireland*.[1] The Northern Ireland Assembly had here been restored after a period of suspension that had been prompted by the First Minister's resignation in protest at the absence of decommissioning of paramilitary weapons (restoration took effect in September 2001; decommissioning commenced shortly afterwards). Under the then applicable provisions of the 1998 Act[2] the Assembly was required to elect, with cross-community support, joint candidates for the posts of First and Deputy First Ministers.[3] Sections 16(8) and 32(3) of the 1998 Act moreover required that the election be held within six weeks of restoration, after which period of time the Secretary of State was required to call fresh Assembly elections if the posts of First and Deputy First Minister could not be filled. On 2 November 2001, the last full working day within the six week period, the candidates, David Trimble and Mark Durkan, failed to be elected to the posts due to an inability to command the requisite Unionist support for their candidatures. In legal proceedings initiated by the (then) deputy leader of the Democratic Unionist Party (Mr Peter Robinson – Northern Ireland's First Minister between 2008–2015), the Secretary of State acknowledged that he was obliged to propose a date for fresh Assembly elections and that he would do so shortly. However, prior to a date being announced there was some intricate politicking within the Assembly whereby some members temporarily re-designated themselves as Unionists with the result that the two candidates were able to be elected with cross-community support on 6 November 2001.[4] Given this development, the Secretary of State announced that Assembly elections would be held on 1 May 2003, which was the date for elections originally specified in the 1998 Act.[5] Peter Robinson thereupon initiated further proceedings to challenge the lawfulness of both the election of the First and Deputy First Ministers and of the Secretary of State's choice of date for Assembly elections.

1   [2002] UKHL 32, [2002] NI 390.
2   Section 16; substituted by ss 16A–16C, *per* s 8 of the Northern Ireland (St Andrews Agreement) Act 2006.
3   'Cross-community support' is defined in s 4(5) as: '(a) the support of a majority of members voting, a majority of the designated Nationalists voting and a majority of the designated Unionists voting; or (b) the support of 60 per cent of the members voting, 40 per cent of the designated Nationalists voting and 40 per cent of the designated Unionists voting'. For the purposes of the election of the First and Deputy First Ministers, (a) applied.
4   All Members of the Assembly must designate themselves as Unionist, Nationalist, or Other when signing the Roll of Membership (1998 Act, s 4(5)). Some members who had designated themselves as 'Other' temporarily re-designated. And note that, where Members now wish to re-designate, they may do so only by becoming a member of a different political party, by ceasing to be a member of any political party, or, where they do not belong to a party, by becoming a member of a political party: 1998 Act, s 4(5A).
5   Section 31(2), as originally enacted.

21.9 Argument in the courts came to centre upon two main points, namely (1) whether the requirement that the election of the First and Deputy First Minister be held within six weeks was mandatory and (2) whether the Secretary of State was obliged, when setting the date for Assembly elections, to choose a date that was 'constitutionally prompt' and not influenced by the Assembly vote of 6 November 2001. In answering both questions in the negative the courts fastened upon the need for political stability in Northern Ireland and for the political choices that had been made to be viewed in that light. In the Northern Ireland High Court and Court of Appeal this was explained in terms of, among other things, public policy justifications for reading time-limits flexibly and the need to interpret the 1998 Act in a way that would not 'imperil' the Belfast Agreement that underlies it.[1] However, it was the majority in the House of Lords that made express use of the language of constitutionalism when holding that neither the election of 6 November 2001 nor the Secretary of State's subsequent choice was unlawful. Lord Bingham, delivering the lead speech of the majority, thus said that it was right that the 1998 Act should be 'interpreted generously and purposively, bearing in mind the values which the constitutional provisions are intended to embody'.[2] Lord Hoffmann likewise said that the Belfast Agreement 'was the product of multi-party negotiations to devise constitutional arrangements for a fresh start in Northern Ireland . . . The 1998 Act is a constitution for Northern Ireland, framed to create a continuing form of government against the history of the territory and the principles agreed in Belfast'.[3]

1   The term was used by Nicholson LJ in the Northern Ireland Court of Appeal, unreported judgment of 21 March 2002.
2   [2002] NI 390, 398 at [11].

³ [2002] NI 390, 402 at [25]. And for more recent judicial recognition of the purposes of the Agreement see *R (Miller) v Secretary of State for Exiting the European Union* [2017] UKSC 5, [2017] 2 WLR 583, para 128, Lord Neuberger: 'The NI Act is the product of the Belfast Agreement and the British-Irish Agreement, and is a very important step in the programme designed to achieve reconciliation of the communities of Northern Ireland'.

21.10 There are two points to be made about the *Robinson* case. The first is that its ascription of constitutional status to the Northern Ireland Act 1998, while not wholly novel in historic terms,[1] elevated the Belfast Agreement and its values to a position of some prominence in the process of judicial reasoning. The implications of this approach were later seen in *Re McComb's Application*,[2] where a former paramilitary prisoner who had been released early under the terms of the Belfast Agreement and Northern Ireland (Sentences) Act 1998 applied to the Department of the Environment for a public service vehicle licence. His application was refused partly because it was found that his previous conviction meant that he was a not a 'fit and proper person to hold the licence' within the meaning of the Road Traffic (Northern Ireland) Order 1981. However, the applicant argued that a distinction should be made between prisoners released under the Agreement and other prisoners and that the decision had failed to take into account the fact that his release from prison was contingent upon the Sentence Review Commissioners being satisfied that he would not be a 'danger to the public'.[3] Granting the application for judicial review, Kerr J, as he then was, accepted that the 'fit and proper' test was different from the 'danger to the public' formulation but that the determination of the Sentence Review Commissioners was a relevant consideration that should have been taken into account (the judge did not accept that this would create a two-tier system of applicants as it was merely one consideration among others). The judge moreover referred to the Belfast Agreement and Lord Hoffmann's comments in *Robinson* when saying that, 'particular attention should be paid to the fact that a prisoner released under the terms of the Northern Ireland (Sentences) Act 1998 has been adjudged not to be a danger to the public'.[4]

¹ See, eg, *Belfast Corporation v OD Cars* [1960] AC 490, 517, Viscount Simmonds, referring to the Government of Ireland Act 1920 as a 'constitutional Act'.
² [2003] NIQB 47.
³ Northern Ireland (Sentences) Act 1998, s 3(6).
⁴ [2003] NIQB 47, paragraph 31. References to the Agreement have also been made in, eg, *Re Parsons' Application for Judicial Review* [2002] NI 378, 388-9, Kerr J (rejecting a challenge to the legality of a 50/50 recruitment quota for the Police Service of Northern Ireland); *Re Sinn Féin's Application for Judicial Review* [2005] NI 412 (Weatherup J referring frequently to the Agreement in the context of a challenge to a decision to reduce financial assistance paid to Sinn Féin: application dismissed); *Re Neill's Application* [2005] NIQB 66, paragraph 35, Girvan J ('The proper approach to the 1998 Act is to regard it as constitutional in nature'); and *Re Coláiste Feirste's Application* [2011] NIQB 98, paras 22, Treacy J stating that 'Article 89 [of the Education (Northern Ireland) Order 1998] is not merely aspirational: it gives statutory expression to the Belfast Agreement'.

21.11 The second point is that the wider context to the case nevertheless revealed the fragility of the constitutional settlement that then pertained – and still does pertain – in Northern Ireland. Although the courts were anxious to afford the local institutions every legal opportunity to function, the political reality was very different indeed and the Assembly soon entered a sustained period of suspension. The subsequent accord reached at St Andrews was therefore something of an exercise in constitutional re-engineering as the parties to it made a number of important changes to the internal design and workings of the institutions. Some of these changes followed from the facts of *Robinson* itself,[1] while others addressed issues that had been litigated in related disputes about the out-workings of the Belfast Agreement.[2] The 1998 Act, in the result, may have been a constitution, but it was one that was open to suspension pending a process of politically driven amendment.[3]

[1] For example, the manner of choosing the First and Deputy First Ministers was changed from election with cross-community support to nomination based on party strength in the Assembly (1998 Act, ss 16A–16C). See, too, the changes to rules of designation, ie a Member of the Assembly is now allowed to re-designate during the life-span of an Assembly only where '(a) (being a member of a political party) he becomes a member of a different political party or he ceases to be a member of any political party; (b) (not being a member of any political party) he becomes a member of a political party' (1998 Act, s 4(5A)).

[2] See, eg, the issue of Ministerial nominations to meetings of the North/South Ministerial Council in *Re De Brun's Application* [2001] NI 442 (First Minister acted unlawfully in refusing nominate Sinn Féin Ministers to meetings), as now read in the light of 1998 Act, s 52A.

[3] Some of the amendments included the imposition of statutory duties on the Executive Committee, for instance as regards the development of an Irish language strategy and an anti-poverty strategy: see ss 28 D and 28E of the 1998 Act. Successful challenges have since been brought against the Executive Committee for its failure to adopt strategies: see respectively, *Re Conradh Na Gaeilge's Application* [2017] NIQB 27 and *Re CAJ's Application* [2015] NIQB 59.

The legality of 'confidence building' measures

21.12 One of the more controversial features of UK government decision-making during earlier periods of suspension caused by political impasse was the above noted use of 'confidence building' measures in an attempt to engender (primarily) unionist support for the institutions.[1] In broad terms, such measures took the form of exercises of power on discrete issues in a manner which would appeal to particular political parties or the communities they represent in order to induce among them a greater acceptance of the new governmental structures. Such decision-making inevitably raised difficult questions about the interface between law and politics, and the courts had to determine when political choices became justiciable matters of law. While the courts here emphasised the need for restraint where there was 'a higher degree of knowledge and expertise on the part of the decider . . . [and where the decision was taken] . . . in accordance with the proper principles',[2] they equally made it clear that they would guard closely those 'proper principles' when political choices, reflecting elements of confidence building, offended public law standards. Several high-profile measures were for that reason held unlawful.

[1] Although for an arguable instance of 'confidence building' with Republicans see *Re Williamson's Application* [2000] NI 281 (challenge to the Secretary of State's decision not to specify the IRA as an organisation which was 'not maintaining a complete and unequivocal ceasefire' for purposes of s 3(8) of the Northern Ireland (Sentences) Act 1998, notwithstanding several instances of violence: application dismissed). See also *R v Downey* (21 February 2014, unreported), discussed at **21.16**.

[2] *Re Williamson's Application* [2000] NI 281, 303-4, Carswell LCJ. This is the so-called 'soft-edged' standard of review: see G Anthony, *Judicial Review in Northern Ireland* (Hart Publishing, Oxford, 2nd edn, 2014) pp 125–126.

21.13 One case that illustrates the point about the courts recognising the need to accommodate the political dimension where legal principle has not been offended is *Re Murphy's Application*.[1] This was a complex case that concerned the legality of flags legislation that mandated that the Union Flag be flown over government buildings in Northern Ireland on those days when it officially flies in the rest of the United Kingdom (the legislation was in the form of an Order in Council made while the Assembly was suspended and regulations made after it had been restored).[2] The proceedings were initiated by a Sinn Féin Member of the Northern Ireland Assembly who argued that the decisions of the Secretary of State when making the legislation were discriminatory; that they were contrary to the notions of equality that run throughout the Belfast Agreement; that the Secretary of State was not legally competent to make the Order and Regulations; and that the Secretary of State had acted pursuant to a secret political deal with David Trimble (the then leader of the then largest Unionist party in the Assembly, the Ulster Unionists). Having rejected the applicant's arguments about discrimination, equality, and competence, the High Court held that it had been open to the Secretary of State to act in pursuit of comments that he may have made to another political leader. Indeed, Kerr J, as he then was, was of the view that such motivation could not, in any event, provide a basis for a legal challenge: 'I accept that, in expressing his intentions to Mr Trimble, the Secretary of State did not do so "for reasons of political expediency to accommodate Mr Trimble and the Ulster Unionist party". Even if he had done so, however, his decision to introduce the Order and to make the Regulations could not be quashed on that account alone. Such a decision is the stuff of politics. It is not subject to judicial review'.[3]

[1]   [2001] NI 425.
[2]   The Flags (Northern Ireland) Order 2000, SI 2000/1347, and the Flags Regulations (Northern Ireland) 2000, SI 2000/347.
[3]   [2001] NI 425, 435, Kerr J.

21.14 The tension between legal principle, political preference and confidence building was, however, more apparent in *Re Duffy*.[1] In this case the Secretary of State for Northern Ireland had appointed to the Parades Commission – the statutory body that is responsible for regulating contentious parades – two members of the Loyal Orders after active approaches had been made to those and other organisations within the Protestant/Unionist community. His decision to do so was prompted in part by a wish to engage that community in dialogue with the Parades Commission, which makes the clear majority of its decisions in relation to parades organised by the Loyal Orders.[2] In the High Court it was held that the Secretary of State had acted unlawfully in doing so as he had failed to give consideration to whether to make active approaches to organisations that were opposed to marching (it was held that this ran contrary to the requirement of community balance that underscores the legislation). While an appeal to the Court of Appeal was allowed – the Court considered that 'the decision in this case was *par excellence* a political one'[3] – the House of Lords held, albeit for different reasons, that there had been an illegality. Noting that the Commission has a duty to seek to resolve contentious disputes by mediation the House of Lords observed that, where that is not possible, the Commission must make determinations that reconcile the wishes of marchers with the wishes of those who do not want to be 'intimidated, insulted or inconvenienced' by a parade.[4] It followed that the

Parades Commission would be able to perform its tasks satisfactorily only where both sides to a dispute accepted that the Commission was independent, objective and impartial in its approach. Given the point, the House of Lords held that no reasonable person with knowledge of the two appointees' background and activities could have supposed that either would have brought an objective or impartial judgment to bear on the problems raised by parades. The House of Lords also held that the decision-making process had failed to take into account all relevant considerations, *viz* how far apparent bias would prevent the appointees playing a full part as Commissioners and whether their appointment would command widespread public acceptance. As Lord Brown put it:

> 'the single critical error made here was in appointing to the Parades Commission two men with an irredeemable conflict of interest rendering them in effect ineligible for the office. They would have been bound to recuse themselves from mediating or adjudicating upon most of the more contentious disputes before the Commission . . . and in any event their very membership of the Commission (whose determinations are assumed to be those of the body as a whole and are issued simply under the hand of the chairman) would inevitably give rise to the perception of bias against the nationalist community'.[5]

[1]   [2008] UKHL 4, [2008] NI 152.
[2]   Public Processions (Northern Ireland) Act 1998.
[3]   [2007] NI 12, 24, paragraph 40, Kerr LCJ.
[4]   [2008] NI 152, 161, paragraph 25, Lord Bingham.
[5]   [2008] NI 152, 172 at [60].

21.15 The Secretary of State was similarly found to have acted unlawfully in *Re Downes' Application*, albeit that the High Court and Court of Appeal in Northern Ireland differed in their approach to the legal significance of 'confidence building' in the case.[1] The application was made by a woman whose husband had been killed by the police in Northern Ireland and who wished to challenge the Secretary of State's decision to appoint a police widow to the position of Interim Victims Commissioner. The appointment, which was made on the basis of the royal prerogative pending the creation of a statutory position,[2] was challenged on a number of grounds that included use of power for an improper purpose and a failure to have due regard for the Code of Practice that governs appointments to public positions. The essence of the applicant's submissions on these points was that the Secretary of State had not adhered to the merit principle when making the appointment but had been influenced to appoint the successful candidate (who had been suggested by the DUP) by a desire to encourage the DUP's participation in the institutions. The High Court agreed that this (and other flaws) rendered the decision unlawful as the 'Secretary of State decided to disregard the accepted merit norms applicable to public appointments in order to secure the appointment of the DUP's nominee who *ex hypothesi* might not have been the best candidate, simply because she was the DUP's candidate'.[3] However, while the Court of Appeal agreed that the Secretary of State had acted unlawfully, it did not follow the reasoning of the trial judge and based its decision, instead, on what it saw as the Secretary of State's failure to consider the terms of the Code. Noting that the Code recognised that 'in certain circumstances absolute merit order [does] not inevitably and invariably dictate the choice of candidate' the Court stated that 'the decision to appoint someone who is able to do the job can co-exist with a selection that is designed to advance another aim'. While this did not mean that the wish to 'secure a political advantage [could be] allowed to predominate over the need to choose a meritorious candidate', it did mean that 'there is nothing objectionable in choosing a candidate whose selection will, incidentally, achieve a desired political objective'.[4] The illegality thus lay in the Secretary of State's failure to take the Code into account as a relevant consideration rather than in any use of power for an improper political purpose.[5]

[1]   [2006] NIQB 77, [2007] NIQB 1, [2009] NICA 26.
[2]   See now the Victims and Survivors (Northern Ireland) Order 2006, SI 2006/2953, NI 17, as read with the Victims and Survivors Act (Northern Ireland) 2008. The legality of the appointments made under the Order was subsequently, and unsuccessfully, challenged: *Re Williamson's Application* [2010] NICA 8.
[3]   [2006] NIQB 77, para 52.
[4]   [2009] NICA 26, paras 48–49.
[5]   Leave to appeal to the Supreme Court was refused.

21.16 A further ruling related to 'confidence building' is *R v Downey*,[1] which was a criminal case that was ultimately concerned with the status of government representations to the effect that known IRA members were not being pursued in relation to certain offences committed during the Northern Ireland conflict. The representations in question had been made at the request of Sinn Féin, who wished to secure guarantees for Republicans who had been 'on the run' at the time of the Belfast Agreement and who were liable to imprisonment if convicted of any outstanding offences (Sinn Féin considered that this was anomalous because the individuals in question would have been eligible for early release under the Belfast Agreement had they been serving prison sentences in 1998).[2] The matter had attracted considerable political attention in 2005 – a government Bill had been introduced in Parliament before being withdrawn – but it thereafter became less prominent and even seemed to have disappeared. However, it later transpired that the government had established a secret administrative scheme whereby Sinn Féin would forward the names of IRA members to the authorities who would thereafter confirm in writing whether the persons in question were being sought for questioning or prosecution. This was intended to consolidate Republican support for the peace process, but the scheme was to prove highly divisive when its details were made public as a result of *R v Downey*. The defendant, who had received a letter from the government,[3] had been arrested in Gatwick Airport while travelling to Greece and was charged in connection with the notorious 1982 IRA bombing of Hyde Park. At his trial, his defence team made an abuse of process application based upon the letter, which had in fact been issued to him in error (the Police Service of Northern Ireland had failed to advise the government that the defendant was being sought by the Metropolitan Police). Granting the application, the trial judge, Sweeney J, held that the error did not detract from the nature of the representation that had been made to the defendant and that it would offend the court's sense of justice to allow the prosecution to proceed in its light. While the judge noted that 'the public interest in ensuring that those who are accused of serious crime should be tried is a very strong one' and that he should keep firmly in mind 'the plight of the victims and their families', he also considered the public interest 'in ensuring that executive misconduct does not undermine public confidence in the criminal justice system and bring it into disrepute, and the public interest in holding officials of the state to promises they have made in the full understanding of what is involved in the bargain'. Having balanced the competing public interests, the judge thus held that the trial could not continue because 'this is one of those rare cases in which, in the particular circumstances, it offends the court's sense of justice and propriety to be asked to try the defendant'.[4]

1   (21 February 2014, unreported).
2   Belfast Agreement, Part 10; and Northern Ireland (Sentences) Act 1998.
3   The letter to him read: 'On the basis of information currently available, there is no outstanding direction for prosecution in Northern Ireland, there are no warrants in existence, nor are you wanted in Northern Ireland for arrest, questioning or charge by the police. The [PSNI] are not aware of any interest in you from any other police force in the United Kingdom. If any other outstanding offence or offences came to light, or if any request for extradition were to be received, these would have to be dealt with in the usual way'.
4   21 Feb 2014, NYR, paras 173–175.

21.17 This was an inevitably controversial outcome and it prompted a number of reviews into the whole matter of the 'on the runs'.[1] Nevertheless, it is to be noted that Sweeney J's ruling centred upon a robust reassertion of the importance of legal principle even in the context of a highly politicised administrative scheme. The *Downey* case may, for that reason, yet come to be regarded as one of the most significant judicial statements about the rule of law in post-conflict Northern Ireland.

1   Most notably, *The Hallett Review: An independent review into the 'On the runs' administrative scheme*, available at http://www.hallettreview.org/

21.18 The *Downey* case is also of note because it touches upon the wider matter of how to deal with the legacy of the Northern Ireland conflict. While *Downey* was of course concerned with the workings of the criminal justice process, the challenge of dealing with the past is a much broader one that has also given rise to inquiries, inquests, and a very large number of applications for judicial review.[1] This piecemeal approach has since attracted a considerable amount of criticism, and there is growing political pressure for the adoption of a more holistic approach that might uncover the fuller 'truth' about the role of state and non-state actors during the conflict. While there has been some political agreement on the structures that might facilitate such an approach,[2] an absence of funding and concerns about imbalances within the process have led to something of a stalemate at the time of writing. It is to be expected that the piecemeal approach will continue pending any political commitment to addressing this most divisive of issues.

1   See, eg, *Re Finucane's Application* [2017] NICA 7.
2   See, in particular, the Stormont House Agreement athttps://www.gov.uk/government/publica tions/the-stormont-house-agreement.

The Ministerial Code

21.19 The final issue to be considered in this section is the judicial approach to the statutory Ministerial Code that now binds Northern Ireland Ministers.[1] As outlined above, the Code is a result of St Andrews and it requires, among other things, that Ministers bring to the attention of the Executive Committee certain matters that are identified in the legislation and the Code. The statutory basis for the Code starts with s 28A(1), which provides that 'a Minister or junior Minister shall act in accordance with the provisions of the Ministerial Code'. Section 28A(5) provides that 'The Ministerial Code must include provision for requiring Ministers or Junior Ministers to bring to the attention of the Executive Committee any matter that ought, by virtue of s 20(3) or (4), to be considered by the Committee'. Those subsections, in turn, deal with functions which require discussion in the Executive Committee and which have been drawn together at paragraph 2.4 of the Ministerial Code under the heading 'Duty to bring matters to the attention of the Executive Committee'. This paragraph of the Code requires that any matter within a list of six shall be brought to the attention of the Executive Committee by the responsible Minister to be considered by the Committee. These include:

'Any matter which:
i)   cuts across the responsibilities of two or more Ministers;
ii)   requires agreement on prioritisation;
iii)   requires the adoption of a common position;
iv)   has implications for the programme for government;
v)   is significant or controversial and is clearly outside the scope of the agreed programme for government; or
vi)   is significant or controversial and which has been determined by the First and Deputy First Minister acting jointly to be a matter that should be considered by the Executive Committee'.

Under s 28A(10) it is indicated that 'a Minister or Junior Minister has no Ministerial authority to take any decision in contravention of a provision of the Ministerial Code made under subsection (5)'. Section 28A is then complemented by s 28B, which allows a minimum of 30 Members of the Assembly to ask for a Ministerial decision to be referred to the Executive Committee where the Members consider that the decision may have been taken in contravention of the Ministerial Code or where it relates to a matter of 'public importance'.[2]

---

[1]   The text of the Code is available at https://www.northernireland.gov.uk/sites/default/files/pu blications/nigov/Northern%20Ireland%20Ministerial%20Code.pdf.
[2]   Note that such referrals can be made only once and within a seven-day time-frame and that the question whether a decision touches upon matters of 'public importance' is one for the Presiding Officer.

21.20 These provisions have given rise to litigation. The leading case remains *Re Solinas' Application*,[1] which concerned the failure of the Minister for Social Development to comply with procedural requirements placed on her by the Executive Committee, thereby allegedly placing her in breach of the Ministerial Code. The decision at issue was that of the Minister to withdraw government funding from a project in a loyalist area because a paramilitary organisation, the Ulster Defence Association (UDA), stood, at least indirectly, to benefit from the project. Subsequent to the project beginning the UDA had been engaged in overt acts of violence and it had later failed to engage in decommissioning of its weapons. The question of whether to withdraw the funding had previously been raised at the Executive Committee and this in effect meant that the Minister was required to take certain steps before doing anything further. These included obtaining legal advice on the legality or otherwise of withdrawing funding; the forwarding of any such advice to the Minister of Finance and Personnel and the First Minister and Deputy First

Minister; and considering the legal advice with the Minister of Finance & Personnel before making any decision. In the event, however, the Minister failed fully to comply with these requirements and announced the withdrawal of the funding even though the Head of the Northern Ireland Civil Service advised her that she would be acting contrary to the Ministerial Code if she did so. In judicial review proceedings brought by an employee of the organisation that administered the government funding Morgan J agreed that the Minister had acted unlawfully. This was because, in his view, the evidence made clear that the Executive Committee had determined how the decision making process was to be carried out and that, by omitting to comply with the various procedural requirements, the Minister had acted in a procedurally improper way. An order of certiorari was issued.

1   [2009] NIQB 43.

21.21 This decision is significant because it demonstrated that the court was prepared to rule on a dispute that had a strong political element that went beyond the interests of the applicant — whose employment was jeopardised by the withdrawal of the financial support for the project — to engage those of the Executive Committee. The Executive Committee itself was represented at the hearing where it relied upon s 28A to argue in favour of Ministerial discipline and collective action and against the ability of the Minister to act on her own without complying with the Executive Committee's requirements. This per-haps foreshadows in Northern Ireland what some commentators have termed 'legal constitutionalism'[1], *viz* a system in which courts play an ever-more important role in controlling government. However, while such constitution-alism may be criticised for the reason that it transfers too much power into the hands of the judges, it should be noted that Morgan J stated in *Re Solinas' Application* that 'there can be political sanctions under the 1998 Act in certain circumstances' and that 'not every breach' of the Ministerial Code 'must lead to the provision of a [legal] remedy'.[2] This would suggest that the courts will remain reluctant to become involved in disputes that are essentially political in nature and where the interests involved are matters of party political prefer-ence. However, where private individuals are directly affected by decisions it would equally appear that the approach of the courts may be very different. As the judge put it: 'This applicant was directly affected by the decision-making in this case as he was at risk of losing his job . . . I consider that where, as here, procedural default is established which directly affects the applicant a practical and effective remedy should normally follow'.[3]

1   On which see A Tomkins, *Public Law* (Oxford, Clarendon Press, 2003).
2   [2009] NIQB 43, paragraph [36].
3   [2009] NIQB 43, paragraph [36].

21.22 There have since been other cases that have reviewed the lawfulness of Ministerial decision-making in the light of s 28A, and more can be expected.[1] This is because of the apparently open-ended nature of much of the Code, particularly where decisions are taken by a Minister alone and where it is arguable that the subject of the decision is one which ought to have been brought before the Executive Committee. Indeed, in this context, the language at paragraph 2.4 of the Ministerial Code, noted at **21.18** above, contains phraseology which clearly invites argument and contention about Ministerial responsibility under the Code. For instance, it is not self-evident when an issue 'cuts across the responsibilities of two or more departments' or is a matter which 'has implications for the programme for government' or is a matter which is 'significant or controversial'. It may very well be that the courts will increasingly be invited to construe the above and other similar phraseology. If the courts are invited to do so, the difficulty will be that, if too wide a definition is provided, the role of the individual Minister may become diminished with the result that the Executive Committee might become inundated with issues.

¹ See, eg, *Re Central Craigavon Ltd's Application* [2010] NIQB 73 and [2011] NICA 17; *Re JR65's Application* [2013] NIQB 101; *Re Minister for Finance and Personnel's Application* [2013] NIQB 137; and *Re Neeson's Application* [2016] NIQB 58.

Devolution Issues

The legal framework

21.23 The above cases have all illustrated, in different ways, some of the difficult and unique questions that can arise in judicial review proceedings brought within the often highly-charged political context of Northern Ireland. Of course, outside such disputes judicial review also provides the forum within which most 'devolution issues' are addressed by the courts. Devolution issues, for these purposes, are defined in para 1 of Sch 10 to the 1998 Act as:

(a) a question whether any provision of an Act of the Assembly is within the legislative competence of the Assembly;

(b) a question whether a purported or proposed exercise of a function by a Minister or Northern Ireland Department is or would be invalid by reason of s 24;

(c) a question whether a Minister or Northern Ireland Department has failed to comply with any of the Convention Rights, any obligation under EU law or any order under s 27 as far as relating to such an obligation; or

(d) any question arising under this Act about excepted or reserved matters.

21.24 It is clear from this definition that the substance of devolution issues will generally be concerned with whether the devolved authorities (the Assembly, the Northern Ireland Ministers and devolved Departments) have acted within their competence. To ascertain whether they have done so involves consideration of the wider scheme of the 1998 Act and, as far as concerns the legislative powers of the Assembly, of s 6. This states:

(1) A provision of an Act is not law if it is outside the legislative competence of the Assembly.

(2) A provision is outside that competence if any of the following paragraphs apply—

(a) it would form part of the law of a country or territory other than Northern Ireland, or confer or remove functions exercisable otherwise than in or as regards Northern Ireland;

(b) it deals with an excepted matter and is not ancillary to other provisions (whether in the Act or previously enacted) dealing with reserved or transferred matters;

    (c)   it is incompatible with any of the Convention rights;

    (d)   it is incompatible with EU law;

    (e)   it discriminates against any person or class of person on the ground of religious belief or political opinion;

    (f)   it modifies an [entrenched] enactment.[1]

---

[1]   Entrenched enactments are defined in s 7; while 'the Convention rights', *per* s 98, has the same meaning as in the Human Rights Act 1998. For the lists of excepted and reserved matters see Schs 2 and 3 respectively.

21.25 The corresponding provision as relates to actions taken by Northern Ireland Ministers or Departments, including actions in the form of making, confirming or approving any subordinate legislation, is section 24. This states:

    (1)   A Minister or Northern Ireland department has no power to make, confirm or approve any subordinate legislation, or to do any act, so far as the legislation or act—

        (a)   is incompatible with any of the Convention rights;

        (b)   is incompatible with EU law;

        (c)   discriminates against a person or class of person on the ground of religious belief or political opinion;

        (d)   in the case of an act, aids or incites another person to discriminate against a person or class of person on that ground; or

        (e)   in the case of legislation, modifies an [entrenched] enactment.[1]

It should be noted that this provision remains central to the legal obligations of Ministers, notwithstanding the changes that were made to the 1998 Act after St Andrews. In other words, while the statutory Ministerial Code that has been considered above provides additional mechanisms for controlling Ministers, it is said to be 'without prejudice to the operation of section 24'.[2]

---

[1]   Entrenched enactments are defined in s 7. And note that sub-s (2) provides that: 'Subsection (1)(c) and (d) does not apply in relation to any act which is unlawful by virtue of the Fair Employment (Northern Ireland) Order 1998, or would be unlawful but for some exception made by virtue of Part VIII of that Order'

[2]   Section 28A(1). On the Code see **21.19–21.22**.

21.26 Where a devolution issue concerns the meaning of an Act of the Assembly or subordinate legislation, section 83 of the 1998 Act imposes an interpretive obligation whereby the courts must try to read the Act in a way that is within the competence of the Assembly or that makes the subordinate legislation valid. Moreover, where a court or tribunal decides that a provision in an Assembly Act is not within competence or a provision of subordinate legislation has been made, confirmed or approved without power, it may remove or limit any retrospective effect of its decision or may suspend the effect of its decision for any period or on any condition to allow the defect to be corrected. In deciding whether to do so, the court or tribunal shall (among other things) have regard to the extent to which persons who are not parties to the proceedings would otherwise be adversely affected.[1]

---

[1]   Section 81(1)–(3).

21.27 There has been little case law under s 83 of the Act itself, although guidance on how to approach the section can be found in Supreme Court rulings on 'devolution issues' that have arisen under the Government of Wales

Act 2006 and the Scotland Act 1998.[1] Here, the Supreme Court has identified three general principles that should inform the judicial interpretation of the various provisions that govern disputes about competence. The first of these is that the courts should always recall that the devolution Acts have been designed by the Westminster Parliament and that the courts should not seek to redraw the parameters of the Acts; the second is that the Acts should be interpreted in the same way as other legislative schemes, bearing in mind the need for a 'constant and predictable' approach to their interpretation; and the third is that the purpose of the devolution Acts – viz 'a generous settlement of legislative authority' – should guide the courts where this is deemed necessary.[2] Read alongside related Supreme Court statements about the democratic legitimacy and importance of the devolved legislatures,[3], this would suggest that the Supreme Court: (a) acknowledges that the devolved legislatures occupy a constitutionally elevated position within the UK constitution, but (b) that fact alone will not lead to a distinct body of jurisprudence on the interpretation of their constitutive Acts.

[1] *A-G v National Assembly for Wales Commission* [2012] UKSC 53, [2013] 1 AC 792 and *Imperial Tobacco Ltd v The Lord Advocate (Scotland)* [2012] UKSC 61, 2013 SC (UKSC) 153.

[2] *Imperial Tobacco Ltd v The Lord Advocate (Scotland)* [2012] UKSC 61, 2013 SC (UKSC) 153, 159, paras 12-15, Lord Hope, citing, among others, *Gallagher v Lynn* [1937] AC 863 and *Martin v Most* 2010 SC (UKSC) 40.

[3] *AXA General Insurance Ltd v Lord Advocate (Scotland)* [2011] UKSC 46, [2012] 1 AC 868.

21.28 The constitutional status of the devolved legislatures was also raised in the seminal *Miller* case, which was heard on appeal by the Supreme Court alongside two references from the Northern Ireland courts (*viz* in the *Agnew* and *McCord* cases).[1] The central issue in *Miller* was not, of course, one of statutory interpretation, but rather whether the government could rely upon the prerogative treaty-making power to trigger Article 50 TEU, or whether it could do so only where an Act of the Westminster Parliament authorised such action. In the corresponding Northern Ireland cases, it had been argued that, if an Act of the Westminster Parliament was required to trigger Article 50 TEU, such legislation could be enacted only after the government had sought the consent of the Northern Ireland Assembly (interventions to like effect were made in the *Miller* case by the Scottish and Welsh Law Officers). In real terms, this was an argument about whether the so-called 'Sewel convention' was a 'constitutional convention' that required legislative consent motions to be passed whenever any Act of the Westminster Parliament would affect the devolved competences, in this instance as a result of EU withdrawal. While the Supreme Court held on the facts of *Miller* that an Act of Parliament was required to trigger Article 50 TEU, it did not accept that there was a judicially enforceable constitutional convention in respect of the powers of the devolved legislatures. In making the point, Lord Neuberger said that 'we do not underestimate the importance of our constitutional conventions, some of which play a fundamental role in the operation of our constitution. The Sewel Convention has an important role . . . But the policing of its scope and the manner of its operation does not lie within the constitutional remit of the judiciary, which is to protect the rule of law'.[2] On this reading, the balance of power within the devolved settlement is squarely a matter for the political powers rather than the courts.

1   *R (Miller) v Secretary of State for Exiting the European Union* [2017] UKSC 5, [2017] 2 WLR 583.
2   [2017] UKSC 5, [2017] 2 WLR 583, para 151.

The procedural regime

21.29 The 1998 Act specifically provides that proceedings for the determination of a devolution issue may be instituted in Northern Ireland by the Advocate-General for Northern Ireland or the Attorney-General for Northern Ireland.[1] Otherwise, it is clear that any person may institute proceedings which encompass or raise a devolution issue, albeit that it is for the court to decide whether the issue is live and whether the contention of the party is frivolous or vexatious.[2] Moreover, where the devolution issue concerns compliance with Convention rights the individual raising it must be a 'victim' of the disputed measure within the meaning of Article 34 ECHR. This reflects the content of section 7 of the Human Rights Act 1998 and a statutory exception to it has been made been only in relation to the Northern Ireland Human Rights Commission.[3]

1   Sch 10, para 4(1). See too the pre-enactment power of the Attorney-General for Northern Ireland to refer to the Supreme Court the question whether a provision of a Bill would be within the legislative competence of the Assembly: 1998 Act, s 11.
2   Sch 10, para 2.
3   1998 Act, s 71(2A)–(2C), as substituted by Justice and Security (Northern Ireland) Act 2007, s 14 and, eg, *Re Northern Ireland Human Rights Commission's Application* [2013] NICA 37. For wider NI case law on HRA, s 7, see, eg, *Re CAJ and Martin O'Brien's Application* [2005] NIQB 25; *Re Northern Ireland Commissioner for Children and Young People's Application* [2009] NICA 10; and *Re JR1's Application* [2011] NIQB 5, paras 38-41, Morgan LCJ.

21.30 Where proceedings encompassing a devolution issue or issues have been initiated, the court or tribunal concerned must give notice of any devolution issue to: (1) the Attorney-General for Northern Ireland; (2) the Advocate-General for Northern Ireland; and (3) the First Minister and Deputy First Minister. The effect of such notice is that it enables each of the office-holders to decide whether they wish to participate as a party to the proceedings in so far as they relate to a devolution issue[1] (there is no need to give notice where they are already a party).[2] Where proceedings for the determination of a devolution issue are initiated by the Advocate-General for Northern Ireland, they may be defended by the Attorney-General for Northern Ireland.[3]

1   1998 Act, Sch 10, paras 5–6. See, too, RCJ Ord 120.
2   1998 Act, Sch 10, para 5.
3   1998 Act, Sch 10, para 4(2).

21.31 In practice, the party initiating the proceedings should draw the attention of the court to the existence or the potential existence of a devolution issue raised by the proceedings so that the court can consider the performance of its obligations to give notice to relevant bodies.[1] It will generally be helpful if the initiating party prepares a draft Notice for the court to issue if it agrees that a devolution issue arises.

1   RCJ Ord 120, r 2.

21.32 Where a devolution issue arises before a court or tribunal, the question of referring the issue to the Court of Appeal should, where appropriate, be addressed. In relation to tribunals there are two possibilities that correspond with the availability of appeals. Hence, where the devolution issue arises before a tribunal from which there is no appeal, that tribunal must refer the matter to the Court of Appeal.[1] Where, in contrast, an appeal is available, the tribunal may refer the devolution issue to the Court of Appeal but it enjoys discretion as to whether to do so.[2]

1   1998 Act, Sch 10, para 8.
2   1998 Act, Sch 10, para 8.

21.33 Other courts, save for the Supreme Court and Court of Appeal, also have a discretion to refer any devolution issue to the Court of Appeal.[1] However, where judicial review proceedings are involved it is likely that the High Court will first resolve the issue and that recourse to the Court of Appeal will occur through the appellate structure.[2] On the other hand, where the Advocate-General for Northern Ireland or the Attorney-General for Northern Ireland are party to proceedings they may require a court or tribunal to refer any devolution issue to the Supreme Court before making any decision.[3] The same persons may likewise refer to the Supreme Court any devolution issue which is not the subject of proceedings.[4]

1   1998 Act, Sch 10, para 7.
2   Appeals to the Court of Appeal in civil matters are without leave: RCJ Ord 53, r 10(b). Appeals in criminal causes or matters lie only to the Supreme Court: Judicature Act (Northern Ireland) 1978, s 41.
3   1998 Act, Sch 10, para 33. For judicial consideration see *Lee v McArthur* [2016] NICA 55.
4   1998 Act, Sch 10, para 34. For judicial consideration see *Lee v McArthur* [2016] NICA 55.

21.34 Where there is a reference to the Court of Appeal, that Court will decide the issue with the possibility of an appeal to the Supreme Court with the leave either of the Court of Appeal or with special leave of the Supreme Court.[1] Where the Court of Appeal is confronted with a devolution issue (other than by reference to it) it may refer the issue to the Supreme Court.[2]

1   1998 Act, Sch 10, para 10.
2   1998 Act, Sch 10, para 9.

Existing experience with devolution issues

21.35 It has been explained above in paragraphs **21.5–21.7** that the process of legislating for Northern Ireland was, until 2007, a 'stop-start' endeavour that involved either the Assembly legislating under the 1998 Act or Northern Ireland legislation being made under the Order in Council procedure contained in the (now repealed) Northern Ireland Act 2000. The latter scenario of course corresponded with periods of particular political instability, but this did not mean that devolution issues could not arise. This was because much of the process of government under the Act of 2000 was carried on by the Northern Ireland Departments, which were responsible for initiating Orders in Council and for taking actions, including the making of subordinate legislation, within the meaning of section 24 of the 1998 Act (on which see **21.25**). Even without the Assembly, much decision-making within the terms of the 1998 Act therefore continued.[1]

1   See G Anthony and J Morison, 'Here, There, and (Maybe) Here Again: The Story of Law-making for Post-1998 Northern Ireland' in R Hazell and R Rawlings (eds) *Devolution, Law Making and the Constitution* (Imprint, 2005), p 155.

21.36 The resulting devolution issues have been relatively small in number and have arisen mainly (though not exclusively) by means of judicial review applications. While there has been no published audit of such issues, two principal trends can be identified. The first is an almost total absence of successful challenges to Acts of the Assembly or Orders in Council, which is doubtless a function of good legal advice during the drafting process and of the effective workings of pre-legislative scrutiny.[1] Indeed, one of the very few cases in which a provision of statute law was considered incompatible with the ECHR was in *Re ES's Application*[2] where article 64(8) of the Children (Northern Ireland) Order 1995 was held incompatible with the provisions of Articles 6 and 8 ECHR (article 64(8) was a part of the regime governing emergency protection orders).[3] Otherwise, the great majority of legislation has not given rise to any devolution issues, or certainly not issues that have transgressed the boundaries of legislative power in the 1998 Act.[4]

1   1998 Act, ss 9–15. A devolution issue arose in *Re Neill's Application* [2005] NIQB 66 and [2006] NICA 5 where the Anti-social Behaviour (Northern Ireland) Order 2004 was challenged, *inter alia*, as having been introduced in breach of the procedures that govern the making of Northern Ireland law that deals with a reserved matter. The application for judicial review was dismissed.
2   [2008] NI 11.
3   See also, eg, Re Northern Ireland Human Rights Commission's Application [2013] NICA 37: paras 14 & 15 of the Adoption (Northern Ireland) Order 1987, as applying to same-sex couples, incompatible with Arts 8 & 14 ECHR.
4   See, eg, *Re CM's Application for Leave* [2013] NIQB 145, where the High Court rejected the argument that a provision of an Act of the Assembly that imposed a two-week time-limit for bringing judicial review proceedings in respect of the decisions of an inquiry was contrary to the common law right of access to a court (the provision in question was section 19 of the Inquiry into Historical Institutional Abuse Act [Northern Ireland] 2013).

21.37 The second concerns the content of devolution issues arising in relation to the actions of Northern Ireland Departments or Ministers, including the making of subordinate legislation. A clear majority of the issues arising here has concerned the compatibility of measures with the Convention rights, and this is something that is consistent with the experience of devolution elsewhere in the United Kingdom.[1] For instance, in one case it was questioned whether a fisheries decommissioning scheme reflected in subordinate legislation made by a Northern Ireland Department breached a Convention right; the court held it did not.[2] In another case, the issue was whether the devolved Education Department had breached Article 14 ECHR when read with the Convention's right to education in arrangements it had made to operate transfer procedure tests for the purpose of admission to post primary schools. Again, no breach was found.[3] Other cases have raised issues about whether a compulsory transfer for a detained patient in Northern Ireland to secure accommodation in Scotland directed by the Department of Health involved a breach of Article 8 ECHR[4] and whether the Department of the Environment had, through its Planning Service, acted contrary to the Convention in the context of the making of planning decisions.[5] These challenges also failed.

1   See, eg, 'Scotland', below.
2   *Re McBride's Application* (29 June 2005, unreported).
3   *Re Newton's Application* [2001] NI 115.
4   *Re O'Sullivan's Application* [2001] NIJB 228.
5   *Re Patrick Green's Application* [2004] NIJB 27. See, also, *Re Stewart's Application* [2003] NI 149.

21.38 Convention rights have not, however, been the sole preserve of devolution issues. For instance, *Re Friends of the Earth's Application* raised the question whether the Department of Regional Development had discharged its obligations under EU law when making agreements and granting consents under the Water and Sewerage Services (Northern Ireland) Order 1973.[1] The High Court held that it had not. And in *Re De Brun's Application*,[2] it was contended that the First Minister had discriminated against his Sinn Féin colleagues when refusing to nominate them to meetings of the North/South Ministerial Council. Although argument on this ground failed, the application for judicial review was granted for other reasons.[3] Moreover, an argument that the First Minister and Deputy First Minister had discriminated contrary to s 76 of the Northern Ireland Act 1998 in the choice of persons to serve as victims commissioners was rejected by the High Court and the Court of Appeal in *Re Williamson's Application*.[4]

1   [2006] NIQB 48.
2   [2001] NI 442.
3   *Viz*, that the First Minister had exercised his statutory powers for a collateral purpose (he had refused nomination in an attempt to pressurise the Republican movement to commence decommissioning).
4   [2009] NIQB 63 and [2010] NICA 8.

21.39 Mention should again be made, here, of the *Miller* case and the related Northern Ireland references that were heard by the Supreme Court in December 2016 (see 21.28).[1] The Northern Ireland references centred upon a number of questions that the High Court in Northern Ireland had referred to the Supreme Court at the request of the Attorney-General for Northern Ireland. While the Supreme Court considered that it was not necessary to answer some of the questions, it did address the important matter of whether there is an enforceable 'constitutional convention' whereby the Northern Ireland Assembly must pass a legislative consent motion before an Act of the Westminster Parliament can affect the devolved competences. On the facts of the case, the Supreme Court did not consider that it had any role to play in 'policing' an 'important' constitutional convention.

1   *R (Miller) v Secretary of State for Exiting the European Union* [2017] UKSC 5, [2017] 2 WLR 583.

Conclusion

21.40 This chapter has provided a brief overview of judicial review and devolution in Northern Ireland. It has traced how the political instability that defined much of the early workings of the 1998 Act has been replaced by a greater institutional accord and by a transfer of further powers to the Northern Ireland Assembly. That transfer of powers has occurred against a backdrop of judicial review case law that has revealed much about how the courts approach (sometimes) difficult questions about the interface between law and politics in post-conflict Northern Ireland. While many of the legal principles that have been applied by the courts have been at one with those that apply elsewhere in the United Kingdom, the context in which they have been used has often been very different. It is thus here that the Northern Ireland case law can be regarded as distinct and of constitutional interest and significance.

JUDICIAL REVIEW AND DEVOLUTION IN SCOTLAND[1]

[1] The author of this section acknowledges the helpfulness, in its revision, of the comments on a draft of Dr Elisenda Casañas Adam. For general accounts of Scottish constitutional arrangements since devolution, see, eg CMG Himsworth and C M O'Neill *Scotland's Constitution: Law & Practice* (3rd edn, 2015); A Page, *Constitutional Law of Scotland* (2015); CMG Himsworth and C R Munro *The Scotland Act 1998* (2nd edn, 2000); and the *Stair Memorial Encyclopaedia: Constitutional Law* (Reissue, 2002).

Introduction

21.41 Institutionally, the Scotland Act 1998 brought the Scottish Parliament and the Scottish Government[2]. Whilst, of course, UK ministers retained many powers in relation to Scotland and the UK Secretaries of State continue to be frequent respondents in the Court of Session, since the creation of the Scottish Government, deriving many powers from new Acts of the Scottish Parliament passed since July 1999 but also inheriting many more powers from UK ministers (principally the Secretary of State for Scotland) in July 1999,[3] the 'Scottish Ministers'[4] have also become respondents (and indeed petitioners) in many cases of judicial review.[5] Acts passed by the Scottish Parliament have also created many new institutions and officials potentially subject to judicial review.[6]

[2] 'Scottish Executive' was the language of the Scotland Act 1998. This was amended to 'Scottish Government' by s 12 of the Scotland Act 2012.
[3] Scotland Act 1998, ss 53–54. Other powers have been conferred by Orders in Council under s 63 of the Scotland Act 1998 (principally the Scotland Act 1998 (Transfer of Functions to the Scottish Ministers etc) Order 1999 (SI 1999/1750)) and others in Acts of the Westminster Parliament.
[4] The term formally prescribed by the Scotland Act 1998, s 44(2). Any member of the Scottish Government is, in law, authorised to exercise powers conferred, by whichever means, on the Scottish Ministers (Scotland Act 1998, s 52(3)).
[5] The Scotland Act 1998 also provides for powers to be conferred (and does itself confer powers) directly upon the First Minister alone (see ss 52(5) and 95) and on the Lord Advocate who, whilst also a member of the Scottish Government, discharges many separately conferred functions (ss 48, 52(5) and (6)). Other institutions and officials created from 1999, which are also, of course, subject to judicial review include the Advocate General for Scotland (the Scottish Law Officer in the UK Government) (s 87) and the Auditor General for Scotland (s 69).
[6] See, eg the Scottish Public Services Ombudsman Act 2002 and *Argyll and Bute Council v Scottish Public Services Ombudsman* 2008 SC 155.

21.42 In addition, however, the new powers conferred on the Scottish Government, but also, more prominently, on the Scottish Parliament, brought the creation by the Scotland Act 1998 of new forms of challenge to the exercise of those powers defined as 'devolution issues'[1] and new procedures for their determination.[2] In particular, these require notice to, and the opportunity for intervention by, the Law Officers, accelerated procedures, and ultimate recourse by reference or appeal to the UK Supreme Court (formerly to the Judicial Committee of the Privy Council (JCPC)). The Scotland Act 2012 created a new category of 'compatibility issues'.[3]

[1]   Scotland Act 1998, s 98.
[2]   Scotland Act 1998, Sch 6.
[3]   See **21.44** below.

Devolution issues and compatibility issues

21.43 'Devolution issues' are defined[1] as the following:

(1)   a question whether an Act of the Scottish Parliament or any provision of an Act of the Scottish Parliament is within the legislative competence of the Parliament;

(2)   a question whether any function (being a function which any person has purported, or is proposing, to exercise) is a function of the Scottish Ministers, the First Minister or the Lord Advocate;[2]

(3)   a question whether the purported or proposed exercise of a function by a member of the Scottish Government is, or would be, within devolved competence;

(4)   a question whether a purported or proposed exercise of a function by a member of the Scottish Government is, or would be, incompatible with any of the Convention rights or with EU law;

(5)   a question whether a failure to act by a member of the Scottish Government is incompatible with any of the Convention rights or with Community (now EU) law;

(6)   any other question about whether a function is exercisable within devolved competence or in or as regards Scotland and any other question arising by virtue of this Act about reserved matters.

[1]   Scotland Act 1998, Sch 6, para 1, as amended by s 36(4) of the Scotland Act 2012 to exclude 'compatibility issues' arising in criminal proceedings. See **21.44** below.
[2]   A question which might arise here is whether the definition of 'devolution issue' would embrace a general point turning on the determination of the correct person to discharge a function but without raising any special question of the transfer of functions under the Scotland Act 1998.

21.44 Now excluded from those defined categories of devolution issue are any questions arising in criminal proceedings in Scotland which relate to the compatibility with Convention rights or with EU law of an Act of the Scottish Parliament or any provision of such an Act; or a function or purported or proposed exercise of a function; or a failure to act. All such issues are now 'compatibility issues', as created by the Scotland Act 2012.[1] Taken with the amendment of s 57 (3) of the 1998 Act and amendments to the Criminal Procedure (Scotland) Act 1995, these changes created a different route for the challenge of the new 'compatibility issues' arising in the criminal courts. The reasons for the adoption of the new procedure included both a sense that Convention rights or EU law failings by the Lord Advocate in prosecutorial capacity should never have been treated as devolution issues in the first place and that they had come numerically to dominate the scene in an inappropriate way.[2]

[1] See s 36(4). In *Kapri v The Lord Advocate representing The Government of the Republic of Albania* 2013 SC (UKSC) 311 the UK Supreme Court held that extradition proceedings were not to be regarded as 'criminal proceedings' for these purposes.
[2] See the report of the (Edward) Expert Group *Section 57(2) and Schedule 6 of the Scotland Act 1998 and the Role of the Lord Advocate* (2010). Because compatibility issues do not arise in a judicial review context, the procedures are not treated in detail here.

21.45 It is further provided that a devolution issue shall not be taken to arise in any proceedings merely because of any contention of a party to the proceedings which appears to the court or tribunal before which the proceedings take place to be frivolous or vexatious.[1]

[1] Scotland Act 1998, Sch 6, para 2.

Special procedural provisions

21.46 Having defined 'devolution issues', Sch 6 to the Act goes on to make four forms of special procedural provision:

(1) by way of the Advocate General for Scotland (the Scottish Law Officer in the UK Government) or the Lord Advocate, as appropriate, proceedings may be brought on behalf of either the UK Government or the Scottish Government to resolve a devolution issue, for example, as to the legislative competence of the Scottish Parliament or the devolved competence of the Scottish Government;

(2) notice must be given to both the Advocate General and the Lord Advocate of any devolution issue raised in proceedings in order to enable either or both to participate in the proceedings;

(3) inferior courts may refer devolution issues to either the Court of Session or the High Court of Justiciary and from those courts devolution issues may pass by reference or appeal to the Supreme Court; in addition

(4) the Lord Advocate or the Advocate General may require any court or tribunal to refer a devolution issue direct to the Supreme Court and they may themselves refer a devolution issue which is otherwise not the subject of proceedings.[1]

[1] For the procedural rules in the Court of Session, see Ch 25A of the Rules of Court: www.scotcourts.gov.uk/docs/default-source/rules-and-practice/rules-of-court/court-of-session/chap25a.pdf?sfvrsn=2. See also Ch 40 of the Criminal Procedure Rules: www.scotcourts.gov.uk/rules-and-practice/rules-of-court/criminal-procedure-rules; and the Supreme Court Rules 2009 (SI 2009/1603).

21.47 As well as this procedural provision in Sch 6, the Act contains some other rules relevant to the judicial review of the acts and decisions of the devolved authorities. Section 99 makes provision for the representation of the rights and liabilities of the Crown in different capacities (ie in right of the Scottish Administration as well as the UK Government); s 101 makes special provision for the interpretation of provisions contained in Bills or Acts of the Scottish Parliament (ASPs) and subordinate legislation of the Scottish Government, ie that such a provision which:

'could be read in such a way as to be outside competence [should] be read as narrowly as is required for it to be within competence, if such a reading is possible, and is to have effect accordingly';[1]

and s 102[2] enables courts and tribunals to vary the retrospective effect of decisions on the invalidity of ASPs; Scottish Government subordinate legislation; or any other purported exercise of a function by a member of the Scottish Government. This power was invoked in all of the only three cases so far in which a provision in an Act of the Scottish Parliament has been held to be invalid.[3]

[1] See *HM Advocate v DS* 2007 SC (PC) 1; *Henderson v HM Advocate* 2011 JC 96; *Salvesen v Riddell* 2013 SC (UKSC) 236.
[2] As amended by the Scotland Act 2012 s 15.
[3] See *Cameron v Procurator Fiscal, Livingston (No 2)* 2013 JC 21; *Salvesen v Riddell* 2013 SC (UKSC) 236. In the latter case, the defect was corrected within the permitted 12 months by the Agricultural Holdings (Scotland) Act 2003 Remedial Order 2014, SSI 2014/98; *Christian Institute v Lord Advocate* 2016 SLT 805.

Cases in which devolution issues arise

21.48 These Scotland Act provisions on devolution issues do not, beyond providing for the proceedings initiated by Law Officers, define the types of proceedings in which such issues may be raised. Potentially, they may arise in any type of case. It might perhaps have been expected, however, that it would be in the course of proceedings for judicial review (especially those raised to challenge decisions of the Scottish Ministers) that devolution issues would in practice most frequently arise. This turned out not to be the case. Prior to the creation of the separate category of 'compatibility issues' by the Scotland Act 2012,[1] numerically, the most significant group of devolution issues were those which arose, on grounds of alleged breaches of Convention rights, in the course of criminal cases prosecuted by the Crown Office on behalf of the Lord Advocate.[2] A rather small number of devolution issues have arisen in judicial review proceedings against the Scottish Ministers and almost all have turned upon questions of Convention rights compatibility. These have included *Lafarge Redland Aggregates Ltd v Scottish Ministers*[3] on delay in planning procedures; *County Properties Ltd v Scottish Ministers*[4] in which it was decided that ministerial decisions on appeal or call-in under the Planning Acts were held not to be incompatible with art 6 of the Convention.[5] In *Napier v Scottish Ministers*[6] it was held that the practice of 'slopping out' in Scottish prisons was contrary to art 3 of the ECHR. In *Scottish Environment Protection Agency v Joint Liquidators of the Scottish Coal Co Ltd*[7] challenges to the Water Environment (Controlled Activities) (Scotland) Regulations 2005 (SSI 2005/3480) and 2011 (SSI 2011/209) were repelled. In *Hunter v Student Awards Agency for Scotland*[8] the Education (Student Loans) (Scotland) Regulations 2007 were held to be unlawfully discriminatory.

[1] See **21.44** above.
[2] Most prominent among these cases in the early years was *Starrs v Ruxton* 2000 JC 218, in which the deployment of temporary sheriffs was outlawed. Later there was *R v HMA* 2003 SC(PC) 21 which, as a JCPC decision, was to be contrasted with the House of Lords decision in *AG's Ref No 2 of 2001* [2004] 2 AC 72, on which see C Himsworth (2004) 8 Ed LR 255. But see too *Spiers v Ruddy* [2008] 1 AC 573.
[3] 2001 SC 298.
[4] 2002 SC 79.

[5]   See also *Alconbury (R (Holding Barnes plc) v Secretary of State for the Environment, Transport and the Regions* [2003] 2 AC 295). See C Himsworth 'Planning Rights Convergence' (2002) 6 Edin LR 253.
[6]   2005 1 SC 229.
[7]   2014 SLT 259.
[8]   2016 SLT 653.

21.49 A more constitutionally significant consequence of these devolution-related developments, however, was the new opportunities which the Scotland Act brought for the use of judicial review for the challenge not merely of new institutions with executive powers but also of the legislative powers of the Scottish Parliament. There have been, over the 18 years of devolution some 17 cases challenging the validity of ASPs – not all in a judicial review context. In *Anderson v Scottish Ministers*,[1] a challenge to the validity of the Parliament's very first ASP was rebuffed – eventually by the JCPC. The Mental Health (Public Safety and Appeals) (Scotland) Act 1999 was challenged on grounds of incompatibility with ECHR, art 5. In *Adams v Advocate General*[2] and also in *Whaley v Lord Advocate*[3] it was the Protection of Wild Mammals (Scotland) Act 2002. In *Flynn v Lord Advocate*[4] the Convention Rights Compliance (Scotland) Act 2001 in *AXA General Insurance Ltd v Lord Advocate (Scotland)*,[5] it was the Damages (Asbestos-related Conditions) (Scotland) Act 2009; in *HM Advocate v DS*[6] it was the Sexual Offences (Procedure and Evidence) (Scotland) Act 2002; in *S v L*[7] the Adoption (Scotland) Act 2007; in *Martin v Most*[8] the Criminal Proceedings etc (Reform) (Scotland) Act 2007; in *Imperial Tobacco Ltd v Lord Advocate*[9] and *Sinclair Collis Ltd v The Lord Advocate*[10] the Tobacco and Primary Medical Services (Scotland) Act 2010; in *Cameron v Cottam (No 2)*[11] and in *Barclay and Bain v HM Advocate*[12] it was the Criminal Justice and Licensing (Scotland) Act 2010; in *AMI v Dunn*[13] the Vulnerable Witnesses (Scotland) Act 2004; in *Salvesen v Riddell*[14] the Agricultural Holdings (Scotland) Act 2003; in *Moohan, Petitioner*[15] the Scottish Independence Referendum (Franchise) Act 2013; in *Scotch Whisky Association v Lord Advocate*[16] the Alcohol Minimum Pricing (Scotland) Act 2012; and in *Christian Institute v Lord Advocate*[17] it was the Children and Young People (Scotland) Act 2014, Pt 4 (named persons). In only three cases (*Cameron v Cottam, Salvesen v Riddell, and Christian Institute v Lord Advocate*) have provisions in ASPs been struck down as incompetent.

[1]   2001 SC 1, 2002 SC(PC) 1.
[2]   2003 SC 171 (OH) and 2004 SC 665 (IH).
[3]   2004 SC 78, 2004 SLT 425.
[4]   2004 SC (PC) 1.
[5]   2012 SC (UKSC) 122.
[6]   2007 (SC)(PC) 1.
[7]   2012 SC 8.
[8]   2010 SC (UKSC) 40.
[9]   2013 SC (UKSC) 213.
[10]   2013 SC 221.
[11]   2013 JC 21.
[12]   2013 JC 40.
[13]   2013 JC 82.
[14]   2013 SC (UKSC) 236.
[15]   2015 SC (UKSC) 1, 2015 SLT 2.
[16]   [2014] CSIH 38; 2016 SLT 1141 (following a preliminary reference to the ECJ).
[17]   2016 SLT 805.

Review of Acts of the Scottish Parliament

21.50 The principal point of interest has been how far the courts would treat the Scotland Act 1998 as a new form of constitutional measure and thus the Scottish Parliament (as a democratically elected legislature) and thus differently from other statutory bodies, with the consequence that ASPs are viewed differently from lesser forms of subordinate legislation in judicial review context.[1] But different judicial styles have been illustrated, for instance, in *Adams v Advocate General*[2] and, more recently, in *AXA General Insurance Ltd, Petitioners*.[3]

[1] On the interpretation of Acts of the Stormont Parliament in Northern Ireland, see, eg *Gallagher v Lynn* [1937] AC 863 and *H Calvert Constitutional Law in Northern Ireland* (1968) Ch 11. For discussion of devolution cases in general, see A Tomkins, 'Confusion and Retreat: the Supreme Court on Devolution', U.K. Const. L. Blog (19 Feb 2015).

[2] 2003 SC 171(OH); 2004 SC 665 (IH).

[3] 2010 SLT 179 (OH); 2011 SC 662 (IH); 2012 SC (UKSC)122.

21.51 An important question which arose in both cases was that of whether it was competent, in the judicial review of ASPs, to challenge their validity on what Lord Nimmo Smith in *Adams* called the 'traditional common law grounds'.[1] In both cases, the petitioners relied in the main on claimed breaches of Convention rights. In *Adams* the validity of the Protection of Wild Mammals (Scotland) Act 2002, which prohibited mounted foxhunting with dogs, was challenged on grounds of breach of art 8 (interference with private life), art 1 First Protocol (possessions) and art 14 (discrimination). In *AXA* the Damages (Asbestos-related Conditions) (Scotland) Act 2009 was challenged on grounds of breach of art 6 (fair procedure etc) and art 1 First Protocol. In neither case was the challenge on these grounds successful. In addition, however, in both cases, the petitioners sought to extend their arguments challenging the ASPs into the familiar grounds of illegality, procedural impropriety and irrationality. On the one hand, in *Adams*, the Lord Ordinary held (and this decision was not directly revisited by the Inner House) that challenge on these grounds was not competent. In *AXA*, however, Lord Emslie held, at first instance, that such challenge *was* competent although he declined to uphold the petitioners' arguments (based on irrationality) in the particular circumstances of the case. Thus much uncertainty arose. In part because the judgments in the two cases reflect an underlying divergence in the general approach to be adopted by courts to the review of ASPs, it will be valuable to provide a brief summary of the arguments upon which the two judges relied. Both sought a proper construction of the Scotland Act. For Lord Nimmo Smith in *Adams*, there was no doubt that the court's general jurisdiction over the Parliament was not excluded by the Scotland Act and to that extent the Parliament was not sovereign. But, despite being subordinate legislation for Human Rights Act purposes, ASPs had far more in common with Acts of the UK Parliament than with subordinate legislation as commonly understood. The Scottish Parliament was a democratically elected representative body. It had a general law-making power, subject to specified restrictions. An ASP was of a character which had far more in common with a public general statute than with subordinate legislation, though it might be preferable to regard it as being *sui generis*. The Scotland Act was clearly intended to provide a comprehensive scheme, not only for the Parliament itself, but also for the relationship between the courts and the Parliament. It therefore followed that traditional common law grounds of judicial review were excluded. There was, he said, 'no room for the implication of common law concepts in considering the legislative competence of the Parliament'.[2]

¹   2003 SC 171 at 202.
²   2003 SC 171 at 201.

21.52 It was with the utmost respect to the Lord Ordinary in *Adams*, said Lord Emslie in *AXA*[1] that he declared himself unable to share his conclusion on the competency of common law grounds of review. In *AXA*, the respondents had conceded that the Scotland Act could not be regarded as embodying 'a comprehensive scheme . . . for the relationship between the courts and the Parliament'. The real question was whether the Act contained anything sufficient, whether by clear words or necessary implication, to oust the fundamental supervisory jurisdiction of the courts at common law and thus — in the absence of any relevant procedural framework — make the Parliament the sole judge of the rationality of its own legislation.[2] Review on grounds of illegality was reinforced by the Scotland Act's own specification of competence limits. On the other hand, review on grounds of procedural impropriety was excluded by s 28(5) of the Act. But was the third head of irrationality excluded?[3] In Lord Emslie's view, there was nothing to suggest that this was the case. Clear and unambiguous terms would be required — in particular if the fundamental rights of the subject (including access to judicial review) were to be overridden.[4] More specifically, however, Lord Emslie selected, as a key feature of the Scotland Act, its treatment of both legislative and executive competence on an apparently equivalent basis. If it had necessarily to be conceded that subordinate legislation and executive acts of the Scottish Ministers were reviewable on common law grounds, then he found it hard to identify any sound basis of construction on which such jurisdiction should be excluded in relation to the Parliament's primary legislative powers.[5] In *Adams*, Lord Nimmo Smith had deliberately refrained from expressing a concluded view on this comparison.[6]

¹   2010 SLT 179 at para 125.
²   Ibid. This was a position for which Lord Emslie found support in the House of Lords decision in *Somerville v Scottish Ministers* 2008 SC (HL) 45, 2007 SLT 1113.
³   Ibid., para 130.
⁴   Ibid., paras 131–132.
⁵   Ibid., paras 137–139.
⁶   See 2003 SC 171 at 201.

21.53 Having decided that review of ASPs on grounds of irrationality was competent, Lord Emslie went on, however, (a) to indicate that it would only be in extreme circumstances that a challenge would be sustained[1] and (b) to conclude that common law irrationality could not be upheld in this case — whether on the basis of a 'premature decision to legislate'; 'controverting established fact or legal principle'; 'irrational generosity'; an 'unconscionable burden on private insurers'; 'alleged 'reconfiguration' of policies'; 'deliberate concealment of a key objective of the Act'; 'unresolved financial uncertainties'; or 'jurisdiction and forum shopping'.[2] This all suggested that a finding of irrationality would be a rare event, even if formally competent.

¹   2010 SLT 179 at paras 142–144.

2   Ibid., paras 227–248.

21.54 Rather separately, in *Adams*, the Second Division of the Inner House appeared to have re-imposed a framework more typical of that appropriate to bodies of a lesser status than the Scottish Parliament when, before going on to assess the specifically Convention rights aspects of the ASP under view, it considered at some length (and favourably to the Parliament in this instance) whether or not the Parliament had before it a 'proper factual basis for the conclusion that mounted foxhunting with dogs was cruel per se'.[1] This led the court to a judgment on the Parliament's approach to the issues before it which might be regarded as unduly intrusive.[2]

1   2004 SC 665 at para 37.
2   See B J Winetrobe, 'The Judge in the Scottish Parliament' [2005] PL 3.

21.55 Returning, however, to *AXA*, important further contributions were made to the question of the review of ASPs on common law grounds by both the First Division and then (determinatively) the Supreme Court. In the Division,[1] a line not dissimilar to that of Lord Emslie was maintained. ASPs were *sui generis*. The traditional grounds of common law judicial review, including irrationality, were not, without modification, apt for Acts of the Scottish Parliament. But this did not mean that challenge on the grounds of irrationality could never, in exceptional circumstances, be sustained. This was not, however, such an exceptional case and the questions at issue were political in character.[2] The Supreme Court[3] (especially at the hand of Lords Hope (at paras 42–52) and Reed (at paras 135–154) advanced upon the deliberations of the lower courts in two principal respects. In the first place, they rejected the competency of challenge to ASPs on the standard common law grounds as constitutionally inappropriate. But, on the other hand, denying that the UK Parliament could have intended to establish a body free to abrogate fundamental rights or to violate the rule of law, they held, in carefully constructed judgments, that review on grounds that those principles had been breached remained an option, although not in the circumstances of *AXA* itself. A marker has been laid down that, in appropriate circumstances yet to be fully defined (but, for Lord Hope, including, for example, the circumstances in which a Scottish Parliament dominated by a single party might abolish the courts' constitutionally fundamental power of judicial review), the Supreme Court may feel compelled to intervene on grounds extending far beyond the limits of legislative competence laid down in the Scotland Acts themselves. Although the justices in *AXA* acknowledged that their discussion of the powers of the Scottish Parliament could not be wholly distinguished from the earlier discussion of possible limits to the powers of the UK Parliament in *R (Jackson) v A-G*,[4] they were careful to avoid a direct comparison.

1   2011 SC 662.
2   Ibid., paras 87–94.
3   2012 SC (UKSC) 122. For the contribution of the case to the law of standing for judicial review, see **22.48** and **22.50**.
4   [2006] 1 AC 262 (esp at the hand of Lord Steyn at para 102).

21.56 In the meantime after a long wait, the first case at the highest level,[1] to raise competence issues (other than in relation to human rights)[2] was decided by the UK Supreme Court in March 2010. In *Martin v Most*.[3] It was held (by a 3–2 majority) that s 45 of the Criminal Proceedings etc. (Reform) (Scotland) Act 2007 which had the effect of raising the maximum punishment for the offence of driving while disqualified under the Road Traffic Offenders Act 1988 and the Road Traffic Act 1988, if prosecuted summarily, from six months imprisonment (or a fine or both) to 12 months' imprisonment (again or a fine or both) was within the competence of the Scottish Parliament. In the first place, all five judges were agreed that, taking into account the purpose tests in s 29(3) and s 29(4) of the Scotland Act,[4] s 45 of the 2007 Act did not relate to a reserved matter. Its purpose was either simply to amend the jurisdiction and sentencing powers of the Scottish courts – not a reserved matter; or, if it did, at first sight, relate to reserved matters because it made modifications of Scots criminal law as it applied to reserved matters, it could be treated as not so relating because its purpose was to make the law apply consistently to reserved matters and otherwise. Thus, looking at s 29 (3)–(4) and Sch 5 alone, s 45 of the 2007 Act was not beyond legislative competence.

[1]   But see also *Logan v Harrower* 2008 SLT 1049.
[2]   There have also been devolution issues raised in cases where there has been a reliance, in whole or in part, on breach of EU law. See *Sinclair Collis Ltd v The Lord Advocate* 2013 SC 221; *Moohan, Petitioner* 2015 SC (UKSC) 1, 2015 SLT 2; *Scotch Whisky Association v Lord Advocate* [2014] CSIH 38. In that last case a reference was made by the Inner House to the ECJ.
[3]   2010 SC (UKSC) 40.
[4]   Different judges placed different degrees of reliance on the two subsections – see Lord Hope at paras 23–33 and Lord Rodger at paras 113–119.

21.57 Different considerations arose, however, in the application of Sch 4. This bars the Scottish Parliament, irrespective of the application of Sch 5, from modifying certain enactments (including, in large measure, the Scotland Act itself and eg the Human Rights Act 1998) and also 'the law on reserved matters' – any enactment the subject-matter of which is a reserved matter (paragraph 2). All members of the Court thought that s 45 of the 2007 Act did indeed modify the law on reserved matters. But this prohibition is restricted in two ways. In the first place it does not apply where modifications are (merely) incidental to or consequential upon provision made which does *not* relate to reserved matters; *and* do not have a greater effect on reserved matters than is necessary to give effect to the purpose of the provision. All but one (Lord Kerr) members of the Court thought that s 45 of the 2007 Act was not saved by virtue of this rule. It was, however, the interpretation and application of the second qualification which divided the Court much more profoundly.

21.58 The restriction of the Parliament's powers in relation to the modification of the law on reserved matters applies, in relation to a rule of Scots private law or Scots criminal law, 'only to the extent that the rule in question is special to a reserved matter'.[1] There is no guidance given in the Act as to what rules may be 'special to a reserved matter'. In the view of the majority of the Court, the modification of the rule defining maximum penalties in summary proceedings (but without modification of the maximum penalty overall) did not involve the modification of a rule special to a reserved matter.[2] In the view of the minority, the modification of road traffic law penalties, whether in relation to summary prosecutions or otherwise, was indeed the modification of a rule special to a reserved matter.[3] In the interpretation of Sch 4 there was no room for the incorporation of the 'purpose' test used in relation to s 29, a test which had indeed been deployed by the majority to distinguish between the adjustment of the overall maximum penalty ('special' to the reserved matter of road traffic and, therefore, incompetent) and the adjustment of the level of fine applicable to a certain type of prosecution (a matter within the general competence of the Scottish Parliament and not 'special').[4]

1   Sch 4, para 2(3). In addition, there is a list of specific rules to which the restriction also applies – none of which was relevant in this case.
2   See, in particular, Lord Hope at paras 34–39 but also Lord Walker at paras 53–60.
3   See, in particular, Lord Rodger at paras 132–141 and his virulent attack on the reasoning of the majority at paras 142–149.
4   See C Himsworth, 'Nothing special about that?' [2010] 14 Edin LR 487.

21.59 *Imperial Tobacco Ltd v The Lord Advocate (Scotland)*[1] was the first case[2] in which provisions in an Act of the Scottish Parliament were challenged on the grounds that they related to specific reservations under the 1998 Act. The UK Supreme Court held that neither s 1 nor s 9 of the Tobacco and Primary Medical Services (Scotland) Act 2010 (which sought to prohibit the display of tobacco products and the use of tobacco vending machines) 'related to' 'the sale and supply of goods to consumers' or 'product safety' which are reserved matters under the Act.[3] Nor did the provisions (in the creation of new criminal offences) 'modify the law on reserved matters.'[4] The case is especially important for the guidance Lord Hope provided on the interpretation of the legislative competence provisions of the Act.[5] Lord Hope referred to three principles that should be followed when undertaking the exercise of determining whether, according to the rules in the 1998 Act, a provision of an Act of the Scottish Parliament is beyond competence.[6] Firstly, the question of competence must be determined in each case according to the particular rules laid down. It is not for the courts to say whether legislation on any particular issue is better made by one Parliament or the other. The statutory language used by the UK Parliament to define the competence was informed by principles that had been applied to resolve questions which had arisen in federal systems but the intention was that it was to the 1998 Act itself, not to decisions in other jurisdictions that one should look for guidance, bearing in mind that a provision may have a devolved purpose and yet be outside competence because it contravenes one of the rules. Second, the rules must be interpreted in the same way as any other rules found in a UK statute. They must be taken to have been intended to create a system that was coherent, stable and workable. Legislation should be construed according to the ordinary meaning of the words used. Third, the description of the 1998 Act as a constitutional statute cannot be taken, in itself, to be a guide to its interpretation.

1   2013 SC (UKSC) 153, 2013 SLT 2.
2   '[R]emarkably', as Lord Hope observed at para 6, having surveyed the range of challenges to Acts of the Scottish Parliament brought on other grounds.
3   1998 Act, Sch 5, ss C7(a) and C8.
4   1998 Act, Sch 4, para 2(1).
5   In several aspects, Lord Hope drew on the comprehensive judgment of Lord Reed in the First Division at 2012 SC 297, 2012 SLT 749 (paras 43-158). He was also to reinforce the principles he had elaborated on in *A-G v National Assembly for Wales Commission* [2013] 1 AC 792.
6   See paras 12–18.

Legislative competence over judicial review

21.60 A consequence of devolution of a different sort comes in the transfer to the Scottish Parliament of legislative competence in relation to judicial review itself. The competence of the Parliament is conferred in general terms[1] as a power to make laws but then by means of a series of constraints imposed by the Scotland Act,[2] the most important of which is the reservation to Westminster of certain areas of competence – 'the reserved matters'.[3] The Scottish Parliament may not legislate in relation to those reserved matters – the question of whether the subject matter of an ASP does indeed relate to a reserved matter being determined 'by reference to the purpose of the provision, having regard (among other things) to its effect in all the circumstances'.[4] Equally, the Scottish Parliament may not legislate in such a way as to modify by amendment or repeal any existing law on reserved matters.[5] Because these restrictions were thought to have the capacity to narrow the powers of the Parliament to legislate in relation to the general law of Scotland (both civil and criminal) in an undesirable way, some further special rules were incorporated into the scheme. The fear was that, because some such general rules of law (for instance in relation to civil or criminal liability) straddled the divide between reserved and devolved matters, the Scottish Parliament might be inhibited from legislating to make general provision for the legal system of Scotland (one of the Parliament's principal *raisons d'être*) because of the danger of impinging (perhaps unintentionally) upon reserved subject matter. Thus a special additional rule was made to the effect that a provision of an ASP which:

'(a) would otherwise not relate to reserved matters, but (b) makes modifications of the Scots private law, or Scots criminal law, as it applies to reserved matters, is to be treated as relating to reserved matters unless the purpose of the provision is to make the law in question apply consistently to reserved matters and otherwise'.[6]

[1]   Scotland Act 1998, s 28(1).
[2]   Scotland Act 1998, s 29.
[3]   Scotland Act 1998, s 29(2)(b) and Sch 5.
[4]   Scotland Act 1998, s 29(3).
[5]   Scotland Act 1998, s 29(2)(c) and Sch 4.
[6]   Scotland Act 1998, s 29(4). Further special provision affecting Scots private and criminal law is made in Sch 4, paras 2 and 3 to the Act. See *Martin v Most* 2010 SC (UKSC) 40 above.

21.61 However, with that special provision in place the remaining important question is that of how Scots private law and Scots criminal law were actually defined for these purposes. The definitions are provided by the Scotland Act 1998 and Scots private law is defined by reference to the general principles of private law, the law of persons, the law of obligations, the law of property and the law of actions.[1] For present purposes, the most interesting additional detail of this definition comes where it is provided that the law of actions includes reference to 'the judicial review of administrative action'.

[1]   Scotland Act 1998, s 126(4).

21.62 The practical consequences of the express inclusion of judicial review in this list may not be altogether clear – quite apart from the initial question arising from the rather old-fashioned and, in a Scottish context, rather ambiguous restriction of the definition to judicial review in a public law context and, within that, to 'administrative' action only.[1] Apart from the procedural rule-making which has been, and remains, in the hands of the Lord President of the Court of Session (now with drafts generated by the Scottish Civil Justice Council), there has in the past been only sporadic legislative intervention into the field of judicial review. Currently, however, the Courts Reform (Scotland) Act 2014 did indeed make significant amendments to the law on judicial review, including providing for time-limits, permission to apply for judicial review and standing.[2]

[1] See **22.11** below.
[2] See CHAPTER **22** below.

WALES

Introduction

21.63 Devolution in Wales has undergone significant developments over the last decade, with the creation of a separate executive government in Wales, and the transfer of further powers, including competence to enact primary legislation to the devolved institutions. The Government of Wales Act 2006 (GOWA) conferred competence on the National Assembly for Wales to make laws in certain specified areas.[1] The Wales Act 2017 will, when the relevant provisions come into force, amend GOWA and will provide competence for the Assembly to make laws in all areas except where the legislation would relate to reserved matters (defined in Sch 7A to GOWA) and subject to certain other limitations discussed below.

[1] The history of devolution in Wales is charted in *Agricultural Sector (Wales) Bill Re, A-G v Counsel General for Wales (A-G for Northern Ireland intervening)* [2014] UKSC 43 at paras 19–2.

The Institutions

The National Assembly for Wales

21.64 There is an elected body, known as the National Assembly for Wales.[1] The Assembly has 60 members, 40 elected by the traditional first past the post method for Assembly constituencies (which at present are the same as the Westminster constituencies) and 20 elected on a regional basis by a system of proportional representation.[2] The Assembly (and the Welsh Government) are declared by statute to be a permanent part of the United Kingdom's constitutional arrangements and, in view of the commitment of the United Kingdom Parliament and Government to those institutions, it is declared that the Assembly and Welsh Government are not to be abolished except on the basis of a decision of the people of Wales voting in a referendum.[3]

[1] See s 1 of GOWA. The Assembly was first created by the Government of Wales Act 1998.
[2] See ss 1(2), 2 and 6 of GOWA.
[3] See s A1 of GOWA as amended by the Wales Act 2017, s 1: this provision will be in force by 1 April 2017.

Extent of legislative competence

21.65 Within the area of its legislative competence, the Assembly may include any provision in an Assembly Act which could be made by an Act of the United Kingdom Parliament.[1] At present, the Assembly has competence to make legislation which relates to one of the subjects listed under the headings in Sch 7 to GOWA or is incidental to, or consequential on, such a provision.[2] The areas where the Assembly may enact legislation include agriculture, economic regeneration, education, environment, health, housing, local government, town and country planning, social welfare (including social services), and the Welsh language. Following the acquisition of direct legislative competence on 5 May 2011, the Assembly embarked upon an extensive legislative programme and, at the time of writing had enacted over 20 Acts, including a Social Services and Well-being (Wales) Act 2014, (which establishes new criteria for entitlement in Wales to adult and child social services), a Planning (Wales) Act 2015, a Human Transplantation (Wales) Act 2013 (which changes the law in Wales on organ and tissue transplantations and presumes a deceased person's consent to transplantation), and a Renting Homes (Wales) Act 2016 (implementing the recommendations of the Law Commission on renting homes). A provision of an Assembly Act will, however, be beyond the Assembly's legislative competence if it exceeds the legislative competence conferred upon the Assembly under Part 4 of GOWA as originally enacted , if it applies otherwise than in relation to Wales,[3] if it breaches certain restrictions contained in Part 2 of Sch 7 to GOWA, or it is incompatible with European Union Law or Convention rights, ie rights derived from the European Convention on Human Rights and incorporated into domestic law by the Human Rights Act 1998.[4]

Once the relevant amendments to GOWA made by the Wales Act 2017 come into force, the Assembly will have competence to make laws in all areas save where the legislation relates to reserved matters as defined in Sch 7A to GOWA and subject to certain other limitations.[5] The reserved matters include matters generally reserved to the United Kingdom Parliament, such as aspects of the constitution (the Crown, the union of the nations of Wales and England, and the UK Parliament), defence, foreign affairs, the single legal jurisdiction (that is, courts, judges, criminal and civil proceedings, pardons, private international law and judicial review of administrative action, and certain tribunals), the civil service and the registration and funding of political parties.[6] There are further categories of reserved matters, which are for the UK Parliament but which contain exceptions about which the Assembly may make laws. Fiscal and economic matters, for example, are reserved to the UK Parliament but there is an exception for devolved taxes and local taxes (such as council tax and non-domestic rates) used to fund local authority expenditure.[7] To fall within the legislative competence of the Assembly, the legislation must also not apply otherwise than in relation to Wales (unless the provision is ancillary to an Act of the Assembly or has no greater effect than is necessary to give effect to the relevant Act of the Assembly), must not extend beyond England and Wales, must not breach any restriction contained in Sch 7B to GOWA and must be compatible with European Union Law and Convention rights.[8]

The legislative process under the current arrangements and the reserved powers model is the same. A Bill is introduced in the Assembly,[9] and becomes an Act of the Assembly when passed by the Assembly and given Royal Assent by the Queen.[10] At present, the Clerk of the Assembly submits the proposed Assembly Act to Her Majesty in Council for approval.[11] In due course, that function will transfer to the Presiding Officer.[12] Certain laws, that is those relating to a protected subject-matter will require a vote of two-thirds of the total number of Assembly members. Protected subject matters include: the name of the Assembly; the franchise and electoral system for Assembly elections; the specification and number of Assembly constituencies; and the number of person who may hold office as a Welsh minister or deputy minister.[13]

The United Kingdom Parliament at Westminster also has power to make laws for Wales and its sovereignty is not altered by GOWA.[14] There are therefore two bodies with the power of making laws in Wales, the United Kingdom Parliament and the Assembly (within its area of legislative competence). Ultimately, the United Kingdom Parliament remains sovereign and could limit or restrict the power of the Assembly to make laws. Section 107(6) of GOWA, however, provides that 'it is recognised that the Parliament of the United Kingdom will not normally legislate with regard to devolved matters without the consent of the Assembly'.[15] The Supreme Court has observed that the effect of such a provision is to recognise the political convention that the UK Parliament does not normally legislate in devolved areas without the consent of the relevant devolved legislature but has indicated that such provisions do not seek to turn that convention into a justiciable rule of law enforceable by the courts.[16]

[1] Section 108(1) of GOWA.
[2] Sections 108(4) and (5) of GOWA.
[3] See s 108(4) of GOWA.
[4] See s 108(6) of GOWA.
[5] See s 108A of, and Sch 7A to, GOWA (as substituted by s 3 of the Wales Act 2017).
[6] See Part 1 of Sch 7A to GOWA.
[7] See Part 2 of Sch 7A to GOWA.
[8] See s 108A of GOWA (as substituted by s 3 of the Wales Act 2017).
[9] See s 110 of GOWA. The bill is then the subject of three-stage consideration by the Assembly in accordance with standing orders made under s 111 of GOWA.
[10] See s 107(2) of GOWA.
[11] See s 115 of GOWA. The office of the Clerk is provided for by s 26 of GOWA.
[12] See s 12 of the Wales Act 2017 amending s 115 of GOWA.
[13] Section 111A of GOWA as amended by the Wales Act 2017.
[14] See s 107(4) of GOWA.
[15] As amended by s 2 of the Wales Act 2017; this section came into force on 31 January 2017.
[16] See *R (Miller) v Secretary of State for Exiting the European Union* [2017] UKSC 5, per Lord Neuberger, giving the judgment of the majority, at paras 148 to 149.

Challenges to Assembly Acts

21.66 The courts will determine whether or not an Assembly Act or Bill, or any provision of such an Act or Bill, is within the Assembly's legislative competence. Guidance on general principles dealing with the resolution of such challenges in the context of the current devolution arrangement, involving the conferment of legislative competence in certain defined areas (under Part 4 of GOWA prior to amendments made by the Wales Act 2017) is to be found in the judgments of the Supreme Court in *A-G v National Assembly for Wales*,[1] and *Agricultural Sector (Wales) Bill, Re, A-G v Counsel General for*

Wales (A-G for Northern Ireland intervening)– Reference by the Attorney General[2] and *Re Recovery of Medical Costs for Asbestos Diseases (Wales) Bill.[3]* The first two of those cases concerned references by the Attorney General on the question of whether provisions of the Local Government Byelaws (Wales) Bill and the Agricultural (Sector) (Wales) Bill respectively were within the legislative competence of the Assembly. The third concerned a reference by the Counsel General of a Bill providing that where a person received treatment from the National Health Service in Wales and then received compensation from an employer, the employer, and insurers of such employers, were liable for the costs of medical care provided for those persons.

The question of whether a provision of a Bill or Assembly Act is within the Assembly's legislative competence is a question of law to be determined by applying the provisions of s 108 of, and Sch 7 to, GOWA. That, in turn, also involves consideration of the purpose of the Assembly Act provision having regard (amongst other things) to its effect in all the circumstances.[4] While the issue of legislative competence will be determined by an interpretation of the specific provisions of GOWA, and the Assembly Act in question, regard may be had to the purpose of GOWA. It is a statute of great constitutional significance whose purpose is to make provision for government of Wales and the transfer of legislative powers to a democratically elected Assembly. That purpose may influence the construction of the words of GOWA.[5] In considering whether a Bill is within the Assembly's legislative competence, the first issue will to be identify the relevant subject within Sch 7. Then the court must consider whether the proposed Assembly Bill relates to that subject. That involves more than a loose or consequential connection and will be determined by having regard to the purpose and effect of the Bill. Finally, the court will need to consider whether or not the Assembly Bill falls within one of the exceptions to the subject listed in the Schedule or within some other exception in GOWA.

Thus, in the *Agricultural Sector (Wales) Bill* reference, the Supreme Court had to determine whether a proposed Assembly Bill established a scheme for the regulation of agricultural wages in Wales. The relevant subject matter in Sch 7 was 'Agriculture'. That, the Supreme Court held, meant the industry or economic activity of agriculture in all its aspects. The purpose of the Bill, as appeared from its provisions and the relevant consultation documents,[6] was to regulate agricultural wages in Wales. That related to agriculture. Schedule 7 did not include any exception indicating that such matters fell outside the legislative competence of the Assembly. Consequently, the Bill fell within the legislative competence of the Assembly. The fact that the subject matter of the Bill could also be described as involving employment and industrial relations which was not a subject within the competence of the Assembly under Sch 7 did not prevent a Bill which did relate to agriculture and where there was no specific exception excluding such matters from the scope of agriculture did not prevent the Bill from relating to agriculture and falling within competence.

In the *Recovery of Medical Costs* case, the Supreme Court had to consider the meaning of 'relates to' a subject. The question arose in the context of a Bill providing that, when a person received treatment for an asbestosis-related disease and that person subsequently received compensation from a former employer, the cost of providing the treatment could be recovered from the employer or its insurers. The only relevant subject matter in Sch 7 of GOWA was the organisation and funding of the health service. The Supreme Court held that the phrase 'related to' meant more than a loose or consequential connection between the legislation and the subject. In the context of this Bill, the Supreme Court held that there needed to be a direct relationship between the service provided and the liability imposed, and the fact that the employer may have been engaged in wrong-doing giving rise to the liability amounted to no more than an indirect relationship. Consequently, the Bill fell outside the legislative competence of the Assembly.[7] These cases concerned the current model of devolution contained in Part 4 of GOWA. They remain relevant as the provisions of the Wales Act 2017 conferring wider legislative competence have not yet come into force and, furthermore, Acts of the Assembly made under the current model of devolution (that is, under Part 4 of GOWA prior to amendment) will be reviewed subject to these principles.

Whilst Assembly Acts and Bills are subject to review to ensure that they are within the legislative competence of the Assembly, they are not subject to review on common law grounds such as irrationality or unreasonableness.[8] Questions of whether a provision of a Bill is within the legislative competence of the Assembly may be referred to the Supreme Court by the Attorney General or the Counsel General[9] or the question of whether a provision of an Assembly Act is within legislative competence may arise in other proceedings. Where the Attorney-General refers a question of competence to the Supreme Court, the proceedings will be served upon the Counsel General.[10]

[1] [2013] 1 A.C. 792.
[2] [2014] UKSC 43.
[3] [2015] A.C. 1016.
[4] See generally the observations of Lord Hope of Craighead in *A-G v National Assembly for Wales Commission* [2013] 1 AC 792 at paras 78 to 81; and per Lord Reed and Lord Thomas in *Agricultural Sector (Wales) Bill – Reference by the Attorney-General* [2014] UKSC 45 at para 6 and in *AXA General Insurance Ltd v Lord Advocate (Scotland)* [2012] 1 AC 868 at para 46 (dealing with the Scottish legislation but similar principles apply to GOWA).
[5] *Agricultural Sector (Wales) Bill – Reference by the Attorney-General* [2014] UKSC 45 at para 50 and see s 108(7) of GOWA.
[6] Ibid at 55–68.
[7] [2015] A.C. 1016 at paras 26 to 34 (per Lord Mance with whom Lord Neuberger and Lord Reed agreed; Lord Thomas and Baroness Hale dissented).
[8] *AXA General Insurance Ltd v Lord Advocate (Scotland)* [2012] AC 868 at para 52 and 147 (see discussion by the Honourable Mr Justice Lewis: '*The AXA Case: the Nature of Devolved Legislation and the Role of the Courts*' in *Landmark Cases in Public Law (eds Juss and Sunkin)*, Hart (2017).
[9] See s 112 of GOWA.
[10] *A-G v National Assembly for Wales Commission* [2013] 1 AC 792 at paras 88 to 100.

21.67 Subordinate legislation made by the Welsh Ministers may also, depending on the statutory provisions conferring the functions or the Order in Council transferring the functions to the Welsh Ministers,[1] need to be laid before the Assembly, or require Assembly approval, or to be subject to annulment by the Assembly. Statute also confers upon the Assembly specific functions to consider and approve particular measures or plans.

[1] See para 9 of Sch 3 to GOWA dealing with Orders made under s 58 of GOWA transferring functions to the Welsh Ministers.

21.68 The Assembly is required to give effect to the principle that the Welsh and English languages are to be treated on a basis of equality, so far as it is appropriate and reasonably practicable to do so, in Assembly proceedings.[1] The English and Welsh texts of any Assembly Measure,[2] Act of the Assembly and subordinate legislation are to be treated as of equal standing.[3]

[1] Section 35(1) GOWA.
[2] Prior to the Assembly acquiring direct legislative competence under Part 4 of GOWA, the Assembly had powers to make a form of legislation, known as Assembly Measures, in areas where a legislative competence order had conferred competence on the Assembly to make such measures.
[3] Section 156 of GOWA.

The Welsh Government

21.69 The Welsh Government[1] comprises the First Minister,[2] the Welsh Ministers, the Deputy Welsh Ministers[3] and the Counsel General.[4] The First Minister and the Welsh Ministers are collectively referred to as the Welsh Ministers.[5] Functions may be conferred or imposed upon the Welsh Ministers either directly by statute or by an Order in Council transferring functions to the Welsh Ministers.[6] Functions are exercisable on behalf of the Crown.[7] It may be that the Carltona principle applies to the Welsh Ministers, as Her Majesty's Ministers exercising functions on behalf of the Crown, so that decisions do not need to be taken personally by the relevant Welsh Minister but may be taken by civil servants acting on behalf of the Welsh Ministers. However, this has not yet been decided by the courts. Certain functions may be made exercisable by the Welsh Ministers and Ministers of the Crown jointly or by the Welsh Ministers after consultation with Ministers of the Crown.

[1] See s 45(1) of GOWA as amended by s 4 of the Wales Act 2014.
[2] Appointed by Her Majesty in accordance with the provisions of ss 47 and 48 of GOWA.
[3] Appointed by the First Minister with the approval of Her Majesty: ss 48 and 50.
[4] Appointed by Her Majesty on the recommendation of the First Minister: see s 49 of GOWA.
[5] Section 45(2) of GOWA.
[6] See s 58 of GOWA. Functions previously transferred to the National Assembly of Wales by Order in Council under s 22 of the Government of Wales Act 1998 have now been transferred to the Welsh Ministers: see para 30 of Sch 11 to GOWA.
[7] Section 57(2) of GOWA.

21.70 A wide array of statutory duties and powers have been conferred upon the Welsh Ministers. They take a wide range of administrative decisions in areas such as agriculture, education, health, social justice and planning and the environment. They also have power to do anything which they consider appropriate to achieve the promotion or improvement of the economic, social or environmental well-being of Wales.[1] The Welsh Ministers also have powers to make subordinate legislation in a wide range of fields. The Welsh Ministers may be, and have been, designated for the purposes of making regulations for the purpose of implementing any European Community law obligation.[2] The Welsh Ministers have no power to make, confirm or approve any subordinate legislation or do any other act in so far as that would be incompatible with either European Community law[3] or the rights guaranteed by the European Convention on Human Rights incorporated in the United Kingdom by the Human Rights Act 1998.[4] Furthermore, if the Secretary of State considers that action proposed by the Welsh Ministers would be incompatible with any international obligation, he may direct that the proposed action is not taken.[5]

1   Section 60 of GOWA.
2   Section 59 of GOWA and s 2(2) of the European Communities Act 1972.
3   Section 80 of GOWA.
4   Section 81 of GOWA.
5   Section 82 of GOWA.

The Administrative Court in Wales[1]

1   See generally, Thomas Glyn Watkin, The Legal History of Wales, (2nd edn), 2012 Chapter 10; D.C. Gardner, *Administrative Law and the Administrative Court in Wales* (2016) (University of Wales Press); David Lloyd Jones, The Machinery of Justice in a Changing Wales, (2010) 16 Transactions of the Cymmrodorion 123.

21.71 With the first phase of devolution under the Government of Wales Act 1998 it was rapidly acknowledged as essential that legal challenges to decisions of the newly created institutions and other public bodies in Wales might be brought, heard and decided in Wales. As a result, arrangements were made for the Administrative Court to sit in Wales. This was the first occasion on which the Administrative Court had sat regularly outside London.

21.72 In the years which followed, a substantial number of applications for judicial review were heard in the Administrative Court sitting in Wales under those arrangements.[1] They covered a wide range of subject matter and included cases against the National Assembly for Wales, the Welsh Ministers and local authorities. Hearings took place principally in the Civil Justice Centre in Cardiff but also in other courts in Wales. In November 2006 in *Condron v National Assembly for Wales*[2] the Court of Appeal observed, in a case concerning planning permission for opencast mining near Merthyr Tydfil which had been heard at first instance and on appeal in London, that it cried out to be heard in Wales both at first instance and on appeal and expressed its considerable regret that that had not occurred. In October 2007, in *R (Deepdock Ltd) v Welsh Ministers*[3] the Administrative Court emphasised that challenges to decisions made in a devolved area by a Welsh national authority, such as the Welsh Ministers, or by a Welsh local authority should ordinarily be heard in Wales unless there is good reason for the hearing to take place elsewhere. These decisions proved important milestones in the development of judicial review in Wales.

1   See, eg *R (South Wales Sea Fisheries Committee) v National Assembly for Wales* (21 December 2001, unreported) (validity of sea fisheries order); *R (Swami Suryananda) v Welsh Ministers* [2007] EWHC 1736 (whether order requiring destruction of a Hindu temple bull compatible with Article 9 ECHR): the Court of Appeal also sat in Cardiff to hear the appeal; see [2007] EWCA Civ 893.
2   [2006] EWCA Civ 1573, per Richards LJ at paragraph 110.
3   [2007] EWHC 3347 (Admin) per HHJ Hickinbottom QC (sitting as a Deputy High Court Judge) at paragraph 20.

21.73 In April 2009 these arrangements were replaced as part of a series of reforms implementing the recommendations of Sir Anthony May's report into administrative justice outside London. These reforms were introduced against the background of the massive increase in the number of public law challenges brought before the courts in recent years.[1] However, their underlying rationale was one of ready access to justice by facilitating the hearing of public law cases outside London.

[1] See generally, Version 3.1. Listing Policy: Administrative Court Office for Wales and the Western Circuit, 8 May 2015.

21.74 Although the resulting structure in Wales is very similar to that adopted in the case of Birmingham, Manchester and Leeds, the other principal centres outside London where it is possible to issue proceedings in the Administrative Court, the arrangements set in place in Wales have an added significance and importance because they operate in the context of Welsh devolution.

21.75 The Administrative Court in its new form opened for business in Wales on 21 April 2009.[1] An essential change brought about by the new arrangements is that the administration of the sittings of the Administrative Court in Wales is now carried out by a team based at the Cardiff Civil Justice Centre, as opposed to the Royal Courts of Justice in London. The new arrangements have the advantage of enabling the Court to operate more efficiently and to provide a speedier service. Judicial supervision of the arrangements in Wales is currently provided by a High Court judge in the Queen's Bench Division who acts as the Administrative Court in Wales Liaison Judge and who oversee Administrative Court sittings and who together with other High Court judges, sits in Wales on public law cases.[2]

[1] Under these arrangements Administrative Court cases originating from the Western Circuit were also issued and heard in the Cardiff Civil Justice Centre. Since the Administrative Court began to sit in Bristol the Administrative Court Office in Cardiff has continued to act as the administrative centre for the Bristol hearing centre. Western Circuit claims are issued and administered in Cardiff but usually heard in Bristol.

[2] The Administrative Court Office in Cardiff now also acts as the Upper Tribunal (Immigration and Asylum Chamber) Office for Wales, for judicial reviews in UTIAC only, as well as the Planning Court Office for Wales.

21.76 Issues of venue are now governed by Practice Direction 54D. The general rule for starting cases is that the claim form in proceedings in the Administrative Court may be issued at the Administrative Court Office of the High Court at the Royal Courts of Justice in London or at the District Registry of the High Court at Birmingham, Cardiff, Leeds or Manchester, unless the claim is one of the excepted classes of claim which may only be started and determined at the Royal Courts of Justice in London.[1] Any claim started in Cardiff will normally be determined at a court in Wales.[2] The classes of claim excluded from the general arrangements under the Practice Direction and which may only be started and determined in London are the following:

(1)   proceedings to which Part 76 or Part 79 applies, and for the avoidance of doubt—
  (a)   proceedings relating to control orders (within the meaning of Part 76);
  (b)   financial restrictions proceedings (within the meaning of Part 79);
  (c)   proceedings relating to terrorism or alleged terrorists (where that is a relevant feature of the claim); and
  (d)   proceedings in which a special advocate is or is to be instructed;

(2)   proceedings to which RSC Order 115 applies;
(3)   proceedings under the Proceeds of Crime Act 2002;
(4)   appeals to the Administrative Court under the Extradition Act 2003;
(5)   proceedings which must be heard by a Divisional Court; and
(6)   proceedings relating to the discipline of solicitors.[3]

If a claim form is issued at an Administrative Court office other than in London and includes one of the excepted classes of claim, the proceedings will be transferred to London.[4]

It should be noted that the Administrative Court in Wales interprets paragraph 3.1(5) as referring to cases which must be heard by a Divisional Court as a result of a statutory provision. Cases of a type which are heard by a Divisional Court by convention or by order under CPR 54.12(6) may be lodged in Cardiff and a Divisional Court will be arranged where appropriate.

Furthermore, cases that must be lodged in London can (and have been) transferred from London to Cardiff for hearing where appropriate.

[1]   Practice Direction 54D, paragraph 2.1.
[2]   Practice Direction 54D, paragraph 2.2.
[3]   Practice Direction 54D, paragraph 3.1.
[4]   Practice Direction 54D, paragraph 3.2.

21.77 Provision is made for the assignment of cases, once commenced, to a different venue, it being expressly stated that such transfer is a judicial act.[1] In this regard, the general expectation is that proceedings will be administered and determined in the region with which the claimant has the closest connection, subject to the following considerations as applicable—

(1)   any reason expressed by any party for preferring a particular venue;
(2)   the region in which the defendant, or any relevant office or department of the defendant, is based;
(3)   the region in which the claimant's legal representatives are based;
(4)   the ease and cost of travel to a hearing;
(5)   the availability and suitability of alternative means of attending a hearing (for example, by videolink);
(6)   the extent and nature of media interest in the proceedings in any particular locality;
(7)   the time within which it is appropriate for the proceedings to be determined;
(8)   whether it is desirable to administer or determine the claim in another region in the light of the volume of claims issued at, and the capacity, resources and workload of, the court at which it is issued;
(9)   whether the claim raises issues sufficiently similar to those in another outstanding claim to make it desirable that it should be determined together with, or immediately following, that other claim; and
(10)   whether the claim raises devolution issues and for that reason whether it should more appropriately be determined in London or Cardiff.[2]

On an application by a party or of its own initiative, the Court, applying the above considerations, may direct that the claim be determined at a venue other than that to which it is currently assigned.[3] Once proceedings have been assigned to Wales, the proceedings will be both administered from Wales and determined by a judge of the Administrative Court at a suitable court within Wales.[4] When giving directions under CPR 54.10, the court may direct that proceedings be reassigned to another region for hearing (applying the considerations in paragraph 5.2). If no such direction is given, the claim will be heard in the same region as that in which the permission application was determined (whether on paper or at a hearing).[5]

The Administrative Court applies a rigorous policy that challenges to decisions of Welsh public authorities should ordinarily be heard in Wales.[6] In particular, the principle established in *R (Deepdock Ltd) v Welsh Ministers* that challenges to decisions made in a devolved area by the Welsh Ministers should ordinarily be heard in Wales, unless there is good reason for the hearing to be elsewhere, remains valid under the Practice Direction. The same approach is followed in the case of Welsh local authorities. In *R (Woolcock) v Bridgend Magistrates' Court*, a challenge to a decision of a magistrates' court in Wales, committing a person for non-payment of council tax owed to the Welsh local authority, which had made the application for committal, was transferred to the Administrative Court in Wales and heard there.[7]

[1] Practice Direction 54D, paragraph 5.1.
[2] Practice Direction 54D, paragraph 5.2.
[3] Practice Direction 54D, paragraph 5.4.
[4] Practice Direction 54D, paragraph 5.5.
[5] Practice Direction 54D, paragraph 5.6.
[6] *R (Condron) v Merthyr Tydfil County Borough Council* [2009] EWHC 1621 (Admin) at paragraph 61; *Jones v DPP* [2011] EWHC 50 (Admin).
[7] *R (Woolcock) v Bridgend Magistrates' Court* [2017] EWHC 34 (Admin.) (per Lewis J. at para. 22.

21.78 The Practice Direction provides that once assigned to a venue, the proceedings will be both administered from that venue and determined by a judge of the Administrative Court at a suitable court within that region. In each case the choice of the appropriate court (from those within Wales which are identified by the Presiding Judges of Wales as suitable for such a hearing) is to be decided, subject to availability, by the considerations under paragraph 5.2, referred to above.[1] Within Wales arrangements have been made for the Administrative Court to sit at any court centre as appropriate. It has sat, for example, in Caernarfon, Carmarthen, Mold, Newport, Rhyl, Swansea, Welshpool and Wrexham, but the great majority of cases are heard in Cardiff. Although proceedings before the Administrative Court in Wales will be issued only in the Civil Justice Centre in Cardiff, proceedings may be lodged at any Queen's Bench District Registry in Wales for transmission to Cardiff for issue. As a matter of listing policy, caseworkers will attempt to list a case in the most geographically appropriate hearing centre, considering judicial availability for that court centre. Only in exceptional circumstances will cases that relate to North Wales not be heard in North Wales.[2]

[1] Practice Direction 54D, paragraph 5.5.
[2] Version 3.1 Listing Policy; Administrative Court Office for Wales and the Western Circuit, 8 May 2015.

21.79 Provision is made for urgent applications. During court hours, where an urgent application needs to be made it will heard by the judge designated to deal with such applications in the Cardiff District Registry. There is a rota of judges to deal with such applications during court hours. The application may be considered on the papers, at an oral hearing in person, or by telephone. In appropriate cases arrangements can be made for the application to be heard by a judge at one of the other designated court centres in Wales. In the first instance, application should be made to the Administrative Court Office in the Cardiff District Registry. Out of hours applications must be made to the duty High Court Judge, the arrangement which operates throughout England and Wales.[1] When an urgent application is made to the Court, this will not by itself decide the venue for the further administration or determination of the claim. The court dealing with the urgent application may direct that the case be assigned to a particular venue. When the Court considering an urgent application does not make such a direction, the claim will be assigned in the first place to London but may be reassigned to another venue at a later date.[2]

[1]   Practice Direction 54D, paragraph 4. The telephone number for out of hours applications is 020 7947 6000.
[2]   Practice Direction 54D, paragraph 5.3.

21.80 Each term at least two nominated High Court Judges, including the Queen's Bench Liaison Judge, hear public law cases in Wales for part of the term. In addition cases before the Administrative Court in Wales may be heard by one of a number of Circuit Judges or Recorders, all of whom are authorised to sit as Deputy High Court Judges in the Administrative Court in London and in Wales.

21.81 The service provided by the new Court in Wales is completely bilingual. All of the court forms relating to public law proceedings are readily available in both English and Welsh. *R (Welsh Language Commissioner) v National Savings and Investments*[1] was the first case before the Administrative Court in Wales which was conducted in the Welsh language.

[1]   [2014] EWHC 488 (Admin).

21.82 In its reconstituted form the Administrative Court is proving an important national resource which makes a major contribution to the administration of justice and to public administration in Wales. One major objective of these arrangements is to ensure ready access to justice in the field of public law and they greatly facilitate the bringing and the efficient management of public law proceedings in Wales. In their application to a devolved Wales they obviously have a further vital dimension and it is to be hoped that they will continue to provide an appropriate framework for legal controls on administrative action as the devolution settlement evolves.

Devolution issues

21.83 There is one category of proceedings, those involving devolution issues, which are dealt with by the provisions of Sch 9 to GOWA. A devolution issues is defined as a question:

(1)   whether an Assembly Measure or Act of the Assembly is within the legislative competence of the Assembly;
(2)   whether any function is exercisable by the Welsh Ministers, First Minister or Counsel General;

(3) whether the exercise of a function by the Welsh Ministers, First Minister or Counsel General is within their powers (including the question of whether the exercise of such a function is compatible with European Union law or a right derived from the European Convention on Human Rights and incorporated into UK law by the Human Rights Act 1998);

(4) whether there has been a failure to comply with a duty imposed Welsh Ministers, First Minister or Counsel General (including duties imposed under European Union law or the Human Rights Act 1998);

(5) whether any failure to act is compatible with a Convention right.[1]

[1] Paragraph 1 of Sch 9 to GOWA.

21.84 There is provision for the notification of devolution issues to the Counsel General and the Attorney General and they are entitled to take part in such proceedings.[1] Where the claimant intends to raise a devolution issue in judicial review proceedings, the claim form must specify the relevant provisions of GOWA and summarise the facts, circumstances and points of law on the basis of which it is said that a devolution issue arises.[2] In practice, in ordinary judicial review proceedings alleging that the Welsh Ministers have acted unlawfully, and whether or not this is a devolution issue, the Welsh Ministers are usually named as the defendant and separate notice to the Counsel General is not usually given. Other litigation, between other parties, including civil litigation between non-public bodies could raise devolution issues. The requirement to notify the Counsel General of a devolution issue, such as, for example, an issue as to whether a provision of an Assembly Measure is within the Assembly's competence, is likely to be of greater importance in such cases. The procedure in relation to references made by the Attorney General alleging that provisions of an Assembly Act are outside the Assembly's competence is discussed above in paragraph **21.66**.

[1] See paragraph 4 of Sch 9 to GOWA.
[2] See paragraph 5.4 of Practice Direction 54A – Judicial Review.

Remedies

21.85 There are additional provisions relating to remedies applicable where a court or tribunal decides that an Assembly Act, or a provision of such an Act, is outside the legislative competence of the Assembly, or that any provision of subordinate legislation is outside the powers of the Welsh Ministers, First Minister or Counsel General. The court or tribunal may make an order removing or limiting the retrospective effect of the court's decision or suspending the effect of the decision for any period and on any conditions to allow the defect to be corrected.[1]

[1] Section 153 of the GOWA.

Chapter 22

JUDICIAL REVIEW IN SCOTLAND

INTRODUCTION

22.1 It is not the purpose of this chapter to provide a full account of the law of judicial review in Scotland.[1] Its aims have necessarily to be more modest. There are very substantial overlaps between the law of England and Wales and the law of Scotland which ensure that much of the rest of this book has equal relevance to both jurisdictions. On the other hand, there are also some important differences and the main aim of this chapter is to explain those differences, principally for the benefit of readers north of the border. There are some divergences between the two systems of judicial review which are of long standing. Other divergences (or reasons for potential divergence) are of more recent origin. At the same time, there have also been signs of a convergence of rules in some areas. These have included deliberate reflection by the judiciary on the case for a greater harmonisation of the law. The divergences and convergences are considered in more detail in later sections of this chapter. It may, however, be helpful to provide a brief sketch at this introductory stage.

¹ For two much more comprehensive accounts, see Lord Clyde and DJ Edwards, *Judicial Review* (2000) and A W Bradley and C M G Himsworth, 'Administrative Law' *Stair Memorial Encyclopaedia Reissue* (2000) (hereafter *Bradley and Himsworth*). For a more general discussion of the Scottish constitutional background, see CMG Himsworth and CM O'Neill, *Scotland's Constitution: Law and Practice* (3nd ed, 2015). See also the Scottish Government's, *Right First Time: a practical guide for public authorities in Scotland to decision-making and the law* (2010). The author of this chapter acknowledges the helpfulness, in its revision, of the comments on a draft of Dr Elisenda Casañas Adam.

22.2 Whilst it has, on the whole, been possible to say that the *grounds* of review have been broadly the same in the two jurisdictions[1] it has also been quite clear that, in matters of procedure and of remedies, the jurisdictions have developed rules along quite different lines deriving from their historically different origins. These are dealt with below.[2] Also deriving from the historically different basis of judicial review in the supervisory jurisdiction of the Court of Session has been a different definition of the scope of review. This led to the reconfirmation in the leading case of *West v Secretary of State for Scotland*[3] of the non-application in Scotland of the jurisprudence in England tending to define the scope of judicial review by reference to a public/private test.[4] The consequences of this divergence are also considered below.[5]

¹ See **22.9** et seq.
² See **22.19** and **22.20**.
³ 1992 SC 385.
⁴ See CHAPTER 5.
⁵ See **22.3**.

22.3 Alongside these established differences of approach, however, have to be considered more recent developments. In the first place, there was the arrival of devolution under the terms of the Scotland Act 1998 which produced new institutions (in particular, the Scottish Parliament and the Scottish Government[1]) and new procedures for judicial challenge.[2] Separate from the general questions of competence of the Scottish Parliament introduced by the Scotland Act 1998 (as since supplemented by the Scotland Act 2012 and the Scotland Act 2016) has been the 'incorporation' by both that Act itself, but more extensively by the Human Rights Act 1998 of the 'Convention rights'[3] contained in the European Convention on Human Rights. The effects of this incorporation are considered in detail in CHAPTER 4 and, for the most part, they are of similar application across the United Kingdom (UK) as a whole. One or two points of special application to Scotland do, however, deserve mention.[4] In the first place, the distinctive application of the Convention rights regime to the Scottish Parliament and Government has led to the consequential designation of the issues raised in challenges to the actions of those bodies as 'devolution issues', producing the different procedural treatment including recourse first to the Judicial Committee of the Privy Council and then, since October 2009, to the UK Supreme Court.[5] Secondly, the parallel introduction of the human rights regimes has generated new questions about how far the responses to human rights issues raised separately in the different UK jurisdictions should be harmonised. There are those who argue that the introduction of the single group of rights deriving from the adherence of the UK rather than its component parts to an international convention policed by a single court in Strasbourg points clearly in the direction of the need, or at least the desirability, of a uniform response by courts across the UK, although the former division of ultimate responsibility between the Judicial Committee of the Privy Council (devolution issues raised in Scotland, Wales or Northern Ireland), the Scottish High Court of Justiciary (Scottish criminal matters not raising devolution issues), and the House of Lords (everything else) militated against any guaranteed uniformity. On the other hand, there are those who have argued that there is nothing which in principle demands any such uniformity of response and that, on the other hand, the option of diversity should wherever possible be sought.[6] On this view there is no reason why either the historic divergences of Scots law from English law or the newfound capacities for difference created for the Scottish Parliament should be undermined by an unnecessarily rigid uniformity of approach to rights issues which increasingly pervade much of the law. There have been few indications of a clear judicial response so far, although, in matters of planning procedures, the House of Lords decision in *R (Alconbury Developments Ltd) v Secretary of State for the Environment, Transport and the Regions*[7] appeared to dictate the outcome in *County Properties Ltd v Scottish Ministers*[8] and in the criminal procedure cases noted above[9] there were strong pressures in the direction of uniformity by the English judges.[10] An important point of difference was established in *Somerville v Scottish Ministers*[11] where the House of Lords held (overturning the Inner House) that the normal 12-month time limit of the Human Rights Act 1998 did not apply to devolution issues raised under the Scotland Act 1998. That led in due course to the passing by the Scottish Parliament of the Convention Rights Proceedings (Amendment) (Scotland) Act 2009 and then to s 14 of the Scotland Act 2012. It is evident that the repeal and replacement of the Human Rights Act 1998, should that be taken forward, would have different consequences for Scotland (and Northern Ireland and Wales) than for England.

[1] Changed from 'Scottish Executive' by the Scotland Act 2012, s 12.
[2] See Chapter **21**.
[3] The terminology used in s 1 (1) of the Human Rights Act 1998 and, by extension, in the Scotland Act 1998 (s 126(1)).
[4] One special feature now of historical interest was that the application of the human rights regime to the Scottish Parliament and Scottish Government (but not to other Scottish institutions) with effect from their creation in 1999 did mean that human rights arguments were available to Scottish litigants more than a year earlier than they became available in England.
[5] A particular consequence of the separate use of the JCPC, but without direct application to judicial review, was the different approaches taken by judges in Scotland and England in cases involving delay in criminal proceedings. See *R v HMA* 2003 SC(PC) 21 and *Attorney General's Reference No 2 of 2001* [2004] 2 AC 72. For discussion, see C Himsworth (2004) 8 Ed LR 255. But see also *Spiers v Ruddy* 2009 SC(PC)1, 2008 SLT 39. The decisions of the UK Supreme Court in *Cadder (Peter) v HM Advocate* 2011 SC (UKSC) 13, 2010 SLT 1125 and *Fraser v HM Advocate* 2011 SC (UKSC) 113, 2011 SLT 515 prompted the introduction of 'compatibility issues'. See Chapter **21**.
[6] On which, see C Himsworth, 'The Hamebringing: Devolving Rights Seriously' in A Boyle et al (eds) *Human Rights and Scots Law* (2002). The creation of the UK Supreme Court brougth the opportunity for greater convergence.
[7] [2003] 2 AC 295.
[8] 2002 SC 79, 2001 SLT 1125. See C Himsworth, 'Planning Rights Convergence' (2002) 6 Edin LR 253.
[9] See note 5 above.
[10] See C Himsworth, 'Jurisdictional Divergences over the Reasonable Time Guarantee in Criminal Trials' (2004) 8 Edin LR 255.
[11] 2008 SC(HL) 45, 2007 SLT 1113.

22.4 In addition to these principal influences upon judicial review in Scotland produced by the Scotland Act, 1998, there are others which may over time affect the context within which judicial review is conducted in Scotland. A brief listing will suffice:

(1)   First, devolution brought the opportunity for the emergence of different conditions for the political accountability of ministers to the Scottish Parliament. Whether this has, in fact, produced a different degree of parliamentary accountability with a consequential effect upon the accountability sought by the courts is still an open question although, in *AXA Insurance Ltd, Petitioners*,[1] Lord Hope did, pertinently, remark that he was not prepared to accept that the dominance over Parliament of a government elected with a large majority could not happen in the United Kingdom's devolved legislatures. In the Scottish Parliament there was a government with a large majority dominating the only chamber and its committees. It is not entirely unthinkable, he said, that a government which has that power might seek to use it to abolish judicial review or to diminish the role of the courts in protecting the interests of the individual. To the extent that the conditions of review of the powers of ministers at Westminster have been said to be defined by the limits of their political accountability,[2] it may be debated whether the conditions of review of Scottish ministers should necessarily be defined in identical terms.

(2)   More specifically, a different judicial approach to the review of subordinate legislation (Scottish Statutory Instruments) might emerge in the light of different practices in the Scottish Parliament, especially on the part of its Delegated Powers and Law Reform Committee.[3] Parliamentary procedures on Scottish Statutory Instruments were reformed by the Interpretation and Legislative Reform (Scotland) Act 2010, which contains variations on the Statutory Instruments Act 1946.

(3)   Even before the arrival of devolution, the context of judicial review in Scotland was, in some measure, distinctive. Thus, for example, the audit of local authorities was conducted on a different basis, and, very importantly, the role of the sheriff in the handling of statutory appeals,[4] mainly but not exclusively from local authorities, produced many differences from English practice. These have been joined by a distinctive new ombudsman – the Scottish Public Services Ombudsman[5] – and new conditions for the future development of administrative tribunals in Scotland. Devolved Scottish tribunals were not subject to the review conducted by Sir Andrew Leggatt.[6] Nor, therefore, were they substantially affected by the Courts, Tribunals and Enforcement Act 2007. On the other hand, the obligation/power to transfer some judicial review cases from the Court of Session to the Upper Tribunal may well have some impact.[7] In practice, such transfers have been extremely rare.[8] More recently, the Tribunals (Scotland) Act 2014 became the basis for the rolling out of a new structure of (First-tier and Upper) Scottish tribunals.

---

[1]   2012 SC(UKSC) 122; 2011 SLT 1061 at para 51.
[2]   See eg *R v Home Secretary, ex p Fire Brigades Union* [1995] 2 AC 513 at 567 (Lord Mustill), since discussed in *R (Miller) v Secretary of State for Exiting the European Union* [2017] UKSC 5 at paras 35, 40 and 250.

3 See C Himsworth, 'Subordinate Legislation in the Scottish Parliament' (2002) 6 Edin LR 356.
4 For an example of the sheriff's continuing jurisdiction, *see Glasgow City Council v Bimendi* 2016 SLT 1063.
5 See Scottish Public Services Ombudsman Act 2002. And see *Argyll and Bute Council v Scottish Public Services Ombudsman* 2008 SC 155; 2008 SLT 168.
6 See Tribunals for Users (2003).
7 Rule of Court 58.5.
8 But see eg A, Petitioner [2014] CSOH 27.

22.5 Returning more specifically to the practice of judicial review in Scotland and to convergence with, or divergence from, that of England and Wales, certain other developments should be noted. Two are attributable directly to the contributions of Lord Hope of Craighead in English cases in the House of Lords. In the first place, his speeches in *R v Bow Street Metropolitan Stipendiary Magistrate, ex p Pinochet (No 2)*[1] and then especially in *Porter v Magill*[2] produced an approach to the law of bias which, in an area where there were emerging differences, there is now a single rule.[3] Second, in *R (Burkett) v Hammersmith and Fulham LBC (No 1)*,[4] Lord Hope did much to integrate, through close comparison of apparently diverse rules, the approach by courts to delay in the initiation of proceedings for judicial review.[5] Another area of interest was that of the concept of the 'non-jurisdictional error of law' where, until *Eba v Advocate General for Scotland*,[6] there appeared to be a divergence between the two jurisdictions.

1 [2000] 1 AC 119.
2 [2002] 2 AC 357.
3 See **22.75**.
4 [2002] 3 All ER 97.
5 See **22.52**.
6 2012 SC (UKSC) 1, 2011 SLT 768.

22.6 Other convergences between Scottish and English practice have occurred since the recommendations of the Report of the (Lord Gill) Scottish Civil Courts Review of 2009 were implemented by s 89 of the Courts Reform (Scotland) Act 2014.[1] Chapter 12 of the Report proposed the introduction of a preliminary permission stage to applications for judicial review, a new time limit for the commencement of proceedings, and new rules on standing, all of which have brought Court of Session practice closer to that of the English Administrative Court. All are mentioned later in this Chapter.[2]

1 With effect (SSI 2015/228) from 22 Sept 2015.
2 And see generally T Kelly 2015 Jur Rev 385.

APPLICATION FOR JUDICIAL REVIEW

22.7 In April 1985[1] a new procedure for invoking the supervisory jurisdiction of the Court of Session was instituted. Its origins were to be found in the speech of the late Lord Fraser in *Brown v Hamilton District Council*[2] in which the House of Lords held the inherent power of review to be exclusive to the Court of Session and thus unavailable in the sheriff court for petitioners in homelessness cases (such as *Brown*) and others in which no statutory procedure for appeal or review was applicable. Lord Fraser urged that there would be advantages in creating a special procedure in the Court of Session which would both make available remedies which were speedy and cheap and at the same time protect public authorities from unreasonable actions.[3] The response came in the appointment by the then Lord President of the Court of Session, Lord Emslie, of a working party chaired by Lord Dunpark with the remit to:

'devise and recommend for consideration a simple form of procedure, capable of being operated with reasonable expedition, for bringing before the court, for such relief as is appropriate, complaints by aggrieved persons . . . '.

Lord Dunpark's Report, with draft rules and commentary appended, was completed in June 1984 and the promulgation of Rule of Court 260B by Act of Sederunt[4] quickly followed. The central recommendations of the Dunpark working party were incorporated. In 1994, the rules of court were revised and consolidated[5] with the rules on judicial review contained in Chapter 58. Incorporating further changes (including the new permission stage), the current consolidation was issued in 2015.[6]

[2]   1983 SC (HL) 1, 1983 SLT 397. See also *Stevenson v Midlothian District Council* 1983 SC, (HL) 50, 1983 SLT 433. And see *Barlow v City of Edinburgh Council* (6 August 2004, unreported).
[3]   1983 SC (HL) 1 at 49; 1983 SLT 397 at 418.
[4]   SI 1985/500. Lord Dunpark's Report was entitled 'Report to the Rt Hon Lord Emslie. Lord President of the Court of Session', by the Working Party on Procedure for Judicial Review of Administrative Action.
[5]   Act of Sederunt (Rules of the Court of Session 1994) 1994, SI 1994/1443.
[6]   6 SSI 2015/228.

22.8 The original Rule 260B provided that:

'An application to the supervisory jurisdiction of the court which immediately before the coming into operation of this rule would have been made by way of summons or petition, shall be made by way of an application for judicial review in accordance with the provisions of this rule.'[1]

This formulation of the scope of the procedure was then expressly qualified in two ways. First, 'petition' was defined to include a summary petition under s 91 of the Court of Session Act 1868 which empowered the court to order specific performance of a statutory duty.[2] Second, however, the rule was stated not to extend to an 'application to the court made, or which could be made, by way of appeal or review under and by virtue of any enactment'.[3] Such applications may, in a broad sense, be made to the 'supervisory jurisdiction' and it was one of the recommendations of the Dunpark working party that the statutory applications be handled under the new judicial review procedure. This recommendation was, however, rejected and these statutory applications, expressly stated in the 1985 rule to include appeals against compulsory purchase orders under the Acquisition of Land (Authorisation Procedure) (Scotland) Act 1947,[4] appeals against structure plans and other planning orders and directions under the Town and Country Planning (Scotland) Act 1972,[5] and against certain orders under the Roads (Scotland) Act 1984[6] continued to be handled by the Inner House rather than a single judge in the Outer House.

[1]   Rule 260B(1).
[2]   Rule 260B(2). The section's consolidated successor is s 45 of the Court of Session Act 1988. Provision is sometimes made in other statutes for enforcement of their terms by procedure

under the Court of Session Act. See eg the Food Safety Act 1990, s 40; the Financial Services and Markets Act 2000, s 1T(3); and the Companies Act 2006, s 1239.
3   Rule 260B(3).
4   Schedule 1, paragraph 15.
5   Sections 232 and 233. See now Town and Country Planning (Scotland) Act 1997, ss 238 and 239.
6   Schedule 2, paragraph 2.

22.9 When the Rules of Court were recast in 1994, the language of the 1985 version was altered but, it is assumed, without effecting substantive change. Chapter 58 is simply stated, in words retained in the most recent formulation of 2015, to apply to an application to the supervisory jurisdiction of the court',[1] ie without reference to the pre-1985 access by way of summons or petition. It is then required that 'an application to the supervisory jurisdiction of the court, including an application under section 45(b) of the Act of 1988 (specific performance of statutory duty) shall be made by petition for judicial review.[2] This is stated not to apply if an 'application is made, or could be made, by appeal or review under or by virtue of any enactment'.[3] The specific references to the Acts of 1947, 1972 and 1984 are omitted. The ways in which these provisions (a) themselves define access to the Court of Session by means of application for judicial review or (b) incorporate previously established principles are discussed below.[4]

1   Rule 58.1(1).
2   Rule 58.(2) and 58.2.
3   Rule 58.3(1).
4   See **22.43**.

22.10 Unlike the position in England, there had been no requirement in Scotland of a leave or permission stage in judicial review procedure. However, the Report of the (Lord Gill) Scottish Civil Courts Review[1] did contain a recommendation that in response to a steady increase in numbers of petitions there should be a requirement to obtain leave to proceed with an application for judicial review. The test to be applied should be whether the petition has a real prospect of success (paragraphs 50–54). The change was adopted into the 2015 version of the Rules of Court.[2]

1   See **22.6** above.
2   See **22.86** below.

SUPERVISORY JURISDICTION OF THE COURT OF SESSION AND THE SCOPE OF JUDICIAL REVIEW[1]

1   For the law of England and Wales on this topic, see Chapter 5. Beyond the scope of this chapter is the international private law question of whether an application for judicial review should be initiated in Scotland or in England and Wales. Whilst, for instance, UK government departments may be reviewable in Scotland, the competence of an application will sometimes turn on the location of the body under review. See eg *Tehrani v Home Secretary* 2007 SC(HL)1; 2006 SLT 1123 in which it was held that an application by a Scottish resident for the review of the Immigration Appeal Tribunal's decision on appeal from an English adjudicator may go to either the Court of Session or the English Administrative Court. See C Himsworth, (2007) 11 Ed LR 277. See also *Struk v Home Secretary* 2004 SLT 468 and *Bank of Scotland v IMRO* 1989 SLT 432 (**22.3.9** below). The approach in England and Wales to territorial jurisdiction is discussed in Chapter 16 above.

22.11 There are some very practical reasons why it is desirable to know with certainty whether or not particular persons and institutions, functions and procedures are susceptible to judicial review in the Court of Session. Upon this may turn the question of whether an issue may or must properly be litigated in the Court of Session or in the sheriff court; the grounds on which the issue will be decided; and the procedure – ordinary or accelerated – to be adopted. As in England, however, there are significant areas of uncertainty about the scope of judicial review – the range of its application to different bodies and their procedures – which reflect, in part, uncertainties in the interpretation of the present rules which govern the court's jurisdiction but which also reflect rather wider uncertainty in principle as to both the historical basis for that jurisdiction and the contemporary theoretical justification for it. At their broadest, these are concerns shared by both Scotland and England but the extent to which shared solutions could or should be achieved is controversial. It is clear, however, that any analysis of the present scope of judicial review in Scots Law should take the rules of court as the starting point.

22.12 It was not the purpose of the 1985 Rules to adjust or even to redefine the jurisdictional competence of the Court of Session in matters of administrative law. This would not itself have been competent under the guise of merely procedural change. It was, however, important. It was, however, necessary to demarcate the sector of the court's business to which the special procedural dispensation would apply and this, as we have seen,[1] was done, in the first instance, by reference to applications previously made by summons or petition to the 'Court of Session's supervisory jurisdiction'. This technique had been suggested by the Dunpark working party but it is interesting to note that their own draft rule had referred to:

> '[the] supervisory jurisdiction of the Court of Session *in relation to acts or decisions of inferior courts, tribunals, public authorities, public bodies or officers acting in a public capacity*' [emphasis added].[2]

[1] See **22.8**. This section of the chapter draws on material contained in the author's article 'Public Employment and the Supervisory Jurisdiction' 1992 SLT (News) 123.

[2] Lord Dunpark's Report (see **22.7** above), p 7. Although the Rules of Court do not define access to judicial review by reference to Dunpark's 'acts or decisions', there is a subsequent reference to 'the decision, act or omission in question' (rule 58.3(4)(c)). If no 'decision' is at stake, but merely a 'statement of intention', review may not be available. See *C v Advocate General for Scotland* 2012 SLT 103. See also the need for a 'real issue' (para **22.49** below).

22.13 Defining the scope of judicial review principally by reference to the extent of the supervisory jurisdiction of the Court of Session but without qualifying reference to 'public authorities' left many questions unanswered. As a creature of judicial development over centuries the exact boundaries of the supervisory jurisdiction had never been precisely defined but this imprecision has been more severely exposed since the introduction of the new procedure because of its attractiveness to litigants and their imaginative counsel eager to exploit its greater speed and simplicity.

22.14 There is, however, a danger that uncertainties at the margins may overshadow the greater areas of certainty at the core of the supervisory jurisdiction. Something approaching a definition appears in the widely-cited words of Lord Kinnear in 1916:

'Wherever any inferior tribunal or any administrative body has exceeded the powers conferred on it by statute to the prejudice of the subject, the jurisdiction of the court to set aside such excess of power as incompetent and illegal is not open to dispute.'[1]

---

1   *Moss' Empires Ltd v Glasgow Assessor* 1917 SC (HL) 1 at 6.

22.15 What amounts to the grounds on which an 'excess of power' may be declared 'incompetent and illegal' is for discussion below.[1] It is clear, however, that the coupling of the formula 'any inferior tribunal or any administrative body' (the institution subject to review) with the need to show it has 'exceeded the powers conferred upon it by statute' (the reviewable functions of that institution) unproblematically characterises most of the applications for judicial review undertaken in recent years. Most have concerned the exercise of their statutory powers by ministers.[2] And there is no good reason why in Scots Law, following the lead in *GCHQ*,[3] powers exercised under the prerogative should not be as reviewable as powers deriving from statute.[4]. With only a little less certainty, some proceedings undertaken since 1985 as ordinary actions and not as applications for judicial review may be readily conceded to fall outside the supervisory jurisdiction. Thus actions against public authorities whose basis is primarily in reparation or in contract (even though turning in part upon the extent of the authorities' powers) are not, and never have been, treated as actions invoking the supervisory jurisdiction.[5] Sometimes, however, the determination of the boundary between the subject matter appropriate for an ordinary action in reparation and a petition for judicial review is not without difficulty.[6] One important issue was, though, resolved by the UK Supreme Court in *Ruddy v Chief Constable, Strathclyde Police*.[7] An Extra Division had held[8] that an action in the sheriff court for assault by police officers including breach of Art 3 ECHR should instead be brought by judicial review.[9] Doubts about this position were expressed by the First Division in *Docherty v Scottish Ministers*[10] and the Supreme Court concluded that it was indeed wrong. The appellant had no need to seek an exercise of the Court of Session's supervisory jurisdiction. The essence of his claim was simply one of damages.[11]

---

1   See 'Grounds of Judicial Review' at **22.54** et seq.
2   An early study showed that, during the first five years of the new procedure, 67% of respondents were local authorities and central government accounted for a further 22%. See Page 'Judicial Review in the Court of Session' in Adler and Millar (eds) *Socio-Legal Research in the Scottish Courts: Volume 2* Scottish Office (1991). A later study found that during 1988–93 45% of respondents to petitions for judicial review were local authorities and 36.4% were central departments. See too Mullen, Pick and Prosser *Judicial Review in Scotland* (1996) and A Page, 'The Judicial Review Caseload: An Anglo-Scottish Comparison' 2015, Jur Rev 337. The Consultation Paper published for the Gill Review (see **22.6** above) reported (Annex D) that, over the period 2002–06, the principal categories of business (although with also a large 'miscellaneous' group) were immigration (almost half of judicial review business by 2006), prisons, licensing, housing, social security and planning. For examples of other respondents and types of review business, see *eg K v Scottish Legal Aid Board* 1989 SLT 617, 1989 SCLR 144; *AB v Scottish Legal Aid Board* 1991 SCLR 702; *Criper v University of Edinburgh* 1991 SLT 129n; *Chalmers v Peterhead Harbour Trustees* 1989 GWD 16–707; *Drummond & Co, WS v Scottish Legal Aid Board* 1990 SLT 633, (and, as *Drummond & Co, W S v Lamb* [1992] 1 All ER 449, (HL)); *Carnegie v Nature Conservancy Council* 1992 SLT 342 (challenging award of expenses by arbiter); *City of Glasgow Council, Petitioners* [2009] CSOH 157 (appointment of arbiter); *Gillies Ramsay Diamond v PJW Enterprises Ltd* 2004 SC 43, 2004 SLT 545 (construction adjudicators); *Re Brackenridge* (21 November 1990, unreported) (challenge to decision of sheriff under Mental Health (Scotland) Act 1984); *Casey v Edinburgh Airport Ltd* 1989 GWD 12–512 (challenging refusal of airport taxi licenses, in

which it was at first argued that the company was not exercising a 'public function'); *Doran v Secretary of State for Scotland* 1990 GWD 26–1431 (accepted that prison governor's decision amenable to review; *Rae v Criminal Injuries Compensation Board* 1997 SLT 291; *Stewart v Secretary of State for Scotland* 1996 SLT 1203 (challenge by sheriff to his own dismissal); *McRae v Parole Board for Scotland* 1997 SLT 97; *Lothian Regional Council v Lord Advocate* 1993 SLT 1132 (Note), *Smith v Lord Advocate* 1995 SLT 379 (Note), *Emms v Lord Advocate* 2008 SLT 2, *Kennedy v Lord Advocate* 2008 SLT 195 and [2009] CSOH 1; *Niven v Lord Advocate* 2009 SLT 876 (involving fatal accident inquiries, including human rights issues in the failure to establish such an inquiry); *Kerr of Argowan v Lord Lyon* 2009 SLT 759 (Lord Lyon); *M,Petitioner* 2006 SLT 907 (Scottish Criminal Cases Review Commission); *Cooper v Forth Ports plc* 2011 SLT 711; *Lutton v General Dental Council* 2011 SLT 671 (Investigating Committee of the General Dental Council; *Rangers Football Club plc, Petitioner* 2012 SLT 1156 (Scottish Football Association; *Cloburn Quarry Co Ltd v HMRC* 2014 SLT 303 (enforcement of aggregates levy); *M v Advocate General for Scotland* 2014 SLT 475 (review of First-tier Tribunal); *M v State Hospitals Board for Scotland* 2014 SLT 905. For questions at the interface between the criminal and civil jurisdiction of the courts, see *Reynolds v Christie* 1988 SLT 68 and *ICL Plastics, Petitioner* 2005 SLT 675 See also *Butt v Scottish Ministers* 2013 JC 274.

3 *Council of Civil Service Unions v Minister for the Civil Service* [1985] AC 374, [1984] 3 All ER 935. See also the extensive discussion of review of the prerogative in *R (Miller) v Secretary of State for Exiting the European Union* [2017] UKSC 5.

4 But see 'The Scope of Judicial Review: Prerogatives and Privileges in Scots Law' 1985 SLT (News) 101. For arguments that the legal status of the Crown should be the same in both jurisdictions, see *Lord Advocate v Dumbarton District Council* [1990] 2 AC 580, 1990 SLT 158 (on immunity from statute). But on crown privilege/immunity see **22.90** and on interdicts against the Crown see **22.85**.

5 See eg *Micosta SA v Shetland Islands Council* 1986 SLT 193; *British Coal Corpn v South of Scotland Electricity Board* 1988 SLT 446 and 1991 SLT 302; *Bonthrone v Secretary of State for Scotland* 1987 SLT 34; *Ross v Secretary of State for Scotland* 1990 SLT 13; *Mearns v Lothian Regional Council* 1991 SLT 338; *Breen v Chief Constable, Dumfries and Galloway Police* 1995 SLT 822; *Armstrong v Moore* 1996 SLT 690; *Mitchell v City of Glasgow Council* 2009 SC(HL) 21, 2009 SLT 247.

6 See *McDonald v Secretary of State for Scotland (No 2)* 1996 SLT 575 and **22.85**.

7 2013 SC(UKSC) 126, 2013 SLT 119.

8 *Ruddy v Chief Constable, Strathclyde Police* 2011 SLT 387.

9 See also *Sidey Ltd v Clackmannanshire Council* 2010 SLT 607.

10 2012 SC 150. See C Himsworth (2012) 16 Edin LR 92.

11 2013 SC (UKSC) 126 at para 15 (Lord Hope). For subsequent proceedings, see Ruddy v Chief Constable, Strathclyde Police 2014 SC 58, 2013 SLT 1199. See too *Kenman Holdings Ltd v Comhairle nan Eilean Siar* [2017] CSIH 10. NB also the amendment of the Rules of Court to enable the transfer of cases between judicial review and ordinary action procedures at **22.90** below.

22.16 Thus far, it may appear that Lord Kinnear's dicta in *Moss' Empires* serve quite well to identify the extent of the court's supervisory jurisdiction and the boundaries between that and the ordinary jurisdiction of the court. At some points, however, those boundaries have proved difficult to maintain. The problem areas may be divided into two broad categories. On the one hand, there are some bodies or institutions which do not appear to fit within Lord Kinnear's rubric and yet have historically been of a type treated, in respect of some at least of their functions, as susceptible to judicial review or, being of recent creation, are considered to satisfy principles assumed to underpin the exercise of the judicial review function. On the other hand, there are also questions about the reviewability of some acts or decisions of bodies which are undoubtedly 'administrative' in character and whose activities are in general reviewable but where those particular acts or decisions probably lie outside the supervisory jurisdiction. Parallel questions of both types are familiar in England but, because the reviewing powers of the courts in the two jurisdictions are built on different foundations, it is by no means inevitable that the same answers will be reached. Indeed, before the landmark 1992 case of *West v Secretary of State for Scotland*[1] which is discussed below it was the complaint of some commentators that an artificial and misplaced tracking of the English approach had been produced in some Scottish decisions. *West* and the cases which have followed have provided very important guidance on how the scope of the supervisory jurisdiction of the Court of Session is to be understood. It will, however, be helpful to understand the reasons why a reformulation of the rules was called for and the difficulties which *West* sought to resolve.

[1]   1992 SC 385, 1992 SLT 636.

22.17   The two boundary questions already referred to will first be considered in the light of the pre-*West* cases decided by the court.[1] The first was that of *Safeway Food Stores Ltd v Scottish Provident Institution*[2] in which decree was granted to reduce the decision of an arbiter. In the course of doing so, however, Lord Mayfield denied that an ordinary action for reduction in the case was incompetent, because displaced by the judicial review procedure under Rule 260B, on the grounds that the action was based on a private arbitration agreement and was neither a statutory nor a public matter. He quoted Lord Diplock in *Council of Civil Service Unions v Minister for the Civil Service* where he stated:

'For a decision to be susceptible to judicial review the decision-maker must be empowered by public law (and not merely, as in arbitration, by agreement between private parties) to make decisions that, if validly made, will lead to administrative action or abstention from action by an authority endowed by law with executive powers.'[3]

On that, it has been observed that:

[w]hatever value that statement may have in relation to English law (where remedies in respect of arbitrations are in any event provided by statute – eg s 23 of the Arbitration Act 1950), it is difficult to see on what basis it can have any validity in relation to Scotland, standing the cases already mentioned.[4]

[1]   For a much fuller account of these issues and one from which the material which follows draws some guidance, see Lord Clyde. 'The Nature of the Supervisory Jurisdiction and the Public/Private Distinction in Scots Administrative Law' in Finnie, Himsworth and Walker (eds) *Edinburgh Essays in Public Law* (1991) EUP. Lord Clyde discusses inter alia the historical connections between invoking the supervisory jurisdiction and applying to the *nobile officium* of the Court of Session. See too *Pringle, Petitioner* 1991 SLT 330, an action not pursued by judicial review.

[2]   1989 SLT 131.

[3]   [1985] AC 374 at 409.

[4]   'Arbitration and Judicial Review' 1990 SLT (News) 113 at 114–115.

22.18   This is a reference to a strong line of authority in Scots Law, represented in particular by *Forbes v Underwood*,[1] from which it is apparent that 'arbiters' joined inferior tribunals in their susceptibility to review.[2] The example of arbitration made two points very nicely. First, where there was strong authority for the subjection to review of certain types of authority or function prior to the introduction of the new procedure in 1985, the strength of that authority should stand, *pace* Lord Mayfield, undiminished. Second, in those circumstances, it would, as a result, be unhelpful to look for guidance south of the border.

¹ (1886) 13 R 465.
² Compare *Carnegie v Nature Conservancy Council* 1992 SLT 342 in which no question of
competency appears to have been raised on an application to review the award of expenses by
an arbiter.

22.19 Another area in which there was some discussion of the scope of the
supervisory jurisdiction was where alleged irregularities by voluntary organisations were challenged by their members¹ and it is possible that a rather
similar line of reasoning justified, in principle, the approach taken in *Bank of
Scotland v Investment Management Regulatory Organisation Ltd (IMRO)*.²
There the main issue became whether, in the light of the Civil Jurisdiction and
Judgments Act 1982, a petition for judicial review of certain actions taken by
the London-based IMRO – a self-regulating organisation for the purposes of
the Financial Services Act 1986 – was competent in Scotland. It was, however,
a necessary part of the argument before the Lord Ordinary, Lord Cullen, and
then of his own decision, that IMRO was at all susceptible to review.
Accepting that it was, Lord Cullen adopted reasoning³ establishing the 'public
nature' of the arrangements for self-regulation made under the 1986 Act and
accepted that IMRO:

> 'was performing public duties as an integral part of the system set up under the Act.
> For this purpose what mattered was the function of the respondent rather than its
> constitution or legal character.'⁴

¹ See, eg *St Johnstone Football Club Ltd v Scottish Football Association Ltd* 1965 SLT 171 (on
which see further **22.39**): *Gunstone v Scottish Women's Amateur Athletic Association* 1987
SLT 611. The latter case was not, however, pursued by application for judicial review.
² 1989 SLT 432.
³ Drawing on *R v Panel on Take-overs and Mergers, ex p Datafin plc* [1987] QB 815, [1987]
1 All ER 564.
⁴ 1989 SLT 432 at 436.

22.20 One of the most contentious issues which defiantly straddled the
boundary of the supervisory jurisdiction of the Court of Session was that of the
review of the employment decisions of public authorities. The same problem
has been seen to arise in England, and for similar reasons. There is an
argument that, when a public authority uses powers, which may or may not
have an explicit statutory underpinning to hire, to fire, to promote or to
discipline an employee, this is an exercise of power adequately governed by
ordinary contract law (whether or not in part statute-based) and enforced
either by courts in the exercise of their ordinary jurisdiction and with recourse
to the remedies available in disputes of that sort or by special tribunals (now
employment tribunals) established for the purpose. However, the attractions to
a potential litigant in extending the basis on which a decision may be
challenged to include forms of procedural impropriety or unreasonableness
available only in judicial review proceedings have led to claims to such
treatment based on the argument that employment disputes in the public sector
(or at least some of them) are different. Whether that difference derives from
an historically distinct basis of public service employment under which the
relationship has been non-contractual or, whilst contractual, overlaid by duties
to act also in the public interest may be unclear but there is no doubt that
recognition has been given to a distinction between some public sector

employment and private employment.[1]

[1] See, on the law of England and Wales, CHAPTER 5 above. See, too, *Malloch v Aberdeen Corpn* [1971] 2 All ER 1278, 1971 SC (HL) 85, *Palmer v Inverness Hospitals Board* 1963 SC 311.

22.21 There were also cases, however, in which the court was unpersuaded that the employment decisions of public authorities should be reviewable. An early, post-1985, decision was that of Lord Allanbridge in *Connor v Strathclyde Regional Council*[1] where a teacher had been refused promotion in circumstances which he claimed to constitute a breach of the rules of natural justice. It was the view of Lord Allanbridge that:

> 'the Court of Session has no power in the exercise of its supervisory jurisdiction to intervene in a situation where there is no element of public law arising which is sufficient to attract public law remedies'.[2]

[1] 1986 SLT 530.
[2] 1986 SLT 530 at 534, adopting reasoning from *R v East Berkshire Health Authority, ex p Walsh* [1985] QB 152, [1984] 3 All ER 425. Compare *Nahar v Strathclyde Regional Council* 1986 SLT 570.

22.22 A return to these issues came in the case of *Tehrani v Argyll and Clyde Health Board (No 2)*[1] There the petitioner, a consultant surgeon, had been dismissed by the respondent health board and he sought reduction of the decision. The dismissal was made following an initial period during which the petitioner was suspended from his hospital duties and a committee of inquiry had been established and had reported. The petitioner's claim was that the decision of the Board to dismiss him summarily on receipt of the committee's report was made unreasonably, a claim upheld in the Outer House by Lord Weir who pronounced decree of reduction. The unreasonableness arose because, in dismissing summarily under one provision of the relevant National Health Service terms and conditions of service, the Board was conscious that the effect of summary dismissal might be to cut out the petitioner's right of appeal to the Secretary of State following dismissal with notice under another such provision. In failing to take full account of the implications of the decision, the Board had failed to take into account something which they should have taken into account. In failing to give clear consideration to the procedural choices before them, the decision of the Board was one which no reasonable board would have come to.[2] However, of more immediate interest here is that, on the route to that conclusion, Lord Weir had to respond to two preliminary arguments from the respondent Board. The first was an argument that the petitioner had failed to have recourse to statutory remedies available to him, an argument he rejected.[3] Second, the Board had argued that the dispute was essentially a matter of private law being concerned with a branch of contract. Such a dispute, it was said, was not open to judicial review.[4]

[1] 1990 SLT 118.
[2] 1990 SLT 118 at 128–130.
[3] 1990 SLT 118 at 124.
[4] 1990 SLT 118 at 124.

22.23 While it was recognised that the supervisory jurisdiction could extend to contracts of employment where an individual's employment was protected by statute, it was maintained that the petitioner's contract with the Board was not so protected. Accordingly, his remedies were either an action of damages at common law for breach of contract or proceedings under the Employment Protection (Consolidation) Act 1978. It was submitted, relying on *R v East Berkshire Health Authority, ex p Walsh*[1] that the modern tendency in case law was to confine judicial review to what were called 'public law' matters. Noting that *Walsh* had already been applied in two cases in the Outer House,[2] Lord Weir nevertheless doubted whether the English distinction in this context between public and private law:

> 'properly or necessarily applies in Scotland. The supervisory jurisdiction of the Court of Session has not in the past been confined to matters of public law and the introduction of judicial review procedure has not affected the extent of this jurisdiction (*O'Neill v Scottish Joint Negotiating Committee for Teaching Staff*, per Lord Jauncey).[3] Rule of Court 260B which created the machinery for judicial review does not refer to any specific distinction between matters of private and public law. Moreover the origin and development of remedies now covered by judicial review in both countries is quite different and I consider that there is danger in applying English authority in this field of law.'[4]

[1] [1985] QB 152, [1984] 3 All ER 425.
[2] *Connor v Strathclyde Regional Council* 1986 SLT 530; *Safeway Food Stores Ltd v Scottish Provident Institution* 1989 SLT 131 above.
[3] 1987 SLT 648.
[4] 1990 SLT 118 at 125.

22.24 In order to establish what was, in his view, the correct approach in the light of Scottish authority, Lord Weir went on to rely on the decision of the House of Lords in *Malloch*[1] to distinguish between, on the one hand, the 'pure master and servant cases' with 'no element of public employment or service, no support by statute, nothing in the nature of an office or a status which is capable of protection' and, on the other, those which do have such an element and which attract 'essential procedural requirements'.[2] Applying this distinction in *Tehrani*, it was Lord Weir's view that those additional 'elements' were indeed to be found in the statutory constitution of, and mode of appointment of, members to the health board and the statutory regulation of the appointment and terms and conditions of officials. Drawing further upon other authorities bearing on the general extent of the supervisory jurisdiction, Lord Weir reinforced his conclusions. The opinion of Lord President Inglis in *Forbes v Underwood*[3] was, in particular, adopted as the 'first full expression of the nature of the supervisory jurisdiction of the Court of Session'.[4] Its importance was that the case concerned 'a matter of purely private law and yet this did not prevent the court from exercising its supervisory jurisdiction'. Lord Weir continued:

> 'The reason it considered it had jurisdiction was on account of the existence of quasi-judicial procedure, namely the arbitration prescribed by the contract. In my view, this case is authority for the proposition that where quasi-judicial machinery is stipulated in a private contract for use in certain circumstances, the court may exercise its supervisory jurisdiction. This proposition applies to the contract between the petitioner and the Board because a quasi-judicial tribunal was set up to consider the allegations made against the petitioner.'[5]

[1] *Malloch v Aberdeen Corpn* [1971] 2 All ER 1278, 1971 SC (HL) 85 especially the speech of Lord Wilberforce.

²   1990 SLT 118 at 125.
³   (1886) 13 R 465.
⁴   1990 SLT 118 at 126.
⁵   1990 SLT 118 at 126.

22.25 Nor could vulnerability to judicial review be confined to the proceedings of the Board's committee of inquiry. Neither logic nor equity could permit review of the committee and not of the Board. The same point had been affirmed in *Palmer*[1] and applied equally in *Tehrani* even though the one case was one based on breach of natural justice and the other was not. 'The concepts of natural justice and "unreasonableness" are both aspects of administrative law and properly open to judicial review and cannot be kept apart artificially'.[2]

¹   See **22.20** above.
²   1990 SLT 118 at 126.

22.26 The reasoning of Lord Weir was, however, firmly rejected by the Second Division. The Lord Justice-Clerk, Lord Ross, traced the emergence of the new procedure for judicial review, concluding that what had been envisaged was a 'special procedure to deal with questions in the public law area'.[1] Despite arguments[2] that the supervisory jurisdiction might also enable the court under private law to review decisions taken by voluntary associations, it was in this case accepted that, for the petitioner to succeed, he must be able to focus upon a matter of public law – a position accepted by the petitioner himself who had also accepted that public law was to be treated as synonymous with administrative law.[3] Lord Ross disagreed with the view taken by the Lord Ordinary of the circumstances which might warrant summary dismissal but, more importantly, of what introduced 'the necessary public element' to render the decision reviewable by judicial review.[4] The fact that 'a particular case is one where the principles of natural justice must be observed does not mean that the case is thereby elevated into the domain of public administrative law'.[5] Preferring the reasoning of the Master of the Rolls in *Walsh* and the interpretation he had placed on *Malloch*, Lord Ross concluded that there were 'no public law elements in the petitioner's case which could give rise to any entitlement to a public law remedy such as judicial review'.[6] The features identified by the Lord Ordinary did not justify that conclusion – although the requirement to observe the rules of natural justice was accepted.

¹   1990 SLT 118 at 131.
²   Supported by *McDonald v Burns* 1940 SC 376; *St Johnstone Football Club Ltd v Scottish Football Association Ltd* 1965 SLT 171 and *Brentnall v Free Presbyterian Church of Scotland* 1986 SLT 471.
³   Invoking, in support of this argument, the *Stair Memorial Encyclopaedia Vol 1*, paragraph 201!
⁴   1990 SLT 118 at 133.
⁵   1990 SLT 118 at 134.
⁶   1990 SLT 118 at 134–135.

22.27 Lord Wylie agreed that the principles of public administrative law had no part to play in the case,[1] the fact that an employer was a public body did not *per se* inject an element of public law into a contract of service; and, again, adopting *Walsh*, disagreed with Lord Weir when he declined to follow English authority because of the distinctive origins and development of the law of judicial review in the two jurisdictions:

> 'I think, however, that he was wrong to do so. The two procedures and the distinctive remedies provided are, of course, different but their purposes and the mischief for which they seek to provide remedies are the same in both jurisdictions . . . I agree with counsel for the respondents that there is no good reason for differences between the two jurisdictions to develop in this field and indeed that it would be regrettable if they did.'[2]

[1]   1990 SLT 118 at 136.
[2]   1990 SLT 118 at 137–138.

22.28 Lord Murray agreed that the Board's arguments should prevail but did so on the basis of quite specific interpretation of the text of the terms and conditions of service of the petitioner – the nexus between the paragraphs stipulating the two modes of dismissal was not close enough to establish the 'administrative element' necessary to make the Board's decision reviewable. He did not, however, draw assistance from *Walsh* in this, and, after rehearsal of some of the arguments presented, expressed his relief that it was not necessary to:

> 'decide between a restrictive and a liberal interpretation of Rule of Court 260B . . . It would be unfortunate if this court had to decide upon that matter without a full consideration of the nature and scope of the supervisory jurisdiction which the Court of Session has exercised in the past and a more detailed consideration of the contents of the Dunpark committee report. I am not persuaded that the Lord Ordinary has been shown to be wrong in his approach to this aspect of the case'.[1]

[1]   1990 SLT 118 at 141.

22.29 *Tehrani* was joined by another case which required discussion in the Inner House of the limits of the supervisory jurisdiction. *Watt v Strathclyde Regional Council*[1] originated in a bitter dispute between teachers and their employing authority and specifically in the wish by Mrs Patsy Watt and others to challenge a decision by an Education Sub-Committee of the Strathclyde Regional Council to introduce revised arrangements (less favourable to teachers) for cover by staff for absent colleagues. The teachers claimed that this move was in contravention of terms statutorily included in all their contracts following a national settlement agreed in 1987 under the auspices of the Scottish Joint Negotiating Committee for Teaching Staff in School Education. The teachers sought judicial review and the case was argued and decided (first by Lord Morison and then in the First Division) simply on the issue of the competency of their application.[2] Reversing the Lord Ordinary, the First Division held the application to be competent. For the Lord President, the justification for this conclusion lay in an appreciation of the 'administrative character' of the decision challenged. The supervisory jurisdiction could not be invoked to provide a remedy for a breach of contract, even if the respondents were a local authority and even if the contracts concerned were to some extent regulated by statute. Looking back, however, to *Moss' Empires*[3] and then to Lord Fraser in *Brown v Hamilton District Council*[4] and *Stevenson v Midlothian District Council*[5] and to *Tehrani*, the Lord President urged that, when considering whether judicial review is available, one should start by asking whether the decision at issue is 'administrative or judicial in character'. In *Watt*, because the attack was directed at the authority's decision itself, not against the consequences (involving breach of contract) flowing from it and because the decision was of general application to all teachers in the region, the decision was clearly one of an administrative character.[6]

1   1992 SLT 324.
2   For subsequent proceedings, see *Bell v Strathclyde Regional Council* 1991 GWD 32–1923.
3   *Moss' Empires Ltd v Glasgow Assessor* 1917 SC (HL) 1.
4   1983 SC, (HL) 1.
5   1983 SC, (HL) 50.
6   Some support derived also from *McClaren v Home Office* [1990] ICR 824, [1990] IRLR 338. See below.

22.30 Lord Clyde took a different route. What was particularly interesting in his reasoning was his incorporation of arguments already developed extra-judicially[1] and which insisted above all upon the rejection of the English public-private distinction to define the limits of judicial review in Scotland and a reliance instead upon the historically developed definition of the supervisory jurisdiction. Thus, although acknowledging that the local authority had indeed made the impugned decision in the exercise of their 'administrative' functions, this was not for him the determining characteristic of the issue. The public and private distinction was only a recent development in England;[2] it *had* indeed been used by Lord Fraser in *Brown* and in *Stevenson* but it did not appear in Rule 260B. The distinction had also been deployed in *Tehrani* but only because of a concession by counsel as to the validity of the distinction:

> The imposition of a requirement to find an element of "public law" for an application under Rule of Court 260B may produce some equalisation of the two systems but only at the cost of an undesirable restriction on the availability of the procedure for judicial review in Scotland.

1   See 'The Nature of the Supervisory Jurisdiction and the Public/Private Distinction in Scots Administrative Law' (eds Finnie, Himsworth and Walker) in *Edinburgh Essays in Public Law* (1991) p 281.
2   See *Davy v Spelthorne Borough Council* [1984] AC 262 at 276 (Lord Wilberforce).

22.31 The supervisory jurisdiction had traditionally been quite general in scope and Lord Kames had indeed related it to a maxim that it was the province of the Court of Session to redress all wrongs for which no other remedy is provided.[1] It was not necessary in this case to explore the general extent of the bodies subject to review. Plainly a local authority's decisions could be reviewed. But the 'element of contract' gave rise to difficulty. *Purely* contractual disputes could not be proper subjects for review but, disowning the public/private distinction, how might one identify the reviewable decisions?

1   See also Edinburgh Essays in Public Law at p 291.

22.32 Unwilling to lay down a general solution in a case only briefly argued and on competency alone, Lord Clyde nevertheless distinguished a number of different situations:

(1)   Some cases of individual employees where contract or employment law 'will provide the appropriate remedies'.

(2)   Some individual cases which 'warrant recourse to the supervisory jurisdiction'. Lord Clyde did not mention *Malloch*[1] but presumably that might be such a case. Nor did he mention, at this point, *Tehrani* which, contrary to the decision actually reached in the case, might surely be another?[2]

(3)   Then, finally, cases where the decision at issue is not one affecting a particular contract but a number of contracts and 'as a matter of general decision in the exercise of their administrative function by a local authority'. If the challenge is made on the 'legality of the decision' and the 'essential remedy sought' is reduction, then the supervisory jurisdiction may be invoked.

[1]   *Malloch v Aberdeen Corpn* [1971] 2 All ER 1278, 1971 SC (HL) 85.
[2]   Elsewhere, Lord Clyde referred to *Tehrani* as distinguishable on the facts, in particular the lack of 'general application' of the Board's decision.

22.33 This was, Lord Clyde decided, the situation in *Watt*. The 'substantial issue' raised was not breach of contract but the legality of a decision of general application. The burden of the attack and the principal remedies sought were 'in substance' an application to the supervisory jurisdiction. On the evidence of *GCHQ*[1] and *McLaren*,[2] English law might reach the same conclusion but Lord Clyde preferred to rest his decision upon 'a consideration of the circumstances of this case, the nature of the decision, the issue raised in the case and the remedies sought' and the 'universal application' of the authority's decision (ie to many teacher contracts in the Region) was a critical consideration. Accepting that access to the supervisory jurisdiction might, in appropriate circumstances, be excluded by the existence of another (statutory) remedy, the requirement to exhaust alternative procedures was not an absolute requirement for the competency of application to the supervisory jurisdiction. In this case not only were 'the convenience and speed of the procedure' of judicial review appropriate where both sides wanted a quick answer but also the 'number of people directly affected' by the authority's decision made the procedure appropriate.

[1]   *Council of Civil Service Unions v Minister for the Civil Service* [1985] AC 374.
[2]   *McClaren v Home Office* [1990] ICR 824, [1990] IRLR 338.

22.34 Whilst *Tehrani* and *Watt* were undoubtedly the cases which, prior to *West*, caused the Court of Session the most anguish in the consideration of the extent of its own supervisory jurisdiction, they joined the earlier cases in presenting a generally confused picture.[1] The court was searching for guiding principles both as to its jurisdiction at large and then as to its application in specific areas, including the vexed matter of 'public employment'.[2] A number of principles or guidelines, at times competing, seemed to be identifiable:

(1)   in the interests of a desirable uniformity, to ensure the development of judicial review in parallel with that in England. That seemed to be the position taken by Lord Wylie in *Tehrani*;

(2)   whilst not necessarily adopting English approaches for their own sake, to adopt the public law/private law divide more familiar in English judicial review. This, as we have seen, had proved attractive to some judges although the dangers of the adoption of distinctions which are English in origin and problematic even in that jurisdiction were

apparent. In particular, the fostering of a public/private distinction appeared to contradict authoritative and historically approved definitions of the extent of the supervisory jurisdiction. The position of 'private' arbiters was the most evidently anomalous;

(3)   in order to avoid the importation of historically unjustified limitations on the supervisory jurisdiction, to adhere to the more broadly cast statements of both the extent of the jurisdiction and of the justifications for it. This was the approach of the Lord Ordinary (Lord Weir) in *Tehrani* and appeared also to be reflected in the views of Lord Morison in *Royal Bank of Scotland plc v Clydebank District Council*[3] who, whilst noting that, following *Tehrani*, the supervisory jurisdiction did not extend 'to review of the operation of a private contract voluntarily and without statutory protection entered into between individual parties, notwithstanding that one of these parties may be a body exercising public functions', denied the authority in Scots Law of distinctions between the field of 'public law' or 'administrative law' and that of 'private law'. This was also the approach adopted by Lord Clyde already referred to.[4] In an important essay he had sought firmly to locate modern perceptions of the supervisory jurisdiction within a tradition which recognised the position of the Court of Session as a supreme court with general powers unconstrained by narrow technicalities and worthy of the injunction of Lord Kames in his *Historical Law Tracts*: 'That it is the province of this court, to redress all wrongs for which no other remedy is provided'. In the light of the problems raised by the other lines of approach, this had evident attractions. It appeared best able to accommodate the historical breadth of the jurisdiction whilst protecting it from narrow technically-drawn distinctions. On the other hand, it was not an approach which offered either judges or lay-people guidance in hard cases. Which 'wrongs' were to be given recognition and accorded a remedy? Had Dr Tehrani suffered a wrong warranting a remedy? Was such a person 'wrongly' treated if denied natural justice but not if the employer acted 'unreasonably'? Unless judges were to exercise almost unlimited discretion, they needed surer guidance than a general ordinance to redress wrongs.

[1]   See also *Jackson v Secretary of State for Scotland* 1992 SC 175 (challenge by suspended prison governor of refusal of his application for medical retirement) where it was noted that the respondent 'expressly refrained' from presenting an argument based on *Tehrani* that the decision was not amenable to judicial review.

[2]   That term itself became problematic since some of the 'public elements' sought in respect of the employment of a *Malloch* or a *Tehrani* might also be sought legitimately in respect of the employee of 'private' bodies. (Compare *Criper v University of Edinburgh* 1991 SLT 129n in which, whilst decided on grounds of relevancy, the competence of the application was, in reliance on *Tehrani*, doubted).

[3]   1991 SLT 635.

[4]   See **22.12** and **22.30**.

22.35 What was needed at this time was the opportunity to take another case to the Inner House in the hope of attracting a general resolution of the issues and this was provided in the form of *West v Secretary of State for Scotland*.[1] A prison officer sought to challenge a refusal to reimburse his removal expenses when transferred from one institution to another. At first instance, Lord Weir, considering himself bound by *Tehrani*, held the petition to be incompetent. He did, on the other hand, welcome the possibility on appeal for a comprehensive reconsideration and statement on the scope of the supervisory jurisdiction. This was indeed produced – in the judgment of the court delivered by the Lord President, Lord Hope. The court held that the petition was incompetent. It related simply to a private dispute between employee and employer and the employer's decision to refuse payment of the removal expenses was not reviewable. In the course of reaching this decision, however, the court took the opportunity to undertake an extensive review of the supervisory jurisdiction both by analysis of underlying principles in decisions since the sixteenth century and then by reference to more recent cases. The conclusions reached by the court were set out first in the form of three propositions (expressed by reference to the old Rule 260B):

'1. The Court of Session has power, in the exercise of its supervisory jurisdiction, to regulate the process by which decisions are taken by any person or body to whom a jurisdiction, power or authority has been delegated or entrusted by statute, agreement or any other instrument.

2. The sole purpose for which the supervisory jurisdiction may be exercised is to ensure that the person or body does not exceed or abuse that jurisdiction, power or authority or fail to do what the jurisdiction, power or authority requires.

3. The competency of the application does not depend upon any distinction between public law and private law, nor is it confined to those cases which English law has accepted as amenable to judicial review, nor is it correct in regard to issues about competency to describe judicial review under Rule of Court 260B as a public law remedy.'

¹   1992 SC 385, 1992 SLT 636.

22.36 Lord Hope then went on to set out, by way of explanation, certain further 'important points':

'(a) Judicial review is available, not to provide machinery for an appeal, but to ensure that the decision maker does not exceed or abuse his powers or fail to perform the duty which has been delegated or entrusted to him. It is not competent for the court to review the act or decision on its merits, nor may it substitute its own opinion for that of the person or body to whom the matter has been delegated or entrusted.

(b) The word "jurisdiction" best describes the nature of the power, duty or authority committed to the person or body which is amenable to the supervisory jurisdiction of the court. It is used here as meaning simply "power to decide", and it can be applied to the acts or decisions of any administrative bodies and persons which similar functions as well as to those of inferior tribunals. An excess or abuse of jurisdiction may involve stepping outside it, or failing to observe its limits, or departing from the rules of natural justice, or a failure to understand the law, or the taking into account of matters which ought not to have been taken into account. The categories of what may amount to an excess or abuse of jurisdiction are not closed, and they are capable of being adapted in accordance with the development of administrative law.

(c) There is no substantial difference between English law and Scots law as to the grounds on which the process of decision making may be open to review. So reference may be made to English cases in order to determine whether there has been an excess or abuse of the jurisdiction, power or authority or a failure to do what it requires.

(d)   Contractual rights and obligations, such as those between employer and employee, are not as such amenable to judicial review. The cases in which the exercise of the supervisory jurisdiction is appropriate involve a tripartite relationship, between the person or body to whom the jurisdiction, power or authority has been delegated or entrusted, the person or body by which it has been delegated or entrusted and the person or persons in respect of or for whose benefit that jurisdiction, power or authority is to be exercised.'[1]

[1]   1992 SC 385 at 412–413.

22.37 It will be observed that this restatement of principles contains not only guidance on the extent of the supervisory jurisdiction but also some relatively uncontroversial material on the grounds of review.[1] In so far as they do deal with the scope of review, however, they resolve some of the difficulties which had been emerging but they have left many issues unclear. Some attracted comment at the time *West* was decided.[2] Others have been exposed in cases which have arisen since *West* and are discussed below. One point which was specifically addressed and resolved in *West*, however, was that decisions of arbiters, however 'private' the context, are reviewable. *Safeway Food Stores* was overruled[3] and the reviewability of arbiters has been reconfirmed in subsequent cases.[4] (This does not, however, extend to arbiters who are *functus officio*.[5]) An independent expert, acting in the role of arbiter, has also been held to be reviewable.[6] Most importantly, and in evident contrast with English practice, adjudicators in proceedings under the Housing Grants, Construction and Regeneration Act 1996 have been held to join arbiters as judicially reviewable.[7] However, in *Gillies Ramsay Diamond v PJW Enterprises Ltd*[8] the Lord Justice Clerk, whilst sustaining the reviewability of such adjudications, also held them to be separately classified as not public law cases and thus to be treated differently in respect of the application of the rules of error of law (paragraph 38). See **22.68** below.

[1]   On which, see **22.54** et seq below.
[2]   See Finnie, 'Triangles as Touchstones of Review', 1993 SLT (News) 51; Wolffe 'The Scope of Judicial Review in Scots Law', [1992] PL 625; Himsworth, 'Public Employment, the Supervisory Jurisdiction and Points West', 1992 SLT (News) 257. For a more recent (and important) assessment, see A McHarg, 'Border Disputes: The Scope and Purposes of Judicial Review' in A McHarg and T Mullen, *Public Law in Scotland* (2006).
[3]   1992 SC 385 at 405.
[4]   See, eg *Shanks & McEwan (Contractors) Ltd v Mifflin Construction Ltd* 1993 SLT 1124; *Haden Young Ltd v William McCrindle & Son Ltd* 1994 SLT 221 and *Witan Properties Ltd v Lord Advocate* [1993] RVR 170. Questions of law arising in an arbitration may also be raised under the Scottish Arbitration Rules in Schedule 1 to the Arbitration (Scotland) Act 2010 (formerly by case stated under s 3(1) of the Administration of Justice (Scotland) Act 1972. See, eg *ERDC Construction Ltd v H M Love & Co (No 2)* 1997 SLT 175; *MacDonald Estates plc v National Carparks Ltd* 2010 SLT 36).
[5]   *Sim Group Ltd v Jack* 2002 SLT 847.
[6]   *AGE Ltd v Kwik Save Stores Ltd* 2001 SLT 841.
[7]   *Naylor v Greenacres Curling Club Ltd* 2002 SLT 1092; *Ballast plc v Burrell Co (Construction Management) Ltd* 2003 SC 279, 2003 SLT 137.
[8]   2004 SC 43; 2004 SLT 545. See also **12.52**.

22.38 The decision in *West* on arbiters was reached in reliance upon *Forbes v Underwood* but it was also this case which was instrumental in the court's broader conclusion that any reliance upon a public/private distinction in determining the limits of the supervisory jurisdiction was wrong. Scots and

English law were in this respect quite different. Reaching this conclusion required the court to reject the suggestions to contrary effect which, as we have seen, were made in cases such as *Tehrani*. The actual decision in *Tehrani* was right but its basis in a public/private distinction was wrong. Among other cases cited, in addition to *Forbes*, in support of this conclusion were the 'religious body' case of *McDonald v Burns*[1] and the 'sporting body' case of *St Johnstone Football Club Ltd v Scottish Football Association*[2] to demonstrate that the supervisory jurisdiction had, in the recent past, been assumed to extend to the review of bodies which were not, in an obvious sense, 'public'. There are, however, a number of reasons why it is necessary to be extremely cautious about how one translates authority on arbiters (compared by Lord Inglis in *Forbes* with 'other public officers')[3] and the very narrowly argued (and in *Scottish Football Association* probably wrongly argued) points about the reviewability of sports regulators[4] or of the Catholic hierarchy (*McDonald v Burns* was primarily an action for decree of removal – eviction – in quite extraordinary circumstances) into wider propositions which reject altogether the usefulness and historical validity of some sort of a public/private distinction.[5]

[1] 1940 SLT 325.
[2] 1965 SLT 171.
[3] (1886) 13 R 465 at 468.
[4] See also *Ferguson v Scottish Football Association* 1996 GWD 11–601; *Fraser v Professional Golfers Assocation* 1999 SCLR 1032.
[5] On this, see full discussion at Himsworth, 'Public Employment, the Supervisory Jurisdiction and Points *West*', 1992 SLT (News) 257 and 'Judicial Review in Scotland' in B Hadfield (Ed) *Judicial Review: A Thematic Approach* (1995).

22.39 The problem is not only one of the interpretation of existing authority but also one of devising alternative criteria for determining the scope of the supervisory jurisdiction and judicial review. On this it will be seen from the court's explanatory points in *West* that its suggested answer was cast in the need for a 'tripartite relationship'. It is for this that *West* has become best known. It has also been the cause of much anguish in its interpretation by others. In paragraph (d) of the 'important points' quoted at 22.37 above, the relevance of a 'tripartite relationship' is apparently confined to contractual (and especially employment) relationships. Before an 'employment' decision can be reviewed it must be seen to derive from a third person or body to whom a jurisdiction, power or authority has been delegated or entrusted. But there are two main difficulties with this. On the one hand, it leaves some apparently reviewable employment situations which lack any obvious tripartite relationship unaccounted for[1] and, on the other, there are other indications within *West* that the tripartite test was intended as a general indication of susceptibility to review and not at all confined to employment situations. If that is the case, then the quest for tripartism becomes very much more problematic. The difficulties involved have been discussed both by commentators[2] and in cases since *West*, in particular *Naik v University of Stirling*[3] and *Joobeen v University of Stirling*.[4] There has been very little sympathy for the prospect of wholesale redefinition of reviewability by reference to elusive and ill-defined inter-institutional triangles.[5] Indeed, there has even been an indication of a wish to return to something resembling a public/private test to determine reviewability in public employment cases. In *Blair v Lochaber District Council*,[6] despite the rejection by Lord Clyde of a public/private test, it seemed to be the absence of the exercise of an 'administrative power' which tipped the scales against review of a local authority's decision to suspend its chief executive from duties.[7] In *Rooney v Chief Constable, Strathclyde Police*[8] in reliance upon *Watt* and *Naik*, it was held that review of the chief constable's decision to accept the petitioner's resignation without adherence to the disciplinary procedures laid down was competent. The question did concern an individual contract but it was nevertheless subject to review. In *Boyle v Castlemilk East Housing Co-operative Ltd*[9] it was accepted that the respondent housing association was reviewable on the basis of its having a 'jurisdiction' and being in a tripartite relationship between the legislature, the householder making a claim for payments from the association, and the association itself. (But does not the extension of a tripartite relationship to include the legislature hold the danger of embracing as reviewable the activities of virtually all statutorily created bodies?) In *Hardie v City of Edinburgh Council*[10] it was held, in a judgment (by Lord Osborne) which ranged widely over the post-*West* cases, that a local authority's removal of a person from a list of supply teachers was reviewable. In *Codona v Showmen's Guild of Great Britain*[11] the reviewability of a decision of the Appeals Tribunal of the Showmen's Guild was not challenged.[12]

[1]   See *Watt v Strathclyde Regional Council* 1992 SLT 324 and *Malloch v Aberdeen Corpn* 1971 SLT 245. Cf *UNISON v Scottish Joint Council* [2006] CSOH 193.
[2]   See **22.38** above.
[3]   1994 SLT 449.
[4]   1995 SLT 120 (Note). For comment on *Naik* and *Joobeen*, see Himsworth, 'Judicial Review in Scotland' above and 'Further *West*? More Geometry of Judicial Review', 1995 SLT (News) 127. Other cases in which *West* has been considered have included *JDP Investments Ltd v Strathclyde Regional Council* 1997 SLT 408 at 413 (disposal of land by local authority) and *Logan v Presbytery of Dumbarton* 1995 SLT 1228.
[5]   See, very importantly, Lord Reed in *Crocket v Tantallon Golf Club* 2005 SLT 663.
[6]   1995 SLT 407. For comment see references in note 4 above.
[7]   In other areas too, the reviewability of decision deriving from a 'contractual' base has been explored. See *Stannifer Developments Ltd v Glasgow Development Agency (No 2)* 1999 SC 156, 1999 SLT 459; *McIntosh v Aberdeenshire Council* 1999 SLT 93; and *Standard Commercial Property Securities Ltd v Glasgow City Council* 2004 SLT 655.
[8]   1997 SLT 1261.
[9]   1998 SLT 56.
[10] 2000 SLT 130.
[11] 2002 SLT 299.
[12] Compare *R v Showmen's Guild of Great Britain, ex p Print* (27 October 1999, unreported). The case did, however, raise questions about the 'error of law' jurisdiction of the court. See **22.65**.

22.40 There has been a return to the reviewability of private sporting clubs. In *Welsh v Committee of the South Western Social and Recreation Club Ltd*[1] it was held to be of 'no moment whether the empowered body operates in the public or private sphere' and that a decision in relation to club membership rights will normally be capable of being the subject of judicial review.[2] In *Irvine v Royal Burgess Golfing Society of Edinburgh*,[3] a case in which a mixture of Scottish and English authority was tendered, the reviewability of the Society was upheld, having in mind the potential seriousness of a decision to suspend from membership.[4] From all of this it is difficult to draw firm conclusions about the rules on the scope of the supervisory jurisdiction of the Court of Session. We should not, however, overstate the extent of the problem. Neither before *West* nor after has there been any question about the competence of an application to the supervisory jurisdiction in the great majority of cases involving public authorities.[5] Pre-*West*, however, there were real doubts about the competence of certain types of application. *West* resolved some of those doubts by the categorical rejection of a public/private test. The abandonment of that test coupled with the problematic adoption of 'tripartism' has left many uncertainties,[6] some of which were well illustrated in *Fotheringham v British Limousin Cattle Society Ltd*[7] in which Lord Eassie, placing some reliance on dicta of Lord Clyde in *McDonald v Secretary of State for Scotland (No 2)*,[8] rejected claims that the respondent society should be subject to review under the supervisory jurisdiction rather than to an ordinary action. The answer lay in 'what the action is truly about'. There is, it seems, an essentialism as to the distinction between types of action which may be an unreliable guide.[9] An interesting recent addition to instances of judicial review at the outer edge of its competence was a case in which, on complicated facts, one co-director of a company sought to review the actions of some others.[10] In the Outer House, it was held that the petition for judicial review was competent. The Inner House, however, reasserted (relying on *West*) the exclusion from judicial review of non-tripartite contractual disputes.[11] For some general insight into the range of bodies reviewed in recent years, see paragraph **22.15** above note 2.

1 25 June 2004, unreported.
2 At **22.27**. The case is also a reminder of need to identify correctly the body whose decision is to be reviewed. One of the reasons why this application failed was that it was brought against the committee rather than the club itself.
3 27 February 2004, unreported. See, also *Crocket v Tantallon Golf Club* 2005 SLT 663. *Wiles v Bothwell Castle Golf Club* 2005 SLT 85; *Smith v Nairn Golf Club* 2007 SLT 909. See S Thomson 2008 SLT(News) 221.
4 At **22.33**.
5 It may be important, nevertheless, to be sure *which* public authority should be the subject of a review. In *Varey v Scottish Ministers* 2000 SLT 1432 the case turned in part upon whether it was really the Scottish Ministers or, alternatively, the Parole Board whose decision was, in the context of the case, under challenge. Holding that it was the Parole Board's decision, review on grounds of breach of human rights was denied because it was made in August 1999, whereas a decision of the Scottish Ministers would at that time have been challengeable.
6 Some of these have been explored with comparative reference to England in D Oliver. *Common Values and the Public-Private Divide* (1999) Annex.
7 2004 SLT 485.
8 1996 SC 113; SLT 575.
9 See also *Aitken, Petitioner* (24 October 2002, unreported).
10 See *G v Watson* 2013 SLT 934. See also para **22.41** below.
11 See *G v Watson* 2014 SLT 1030. See also *Gray v Braid Logistics (UK) Ltd* 2015 SC 222; *Dryburgh v NHS Fife* [2016] CSOH 116.

MANDATORY TO PROCEED BY JUDICIAL REVIEW

22.41 Despite these difficulties in defining, by reference to the supervisory jurisdiction of the Court of Session, the general scope of judicial review and, subject to what is said below concerning the exclusion of review, the use of the procedure is, where it is appropriate, mandatory. Rule 58.1(2) provides that an application to which it applies *must* (formerly, 'shall') be made by petition for judicial review. Thus, in *McDonald v Secretary of State for Scotland*[1] an action of declarator, interdict and damages raised by a prisoner against the Secretary of State was held to have been inappropriately raised in the sheriff court. The case primarily concerned whether or not standing orders made by the Secretary of State were valid and was, therefore, on the basis of the pleadings themselves, one which could competently proceed only by way of judicial review in the Court of Session.[2] In *Sleigh v City of Edinburgh District Council*,[3] it was held that a petition for interdict initiated by some of the council's own members to challenge a decision of the council should have been done by petition under the then Rule 260B. On the other hand, it was held in *Hands v Kyle and Carrick District Council*[4] that an action for declarator as to the petitioner's rights under an existing planning permission was competent because the issue in the case was 'not as to the validity of a decision, but as to the legal effect of decisions which were not themselves questioned'.[5] A question not yet resolved, it seems, is whether it is ever legitimate to raise by ordinary action of reduction issues which appear to lie within the supervisory jurisdiction of the court. Rule 58.1(2) appears to preclude this, but *Gunstone v Scottish Women's Amateur Athletic Association*,[6] *Lennox v Scottish Branch of the British Show Jumping Association*[7] and *Brown v Executive Committee of the Edinburgh District Labour Party*[8] (in which the remedies sought were suspension and interdict) seem to be counter examples. In *Kirkwood v City of Glasgow District Council*,[9] Lord Weir appeared to refer to the availability of a choice in the matter,[10] although this does seem to defy the terms of the Rule of Court. *Kirkwood* was a case in which an action of reduction was brought in an attempt to reduce a decree of the sheriff court. In *Bell v Fiddes*[11] Lord Marnoch went even further and seemed to deny the possibility of using a petition for judicial review to seek reduction of a decree of an inferior court. His decision appears to have been based on ill-advised concessions by the petitioners and also upon the existence of other rules of court, especially Chapter 53 concerning actions of reduction. With respect, however, this line of approach seems wrong. Plainly, actions of reduction may competently be raised in relation to matters in other areas which are not subject to the supervisory jurisdiction of the court. *All* applications to the supervisory jurisdiction, however, should, in terms of Rule 58.1(2), be brought by petition for judicial review – an approach apparently supported by the Second Division in *Gupta's Trustee v Gupta*.[12] There was a return to this question in *Glasgow City Council, Petitioners*[13] in which it was held that, whilst in circumstances such as those in *Bell v Fiddes* and the absence of an issue subject to the supervisory jurisdiction of the court, reduction by the alternative procedure under Chapter 53 was wholly appropriate, any petition to that jurisdiction *must* be brought by judicial review.[14] In November 2012 an important procedural change was made to permit the judge in proceedings started as an application for judicial review to transfer the case and appoint it to proceed as an ordinary action (and vice versa).[15] Although this rule change provides only a procedural facility, and no blurring of the different characteristics of judicial review and ordinary actions, such a blurring seems to have been implied, if only at (the then) first order stage, at first instance in *G v Watson*.[16]

1   1996 SC 113; and, as (No 2), 1996 SLT 575.
2   1996 SLT 575 at 557 (Lord Weir). See also Lord Clyde at 577–578.
3   1988 SLT 253.
4   1988 SCLR 470.
5   1988 SCLR 470 at 473. Cf *Munro v Edinburgh and District Trades Council Social Club* 1989 GWD 6–240. See, too *National Association of Schoolmasters and Union of Women Teachers v Scottish Joint Negotiating Committee for Teaching Staff in School Education* 1987 GWD 8–246 in which a petition for suspension and interdict in respect of a proposed meeting of the Committee was refused, notwithstanding debate as to whether the appropriate means of procedure was by petition for judicial review. Similar questions have arisen in relation to the

use of s 45(b) of the Court of Session Act 1988 to compel performance of a statutory duty. See
Magnohard Ltd v UK Atomic Energy Authority 2004 SC 247, 2003 SLT 1083: and *McKenzie
v Scottish Ministers* 2004 SLT 1236.

6   1987 SLT 611.
7   1996 SLT 353.
8   1995 SLT 985.
9   1988 SLT 430.
10 1988 SLT 430 at 431.
11 1996 SLT 51 (Note).
12 1996 SLT 1098 at 1099, following *Lord Advocate v Johnston* 1983 SLT 290. See also *R v
    Secretary of State for Scotland* 1996 GWD 25–1447. For comment see also Holligan, 'Aspects
    of Appeals from the Sheriff Court' 1997 SLT (News) 40 and Himsworth, 'Public Employment,
    the Supervisory Jurisdiction and Points *West*' 1992 SLT (News) 257 at 260.
13 2004 SLT 61.
14 In so deciding, Lord Menzies expressed his disagreement with the contrary opinion expressed
    in *Saunders, Petitioner* 1999 SC 564. See also *SD, Petitioner* 2011 SLT 101. In *Glasgow
    City Council, Petitioners* 2013 SLT 917, it was said (para 18), in the course of rejecting an
    application for reduction of the children's reporter's refusal to hold a hearing because an
    earlier decision of a sheriff was a nullity, that the proper course would have been for the
    reporter to seek review of the sheriff's decision in the first place.
15 See now rules of court 58.15 and 58.16, **22.90** below and *Shedadh v Advocate General for
    Scotland* 2012 SLT 205; *S v SSHD* 2014 SLT 199 and 2014 SLT 1120 (IH).
16 2013 SLT 934. But see **22.40** above for *G v Watson* 2014 SLT 1030.

22.42 Another boundary issue which has never been fully resolved is that
involving the distinction to be drawn between what is now, with greater
confidence since *West*, described as the 'supervisory jurisdiction' of the court
and other aspects of its 'super-eminent jurisdiction' such as, in particular, its
nobile officium.[1] Both in *Forbes v Underwood*[2] and, much more recently, in
Royal Bank of Scotland plc v Clydebank District Council,[3] these jurisdictions
have been viewed as virtually synonymous[4] but petitions to the Inner House
invoking the *nobile officium* have survived the making of Rule 260B and its
successor.[5] It is not clear why the (unsuccessful) attempt to compel an arbiter
to state a case in *Edmund Nuttall Ltd v Amec Projects Ltd*[6] was made by
recourse to the *nobile officium* rather than by judicial review. That procedure
by way of judicial review is, where appropriate, stated to be mandatory does
not, therefore, remove the boundary questions which arise at the limits of the
supervisory jurisdiction. If anything, it tends to generate new ones. It may also,
because of the compulsory integration of actions for separate specific remedies
and procedures which were previously separate, produce new procedural
issues in need of resolution.[7]. One option which remains unaffected by either
the redefinition of the supervisory jurisdiction or the procedures for judicial
review arises where the challenge to an act or decision is raised not proactively
but defensively, either in response to a criminal charge[8]or *ope exceptionis* as a
defence to a civil action.[9] A consequence of having the opportunity to
challenge a decision (of a construction adjudicator) both in judicial review and
as a defence to an ordinary action has sometimes produced cases in which the
two are considered and determined in parallel.[10]

1   For discussion at the *nobile officium* in the House of Lords and the encouragement given by
    that court to the Court of Session to deploy its powers, see *Davidson v Scottish Ministers (No
    2)* 2004 SLT 895.
2   (1886) 13 R 465 at 468.
3   1992 SLT 356 at 365.
4   See also Lord Clyde, 'The Nature of the Supervisory Jurisdiction and the Public/Private
    Distinction in Scots Administrative Law' (**22.17** above).

[5] See eg *Pringle, Petitioner* 1991 SLT 330; *Sloan, Petitioner* 1991 SLT 527; *H, Petitioner* 1997 SLT 3; *M v S* [2009] CSIH 44, 2009 Fam LR 149. Provision for applications to the nobile officium is made by Rule 14.3(d). For *nobile officium* practice in general, see S Thomson, *The Nobile Officium* (2015).

[6] 1992 SC 133.

[7] For example, *MacGillivray v Johnston (No 2)* 1994 SLT 1012. See also HM Advocate v McCrossan 2013 SLT 1026

[8] One surviving anomaly may have been encountered in *L v Angus Council* 2012 SLT 304 where it was held that an ordinary action for declarator was required, rather than judicial review, for the determination of a person's age (para 25).

[9] For example, *Vaughan Engineering Ltd v Hinkins of Frewins Ltd* 2003 SLT 428.

[10] *Curot Contracts Ltd (t/a Dimension Shop Fitting) v Castle Inns (Stirling) Ltd (t/a Castle Leisure Group)* 2009 SLT 62; and *Barr Ltd v Klin Investment UK Ltd* [2009] CSOH 104. For discussion, see C Himsworth, 'Inter-Jurisdictional Error of Law in the Review of Construction Adjudication' 2010 Jur Rev 307.

ALTERNATIVE STATUTORY REMEDIES AND THE STATUTORY EXCLUSION OF JUDICIAL REVIEW[1]

[1] Sometimes the interface of the supervisory jurisdiction and the non-statutory action for damages is discussed in terms of the existence or not of an 'alternative remedy'. See, eg *Aitken, Petitioner* (24 October 2002, unreported) at **22.40** above; and *Anderson v Shetland Islands Council* 2010 SC 246 2011 SLT 196. One consequence of *McCue v Glasgow City Council* 2014 SLT 891(see **22.45**, note 2) may be that the designation 'statutory remedies' will have to be reconsidered.

22.43 The effect of Rule 58.3(1) is not completely clear. As already mentioned[2] Rule 260B used to provide that the procedure for application for judicial review did not apply to specified applications made to the Court of Session under the Acquisition of Land (Authorisation Procedure) (Scotland) Act 1947, the Town and Country Planning (Scotland) Act 1972[3] and the Roads (Scotland) Act 1984. This did not mean that no orders and decisions made under those Acts could be challenged by judicial review. Those for which no statutory appeal is provided may be reviewed.[4] A feature of the special appeals under these Acts is that they are made subject to strict time limits, following which further challenge in a court is excluded. In this respect, they join other circumstances in which statute purports expressly to exclude challenge of a decision in the courts, either absolutely or after the opportunity for a time-limited statutory appeal[5] and, in this area, Scottish practice appears to be not notably different from that in England,[6] although the case of *McDaid v Clydebank District Council*[7] did seem to expand the opportunity for challenge by judicial review of an enforcement notice subject to a time-limited appeal.[8] In addition to the appeals under the three named statutes, it was also plain that applications expressly made under other enactments were not to proceed by way of the judicial review procedure. Frequently, for instance, statutory appeals are made to the Court of Session, after initial appeal to the sheriff, under the Licensing (Scotland) Act 2005, the Betting, Gaming and Lotteries Act 1963, or the Gaming Act 1968.[9] These cannot be taken by judicial review but, once again, the possibility remains of the judicial review of licensing decisions for which no statutory appeal is provided.[10] In *Mitchell and Butlers Ltd v Aberdeen City LB*[11] *there* was an application for review of a *policy* (on minimum pricing of alcohol) rather than an actual licensing decision.

² See **22.41**.
³ Now consolidated in the Town and Country Planning (Scotland) Act 1997, ss 238 and 239.
⁴ See, eg *Glasgow City District Council v Secretary of State for Scotland* 1990 SLT 343 (compulsory purchase); *Royal Bank of Scotland v Clydebank District Council* 1991 SLT 635 (compulsory purchase); *Lakin Ltd v Secretary of State for Scotland* 1988 SLT 780 (planning); *Re Upper Drum Fishings* (22 May 1986, unreported)(planning); *Donald v Marquetty* (13 November 1986, unreported)(planning); *Inverness, Loch Ness and Nairn Tourist Board v Highland Regional Council* 1988 GWD 6–219 (planning); *Kirkcaldy District Council v Fife Regional Council* 1987 GWD 29–1120 (planning); *Re Miller Group Ltd* (28 December 1989, unreported)(planning); *Strathclyde Regional Council v Secretary of State for Scotland* 1991 SLT 796, 1991 SCLR 311 (planning); *Pickering v Kyle and Carrick District Council* 1991 GWD 7–361 (planning). *Lochore v Moray District Council* 1992 SLT 16, 1991 SCLR 741. For detailed discussion of judicial review in Scots planning law, see J Rowan-Robinson et al Scottish Planning Law and Procedure (2001).
⁵ For full treatment, see Bradley and Himsworth, paragraphs 117–120.
⁶ See CHAPTER **18**.
⁷ 1984 SLT 162.
⁸ But see *Martin v Bearsden and Milngavie District Council* 1987 SLT 300; *Pollock v Secretary of State for Scotland* 1993 SLT 1173.
⁹ Quite separately, references may be made to the Court of Session by way of a special case under s 27 of the Court of Session Act 1988 (see, eg *Piggins & Rix Ltd v Montrose Port Authority* 1995 SLT 418).
¹⁰ See, eg *Mecca Leisure Ltd v City of Glasgow District Council* 1987 SCLR 26; *Purdon v Glasgow District Licensing Board* 1988 SCLR 466; *Bury v Kilmarnock and Loudon District Licensing Board* 1989 SLT 110; *Centralbite Ltd v Kincardine and Deeside District Licensing Board* 1990 SLT 231; *Bantop Ltd v City of Glasgow District Licensing Board* 1990 SLT 366; *Cooper v City of Edinburgh District Licensing Board* 1990 SLT 246 and 1991 SLT 47; *Elder v Ross and Cromarty District Licensing Board* 1990 SLT 307; *Glasgow City Council, Petitioners* 2004 SLT 61.
¹¹ 2005 SLT 13.

22.44 The reference to the three specific statutory appellate mechanisms was dropped from the 1994 rules of court but it may be assumed that their exclusion from the judicial review procedure is ensured by the general language of Rule 58.3(1).[1] This excludes from the review procedure an application which 'is made, or *could* be made, by appeal or review under or by virtue of any enactment'. The effect of this is presumably to reinforce the Court of Session's long-standing reluctance to permit the use of judicial review where an alternative statutory remedy is provided. Statutory remedies must first be exhausted.[2] The rule might, however, appear to operate at a procedural level only by confining its terms to a remedy by way of appeal or review in the Court of Session itself.[3] The routine exclusion of judicial review where a statutory appeal lies to *another* court or tribunal (and raising, therefore, not merely the question of the procedural route to the Court of Session) was impliedly ensured by the former Rule 260B(1) in its restriction of the judicial review procedure to situations in which, prior to April 1985, an application would have been made to the supervisory jurisdiction.[4] It is assumed that, although the same formula is not used in Rule 58.1, the same effect is retained.

¹ More or less retaining the wording of the former Rule 260B(3).
² It should also be noted, however, that the court has a general dispensing power under Rule of Court 2.1 to permit eg judicial review to continue even if an alternative procedure was considered to be appropriate – see *Glasgow City Council, Petitioners* 2004 SLT 61 at 69.
³ See (in relation to an earlier version of the rule) *London and Clydeside Estates Ltd v Secretary of State for Scotland* 1987 SLT 459; *Simpson v IRC* 1992 SLT 1069 (Note). See also *Strathclyde Buses Ltd v Strathclyde Regional Council* 1994 SLT 724. Most such statutory

appeals are to the Inner House but compare *Kilmarnock and Loudon District Council v Young* 1993 SLT 505 (appeal under Burial Grounds (Scotland) Act 1855-since repealed by the Burial and Cremation (Scotland) Act 2016.).

4   On this limited ambit of Rule 260B(3), see *Tarmac Econowaste Ltd v Assessor for Lothian Region* 1991 SLT 77 at 78. See also *Accountant in Bankruptcy v Allans of Gillock Ltd* 1991 SLT 765. For discussion of its application in circumstances where an appeal lies to the Court of Session from another tribunal, see *Nahar v Strathclyde Regional Council* 1986 SLT 570.

22.45 A restatement of the operation of the traditional Scottish principle that the court will not grant redress in the exercise of its supervisory power where all statutory remedies have not been exhausted appears in the opinion of the Lord Ordinary (Lord Clyde) in *Tarmac Econowaste Ltd v Assessor for Lothian Region.*[1] Applications to the court in this situation are in general incompetent[2] and only if the statutory procedure has been exhausted is a common law remedy competent.[3] On the other hand, the general principle is not absolute but admits of exceptions. In the widely-cited language of Lord Justice-Clerk Wheatley, these arise in 'exceptional' or 'special' circumstances.[4] What amounts to such exceptional or special circumstances is not completely clear, but it appears that judicial review is, for instance, competent, where fraud has been alleged or where the complainer has been prevented from pursuing a statutory appeal through a procedural irregularity.[5] In *Kirkwood v City of Glasgow District Council,*[6] Lord Weir stated two important qualifications to the grant of a remedy. It would not be available where the departure from normal procedure was in circumstances within the knowledge and control of the party to avoid nor where any other means of review were prescribed but the party has failed to take advantage of them.[7] (See also *Ingle v Ingle's Trustee.*[8]) In *Glasgow City Council, Petitioner*[9] it was stated, following *Ingle*, that an application to the supervisory jurisdiction involves the exercise of the court's equitable discretion in each case. If a petitioner has an 'obvious and clearly available effective alternative remedy' the court will normally decline to exercise its supervisory jurisdiction. 'Moreover, a respondent cannot escape this jurisdiction by pointing to some arcane or rarely used means of appeal of doubtful efficacy'.[10] On the other hand, in *Mackinnon v Argyll and Bute Council*[11] it was held that the remedy by way of the appointment of an arbiter under s 163(3) of the Roads (Scotland) Act 1984 was not sufficient to exclude judicial review. In *Choi v Secretary of State for the Home Department*[12] it was held that 'the accumulation of grounds averred both of procedural impropriety and of irrationality' could constitute special circumstances permitting judicial review rather than restriction to a statutory remedy.[13] Another circumstance is where an appeal against an individual decision would be an inadequate form of challenge to a general policy decision.[14] Lord Wheatley himself referred to an averment of ultra vires as the basis for recourse to the common law remedy. In *M v Home Secretary*[15] the availability of an appeal to the First-tier Tribunal was sufficient to exclude review.

1   1991 SLT 77 at 78–79.
2   See *Dante v Assessor for Ayr* 1922 SC 109, *sub nom Dante v Magistrates of Ayr* 1922 SLT 74; *Bellway v Strathclyde Regional Council* 1979 SC 92, 1980 SLT 66; *Inverclyde District Council v Inverkip Building Co Ltd* 1981 SC 401, 1982 SLT 401; *Bovis Homes (Scotland) Ltd v Inverclyde District Council* 1982 SLT 473; *O'Neill v Scottish Joint Negotiating Committee* 1987 SCLR 275; *Pollock v Secretary of State for Scotland* 1993 SLT 1173. *Falconer v South Ayrshire Council* 2002 SLT 1033. See also *W v Scottish Ministers* 2010 SLT 65, but with a novel hint (at para 19) of exclusion by possible availability of an ombudsman remedy;

Wallace, Petitioner [2012] CSOH 195; and *Archid Architecture and Interior Design v Dundee City Council* 2014 SLT 81, and *McCue v Glasgow City Council* 2014 SLT 891 (non-statutory complaints procedure as surprisingly the alternative remedy). But see also *Smart's Guardian v Fife Council* 2016 SLT 384.

3   *Abercromby v Badenoch* 1909 2 SLT 114. It appears to be permissible for the court to proceed to decide the substantive issue raised by a petition, despite doubts aired but not pressed as to its competency. See *Short's Trustee v Keeper of the Registers of Scotland* 1993 SLT 1291.

4   *British Railways Board v Glasgow Corpn* 1976 SC 224 at 239. See also *Tehrani v Argyll and Clyde Health Board (No 2)* 1990 SLT 118 at 124; *Kennedy Petitioner* 1988 SCLR 149; *Alagon v Secretary of State for the Home Department* 1995 SLT 381; *Sangha v Secretary of State for the Home Department* 1997 SLT 545. For a full discussion, see Bradley and Himsworth, paragraphs 117–118.

5   See *Tarmac Econowaste Ltd v Assessor for Lothian Region* 1991 SLT 77 at 79 and the cases there cited.

6   1988 SLT 430.

7   1988 SLT 430 at 431.

8   1997 SLT 160. See, too, *Prestige Assets Ltd v Renfrewshire Council* 2003 SC 88.

9   2004 SLT 61.

10 At **22.31**. See also *Shiels v City of Edinburgh Council* 1999 Fam LR 92. In *Welsh v Committee of the South Western Social and Recreation Club Ltd* 2004 GWD 23–492 it was held that the petitioner's application was excluded by the existence of an appeal under s 60(7)(b)(ii) of the Industrial and Provident Societies Act 1965 but not, as urged by the respondent, of the 'alternative' of an apology and resignation from the Club.

11 2001 SLT 1275.

12 1996 SLT 590.

13 1996 SLT 590 at 595. See also *Phillips v Strathclyde Joint Police Board* 2004 SC 728, 2004 SLT 73.

14 See *City Cabs (Edinburgh) Ltd v City of Edinburgh District Council* 1988 SLT 184.

15 2014 SLT 649. See also *B v Home Secretary* 2016 SLT 1220 (para 73).

22.46 Further difficulties were discussed in *Mensah*[1] where Lord Coulsfield held that 'the general principle does not normally go so far as to exclude the jurisdiction of the court to grant redress on the ground of fundamental invalidity (unless, of course, the statute so provides)'.[2] It has also been held that the right of an individual to petition for review in reliance upon s 45 of the Court of Session Act 1988 will be excluded only on clear statutory provision.[3] It will, however, be recalled that, under Rule 58(2), applications under s 45(b) of the Court of Session Act 1988 are expressly included within the procedural ambit of judicial review[4] and, the exclusions provided under Rule 58.3(1) must be read subject to that provision. Thus, not only should applications made directly in reliance upon s 45 proceed by judicial review,[5] but also those made under some other statute which itself provides for enforcement by way of a s 45 petition. These are presumably not excluded by Rule 58.3(1). On the other hand, it may be debatable whether the express provision made by some of those same statutes for the enforcement by interdict of directions and other obligations imposed by ministers[6] excludes proceeding by way of application for judicial review. One consequence noted by Lady Paton in *Magnohard v UK Atomic Energy Authority*[7] of taking applications under s 45(b) as applications for judicial review is that such applications could not be resorted to until all other statutory remedies had been exhausted.[8]

1   *Mensah v Home Secretary* 1992 SLT 177.

2   Relying, inter alia, on *Lord Advocate v Police Comrs of Perth* (1869) 8 M 244. See, also, *Grubb v Jones* 2003 SLT 1101; *Ho,Ho,Hong and Chin v Lord Advocate* 2004 SC 1, 2003 SLT 867.

3   See *T Docherty Ltd v Burgh of Monifieth* 1970 SC 200, 1971 SLT 13; *Walker v Strathclyde Regional Council* 1986 SLT 523.

4   See **22.9**.

⁵ See *Magnohard Ltd v UK Atomic Energy Authority* 2004 SC 247, 2003 SLT 1083 paragraphs 118–131. But see also *McKenzie v Scottish Ministers* 2004 SLT 1236.
⁶ See, eg Outer Space Act 1986, s 8(3);.
⁷ 2004 SC 247, 2003 SLT 1083.
⁸ 2004 SC 247 at paragraph 127. But, again, see *McKenzie v Scottish Ministers* 2004 SLT 1236.

22.47 New questions were raised[1] when it was sought to review unappealable decisions of the new Upper Tribunal (typically decisions to refuse leave to appeal from a first-tier tribunal). The options ranged from the application of the normal principles of review applicable to any statutory body through to the possibility, in the light of the Upper Tribunal's special character, of no review at all. Between the two was the possibility of a compromise solution, a less intrusive form of review, and it was this that was adopted by the Supreme Court,[2] with care taken to ensure that the same principles would apply in the two jurisdictions.[3] The form of words used to encapsulate the new 'benchmark' was adopted, by 'analogy', from the language already used to identify the circumstances in which 'second appeals' could be taken from the Upper Tribunal to the Inner House or Court of Appeal under the Tribunals, Courts and Enforcement Act 2007, and had two limbs. The case had to involve either 'some important point of principle or practice' or 'some other compelling reason' to justify its further consideration.[4] Lord Hope went on, however, to say that he was leaving it to the Court of Session to give such further guidance as might be needed for the implementation of the new approach, whilst also giving some advice on how to proceed.[5] After an initial period of uncertainty, some guidance was offered by the Second Division in *SA v Secretary of State for the Home Department*[6].On the implementation of the Court of Session Act 1988, s 27B from 22 September 2015, the *Eba* screening process migrated into an adapted permission stage.[7] See 22.92.

¹ As they were also in England and Wales. See Chapter 19 and Chapter 20.
² *Eba v Advocate General for Scotland* 2012 SC (UKSC) 1 (for Scotland) on appeal from the First Division at 2011 SC 70, 2010 SLT 1047 and *R (Cart) v Upper Tribunal* [2012] 1 AC 663 (for England and Wales).
³ Lord Hope in *Eba* at paras 38–47.
⁴ Lord Hope in *Eba* at para 48.
⁵ *Eba* para 49.
⁶ 2013 SLT 1132. See also *EP v Secretary of State for the Home Department* 2014 SC 706.
⁷ See eg *Mdluli, Petitioner* 2014 SLT 483. *CF, Petitioner* [2016] CSOH 28. See also C Himsworth, 'Doing Judicial Review in the Post-*Eba* Era' (2014) 18 Edin LR 395.

STANDING TO APPLY FOR JUDICIAL REVIEW

22.48 Suddenly, on 12 October 2011, the UK Supreme Court swept away a century of Scottish practice by changing the rules on standing to apply for judicial review.[1] This was followed by rule changes in consequence of the Courts Reform (Scotland) Act 2014. The effects of those changes are considered below.[2] The historically approved terminology in Scotland was by reference to the requirement that, in all areas of the law, 'a litigant, and in particular a pursuer, must always qualify title and interest.' Questions surrounding the way in which that cryptic requirement was to be satisfied in an administrative law context were troublesome as the policy issues of access to the courts, familiar too in other jurisdictions, had to be addressed. Nor, in Scotland, were the questions of title and interest removed or modified by the procedural changes introduced in 1985. Despite suggestions at the time that the occasion of the rule changes might be used also to modify the rules on standing and subsequent arguments that, by implication, a modification may in fact have been achieved (in the direction of liberalisation), it had to be assumed that no such change was made. For a full account of the former rules, see the 5th edition of this book at paras 22.6.1–22.6.7.

[1] *AXA General Insurance Ltd v Lord Advocate (Scotland)* 2012 SC (UKSC) 122, 2011 SLT 106. The case involved the review of an Act of the Scottish Parliament and is, therefore, dealt with more fully in Chapter 21.

[2] It should be noted that statutory provision in relation to the requirements of title and interest have been made in specific cases. The Local Government Act 1988, s 19(7) provides that 'in proceedings for judicial review, the persons who have . . . in Scotland, title and interest in the matter shall include any potential contractor . . . or former potential contractor'. Cf *Kershaw v City of Glasgow District Council* 1992 SLT 71. The 1988 Act is not unique in continuing to contain a reference to the old test of standing. Presumably, all should be amended.

22.49 The Report of the (Gill) Scottish Civil Courts Review[1] proposed major changes. The Review Committee were persuaded that, on balance, the current law on standing had been too restrictive and that the separate tests of title and interest should be replaced by a single test: whether the petitioner has demonstrated a sufficient interest in the subject matter of the proceedings (paragraph 25). Section 89 of, the Courts Reform (Scotland) Act 2014 gave effect to that recommendation from its implementation (SSI 2015/247) on 22 September 2015.

[1] See **22.6** above.

22.50 In the meantime, however, the UK Supreme Court had made its own radical reforming contribution, already mentioned Called upon to address the standing not of the petitioner insurance companies in *AXA General Insurance Ltd v Lord Advocate (Scotland)*[1] to make their application for judicial review, but rather that of the victims of pleural plaques (who stood to benefit from the terms of the Damages (Asbestos-related Conditions) (Scotland) Act 2009 being challenged in the proceedings) to enter the proceedings as persons 'directly affected',[2] The court, especially in the judgment of Lord Reed (at paragraphs 155-175)[3] took the opportunity (a) to treat the two standing tests as the same – as Lord Hope said, 'two sides of the same coin' (paragraph 61) – and (b) to reformulate the rule. The time had come for a change and it was the role of the courts to make it (see Lord Reed paragraph 171). In the light of the changes brought about by the adoption of the judicial review procedures in 1985, the decision in *West*,[4] and the recent substantial growth in the number of applications and the emerging inappropriateness of the narrow (especially in contrast with England) focus of the existing private law Scottish rules on title and interest, there was a need to adopt a new rule (whose content in detail would not be spelled out) requiring a person with 'sufficient interest' (paragraphs 62 and 171) to be directly affected by the subject matter of the proceedings.

[1] 2012 SC (UKSC) 122, 2011 SLT 106.
[2] Under (new) rule 58.8(2). See **22.92** below.
[3] With the strong support of Lord Hope at paras 53–64.
[4] *West v Secretary of State for Scotland* 1992 SC 385.

22.51 Initially, a rather hesitant start was made to the exploitation by the courts of the changes pioneered by the Supreme Court. In *Christian Institute v Lord Advocate*,[1] Lord Pentland, in the Outer House, held that, in their challenge to the 'named persons' legislation of the Scottish Parliament, the Christian Institute and other organisations did not have 'sufficient interest' in the proceedings. They were not 'in any realistic sense directly affected'. They had not, for instance, contributed to the legislative scrutiny of the Act under review. Nor did they demonstrate sufficient levels of expertise and knowledge to claim to act in a representative capacity.

[1] 2015 SLT 72. The question of standing was not, however, further pursued. For the case as eventually decided by the Supreme Court, see CHAPTER 21 at 21.49.

MORA, TACITURNITY AND ACQUIESCENCE

22.52 A proposal considered but rejected by the Dunpark Committee was for the imposition of a 'time limit of three months after the last act or decision challenged'[1] within which an application for judicial review would need to be lodged. That is a proposal which was revived in the Report of the (Gill) Scottish Civil Courts ReviewSee 22.6 above. It may be noted in passing that the case for time limits in judicial review in both England and Scotland has been made with[2] which recommended that the common law plea of mora, taciturnity and acquiescence should be replaced by a rule requiring petitions to be brought promptly and, in any event, within a period of three months, subject to extension at the discretion of the court (paragraphs 38–39). The Courts Reform (Scotland) Act 2014 contains a provision which requires applications to be made (in the absence of a statutory specification of a period shorter than three months) before the end of the period of three months beginning with the date on which the grounds giving rise to the application first arise or such longer period as the court considers equitable having regard to all the circumstances.[3] Until the implementation of the 2014 Act on 22 September 2015 access to judicial review was unrestricted by any particular time-limit, which entailed instead the use of the general common law plea of 'mora, taciturnity and acquiescence', around which a rich jurisprudence was developed by the courts. For a full account, reference should be made to paras 22.7.1–22.7.3 of the 5th edition of this work. It may be assumed that, with the new time limit in operation, the relevance of the cases in which the old rules of mora were developed will fade.[4] On the other hand, the common law tests have not been explicitly overridden and might yet be revived in some (as yet unguessable) circumstances. It is, for instance, possible that, when courts are required to determine when a longer time limit under the new rule might be considered equitable, the old principles of mora may be invoked as a guide.[5] Equally, it is conceivable that an application, even though made within the statutory time limit, might be considered to have (by mora) improperly delayed.

[1] Dunpark Report (see **22.7** above), paragraph 8.
[2] the review of public bodies in mind and the desirability of giving them some protection from delayed applications. That rationale would have supported the Dunpark Committee proposals because their rule change would indeed have been directed at public authorities. The Gill Review proposals, on the other hand, were made (with perhaps less justification) in the knowledge that modern judicial review in Scotland is not confined to public sector respondents.

3   See 22.87 below
4   Principal later cases included: *Somerville v Scottish Ministers* 2007 SC 140, 2007 SLT 96; *Portobello Park Action Group Association v City of Edinburgh Council* 2013 SC 184, 2012 SLT 1137; *Kenman Holdings Ltd v Comhairle nan Eilean Siar* [2017] CSIH 10.
5   In *Quissongo v Glasgow City Council* [2016] CSOH 135 (para 15) the point was taken, in a discussion of the rules of mora, that, had the application been commenced four days later, it would have been caught by the new rule.

GENERAL POWERS OF THE COURT

22.53 Chapter 58 of the Rules of Court makes general provision for the powers of the court in judicial review proceedings, powers intended to confer considerable flexibility. Thus the court may, in exercising its supervisory jurisdiction, grant or refuse a petition for judicial review or any part of it, with or without conditions and may make: any order that could be made if sought in any action or petition including, in particular an interim order or any of the following orders: an order for reduction, declarator, suspension, interdict,[1] implement, restitution, payment (whether of damages or otherwise).[2]

1   Subject, in the case of the Crown, to the Crown Proceedings Act 1947, ss 21 and 43 which ostensibly prohibit interdicts against the Crown. But see **22.85**.
2   For further consideration of remedies, see 'Remedies in Judicial Review' at **22.82**.

THE GROUNDS OF JUDICIAL REVIEW

Introduction

22.54 Although it might be expected that discussion of the grounds of review would constitute a dominant part of an account of judicial review – this is indeed the case in this book at large – two reasons combine to justify briefer treatment in this chapter. The first is that Scottish authorities are agreed that, taken as a whole, the grounds of review are, and should be, the same in Scotland as in England. The second is that the grounds themselves are treated so comprehensively elsewhere in the book that repetition of that material is wholly unnecessary. Thus, the bulk of the material relevant to practitioners north, as south, of the border is to be found in relation to the grounds of review in CHAPTERS 6 to 13 above. This section serves to extend the reference made to decisions in the Court of Session and thus to illustrate the use made in the Scottish system of principles common to both.[1]

1   For the fullest account reference should be made to Bradley and Himsworth, paragraphs 15–92. As to the applicability (or not) of the 'common law grounds of review' to the review of Acts of the Scottish Parliament, see *Adams v Scottish Ministers* 2003 SC 171, 2003 SLT 366; and *AXA General Insurance Ltd v Lord Advocate* 2012 SC (UKSC) 122, 2011 SLT 106 discussed at **21.55**.

Similarity of general principles

22.55 Whilst there has been good reason to be cautious of claims to a basic similarity of approach between England and Scotland in some other aspects of administrative law and of judicial review in particular, there is authority at the highest level that the rules governing the grounds of review themselves are the same. Most prominent are the dicta of Lord Fraser in *Brown v Hamilton District Council*:[1]

'It is not necessary for me to consider the grounds on which judicial review may be open. The decisions in the English cases of *Associated Provincial Picture Houses Ltd v Wednesbury Corporation*,[2] and *Anisminic Ltd v Foreign Compensation Commission*,[3] so far as they relate to matters of substance and not of procedure, are accepted as being applicable to Scotland, see *Watt v Lord Advocate*.[4] There is no difference of substance between the laws of the two countries on this matter, although, in order to avoid confusion, it has to be remembered that the word "review" is commonly used in Scottish cases to describe a process which in England would be called "appeal" and is not restricted to procedure corresponding to the English procedure of judicial review'.[5]

[1] 1983 SC (HL) 1 at 42.
[2] [1948] 1 KB 223.
[3] [1969] 2 AC 147.
[4] 1979 SC 120.
[5] In the light of the subsequent divergence between the two jurisdictions on the application of *Anisminic* and *Watt* (see 'Excess of Jurisdiction' at 22.12) there was some irony in the reference to the two cases. See, too, *Elder v Ross and Cromarty District Licensing Board* 1990 SLT 307 at 311 but see also the cautionary words (on the effect of English procedures on substance) of Lord Clyde in *Stewart v Monklands District Council* 1987 SLT 630 at 633.

22.56 This position was reconfirmed in *West* where it was explained that:

'[there is] no substantial difference between English law and Scots law as to the grounds on which the process of decision-making may be open to review. So reference may be made to English cases in order to determine whether there has been an excess or abuse of the jurisdiction, power or authority or a failure to do what it requires'.[1]

The effect of this willed harmonisation of the law has indeed been to make the classic English authorities, above all *Associated Provincial Picture Houses Ltd v Wednesbury Corporation*,[2] as readily cited in argument and judgment in the Court of Session as in the English courts. It has also been noted, however, that this imposes an obligation upon the Court of Session, as on the Administrative Court, to take account of developments in the law – to contribute, indeed, to those developments – and not to adhere slavishly to principles more familiar at an earlier stage in administrative law.[3]

[1] *West v Secretary of State for Scotland* 1992 SC 385 at 413.
[2] [1948] 1 KB 223, [1947] 2 All ER 680.
[3] See, for example, Lord Dervaird who warned against the use of the language of 'unfettered discretion' which, he said, 'fits unhappily with more recent developments in administrative law in England'. See *Bantop Ltd v City of Glasgow District Licensing Board* 1990 SLT 366 at 369. It was in *Somerville v Scottish Ministers* 2008 SC (HL) 45, 2007 SLT 1113 that the House of Lords pronounced on the status of proportionality.

22.57 One area in which quite a sharp divergence between English and Scottish practice was in danger of opening up was the relevance to judicial review of the European Convention on Human Rights prior to its 'incorporation'.[1] However, the passing of the Human Rights Act 1998 produced a new convergence in that area. Where bodies of substantive law have been amassed in large numbers of English cases in particular areas, these bodies of law have been quite freely adopted by the Court of Session.

¹   See, especially, *Kaur v Lord Advocate* 1980 SC 319. But see also *T, Petitioner* 1996 SCLR 897 in which the court eventually recognised the use of the ECHR as an interpretational aid. For an acknowledgement of the same principle in relation to the Aarhus Convention, see *Forbes v Aberdeenshire Council* [2010] CSOH 1 at paragraph 11.

22.58 Most prominent among trans-border receptions has been that of Lord Diplock's tripartite classification of the grounds of review – illegality, irrationality and procedural impropriety – formulated in his speech in *Council of Civil Service Unions v Minister for the Civil Service* (the 'GCHQ case').¹ It was approved in *Edinburgh City District Council v Secretary of State for Scotland.*² Since then, the GCHQ classification has been widely cited, with approval, in the Court of Session. A prominent early example was *Lakin Ltd v Secretary of State for Scotland.*³ In that case, it was observed that the three heads of challenge were not to be regarded as either exhaustive or mutually exclusive,⁴ although there has also been the occasional tendency in the direction of 'watertight compartments'. Conceding that there is 'an evolutionary process at work' in the development of grounds of view, it has been urged that this:

> 'does not avoid the need for analysis and classification of the grounds of decision at any point in the development of the law . . . . Lord Diplock's classification reflected the result of a process of analysis and classification at the stage at which he considered the matter. That classification is part of the law of Scotland . . . An authority may deviate from the path of duty in a number of ways simultaneously. But the essence of the matter is that there are separate grounds, and that they provide a proper focus for analysis of the facts of particular cases, notwithstanding that the content of the classes may be developed, or other classes added.'⁵

¹   [1985] AC 374 at 410–411.
²   1985 SLT 551. For further discussion of the case, see **22.73**.
³   1988 SLT 780.
⁴   1988 SLT 780 at 799 (Lord Mayfield).
⁵   *Pickering v Kyle and Carrick District Council* 1991 GWD 7–361 (Lord Morison). See also *Shetland Line 1984 Ltd v Secretary of State for Scotland* 1996 SLT 653 at 658.

22.59 The three GCHQ grounds of review are now briefly considered (including mention of disproportionality as a possible ground of review), followed by a note on the fourth ground of 'incompatibility with Convention Rights'.

Illegality¹

¹   For the law of England and Wales on this topic, see CHAPTER 7.

22.60 In most respects, challenge on the ground of 'illegality' may be presented as a fairly uncontroversial successor to review on the grounds that an authority has 'exceeded its powers' or 'done the wrong thing'. The problem of the interpretation of statutory powers – whether express powers or powers to be implied from the language of the statute – remains but there is little doubt that the issues in the classic case of *Dundee Harbour Trustees v Nicol*² and, more recently, of *Graham v Glasgow Corporation.*³ *Glasgow Corporation v Flint*⁴ and *McColl v Strathclyde Regional Council*⁵ can be readily classified as issues of 'legality' in Lord Diplock's scheme. The two-stage challenge to trans-Atlantic air traffic distribution rules falls into the same category.[6] Another important instance of 'doing the wrong thing' was the attempt to avoid the full procedural consequences of a rail closure by the provision instead of 'ghost trains' as substitute rail services.[7] In *Fayed v Advocate General for Scotland*[8] 'forward tax agreements' entered into by the Inland Revenue were held to be ultra vires and unenforceable.

[2]   1915 SC (HL) 7.
[3]   1936 SC 108.
[4]   1966 SC 108.
[5]   1983 SC 225.
[6]   *Air 2000 Ltd v Secretary of State for Transport* 1989 SLT 698; *Air 2000 Ltd v Secretary of State for Transport (No 2)* 1990 SLT 335.
[7]   *Highland Regional Council v British Railways Board* 1996 SLT 274.
[8]   2004 SLT 798.

22.61 'Illegality' must be assumed to encompass (because they would otherwise be difficult to accommodate within the tripartite scheme) those aspects of 'non-irrational' unreasonableness discussed by Lord Greene in *Associated Provincial Picture Houses Ltd v Wednesbury Corporation*[1] as the adoption of an improper purpose in the exercise of discretion or decision-making on the basis of irrelevant considerations.[2] *Wednesbury* has itself been widely cited and approved in the Scottish Courts. Its tests of reasonableness were authoritatively restated by the First Division in the planning case of *Wordie Property Co Ltd v Secretary of State for Scotland*:[3]

'A decision of the Secretary of State acting within his statutory remit is ultra vires if he has improperly exercised the discretion confided to him. In particular it will be ultra vires if it is based upon a material error of law going to the root of the question for determination. It will be ultra vires, too, if the Secretary of State has taken into account irrelevant considerations or has failed to take account of relevant and material considerations which ought to have been taken into account. Similarly it will fall to be quashed on that ground if, where it is one for which a factual basis is required, there is no proper basis in fact to support it. It will also fall to be quashed if it, or any condition imposed in relation to a grant of planning permission is so unreasonable that no reasonable Secretary of State could have reached or imposed it.[4]

Although a statutory appeal under the planning legislation, *Wordie* has been widely adopted in judicial review cases.[5]

[1]   [1948] 1 KB 223, [1947] 2 All ER 680.
[2]   See *Edinburgh City District Council v Secretary of State for Scotland* 1985 SLT 551 at 555 (Lord Jauncey) but cf eg *Edinburgh Property Management Association, City of Edinburgh District Council* 1987 GWD 38–1348.
[3]   1984 SLT 345.
[4]   1984 SLT 345 at 347–348 (Lord Emslie). The test of irrationality/unreasonableness is treated below at **22.70**.
[5]   See, eg *Strathclyde Passenger Executive v McGill Bus Service Ltd* 1984 SLT 377; *Mecca Leisure Ltd v City of Glasgow District Council* 1987 SCLR 26; *Lowrie v Secretary of State for Scotland* 1988 SCLR 614; *Elder v Ross and Cromarty District Licensing Board* 1990 SLT 307; *Centralbite Ltd v Kincardine and Deeside District Licensing Board* 1990 SLT 231; *Association of Optical Practitioners Ltd v Secretary of State for Scotland* (10 October 1985, unreported); *Ian Monachan (Central) Ltd v Lanarkshire Health Board* 1990 GWD 40–2299; *Clydesdale District Council v Law Mining Ltd* 1991 SCLR 236; *Thornbank Developments (Galashiels) Ltd v Secretary of State for Scotland* 1991 SCLR 532; *Glasgow for People v Secretary of State for Scotland* 1991 SCLR 775; *Central Regional Council v Secretary of State for Scotland* 1991 SCLR 348; *North Uist Fisheries Ltd v Secretary of State for Scotland* 1992 SC 33; *Shetland Line (1984) Ltd v Secretary of State for Scotland* 1996 SLT 653; *Rae v*

Criminal Injuries Compensation Board 1997 SLT 291; *Standard Commercial Property Securities Ltd v Glasgow City Council* 2004 SLT 655; *Cooper v Forth Ports plc* 2011 SC 760; 2011 SLT. 711.

22.62 Many cases have involved challenge based on abuse of discretion within the categories defined in *Wednesbury* and *Wordie*. Thus, in *City Cabs (Edinburgh) Ltd v City of Edinburgh District Council*,[1] the failure to take account of relevant information was the basis for the reduction of the Council's decision. It was not sufficient that the Council's officials in the department of administration had considered the information. 'If information is of such a nature that it ought to be considered by the administrative body in reaching its decision, it ought to be considered by those persons to whom the task of making the decision falls'.[2] In *Bury v Kilmarnock and Loudon District Licensing Board*[3] the Board's decision to refuse to hear an application because the refusal was itself based on a blanket refusal to hear applications in cases of non-representation and non-attendance was struck down. Such a blanket decision was a:

'negation of the discretion which the statute requires to be exercised . . . In the absence of any more particular reason for declining to deal with the application, it appears to me that the decision which the respondents took was not a reasoned, or reasonable one'.[4]

[1] 1988 SLT 184.
[2] 1988 SLT 184 at 188 (Lord Cullen). Cf *Thomson v Motherwell District Council* 1989 SCLR 175. See also *Glasgow City District Council v Secretary of State for Scotland* 1990 SLT 343; *McTear v Scottish Legal Aid Board* 1997 SLT 108.
[3] 1988 SCLR 436.
[4] 1988 SCLR 436 at 438. Cf *Christie v Strathclyde Regional Council* 1987 GWD 22–819.

22.63 The extent to which a policy legitimately adopted may constrain the exercise of a discretionary power has been described in the following terms:

'Where a statutory body having discretionary power is required to consider numerous applications there is no objection to it announcing that it proposes to follow a certain general policy in examining such applications. Indeed, in certain circumstances it may be desirable to achieve a degree of consistency in dealing with applications of similar character. Moreover, there is nothing wrong with policies being made public so that applicants may know what to expect. However, such a declared policy may be objectionable if certain conditions are not fulfilled. A policy must be based on grounds which relate to and are not inconsistent with or destructive of the purposes of the statutory provisions under which the discretion is operated. Moreover, the policy must not be so rigidly formulated so that, if applied, the statutory body is thereby disabled from exercising the discretion entrusted to it. Finally, the individual circumstances of each application must be considered in each case whatever the policy may be. It is not permissible for a body exercising a statutory discretion to refuse to apply its mind to that application on account of an apparent conflict with policy.'[1]

[1] Lord Weir in *Elder v Ross and Cromarty District Licensing Board* 1990 SLT 307 at 311. See also *Inverness, Loch Ness and Nairn Tourist Board v Highland Regional Council* 1988 GWD 6–219; *Texaco Ltd v North Lanarkshire Licensing Board* 1998 SC 408; *Texaco Ltd v West Fife Licensing Board* 1998 SC 470; *Abadoa v Home Secretary* 1998 SC 504; *Ahmed v North Lanarkshire Council* 1999 SCLR 585; *Westerhall Farms v Scottish Ministers* (25 April 2001, unreported). Cf *Potter v Scottish Ministers* 2010 SLT 779.

22.64 In *Gerry Cottle's Circus Ltd v City of Edinburgh District Council*,[1] the Council's refusal of an entertainment licence was reduced because its sole reason for the refusal was to uphold its policy against performing animals, an improper policy in the light of the Council's other statutory licensing powers. In *La Belle Angele v City of Edinburgh Licensing Board*[2] it was held that instances of illegal flyposting could not be viewed as a public nuisance and were, therefore, not a relevant consideration in relation to an application for extended permitted hours for licensed premises. The question of the relevance of availability of resources to the obligation to discharge statutory functions has been raised in *MacGregor v South Lanarkshire Council*[3] (held irrelevant) and the resources of an applicant for residential accommodation *Robertson v Fife Council*[4] (also held irrelevant). The special category of abuse of discretion based on breach of fiduciary duty to its ratepayers (and, by extension, those who pay poll tax or council tax) to a local authority received some recognition by the Court of Session.[5]

[1]   1990 SLT 235.
[2]   2001 SLT 801. See also *Cooper v Forth Ports plc* 2011 SLT 711.
[3]   2001 SLT 233.
[4]   2002 SC(HL) 145; 2002 SLT 951.
[5]   *Commission for Local Authority Accounts v Stirling District Council* 1984 SLT 442. But see Himsworth 'The Fiduciary Duties of Local Authorities in Scotland' 1982 SLT (News) 241 and 249.

Excess of jurisdiction

22.65 It will be observed that, up to this point in this section, there has been no difficulty in relating Scottish decisions to equivalent decisions in England and discussing both under the general umbrella of Lord Diplock's classification. However, one area of difference appeared, until recently, to have been maintained in the adherence by the Scottish courts to a distinction between those errors of law which took the decision-maker outside his jurisdiction and were thus reducible in review proceedings and those within the jurisdiction which were not.[1] Since *Watt v Lord Advocate*,[2] it was assumed that only misinterpretations of the law producing jurisdictional error were reviewable and, after *GCHQ*, the question was bound to arise as to whether Lord Diplock's 'illegality' should be similarly construed as relating to jurisdictional errors of law only. In contrast with the position reached in England,[3] the answer seemed to be that it should. In *O'Neill v Scottish Joint Negotiating Committee for Teaching Staff*[4] Lord Jauncey said:

> 'However, Lord Greene's dictum [that "a person entrusted with a discretion must, so to speak, direct himself properly in law"] must be read in the light of the principle that a tribunal or arbiter acting otherwise properly is entitled to reach a wrong decision in law. Thus Lord Greene's reference to a person directing himself properly in law does not mean that a person acting properly within his jurisdiction is not entitled to a mistake in applying general law. The mistake he must not make is in applying the law which determines his jurisdiction.
>
> Similarly when Lord Diplock in *CCSU v Minister for Civil Service* said that "the decision-maker must understand correctly the law that regulates his decision-making power and give effect to it",[5] he was not, as I understand it, departing from the principle stated at the beginning of this paragraph.

In *Watt v Lord Advocate*, the Lord President drew the sharp distinction between a decision-maker who misconstrued certain statutory provisions in the course of trying to answer the right question and one who misconstrued the question which he had to answer. It is to the latter situation and not to the former that I understand the dicta of Lord Greene and Lord Diplock to apply'.[6]

[1] A convergence by adoption of the English approach had, however, been advocated. See Lord Clyde and D J Edwards, *Judicial Review* (2000) paragraph 22–20 et seq.
[2] 1979 SC 120.
[3] See **6.7** et seq and **7.19** et seq above.
[4] 1987 SLT 648.
[5] At 410.
[6] At 651.

22.66 Lord Jauncey's determination that *Watt* survived *GCHQ* and that both *GCHQ* and *Wednesbury*, on the matter of distinguishing ultra vires and intra vires errors of law, had to be read subject to *Watt* was echoed in other cases.[1]

[1] See eg *Civil Aviation Authority v Argyll and Bute Valuation Appeal Committee* 1988 SLT 119; *Cooper v City of Edinburgh District Licensing Board* 1990 SLT 246; *Rae v Criminal Injuries Compensation Board* 1997 SLT 291. For fuller discussion, see the 'Judicial Review in Scotland' chapter in earlier editions of this book.

22.67 The specialised area of challenge to the decisions of adjudicators under the Housing Grants, Construction and Regeneration Act 1996 is also of interest. Broadly, similar principles were applied in Scotland, where cases generally arose as applications for judicial review, and in England, where they arise in actions to enforce the decisions of adjudicators. There the English courts appeared to have joined the Scottish courts in adopting a jurisdiction-based test: see, for example, *Bouygues (UK) Ltd v Dahl-Jensen (UK) Ltd*[1] But see also *Gillies Ramsay Diamond v PJW Enterprises Ltd*[2] in which the Lord Justice Clerk appeared to acknowledge the general relevance of post-*Anisminic* developments but insisted that, at least in respect of construction adjudicators which he classified as being not 'statutory decision-makers', only ultra vires errors were fatal to the decision.[3]

[1] [2001] 1 All ER (Comm) 1041.
[2] 2004 SC 430.
[3] See Lord Hope of Craighead, 'Arbitration' *SME (Reissue)*, and also *Lesotho Highlands Development Authority v Impreglio SpA* [2006] 1 AC 221 where the House of Lords held that the rules on error of law in judicial review were irrelevant to the challenge of decisions of arbitrators.

22.68 Whatever the continuing position in relation to arbitration and construction adjudication, however, the general law on error of law in judicial review in Scotland was suddenly changed by the intervention of Lord Hope in *Eba v Advocate General for Scotland*.[1] He simply declared, stressing that the substantive grounds of review were the same in the two jurisdictions, that the time had come for it to be declared that Lord Emslie's dictum in *Watt v Lord Advocate* was incompatible with what was decided in *Anisminic*.[2] The traditional distinction between *ultra vires* and *intra vires* errors was thereby abolished. Whether, however, the law has indeed become the same as in England may be in doubt because, instead of holding that all reviewable errors of law are ultra vires, Lord Hope appeared to retain a concept of reviewable non-jurisdictional error.[3]

1   2012 SC (UKSC) 1, 2011 SLT 768. On the principal contribution of the case to the review of the Upper Tribunal, see **22.47.**
2   Para 34.
3   See C Himsworth, 'Jurisdictional Aspects of Judicial Review in Scots Law' 2015 Jur Rev 353. See also *Ashley, Petitioner* [2016] CSOH 78.

Irrationality[1]

1   For the law of England and Wales on this topic, see CHAPTER 8. For challenge to Acts of the Scottish Parliament on grounds of irrationality, see *AXA General Insurance Ltd, Petitioners* 2012 SC (UKSC) 1, 2011 SLT 768 at **21.50.**

22.69 Lord Diplock's second ground of review – irrationality – was, he recognised, a recasting of the familiar *Wednesbury* unreasonableness in the form where the basis of invalidity of a decision is that it is so unreasonable that no reasonable body of the sort concerned would make it.[2] The test which requires to be satisfied has been described as an 'exacting one'.[3] It is concerned with the substance of the decision itself rather than simply the way it was made.[4] Recent Scottish cases have produced a number of examples of the attempted but unsuccessful use of this ground of challenge.[5] In *Shetland Line (1984) Ltd v Secretary of State for Scotland*[6] it was held that, although an irrational decision might also be categorised as 'unfair', unfairness as a separate ground of challenge was to be confined to procedural rather than substantive unfairness. Furthermore, although irrationality might well involve an error of fact, the error must relate to relevant facts available at the time of the decision and not be judged with benefit of hindsight.[7] In *McTear v Scottish Legal Aid Board*[8] it was observed that, if the Board had based a legal aid decision solely on cost, such a decision could be 'categorised as unreasonable in the *Wednesbury* sense'.[9]

2   *Council of Civil Service Unions v Minister for the Civil Service* [1985] AC 374 at 410.
3   *K v Scottish Legal Aid Board* 1989 SCLR 144 at 145. See also *AB v Scottish Legal Aid Board* 1991 SCLR 702 and *Donald v Marquetty* (13 November 1986, unreported).
4   See CHAPTER 8 above. Whilst the distinctions made between different categories of *Wednesbury* unreasonableness may be broadly relied on in Scotland, it is not clear how the statutory tests of 'unreasonableness' incorporated into eg the Licensing (Scotland) Act 1976, s 39 and the Civic Government (Scotland) Act 1982, Sch 1 are to be viewed. It is, however, clear that they are not to be read as confined to 'irrational' unreasonableness. See *Noble Organisation Ltd v City of Glasgow District Council (No 3)* 1991 SLT 213 at 217–218. Sometimes the language of irrationality and procedural unfairness does seem to overlap. See, eg *Ahmad v Home Secretary* 2001 SLT 282; *MacIntyre v Crofters Commission* 2001 SLT 929.
5   See, eg *McAlinden v Bearsden and Milngavie District Council* 1986 SLT 191; *Harvey v Strathclyde Regional Council* 1989 SLT 612; *Cooper v City of Edinburgh District Licensing Board* 1990 SLT 246 and 1991 SLT 47; *Kirkcaldy District Council v Fife Regional Council* 1987 GWD 29–1120; *McIntyre v Western Isles Islands Council* 1988 GWD 25–1075; *Re Miller Group* (28 December 1989, unreported); *Doran v Secretary of State for Scotland* 1990 GWD 26–1431; *Leech v Secretary of State for Scotland* 1992 SC 89, 1993 SLT 365; *Singh v Secretary of State for the Home Department* 1993 SC (HL) 1; *Banks v Scottish Legal Aid Board* 1996 GWD 17–1008; *K v Murphy* 1997 SLT 248; *Rae v Criminal Injuries Compensation Board* 1997 SLT 291; *Bonnes v West Lothian District Council* 1997 SLT 398; *City of Aberdeen Council v Local Government Boundary Commission for Scotland* 1998 SLT 613; *Blue Circle Industries plc v Scottish Ministers* 2002 SLT 894; *Eriden Properties LLP v Falkirk Council* 2007 SLT 966.
6   1996 SLT 653.
7   1996 SLT 653 at 658.

22.70 *Purdon v Glasgow District Licensing Board*[1] was one case in which Lord Diplock's test of irrationality (as the 'revised *Wednesbury* test') was explicitly applied, but again with the result that the Board's decision (to postpone consideration of a licensing application) should stand. The case is interesting for Lord Davidson's discussion of the inference to be drawn from the lack of reasons for the decision under challenge:

> 'In an application for judicial review the onus rests upon [the petitioner] to demonstrate that the decision challenged is irrational. In my opinion the absence of reasons can help an applicant only if on a consideration of the whole averments the court inclines to the conclusion that there is no material upon which a rational refusal could be based'.[2]

[1]   1988 SCLR 466.
[2]   1988 SCLR 466 at 469. See also *Mecca Leisure Ltd v City of Glasgow District Licensing Board* 1987 SLT 483.

22.71 In *Stewart v Monklands District Council*[1] Lord Clyde cautioned against viewing the decisions of an authority on a spectrum at the end of which was the decision which it was 'just conceivable' the authority could make, and beyond which lay the area of perversity or *Wednesbury* unreasonableness. 'It may be preferable', he said, 'to formulate the test in terms of whether the authority was entitled to reach its decision rather than concentrate on the case which lies at the extreme end of all possible cases which are within the area of entitlement'.[2] In some cases the challenge on grounds of unreasonableness has succeeded. Thus in *Kelly v Monklands District Council*,[3] Lord Ross was of the view that, following the *Wednesbury* principles,[4] the local authority's decision that two 16-year-old girls were not, in their particular circumstances, 'vulnerable' in terms of the then Housing (Homeless Persons) Act 1977 was a conclusion at which no reasonable authority could have arrived.[6]

[1]   1987 SLT 630.
[2]   1987 SLT 630 at 633.
[3]   1986 SLT 169.
[4]   As articulated also in *Wordie Property Co Ltd v Secretary of State for Scotland* 1984 SLT 345.
[6]   1986 SLT 169 at 171.

22.72 In the very different field of valuation for rating it has been interesting to see the decisions of two valuation appeal committees not to refer valuation appeals to the Lands Tribunal for Scotland struck down on grounds of *Wednesbury* unreasonableness and *GCHQ* irrationality.[1] In *James Aitken & Sons (Meat Producers) v City of Edinburgh District Council*[2] it was successfully argued that a purported grant of planning permission was invalid because it was made whilst an earlier application by the same applicants for permission to develop the same site was awaiting decision on appeal to the Secretary of State. No reasonable authority charged with the duties under the Planning Acts would have acted in this manner.[3] In *Woods v Secretary of State for Scotland*[4] it was held to be wholly irrational for the respondent to refuse to pay a student's university fees if the refusal were based on an alleged failure to meet an administrative deadline and an unwillingness to make an exception because that would be 'unjust to those whose similar cases have been rejected in the past'. In *La Belle Angele v City of Edinburgh Licensing Board*[5] it was held to be irrational for the board to have sought to distinguish the justification for a 2.00 am licensing extension (which it imposed) from a 3.00 am extension (sought by the applicant). In *Standard Commercial Property Services Ltd v Glasgow City Council*[6] it was held to be not irrational to choose a 'preferred developer' on the terms and conditions on which this was done.[7]

1   See *ICI plc v Central Region Valuation Appeal Committee* 1988 SLT 106 and *Civil Aviation Authority v Argyll and Bute Valuation Appeal Committee* 1988 SLT 119.
2   1990 SLT 241, 1989 SCLR 674.
3   See also *Trusthouse Forte (UK) Ltd v Perth and Kinross District Council* 1990 SLT 737, 1991 SCLR 1; *Bett Properties Ltd v Scottish Ministers* 2001 SLT 1131.
4   1991 SLT 197.
5   2001 SLT 801.
6   2007 SC (HL) 33, 2006 SLT 1152.
7   See also *Coyle v Auditor of the Court of Session* 2006 SLT 1045; *Glasgow City Council v Scottish Information Commissioner* [2009] CSIH 73.

Irrationality and delegated legislation[1]

1   For the inapplicability of the ground of irrationality to the review of Acts of the Scottish Parliament, see CHAPTER 21. For the UK Supreme Court's response to the non-making of regulations and its relationship to the non-making of commencement orders, see *M v Scottish Ministers* 2013 SC(UKSC) 139, 2013 SLT 57 and C Himsworth (2014) 18 Edin LR 109.

22.73 The debate in the English courts as to whether, and if so in what terms, the scope for challenge on grounds of irrationality should be narrowed in the case of statutory instruments and other measures which are open to scrutiny by one or both Houses of Parliament has been recorded elsewhere.[2] The same issue was raised in *Edinburgh City District Council v Secretary of State for Scotland*[3] before it reached the House of Lords in *Nottinghamshire County Council*.[4] The *Edinburgh District Council* case concerned a challenge to an order made by the Secretary of State restricting transfers from their then 'rate funds' of local housing authorities to their housing revenue accounts. The limits were imposed by statutory instrument subject to annulment by resolution of either House and it was the view of Lord Jauncey (upheld by the Second Division) that such an instrument could be struck down only in the case of a 'patent defect' in that it purported to do what was not authorised by the enabling statute or where the procedure followed in making the instrument departed from the requirements of the enabling statute[5] and not, therefore, on grounds of irrationality.[6] In the later case of *Sutherland District Council v Secretary of State for Scotland*,[7] decided after and incorporating reference to *Nottinghamshire County Council*, Lord Clyde noted the agreement with Lord Jauncey's opinion expressed by the Second Division in *City of Edinburgh* but observed that he did not find in their opinions so express or absolute a restriction on the grounds of review. There appears every reason to believe that, although the final outcome seems not yet certain, the courts in both jurisdictions are adopting a similar approach to the issue.[8] In *East Kilbride District Council v Secretary of State for Scotland*[9] Lord Penrose acknowledged the differences which had earlier emerged and that, although on one view 'manifest absurdity' could not be used as a ground for review in Scotland, it might nevertheless have a place in theoretical analysis. However, '[a]pplied objectively, a test of manifest absurdity must be expected to be satisfied only in the most extreme and extraordinary of circumstances, and wholly beyond the scope for differences in matters of judgment and opinion'.[10]

2   See Chapter 8.
3   1985 SLT 551.
4   *Nottinghamshire County Council v Secretary of State for the Environment* [1986] AC 240 discussed at [1986] PL 374.
5   Cf Lord Diplock in *Hoffmann-La Roche & Co AG v Secretary of State for Trade and Industry* [1975] AC 295 at 365.
6   For a fuller discussion of the case, see C M G Himsworth, 'Defining the Boundaries of Judicial Review' 1985 SLT (News) 369.
7   1988 GWD 4–167.
8   See *R v Secretary of State for the Environment, ex p Hammersmith and Fulham London Borough Council* [1990] 3 All ER 589 (discussed at [1991] PL 76; *Leech v Secretary of State for Scotland* 1991 SLT 910 (affirmed at 1992 SC 89, 1993 SLT 365).
9   1995 SLT 1238.
10   1995 SLT 1238 at 1247.

Disproportionality[1]

1   For the law of England and Wales on this topic, see Chapter 8 et seq.

22.74 It was in the Scottish case of *Somerville v Scottish Ministers*[2] that the House of Lords acknowledged the uncertain status of disproportionality as an independent ground of review (independent, that is, of the 'balancing' involved in human rights adjudication) but declined to produce an authoritative answer.[3] Disproportionality has, on the other hand, been introduced as a ground of appeal in sheriff appeals under the Licensing (Scotland) Act 2005.[4]

2   2008 SC (HL) 45; 2007 SLT 1113.
3   Ibid at paragraphs 53–56. See also, under reference to *R (Khatun) v Newham LBC* [2005] 1 QB 37 and *Pham v Home Secretary* [2012] 1 AC 621, *Gage v Scottish Ministers* 2016 SLT 424.
4   Section 131(3). See C Himsworth, 'Licensing and Disproportionality' 2009 Jud Rev 289.

Procedural impropriety

22.75 The emergence and development of the principles of natural justice and their broadening into principles of fairness as a ground for challenge in judicial review proceedings in England and Wales have already been fully described.[1] Lord Diplock's third head of 'procedural impropriety' takes account of the broadening of the scope and application of these principles, together with those situations in which procedural requirements expressly laid down by statute have been breached. Whilst the general assumptions of parallel development of the law north and south of the border hold good in this area, there was, until quite recently, one aspect of apparent divergence. As earlier noted,[2] however, Lord Hope in *Porter v Magill*[3] adjusted the earlier English test for bias in *R v Gough*[4] to produce a test which he believed to apply equally in both jurisdictions:[5] 'The question is whether the fair-minded and informed observer, having consulted the facts would conclude that there was a real possibility that the tribunal was biased'.[6] The test was adopted by the First Division in *Singh v Home Secretary*[7] and *Secretary of State for Work and Pensions v Gillies*[8] and by the House of Lords in *Davidson v Scottish Ministers*

(No 2).[9] In *Helow v AG for Scotland*[10] the House of Lords held that there was no reason for a fair-minded observer to conclude that there was a real possibility of unconscious influence arising from a judge's membership of an organistion, some of whose members sometimes expressed extreme views.[11] In *Congregation of the Poor Sisters of Nazareth v Scottish Ministers*[12] it was held that, where an advocate was to be appointed as chair of an inquiry into historical child abuse, there was no apparent bias deriving from her prior involvement in a damages case.

[1] See CHAPTERS 10, 11 and 12. For a full Scottish account, see *Bradley and Himsworth*, paragraphs 52–92.

[2] See 22.5.

[3] [2002] 2 AC 357 at paragraph 103.

[4] [1993] AC 646.

[5] For recent Scottish cases, see eg *Bradford v McLeod* 1986 SLT 244; *London and Clydesdale Estates Ltd v Secretary of State for Scotland* 1987 SLT 495; *Samuel Smith Old Brewery (Tadcaster) v City of Edinburgh Council* 2001 SLT 977; *Rimmer, Petitionerr* 2002 SCCR 126; *Robson v Law Society of Scotland* 2005 SC 125; *William Hill Organisation Ltd v City of Glasgow LB* 2005 SC 102.

[6] See also *Lawal v Northern Spirit Ltd* [2004] 1 All ER 187.

[7] 24 December 2003, unreported.

[8] 2004 SLT 14 at 20–21. See also 2006 SC(HL) 71; 2006 SLT 77.

[9] 2005 1 SC(HL) 7, [2004] SLT 895. See also *Pentland-Clark, Petitioner* 2011 SLT 795.

[10] 2009 SC(HL)1, 2008 SLT 967.

[11] See also *O'Neill v HM Advocate (Scotland)* 2013 SC (UKSC) 266, 2013 SLT 888.

[12] 2015 SLT 445.

22.76 Important 'fair hearing' cases[1] include *Errington v Wilson*,[2] a successful challenge sustained in the Inner House against a decision of a justice of the peace under the Food Safety Act 1990. In the circumstances, the refusal to allow cross-examination of expert witnesses was a breach of the rules of natural justice. It was not necessary to aver prejudice. In *Young v Criminal Injuries Compensation Board*,[3] relief was denied on the grounds that natural justice did not require, in the context of the scheme under review, a right to an oral hearing. There was a distinction between 'a right to a hearing and a right to be heard'.[4] In *Rape Crisis Centre v Home Secretary*,[5] a case decided principally on title and interest,[6] it was held that the petitioners had no right to be heard prior to the Home Secretary's decision to admit the boxer Frank Tyson to the country. In *M v Advocate General for Scotland*,[7] in a review of a First-tier Tribunal, the case 'almost cried out for an oral hearing'.

[1] Others include *Murphy v General Teaching Council for Scotland* 1997 SC 172; *Stewart v Secretary of State for Scotland* 1998 SLT 385 (HL); *City of Glasgow District Council v Secretary of State for Scotland* 1998 SLT 283; *Hardie v City of Edinburgh Council* 2003 SLT 1112; *Irvine v Royal Burgess Golfing Society of Edinburgh* (27 February 2004, unreported).

[2] 1995 SLT 1193.

[3] 1997 SLT 297.

[4] 1997 SLT 297 at 301. See also *Craig v Parole Board for Scotland* 2013 SLT 953.

[5] 2000 SC 527, 2001 SLT 389.

[6] See 22.49.

[7] 2014 SLT 475, para 23.

22.77 In situations in which reasons for decisions are required, the quality of those reasons has been assessed against the test that there be no 'real and substantial doubt' as to what they are.[1] Reasons must be readily understood and readily related to the matters which the decision-maker is required to consider.[2] Particular care to give specific attention to the material facts and the conclusions drawn from them was required where an appellate body reached a decision different from the original decision-maker. It was not sufficient merely to paraphrase the appropriate regulations.[3] There has been some discussion of the circumstances in which, despite the absence of a statutory requirement to state reasons for a decision, reasons may nevertheless be required.[4] In *Lawrie v Commission for Local Authority Accounts*,[5] however, it was held not to be necessary for the Commission to state reasons for its findings. It was not a 'fully judicial body' nor was there any real uncertainty as to the issue to which the Commission had addressed its mind nor as to the basis of fact for its conclusions.[6] In circumstances where reasons were given there was no need to give them, they could be subject to scrutiny but, provided the reasons did not disclose that the decision was flawed, the decision-maker did not render his decision liable to be set aside by giving reasons which did not adequately explain his decision.[7] In *Scottish Ministers v Scottish Information Commissioner*[8] it was held, in an appeal against decisions of the Commissioner requiring the Scottish Ministers to release documents that a general duty to provide adequate reasons for a decision was tempered by a need to avoid the improper disclosure of information.

[1] *Wordie Property Co Ltd v Secretary of State for Scotland* 1984 SLT 345. See also MacLeod v Banff and Buchan District Housing Benefit Review Board 1988 SLT 753; K v Secretary of State for the Home Department 1988 GWD 13–572; Akram, Petitioner 1989 GWD 39–1816; Ian Monachan Central Ltd, Petitioners 1991 SLT 494; Mensah v Home Secretary 1992 SLT 177; Brechin Golf and Squash Club v Angus District Licensing Board 1993 SLT 547; Malcolm v Tweeddale District Housing Benefit Review Board 1994 SLT 1212; Young v Criminal Injuries Compensation Board 1997 SLT 297; Singh v Home Secretary 1998 SLT 1370; Perth and Kinross Council v Secretary of State for Scotland 1999 SC 144; Gallacher v Stirling Council 2001 SLT 94; Buchan v West Lothian Council 2001 SLT 1452; Amara, Petitioner (11 Jan 2002, unreported); Adams v South Lanarkshire Council 2003 SLT 145; Di Ciacca v Scottish Ministers 2003 SLT 1031; Glasgow City Council, Petitioners 2004 SLT 61; Campbell, Petitioner 2009 231; Kelly v Shetland HB 2009 SC 248; J R Buzzworks Leisure Ltd v South Ayrshire Licensing Board 2012 SLT 442.

[2] *Deane v Lothian Regional Council* 1986 SLT 22. In *Chief Constable, Lothians and Borders Police v Lothian and Borders Police Board* 2005 SLT 315, the failure to provide statutorily required reasons should result in the quashing of the decision, producing the need for a rehearing of the issue with a freshly constituted tribunal.

[3] *Safeway Stores plc v National Appeal Panel* 1996 SC 37, 1996 SLT 235.

[4] For discussion of the law of England and Wales on this issue, and on the adequacy of reasons, see CHAPTERS 8, 9 and 11.

[5] 1993 SLT 1185.

[6] 1993 SLT 1185 at 1192. See also *JAE (Glasgow) Ltd v City of Glasgow District Licensing Board* 1994 SC 290; Bass Taverns Ltd v Clydebank District Licensing Board 1995 SLT 1275; Dundee United Football Co Ltd v Scottish Football Association 1998 SLT 1244 (Note). See, too, Munro. 'The Duty to give Reasons for Decisions' 1995 SLT (News) 5.

[7] *Gallacher v Stirling Council* 2001 SLT 94.

[8] 2007 SLT 274.

22.78 In *Ryrie (Blingery) Wick v Secretary of State for Scotland*,[1] the Secretary of State's decision to revoke the petitioners' grant under the Agriculture and Horticulture Grant Scheme 1980 was reduced on the grounds that he had failed to supply to the petitioners, in accordance with the Agriculture Act 1970, a copy of the report on which the revocation was based. Drawing in part on *London and Clydeside Estates Ltd v Aberdeen District Council*[2] Lord Cullen relied (perhaps more heavily than did the speeches and especially that of Lord Hailsham in *London and Clydeside*) upon the distinction between 'mandatory' and 'directory' procedural requirements to hold the Secretary of State's error to be in breach of a mandatory requirement and, therefore, fatal to the decision.[3] In *Abbas v Home Secretary*[4] it was held not to be improper for the respondent to deny legal representation before the extra-statutory advisory panel established to hear representations from persons aggrieved by his decision to deport them in the interests of national security under the Immigration Act 1971. In *Glasgow City Council v Scottish Information Commissioner*[5] it was held that the withholding by the Commissioner of information about his investigations was unfair.

[1] 1988 SLT 806. See, also, *Coakley v Secretary of State for Transport* 2004 SC 398.
[2] [1979] 3 All ER 876, 1980 SC (HL) 1.
[3] For another important decision by Lord Cullen (in relation to consultation on a planning application), see *Lochore v Moray District Council* 1991 SCLR 741. Cf *Chalmers v Peterhead Harbour Trustees* 1989 GWD 16–707; *Winter v Walker* 1989 GWD 33–1531; *Johnstone v Secretary of State for Scotland* 1990 GWD 30–1711; See also *Monklands District Independent Taxi Owners Association v Monklands District Council (No 2)* 1997 SLT 7 at 9.
[4] 1993 SLT 502.
[5] 2010 SLT 9.

Legitimate expectation

22.79 The development of the concept of the legitimate or reasonable expectation in English jurisprudence has already been traced.[1] It is a concept fraught with ambiguity – especially as to whether or not both substantive[2] and procedural expectations are embraced and also as to its employment in aid of *locus standi* as well as in aid of a ground of review. Whilst reference to legitimate expectations is included at this point, the use of the concept in the Court of Session has retained much of this ambiguity. The tests enunciated by Lord Fraser and Lord Diplock in *GCHQ*[3] were deployed by Lord Allanbridge in *Connor v Strathclyde Regional Council*[4] where the petitioner was held to enjoy the 'legitimate expectation' of appearance before a selection board although, fatally for the petition, not a board which would act in accordance with the rules of natural justice.[5] In *Strathkelvin District Council v Secretary of State for the Environment*[6] the petitioner authority made no headway in seeking to establish that an undertaking made on behalf of the Secretary of State for the Environment to consult with planning authorities prior to the disposal of Crown Land created a 'legitimate expectation' of consultation prior to a particular disposal. In so holding, Lord Jauncey was relying upon the need, on his interpretation of Lord Diplock in *GCHQ*, to establish not only the express or implied right to a hearing or consultation but also the existence of a relevant 'benefit or advantage'. The District Council could not claim a 'benefit or advantage' equivalent to the benefits of trade union membership, as claimed in *GCHQ*.[7]

[1] See **7.64** et seq and CHAPTERS 8, 9 and 11.
[2] On which, see the (pre-Coughlan) case of *McPhee v North Lanarkshire Council* 1998 SLT 1317.
[3] *Council of Civil Service Unions v Minister for the Civil Service* [1985] AC 374 at 401 and 408–409.
[4] 1986 SLT 530.
[5] See **22.21**.
[6] 1987 GWD 9–258.

⁷ See too *Inverness, Loch Ness and Nairn Tourist Board v Highland Regional Council* 1988 GWD 6–219; *Kincardine and Deeside District Council v Forestry Comrs* 1991 SCLR 729, 1992 SLT 1180.

22.80 Probably the most serious, and successful, application of the concept of 'legitimate expectation' in combination with other aspects of procedural fairness came in *Lakin Ltd v Secretary of State for Scotland*.[1] The Second Division conducted a substantial survey of the grounds of judicial review and especially those proposed by Lord Diplock in *GCHQ*, the acceptance of his classification as a part of the law of Scotland in *Edinburgh City District Council*:[2] the distinctions to be drawn between (substantially) fair decisions and decisions made (procedurally) fairly; and the relationship between procedural unfairness and the abuse of power deriving from a failure to make a decision on the basis of relevant considerations or a proper purpose.[3] In argument, it was contended that the Secretary of State's failure to call in a major planning application on one site (the superstore site recognised as the alternative to a second in respect of which the petitioner's own application had been refused) was in breach of a legitimate expectation to a hearing on appeal which should not be made meaningless by the prior grant of permission on the first site. This argument was accepted by the court and the Secretary of State's decision was reduced on the grounds of procedural impropriety or unfairness.[4] In a later case, *Lakin* was distinguished to deny that a district council which, as planning authority, had promised not to allow development on one part of a site without considering the effect on development of the other, was acting in breach of the 'legitimate expectation' of the petitioner to that effect.[5] In *Fayed v Commissioners of Inland Revenue*[6] it was held that there could be no legitimate expectation in respect of the implementation of a 'forward tax agreement' subsequently held to be unlawful.[7]

¹ 1988 SLT 780. For a subsequent inter-superstore dispute see *Asda Stores Ltd v Secretary of State for Scotland* 1999 SLT 503. See also *Bett Properties Ltd v Scottish Ministers* 2001 SC 238.
² *Edinburgh City District Council v Secretary of State for Scotland* 1985 SLT 551.
³ 1988 SLT 780 at 787–788, Lord Ross.
⁴ 1988 SLT 780; see, especially, Lord Ross at 790–93. Cf *Pickering v Kyle and Carrick District Council* 1991 GWD 7–361.
⁵ *Re Miller Group Ltd* (28 December 1989, unreported).
⁶ 2004 SLT 798.
⁷ See **22.60**. Other recent cases in which breach of a legitimate expectation has been argued have included *Clyde Solway Consortium v Scottish Ministers* 2001 SLT 1455; *Danskin v Council of the Law Society of Scotland* 2002 SLT 900; *Devine v McPherson* 2002 SLT 213; *Ibrahim v Home Secretary* 2002 SLT 1150; *Shetland Islands Council v Lerwick Ports Authority* [2007] CSOH 5 (which contains a substantial review of the authorities by Lord Reed), *Fargie, Petitioner* 2008 SLT 949; *Kerr of Ardgowan v Lord Lyon* 2009 SLT 759; *Archid Architecture and Interior Design v Dundee City Council* 2014 SLT 81; *M v Home Secretary* 2014 SLT 649.

Incompatibility with Convention rights

22.81 The impact of the implementation of the Human Rights Act 1998 (HRA 1998) on judicial review and, in particular, the creation by s 6 of the Act of what is in effect a new ground of review have been considered extensively in CHAPTER 4. The general effect of the HRA 1998 may be assumed to be broadly the same in Scotland as in England and Wales and the content of CHAPTER 4 may, therefore, be treated as authoritative in Scotland, in the same way as other chapters on the grounds of review. There are, however, certain differences, most but not all of which derive from the application of the Scotland Act 1998.[1] The general requirement for public authorities to act compatibly with Convention rights under the HRA 1998 with effect from 2 October 2000 was introduced as a requirement imposed on the Scottish Government and the Scottish Parliament from prescribed dates in 1999, producing a temporary divergence between the two jurisdictions.[2] On a continuing basis, however, the requirements of the two Acts have now to be read in parallel, with the effect, in particular, that human rights cases in relation to the Government and the Parliament must be treated procedurally as 'devolution issues' (whether in relation to civil or criminal matters) under the Scotland Act, with ultimate recourse to the UK Supreme Court.[3] The effect of s 57(2) of the Scotland Act 1998 which provides that a member of the Scottish Government 'has no power to make any subordinate legislation, or to do any other act' which is incompatible with Convention rights has been interpreted as imposing a stronger obligation than the HRA 1998 operating alone to comply with art 6 of the European Convention on Human Rights (ECHR) requirements to avoid delay in criminal trials.[4] In relation to matters within the competence of the Scottish Parliament, the opportunity to make remedial orders under the HRA 1998 falls to the Scottish Ministers. Unrelated to the Scotland Act, is the different relationship in Scotland between the HRA restriction to 'public authorities' and the scope of judicial review. The meaning of 'public authority' itself may be assumed to be the same in both jurisdictions.[5] The fact that the supervisory jurisdiction of the Court of Session is not confined to public bodies produces a situation in which judicial review is more readily available against respondents which are *not* also embraced by the 'public authority' test of the HRA 1998.[6] On substantive human rights, Scottish judicial review cases have ranged widely to include cases on arts 2[7], 3,[8] 5,[9] 6,[10] 8[11], 14[12] of the ECHR and First Protocol, art 1,[13] First Protocol, art 2,[14] First Protocol, art 3.[15] On the question of 'anxious scrutiny' by the court in cases involving Convention rights, as discussed in *ZT (Kosovo) v Home Secretary*,[16] see *S v Home Secretary*.[17]

---

[1]   See CHAPTER 21.

[2]   The principle that the HRA 1998 can have no retrospective effect (*R v DPP, ex p Kebeline* [2000] 2 AC 326) has been accepted in Scotland (see eg *Al Fayed v Advocate General for Scotland* 2004 SLT 798 paragraph 121). In *Singh v Home Secretary* 2004 SC 416, 2004 SLT 1058, a rather different point of timing was taken where the act challenged took place on 21 November 1997 and the case turned on the issue of apparent bias. The respondent argued successfully that this should be determined by the standards of the time but failed to persuade the First Division that those standards would be any lower than the standards as subsequently influenced by the incorporation of the Convention. See also *Varey v Scottish Ministers* 2000 SLT 1432.

[3]   Section 98 and Sch 6. But, for the non-application of the HRA's 12-month time bar to devolution issues, (see *Somerville v Scottish Ministers* 2008 SC(HL) 45, 2007 SLT 1113. See CHAPTER 21.

[4]   See cases cited at **22.3** above.

[5]   *L v Birmingham City Council* [2008] 1 AC 95. But see also the Health and Social Care Act 2008, s 145.

[6]   Cf the English (adjudication) case of *Austin Hall Building Ltd v Buckland Securities Ltd* [2001] BLR 272.

[7]   *Niven v Lord Advocate* 2009 SLT 876; *Ems, Petitioner* 2011 SC 433, 2011 SLT 354.

[8]   *Napier v Scottish Ministers* 2005 SC 229; *Dundee City Council v GK* 2006 SC 326; *DJS v Criminal Injuries Compensation Appeal Panel* 2007 SC 748; *M v State Hospitals Board for Scotland* 2015 SC 112, 2014 SLT 905; *Johnstone v Scottish Ministers* 2015 SLT 743.

9   *Dutch v Parole Board for Scotland* 2014 SLT 285; *Duncan v Scottish Ministers* 2014 SLT 531; *Brown v Parole Board for Scotland* 2015 SLT 568; *AG v Scottish Ministers* [2017] CSOH 10; *Ansari v Aberdeen City Council* [2017] CSIH 5.

10 *Singh v Home Secretary* 2004 SC 416, 2004 SLT 1058; *Tehrani v UK Central Council for Nursing, Midwifery and Health Visiting* 2001 SLT 879; *County Properties Ltd v Scottish Ministers* 2002 SC 79; *Lafarge Redland Aggregates Ltd v Scottish Ministers* 2001 SC 298; *Samuel Smith Old Brewery (Tadcaster) v City of Edinburgh Council* 2001 SLT 977; *Harris v Appeal Committee of the Institute of Chartered Accountants of Scotland* 2005 SLT 487; *Martin v Greater Glasgow Primary Care NHS Trust* 2009 SC 417. There have, in addition, been many challenges in Scottish criminal cases, based on the role of the Lord Advocate. See, in particular, *Starrs v Ruxton* 2000 JC 208 and *R v HMA* 2003 SC (PC) 21.

11 *Wright v Scottish Ministers* 2005 SC 453; *Potter v Scottish Ministers* 2007 SLT 1019; *Potter v Scottish Ministers* 2010 SLT 779; *Greens*, Petitioner2011 SLT 549; *J v Lord Advocate* 2013 SLT 347; *M v State Hospital Board for Scotland* 2014 SLT 905; *Beggs v Scottish Ministers* [2016] CSOH 153.

12 *Hunter v Student Awards Agency for Scotland* 2016 SLT 653.

13 *Adams v South Lanarkshire Council* 2003 SLT 145; *Di Ciacca v Scottish Ministers* 2003 SLT 1031; *Al Fayed v Advocate General for Scotland* 2004 SLT 798; *McCall v Scottish Ministers* 2006 SC 266, 2006 SLT 365.

14 *Dove v Scottish Ministers* 2002 SLT 1296.

15 *Smith v Scott* 2007 SC 345; *XY v Scottish Ministers* 2007 SC 631; *Moohan*, Petitioner 2015 SC (UKSC) 1, 2015 SLT 2; *Ross v Lord Advocate* 2015 SLT 617; *O'Neill v Scottish Ministers (No 1)* 2015 SLT 811; *O'Neill v Scottish Ministers (No 2)* 2015 SLT 820; *Johnstone v Scottish Ministers* 2015 SLT 743; *Beggs v Scottish Ministers* 2015 SLT 487.

16 [2009] 3 All ER 970.

17 2015 SLT 651.

REMEDIES IN JUDICIAL REVIEW[1]

1   The validity of acts and decisions subject to review under the supervisory jurisdiction may also be challenged as a defence in criminal proceedings (see eg *MacGillivray v Johnston (No 2)* 1994 SLT 1012) and *ope exceptionis* in civil proceedings (see, especially, *Vaughan Engineering Ltd v Hinkins & Frewin Ltd* 2003 SLT 428). See **22.40**.

22.82 It was the view of the Dunpark working party that, for the new judicial review procedure to be effective, 'the judge must have the power to grant any decree or make any order which he considers necessary or reasonable in the interests of justice'. 'We think it important', they continued: 'that every possible remedy should be made available in this process so that no ancillary litigation should be necessary'.[2] They were, in particular, concerned to ensure that remedies, not previously appropriate in petition proceedings (such as damages and restitution) should be available[3] and it has already been noted that a very broad formula was adopted in the new rule.[4] In part, no doubt, because of these steps taken to ensure flexibility in the availability of remedies (and also because only a small proportion of petitions have been granted), there appears to have been only limited debate in cases since 1985 about the proper scope of remedies and their use.[5]

2   Dunpark Report (see **22.7** above).

3   Dunpark Report at p 10.

4   It should also be noted that the list of remedies specified does not purport to be comprehensive. For fuller discussion of remedies, see *Bradley and Himsworth*, paragraphs 117–152. For the separate recourse to the *nobile officium* of the Court of Session, see paragraph 34 (and para **22.42** above). Remedies available on judicial review under the law of England and Wales are discussed in CHAPTERS **16** and **17**.

22.83 It has been declared that the rule of court 'provides no remedy or relief which did not already exist'.[1] Whilst the rule gives the court 'a discretion in the selection of the remedy so that the matter does not wholly depend upon the particular remedies sought in the petition',[2] the court 'should not compel a petitioner to accept a remedy not sought and not desired by him or her'.[3] Whatever the discretion generally available to the court in the choice of remedy to be awarded, it has been powerfully denied that, in a case where a petitioner's rights have been held to have been infringed, the grant of a remedy should be treated as discretionary and refused, for instance, on the grounds of great inconvenience or pecuniary loss to somebody else.[4] On the other hand, reduction of a decision has been refused in circumstances where a decision was made in error of law but, although therefore reached by the wrong route and for the wrong reasons, was in fact the correct result.[5] It has also been held that the court has an inherent jurisdiction to refuse to grant decree of reduction where no practical result would be achieved.[6] One example of the flexible availability of remedies is the competency, where appropriate, of the award of a bare declarator in judicial review proceedings.[7] Once made, an order may, if necessary, be enforced in further proceedings. For a refusal of such enforcement, however, on the grounds that the respondent has since justified its original decision on an alternative statutory basis see *McKeller v Aberdeen City Council (No 2)*.[8]

1   *O'Neill v Scottish Joint Negotiating Committee for Teaching Staff* 1987 SCLR 275 at 277.
2   *Sutherland District Council v Secretary of State for Scotland* 1988 GWD 4–167.
3   *Mecca Leisure Ltd v City of Glasgow District Council* 1987 SCLR 26 at 32.
4   *Hanlon v Traffic Commissioners* 1988 SLT 802 at 806, following *Bank of Scotland v Stewart* (1891) 18 R 957; cf *Kincardine and Deeside District Council v Forestry Commissioners* 1991 SCLR 729. See also *Samuel Smith Old Brewery (Tadcaster) v City of Edinburgh Council* 2001 SLT 977 where reliance seems to have been placed upon English authorities (at paragraph 24)).
5   *Andrew v City of Glasgow District Council* 1996 SLT 814. See also *Dillon v Secretary of State for the Home Department* 1997 SLT 842.
6   *King v East Ayrshire Council* 1998 SC 182 at 194. See also *Walker v City of Aberdeen Council* 1998 SLT 427; *Uprichard v Fife Council* 2000 SCLR 949; *Samuel Smith Old Brewery (Tadcaster) v City of Edinburgh Council (No 2)* 2001 SLT 977.
7   *Ross v Lord Advocate* 1986 SLT 602; *Sutherland District Council v Secretary of State for Scotland* 1988 GWD 4–167; *Magnohard Ltd v UK Atomic Energy Authority* 2004 SC 247, 2003 SLT 1083. For a full treatment of the declarator, see Lord Clyde. 'The Action of Declarator in Scotland' in I Zamir and Lord Woolf, The Declaratory Judgment (2nd edn. 1993).
8   2005 1 SC 186, 2005 SLT 95.

22.84 The issue which has perhaps attracted most difficulty has been in those cases where the court has had to devise the most appropriate form of positive order where this is required. An example of this is where, to accompany the reduction of a decision of a licensing board, it has been held appropriate to order the board to meet again to reconsider the petitioner's application.[1] In *McDonnell, Petitioner*[2] reduction was granted but no additional order, on an undertaking by the respondent board to hold a further hearing. In a hearing of a petition to reduce two decisions by a local authority to refuse repairs grants, it was agreed that, if reduction had been granted it would have been appropriate to issue a further order ordaining the respondents to approve the applications.[3] Whilst in *Lakin v Secretary of State for Scotland*,[4] the minister was ordered to call in a planning application,[5] that case was distinguished in a later case where it was held that it would be inappropriate to order a regional council to call in an application, especially where the call-in might be taken on appeal to the Secretary of State – producing the 'constitutional novelty' of the minister's hearing, in effect, an appeal from the court's decision.[6] Care was taken in *Wood v Dumbarton District Council*[7] to order specific performance of a duty to supply information to a community charges registration officer in terms which allowed reasonable time, which were no wider than the terms of the requirement originally imposed on the respondents and which did not relate to duties which were not yet incumbent upon them.[8] Doubt has been expressed about the competence of the use of an interdict to secure positive action.[9]

1   See *Bury v Kilmarnock and Loudon District Licensing Board* 1989 SLT 110; *Centralbite v Kincardine and Deeside District Licensing Board* 1990 SLT 231; *Bantop Ltd v City of Glasgow District Licensing Board* 1990 SLT 366. See also *Mecca Leisure Ltd v City of Glasgow District Council* 1987 SCLR 26.
2   1987 SLT 486.
3   *Milner v City of Glasgow District Council* 1990 SLT 361 but see also *Wincentzen v Monklands District Council* 1988 SLT 259 (orders to follow reduction of homelessness decision); *CRS Leisure Ltd v Dumbarton District Licensing Board* 1989 SCLR 566 (consideration of consequences of reduction of one decision for validity and effect of another). In *North Rotunda Casino Ltd v Glasgow City Licensing Board* 2002 SLT 974, it was considered that where a qualified approval of a licence was held to be ultra vires and unlawful it would not be right for the court, at its own hand, to substitute an unqualified approval. It should remit to the licensing board.
4   1988 SLT 780.
5   See **22.80**.
6   *Miller Group, Petitioners* (28 December 1989, unreported).
7   1991 SLT 586.
8   Cf *Walker v Strathclyde Regional Council* 1986 SLT 523.
9   *Edinburgh Property Management Association v City of Edinburgh District Council* 1987 GWD 38–1348 following *Grosvenor Developments (Scotland) plc v Argyll Stores Ltd* 1987 SLT 738. For the wider implications of that case, see N R Whitty, 'Positive and Negative Interdicts' 1990 JLSS 453 and 510.

22.85 An area of divergence between England and Scotland appeared to be opening up in relation to remedies against the Crown. The *Factortame* case[1] now serves to ensure that contrary to the provisions of the Crown Proceedings Act 1947[2] which purport to prevent interdicts against the Crown, such interdicts must be made available when necessary to enforce a Community right. For England, *M v Home Office*[3] probably expanded the scope of *Factortame* to cover non-EU matters, but in Scotland, that approach had been rejected and the applicability of the Crown Proceedings Act reaffirmed.[4] In *Davidson v Scottish Ministers*,[5] however, the House of Lords held that, in what Lord Hope called 'public law proceedings',[6] interdict and other coercive remedies were competent. In the meantime, it has been observed that, in immigration cases, the competency of granting interim liberation against the Crown has never been challenged.[7] Cases involving challenge to the decisions of immigration appeal tribunals have raised questions about what would be an appropriate order in the event of success. The decision of the tribunal would be reduced but, even if defective, not that of the adjudicator.[8] A deportation order made in consequence of the tribunal's decision may, however, appropriately be reduced.[9] The award of damages following upon successful applications for judicial review appears not to have occurred at all often.[10] Separately it may be noted that general recognition of the application of the *Carltona* principle to acts of the Scottish Ministers was given by the House of Lords in *Beggs v Scottish Ministers*.[11]

1   *R v Secretary of State for Transport, ex p Factortame Ltd (No 2)* [1991] 1 AC 603. See **14.6** et seq.

2   For Scotland, ss 21 and 43.

3   [1994] 1 AC 377. See Chapter **14**.

4   See *McDonald v Secretary of State for Scotland* 1994 SLT 692; *Davidson v Scottish Ministers (No 1) (also known as Scott v Scottish Ministers)* 2002 SCLR 166; *Davidson v Scottish Ministers (No 2)* 2001 SC 205, 2003 SC 103, 2002 SLT 1231; *McKenzie v Scottish Ministers (No 2)* 2004 SLT 1236. But see also *Millar & Bryce Ltd v Keeper of the Registers of Scotland* 1997 SLT 1000.

5   2006 SC (HL) 41, 2006 SLT 110. For comment, see C Himsworth, (2006) 10 Ed LR 282.

6   Ibid., at paragraph 53.

7   *Duncan v Scottish Ministers* (20 July 2004, unreported).

8   *Akram v Immigration Appeal Tribunal* 1990 SC 1, following Singh v Immigration Appeal Tribunal [1986] 2 All ER 721, [1986] 1 WLR 910.

9   As in K v Secretary of State for the Home Department 1988 GWD 13–572.

10   But see *Kelly v Monklands District Council* 1986 SLT 169; *Mallon v Monklands District Council* 1986 SLT 347 and B v Forsey 1988 SLT 572. See too Anderson v Scottish Information Commissioner [2010] CSIH 15; *M v State Hospitals Board for Scotland* 2013 SLT 1001 in which, although a ban on smoking was held to be an infringement of ECHR Arts 8 and 14, damages were refused because, in an application to challenge a smoking ban, the petitioner had gained significant health and financial benefits by not smoking. (But see also *M v State Hospitals Board for Scotland* 2015 SC 112, 2014 SLT 905 where the Outer House decision was reversed but the finding of no entitlement to damages was upheld).

11   2007 SLT 235.

PROCEDURE[1]

1   For procedure under the law of England and Wales, see Chapters **19** and **20**, and **21.71** et seq.

General

22.86 Reference has already been made[2] to the procedural changes recommended by the Gill Review of 2009 and to the enactment of the Courts Reform (Scotland) Act 2014. Most important has been the introduction of new rules on standing, a time limit for the commencement of proceedings and a new permission stage in applications for judicial review. When the time came for the implementation of these changes by amendment of the Rules of Court, the opportunity was taken for a complete revision of Chapter 58 (Judicial Review), effected by Act of Sederunt (Rules of the Court of Session 1994 Amendment) (No 3) (Courts Reform (Scotland) Act 2014) 2015.[3] Practice Note No 5 of 2015 was issued to take effect from the same date. A summary of the principal features of the new rules (incorporating reference to the new ss 27A, 27B, 27C and 27D of the Court of Session act 1988, as inserted by s 89 of the 2014 Act) follows.

2   See **22.6**. For the (Gill) Scottish Civil Courts Review, a consequence of the introduction of a leave stage in the Court of Session (see **22.10** above for that recommendation) would be increased opportunities for judicial case management (paragraph 58).

3   SSI 2015/228.

The Petition

22.87 An application to the supervisory jurisdiction of the Court of Session must be made by petition for judicial review[1]. A petition may not be externally imposed,lodged in respect of an application which case the precise date of the could be made by appeal or review under or by virtue of any enactment.[2] An application must be made (for these purposes, the lodging of the petition) before the end of the period of three months beginning with the date on which the grounds giving rise to the application first arose or such longer period as the court considers equitable having regard to all the circumstances, except where an earlier date is statutorily prescribed.[3] It should be observed that the statute imposes no added obligation to initiate proceedings 'promptly'; nor is any further guidance offered on what is to be considered 'equitable' beyond the three-month time limit. It is likely that the earlier jurisprudence of the court on mora (not expressly displaced by the Act) will continue to be invoked by respondents seeking to repel petitions lodged within the time limit, but arguably following undue delay; or by petitioners seeking to establish grounds for an equitable extension.

[1] Rule 58.1(1),(2).
[2] Rule 58.3 (1) and see **22.43**.
[3] 1988 Act, s 27A and Rule 58.3(2). For a separate statutory rule see *Tor Corporate AS v Sinopec Group Star Petroleum Corporation Ltd 2008 SC 303, 2008 SLT 97*. Transitional provision was made (by SSI 2015/247) for all applications lodged after 22 September 2015 in respect of grounds arising before 22 September, to be deemed to have arisen on 22 September. See eg *CF, Petitioner* [2016] CSOH 28; *Shearer, Petitioner* [2016] CSOH 62.

22.88 A petition must be made in the prescribed form[1] and must have lodged with it all relevant documents and a schedule of documents not in the petitioner's possession or control.[2] The rules also state that 'where the decision, act or omission in question and the basis of the challenge is not apparent from the documents lodged with it an affidavit stating the terms of that decision, act or omission and the basis of the challenge.' It may be noted that the rules make no prior reference to a 'decision, act or omission'. Nor do they illuminate what may be the 'terms' of an 'omission'.[3]

Once the petition has been lodged, the Lord Ordinary must make an order specifying such intimation, service and advertisement as may be necessary and dates for service and for responses by respondents or interested parties.[4]

In addition, a 'party' (undefined in the rule) may, at this stage by motion, seek any of a number of 'things' listed in Rule 58.4(5) which, having 'regard to the need for the speedy determination of the petition', the Lord Ordinary may order. The 'things' (a closed list) include adjustments to the service requirements, an extension to the three-month time limit,[5] urgent consideration of the petition, and a sist for legal aid.

[1] Rule 58.3 (3).
[2] As to the production of documents, similar rules on Crown privilege/public interest immunity apply in Scotland and in England (see Chapter **14**). See, however *Parks v Tayside Regional Council* 1989 SLT 345 which confines the claim to public interest immunity as such to central departments. See also *Pearson v Educational Institute of Scotland* 1997 SC 245 and see also, on crown immunity in general, *Somerville v Scottish Ministers* 2008 SC(HL) 45, 2007 SLT 1113; and *AI Megrahi v HMA* 2008 SLT 333.
[3] Rule 58.3(4).

22.89 In addition, the judge may make an interim order.[1] Under the 'old' procedure, in advance of the first hearing of *AXA General Insurance Ltd, Petitioners*[2] sought a first order and, at that point, moved for interim interdict to prevent the Scottish Ministers from making the commencement order required to bring the Damages (Asbestos-related Conditions) (Scotland) Act 2009 into effect. The petitioners argued, on the matter of balance of convenience, that, if the Act were brought into force before the challenge to its lawfulness was resolved, there would be a great deal of unnecessary expense (including legal expense) and inconvenience. It was understood that 400 claims had been intimated but not started whilst a further 600 or so had been sisted and it could be expected that all these actions might be launched and defences would have to be prepared.[3] On the other hand, the respondents predicted that all actions would be sisted pending resolution of the lawfulness challenge.[4] These conflicting predictions of probable events, the Lord Ordinary (Lord Glennie) regarded as fairly evenly balanced.[5] However, he (a) expressed a reluctance to defer a decision on the interim interdict until the time the commencement order might have been made;[6] and (b) concluded that there was no strong reason of convenience for stopping the Act coming into force and that he was reluctant to interfere with the democratic process.[7] He took into account the strength of the petitioners' case and its likelihood of success as an element in assessing the balance of convenience. His view was that the *prima facie* case (based on Convention rights and common law judicial review) was not a particularly strong one and was insufficient to overcome his reluctance to interfere with the democratic process.[8] In *Fox Solicitors Ltd v Advocate General for Scotland*[9] interim interdict to prevent the making of the order under challenge was refused in the light of an undertaking by the Lord Chancellor to reimburse any losses incurred in the event of a finding of invalidity (and also because of the possible impact of an interim interdict on English proceedings). In *Coburn Quarry Co Ltd v HMRC*,[10] special EU considerations were raised in relation to the enforcement by the HMRC of aggregates levy.

An interim order which has frequently been both sought and granted has been interim liberation in immigration cases.[11]

On the 'balance of convenience' before grant of an interim interdict, see *Falkirk Regional Council v Central Regional Council* 1997 SLT 1242; *Secretary of State for Scotland v Highland Council* 1998 SLT 222; *Westerhall Farms v Scottish Ministers* (25 April 2001 unreported); *Beggs v Scottish Ministers* 2004 SLT 755; *Callison v Scottish Ministers* (25 June 2004 unreported); *Duncan v Scottish Ministers* (20 July 2004 unreported). For proceedings to recall an interim interdict, see *Monklands District Taxi Owners Association v Monklands District Council* 1996 SLT 182; *L v Angus Council* 2011 SLT 853. It is competent for a caveat in appropriate terms to be lodged by a potential respondent ensuring a hearing before the grant of a first order. See *Kelly v Monklands District Council* 1986 SLT 165. For the award of an interim order *ad factum praestandum* under s 47(2) of the Court of Session Act 1988, see *Millar & Bryce Ltd v Keeper of the Registers of Scotland* 1997 SLT

1000.

2 [2009] CSOH 57.
3 Ibid paragraph 15.
4 Ibid paragraph 16.
5 Ibid paragraph 18.
6 Ibid paragraph 17.
7 Ibid paragraph 18.
8 Ibid paragraph 19, in reliance on *Infant and Dietetic Foods Assn Ltd v Scottish Ministers* 2008 SLT 137 (Lord McPhail at paragraph 30) and *R v Secretary of State for Transport, ex p Factortame (No 2)* [1991] AC 603 (Lord Goff of Chieveley at 674).
9 2013 SLT 1169.
10 2014 SLT 303
11 See eg *SSA (Pakistan) v Home Secretary* [2013] CSOH 33. For discussion of earlier practice see Mullen, Pick and Prosser Judicial Review in Scotland (1996), pp 32–36. On the other hand, the Gill Report (see **22.6**) stated (paragraph 49) that petitioner practice had more recently tended to be to avoid application for interim orders and thus avoid triggering caveats and having the petition dismissed at (the then) first order stage.

22.90 Normally, a petition proceeds to the permission stage (see below) but it may be diverted by the Lord Ordinary: (a) to the Upper Tribunal – either compulsorily or in the exercise of the Lord Ordinary's discretion, under s 20(1)(a),(b) of the Tribunals, Courts and Enforcement Act 2007; or (b) to proceed as an ordinary action, 'if satisfied that it should proceed in that way'.[1]

In addition, any person *not* specified for service in the first order may nevertheless seek to enter the process, as a person 'directly affected by any issue raised', by enrolling a motion for leave to enter. If that motion is granted the general rules apply, with any necessary modifications, to such a person.[2]

Provision has also been made for 'public interest intervention' by a person not otherwise entitled to apply for leave to enter the process where the court is satisfied that:

(1) the proceedings do raise a matter of public interest;
(2) the applicant's propositions are likely to assist the court; and
(3) the intervention will not unduly delay or otherwise prejudice the rights of the parties.[3]

1 Rule 58.16. It should be noted that, under Rule 58.15, causes may be transferred in the opposite direction, from an action to petition for judicial review. For a complex instance, see eg *S (or NS) v Home Secretary* 2015 SC 295, 2014 SLT 1120.
2 Rule 58.814. In *AXA General Insurance Ltd, Petitioners* 2010 SLT 197 this rule was used to admit to the process individuals who would have been affected by the annulment of the Act under challenge. See also [2010] CSOH 36. Subsequently, the UK Supreme Court decided that, by equiparating the general rules on standing with being 'directly affected' for the purposes of this rule, the test was that of a person's 'sufficient interest' in the proceedings. See 2012 SC (UKSC) 122, 2011 SLT 106 and **22.48** above. See also *MacReath, Petitioner* 2012 SLT 1195; *Sustainable Shetland v Scottish Ministers* [2013] CSIH 116.
3 Rule 58.17. See *Sustainable Shetland v Scottish Ministers* [2013] CSIH 116; *Scotch Whisky Association, Petitioner* [2014] CSIH 38. And see T Mullen, 'Protective Expenses Orders and Public Interest Litigation' (2015) 19 Ed LR 36.

22.91 Until recently, there was little recognition in the Court of Session[1] of the equivalent of the device known in England as costs capping orders (previously protective costs orders).[2] There have, however, been two developments. In the first place, without any reform, *McGinty, Petitioner*[3] recognised the court's capacity to make a protective expenses order. Secondly, there was a recommendation in the Report of the (Gill) Scottish Civil Courts Review that such orders should be placed on a more secure basis (paragraphs 59–78)and, in due course, specific provision was made, in relation to environmental cases only, by the insertion into the Rules of Court of a new Chapter 58A.[4]

1   But see *McArthur v Lord Advocate* 2006 SLT 170.
2   See CHAPTER 19.
3   [2010] CSOH 5.
4   For comment see K Campbell 2014 SLT (News) 19. and T Mullen, 'Protective Expenses Orders and Public Interest Litigation' (2015) 19 Ed LR 36. See also *Road Sense v Scottish Ministers* 2011 SLT 889. But see too *Carroll v Scottish Borders Council* 2014 SLT 659; *Friends of Loch Etive, Petitioners* [2014] CSOH 116; *Gibson v Scottish Ministers* 2016 SC 454, 2016 SLT 319.

The Permission Stage

22.92 The Court of Session Act 1988, s 27B provides:

(1)   No proceedings may be taken in respect of an application to the supervisory jurisdiction of the court unless the court has granted permission for the application to proceed.

(2)   Subject to subs (3)[1], the court may grant permission under subsection (1) for an application to proceed only if it is satisfied that:

    (a)   the applicant can demonstrate a sufficient interest in the subject matter of the application,[2] and

    (b)   the application has a real prospect of success.

(3)   The court may grant permission under sub-section (1) for an application to proceed—

    (a)   subject to such conditions as the court thinks fit,

    (b)   only on such of the grounds specified in the application as the court thinks fit.

A person served with the petition 'who intends to participate in the decision whether permission should be granted',[3] must lodge answers. Alternatively, a person not wishing to participate in the permission stage may instead notify the court (and petitioner) of an intention instead to contest the petition, if permission is granted.[4]

Within 14 days from the end of the period for lodging answers, the Lord Ordinary must decide whether to grant permission for an application to proceed or order an oral hearing for the purpose of deciding.[5] Reasons for a refusal must be given.[6] If permission is refused without an oral hearing, a request to review such a decision may be made. If granted, the hearing must be held within seven days before another Lord Ordinary.[7]

In the early case of *M v Home Secretary*[8] the focus was on the 'real prospect of success' test. Largely rejecting *Pepper v Hart* arguments that direct account should be taken of ministerial statements, and, without much fuller discussion, English leave authorities, Lady Wolffe drew some support from the 'protective expenses order' case of *Carroll v Scottish Borders Council*[9] to the effect that the test imposed 'a fairly low hurdle' and then from the Gill Review that the mischief addressed was 'preventing unmeritorious claims proceeding' to agree with Lord Woolf in *Swain v Hillman*[10] that: 'The words "no real prospect of succeeding" do not need amplification, they speak for themselves. The word "real" distinguishes fanciful prospect of success and they direct the court to the need to see whether there is a "realistic" as opposed to a "fanciful" prospect of success' [para 37].[11] Questions have arisen, in proceedings to amend pleadings (under Rule 24) about the need to ensure the application of the 'real prospects' test.[12]

If, following a hearing, permission is refused or granted subject to conditions or only on particular grounds, an appeal lies to the Inner House.

1 Sub-section (3) provides the special (Eba) rules which apply to reviews of the Upper Tribunal. See 22.47. In addition to the standard grounds for permission, the applicant must demonstrate either that the application would raise an important point of principle or practice or that there is some other compelling reason for the application to proceed.
2 See **22.48**.
3 Rule 58.6(1). It is a curious formulation. Parties may participate in or at the permission stage, but scarcely in the decision.
4 Rule 58.6(2). But (para (3)) the Lord Ordinary or Inner House may subsequently order otherwise.
5 Rule 58.7(1).
6 Rules 58.7(2), 59(2).
7 1988 Act s 27C and Rule 58(8). See eg RA, Petitioner [2016] CSOH 182.
8 2016 SLT 280.
9 2014 SLT 659.
10 [2001] 1 All ER 91.
11 See also *CF, Petitioner* [2016] CSOH 28.
12 See *B v Home Secretary* 2016 SLT 1220; *RA, Petitioner* [2016] CSOH 182.

22.93 When permission is granted, the Keeper of the Rolls must, in consultation with the Lord Ordinary, fix a date (no later than 12 weeks from the permission date) for the substantive hearing, and, unless this is considered unnecessary by the Lord Ordinary, a date (within six weeks) for the prior procedural hearing. Both periods may be extended by the Lord Ordinary if he is satisfied that is necessary.[1] In any case, the Lord Ordinary is obliged to 'make such orders for further procedure as are appropriate for the speedy determination of the petition'. In particular, there may be ordered a range of requirements in relation to further service, answers, documents, authorities, notes of arguments, statements of issues and facts founded upon.[2]

At the procedural hearing, if ordered, the Lord Ordinary must ascertain whether such orders have been complied with and the parties' readiness to proceed, and make any further appropriate procedural orders.[3]

At the substantive hearing, the Lord Ordinary must hear the parties and then grant or refuse any part of the petition, with or without conditions, and make any remedial order, whether or not sought in the petition.[4]

1 Rule 58.11(1).
2 Rule 58.11(2), (3).
3 Rule 58.12.
4 Rule 58.13. For discussion of the available listed (a closed list) remedies, see **22.82**.

22.94 In an early case arising under the new procedural rules, it fell to Lady Wolffe in the Outer House to offer guidance on how they might be deployed to best effect. In *M v Home Secretary*[1] at a procedural hearing on three petitions, Lady Wolffe was highly critical of a number of failures to observe requirements laid down at the permission stages. Documents had not been lodged or they had been inadequately marked up. In addition, none of the counsel appearing were the counsel principally instructed. She explained what the court was entitled to expect, against the background that 'the emphasis is on a focused, disciplined analysis of the issues at an early stage and which are to be resolved by a swift and efficient judicial procedure' [6]. To that end the court's requirements to lodge notes of argument and/or statements of issues and to lodge (joint) bundles of documents, with passages duly marked up had to be produced, with liaison between them, as necessary. Bundles should be assembled according to some ordering principle (without duplication) and duly paginated. And all of this had to be in time for the judge to review the authorities beforehand. In general, instructed counsel should appear at the procedural hearing unless that is impossible, in which case the representative must be properly briefed [6–10].

Procedural guidance had previously been given on the basis of earlier versions of the rules by (1) Lord Clyde in *Inverness, Loch Ness and Nairn Tourist Board v Highland Regional Council*[2] as to how parties might most usefully contribute to an efficient handling of a case at (the then) first hearing. They should discuss in advance the scope of the hearing. Particularly if a final determination was sought at that stage, they should agree on the extent to which facts are in dispute and the extent to which documents can be accepted in evidence. Such agreement should be formally recorded in a joint minute to avoid misunderstanding; and (2) by Lord Hope in *Somerville v Scottish Ministers*.[3] Concerns were expressed about delays caused in the case by lengthy and unclear pleadings. Lord Hope advised that:

> 'the degree of precision and detail in written pleadings that has traditionally been looked for in other forms of action in Scotland is not to be looked for in petitions for judicial review . . . The requirement is simply this. The factual history should be set out succinctly and the issues of law should be clearly identified. The aim is to focus the issues so that the court can reach a decision upon them, in the interests of sound administration and the public interest, as soon as possible.'[4]

[1] 2016 SLT 280.
[2] 1988 GWD 6–219.
[3] 2008 SC (HL) 45, 2007 SLT 1113.
[4] Ibid at paragraph 65. See also *Anderson v Shetland Islands Council* 2011 SLT 196.

Reclaiming

22.95 An appeal may be made by reclaiming motion to the Inner House[1] and thereafter to the UK Supreme Court.[2] However, reclaiming motions against procedural orders (ie other than against the determination of an application itself) may be made only with the leave of the judge.[3] Such leave must be applied for by way of motion not later than 14 days after the making of the order in question.

[1] Court of Session Act 1988, s 28. Rule 38.1–38.2. Not all decisions at first instance attract a written judgment. A subsequent reclaiming motion may, however, provide the need for the production of written reasons at a later date. See eg *Re Mundie* (30 August 1989, unreported).
[2] Court of Session Act 1988, s 40. That section was amended by s 117 of the Courts Reform (Scotland) Act 2014 to require that appeals (not only in judicial review but generally) to the Supreme Court can be taken only with the leave of either the Court of Session or the Supreme Court. That followed complaints from the Supreme Court about abuse of the

previous procedure in cases including *Uprichard v Scottish Ministers* 2013 SC(UKSC)219, 2013 SLT 1218.

3   Rule 38.2(6) and see refusal of leave to reclaim against refusal of adjournment in *Casey v Edinburgh Airport Ltd* 1989 GWD 12–512. On refusal of leave to reclaim to ensure rapid progress to a hearing, see *Kelly v Monklands District Council* 1986 SLT 165.

Index

A

Index